MULTIMEDIA ANCILLARIES ON CD-ROM

Text specific!
PsychNow!™: Interactive Experiences in Psychology
by Joel Morgovsky, Brookdale Community College; Lonnie Yandell, Belmont University; Elizabeth Lynch, Glendale College; Tamara Ferguson, Utah State University; William McVaugh, Weber State University; and project consultant Dennis Coon (ISBN: 0-314-07220-9)

This dynamic CD-ROM is directly correlated to your textbook. Whenever you see a CD-ROM logo in your book, you will know that a relevant interactive module awaits you in *PsychNow!* This CD-ROM for Macintosh and Windows gives you an exciting, multimedia experience that goes beyond the boundaries of the classroom to let you explore the concepts of psychology as never before. Stunning graphics and animations, interesting video clips, and interactive exercises bring the theories of psychology to life. With *PsychNow!*, you can do more than just read about a topic—you can watch, listen, and react to it. *PsychNow!* contains 39 fully interactive modules designed to pique your curiosity and enhance your understanding of core concepts.

Each module includes up to three activities in the *Explore*, *Lesson*, and *Apply* features. Using *PsychNow!*, you can participate in memory exercises, see video clips that demonstrate Piaget's stages of cognitive development, create facial expressions based on Paul Ekman's cross-cultural research, and much more!

Text specific!
The Integrator™ for Introductory Psychology, 2.0
by Arthur J. Kohn and Wendy Kohn (ISBN: 0-534-34924-2)

This CD-ROM for Macintosh and Windows offers dramatic new ways for instructors to teach and students to learn! With a click of the mouse, you can reinforce your learning or explore independently by calling up interactive experiments, animations, homework assignments, video clips, transparencies, audio clips, dynamic images, demonstrations, study pages, and interactive surveys. For each chapter of your text, you can interact with three linked review and testing modules: the "Glossary Module," which provides a complete list of terms and definitions, including audio pronunciation; the "Study Module," which requires you to recall key terms and concepts; and the "Quiz Module," which provides a set of 10 randomized questions for each quiz. Version 2.0 features new activities, study pages, demonstrations, and videos added in the areas of Learning, Biological Psychology, Cognition and Language, Motivation, Memory, Intelligence, Development, Therapy, Social Psychology, and Emotions/Health/Stress.

MORE BOOKS AND SOFTWARE

College Survival Guide: Hints and References to Aid College Students, Fourth Edition
by Bruce M. Rowe, Los Angeles Pierce College (ISBN: 0-534-35569-2)

This new edition of Rowe's helpful guide for college students provides tips on managing time, studying, taking exams, and more.

Cross-Cultural Perspectives in Introductory Psychology, Third Edition
by William Price, North County Community College, and Rich Crapo, Utah State University (ISBN: 0-534-35570-6)

This timely revision contains articles on American ethnic groups as well as other cultures around the world and is an ideal companion volume to Dennis Coon's text. Where appropriate in the standard curriculum of the introductory course, the authors include a cross-cultural reading or vignette that will enrich the traditional material of the course.

Writing Papers in Psychology: A Student Guide, Fourth Edition
by Ralph L. Rosnow, Temple University, and Mimi Rosnow (ISBN: 0-534-34826-2)

This new edition of the Rosnows' valuable "how to" manual for writing term papers and research reports has been updated to reflect the latest APA guidelines for formatting references. The book covers each task with examples and hints and includes two complete writing samples, one report and one research paper.

MindScope Software
by Robert Hendersen (ISBN: 0-314-06173-8)

This software includes 20 experiments which help you discover and analyze aspects of your own behavior that might otherwise be hidden from you. Each experiment is one that you perform on yourself. You generate the results from your own performance in the tasks that comprise the exercise. A 200-page student manual is also included.

Psych Lab I and II
Created by Roger Harnish of the Rochester Institute of Technology, these interactive software programs provide psychology demonstrations and simulations and are available for DOS and Macintosh.
PsychLab I (ISBN: 0-534-15344-5 for DOS; 0-534-13619-2 for Macintosh);
PsychLab II (ISBN: 0-534-13618-4 for DOS; 0-534-15349-6 for Macintosh)

Introduction to Psychology

Exploration and Application

Introduction to Psychology
Exploration and Application
Eighth Edition

Dennis Coon

Brooks/Cole Publishing Company

I(T)P® *An International Thomson Publishing Company*

Pacific Grove • Albany • Belmont • Bonn • Boston • Cincinnati • Detroit • Johannesburg • London
Madrid • Melbourne • Mexico City • New York • Paris • Singapore • Tokyo • Toronto • Washington

Sponsoring Editor: *Denis Ralling*
Marketing Team: *Lauren Harp, Marcy Perman,*
  Margaret Parks, Alicia Barelli
Editorial Assistant: *Stephanie Andersen*
Production Editor: *Karen Ralling*
Permissions Editor: *Mary Kay Hancharik*
Senior Designer: *Kelly Shoemaker*
Interior Design: *Vargas/Williams Design*
Interior Illustration: *Rolin Graphics Inc.*

Cover Illustration: *Jim Alford*
Cover Design: *Laurie Albrecht*
Art Coordinator: *Lisa Torri*
Art Editor: *Kathy Joneson*
Photo Editor: *Bob Western*
Photo Researcher: *Sue C. Howard*
Typesetting: *Graphic World Inc.*
Cover Printing: *Phoenix Color Corporation*
Printing and Binding: *R. R. Donnelley & Sons*

For more information, contact:

BROOKS/COLE PUBLISHING COMPANY
511 Forest Lodge Road
Pacific Grove, CA 93950
USA

International Thomson Publishing Europe
Berkshire House 168-173
High Holborn
London WC1V 7AA
England

Thomas Nelson Australia
102 Dodds Street
South Melbourne, 3205
Victoria, Australia

Nelson Canada
1120 Birchmount Road
Scarborough, Ontario
Canada M1K 5G4

International Thomson Editores
Seneca 53
Col. Polanco
11560 México, D. F., México

International Thomson Publishing GmbH
Königswinterer Strasse 418
53227 Bonn
Germany

International Thomson Publishing Asia
221 Henderson Road
#05-10 Henderson Building
Singapore 0315

International Thomson Publishing Japan
Hirakawacho Kyowa Building, 3F
2-2-1 Hirakawacho
Chiyoda-ku, Tokyo 102
Japan

Printed in the United States of America

10 9 8 7 6 5 4 3 2

Library of Congress Cataloging-in-Publication Data

Coon, Dennis.
    Introduction to psychology: exploration and application/Dennis
Coon.—8th ed.
        p.   cm.
    Includes bibliographical references and indexes.
    ISBN 0-534-34966-8
    1. Psychology.   I. Title.
BF121.C625   1998   97-34738
150—dc21   CIP

For my parents

My first psychology course was taught by a woman whose intellect, warmth, and wisdom had a lot to do with my decision to major in psychology. In the years that followed, I was inspired and challenged by other gifted teachers. Their voices, as well as my own, can be heard throughout this book.

About the Author

After earning a doctorate in psychology from the University of Arizona, Dennis Coon taught for 22 years at Santa Barbara City College, California. Throughout his career, Dr. Coon has especially enjoyed the challenge of teaching introductory psychology. He and his wife Sevren recently returned to Tucson, where he continues to teach, write, edit, and consult.

Dr. Coon is the author of **Introduction to Psychology,** as well as **Essentials of Psychology**. Together, these texts have been used by nearly 2 million students. Dr. Coon frequently serves as a reviewer and consultant to publishers, and he edited the best-selling trade book, **Choices**. He also helped design modules for **PsychNow!**, Brooks/Cole's interactive CD-ROM.

In his leisure hours, Dr. Coon enjoys hiking, photography, painting, woodworking, and music. He also designs, builds, and plays classical and steel string acoustic guitars. He has published articles on guitar design and occasionally offers lectures on this topic, in addition to his more frequent presentations on psychology. His recent return to Arizona has made it possible for him to fulfill a lifelong dream of using operant conditioning to teach scorpions to tap dance.

Contents in Brief

Contents

Chapter 2

Chapter 3

Chapter 4

Child Development 85

Chapter 5

From Birth to Death: Life-Span Development 128

Chapter 6

Sensation and Reality 168

Chapter 7

Chapter 8

Chapter 9

Conditioning and Learning   276

Chapter 10

Memory 314

Chapter 11

Cognition and Creativity   347

Chapter 12

Intelligence   380

Chapter 13

Motivation and Emotion 406

Chapter 14

Health, Stress, and Coping 449

Chapter 15

Gender and Sexuality 485

Chapter 16

Personality   518

Preview: The Hidden Essence   518
Chapter Survey   519

Chapter 17

Abnormal Behavior: Deviance and Disorder 557

Chapter 18

Major Mental Disorders 584

Chapter 19

Chapter 20

Chapter 21

Chapter 22

Applied Psychology 706

Preface to the Eighth Edition

To the Student

Psychology is a large and rapidly growing field. It is at once familiar, exotic, commonplace, surprising, and challenging. Most of all, psychology is changing. Indeed, this book can be no more than a "snapshot" of a colorful passing scene. And yet, change makes psychology especially fascinating: What, really, could be more intriguing than our evolving understanding of human behavior?

Psychology is about each of us. Psychology asks, "How can we step outside of ourselves for a more objective look at how we live, think, and act?" Psychologists believe the answer is through careful thought, observation, and inquiry. As simple as that may seem, it is the guiding light for everything that follows in this book.

I sincerely hope that you will find psychology as fascinating as I do. In this text, I have done all that I could imagine to make your first encounter with psychology enjoyable and worthwhile.

To help you get off to a good start, a short Introduction precedes Chapter 1. The Introduction describes study skills you can use to get the most out of this text and your psychology course. In the chapters that follow, I hope the delight I have found in my own students' curiosity, insights, imagination, and interests will be apparent. Please view this book as a long letter from me to you. It is, in a very real sense, written about you, for you, and to you.

To the Instructor

This book is designed to promote an interest in human behavior, to facilitate learning, and to encourage critical thinking. If you are already familiar with its format, a description of Eighth Edition changes follows shortly. If the text is unfamiliar, a brief sketch of its design and underlying philosophy is in order.

A Book for Students

Selecting a textbook is half the battle in teaching a successful course. A good text does much of the work of imparting information to students. This frees class time for discussion and leaves students asking for more. When a book overwhelms students or cools their interest, teaching and learning become uphill battles. For this reason, I have worked hard to make this a clear, readable, and interesting text.

I believe an important question to ask of the introductory course is, "What will students remember next year, or in 10 years?" Consequently, *Introduction to Psychology* gives students a clear grasp of major concepts, without burying them in details. At the same time, it provides a broad overview that reflects psychology's diversity. I think students will find this book full of intellectual challenge, and teachers will find traditional topics covered to their satisfaction. In addition, I have made a special effort to relate psychology to common experiences and the practical problems of daily life.

A major feature of this book is the *Applications* section in each chapter. These high-interest features bridge the gap between theory and practical applications. I believe students have every right to ask, "Does this mean anything to me? Can I use it? Why should I learn it if I can't?" Applications sections spell out how students can use the principles of psychology. By doing so, they breathe life into its concepts.

At the end of each chapter you will find a separate *Exploration*. These brief articles cover controversies, current issues, topics from psychology's frontiers, or subjects likely to promote critical thinking and discussion. In essence, they serve as supplemental readings within the text, to provide a taste of changing issues and ideas in psychology. Because Explorations conclude each chapter, they are easy to assign or delete at your discretion.

A Format for Learning

Before this book first appeared, psychology texts made surprisingly little use of cognitive principles to teach psychology. My use of learning aids is based on a belief that students can be guided into more effective study and reading habits while learning course content.

Each chapter of this text is built around the well-known SQ3R study-reading formula. In addition to helping students learn psychology, this format promotes valuable study skills. Student reactions to it have been very positive, with many students reporting that they transfer SQ3R techniques to other texts as well.

Notice how the time-tested steps of the SQ3R method—*survey, question, read, recite, and review*—underlie the design of each chapter.

Survey A short *Preview* arouses interest, gives an overview of the chapter, and focuses attention on the task at hand. Next, a boxed *Chapter Survey* relates "Key Questions" to "Key Topics" that will appear in the chapter. This juxtaposition of questions and topics spotlights major issues, so that students will read with a purpose.

Question Throughout each chapter, *Guide Questions* act as advance organizers that prime students to look for important ideas as they read. This helps ensure that reading is an active learning experience. Guide Questions also create a dialogue in which student questions and reactions are anticipated. This clarifies difficult points—in a lively give-and-take between questions and responses.

Read The readability of each chapter has been carefully controlled for maximum student involvement and comprehension. I have made every effort to keep the text as clear and accessible as possible. To further facilitate comprehension, the text employs a full array of traditional learning aids. These include boldface type and phonetic pronunciations for important terms, bullet summaries, a detailed glossary, summary tables, a complete index, and a robust illustration program. In addition, figure and table references in the text are marked with small geometric shapes so that students can easily return to the point where they were reading. This feature also allows readers to start with a figure or table and easily find the place in the text where it is discussed.

An *integrated running glossary* provides precise definitions to enhance reading comprehension. When they first appear, important terms are boldfaced and accompanied by an italicized definition. In this way, students get clear definitions when and where they need them—in the general text itself.

At several points in each chapter, special accentuated *highlights* discuss recent research, interesting topics, and original viewpoints. All highlights are placed exactly where they should be read. Students do not need to search for a separate "box" of information. Highlights are stimulating but non-intrusive supplements to the main text. I have classified them as follows: "A Closer Look," "Focus on a Controversy," "Research Frontier," "Cultural Diversity," "Using Psychology," "Research Classic," "Critical Thinking," "Fact or Fallacy?," "Try It Yourself," and "Rate Yourself." As these headings imply, highlights enrich each chapter and encourage critical thinking.

Recite Every few pages, a *Learning Check* allows students to test their understanding and recall of the preceding discussion. Learning Checks are short, non-comprehensive quizzes that require students to stop and actively process information. Students who miss any questions are encouraged to backtrack and clarify their understanding before reading more. Completing each Learning Check serves as a form of recitation to enhance learning. It also provides feedback so that students can gauge their progress.

A course in psychology naturally contributes to the development of critical thinking abilities. To further facilitate critical thinking, each Learning Check includes a *Critical Thinking Question*. These stimulating questions challenge students to think critically and analytically about psychology. Each question includes a brief answer with which students can compare their own thoughts. Many of these answers are based on recent research and are informative in their own right.

Review As mentioned earlier, an Applications section completes the core of each chapter. Applications show students how psychological concepts relate to practical problems, including problems in their own lives. Through these discussions, students review and extend the ideas they have learned. Applications help reinforce and consolidate learning by illustrating psychology's practicality.

An Exploration follows each Applications section. In most cases, students must be familiar with chapter concepts to fully appreciate an Exploration. This again motivates them to review what they have learned and to broaden their understanding.

To complete the review phase of the SQ3R method, a point-by-point *Chapter Summary* provides a concise synopsis of all major topics. The Chapter Summary is organized around the same Key Questions found in the Chapter Survey. This brings the SQ3R process full-circle and provides closure with respect to the learning objectives of each chapter.

Critical Thinking

The active, questioning nature of the SQ3R method is, in itself, an inducement to think critically. Many of the Guide Questions that introduce topics in the text act as models of critical thinking. More important, the Applications section of Chapter 1 specifically discusses critical thinking skills. The discussion of research methods in Chapter 2 is actually a short course on how to think clearly about behavior. Chapter 11, "Cognition and Creativity," also discusses many topics that focus on thinking skills. The Explorations in several chapters critically evaluate controversial topics. Throughout the text, many highlights present topics that students should approach with healthy skepticism. As mentioned earlier, every Learning Check includes a Critical Thinking Question. Taken together, these features will help students gain thinking skills of lasting value.

Human Diversity

Student populations increasingly reflect the multicultural, multifaceted nature of contemporary society. The Eighth Edition of *Introduction to Psychology* includes numerous discussions of human diversity, including differences in race, ethnicity, culture, gender, abilities, sexual orientation, and age. Too often, such differences needlessly divide people into opposing groups. My intent throughout the text is to discourage stereotyping, prejudice, discrimination, and intolerance. Numerous topics and examples in the Eighth Edition encourage students to appreciate social, physical, and cultural differences and to accept them as a natural part of being human.

What's New in the Eighth Edition?

The publication of this book marks the twentieth anniversary of *Introduction to Psychology*. Thanks to the vitality of the field, and suggestions from colleagues and reviewers, this edition has improved in many ways.

■ The developmental chapters, which were formerly mid-text, now appear near the front of the book (Chapters 4 and 5). Human development is not only a good, foundational topic to cover early, it also helps avoid an excessively long stretch of chapters devoted to basic processes early in the course.

■ The chapter on intelligence and intelligence testing now follows the cognition chapter. A greater emphasis on cognitive approaches to intelligence dictated this new pairing of topics.

■ The prevalence of STDs, AIDS, teenage pregnancies, and sexual dysfunctions, and a surprising degree of ignorance about human sexuality, persuaded me to move the sexuality chapter to a more prominent position in the text. The chapter now follows a discussion of health, stress, and coping.

■ A new feature, called the Chapter Survey, follows the chapter Preview. The Chapter Survey combines elements of "In this Chapter" and "Survey Questions" from the previous edition. My goal in the Chapter Survey is to help students form a cognitive map of the chapter before they begin reading.

■ Guide Questions, which are a key element of the SQ3R format, are retained in this edition. However, I have attempted to make them more subtle by deleting the word "Question:" that used to precede them. This treatment still prompts students to actively search for information, but it allows the reading to flow more smoothly.

■ A prominent change in this edition is the shift from a margin glossary to a fully integrated running glossary. Blending the glossary into the general text has added greatly to its precision. No longer are students forced to infer meanings from context or look for a separate definition in the margin. Now, important terms are clearly defined where they first appear.

■ More than ever, I've made a special effort to make this edition of the text gender neutral and sensitive to diversity issues. All pronouns and examples involving females and males are equally divided by gender. In artwork, photographs, and examples, I have tried to portray the rich diversity of humanity.

■ The text's contribution to critical thinking skills continues to grow stronger. An enlarged discussion of critical thinking comprises the Applications section of Chapter 1. Several new and revised highlights challenge students to think critically about topics they may have seen presented non-critically in the news.

■ All chapters benefit from new and/or improved art and photographs, as well as several new cartoons.

■ Many new tables complement the text.

■ This edition features 22 new highlights, plus updates and revisions of several more.

■ Chapters 1, 9, and 22 have been significantly reorganized.

■ Although the book contains more information than before, it is shorter in words. Tighter editing has allowed the use of a larger, more readable typeface throughout the text.

■ I have deleted the appendix on careers in psychology, which has been replaced by an excellent booklet titled *Psychology: Careers for the 21st Century*. Through an exclusive agreement with the American Psychological Association, Brooks/Cole is able to offer the booklet shrink-wrapped with this text at no additional cost to students.

■ By popular request, I have added Learning Checks to the statistics appendix.

■ A new appendix on the use of electronic media in psychology introduces students to electronic databases, psychological information on the Internet, CD-ROMs, and more.

The comments that follow provide more details about some of the changes listed here.

New Topics and Updated Coverage

In addition to the changes and improvements already noted, my general goal for this revision was to report psychology's latest ideas, insights, and findings. As this defines a deluge of information, I tried to be very selective about what I included. To make the grade, information had to be conceptually significant or inherently fascinating—or preferably both. Almost every chapter of this text contains new ideas that I believe meet these criteria. I have drawn on hundreds of new references (many as recent as 1997 and some in press) for this revision.

New Appendix As mentioned, a new appendix, "Using Electronic Media in Psychology," by Karen Casto, appears in this edition. Appendix B describes a variety of electronic resources in psychology. Students will learn how to retrieve psychological information from the Internet, gophers, FTP sites, the Wide Area Information Server, bulletin boards, online databases, and CD-ROM databases. Multimedia CD-ROMs are also discussed, including *PsychNow!*, which was designed for use in conjunction with this text.

More than ever, electronic media have become important gateways to psychology. Appendix B tells students how to find and use these resources. To help students get started, a World Wide Web site has been created to accompany the appendix. This site contains additional information about electronic media. More important, it provides direct links, via the Internet, to many of the sites discussed in the appendix.

New Highlights   Over the years, I have used highlights to report very recent research, controversies, issues, and findings. My review of the literature this past year proved to be bountiful. In addition to updating many existing highlights, I was able to create 22 that are entirely new, including the following titles:

Ch. 1   Psychologists: Perceptions and Realities
Ch. 3   His and Her Brains?
Ch. 5   The "Be-Good" Drug
Ch. 6   Are You a Supertaster?
             Dynamic Touch
Ch. 7   Who's Flying this Thing?
Ch. 8   Designer Drugs—Agony or Ecstasy?
             New Strategies to Stop Smoking
Ch. 10   How's Your Memory?
Ch. 11   Which Parent?
Ch. 12   Inspecting Intelligence
Ch. 13   Melatonin—Nighttime in a Jar?
             Self-Confidence—Keeping Your Eye on the
               Goal
             Emotional Intelligence—The Fine Art of Self-
               Control
Ch. 15   What Do Women Want?
Ch. 16   Tell It to the Computer
Ch. 20   Gendered Friendships
Ch. 21   Consumer Psychology
             Choking on Stereotypes
Ch. 22   Reduce, Reuse, Recycle
             The School of the Future
             Death-Qualified Juries

Chapter Notes

With respect to more detailed updates, I am pleased to report that every chapter of the Eighth Edition has been enhanced. The following annotations spotlight some of the new topics that appear in this edition.

Introduction, The Psychology of Studying   This material was formerly part of Chapter 1. Its new placement introduces students to a variety of study skills *before* they begin reading topical chapters. The Introduction has been rewritten for clarity and brevity and includes some new information on test-taking skills.

Chapter 1, The Search for Understanding   This reorganized chapter provides a more dynamic introduction to psychology and psychologists. It begins with a greater emphasis on human behavior, empiricism, and the scope of psychology. The chapter also includes brief new coverage of

the science and profession of psychology and the psychology of gender. Expanded captions give added biographical information about prominent historical psychologists. The chapter includes a new highlight, "Psychologists: Perceptions and Realities." Also, a new Applications section offers an expanded discussion of critical thinking skills.

Chapter 2, Research Methods and Critical Thinking   The role of publication and the public availablity of information have been added to coverage of the scientific method. The Exploration on misinformation in the popular press has been updated.

Chapter 3, The Brain, Biology, and Behavior   This chapter includes research updates, improved art, and a new highlight, "His and Her Brains?" A revised highlight discusses brain grafts and the repair of spinal cord injuries. New information on the amygdala and fear also appears in this chapter.

Chapter 4, Child Development   This chapter features a new highlight on postpartum depression, plus research updates on motor development, infant emotions, temperament, pregnancy and childbirth, attachment and day care, cognitive abilities in early infancy, moral development, deprivation, and enrichment.

Chapter 5, From Birth to Death: Life-Span Development   A new highlight, "The 'Be-Good' Drug," addresses the Ritalin controversy. New information is included on wellbeing at mid-life and Levinson's study of mid-life transitions for women. Research updates cover ADHD, stuttering, autism, child abuse, mid-life adjustment, successful aging, bereavement, grief, and euthanasia.

Chapter 6, Sensation and Reality   This chapter features two new highlights, "Are You a Supertaster?" and "Dynamic Touch." Also, students will find updates on subliminal persuasion, tunnel vision, cochlear implants, tinnitus, olfaction, and taste.

Chapter 7, Perceiving the World   A highlight on human factors engineering, "Designing for Human Use," has been moved to this chapter from Chapter 22. The new highlight "Who's Flying this Thing?" discusses the role of active control in perception. New art enhances discussions of shape constancy, linear perspective, light and shadow, stroboscopic movement, attention, and the Müller-Lyer illusion. Research updates enhance discussions of pictorial depth, habituation, eyewitness credibility, and evidence for and against extrasensory perception.

Chapter 8, States of Consciousness   Two interesting new highlights appear in this chapter: "Designer Drugs—Agony or Ecstasy?" and "New Strategies to Stop Smoking." Research updates appear throughout the chapter on sleep, dreaming, hypnosis, sensory deprivation, marijuana, lucid dreaming, and early predictors of drug use. Students will also find new information on crystal methamphetamine, Rohypnol, MDMA, barbiturates, tranquilizers, SIDS, and second-hand smoke.

Chapter 9, Conditioning and Learning A reorganized, shortened, and streamlined discussion of conditioning and learning makes these difficult topics more accessible to students. Improved art appears in several figures and revised art clarifies the mechanisms of classical and operant conditioning. A new table helps students identify key elements of classical conditioning.

Chapter 10, Memory A new highlight, "How's Your Memory?," induces a false memory. This experience allows students to better appreciate the fallibility of memory and the frequency with which pseudo-memories occur. This chapter also contains new information on constructive processing of memories, including the existence of a self-serving bias in memory distortions. A new exercise elicits the tip-of-the-tongue state so that students can experience it directly. An enlarged and updated discussion addresses the question of whether exceptional memory derives from learned strategies, innate capacities, or both. Research updates appear throughout the chapter, including the topics of repression, flashbulb memories, rehearsal, organization, and memory cues.

Chapter 11, Cognition and Creativity This chapter begins with an updated Preview on human intelligence versus machine intelligence. A new highlight, "Which Parent?," provides insight into how framing affects decision making. Chapter 11 also features new examples of insightful solutions and new art that presents some interesting insight problems. A reorganized and updated discussion of creativity includes a new table that differentiates convergent and divergent thinking. The concluding Exploration presents new information on animal intelligence and tool use.

Chapter 12, Intelligence The Preview for this chapter includes an update on the savant syndrome. An important new section discusses the neural basis of intelligence. A new highlight, "Inspecting Intelligence," explains how inspection time is used to measure the speed of neural processing. This new section also includes discussions of metacognitive skills, cognitive models of intelligence, and Gardner's theory of multiple intelligences. The discussion of organic retardation now covers the fragile-*X* syndrome. A revised Applications section critiques *The Bell Curve* and the idea that group differences in average IQ are genetic.

Chapter 13, Motivation and Emotion This chapter features three new highlights: "Melatonin—Nighttime in a Jar?," "Self-Confidence—Keeping Your Eye on the Goal," and "Emotional Intelligence—The Fine Art of Self-Control." Important updates address the mechanisms of hunger, including the latest information on the role of

glucagon-like peptide 1 (GLP-1) and leptin in the control of eating. A brief new discussion links intrinsic motivation and creativity. Updates clarify the impact of circadian rhythms and jet lag. New information appears on the cerebral hemispheres and emotion, as well as the amygdala and fear. An updated Applications presents the principles of behavioral weight management.

Chapter 14, Health, Stress, and Coping In Chapter 14 students will find new information on behavioral risk factors, health-promoting behaviors, and life skills training. Three new tables list typical signs and symptoms of stress, the 10 most stressful jobs, and examples of daily hassles. Also included are updates on the college blues, life events and health, biofeedback, and writing as a means of stress reduction.

Chapter 15, Gender and Sexuality A new table (with pronunciations) accompanies anatomical art and describes the functions of basic reproductive structures. A new highlight, "What Do Women Want?," explores differences between subjective feelings of sexual arousal and actual physical arousal. An updated discussion explores the nature and magnitude of gender differences. The highlight on genetics and sexual orientation has been updated. A new table lists the most common STDs, their symptoms, prevention, and treatment. The discussion of HIV/AIDS has been updated and is followed by a revised and expanded discussion of safer sex practices. A new table details the most common excuses given for not practicing safer sex. The Applications includes new information on sexual dysfunctions and ways to maintain sexual satisfaction in relationships.

Chapter 16, Personality A new highlight, "Tell It to the Computer," examines the use of computerized diagnostic interviews in psychological and psychiatric clinics. New art clarifies the concept of personality types and revised art adds new detail to the presentation of the "Big Five" personality model. A brief new discussion shows how self-esteem relates to self-concept. Also included are small updates of twin research, Freudian theory, honesty testing, the Rorschach, self-actualization, and self-monitoring.

Chapter 17, Abnormal Behavior: Deviance and Disorder This chapter begins with a revised introduction to psychopathology. A new table simplifies recognition of major DSM categories. The chapter also contains new information on Theodore Kaczynski and personality disorders, under-arousal of the psychopathic brain, and the tactics of child molesters. Research updates cover the topics of rape, PTSD, and somatoform disorders. A new section adds cognitive explanations to the discussion of anxiety disorders.

Chapter 18, Major Mental Disorders In addition to research updates, this chapter includes a new table that lists common warning signs for psychosis and major mood disorders. Revised art presents updated estimates of the heritability of schizophrenia and new art illustrates the dopamine hypothesis with respect to schizophrenia and antipsychotic drugs. Another new figure clarifies the stress-vulnerability model of psychopathology. The discussion of seasonal affective disorder contains a new list of primary symptoms. A new table gives examples of commonly prescribed psychiatric drugs and their desired effects.

Chapter 19, Therapies   This chapter features an expanded discussion of media psychologists, as well as new information on telephone counselors and "cybertherapists" accessed through the Internet. Intriguing information on treating phobias with virtual reality exposure is also new to this chapter. A revised and updated highlight on eye movement desensitization and reprocessing makes note of questions that have been raised about this emerging therapy. Chapter 19 also benefits from brief updates on psychoanalysis, short-term dynamic therapy, rational-emotive behavior therapy, group therapies, the effectiveness of psychotherapy, self-help groups, self-help books, and locating a competent therapist.

Chapter 20, Social Behavior   A new highlight, "Gendered Friendships," compares male and female friendship patterns. Research updates refresh discussions of the following topics: touch and status, self-handicapping, male and female standards for success, interpersonal attraction, mate selection, romantic love, love and attachment, conformity, groupthink, and social traps.

Chapter 21, Attitudes, Culture, and Human Relations   Two new highlights enhance this chapter. The first is "Consumer Psychology," which is derived from material formerly in Chapter 22. A second new highlight, "Choking on Stereotypes," explains how stereotype threat can impair academic performance. A new table describes commonly used strategies for reducing cognitive dissonance. Other improvements include updates on the biology of aggression, televised violence, aggressive pornography, and preventing violence. A brief new discussion explains how to improve the chances of getting help in an emergency.

Chapter 22, Applied Psychology   This chapter begins with a revised Preview. The highlight on personal interviews has also been updated. Three highlights are entirely new: "Reduce, Reuse, Recycle" describes strategies to promote recycling; "The School of the Future" explores the benefits of full-service schools; and "Death-Qualified Juries" examines the inherent bias found in death-penalty juries. Other new material presents techniques for promoting peak performance in sports. The chapter concludes with an updated Exploration on space psychology, including multicultural factors that may affect the International Space Station. New information is also included concerning self-managed work groups, job enrichment, sustainable world population levels, noise pollution, architectural depth, jury behavior, and mental practice.

Appendix B, Using Electronic Media in Psychology   This entirely new appendix shows students how to use electronic databases and the Internet to explore topics in psychology.

Teaching and Learning Supplements

Teaching the introductory course is always challenging. I am happy to report that an enlarged and improved array of supplements accompanies the Eighth Edition of *Introduction to Psychology*. These materials are designed to make teaching and learning more effective. Many are available free to adopters or students. Others can be packaged with this text at discounted cost. For more information on any of the listed resources, please call the Brooks/Cole Marketing Department at 800-354-0092.

Student Support Materials

Introductory students must contend with a multitude of abstract concepts, which can make a first course in psychology difficult. The materials listed here are designed to greatly improve students' chances for success.

Study Guide   To facilitate learning, the *Study Guide* provides abundant opportunities for practice, self-testing, and elaborative rehearsal. The *Study Guide* (ISBN: 0-534-35402-5) is structured around the SQ3R method and is closely coordinated with this text. Each chapter includes the following sections: "Chapter Overview" (a concise chapter summary), "Recite and Review" (a survey of major terms and concepts), "Relate" (matching items), "Check Your Memory" (true-false items), "Final Survey and Review" (fill-in-the-blank questions) and a "Mastery Test" (multiple-choice questions similar to in-class test items).

Mastery Study Guide   Tom Bond's *Mastery Study Guide* (ISBN: 0-534-35401-7) offers a very thorough review and a chance to practice concepts presented in the text. The MSG includes a list of important terms and individuals, learning objectives (with space for student responses), two tests ("Do You Know the Information?," "Can You Apply the Information?"), and a fill-in-the-blanks Chapter Review.

Electronic Study Guide   The ESG (Macintosh, ISBN: 0-534-35567-6; Windows, ISBN: 0-534-35568-4) provides questions and answers in an interactive format. The ESG reinforces students for correct answers and provides helpful cues for incorrect answers.

ESL/Developmental Reader's Guide   For some students,

language and culture can be major barriers to full comprehension. The *ESL/Developmental Reader's Guide* (ISBN: 0-534-35403-3) helps clarify idioms and special phrases, cultural and historic allusions, and difficult vocabulary. All terms and phrases in the manual are page-referenced to the text and followed by concise definitions. Like a helpful tutor, the *ESL/Developmental Reader's Guide* can answer questions about the meaning of unfamiliar terms and expressions. It is especially suitable for ESL or developmental-skills students.

Chapter Quizzes This collection (ISBN: 0-534-35568-8) is available shrink-wrapped free with the text. It provides one page per chapter of multiple-choice questions that students can use to evaluate their understanding and prepare for tests.

Multimedia CD-ROMs

CD-ROMs have made it possible for students to directly experience some of the phenomena they are studying. The following CDs from Brooks/Cole provide a wealth of engaging, informative, and highly interactive exercises.

PsychNow!: Interactive Experiences in Psychology
This exciting new CD-ROM (ISBN: 0-314-07220-9) was created by Joel Morgovsky, Lonnie Yandell, Elizabeth Lynch, Tamara Ferguson, William McVaugh, and project consultant Dennis Coon. *PsychNow!* was specifically designed to accompany this text. As students read, CD-ROM logos alert them whenever a relevant interactive module can be found on *PsychNow!*.

PsychNow! provides students with a dynamic, multimedia experience that goes beyond the boundaries of the classroom, allowing them to explore psychology like never before. Stunning graphics and animations, interesting video clips, and interactive exercises bring psychology to life. With *PsychNow!*, students can do more than just read about a topic—they can read, watch, listen, react, and reflect on the meaning of their own responses. *PsychNow!*, which is available for Macintosh and Windows, contains 39 fully interactive modules that will pique students' curiosity and enhance their understanding. Each module includes up to three activities in the "Explore," "Lesson," and "Apply" features. By using *PsychNow!*, students can participate in memory exercises, see video clips that demonstrate Piaget's stages of cognitive development, create facial expressions based on Paul Ekman's cross-cultural research, and much more.

While *PsychNow!* can be used alone, it is also available in a discount bundle for students when packaged with this textbook (ISBN: 0-534-80762-3).

The Integrator for Introductory Psychology, 2.0 Arthur
J. Kohn and Wendy Kohn created this CD-ROM for Windows and Macintosh to provide new ways for instructors to teach and students to learn. With a click of the mouse, students can reinforce their learning or explore independently by calling up interactive experiments, animations,

homework assignments, video clips, transparencies, audio clips, dynamic images, demonstrations, study pages, and interactive surveys. For each chapter of this text, students can interact with three linked review and testing modules. The "Glossary Module" provides a complete list of terms and definitions, including audio pronunciations. The "Study Module" requires students to recall key terms and concepts. The "Quiz Module" provides a set of 10 randomized questions for each quiz.

The Integrator (ISBN: 0-534-34924-2) also includes *LectureMaker*, a program that allows professors to prepare professional multimedia lectures quickly and easily. The *LectureMaker* tool enables you to export multimedia elements to popular presentation packages, such as *PowerPoint*, *Persuasion*, and *Astound*.

Psyk.trek: A Multimedia Introduction to Psychology
This CD-ROM for Windows and Macintosh (ISBN: 0-534-34286-8) covers the core topics of introductory psychology and can be used with any introductory text. Students using *Psyk.trek* will find studying fun, as they create illusions, run simulated experiments, view videos, and quiz themselves on the content of the introductory psychology course.

Internet Resources

The Internet has provided new opportunities for exchanging information and enhancing education. In psychology, Brooks/Cole is at the forefront in making use of this exciting technology.

The Brooks/Cole Psychology Study Center on the World
Wide Web As users of this text, you and your students will have access to the Coon, Eighth Edition, section of the Brooks/Cole Psychology Study Center. This Web site includes the following features for instructors and students:

- *Bulletin Boards.* This area allows users to chat with students and instructors from around the world via our threaded discussion forums in the Psychology Discussion Area. Students and professors can post their psychology related queries here and check back for answers from fellow users.

- *Internet Links.* Direct links to related psychology resources are organized by subject area, making it easy to locate and identify relevant sites. Brief annotations are provided to guide users to information relevant to their interests.

- *Hot Topics.* In this area, users will find topics of current interest for discussion on the bulletin boards. Instructors and students can contribute their own "hot topics." These topics change monthly.

- *Point-Counterpoint.* Two colleagues debate a controversial issue in these lively point-of-view pieces. Topics can range from the use of animals in psychological research to the effectiveness of therapy. These topics also change every month.

- *Author Symposia.* Drop into a symposium to see the latest research from one of your colleagues (with links to appropriate journals) or to see the text of papers and presentations that you might have missed.

- *News Updates and Internet Activities.* This area explores current psychological topics in the news, provides analysis, and relates the information to material in this text. In addition, professors who are using the Internet in the classroom offer teaching tips and activities that students can do on the Web.

In addition to the preceding open resources, two password-protected sites are available to instructors only.

- *Instructor Resources.* This site features pedagogical tips, suggested classroom activities, lecture topics, and download-able images for integration into your course.
- *Bulletin Boards.* This is a password-protected chat area for instructors only.

The following specialized sites for students can also be accessed at the Brooks/Cole Psychology Study Center.

- *Interactive Activities for Students.* This password-protected section offers online activities that allow students to take a "hands-on" approach to understanding and appreciating psychology's concepts.
- *Online Student Tutorial Quizzes.* These chapter-by-chapter quizzes allow students to test their understanding of concepts and facts. Rejoinders help students understand both correct and incorrect answers. Ten questions are provided per chapter and students can track their progress via a running scoreboard.
- *Online Practice Tests.* In addition to the Tutorial Quizzes, students can take a 15-question practice test for each chapter. Results can be sent via e-mail to the instructor.

Essential Teaching Resources

As every professor knows, teaching an introductory psychology course is a tremendous amount of work. The supplements listed here should not only make life easier for you, they should also make it possible for you to concentrate on the more creative and rewarding facets of teaching.

Instructor's Manual The *Instructor's Manual* (ISBN: 0-534-35399-1) for this edition was revised by psychologist and master teacher Sandra Ciccarelli. The manual includes updated learning objectives, film suggestions, demonstrations, supplemental lectures, classroom exercises, discussion ideas, and suggested readings.

Test Bank The *Test Bank* (ISBN: 0-534-35400-9) includes more than 4,000 multiple-choice questions organized by learning objectives, with correct answers and page references to the main text. The test items, which were meticulously updated by Robert Leduc and Teresa Scardino, are classified by question type (factual, conceptual, or applied).

WESTEST 3.2 Computerized Testing This user-friendly electronic testing system allows you to create, edit, store, and print exams directly to word processor format. This improved version of WESTEST is more intuitive and less demanding of technical computer skills. New questions may be added and existing questions may be edited directly on-screen, similar to a word processor. Exam questions can be arranged automatically by type, randomly, or directly on-screen using the drag and drop feature. Available for Windows (ISBN: 0-534-35493-9) and Macintosh (ISBN: 0-534-35492-0).

For your convenience, complimentary Telephone Testing, or "tele-testing," is also available. ITP Technology Services will construct a test for any instructors who have adopted *Introduction to Psychology: Exploration and Application.* Technology Services requests a minimum of 48 hours notice to construct these complimentary tests. For tele-testing, call the Academic Resource Center at 800-423-0563.

Transparency Acetates A revised set of transparencies (ISBN: 0-534-35404-1) will again be available to illustrate and enliven lectures. These text-specific transparencies contain over 140 tables, graphs, charts, and drawings—most in color. All of the acetates are reproduced from figures and tables in this text.

The *Brooks/Cole Introductory Psychology Transparencies* is a second set of 95 full-color acetates. This collection (ISBN: 0-534-13013-5) illustrates a range of topics for the introductory course. It can be used to supplement the text-specific package.

Images of Psychology: Videodisc Library of Human Behavior This two-disc set provides nearly two hours of video footage to help you prepare exciting classroom presentations. All of the videos have been carefully chosen to support major concepts in the introductory course. Several segments were designed and recorded specifically for this disc. Video clips range from two to six minutes in length and cover a wide variety of topics. The clips feature material such as original research footage, classic experiments, interviews with prominent psychologists, and investigations of psychological phenomena. The *Videodisc Library* also contains a large collection of still-frame art, charts, tables, animated sequences, and on-screen quizzes.

Videodisc materials can be accessed instantly, in any order, by simply entering a frame number, or scanning a barcode. Brooks/Cole's companion *Lecture Builder* software allows you to prepare entire laser disc lectures and play them back in class. *Lecture Builder* is available for both Macintosh and Windows environments. The *Images of Psychology Videodisc Library* includes an annotated *Instructor's Manual* by Lonnie Yandell. The manual lists all frames and video segments, describes their contents, and gives suggestions for their use.

ASTOUND Presentation Software This state-of-the-art multimedia presentation package provides you with visual support in the classroom. Custom presentations contain lecture material from the textbook, including text, art, photos, problems, and chapter outlines. You can use these presentations "as is," or customize the material to create your own unique presentations that include text, graphics, animations, and sound. Available for Macintosh (ISBN: 0-314-09069-X) or Windows (ISBN: 0-314-09070-3).

Animations Plus! Videodisc   Produced by Brooks/Cole, this videodisc includes a collection of animations as well as still frame reviews and quizzes, diagrams, and video segments. The videodisc comes with an *Instructor's Guide* including bar codes for easy reference. (Videodisc, ISBN: 0-534-15351-8; accompanying *Instructor's Guide*, ISBN: 0-534-15353-4.)

Videotapes and Films

Brooks/Cole offers a variety of videotapes and films to enhance classroom presentations. Many video segments in the Brooks/Cole collection pertain directly to major topics in this text, making them excellent lecture supplements.

Brooks/Cole Film and Video Library for Introductory Psychology   Adopters of this text can choose from a variety of up-to-date video and film options. Please contact Brooks/ Cole Marketing (800-354-0092) for information about the availability of videos or to request specific titles. The *Film and Video Library* includes:

- The Pennsylvania State University's *PCR: Films and Videos in the Behavioral Sciences.* Adopters receive a set of three complimentary film/video rental vouchers and can choose from the world's largest collection of films and videos on human behavior.
- *The Brain* videotapes. This collection consists of 30 video modules. The collection and a faculty guide were prepared by Frank Vattano of Colorado State University in conjunction with the Annenberg/CPB Project Video Collection.
- *The Mind* videotapes. Thirty-eight brief video modules provide examples of important concepts in introductory psychology. The accompanying faculty guide was prepared by Frank Vattano in cooperation with WNET, New York.
- *Seeing Beyond the Obvious: Understanding Perception in Everyday and Novel Environments.* This videotape provides an introduction to basic concepts of visual perception. It was created by NASA Ames Research Center in conjunction with the University of Virginia.
- *Discovering Psychology* videotapes. The 26 half-hour programs in this series integrate historical and contemporary perspectives on the field of psychology. Phillip Zimbardo hosts each program from the Annenberg/CPB Collection.
- *Films for the Humanities and Sciences.* Adopters can choose one video from a selection that includes "Further Approaches to Learning," "Memory: Fabric of the Mind," and "Dreams: Theater of the Night."

Brooks/Cole-CNN Introductory Psychology Video   This exclusive videotape includes 20–30 clips (each between one and two minutes in length). The collection will be available beginning early in 1998. Call Brooks/Cole marketing for more information at 800-354-0092.

Grade Improvement: Taking Charge of Your Learning Videotape   This 20-minute video (ISBN: 0-314-05881-8) uses an upbeat and entertaining delivery to show first-year and re-entry students strategies they can use to enjoy greater success in college. Students will learn proven techniques for choosing an approach to learning, time management, class preparation, effective test taking and more. Above all else, the presentation stresses that students must be actively involved in their learning.

Psychology/Careers for the Twenty-First Century Videotape   Brooks/Cole has an exclusive agreement to offer this dynamic 13-minute video produced by the APA. It is available free to adopters of this text. The videotape (ISBN: 0-534-34293-0) gives viewers an overview of emerging growth opportunities in psychology and advice about how to choose a career path.

Technical Support   ITP Technology Services provides technical support and customer service for Brooks/Cole software, multimedia, and computerized testing. For assistance, call the Academic Resource Center at 800-423-0563.

Supplementary Books and Software

No text can cover all of the topics that might be included in an introductory psychology course. If you would like to enrich your course, or make it more challenging, the titles listed here may be of interest.

Readings in Introductory Psychology   This fine collection of articles, edited by Kathleen McDermott and Henry L. Roediger III, is an ideal way to engage students and stimulate discussion. The articles, which are drawn from newspapers and popular magazines, are highly readable and informative. Sixteen reports address recent findings and issues in 13 major areas of psychology (ISBN: 0-314-09382-6).

College Survival Guide   The new Fourth Edition of Bruce Rowe's *College Survival Guide: Hints and References to Aid College Students* (ISBN: 0-534-35569-2) is designed to help students succeed. Rowe provides valuable tips on how to finance an education, how to manage time, how to study for and take exams, and more. Other sections focus on maintaining concentration, credit by examination, use of the credit/no credit option, cooperative education programs, and the importance of a liberal arts education.

Cross-Cultural Perspectives in Psychology   How well do the concepts of psychology apply to various cultures? What can we learn about human behavior from cultures different from our own? These questions lie behind a collection of original articles written by William F. Price and Rich Crapo. The new Third Edition of *Cross-Cultural Perspectives in Psychology* (ISBN: 0-534-35570-6) contains articles on North American ethnic groups as well as cultures from around the world. It is an ideal way to enrich your course with additional multicultural perspectives. Each article begins with an intriguing question about behavior, which is then explored through cross-cultural research. The articles in this book will challenge students to examine the assumptions they make about behavior.

Writing Papers in Psychology The Fourth Edition of *Writing Papers in Psychology: A Student Guide* (ISBN: 0-534-34826-2), by Ralph L. Rosnow and Mimi Rosnow, is a valuable "how to" manual for writing term papers and research reports. This new edition has been updated to reflect the latest APA guidelines for formatting references. The book covers each task with examples, hints, and two complete writing samples. Citation ethics, how to locate information, and new research technologies are also covered.

Challenging Your Preconceptions: Thinking Critically about Psychology This paperbound book (ISBN: 0-534-19972-0), written by Randolph Smith, helps students strengthen their critical thinking skills. Psychological issues such as hypnosis and repressed memory, statistical seduction, the validity of pop psychology, and other topics are used to illustrate the principles of critical thinking.

People: Psychology from a Cultural Perspective David Matsumoto's unique book (ISBN: 0-534-19338-2) discusses similarities and differences in research findings in the United States and other cultures. By doing so, it helps students see psychology and their own behavior from a broader, more culturally-aware perspective.

Three Psychologies: Perspectives from Freud, Skinner, and Rogers In this popular and critically acclaimed book (ISBN: 0-534-26616-9), Robert Nye presents the essential ideas of Freud, Skinner, and Rogers. Comparing and contrasting the ideas of these three theorists will help students appreciate the contribution each made to psychological thought.

The 'Net, the Web, and You This paperback by Daniel Kurland offers a brief, comprehensive, easy-to-understand introduction to the Internet. It is useful for any course that requires students to use the Internet for research or inquiry (ISBN: 0-534-51281-X).

Psychology: Careers for the 21st Century Brooks/Cole is able to offer this informative booklet (ISBN: 0-534-34292-2) to students by exclusive agreement with the American Psychological Association. It describes the field of psychology, as well as how to prepare for a career in psychology. This 30-page pamphlet can be shrink-wrapped with this text at no additional cost to students.

Mind Scope Software This program was created by Robert W. Hendersen. *Mind Scope* (ISBN: 0-314-06173-8) consists of 14 computerized exercises in perception, learn-ing, memory, and cognition. The series helps students discover and analyze aspects of their own behavior that might otherwise be hidden from them. In each exercise, students perform a task and record their own responses. By analyzing the results, students are able to see psychological processes illustrated by their own behavior. *Mind Scope* will run on any IBM-compatible microcomputer. A 200-page student manual is also included.

Psych Lab I and II This software, created by Roger Harnish, provides interactive psychology demonstrations and simulations. Versions are available for both DOS and Macintosh. *PsychLab I* (ISBN: 0-534-15344-5 for DOS; 0-534-15349-6 for Macintosh) includes eight easy-to-use interactive demonstrations on the following topics: hemispheric specialization, Weber's Law, optical illusions, classical conditioning, levels of processing, pressure and performance, problem solving, and emotional expression. *PsychLab II* (ISBN: 0-534-13618-4 for DOS; 0-534-13619-2 for Macintosh) features six interactive demonstrations, experiments, and tutorials about the following subjects: brain anatomy, brain memorizing, classical conditioning, operant conditioning, shaping, and an ESP simulation.

Summary

I sincerely hope that teachers and students will consider this book and its supporting materials a refreshing change from the ordinary. Writing and revising it has been quite an adventure. In the pages that follow, I think the reader will find an attractive blend of the theoretical and the practical, plus many of the most exciting ideas in psychology.

Acknowledgments

Psychology is a cooperative effort requiring the talents and energies of a large community of scholars, teachers, researchers, and students. As with earlier versions of this text, this edition reflects the efforts of a large number of people.

I would like to thank first the many students who sent comments, suggestions, and letters of encouragement.

To the professional reviewers who gave their time and expertise, I extend my sincere thanks. I deeply appreciate the contributions of all those who have, over the years, supported this text's evolution. I especially wish to thank the following professors, who helped make this edition a reality.

Derek Cadman
El Camino Community College

Eugenio J. Galindro
El Paso Community College

Michael B. Guyer
John Carroll University

Raquel Henry
Kingwood College

James A. Johnson
Sam Houston State University

Yancy B. McDougal
University of South Carolina-Spartanburg

Edward Mosley
Pasiac County Community College

Steve G. Ornelas
Central Arizona College

Debra Parish
Tomball College

Jeffrey Rudski
Mulhenberg College

Donald M. Stanley
North Harris County Community College

Christopher Taylor
University of Arizona

Paul E. Turner
David Lipscomb University

Paul J. Wellman
Texas A&M University-College Station

Kaye D. Young
North Iowa Area Community College

I would also like to thank the psychologists whose work and advice has so obviously enhanced this text and its supporting materials: Wayne Bartz, Brian Bate, Tom Bond, Karen Casto, Sandra Ciccarelli, Rich Crapo, David Gershaw, Roger Harnish, Robert Hendersen, Arthur Kohn, Wendy Kohn, Linda Kovacs, Robert Leduc, Elizabeth Lynch, Joel Morgovsky, William Price, Bruce Rowe, Teresa Scardino, and Lonnie Yandell. It has been a pleasure working with such gifted colleagues.

The complexity of revising *Introduction to Psychology* and its supplements continues to be a formidable challenge. The Eighth Edition reflects the talents of many people. I am indebted to Karen Ralling for her many hours of dedicated work. Special thanks to Kelly Shoemaker for ensuring that this edition is graced by an attractive design, and to Bob Western for providing excellent photos. I greatly appreciate the efforts of Faith Stoddard, Margaret Parks, Marcy Perman, and Lauren Harp, who have energetically supported this book and my efforts. Many, many thanks to Victoria Knight, Craig Barth, and Bill Roberts, whose resourcefulness, vision, and leadership eased the transition and helped keep the dream alive. These individuals and many others at Brooks/Cole have made this text a reality.

Finally, I want to express my sincere gratitude to Denis Ralling for excellent, multifaceted editorial guidance and support.

Last of all, I would like to thank my wife Sevren, whose understanding, emotional support, and countless hours of help made this book possible.

Dennis Coon

Introduction

The Psychology of Studying

Even if you're already doing well in school, you may be able to improve your study skills. Would you like to learn more in less time? There is a good chance you can if you apply the methods described here. Studies have shown that students who get good grades tend to work *smarter*, not just longer (Dickinson & O'Connell, 1990; Hill, 1990).

The SQ3R Method—How To Tame a Textbook

Have you ever finished a reading assignment and then discovered that you could remember little about it? This problem plagues students everywhere. But fortunately, an excellent solution exists. Educator Francis Robinson developed a superb technique called the **SQ3R method,** *which stands for survey, question, read, recite, and review.* Robinson's method is a way of studying as you read. Following its steps can help you understand ideas quickly, remember more, and review effectively (Robinson, 1970):

S = *Survey.* Look ahead through a chapter before you begin reading. As you do, read only topic headings, captions for illustrations, and any chapter summary or review. This step should give you an overall picture of what lies ahead.

Q = *Question.* To focus your attention as you read, turn each topic heading into one or more questions. For example, the heading "Stages of Sleep" could raise these questions: "Is there more than one stage of sleep?" "What are the stages of sleep?" "How do they differ?" Asking questions will increase your interest and help relate new ideas to what you already know.

R1 = *Read.* The first R in SQ3R refers to *read.* As you read, try to answer the questions you asked. Read in short "bites," from *one topic heading* to the next, then stop. (If the material is very difficult, you may even want to read only a paragraph or two at a time.)

R2 = *Recite.* After you have read a small amount, you should

Effective studying is planned and systematic. The number of hours you spend studying is less important than the quality and efficiency of your learning strategies (Woehr & Cavell, 1993).

Figure I–1 ◆ The SQ3R method promotes active learning and information processing. You should begin with a survey of the chapter, proceed through cycles of questioning, reading, and reciting, and conclude with a review of the chapter.

stop and *recite*. That is, try to silently answer your questions. Or better yet, summarize what you've read in brief notes. Doing so can significantly improve your test scores (Radmacher & Latosi-Sawin, 1995).

If you can't summarize main ideas in your own words, scan back over the section until you can. Until you can remember what you just read, there's little point to reading more.

After you have read a short "bite" of information, turn the next topic heading into questions. Then read to the following heading. Again, you should look for answers as you read and recite before moving on. Repeat the question-read-recite cycle until you've read the entire chapter.

R3 = *Review*. When you've finished reading, skim back over the chapter, or read your notes. Then check your memory by reciting and quizzing yourself again. Or better yet, get someone to ask you questions about each topic. Try to make frequent review a key element of your study habits. (See Figure I–1 ◆.)

Does this method really work?

Experiments show that using the SQ3R method improves both reading comprehension and grades. Simply reading straight through a chapter often leads to a case of intellectual "indigestion." That's why it's important that you stop often to think, question, recite, review, and "digest" information (Chastain & Thurber, 1989; Martin, 1985).

Relate　A point to keep in mind is that new ideas are easiest to remember when you relate them to personally meaningful information. As you review a chapter, try to associate facts, terms, and concepts with familiar ideas. As a reminder, you may want to add a fourth R—for *relate*—to the SQ3R method.

How to Use This Text

You can apply the SQ3R method to any book. However, as you may have guessed, its steps are built into this text to help you use them. Each chapter opens with a *Preview*, plus a short overview called the *Chapter Survey*. Questions in the Chapter Survey will help you identify main points to watch for as you read.

You can use the Chapter Survey to form a "mental map" of each chapter. Before you begin reading, however, take a

minute or two to make your own survey. As you read, additional questions in the text will help clarify ideas and focus your attention, to improve learning and memory (Melton, 1978; Wade & Trathen, 1989).

Every few pages, *Learning Checks* will allow you to recite and test your memory of important points. (Again, you should also take notes or recite on your own.) If you have only a few minutes to study, or if you would like to study chapters in smaller sections, Learning Checks make good stopping points.

To add to your enjoyment of psychology, you'll find an *Applications* section near the end of each chapter. Applications are filled with practical information that you can put to use. Then, to extend your knowledge, a short *Exploration* covers an interesting topic related to the core of the chapter. Finally, a *Chapter Summary* restates key ideas so you can do a final review.

As you read, new terms are defined where they first appear in the text. Important terms are printed in **boldface type** and some are followed by pronunciations. (Capital letters show which syllables are accented.) As a further study aid, a *glossary*, or "mini-dictionary," of terms appears near the end of this book. Perhaps you should take a moment to find it now.

Table I–1 ■ summarizes how this text helps you apply the SQ3R method. The listed features should make learning psychology enjoyable and effective, but there is still more you can do on your own.

Effective Note-Taking— Good Students, Take Note!

The SQ3R method may be good for reading, but what about taking notes in class when it's difficult to know what's important?

Effective note-taking requires *active* listening. **Active listeners** *control their attention* to avoid distractions and daydreaming. Here's a listening/note-taking plan that works for many students. The important steps are summarized by the letters LISAN, pronounced like the word *listen* (Carmen & Adams, 1985).

L = *Lead. Don't follow.* Try to anticipate what the instructor will say by using questions as guides. Questions can come from the instructor's study guides or reading assignments.

I = *Ideas.* Every lecture is based on a core of important ideas. Usually, an idea is introduced and examples or explanations are given. Ask yourself often, "What is the main idea now? What ideas support it?"

S = *Signal words.* Listen for words that tell you the direction the instructor is taking. For instance, here are some groups of signal words:

There are three reasons why . . .	Here come ideas
Most important is . . .	Main ideas
On the contrary . . .	Opposite idea
As an example . . .	Support for main idea
Therefore . . .	Conclusion

A = *Actively listen.* Sit where you can hear and where you can be seen if you need to ask a question. Look at the instructor while he or she talks. Bring questions you want answered from the last lecture or from your reading. Raise your hand at the beginning of class or approach your instructor before the lecture begins. Do anything that helps keep you active and alert.

N = *Note-taking.* As you listen, write down only key points. Listen to everything, but be selective. If you are too busy writing, you may not grasp what is being said.

There is something more you should know: A revealing study found that most students take reasonably good notes—and then don't use them! Most students wait until just before exams to review their notes (Palkovitz & Lore, 1980). By then the notes have lost much of their meaning. If you don't want your notes to seem like hieroglyphics or "chicken scratches," it pays to review them *on a regular basis*—daily is not too often.

Using and Reviewing Your Notes

When you review, you will learn more if you take the extra steps listed here (Kiewra et al., 1991; King, 1992, 1995).

- Return to your notes as soon as you can and improve them by filling gaps and finishing incomplete thoughts.
- Look for connections among ideas. Try to see how the concepts in your notes relate to one another.
- Make an effort to link lecture information with previously acquired knowledge. Relate new ideas to what you already know.
- Summarize your notes. Boil them down and *organize* them.
- Make up questions about lecture material from your notes and make sure you can answer them.

Summary The letters LISAN are a guide to active listening, but remember that listening and taking good notes is not enough. You must also review, organize, relate, extend, and think about new ideas. Doing so will deepen your understanding and help you build connections in memory.

Study Habits—Avoiding the Last-Minute Blues

Virtually every topic is interesting to someone, somewhere. Although I may not be interested in the sex life of the South American tree frog, a biologist might be fascinated. If you wait for your teachers to "make" their courses interesting, you are missing the point. Interest is a matter of *your attitude*. Students and teachers *together* make a class rewarding. It's a big mistake to blame poor performance on circumstances "beyond your control." Students who believe that success is due to effort and motivation do better in the long run (Noel et al., 1987).

With the preceding in mind, let's consider a few things you can do to improve your study habits.

Study in a Specific Place It goes almost without saying that you should study in a quiet, well-lighted area free of distractions. If possible, you should also have at least one place where you only study. Do nothing else at that spot: Keep magazines, radios, friends, pets, posters, games, puzzles, food, lovers, sports cars, elephants, pianos, televisions, hang gliders, kazoos, and other distractions out of the area. In this way, studying will become strongly linked with one specific place (Beneke & Harris, 1972). Then, rather than trying to force yourself to study by "willpower," all you have to do is go to your study area. Once there, you'll find it relatively easy to get started.

Use Spaced Study Sessions It is quite reasonable to review intensely before an exam. However, you are asking for trouble if you are actually learning information for the first time ("cramming"). Research suggests that spaced practice is more efficient (Naveh-Benjamin, 1990). **Spaced practice** *consists of a large number of relatively short study sessions*, rather than one or two long ones (called massed practice). (It might be worth remembering that if you "massed up" your studying, you probably messed it up too.) Your first hour of study on any particular topic is usually the most efficient.

Cramming places a tremendous burden on memory. It is far better to learn small amounts on a daily basis and to review frequently. It also makes sense to reward yourself with a treat of some kind after each study session, to keep yourself motivated between tests.

Try Mnemonics Learning has to start somewhere, and memorizing is often the first step. Psychologists now know a great deal about how to improve memory. Since many of the important points are summarized in Chapter 10, let's consider just one technique here.

A **mnemonic** (nee-MON-ik) *is a memory aid*. Most mnemonics link new information to ideas or images that are easy to remember. For example, imagine that you want to remember that the Spanish word for duck is *pato* (pronounced POT-oh). To use a mnemonic, you could picture a duck in a pot or a duck wearing a pot for a hat (Pressley, 1987). Or, to remember that the cerebellum controls coordination, you might picture someone named "Sarah Bellum" who is very coordinated. Obviously, there are many

Mnemonics make new information more familiar and memorable. Forming an image of a duck wearing a pot for a hat might help you remember that *pato* is the Spanish word for duck.

ways to create mnemonics. If you would like to learn more, look ahead to Chapter 10.

Test Yourself Many students overlook one of the best ways to improve grades: When studying, you can arrange to take several practice tests before the real one in class. In other words, studying should include **self-testing**, *in which you pose questions to yourself* by the use of flash cards, Learning Checks, a study guide, or other means. As you study, ask as many questions as you can and be sure you can answer them. Studying without testing yourself is like practicing for a basketball game without shooting any baskets.

To make self-testing more convenient, your professor may make a *Study Guide* or a separate booklet of *Practice Quizzes* available with this text. You can use either one to review for tests.

Overlearn Here is something else to keep in mind: Many students *underprepare* for exams, and most *overestimate* how well they will do (Murray, 1980). A solution to both problems is **overlearning**, *in which you continue studying beyond bare mastery of a topic*. In other words, you should reserve time for extra study and review *after* you think you are prepared for a test.

Here's another reason for overlearning. Students who expect to take an essay test (usually the hardest kind) do better on essay, multiple-choice, and short-answer tests (Foos & Clark, 1984). Before tests, students always ask, "Will it be an essay or multiple choice?" But as the study shows, *it is best to approach all tests as if they were essays*. By doing so, you will learn information more completely, so you really "know your stuff."

All of these study techniques are fine. But what can I do about procrastination?

Procrastination

A tendency to procrastinate is almost universal among college students. (When campus workshops on procrastination are offered, many students never get around to signing up!) High levels of procrastination are associated with lower grades (Wesley, 1994). Even when procrastination doesn't lead to failure, it can cause much suffering. Procrastinators put off work until the last moment, work only under pressure, skip classes, give false reasons for late work, and feel ashamed of their last-minute efforts (Burka & Yuen, 1983).

Why do so many students procrastinate?

It is fairly natural to put off long-range assignments, at school and elsewhere. However, there are added reasons for student procrastination. Psychologists Jane Burka and Lenora Yuen observe that many students equate performance in school with their *personal worth*. By procrastinating, students can blame poor work on a late start, rather than a lack of ability (Ferrari, 1991). After all, it wasn't their best effort, was it?

Perfectionism is a related problem. If you have high expectations for yourself, you may find it hard to start an assignment. Students with high standards expect the impossible from themselves and end up with all-or-nothing work habits (Burka & Yuen, 1983). This is especially true if you are very sensitive about what others think of you (Clark & Hill, 1994; Ferrari, 1992).

Time Management Burka and Yuen say that most procrastinators must eventually face the self-worth issue. Nevertheless, progress can be made by learning better study skills and effective time management. Since we have already discussed study skills, let's consider time management.

A **formal time schedule** *is a written plan that allocates time for study, work, and leisure activities.* Such plans can do much to prevent procrastination and maintain motivation. To prepare your schedule, make a chart showing all of the hours in each day of the week. Then fill in times that are already committed: sleep, meals, classes, work, team practices, lessons, appointments, and so forth. Next, fill in times when you will study for various classes, and label them. Finally, label the remaining hours as open and free times.

The beauty of keeping a schedule is that you know you are making an honest effort. In addition to getting more done, you will avoid the trap of yearning to play while you work and feeling guilty when you play. The key to time management is to treat your study times as serious commitments, like class meetings or a job. Be sure to respect your free times, too, so you don't get stale or discouraged. And remember this: Students who practice good time management *do* get better grades (Britton & Tesser, 1991).

Goal Setting Many students find it helpful to set **specific goals** *that are clear-cut and measurable* (Schunk, 1990). If you have trouble staying motivated, it's a good idea to set goals for the semester, the week, the day, and even for single study sessions. Be realistic about your goals, but don't underestimate yourself either. By increasing your efforts at the beginning of a semester, you can greatly reduce the "pain" and stress you will experience later (Brown, 1991).

Students who procrastinate do better when they are given frequent smaller assignments (Rothblum, Solomon, & Murakami, 1986). If your professors don't give frequent assignments, set up your own day-to-day goals. An example would be reading, studying, and reviewing eight pages a day to complete a 40-page chapter in five days. Many small steps can add up to an impressive journey.

Quality Time Effort has nearly as much impact on grades as how "smart" you are does. However, remember that good students work more *efficiently*, not just more hours. Many study practices are notoriously inefficient. For example, all of the following are time-consuming, but weak, study methods: re-copying lecture notes; studying only lecture notes and not the textbook; outlining textbook chapters; answering study questions with the textbook open; and "group study" (which often becomes a party or a social event). Students who get the best grades emphasize *quality*: They study their books and notes in depth and attend classes regularly (Woehr & Cavell, 1993).

Taking Tests—Are You "Test Wise"?

If I have read and studied effectively, is there anything else I can do to improve my grades?

Learning is only a first step. You must then be able to show what you know on tests. Here are some suggestions for improving your test-taking skills.

General Test-Taking Skills

You'll do better on all types of tests if you observe the following guidelines (Wood & Willoughby, 1995).

1. Read all directions and questions carefully; they may give you good advice or clues for the test.
2. Quickly survey the test before you begin.
3. Answer easy questions before spending time on more difficult ones.
4. Be sure to answer all questions.
5. Use your time wisely.
6. Ask for clarification whenever necessary.

Several additional strategies can help you do better on objective tests.

Objective Tests Objective tests (multiple choice and true-false items) require you to recognize a correct answer among wrong ones or a true statement against a false one. If you are taking an objective test, try this:

1. First, relate the questions to what you know about the topic. Then, read the alternatives to see if any match the answer you expected to find. If none match, reexamine the alternatives and look for a partial match.
2. Read *all* the choices for each question before making a decision. If you immediately think that *a* is correct, for instance, and stop reading, you might miss seeing a choice like "both *a* and *d*" that is a better answer.
3. Read rapidly and skip items you are uncertain about. Later questions may give you "free information" that will help you answer difficult items.
4. Eliminate certain alternatives. With a four-choice multiple-choice test, the odds are one in four that you could

guess right. If you can eliminate two alternatives, your guessing odds improve to 50-50.

5. Unless there is a penalty for guessing, be sure to return and answer any skipped items. Even if you are not sure of the answer, you may be right. If you leave a question blank, it is automatically wrong.

When you are forced to guess, don't make the mistake of choosing the longest answer or the letter you've used the least. Both strategies lower scores more than random guessing does (Shatz, 1986).

6. There is a bit of folk wisdom that says "Don't change your answers on a multiple-choice test. Your first choice is usually right." Careful study of this idea has shown it is *false*.

If you change answers you are three times more likely to gain points than to lose them (Geiger, 1991). This is especially true if you feel *very* uncertain of your first answer. ("When in doubt, scratch it out!") When you have doubts, your second answer is more likely to be correct (Ramsey et al., 1987).

7. Remember that you are searching for the one *best* answer to each question. Some answers may be partly true, yet flawed in some subtle way. When you are in doubt, try rating each multiple-choice alternative on a 1-to-10 scale. The answer with the highest rating is the one you are looking for.

Essay Tests   Essay questions are a weak spot for students who lack organization, fail to support main ideas, or don't write directly to the question. When you take an essay exam try the following:

1. Read the question carefully. Make sure that you note key words, such as *compare, contrast, discuss, evaluate, analyze,* and *describe*. These words all demand a certain emphasis in your answer.

2. Think about your answer before putting words on paper. It's a good idea to make a brief list of the point you want to make. Just list them as they come to mind. Then rearrange your ideas in the order you want to write them. Elaborate plans or outlines are not necessary and will not improve your grade (Torrance, Thomas, & Robinson, 1991).

3. Don't beat around the bush or pad your answer. Be direct. Make a point and support it. Get your list of ideas into words.

4. Look over your essay for errors in spelling and grammar. Save this for last. Your *ideas* are of first importance. You can work on spelling and grammar separately if they affect your grades. (For your convenience, Figure I–2 ◆ provides a checklist summary of the main study skills we have covered.)

A Final Word

There is a distinction in Zen between "live words" and "dead words." Live words come from personal experiences;

Figure I–2   ◆   Study skills ckecklist.

dead words are "about" a subject. This book can only be a collection of dead words without your personal involvement. It is designed to help you learn psychology, but it cannot do it for you. You will find many helpful, useful, and exciting ideas in the pages that follow. To make them yours, you must set out to *actively* learn as much as you can. The ideas presented here should get you off to a good start. Good luck!

For more information, consult any of the following books.

Annis, L. F. *Study Techniques*. Dubuque, IA: Brown, 1983.

Burka, J. B., and L. M. Yuen. *Procrastination: Why You Do It; What To Do About It*. Menlo Park, CA: Addison-Wesley, 1983.

Campanelli, J. F., and J. L. Price. *Write in Time: Essay Exam Strategies*. Ft. Worth, TX: Holt, Rinehart, & Winston, 1991.

Carman, R. A., and W. R. Adams. *Study Skills: A Student's Guide for Survival*. New York: Wiley, 1985.

Deese, J., and E. K. Deese. *How to Study*. New York: McGraw-Hill, 1979.

Rosnow, R. L., and M. Rosnow. *Writing Papers in Psychology: A Student Guide*. Pacific Grove, CA: Brooks/ Cole, 1995.

Rowe, B. *College Survival Guide: Hints and References to Aid College Students*. St. Paul: West, 1995.

1. The three *R*s in SQ3R stand for "read, recite, and review." T or F?

2. When using the LISAN method, students try to write down as much of a lecture as possible so that their notes are complete. T or F?

3. Spaced study sessions are usually superior to massed practice. T or F?

4. According to recent research, you should almost always stick with your first answer in multiple-choice tests. T or F?

5. To use the technique known as overlearning, you should continue to study after you feel you have begun to master a topic. T or F?

6. Procrastination is related to seeking perfection and equating self-worth with grades. T or F?

Answers:

1. T 2. F 3. T 4. F 5. T 6. T

The Search for Understanding

Preview

Why Study Psychology?

Y ou are a universe, a collection of worlds within worlds. Your brain is possibly the most complicated device in existence. Through its action you are capable of art, music, science, war, philosophy, love, hatred, and charity. You are the most challenging riddle ever written, a mystery at times even to yourself. Your thoughts, emotions, and actions, your behavior and conscious experience, are the subject of this book.

Look around you. Newspapers, radio, magazines, television, and even the Internet abound with psychological information. Psychology is an ever-changing panorama of people and ideas. You can hardly call yourself educated without knowing something about it.

There is another reason for studying psychology. Socrates said, "Know thyself," and while we must envy those who have walked on the moon or cruised the ocean's dream-like depths, the ultimate frontier still lies close to home. What, really, could be more fascinating than a journey of self-discovery?

In a sense, this book is a travel guide. Psychologists can't claim to have "the answers" to all your questions. But we can show you the landscape already explored. More important, psychology can aid your own search for understanding. Ultimately, the answers must be your own, but studying psychology is a rich starting point.

Chapter Survey

Theme: Psychology is both a profession and a natural science.

Key Questions:

Key Topics to Watch for:

What is psychology?	A definition of psychology Psychology's scientific basis
What do psychologists hope to achieve?	Major areas of psychological research Psychology's four basic goals
How did psychology emerge as a field of knowledge?	Important persons in psychology's history Ideas that shaped modern psychology
What are the major perspectives in psychology?	Five ways to view behavior
What roles and specialties are found in psychology and related fields?	Education and licensing of psychologists Kinds of psychologists and what they do
What is critical thinking?	Basic principles of critical thinking
How does psychology differ from false explanations of behavior?	A critique of pseudo-psychologies

Psychology—Spotlight on Behavior

Snapshot: A clinical psychologist devises new ways to treat people who suffer from terrifying nightmares.

Snapshot: A biopsychologist uses computerized brain scans to study vision.

Snapshot: An educational psychologist helps children overcome reading disabilities that could handicap them for life.

Snapshot: A personnel psychologist uses personality tests to help select future police officers.

Snapshot: An experimental psychologist provides striking new insights into how memory operates.

As these images suggest, psychology is an extremely broad field. Psychology is about memory, stress, therapy, love, persuasion, hypnosis, perception, death, conformity, creativity, learning, personality, aging, intelligence, sexuality, emotion, and many, many more topics.

Psychology has become such an enormous and colorful beast that no short description can do it justice. By the time you have read this entire book, you will begin to have an overall picture of what psychology is and what psychologists do.

A Science and Profession   As you may have guessed from our first "snapshots," psychology is both a *science* and a *profession*. Some psychologists are scientists, who do research to enrich human knowledge. Others are practitioners, who apply psychology to solve problems in mental health, education, business, sports, law, and medicine. Many psychologists are both scientists and practitioners.

Later in this chapter we will return to the profession of psychology. For now, let's focus on how psychological knowledge is created.

Defining Psychology

The word *psychology* comes from the roots *psyche*, which means "mind" and *logos*, meaning "knowledge or study." However, the "mind" is notoriously difficult to observe. That's why **psychology** is defined as *the scientific study of human and animal behavior*.

What does behavior refer to in the definition of psychology?

Behavior   Anything you do—eating, sleeping, talking, thinking, or sneezing—is a behavior. So is dreaming, gambling, watching TV, learning Spanish, basket weaving, or reading this book. Of course, we are interested in **overt behaviors** (*observable actions and responses*). However, psychologists also study **covert behaviors**, *which are private, internal activities*, such as thinking or remembering (Kelly & Saklofske, 1994).

Overt behavior can be studied by direct observation. But how do we study mental activities? Often it takes skillful detective work to *deduce* what is happening internally from what can be observed directly. For example, try answering these questions: Is a horse bigger than a mouse? Is a collie bigger than a German shepherd?

If you are like most people, you answered the first question faster than the second. Why? Most people form mental images of the animals to compare their sizes. A slower answer, therefore, suggests that it is more difficult to compare mental images that are similar in size (Moyer & Bayer, 1976). Although we couldn't actually observe thinking, we were able to learn something interesting about it just the same. When a number of indirect observations consistently point to a conclusion, we can be reasonably certain it is correct.

Psychologists are highly trained professionals. In addition to the psychological knowledge they possess, psychologists learn specialized skills in counseling and therapy, measurement and testing, research and experimentation, statistics, diagnosis, treatment, and many other areas.

Empiricism

Psychologists are keenly aware that opinions, or claims made by "authorities," may be wrong. Psychologists therefore have a special respect for **empirical evidence** (*information gained from direct observation and measurement*). Whenever possible, psychologists settle differences by collecting **data** (*observed facts*) (Kimble, 1989). Gathering data allows us to compare observations and draw accurate conclusions. Would you say it's true, for instance, that "You can't teach an old dog new tricks"? Why argue about it? A psychologist would get 10 "new" dogs, 10 "used" dogs, and 10 "old" dogs and then try to teach them all new tricks to find out!

The heart of the empirical attitude is summarized by the phrase, "Let's take a look" (Stanovich, 1996). Here's an example: Have you ever wondered if drivers become more hostile when the weather gets hot and uncomfortable? Psychologists Douglas Kenrick and Steven MacFarlane (1986) decided to collect some data to investigate. Kenrick and MacFarlane parked a car at a green light in a one-lane intersection, in Phoenix, Arizona, in temperatures ranging from 88° to 116°. Then they recorded the number of times other drivers honked at the stalled car, and how long they honked.

The results are shown in Figure 1–1 ◆. As you can see, higher temperatures were closely related to an increase in the amount of time spent leaning on the horn (which may be why cars come equipped with horns and not cannons). While these findings are not surprising, they do add to our understanding of links between discomfort and aggression.

An empirical approach seems natural in fields like biology and physics. Yet, in psychology, we are often tempted to accept what seems reasonable, rather than what *is*. For example, see if you can tell, from your own experience or common sense, which of the items in a brief psychology quiz are true. After you've completed the quiz we will compare your answers with those arrived at empirically.

Psychology Quiz

Are these ideas true or false?

1. If you happened to step on a nail, you would feel it instantly. True or false? (Chapter 3)

2. A one-eyed man could not land an airplane. True or false? (Chapter 7)

3. The apparent size of the moon is greatly magnified by the atmosphere when the moon is low in the sky. True or false? (Chapter 7)

Figure 1–1 ◆ Results of an empirical study. The graph shows that horn honking by frustrated motorists becomes more likely as air temperature increases. This suggests that physical discomfort is associated with interpersonal hostility. Riots and assaults also increase during hot weather. Here we see a steady rise in aggression as temperatures go higher. However, research done by other psychologists has shown that hostile actions that require physical exertion, such as a fist fight, may become *less* likely at very high temperatures. (Data from Kenrick & MacFarlane, 1986.)

4. When hypnotized, witnesses to crimes can be made to have perfect memory of what they saw. True or false? (Chapter 10)

5. Brain activity almost ceases at various times during sleep. True or false? (Chapter 8)

6. Punishment is the most effective way to reinforce the learning of new habits. True or false? (Chapter 9)

7. All memories are permanent, if only there were some way to retrieve them. True or false? (Chapter 10)

8. People who have high IQs are also usually highly creative. True or false? (Chapter 12)

9. The lie detector (polygraph) is highly accurate at identifying attempts to deceive. True or false? (Chapter 13)

10. Stress is almost always bad for you. True or false? (Chapter 14)

11. Intelligence is completely inherited from one's parents. True or false? (Chapter 12)

12. Those who threaten suicide rarely actually commit suicide. True or false? (Chapter 17)

13. Schizophrenics have two or more distinct personalities. True or false? (Chapter 17)

14. If your car breaks down, you are more likely to get help from a passerby on a busy highway than on a lightly traveled country road. True or false? (Chapter 21)

Scoring the quiz is easy. Empirical research has shown that all of the statements are *false*. (To find out why, you may want to look ahead at the chapters cited in parentheses.) If you missed some questions, don't despair. The point is simply this: Psychology became a science when psychologists began to make observations and seek evidence, and you will become a better observer of human behavior if you do the same.

Scientific Observation   Empiricism alone is not enough to make a science. What sets psychology apart is that it applies the scientific method to behavioral questions. True **scientific observation** *is structured so that it answers questions about the world* (Stanovich, 1996). To return to an earlier example, little would be gained if you drove around a city and made haphazard observations of horn honking. To be scientific, observations must be carefully planned and recorded. In the next chapter we will look more closely at how this is done.

Studying certain topics in psychology is still difficult. Sometimes this stems from ethical or practical concerns. More often, questions go unanswered for lack of a suitable **research method** (*a systematic procedure for answering scientific questions*). For example, at one time we had to accept the reports of people who say they never dream. Then the EEG (electroencephalograph, or brain-wave machine) was developed. The EEG can reliably reveal when a person is dreaming. People who "never dream," it turns out, dream frequently. If they are awakened during a dream they vividly remember it. Thus, use of the EEG made the study of dreaming more scientific.

Psychological Research

As you can see, it often takes creativity to find new methods for answering age-old questions. The effort is worthwhile, though. What we know today adds up to a large and highly useful body of knowledge.

What kinds of topics would a research psychologist study?

Here is a sampling of typical research topics.

Developmental Psychology   "In general, **developmental psychologists** *study the course of human growth and development, from conception until death.* I'm especially interested in early childhood. My colleagues and I seek the principles whereby a child develops the ability to think, speak, perceive, and act. Currently, I am studying the effects of stimulating childhood environments on the development of intelligence."

Learning   "I'm also interested in how people get to be the way they are, but in a more abstract sense. I believe that most human behavior is learned. Like other **learning theorists,** *I study how and why learning occurs in humans and animals.* Right now I'm using pigeons to investigate the effects of reinforcement patterns on learning."

The scientific study of dreaming was made possible by use of the EEG, a device that records the tiny electrical potentials generated by the brain as a person sleeps. The EEG converts these electrical potentials to a written record of brain activity. Certain shifts in brain activity, coupled with the presence of rapid eye movements, are strongly related to dreaming. (See Chapter 8 for more information.)

Personality "In many ways my area is both the most rewarding and the most frustrating. **Personality theorists** *study personality traits and dynamics.* We draw on other research areas, as well as our own work, to understand personality structure, motivation, and individual differences. I am particularly interested in the personality profiles of highly creative college students."

Sensation and Perception "How do we come to know the world? How does information 'get into' our nervous systems? How is it processed into meaningful patterns? These are my concerns. **Sensation and perception psychologists** *study the sense organs and the process of perception.* I am using an information-processing theory to study the visual recognition of faces."

The variety and complexity of human behavior make psychological investigation challenging. How would you explain the behaviors shown here?

Comparative Psychology "Comparative psychologists *study and compare the behavior of different species, especially animals.* Personally, I am fascinated by the echolocation abilities of porpoises. In a typical study, we ask porpoises to select between different shapes underwater, while blindfolded. If they choose the right target we reward them with food. Their ability to discriminate in this way is superb."

Biopsychology "The brain and nervous system are my meat . . . so to speak. I believe that ultimately all other areas in psychology—learning, perception, even personality and abnormal behavior—will be explained by the action of nerve cells and brain chemicals. **Biopsychologists** *study the relationship between behavior and biological processes, especially activities in the nervous system.* I've been doing some exciting research on hunger. Altering the hypothalamus in the brain will cause a rat to eat and gain weight until it looks like a furry water balloon. If I remove an area just a few millimeters away, the rat will starve if not force-fed."

The Psychology of Gender "**Gender psychologists** *study differences between females and males and how they develop.* I want to understand how gender differences are influenced by factors such as biology, child rearing, education, and stereotypes. Much of my research has centered on how we learn basic 'male' and 'female' identities. For example, I've observed that girls are praised for playing with 'nurturing,' or 'female' toys, whereas boys are belittled for doing the same thing."

Social Psychology "**Social psychologists** *are interested in human social behavior,* such as attitudes, social influence, riots, conformity, leadership, racism, friendship, and many other topics. My own interest is interpersonal attraction. I place two strangers together in a room for a short time and investigate factors that affect their degree of attraction toward each other."

Cultural Psychology "**Cultural psychologists** *study the ways in which culture affects human behavior.* The language you speak, the foods you eat, how your parents disciplined you, what laws you obey, who you regard as 'family,' whether you eat with a spoon or your fingers—these and countless other details of behavior are strongly influenced by culture. For the last 5 years I have been comparing early child development in North America, Mexico, India, and Central Africa." This small sample should give you an idea of the diversity of psychological research. It also hints at some of the kinds of information covered later in this book.

Research involving animals was mentioned in some of the preceding examples. Why is that?

Animals and Psychology It may surprise you to learn that as a group, psychologists are interested in natural laws governing the behavior of *any* living creature—from flatworms to humans. Indeed, comparative psychologists often

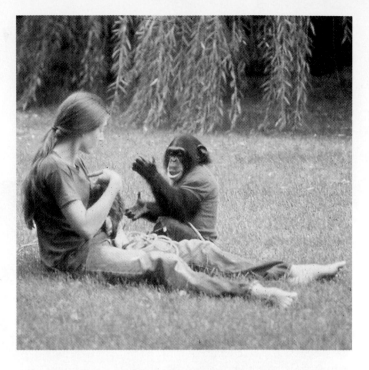

Some of the most interesting research with animals has focused on attempts to teach primates to communicate using sign language. Such research has led to better methods for teaching language to aphasic children (children with serious language impairment). (See Chapter 11 for more information.)

spend their entire careers studying rats, cats, dogs, turtles, chimpanzees, or other animals. In general, animals are the subject of about 8 percent of all psychological research (American Psychological Association, 1995).

Animal models are used in psychology *to discover principles that apply to human behavior.* Studies of obesity, memory, stress, psychosis, therapy, aging, and many other topics, have been enriched by animal research. More importantly, animal models provide the *only* information available on some subjects. For instance, most of what is known about the brain is based on animal research.

Psychology also benefits animals. Behavioral research has helped identify ways to avoid the killing of coyotes, crows, deer, and other animals that destroy crops or livestock. Likewise, the proper care of endangered species in zoos relies on behavioral research (Miller, 1985b). For such reasons, animals are very much a part of psychology. In fact, a government panel (which included animal welfare advocates) concluded that in psychology there is often no substitute for ethically done animal research (Fisher, 1986). (The animal rights movement and the ethics of animal research are discussed in the "Exploration" section of Chapter 2.)

Psychology's Goals What do psychologists hope to achieve? In general, the goals of psychology as a science are to *describe, understand, predict,* and *control* behavior. Beyond that, psychology's ultimate goal is to gather knowledge to benefit humanity (Kimble, 1989).

Description What do psychology's goals mean in practice? Assume that we would like to answer the following questions: What happens when the right side of the brain is injured? Is there more than one type of memory? How does creative problem solving differ from ordinary thinking? Do autistic children react abnormally to their parents? The answer to each question requires a careful description of behavior. **Description,** *or naming and classifying,* is typically based on making a detailed record of behavioral observations.

But a description doesn't explain anything, does it?

Right. Useful knowledge begins with accurate description, but descriptions fail to answer the important "why" questions. *Why* do more women attempt suicide, and *why* do more men complete it? *Why* are people more aggressive when they are uncomfortable? *Why* are bystanders often unwilling to help in an emergency?

Understanding Psychology's second goal is met when we can explain an event. That is, **understanding** usually means we can *state the causes of a behavior.* Take our last "why" question as an example. Research on "bystander apathy" has shown that people often fail to help when *other* possible helpers are nearby. Why? Because a "diffusion of responsibility" occurs, so no one feels required to pitch in. Generally, the larger the number of potential helpers present, the less likely it is that help will be given (Darley & Latané, 1968). Now we can explain a perplexing problem. (See Chapter 21 for more details.)

Prediction Psychology's third goal, **prediction,** *is the ability to accurately forecast behavior.* Notice that our explanation of bystander apathy makes a prediction about the chances of getting help. Anyone who has been stranded by car trouble on a busy freeway will recognize the accuracy of this prediction.

Behavioral predictions are often quite useful. For instance, research predicts that you will suffer less jet lag if you fly east early in the day and west late in the day. (See Chapter 8 to learn why.) Prediction is especially important in **psychometrics** (*mental measurement*). Experts in this area use tests to predict success in school, work, or a career.

Description, explanation, and prediction seem reasonable, but is control a valid goal for psychology?

Control Psychology's most misunderstood goal is control, probably because it seems to threaten personal freedom. However, **control** simply means *altering conditions that influence behavior in predictable ways.* If a psychologist suggests changes in a classroom that help children learn better, she has exerted control. If she helps a person overcome a crippling fear of heights, control is involved. Control is also an element of designing airplanes to reduce pilot errors. Clearly, psychology can change behavior. But, as is true of other types of knowledge, psychological principles must be used wisely and humanely (Kipnis, 1987).

In summary, psychology's goals are a natural outgrowth of our desire to understand behavior. For the many topics studied in psychology, the goals boil down to asking:

What is the nature of this behavior? (description)

Why does it occur? (explanation)

Can we predict when it will occur? (prediction)

What conditions affect it? (control)

Some psychologists specialize in administering, scoring, and interpreting psychological tests, such as tests of intelligence, creativity, personality, or aptitude.

To improve your memory of this chapter, see if you can answer these questions. If you miss any, skim over the preceding material before continuing, to make sure you understand what you have just read.

1. Psychology is the _____ study of the _____ of humans and animals.

2. Information gained through direct observation and measurement is called _____ evidence.

3. In psychological research animal _____ may be used to discover principles that apply to human behavior.

Match the following research areas with the topics they cover.

4. _____ Developmental psychology   **A.** Attitudes, groups, leadership

5. _____ Learning   **B.** Conditioning, memory

6. _____ Personality   **C.** The psychology of law

7. _____ Sensation and perception   **D.** Brain and nervous system

8. _____ Biopsychology   **E.** Child psychology

9. _____ Social psychology   **F.** Individual differences, motivation

10. _____ Comparative psychology   **G.** Animal behavior

                              H. Processing sensory information

11. Which of the following questions relates most directly to the goal of understanding behavior?
    a. Do the scores of men and women differ on tests of thinking abilities?
    b. Why does a blow to the head cause memory loss?
    c. Will productivity in a business office increase if room temperature is raised or lowered?
    d. What percentage of college students suffer from test anxiety?

12. All sciences are interested in controlling the phenomena they study. True or false?

Answers:

1. scientific, behavior 2. empirical 3. model 4. E 5. B 6. F 7. H 8. D 9. A 10. G 11. b 12. F (Astronomy and archaeology are examples of sciences that do not share psychology's fourth goal.)

A Brief History— Psychology's Family Album

Psychology has a long past but a short history. Psychology's past is centuries old because it includes **philosophy,** *the study of knowledge, reality, and human nature.* In contrast, psychology's history is short, beginning only about 100 years ago. As sciences go, psychology is the new kid on the block: Easily 9 out of 10 persons to ever work in the field are alive today. Of course, to some students any history is "not short enough"! Yet, the ideas in psychology's past are intimately tied to the present. To understand where psychology is now, let's take a brief look at its short history.

1B *PsychNow!*

Into the Lab Psychology's history as a science began in 1879 in Leipzig, Germany. There, the "father of psychology," **Wilhelm Wundt** (VILL-helm Voont), *set up the first psychological laboratory to study conscious experience.* How, he wondered, are sensations, images, and feelings formed? To find out, Wundt observed and carefully measured *stimuli* of various kinds (lights, sounds, weights). A **stimulus** *is any physical energy that has some effect on an organism and that evokes a response* (stimulus: singular; stimuli [STIM-you-lie]: plu-

ral). Wundt then used **introspection,** *or "looking inward,"* to probe his reactions to various stimuli. If you stop reading for a moment, and examine your own thoughts, feelings, and sensations, you will have used introspection. Wundt called his own approach **experimental self-observation,** *because it combined trained introspection with objective measurement.* Over the years, he studied vision, hearing, taste, touch, reaction time, memory, time perception, and many other subjects (Lieberman, 1979). By insisting on careful observation and measurement, Wundt got psychology off to a good start.

Structuralism

Wundt's ideas were carried to the United States by one of his students, a man named Edward B. Titchener (TICH-in-er). In America, Wundt's ideas became known as *structuralism* because they dealt with the structure of mental life. That is, the **structuralists** *hoped to analyze experience into basic "elements" or "building blocks."*

How could they do that? You can't analyze experience like you can a chemical compound, can you?

Perhaps not, but the structuralists tried, mostly by using introspection. In this approach, an observer might heft an apple and then decide that she or he had experienced the

Wilhelm Wundt, 1832–1920. Wundt is credited with making psychology an independent science, separate from philosophy. Wundt's original training was in medicine, but he became deeply interested in psychology. In his laboratory, Wundt investigated how sensations, images, and feelings combine to make up personal experience.

William James, 1842–1910. William James was the son of philosopher Henry James, Sr., and the brother of novelist Henry James. During his long academic career, James taught anatomy, physiology, psychology, and philosophy at Harvard University. James believed strongly that ideas should be judged in terms of their practical consequences for human conduct.

elements "hue" (color), "roundness," and "weight." Another example of the kind of question that might have interested a structuralist is, What basic tastes mix together to create complex flavors as different as liver, lime, bacon, or burnt-almond fudge?

It soon became clear that introspection was a poor way to answer many questions, because the structuralists frequently *disagreed*. And when they did, there was no way to settle differences. If two researchers came up with different lists of basic taste sensations, for example, who could say which was right? Despite such limitations, "looking inward" still has a role. Studies of hypnosis, meditation, drug effects, problem solving, moods, and many other topics would be incomplete if people did not describe their private experiences (*e.g.*, Mayer & Hanson, 1995).

Functionalism William James, an American scholar, broadened psychology to include animal behavior, religious experience, abnormal behavior, and other interesting topics. James' first book, *Principles of Psychology* (1890), helped establish psychology as a serious discipline. It was so brilliant that it is still in print today.

The term **functionalism** comes from an interest in *how the mind functions to adapt us to our environment.* To James, consciousness was an ever-changing *stream* or *flow* of images and sensations—not a set of lifeless building blocks, as the structuralists claimed.

The functionalists were influenced by Charles Darwin, who deduced that creatures evolve in ways that favor their survival. According to Darwin's principle of **natural selection**, *physical features which help animals adapt to their environments are retained in evolution.* Similarly, the functionalists wanted to find out how human behaviors, such as thinking, perception, habits, and emotions aid survival. In short, they wanted to study the mind *in use.*

What effect did functionalism have on modern psychology?

Functionalism brought the study of animals into psychology. It also promoted **educational psychology,** *which is the study of learning, teaching, classroom dynamics, and related topics.* Learning makes us more adaptable, and the functionalists sought ways to improve education. Functionalism also spurred the rise of **industrial psychology,** *the study of people at work.* (See Chapter 22.)

Behaviorism Functionalism was soon challenged by **behaviorism,** *the study of overt, observable behavior.* Behaviorist John B. Watson objected to defining psychology as the study of the "mind" or "conscious experience." "Introspection," he said, "is unscientific." Watson realized that he could study animal behavior even though he couldn't ask animals questions, or know what they were thinking. He simply observed the relationship between **stimuli** (*events in the environment*) and an animal's **responses** (*any muscular action, glandular activity, or other identifiable behavior*). Why not, he argued, apply the same objectivity to studying humans (Watson, 1994)?

Watson soon adopted Russian physiologist Ivan Pavlov's (ee-VAHN PAV-lahv) concept of conditioning to explain most behavior. A **conditioned response** *is a learned reaction to a particular stimulus.* Watson enthusiastically proclaimed, "Give me a dozen healthy infants, well-formed, and my own special world to bring them up in and I'll guarantee to take any one at random and train him to become any type of specialist I might select—doctor, lawyer, artist, merchant-chief, and yes, beggarman and thief" (Watson, 1913).

Would most psychologists agree with Watson's claim?

Today, most would consider it an overstatement. Just the same, behaviorism profoundly affected psychology by helping to make it a natural science, rather than a branch of philosophy (Richelle, 1995).

One of the best-known modern behaviorists, B. F. Skinner (1904–1990), said, "In order to understand human behavior we must take into account what the environment does to an organism before and after it responds. Behavior is shaped and maintained by its consequences" (Skinner, 1971). As a "radical behaviorist," Skinner believed that mental events are unnecessary to explain behavior (Richelle, 1995).

John B. Watson, 1878–1958. Watson's intense interest in observable behavior began with his doctoral studies in biology and neurology. Watson became a psychology professor at Johns Hopkins University in 1908 and advanced his theory of behaviorism. He remained at Johns Hopkins until 1920 when he left for a career in the advertising industry!

B. F. Skinner, American Behaviorist

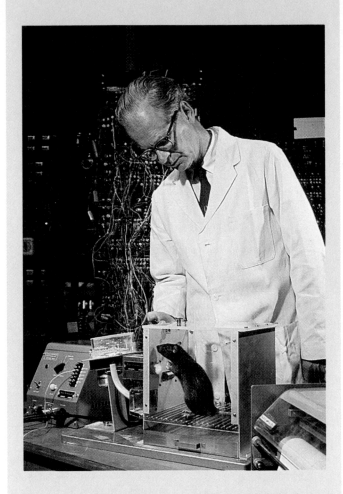

B. F. Skinner, 1904–1990. Skinner studied simple behaviors under carefully controlled conditions. In addition to advancing psychology, he hoped that his radical brand of behaviorism would improve human life. Skinner was the first person to receive the American Psychological Association's citation for lifetime contributions to psychology.

Burrhus Frederic Skinner, who died in 1990 at age 86, was fascinating and controversial. Skinner believed that our behavior is controlled by rewards, or positive reinforcers.

To study learning, Skinner created his famous conditioning chamber or "Skinner Box" (Fig. 1–2 ◆). With it, Skinner could present stimuli to laboratory animals and record specific responses (see Chapter 9, "Operant Conditioning"). Many of Skinner's ideas about learning grew out of work with rats and pigeons.

Figure 1–2 ◆ The Skinner Box is used to study learning in simplified animal experiments.

Nevertheless, he believed that the same laws of behavior apply to all organisms, including humans.

Skinner was convinced that we could benefit from a "designed culture," in which positive reinforcement would encourage desirable behavior. (Contrary to common belief, Skinner disliked the use of punishment.) It is essential, he said, to change our behavior before overpopulation, pollution, or nuclear war shatters humanity. Too often, he believed, misguided rewards lead us into destructive actions.

Among the general public, B. F. Skinner was perhaps best known as the man who taught pigeons to play table tennis (see Chapter 9), as the inventor of teaching machines, and as the creator of a mechanical "baby tender" that looked suspiciously like a big Skinner Box. Skinner's own daughter Deborah lived for 2 1/2 years in the baby tender—a crib-sized chamber with warm filtered air, sound-absorbing walls, special toys, and a large window on one side. "How dehumanizing!" said the critics. But contrary to news reports, Deborah was frequently taken out of the box for cuddling and play. As an adult, she said, "I think I was a very happy baby. Most of the criticisms of the box are by people who don't understand what it was." The same is true of many criticisms of Skinner, which are often based on a misunderstanding of his ideas (DeBell & Harless, 1992).

Of course, not all critics have misunderstood Skinner. The behaviorist emphasis on visible behavior does tend to ignore thinking. This has led some observers to the tongue-in-cheek charge that Skinnerian psychology has "lost consciousness." However, many such criticisms are answered by **cognitive behaviorism,** *a broader view that combines thinking and environmental control to explain behavior.*

(Sperry, 1995). Nevertheless, strict behaviorism is alive and well and has many advocates.

Behaviorists deserve credit for discovering much of what we know about learning, conditioning, and the proper use of reward and punishment. Behavior modification is another valuable product of behaviorism. In **behavior modification,** *learning principles are used to change problem behaviors* such as overeating, unrealistic fears, or temper tantrums. (See Chapter 19 for more information.)

Gestalt Psychology Imagine that you have just played "Happy Birthday" on a tuba. Next you play it on a high-pitched violin. None of the sounds made by the tuba are duplicated by the violin. Yet, the melody will still be recognizable—as long as the *relationship* between notes is the same. Now, what if you played the original notes in the correct order, but at a rate of one per hour? What would we have? Nothing. The separated notes would no longer be a melody. Perceptually, the melody is somehow more than the individual notes that define it. It was observations such as these that launched the *Gestalt* school of thought. **Gestalt psychology** *emphasizes the study of thinking, learning, and perception in whole units, not by analysis into parts.* The Gestaltists' slogan was "The whole is greater than the sum of its parts." (See Figure 1–3 ◆.)

The German word *Gestalt* (geh-SHTALT) means "form," "pattern," or "whole." The Gestalt viewpoint was first advanced by Max Wertheimer (VERT-hi-mer), a German psychologist. It is a mistake, he said, to analyze psychological events into pieces, or "elements," as the structuralists did. As with a melody, many experiences resist analysis into smaller units. For this reason, the Gestalt viewpoint remains influential in the study of perception and

Max Wertheimer, 1880–1941. Wertheimer first proposed the Gestalt viewpoint to help explain perceptual illusions. He later promoted Gestalt psychology as a way to understand not only perception, problem solving, thinking, and social behavior, but also art, logic, philosophy, and politics.

Mary Calkins, 1863–1930.

Figure 1–3 ◆ The design you see here is entirely made up of the two elements shown below it. If you stare at the design for a moment, you should quickly see that as a whole it contains patterns and complexities that greatly exceed the sum of its parts.

personality. It is also the basis for a type of psychotherapy. If you are curious about what Gestalt therapy is like, look ahead to Chapter 19.

Were all the early psychologists men? So far, no women have been mentioned.

For the most part, men dominated science and education at the turn of the century. Nevertheless, women were active in psychology from its beginning.

Women in Psychology

Histories of psychology are rich in "forefathers" but seldom mention women. In fact, women were actively discouraged from seeking advanced degrees in the late 1800s (Bohan, 1990). Even so, by 1906 in America about 1 psychologist in every 10 was a woman. Who were these "foremothers" of psychology? Three who

became well known are Mary Calkins, Christine Ladd-Franklin, and Margaret Washburn.

Mary Calkins did valuable research on memory. She was also the first woman president of the American Psychological Association, in 1905. Christine Ladd-Franklin studied color vision. In 1906 she was ranked as one of the 50 most important psychologists in America. In 1908, Margaret Washburn published an influential textbook on animal behavior, titled *The Animal Mind.*

The first woman to be awarded a Ph.D. in psychology was Margaret Washburn, in 1894. Over the next 15 years many more women followed her pioneering lead. Today, 2 out of 3 graduate students in

Christine Ladd-Franklin, 1847–1930.

Margaret Washburn, 1871–1939.

Sigmund Freud, 1856–1939. For over 50 years, Freud probed the unconscious mind. In doing so, he altered modern views of human nature. His early experimentation with a "talking cure" for hysteria is regarded as the beginning of psychoanalysis. Through psychoanalysis, Freud added psychological treatment methods to psychiatry.

psychology are women. And, in recent years, nearly 75 percent of all college graduates with a major in psychology have been women. Clearly, psychology has become fully open to both men and women. (Sources: Furumoto & Scarborough, 1986; Howard et al., 1986; Madigan & O'Hara, 1992; Martin, 1995.)

Psychodynamic Psychology As the mainstream of psychology grew more scientific, an Austrian physician named Sigmund Freud was developing his own theory of behavior. Freud's point of departure was his belief that mental life is like an iceberg: only a small portion is exposed to view. According to Freud, a part of the mind called the **unconscious** *lies outside of personal awareness.* Freud believed our behavior is constantly influenced by unconscious thoughts, impulses, and desires. This idea added a new dimension to art, literature, and history, as well as psychology.

Freud theorized that many unconscious thoughts are of a threatening, sexual, or aggressive nature. Hence, they are **repressed** (*actively held out of awareness*). But sometimes, he said, they are revealed by dreams, emotions, or slips of the tongue. ("Freudian slips" are often humorous, as when a student who is tardy for class says, "I'm sorry I couldn't get here any later.") Freud also insisted that all thoughts, emotions, and actions are *determined* (nothing is an accident). He brought new awareness of the importance of childhood in later personality development ("The child is father to the man"). Most of all, perhaps, Freud is known for creating **psychoanalysis,** *a method of psychotherapy that explores unconscious conflicts and emotional problems* (see Chapter 19).

Freud had not held sway for very long before some of his students began to break away from him. These psychologists modified Freud's ideas and became known as neo-Freudians

(*neo* means "new" or "recent"). **Neo-Freudians** *accept the broad features of Freud's theory but revise parts of it.* Some well-known neo-Freudians are Alfred Adler, Anna Freud (Freud's daughter), Karen Horney (HORN-eye), Carl Jung (yoong), and Otto Rank (rahnk). Today, Freud's ideas have been altered and adapted to the point that few strictly psychoanalytic psychologists are left. However, Freud's legacy is still evident in various **psychodynamic theories,** *which emphasize internal motives, conflicts, and unconscious forces.*

Humanistic Psychology

A fairly recent view known as **humanism** *focuses on understanding human experience.* Humanism is sometimes called the "third force" in psychology (psychodynamic psychology and behaviorism are the other two). In general, humanistic psychologists are interested in human problems, potentials, and ideals.

How is the humanistic approach different from others?

Psychologists Carl Rogers, Abraham Maslow, and others developed humanism as a reply to the negativity they saw in earlier views. Humanists reject the Freudian idea that personality is ruled by unconscious forces. They are also uncomfortable with the behavioristic idea that we are controlled by the environment. Both views have a strong undercurrent of **determinism,** *the idea that behavior is determined by forces beyond our control.* In contrast, the

Table 1–1 ■ The Early Development of Psychology

Approximate Origin	Date	Notable Events
Experimental psychology	1875	■ First psychology course offered by William James
	1878	■ First American Ph.D. in psychology awarded
	1879	■ Wilhelm Wundt establishes first psychology laboratory in Germany
	1883	■ First American psychology lab founded at Johns Hopkins University
	1886	■ First American psychology textbook published by John Dewey
Structuralism	1898	■ Edward Titchener advances psychology based on introspection
Functionalism	1890	■ James publishes *Principles of Psychology*
	1892	■ American Psychological Association founded
Psychoanalytic psychology	1895	■ Sigmund Freud publishes first studies
	1900	■ Freud publishes *The Interpretation of Dreams*
Behaviorism	1906	■ Ivan Pavlov reports his research on conditioning
	1913	■ John Watson presents behavioristic view
Gestalt psychology	1912	■ Max Wertheimer and others advance Gestalt viewpoint
Neo-Freudianism	1914	■ Carl Jung breaks with Freud

humanists stress **free will,** *the human ability to make choices.* Humanists do admit that past experiences affect personality. However, they also believe that people can freely *choose* to live more creative, meaningful, and satisfying lives.

Humanists helped stimulate interest in psychological needs for love, self-esteem, belonging, self-expression, creativity, and spirituality. Such needs, they believe, are as important as our biological needs for food and water. For example, newborn infants deprived of human love may die just as surely as they would if deprived of food.

How scientific is the humanistic approach?

Humanists collect data and seek evidence to support their ideas, but they tend to be less interested in treating psychology as an objective, behavioral science. Instead, they stress the importance of such subjective factors as one's self-image, self-evaluation, and frame of reference. **Self-image** *is your perception of your own body, personality, and capabilities.* **Self-evaluation** *refers to the positive and negative feelings you have about yourself.* A **frame of reference** *is a mental or emotional perspective used for evaluating events.* Thus,

humanists seek to understand how people perceive themselves and experience the world.

A unique feature of the humanistic approach is Maslow's self-actualization concept. **Self-actualization** *is the process of developing one's potential fully and becoming the best person possible.* According to the humanists, everyone has this potential. The humanists seek ways to help it emerge. (Return to Table 1–1 ■ for a summary of psychology's early development.)

Psychology Today—Five Views of Behavior

At one time, schools of thought in psychology were almost like political parties. Loyalty to each view was fierce, and clashes were common. Today, viewpoints such as functionalism and Gestalt psychology have been incorporated into

Abraham Maslow, 1908–1970. As a founder of humanistic psychology, Maslow was interested in studying people of exceptional mental health. Such self-actualized people, he believed, make full use of their talents and abilities. Maslow offered his positive view of human potential as an alternative to the schools of behaviorism and psychoanalysis.

newer, broader perspectives. Also, some early schools of thought, such as structuralism, have disappeared entirely. Certainly, loyalties and specialties still exist. But many psychologists now are **eclectic** (ek-LEK-tik: *drawing from many sources*) and embrace a variety of theoretical views. Even so, five major perspectives are evident in modern psychology. These are the *behavioristic, humanistic,* and *psychodynamic* views, plus the increasingly important *cognitive* and *biopsychological* perspectives (Table 1–2 ■).

The value of biological approaches for understanding behavior has risen dramatically. As noted earlier, biopsychologists believe that eventually we will be able to explain all behavior in terms of physical mechanisms, such as brain activity and genetics. This optimism is based on exciting new knowledge about how the brain relates to thinking, feelings, perception, abnormal behavior, and other important topics.

A similar trend is occurring in cognitive psychology. Cognition means "thinking" or "knowing." **Cognitive psychologists** *study thoughts, expectations, memory, language, perception, problem solving, consciousness, creativity, and other mental processes.* Some of these topics were neglected for so many years that psychology can be said to have recently "regained consciousness." Computer models of human thinking have been especially important in spurring recent advances in cognitive psychology.

Table 1–2 ■ Five Ways to Look at Behavior

PSYCHODYNAMIC VIEW

Key Idea: *Behavior is directed by forces within one's personality which are often hidden or unconscious.*

Emphasizes internal impulses, desires, and conflicts—especially those that are unconscious; views behavior as the result of clashing forces within personality; somewhat negative, pessimistic view of human nature.

BEHAVIORISTIC VIEW

Key Idea: *Behavior is shaped and controlled by one's environment.*

Emphasizes the study of observable behavior and the effects of learning; stresses the influence of external rewards and punishments; neutral, scientific, somewhat mechanistic view of human nature.

HUMANISTIC VIEW

Key Idea: *Behavior is guided by one's self-image, by subjective perceptions of the world, and by needs for personal growth.*

Focuses on subjective, conscious experience, human problems, potentials, and ideals; emphasizes self-image and self-actualization to explain behavior; positive, philosophical view of human nature.

BIOPSYCHOLOGICAL VIEW

Key Idea: *Human and animal behavior is the result of internal physical, chemical, and biological processes.*

Seeks to explain behavior through activity of the brain and nervous system, physiology, genetics, the endocrine system, biochemistry, and evolution; neutral, reductionistic, mechanistic view of human nature.

COGNITIVE VIEW

Key Idea: *Much human behavior can be understood in terms of the mental processing of information.*

Concerned with thinking, knowing, perception, understanding, memory, decision making, and judgment; explains behavior in terms of information processing; neutral, somewhat computer-like view of human nature.

Behavior in Perspective

Each of the five major perspectives adds to our understanding of human behavior. Consider, for example, a student who has become deeply depressed during her first year at college. Marcia's grades have fallen, she sleeps all the time, and she barely speaks to other students. Let's see what each viewpoint might say about Marcia's depression.

Psychodynamic psychologist: "It's interesting that Marcia broke up with her boyfriend shortly before she became depressed. Depression is often related to loss. Marcia may be unconsciously turning feelings of loss, anger, or rejection into self-blame and self-hate."

Behaviorist: "I've noticed that Marcia's grades were mediocre before her depression began and that they have dropped further. When rewards, such as grades, affection, friendship, or approval are withdrawn, studying and other activities can grind to a halt. As Marcia became depressed, her behavior may have changed in ways that made it even less likely that she would be rewarded with successes, praise, and affection."

Humanistic psychologist: "Because Marcia got good grades in high school, she may have been unprepared for the difficulty of college. If being intelligent and competent is important to her self-image, she may be threatened by her poor performance. The break-up with her boyfriend could be a similar threat. I believe that she may be feeling depressed, vulnerable, and confused because of such threats to her self-image and self-esteem."

Biopsychologist: "Heredity can influence whether a person is prone to depression. I would like to know if there is a history of depression in Marcia's family. Also, depression can be caused by changes in brain chemistry, regardless of a person's life circumstances. Marcia might have a medical problem that needs treatment."

Cognitive psychologist: "Marcia's depression might be explained by her thinking patterns. For example, she could be magnifying the importance of bad things that have happened to her recently. She may also have unrealistic beliefs that lead to depression, such as, 'I must be completely competent and achieving to be a worthwhile person,' or 'I must always be loved and approved by every significant person in my life.' "

As you can see, it is helpful to view human behavior from more than one perspective. This is also true in another sense. We are rapidly becoming a multicultural society, made up of people from many different nations. How has this affected psychology?

The Challenge of Human Diversity

Much of what we think, feel, and do is influenced by the social and cultural worlds in which we live. For instance, imagine that you are a psychologist. Your client, Linda, who is a Native American, tells you that spirits live in the trees near her home. Is Linda suffering from a delusion? Is she abnormal?

To fully understand human behavior, personal differences based on age, race, culture, ethnicity, gender, and sexual orientation must be taken into account.

Obviously, you will misjudge Linda's mental health if you fail to take her cultural background into account.

Human diversity teaches us to be wary of using false standards when comparing groups. For example, let's say an observer notes that child-rearing practices in Culture A are very "indulgent." What does that tell us? Is child care *inferior* in Culture A? Actually, it probably means that the observer used his or her own culture as a standard. Child rearing in Culture A may be more relaxed than it is in our own, but it could be less indulgent than child care in many other cultures.

Age, race, ethnicity, gender, religion, and sexual orientation all have an impact on our behavior patterns. Yet all too often, the unstated standard for judging what is "average" or "normal" is the behavior of white, middle-class males. To understand human behavior, psychologists need to know how people differ, as well as the ways in which we are all alike. For the same reason, an appreciation of human diversity can enrich your life, as well as your understanding of psychology. (Sources: Denmark, 1994; Graham, 1992; Sampson, 1993; Shweder & Sullivan, 1993; Tavris, 1992.)

In a moment, we will further explore what psychologists do and identify some of their specialties. First, see if you can correctly match the items in the following Learning Check.

Match:

1. _____ Philosophy
2. _____ Wundt
3. _____ Structuralism
4. _____ Functionalism
5. _____ Behaviorism
6. _____ Gestalt
7. _____ Psychodynamic
8. _____ Humanistic
9. _____ Cognitive
10. _____ Washburn
11. _____ Biopsychology

A. Against analysis; studied whole experiences
B. "Mental chemistry" and introspection
C. Emphasizes self-actualization and personal growth
D. Interested in unconscious causes of behavior
E. Gave rise to educational and industrial psychology
F. First woman Ph.D. in psychology
G. Studied stimuli and responses, conditioning
H. Part of psychology's "long past"
I. Concerned with thinking, language, problem solving
J. Used "experimental self-observation"
K. Relates behavior to the brain, physiology, and genetics
L. Also known as engineering psychology

12. Modern sciences like psychology are built on observations that can be verified by two or more independent observers. Did structuralism meet this standard?

Answers:

12. No, it did not. The downfall of structuralism was that each observer examined the contents of his or her own mind—which is something that no other person can observe.

1. H 2. J 3. B 4. E 5. G 6. A 7. D 8. C 9. I 10. F 11. K

Psychologists—Guaranteed Not to Shrink

What is the difference between a psychologist and a psychiatrist? About $30 an hour. (And going up.)

Confusion often exists about the differences among psychologists, psychiatrists, psychoanalysts, counselors, and other mental health professionals. It is quite inaccurate to think of them all as "shrinks." Each title reflects distinct differences in training and emphasis.

A **psychologist** *is highly trained in the methods, factual knowledge, and theories of psychology.* Psychologists usually have a master's degree or a doctorate. These degrees typically require from 3 to 8 years of postgraduate training in theory and research methods. Psychologists may teach, do research, give psychological tests, or serve as consultants to business, industry, government, or the military.

A Closer Look:

Psychologists—Perceptions and Realities

A recent survey of what people know about psychologists revealed some common misunderstandings.

Public perception: Most psychologists work in private practice.
Reality: Only 1 psychologist out of 4 works in private practice. Most psychologists are employed by schools, businesses, social agencies, and other organizations.

Public perception: Most psychologists work in clinics or hospitals.
Reality: Only 13 percent of psychologists work in clinics or hospitals. The interests and specialties of psychologists are extremely varied. They are not all therapists.

Public perception: Most practicing psychologists do not hold doctoral degrees.
Reality: Doctoral-level training is required to obtain a license to practice psychology. Most professional psychologists hold doctoral degrees.

Public perception: A psychologist's job is to help people.
Reality: In this instance, the public view is mostly correct. About 75 percent of all psychologists do help people directly. In addition, nearly all psychologists aid people in one way or another. For example, research psychologists help people by providing valuable information about human behavior (Peterson, 1995).

Psychologists interested in emotional problems specialize in clinical or counseling psychology (see Table 1–3). **Clinical psychologists** *treat psychological problems or do research on clinical topics.* **Counseling psychologists** *treat milder emotional and behavioral disturbances.* Counseling psychology used to be limited to problems such as adjustment at work or school. Now, however, many counseling psychologists are mainly doing psychotherapy. As a result, differences between counseling and clinical psychology are beginning to fade (Tyler, 1992).

To enter the profession of psychology, it is best to have a doctorate (Ph.D., Psy.D., or Ed.D.). Most clinical psychologists hold a Ph.D. degree and follow a **scientist-**

practitioner model, *in which they are trained to do either scientific research or therapy* (O'Sullivan & Quevillon, 1992). Many do both. Other clinical psychologists earn the Psy.D. (Doctor of Psychology) degree, which emphasizes practical clinical skills, rather than research (Hershey, Kopplin, & Cornell, 1991).

What kinds of positions are available to people with master's degrees in psychology?

Earning a doctoral degree opens doors to the widest range of employment. However, many master's-level psychologists find jobs in specialties such as human factors engineering, school psychology, psychometrics, industrial psychology, general psychology, and community college teaching (Murray, 1995).

Other Mental Health Professionals

A **psychiatrist** *is a medical doctor who specializes in treating mental disorders.* Psychiatrists are usually "talking doctors" who spend much of their time doing psychotherapy. However, they may also use medical procedures and prescribe drugs, which is something a psychologist cannot do. This distinction may disappear, however. A majority of psychologists believe that they should be granted prescription privileges after receiving additional training. Those who support this change point out that psychologists now do everything psychiatrists do, except prescribe drugs. It will be interesting to see if lawmakers agree (DeLeon, Sammons, & Sexton, 1995).

To be a psychoanalyst, you must have a moustache and goatee, spectacles, a German accent, and a well-padded couch—or so the TV and movie stereotype goes. Actually, to become a **psychoanalyst**, *you must have an M.D. or Ph.D. degree plus further specialized training in the theory and practice of Freudian psychoanalysis.* In other words, either a physician or a psychologist may become an analyst by completing more training in a specific type of psychotherapy. Analysts typically undergo psychoanalysis themselves before applying the method to others.

Is psychoanalysis widely used?

Traditional Freudian analysis is expensive and time consuming. As a result, psychoanalysts are becoming a rare breed, and fewer clients seek analysis. Many modern psychotherapists prefer a flexible and eclectic approach, rather than applying only a single method of therapy.

In many states, counselors also do mental health work. A **counselor** *is an adviser who helps solve problems with marriage, career, school, work, or the like.* To be a licensed counselor (such as a marriage and family counselor, a child counselor, or a school counselor) typically requires a master's degree plus one or two years of full-time supervised counseling experience. Almost all of a counselor's postgraduate education is related to practical helping skills. Counselors are not as highly trained as counseling psychologists or clinical psychologists and do not treat serious mental disorders.

Psychiatric social workers play an important role in many mental health programs. **Psychiatric social workers** *apply social science principles to help patients in clinics and hospitals.* Most psychiatric social workers hold an M.S.W. (Master of Social Work) degree. Often, they assist psychologists and psychiatrists as part of a team. Their typical duties include evaluating patients and families, conducting group psychotherapy, or visiting a patient's home, school, or job to alleviate problems.

Does a person have to have a license to practice psychology?

The Profession of Psychology

Before the American Psychological Association (APA) began a push for licensing and certification, it was possible in many states for anyone to purchase an inexpensive license and "hang out a shingle" as a "psychologist." Now a person must meet rigorous educational requirements to be legally called a psychologist. To work as a clinical or counseling psychologist, she or he must have a license issued by a state examining board. However, the law does not prevent you from calling yourself anything else you choose—psychotherapist, rebirther, primal feeling facilitator, cosmic aura balancer, or Rolfer—or from selling your "services" to anyone willing to pay. Beware of people advertising under such self-proclaimed titles. Even if their intentions are honorable, their training may be limited or non-existent. A fully trained, certified psychologist who chooses to use a particular type of therapy is not the same as someone "trained" solely in that technique.

Ethics Psychology, like medicine, has unfortunately attracted a fringe of opportunists, quacks, and charlatans who take advantage of human needs, fears, and suffering. (See this chapter's Exploration section.) What happens when the escapades of these "not-really psychologists" make the news or when a friend or relative has a bad experience with one? Often, psychologists take the blame. This is truly unfortunate. Most psychologists take pride in following a professional code established by the APA that stresses (1) high levels of competence, integrity, and responsibility; (2) respect for people's rights to privacy, dignity, confidentiality, and personal freedom; and above all, (3) protection of the client's welfare. Psychologists are also expected to use their knowledge to contribute to the welfare of society. Many do volunteer work in the communities in which they live ("Ethical," 1992).

Specialties in Psychology

Do all psychologists do therapy and treat abnormal behavior?

No. Only about 55 percent are clinical and counseling psychologists. The rest are found in a large number of other specialties. At present, there are 47 divisions of the APA, each reflecting special skills or areas of interest. Some of the major specialties are listed in Table 1–3 ■ (also see Figure 1–4 ◆). Over 40 percent of all psychologists are employed full-time at colleges or universities. In these settings they teach and may also do research, consulting, or therapy. Some do **basic research,** *in which they seek knowledge for the sake of knowledge.* For example, a psychologist might study memory purely out of interest in understanding how it works. Others do **applied research** *to solve immediate practical problems,* such as finding ways to improve the memory of eyewitnesses to crimes.

Table 1–3 ■ Kinds of Psychologists and What They Do

Specialty	Typical Activities
Clinical or counseling psychologist	(A*) Does psychotherapy and personal counseling, helps with emotional and behavioral problems, researches clinical problems, and develops methods of treatment
Industrial-organizational psychologist	(A) Selects job applicants, does skills analysis, evaluates on-job training, improves work environments and human relations in work setting
Educational psychologist	(A) Conducts research on classroom dynamics, teaching styles, and learning variables; develops educational tests, evaluates educational programs, acts as consultant for schools
Consumer psychologist	(A) Researches and tests packaging, advertising, and marketing methods; determines characteristics of product users, conducts public opinion polling
School psychologist	(A) Does psychological testing, referrals, emotional and vocational counseling of students; detects and treats learning disabilities; improves learning and motivation in the classroom
Developmental psychologist	(A,B) Carries out basic and applied research on child development, adult developmental trends, and aging; does clinical work with disturbed children; acts as consultant to preschools, programs for the aged, and so forth
Engineering psychologist	(A) Does applied research on design of machinery, controls, airplanes, automobiles, and so on for business, industry, and the military
Medical psychologist	(A) Studies the relationship between stress, personality, and disease (heart attacks, high blood pressure, ulcers); manages emotional problems associated with illness or disability
Environmental psychologist	(A,B) Studies the effects of urban noise pollution, crowding, attitudes toward environment, and human use of space; acts as consultant for design of industrial environments, schools, housing for elderly, and urban architecture
Forensic psychologist	(A) Studies problems of crime and crime prevention, rehabilitation programs in prisons, courtroom dynamics, psychology and law; selects candidates for police work
Community psychologist	(A) Treats whole neighborhoods or communities as "clients" by emphasizing prevention, education, and consultation to promote community mental health
Experimental psychologist	(B) Applies scientific research methods to study of human and animal behavior; may conduct research in the areas of comparative animal behavior, learning, sensation/perception, personality, biopsychology, motivation/emotion, social behavior, or cognition

*Research is typically: applied (A); basic (B); or both.

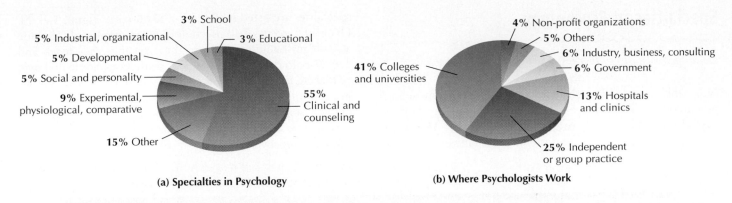

3% School
5% Industrial, organizational
5% Developmental
5% Social and personality
9% Experimental, physiological, comparative
15% Other
3% Educational
55% Clinical and counseling

(a) Specialties in Psychology

4% Non-profit organizations
5% Others
6% Industry, business, consulting
6% Government
41% Colleges and universities
13% Hospitals and clinics
25% Independent or group practice

(b) Where Psychologists Work

Figure 1–4 ◆ **(a)** Specialties in psychology. Percentages are approximate. **(b)** Where psychologists work (from Pion, 1991). The percentages shown here are based on membership in the American Psychological Association. The APA welcomes both scientists and practitioners. However, some psychological researchers belong to other organizations, such as the American Psychological Society. As a result, the percentage of clinical and counseling psychologists working in the United States may be a little lower than shown in chart *a*. Nevertheless, it is accurate to say that most psychologists specialize in applied areas and work in applied settings.

Some, of course, do research of both types. In the next chapter we'll take a closer look at how psychologists do research.

In addition to the specialties listed in Table 1–3, it shouldn't be long before job titles such as the following become more common: shyness counselor, thanatologist, retirement counselor, jury selection specialist, weight-control counselor, stress-reduction counselor, executive recruiter, and sleep disorders therapist. In short, psychology should remain a stimulating and innovative field for years to come.

A good summary of our discussion so far is provided by psychologists Gary VandenBos and Brenda Bryant:

> Psychologists are explorers and discoverers. They explore the reactions of human beings to small frustrations and great successes, to pleasing colors and the aftermath of disaster,

always looking for answers to how and why people think, feel, and behave as they do. . . . The psychologist, regardless of where she or he may work, is always applying what is known in an effort to resolve the unknown. The psychologist, no matter how small the question being asked may appear to be, is looking for the larger answer. (VandenBos & Bryant, 1987)

A Look Ahead

To help you get the most out of psychology, each chapter of this text includes an "Applications" section like the one that follows. These sections discuss ideas you can actually use, now or in the future. Our first Applications section explains how to think more analytically about human behavior. After that, a final "Exploration" section provides a look at some decidedly unscientific explanations of behavior.

Learning Check	**Critical Thinking**

See if you can answer these questions before continuing.

1. Which of the following can prescribe drugs?
   a. a psychologist **b.** a psychiatrist **c.** a psychotherapist **d.** a counselor **e.** all of the preceding

2. A psychologist who specializes in treating human emotional difficulties is called a
   _____ psychologist.

3. Roughly 40 percent of psychologists specialize in counseling psychology. T or F?

4. Who among the following would most likely be involved in the detection of learning disabilities?
   a. a consumer psychologist **b.** a forensic psychologist **c.** an experimental psychologist
   d. a school psychologist

5. If the majority of psychologists work in applied settings, why is basic research still of great importance?

Answers:
that leads to useful applications. basic science form the knowledge base from basic psychological research in biology. Discoveries in same way that physicians benefit from basic psychological research benefit 4. d 5. Because practitioners benefit 1. b 2. clinical or counseling 3. F

Most of us would be skeptical when buying a used car. But all too often, we may be tempted to "buy" outrageous claims about topics such as "channeling," dowsing, the occult, the Bermuda Triangle, hypnosis, UFOs, numerology, and so forth. Likewise, most of us easily accept our ignorance of sub-atomic physics. But because we deal with human behavior every day, we tend to think that we already know what is true and what is false in psychology.

For these, and many more reasons, learning to think critically is one of the lasting benefits of getting an education. Facts and theories may change. Thinking and problem-solving skills last a lifetime.

In the broadest terms, **critical thinking** *refers to an ability to evaluate, compare, analyze, critique, and synthesize information.* Critical thinkers are willing to ask hard questions and challenge conventional wisdom. For example, many people believe that punishment (a spanking) is a good way to reinforce learning in children. A critical thinker would immediately ask: "Does punishment work? If so, when? Under what conditions does it not work? What are its drawbacks? Are there better ways to guide learning?" (Halonen, 1986). (Punishment is actually a poor way to discipline children, see chapter 5 for details.)

Thinking about Behavior

The core of critical thinking is a willingness to actively evaluate ideas. It is, in a sense, the ability to stand outside yourself and reflect on the quality of your own thoughts. Critical thinkers analyze the evidence supporting their beliefs and probe for weaknesses in their reasoning. They question assumptions and look for alternate conclusions. True knowledge, they recognize, comes from constantly revising and enlarging our understanding of the world.

Critical thinking is built upon four basic principles (Gill, 1991; Shore, 1990):

1. *Few "truths" transcend the need for empirical testing.* It is true that religious beliefs and personal values may be held without supporting evidence. But most other ideas can be evaluated by applying the rules of logic and evidence.

2. *Evidence varies in quality.* Judging the quality of evidence is crucial. Imagine that you are a juror in a courtroom, judging claims made by two battling lawyers. To judge correctly, you can't just weigh the evidence. You must also critically evaluate the *quality* of the evidence. Then you can give greater weight to the most credible facts.

3. *Authority or claimed expertise does not automatically make an idea true.* Just because a teacher, guru, celebrity, or authority is convinced or sincere doesn't mean you should automatically believe them. It is unscientific and self-demeaning to just take the word of an "expert" without asking, "What evidence convinced her or him? How good is it? Is there a better explanation?"

4. *Critical thinking requires an open mind.* Be prepared to consider daring departures and go wherever the evidence leads. However, it is possible to be so "open-minded" that you simply become gullible. Critical thinkers try to strike a balance between open-mindedness and healthy skepticism. Being open-minded means that you consider all possibilities before drawing a conclusion. It is the ability to change your views under the impact of new and more convincing evidence.

Evaluating Claims and Evidence

An anxious mother watches her son eat a candy bar and says, "Watch, it's like lighting a fuse on a skyrocket. He'll be bouncing off the walls in a few minutes." Is she right? Will a "sugar buzz" make her son "hyper." How would you evaluate the claim that sugar adversely affects behavior? Here are some basic steps.

1. *State the claim clearly. What are its implications?* It's important to spell out what you would expect to see if the claim is true.

2. *Gather evidence.* Look for evidence relevant to the claim. Also, be sure to collect evidence both for and against the claim. Evidence may come from many sources, such as casual observations, opinions of authorities, published studies, or direct scientific observation.

3. *Evaluate the evidence.* Is the evidence you found consistent with the claim? If the information is conflicting, what conclusion does the strongest evidence support? (In general, scientific observations provide the highest-quality evidence.)

4. *Draw a conclusion.* If you have carefully evaluated the arguments and evidence bearing on a claim, you should have little trouble drawing a valid conclusion.

A Case Study of Critical Thinking

To see how the preceding steps apply, let's return to the question about sugar. What we want to know is, Does eating excessive amounts of sugar adversely affect children's behavior? What are the implications of this claim? If it is true, children who eat sugar should display measurable changes in behavior.

Anecdotal Evidence   What evidence is there to support the claim? It should be easy to find parents who will attest that their children become high-strung, inattentive, or unruly after eating sugar. However, parents are not likely to be objective observers. Beliefs about "sugar highs" are common and could easily color parents' views.

Casual Observation   Perhaps it would help to observe children directly. Let's say you decide to watch children at a birthday party, where you know large amounts of sugary foods will be consumed. As predicted by the claim, children at the party become loud and boisterous after eating cake, ice cream, and candy. How persuasive is this evidence? Actually, it is seriously flawed. Birthday parties expose children to bright lights, loud noises, and unfamiliar situations. Any of these conditions, and others as well, could easily explain the children's "hyper" activity.

Authority   For nearly 50 years many doctors, teachers, nutritionists, and other "experts" have emphatically stated that sugar causes childhood misbehavior. Should you believe them? Unfortunately, most of these "expert" opinions are based on anecdotes and casual observations that are little better than those we have already reviewed.

Formal Evidence   The truth is, parents, casual observers, and many authorities have been wrong. Dr. Mark Wolraich and his colleagues recently reviewed 23 scientific studies on sugar and children. In each study, children consumed known amounts of sugar and were then observed or tested. The clear-cut conclusion in all of the studies was that sugar does not affect aggression, mood, motor skills, or cognitive skills (Wolraich, Wilson, & White, 1995).

Studies like those we just reviewed tend to be convincing because they are based on systematic, controlled observation. To evaluate psychological questions you will often have to rely on similar published evidence. But don't just accept the investigators' conclusions. It is important to review the evidence yourself and decide if it is convincing. (Appendix B of this book explains how you can use the Internet and other electronic resources to locate studies on various topics.)

Summary

How do the principles of critical thinking apply to everyday questions about behavior?

To apply critical thinking on a day-to-day basis you should be prepared to ask the following questions over and over again (Bartz, 1990):

1. What claims are being made?
2. What test of these claims (if any) has been made?
3. Who did the test? How good is the evidence?
4. What was the nature and quality of the tests? Are they credible? Can they be repeated?
5. How reliable and trustworthy were the investigators? Do they have conflicts of interest? Do their findings appear to be objective? Has any other independent researcher duplicated the findings?
6. Finally, how much credence can the claim be given? High, medium, low, provisional?

A course in psychology naturally enriches thinking skills. To add to the process, all upcoming Learning Checks include Critical Thinking questions like the ones you have already seen here. Tackling these exercises will sharpen your thinking skills and make learning more lively. For an immediate thinking challenge, the next section offers a critical look at several non-scientific systems that claim to explain behavior.

Learning Check

1. An important aspect of _____ _____ is to seek evidence for and against an idea and to also evaluate the _____ of that evidence.
2. Most truths transcend the need for empirical testing. T or F?
3. To effectively evaluate a claim you must be able to clearly state its _____.
4. Evidence derived from _____ _____ is usually of the highest quality because it is based on systematic investigation.

Critical Thinking

5. In studies of the effects of sugar, some children are fed diets that are low in sugar. Typically, aspartame is used to artificially sweeten the foods in these diets. Why is it important for the low-sugar diet to include sweet flavors?

Answers:
1. critical thinking, quality 2. F 3. implications 4. scientific observation 5. So that the children being tested won't know their food is low in sugar. Otherwise, they might be affected by their own expectations concerning the effects of eating sugar.

Exploration

Pseudo-psychologies—Palms, Planets, and Personality

A **pseudo-psychology** (SUE-doe-psychology) *is any unfounded system that resembles psychology.* Many pseudo-psychologies offer elaborate schemes that give the appearance of science, but are actually false. (*Pseudo* means "false.") Pseudo-psychologies change little over time because their followers do not seek new data. In fact, pseudo-psychologists often go to great lengths to avoid evidence that contradicts their beliefs (Kelly & Saklofske, 1994). Scientists, in contrast, actively look for contradictions as a way to advance knowledge (see Table 1–4 ■). They must be skeptical critics of their own theories (Woodward & Goodstein, 1996).

Unlike the real thing, pseudo-psychologies are not based on empirical observation or scientific testing. For instance, **palmistry** *is a false system that claims lines on the hand reveal personality and predict the future.* Despite the overwhelming evidence against this, palm-

Phrenology was an attempt to assess personality characteristics by examining various areas of the skull. Phrenologists used charts such as the one shown here as guides. Like other pseudo-psychologists, phrenologists made no attempt to empirically verify their concepts.

ists can still be found separating the gullible from their money in many cities. A similar false system is **phrenology,** *which claims that personality traits are revealed by the shape of the skull.* Phre-

nology was popularized in the nineteenth century by Franz Gall, a German anatomy teacher. Modern research has long since shown that bumps on the head have nothing to do with talents or

Table 1–4 ■ Some Key Differences Between Scientists and Pseudo-Scientists

	Scientist	Pseudo-Scientist
Admits own ignorance, accepts need for more research	Yes	No
Advances knowledge by posing and solving new problems	Yes	No
Welcomes new hypotheses and methods	Yes	No
Theories and hypotheses are testable	Yes	Sometimes
Systematically tests concepts by gathering data	Yes	No
Looks for examples that contradict his or her beliefs	Yes	No
Applies objective checking procedures	Yes	No
Settles disputes by experimentation or systematic data collection	Yes	No
Suppresses or distorts unfavorable data	No	Yes
Seeks criticism from others	Yes	No

Adapted from Bunge, 1984.

abilities. In fact, the phrenologists were so far off that they listed the brain area for hearing as a center for "combativeness"!

At first glance, a pseudo-psychology called graphology might seem more reasonable. **Graphologists** *claim that personality traits are revealed by handwriting.* Based on such claims, some companies use graphologists to select job candidates. This is troubling because studies show that graphologists score close to zero on tests of accuracy in rating personality (Ben-Shakhar et al., 1986). In fact, graphologists do no better than untrained college students in rating personality and job performance (Neter & Ben-Shakhar, 1989; Rafaeli & Klimoski, 1983). (By the way, graphology's failure at revealing personality should be separated from its proven value for detecting forgeries.)

Like other pseudo-psychologies, graphology might seem harmless enough. However, this false system has been used to determine who is hired, given bank credit, or selected for juries. In these and similar situations, where fairness is important, pseudo-psychologies do, in fact, harm people (Barker, 1993; Beyerstein & Beyerstein, 1992).

If pseudo-psychologies have no scientific basis, how do they survive and why are they popular? There are several reasons, all of which can be demonstrated by a critique of astrology.

Problems in the Stars

Astrology is probably the most popular pseudo-psychology. **Astrology** *holds that the positions of the stars and planets at the time of one's birth determine personality traits and affect behavior.* Like other pseudo-psychologies, astrology has repeatedly been shown to have no scientific validity (Kelly & Saklofske, 1994; Stewart, 1996).

The objections to astrology are numerous and devastating:

1. The zodiac has shifted by one full constellation since astrology was first set up. However, most astrologers simply ignore this shift. (In other words, if astrology calls you a Scorpio you are really a Libra, and so forth.)

2. There is no connection between the "compatibility" of couples' astrological signs and their marriage and divorce rates.

3. Studies have found no connection between astrological signs and leadership, physical characteristics, career choices, or personality traits.

4. The force of gravity exerted by the physician's body at the moment of birth is greater than that exerted by the stars. Also, astrologers have failed to explain why the moment of birth should be more important than the moment of conception.

5. A study of over 3,000 predictions by famous astrologers found that only a small percentage were fulfilled. These "successful" predictions tended to be vague ("There will be a tragedy somewhere in the east in the spring") or easily guessed from current events. (Sources: "Astrology and Astronomy," 1983; Culver & Ianna, 1979; Kelly & Saklofske, 1994; Pasachoff, 1981; Stewart, 1996.)

In short, astrology doesn't work.

Then why does astrology often seem to work?

The following discussion tells why.

Uncritical Acceptance If you have ever had your astrological chart done, you may have been impressed with its apparent accuracy. However, such perceptions are typically based on **uncritical acceptance** (*the tendency to believe positive or flattering descriptions of yourself*). Many astrological charts are made up of mostly flattering traits. Naturally, when your personality is described in *desirable* terms, it is hard to deny that the description has the "ring of truth." How much acceptance would astrology receive if the characteristics of a birth sign read like this:

> **Virgo:** You are the logical type and hate disorder. Your nitpicking is unbearable to your friends. You are cold, unemotional, and usually fall asleep while making love. Virgos make good doorstops.

Positive Instances Even when an astrological description contains a mixture of good and bad traits it may seem accurate. To find out why, read the following personality description.

Your Personality Profile

You have a strong need for other people to like you and for them to admire you. You have a tendency to be critical of yourself. You have a great deal of unused energy which you have not turned to your advantage. While you have some personality weaknesses, you are generally able to compensate for them. Your sexual

Would you hire this man? Here's a sample of your author's handwriting. What do you think it reveals? Your interpretations are likely to be as accurate (or inaccurate) as those of a graphologist.

adjustment has presented some problems for you. Disciplined and controlled on the outside, you tend to be worrisome and insecure inside. At times you have serious doubts as to whether you have made the right decision or done the right thing. You prefer a certain amount of change and variety and become dissatisfied when hemmed in by restrictions and limitations. You pride yourself on being an independent thinker and do not accept other opinions without satisfactory proof. You have found it unwise to be too frank in revealing yourself to others. At times you are extroverted, affable, sociable, while at other times you are introverted, wary, and reserved. Some of your aspirations tend to be pretty unrealistic.*

Does this describe your personality? A psychologist read this summary individually to college students who had taken a personality test. Only 5 students out of 79 felt that the description failed to adequately capture their personalities. Another study found that people rated this "personality profile" as more accurate than their actual horoscopes (French et al., 1991).

Reread the description and you will

---

* Reprinted with permission of author and publisher from: R. E. Ulrich, T. J. Stachnik, and N. R. Stainton, "Student acceptance of generalized personality interpretations," *Psychological Reports*, 13, 1963, 831–834.

© 1993 WASHINGTON POST WRITERS GROUP

see that it contains both sides of several personality dimensions ("At times you are extroverted . . . while at other times you are introverted . . ."). Its apparent accuracy is an illusion based on the **fallacy of positive instances,** *in which we remember or notice things that confirm our expectations and forget the rest.* The pseudo-psychologies thrive on this effect. For example, you can always find "Leo characteristics" in a Leo. If you looked, however, you could also find "Gemini characteristics," "Scorpio characteristics," or whatever.

The Barnum Effect Pseudo-psychologies also take advantage of the **Barnum effect,** *which is a tendency to consider personal descriptions accurate if they are stated in very general terms.* P. T. Barnum, the famed circus showman, had a formula for success: "Always have a little something for everybody." Like the all-purpose personality profile, palm readings, fortunes, horoscopes, and

other products of pseudo-psychology are stated in such general terms that they can hardly miss. There is always "a little something for everybody." To observe the Barnum effect, read *all 12* of the daily horoscopes found in newspapers for several days. You will find that predictions for other signs fit events as well as those for your own sign do.

Astrology's popularity shows the difficulty many people have separating valid psychology from systems that seem valid but are not. The goal of this discussion, then, has been to make you a more critical observer of human behavior and to clarify what is, and what is not, psychology. In the meantime, here is what the "stars" say about your future:

Emphasis now on education and personal improvement. A learning experience of lasting value awaits you. Take care of scholastic responsibilities before engaging in recreation. The word *psychology* figures prominently in your future.

Learning Check

1. _____ is the out-dated theory that personality is revealed by the skull. It was popularized by Franz _____.

2. The fallacy of positive instances refers to graphology's accepted value for the detection of forgeries. T or F?

3. Personality descriptions provided by pseudo-psychologies are stated in general terms, which provide "a little something for everybody." This fact is the basis of the
   a. palmist's fallacy   b. uncritical acceptance pattern   c. fallacy of positive instances
   d. Barnum effect

4. So called "psychic hotlines" typically dispense lots of flattering information to callers. Obviously the "psychics" are relying on _____ to create an illusion of accuracy.
   a. graphology   b. uncritical acceptance   c. analysis of the zodiac   d. the Barnum effect

Critical Thinking

5. Each New Year's Day, phony "psychics" make predictions about events that will occur during the coming year. The vast majority of these predictions are wrong, but the practice continues each year. Can you explain why?

Answers:

1. Phrenology, Gall 2. F 3. d 4. b 5. Because of the fallacy of positive instances, people only remember predictions that seemed to come true and forget all of the errors. Incidentally, "predictions" that appear to be accurate are usually easily deduced from current events or are stated in very general terms to take advantage of the Barnum effect.

Chapter Summary

What is psychology?

◆ Psychology is the scientific study of behavior.
◆ Whenever possible, psychologists seek **empirical** (objective and observable) **evidence** based on **scientific observation.**

What do psychologists hope to achieve?

◆ Some major areas of research in psychology are comparative, learning, sensation, perception, personality, biopsychology, motivation and emotion, social, cognitive, developmental, the psychology of gender, and cultural psychology.
◆ Psychologists study animals as well as people.
◆ Psychologists may be directly interested in animal behavior or they may study animals as **models** of human behavior.
◆ As a science, psychology's goals are to **describe, understand, predict,** and **control** behavior.

How did psychology emerge as a field of knowledge?

◆ Historically, psychology is an outgrowth of **philosophy,** an "armchair" approach to understanding human behavior.
◆ The first psychological laboratory was established in Germany by **Wilhelm Wundt,** who tried to apply scientific methods to the study of conscious experience.
◆ The first school of thought in psychology was **structuralism,** a kind of "mental chemistry" based on Wundt's ideas and the method of **introspection.**
◆ Structuralism was followed by **functionalism, behaviorism,** and **Gestalt** psychology.
◆ The **psychodynamic** approach emphasizes unconscious determinants of behavior. Freud's **psychoanalytic psychology** is an early example of a psychodynamic approach.

◆ A more recent development is **humanistic** psychology, which emphasizes subjective experience, human potentials, and personal growth.

What are the major perspectives in psychology?

◆ Five main streams of thought in modern psychology are **behaviorism, humanism,** the **psychodynamic** approach, **biopsychology,** and **cognitive** psychology.
◆ Today, there is a strong trend toward an eclectic blending of the best features of many viewpoints within psychology.

What roles and specialties are found in psychology and related fields?

◆ Although **psychologists, psychiatrists, psychoanalysts,** and **counselors** all work in the field of mental health, their training and methods differ considerably.
◆ **Clinical** and **counseling** psychologists, who do psychotherapy, represent only two of dozens of specialties in psychology.
◆ Other representative areas of specialization are **industrial, educational, consumer, school, developmental, engineering, medical, environmental, forensic, community, psychometric,** and **experimental** psychology.
◆ Psychological research may be **basic** or **applied.**

What is critical thinking?

◆ **Critical thinking** is the ability to evaluate, compare, analyze, critique, and synthesize information.
◆ To judge the validity of a claim, it is important to gather evidence for and against the claim and to evaluate the *quality* of the evidence.

How does psychology differ from false explanations of behavior?

◆ Numerous **pseudo-psychologies** exist. These false systems are frequently confused with valid psychology.
◆ Belief in pseudo-psychologies is based in part on **uncritical acceptance,** the **fallacy of positive instances,** and the **Barnum effect.**

Research Methods and Critical Thinking

Preview

From Common Sense to Controlled Observation

Comment overheard on campus: "I don't know why he bothers taking psychology, it's just common sense." Is psychology common sense? Is common sense a good source of information?

Consider some commonsense statements. Let's say that your grandfather has gone back to college. What do people say? "Ah . . . never too old to learn." And what do they say when he loses interest and quits? "Well, you can't teach an old dog new tricks." Let's examine another commonsense statement. It is frequently said that "absence makes the heart grow fonder." Those of us separated from friends and lovers can take comfort in this knowledge—until we remember "Out of sight, out of mind"! Much of what passes for common sense is equally vague and inconsistent. Notice also that most of these *B. S.* statements work best after the fact. (*B. S.*, of course, stands for *Before Science*.)

Common sense is not without value. Without it, many of us would be dead. Yet, common sense can prevent us from seeking better information or seeing the truth. Albert Einstein said, "Common sense is the layer of prejudice laid down in our minds before we are 18." During the scientific revolution, people laughed at the idea that the world is round. (Anyone with eyes could see it wasn't.) They laughed at Pasteur when he proposed that microbes cause disease. (How could creatures too small to be seen kill a human?) Scientific ideas such as these directly contradicted the common sense of their times. Now few people argue with the findings of sciences such as chemistry, physics, and biology. But many still write off psychology as "just common sense."

Jab a hat pin into your finger. The sensation of pain seems instantaneous. We can go no further with personal observation. However, by using electrical recorders, psychologists have found that nerve impulses travel at a maximum of 120 meters per second. That's fast, but certainly not instantaneous. Pain messages from the finger take at least a hundredth of a second to reach the brain.

As you can see, psychologists use careful measurement and specialized research techniques to avoid the pitfalls of "common sense." Their techniques are the topic of this chapter.

Chapter Survey

Theme: Scientific observation is the most powerful way to answer questions about behavior.

Key Questions:

Why is the scientific method important to psychologists?	
How do psychologists collect information?	
How is an experiment performed?	
What other research methods do psychologists use?	
How dependable is psychological information found in the popular press?	
What ethical questions does psychological research raise?	

Key Topics to Watch for:

Six elements of the scientific method

Five major research methods
Naturalistic observation
Correlational studies and types of relationships

Types of variables and the logic of experiments
Placebo effects and double-blind studies

The clinical method and the survey method

Tips on how to critically evaluate information in the media

The effects of deception, loss of privacy, and potential harm
The ethics of animal research

Scientific Research— How to Think Like a Psychologist

It is a strange medical fact that if you ate Frosted Flakes cereal as a child your current chance of having cancer is half that of adults who never ate the cereal. Does this mean that doctors should prescribe Frosted Flakes to growing children? Only a scientifically naive person would think so. The apparent link between diet and cancer is actually related to an age bias. Older people naturally have higher cancer rates. They also never ate Frosted Flakes. That's because Frosted Flakes *weren't available* when they were young. Thus, Frosted Flakes *appear* to be related to cancer, when age is the real connection (Tierny, 1987).

In many ways, psychologists must avoid similar traps of faulty observation. To do so, they use the **scientific method,** *which is based on solid evidence, accurate description and measurement, precise definition, controlled observation, and repeatable results.*

The Scientific Method

Observation, or *carefully recording facts and events,* is the heart of all sciences. In its ideal form the scientific method has six elements:

1. Observation
2. Defining a problem
3. Proposing a hypothesis
4. Gathering evidence/testing the hypothesis
5. Publishing results
6. Theory building

What exactly is a hypothesis?

Hypothesis Testing A **hypothesis** (hi-POTH-eh-sis) *is a tentative explanation of an event or relationship.* In common terms, a hypothesis is a *testable* hunch or educated guess about behavior. For example, after observing others you might hypothesize that "Frustration encourages aggression." How would you test this hypothesis? First you would have to decide how you are going to frustrate people. (This part might be fun.) Then you would need to find a way to measure whether or not they become more aggressive. (Not so much fun if you plan to be nearby.) Your observations would then provide evidence to confirm or disconfirm the hypothesis.

Applying the scientific method to the study of behavior requires careful observation. Here, a psychologist videotapes a session in which a child's thinking abilities are being tested.

Operational Definitions Since we cannot see or touch frustration, it must be defined *operationally*. An **operational definition** *states the exact procedures used to represent a concept.* Operational definitions allow abstract ideas to be tested in real-world terms. (See Figure 2–1 ◆.) For example, you might define frustration as "interrupting an adult before he or she can finish a puzzle and win a $100 prize." And aggression might be defined as "the number of times a frustrated individual insults the person who prevented work on the puzzle."

Clever Hans Several major steps of the scientific method can be illustrated with the story of Clever Hans, a "wonder horse" (Rosenthal, 1965). Clever Hans seemed to solve difficult math problems, which he answered by tapping his foot. If you asked Hans, "What is 12 times 2, minus 18," Hans would tap his foot six times. Hans was so astonishing that an inquiring scientist decided to discover if Hans actually did arithmetic. Assume that you are the scientist and that you are just itching to find out how Hans *really* does his trick.

Can a Horse Add?

Your investigation of Hans' math skills would probably begin with careful *observation* of both horse and owner while Hans was performing. Assume that these observations fail to reveal any obvious cheating. Then the *problem* becomes more clearly *defined:* What signals Hans to start and stop tapping his foot? Your first *hypothesis* might be that the owner is giving Hans a signal. Your proposed *test* would be to make the owner leave the room. Then someone else could ask Hans questions. Your test would either confirm or deny the owner's role. This *evidence* would support or eliminate the cheating hypothesis. By changing the conditions under which you observe Hans, you

have *controlled* the situation to gain more information from your observations.

Incidentally, Hans could still answer when his owner was out of the room. But a brilliant series of controlled observations revealed Hans' secret. If Hans couldn't see the questioner, he couldn't answer. It seems that questioners always *lowered their heads* (to look at Hans' foot) after asking a question. This was Hans' cue to start tapping. When Hans had tapped the correct number, a questioner would always *look up* to see if Hans was going to stop. This was Hans' cue to stop tapping!

What about theory formulation?

Theories Since Clever Hans' ability to do math was an isolated problem, no theorizing was involved. However, in actual research, theory building is quite important. A **theory** *interrelates concepts and facts in a way that summarizes a large number of observations.* Good theories explain existing data, predict new observations, and guide further research (Fig. 2–2 ◆). Without theories of forgetting, personality, stress, mental illness, and the like, psychologists would drown in a sea of disconnected facts.

Conceptual Level

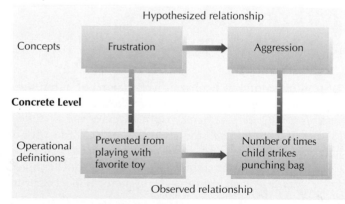

Figure 2–1 Operational definitions are used to link concepts with concrete observations. Do you think the examples given are reasonable operational definitions of frustration and aggression? Operational definitions vary in how well they represent concepts. For this reason, many different experiments may be necessary to draw clear conclusions about hypothesized relationships in psychology.

Figure 2–2 ◆ Psychologists use the logic of science to answer questions about behavior. Specific hypotheses can be tested in a variety of ways, including naturalistic observation, correlational studies, controlled experiments, clinical studies, and the survey method. Psychologists revise their theories to reflect the evidence they gather. New or revised theories then lead to new observations, problems, and hypotheses.

A good scientific theory, like a good hypothesis, must be **falsifiable** (*defined so that it can be disconfirmed*). For instance, if you hypothesize that "All dreams occur during rapid-eye-movement sleep," then recording even one dream at any other time will disconfirm the hypothesis. True science focuses on solvable problems. It avoids pie-in-the-sky theories that cannot be tested (Stanovich, 1996).

Publication   Scientific information must also be *publicly available*. The results of scientific studies are usually published in professional journals. (See Table 2–1 ■.) That way, anyone willing to make the appropriate observations can see whether or not a claim is true (Schick & Vaughn, 1995).

Do you remember news reports about an amazing breakthrough in physics called "cold fusion"? This mysterious process was supposed to produce immense amounts of cheap energy. But don't start leaving all your lights on. Independent scientists who tried to produce cold fusion failed, time after time. If the original study hadn't been published, it might have taken years to show that cold fusion was bogus.

Summary   Now let's summarize with a more realistic example of psychological research. All the basic elements of the scientific method are found in the example that follows.

Observation: Suzanne, a psychologist, observes that some business managers seem to experience less work-related stress than others do.

Defining a Problem: Suzanne's problem is to identify the ways in which high-stress and low-stress managers are different.

Observation: Suzanne carefully questions managers about how much stress they experience. These additional observations suggest that low-stress managers feel they have more control over their work.

Proposing a Hypothesis: Suzanne hypothesizes that having control over difficult tasks reduces stress.

Gathering Evidence/Testing the Hypothesis: Suzanne designs an experiment in which people must solve a series of very difficult problems. In one group, people solve the problems at a forced pace, dictated by Suzanne. In another group, they are allowed to set the pace themselves. While working, the second group reports lower stress levels than the first did. This suggests that Suzanne's hypothesis is correct.

Publishing Results: In a scholarly article, Suzanne carefully describes the question she investigated, the methods she used, and the results of her experiment. The article is published in the *Journal of Clinical Psychology*.

Theory Building: Drawing on the results of similar experiments, Suzanne and other psychologists create a theory to explain why having control over a task helps reduce stress.

Research Methods

In their search for accurate information and useful theories, psychologists gather evidence and test hypotheses in many ways: They *observe behavior as it unfolds in natural settings* (**naturalistic observation**); they *make measurements to discover relationships between events* (**correlational method**); they use the powerful technique of *controlled experimentation* (**experimental method**); they *study psychological problems and therapies in clinical settings* (**clinical method**); and they *use questionnaires and surveys to poll large groups of people* (**survey method**). Let's see how each of these is used to advance psychological knowledge.

Naturalistic Observation— Psychology Steps Out!

Instead of waiting to haphazardly encounter an interesting event, psychologists may *actively observe* behavior in a **natural setting** (*the typical environment in which a person or animal lives*). A good example of this style of research is the work of Jane Goodall. She and her staff have been observing chimpanzees in Tanzania since 1960. A quote from her book, *In the Shadow of Man*, captures the excitement of a scientific discovery:

> Quickly focusing my binoculars, I saw that it was a single chimpanzee, and just then he turned my direction. . . . He was squatting beside the red earth mound of a termite nest, and as I watched I saw him carefully push a long grass stem into a hole in the mound. After a moment he withdrew it and picked something from the end with his mouth. I was too far away to make out what he was eating, but it was obvious that he was

Table 2–1 ■   Outline of a Research Report

Abstract   Research reports begin with a very brief summary of the study and its findings. The abstract allows you to get an overview without reading the entire article.

Introduction   The introduction describes the question to be investigated. It also provides background information by reviewing prior studies on the same or related topics.

Method   This section explains how and why observations were made. It also describes the specific procedures used to gather data so that other researchers can duplicate the study.

Results   The outcome of the investigation is presented. Data may be graphed, summarized in tables, or statistically analyzed.

Discussion   The results of the study are discussed in relation to the original question. Implications of the study are explored and further studies may be proposed.

actually using a grass stem as a tool (Fig. 2–3 ◆). (van Lawick-Goodall, 1971)

Notice that naturalistic observation only provides *descriptions* of behavior. In order to *explain* observations we may need information from other research methods. Just the same, Goodall's discovery forced scientists to recognize that humans are not the only tool-making animals.

Chimpanzees in zoos use objects as tools. Doesn't that demonstrate the same thing?

Not necessarily. Naturalistic observation allows us to study behavior that hasn't been tampered with by outside influences. Only by observing chimps in their natural environment can we tell if they use tools without human interference.

Limitations

Doesn't the presence of human observers in an animal colony affect the animals' behavior?

Yes. A major problem with naturalistic studies is the effect of the observer on the observed. The **observer effect** *refers to changes in a subject's behavior brought about by an awareness of being observed.* Naturalists studying animal colonies must be very careful to keep their distance and avoid "making friends" with the animals. Likewise, if you were interested in

Figure 2–3 ◆ A special moment in Jane Goodall's naturalistic study of chimpanzees. A chimp uses a grass stem to extract a meal from a termite nest. Goodall's work also documented the importance of long-term emotional bonds between chimpanzee mothers and their offspring, as well as fascinating differences in the behavior and "personalities" of individual chimps (Goodall, 1990). (Photo by Baron Hugo van Lawick. C National Geographic Society.)

student-teacher interactions, you couldn't simply walk into a classroom and begin taking notes. A stranger in the room might affect both the students and the teacher. Whenever possible, this problem is minimized by *concealing the observer.*

Observer bias is a related problem in which *observers see what they expect to see or record only selected details.* Teachers in one study were told to watch elementary school children (all normal) who had been labeled as either learning disabled, mentally retarded, emotionally disturbed, or normal. The results were troubling: Ratings teachers gave the children differed markedly, depending on the labels used (Foster & Ysseldyke, 1976).

The Anthropomorphic Error A special trap that must be avoided while observing animals is the **anthropomorphic fallacy** (AN-thro-po-MORE-fik). This is *the error of attributing human thoughts, feelings, or motives to animals*—especially as a way of explaining their behavior (Blumberg & Wasserman, 1995).

Why is it risky to attribute motives or emotions to animals?

The temptation to assume that an animal is "angry," "jealous," "bored," or "guilty" can be strong, but it can lead to false conclusions. As an example, let's say I observe gorillas in the wild (where food is plentiful) and conclude that by nature gorillas are not very "greedy." You, on the other hand, place two hungry gorillas in a cage with a banana, stand back to watch the action, and conclude that gorillas are in fact *very* "greedy." Actually, all we have observed is that competition for food is related to the amount of food available. Allowing the human concept of greed into the picture just clouds our understanding of gorilla behavior.

Recording Observations

Psychologists doing naturalistic studies make a special effort to minimize bias by keeping a *formal log of data and observations,* called an **observational record.** In some cases, videotape recordings provide the best records of all (Pepler & Craig, 1995).

Despite its problems, naturalistic observation can supply a wealth of information and raise many interesting questions. In most scientific research it is an excellent starting point.

Correlational Studies— In Search of the Perfect Relationship

Let's say a psychologist notes an association between the IQs of parents and their children, or between beauty and social popularity, or between anxiety and test performance, or even between crime and the weather. In each instance, two observations or events are **correlated** (*linked together in an orderly way*). A **correlational study** *finds the degree of relationship, or correlation, between two existing traits, behaviors, or events.*

Unlike naturalistic observation, correlational studies can be done either in the lab or in the natural environment. First, two factors of interest are measured. Then a statistical technique is used to find their degree of correlation. (See Appendix A for more information.) For example, we could find the correlation between the number of hours slept at night and afternoon sleepiness. If the correlation is large, knowing how long a person sleeps at night would allow us to predict his or her degree of afternoon sleepiness. Likewise, afternoon sleepiness could be used to predict the duration of nighttime sleep.

Correlation Coefficients

How is the degree of correlation expressed?

The *strength and direction of a relationship* can be expressed as a **coefficient of correlation.** This is simply a number falling somewhere between +1.00 and −1.00 (see Appendix A). If the number is zero or close to zero, the association between two measures is weak or nonexistent. For example, the correlation between shoe size and intelligence is zero. (Sorry, size 12 readers.) If the correlation is +1.00, a *perfect positive relationship* exists; if it is −1.00, a *perfect negative relationship* has been discovered.

Correlations in psychology are rarely perfect. But the closer the correlation coefficient is to +1.00 or −1.00, the stronger the relationship. For example, identical twins tend to have almost identical IQs. In contrast, the IQs of parents and their children are only generally similar. The correlation

between the IQs of parents and children is .35; between identical twins it's .86.

What do the terms "positive" and "negative" correlation mean?

A **positive correlation** *shows that increases in one measure are matched by increases in the other (or decreases correspond with decreases).* For example, there is a positive correlation between high school grades and college grades; students who do better in high school tend to do better in college (and the reverse). In a **negative correlation,** *increases in the first measure are associated with decreases in the second* (Fig. 2–4 ◆). We might observe, for instance, that the higher the air temperature, the lower the activity level of animals in a zoo.

Would that show that air temperature causes changes in activity level?

It might seem so, but we cannot be sure without performing an experiment.

Correlation and Causation Correlational studies help us discover relationships and make predictions. However, correlation *does not demonstrate causation.* (There is an exception, but it involves an advanced technique beyond the scope of this book.) Just because two things *appear* to be related does not mean that **causation** (*a cause-and-effect connection*) exists. The animals' activity might be affected by seasonal changes in weight, hormone levels, or even the feeding schedule at the zoo.

Here is another example of mistaking correlation for causation: What if a psychologist discovers that the blood of schizophrenic patients contains a certain chemical not found in normal people? Does this show that the chemical *causes* schizophrenia? It may seem so, but schizophrenia could cause the chemical to form. Or, both schizophrenia and the

Correlation

Perfect	Strong	Medium	Weak	Zero	Weak	Medium	Strong	Perfect
−1.00	−.75	−.50	−.25	0.0	+.25	+.50	+.75	+1.00

Perfect negative relationship   Medium negative relationship   No relationship   Medium positive relationship   Perfect positive relationship

Figure 2–4 ◆ The correlation coefficient tells how strongly two measures are related. These graphs show a range of relationships between two measures, A and B. If a correlation is negative, increases in one measure are associated with decreases in the other. (As B gets larger, A gets smaller.) In a positive correlation, increases in one measure are associated with increases in the other. (As B gets larger, A gets larger.) The center-left graph ("medium negative relationship") might result from comparing anxiety level (B) with test scores (A): Higher anxiety is associated with lower scores. The center graph ("no relationship") would result from plotting a person's shoe size (B) and his or her IQ (A). The center-right graph ("medium positive relationship") could be a plot of the number of hours pilots went without sleep (B) and the number of errors each made when tested on a flight simulator (A). In this case, longer periods without sleep are associated with a greater number of errors.

chemical might be caused by some unknown third factor, such as the typical diet in mental hospitals.

Just because one thing *appears* to cause another does not *confirm* that it does. This fact can be seen clearly in the case of obviously non-causal relationships. For example, there is a correlation between the number of churches in American cities and the number of bars; the more churches, the more bars. Does this mean that drinking makes you religious? Does it mean that religion makes you thirsty? No one, of course, would leap to such conclusions about cause and effect. But in less obvious situations, it's tempting. (The real connection is simply this: the number of churches and the number of bars are both related to the population size of cities.)

Relationships in Psychology

Do students who study more get better grades? To answer this question we could record how long a number of students study each week. Then we could match hours studied with grades earned. Suppose we find that low study times correspond to low grades. Likewise, high amounts of studying are associated with high grades. If this were the case, there would be a *positive relationship* between studying and grades. Similarly, we might discover that students who watch many hours of television tend to get lower grades than those who watch few hours. (This is the well-known TV zombie effect.) This time, a *negative relationship* would exist. That is, low viewing times go with high grades, and high viewing times go with low grades. Obviously, these examples are only hypothetical. However, when real patterns can be identified, they have great value. Relationships summarize large amounts of data and allow us to make accurate predictions.

Graphical Data   Drawing graphs of relationships can help clarify their nature. For instance, Figure 2–5 ◆ shows the results of a memory experiment. Before being tested, subjects learned from one to 20 word lists. The question was, How well would they remember the last list? The graph shows that when participants learned only one list, they remembered 80 percent of it. When they learned 4 lists, their scores on the last list dropped to 43 percent (blue arrows). When they memorized 10 other lists, their recall fell even more, to 22 percent (red arrows). Overall, there was a negative relationship between the number of lists memorized and recall of the last list. (The meaning of this finding is discussed in Chapter 10. For now, let's just say that you shouldn't memorize the telephone book before studying for a test.)

Some graphs reveal **linear** (*straight-line*) **relationships.** Others are **curvilinear** (kur-vih-LIN-ee-er) and *consist of a curved line*, like Figure 2–5. In either case, relationships need not be perfect to be useful. Suppose, for instance, that we randomly select 10 people. We then compare the years of college completed with each person's income at age 25. Results like those shown in Figure 2–6 ◆, would make it clear that there is a strong positive relationship between education and earnings. Remember that such correlations do not prove education increases earnings. Nevertheless, a pattern like this might be of great interest to a high school student thinking about whether to attend college.

The shaded area and the colored line in Figure 2–6 show that the relationship is approximately linear, but not perfect. (If it were perfect, all the dots would lie on the colored line.) The correlation coefficient (*r*) also shows that the relationship is strong, and positive, but not perfect. (How often do you find a perfect relationship?) If the relationship *were* perfect, the coefficient would be 1.00.

For comparison, Figure 2–7 ◆ plots more hypothetical

Figure 2–5 ◆ Effects of interference on memory. A graph of the approximate relationship between percentage recalled and number of different word lists memorized. (Adapted from Underwood, 1957.)

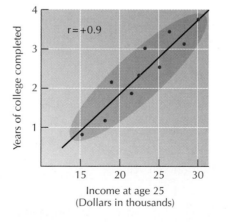

Figure 2–6 ◆ The relationship between years of college completed and personal income (hypothetical data).

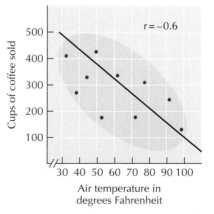

Figure 2–7 ◆ The relationship between air temperature and amount of coffee consumed (hypothetical data).

data. Assume that the manager of a college cafeteria has recorded the amount of coffee sold on 10 different days, as well as the air temperature on each day. Notice again that the relationship appears to be linear. However, this time it is negative. Also note how the shaded area and the correlation coefficient both indicate a weaker relationship. Even so, knowing the correlation between temperature and coffee drinking would help anyone planning how much "mud" to brew each morning.

On a higher plane, psychologists seek to identify relationships concerning memory, perception, stress, aging, therapy, and a host of similar topics. Much of this book is a summary of such relationships.

The best way to be confident that a cause-and-effect relationship exists is to perform a controlled experiment. You'll learn how in the next section. But before you read more, check your progress by answering the questions that follow.

Learning Check	Critical Thinking
1. Most of psychology can rightfully be called common sense because psychologists prefer naturalistic observation to controlled observation. T or F?	7. Correlation coefficients measure the strength of linear (straight-line) relationships. Why might it be a mistake to assume that a low correlation means two variables are unrelated?
2. A hypothesis is any careful observation made in a controlled experiment. T or F?	
3. Two problems in naturalistic observation are a. getting subjects to cooperate and identifying correlations b. defining a problem and proposing a hypothesis c. the effects of the observer and observer bias d. running the experiment and making careful records	
4. Correlation typically does not demonstrate causation. T or F?	**Answers:**
5. Which correlation coefficient represents the strongest relationship? a. −0.86 b. +0.66 c. +0.10 d. +0.09	1. F 2. F 3. c 4. T 5. a 6. curvilinear 7. Because the relationship could be very strong, yet curvilinear. In such cases, a psychologist might find that the correlation coefficient is zero, even though a significant relationship exists.
6. A relationship that does not form a straight line when it is graphed is described as _____ .	

The Psychology Experiment—Where Cause Meets Effect

The most powerful research tool is an **experiment** (*a formal trial undertaken to confirm or disconfirm a hypothesis*). Psychologists carefully control experimental conditions to identify cause-and-effect relationships. To perform an experiment you would do the following:

1. Directly vary a condition you think might affect behavior.

2. Create two or more groups of subjects. These groups should be alike in all ways *except* the condition you are varying.

3. Record whether varying the condition has any effect on behavior.

Assume, for example, that you want to find out if hunger affects memory. First, you would form two groups of people. Then you could give the members of one group a memory test while they are hungry. The second group would take the same test after eating a meal. By comparing average memory scores for the two groups, you could tell if hunger affects memory.

As you can see, the simplest psychological experiment is based on two groups of **subjects** (*animals or people whose behavior is investigated*). One group is called the *experimental group;* the other becomes the *control group.* The control group and the experimental group are treated exactly alike except for the condition you intentionally vary. This condition is called the *independent variable.*

Variables and Groups

A **variable** *is any condition that can change*, and that might affect the outcome of the experiment. Identifying causes and effects in an experiment involves three types of variables:

1. **Independent variables** *are the conditions altered or varied by the experimenter.* The size, amount, or value of an independent variable is set by the experimenter and does not depend on any other condition. Independent variables are suspected *causes* for differences in behavior.

2. **Dependent variables** *measure the results of the experiment.* Dependent variables reveal the *effects* that independent

variables have on *behavior*. Such effects are often revealed by measures of performance, such as test scores.

3. Extraneous variables *are conditions that a researcher wishes to prevent from affecting the outcome of the experiment.*

We can apply these terms to our hunger/memory experiment in this way: Hunger is the independent variable—we want to know if hunger affects memory. Memory (defined by scores on the memory test) is the dependent variable—we want to know if the ability to memorize depends on how hungry a person is. All other conditions that could affect memory scores, such as hours slept the night before the test, intelligence, or difficulty of the questions, are extraneous variables.

As you can see, an **experimental group** *consists of subjects exposed to the independent variable* (hunger in the preceding example). Members of the **control group** *are exposed to all conditions except the independent variable.*

Let's examine another simple experiment. Suppose you notice that you seem to study better while listening to music. This suggests the hypothesis that music improves learning. We could test this idea by forming an experimental group that studies with music. A control group would study without music. Then we could compare their scores on a test.

Is a control group really needed? Can't people just study with music on to see if they do better?

Without a control group it would be impossible to tell if music had any effect on learning. The control group provides a *point of reference* for comparison with scores of the experimental group. If the average test score of the experimental group is higher than that of the control group, we can conclude that music improves learning. If the average is lower than the control group's average, we will know that music slows learning. If there is no difference, we know that the independent variable has no effect on learning.

In the experiment described, the amount learned (indicated by scores on the test) is the *dependent variable*. We are asking the question, Does the independent variable *affect* the dependent variable? (Does music affect or influence learning?) Another way to think of this is that the results of an experiment are measured by the dependent variable, which *depends* on the independent variable. (The amount learned depends on whether or not music accompanies study.)

How do we know that the people in one group aren't more intelligent than those in the other group?

Experimental Control It's true that personal differences among subjects might influence the outcome of an experiment. However, these can be controlled by *randomly assigning* subjects to the two groups. **Random assignment** *means that a subject has an equal chance of being a member of either the experimental group or the control group.* Random assignment helps ensure that personal differences are evenly balanced across the two groups. In our musical experiment, random assignment could be done by simply flipping a coin

CONTROL GROUP   OUT OF CONTROL GROUP

COURTESY OF PETER S. MUELLER

for each subject: Heads, and the subject is in the experimental group; tails, it's the control group. Even in fairly small groups, this results in few differences in the number of people in each group who are geniuses or dunces, hungry, hung over, tall, music lovers, or whatever.

Other *extraneous*, or outside, variables—such as the amount of study time, the sex of subjects, the temperature in the room, the time of day, the amount of light, and so forth—must also be prevented from affecting the outcome of an experiment. But how? Usually this is done by making all conditions except the independent variable *exactly* alike for both groups. When all conditions are the same for both groups—*except* the presence or absence of music—then a difference in the amount learned *must* be caused by the music (Fig. 2–8 ◆).

Cause and Effect Now let's summarize more formally. In a psychology experiment two or more groups of subjects are treated differently with respect to the independent variable. In all other ways they are treated the same. That is,

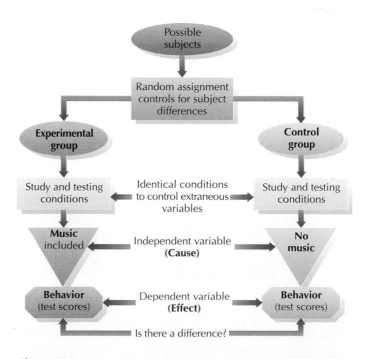

Figure 2–8 ◆ Elements of a simple psychological experiment to assess the effects of music during study on test scores.

extraneous variables are equalized for all groups in the experiment. This prevents conditions we are not interested in from affecting the results of the experiment. The effect of the independent variable (or variables) on some behavior (the dependent variable) is then measured. In a carefully controlled experiment, differences in the independent variable are the only possible *cause* for any *effect* noted in the dependent variable. This allows clear cause-and-effect connections to be identified (Fig. 2–9 ◆).

Experiments seem to set up artificial situations. Do experimental findings have anything to do with the real world?

Field Experiments

Being able to "custom design" conditions in a laboratory experiment has many advantages. But there is also a degree of artificiality. An alternative is the **field experiment**, *which uses natural settings* in the "real world" as a laboratory. Here is an illustration:

One Good Flat Deserves Another

James Bryan and Mary Test (1967) wanted to know, Are people are more likely to help someone in distress if they have just seen someone else receiving help? To find out, they parked a Ford Mustang with a flat tire on a busy street. An inflated tire leaned against the car, and a young woman stood nearby. Of the 2,000 cars that passed, only 35 stopped in this control condition. In the experimental condition, a second car was parked one-quarter mile back from the test car. A woman stood watching as a man changed a tire on the second car. Of the 2,000 vehicles that first passed this staged helping scene, 58 stopped to help the woman in the test car.

Such "real-life" experiments are popular among psychologists as a way to bridge the gap between laboratory studies and everyday life. You may have even taken part in an experiment without knowing it!

Figure 2–9 ◆ Experimental control is achieved by balancing or equalizing extraneous variables for the experimental group and the control group. Then, when the independent variable is applied to the experimental group, any change in the dependent variable must be caused by the independent variable.

Is the difference between 35 helpers and 58 helpers really enough to draw a conclusion?

Significance How can we tell if the independent variable made a difference? The problem is handled statistically. Reports in psychology journals almost always include the statement, "Results were **statistically significant**." What this means is that the obtained results *would occur very rarely by chance alone*. To be statistically significant, a difference must be large enough so that it would occur by chance in less than 5 experiments out of 100. (See Appendix A for more information.) Of course, research findings also become more convincing when they can be duplicated or repeated.

Critical Thinking

Replication and Parascience

The question, "Could you repeat that, please?" takes on special meaning in psychology. A key element in any science is the ability to **replicate** (*repeat*) observations or experiments to confirm prior conclusions. In contrast, a failure to replicate observations is a major flaw of **parascience** (*that which resembles science, but is not truly scientific*). A good example is the idea that plants have feelings. This claim, which received wide media coverage, was largely based on "experiments" performed by Cleve Backster, a polygraph expert. (The polygraph is commonly referred to as a lie detector; see Chapter 13.)

Backster claimed that plants wired to a lie detector responded to music, threats (such as a lighted match), and other stimuli. However, when scientists tried to repeat the experiments, using either identical or improved methods, the results were completely negative (Galston & Slayman, 1983).

A long list of other purported wonders—from "pyramid power" to dowsing to moon madness—have likewise disappeared in the light of careful scrutiny. Psychology, too, has admittedly had its share of unrepeatable results. However, what separates psychology and other sciences from parascience is that they are self-correcting.

When a finding cannot be repeated, the scientific response is, "We don't believe the result." Maintaining such high standards can be frustrating at times. Among other things, it requires a willingness to change one's beliefs as new or better evidence comes along. Yet, the end result is highly satisfying. High standards of evidence and a demand for repeatability ensure that science moves slowly, but surely, toward the truth (Lett, 1990).

Placebo Effects—Sugar Pills and Saltwater

Assume that we want to perform an experiment to see if amphetamine (a powerful central nervous system stimulant) affects learning. An accurate test of the drug will *not* occur if, before studying, members of the experimental group are given an amphetamine pill and control group members get nothing.

Why not? The experimental group gets the drug and the control group doesn't. If there is a difference in learning scores, it must be due to the action of the drug, right?

No, because an error has been made: The drug is not the only difference between the groups. Members of the experimental group swallow a pill, and control subjects do not. Without using a *placebo* (plah-SEE-bo), it is impossible to tell if the drug affects learning. It might be that those who swallow a pill *expect* to do better. This alone might alter their performance, even if the pill has no chemical effect.

What is a placebo? Why would it make a difference?

A **placebo** *is a fake pill or injection.* A placebo's benefits come from what it suggests to a person, rather than from what it contains. Sugar pills and saline (saltwater) injections are common placebos.

Although they have little or no direct chemical effect, placebos can have a tremendous *psychological* impact. The **placebo effect** (*changes in behavior caused by belief that one has taken a drug*) can be powerful. For instance, an injection of saline solution is 70 percent as effective as morphine in reducing pain. This fact is well known to physicians. For years they have prescribed placebos for complaints that seem to have no physical basis.

The placebo effect is based on expectations, but it is not entirely imaginary. Placebos relieve pain by causing the pituitary gland to release **endorphins.** These chemicals *are similar to painkilling opiate drugs such as morphine.* The body also naturally releases endorphins at times of stress and bodily injury (Lipman et al., 1990).

Controlling Placebo Effects

To control for placebo effects, a psychologist doing drug research could use a **single-blind experiment.** In this case, *subjects do not know if they are receiving a real drug or a placebo.* All subjects get a pill or injection. Members of the experimental group get a real drug and the control group gets a placebo. Because subjects are *blind* as to whether they received the drug, any difference between the two groups must be caused by the drug.

Keeping subjects "blind" is not necessarily enough. In a **double-blind experiment** *neither subjects nor experimenters*

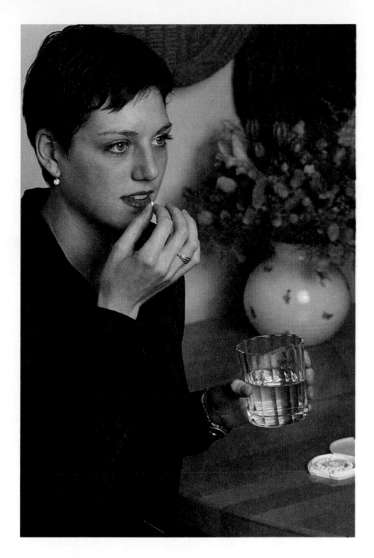

The placebo effect is a major factor in medical treatments. Would you also expect the placebo effect to occur in psychotherapy? (It does, which complicates studies on the effectiveness of new therapies.)

know which subjects are receiving drugs and which are receiving placebos. Double-blind experiments prevent researchers from unconsciously influencing subjects' reactions. Typically, someone else prepares the pills or injections, so the experimenters don't know until after testing who got what.

How could a researcher influence subjects?

The Experimenter Effect

Psychologists face an interesting problem not shared by physicists and chemists. Humans are very sensitive to hints from experimenters about what is expected of them (Rosenthal, 1976).

The **experimenter effect** (*changes in subjects' behavior caused by the unintended influence of an experimenter*) even applies outside the laboratory. Psychologist Robert

Rosenthal (1973) reports a typical example of how expectations can influence people: At the U.S. Air Force Academy Preparatory School 100 airmen were randomly assigned to one of five math classes. Their teachers were unaware of this random assignment. Instead, the teachers were told that their students were selected for high or low ability. Students in the classes labeled "high ability" improved much more in math scores than those in "low-ability" classes. Yet, initially, the classes all contained students of equal ability.

Apparently, the teachers subtly communicated their expectations to students through tone of voice, body language, and encouragement or criticism. This, in turn, created a *self-fulfilling prophecy* that affected the students. A **self-fulfilling prophecy** is *a prediction that prompts people to act in ways that make the prediction come true*. In this instance, students tended to perform as they were expected to perform. Even though educators should know better, self-fulfilling prophecies continue to influence large numbers of students (Jussim & Eccles, 1992).

In short, people sometimes become what we prophesy for them. It is wise to remember that others tend to live *up* or *down* to our expectations of them.

Learning Check	Critical Thinking

Learning Check

1. Anything that can change (vary) and that might affect the behavior of subjects is called a
_____.

2. To understand cause and effect, a simple psychological experiment is based on creating two groups: the _____ group and the _____ group.

3. There are three types of variables to consider in an experiment: _____ variables (which are manipulated by the experimenter); _____ variables (which measure the outcome of the experiment); and _____ variables (factors not of interest in a particular experiment).

4. A researcher performs an experiment to learn if room temperature affects the amount of aggression displayed by college students under crowded conditions in a simulated prison environment. In this experiment, the independent variable is
   a. room temperature   b. the amount of aggression   c. crowding
   d. the simulated prison environment

5. A procedure used to control both the placebo effect and the experimenter effect in drug experiments is the
   a. correlation method   b. extraneous prophecy   c. double-blind technique
   d. random assignment of subjects

Critical Thinking

6. People who believe strongly in astrology have personality characteristics that actually match, to a degree, those predicted by their astrological signs. Can you explain why this occurs?

Answers:

1. variable 2. experimental, control 3. Independent, dependent, extraneous 4. a 5. c 6. A recent study showed that belief in astrology can create a self-fulfilling prophecy in which people alter their behaviors and self-concepts to match their astrological signs (van Rooij, 1994).

The Clinical Method— Data by the Case

Many experiments that might be revealing are impractical, unethical, or impossible to perform. In instances such as these, information may be gained from a **case study** (*an in-depth focus on all aspects of a single subject*). Clinical psychologists rely heavily on case studies.

Case studies may sometimes be thought of as **natural clinical tests** (*accidents or other natural events that provide psychological data*). Gunshot wounds, brain tumors, accidental poisonings, and similar disasters have provided much information about the human brain. One remarkable case from the history of psychology is reported by Dr. J. M. Harlow (1868). Phineas Gage, a young foreman on a work crew, had a 13-pound steel rod blown through the front of his brain by an excavating charge (Fig. 2–10 ◆). Amazingly,

he survived the accident, and within 2 months Gage could walk, talk, and move about normally. But the injury forever changed his personality. Instead of the honest and dependable worker he had been before, Gage became a surly, foul-mouthed liar. Dr. Harlow carefully recorded all details of what was perhaps the first in-depth case study of an accidental **frontal lobotomy** (*the destruction of front brain matter*).

Over 120 years later, a Los Angeles carpenter named Michael Melnick was the victim of a similar freakish accident. Melnick fell from the second story at a construction site and impaled his head on a steel reinforcing rod. Incredibly, he recovered completely, with no sign of lasting ill effects ("Man tells," 1981). Melnick's very different reaction to a similar injury shows why psychologists prefer controlled experiments and often use lab animals for studies of the brain. Case studies lack formal control groups. This, of course, limits the conclusions that can be drawn from clinical observations. Nonetheless, when a purely psycho-

Figure 2–10 ◆ Some of the earliest information on the effects of damage to frontal areas of the brain came from a case study of the accidental injury of Phineas Gage.

logical problem is under study, the clinical method may be the *only* source of information.

A classic psychological case study is *The Three Faces of Eve* (Thigpen & Cleckley, 1957). Eve White was a mild, restrained suburban housewife. In the course of psychotherapy, Eve revealed a second, separate personality. This second personality, Eve Black, was the antithesis of Eve White. Eve Black was childish, mischievous, and erotically flirtatious. Eve Black knew about Eve White and openly talked about the times she had disobeyed her parents or gotten drunk and had then "gone into" Eve White. After Eve Black's escapades, Eve White faced her punishment or bore her hangover. But she did so with bewilderment because she didn't know of Eve Black's existence. Eventually, this duality was resolved when a third personality—who called herself Jane—emerged. Jane ultimately separated from Eve White's husband. She then began a relatively stable new life marked by the slow development of several other personalities. Now in her late 50s, the former Eve White no longer suffers from *multiple personality disorder.*

The careful recording of all pertinent facts in cases like Eve's is essential to psychology. Multiple personality is a rare event, which cannot be produced experimentally. (Multiple personality is discussed further in Chapter 17.)

Survey Method—Here, Have a Sample

Sometimes psychologists would like to ask everyone in the world a few well-chosen questions: "Have you ever smoked marijuana?" "Have you engaged in premarital sexual intercourse?" "What is your marital status now, and were your parents ever separated or divorced?" "Do you favor legal abortion?" The answers to questions such as these can reveal much about significant psychological events in people's lives. But because it is impractical to question everyone, psychologists use *public polling techniques to answer psychological questions*, an approach called the **survey method.**

In a survey, people in a representative sample are asked a series of carefully worded questions. A **representative sample** *is a small group that accurately reflects a larger population.* Such samples include the same proportion of men, women, young, old, professionals, blue-collar workers, Republicans, Democrats, whites, blacks, Latinos, Asians, and so on, as found in the population as a whole. A **population** *is an entire group of animals or people belonging to a particular category* (for example, all college students or all married women). Ultimately, we are interested in entire populations. But by selecting a smaller sample, we can draw conclusions about the entire group without polling each and every person. Representative samples are often obtained by *randomly* selecting who will be included (Fig. 2–11 ◆).

Survey questions must be carefully phrased because wording can greatly affect how people answer. In a survey conducted in 1991, during the Persian Gulf War, people were asked if they were concerned about the "collateral damage" caused by bombing in Iraq. When this military euphemism for civilian deaths was used, 55 percent of those polled said they were concerned. In contrast, when people were asked if they were concerned about "the number of civilian casualties and other unintended damage," 82 percent said yes (Rosenstiel, 1991).

A careful survey can provide an accurate picture of how the general population feels about current issues. However, some psychologists have questioned—tongue in cheek—claims that psychology's conclusions apply to people in general. The distinguished psychologist Edward Tolman once noted that much of psychology is based on two sets of subjects: rats and college sophomores. Tolman urged his colleagues to remember that rats certainly are not people and that college sophomores may not be!

In recent years, 93 percent of human subjects in psychology experiments were recruited from introductory psychology courses (Sieber & Saks, 1989). The majority of these subjects were white members of the middle class (Graham, 1992). This doesn't automatically invalidate the results of psychology experiments. But it may place some limitations on their meanings.

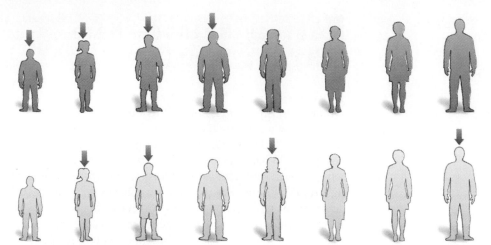

Figure 2-11 ◆ If you were conducting a survey in which a person's height might be an important variable, the upper, non-random sample would be very unrepresentative. The lower sample, selected using a table of random numbers, better represents the group as a whole.

Cultural Diversity

Is There a Gender Bias in Psychological Research?

Many doctors recommend that adults take an aspirin a day to help prevent heart attack. Both men and women are given this advice. The problem? Not a single woman was included in the sample on which the advice is based. Although females make up more than half the population, they continue to be neglected in psychological and medical research (Denmark, 1994).

Gender bias *is a tendency for researchers to base conclusions solely on subjects of one gender,* usually males. Owing to a gender bias, researchers must often *assume* that conclusions based on men also apply to women. But without directly studying women, it is impossible to know how often this assumption is wrong. A related problem occurs when researchers combine results from men and women. Doing so can hide important male-female differences. Similar biases exist concerning the race, ethnicity, age, and sexual orientation of participants in psychological research (Denmark, 1994).

The solution to such problems is straight-forward: Whenever possible, researchers need to include a wider array of people in their studies. In recognition of human diversity, many researchers are doing just that.

How accurate is the survey method?

Modern surveys like the Gallup and Harris polls are quite accurate. The Gallup poll has erred in its election predictions by an average of only 1.5 percent since 1954. This high level of accuracy has not always existed. During the 1936 U.S. presidential election, a well-known magazine, the *Literary Digest*, predicted that Alfred Landon would defeat Franklin Roosevelt by a large margin. Roosevelt defeated Landon by a landslide!

How could the poll have been so wrong?

The answer lies in the way the sample was taken. Most people in the poll were contacted by *telephone*. In 1936, during the Great Depression, people who had phones were much more wealthy than average, and the wealthy favored Landon. Thus, the sample was *biased*. A **biased sample** *does not accurately reflect the population from which it was drawn.* Today, similar problems afflict surveys done by magazines and on-line information services, such as Prodigy and CompuServe. If only subscribers can be polled, the resulting sample may be biased. A survey on the use of illicit drugs conducted by *Cosmopolitan* and *Rolling Stone* would probably produce very different results—neither of which would represent the general population.

Even when questions are carefully stated and the sample is representative, a survey may be limited by another problem. If a psychologist were to ask you detailed questions about your sexual history and current sexual behavior, how accurate would your replies be? Would you be self-conscious and perhaps not completely frank? Or might you have a tendency to exaggerate? Replies to survey questions are not always *accurate* or *truthful*. Many people show a distinct **courtesy bias** (*a tendency to give answers that are "polite" and socially acceptable*). For example, pollsters working on an election found that black persons talking to white interviewers were less likely to admit support for an African-American candidate. Similarly, white persons talking to black interviewers were more likely to claim support for the African-American candidate (McKean, 1984).

Despite their limitations, surveys frequently produce useful information. For instance, in recent years working women have complained of sexual harassment at their jobs. How widespread is this problem? In 1981, psychologist Barbara Gutek found that 53 percent of women had experienced some form of sexual harassment at work (Gutek, 1981). A more recent survey obtained a figure of 45 percent (Janus & Janus, 1993). These results suggest that sexual harassment has declined slightly, perhaps because of greater public awareness of the problem. Although such information does not solve the problem of sexual harassment, it is a first step toward understanding it and remedying it.

Summary—Science and Critical Thinking

Is so much emphasis on research really necessary in psychology?

In a word, yes. As we have seen, science is a powerful way of asking questions about the world and getting trustworthy answers. More importantly, we might ask, What is the alternative to using the scientific method? In most areas of knowledge, wiping out scientific advances would mean a return to the Dark Ages. Your awareness of this fact, along with your understanding of research methods, should help make you a more critical observer of human behavior. Table 2–2 ■ summarizes many of the important ideas we have covered.

In many ways, scientific thinking is a refinement of the critical thinking skills described in Chapter 1. Of course, thinking critically about behavior is not easy. A special trap to watch for is called the **my-side bias,** which is the *tendency to pay more attention to evidence that supports your existing beliefs and to avoid contradictory evidence.* To minimize the my-side bias, critical thinkers actively look for reasons why their ideas might be wrong or incomplete (Baron, 1993).

As you seek to understand your own behavior and that of others, it is valuable to ask yourself frequently: "How might my initial conclusions be wrong? What counter-arguments can I identify? What contradictory evidence might cause me to draw a new conclusion? Remember, too, that critical thinking can help you resist persuasion based on faulty logic, irrational thinking, or invalid conclusions. Searching for contradictory evidence and arguments is a wonderful antidote to misguided persuasion by advertisers, gurus, pundits, politicians, "experts," medical quacks, and sometimes, even psychologists and educators!

A Look Ahead   To complete our discussion, this chapter's Applications section offers a critical look at information reported in the popular press. Unfortunately, these reports

Table 2–2 ■ **Comparison of Psychological Research Methods**		
	Advantages	**Disadvantages**
Naturalistic observation	Behavior is observed in a natural setting; much information is obtained, and hypotheses and questions for additional research are formed	Little or no control is possible; observed behavior may be altered by the presence of the observer; observations may be biased; causes cannot be conclusively identified
Correlational method	Demonstrates the existence of relationships; allows prediction; can be used in lab, clinic, or natural settings	Little or no control is possible; relationships may be coincidental; cause-and-effect relationships cannot be confirmed
Experimental method	Clear cause-and-effect relationships can be identified; powerful controlled observations can be staged; no need to wait for natural event	May be somewhat artificial; some natural behavior not easily studied in laboratory (field experiments may avoid these objections)
Clinical method	Takes advantage of "natural clinical trials" and allows investigation of rare or unusual problems or events	Little or no control is possible; does not provide a control group for comparison, subjective interpretation is often necessary, a single case may be misleading or unrepresentative
Survey method	Allows information about large numbers of people to be gathered; can address questions not answered by other approaches	Obtaining a representative sample is critical and can be difficult to do; answers may be inaccurate; people may not do what they say or say what they do

abound with sloppy thinking, misinformation, and pie-in-the-sky theories. The first words to spring to your lips when you read outlandish claims should be, "Prove it." The Applications section gives some pointers on what to look for.

After that, we'll explore the ethics of psychological research. You should find these topics an interesting way to conclude our survey of research in psychology.

Learning Check

1. Case studies can often be thought of as natural tests and are frequently used by clinical psychologists. T or F?

2. For the survey method to be valid, a representative sample of people must be polled. T or F?

3. The phenomenon of multiple personality would most likely be investigated by use of
   a. a representative sample **b.** field experiments **c.** the double-blind procedure **d.** case studies

4. A problem with the survey method is that answers to questions may not always be
   _____ or _____ .

5. People who abuse certain "designer drugs" develop neurological symptoms similar to Parkinson's disease. Studying damage to the brains of these people would provide a _____ _____ test of theories about the causes of Parkinson's.

Critical Thinking

6. A psychologist conducting a survey at a shopping mall (The Gallery of Wretched Excess) flips a coin before stopping passersby. If the coin shows heads, he interviews the person; if it shows tails he skips that person. Has the psychologist obtained a random sample?

Answers:

1. T 2. T 3. d 4. accurate, truthful 5. natural clinical 6. The psychologist's coin flips might produce a reasonably good sample of people at the mall. The real problem is that people who go to the mall may be mostly from one part of town, from upper income groups, or from some other non-representative group. The psychologist's sample is likely to be seriously flawed.

*P*sychology is discussed extensively in magazines and newspapers. Unfortunately, much of what you will read is based on wishful thinking rather than science. Here are some suggestions for separating high-quality information from misleading fiction.

Suggestion 1: Be skeptical. Reports in the popular press tend to be made uncritically and with a definite bias toward reporting "astonishing" findings. Remember, saying "That's incredible" means "That's not believable"—which is often true.

Example 1: Some years ago, numerous articles appeared concerning "dermo-optical perception." According to these reports, people had been found who could use their fingertips to identify colors and read print (even under glass) while blindfolded. Many articles referred to the existence of a "sixth sense" or "X-ray eyes."

In reality, such "abilities" are based on what stage magicians call a "nose peek." It is impossible to prepare a blindfold (without damaging the eyes) that does not leave a tiny space on each side of the nose through which a person can peek. In accordance with this criticism, the phenomenal abilities reported in the first dermo-optical perception experiments disappeared each time the opportunity to peek was controlled.

Example 2: In 1994 the *National Enquirer* reported that "Top University Researchers Reveal . . . 8 Million Americans may have been abducted by UFOs." However, one of the researchers cited in the article had actually concluded "the public can rest assured that there is no evidence that millions of Americans are being abducted." In other words, the *Enquirer* story completely *reversed* the real findings. You'll find similar misinformation and sensationalism throughout the popular media. Be on guard.

Suggestion 2: Consider the source of information. It should come as no surprise that information used to sell a product often reflects a desire for profit rather than the objective truth. Here is a typical advertising claim: "Government tests have proved that no pain reliever is stronger or more effective than Brand X aspirin." A statement like this usually means that there was *no difference* between the product and others tested. No other pain reliever was stronger or more effective. But none was weaker either.

Keep the source in mind when reading the claims of makers of home biofeedback machines, sleep-learning devices, subliminal tapes, and the like. Remember that psychological services may be merchandised as well. Be wary

of expensive courses that promise instant mental health and happiness, increased efficiency, memory, ESP or psychic ability, control of the unconscious mind, an end to smoking, and so on. Usually they are promoted with a few testimonials and many unsupported claims.

Psychic claims should be viewed with special caution. Stage mentalists make a living by deceiving the public. Understandably, they are highly interested in promoting belief in their non-existent powers. Psychic phenomena, when (and if) they do occur, are quite unpredictable. It would be impossible for a mentalist to do three shows a night, six nights a week without consistently using deception.

I've seen some amazing things on TV. Could you give an example of how I may have been fooled?

Here is a typical stage mentalist's routine. The mentalist picks an audience member "at random" and begins telling him personal things that "the mentalist could not possibly know." How does the mentalist do it? Easy! One of the mentalist's assistants stood in line outside the theater and eavesdropped on conversations before the show. The assistant then made careful note of where the audience member was seated. The seating location and the overheard information were then passed to the mentalist. The mentalist then announces, "You have an aunt . . . Aunt Bessy . . . she has been very ill . . . you were thinking about her earlier this evening . . . you had a flat tire on the way here this evening."

Suggestion 3: Ask yourself if there was a control group. The key importance of a control group in any experiment is frequently overlooked by the unsophisticated—an error to which you are no longer susceptible! The popular press is full of reports of "experiments" performed without control groups: "Talking to Plants Speeds Growth"; "Special Diet Controls Hyperactivity in Children"; "Food Shows Less Spoilage in Pyramid Chamber"; "Graduates of Firewalking Seminar Risk Their Soles."

Consider the last example for a moment. In recent years, expensive commercial courses have been promoted to teach people to walk barefoot on hot coals. (Why anyone would want to do this is itself an interesting question.) Firewalkers supposedly protect their feet with a technique called "neurolinguistic programming." Many people have paid good money to learn the technique, and most do manage a quick walk on the coals. But is the technique necessary? And is anything remarkable happening? We need a comparison group!

Fortunately, physicist Bernard Leikind has provided one.

Leikind showed with volunteers that anyone (with reasonably callused feet) can walk over a bed of coals without being burned. The reason is that the coals, which are light, fluffy carbon, transmit little heat when touched. The principle involved is similar to briefly putting your hand in a hot oven. If you touch a pan, you will be burned because metal transfers heat efficiently. But if your hand stays in the heated air you'll be fine because air transmits little heat (Mitchell, 1987). Mystery solved.

Suggestion 4: Look for errors in distinguishing between correlation and causation. As you now know, it is dangerous to presume that one thing *caused* another just because they are corre-

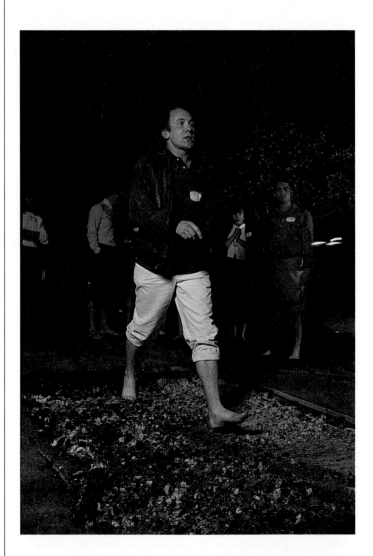

Firewalking is based on simple physics, not on any form of supernatural psychological control. The temperature of the coals may be as high as 1200° F. However, coals are like the air in a hot oven: they are very inefficient at transferring heat during brief contact.

lated. In spite of this, you will see many claims based on questionable correlations. Recently, a nutritionist was quoted in the news as saying that drinking excessive amounts of milk may cause juvenile delinquency. (This must have been a real hit with the National Dairy Association.) On what did he base this conclusion? Adolescent males who are often in trouble, he said, drink greater than average amounts of milk.

In no way does this correlation demonstrate that milk causes delinquency. It could easily be, for instance, that young males who mature early are more likely to be aggressive or get into trouble. Maturing early involves rapid growth. And rapid growth promotes hunger. It is entirely possible that this is the only link between milk and delinquency. Or perhaps some other unknown factor is involved.

Here's another example of mistaking correlation for causation. Jeanne Dixon, an astrologer, once answered a group of prominent scientists—who had declared that there is no scientific foundation for astrology—by saying, "They would do well to check the records at their local police stations, where they will learn that the rate of violent crime rises and falls with lunar cycles" (Dixon, 1975). Dixon, of course, believes that the moon affects human behavior.

If it is true that violent crime is more frequent at certain times of the month, doesn't that prove her point?

Far from it. Increased crime could be due to darker nights, the fact that bills fall due at the first of the month, or any number of similar factors. More importantly, direct studies of the alleged "lunar effect" have shown that it doesn't occur (Rotton & Kelly, 1985). Moonstruck criminals, along with "moon madness," are a fiction (Coates, Lehle, & Cottington, 1989).

Suggestion 5: Be sure to distinguish between observation and inference. If you see a person *crying* is it correct to assume that she or he is *sad?* Although it seems reasonable to make this assumption, it is actually quite risky. We can observe objectively that the person is crying, but to *infer* sadness may be in error. It could be that the individual has just peeled five pounds of onions. Or maybe he or she just won a million-dollar lottery or is trying contact lenses for the first time.

Psychologists, politicians, physicians, scientists, and other experts often go far beyond the available facts in their claims. This does not mean that their inferences, opinions, and interpretations have no value; the opinion of an expert on the causes of mental illness, criminal behavior, learning problems, or whatever can be revealing. But be careful to distinguish between fact and opinion.

Suggestion 6: Beware of over-simplifications, especially those motivated by monetary gain.   Courses or programs that offer a "new personality in three sessions," "six steps to love and fulfillment in marriage," or newly discovered "secrets of unlocking the powers of the mind" should be immediately suspect.

An excellent example of over-simplification is provided by a brochure entitled, "Dr. Joyce Brothers Asks: How Do You Rate as a 'Superwoman'?" Dr. Brothers, a "media" psychologist who has no private practice and is not known for research, wrote the brochure as a consultant for the Aerosol Packaging Council of the Chemical Specialties Manufacturers Association. A typical suggestion in this brochure tells how to enhance a marriage: "Sweep him off to a weekend hideaway. Tip: When he's not looking spray a touch of your favorite *aerosol* cologne mist on the bedsheets and pillows" (italics added). Sure, Joyce.

Suggestion 7: Remember, "for example" is no proof.   After reading this chapter you should be sensitive to the danger of selecting single examples. If you read, "Law student passes state bar exam using sleep-learning device," don't rush out to buy one. Systematic research has shown that these devices are of little or no value (Druckman & Bjork, 1994; Wood et al., 1992). A corollary to this suggestion is to ask, Are the reported observations important or widely applicable?

Examples, anecdotes, single cases, and testimonials are all potentially deceptive. Unfortunately, *individual cases* tell nothing about what is true *in general* (Stanovich, 1996). For instance, studies of large groups of people show that smoking increases the likelihood of lung cancer. It doesn't matter if you know a lifelong heavy smoker who is 94 years old. The general finding is the one to remember.

Summary   We are all bombarded daily with such a mass of new information that it is difficult to absorb it. The available knowledge, even in a limited area like psychology, biology, medicine, or contemporary rock music, is so vast that no single person can completely know and comprehend it. With this situation in mind, it becomes increasingly important that you become a critical, selective, and informed consumer of information.

Learning Check

1. Newspaper accounts of dermo-optical perception have generally reported only the results of carefully designed psychological experiments. T or F?

2. Stage mentalists and psychics often use deception in their acts. T or F?

3. Blaming the lunar cycle for variations in the rate of violent crime is an example of mistaking correlation for causation. T or F?

4. To investigate possible links between drinking milk and delinquent behavior, it would be desirable to create an experimental group that consumes large amounts of milk and a control group that drinks none. T or F?

Critical Thinking

5. In what way is reading the popular press like being a jury member in a courtroom trial?

Answers:

1. F 2. T 3. T 4. T 5. In both instances it is important to not only study the evidence supporting various claims, but also to evaluate the quality of that evidence.

Some years ago, social psychologist Philip Zimbardo and his associates set up a simulated prison at Stanford University. Their goal was to probe the effects of imprisonment on otherwise healthy individuals. Students were recruited to play the roles of prisoners and guards. Much to everyone's surprise, the 2-week experiment had to be called off 6 days after it began. The "guards" had become so sadistic that 4 of the 10 "prisoners" suffered severe emotional reactions, including crying, depression, anxiety, and rage (Zimbardo et al., 1973). (This experiment is discussed further in Chapter 20.)

The Stanford prison experiment is only one of several to raise serious ethical questions. Were the participants permanently harmed? Did the information gained justify the emotional costs? Are such experiments dehumanizing? Questions like these draw attention to three issues to which researchers must be particularly sensitive. These are: *deception, invasion of privacy,* and *lasting harm.* Each issue is illustrated by the following experiments. See if you think they are ethical.

Deception

To obtain genuine reactions, the true purpose of many experiments is hidden by deception. For example, a researcher interested in guilt once led subjects to believe they had broken an expensive piece of machinery. During the experiment, a machine suddenly popped loudly, released a plume of smoke, and sputtered to a stop. As embarrassed subjects were about to leave, the experimenter asked them to sign a petition he was circulating. The petition called for doubling tuition fees at the school. Almost all control subjects had refused to sign the same petition. However, because of their guilt, more than 50 percent of the experimental subjects

signed (Rubin, 1970a). Was deception really necessary to answer the researcher's question?

Invasion of Privacy

To what extent should invasions of privacy be allowed in psychological research? One study that has been both criticized and defended involved secret observation of men in a rest room. Psychologist Eric Knowles was interested in the stress caused by "personal space" invasions. An observer concealed himself in a toilet stall in a public rest room and used a hidden periscope to monitor activity at the urinals. As predicted, urination took longer to begin when an assistant occupied a urinal next to the unsuspecting subject (Koocher, 1977; Middlemist et al., 1976). This finding is interesting, but does it justify the invasion of privacy used to obtain it?

Lasting Harm

Do psychological experiments ever do lasting harm to participants? This is perhaps the most serious ethical question of all. A classic experiment on obedience to authority illustrates the problem. In the study, subjects thought they were giving painful and dangerous electrical shocks to another person (Milgram, 1974). (No shocks were actually given; see Chapter 20.) Belief that they were hurting someone proved extremely stressful for most subjects. Many left the experiment shaken and upset. Some presumably suffered guilt and distress for some time afterward.

This experiment may sound clearly unethical, but the researcher, Stanley Milgram, did follow-up studies on the participants. Most felt positive about their experience and claimed they were glad they had taken part. Many added that they had learned something of value about themselves. But what about

the few who felt otherwise? As in medical research, there are no easy answers to the ethical questions raised by psychology.

Most students find the studies just described interesting and informative. How can the search for knowledge be properly balanced with human rights? As a reply to this question, ethical guidelines of the American Psychological Association state: "Psychologists must carry out investigations with respect for the people who participate and with concern for their dignity and welfare." To ensure that this is the case, most college psychology departments have ethics committees that oversee proposed research. Nevertheless, no easy answers exist for the ethical questions raised by some research. How do *you* think a psychologist should decide if his or her research is ethical?

Becoming a Subject

The ethics of research may turn out to be highly pertinent for many students. As mentioned earlier, college students frequently serve as subjects in psychology experiments. If you become a subject, what should you expect? First of all, count on having an interesting educational experience. There is no better way to learn how research is done than to observe it firsthand. Beyond that, you have a right to expect that your reactions will remain confidential; that you will be debriefed about the purpose of the research; that you will receive an interpretation of your responses or test results; and finally, that the results of the research project will be made available to you (Blanck et al., 1992; Fisher & Fyrberg, 1994). (See Table 2–3 ■.)

Psychological research can be truly fascinating. If you do participate as a subject, you may be inspired to try experiments or answer questions of your

Table 2–3 ■ **Basic Ethical Guidelines for Psychological Researchers**

- Do no harm.
- Accurately describe risks to potential subjects.
- Ensure that participation is voluntary.
- Minimize any discomfort to participants.
- Maintain confidentiality.
- Do not unnecessarily invade privacy.
- Use deception only when absolutely necessary.
- Remove any misconceptions caused by deception (debrief).
- Provide results and interpretations to participants.
- Treat participants with dignity and respect.

own. Many careers in psychology were launched in just this way.

The Ethics of Animal Research

Research with animals can also raise difficult ethical questions. In recognition of this fact, Principle 10 of the *Ethical Principles of Psychologists* states:

> An investigator of animal behavior strives to advance understanding of basic behavioral principles and/or to contribute to the improvement of human health and welfare. In seeking these ends, the investigator ensures the welfare of animals and treats them humanely. Laws and regulations notwithstanding, an animal's immediate protection depends upon the scientist's own conscience. ("Ethical," 1992)

Behind this statement lies a storm of controversy. Opinions about the ethics of animal research range widely—from medical researchers who routinely conduct animal experiments to vegetarian animal rights activists who raid labs to "liberate" animals. It is not possible here to discuss all of the arguments for and against animal research. However, a brief sketch of the debate may serve as a starting point for further thought.

At one extreme, members of the animal liberation movement believe that animals have a right to live without human interference. Animal liberators oppose animal research of all kinds, the raising of animals for food, hunting, rodeos, zoos, and circuses. They regard behavioral research as worthless and cruel, and want to abolish it entirely (Herzog, 1990). At the other extreme are scientists who believe human welfare always takes precedence over animal welfare. These individuals feel that they have a moral imperative to improve the human condition and save human lives. Doing so, they believe, inescapably involves animal research ("Scientists," 1989).

Is there a middle ground?

The majority of scientists, 80 percent of the general public, and many animal welfare advocates, take a more moderate position. These individuals accept the necessity for scientific experiments. They note, for instance, that creating vaccines to end the crippling polio epidemics of the 1950s would have been impossible without animal research. They also recognize that animals, as well as humans, benefit from knowledge gained from scientific research. Moderates primarily seek to ensure humane treatment of animals and to minimize the use of animals where possible. As animal activist Phyllis Macy (1990) says:

> What is called for here is not the cessation of research with animals, but a different attitude toward their use. . . . Research with animals should above all be humane. This means respecting another creature's aspirations for life and capacity for pain. On this variable, all animals, including humans, are equal. We earn respect for ourselves by respecting life around us.

It is probably fair to say that the animal rights movement has called needed attention to the abuse of animals for such purposes as testing cosmetics and other commercial products. It has also encouraged development of alternatives to animal research. Part of the middle ground in this debate, if indeed one exists, is the agreed-upon value of finding alternatives that minimize the use of animals. For example, it may be possible to use computer simulations of animal behavior for teaching and preliminary research. Also, use of animals could be limited to critical studies. But, again questions arise: Who is to say what research is worthwhile? Is it possible to guess where new knowledge will lead? Might a seemingly minor finding eventually unleash a breakthrough?

Think About It No easy answers exist for the ethical questions raised by animal research. However, as noted in Chapter 1, a government report on behavioral research concluded, "The chance that alternatives will completely replace animals in the future is nil" ("Research," 1989). In light of this, how would you answer the following questions?

- When is the use of animals necessary? When are replacements acceptable?
- If use of animals is necessary, can their numbers be reduced?
- If use of animals is necessary, and the numbers cannot be decreased, what are the moral and ethical implications?
- Could animal subjects be treated more humanely than they are now?
- What groups are best qualified to make decisions in this area? ("Animal rights," 1990.)

Learning Check

1. Deception is regarded as a necessary part of almost all psychology experiments. T or F?

2. Most of the subjects who participated in Milgram's obedience experiment felt that they had not been harmed. T or F?

3. The major ethical question raised by the Stanford prison experiment concerned an invasion of privacy. T or F?

4. In the United States, the American Psychological Association must rule on whether or not an experiment is ethical before it is performed. T or F?

5. Principle 10 of the *Ethical Principles of Psychologists* states that humane treatment of animals ultimately depends on each scientist's own conscience. T or F?

Critical Thinking

6. Perhaps the most basic of all ethical requirements in psychological research involves the accurate reporting of results. Can you explain why?

Answers:

1. F 2. T 3. F 4. F 5. T 6. To advance scientific knowledge and human welfare, psychologists must report the results of their studies honestly—even when the results contradict the researcher's beliefs or expectations. It takes a high level of integrity to do psychological research and follow the evidence wherever it leads.

Chapter Summary

Why is the scientific method important to psychologists?

◆ The **scientific method** is used to improve on common sense and avoid the pitfalls of informal observation.

◆ Important elements in a scientific investigation include **observing, defining a problem,** proposing a **hypothesis, gathering evidence/testing the hypothesis, publishing the results,** and forming a **theory.**

◆ Before they can be investigated, psychological concepts must be given **operational definitions.**

How do psychologists collect information?

◆ Naturalistic observation is a starting place in many investigations. Three problems with this approach are the effects of the observer on the observed, observer bias, and an inability to explain observed behavior.

◆ In animal studies, the **anthropomorphic fallacy** can lead to false conclusions. This error is the tendency to treat animals as if they had human characteristics.

◆ In the **correlational method,** relationships between two traits, responses, or events are measured.

◆ A **correlation coefficient** is computed to gauge the strength of the relationship. Correlations allow prediction, but they are usually insufficient to demonstrate cause-and-effect connections.

◆ **Relationships** in psychology may be **positive** or **negative, linear** or **curvilinear.** Relationships are often clarified by graphing.

◆ Cause-and-effect relationships are best identified by **controlled experiments.**

How is an experiment performed?

◆ In an experiment, two or more groups of subjects are formed. These groups differ only with regard to the **independent variable** (condition of interest as a cause in the experiment).

◆ Effects on the **dependent variable** are then measured. All other conditions **(extraneous variables)** are held constant.

◆ It must be possible to **replicate** (repeat) observations or experiments for them to be meaningful.

◆ In experiments testing drugs, a **placebo** (fake pill or injection) must be used to control for the effects of expectations.

◆ Drug research also frequently employs a **double-blind** procedure so that neither subjects nor experimenters know who is receiving a drug.

◆ A related problem is the **experimenter effect.** This is the tendency for experimenters to subtly and unconsciously influence the outcome of an experiment.

◆ Expectations can create a **self-fulfilling prophecy,** in which a person changes in the direction of the expectation.

What other research methods do psychologists use?

◆ The **clinical method** employs **case studies,** which are in-depth records of a single subject. Case studies provide important information on topics that would not be studied any other way.

◆ In the **survey method,** people in a **representative sample** are asked a series of carefully worded questions. Responses to these questions provide information on the attitudes and psychological functioning of large groups of people.

How dependable is psychological information found in the popular press?

◆ Information in the popular media varies greatly in quality and accuracy.

◆ It is wise to approach such information with skepticism and caution. This is especially true with regard to the **source of information, uncontrolled observation, correlation and causation, inferences, oversimplification,** and **single examples.** Critical thinking will help you cut through the misinformation.

What ethical questions does psychological research raise?

◆ Psychological research raises a number of ethical questions. Three **ethical issues** of particular importance in human research are: **deception, invasion of privacy,** and **lasting harm.**

◆ Animal research also poses ethical dilemmas. Debates concerning animal welfare are based on personal values and morals and are therefore not easily resolved. The American Psychological Association strongly endorses the humane treatment of research animals.

The Brain, Biology, and Behavior

Preview

Worlds within Worlds within Worlds

I magine yourself smaller than the period at the end of this sentence. Then join me as we enter a bizarre microscopic world. Surrounding us is a tangle of spidery branches, delicate fibers, and transparent globes. As we watch, pulsing waves of electrical energy flash by, scattering everywhere. Meanwhile, all is bathed in a swirling sea of exotic chemicals. We are indeed in a strange realm. Yet there is beauty here, and mind-bending complexity— for we have just entered that most amazing of all computers, the human brain.

Crack open the fragile shell of the skull and you find, in the truest sense, "worlds within worlds within worlds." The human brain is the size of a large grapefruit. Weighing a little over 3 pounds, it consists of some 100 billion **neurons** (NEW-rons: *individual nerve cells*).

Neurons carry and process information. They also activate muscles and glands. Thus, everything you think, do, or feel can be traced back to these tiny cells. The mass of neurons we call the brain allows humans to make music of exquisite beauty, to seek a cure for cancer, or to read a book like this one. Each neuron in the brain's "enchanted loom" is linked to as many as 15,000 others. This network makes it possible to combine and store an exceedingly large amount of information. In fact, there may be more *possible* pathways between neurons in a single human brain than there are atoms in the entire universe!

Scientists have long known that the brain is the organ of consciousness and action. Yet only recently have they been able to demonstrate it directly. To prove the point, researcher José Delgado once entered a bullring with a cape and a radio transmitter. The bull charged. Delgado retreated. At the last instant the speeding bull stopped short. Why? Because Delgado's radio activated electrodes (metal wires) implanted deep within the bull's brain. These, in turn, stimulated "control centers" that brought the bull to a halt.

Biopsychology *is the study of how biological processes, especially activity in the brain and nervous system, relate to behavior.* Clearly, answers to many age-old questions of mind, consciousness, and knowledge lie buried within the brain (Carlson, 1994). Let us enter this fascinating realm for a closer look at our biological heritage and human potential.

Chapter Survey

Theme: Brain activity is the source of human consciousness, intelligence, and behavior.

Key Questions:

How do nerve cells operate and communicate?	
What are the functions of major parts of the nervous system?	
How is the brain organized and what do its higher structures do?	
Why are the brain's association areas important? What happens when they are injured?	
What kinds of behaviors are controlled by the subcortex?	
Does the glandular system affect behavior?	
In what ways do right- and left-handed individuals differ?	
How do biopsychologists study the brain?	

Key Topics to Watch for:

Neurons, nerve impulses, and neurotransmitters
Divisions of the nervous system
The cerebral cortex
Right and left brain hemispheres
Lobes of the cortex
Associative areas
Aphasias and agnosias
The medulla, cerebellum, and reticular formation
The thalamus and hypothalamus
The limbic system and emotion
Endocrine glands and hormones
Handedness, brain dominance, and laterality
Traditional research methods
Computer-enhanced brain images

Neurons—Building a "Biocomputer"

As biopsychologist Paul MacLean once remarked, the towering question today is whether we can master the brain before we blow ourselves to smithereens through our mastery of physics and chemistry. Unraveling the mysteries of the brain begins with neurons, the basic units of the human "biocomputer." A single neuron is not very smart. Yet, when neurons join in vast networks, they produce intelligence and consciousness.

How do neurons carry information?

Parts of a Neuron

Long "chains" of neurons make up the nervous system. No two neurons are exactly alike in size or shape, but most have four basic parts (Fig. 3–1 ◆). Notice first the *dendrites* (DEN-drytes), which look like the roots of a tree. **Dendrites** *specialize in receiving messages from other neurons*. The **soma** (SOH-mah: *cell body*), also accepts incoming information, which it collects and combines. Every so often, these messages cause the soma to send a nerve impulse down a thin fiber called the *axon* (AK-sahn). The **axon** *carries information away from the cell body*.

Most axons end in **axon terminals** (*branches*) that link with the dendrites and somas of other neurons. These links

allow information to pass from neuron to neuron. Some axons are only 0.1 millimeter long. (That's about the width of a pencil line.) Others stretch up to a meter through the nervous system. Like miniature cables, axons carry messages from sensory organs to the brain, from the brain to muscles or glands, or simply from one neuron to the next.

The Nerve Impulse

Each neuron is like a tiny biological battery. *Electrically charged molecules* called **ions** (EYE-ons) are found in differing numbers inside and outside of the cell. As a result, a tiny electrical charge exists across the **cell membrane** (*outer casing*). If you could put one end of a tiny wire inside the axon and the other end outside, you would find a small difference in voltage, just as if you had touched the ends of a flashlight battery. The inside of human neurons measures about minus 70 millivolts compared to outside the cell (Fig. 3–2 ◆). (A millivolt is one thousandth of a volt.)

The electrical charge of a neuron at rest is called the **resting potential**. Messages arriving from other neurons alter the resting potential until it reaches a **threshold** (*trigger point*) for firing. The threshold for human neurons is about minus 50 millivolts (see Fig. 3–2). When a neuron reaches this point, an **action potential**, *or nerve impulse*, sweeps down the axon (Fig. 3–3 ◆).

The action potential occurs because **ion channels** (*tiny molecular tunnels*) pierce the axon membrane. These channels are normally closed by molecules that act like "gates"

Figure 3–1 ◆ An example of a neuron, or nerve cell, showing several of its important features. The right foreground shows a nerve cell fiber in cross section, and the upper left inset gives a more realistic picture of the shape of neurons. The nerve impulse usually travels from the dendrites and soma to the branching ends of the axon. The neuron shown here is a motor neuron. Motor neurons originate in the brain or spinal cord and send their axons to the muscles or glands of the body.

Synapse (see Fig. 3–5 for an enlarged view)

Other neuron

Axon terminals

Nerve impulse

Myelin

Neurilemma

Nerve impulse

Soma (cell body)

Axon

Axon collateral (branch)

Nerve cell fiber

Myelin sheath

Axon

Dendrites

Membrane potential (in millivolts)

+30

0

−50

−70

Resting potential

Action potential

Negative after-potential

Threshold

Time

Axon

Figure 3–2 ◆ Activity in an axon can be measured by placing electrical probes inside and outside the axonal membrane. At rest, the inside of an axon is about minus 60 to 70 millivolts, compared with the outside. Electrochemical changes in a nerve cell generate an action potential. When positively charged sodium ions (Na^+) rush into the cell, its interior briefly becomes positive. This is the action potential. After the action potential, an outward flow of positive potassium ions (K^+) restores the negative charge inside the axon. (See Figures 3–3 and 3–4 for further explanation.)

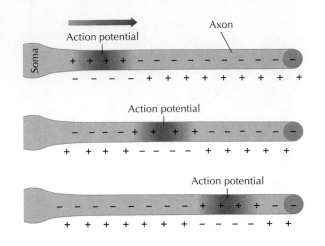

Figure 3–3 ◆ The inside of an axon normally has a negative electrical charge. The fluid surrounding an axon is normally positive. As an action potential passes along the axon, these charges reverse, so that the interior of the axon briefly becomes positive.

or "doors." During an action potential, the gates pop open and allow sodium ions (Na⁺) to rush into the axon (Carlson, 1994). This happens first near the soma. Then, as the action potential moves along, the gates open, one after another, down the length of the axon (Fig. 3–4 ◆). At this very instant, millions of action potentials are firing in your brain.

The action potential is an **all-or-nothing event** (*an impulse occurs completely or not at all*). You might find it helpful to picture the axon as a row of dominoes set on end. Tipping

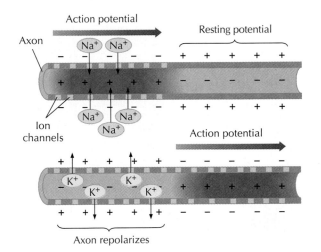

Figure 3–4 ◆ Cross-sectional views of an axon. The right end of the top axon is at rest, with a negatively charged interior. An action potential begins when the ion channels open and sodium ions (Na⁺) enter the axon. In this drawing the action potential would travel rapidly along the axon, from left to right. In the lower axon the action potential has moved to the right. After it passes, potassium ions (K⁺) flow out of the axon. This quickly renews the negative charge inside the axon, so it can fire again. Sodium ions that enter the axon during an action potential are pumped back out more slowly. Their removal restores the original resting potential.

over the dominoes is an all-or-nothing act. Once the first domino drops, a wave of falling blocks will zip rapidly to the end of the line. Similarly, when a nerve impulse is triggered near the soma, a wave of activity (the action potential) travels down the length of the axon.

After each nerve impulse, *the cell briefly drops below its resting level.* This **negative after-potential** occurs because potassium ions (K⁺) flow out of the neuron while the membrane gates are open (Fig. 3–4). After a nerve impulse, the neuron recharges. This occurs as displaced ions move back inside and outside the cell membrane. In our model, the row of dominoes is quickly set up again, beginning at the soma. Soon, the axon is ready for another wave of activity.

It takes about one thousandth of a second for a neuron to fire an impulse and return to its resting level. For this reason, only about 1,000 nerve impulses per second are possible. However, firing rates of 1 per second to 400 per second are more typical.

How fast do nerve impulses travel along the axon?

Impulses travel at about 2.5 meters (roughly, 8 feet) per second in small, thin axons. In large axons the rate can be up to 100 meters per second (about 225 miles per hour). The larger the diameter of an axon, the faster it conducts. The speed of nerve impulses is also higher when *myelin* (MY-eh-lin) is present. **Myelin** *is a fatty layer that covers some axons.* Where the myelin is broken by small gaps, nerve impulses can move faster by jumping from gap to gap.

As you can see, nerve impulses are far from instantaneous. If someone steps on your toes, it takes one fiftieth of a second for your brain to get the message!

How does information move from one neuron to another?

Synapses and Neurotransmitters

We have seen that the nerve impulse is primarily an electrical event. That's why electrically stimulating the brain affects behavior. (A good example is José Delgado's "electronic bullfighting" described in the Preview.) In contrast, communication between neurons is primarily *chemical*.

The microscopic space between two neurons, over which messages pass, is called a **synapse** (SIN-aps) (Fig. 3–5 ◆). When a nerve impulse reaches the tips of the axon terminals, it causes *neurotransmitters* (NUE-roh-TRANS-mit-ers) to be released into the synaptic gap. **Neurotransmitters** *are chemicals that alter activity in other neurons.* Transmitter molecules cross the gap and attach to special *receptor sites* on the soma or dendrites of the next neuron (Fig. 3–5). **Receptor sites** *are tiny areas on the surface of a cell that are sensitive to neurotransmitters.* Transmitters also activate receptor sites on muscles and glands.

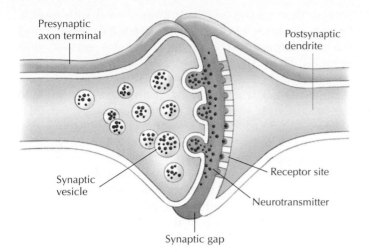

Figure 3–5 ◆ A highly magnified view of a synapse like that shown in Figure 3–1. In a typical chemical synapse, neurotransmitters are stored in tiny sacs called synaptic vesicles. When a nerve impulse arrives at an axon terminal, the vesicles move to the surface and release neurotransmitters. These transmitter molecules cross the synaptic gap to affect the next neuron. The size of the gap is exaggerated here; it is actually only about one millionth of an inch. Transmitter molecules vary in their effects: Some excite the next neuron and some inhibit its activity. In insects and lower animals electrical synapses sometimes occur. In this case, a nerve impulse in one neuron may directly alter the electrical charge in the next neuron, without any reliance on chemical messengers (Agnati et al., 1992).

Does the release of a neurotransmitter immediately trigger an action potential in the next neuron?

Not always. Transmitters may *excite* the next neuron (move it closer to firing) or *inhibit* it (make an impulse less likely). At any instant, a neuron may receive messages from hundreds or thousands of other neurons. If several "exciting" messages arrive close in time, and they are not canceled by "inhibiting" messages, the neuron reaches its trigger point. This means that chemical messages are *combined* before a neuron "decides" to fire its all-or-nothing action potential. Multiply these events by 100 billion neurons and 100 trillion synapses and you have an amazing computer—one that fits into a space smaller than a shoe box.

There are now more than 30 known or suspected neurotransmitters in the brain. Among the more important "chemical messengers" are acetylcholine, adrenaline, noradrenaline, serotonin, dopamine, histamine, and various amino acids. So, in addition to acting like an electronic computer, the brain is also a sort of chemical factory. The large variety of transmitter chemicals is one reason why thousands of drugs affect behavior.

Many drugs operate by imitating, duplicating, or blocking the actions of neurotransmitters. For example, a transmitter called **acetylcholine** (ah-SEET-ul-KOH-leen) *normally activates muscles.* However, the drug **curare** (cue-RAH-ree) *competes with acetylcholine by attaching to receptor sites on muscles.* This prevents acetylcholine from reaching the sites. As a result, a person or animal given curare will be paralyzed—a fact known to South American Indians of the Amazon River Basin, who use curare as an arrow poison.

Neural Regulators Recent discoveries have revealed a new class of brain transmitters called **neuropeptides** (NUE-roh-PEP-tides), *which regulate the activity of other neurons.* An example of a brain peptide in action is shown in Figure 3–6 ◆. As you can see, some neurons have specific receptor sites for opiate drugs such as morphine (Agnati et al., 1992).

Why would the brain have opiate receptors? After all, the human body isn't born with opium in it.

This is exactly the question that started a search for brain peptides. Scientists found that *the brain produces opiate-like neural regulators* called **enkephalins** (en-KEF-ah-lins) to relieve pain and stress. Related, *opiate-like chemicals* called **endorphins** (en-DORF-ins) *are released by the pituitary gland.* It now appears that phenomena as diverse as "runner's high," the placebo effect, and acupuncture may be explained by the action of enkephalins and endorphins. (See Chapter 6 for more information.)

When you accidentally touch something hot, your hand jerks away. The neural messages for this action are carried by neurotransmitters. At the same time, pain may cause the brain to release enkephalins and endorphins. These chemical regulators reduce the pain so that it is not too disabling.

Relaying messages across synapses is fast and efficient. Information travels in well-defined pathways, like train tracks connecting cities. In contrast, neuropeptides seem to "leave the track" in order to influence surrounding nerve cells. The action of neuropeptides is more like a radio broadcast: When a peptide is released, *large groups of neurons may be affected*, a process called **volume transmission** (Agnati et al., 1992).

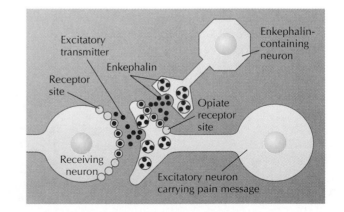

Figure 3–6 ◆ This simplified diagram shows how natural opiates may operate in the brain to relieve pain. Neurons carrying pain messages appear to have receptor sites for opiate-like transmitters called enkephalins. Release of enkephalins by "regulator" neurons suppresses activity in pain-carrying neurons. This suppression blocks or reduces the flow of pain messages.

Rather than merely crossing the synaptic gap, some neuropeptides are carried through the fluid-filled space surrounding neurons. Messages carried in this way can be received by any nerve cell that has an appropriate receptor. A neuropeptide can affect the neuron that released it (autoregulation), a neighboring cell, or a distant cell (Fig. 3–7 ◆).

Neuropeptides can have long-term effects on how excitable a target neuron is. The neuron's metabolism or growth may even be affected. In these ways, release of peptides from a few neurons can alter the pattern of activity in large areas of the brain. By regulating the general level of activity in brain circuits, neuropeptides appear to influence sleep and wakefulness, alertness, moods, memory, pain, hunger, pleasure, sexual behavior, and other basic processes (Agnati et al., 1992). Ultimately, brain peptides may help explain depression, schizophrenia, drug addiction, and other puzzling problems.

because they consist mainly of axons coated with myelin. Outside the brain and spinal cord, a *thin layer of cells* called the **neurilemma** (NUE-rih-LEM-ah) also encases most nerve cell fibers. (Return to Figure 3–1.)

The neurilemma forms a "tunnel" for damaged nerve cell fibers to follow as they repair themselves. If you were to accidentally sever a finger and have it sewn back on, there is a good chance the nerves would regenerate. In fact, you could expect feeling to creep back at a rate of about 1 millimeter per day.

The brain and spinal cord cannot normally grow new neurons to replace any that are lost, so they must last a lifetime. If the spinal cord is torn, cut, or crushed, a person may permanently lose use of the body below the point of injury. Also, if the cell body of *any* neuron is destroyed, the cell's axon and dendrites will die, too. This is the cause of polio, a crippling disease in which neurons that control

The Nervous System— Wired for Action

Picture two people playing catch with a Frisbee. To toss the Frisbee or catch it, a huge amount of information must be sensed, interpreted, and then directed to countless muscle fibers. The neural circuits of the body are ablaze with activity. Let's explore the "wiring diagram" that makes this possible.

Neurons and Nerves

Are neurons the same as nerves?

No. Neurons are tiny individual cells. You can see a nerve with the unaided eye. Rather than being single cells, **nerves** *are large bundles of axons and dendrites.* Some nerves are white

Each year spinal cord injuries rob many thousands of people, like actor Christopher Reeve, of the ability to move. Yet, there is growing hope that nerve grafting techniques may someday make it possible for some of these people to walk again.

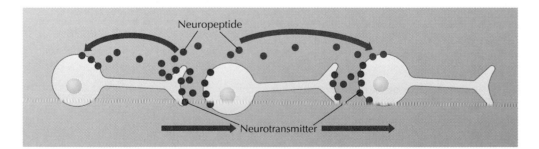

Figure 3–7 ◆ Some neurons release only neurotransmitters. These nerve cells create fast, reliable message pathways in the brain. Other neurons release neuropeptides, which directly regulate the activity of specific target neurons. (See Figure 3–6.) A third class of neurons releases both neurotransmitters and neuropeptides. As you would expect, the neurotransmitters are released directly into the synaptic gap. Neuropeptides, in contrast, are released at some distance from the synapse. As the drawing shows, brain peptides can travel through the extracellular fluid surrounding neurons. Although they move slowly, neuropeptides can have far-reaching effects on neighboring neurons, resulting in changes in emotion and behavior (Agnati et al., 1992).

muscles are destroyed. However, fascinating exceptions to the preceding statements are beginning to appear.

Brain Grafts and Nerve Regeneration

Transplanting brain tissue may sound like science fiction. Nevertheless, some brain grafts are already being done. It seems likely that grafts will someday be used to correct a variety of nervous system diseases and injuries.

If brain cells that die are lost forever, can they be replaced artificially? In some cases the answer is yes. Damage can sometimes be repaired with grafts of healthy brain cells (Kimble, 1990). In one experiment, the brains of rats were damaged in an area that affects learning. Some of the rats then received implants of healthy brain tissue in the damaged region. Others remained untreated. Next, a maze-learning test was conducted, with encouraging results: Rats that received implants did significantly better than those left untreated (Labbe et al., 1983). In addition, the grafts appeared to have "taken," or actually linked up with existing brain tissue.

Implants may also provide a cure for some brain-centered diseases. For instance, the crippling effects of Parkinson's disease are caused by a loss of brain cells that release dopamine. (Recall that dopamine is a transmitter substance.) In recent years, a number of human patients with severe Parkinson's disease have had dopamine-producing cells grafted into their brains. Some of these patients have improved greatly (Lindvall, 1994).

A problem with brain grafts is that they are unlikely to be accepted by the body unless immature fetal cells are used. However, reliance on fetal cells raises grave ethical concerns. Is there a way to resolve this dilemma? In a stunning breakthrough, researchers have succeeded in growing normal, mature brain cells in the laboratory (Ronnett et al., 1990). Thus, cultured neurons may soon be available to help repair brain injuries and to treat Parkinson's disease (Fig. 3–8 ◆).

Obviously, it's a little early to think about seeking a brain graft to get you through final exams. Transplants remain highly experimental. Just the same, brain grafting may make it possible to repair some brain and spinal injuries that are now irreversible. Imagine what that could mean to a person confined to a wheelchair or someone suffering the after-effects of a stroke.

Progress is also being made in coaxing regrowth of damaged neurons in the brain and spinal cord. Scientists were recently able to partially repair severed spinal cords in rats. First they closed the gap with nerve fibers from outside the spinal cord. Then they bio-

Figure 3–8 ◆ Scientists predict that damaged neurons in the brain and spinal cord will someday be regenerated with a combination of growth-promoting substances and chemicals that block growth inhibitors. Here, a cultured nerve cell bathed in nerve growth factor (a growth-promoting protein) has been coaxed into sprouting new nerve endings (Weiss, 1989).

chemically coaxed the severed spinal nerve fibers to grow through the "tunnels" provided by the implanted fibers. Within 2 months, the rats had regained partial use of their hind legs (Cheng, Cao, & Olson, 1996).

Although it is unwise to raise false hopes, such studies suggest that regrowth and repair of the nervous system is slowly moving closer to reality (Baisden, 1995).

The Nervous System

The nervous system is a single unified structure. Dividing it into smaller parts, however, makes it easier to understand. As seen in Figures 3–9 ◆ and 3–10 ◆, the **central nervous system (CNS)** *consists of the brain and spinal cord.* The CNS can be distinguished from the **peripheral nervous system (PNS),** *which is composed of nerves that carry information to and from the CNS.* The brain is the central "computer" of the nervous system. It communicates with the rest of the body through the spinal cord and the peripheral nervous system (and in other ways as well).

How are the CNS and the peripheral nervous system related?

The Peripheral Nervous System The peripheral system has two subparts: (1) the **somatic system,** *which carries messages to and from the sense organs and skeletal muscles* and (2) the **autonomic system,** *which serves the internal organs and glands of the body.* In general, the somatic system controls voluntary behavior. The autonomic system controls involuntary activities. Thus, messages carried by the somatic

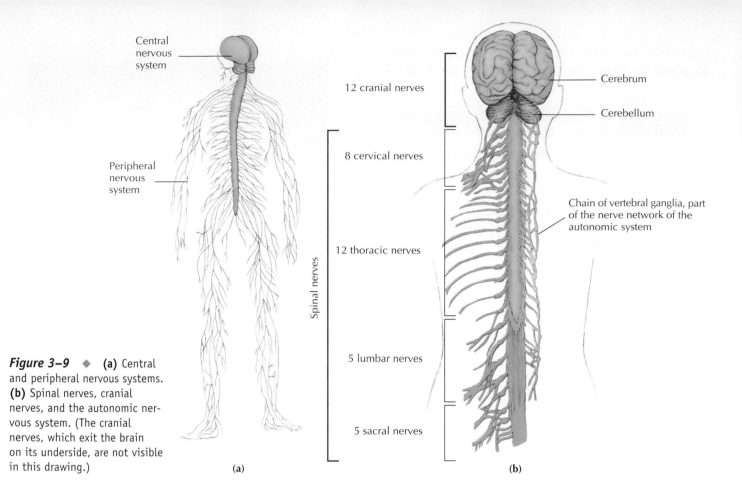

Central nervous system

Peripheral nervous system

12 cranial nerves

8 cervical nerves

Spinal nerves

12 thoracic nerves

5 lumbar nerves

5 sacral nerves

Cerebrum

Cerebellum

Chain of vertebral ganglia, part of the nerve network of the autonomic system

Figure 3–9 ◆ **(a)** Central and peripheral nervous systems. **(b)** Spinal nerves, cranial nerves, and the autonomic nervous system. (The cranial nerves, which exit the brain on its underside, are not visible in this drawing.)

(a)

(b)

system can make your hand move, but they cannot change your heart rate. Likewise, messages carried by the autonomic system can stimulate digestion, but they cannot make you write a letter.

The autonomic nervous system (ANS) can be subdivided into the *sympathetic* and *parasympathetic* branches. Both branches are related to emotional responses, such as crying, sweating, heart rate, and other involuntary behavior

Figure 3–10 ◆ Subparts of the nervous system.

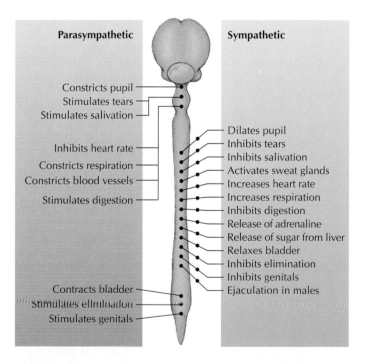

Parasympathetic

Constricts pupil
Stimulates tears
Stimulates salivation

Inhibits heart rate
Constricts respiration
Constricts blood vessels
Stimulates digestion

Contracts bladder
Stimulates elimination
Stimulates genitals

Sympathetic

Dilates pupil
Inhibits tears
Inhibits salivation
Activates sweat glands
Increases heart rate
Increases respiration
Inhibits digestion
Release of adrenaline
Release of sugar from liver
Relaxes bladder
Inhibits elimination
Inhibits genitals
Ejaculation in males

Figure 3–11 ◆ Sympathetic and parasympathetic branches of the autonomic nervous system. Both branches control involuntary actions. The sympathetic system generally activates the body. The parasympathetic system generally quiets it. The sympathetic branch relays through a chain of ganglia (clusters of cell bodies) outside the spinal cord.

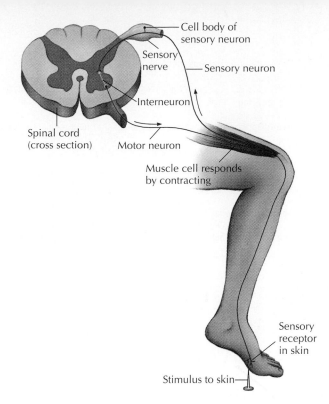

(Fig. 3–11 ◆). The ANS, along with the somatic system, coordinates the inner and outer worlds of the body. If a large and angry-looking dog lunges at you, the somatic system helps control your muscles for running. At the same time, the autonomic system raises blood pressure, quickens your heart, and so forth.

How do the branches of the autonomic system differ?

The **sympathetic branch** *is an "emergency" system that prepares the body for "fight or flight" during times of danger or emotion.* In essence, it arouses the body for action. The **parsympathetic branch** *quiets the body and returns it to a lower level of arousal.* The parasympathetic branch is most active soon after a stressful or emotional event (Thompson, 1985). It also helps maintain vital functions such as heart rate, breathing, and digestion at moderate levels. Of course, both branches of the ANS are always active. Their combined activity determines if the body is aroused or quieted. (See Chapter 13 for more information on the autonomic system.)

The Spinal Cord The spinal cord is responsible for some low-level behaviors, such as reflexes. It also acts like a cable connecting the brain to other parts of the body. If you were to cut through the spinal cord, you would see columns of **white matter** *in areas where myelin is present.* This tissue is made up of axons that leave the spinal cord, where they form peripheral nerves. Return to Figure 3–10b and you will see that there are 30 pairs of these *spinal nerves* leaving the spinal cord, plus one pair leaving the bottom tip. The **spinal nerves** *carry sensory and motor messages to and from the spinal cord.* In addition, 12 pairs of **cranial nerves** *leave the brain directly.* Together, these nerves keep the entire body in communication with the brain.

How is the spinal cord related to behavior?

The simplest behavior pattern is a **reflex arc,** *in which a stimulus provokes an automatic response.* Such reflexes occur within the spinal cord, without any help from the brain (see Fig. 3–12 ◆). Imagine that one of our Frisbee players steps on a thorn. Pain is detected in the foot by a **sensory neuron** (*a nerve cell that carries messages from the senses toward the CNS*). An action potential is fired off to the spinal cord.

Inside the spinal cord, the sensory neuron synapses with a **connector neuron** (*a nerve cell that links two others*). The connector neuron activates a **motor neuron** (*a cell that carries commands from the CNS to muscles and glands*). The muscle

Figure 3–12 ◆ A simple sensory-motor (reflex) arc. A simple reflex is set in motion by a stimulus to the skin (or other part of the body). The nerve impulse travels to the spinal cord and then back out to a muscle, which contracts. Reflexes provide an "automatic" protective device for the body.

fibers are made up of **effector cells** (*cells capable of producing a response*). The muscle cells contract and cause the foot to withdraw.

Note that brain activity is not required for a reflex arc. The body can react to protect itself without calling on the brain. (However, the spinal cord informs the brain of the action it has taken.) In reality, even a simple reflex usually triggers more complex activity. For example, muscles of the limb on the opposite side of the body must contract to support a shift in weight. Even this can be done by the spinal cord, but it involves many more cells and several spinal nerves.

Perhaps you have realized how adaptive it is to have a spinal cord capable of responding on its own. Such automatic responses leave the brain of our Frisbee ace free to deal with more important information—such as the location of trees, lampposts, and attractive onlookers—as he or she makes a grandstand catch.

Learning Check	Critical Thinking

Before reading further, see if you can answer these questions.

1. The _____ and _____ are receiving areas where information from other neurons is accepted.

2. Nerve impulses are carried down the _____ to the _____ _____.

3. The point of interchange between two neurons is called a myelin. T or F? _Synapse_

4. The _____ potential becomes an _____ potential when a neuron passes the threshold for firing.

5. Neuropeptides are transmitter substances that help regulate the activity of neurons. T or F?

6. The somatic and autonomic systems are part of the _____ nervous system.

7. Sodium and potassium ions flow through ion channels in the synapse to trigger a nerve impulse in the receiving neuron. T or F?

8. The simplest behavior sequence is a _____ _____.

9. The parasympathetic nervous system is most active during times of high emotion. T or F?

10. Why do you think that brain cells are not replaced when they are damaged, like other cells in the body are?

The Cerebral Cortex— My, What a Big Brain You Have!

In many ways humans are pretty unimpressive creatures. Fragile, weak, born naked and helpless, humans are excelled by animals in almost every category of strength, speed, and sensory sensitivity. The one area in which humans excel is intelligence.

Do humans have the largest brains?

Surprisingly, no. Elephant brains weigh 13 pounds, and whale brains, 19 pounds. At 3 pounds, the human brain seems puny—until we figure the proportion of brain weight to body weight. We then find that an elephant's brain is 1/1000 of its weight; the ratio for sperm whales is 1 to 10,000. The ratio for humans is 1 to 60. If someone tells you that you have a "whale of a brain" be sure to find out if they mean size or ratio!

What about dolphins?

The only other creatures that compare well to humans in both brain size and *brain-body ratio* are dolphins and porpoises. It is possible, although not established, that these animals may be as intelligent as humans (or more so). Researchers have shown that dolphins communicate with sounds as complex as our own (Wursig, 1979). However, dolphins may use larger portions of their brains for swimming and "lower" sensory-motor functions.

So, relatively speaking, humans have very highly developed brains. More importantly, as we move from lower to higher animals, an ever-increasing proportion of the brain is devoted to the **cerebrum** (SER-eh-brum or ser-REE-brum: *two large hemispheres that cover the upper part of the brain*) (see Fig. 3–13 ◆). The cerebrum is the highest brain

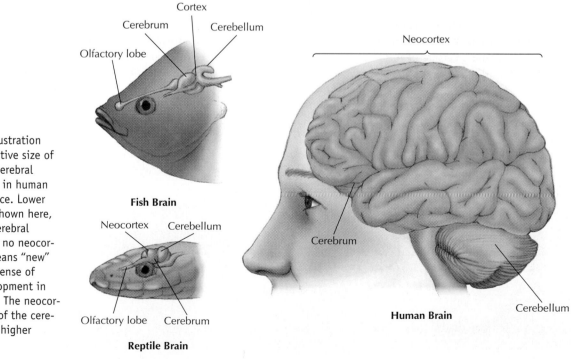

Figure 3–13 ◆ An illustration showing the increased relative size of the human cerebrum and cerebral cortex, a significant factor in human adaptability and intelligence. Lower animals, such as the fish shown here, have only small areas of cerebral cortex, and they may have no neocortex. The term *neocortex* means "new" cortex. It is "new" in the sense of being a more recent development in the evolution of the brain. The neocortex makes up a large area of the cerebral cortex in humans and higher animals.

area in humans. Its *outer layer,* or "bark," is known as the **cerebral cortex** (seh-REE-brel or ser-EH-brel). Although the cerebral cortex is only about 3 millimeters thick (one tenth of an inch), it contains no less than 70 percent of the neurons in the central nervous system.

Corticalization The cerebral cortex looks a little like a giant, wrinkled walnut. It covers most of the visible portions of the brain with a mantle of **gray matter** (*spongy tissue made up mostly of cell bodies*). The cortex in lower animals is small and smooth; in humans it is highly convoluted and the largest brain structure. The fact that humans are more intelligent than other animals is related to this **corticalization** (KORE-tih-kal-ih-ZAY-shun), *or increase in the size and wrinkling of the cortex.*

Does having a larger brain make a person smarter?

Several recent studies have found positive correlations between intelligence and the size of higher brain structures (Andreasen et al., 1993; Rushton, 1995; Wickett, Vernon, & Lee, 1995). These findings imply that differences in brain size may partly explain differences in intelligence. It is a mistake, however, to think that brain size alone determines human intelligence.

Critical Thinking

The Brain at Work

According to folklore, a person with a large head and a high forehead is likely to be intelligent. But brain efficiency probably has as much to do with intelligence as brain size does (Gazzaniga, 1995).

Psychologist Richard J. Haier and his colleagues found that the brains of people who perform well on mental tests consume less energy than the brains of poor performers (Haier et al., 1988). Haier measured brain activity with a technique called *positron emis-*

sion tomography (tuh-MOG-ruh-fee), or PET. A **PET scan** *records the amount of glucose (sugar) used by brain cells.* By using harmless, radioactively labeled glucose, it is possible to record an image of how hard the brain is working (Fig. 3–14 ◆). (See this chapter's Exploration for more information.)

What did PET scans reveal when subjects took a difficult reasoning test? Researchers found that the brains of those who scored *lowest* on the test used the *most* glucose. Although we might assume that smart brains are hard-working brains, the reverse appears to be true. Brighter subjects actually used less energy to get the right answers. Haier believes this shows that intelligence is related to brain efficiency: Less efficient brains work harder and still accomplish less. We've all had days like that!

Cerebral Hemispheres The cortex is composed of two sides, or **hemispheres** (*half-globes*). The two hemispheres are connected by a *thick band of fibers* called the **corpus callosum** (KORE-pus kah-LOH-sum) (Fig. 3–15 ◆). Surprisingly, the two halves control opposite sides of the body. The left side of the brain mainly controls the right side of the body. The right half of the brain mainly controls left body areas. Thus, if a person has an injury or stroke that damages the right hemisphere, we can expect parts of the left side of the body to be paralyzed or to lose sensation. The reverse occurs for damage to the left hemisphere.

Hemispheric Specialization

We turn now to some remarkable findings. In 1981, biopsychologist Roger Sperry (1914–1994) won a Nobel Prize for his work on the special abilities of the cerebral hemispheres. Sperry and other scientists have shown that the right and left brain differ on tests of language, perception, music, and other capabilities.

Figure 3–14 ◆ In the images you see here, red, orange, and yellow indicate high consumption of glucose; green, blue, and pink show areas of low glucose use. The PET scan of the brain on the left shows that a man who solved 11 out of 36 reasoning problems burned more glucose than the man on the right, who solved 33.

Figure 3–15 ◆ The corpus callosum is the major "cable system" through which the right and left cerebral hemispheres communicate. A recent study found that the corpus callosum is larger in classically trained musicians than it is in non-musicians. When a person plays a violin or piano, the two hemispheres must communicate rapidly as they coordinate the movements of both hands. Presumably, the size of the corpus callosum can be altered by early experience, such as musical training.

How is it possible to test only one side of the brain?

One way is to work with people who have had a **"split-brain" operation**, *a rare type of surgery in which the corpus callosum is cut to control severe epilepsy.* The result is essentially a person with two brains in one body. After the surgery, it is a simple matter to route information to one hemisphere or the other (see Fig. 3–16 ◆).

"Split Brains" In both animals and humans, separating the hemispheres doubles consciousness. As Sperry (1968) said, "In other words, each hemisphere seems to have its own separate and private sensations; its own perceptions; its own concepts; and its own impulses to act."

How does a split-brain person function after the operation?

Having two "brains" in one body can create quite a dilemma. When one split-brain patient tried to dress himself he sometimes pulled his pants down with one hand and up with the other. Once, the patient grabbed his wife with his left hand and shook her violently. Gallantly, his right hand came to her aid and grabbed the belligerent left hand (Gazzaniga, 1970). Despite such conflicts, it is far more typical for split-brain patients to act completely normal. The reason is that both halves of the brain have about the same experience at the same time. Also, if a conflict arises, one hemisphere usually overrides the other.

Split-brain effects become most apparent in specialized testing. For example, a dollar sign can be flashed to the right brain and a question mark to the left brain. (Figure 3–16 shows how this is possible.) Next, the person is asked to draw what she or he saw, using the left hand, out of sight. The left hand draws a dollar sign. If the person

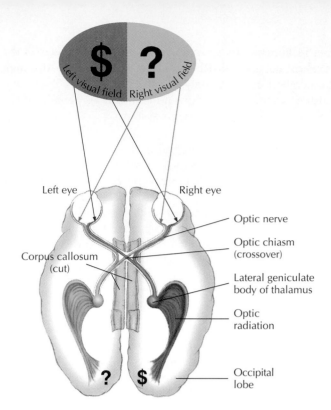

Figure 3–16 ◆ Basic nerve pathways of vision. Notice that the left portion of each eye connects only to the left half of the brain; likewise, the right portion of each eye connects to the right brain. When the corpus callosum is cut, a "split brain" results. Then visual information can be directed to one hemisphere or the other by flashing it in the right or left visual field as the person stares straight ahead.

is then asked to point with the right hand to a picture of what the hidden left hand drew, he or she will point to a question mark (Sperry, 1968). In short, for the split-brain person, one hemisphere may not know what is happening in the other. This has to be the ultimate case of the "right hand not knowing what the left hand is doing"! Figure 3–17 ◆ provides another example of split-brain testing.

Earlier it was stated that the hemispheres differ in abilities; in what ways do they differ?

Right Brain/Left Brain The brain divides its work in interesting ways. For example, language is a specialty of the left hemisphere. Roughly 95 percent of all adults use the left brain for speaking, writing, and understanding language. (The figures are 97 percent for right-handed persons and 68 percent for left-handers—see the Applications section for details.) In addition, the left hemisphere is superior at math, at judging time and rhythm, and at ordering complex movements (especially those needed for speech).

In contrast, the right hemisphere responds to only the simplest language and numbers. Working with the right brain is a little like talking to a child who only understands a dozen words or so. To answer questions, the right

Left Brain

- Language
- Speech
- Writing
- Calculation
- Time sense
- Rhythm
- Ordering of complex movements

Right Brain

- Non-verbal
- Perceptual skills
- Visualization
- Recognition of patterns, faces, melodies
- Recognition and expression of emotion
- Spatial skills
- Simple language comprehension

Left Hemisphere

I see a circle.

Right Hemisphere

I see nothing.

Figure 3–17 ◆ If a circle is flashed to the left brain and a split-brain patient is asked to say what she or he saw, the circle is easily named. The person can also pick out the circle by touching shapes with the right hand, out of sight under a tabletop (shown semi-transparent in the drawing). However, the left hand will be unable to identify the shape. If a triangle is flashed to the right brain, the person cannot say what was seen (speech is controlled by the left hemisphere). The person will also be unable to identify the correct shape by touch with the right hand. Now, however, the left hand will have no difficulty picking out the hidden triangle. Separate testing of each hemisphere reveals distinct specializations, as listed above. (Figure adapted from an illustration by Edward Kasper in McKean, 1985.)

hemisphere must point to objects or make other non-verbal responses (see Fig. 3–17).

At one time the right brain was regarded as the "minor" hemisphere. But we now know that it has talents of its own. The right hemisphere is superior at perceptual skills such as recognizing patterns, faces, and melodies. It is also involved in detecting and expressing emotion (Christianson et al., 1995). The right brain is better at visualization, spatial skills, and manipulation, such as arranging blocks to match a pattern, putting together a puzzle, or drawing a picture (Hellige, 1990).

Right brain superiority at spatial tasks leads to another intriguing observation. A common test of spatial ability involves solving a geometric puzzle. On this test the split-brain patient's left hand can typically perform quite well, but the right hand cannot. If the right hand fails to solve the problem, the left hand will "correct" the right (Ornstein, 1972). It's as if you know the answer to a problem and watch me making mistakes, and cannot refrain from telling me the answer.

Do people normally solve puzzles with just the right hemisphere? Do they do other things with only the left?

No. The entire brain is active at all times. It's true that some tasks may make *more* use of one hemisphere or the other. But both hemispheres are activated for virtually all tasks. What changes is the *balance* of activity between the two hemispheres (see "Using Psychology: The Risky Side of the Brain"). There is no scientific basis for the idea that people rely on only one hemisphere or the other for thinking (Hellige, 1990).

It is possible, of course, to prefer right- or left-brain modes of thought. One study found that students who prefer

right-brain thinking tend to major in such subjects as music, journalism, art, oral communication, and architecture. A left-brain preference was associated with majors in such subjects as management, computer science, mathematics, nursing, criminal justice, and education (Monfort et al., 1990).

In general, the left hemisphere is mainly involved with *analysis* (breaking information into parts). It also processes information *sequentially* (in order, one item after the next). The right hemisphere appears to process information simultaneously and *holistically* (all at once) (Springer & Deutsch, 1993). However, in most "real world" tasks, the hemispheres share the work. Each does the parts it does best and shares information with the other side of the brain. That's why popularized courses that claim to teach "right-brain thinking" ignore the fact that everyone already uses the right brain for thinking (Hellige, 1990).

The Risky Side of the Brain

If you pay attention to information from your right ear or the right side of vision, your left brain will become more active. The reverse is true for leftward attention and right-brain activity (De Toffol et al., 1992).

How could you apply these facts in everyday life? One way is to attend to information from the right side when you want to emphasize the talents of the left hemisphere. For example, to judge the timing or rhythm of a musical passage, turn your right ear toward the music. To better appreciate its melody, turn your left ear toward the music. Here's another example: To evaluate a drawing, place the drawing to the left in your visual field. (That is, look to the right of the drawing.) Doing so will facilitate right-hemisphere processing and improve your sensitivity to shapes. (Refer to the specialized abilities in Figure 3–17 for other possibilities.)

One of the most useful differences between the right and left hemispheres involves decision making. Psychologist Roger Drake and others have found that people are more willing to make risky decisions when their left hemisphere is more active than the right. The right hemisphere is associated with a more cautious cognitive style (Drake & Seligman, 1989; Drake & Ulrich, 1992; Miller & Milner, 1985).

Professor Drake suggests that when you want to persuade a friend to be careful, you should speak to the person from his or her left side. That way, you will activate the more cautious right hemisphere. On other occasions you may want to advise a friend to take more risks, such as joining a club, seeking out new friends, or applying for a job. At such times you will be more effective if you place yourself on your friend's right side. Doing so will emphasize stimuli that activate the left hemisphere and the tendency to take a risk (Drake, 1994).

Lobes of the Cerebral Cortex

In addition to the hemispheres, the cerebral cortex can be divided into several **lobes** (*smaller areas bordered by major fissures*) (see Fig. 3–18 ◆).

What is known about the function of the lobes?

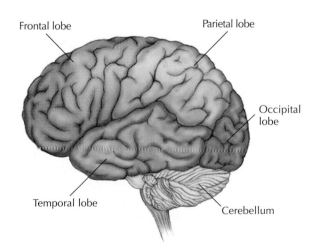

Frontal lobe

Parietal lobe

Occipital lobe

Temporal lobe

Cerebellum

Figure 3–18 ◆ The lobes of the cerebral cortex are defined by several larger and more prominent fissures on the surface of the cerebrum.

The lobes have been "mapped" by clinical and experimental studies. For example, the surface of the cortex can be activated by touching it with a small **electrode** (*electrified needle or wire*). When this is done to a patient undergoing brain surgery (using only local painkillers), the patient can report what effect the stimulation had. (This chapter's Exploration tells more about methods of brain mapping.) The functions of the cortex have also been identified by clinical studies of changes in personality, behavior, or sensory capacity caused by brain diseases or injuries. Let us consider the outcome of such studies (see Fig. 3–19 ◆).

The Occipital Lobes At the back of the brain, we find the **occipital lobes** (awk-SIP-ih-tal), *the primary visual area of the cortex*. Patients with **tumors** (*cell growths that interfere with brain activity*) in the occipital lobes experience blind spots in their vision.

Do the visual areas of the cortex correspond directly to what is seen?

Visual images are mapped onto the cortex, but the map is greatly stretched and distorted (Carlson, 1994). It is important to avoid thinking of the visual area as being like a TV screen in the brain. Visual information creates complex patterns of activity in nerve cells; it does *not* make a TV-like image.

The Parietal Lobes *Bodily sensations register in the* **parietal lobes** (puh-RYE-ih-tal), located just above the occipital lobes. Touch, temperature, pressure, and other *somatic sensations are channeled to the* **somatosensory area** (SO-mat-oh-SEN-so-ree) on the parietal lobes. The correspondence between areas of the parietal lobes and parts of the body is not perfect. The distorted body in Figure 3–19 shows that the cortex maps the *sensitivity* of body areas, not their size. For example, the lips are large in the drawing because of their great sensitivity, while the back and trunk, which are less sensitive, are much smaller.

The Temporal Lobes The temporal lobes are located on each side of the brain. *Auditory information projects directly to the* **temporal lobes,** making them the main site where hearing registers. If we were to stimulate the **primary auditory area** of a temporal lobe, *our subject would "hear" a series of sounds*. These sounds would increase in pitch as we moved from the top to the bottom. Stimulating in another direction, we would find an orderly change in loudness (Carlson, 1994). This indicates that sound qualities are clearly mapped on the cortex.

For most people, the left temporal lobe also contains a language "center." (For 5 percent of all people, the area is on the right temporal lobe.) Damage to the temporal lobe can severely limit ability to use language. (More on this later.)

The Frontal Lobes The **frontal lobes** *are associated with higher mental functions and the control of movement.* An important arch of tissue over the top of the brain, called the **motor cortex,** *directs the body's muscles.* If this area is stimulated with an electrical current, various parts of the

Primary Motor

Wrist
Hand
Little
Ring
Middle
Index
Thumb
Neck
Brow
Eyelid and eyeball
Face
Lips
Vocalization
Jaw
Tongue
Salivation
Mastication
Swallowing

Elbow
Shoulder
Trunk
Hip
Knee
Ankle
Toes
Fingers

Left
hemisphere

Temporal lobe

Primary Somatosensory

Head
Neck
Trunk
Hip
Leg
Foot
Toes
Genitalia

Shoulder
Arm
Forearm
Elbow
Wrist
Hand
Little
Ring
Middle
Index
Thumb
Fingers
Eye
Nose
Face
Upper lip
Lips
Lower lip
Teeth, gums, and jaw
Tongue
Pharynx
Intra-abdominal
organs

Left
hemisphere

Temporal lobe

Association
Motor
Somatosensory
Association

Frontal lobe
Broca's area
Olfactory bulb
Temporal lobe
Auditory
Association
Visual

Parietal lobe
Wernicke's area
Occipital lobe
Cerebellum

Pons
Medulla
Spinal cord

Figure 3–19 ◆ The lobes of the cerebral cortex and the primary sensory, motor, and association areas on each. The top diagrams show (in cross section) the relative amounts of cortex "assigned" to the sensory and motor control of various parts of the body. (Each cross section, or "slice," of the cortex has been turned 90 degrees so that you see it as it would appear from the back of the brain.)

body will twitch. Like the somatosensory area, the motor cortex corresponds to the importance of bodily areas, not to their size. The hands, for example, get more area than the feet (see Fig. 3–19). The large area of motor cortex devoted to our hands is what makes them so dexterous.

More complex behaviors are also related to the frontal lobes. Damage to the frontal lobes in humans tends to alter personality and emotionality. Intellectual tasks based on reasoning or planning also rely on the frontal lobes. Patients with frontal lobe damage often get "stuck" on such tasks and repeat the same wrong answers over and over (Goel & Grafman, 1995). Frontal lobe damage in childhood leads to a lowered adult IQ and significant social impairment (Kolb, 1989).

The sensory and motor areas leave a lot of the cortex unaccounted for. What do the remaining areas do?

Associative Areas In the human brain, primary sensory and motor areas make up only a small part of the cerebral cortex. *All other cortical areas,* including parts of all the lobes, are called the **association cortex.** The size and relative amount of association cortex increase strikingly as one ascends the evolutionary scale.

The association cortex seems to process and combine information from the various senses. It is probably also related to higher mental abilities. The frontal lobe's link with thinking skills is a good example of such abilities. Additional clues to the workings of the association cortex come from studies of humans with brain injuries.

Brain Injuries

As mentioned earlier, damage to the right brain may paralyze the left side of the body; this is reversed for damage to the left brain. Damage to the right hemisphere may also cause a curious problem called **neglect,** *in which patients pay no attention to the left side of visual space.* Often, the patient will not eat food on the left side of a plate. Some even refuse to acknowledge a paralyzed left arm as their own. (See Figure 3–20 ◆.) Surprisingly, left-hemisphere damage usually does not produce similar neglect of the right side of space (Springer & Deutsch, 1993).

Model | Patient's copy

Figure 3-20 ◆ Spatial neglect. A patient with right-hemisphere damage was asked to copy three model drawings. Notice the obvious neglect of the left side in his drawings. Similar instances of neglect occur in many patients with right-hemisphere damage. (From *Left Brain, Right Brain,* Revised Edition by S. P. Springer and G. Deutsch, copyright 1981, 1985, 1989, 1993. Reprinted with the permission of W. H. Freeman and Company.)

Brain injuries may also impair the special abilities of the hemispheres. A person with damage in the left brain may lose the ability to speak, read, write, or spell. Yet, the same person may draw or hum with skill. Persons with right-brain damage may get lost while driving or have difficulty understanding diagrams and pictures. Yet, they can speak and read as before.

Regarding emotions, a person with left-brain damage may not understand what you say, but she or he will pick up your emotional tone. With right-hemisphere damage, the person can understand what is said, but may not recognize if it is spoken in an angry or humorous way (Springer & Deutsch, 1993).

Is it fair to say that damage to the left hemisphere is generally more serious?

Generally it is, because speech and language are so essential. However, if you are an artist, the right brain may be the "major hemisphere" from your point of view. It has been observed, for instance, that painters can still paint after left-brain damage. But an artist with right-brain damage may neglect the left side of the canvas, distort outlines, or portray bizarre and repulsive subject matter. Also, because the right hemisphere is important for recognizing faces and emotion, damage to the right side of the brain can seriously impair a person's ability to relate to others.

Aphasia Two areas of the cortex are particularly related to language. One, called **Broca's area** (BRO-cahs), *lies on the left frontal lobe.* The second, known as **Wernicke's area** (VER-nick-ees), *is found on the left temporal lobe* (see Fig. 3–19). Injury to either area can cause **aphasia** (ah-FAZE-yah: *an impaired ability to use language*).

What kinds of impairment take place?

Persons with damage in Broca's area can read and understand the speech of others, but they have great difficulty speaking or writing themselves. Typically, their grammar and pronunciation are poor and their speech is slow and labored. For example, the person may say "bife" for bike, "seep" for sleep, or "zokaid" for zodiac. Generally the person knows what he or she wants to say but can't seem to utter the words (Geschwind, 1979).

Cultural Diversity

His and Her Brains?

A patient has had a stroke. It looks like Broca's area was damaged. As expected, the patient's speech is impaired. Will the patient recover any language skills? It may depend on his or her sex.

When Broca's area is damaged, women typically regain more of their lost abilities than men do. Why should this be so? Let's look at some male and female brains for an answer.

Recently, researchers used brain imaging to observe brain activity while people did language tasks. As they worked, both men and women showed increased activity in Broca's area, on the left side of the brain. This is exactly what we would expect. However, to the scientists' surprise, both the left *and the right* brain were activated in more than half the women tested. Apparently, male and female brains tend to differ in ways that can affect speech and language (Shaywitz, Fletcher, & Shaywitz, 1995; Shaywitz & Gore, 1995). (See Figure 3–21 ◆.)

Using both sides of the brain for language may be a big advantage. When Broca's area is damaged, some women can use the right side of their brains to compensate for the loss. Men with similar damage have little chance of improving. Thus, when a man says, "I have half a mind to tell you what I think," he may be stating a curious truth.

In Wernicke's aphasia, problems center on the *meaning* of words, not grammar or pronunciation. Whereas someone with Broca's aphasia might say "tssair" when shown a picture of a chair, a Wernicke's patient might say "stool." People with Wernicke's aphasia often speak in incredibly roundabout ways to avoid using certain nouns. While discussing

Figure 3–21 ◆ Language tasks activate the left side of the brain in men and both sides in many women.

her son's career, one patient said, "Well he was two years away, away down for nothing. He didn't do it and got out and said I want to go over there and . . . how to do things, what he's doing now" (Goodglass, 1980).

It is obvious that both Broca's area and Wernicke's area are crucial for normal language use. It is not surprising to find that they are interconnected in the brain.

"Mindblindness" One of the most fascinating results of brain injury is **agnosia** (ag-KNOW-zyah: *an inability to identify seen objects*). This condition is sometimes referred to as "mindblindness." If shown a candle, someone with an agnosia might describe it as a long narrow object tapering at the top. The person might even draw it accurately and still fail to name it. However, if the person is allowed to feel the candle, she or he will name it immediately (Warrington & McCarthy, 1995). The person can still see color, size, and shape. He or she

just can't perceive the meanings of objects (De Haan et al., 1995).

Are agnosias limited to objects?

No. A fascinating form of "mindblindness" is **facial agnosia,** *the inability to identify familiar persons.* One patient with facial agnosia was unable to recognize her husband or mother when they visited her in the hospital, and she could not identify pictures of her children. However, when visitors spoke she knew them immediately from their voices (Benton, 1980).

Areas devoted to recognizing faces lie on the underside of the occipital lobes. These areas appear to have no other function. Why would part of the brain be set aside solely for identifying faces? From an evolutionary standpoint it is not really so surprising. After all, we are social animals, for whom facial recognition is very important. This specialization is one more example of what a marvelous organ of consciousness we possess.

Learning Check

See if you can successfully match the following.

1. _____ Corpus callosum
2. _____ Occipital lobes
3. _____ Parietal lobes
4. _____ Temporal lobes
5. _____ Frontal lobes
6. _____ Association cortex
7. _____ Aphasias
8. _____ Corticalization
9. _____ Left hemisphere
10. _____ Right hemisphere
11. _____ "Split brain"
12. _____ Agnosia

A. Visual area
B. Language, speech, writing
C. Motor cortex and abstract thinking
D. Spatial skills, visualization, pattern recognition
E. Speech disturbances
F. Causes sleep
G. Increased ratio of cortex in brain
H. Bodily sensations
I. Treatment for severe epilepsy
J. Inability to identify seen objects
K. Fibers connecting the cerebral hemispheres
L. Cortex that is not sensory or motor in function
M. Hearing

Critical Thinking

13. If you wanted to increase the surface area of the cerebrum so that more cerebral cortex would fit within the skull, how would you do it?

Answers:

13. One solution would be to gather the surface of the cortex into folds, just as you might if you were trying to fit a large piece of cloth into a small box. This, in fact, is probably why the cortex is more convoluted (folded or wrinkled) in higher animals.

7. E 8. G 9. B 10. D 11. I 12. J
1. K 2. A 3. H 4. M 5. C 6. L

The Subcortex—At the Core of the (Brain) Matter

What do brain areas below the cortex do?

A person can lose large portions of the cerebrum and still survive. As a matter of fact, if damage is limited to the less crucial areas of the cortex, little visible change may take place. Not so with the brain areas below the cortex. Most are indispensable and damage may endanger a person's life.

Why are the lower brain areas so important?

The **subcortex** *lies below the cerebral cortex* and is completely covered by it. The subcortex can be divided into the *brainstem* (or *hindbrain)*, the *midbrain,* and the *forebrain.* (The forebrain also includes the cerebral cortex, which we have already discussed because of its size and importance.) For our purposes the **midbrain** can be viewed as *a link between the forebrain and the brainstem.* Therefore, let us focus on the remainder of the subcortex to appreciate its importance (see Fig. 3–22 ◆).

The Hindbrain

As the spinal cord enters the skull to join the brain, it widens into the brainstem. The **brainstem** *consists mainly of the medulla* (meh-DUL-ah) *and the cerebellum* (ser-ah-BEL-uhm). The **medulla** *contains centers important for the reflex control of vital life functions,* including heart rate, breathing, swallowing, and the like. Various drugs, diseases, or injuries can disrupt the medulla and end or endanger life. That's why a karate chop to the back of the neck can be extremely dangerous.

The cerebellum, which looks like a miniature cerebral cortex, lies at the base of the brain. The **cerebellum** *primarily regulates posture, muscle tone, and muscular coordination.* The cerebellum also plays a role in the storage of memories for skills and habits (Thompson, 1991). (See Chapter 10 for more information on "skill memory.")

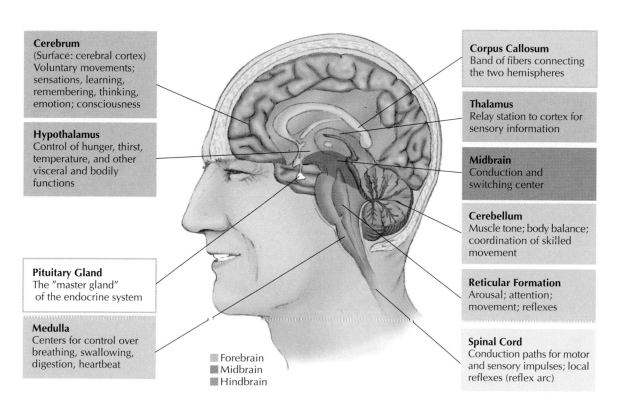

Cerebrum
(Surface: cerebral cortex)
Voluntary movements; sensations, learning, remembering, thinking, emotion; consciousness

Hypothalamus
Control of hunger, thirst, temperature, and other visceral and bodily functions

Pituitary Gland
The "master gland" of the endocrine system

Medulla
Centers for control over breathing, swallowing, digestion, heartbeat

Corpus Callosum
Band of fibers connecting the two hemispheres

Thalamus
Relay station to cortex for sensory information

Midbrain
Conduction and switching center

Cerebellum
Muscle tone; body balance; coordination of skilled movement

Reticular Formation
Arousal; attention; movement; reflexes

Spinal Cord
Conduction paths for motor and sensory impulses; local reflexes (reflex arc)

Forebrain
Midbrain
Hindbrain

Figure 3–22 ◆ This simplified drawing shows the main structures of the human brain and describes some of their most important features. (You can use the color code in the foreground to identify which structures are parts of the forebrain, midbrain, and hindbrain.)

What happens if the cerebellum is injured?

Without an intact cerebellum, tasks like walking, running, or playing catch are impossible. The first symptoms of a crippling disease called *spinocerebellar degeneration* are tremor, dizziness, and muscular weakness. Eventually, victims have difficulty standing, walking, or even feeding themselves.

Reticular Formation A *network of fibers and cell bodies* called the **reticular** (reh-TICK-you-ler) **formation (RF)** lies within a cavity inside the medulla and the brainstem. The RF influences messages entering and leaving the brain. As a result, the **RF** *affects attention, movement, some reflexes, and alertness.*

As nerve impulses flow into the brain, the RF gives priority to some messages, while excluding others. In this way, the RF influences *attention.* The reticular formation also modifies out-going commands to the body. Muscle tone, posture, and movements of the eyes, face, head, body, and limbs are all affected by the RF. In addition, the RF controls reflexes involved in breathing, sneezing, coughing, and vomiting (Stalheim-Smith & Fitch, 1993).

Maintaining vigilance, alertness, and wakefulness is another important task of the reticular formation (Carlson, 1994). Incoming messages from the sense organs branch into a part of the RF called the **reticular activating system (RAS).** The RAS *bombards the cortex with stimulation, keeping it active and alert.*

Researchers have found that destroying a small area of the RAS causes a coma resembling sleep. In contrast, electrical stimulation of the RAS instantly awakens sleeping animals. The reticular formation is also very responsive to stimulant drugs, such as amphetamine, which produce arousal and wakefulness (Carlson, 1994).

A sleepy driver who snaps to attention when an animal appears in the road can thank the RAS for arousing the rest of the brain. If you're getting sleepy while reading this chapter, try pinching your ear—a little pain will cause the RAS to momentarily arouse your cortex.

The Forebrain

Like gemstones of nerve tissue, two of the most important parts of the body lie buried deep within the brain. The *thalamus* (THAL-uh-mus) and an area just below it called the *hypothalamus* (HI-po-THAL-uh-mus) are part of the forebrain (see Fig. 3–22).

How could these be any more important than other areas already described?

The **thalamus** *acts as a final "switching station" for sensory messages on their way to the cortex.* Information from vision, hearing, taste, and touch relay through this small, football-shaped structure. Sensory messages undergo initial analysis there as well. Injury to even small areas of the thalamus can cause deafness, blindness, or loss of any other sense, except smell. (Sensory information from the sense of smell is sent directly to the cortex, on the underside of the brain, without passing through the thalamus.)

The human hypothalamus is about the size of a small grape. Small as it may be, the **hypothalamus** *is a kind of master control center for emotion and many basic motives* (Carlson, 1994). The hypothalamus affects behaviors as diverse as sex, rage, temperature control, hormone release, eating and drinking, sleep, waking, and emotion. The hypothalamus is a "crossroads" that connects with many areas of the cortex and subcortex. As such, it acts as a "final path" for many kinds of behavior leaving the brain. You might think of the hypothalamus as the last area in the brain where many behaviors are organized or "decided on." (See Chapter 13 for a discussion of the role of the hypothalamus in hunger and thirst.)

The Limbic System The hypothalamus, parts of the thalamus, and several structures buried within the cortex form the *limbic system* (Fig. 3–23 ◆). The **limbic system** *has a major role in producing emotion and motivated behavior.* Rage, fear, sexual response, and other instances of intense arousal can be obtained from various points in the limbic system. For example, cats can be made aggressive by electrically stimulating the limbic system. Typically, they will crouch, hiss, expose their claws, lean forward, and tense their muscles—all characteristic of defense or attack. More information on research of this type follows.

Figure 3–23 ◆ Parts of the limbic system are shown in this highly simplified drawing. Although only one side is shown, the hippocampus and the amygdala extend out into the temporal lobes at each side of the brain. The limbic system is a sort of "primitive core" of the brain strongly associated with emotion.

Electrical Stimulation of the Brain

Electrical stimulation of the brain (ESB) *is the direct electrical stimulation and activation of brain tissue.* ESB is used to explore brain-behavior connections. It allows an animal (or person) to function normally while various brain areas are turned "on" or "off." As we saw in the Preview, ESB can even be done at a distance, with a radio transmitter and receiver.

ESB begins with the implantation of thin metal electrodes deep within the brain. Each electrode activates a specific brain area. ESB calls forth behavior with astonishing power. Instantly it can bring about aggression, alertness, escape, eating, drinking, sleeping, movement, euphoria, memories, speech, tears, and more.

Electrical activation of parts of the limbic system often produces emotional responses. During medical testing, one woman reacted with a sudden outburst of fear and anger when the amygdala (ah-MIG-dah-luh) was stimulated, saying "I feel like I want to get up from this chair! Please don't let me do it! I don't want to be mean! I want to get something and just tear it up!" (King, 1961). When the temporal lobe was activated, another patient giggled, became flirtatious, and said she enjoyed the stimulation very much. Soon, she expressed a desire to marry the therapist! When stimulation ceased, she again became quiet, reserved, and proper.

It might seem that ESB could be used to control a person like a robot. But the details of emotions and behaviors elicited by ESB are modified by personality and the situation. Fortunately, it would be impossible for a ruthless dictator to enslave people by "radio controlling" their brains.

ESB is best thought of as a tool for probing the brain, and, in the future, as a potential treatment for epilepsy, uncontrollable violence, and other brain-based problems. Using ESB, researchers are creating a three-dimensional brain map or "atlas." The atlas shows the sensory, motor, and emotional responses that can be elicited from various parts of the brain. It promises to be a valuable guide for medical treatment, as well as for exploring the brain (Yoshida, 1993).

During evolution, the limbic system was the earliest layer of the forebrain to develop. In lower, relatively primitive animals, the limbic system helps organize the appropriate response to stimuli: feeding, fleeing, fighting, or reproduction (Thompson, 1985). In humans, the link to emotion remains. The **amygdala,** in particular, *is strongly related to fear.* The amygdala provides a "quick pathway" to the cortex. It allows us to respond to dangerous stimuli before we fully know what is going on. In situations where true danger exists, such as in military combat, this rapid response may aid survival. However, disorders of the brain's fear system can be quite disruptive. An example is the military veteran who involuntarily dives into the bushes when he hears a car backfire (LeDoux, 1996).

Some parts of the limbic system have taken on additional, higher-level functions. For example, one part called the **hippocampus** (HIP-oh-CAMP-us) *is important for forming lasting memories* (Squire, 1992). The hippocampus lies at the core of the temporal lobes, which may explain why stimulating the temporal lobes can produce memory-like or dream-like experiences. (See Chapter 10 for more information on this point.)

One of the most exciting discoveries in biopsychology was the finding that animals will learn to press a lever to deliver a rewarding dose of electrical stimulation to the limbic system (Olds & Milner, 1954). Since the original discovery, many additional areas of the limbic system have been shown to act as reward, or "pleasure," pathways in the brain. Many are found in the hypothalamus, where they overlap with areas associated with drives such as thirst, sex, and hunger (Olds, 1977). (See Chapter 9.) Commonly abused drugs, such as cocaine, amphetamine, heroin, nicotine, marijuana, and alcohol, activate many of the same pleasure pathways. This appears to explain, in part, the rewarding properties of such drugs (Wise & Rompre, 1989).

Punishment, or "aversive," areas have also been found in the limbic system. When these areas are stimulated, animals show discomfort and will work to turn off the stimulation. Since a great deal of human and animal behavior is based on seeking pleasure and avoiding pain, these discoveries continue to fascinate psychologists.

The Brain in Perspective—Beyond the Biocomputer

We have seen that the human brain is an impressive assembly of billions of sensitive cells and nerve fibers. The brain controls vital bodily functions, keeps track of the external world, issues commands to the muscles and glands, responds to current needs, creates the magic of consciousness, and regulates its own behavior—*all* at the same time. Each of these basic needs is met by the action of one or more of the three main brain divisions: Control of vital bodily functions is carried out by the hindbrain (with some assistance from the hypothalamus in the forebrain); gathering sensory information and issuing motor commands takes place at all three levels of the brain; and response selection, learning, memory, and higher thought processes are controlled by the forebrain, particularly the cortex and its association areas.

Redundancy A final note of caution is now in order. For the sake of simplicity we have assigned functions to each "part" of the brain as if it were a computer. This is only a half-truth. In reality the brain is a vast information-processing system. Incoming information scatters to structures all over the brain and converges again as it goes out to muscles and glands. The overall system acts in ways that go far beyond any view that considers only "parts" or "brain centers" (Thompson, 1985). To say the least, the brain is much, much more complicated than implied here.

One reason the brain is so complex is because it has tremendous **redundancy,** *or duplication,* throughout. The brain may use dozens of areas to do what any one area could manage alone. Because of such redundancy, the brain has an impressive ability to compensate for some types of injury.

Does it make any difference at what age a person experiences a brain injury?

Plasticity Yes. In response to brain damage, children often show greater **plasticity** (*flexibility of brain organization*) than adults. For example, when there is severe damage to the left hemisphere, children under age 2 usually can shift language processing to the right side of the brain. If damage occurs between ages 2 and 5, language areas remain in the left brain but shift to new locations (Kolb, 1989). A more dramatic example of plasticity occurs when a person is born without a corpus callosum. As adults, these people can answer questions from both hemispheres, write with both hands, draw with both hands, and solve block-design puzzles with both hands (Sperry, 1974). In general, brain plasticity appears to be based on increased branching of dendrites (Kolb, 1989). After age 10, such plasticity becomes rare.

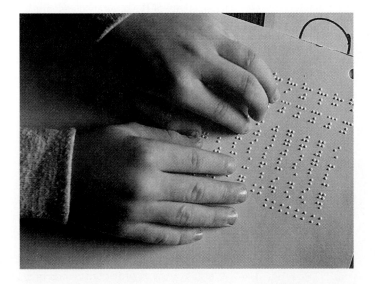

A recent study of blind people found that they show a high level of activity in the visual area of the brain when reading Braille, a remarkable example of brain plasticity and reorganization (Sadato, Pascual-Leone, & Hallett, 1996).

Potential In the final analysis, the brain is both highly vulnerable and amazingly resilient. Brain damage before age 5 almost always lowers adult IQ (Kolb, 1989). Yet, in one astounding case a child had the entire left hemisphere of his brain removed at age 5. As an adult he was paralyzed on the right side and blind in his right visual field. But he was able to speak, read, write, and comprehend so well that he maintained a double major in college and has an above-average IQ (Smith & Sugar, 1975). Such recoveries suggest that full use of the brain's potential may still lie ahead. At the same time that injuries help us understand the brain's limitations, they also raise questions about how the undamaged brain might be used more fully. Perhaps future breakthroughs will allow us to enhance memory, intelligence, or thinking abilities. For now, it is exciting to think that the brain hasn't yet yielded all its secrets.

The Endocrine System— Slow but Sure Messenger Service

The nervous system is not the only communication network in the body. The *endocrine system* (IN-duh-krin) is the second great communication system. The **endocrine system** is made up of a number of *glands that pour chemicals directly into the bloodstream or lymph system* (see Fig. 3–24 ◆). These chemicals, called **hormones,** are carried throughout the body, where they *affect internal activities and behavior.* Hormones are chemically related to neurotransmitters. Like transmitters, hormones activate cells in the body. To respond, the cells must have receptor sites for the hormone (Carlson, 1994).

How do hormones affect behavior?

Although we are seldom aware of them, hormones affect us in a multitude of ways. Here is a brief sample: Hormone output from the adrenal glands rises during stressful situations; androgens ("male" hormones) are related to the sex drive in both males and females; hormones secreted during times of high emotion intensify memory formation; at least some of the emotional turmoil of adolescence is due to elevated hormone levels; different hormones predominate when you are angry, rather than fearful. Since this is just a sample, let's consider some additional effects hormones have on the body and behavior.

The *pituitary* is a pea-sized structure hanging from the base of the brain (return to Fig. 3–24). One of the pituitary's more important roles is regulation of growth. During childhood, the pituitary secretes a hormone that speeds body development. If too little **growth hormone** is released, a person may remain far smaller than average. Too much

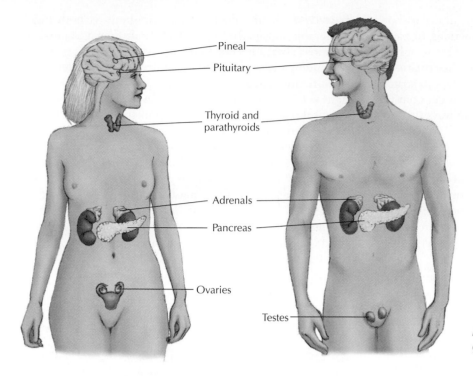

Figure 3–24 ◆ Locations of the endocrine glands in the male and female.

growth hormone produces **giantism** (*excessive bodily growth*). Secretion of too much growth hormone late in the growth period causes **acromegaly** (AK-row-MEG-uh-lee) *a condition in which the arms, hands, feet, and facial bones become enlarged*. Acromegaly produces unusually prominent facial features, which some people have used as a basis for careers as character actors, wrestlers, and the like.

Underactivity of the pituitary gland may produce a dwarf; overactivity a giant.

A Tall Question

Children who lag far behind in growth may suffer lasting emotional scars from rejection by peers or adults. One common cause of limited growth is insufficient growth hormone. If this condition is not treated, a child may fall 6 to 12 inches behind age-mates in height. As adults, some will be **hypopituitary dwarfs** (HI-po-pih-TU-ih-ter-ee). *Such individuals are perfectly proportioned, but tiny.* Should they receive medical treatment?

For many years, dwarfism could be treated only with injections of human growth hormone. Supplies were extracted from the pituitary glands of human cadavers—a painstaking and expensive process. Now, a cheaper synthetic growth hormone is available. (Treatment still costs about $15,000 per child per year.) Regular injections of growth hormone can raise a hypopituitary child's height by several inches, usually to the short side of average. Treatment, however, can last from 3 to 7 years, and cost from $45,000 to $105,000.

Growth hormone therapy is usually safe. However, it does raise ethical concerns. Some experts believe that it is wrong to treat shortness as a medical problem. Also, some parents and children are bitterly disappointed when the child fails to grow as much as expected. In addition, some short children adjust poorly to becoming more "ordinary." Many go from playing with younger children to being ignored by age-mates.

The greatest risk comes from parents who pressure physicians to increase the growth of "normal short" children. If a child's body produces normal amounts of growth hormone, drugs typically will not make the child taller as an adult. Such children grow *faster* when given growth hormone, but not taller. Nevertheless, thousands of "normal short" children are being given growth hormone injections.

With all this in mind, perhaps it is fair to say that the success of growth hormone therapy should be measured by increased emotional well-being—not merely by an increase in stature (Adler, 1992; Franklin, 1984; Roan, 1993).

The pituitary also regulates the functioning of other glands (especially the thyroid, adrenal glands, and ovaries or testes). These glands in turn regulate such bodily processes as metabolism, responses to stress, and reproduction. In women, the pituitary controls the production of milk during pregnancy. The **pituitary** *is often called the "master gland" because its hormones influence other endocrine glands.* But the master has a master: The pituitary is directed by the hypothalamus, which lies directly above it. In this way, the hypothalamus affects glands throughout the body. This, then, is the major link between the brain and the glandular system (Carlson, 1994).

The *pineal gland* (pin-EE-ul), was once considered a useless remnant of evolution. In certain fishes, frogs, and lizards, the gland is associated with a well-developed light-sensitive organ, or so-called "third eye." In humans, the function of the pineal gland is just now coming to light (so to speak). The **pineal gland** *releases a hormone called* melatonin (mel-ah-TONE-in) *in response to daily variations in light.* Melatonin levels in the bloodstream rise at dusk and peak around midnight. They fall again as morning approaches. This light-driven cycle helps control body rhythms and sleep cycles. People who are totally blind sometimes suffer from sleep disorders because their melatonin cycle is upset. (See Chapter 13 for information on melatonin and jet lag.)

The **thyroid gland,** located in the neck, *regulates metabolism.* Because **metabolism** is the *rate at which energy is produced and expended in the body,* the thyroid can have a sizable effect on personality. A person suffering from **hyperthyroidism** (*an overactive thyroid*) tends to be thin, tense, excitable, and nervous. An *underactive thyroid* (**hypothyroidism**) in an adult can cause inactivity, sleepiness, slowness, and overweight. In infancy, hypothyroidism limits development of the nervous system, leading to severe mental retardation (see Chapter 12).

When you are frightened or angry, a number of important actions take place in your body to prepare it for action: Your heart rate and blood pressure rise; stored sugar is released into the bloodstream for quick energy; the muscles tense and receive more blood; and blood is prepared to clot more quickly in case of injury. As we discussed earlier, these changes are brought about by the autonomic nervous system. Specifically, the sympathetic branch of the ANS causes the hormones *adrenaline* and *noradrenaline* to be released by the adrenal glands. **Adrenaline,** which is associated with fear, *tends to arouse the body.* **Noradrenaline** *also tends to arouse the body,* but it is associated with anger. (As mentioned earlier, both substances also act as neurotransmitters.)

The **adrenal glands** *are located just under the back of the rib cage, atop the kidneys.* The **adrenal medulla,** *or inner core of the adrenal glands, is the source of adrenaline and noradrenaline.* The **adrenal cortex,** *or outer "bark" of the adrenal glands, produces a set of hormones called corticoids* (KOR-tih-coids). One of their jobs is to regulate salt balance in the body. A deficiency of certain corticoids can evoke a powerful craving for the taste of salt in humans. The corticoids also help the body adjust to stress, and they are a secondary source of sex hormones. (For a full discussion of the role of sex glands in development, see Chapter 15.)

An oversecretion of the adrenal sex hormones can cause **virilism** (*exaggerated male characteristics*). For instance, a woman may grow a beard or a man's voice may become so low it is difficult to understand. Oversecretion early in life may cause **premature puberty** (*full sexual development during childhood*). One of the most remarkable cases on record is that of a 5-year-old Peruvian girl who gave birth to a son (Strange, 1965).

While we are on the topic of sex hormones, there is a related issue worth mentioning. One of the principal androgens or "male" hormones is testosterone, which is supplied in small amounts by the adrenal glands. (The testes are the main source of testosterone in males.) Perhaps you have heard about the use of anabolic steroids by athletes who want to "bulk up" or promote muscle growth. Most of these drugs are synthetic versions of testosterone.

Although many athletes believe otherwise, there is no evidence that steroids improve performance, and they may cause serious side effects. Problems include voice deepening or baldness in women and shrinkage of the testicles, sexual impotence, or breast enlargement in men. Also common are an increased risk of heart attack and stroke, liver damage, and stunted growth when steroids are used by younger adolescents. For some users steroids may cause mania or suicidal depression, antisocial behavior ("roid rage"), and near-psychotic reactions (Harrison & Katz, 1987). Understandably, all major sports organizations ban the use of anabolic steroids.

In this brief discussion of the endocrine system we have considered only a few of the more important glands. Nevertheless, this should give you an appreciation of how completely behavior and personality are tied to the ebb and flow of hormones in the body.

A Look Ahead   In the upcoming Applications section, we will return to the nervous system to see how hand preference relates to the brain. You'll also find out if being right- or left-handed affects your chances of living to a ripe old age. The final Exploration contrasts time-tested research methods with trailblazing new ways to explore the brain. Included are some fascinating images of the brain's inner workings.

Professional football player Lyle Alzado used anabolic steroids throughout his athletic career. Alzado died of brain cancer, which he attributed to his abuse of steroids.

Learning Check

Here is a chance to check your memory of the preceding discussions.

1. Three major divisions of the brain are the brainstem or _____ , the _____ , and the _____ .

2. Reflex centers for heartbeat and respiration are found in the
   a. cerebellum   **b.** thalamus   **c.** medulla   **d.** RF

3. A portion of the reticular formation, known as the RAS, serves as an _____ system in the brain.
   a. activating   **b.** adrenal   **c.** adjustment   **d.** aversive

4. The _____ is a final relay, or "switching station," for sensory information on its way to the cortex.

5. ESB is done primarily by electrically stimulating the spinal cord.   T or F?

6. Stimulation of the amygdala causes a person to become hostile and aggressive.   T or F?

7. "Reward" and "punishment" areas are found throughout the _____ system, which is also related to emotion.

8. Undersecretion from the thyroid can cause
   a. dwarfism   **b.** giantism   **c.** overweight   **d.** mental retardation

9. The body's ability to resist stress is related to the action of the adrenal _____ .

Critical Thinking

10. If your brain were removed, replaced by another, and moved to a new body, which would you consider to be yourself, your old body with the new brain, or your new body with the old brain?

Answers:

1. hindbrain, midbrain, forebrain 2. c 3. a 4. thalamus 5. F 6. T 7. limbic 8. c, d (in infancy) 9. cortex 10. While there is no "correct" answer to this question, your personality, knowledge, personal memories, and self-concept all derive from brain activity—which makes a strong case for your old brain in a new body being more nearly the "real you."

*I*n the English language, "what's right is right," but what's left may be wrong. We have left-handed compliments, people with "two left feet," those who are left behind, left out, and . . . left-handed. On the other hand (so to speak), we have the right way, the right angle, the "right-hand man" (or woman), righteousness, and . . . the right-handed.

The Sinister Hand Left-handedness has a long and undeserved bad reputation. Southpaws have been accused of being clumsy, stubborn (for refusing to use their right hand), and maladjusted. But as any lefty will tell you, and psychology has confirmed, none of this is true. The supposed clumsiness of lefties is merely a result of living in a right-handed world: If it can be gripped, turned, folded, held, or pulled, it's probably designed for the right hand. Even toilet handles are on the right side.

What causes **handedness** (*a preference for the right or left hand*)? Why are there more right-handed than left-handed people? How do left-handed and right-handed people differ? Does being left-handed create any problems—or benefits? The answers to most of these questions lead us back to the brain, where handedness begins. Let's see what research has revealed about handedness, the brain, and you.

Hand Dominance Take a moment and write your name on a sheet of paper, first using your right hand and then your left. You were probably much more comfortable writing with your dominant hand. This is interesting because there's no real difference in the dexterity of the hands themselves. The agility of your dominant hand is an outward expression of superior motor control on one side of the brain.

The preceding exercise implies that you are either entirely right- or left-handed. But handedness is a matter of degree (Coren, 1992). To better assess your handedness, circle an answer for each of the questions that follow.

Are You Right- or Left-Handed?

1. Which hand do you normally use to write? Right (Left) Either
2. Which hand would you use to throw a ball at a target? (Right) Left Either
3. Which hand do you use to hold your toothbrush? Right (Left) Either
4. Which hand do you use to hold a knife when cutting food? (Right) Left Either
5. With which hand do you hold a hammer when hitting a nail? (Right) Left Either

6. When you thread a needle, which hand holds the thread? Right (Left) Either

To find your score, count the number of "Rights" you circled and multiply by 3. Then multiply the number of "Eithers" by 2. Next count the number of "Lefts" you circled. Now add all three totals and compare the result with the following scale (adapted from Coren, 1992).

17-18	Strongly right-handed
15-16	Moderately right-handed (mixed)
13-14	Mildly right-handed (mixed)
12	Ambidextrous
10-11	Mildly left-handed (mixed)
8-9	Moderately left-handed (mixed)
6-7	Strongly left-handed

A majority of people (about 77 percent) are strongly right- or left-handed. The rest show some inconsistency in hand preference. As Table 3–1 ■ indicates, such differences can affect performance in some sports.

If a person is strongly left-handed does that mean the right hemisphere is dominant?

Not necessarily. It's true that the right hemisphere controls the left hand, but a left-handed person's *language-producing*, **dominant hemisphere** may be on the opposite side of the brain.

Brain Dominance About 97 percent of right-handers process speech in the left hemisphere and are left-brain dominant

Table 3–1 ■ Sports and Handedness

Sport	Handedness Advantage
Boxing	Left
Fencing	Left
Basketball	Mixed and ambidextrous
Ice hockey	Mixed and ambidextrous
Field hockey	Mixed and ambidextrous
Tennis	Strong left or strong right
Squash	Strong left or strong right
Badminton	Strong left or strong right

Coren, 1992.

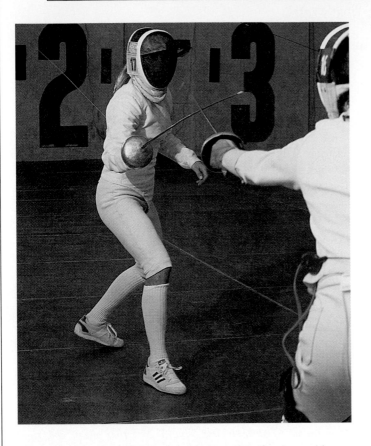

Left-handers have an advantage in sports such as fencing and boxing. Most likely, their movements are less familiar to opponents, who usually face right-handers. Contrary to what many people believe, left-handers have no overall advantage in baseball (Coren, 1992).

(Fig. 3–25 ◆). A good 68 percent of left-handers produce speech from the left hemisphere, just as right-handed people do. About 19 percent of all lefties and 3 percent of righties use their right brain for language. Some left-handers (approximately 12 percent) use both sides of the brain for language processing. All totaled, 94 percent of the population uses the left brain for language (Coren, 1992).

Is there any way for a person to tell which of his or her hemispheres is dominant?

One interesting clue is based on the way you write. Right-handed individuals who write with a straight hand, and lefties who write with a hooked hand, are usually left-brain dominant for language. Left-handed people who write with their hand below the line, and righties who use a hooked position, are usually right-brain dominant (Levy & Reid, 1976). Are your friends right brained or left brained? (See Figure 3–26 ◆.)

Before you leap to any conclusions, be aware that writing position is not foolproof. The only sure way to determine brain dominance is to do a medical test that involves briefly anesthetizing one cerebral hemisphere at a time (Springer & Deutsch, 1993).

How common is left-handedness, and what causes it?

Handedness   In most animal groups—even monkeys—there is a 50-50 split of right- and left- "handedness." Among humans the split is about 90-10, favoring right-handedness. The prevalence of right-handedness in humans probably reflects the left brain's specialization for producing language (Coren, 1992).

In the past, many left-handed children were forced to use the right hand for writing, eating, and other skills. But as fetal ultrasound images show, clear hand preferences are apparent even before birth (Hepper, 1990). (See Figure 3–27 ◆.) This suggests that handedness cannot be dictated. Parents should never try to force a left-handed child to use the right hand. To do so may invite speech or reading problems.

Is handedness inherited from parents?

Hand preferences are not directly inherited like eye color or skin color. What is inherited is the *degree* of handedness. If your parents are strongly handed you probably have a strong hand preference too—even though your dominant

Entire Population   **Right-handers**   **Left-handers**

Left **94%**   Left **97%**   Left **68%**
                                                                                          Right **19%**

Right **5%**   Right **3%**   Bilateral **12%**
Bilateral **1%**

Figure 3–25   ◆   Language is controlled by the left side of the brain in the majority of right- and left-handers.

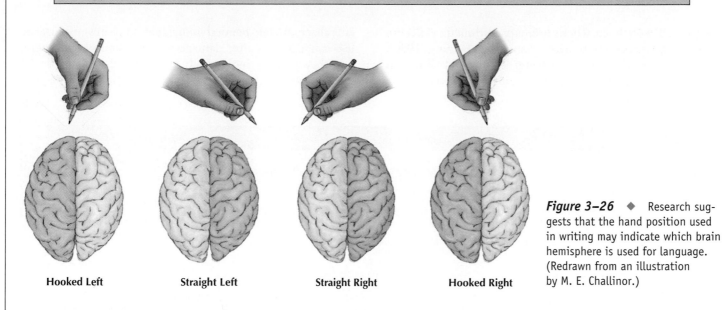

Hooked Left   Straight Left   Straight Right   Hooked Right

Figure 3–26 ◆ Research suggests that the hand position used in writing may indicate which brain hemisphere is used for language. (Redrawn from an illustration by M. E. Challinor.)

hand may not match theirs. If your parents are ambidextrous or mixed handed, you probably are too (Coren, 1992).

Are there any drawbacks to being left-handed?

A minority of lefties owe their hand preference to birth traumas (such as prematurity, low birth weight, and breech birth). These individuals have a higher incidence of allergies, learning disorders, and other problems (Betancur et al., 1990). But genetic left-handedness, which accounts for most lefties, is unrelated to general intelligence (McManus et al., 1988).

Many people have been alarmed by news reports that lefties tend to die younger than right-handed persons (Coren

Figure 3–27 ◆ In this ultrasound image, a four-month-old fetus sucks her right thumb. A study by psychologist Peter Hepper suggests that she will continue to prefer her right hand after she is born and that she will be right-handed as an adult.

& Halpern, 1991). However, three rather decisive studies have found no difference in the age at which left- and right-handed persons die (Harris, 1993a, 1993b; Salive et al., 1993). More importantly, there are some clear advantages to being left-handed.

Advantage Left Throughout history a notable number of artists have been lefties, from Leonardo da Vinci and Michelangelo to Pablo Picasso and M. C. Escher. Conceivably, since the right hemisphere is superior at imagery and visual abilities, there is some advantage to using the left hand for drawing or painting (Springer & Deutsch, 1993). At the least, lefties are definitely better at visualizing three-dimensional objects. This may be why there are more left-handed architects, artists, and chess players than would be expected (Coren, 1992).

Lateralization *refers to specialization in the abilities of the brain hemispheres.* One striking feature of lefties is that they are generally less lateralized than the right-handed (Hellige, 1990). In fact, even the physical size and shape of their cerebral hemispheres are more alike. If you are a lefty you can take pride in the fact that your brain is less lopsided than most! In general, left-handers are more symmetrical on almost everything, including eye dominance, fingerprints—even foot size (Corballis, 1980).

In some situations less lateralization may be a real advantage. For instance, individuals who are moderately left-handed or ambidextrous seem to have better than average pitch memory, which is a basic musical skill. Correspondingly, more musicians are ambidextrous than would normally be expected (Springer & Deutsch, 1993).

Math abilities may also benefit from fuller use of the right hemisphere. Students who are extremely gifted in math are much more likely to be left-handed or ambidextrous

(Benbow, 1986). Even where ordinary arithmetic skills are concerned, lefties seem to excel (Annett & Manning, 1990).

The clearest advantage of being left-handed shows up when there is a brain injury. Because of their milder lateralization, left-handed individuals typically experience less language loss after damage to either brain hemisphere, and they recover more easily (Geschwind, 1979). Maybe having "two left feet" isn't so bad after all.

Learning Check

1. About 97 percent of left-handed people process language on the left side of the brain, the same as right-handed people do. T or F?

2. Left-handed individuals who write with their hand below the line are likely to be right-brain dominant. T or F?

3. Most animals, like most humans, show a preference for the right limb. T or F?

4. In general, left-handed individuals show less lateralization in the brain and in fact throughout the body. T or F?

5. Recent studies have shown conclusively that left-handed people tend to die younger than members of the right-handed population. T or F?

Critical Thinking

6. Reports that left-handed people tend to die younger were flawed in an important way: The average age of people in the left-handed group was younger than that of subjects in the right-handed group. Why would this make a difference in the conclusions drawn?

Answers:

1. F 2. T 3. F 4. T 5. F

6. Because we can't tell if handedness or average age accounts for the difference in death rates. For example, if we start with a group of 20- to 30-year-old people, in which some die, the average age of death has to be between 20 and 30. If we start with a group of 30- to 40-year-old people, in which some die, the average age of death has to be between 30 and 40. Thus, the left-handed group might have an earlier average age at death simply because members of the group were younger to start with.

---

*O*n the table in front of you lies a small, mysterious, and powerful computer. Your assignment is to discover how it works. How will you proceed? It's a challenge much like the one scientists face in studying the brain. You'll find a box of tools and a flashlight next to the computer. Ready. Begin.

The Computer   Your first step might be to take apart the computer. This would allow you to tell in general what is connected with what.

The Brain   Similarly, researchers use **dissection** (dih-SEK-shun: *separation into parts*) to identify major brain parts and pathways. Dissection is often aided by **staining** (*chemically treating*) thin slices of brain tissue to make smaller details visible. However, like taking a computer apart, dissection and staining tell relatively little about the purpose or *function* of parts of the brain.

The Computer   What parts of the computer supply its memory? Control its keyboard? Activate its screen? Do the computing? To begin answering such questions, you could remove one part at a time. By observing what effect this has you could learn something about each part's purpose.

The Brain   Using similar logic, many studies are based on **ablation** (ab-LAY-shun: *surgical removal*) of parts of the brain. (Don't try this at home.) When ablation is followed by a change in behavior or capacity, we gain insight into the purpose of the missing structure. But it may take many studies before we can be confident about the function of each part.

The Computer   In time, it will become

instructive to cut only a single wire or to remove only one tiny electrical part of the computer.

The Brain   *Deep lesioning* (LEE-zhun-ing) is the comparable procedure in brain research. In **deep lesioning,** *a thin wire electrode is used to destroy a small amount of brain tissue*. After the electrode is lowered into a selected target area inside the brain an electric current passes through its tip (Fig. 3–28 ◆). Again, observed changes in behavior give clues about the function of the lesioned area. Using a weaker current, it is also possible to *activate* target areas, rather than remove them. This is called ESB, as described earlier.

The Computer   As you delve deeper, you may want to measure electrical activity in various circuits of the computer *while it is on and functioning*.

The Brain   Likewise, researchers use electrodes to record the firing of large populations of neurons within the brain. Even more revealing, perhaps, are *micro-electrode recordings*. A **micro-electrode** *is a tiny glass tube filled with a salty, electrically conducting fluid*. The tip of a micro-electrode is small enough to detect the activity of a *single* neuron.

Watching the action potentials of a single neuron provides a fascinating, fine-grain glimpse into the origins of behavior.

Up to this point, our "mystery computer" has merely served as a model to clarify the nature of conventional brain research. The remainder of this Exploration explains how computers are being used to create vivid images of the brain and its activity.

New Images of the Living Brain

Many of the brain's riddles have been solved with the methods just described. Yet, each technique lets us see only a small part of the whole picture. What would it be like to be able to "peek" inside an intact brain while a person is thinking, perceiving, and reacting? Computer-enhanced images are now making this age-old dream possible. Let's look through some of these newly opened "windows" into the human bio-computer.

CT Scan   Computerized X-ray scanning has revolutionized the study of brain diseases and injuries. At best, conventional X-rays produce only shadowy

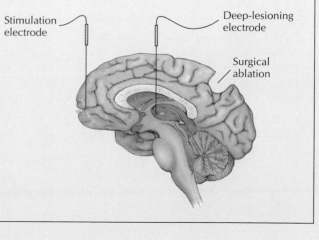

Figure 3–28 ◆ The functions of brain structures can be explored by selectively activating or removing them. Brain research is often based on electrical stimulation, but chemical stimulation is also used at times.

Figure 3–29 ◆ An MRI scan shows a tumor in the cerebrum (see arrow). Notice how it is possible to display a precise "slice" from the middle of the three-dimensional MRI data.

Figure 3–30 ◆ A conventional EEG record of brain-wave patterns.

images of the brain. **Computed tomographic (CT) scanning** *is a computer-enhanced X-ray image.* CT scans do a much better job of making the brain visible. In a CT scan, X-ray information is collected by a computer and formed into an image. A CT scan can reveal the effects of strokes, injuries, tumors, and other brain disorders (Larson, 1990). These, in turn, can be related to changes in a person's behavior.

MRI Scan Magnetic resonance imaging **(MRI)** *uses a magnetic field to produce an image of the body's interior.* During an MRI scan, a detector records how hydrogen atoms within the body respond to a powerful magnetic field. Computer processing then creates a three-dimensional representation of the brain or body. Any two-dimensional plane, or slice, of the body can be selected electronically from the MRI data and displayed as an image on a computer screen (Larson, 1990). This allows scientists to peer into the living brain almost as if it were transparent (Fig. 3–29 ◆).

A **functional MRI** goes one step further by *making brain activity visible.* For example, the motor cortex will be highlighted in a functional MRI image when a person taps her fingers. Such images are allowing scientists to pinpoint areas in the brain responsible for thoughts and actions (Naeye, 1994).

Electroencephalography (EEG) Electroencephalography (ee-LEK-tro-in-SEF-ah-LOG-ruh-fee) *measures the waves of electrical activity produced by the brain.* Small disk-shaped metal electrodes are placed at various locations on the scalp. Electrical impulses from the brain are detected and sent to an **electroencephalograph (EEG)**. The EEG *amplifies these very weak signals (brain waves) and records them on a moving sheet of paper* (Fig. 3–30 ◆). Various brain-wave patterns can help identify the presence of tumors, epilepsy, and other diseases. The EEG also reveals changes in brain activity during sleep, daydreaming, hypnosis, and other mental states (see Chapter 8).

For all its value, an "old-fashioned"

EEG is like trying to guess what's happening inside a busy factory by standing outside with your ear pressed against the wall. The EEG allows us to detect an overall rise or fall of brain activity, but only very general patterns are apparent.

MANSCAN Computers have recently brought the EEG a step closer to the dream of "seeing" brain activity. Neuroscientist Alan Gevins (1989) and his colleagues have developed a new technique they call the **mental activity network scanner,** or MANSCAN. It consists of a soft helmet that *records EEG data from 124 points,* rather than the typical 16 to 30. A computer tracks brain-wave activity and maps it onto a three-dimensional MRI scan of the brain (Weiss, 1990). While a person performs a mental task, MANSCAN takes 250 "snapshots" of brain waves per second. After processing and analysis, the computer creates a diagram of brain activity (Fig. 3–31 ◆). MANSCAN is providing new information on memory, mental fatigue, coordination, and language use (Gevins et al., 1990).

Figure 3–31 ◆ *(Top)* The MANSCAN device records EEG data from 124 points on the head. *(Bottom)* A computer combines EEG data with an MRI scan to produce three-dimensional "maps" of thinking and other brain activity. Colors are used to show the time delay between points of peak activity. Wider arrows indicate greater similarity of activity between two points. In this example, notice how different the patterns are for a task requiring immediate memory *(right)* and one not requiring it *(left)*.

Figure 3–32 ◆ These PET images show scans of the left side of the brain made while a person heard a word, saw a word, repeated a word aloud, and said a word related to the one that was seen (Petersen et al., 1988).

PET Scan Positron emission tomography (PET) images of the brain are perhaps the most remarkable of all. As described earlier, a **PET scan** *detects positrons (sub-atomic particles) emitted by weakly radioactive glucose (sugar) as it is consumed by the brain.* Since the brain runs on glucose, a PET scan shows which brain areas are using more energy. Higher energy use is assumed to correspond with higher activity. By placing positron detectors around the head and sending data to a computer it is possible to create a moving, color picture of changes in brain activity (Fig. 3–14 is a good example).

Rainbow-hued PET scan images are mapping human brain activity with a precision never before possible. In a further refinement, tiny amounts of a radioactive oxygen compound are injected into a person's bloodstream. This "tagged" oxygen remains active for only a few minutes. Tagged glucose, in comparison, is active for several hours.

Each dose of oxygen allows a brief PET scan to be made. Each of these "snapshots" of the brain can be compared with others in a way that isolates a fleeting moment of brain activity. As you can see in Figure 3–32 ◆, tagged-oxygen PET scans reveal that very specific brain areas are active when you are reading a word, hearing a word, saying a word, or thinking about the meaning of a word. PET images of this type can also be superimposed on an MRI scan. The MRI scan shows the brain in detail and the

PET scan tells which areas are linked with various abilities (Fig. 3–33 ◆).

Images of the Future Neuroscientists are still learning how to make full use of computerized imaging techniques. At the same time, newer techniques are being added to their arsenal. One is called MEG, which stands for magnetoencephalography. A MEG scan uses exotic electronic devices to detect the exceedingly weak magnetic fields created when neurons fire (Heppenheimer, 1990). MEG is giving the clearest views yet of human brain activity. It is just a matter of time until even brighter beacons are flashed into the shadowy inner world of thought.

Figure 3–33 ◆ The bright spots you see here were created by a PET scan. They are similar to the spots in Figure 3–32. However, here they have been placed over an MRI scan so that the brain's anatomy is visible. The three bright spots are areas in the left brain related to language. The spot on the right is active during reading. The top-middle area is connected with speech. The area to the left, in the frontal lobe, is linked with thinking about a word's meaning (Montgomery, 1989).

Learning Check

1. In brain research, making a micro-electrode recording is the first step in deep lesioning studies. T or F?

2. Both CT scans and MRI scans are based on X-ray data that is assembled into an image by a computer. T or F?

3. The MANSCAN technique combines EEG information with an MRI scan. T or F?

4. In a PET scan, brain areas that are using more glucose or oxygen are assumed to be more active than surrounding areas. T or F?

Critical Thinking

5. Deep lesioning is used to ablate an area in the hypothalamus of a rat. After the operation, the rat seems to lose interest in food and eating. Why would it be a mistake to conclude that the ablated area is a "hunger center"?

Answers:

1. F 2. F 3. T 4. T 5. Because other factors might explain the apparent loss of appetite. For example, the taste or smell of food might be affected, or the rat might simply have difficulty swallowing. It is also possible that hunger originates elsewhere in the brain and the ablated area merely relays messages that cause the rat to eat.

Chapter Summary

How do nerve cells operate and communicate?

◆ The brain and nervous system are made up of linked nerve cells called **neurons.** Neurons are arranged in long chains and dense networks. They pass information from one to another through **synapses.**

◆ The basic conducting fibers of neurons are **axons,** but **dendrites** (a receiving area), the **soma** (the cell body and also a receiving area), and **axon terminals** (the branching ends of an axon) are also involved in communication.

◆ The firing of an **action potential** (nerve impulse) is basically electrical, whereas communication between neurons is chemical or electrical. Chemical synapses are most numerous in nature, but some electrical synapses exist.

◆ In chemical synapses, neurons release chemicals called **neurotransmitters.** These cross to **receptor sites** on the receiving cell, causing it to be excited or inhibited.

◆ Transmitters called **neuropeptides** appear to regulate activity in the brain. Through **volume conduction** their effects can be widespread.

◆ **Nerves** are made of axons and associated tissues. Neurons and nerves in the peripheral nervous system can often **regenerate;** damage in the central nervous system is *permanent*, unless a repair is attempted by **grafting** or implanting healthy tissue.

What are the functions of major parts of the nervous system?

◆ The nervous system can be divided into the **central nervous system** (the brain and spinal cord) and the **peripheral nervous system,** which includes the **somatic** (bodily) and **autonomic** (involuntary) nervous systems.

◆ The autonomic system has two divisions: the **sympathetic** (emergency, activating) branch and the **parasympathetic** (sustaining, conserving) branch.

How is the brain organized and what do its various areas do?

◆ The human brain is marked by advanced **corticalization,** or enlargement of the **cerebral cortex.**

◆ The **left cerebral hemisphere** contains speech or language "centers" in most people. It also specializes in writing, calculating, judging time and rhythm, and ordering complex movements.

◆ The **right hemisphere** is largely non-verbal. It excels at spatial and perceptual skills, visualization, and recognition of patterns, faces, and melodies.

◆ "Split brains" have been created in animals and humans by cutting the **corpus callosum.** The split-brain individual shows a remarkable degree of independence between the right and left hemispheres.

◆ The most basic functions of the **lobes** of the cerebral cortex are as follows: **occipital** lobes—vision; **parietal** lobes—bodily sensation; **temporal** lobes—hearing and language; **frontal** lobes—motor control, speech, and abstract thought. Damage to any of these areas will impair the named functions.

Why are the brain's association areas important? What happens when they are injured?

◆ There are a number of **association areas** on the cortex that are neither sensory nor motor in function. These are related to more complex skills such as language, memory, recognition, and problem solving.

◆ Damage to either **Broca's area** or **Wernicke's area** causes speech and language problems known as **aphasias.**

◆ Damage in other areas may cause **agnosia,** the inability to identify objects by sight.

What kinds of behaviors are controlled by the subcortex?

◆ The brain as a whole can be subdivided into three general areas: the **forebrain, midbrain,** and **hindbrain.** The **subcortex** includes several crucial brain structures found at all three levels, below the cortex.

◆ The **medulla** contains centers essential for reflex control of heart rate, breathing, and other "vegetative" functions.

◆ The **cerebellum** maintains coordination, posture, and muscle tone.

◆ The **reticular formation** directs sensory and motor messages, and part of it, known as the **RAS,** acts as an activating system for the cerebral cortex.

◆ The **thalamus** carries sensory information to the cortex. The **hypothalamus** exerts powerful control over eating, drinking, sleep cycles, body temperature, and other basic motives and behaviors.

◆ The **limbic system** is strongly related to emotion. It also contains distinct reward and punishment areas and an area known as the **hippocampus** that is important for forming memories.

◆ Electrical stimulation of the brain **(ESB)** has been used to study the functions of various areas. ESB holds promise as a medical treatment. It is unlikely that it could be used to forcibly control behavior.

Is behavior affected by the glandular system?

◆ The **endocrine system** provides **chemical** communication in the body through the release of **hormones** into the bloodstream. Endocrine glands influence moods, behavior, and even personality.

◆ Many of the endocrine glands are influenced by the **pituitary** (the "master gland"), which is in turn influenced by the hypothalamus. Thus, the brain controls the body through the fast nervous system and the slower endocrine system.

In what ways do right- and left-handed individuals differ?

◆ Hand dominance ranges from strongly left- to strongly right-handed, with mixed handedness and ambidexterity in between. Ninety percent of the population is basically right-handed, 10 percent left-handed.

◆ The vast majority of people are right-handed and therefore left-brain dominant for motor skills. Ninety-seven percent of right-handed persons and 68 percent of the left-handed also produce speech from the left hemisphere.

◆ In general, the left-handed are less strongly **lateralized** in brain function than are right-handed persons.

How do biopsychologists study the brain?

◆ Conventional brain research relies on dissection, staining, ablation, deep lesioning, electrical recording, electrical stimulation, micro-electrode recording, EEG recording, and clinical studies.

◆ Computer-enhanced techniques are providing three-dimensional images of the living human brain and its activity. Examples of such techniques are CT and MRI scans, the MANSCAN technique, PET scans, and MEG.

Child Development

Preview

Alien Minds

You may not have noticed. Not everyone has. There are alien creatures among us. More arrive daily. They look a lot like you and me, but they're smaller, and they think differently. Their speech is strange. They ask many questions. It's obvious they are trying to understand how we live. Their goal is to inhabit the planet Earth in our place. Who are these creatures? Where are they from? You need not be alarmed: They come not from outer space, but from inner space. They are the product of life perpetuating life. They are children.

Studying children helps answer the question, How did I become the person I am today? This makes children captivating, but there is another reason for interest: A child's understanding of the world is *qualitatively* different from yours and mine. Entering a child's awareness has much of the intrigue of meeting a person from another culture—or another planet! In short, children are extremely interesting creatures. A tremendous amount of psychological research has focused on them.

What branch of psychology studies children?

Children are the heart of **developmental psychology** (*the study of progressive changes in behavior and abilities*). Be aware, however, that human development reaches beyond childhood to include every stage of life from conception to death (or "the womb to the tomb").

An entire lifetime of development includes many topics—so many in fact, that some appear in other chapters. In this chapter, we will discuss the first years of life. The next covers development over an entire life span, plus specific problems that occur at various ages.

Human development is a story of growth and transformation. Perhaps learning about development will contribute to your own development. Find out by reading more!

Key Questions:

Key Topics to Watch for:

Key Questions	Key Topics to Watch for
What can newborn babies do?	The sensory, motor, and mental capacities of neonates
What influence does maturation have on early development?	The effects of maturation on motor skills, emotions, and learning
How do heredity and environment affect development?	DNA and the mechanisms of heredity How children differ in temperament Nature-nurture interactions Prenatal influences and the effects of birth
How important are parenting styles?	Maternal and paternal influences The parenting styles of fathers and mothers
Of what significance is a child's emotional bond with parents?	Social awareness, critical periods, imprinting, and attachment
How do children acquire language and thinking abilities?	Early communication, language development, and parentese Piaget's stages of cognitive development
How do children develop morals and values?	Moral dilemmas, moral reasoning, and stages of moral development
What are the effects of a poor early environment?	The impact of early deprivation
What can be done to enhance early development?	Enriched environments How to facilitate early development
How has new genetic knowledge affected parenthood?	Assisted conception, sex selection, eugenics, and genetic counseling

The Newborn Baby— The Basic Model Comes with Options

At birth the human **neonate** (NEE-oh-NATE: *newborn infant*) is completely dependent on others and will die if not given care. Newborn babies cannot lift their heads, turn over, or feed themselves. Does this mean they are inert and unfeeling? Definitely not! Neonates can see, hear, smell, taste, and respond to pain and touch. Although their senses are less acute at birth, babies are immediately responsive (Bernt, 1992). Neonates will follow a moving object with their eyes and will turn in the direction of sounds. Within *hours* after they are born, babies begin to prefer seeing their mother's face, rather than a stranger's (Walton, Bower, & Bower, 1992).

Neonates also display a number of adaptive *reflexes*. To elicit the **grasping reflex,** press an *object in the neonate's palm and she will grasp it* with surprising strength. Many infants, in fact, can hang from a raised bar, like little trapeze artists. The grasping reflex aids survival by helping infants avoid falling. The **rooting reflex** (*reflexive head turning and nursing*) can be demonstrated by touching a baby's cheek. Immediately, he will turn toward your finger, as if searching for something.

How is such turning adaptive?

The rooting reflex helps infants to find a bottle or breast. Then, when a nipple touches the infant's mouth, the **sucking reflex** (*rhythmic nursing movements*) helps her obtain needed food. At the same time, food rewards nursing. As a result, nursing rapidly increases in vigor during the first days after birth. Thus, we see that learning begins at once in the newborn.

The **Moro reflex** is also interesting. If a baby's position is changed abruptly or he is startled by a loud noise, he will make *movements similar to an embrace*. These movements have been compared to the ones used by baby monkeys to cling to their mothers. (It is left to the reader's imagination to decide if there is any connection.)

We are tempted to think of newborn babies as mere bundles of reflexes. But infants can respond in ways that are more subtle than once imagined. For example, Andrew Meltzoff and Keith Moore (1977, 1983) found that babies are born mimics. Figure 4–1 ◆ shows Meltzoff as he sticks out his tongue, opens his mouth, and purses his lips at a 20-day-old girl. Will she imitate him? Videotapes made of babies confirmed that they imitate adult facial gestures. As early as 9 months of age, infants can imitate actions a full day after seeing them (Heimann & Meltzoff, 1996). Such mimicry is obviously an aid to rapid learning in infancy.

How intelligent are newborn babies?

Child psychologist Jerome Bruner (1983) believes babies are smarter than most people think. Bruner cites an experiment in which 3- to 8-week-old babies seemed to understand that a person's voice and body are connected. If babies heard their mother's voice coming from where she was standing, they remained calm. If her voice came from a loudspeaker several

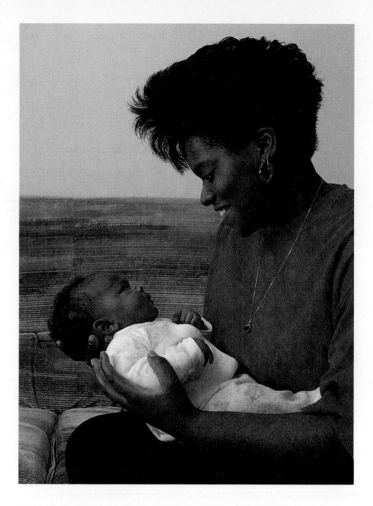

Newborn babies display a special interest in the human face. A preference for seeing their mother's face develops rapidly and encourages social interactions between mother and baby.

feet away, the babies became agitated and began to cry. Another sign of infant awareness is the fact that newborn babies appear to remember simple speech sounds up to a day after first hearing them (Swain, Zelazo, & Clifton, 1993). Clearly, the human mind is active from birth onward (more on this later).

Tests of infant vision offer a further look into the private world of the neonate.

How is it possible to test a baby's vision?

Working with infants always requires imagination because they cannot talk. Robert Fantz invented a device called a **looking chamber** *to test infant vision* (Fig. 4–2a ◆). A child is placed on his or her back inside the chamber, facing a lighted area above. Next, two objects are placed in the chamber. By observing the movements of the infant's eyes and the images they reflect, researchers can tell what the infant is looking at. Testing of this type shows that adult vision is about 30 times sharper, but babies can see large patterns, shapes, and edges (Bernt, 1992).

Fantz found that 3-day-old babies prefer complex patterns, such as checkerboards and bull's eyes, to simpler colored rectangles. Other psychologists have learned that infants are more excited by circles and curves and that they will look longer at bright lights (Fig. 4–2b ◆) (Brown, 1990). Within hours after they are born, babies are aware of changes in the position of objects (Slater et al., 1991). Findings such as these demonstrate (as a friend of the author's once put it) that "There really is a person inside that little body."

Of greater interest is the finding that infants will spend more time looking at a human face pattern than at a scrambled face or a colored oval (Fig. 4–2c ◆). When real human faces were used, Fantz found that familiar faces are

Figure 4–1 ◆ Infant imitation. In the top row of photos, Andrew Meltzoff makes facial gestures at an infant. The bottom row records the infant's responses. Videotapes of Meltzoff and of tested infants helped ensure objectivity. (Photos courtesy of Andrew N. Meltzoff.)

Child Development | **87**

(a)

(b)

(c)

Figure 4–2 ◆ **(a)** Eye movements and fixation points of infants are observed in Fantz's "looking chamber." **(b)** Thirteen-week-old infants prefer concentric and curved patterns like those on the left to non-concentric and straight-line patterns like those on the right. **(c)** Infants tested in a looking chamber look at the normal face longer than at the scrambled face and at both faces longer than at the design on the right. (Photo courtesy of David Linton. Drawing from "The Origin of Form Perception" by Robert L. Fantz, Copyright c 1961 by Scientific American, Inc. All rights reserved.)

preferred to unfamiliar faces. However, this preference reverses at about age 2. At that time, unusual objects begin to hold greater interest for the child. For instance, Jerome Kagan (1971) showed three-dimensional face masks to 2-year-olds. Kagan found that the toddlers were fascinated by a face with eyes on the chin and a nose in the middle of the forehead. He believes the babies' interest came from a need to understand why the scrambled face differed from what they had come to expect.

Maturation

The emergence of many abilities closely parallels **maturation** (*physical growth and development of the body, especially the brain and nervous system*). Maturation particularly underlies the unfolding of motor abilities, such as crawling and walking. Of course, the *rate* of maturation varies from child to child. Nevertheless, the *order* is virtually universal. For instance, the strength and coordination a child needs to sit without support appears before that needed for crawling. Therefore, infants the world over typically sit before they

crawl (and crawl before they stand, stand before they walk, and so on) (Fig. 4–3 ◆).

What about my weird cousin Emo who never crawled?

Like cousin Emo, a few children substitute rolling, creeping, or shuffling for crawling. A very few move directly from sitting to standing and walking (Robson, 1984). Even so, an orderly sequence of motor development remains evident. In general, increased muscular control proceeds in a pattern that is **cephalocaudal** (SEF-eh-lo-KOD-ul: *from head to toe*) and **proximodistal** (PROK-seh-moe-DIS-tul: *from the center of the body to the extremities*). Even if cousin Emo flunked Elementary Crawling, his motor development followed the standard top-down, center-outward pattern.

While maturation is certainly important, motor skills don't simply "emerge." Infants must *learn* to control their actions. Babies actively explore movements, selecting those that work. A baby's first efforts may be approximate—a wobbly crawl or some shaky first steps. However, with practice, babies "tune" their movements to be smoother and more effective. Such learning is evident in the very first months of life (Thelen, 1995). (See Figure 4–4 ◆.)

1. Fetal posture
(newborn)

2. Holds chin up
(1 month)

3. Holds chest up
(2 months)

4. Sits when supported
(4 months)

5. Sits alone
(7 months)

6. Stands holding furniture
(9 months)

7. Crawls
(10 months)

8. Walks if led
(11 months)

9. Stands alone
(11 months)

10. Walks alone
(12 months)

Figure 4–3 ◆ Motor development. Most infants follow an orderly pattern of motor development. Although the order in which children progress is similar, there are large individual differences in the ages at which each ability appears. The ages listed are averages for American children. It is not unusual for many of the skills to appear 1 or 2 months earlier than average or several months later (Frankenberg & Dodds, 1967; Harris & Liebert, 1991). Parents should not be alarmed if a child's behavior differs somewhat from the average.

Emotion   Do babies express emotions? The traditional view is that **general excitement** (widespread arousal) is the only emotion newborn infants express. However, as any parent can tell you, emotional life blossoms rapidly. One researcher (Bridges, 1932) observed a large number of babies and found that all the basic human emotions emerge before age 2. According to Bridges, emotions appear in a consistent order, beginning first with a split between pleasant and unpleasant emotions (Fig. 4–5 ◆).

Many experts continue to believe that emotions unfold slowly, as the nervous system matures (Camras, Sullivan, & Michel, 1993; Matias & Cohen, 1993). However, psychologist Carroll Izard believes he has evidence that infants can express several basic emotions as early as 2.5 months of age. Izard looked carefully at the faces of babies and found that emotions abound during infancy. (See Figure 4–6 ◆.) The most common infant expression, he found, is not excitement, but *interest*—followed by *joy, anger,* and *sadness* (Izard et al., 1995).

If Izard is right, then emotions are primarily innate and have a strong biological-evolutionary basis. Perhaps that's why smiling is one of a baby's most common reactions. Smiling probably helps babies survive by eliciting affection and other positive reactions from caregivers (Izard et al., 1995).

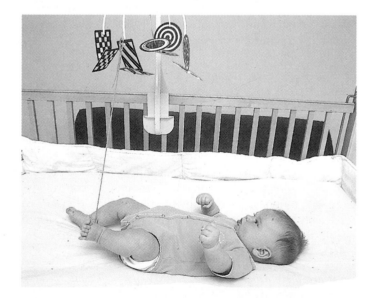

Figure 4–4 ◆ Psychologist Carolyn Rovee-Collier has shown that babies as young as 3 months old can learn to control their movements. In her experiments, babies lie on their backs under a colorful crib mobile. A ribbon is tied around the baby's ankle and connected to the mobile. Whenever babies spontaneously kick their legs, the mobile jiggles and rattles. Within a few minutes, infants learn to kick faster. Their reward for kicking is a chance to see the mobile move (Hayne & Rovee-Collier, 1995).

Child Development   **89**

Figure 4–5 ◆ The traditional view of infancy holds that emotions are rapidly differentiated from an initial capacity for excitement. (After K. M. B. Bridges, 1932. Reprinted by permission of the Society for Research in Child Development, Inc.)

Initially, smiling is just a reflex response to comfort or pleasure. However, by the age of 10 months, babies *smile more frequently when another person is nearby* (Jones, Collins, & Hong, 1991). This **social smile** encourages parents to pay attention to infants and give them affection. Negative emotions also have value. When new parents see and hear a crying baby, they feel annoyed, irritated, disturbed, or unhappy. Such reactions encourage parents to tend to a baby's needs, again increasing its chances for survival. Babies the world over, it seems, rapidly become capable of letting others know what they like and dislike. (Prove this to yourself sometime by driving a baby buggy.)

Readiness At what ages are children ready to feed themselves, to walk alone, or say goodbye to diapers? Such milestones tend to be governed by a child's *readiness* for rapid learning. The principle of **readiness** (also known as the **principle of motor primacy**) states that *minimum levels of physical maturation must precede the learning of certain skills.* It is impossible, for instance, to teach children to walk or use a toilet before they have matured enough to control the necessary muscles. Parents invite failure when they try to force a child to learn skills too early. They also run a risk of needlessly frustrating the child (Luxem & Christophersen, 1994).

Then are there definite ages at which children become ready to learn particular skills?

No. Readiness usually emerges over a period of weeks or months. Training that begins too early will not succeed; training early in a transition period may succeed, but it will be inefficient; and training when a child is maturationally ready produces rapid learning.

Parents are sometimes tempted to hurry a child along. However, much needless grief can be avoided by respecting

(a)   (b)

(c)   (d)

Figure 4–6 ◆ Infants display many of the same emotional expressions as adults do. Carroll Izard believes such expressions show that distinct emotions appear within the first months of life. Other theorists argue that specific emotions come into focus more gradually, as an infant's nervous system matures. Either way, parents can expect to see a full range of basic emotions by the end of a baby's first year. Over the first two years, children become increasingly active in initiating emotional exchanges with parents (Grolnick, Cosgrove, & Bridges, 1996).

a child's personal rate of growth. Consider the eager parents who toilet train an 18-month-old child in 10 trying weeks of false alarms and "accidents." If the parents had waited until the child was 24 months old, they might have succeeded in just 3 weeks. Parents may control when toilet training starts, but maturation tends to dictate when it will be completed (Luxem & Christophersen, 1994). (Around 30 months is average for completion.) So why fight nature? (The wet look is in.)

Human infants are transformed from helpless babies to independent persons with dazzling speed. Early growth is extremely rapid. By the third year of life, the child stands, walks, talks, explores, and has a unique personality. At no other time after birth does development proceed more rapidly. During this period, the child's development is shaped by a potent mixture of heredity and environment. Before we explore that topic, Table 4–1 ■ summarizes some of the implications of the preceding discussion.

Heredity and Environment—The Nurture of Nature

Which has a greater effect on development, heredity or environment?

Psychologists have debated—sometimes heatedly—the relative impact of nature versus nurture on behavior. **Heredity** ("nature") refers to *the genetic transmission of physical and psychological characteristics from parents to offspring.* The potent effects of heredity certainly can't be denied. An incredible number of personal features are determined at **conception,** *when a sperm and an ovum (egg) unite.* It is estimated that the genetic information in each human cell would fill thousands of 1,000-page books—and that's in fine print!

How does heredity operate?

Heredity

The nucleus of every cell contains 46 **chromosomes** (*thread-like "colored bodies" that transmit the coded instructions of heredity*) (Fig. 4–7 ◆). An exception is sperm cells and ova, each of which contains only 23 chromosomes. Thus, humans normally receive 23 chromosomes from their mother and 23 from their father. Chromosomes are made up of **DNA,** *deoxyribonucleic acid* (dee-OX-see-RYE-bo-new-KLEE-ik). DNA is a long, ladder-like chemical structure assembled from smaller molecules (Fig. 4–8 ◆). The order of these molecules, or *organic bases,* acts as a code for genetic information.

The DNA in each cell contains 300 billion base pairs. That's enough to provide all the instructions needed to make a human—with room left over to spare. **Genes** are *small areas of the DNA code.* Each gene, which can be up to 30,000 base pairs long, carries instructions that affect a particular process or personal characteristic. Every human cell has roughly 100,000 genes. In some cases, a single gene is responsible for a particular inherited feature, such as eye color. Most characteristics, however, are **polygenic** (pol-ih-JEN-ik), or *determined by many genes working in combination.*

Genes may be dominant or recessive. When a gene is **dominant,** the trait it controls *will be present every time the gene is present.* When a gene is **recessive,** it must be *paired with a second recessive gene before its effect will be expressed.* Here's an example: We receive one half of our chromosomes (and genes) from each parent. If you were to get a brown-eye gene from your father and a blue-eye gene from your mother, you would be brown-eyed, because brown-eye genes are dominant.

If brown-eye genes are dominant, how is it that two brown-eyed parents sometimes have a blue-eyed child?

Table 4–1 ■ The Neonate: Implications for Parents and Caregivers
▪ From birth onward, infants are responsive to their immediate surroundings and to other people. Mental life and intellectual development also begin immediately. Learning doesn't start in preschool or kindergarten.
▪ Maturation proceeds at its own pace and in an orderly sequence. Caregivers should be sensitive to a child's level of development and avoid forcing the pace of learning. The principle of readiness applies to many early skills.
▪ Even infants under the age of 1 year have feelings and emotional experiences.

Figure 4–7 ◆ This image, made with a scanning electron microscope, shows several pairs of human chromosomes. (Colors are artificial.)

Figure 4–8 ◆ (*Top left*) The order of the linked molecules (organic bases) that make up the "rungs" on DNA's twisted "molecular ladder" serve as a code for genetic information. The order of the code provides a genetic blueprint that is unique for each individual (except identical twins). The drawing shows only a small section of a DNA strand. An entire strand of DNA is composed of billions of smaller molecules. (*Bottom left*) The nucleus of each cell in the body contains chromosomes made up of tightly wound coils of DNA. (Don't be misled by the drawing: Chromosomes are microscopic in size and the chemical molecules that make up DNA are even smaller.)

If each parent has two brown-eye genes, the couple's children can only be brown-eyed. But what if each parent has one brown-eye gene and one blue-eye gene? In that case the parents would both have brown eyes, but there is 1 chance in 4 that their children will get two blue-eye genes and have blue eyes (Fig. 4–9 ◆).

Sex is also genetically determined—in this case by two specialized chromosomes. A child who inherits two **X chromosomes** will normally be a *female*. An *X* chromosome paired with a **Y chromosome** normally yields a *male*. The woman's ovum always provides an *X* chromosome, since she has two *X*'s in her own genetic makeup. In contrast, one half of the male's sperm carry *X* chromosomes and the other half *Y*'s. There is evidence that just one gene on the *Y* chromosome initiates the events that make a male baby. (Gender can be more complex than implied here. See Chapter 15 for more information.)

Whether you have *XX* or *XY* chromosomes may affect more than your gender. Some traits are **sex linked,** or *carried by recessive genes on an X or Y chromosome.* An example is color blindness, which is carried on an *X* chromosome and given from mother to son. Sex-linked traits are also carried by *Y* chromosomes, but this is exceedingly rare.

Nature Hereditary instructions influence events from conception to **senescence** (seh-NESS-ens: *aging*) and death (see Table 4–2 ■). That's why the **human growth sequence** (*overall pattern of physical development*) is universal. Heredity also determines eye color, skin color, and susceptibility to some diseases. It underlies maturation and motor development. Heredity exerts considerable influence over body size and shape, height, intelligence, athletic potential, personal-

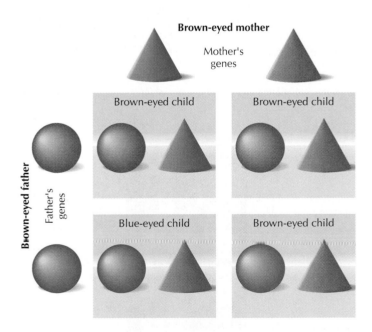

Figure 4–9 ◆ Gene patterns for children of brown-eyed parents, where each parent has one brown-eye gene and one blue-eye gene. Since the brown-eye gene is dominant, only 1 child in 4 will be blue eyed.

Table 4–2 ■ Human Growth Sequence

Period	Duration	Descriptive Name
Prenatal period	From conception to birth	
Germinal period	First two weeks after conception	Zygote
Embryonic period	2–8 weeks after conception	Embryo
Fetal period	From 8 weeks after conception to birth	Fetus
Neonatal period	From birth to a few weeks after birth	Neonate
Infancy	From a few weeks after birth until child is walking securely; some children walk securely at less than a year, while others may not be able to until age 17–18 months	Infant
Early childhood	From about 15–18 months until about 2–2½ years	Toddler
	From age 2–3 to about age 6	Preschool child
Middle childhood	From about age 6 to about age 12	School-age child
Pubescence	Period of about 2 years before puberty	
Puberty	Point of development at which biological changes of pubescence reach a climax marked by sexual maturity	
Adolescence	From the beginning of pubescence until full social maturity is reached (difficult to fix duration of this period)	Adolescent
Adulthood	From adolescence to death; sometimes subdivided into other periods as shown at left	Adult
Young adulthood (19–25)		
Adulthood (26–40)		
Maturity (41 plus)		
Senescence	No defined limit that would apply to all people; extremely variable; characterized by marked physiological and psychological deterioration	Adult (senile), "old age"

*Note: There is no exact beginning or ending point for the various growth periods. The ages are approximate, and each period may be thought of as blending into the next. (Table courtesy of Tom Bond.)

ity traits, sexual orientation, and a host of other details (Rose, 1995). Some genes affect events that will not occur in a person's life for 80 or 90 years (Konner, 1991). Score 1 for those who favor heredity as the more important factor in development!

Environment

Environment ("nurture") refers to the *sum of all external conditions affecting development*. Does the powerful impact of heredity mean that environment takes a back seat? Definitely not. Humans today are physically very similar to cave dwellers who lived 30,000 years ago. A bright baby born today could become almost anything—a computer programmer, an engineer, a gangsta rapper, or a biochemist who likes to paint in watercolors. But an Upper Paleolithic baby could not possibly have grown into anything except a hunter or food gatherer. Score 1 for the environmentalists!

Nature-Nurture Interactions The outcome of this debate is clear: *both* heredity and environment are important. The two are, in fact, inseparable. As a person grows, there is a constant interplay, or *interaction*, between nature and nurture. Heredity provides a framework of personal potentials and limitations. These, in turn, are altered by

Identical twins. Twins who share identical genes (identical twins) demonstrate the powerful influence of heredity. Even when they are reared apart, identical twins are strikingly alike in motor skills, physical development, and appearance (Horn et al., 1976). At the same time, twins are less alike as adults than they were as children, which shows environmental influences are at work (McCartney, Bernieri, & Harris, 1990).

learning, nutrition, disease, culture, and other environmental factors. By themselves, hereditary instructions are meaningless. The development of hereditary tendencies depends on the quality of the environments in which a child lives, learns, and grows (Baker & Clark, 1990; Lipsitt, 1990).

How soon after birth do hereditary differences in behavior appear?

Some appear immediately. Newborn babies differ noticeably in **temperament** (*the physical core of personality*). Heredity significantly affects an infant's sensitivity, irritability, distractibility, and typical mood (Braungart et al., 1992).

Here's an interesting test: Give a newborn baby a pacifier. How long does it take her to become calm and quiet? If she takes longer than average to soothe now, she will probably be more active, exploratory, and distractible than average at 12 months of age (Riese, 1995). Thus, from birth onward, babies are unique individuals.

On the basis of temperament, babies can be separated into three major categories. **Easy children** (about 40 percent of those observed) are *relaxed and agreeable*. **Difficult children** (about 10 percent) are *moody, intense, and easily angered*. **Slow-to-warm-up children** (about 15 percent) are *restrained and unexpressive*, or shy. The remaining children do not fit neatly into any single category (Chess & Thomas, 1986). (Perhaps we should call them "generic" children?)

Because of inborn differences in readiness to smile, cry, vocalize, reach out, or pay attention, babies rapidly become *active participants* in their own development—especially

their social development. Growing infants alter parents' behavior at the same time they are changed by it. For example, Amy is an easy baby who smiles frequently and is easily fed. This encourages touching, feeding, and affection from her mother. The mother's responses, in turn, reward Amy and cause more smiling and other positive reactions. A dynamic *relationship* has been created between mother and child.

A person's **developmental level** is his or her *current state of physical, emotional, and intellectual development*. To summarize, we might say that three factors combine to determine your developmental level at any stage of life. These are *heredity*, *environment*, and your *own behavior*, each tightly interwoven with the others. (See Table 4–3 ■.)

Table 4–3 ■ Heredity and Environment: Implications for Parents and Caregivers
■ At any given time a child's development reflects the joint effects of heredity and environment. However, caregivers can only influence environment.
■ Children vary in temperament. Caregivers should be sensitive to such differences and accept them as natural.
■ Parenting is a serious responsibility, especially during the first years of life, which has far-reaching effects.

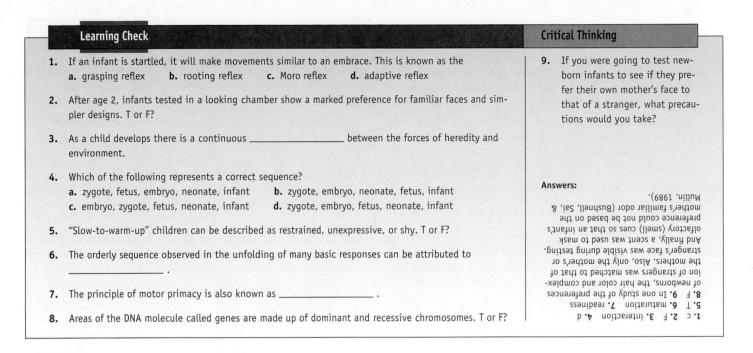

Early Environment—As the Twig Is Bent

Normally the **intrauterine environment** (*interior of the womb*) is highly protected and stable. But during periods of embryonic and fetal growth it's possible for environmental effects to reach the developing child.

Prenatal Influences

If a mother's health or nutrition is poor, if she contracts certain diseases, such as German measles or syphilis, uses drugs, or is exposed to X-rays or atomic radiation, the fetus may be harmed (Rosenblith, 1992). The result is a **congenital problem** (*a defect that originated during prenatal development*). Congenital problems (or "birth defects") are different from **genetic problems,** *which are inherited from parents.* (You will find more information on genetic problems in this chapter's Exploration.)

How is it possible for the embryo or the fetus to be harmed?

Effects of Drugs   No direct intermixing of blood takes place between a mother and her unborn child. Nevertheless, some substances—especially drugs—do reach the fetus. If the mother is addicted to morphine, heroin, or methadone, the infant may be born with a drug addiction. Some drugs that reach the fetus are known to be **teratogens** (teh-RAT-uh-jens: *substances capable of causing birth defects*). For example,

just one hit of cocaine taken by a pregnant woman can cause defects in her fetus. Cocaine penetrates the brain of the fetus and reduces oxygen flow (Heyser et al., 1992).

At birth, "crack" babies are very excitable and jittery if their mother recently used cocaine (Lester et al., 1991). Otherwise, they are sluggish and depressed. By the time cocaine babies start school, they often suffer from tremors, hyperactivity, listlessness, slowed language learning, and disorganized thinking. Many will never be normal. Even when prenatal drug damage is absent, the chaotic home

Due to the rapid growth of basic structures, the developing fetus is sensitive to a variety of diseases, drugs, and sources of radiation. This is especially true during the first trimester (3 months) of gestation (pregnancy).

environment of crack-addicted mothers can have a devastating effect (Hawley, 1996).

Most common prescription drugs also reach the fetus. All of the following substances are potentially damaging: general anesthetics, cortisone, tetracycline, excessive amounts of vitamins A, D, B_6, and K, cocaine, some barbiturates, opiates, tranquilizers, steroids, and synthetic sex hormones (Rosenblith, 1992). Even aspirin, a seemingly safe drug, has been linked with lowered infant IQs when taken prenatally (Streissguth et al., 1987). In short, when a pregnant mother takes drugs, her unborn child does too.

What about alcohol and tobacco?

Repeated heavy drinking by pregnant women causes the **fetal alcohol syndrome (FAS)**. Affected infants have *low birth weight, bodily defects, facial malformations, and many are mentally retarded.* Miscarriages and premature births are also common. During pregnancy, frequent drinking of even small amounts of alcohol, or a single "binge" of five or more drinks, can cause fetal brain damage. Considering the risks, the best advice for pregnant women is to entirely avoid drinking alcohol. The tragedy of FAS is that it is completely preventable (Short & Hess, 1995).

Tobacco is also damaging. A pregnant woman who smokes two packs of cigarettes a day blocks off about 25 percent of the oxygen supply to the fetus. Heavy smokers run a higher risk of miscarrying or giving premature birth to underweight babies (Rosenblith, 1992). The infant death rate is 27 percent higher if a woman smokes during pregnancy. Children of smoking mothers score lower in

Some of the typical features of children suffering from fetal alcohol syndrome include a small non-symmetrical head, a short nose, a flattened area between the eyes, oddly shaped eyes, and a thin upper lip. Many of these features become less noticeable by adolescence. However, mental retardation and other problems commonly follow the FAS child into adulthood. The infant shown here represents a moderate example of FAS.

language development and general mental ability (Fried et al., 1992). Of the many reasons for not smoking, pregnancy appears to be one of the most compelling.

Childbirth

More than ever, parents can choose how their children will be born. Should it be a conventional hospital birth? Should they try natural childbirth? Should the father be present? In recent years, researchers have carefully probed the effects of such choices. Let's briefly explore what they have learned.

Conventional Delivery In a traditional **medicated birth** *the mother is assisted by a physician and given drugs to relieve pain.* Until recently, this was the rule for hospital births. The drugs used range from local analgesics (painkillers) to general anesthetics, which cause a loss of consciousness.

Increasingly, doctors and parents have come to realize that general anesthesia has major drawbacks. For one thing, drugs dull or block the mother's awareness of birth. They also reduce oxygen flow to the fetus and often require a forceps delivery (in which the baby is pulled through the birth canal). In many cases, infants are born partially anesthetized. For such reasons, babies tend to lag in muscular and neural development if their mothers were heavily anesthetized.

In the last 10 years there has been a marked move away from the use of general anesthesia during birth. Nevertheless, 95 percent of all deliveries in the United States and Canada use some form of painkiller. Certainly, mothers should not feel guilty if they need pain relief. Drugs injected into the spinal cord (a *spinal block*) can greatly reduce pain without affecting the child or the mother's alertness. However, it appears wise to use general anesthetics as little as possible.

Other practices that promote successful pregnancies and healthy babies include (Bradley, 1995):

- Maintaining good nutrition during pregnancy
- Learning relaxation and stress reduction techniques to ease the transition to motherhood
- Avoiding teratogens and other harmful substances
- Getting adequate exercise during pregnancy
- General education about pregnancy and childbirth

Prepared Childbirth What can parents do to give babies the best possible start in life, while avoiding over-medicated births? In **natural,** or **prepared, childbirth,** *parents learn specific techniques to manage discomfort and facilitate labor.* The most popular approach is the *Lamaze method* (la-MAHZ), developed by French physician Ferdinand Lamaze.

Early in pregnancy, Lamaze instructors explain the entire birth process to couples. Women who understand what is happening in their bodies tend to have fewer fears and less anxiety. Expectant mothers then learn methods of breathing and muscular control to reduce pain. Another important element is training the father or a friend to give emotional support to the mother during childbirth.

Natural childbirth typically shortens labor and reduces pain. It makes birth a celebration of life, rather than a medical problem. Accordingly, parents are more likely to experience birth as a time of great joy (Mackey, 1995).

As the following highlight explains, mothers continue to need emotional support *after* giving birth, not just during the big event.

A Closer Look

Understanding Postpartum Depression

Two weeks after her child was born, Cheryl realized something was wrong. She could no longer ignore that she was extremely irritable, fatigued, tearful, and depressed. "Shouldn't I be happy?" she wondered. "What's wrong with me?"

Many women are surprised to learn that they face an increased risk of depression after giving birth. The two most common forms of the problem are *maternity blues* and *postpartum depression*. (The term *postpartum* refers to the time period following childbirth.)

An estimated 50 to 80 percent of all women experience **maternity blues,** *a mild depression that usually lasts from 24 to 48 hours after childbirth*. These "third-day blues" are marked by crying, fitful sleep, tension, anger, and irritability. For most women, these reactions are a normal part of adjusting to childbirth. Their depression is usually brief and not too severe.

For some women, maternity blues can be the beginning of a more lasting depression. As many as 12 percent of all women who give birth develop **postpartum depression,** *a moderately severe depression that begins within 3 months following childbirth*. Typical signs of postpartum depression are mood swings, despondency, feelings of inadequacy, and an inability to cope with the new baby. Depression of this kind may last anywhere from 2 months to about a year. Stress and anxiety before birth and negative attitudes toward child rearing increase the risk. Hormone changes can also be a factor: After a woman gives birth, her estrogen levels may drop, altering her mood.

How can we prevent postpartum depression? The amount of social support a woman receives appears to be an important factor. Women who become depressed tend to perceive their husbands as unsupportive. Therefore, educating prospective parents about postpartum depression and the value of mutual support may be helpful. Simply providing adequate maternity leaves for working parents could also lower the risk of depression. (Sources: Demyttenaere et al., 1995; Gilbert, 1996; Hyde et al., 1995; Zelkowitz & Milet, 1995)

How important is it for fathers to participate in the birth process?

Men generally make a better transition to parenthood when they help prepare for childbirth. During birth, a father may form lifelong memories that will affect his willingness to love and care for his child.

While participating in the birth is valuable, a father's *attitude* is probably more important. Fathers who *want* to be present during delivery show greater interest in their infants and are more likely to help care for them (Grossman &

Changing attitudes toward childbirth have encouraged mothers and fathers to actively prepare for birth and to participate more fully in caring for the newborn.

Volkmer, 1984). This is true whether or not the father was actually able to attend the birth.

Many hospitals now have home-like **birthing rooms** *designed to minimize the medical aspects of childbirth.* These facilities allow fathers to stay at the hospital so they can participate in the birth and care for the newborn. Even traditional delivery rooms are allowing fathers to observe the birth and coach the mother through labor. In some cases, the father cuts the umbilical cord and gives the infant its first bath. In many hospitals, babies spend their first night with parents in the birthing room. Home births, assisted by physicians or licensed midwifes, are also more common. Clearly, such changes are making birth more psychologically rewarding for mothers, fathers, and babies.

Maternal and Paternal Influences

In time, a child's environment expands to include the effects of culture, subculture, family, school, television, friends, and peers. However, for the first few years of life, the most important influences come from caregivers. The quality of mothering and fathering is therefore of prime importance.

How important are parenting styles?

One revealing study focused on **maternal influences** (*the sum of all effects a mother has on her child*). Researchers began by selecting children who were very competent ("A" children) or low in competence ("C" children). As they observed younger children, it became apparent that A and C patterns were already set by age 3.

To learn how this was possible, psychologists visited homes and observed children under age 3 and their mothers (White & Watts, 1973). The **caregiving styles** (*patterns of parental care*) they found ranged from the "super mother" to the "zoo-keeper mother." Super mothers went out of their way to provide children with educational experiences and allowed them to initiate activities. This caregiving style produced A children, competent in most areas of development. At the other end of the spectrum, zoo-keeper mothers gave their children good physical care, but interacted with them very little. Their child-care routines were rigid and highly structured. The result was C children who approached problems inflexibly.

More recent studies mirror the earlier findings: Optimal caregiving is characterized by **proactive maternal involvement** (*warm, educational interactions between mother and child*) (Pettit & Bates, 1989). Proactive mothers talk to babies more and encourage them to explore their surroundings (Olson, Bates, & Kaskie, 1992). This caregiving style speeds mental growth and minimizes behavior problems.

Optimal caregiving also depends on **goodness of fit** (*the degree to which parents and children have complementary temperaments*) (Chess & Thomas, 1986). For instance, a slow-to-warm-up child with impatient parents will probably have more problems than he would if his parents were easy-going. A similar point is made by a study of 12-year-old children. Those who scored high in intellectual ability and self-esteem had mothers who were *responsive* to them during childhood (Beckwith, Rodning, & Cohen, 1992). **Parental responsiveness** refers to *caregiving that is sensitive to a child's feelings, needs, rhythms, and signals.* For example, at one month of age, high quality parenting will focus on touching, holding, feeding, and stimulating a baby. With a one-year-old, give-and-take interactions and promoting emerging skills becomes more important. Thus, effective mothers alter

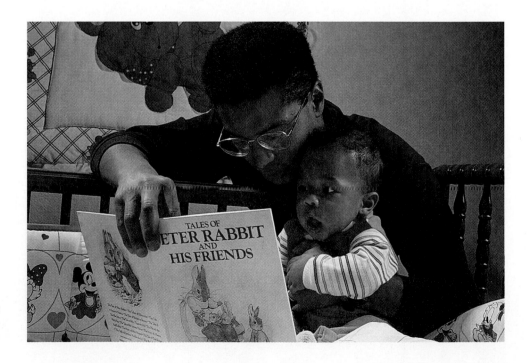

Fathering typically makes a contribution to early development that differs in emphasis from mothering.

Figure 4–10 ◆ Mother-infant and father-infant interactions. These graphs show what occurred on routine days in a sample of 72 American homes. The graph on the left records the total amount of contact parents had with their babies, including such actions as talking to, touching, hugging, or smiling at the infant. The graph on the right shows the amount of caregiving (diapering, washing, feeding, and so forth) done by each parent. Note that in both cases mother-infant interactions greatly exceed father-infant interactions. (Adapted from Belsky et al., 1984.)

their own behavior to meet children's changing needs at each stage of development (Heermann, Jones, & Wikoff, 1994).

Taken together, such findings support two beliefs long held by psychologists. First, mothering *does* make a difference. Second, early development has lasting effects on a person.

Aren't you overlooking the effects of fathering?

Yes. Fathers add significantly to an infant's social, emotional, and intellectual growth. In fact, fathers make a unique contribution by interacting with infants in ways that differ from those typical of mothers. Studies of **paternal influences** (*the sum of all effects a father has on his child*) reveal that fathers tend to act as *playmates* for infants.

Fathers typically spend 4 or 5 times more hours playing with infants than they do in caregiving (Parke & Sawin, 1977). It's true that fathers have become more involved in child care during the last decade. Just the same, mothers spend much more time feeding, dressing, grooming, disciplining, teaching, and caring for children (de Luccie & Davis, 1991). Altogether, fathers only interact with children below the age of 6 for an average of 26 minutes a day (Gottfried & Gottfried, 1988).

It might seem that the father's role as a playmate makes him less important. Not so. From birth onward, fathers pay more visual attention to children than mothers do. Fathers are much more tactile (lifting, tickling, and handling the baby), more physically arousing (engaging in rough-and-tumble play), and more likely to engage in unusual play (imitating the baby, for example) (Crawley & Sherrod, 1984). Mothers speak to infants more, play more conventional games (such as peekaboo), and as noted, spend more time in caregiving (Fig. 4–10 ◆).

Overall, fathers can be as affectionate, sensitive, and responsive to their children as mothers are. Nevertheless, infants tend to get very different views of males and females. Females, who offer comfort, nurturance, and verbal stimulation, tend to be close at hand. Males come and go, and when they are present, action, exploration, and risk taking prevail. It's no wonder, then, that maternal and paternal caregiving styles have a major impact on children's sex role development (Siegal, 1987; Silverstein, 1991).

Children are very adaptable. It is therefore tempting to assume that parenting only needs to be "adequate" or just "good enough" for a child to develop normally. It's true, of course, that many children do well with little more than routine care. Nevertheless, excellent parenting tends to optimize children's development. Active, high-quality caregiving is well worth the effort (Baumrind, 1993). (See Table 4–4 ■.)

BY PERMISSION OF JERRY SCOTT & RICK KIRKMAN AND CREATORS SYNDICATE

Table 4-4 ■ Early Environment: Implications for Parents and Caregivers

- Prenatal development is a time of great vulnerability, especially if a mother smokes, takes drugs, or abuses alcohol.
- While some methods of birth may have advantages, it is more important that parents are emotionally involved in the process and have a good attitude toward the birth of their child.
- Caregiving styles have major effects on infant development. Optimal development occurs when parents are responsive to their children and actively involved in their progress.

Social Development— Baby, I'm Stuck on You

Like all humans, infants are social creatures. Let's explore the origins of infant social life. Early **social development** *lays a foundation for later relationships* with parents, siblings, friends, relatives, and schoolmates. Two major steps toward entering the social world are gaining self-awareness and becoming aware of others.

Self-Awareness When you look in a mirror, you recognize the image staring back as your own—except, perhaps, early on Monday mornings. At what age did this sense of recognition first emerge? Like many events in development,

self-awareness (*consciousness of oneself*) depends on maturation of the nervous system.

How is self-awareness demonstrated in a baby?

In an experiment that must have been fun to do, mothers of children 9 to 24 months old secretly rubbed a spot of rouge on their child's nose. Each child was then placed in front of a mirror. The question was, "At what age would children notice the red spot, indicating they recognized the mirror image as their own?" The probability that a child would touch his or her nose was very low at 9 months. However, it jumped dramatically during the second year.

In an even stronger test of self-recognition, infants were shown videotaped images of themselves on a TV. Most infants had to be 15 months old before they recognized themselves (Lewis & Brooks-Gunn, 1979). Self-awareness, then, closely parallels maturation. Typically, it appears sometime after an infant's first birthday. When coupled with an increased interest in others, self-awareness begins to form the core of social development (Asendorpf, 1996; Kagan, 1991).

Social Referencing At about the same time that self-awareness develops, infants become more aware of others. Have you noticed that adults sometimes glance at the facial expressions of others to decide how to respond to them? **Social referencing** (*observing others to obtain information or guidance*) can also be observed in babies. For example, most one-year-old babies glance at their mothers when placed in an unfamiliar situation (Diekstein & Parke, 1988; Walden & Ogan, 1988).

In one study of social referencing, babies were placed on a visual cliff. (A visual cliff is pictured in Chapter 7.) The deep side of the cliff was just high enough so that the babies

A sense of self, or self-awareness, develops at about age 18 months. Before children develop self-awareness, they do not recognize their own image in a mirror. Typically, they think they are looking at another child. Some children hug the child in the mirror or go behind it looking for the child they see there (Lewis, 1995).

were tempted to cross it, but did not. (If a visual cliff is very high, babies generally will not cross it, even if coaxed onto the glass.) Most babies placed on the edge of the cliff repeatedly looked at their mothers. As they did, the mothers made faces at them. (All for science, of course.) When the mothers posed faces of joy or interest, most babies crossed the deep side of the cliff. When they posed fear or anger, few babies crossed (Sorce et al., 1985). Thus, by the end of their first year, infants are aware of the facial expressions of others and seek guidance from them—especially from mother (Hirshberg & Svejda, 1990). Again, we see the roots of an important social skill.

The real core of social development is found in the emotional bonds that babies form with their caregivers. Before we consider this topic directly, let's look at some related animal behavior to see what we can learn from it.

Critical Periods and Imprinting

Why do experiences early in life tend to have such lasting effects?

Part of the answer lies in the existence of critical periods for acquiring behaviors. A **critical period** *is a time of increased sensitivity to environmental influences* (both positive and negative). Events occurring at these times may have dramatic effects long after the sensitive period has passed (Bornstein, 1989). For example, the critical period for mastering a second language is before puberty—the earlier the better (Johnson & Newport, 1989).

Often, certain events must occur during a critical period for a person or an animal to develop normally. To illustrate, Konrad Lorenz (1903–1989), an ethologist who studied animal behavior, decided to find out why baby geese follow their mothers. The accepted explanation was, "It's instinctive," but Lorenz showed otherwise.

Mother Lorenz

Normally, the first large moving object a baby goose sees is its mother. Lorenz hatched geese in an incubator, so the first moving object they saw was him. From then on, these baby geese followed Lorenz. They even reacted to his call as if he were their mother. (Lorenz, 1937)

Imprinting As you can see, baby geese aren't born knowing that they should follow their mothers. Instead, they are born with a tendency to follow large moving objects. Normally that will be their mother. But it need not be. Mother-goose following is acquired during a critical period by exposure to an adult goose (or whatever else happens to be around). The *rapid and early learning of permanent behavior patterns* of this type is called **imprinting.**

In most birds, the critical period for imprinting is very brief. For instance, if newly hatched ducklings don't imprint on their mother (or some other object) within 30 hours, they never will (Hess, 1959). (Ducklings have been imprinted on decoys, rubber balls, wooden blocks, and other unlikely

"Mother" Lorenz leads his charges. The goslings have imprinted on Lorenz because he was the first moving object they saw after they hatched.

objects.) In many animals, imprinting has lifelong consequences (Lorenz, 1962).

Revenge of the Jackdaw

Imprinting normally serves to attach a young animal to its mother. It also guides the selection of a mate of the same species at sexual maturity. In another of Lorenz's experiments, a jackdaw (European starling) imprinted on him. When the bird reached sexual maturity, Lorenz became the target of its mating ritual. Part of this ritual involves stuffing worms into the mouth of the intended mate—as a surprised Lorenz learned while asleep on the lawn one day. When Lorenz refused its gift, the jackdaw stuffed a worm in Lorenz's ear. (Showing, perhaps, that it's not nice to fool Mother Nature!)

Attachment

Does imprinting occur in humans?

True imprinting is limited to birds and some other animals. However, human infants do form an **emotional attachment** (*close emotional bond*) to their **primary caregivers** (*usually parents*). There is a critical period (roughly the first year of life) during which this must occur for healthy development. Attachment helps keep babies close to their mothers, who provide safety, stimulation, and a secure "home base" from which a baby can go exploring. Mothers begin to cultivate attachment within hours of giving birth. For example, they touch their own infants more and hold them closer than they do other babies (Kaitz et al., 1995).

A direct sign that an emotional bond has been formed appears at around 8 to 12 months of age. At that time, babies display **separation anxiety** (*crying and signs of fear*) when they are *left alone or left with a stranger.*

According to psychologist Mary Ainsworth, the quality of attachment is revealed by how babies act when their mothers return after a brief separation. Infants who are **securely attached** have a *stable and positive emotional bond.* They are upset by the mother's absence and they seek to be near her when she returns. **Insecure-avoidant** infants have an *anxious emotional bond.* They tend to *turn away* from their mother when she returns. **Insecure-ambivalent** attachment is also an *anxious emotional bond.* In this case, babies are ambivalent: they both *seek to be near the returning mother, and angrily resist contact* with her. Studies of several cultures suggest that these attachment patterns are universal. However, the percentage of children falling into each category differs from culture to culture (Sagi, 1990).

Attachment can have lasting effects. Infants who are securely attached at the age of one year show more resiliency, curiosity, problem-solving ability, and social competence in preschool (Collins & Gunnar, 1990). The key to secure attachment is a mother who is *accepting and sensitive to her baby's signals and rhythms* (Isabella, 1993; Susman-Stillman et al., 1996). Poor attachment occurs when a mother's actions are inappropriate, insufficient, intrusive, overstimulating, or rejecting. An example is the mother who tries to play with a drowsy infant or who ignores a baby who is looking at her and vocalizing (Isabella & Belsky, 1991).

What about attachment to fathers?

Fathers of securely attached infants tend to be outgoing, agreeable, and happy in their marriage. In general, a warm family atmosphere tends to produce secure children (Belsky, 1996).

Does day care for young children interfere with the quality of attachment?

Day Care Authorities generally agree that *high-quality* day care does not have harmful effects on preschool children (Belsky et al., in press; Hagekull, 1995). Overall, there are no differences in children with home care versus day care, *if* both are of good quality (Scarr & Eisenberg, 1993). Poor-quality care, however, can be risky (Fig. 4–11 ◆).

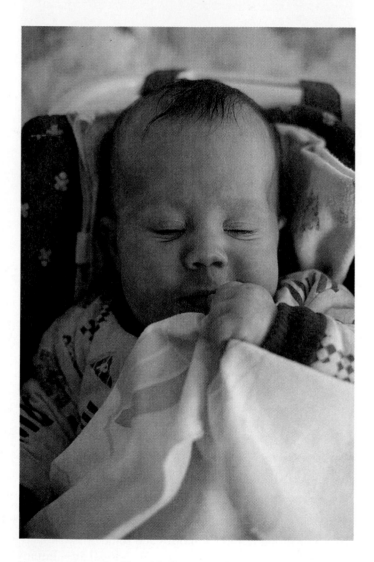

Most parents are familiar with the storm of crying that sometimes occurs when babies are left alone at bedtime. Bedtime distress is a mild form of separation anxiety. As many parents also know, it is often eased by the presence of "security objects," such as a stuffed animal or favorite blanket. Interestingly, children in cultures where infants and toddlers sleep with their parents show few signs of bedtime distress. Parents in the United States usually want their infants to sleep alone, to promote independence. In many cultures, parents choose to sleep near their infants to promote closeness with them. Either approach is valid (Morelli et al., 1992).

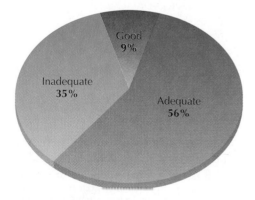

Figure 4–11 ◆ In 1994, the Families Work Institute completed a 5-year study of child care. The study focused on care based in homes other than the child's (rather than day-care centers). In most cases, parents paid for this care, although many of the caregivers were unlicensed. As you can see, child care was "good" in only 9 percent of the homes. In 35 percent of the homes it was rated as inadequate. Wise parents carefully evaluate and monitor the quality of day care their children are receiving (Mehren, 1994).

Children who spend too much time in low-quality day care tend to be more insecure and aggressive with other children (Schachere, 1990). High-quality care, on the other hand, can actually enhance children's social and mental skills (Howes & Smith, 1995; Volling & Feagans, 1995).

Working parents are understandably concerned about what *quality* in child care means. The most important elements are a small number of children per caregiver, small overall group size, trained caregivers, and a stable day care experience (Clarke-Stewart, Gruber, & Fitzgerald, 1994). (Also, avoid any child-care center with the words *zoo, menagerie,* or *stockade* in its name.)

What effect does the arrival of a second child have on attachment?

A recent study confirmed what many parents have observed: Attachment security drops for a firstborn child when a second baby arrives. Wise parents, therefore, make a special effort to involve their firstborn child in the excitement of the "new arrival" and give the firstborn extra attention and affection (Teti, 1996).

In recent years a controversy has raged over whether attachment is influenced by events that occur immediately after birth. For your interest, a discussion of "mother-infant bonding" follows.

In one hospital ward, mothers get a brief glimpse of their newborns shortly after birth, followed by 30-minute visits every 4 hours. In a second ward, "extended-contact" mothers are given their babies for 1 hour during the first 3 hours after birth and for an extra 5 hours of contact each afternoon for the first 3 days after delivery. Does the extra contact have any effect?

An initial series of studies reported by Marshall Klaus and John Kennell (1982) seemed to suggest that close early contact between a mother and her infant has lasting benefits. According to Klaus and Kennell, the first few hours after birth are a sensitive period. Therefore, mother-child pairs who spend extra time together form a stronger emotional bond. This is especially true, they believe, if skin-to-skin touching is part of early contact.

Klaus and Kennell reported that "bonded" babies are more alert and responsive, as well as healthier and brighter than those denied extra contact.

Were they right?

Probably not. More careful studies have generally failed to support the bonding concept (Rosenblith, 1992). While long-term infant attachments are a reality, instantaneous "bonding" appears to be a myth (Eyer, 1994).

Skeptics point out that adopted children, premature babies, and babies born by cesarean section (surgical birth) all develop normal, affectionate bonds with their mothers. Even Klaus and Kennell now acknowledge that it is unlikely that something as important as emotional attachment would depend *solely* on the first few hours of life (Klaus & Kennell, 1984). Humans are highly adaptable, and there are many opportunities for attachment during the first year of life.

Even if early contact is unnecessary, allowing mother, father, and infant to be together during the first few hours following birth is humane and natural. So, while most evidence suggests that early contact is *not* necessary, it is undoubtedly a positive, emotionally satisfying experience (Rosenblith, 1992).

Ultimately, it is less important *when* secure attachment occurs, than *if* it occurs. In addition, it is valuable to remember that children thrive when they have good relationships with *both* parents (Eyer, 1993).

Motherless Monkeys Infant attachments, like imprinting, can have lasting effects. Harry Harlow (1966, 1967) showed that baby rhesus monkeys separated from their mothers and raised in isolation become troubled adult animals. These "motherless monkeys" never develop normal sexual behaviors and they make very poor mothers if mated. They are coldly rejecting or indifferent to their babies and may brutalize or injure them. A similar pattern may explain why some human parents abuse, reject, or physically injure their children. A sizable percentage of abusive parents were themselves rejected or mistreated as children. Some types of antisocial behavior may also trace back to poor attachment (Magid, 1988). Children with severe attachment problems do not learn to trust others or care about them. As a result, many are cruel, angry, and self-destructive.

A baby's **affectional needs** (*needs for love and affection*) are every bit as important as more obvious needs for food, water, and physical care. All things considered, creating a bond of trust and affection between the infant and at least one other person is a key development during the first year of life. Parents are sometimes afraid of "spoiling" babies with too much attention, but for the first year or two this is nearly impossible (Konner, 1991). As a matter of fact, a later capacity to experience warm and loving relationships may depend on it. (See Table 4–5 ■.)

1. The intrauterine environment is so protected that it has little effect on a person's development. T or F?

2. Two important elements of effective mothering are _____ maternal involvement and parental _____ to a child's feelings, needs, rhythms, and signals.

3. Patterns of paternal behavior typically differ little from maternal caregiving patterns. T or F?

4. Clear signs of self-awareness or self-recognition are evident in most infants by the time they reach 8 months of age. T or F?

5. Social _____ of parents' facial expressions is evident in infants by the time they are 1 year old.

6. A duckling can be imprinted after the critical period has passed if special attention is given to its affectional needs. T or F?

7. The development of separation anxiety in an infant corresponds to the formation of an attachment to parents. T or F?

8. Research has shown conclusively that mother-infant contact immediately after birth is essential for optimal development. T or F?

9. In Mary Ainsworth's system for rating the quality of attachment, secure attachment is revealed by a lack of distress when an infant is left alone with a stranger. T or F?

10. Attachment quality is usually attributed to the behavior of parents or caregivers. How might infants contribute to the quality of attachment?

Answers:

1. F 2. proactive, responsiveness 3. F 4. F 5. referencing 6. F 7. T 8. F 9. F 10. An infant's behavior patterns, temperament, and emotional style may greatly influence parents' behavior. As a result, infants can affect attachment as much as parents do (Oatley & Jenkins, 1992).

Table 4–5 ■ Social Development: Implications for Parents and Caregivers

- The quality of a child's relationships with caregivers is a key to healthy development in most areas of competence.
- Secure emotional attachments are fostered by consistent care and by parents who are sensitive to a baby's signals and rhythms.
- High-quality day care is not harmful to preschool children. Poor-quality care, either inside or outside the home, can be harmful.

Language Development— Fast-Talking Babies

There's something almost miraculous about a baby's first words. It's easy to understand why parents get so excited when they first hear the sounds *ma-ma* or *da-da*. As infants, how did we manage our leap into the world of language? It will soon be apparent that social interaction provides a foundation for language learning. But before we explore that connection, let's begin with a survey of language development.

Language Acquisition The development of speech is closely tied to maturation. As any parent can tell you, babies can cry from birth on. By 1 month of age, infants can control crying well enough to use it to gain attention. At about 1 month, parents can also tell the nature of an infant's needs from the tone of the crying. Around 6 to 8 weeks of age, babies begin **cooing** (*the repetition of vowel sounds like "oo" and "ah"*).

By 6 months of age, the nervous system has matured enough to allow children to grasp objects, to smile, laugh, sit up, and **babble.** In the babbling stage, *consonants are combined with vowels to produce meaningless language sounds*. Environmental influences at this time are revealed by the fact that children babble more when parents talk to them (Bernt, 1992).

At about 1 year of age, children can stand alone for a short time and respond to words such as *no* or *hi*. Soon afterward, the first connection between words and objects forms, and children may address their parents as "Mama" or "Dada." By age 1½ to 2 years, children have learned to stand and walk alone. By then, their vocabulary may include from 24 to 200 words. At first there is a **single-word stage,** during which the child says *one word at a time* such as "go," "juice," or "up." Soon after, words are arranged in *simple two-word sentences* called **telegraphic speech:** "Want-Teddy," "Mama-gone." Just before age 2, the child's comprehension and use of words takes a leap forward (Reznick & Goldfield, 1992). From this point on, vocabulary and language skills grow at a phenomenal rate. By first grade, the child can understand around 8,000 words and use about 4,000.

BY PERMISSION OF JERRY SCOTT & RICK KIRKMAN AND CREATORS SYNDICATE

The Roots of Language

In a fascinating study, researchers Louis Sander and William Condon (1974) filmed newborn infants as the babies listened to various sounds. A frame-by-frame analysis of the films showed something astonishing: Infants move their arms and legs in synchrony to the rhythms of human speech. Random noise, rhythmic tapping, or disconnected vowel sounds will not produce this "language dance." Only the natural rhythms of speech have this effect.

Why should day-old infants "dance" to speech but not other sounds? One possibility is that language recognition is innate. Linguist Noam Chomsky (1975, 1986) has long claimed that humans have a **biological predisposition** (*hereditary readiness*) to develop language. According to Chomsky, language organization is inborn, much like a child's ability to coordinate walking. If such inborn language recognition does exist, it may explain why children around the world use a limited number of patterns in their first sentences. Typical patterns include (Mussen et al., 1979):

Identification:	"See kitty."
Non-existence:	"Allgone milk."
Possession:	"My doll."
Agent-Action:	"Mama give."
Negation:	"Not ball."
Question:	"Where doggie?"

Does Chomsky's theory explain why language develops so rapidly?

Perhaps. But many psychologists feel that Chomsky underestimates the importance of learning (Bruner, 1983). **Psycholinguists** (*specialists in the psychology of language*) have shown that language is not magically "switched on" by adult speech. Imitation of adults and rewards for correctly using words (as when a child asks for a cookie) are an important part of language learning. Also, when a child makes a language error, parents typically repeat the child's sentence, with needed corrections (Bohannon & Stanowicz, 1988). More important is the fact that parents and children begin to communicate long before the child can speak. Months of shared effort precede the child's first word (Miller, 1977). From this point of view, the filmed infants' behavior reflects a readiness to interact *socially* with parents, not innate language recognition. The next section explains why.

How do parents communicate with infants before they can talk?

Early Communication Parents go to a great deal of trouble to get babies to smile and vocalize (Fig. 4–12 ◆). In doing so, they quickly learn to change their actions to keep the infant's attention, arousal, and activity at optimal levels (Brazelton et al., 1974). A familiar example is the "I'm-Going-to-Get-You Game." In it, the adult says, "I'm gonna getcha. . . . I'm gonna getcha. . . . I'm gonna getcha. . . . Gotcha!" Through such games, adults and babies come to share similar rhythms and expectations (Stern, 1982). Soon a system of shared **signals** is created, such as *touching*,

85
Medium high positive

50
Neutral attention

20
Avert

Figure 4–12 ◆ Infant engagement scale. These samples from a 90-point scale show various levels of infant engagement, or attention. Babies participate in prelanguage "conversations" with parents by giving and withholding attention and by smiling, gazing, or vocalizing. (From Beebe et al., 1982.)

vocalizing, gazing, and smiling. These help lay a foundation for later language use. Specifically, signals establish a pattern of "conversational" **turn-taking** (*alternate sending and receiving of messages*).

Mother	Ann
	(smiles)
"Oh what a nice little smile!"	
"Yes, isn't that nice?"	
"There."	
"There's a nice little smile."	(burps)
"Well, pardon you!"	
"Yes, that's better, isn't it?"	
"Yes."	(vocalizes)
"Yes."	(smiles)
"What's so funny?"	

Although such exchanges may look meaningless, they represent real communication. A baby's vocalizations and attention provide a way of interacting emotionally with parents. Even infants as young as 3 months make more speech-like sounds when an adult engages them in a turn-taking pattern of interaction (Bloom et al., 1987). (For another perspective on turn-taking, see Figure 4–13 ◆.) Overall, the more time parents spend interacting with children, the faster they learn to talk (Hart & Risley, 1992; Tamis-LeMonvda & Bornstein, 1994). The more often adults label objects, the faster a child's vocabulary grows

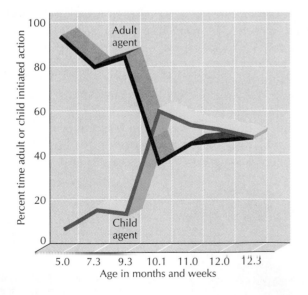

Figure 4–13 ◆ This graph shows the development of turn-taking in games played by an infant and his mother. For several months Richard responded to games such as peekaboo and "hand-the-toy-back" only when his mother initiated action. At about 9 months, however, he rapidly began to initiate action in the games. Soon, he was the one to take the lead about one half of the time. Learning to take turns and to direct actions toward another person underlie basic language skills. (From Bruner, 1983.)

(Poulin-Dubois, Graham, & Sippola, 1995). Babies who most readily imitate new words learn language the fastest (Masur, 1995). Clearly, the roots of language lie in social relationships.

Parentese Parents help children learn language with *an exaggerated pattern of speaking* called **caretaker speech.** When talking to infants, parents around the world raise their tone of voice, use short, simple sentences, and repeat themselves more. They also slow their rate of speaking, and use exaggerated voice inflections: "Did Jenny eat it A-L-L UP?"

What is the purpose of such changes?

Parents are trying to help their children identify key features of language. When a baby is still babbling, parents tend to use long, adult-style sentences. But as soon as a baby says its first word they switch to caretaker speech (also known as caregiver speech or parentese).

In addition to being simpler, parentese has a distinct "musical" quality all its own (Fernald & Mazzie, 1991). No matter what language mothers speak, the melodies, pauses, and inflections they use to comfort, praise, or give warning are universal. Psychologist Anne Fernald has found that mothers of all nations talk to their babies with similar changes in pitch. For instance, we praise babies with a rising, then falling pitch ("BRA-vo!" "GOOD girl!"). Warnings are delivered in a short, sharp rhythm ("Nein! Nein!" "Basta! Basta!" "Not! Dude!"). To give comfort, parents use low, smooth, drawn-out tones ("Oooh poor baaa-by." "Oooh pobrecito."). A high-pitched, rising melody is used to call attention to objects ("See the pretty BIRDIE?") (Fernald, 1989).

Caretaker speech helps parents get babies' attention, communicate with them, and teach them language (Kaplan et al., 1995). Later, as a child's speaking improves, parents tend to adjust their speech to the child's level of language ability. Especially from age 1½ to 4, parents seek to clarify what a child says and prompt the child to say more. Two typical strategies are (Newman & Newman, 1978):

Expansion:	*Child:*	Doggie bite.
	Parent:	Yes, the dog bit *the toy*.
Prompting:	*Child:*	Doggie briggle.
	Parent:	What did the doggie do?

In summary, some elements of language are innate. All normal children learn language, unless they grow up in an extremely abnormal environment. Nevertheless, our inherited tendency to learn language does not determine if we will speak English, German, Spanish, or Russian. Environmental forces also influence whether a person develops simple or sophisticated language skills. Clearly, a full flowering of speech requires careful cultivation. (See Table 4–6 ■.)

Now that we have our subjects (babies) talking, let's move on to a broader view of intellectual development.

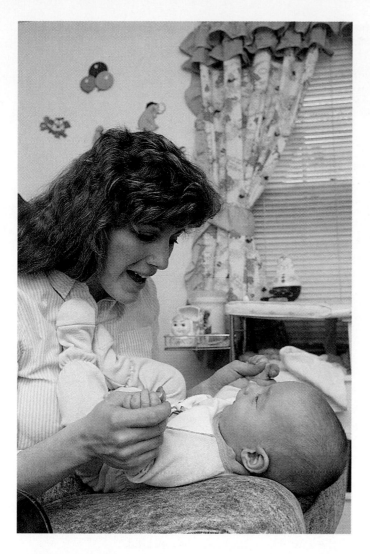

As with caretaker speech, parents use a distinctive style when singing to an infant. Even people who speak another language can tell if a tape-recorded song was sung to an infant or an adult. Likewise, lullabies remain recognizable when electronic filtering removes words (Trehub et al., 1993a, 1993b).

Table 4–6	Language Development: Implications for Parents and Caregivers

- The pace of language learning is closely related to maturation and need not be "hurried."
- Non-verbal communication sets the stage for acquiring language. Children gain language ability when parents engage them in exchanges that involve signaling, turn-taking, and non-verbal communication.
- In the early stages of language learning, caregivers can help their children by using simplified grammar and accentuated voice inflections ("parentese"). As children become more verbal, expanding, prompting, and restating can facilitate language learning.

Cognitive Development— How Do Children Learn to Think?

How different is a child's understanding of the world from that of an adult?

Generally speaking, their thinking is less abstract. Children use fewer generalizations, categories, or principles. They also tend to base their understanding on particular examples, immediate sensations, and objects they can see or touch.

Before the age of 6 or 7, thinking is very concrete. Younger children cannot make **transformations** in which they must *mentally change the shape or form of a substance (such as clay or water)*. If you show a young child a short, wide glass full of milk and a tall, narrow glass (also full), the child will tell you that the taller glass contains more milk. Children will tell you this even if they watch you pour milk from the short glass into an empty, tall glass. They are not bothered by the fact that the milk appears to be transformed from a smaller to a larger amount. Instead, they respond only to the fact that *taller* seems to mean *more*. (See Figure 4–14 ◆.) After about age 7, children are no longer fooled by this situation. Perhaps that's why 7 has been called the "age of reason." From age 7 on, we see a definite trend toward more logical, adult-like thought (Flavell, 1992).

Is there any pattern to the growth of intellect in childhood?

According to the Swiss psychologist and philosopher Jean Piaget (1951, 1952) there is.

Piaget's Theory of Cognitive Development

Jean Piaget (Jahn pea-ah-JAY) believed that all children pass through a series of distinct stages in intellectual development. Many of his ideas came from observing his own children as they solved various thought problems. (It is tempting to imagine that Piaget's illustrious career began one day when his wife said to him, "Watch the children for a while, will you, Jean?") Piaget's observations convinced him that intellect grows through processes of *assimilation* and *accommodation*.

Assimilation is the *use of existing mental patterns in new situations*. Let's say that a plastic hammer is Benjamin's favorite toy. Benjamin holds the hammer properly and loves to pound on blocks with it. For his birthday Benjamin gets an oversized toy wrench. If he uses the wrench for pounding, it has been assimilated to an existing mental structure.

In **accommodation,** *existing ideas are modified to fit new requirements*. For instance, a younger child might think that a dime is worth less than a (larger) nickel. As the child begins to spend money, she or he will be forced to alter ideas about

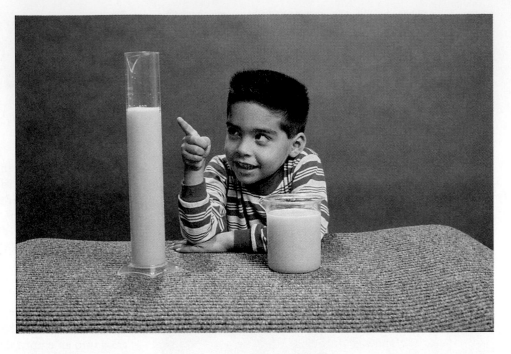

Figure 4-14 ◆ Children under age 7 intuitively assume that a volume of liquid increases when it is poured from a short, wide container into a taller, thinner one. This boy thinks the tall container holds more than the short one. Actually, each has the same amount of liquid in it. Children base such judgments on the height of the liquid, not its volume.

what "more" and "less" mean. Thus, new situations are assimilated to existing ideas, and new ideas are created to accommodate new experiences.

Piaget's theories have had a profound effect on our thinking about children (Beilin, 1992). The following is a brief summary of what he found.

The Sensorimotor Stage (0–2 Years) In the first 2 years of life, a child's mental development is largely *non-verbal*.

Jean Piaget—philosopher, psychologist, and keen observer of children.

The child is mainly concerned with learning to coordinate *purposeful movements* with information from the senses. Also, **object permanence** (*an understanding that objects continue to exist when they are out of sight*) emerges at this time. By about age 1½, the child begins to actively pursue disappearing objects, such as a ball rolling behind a sofa. Younger infants, Piaget believed, behave as if hidden objects cease to exist. By age 2, the child can anticipate the movement of hidden objects. For example, when watching an electric train the child looks ahead to the end of a tunnel, rather than staring at the spot where the train disappeared.

In general, developments in this stage indicate that the child's conceptions are becoming more *stable*. Objects cease to appear and disappear magically, and a more orderly and predictable world replaces the confusing and disconnected sensations of infancy.

The Preoperational Stage (2–7 Years) During the preoperational period, children begin to think *symbolically* and use language. But the child's thinking is still very **intuitive** (*it makes little use of reasoning and logic*). For example, after lifting a Styrofoam cup, 75 percent of 4- to 6-year-olds will say the cup has no weight! Most preoperational children judge weight intuitively (by the way an object feels) (Smith, Carey, & Wiser, 1985).

During the preoperational period, use of language is not always as sophisticated as it might seem. For instance, children tend to confuse words with the objects they represent. If the child calls a toy block a "car" and you make a "train" with it, the child may be upset. To children, the name of an object is as much a part of the object as its size, shape, and color. That's why an insulting name may hurt a preoperational child as much as "sticks and stones." Consider one rather protected youngster who was angered by her older brother. Searching for a way to retaliate against her larger and stronger foe, she settled on, "You panty-girdle!" It was the worst thing she could think of saying.

During the preoperational stage, the child is also quite **egocentric** (*unable to take the viewpoint of other people*). The child's ego seems to stand at the center of his or her world. To illustrate, show a child a two-sided mirror. Then hold it between the two of you so the child can see herself in it. If you ask her what she thinks *you* can see, she imagines that you see *her* reflected image instead of your own.

The concept of egocentrism helps us to understand why children can seem exasperatingly selfish or uncooperative at times. A child who blocks your view by standing in front of a television assumes that you see the same thing he does. If you ask him to move so you can see, he may move so that he can see better! The child is not being selfish in the ordinary sense. He just doesn't realize that your view differs from his.

The Concrete Operational Stage (7–11 Years)
An important development during this stage is mastery of **conservation** (*the concept that volume remains unchanged when the shape of objects changes*). Children have learned conservation when they understand that rolling a ball of clay into a "snake" does not increase the amount of clay. Likewise,

Crossing a busy street can be dangerous for the preoperational child. Because their thinking is still egocentric, younger children cannot understand why the driver of a car can't see them if they can see the car. Children under the age of 7 also cannot consistently judge speeds and distances of oncoming cars. Adults can easily overestimate the "street smarts" of younger children. It is advisable to teach children to cross with a light, in crosswalks, or with assistance.

pouring liquid from a tall, narrow glass into a shallow dish does not reduce the amount of liquid. In each case the volume remains the same despite changes in shape or appearance. The original amount is *conserved* (return to Fig. 4–14).

During the concrete operational stage, children begin to use concepts of time, space, and number. The child can think logically about very concrete objects or situations, categories, and principles. Such abilities explain why children stop believing in Santa Claus when they reach this stage. Because they can conserve volume, they realize that Santa's sack couldn't possibly hold enough toys for millions of girls and boys (Fehr, 1976). Similarly, 65 percent of children aged 5 to 7 believe that the Tooth Fairy is real (Croll, 1986). Around the ages of 7 to 8, however, most children begin to realize this is a fantasy.

Another important development at this time is the ability to *reverse* thoughts or operations. A conversation with a 4-year-old boy (still in the preoperational stage) shows what happens when thinking *lacks* reversibility (Phillips, 1969).

"Do you have a brother?"
"Yes."
"What's his name?"
"Jim."
"Does Jim have a brother?"
"No."

Reversibility of thought allows children *in the concrete operational stage to recognize that if 4 × 2 = 8, then 2 × 4 does, too.* Younger children must memorize each relationship separately. Thus, a preoperational child may know that $4 \times 9 = 36$, but may not realize that 9×4 also equals 36.

The Formal Operations Stage (11 Years and Up)
Sometime after about the age of 11, children begin to break away from concrete objects and specific examples. Thinking is based more on **abstract principles** (*symbolic ideas*). Children can think about their thoughts, and they become less egocentric. Older children and young adolescents also gradually become able to consider **hypothetical possibilities** (*suppositions, guesses, or projections*). For example, if you ask a younger child, "What do you think would happen if it suddenly became possible for people to fly?" the child might respond, "People can't fly." Older children are able to consider the possibilities and discuss their implications.

Full adult intellectual ability is attained during the stage of formal operations. Older adolescents are capable of inductive and deductive reasoning and they can comprehend math, physics, philosophy, psychology, and other abstract systems. Of course, not everyone reaches this level of thinking. Also, many adults can think formally about some topics, but their thinking becomes concrete when the topic is unfamiliar. This implies that formal thinking may be more a result of culture and learning than maturation. In any case, after late adolescence, improvements in intellect are based on gaining knowledge, experience, and wisdom, rather than on a boost in basic thinking capacity.

For your convenience, here's a brief summary of each Piagetian stage. These stages may be easier to remember if we relate them to a single example. What would happen at each stage if we played a game of *Monopoly* with the child?

Sensorimotor stage *The stage during which sensory input and motor responses become coordinated.*
Monopoly Game The child puts houses, hotels, and dice in his mouth and plays with "Chance" cards.

Preoperational stage *The period of cognitive development when children begin to use language and think symbolically, yet remain intuitive and egocentric.*
Monopoly Game The child plays *Monopoly*, but makes up her own rules and cannot understand instructions.

Concrete operational stage *The period of cognitive development during which children begin to use concepts of time, space, volume, and number, but in ways that remain simplified and concrete.*
Monopoly Game The child understands basic instructions and will play by the rules, but is not capable of hypothetical transactions dealing with mortgages, loans, and special pacts with other players.

Formal operations stage *The period of intellectual development marked by a capacity for abstract, theoretical, and hypothetical thinking.*
Monopoly Game The child no longer plays the game mechanically; complex and hypothetical transactions unique to each game are now possible.

Piaget Today Piaget's theory remains a valuable "road map" for understanding how children think. But some research suggests that intellectual growth is not as strictly age and stage related as Piaget claimed. Today, many psychologists are convinced that Piaget gave too little credit to the effects of learning. For example, children of pottery-making parents can correctly answer questions about the conservation of clay at an earlier age than Piaget would have predicted (Bransford et al., 1986).

According to learning theorists, children continuously gain specific knowledge; their mental abilities do not make sudden shifts in character each time they enter a new stage (Carey, 1986). Yet, brain growth does occur in cycles that correspond with Piaget's stages (Thatcher et al., 1987). Thus, the truth may lie somewhere between Piaget's stage

| Table 4–7 ■ | Cognitive Development: Implications for Parents and Caregivers |

- Children's cognitive development follows the general pattern described by Piaget.
- In some areas, infants and younger children are capable of a level of thinking that Piaget did not believe possible.
- Understanding a child's view of the world is aided by taking the child's level of cognitive development into account.
- Caregivers should offer encouragement and learning opportunities appropriate for the child's level of development.

theory and modern learning theory. On a broad scale, many of Piaget's *observations* have held up well. However, his *explanations* for the growth of thinking abilities in childhood continue to be debated. (See Table 4–7 ■.)

Where early infancy is concerned, even Piaget's observations may need to be revised. As discussed in the following highlight, Piaget may have greatly underestimated the thinking abilities of infants.

Piaget believed that infants under the age of one year cannot think. Babies, he said, have no memory of people and objects that are out of sight. Yet, new evidence suggests that infants begin forming representations of the world very early in life. Researchers have shown that babies as young as 3 months of age know that objects are solid and do not disappear when out of view (Baillargeon & DeVos, 1992; Johnson & Nanez, 1995). By age 4 months, infants can learn to recognize pictures of cats among pictures of lions or dogs (Eimas, Quinn, & Cowan, 1994). At age 6 to 8 months babies have memories that Piaget didn't see until 18 months (Hayne & Rovee-Collier, 1995; Raymond, 1991; Shields & Rovee-Collier, 1992).

Why did Piaget underestimate the abilities of infants?

Most likely, Piaget mistook babies' limited *physical* skills for *mental* incompetence. Piaget's tests required babies to search for objects or reach out and touch them. Newer, more sensitive methods are uncovering abilities Piaget could not have detected (Mandler, 1990). One of the more revealing methods takes advantage of the fact that babies, like adults, are surprised when they see something "impossible" or

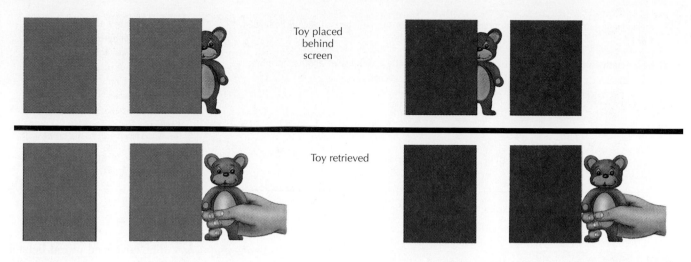

Toy placed behind screen

Toy retrieved

Figure 4–15 ◆ The left two panels show a possible event, in which an infant watches as a toy is placed behind the right of two screens. After a delay of 70 seconds, the toy is brought into view from behind the right screen. In the right two panels, an impossible event occurs. The toy is placed behind the left screen and retrieved from behind the right. (A duplicate toy was hidden there before testing.) Eight-month-old infants react with surprise when they see the impossible event staged for them. Their reaction implies that they remember where the toy was hidden. Infants appear to have a capacity for memory and thinking that greatly exceeds what Piaget claimed is possible during the sensorimotor period. (Adapted from Baillargeon et al., 1989.)

unexpected occur. To make use of this effect, psychologist Renee Baillargeon (1991) puts on little "magic shows" for infants. In her "theater" babies watch as possible and impossible events occur with toys or other objects. Some 3-month-old infants act surprised and gaze longer at impossible events. An example is seeing two solid objects appear to pass through each other. By the time they are 8 months old, babies can remember where objects are (or should be) for at least one minute (Fig. 4–15 ◆). Children as young as 11 months old can remember and imitate simple two-step actions, such as

setting up a small ramp and then placing a toy car at the top (Bauer, 1996).

Piaget believed that abilities like those described in Figure 4–15 emerge only after a long sensorimotor period of development. However, evidence continues to mount that babies are born with a capacity to form concepts about the world, or acquire this ability early in life (Eimas, Quinn, & Cowan, 1994). It looks as if further study is likely to refine and amend the ideas that grew from Piaget's fateful decision to "watch the children for awhile."

Learning Check

Critical Thinking

Match each item with one of the following Piagetian stages.

A. Sensorimotor   B. Preoperational   C. Concrete operational   D. Formal operations

1. _____ egocentric thought

2. _____ abstract or hypothetical thought

3. _____ purposeful movement

4. _____ intuitive thought

5. _____ conservation

6. _____ reversibility

7. _____ object permanence

8. _____ non-verbal development

9. Assimilation refers to applying existing thought patterns or knowledge to new situations. T or F?

10. The development of speech and language usually occurs in which order?
   a. crying, cooing, babbling, telegraphic speech
   b. cooing, crying, babbling, telegraphic speech
   c. babbling, crying, cooing, telegraphic speech
   d. crying, babbling, cooing, identification

11. Prelanguage turn-taking and social interactions would be of special interest to a psycholinguist. T or F?

12. Newer methods for testing infant thinking abilities frequently make note of whether an infant is _____ by seemingly _____ events.

13. As discussed earlier, infants show a preference for familiar faces. After age 2, however, unusual or surprising objects tend to gain the toddler's interest. At what Piagetian stage does this change take place?

Answers:
1. B 2. D 3. A 4. B 5. C 6. C 7. A 8. A 9. T 10. a 11. T 12. surprised, impossible 13. As the child enters the preoperational stage.

Moral Development— Growing a Conscience

A person with a terminal illness is in great pain. She is pleading for death. Should extraordinary medical efforts be made to keep her alive? If a friend of yours desperately needed to pass a test and asked you to help him cheat, would you do it? These are *moral* questions, or questions of conscience. How are moral values acquired? Psychologist Lawrence Kohlberg (1981a) believed that they are learned, in part, as children develop the ability to think and reason.

What did he base this belief on?

Moral Dilemmas

Through **moral development** we acquire *values, beliefs, and thinking abilities that guide responsible behavior.* To study moral development, Kohlberg posed dilemmas to children of different ages. The following is one of the *moral dilemmas* he used (Kohlberg, 1969, adapted).

> A woman was near death from cancer, and there was only one drug that might save her. It was discovered by a druggist who was charging 10 times what it cost to make the drug. The sick woman's husband could only pay $1,000, but the druggist wanted $2,000. He asked the druggist to sell it cheaper or to let him pay later. The druggist said no. So the husband became desperate and broke into the store to steal the drug for his wife. Should he have done that? Was it wrong or right? Why?

Each child was asked what action the husband should take. Kohlberg classified the reasons given for each choice and identified three levels of moral development. Each is based not so much on the choices made, but on the reasons given for the choices.

At the **preconventional level,** moral thinking is determined by *the consequences of actions* (punishment, reward, or an exchange of favors). In the **conventional level,** actions are directed by *a desire to conform to the expectations of others*

or to accepted rules and values. The advanced moral behavior found at the **postconventional level** is directed by *self-accepted moral principles*. In addition to the three major levels, Kohlberg identified six stages of moral development (Table 4–8 ■). In time, Kohlberg found it necessary to combine stages 5 and 6 because it proved difficult, in practice, to separate them (Kohlberg, 1981b). He remained firm in his belief, however, that morality develops in preconventional, conventional, and postconventional phases.

Does everyone eventually reach the highest level?

People advance through the stages at different rates and many fail to reach the postconventional stage. In fact, many do not even reach the conventional level. For instance, a survey in England revealed that 11 percent of men and 3 percent of women would commit murder for $1 million if they were assured of getting away with the crime ("They'd kill," 1991).

The preconventional stages (1 and 2) are most characteristic of young children and delinquents (Nelson, Smith, & Dodd, 1990). Conventional, group-oriented morals of stages 3 and 4 are characteristic of older children and most adults. Kohlberg estimated that only about 20 percent of the adult population achieves postconventional morality, representing self-direction and higher principles.

Morality in the Real World To illustrate the importance of moral development, let us compare two very different individuals. First let's apply Kohlberg's analysis to statements attributed to Nazi officer Adolf Eichmann, accused of sharing responsibility for the deaths of millions of Jews in Germany during World War II:

> In actual fact, I was merely a little cog in the machinery that carried out the directives of the German Reich [stage 1]. It was really none of my business [stage 2]. Yet what is there to "admit"? I carried out my order [stage 1]. (Kohlberg, 1969)

Compare this to the words of Mahatma Gandhi, the famous leader who protested British rule of India. Gandhi once addressed a British court:

> I had to either submit to a system which I considered had done

Table 4–8 ■ Kohlberg's Stages of Moral Development

PRECONVENTIONAL

Stage 1: Punishment orientation. Actions are evaluated in terms of possible punishment, not goodness or badness; obedience to power is emphasized.
Example: "He shouldn't steal the drug because he could get caught and sent to jail" (avoiding punishment).

Stage 2: Pleasure-seeking orientation. Proper action is determined by one's own needs; concern for the needs of others is largely a matter of "You scratch my back and I'll scratch yours," not of loyalty, gratitude, or justice.
Example: "It won't do him any good to steal the drug because his wife will probably die before he gets out of jail" (self-interest).

CONVENTIONAL

Stage 3: Good boy/good girl orientation. Good behavior is that which pleases others in the immediate group or which brings approval; the emphasis is on being "nice."
Example: "He shouldn't steal the drug because others will think he is a thief. His wife would not want to be saved by thievery" (avoiding disapproval).

Stage 4: Authority orientation. In this stage the emphasis is on upholding law, order, and authority, doing one's duty, and following social rules.
Example: "Although his wife needs the drug, he should not break the law to get it. Everyone is equal in the eyes of the law, and his wife's condition does not justify stealing" (traditional morality of authority).

POSTCONVENTIONAL

Stage 5: Social-contract orientation. Support of laws and rules is based on rational analysis and mutual agreement; rules are recognized as open to question, but are upheld for the good of the community and in the name of democratic values.
Example: "He should not steal the drug. The druggist's decision is reprehensible, but mutual respect for the rights of others must be maintained" (social contract).

Stage 6: Morality of individual principles. Behavior is directed by self-chosen ethical principles that tend to be general, comprehensive, or universal; high value is placed on justice, dignity, and equality.
Example: "He should steal the drug and then inform the authorities that he has done so. He will have to face a penalty, but he will have saved a human life" (self-chosen ethical principles).

irreparable harm to my country, or incur the risk. . . . I am here, therefore, to invite and cheerfully submit to the highest penalty that can be inflicted upon me for what in law is a deliberate crime and what appears to me to be the highest duty of a citizen.

Gandhi, like other great leaders (Lincoln, Martin Luther King, Desmond Tutu, Nelson Mandela), was clearly operating at a postconventional level of morality in his political life.

Moral development is a promising topic for further study. As an example, consider the work of psychologist Carol Gilligan.

Justice or Caring? Gilligan (1982) noticed that Kohlberg's system is concerned mainly with the ethics of *justice*. Based on studies of women who faced real-life dilemmas, Gilligan argues that there is also an ethic of *caring* and responsibility to others. As one illustration, Gilligan presented the following story to 11- to 15-year-old American children.

The Porcupine and the Moles

Seeking refuge from the cold, a porcupine asked to share a cave for the winter with a family of moles. The moles agreed. But because the cave was small, they soon found they were being scratched each time the porcupine moved about. Finally, they asked the porcupine to leave. But the porcupine refused, saying, "If you moles are not satisfied, I suggest that you leave."

Gilligan found that boys who read this story tend to opt for justice in resolving the dilemma: "It's the moles' house. It's a deal. The porcupine leaves." In contrast, girls tend to look for solutions that would keep all parties happy and comfortable, such as "Cover the porcupine with a blanket."

Gilligan's point is that male psychologists have, for the most part, defined moral maturity in terms of justice and autonomy. From this perspective, women's concern with relationships can look like a weakness rather than a strength. (A woman who is concerned about what pleases or helps others would be placed at stage 3 in Kohlberg's system.) But Gilligan believes that caring is also a major element of moral

Each of us faces moral dilemmas, both large and small, every day. Dishonesty on taxes, sexual faithfulness, abortion, speeding, found valuables, temptations to lie, honesty in business—these and many other situations raise moral questions. A moral dilemma familiar to most students involves being unprepared for an exam. Sadly, the majority of American children function at the preconventional level of moral development at school: A 1990 poll found that two thirds would cheat to pass an important exam.

development and she suggests that males may lag in achieving it (Gilligan & Attanucci, 1988).

Does the evidence support Gilligan's position?

Several studies have found little or no difference in men's and women's moral reasoning abilities (Mednick, 1989; Wilson, 1995). Indeed, both men and women may use caring *and* justice to make moral decisions. The choice of a moral yardstick appears to depend on the *situation* a person faces (Wark & Krebs, 1996). Gilligan does deserve credit, nevertheless, for identifying a second major way of judging morality.

Whatever the outcome of such debates, studying moral development seems highly worthwhile. Many of the problems facing us today—overpopulation, environmental destruction, crime, prejudice—are essentially problems of individual conscience. (See Table 4–9 ■.)

We have now examined development in several major areas. To conclude our discussion, the next section describes

the effects of *deprivation* and *enrichment*. These are conditions that can affect nearly all facets of a child's early years.

Deprivation and Enrichment— In Search of Tender Loving Care

At birth, the brain of a newborn baby has fewer **synapses** (*connections between nerve cells*) than adult brains do. The same is true of the number of **dendrites** (*nerve cell branches*) in the newborn brain (see Figure 4–16 ◆). However, during the first 2 years of life, an explosion in the number of synapses takes place. Simultaneously, there is a rapid "pruning" away of connections that are not used. As a result, early learning experiences can literally shape the structure of the developing brain. That's why the quality of a child's learning environment can have such a lasting impact. This is especially true of environments that can be described as *enriched* or *deprived*.

Early Deprivation

News item: "Wild Child Raised by Apes Found in Africa." Over the years there have been several reported discoveries of "feral children." Supposedly, these children grow up in the care of animals and act like animals when found. Actually, there is little evidence that such children have existed. Moreover, we needn't go this far afield to see the destructive effects of early **deprivation** (*a lack or withholding of normal stimulation, nutrition, comfort, or love*).

Many children have spent the first 5 or 6 years of life in closets, attics, and other restricted environments. When

Table 4–9 ■ Moral Development: Implications for Parents and Caregivers

- Moral behavior is based, in part, on a child's capacity to reason about moral choices. For this reason, younger children tend to make simplified moral choices.
- Achieving justice is a dominant moral standard, but children may benefit from learning other ways of defining moral behavior.
- Parents act as models of moral behavior for their children. Parents can teach moral reasoning by example and by asking their children to reason about moral dilemmas and choices.

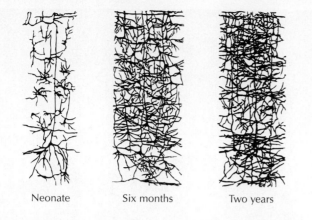

| Neonate | Six months | Two years |

Figure 4-16 ◆ A rapid increase in brain synapses continues until about age 4. At that point, children actually have more brain synapses than adults do. Then, after age 10, the number slowly declines, reaching adult levels at about age 16. (From Conel, 1939–1963).

discovered, these children are usually mute, severely retarded, and emotionally damaged. Some suffer from **deprivation dwarfism**—*stunted growth associated with isolation, rejection, or general deprivation* (see boxed news excerpt). Special efforts to teach such children to speak and behave normally are often of limited success. Examples such as these, as well as the earlier discussion of attachment, suggest that in many ways the first 3 years of life are a *relatively critical period* in development.

"Closet Child" Now with Loving Parents

LONG BEACH (AP)—Becky's story began to unfold when the Sheriff's Department responded to a tip like hundreds of others. They found Becky in urine-soaked clothes, asleep on a hard cot in her parents' bedroom.

"She was almost like an animal," one of the deputies reported.

Her world then was the bedroom and its closet, in which she was kept for untold hours. Now Becky lives in a spacious foster home.

Since Becky's rescue, she has gained 12 pounds and grown 6 inches. But she is still a mite, for she weighed only 24 pounds and stood only 32 inches tall last April.

When she was found, Becky couldn't even crawl; now she walks. Then, she knew only a few words—now she speaks in sentences. She is, except for the hurt in her eyes, like almost any toddler.

But Rebecca is no toddler. She is 9 years old, and her pediatrician says she may never catch up.

What aspects of deprivation are responsible for the damage done?

An early hint came when psychoanalyst René Spitz (1945)

compared two groups of infants. One group was made up of healthy and lively babies in an institution Spitz called the "nursery." A second group of babies in a "foundling home" suffered from **hospitalism** (*deep depression marked by weeping and sadness*). The foundling home babies rocked back and forth mechanically, appeared to be retarded, showed little interest in other humans, and died at an alarmingly high rate.

Spitz compared conditions at the two institutions and found some striking differences. At the nursery, each baby had a separate attendant. At the foundling home, there were eight babies to a nurse. In view of this, Spitz concluded that the foundling home babies were "wasting away" because they lacked dependable "mother figures."

In other words, the babies failed to form an attachment to an adult, right?

Yes. Attachment failures can be a major element in early deprivation. Consider, for example, the plight of children raised in severely overcrowded Romanian orphanages. These children received almost no attention from adults for the first year or more of their lives. Some have now been adopted by Canadian families, where many are making progress toward normalcy. However, the children still tend to remain poorly attached to their adoptive parents. Many, for instance, will readily wander off with strangers (Chisholm et al., 1995).

A second major factor in many cases of deprivation is a lack of **perceptual stimulation** (*varied, patterned, and meaningful sensory input*). All of Spitz's "wasted" babies received good physical care. However, they were kept in bare rooms in cribs with sheets hung on the sides that allowed them to see only the blank ceiling. Their only contact with others came when they were quickly fed or changed. To put it mildly, there was *nothing happening* for these children: no variety, no input, no cuddling, no attention, and most of all, no stimulation. This was deprivation in the fullest sense of the word.

Perceptual, intellectual, and emotional deprivation can occur in any family, at any income level. However, when families must cope with poverty, the risk that children will be victims of deprivation is magnified.

A Closer Look

The Impact of Poverty

Psychologists have long known that poverty is associated with retarded emotional and intellectual development. By the age of 5, poor children have lower IQs and they are more fearful, unhappy, and prone to aggressive behavior. But these observations leave an important question unanswered: Exactly how does poverty contribute to such problems?

Basically, researchers have found that poverty

wears down families. Unemployment, decaying neighborhoods, crime, and social disorder all take a toll on parenting. Even when parents have the best intentions, poverty can lead to many kinds of deprivation.

The longer a family remains poor, the less likely parents are to express love and warmth toward their children. The longer they are poor, the more likely parents are to use harsh discipline. Fighting and conflict are common in poor families. Stimulating language environments are not. Most important, children living in poverty tend to be deprived of learning opportunities, both at home and in inferior schools.

None of these observations suggests that poor parents intentionally deprive their children. Typically, when family income increases, parents use the extra money to enhance their children's lives. How, then, can the odds of success be improved for poor children? According to a major study done by the Carnegie Corporation, the most important steps are:

- Educate parents about caregiving
- Make sure that quality child care is available to working parents
- Promote physical health and safety for all children
- Get communities involved in supporting young children and their families

Almost everyone knows that good nutrition is important in early childhood. As this discussion suggests, it is equally important to nourish the mind. (Sources: Carnegie Corporation, 1994; Dodge, Pettit, & Bates, 1994; Duncan, Brooks-Gunn, & Klebanov, 1994; Garrett, Ng'andu, & Ferron, 1994; Korenman, Miller, & Sjaastad, 1995.)

Early Stimulation

Animal experiments have confirmed the destructive effects of poor stimulation in infancy. For example, Harry Harlow separated infant rhesus monkeys from their mothers at birth. The real mothers were replaced with **surrogate** (*substitute*) **mothers.** These replicas were approximately the same size and shape as real monkeys. Some of the surrogates were made of cold, unyielding wire. Others were covered with soft terry cloth (Fig. 4–17 ◆). When the infants were given a choice between the two mothers, they consistently chose to spend most of their time clinging to the cuddly terry-cloth mother. This was true even when the wire mother held a bottle, making her the source of food.

The "love" and attachment displayed toward the cloth mothers was identical to that shown toward natural mothers. When frightened by rubber snakes, wind-up toys, and other "fear stimuli," the infant monkeys ran to their cloth mothers and clung to them for security (Harlow & Zimmerman,

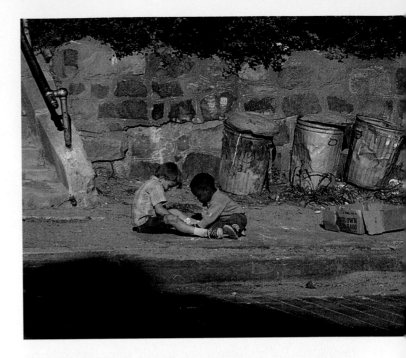

Children who grow up in poverty run a high risk of experiencing many forms of deprivation. There is evidence that lasting damage to social, emotional, and cognitive development occurs when children must cope with severe early deprivation.

1958). Harlow concluded that an important dimension of early stimulation is **contact comfort** (*a pleasant and reassuring feeling infants get from touching something soft and warm, usually their mother*). Harlow's findings are backed up by human research, as well. For example, premature babies benefit physically and emotionally from affectionate touching and massage by parents (de Roiste & Bushnell, 1996; Schok & Samuels, 1992). Indeed, touch is an effective way to gain attention and elicit positive emotions from all babies (Pelaez-Nogueras et al., 1996).

Contact comfort is part of the rationale for advocating breast-feeding of infants. Breast-feeding almost guarantees that a baby will receive adequate touching and handling. It also aids attachment and early cognitive development (Jensen et al., 1981; Morrow-Tlucak, Haude, & Ernhart, 1988). Even without such advantages, breast-feeding is advisable. For the first few days after giving birth, mothers produce **colostrum** (kuh-LOSS-trum: *a fluid rich in proteins*), rather than milk. Colostrum carries antibodies from the mother to the newborn. These antibodies help prevent certain infectious diseases. Colostrum is also easier for the newborn to digest than cow's milk and many infant formulas.

What about the mother who can't breast-feed or who prefers not to?

The advantages of breast-feeding are not paramount. If a mother is aware of the importance of touching and cuddling, bottle feeding need not be psychologically inferior. A

Figure 4-17 ◆ An infant monkey clings to a cloth-covered surrogate mother. Baby monkeys become attached to the cloth "contact-comfort" mother but not to a similar wire mother. This is true even when the wire mother provides food. (Photo courtesy of Harry Harlow, University of Wisconsin Primate Laboratory.)

mother's warmth or coldness, relaxation or tension, and acceptance or rejection are more important than the choice of breast or bottle. As mentioned earlier, being sensitive to a baby's feeding rhythms is a key to healthy infant attachment.

Contact comfort may also underlie the tendency of many children to become attached to inanimate objects, such as blankets or stuffed toys. This does not appear to be a cause for alarm, however. A study of 2- to 3-year-old "blanket-attached" children found that they were no more insecure than others (Passman, 1987). (So, maybe Linus is okay after all.)

Enrichment   If too little stimulation limits development, can abundant stimulation enhance it? Attempts to answer this question have made use of **enriched environments,** which are *deliberately made more novel, complex, and stimulating.* Enriched environments may be the "soil" from which brighter children grow. To illustrate, let us begin with an experiment in which rats were raised in an enriched environment (Krech et al., 1962).

Building Bigger and Better Brains

One group of infant rats was raised in *stimulus-poor* conditions inside adequate, but unstimulating cages. These gray-walled cages contained nothing to explore or investigate. The second group was housed in a sort of "rat wonderland." The walls of this *stimulus-enriched* environment were decorated with colored patterns and each cage was filled with platforms, ladders, and cubbyholes. When the rats reached adulthood, their ability to learn mazes was tested. The stimulated rats dramatically out-performed their deprived relatives. In addition, rats living in enriched environments typically have larger, heavier brains, with a thicker cortex (Benloucif, Bennett, & Rosenzweig, 1995).

Extra touching, massage, and human contact is especially beneficial for premature and low-birth-weight infants.

It may be a long leap from rats to people, but it is hard to overlook an increase in brain size caused by sensory stimulation. If stimulation can enhance the "intelligence" of a lowly rat, it seems reasonable to assume that human infants also benefit from enrichment.

Is there any evidence that this is actually the case?

As might be expected, it is much harder to demonstrate in humans. In Chapter 12 you will find a full discussion of the effects of environment on intelligence. For now, let's examine two examples of enrichment applied to humans.

Infants like to reach out and touch things, but normally it takes about 5 months after birth for this skill to develop. In an experiment, newborn infants were given several kinds of extra stimulation each day for several months (White & Held, 1966). Each child in the stimulus enrichment condition was handled an extra 15 minutes daily. Each was placed in a position that allowed visual exploration outside the crib. White crib sheets were replaced by patterned sheets with colorful animal designs. A collection of bright and colorful objects was hung over each child's crib. As limited as these changes may seem, they caused *visually directed reaching* to occur an average of 6 weeks early. This may not sound like an earth-shaking improvement in adult terms, but to an infant it is a substantial acceleration in development.

The preceding is only one of many experiments showing a positive relationship between stimulation and improved abilities. One of the most encouraging examples can be found in **early childhood education programs,** *which provide stimulating intellectual experiences for disadvantaged children.* For example, the Head Start program helps children "learn to learn" before they enter school. Studies confirm that Head Start children show real improvements in their abilities and school performance (Lee, Brooks-Gunn, & Schnur, 1988; Campbell & Ramey, 1994). This is especially true for the most needy children.

Programs like Head Start can't work miracles, but they

Table 4–10 ■ Deprivation and Enrichment: Implications for Parents and Caregivers

- All of early childhood should be viewed as a relatively critical period in development.
- Infants and young children thrive in enriched, stimulating environments.
- Touch and human contact are important elements of infant development.
- Children need a sense of security, belonging, and support; they need to feel loved.

---

can prepare children for school. They also teach children social and emotional skills that may help them cope better with life (Zigler & Styfco, 1994). As teens, former Head Start participants are less likely to drop out of school, get arrested, or get pregnant, among other things (Zigler & Muenchow, 1992).

Summary   Most people recognize that babies need lots of "tender loving care" for their physical needs. But as our discussion has shown, tender loving care should include a baby's psychological needs as well. In general, the effects of deprivation and enrichment appear to apply to *all* of the categories of development discussed earlier in this chapter. It would be a good idea to place perceptual and intellectual stimulation, affectionate touching, and personal warmth high on any list of infant needs. (See Table 4–10 ■.)

A Look Ahead   The first years of life are a magic and sensitive time. What can parents do to make the most of this period? The Applications section that follows gives some practical advice. After that, an Exploration delves into recent advances in genetics and reproductive technologies that are sure to affect our lives.

Learning Check	**Critical Thinking**

1. According to Kohlberg, the conventional level of moral development is marked by a reliance on outside authority. T or F?

2. Self-interest and avoiding punishment are elements of postconventional morality. T or F?

3. About 80 percent of all adults function at the postconventional level of moral reasoning. T or F?

4. Gilligan regards gaining a sense of justice as the principal basis of moral development. T or F?

5. Harlow's "motherless monkeys" became attached to the wire surrogate mother if it fed them. T or F?

6. René Spitz attributed hospitalism to an absence of perceptual stimulation. T or F?

7. Bottle feeding prevents a mother from providing an adequate amount of contact comfort for an infant. T or F?

8. Early childhood education programs can be characterized as attempts to enrich the environments of deprived children. T or F?

9. Some of Carol Gilligan's work involved presenting real-life dilemmas concerning abortion to a group of women. Why might any conclusions drawn from such studies be open to question?

Answers:

1. T 2. F 3. F 4. F 5. F 6. F 7. F 8. T 9. To identify differences between men's and women's moral reasoning, men and women must face the same dilemma; Gilligan, therefore, cannot draw firm conclusions about how men might react, based on the dilemma she presented to women (Mednick, 1989).

*D*erek's room looks like an overstocked toy store. The walls are covered with posters. Model airplanes, rockets, a pterodactyl, and a miniature solar system dangle from the ceiling. Expensive playthings cover the floor.

For several hours a day, Derek's mother plays classical music for him—through his own stereo system. Each evening, Derek watches educational videotapes about animals, premath skills, and nuclear physics. Every day, Derek's mother drills him with flash cards in hopes that he will learn to read before any of the neighbor children. Derek is taking swimming lessons at a local pool.

Derek is 2½. At present his favorite toy is a fake cellular phone.

Derek's parents obviously mean well. But are they really enriching his early development? Let's put it this way: By the time he is 5, if Derek's parents ask him to change a light bulb, he will hold it in the socket and wait for the world to revolve around him.

Facilitating Early Development

Understandably, parents want to see their children's potentials develop fully. As discussed earlier, proactive parental involvement can greatly benefit a child. It is easy, however, to go overboard and overwhelm a child. "Enrichment" that does not match a child's needs is of little value. How can parents strike a balance between enrichment and "pushing" their children? As a start, it helps to have appropriate goals for infancy. Child expert Burton White (1990) believes that for the first year or so of life the three goals for healthy development are:

1. Giving the infant a feeling of being loved and cared for.
2. Encouraging interest in the outside world.
3. Helping the infant develop specific skills.

Let's see how these goals apply to parental behavior. (For an excellent description of early development, and practical advice for effective parenting, consult White's book, *The First Three Years of Life*.)

Attachment Letting infants know they are loved and cared for helps build secure mother-infant and father-infant bonds. The importance of giving babies good physical care is self-evident. Beyond that, parents should touch, hold, and handle their infant frequently. They should also attend promptly to a baby's cries as often as possible.

Parents sometimes believe that they should let babies "cry it out" to avoid spoiling them. There will, of course, be times when nothing will console an unhappy, but otherwise

healthy baby. But for the first year of life, it is best to respond promptly to a baby's signs of discomfort. Infants are better off in the long run if they are tended and comforted in a loving way (White, 1990). This helps them feel secure and it strengthens emotional bonds with parents.

Overindulgence As mentioned earlier, spoiling very young infants is nearly impossible. As children grow more mobile and independent, however, overindulgence becomes a risk. From about age 2 on, parents are asking for trouble if they do everything, and buy everything they can for a child, no matter what. Another clear sign of overindulgence is giving in to the child's demands, even when they go against your better judgment. Effective parents are very loving and even quite indulgent. What spoils a child is a lack of firm age-appropriate limits and guidelines for acceptable behavior. (Information on setting and maintaining such limits is discussed in the Applications section of Chapter 5.)

The Outside World During the first year, you can promote exploration of the world by involving babies in activities that interest *them*. Parents must pay close attention to a baby's signals, likes, and dislikes, as well as what holds the baby's attention. Burton White (1990) recommends using an infant seat to keep the baby near you as you move around the house. That way, the baby gets a change of scene and you get to interact with her or him more often.

To further encourage exploration, try to minimize the use of restrictive devices. Playpens, jump seats, and gates should not be used for long periods, if at all. Restricting exploration tends to stifle a child's natural curiosity.

Your attitude toward a child's *investigation* of the world can contribute greatly to intellectual growth. The child who repeatedly hears, "Don't touch that" (chair, handle, trash, radio, pencil, flower) or "I told you not to" (go up there, play with that, leave this spot, get dirty, and so forth) may become passive and intellectually dulled (Carew et al., 1976). Placing virtually all common objects off-limits for a child is a serious mistake. When children begin to crawl and walk, it is better to "child-proof" a house than to strictly enforce rules about what the child cannot touch.

Respecting Individual Variation A major element of good child rearing in infancy consists of facilitating the normal pattern of emerging skills. If an infant lags far behind expected milestones in development, parents should take note and find out why (White, 1990). However, within normal ranges it is valuable to remember that individual differences in maturation rates are the rule.

Aware parents recognize that the **statistical child** (*average child*) is a convenient fiction. Developmental norms cited in books give the *average* ages at which abilities appear. There is always a *wide range of normal variation* around each average. Thus, we can expect plateaus, reversals, and periods of rapid advancement in the development of a particular child. This applies not only to the emergence of motor skills, such as crawling and walking, but also to language development and the stages of cognitive development. Parents should try to respect a child's uniqueness in all areas. This means resisting the temptation to compare the child with others—particularly in the child's presence. Each child is an individual and should be judged as such.

Enrichment

As we have noted, babies crave stimulation. By keeping this in mind, parents can do much to provide varied sensory experiences during infancy. A baby should be surrounded by colors, music, people, and things to see, taste, smell, and touch. Babies are not vegetables. It makes perfect sense to take them outside, to hang mobiles over their cribs, to place mirrors nearby, or to rearrange their rooms now and then.

It also makes sense to talk to infants, from birth onward. Try to talk about present events, such as what you are doing, objects the baby is looking at, and parts of the baby's body you are touching. As you interact with a baby, be sure to respond to his or her coos, gurgles, and other vocalizations—not just to crying (White, 1990). Remember, the more time babies spend interacting with parents, the faster they develop language and thinking abilities (Hart & Risley, 1992).

Throughout a baby's second year it is very important to watch for signs of hearing loss, which can have a devastating effect on cognitive development. To test for hearing loss, the baby's mother should call to her or him in a normal voice from 6–10 feet away. As she calls repeatedly for about a minute, the baby should turn accurately toward her voice. If the baby does not, or if you have doubts about an infant's hearing, seek professional advice (White, 1990).

Responsiveness

Most parents could put far more imagination into enriching an infant's surroundings than they typically do. The presence of stimulating play materials in the home, together with responsive parents, is strongly related to how quickly children progress (Bradley et al., 1989; Luster & Dubow, 1992).

How should parents decide if enrichment is being overdone?

The answer depends more on *quality* than quantity. Remember that the goal in enrichment is to create a world that *responds* to infants—not one that bombards them with stimuli. Elaborately enriched environments are unnecessary and can be upsetting to a baby (White, 1990).

The concept of *responsiveness*, mentioned earlier, applies to toys and objects, as well as parents' behavior. Toys that respond to a child's actions, such as balls, rattles, mirrors—even a spoon and a pie tin—help speed infant learning. Such toys allow children to observe the cause-and-effect results of their own behavior. As psychologist Paul Chance points out, the least responsive toy available is probably a $500 color television, while one of the most responsive is a $1 rubber ball (Chance, 1982).

Drawbacks of Forced Teaching   Of special concern are misguided attempts to push development and produce "super babies." It's worth saying again that flooding an infant with stimuli, flash cards, and exercises is not enriching. Neither is **forced teaching** (*accelerated learning at a pace dictated by an adult*). Forcing children to learn reading, pre-math skills, gymnastics, swimming, musical skills, and the like can bore or oppress them. These practices, which are sometimes called "hothousing," are like trying to force plants to bloom prematurely (Hyson et al., 1991).

Forced teaching is expensive and unnecessary (White, 1990). Parents who approach play and learning as if their preschooler is on the fast track for Harvard are filling their own needs at the expense of the child (Alvino et al., 1996). True enrichment is responsive to the child's curiosity and interests. It does not make the child feel pressured to perform. Many of the things Derek's parents did (in the opening vignette) would be perfectly appropriate for an older child—especially when the child's own interests are taken into account. The next section offers some further guidelines for parents.

Piaget Revisited

Piaget's theory suggests that the ideal way to guide intellectual development is to provide experiences that are only slightly novel, unusual, or challenging. Remember, a child's intellect develops mainly through accommodation. As old concepts and thinking habits become obsolete, they are discarded or adapted to fit new demands.

To stretch a child's intellect, demands must be made, but experiences that are too far beyond the familiar may cause frustration and withdrawal. Therefore, gradually expanding beyond a child's current level of comprehension is usually most productive. Effective parents typically follow a *one-step-ahead strategy* when adapting their instruction to an infant's current abilities (Heckhausen, 1987).

In addition, Piaget's work shows the importance of relating to a child on the right level. If you give a physical explanation when a very young child asks, "Why does the sun come up in the morning?" you may have missed the point. Answering in terms of the child's egocentric viewpoint is often more meaningful. An answer such as, "So you will know it's time to get up" is completely satisfactory for a young child. Later, explanations can be made increasingly abstract and accurate.

Are there any guidelines for relating to children at their own level?

In a delightful book entitled *Using Psychology*, psychologist Morris Holland offers some suggestions about how best to relate to children at different stages of intellectual development. The following points are drawn from his discussion (Holland, 1975).

1. **Sensorimotor stage (0–2).** Active play with a child is most effective at this stage. Encourage explorations in touching, smelling, and manipulating objects. Peekaboo is a good way to establish the permanence of objects.

2. **Preoperational stage (2–7).** Although children are beginning to talk to themselves and act out solutions to problems, touching and seeing things will continue to be more useful than verbal explanations. Concrete examples will also have more meaning than generalizations. The child should be encouraged to classify things in different ways. Learning the concept of conservation may be aided by demonstrations involving liquids, beads, clay, and other substances.

3. **Concrete operational stage (7–11).** Children in this stage are beginning to use generalizations, but they still require specific examples to grasp many ideas. Expect a degree of inconsistency in the child's ability to apply concepts of time, space, quantity, and volume to new situations.

4. **Formal operations stage (11–adult).** At this point, it becomes more realistic to explain things verbally or symbolically. Helping the child to master general rules and principles now becomes productive. Encourage the child to create hypotheses and to imagine how things could be.

Keeping this general outline in mind should help you adjust to the changing patterns of intellect displayed by developing children.

Learning Check	Critical Thinking
1. The idea that the particular child is different from the "statistical child" applies to language development and cognitive skills, but not to motor development. T or F?	6. Forced teaching ignores what principle of early maturation and development?
2. Parental overindulgence is likely to occur when parents fail to set firm age-appropriate guidelines for their children's behavior. T or F?	
3. To promote accommodation, it is best to provide information or experiences only moderately beyond a child's current level of comprehension. T or F?	
4. Playing peekaboo is a good way to help the sensorimotor child master the concept of conservation. T or F?	**Answers:**
5. A key element of enrichment in infancy and early childhood is the concept of _____ .	1. F 2. T 3. T 4. F 5. responsiveness 6. Readiness.

*I*n his famous novel, *Brave New World,* Aldous Huxley described a futuristic society in which "baby factories" produce thousands of duplicate humans to do society's labor. Huxley, writing in the 1930s, envisioned a future in which biological engineering would be used for sinister and totalitarian ends. Now that the future has arrived, we find instead that some of the advances Huxley anticipated have made it possible for previously infertile couples to have children. And yet, as is often true, new solutions create new problems. In this Exploration we will briefly describe some recent developments in medicine and genetics that raise interesting social, psychological, and ethical questions.

In the recent past, adoption was the only alternative for infertile couples. Now, couples have an array of new options. Let's investigate two that are of special interest.

Artificial Insemination   If her husband is sterile, a woman can undergo **artificial insemination** (*medically engineered pregnancy*). In this procedure, sperm cells from an anonymous donor are used to impregnate the woman. Donors are selected so that their eye and hair color, height, and so on, match the husband's as closely as possible. For emotional reasons, some of the husband's sperm cells are sometimes mixed with the donor sperm so that it is impossible to tell who was actually the father. (Men who are sterile often produce sperm, but their sperm count is too low for them to father a child.)

Test-Tube Babies   In vitro fertilization (*fertilization of an ovum outside a woman's body*) has made it possible for some infertile couples to bear children who share both the mother's and father's genes. To produce a "test-tube" baby, egg cells are surgically collected from the mother's ovary. The egg cells are placed in a petri dish of nutrients and the father's sperm cells are added (Fig. 4–18 ◆). (A womb with a view!) After an egg cell is fertilized and begins dividing, it is implanted in the mother's womb, where it develops normally. In a new variation on in vitro fertilization, an unrelated woman may donate an egg cell to the infertile couple. The egg cell is then fertilized with the husband's sperm and implanted in the wife's uterus. Infertile couples who are considering this technique should be warned, however. Even using the latest methods, only 15 percent of in vitro attempts are successful, and the cost ranges from $8,000 to $13,000.

Questions and Controversies

The procedures outlined here raise a number of practical, emotional, moral, and even religious issues. Many will no doubt occur to you. A few that may not are listed here.

Many donors for artificial insemination are used repeatedly. One clinic reported that a single donor fathered 50 babies. What if this donor harbored a genetic disease or defect? What if children fathered by the same donor were to meet and marry? Since they would be half

Figure 4–18 ◆   During in vitro fertilization, ova from the woman or a donor are mixed with sperm from the man or a donor. In the advanced technique shown here, a sperm cell is placed inside an ovum. If both the egg and sperm are donated, both nominal parents are genetically unrelated to the "test-tube" baby.

brother and sister, their offspring would run a high risk of having genetic defects. What rules of testing and record keeping should apply to artificial insemination by donor?

Many scientists believe that handling egg cells for in vitro fertilization may increase the risk of deformities in babies. If a child is born with a defect, is the physician responsible? Frequently, more than one egg is fertilized. Should they be donated to another infertile couple? Is letting them die an abortion? Should in vitro fertilization be allowed if the man and woman are not married? If they divorce, who should get "custody" of the ova?

In two very important ways, assisted conception has not been a problem. A recent study found that the quality of parenting in families with assisted conception was *superior* to that of families with naturally conceived or adopted children. Also, assisted conception had no effect on children's emotions, behavior, or relationships with parents (Golombok et al., 1995).

Sex Selection   Another recent development that may have an impact on parenthood is the possibility of selecting an infant's sex prior to conception. The procedure involves separating *X*- and *Y*-bearing sperm and then artifi-cially fertilizing the egg cell with all male-producing or all female-producing sperm.

Currently, sex selection techniques cannot *guarantee* to produce a child of the desired sex. Sex selection is also relatively expensive (about $500), and some couples may be discouraged by the need for artificial insemination. A further worry is that two thirds of all childless couples say they would prefer to have a boy as a first child.

If large numbers of couples select their children's sex, would there be an excess of male births?

Seventy-three percent of all potential parents who would be willing to use sex-selection technology say they would choose sons (Steinbacher & Gilroy, 1990). If many couples were to make this choice, the male-female population balance would be upset. Birth rate and population growth would slow dramatically once 70 percent of the population became male. (Also, of course, beer sales would skyrocket.)

Genetics and Parenthood

In recent years, having children has been influenced by an improved understanding of human genetics and problems that "run in the family." Increasingly, it has become possible to identify genetic disorders such as sickle cell anemia, hemophilia, cystic fibrosis, muscular dystrophy, albinism, and some forms of mental retardation.

Scientists are currently hard at work on a giant project to identify, in order, every gene on every human chromosome. The result will be a map of the **human genome** (JEEN-ome), or *entire set of human genes.* Having, in essence a "full set of instructions for making a human" will allow advanced identification of genetic diseases and new tests to detect those diseases in people. It will take at least another decade to produce a complete blueprint of all human genes. At that point, doctors, biologists, and you and I will face a host of new ethical and practical dilemmas to resolve.

Genetic Counseling   Today, prospective parents who suspect that they may be carriers of genetic disorders may seek **genetic counseling** (*guidance and testing of prospective parents*). By examining the family history of each future parent, and in some cases by directly mapping chromosomes, geneticists can calculate the risk of a genetic disorder.

What can a couple do if the risk of a genetic defect is high?

Knowing the risks, parents can choose

Strands of DNA can be chemically broken into shorter segments which (after further manipulation) can be displayed for analysis. The pink-glowing pieces of DNA you see here are enlarged many times.

not to have a child; or, if the odds are in their favor, they may elect to take the chance. Even when there is a reasonable likelihood of a genetic disorder, some couples elect to have children. If pregnancy occurs, however, they then have a test performed to detect the genetic defect. Such prenatal testing is done by **amniocentesis** (AM-nee-oh-SEN-tee-sis: *taking a sample of amniotic fluid from the mother's womb*). This procedure allows determination of fetal sex as well as detection of many genetic defects.

Amniocentesis is usually done at about the 15th week of pregnancy. An alternate procedure, called **chorionic villus sampling,** can be done between 6 and 8 weeks of pregnancy. This technique *takes a small piece of the placenta for analysis*. Either method allows couples who do not object to abortion to terminate the pregnancy when a serious genetic defect is detected. Parents who consider abortion unacceptable still have the advantage of forewarning so

that they may prepare the best possible care for the child.

One of the challenges of genetic counseling today is that new tests are making it possible to identify genetic problems long before any cures will be available (Kenen & Smith, 1995).

The Future

Recent advances in genetics, the exploding knowledge about how DNA controls heredity, and mapping of the human genome will bring profound changes to the human condition. Let's sample some of the possibilities.

Eugenics   Domestic plants and animals have been improved more in the past 50 years than in the previous 5,000. This improvement has been accomplished primarily through **eugenics** (you-JEN-iks: *selective breeding for desirable characteristics*). Some extremists have already proposed that eugenics be applied to

humans. But the very idea is loaded with ethical problems. How would we decide what characteristics are desirable? And who would decide who can have children and who cannot? Typically, eugenic arguments are applied to the least powerful individuals in any society (Smith, 1995).

In practice, it is unlikely that widespread human eugenics will ever be practiced. On the other hand, some genetic diseases will almost certainly be "cured." Even without such direct efforts, the steady use of genetic counseling could have a eugenic effect on future generations.

Genetic Engineering   It is now becoming possible to remove defective genes and replace them with normal ones. Could such genetic engineering also be used to produce beauty, intelligence, resistance to aging, or superhuman athletic potential? In theory yes, but practically speaking, probably not. Literally thousands of

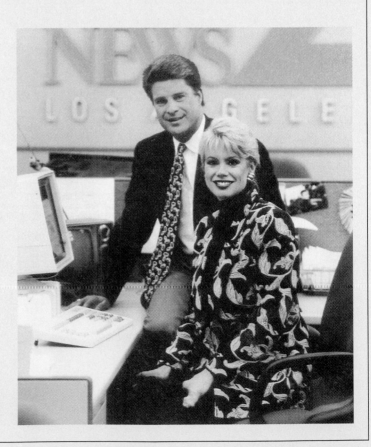

Bree Walker Lampley, a TV celebrity in Los Angeles, has a genetic condition that causes deformity of the hands and feet. Before she became pregnant, she knew she had a 50 percent chance of giving birth to a baby with the same trait. Despite public criticism, she had a baby (who did, in fact, inherit her genetic condition). The social pressures she faced illustrate the dilemmas people who carry genetic defects often face (Rennie, 1994).

genes affect such qualities, not to mention the effects of environment. For this reason, limited genetic engineering involving one or two genes may soon be used to combat specific diseases such as diabetes or cancer, and inherited disorders. Tampering with genes on a major scale is not likely in the near future. **Cloning,** *the production of an entire organism from a single cell,* is also likely to remain science fiction (where humans are concerned) for the immediate future. While it is true that a sheep was successfully cloned in 1997, there is no medical or scientific reason why anyone would attempt to clone a human.

Gene Cards One authority on genetic engineering and genetic defects predicts that people will one day carry a "gene identity card" based on blood tests made during childhood. These would show what hereditary diseases a person is predisposed to, or which problems may be passed on in childbearing when combined with the gene pattern of a mate (Milunsky, 1992).

Rapid advances in techniques that affect heredity and conception have an important place in the understanding of behavior. And as we have seen, such changes raise a number of important psychological and ethical questions. Brace yourself, the brave new world of genetics is here.

Learning Check

1. The procedure known as in vitro fertilization involves fertilizing a woman with donor sperm. T or F?

2. Test-tube babies are produced by fertilizing an egg cell outside of the body. T or F?

3. Current sex selection procedures can consistently produce male offspring, but they cannot guarantee female babies. T or F?

4. Amniocentesis is primarily used to select sex before birth. T or F?

5. The term *eugenics* refers to the production of an entire organism from a single cell. T or F?

Critical Thinking

6. Many people who should seek genetic screening choose not to be tested. Why do you think people resist testing?

Answers:

1. F 2. T 3. F 4. F 5. F 6. The most typical reasons given are that: People would rather not know they carry a defect because it would mean their children might be at risk too; they fear being stigmatized; they worry that their health insurance may be affected; and they are concerned that they may be turned down for future employment.

Chapter Summary

What can newborn babies do?

◆ The human **neonate** has a number of *adaptive reflexes*, including the **grasping, rooting, sucking,** and **Moro reflexes.** Neonates show immediate evidence of learning and of appreciating the consequences of their actions.

◆ Tests in a **looking chamber** reveal a number of visual preferences in the newborn. The neonate is drawn to complex, circular, curved, and brightly lighted designs.

◆ Infants prefer human face patterns, especially familiar faces. In later infancy, interest in the unfamiliar emerges.

What influence does maturation have on early development?

◆ **Maturation** of the body and nervous system underlies the orderly *sequence* of motor, cognitive, language, and emotional development. The *rate* of maturation, however, varies from person to person. Also, learning contributes greatly to the development of basic motor skills.

◆ Many early skills are subject to the principle of **readiness** (or **motor primacy**).

How do heredity and environment affect development?

◆ The *nature-nurture controversy* concerns the relative contributions to development of **heredity** (nature) and **environment** (nurture).

◆ Hereditary instructions are carried by the **chromosomes** and **genes** in each cell of the body. Most characteristics are **polygenic** and reflect the combined effects of **dominant** and **recessive** genes.

◆ Heredity affects a large number of personal characteristics and it organizes the general **human growth sequence.**

◆ Heredity is also involved in differences in **temperament** present at birth. Most infants fall into one of three temperament categories: *easy* children, *difficult* children, and *slow-to-warm-up* children.

◆ Most psychologists accept that heredity and environment are inseparable and *interacting* forces. A child's **developmental level** therefore reflects *heredity, environment,* and the effects of the child's *own behavior.*

◆ *Prenatal development* is subject to environmental influences in the form of diseases, drugs, radiation, and the mother's diet, health, and emotions. Various **teratogens** can cause prenatal damage to the fetus, resulting in **congenital problems,** or "birth defects."

◆ Healthy children are produced by both **conventional birth** and by **natural (prepared) childbirth.** However, prepared births do have the advantage of minimizing the use of anesthetics. The father's presence at birth appears to be desirable, although his attitude toward birth may be of more basic importance.

How important are parenting styles?

◆ Studies of parents and their children suggest that **caregiving styles** have a substantial impact on emotional and intellectual development.

◆ Whereas mothers typically emphasize caregiving, fathers tend to function as a playmate for the infant.

◆ Optimal caregiving includes **proactive maternal involvement,** a **good fit** between the temperaments of parent and child, and **responsiveness** to a child's needs and signals.

Of what significance is a child's emotional bond with parents?

◆ **Self-awareness** and **social referencing** are elements of early social development.

◆ A variety of **critical periods** exist in development, as illustrated by **imprinting** in animals. **Emotional attachment** of human infants to their caregivers is a critical early event.

◆ Infant attachment is reflected by **separation anxiety.** The quality of attachment can be classified as **secure, insecure-avoidant,** or **insecure-ambivalent.**

◆ *High-quality* day care does not appear to harm children.

◆ Although the issue is debated, it is doubtful that immediate *mother-infant contact* is crucial for forming lasting emotional bonds.

How do children acquire language and thinking abilities?

◆ *Language development* proceeds from control of **crying,** to **cooing,** then **babbling,** the use of **single words,** and then to **telegraphic speech.**

◆ The underlying patterns of telegraphic speech suggest a **biological predisposition** to acquire language. This innate predisposition is augmented by learning.

◆ **Prelanguage communication** between parent and child involves *shared rhythms,* non-verbal *signals,* and *turn-taking.*

◆ The intellect of a child is *less abstract* than that of an adult. Jean Piaget theorized that intellectual growth occurs through a combination of **assimilation** and **accommodation.**

◆ Piaget also held that children go through a fixed series of **cognitive stages.** The stages and their approximate age ranges are: **sensorimotor (0–2), preoperational (2–7), concrete operational (7–11),** and **formal operations (11–adult).**

◆ Learning principles provide an alternate explanation that assumes that cognitive development is continuous, it does not occur in stages.

◆ Recent studies of infants under the age of one year suggest that they are capable of thought beyond that observed by Piaget.

How do children develop morals and values?

◆ Lawrence Kohlberg theorized that **moral development** passes through a series of stages revealed by moral reasoning.

◆ Kohlberg identified **preconventional, conventional,** and **postconventional** levels of moral reasoning.

◆ Some psychologists have questioned whether measures of moral development should be based only on a morality of justice. Adults appear to base moral choices on either justice or caring, depending on the situation.

What are the effects of a poor early environment?

◆ During the first few years of life, rapid changes in connections between brain cells tend to amplify the impact of early learning environments.

◆ Early *perceptual, intellectual,* and *emotional* **deprivation** seriously retards development. Even physical growth may be affected, as is the case in **deprivation dwarfism.**

◆ Poverty greatly increases the likelihood that children will experience various forms of deprivation.

◆ Research on deprivation suggests secure attachment and perceptual stimulation are essential for normal development.

◆ Work with subhuman primates (monkeys) has also pointed to **contact comfort** as an important source of infant stimulation and attachment.

◆ Deliberate **enrichment** of the environment in infancy and early childhood has a beneficial effect on development.

What can be done to enhance early development?

◆ Parents should take steps to encourage secure infant attachment.

◆ Effective parents avoid overindulgence while encouraging exploration of surroundings.

◆ Parents must respect individual differences and be aware of the distinction between the **statistical child** and a **particular child.**

◆ It is desirable to provide enrichment that is *responsive* to a child's interests and needs, and takes into account the child's level of cognitive development.

◆ Parents should avoid forced teaching.

How has new genetic knowledge affected parenthood?

◆ Many recent developments in genetics and reproduction raise ethical and social questions. Examples of such developments are **artificial insemination, in vitro fertilization, sex selection techniques, amniocentesis, chorionic villus testing, eugenics, cloning,** and **genetic counseling.**

5

From Birth to Death: Life-Span Development

Preview

The Time Machine

Time machines exist only in movies and science fiction. What if they were real? What could you learn about your life from one? Let's say that we have just such a machine. It can show an entire lifetime on a screen, forward or backward. Watch closely, here's an overview of your life: There you are taking your first breath. What a beautiful baby! Zzzzip. And there you are taking your last breath. Oops! That was a little too fast. I think we missed some important stuff in the middle. Maybe we should slow down and try it again.

Here we go: There you are at birth. Oh, and there's the birth of your first child. Hmm, now you're on the beach in Pago Pago. You seem to be coping well with middle age. Okay, who are all those people congratulating you? It must be your retirement party. Look, there's another party. Except I don't see you anywhere. And no one seems to be having a very good time. Uh oh, I think maybe we're at the end of the tape again. Sorry about that.

I guess that was still too fast. Maybe we should slow down even more. I'll reset the machine at zero. On second thought, maybe you should just read this chapter.

In the following pages we will examine development from a **life-span perspective.** Life-span psychologists *study both continuity and change in behavior during a lifetime* (Baltes, 1987). Every life is marked by a number of **developmental milestones.** These are *notable events, markers, or turning points in personal development.* Some examples include graduating from school, voting for the first time, getting married, watching a child leave home, (or move back!), the death of a parent, becoming a grandparent, retirement, and one's own death (Kimmel, 1990).

It is not practical here to describe all of the significant events of a lifetime. We will, nevertheless, touch on several of the major milestones, challenges, and problems you are likely to encounter from childhood to old age.

Theme: Development over a lifetime reflects a delicate balance between stability and change.

Key Questions:	Key Topics to Watch for:
What are the typical tasks and dilemmas through the life span?	Erikson's stages of life
What is the nature of effective parenting?	Authoritarian, permissive, and authoritative parenting
What are some of the more serious childhood problems?	Normal problems of childhood Serious childhood disorders The tragedy of child abuse
Why is adolescent development especially challenging?	Adolescence and puberty Early versus late maturation The search for identity
How do people select careers for themselves?	Stages and phases of career development
What happens psychologically during adulthood?	Typical patterns of adult development
What are the psychological challenges of aging?	Biological aging, activity and disengagement, ageism
How do people typically react to death and bereavement?	Reactions to impending death Bereavement and grief
How do effective parents discipline their children?	Principles of effective parenting Communication with children
In what ways are attitudes toward death changing?	The hospice movement, living wills, euthanasia, and cryonics

The Cycle of Life— Rocky Road or Garden Path?

If you take pride in being one of a kind, you have good reason. There is no such thing as a "typical person" or a "typical life." Nevertheless, there are broad similarities in the universal **life stages** *of infancy, childhood, adolescence, young adulthood, middle adulthood, and old age.* Each stage confronts a person with new **developmental tasks** *that must be mastered for optimal development.* Examples are learning to read in childhood, adjusting to sexual maturity in adolescence, and establishing a vocation as an adult (Havighurst, 1979).

In an influential book entitled *Childhood and Society* (1963), personality theorist Erik Erikson (1903–1994) suggests that we face a specific *psychosocial dilemma,* or "crisis," at each stage of life. A **psychosocial dilemma** *is a conflict between personal impulses and the social world.* Resolving each dilemma creates a new balance between a person and society. A string of "successes" produces healthy development and a satisfying life. Unfavorable outcomes throw us off balance, making it harder to deal with later crises. Life becomes a "rocky road" and personal growth is stunted. Table 5–1 lists Erikson's dilemmas. A brief description of each follows.

What are the major developmental tasks and life crises?

Stage One, First Year of Life: Trust versus Mistrust
During the first year of life, children are completely dependent on others. Erikson believes that a basic attitude of trust or mistrust is formed at this time. **Trust** *is established when babies are given adequate warmth, touching, love, and physical care.* **Mistrust** *is caused by inadequate or unpredictable care and by parents who are cold, indifferent, or rejecting.* Basic mistrust may later cause insecurity, suspiciousness, or an inability to relate to others. Notice that trust comes from the same conditions that help babies become securely attached to their parents (see Chapter 4).

Stage Two, 1–3 Years: Autonomy versus Shame and Doubt
In stage two, growing self-control is expressed by children's climbing, touching, exploring, and general desire to do things for themselves. Parents help foster a sense of **autonomy** *by encouraging children to try new skills.* However, the child's crude efforts often result in spilling, falling,

Table 5–1 ■ Erikson's Psychosocial Dilemmas	
Age	**Characteristic Dilemma**
Birth to 1 year	Trust versus mistrust
1 to 3 years	Autonomy versus shame and doubt
3 to 5 years	Initiative versus guilt
6 to 12 years	Industry versus inferiority
Adolescence	Identity versus role confusion
Young adulthood	Intimacy versus isolation
Middle adulthood	Generativity versus stagnation
Late adulthood	Integrity versus despair

Personality theorist Erik Erikson (1903–1994) is best known for his life-stage theory of human development. His last book, *Vital Involvement in Old Age,* published in 1986, described his ideas about successful aging.

wetting, and other "accidents." Thus, parents who *ridicule or overprotect* their children, may cause them to **doubt** their abilities and feel **shame** about their actions.

Stage Three, 3–5 Years: Initiative versus Guilt In stage three the child moves beyond simple self-control and begins to take initiative. Through play, the child learns to make plans and carry out tasks. Parents reinforce **initiative** *by giving children freedom to play, ask questions, use imagination, and choose activities.* Pretend play during this period also helps children practice social skills and roles (Connolly, Doyle, &

Reznick, 1988). Feelings of **guilt** about initiating activities are formed if parents *criticize severely, prevent play, or discourage a child's questions.*

Stage Four, 6–12 Years: Industry versus Inferiority
Many events of middle childhood are symbolized by that fateful day when you first entered school. With dizzying speed your world expanded beyond your family, and you faced a whole series of new challenges.

Erikson describes the elementary school years as the child's "entrance into life." In school, children begin to learn skills valued by society, and success or failure can affect feelings of adequacy. Children learn a sense of **industry** *if they win praise for productive activities,* such as building, painting, cooking, reading, and studying. If a child's *efforts are regarded as messy, childish, or inadequate,* feelings of **inferiority** result. For the first time, teachers, classmates, and adults outside the home become as important as parents in shaping attitudes toward oneself.

Stage Five, Adolescence: Identity versus Role Confusion
Adolescence is often a turbulent time. Caught between childhood and adulthood, the adolescent faces some unique problems. Erikson considers a need to answer the question, "Who am I?" the primary task during this stage of life. Mental and physical maturation brings new feelings, a new body, and new attitudes (Fig. 5–1 ◆). The adolescent must build a consistent **identity** out of self-perceptions and relationships with others. Conflicting experiences as a student, friend, athlete, worker, son or daughter, lover, and so forth, must be integrated into a *unified sense of self* (more on this later). Persons who fail to develop a sense of identity suffer from **role confusion,** *an uncertainty about who they are* and where they are going.

According to Erikson, children aged 3 to 5 learn to plan and initiate activities through play.

Figure 5–1 ◆ Dramatic differences in physical size and maturity are found in adolescents of the same age. The girls pictured are all 13, the boys 16. Maturation that occurs earlier or later than average can affect the "search for identity." (Adapted from "Growing Up" by J. M. Tanner. Copyright © September 1973 by Scientific American, Inc. All rights reserved.)

What does Erikson believe is the major conflict in early adulthood?

Stage Six, Young Adulthood: Intimacy versus Isolation
In stage six, the individual feels a need for *intimacy* in his or her life. After establishing a stable identity, a person is prepared to share meaningful love or deep friendship with others. By **intimacy,** Erikson means *an ability to care about others and to share experiences with them.* In line with Erikson's view, 75 percent of college-age men and women rank a good marriage and family life as their primary adult goal (Bachman & Johnson, 1979). And yet, marriage or sexual involvement is no guarantee that intimacy will prevail: Many adult relationships remain superficial and unfulfilling. Failure to establish intimacy with others leads to a deep sense of **isolation** (*feeling alone and uncared for in life*). This circumstance often sets the stage for later difficulties.

Stage Seven, Middle Adulthood: Generativity versus Stagnation
According to Erikson, an interest in guiding the next generation is the main source of balance in mature adulthood. This quality, called **generativity,** is expressed by

caring about oneself, one's children, and future generations. Generativity may be achieved by guiding one's own children or by helping other children (as a teacher, clergyman, or coach, for example). Productive or creative work can also express generativity. In any case, a person's concerns and energies must broaden to include the welfare of others and society as a whole. Failure in this is marked by a **stagnant** *concern with one's own needs and comforts.* Life loses meaning, and the person feels bitter, dreary, and trapped (Peterson & Klohnen, 1995).

What does Erikson see as the conflicts of old age?

Stage Eight, Late Adulthood: Integrity versus Despair
Old age is a time of reflection. According to Erikson, a person must be able to look back over life with acceptance and satisfaction. The person who has lived richly and responsibly develops a sense of **integrity** (*self-respect*). This allows the person to face aging and death with dignity. If previous life events are viewed with regret, the elderly person experiences **despair** (*heartache and remorse*). In this case, people feel that life has been a series of missed opportunities,

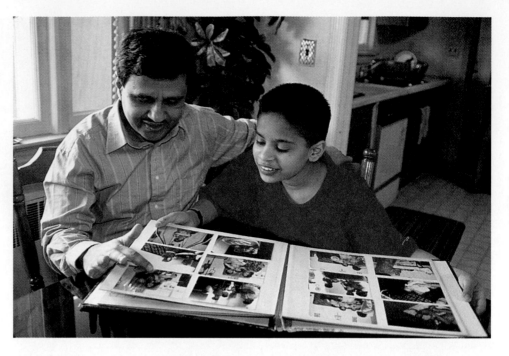

According to Erikson, an interest in future generations characterizes optimal adult development.

that they have failed, and that it is too late to reverse what has been done. Aging and the threat of death then become sources of fear and depression.

To squeeze the events of a lifetime into a few pages, we must ignore countless details. Although much is lost, the net effect is a clearer picture of an entire life cycle. Is Erikson's description an exact map of your future? Probably not. The dilemmas Erikson described do not inevitably occur at the listed ages. Also, some may be repeated at various points in life. A 50-year-old widow, for instance, may be faced with an intimacy crisis at the same time as her 25-year-old daughter (Whitbourne, 1986).

Still, the dilemmas we have discussed reflect typical psychological events in the lives of many people. Knowing about them may allow you to anticipate changes and trouble spots in life. You may also be better prepared to understand the problems and feelings of friends and relatives at various stages in the life cycle. (Table 5–2 ■ summarizes the primary dilemma in each of Erikson's stages.)

Having completed our whirlwind birth-to-death tour, we will revisit several life stages for a closer look at some of their challenges, milestones, tasks, and problems. Before we begin, it might be a good idea to complete the Learning Check that follows.

Table 5–2　■　Core Conflicts in Erikson's Psychosocial Dilemmas

Trust versus mistrust　A conflict early in life centered on learning to trust others and the world.

Autonomy versus shame and doubt　A conflict created when growing self-control (autonomy) is pitted against feelings of shame or doubt.

Initiative versus guilt　A conflict centered around learning to take initiative instead of feeling guilty about one's actions.

Industry versus inferiority　A conflict in middle childhood in which feelings of inferiority develop if industrious behavior is discouraged.

Identity versus role confusion　A major conflict of adolescence, involving the need to establish a consistent personal identity.

Intimacy versus isolation　The challenge in early adulthood of establishing intimacy with friends, family, a lover, or a spouse.

Generativity versus stagnation　A conflict of middle adulthood in which stagnant self-interest is pitted against interest in future generations.

Integrity versus despair　A conflict in old age between a sense of personal integrity versus despair over regretted life events.

Check your memory of Erikson's psychosocial dilemmas by seeing if you can correctly fill in the blanks.

Stage	Crisis	Favorable Outcome
First year of life	1. _____ vs. 2. _____	Faith in the environment and in others
Ages 1–3	Autonomy vs. 3. _____	Feelings of self-control and adequacy
Ages 3–5	4. _____ vs. guilt	Ability to begin one's own activities
Ages 6–12	Industry vs. 5. _____	Confidence in productive skills, learning how to work
Adolescence	6. _____ vs. role confusion	An integrated image of oneself as a unique person
Young adulthood	Intimacy vs. 7. _____	Ability to form bonds of love and friendship with others
Middle adulthood	Generativity vs. 8. _____	Concern for family, society, and future generations
Late adulthood	9. _____ vs. 10. _____	Sense of dignity and fulfillment, willingness to face death

11. Trying to make generalizations about development throughout life is complicated by at least one major factor. What do you think it is?

Answers:

1. trust 2. mistrust 3. shame or doubt 4. initiative 5. inferiority 6. identity 7. isolation 8. stagnation 9. integrity 10. despair 11. Different cohorts (groups of people born in the same year) live in different historical times. People born in various decades may have very different life experiences. This makes it difficult to identify universal patterns.

Problems of Childhood—Why Parents Get Gray Hair

Can you remember a time in childhood when your actions led to a disaster or a near disaster? It shouldn't be hard. It's a wonder that many of us survive childhood at all. Where I grew up, digging underground tunnels, wiggling down chimneys, hopping on trains, jumping off houses, crawling through storm drains, making bombs—and worse—were common childhood adventures.

Parenting Styles

If initiative and industry are important in childhood, what limits should parents place on a child's freedom to explore the world?

An answer is provided by psychologist Diana Baumrind (1980, 1991), who has studied the effects of three major styles of parenting. According to Baumrind, each style tends to have a distinct effect on children's behavior. See if you recognize the styles she describes.

Authoritarian parents *enforce rigid rules and demand strict obedience to authority.* Typically they view children as having few rights but adult-like responsibilities. The child is expected to stay out of trouble and to accept, without question, what parents regard as right or wrong. ("Do it because I say so.") The children of authoritarian parents are usually obedient and self-controlled. But they also tend to be emotionally stiff, withdrawn, apprehensive, and lacking in curiosity.

Overly permissive parents *give little guidance, allow too much freedom, or don't hold children accountable for their actions.* Typically, the child has rights similar to an adult's but few responsibilities. Rules are not enforced, and the child usually gets his or her way. ("Do whatever you want.") Permissive parents tend to produce dependent, immature children who misbehave frequently. Such children are aimless and likely to "run amok."

Baumrind describes **authoritative parents** as those who supply *firm and consistent guidance, combined with love and affection.* Such parents balance their own rights with those of their children. They control their children's behavior, but in a caring, responsive, non-authoritarian way. ("Do it for this reason.") Effective parents are firm and consistent, not harsh or rigid. In general, they encourage the child to act responsibly, to think, and to make good decisions. This style produces children who tend to be competent, self-controlled, independent, assertive, and inquiring (Baumrind, 1991).

As an added guide to parenting, it may help to remember that stress is a normal part of life—even in childhood. Certainly this does not mean that parents should go out of

"All right now, give Mommy the super-glue."

their way to stress a child. However, it does suggest that children need not be completely sheltered from distress. Overprotection, or "smother love," can be as damaging as overstressing a child. (**Overprotection** refers to *excessively shielding a child from ordinary stresses.*)

Most children do a good job of keeping stress at comfortable levels when *they* initiate an activity (Murphy & Moriarty, 1976). At a public swimming pool, for instance, some children can be observed making death-defying leaps from the high dive, while others stick close to the wading area. If no immediate danger is present, it is reasonable to let children get stuck in trees, make themselves dizzy, squabble with neighborhood children, and so forth. Getting into a few scrapes can help prepare a child to cope with later stresses. (Just think, if your author hadn't crawled through a few storm pipes, his adult interest in plumbing the depths of the psyche might have gone down the drain.)

How can you tell if a child is being subjected to too much stress?

Normal Childhood Problems

Child specialist Stella Chess has identified difficulties experienced at times by almost every child. These can be considered normal reactions to the unavoidable stress of growing up.

1. All children experience occasional *sleep disturbances*, including wakefulness, frightening dreams, or a desire to get into their parents' bed.

Most children do a good job of keeping stress at comfortable levels when they initiate an activity.

2. *Specific fears* of the dark, dogs, school, or a particular room or person are also common.

3. Most children will be *overly timid* at times, allowing themselves to be bullied by other children into giving up toys, a place in line, and the like.

4. Temporary periods of *general dissatisfaction* may occur, when nothing pleases the child.

5. Children also normally display periods of *general negativism* marked by tantrums, refusal to do anything requested, or a tendency to say no on principle.

6. Another normal problem is *clinging*, in which children refuse to leave the sides of their mothers or do anything on their own.

7. Development does not always advance smoothly. Every child will show occasional *reversals* or *regressions* to more infantile behavior (Chess, Thomas, & Birch, 1976).

An additional problem common to the elementary school years is **sibling rivalry** (*competition among brothers and sisters*).

It is normal for a certain amount of jealousy, rivalry, and even hostility to develop between siblings. Some sibling conflict may even be constructive. A limited amount of aggressive give-and-take between siblings provides an opportunity to learn emotional control, self-assertion, and good sportsmanship (Bank & Kahn, 1982). Parents can help keep such conflicts within bounds by not "playing favorites" and by resisting the temptation to compare one child with another. Supportive and affectionate fathering, in particular, seems to minimize conflicts and jealousy among siblings (Rolling & Belsky, 1992).

Parents should also expect to see some **childhood rebellion** (*open defiance of adult authority*). Most school-age children rebel at times against the rules and limitations imposed by parents. Being with other children offers a chance to "let off steam" by doing some of the things the adult world forbids. It is normal for children to be messy, noisy, hostile, or destructive to a moderate degree.

Keep in mind that "normal problems" that intensify or last for long periods may become serious disturbances. Some examples of more serious problems are identified in the following sections.

Serious Childhood Problems—Off to a Bad Start

By the time he was 5, Billy resembled a parent's worst nightmare. Billy threw uncontrollable temper tantrums and never seemed to sleep. He had not learned to talk. He got into closets and tore up his mother's dresses and urinated on her clothes. He smashed furniture and spread soap powder and breakfast food all over the floors. He attacked his mother at every opportunity, once going for her throat with his teeth. He tried to stuff his baby brother in a toy box. When Billy's parents bought him a doll they called by his brother's name, they began finding the doll pushed head down in the toilet bowl.

Billy refused to eat anything but cold, greasy hamburgers from a certain drive-in. To get through a week, his parents were forced to buy the hamburgers by the sack and hide them around the house, so Billy wouldn't eat them all at once. When his parents went out driving they had to detour around drive-ins to prevent Billy from frothing at the mouth and trying to jump out the window (Moser, 1965). Billy, you may note, was not an average 5-year-old.

What was his problem?

Billy was an *autistic* child. His problem is rare. Few children get off to as bad a start in life as Billy. Such severe disturbances affect only a minority of children. Nevertheless, the number of children with serious emotional and behavioral problems is larger than most people realize.

What is the nature of these problems?

Toilet-Training Disturbances

Difficulty sometimes centers on toilet training or bowel and bladder habits. The two most common problems are **enuresis** (EN-you-REE-sis: *lack of bladder control*) and **encopresis** (EN-coh-PREE-sis: *lack of bowel control*). Enuresis is more common than encopresis and many times more common among males than females.

Both wetting and soiling are sometimes an expression of frustration or pent-up hostility. But parents should not be overly alarmed by some delays in toilet training or by a few "accidents." As mentioned in Chapter 4, 30 months is the average age for completing toilet training. It is not unusual, however, for some children to take 6 months longer (age 3).

Persistent toilet training problems may be purely physical. Many bed-wetters, for instance, have difficulty because they become extremely relaxed when asleep. These children can be helped by limiting how much they drink during the evening. They should also use the toilet before going to bed, and they can be rewarded for "dry" nights. For older children, learning various self-control strategies is effective (Ronen & Wozner, 1995). Understanding, tact, and sympathy can do much to alleviate mild disturbances. Where more serious problems exist, parents should seek professional help.

Feeding Disturbances

Feeding disturbances take a variety of forms. The disturbed child may vomit or refuse food for no reason or may drastically overeat or undereat. **Overeating** (*eating in excess of daily caloric needs*) can be a serious problem. Some parents overfeed simply because they consider a fat baby healthy or desirable. Others, who feel unloved, may compensate by showering the child with "love" in the form of food. Whatever the case, overfed children develop eating habits and conflicts that have lifelong consequences.

Serious cases of undereating, or self-starvation, are called **anorexia nervosa** (AN-or-REX-yah ner-VOH-sah: *nervous loss of appetite*). The victims of anorexia nervosa are mostly adolescent females. Many seem to have conflicts about maturing sexually. By starving themselves, girls can limit figure development and prevent menstruation. This delays the time when they must face adulthood. As we will discuss in Chapter 13, pressures to conform to unrealistic standards of beauty also contribute to self-starvation (Nagel & Jones, 1992).

Pica (PIE-ka: *a craving for unnatural foods*) is another childhood eating difficulty. Some children go through a period of intense appetite during which they eat or chew on all sorts of inedible substances, such as plaster and chalk. Some children try to eat things like buttons, rubber bands, mud, or paint flakes. The latter can be quite dangerous because paint may contain lead, which is highly poisonous.

Speech Disturbances

Delayed speech (*learning to talk after the normal age for language development*) can be a serious handicap. An example is Tommy, who at age 5 was still using telegraphic speech: "Me go. Outdoor. Mama in car now. Dink Tommy cup." Delayed speech is sometimes caused by too little intellectual stimulation in early childhood. Other possible causes are parents who discourage the child's attempts to grow up, childhood stresses, mental retardation, and emotional disturbances.

Stuttering (*chronic stumbling in speech*) is a second major language problem. In the past, many parents were made to feel that they had somehow "caused" stuttering. Now, researchers believe the problem involves speech-timing mechanisms in the brain (Wieneke, Janssen, & Brutten, 1995). Stuttering is 4 times more common in males and seems to be partially inherited (Felsenfeld, 1996).

While parents may not cause stuttering, they can certainly make it worse. Children who fear that they are about to stutter are, in fact, more likely to stutter. That's why parents should avoid criticizing speech difficulties. With support from parents, and formal speech therapy, many children do overcome stuttering (Wagaman et al., 1995).

Learning Disorders

Soon after Gary entered school, he became shy and difficult. Gary's teacher suspected a learning disorder, and a specialist confirmed it. **Learning disorders** *include problems with reading, math, or writing.* A learning disorder may exist when school achievement is much lower than we would expect for a child's age and intelligence (DSM-IV, 1994). Gary's specific problem was **dyslexia** (dis-LEX-yah), *an inability to read with understanding.* Because of it, he often felt confused and "stupid" in class, although his intelligence was normal.

Approximately 10 to 15 percent of school-age children have some dyslexia, or "word blindness." When dyslexic children try to read, they often reverse letters (such as seeing *b* for *d*) and words (*was* and *saw*, for example). Some also try to read from right to left. Dyslexia appears to be caused by a malfunction of language processing areas on the left side of the brain (Hynd & Semrud-Clikeman, 1989). Dyslexia is typically treated with exercises in hearing, touch, and vision that improve reading comprehension.

Attention-Deficit Hyperactivity Disorder

One of the most significant childhood problems is **attention-deficit hyperactivity disorder** (**ADHD**) (Erk, 1995). The ADHD child is *constantly in motion and cannot concentrate.* The child talks rapidly, cannot sit still, rarely finishes work, acts on impulse, and cannot pay attention. ADHD afflicts 4 to 6 percent of all children and some adults.

Five times as many boys as girls have the problem. Unless it is carefully managed, ADHD can lead to school drop-outs and lifelong problems with antisocial behavior (Faigel et al., 1995).

What causes attention-deficit hyperactivity disorder?

Specific areas of the brain associated with language, motor control, and attention are smaller than normal in ADHD children. Something appears to interfere with normal growth in these areas before birth (Riccio et al., 1993). ADHD tends to run in families, which suggests it may be hereditary. In one striking example, doctors found that an 8-year-old boy, his father, and his grandfather all suffered from the problem (Zametkin, 1995).

Many parents believe that hyperactive behavior is triggered by eating sugar. However, as discussed in Chapter 1, sugary diets have no effect on the behavior of either normal or hyperactive children. "Sugar highs" are a myth (Wolraich, Wilson, & White, 1995).

How is ADHD treated?

Treatment for ADHD includes drugs, behavioral management approaches, and family counseling. Physicians typically use the stimulant drug Ritalin (methylphenidate) to control ADHD. It might seem that stimulants would make hyperactivity worse. But the drugs actually have a calming effect. Most likely, this is because they lengthen the ADHD child's attention span and reduce impulsiveness (Faigel et al., 1995).

Focus on a Controversy

The "Be-Good" Drug

Ritalin is a potent, amphetamine-like drug that can cause withdrawal symptoms. In view of this, it is remarkable that 5 percent (1 in 20) of all school-age boys in the U.S. take Ritalin for ADHD. The drug's possible side effects include insomnia, weight loss, irritability, depression, and a slowing of physical growth. Some children have been known to abuse Ritalin's stimulant effect by taking several doses at once.

The greatest controversy stems from concerns that Ritalin is overused. Many experts believe that drugs are sometimes being prescribed for ordinary misbehavior, not because a child actually suffers from ADHD. Ritalin does seem to be effective when the diagnosis of ADHD is accurate. The problem is that doctors, parents, and teachers may be tempted to use drugs to control children who are merely disobedient. (Sources: Guffey, 1992; Hancock, 1996; Leutwyler, 1996.)

The ADHD child's inability to hold still and pay attention can seriously disrupt learning.

Few specialists today would recommend the use of drugs to treat ADHD without also providing therapy for behavioral and emotional problems. For many children, behavior modification is as effective as drug treatment (Carlson et al., 1992). **Behavior modification** *is the application of learning principles to change or eliminate maladaptive or abnormal behavior.* (See Chapter 19 for more information.) The basic idea is to reward the ADHD child for being calm and paying attention. Children are also taught how to monitor their own behavior and how to ignore distractions. When children learn self-control in this way, improvements are more lasting than they are with drug treatment alone (Franks, 1987).

Childhood Autism

Children who suffer from **autism** (AW-tiz'm) *display an extreme preoccupation with their own thoughts, fantasies, and private impulses.* Autism is one of the most severe childhood problems. It affects 1 in 2,500 children, boys 4 times more often than girls. The autistic child is locked into a private world and appears to have no need for affection, or contact with others. Autistic children sometimes do not even seem to know or care who their parents are (Sigman, 1995).

In addition to being extremely isolated, the autistic child may throw gigantic temper tantrums—sometimes including self-destructive behavior such as head banging. Many autistic children are mute. If they speak at all, they may infuriatingly *parrot back everything said,* a response known as **echolalia** (EK-oh-LAY-li-ah). Some autistic children also engage in repetitive actions such as rocking, flapping their arms, or waving their fingers in front of their eyes. Additionally, they may show no response to an extremely loud noise (sensory blocking) or they may spend hours watching a water faucet drip (sensory "spin-out"). Finally, the autistic don't seem to understand what other people are thinking—or even that they do think. This impairment makes autistic persons very inept in social situations (Firth, 1993).

Do parents cause autism?

At one time experts blamed parents for autism. It is now recognized that autism is caused by congenital defects in the nervous system. That's why even as babies, autistic children are aloof and do not cuddle or mold to their parents' arms. Medical scans reveal that the brains of autistic adults are larger than normal. This suggests that something goes wrong during development of the autistic brain (Piven, Arndt, & Palmer, 1995).

Can anything be done for an autistic child?

Even with help, only about 25 percent of all autistic children approach normalcy and only 2 percent are able to live independently. Nevertheless, almost all autistic children can make progress with proper care. When treatment is begun early, behavior modification has been particularly successful.

Do you remember Billy, the autistic child described earlier? Billy was one of the first patients in a pioneering program designed by psychologist Ivar Lovaas. Billy was selected for the program because of his unusual appetite for hamburgers. Teaching Billy to talk illustrates one aspect of his treatment. It began with his learning to blow out a match—making a sound like "who." Each time he made the "who" sound, Billy was rewarded with a bite of his beloved hamburgers. Next he was rewarded for babbling meaningless sounds. If he accidentally said a word, he was rewarded. After several weeks, he was able to say words such as *ball, milk, mama,* and *me.* By this painstaking process, Billy was eventually taught to talk. (This process is called operant shaping; it is discussed further in Chapter 9.)

In a behavior modification program, each of an autistic child's maladaptive behaviors is altered using reward and punishment. In addition to food, therapists have found that sensory stimulation, such as tickling or music, is often very reinforcing for autistic children (Rincover & Newsom, 1985). And strangely enough, following actions such as head banging and hand biting with punishment can bring a swift end to self-destructive behavior (Haywood et al., 1982). When such efforts are combined with home treatment by parents, considerable progress can be made. A few children, in fact, approach near-normal functioning (McEachin, Smith, & Lovaas, 1993).

Autism and other severe childhood problems are a monumental challenge to the ingenuity of psychologists, educators, and parents. However, great strides have been made in the last few years. There is reason to believe that in the future even more help will be available to children who get a bad start in life.

Child Abuse—Cycles of Violence

Sadly, no account of problems in development would be complete without a brief discussion of **child abuse** (*physical or emotional harm caused by violence, mistreatment, or neglect*). Much as we might like to believe otherwise, child abuse is widespread. From 3.5 to 14 percent of all children are physically abused by parents. Even if the lower figure is right, that would mean that 2 million children are physically battered each year in the United States and Canada alone. In about one third of all cases of physical abuse, the child is seriously injured. Every year thousands of children are killed by their own parents (Finkelhor & Dziuba-Leatherman, 1994).

Characteristics of Abusive Parents

What are abusive parents like?

Abusive parents are usually young (under 30) and from lower income levels. However, professionals who treat child abuse see parents of all ages and incomes.

Abusive parents often have a high level of stress and frustration in their lives. Typical problems include depression, loneliness, marital discord, unemployment, drug abuse, divorce, family violence, heavy drinking, and work anxieties ("A Nation's," 1995; Famularo et al., 1992).

Some parents are aware they are mistreating a child but are unable to stop. Other abusive parents literally hate their children or are disgusted by them. The child's sloppiness, diapers, crying, or needs are unbearable to the parent. An abusive mother is likely to believe her child is *intentionally* annoying her (Bauer & Twentyman, 1985). In many cases, troubled parents expect the child to love them and make them happy. When the child (who is usually under 3 years old) cannot meet such unrealistic demands, the parent reacts with lethal anger.

Cycles of Violence   The core of much child abuse is a cycle of violence that flows from one generation to the next. Roughly one third of all parents who were abused as children mistreat their own children (Knutson, 1995). A second third do not routinely abuse their children, but they are likely to do so when stressed (Oliver, 1993). Such parents simply never learned to love, communicate with, or discipline a child. When does the cycle of violence begin? Sad to say, it shows up almost immediately:

Abusive Toddlers

In a study, abused 1- to 3-year-olds were observed as they interacted with playmates. The question of interest was, How do abused children react when another child is crying or distressed? In almost every instance, abused children responded to distress with fear, threats, or physical assault. (Main & George, 1985)

In short, abused children rapidly become abusive children. Later, many become abusive adults (Oliver, 1993).

How do caring parents who were abused as children differ from abusive parents who continue the cycle of violence?

Adults who break the abuse cycle are more likely to have received emotional support from a non-abusive adult during childhood or to have been in therapy. They also tend to have an emotionally supportive mate (Egeland, Jacobvitz, & Sroufe, 1988). Without such support, childhood abuse greatly increases the lifetime risk of emotional problems, substance abuse, sexual difficulties, and violence (Malinosky-Rummell & Hansen, 1993; Mullen et al., 1996).

What can be done about child abuse?

Preventing Child Abuse

Many public agencies now have teams to identify battered or neglected children. However, legal "cures" for child abuse are not very satisfactory. The courts can take custody of a child, or parents may volunteer to place the child in a foster home. Foster care may be an improvement, but it can just as easily further traumatize the child. In some cases the child is allowed to remain with the parents, but under court supervision. Even then, there is a chance of further injury, unless the parents get help. Some of the most effective programs teach parents childcare skills and how to manage stress (Wolfe & Wekerle, 1993).

Self-help groups staffed by former child abusers and concerned volunteers are also a major aid. One such group is Parents Anonymous, a national organization of parents determined to help each other stop abusing children. Local groups set up networks of members that parents can call in an abuse crisis. Participating parents learn how to curb violent impulses and how to cope with their children.

Experts recommend that a parent who is tempted to shake or strike a crying infant should try any of the following (Evans, 1993):

- Leave the room and call a friend.
- Put on some soothing music.
- Take 10 deep breaths and calm yourself; then take 10 more.
- Move to another room and do some exercise.
- Take a shower.

- Sit down, close your eyes, and vividly imagine yourself in a pleasant place.

- If none of the preceding strategies work, seek professional help. (Telephone numbers are listed at the end of this chapter.)

Dangerous Attitudes Another way of preventing child abuse is by changing attitudes. Despite newspaper and TV coverage of the problem, many parents believe it is their "right" to slap or hit their children. A survey of parents found that physical punishment is widely accepted. In a 1994 *USA Today* poll, 67 percent of adults agreed that, "a good, hard spanking" is sometimes necessary to discipline a child. For many parents, "sometimes" occurs quite often: Parents report spanking their children an average of 2.5 times a week (Holden, Coleman, & Schmidt, 1995).

As a society we seem to say, "Violence is okay if the child isn't injured; if the child is injured, then it's child abuse." Of course, when the child is injured, it's too late to take back the violence. By condoning punishment that borders on abuse, we greatly raise the chances of injury. The best solution to physical abuse, then, may lie in rethinking attitudes toward physical punishment and toward the rights of children. It is also important to remember that emotional abuse can be just as damaging as physical abuse. Parents inflict long-lasting emotional scars when they persistently humiliate, intimidate, or terrorize their children.

To face the problem squarely, we must realize that the line between acceptable discipline and child abuse is easily blurred. Fortunately, public opinion regarding spanking is starting to shift. Several states have banned spanking in schools. However, child victimization will continue as long as we as a society tolerate it (Finkelhor & Dziuba-Leatherman, 1994).

Widespread acceptance of physical punishment creates an atmosphere in which angry parents can easily lose control and abuse their children. Even parents who would never strike a child may fall prey to the "shaken baby syndrome." In such cases, an angry parent violently shakes an infant (often one that won't stop crying). The result can be brain injuries that cause mental retardation, blindness, or even death.

Learning Check	Critical Thinking
See if you can answer these questions before you continue reading.	8. Several Scandinavian countries have made it illegal for parents to spank their own children. Does this infringe on the rights of parents?

Learning Check

See if you can answer these questions before you continue reading.

1. Occasional reversals and regressions to more infantile behavior are sure signs that a significant childhood problem exists. T or F?

2. Sleep disturbances and specific fears can be a sign of significant childhood problems when they are prolonged or exaggerated. T or F?

3. A moderate amount of sibling rivalry is considered normal. T or F?

4. Encopresis is the formal term for lack of bladder control. T or F?

5. The ADHD child is lost in his or her own private world. T or F?

6. According to Diana Baumrind's research, effective parents are authoritarian in their approach to their children's behavior. T or F?

7. Approximately 30 percent of all parents who were abused as children mistreat their own children. T or F?

Critical Thinking

8. Several Scandinavian countries have made it illegal for parents to spank their own children. Does this infringe on the rights of parents?

Answers:

1. F 2. T 3. T 4. F 5. F 6. F 7. T 8. Such laws are based on the view that it should be illegal to physically assault any person, regardless of their age. While parents may believe they have a "right" to spank their children, it can be argued that children need special protection because they are small, powerless, and dependent.

Adolescence—The Best of Times, the Worst of Times

Adolescence is a time of change, exploration, exuberance, and youthful searching. It can also be a time of worry and problems, especially in today's world. It might even be fair to describe adolescence as "the best of times, the worst of times." Just in case you weren't taking notes in junior high, let's survey the challenges of this colorful chapter of life.

Adolescence and Puberty

Adolescence *is the culturally defined period between childhood and adulthood.* Socially, the adolescent is no longer a child, yet not quite an adult. Almost all cultures recognize this transitional status. However, the length of adolescence varies greatly from culture to culture. For example, most 14-year-old girls in North America live at home and go to school. In contrast, many 14-year-old females in rural villages of the Near East are married and have children (Santrock, 1995). In our culture, 14-year-olds are adolescents. In others, they may be adults.

Many people confuse adolescence with puberty. However, puberty is a *biological* event, not a social status. During **puberty,** hormonal changes promote *rapid physical growth and sexual maturity.* Interestingly, the peak **growth spurt** (*accelerated growth rate*) during puberty occurs earlier for girls than for boys (Fig. 5–2 ◆). This difference accounts for the 1- to 2-year period when girls tend to be taller than boys. (Remember going to dances where the girls towered over the boys?) For girls the onset of puberty typically occurs between 11 and 14 years of age. For most boys the age range is 13 to 16 years (Kaluger & Kaluger, 1984).

Biologically, most people reach reproductive maturity in the early teens. Social and intellectual maturity, however, may still lie years ahead. Young adolescents often make fateful decisions that affect their entire lives, even though they are immature in cognitive development, knowledge, and social experience. The tragically high rates of teenage pregnancy and drug abuse in many western nations are prime examples. The younger an adolescent becomes sexually active, delinquent, or involved with drugs, the more the resulting damage (White & DeBlassie, 1992).

When you were going through puberty, did you ever spend *hours* preparing to attend a party, dance, or other social event? If you did, you weren't alone. Puberty tends to dramatically increase body awareness and concerns about physical appearance. About one half of all boys and one third of all girls report being dissatisfied with their appearance during early adolescence (Rosenbaum, 1979). In many instances, such feelings are related to the *timing* of puberty.

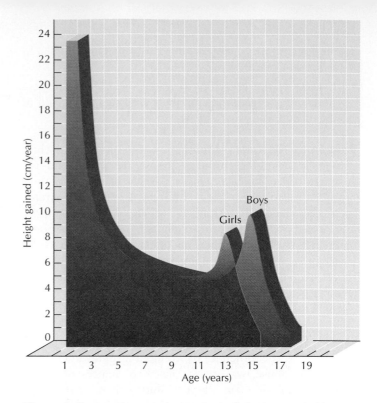

Figure 5–2 ◆ The typical rate of growth for boys and girls. Notice that growth in early adolescence equals that for ages 1 to 3. Note too the earlier growth spurt for girls.

Girls who are temporarily "too tall," boys who are "too small," and both boys and girls who lag in sexual development are likely to be upset about their bodies (Petersen et al., 1991).

How much difference does the timing of puberty make?

Early and Late Maturation Because puberty involves so many rapid changes, it can be stressful for just about anyone. When puberty comes unusually early or late, its impact may be magnified—for both good and bad.

For boys, maturing early is generally beneficial. Typically, it enhances their self-image and gives them an advantage socially and athletically (Petersen, 1987). For such reasons, early maturing boys tend to be more poised, relaxed, dominant, self-assured, and popular with their peers (Santrock, 1995). Many late maturing boys are anxious about being behind in development. However, after they catch up they tend to be more eager, talkative, self-assertive, and tolerant of themselves than average maturers.

For girls, the advantages of early maturation are less clear-cut. In elementary school, developmentally advanced girls tend to have *less* prestige among peers. They also have poorer self-images (Alsaker, 1992). Presumably, this is because they are larger and heavier than their classmates. By junior high, however, early development includes secondary sexual characteristics. This leads to a more positive body image, *greater* peer prestige, and adult approval (Brooks-Gunn & Warren, 1988). In contrast, later maturing girls

Typical clothing worn by young adolescents 40 years ago and today.

have the possible advantage of usually growing taller and thinner than early maturing girls. Other relevant findings are that early maturing girls date sooner and are more independent and more active in school; they are also more often in trouble at school (Siegel, 1982).

As you can see, there are costs and benefits associated with both early and late puberty. One added cost of early maturation is that it may force premature identity formation (Siegel, 1982). When a teenager begins to look like an adult, she or he may be treated like an adult. Ideally, this change can encourage greater maturity and independence. But what happens when a person is treated as an adult before he or she is emotionally ready? Then the search for identity may end too soon, leaving the person with a distorted, poorly formed sense of self.

Focus on a Controversy

Hurried into Adulthood?

Psychologist David Elkind (1981) believes that many parents are hurrying their children's development. Elkind is concerned about parents who try to raise their babies' IQs, force them to "read" flash cards, or have them swimming and doing gymnastics before they are 3 months old. Such pushing, he believes, partly explains why more children have recently begun to show serious stress symptoms. Moreover, hurried children are turning into hurried teenagers—urged by parents and the media alike to grow up fast. Elkind believes that too many teenagers are left without the guidance, direction, and support they need to become healthy adults (Elkind, 1984). In part, this occurs because many parents are too busy dealing with demands outside the family and expect their children to "take care of themselves" (Elkind, 1995).

Elkind's main point is that today's teenagers have adulthood thrust on them too soon. Violence, drug abuse, X-rated movies, youth crime, teenage pregnancy, divorce and single parent families, date rape, aimless schools—all this, and more, strikes Elkind as evidence that there is no place for teenagers in today's society.

According to Elkind, the traditional **social markers** of adolescence have all but disappeared. (Markers are *visible or tangible signs that indicate a person's social status or role*—such as a driver's license or a wedding ring.) As an example, Elkind notes that clothing for children and teenagers is increasingly adult-like. Girls especially are urged to wear seductive clothing and revealing swimsuits.

Clearly, Elkind is stating a clinical opinion. It's possible that his view exaggerates the problem somewhat—indeed, much of what he says is debatable. Nevertheless, his portrayal of hurried adolescents as "all grown up with no place to go" is highly thought provoking.

Search for Identity

As discussed earlier, many psychologists regard identity formation as a key task of adolescence. To be sure, problems of identity occur at other times too. But in a very real sense, puberty signals that it's time to begin forming a new, more

From Birth to Death: Life-Span Development   **141**

mature self-image. Many problems during adolescence stem from unclear standards about the role young people should play within society. Are they adults or children? Should they be autonomous or dependent? Should they work or play? Such ambiguities make it difficult for adolescents to form clear images of themselves and of how they should act (Alsaker, 1995).

Answering the question, "Who am I?" is also spurred by cognitive development. After adolescents have attained the stage of formal operations, they are better able to ask questions about their place in the world and about morals, values, politics, social relationships, and private thoughts. Then too, being able to think about hypothetical possibilities allows the adolescent to contemplate the future and ask more realistically, "Who will I be?" (Suls, 1989).

David Elkind has noted an interesting pattern in adolescent thought. According to Elkind (1984), many teenagers are preoccupied with **imaginary audiences** (*people they imagine are watching them*). In other words, teenagers may act like others are aware of their thoughts and feelings. Sometimes this leads to painful self-consciousness—as in thinking that *everyone* is staring at a bad haircut you just received. The imaginary audience also seems to underlie attention-seeking "performances" involving outlandish dress or behavior. In any case, adolescents become very concerned with controlling the impressions they make on others (Santrock, 1995). For many, being "on stage" in this way helps define and shape an emerging identity.

What effects do parents have on identity formation?

Parents and Peers The adolescent search for identity frequently leads to conflict with parents. This is especially true in early adolescence (Eccles et al., 1993). However, some disagreement with parents is probably necessary for growth of a separate identity. A complete lack of conflict may mean that the adolescent is afraid to seek independence.

Actually, adolescents and parents usually agree to a large degree about basic topics such as religion, marriage, and morals. The biggest conflicts tend to be over superficial differences in styles of dress, manners, social behavior, and the like. Adolescents naturally desire more freedom, but they do not want their parents to abruptly abandon them. Teenagers do best when they are given gradual increases in personal freedom and more opportunities to make decisions. Problems occur when parents crack down too hard or throw their hands up and surrender control over an adolescent's behavior (Eccles et al., 1993).

In high school were you a jock, preppy, brain, hacker, surfer, cowboy, punk, mod, rapper, druggy, warthog, dervish, gargoyle, or aardvark? (Well, okay, I made up the last four—the rest are real.) Increased identification with *peer groups* is quite common during adolescence. A **peer group** *consists of people who share similar social status*. To an extent, membership in such groups gives a measure of security and a sense of identity apart from the family. Beyond this, group

I never really knew my father; he was always videotaping me.

© 1993 CHRONICLE FEATURES

membership provides practice in belonging to a social network. Children tend to see themselves more as members of families and small friendship groups, not as members of society as a whole. Therefore, gaining a broader, member-of-society perspective can be a major step toward adulthood (Hill, 1993).

Membership in friendship groups, cliques, "posses," or "crews" helps adolescents build an identity apart from their relationship to parents. However, over-identification with a clannish group that rejects anyone who looks or acts different can limit personal growth.

But aren't groups also limiting?

Yes, they are. Conformity to peer values peaks in early adolescence, but it remains strong at least through high school (Newman, 1982). Throughout this period there is always a danger of allowing group pressure to **foreclose** (*shut down*) personal growth (Newman & Newman, 1987). By the end of high school, many adolescents have not yet sufficiently explored various interests, values, vocations, skills, or ideologies on their own. Perhaps this is why many students view moving on to work or college as a chance to break out of earlier roles—to expand or reshape personal identity. For many who choose college, the effect may be more a matter of placing further changes in identity on hold. By doing so, college students keep open the possibility of changing majors, career plans, personal style, and so on. Typically, commitment to an emerging adult identity grows stronger in later college years (Santrock, 1995).

Minority Youth and the Search for Identity

As they define an adult identity, minority youths often face a barrage of prejudice and negative stereotypes from the majority culture (Spencer, 1990). In many ways, society seems to say to them, "You are invisible," "You are bad," or "You are not one of us." This discourages contact with members of the majority culture and limits the "trying on" of various identities and values.

For such reasons, and others as well, minority adolescents run a high risk of adopting a personal identity prematurely (Spencer & Markstron-Adams, 1990). The danger in this is that it severely limits the exploration of various life paths. Too often, these "foreclosed" identities take forms such as gang member, school drop-out, unskilled laborer, unmarried parent, or "second-class citizen."

Minority youths, of course, share the same hopes, dreams, and aspirations as any other social group. As psychologist Margaret Beale Spencer (1990) says, "Broader American culture could be enriched by the talents, creativity, and intelligence of minority youngsters who have been provided the opportunity to reach their potentials." Before that can happen, minority youths need to feel that they have a positive role to play in society. Enhanced group pride, educational opportunities, positive models, and a more tolerant society could do much to keep a broad range of options open to *all* of today's adolescents (Blechman, 1992).

The search for identity may intensify during adolescence, but it does not end there. For example, the process of selecting a career often starts in childhood and continues into young adulthood. In the next section we will take a brief look at this interesting aspect of personal development.

Vocational Choice— Charting a Course in the World of Work

John was always an excellent student, but his real love was sports. Being on the track team was, in fact, the high point of his college career. (About 7 feet high, to be exact. John was a high-jumper.) After he graduated, John was hired by a large accounting firm at an enviable starting salary. Yet within 2 years, John knew he had made a mistake. Accounting left him dissatisfied, restless, and often bored.

In college, John's career choice seemed highly practical. Now he was miserable. What could he do about it? John decided to take a chance. He quit his job, and after several years of additional education, financial hardship, and personal sacrifice, he accepted his first college coaching position.

Vocational Choice

As John's story illustrates, vocational decisions are neither permanent nor easily undone. Usually, by the time a person has selected a career path, it takes a big effort to change course. Moreover, changing careers can be a major risk. (What if John had discovered that he also disliked coaching?) The reality that John faced is illustrated by a survey in which 44 percent of those polled said that for better or worse, they felt "locked into" their current jobs (Renwick & Lawler, 1979). Clearly, there is value in making good vocational choices, and in making them early, if possible.

Career Development Career development refers an *entire career path*, from choosing an initial occupation through retirement. John's abrupt change is somewhat unusual. For people who enter professions, career development tends to flow through four broad phases (Fig. 5–3 ◆). These are: (1) the **exploration phase,** *during which an initial search for a career is made*; (2) the **establishment phase,** *during which the person finds a job, enters a career, develops competence, and gains status*; (3) the **midcareer phase,** *which is a stable period of high productivity and acceptance by co-workers*; and (4) the **later career phase,** *a time before retirement when the individual serves as a respected expert* and often as a mentor (role model and guide) for younger workers (Van Maanen & Schein, 1977).

Figure 5–3 ◆ A model of career development. The exploration phase can be divided into three substages of vocational choice.

Of the four phases, the one most likely to be of immediate relevance to you is exploration. Let's probe this phase in more depth.

How do most people choose their vocations?

During the exploration phase, most people go through a recognizable series of stages as they choose a vocation (Ginzberg, 1984).

In the **fantasy stage,** children under age 10 simply *imagine what they want to be when they grow up.* The roles they fantasize—such as president, pilot, rock star, rodeo rider, or TV announcer—may be unrealistic, but they do show that children realize that they will need to work someday.

During the **tentative stage** (roughly, ages 10 to 18) adolescents *begin to form more realistic, if somewhat general, ideas about what they want to do.* However, their plans may shift several times during this period, and they typically remain tentative. Toward the end of high school, many students begin to more fully appreciate the importance of choosing a vocation. They also become aware that there are limits to their options and barriers to certain careers.

After high school, various social and practical pressures lead most people to narrow their range of vocational options. During this **realistic stage,** *the first steps are taken to find out what specific jobs are like and to prepare for one.* At this time, many college students use course work to discover what they are good at and what holds their interest.

By the early 20s, most people begin to carry out their vocational plans. This involves completing necessary training and landing that important first job.

The preceding description implies that most people carefully choose a vocation or career. Actually, vocational choice is frequently rather haphazard (Janis & Wheeler, 1978). For example, it is not unusual for students to allow a tentative choice of a major to determine school course work. Soon, they find themselves channeled into a career path—without really having made a clear decision.

How would a person go about improving the quality of his or her vocational choice?

To begin with, it helps to recognize that our attraction to certain jobs or careers is influenced by many factors. Some of the more important influences are socioeconomic status, intelligence, school achievement, family background, gender, and personal interests (Kaplan & Stein, 1984). As much as these factors may influence your own choice, it is also important to realize that you have the potential to succeed in a variety of occupations. In fact, the best single predictor of what job category you will enter is your **vocational aspiration,** which is simply *what you tell yourself you would like to do.*

The world of work is complex and rapidly changing. In the face of such changes, it is becoming more important to make careful, informed decisions about what kind of work to pursue. To make sure your vocational choice will be realistic and personally rewarding, you must (1) gain an accurate understanding of various occupations and (2) get a clear picture of your own interests, needs, and goals.

That seems obvious. But how?

Vocational Counseling A good way to improve occupational choice is to consult a **vocational counselor.** These professionals are *counseling psychologists who specialize in matching people with jobs.* A vocational counselor can help you clarify your career goals, and she or he can administer vocational interest and aptitude tests to guide your choice. Many colleges now have **career centers,** *which offer testing and career guidance.* These centers also typically hold a wealth of information about various jobs and careers. Many offer computerized programs that guide students through the initial steps of career decision making (Katz, 1993).

If formal guidance is unavailable, you will have to serve as your own "vocational counselor." A good way to start is to consult the *Occupational Outlook Handbook,* available in most libraries. This book provides objective information about the outlook for various occupations. The *Handbook* includes job descriptions, information on training requirements, average earnings, and the number of jobs likely to be available in coming years. A simple look at such facts could prevent many students from pursuing over-populated careers (law, for instance).

To find out what a particular job is really like may require more initiative. In many occupations the nature of the work is not what it seems from the outside. For instance, medical students are often dismayed when they first begin to realize that disease is ugly and that many medical procedures are distasteful. To find out beforehand what an occupation is like, it is advisable to talk to several people in that line of work. Be sure to ask your informants what they dislike about their jobs, as well as what they like. If possible, you might even spend a day observing people in an occupation that interests you.

Beginning a career is only one of the major challenges of adulthood. We'll explore others in a moment. Before you read more, here's a chance to check your progress.

Learning Check

1. In most societies, adolescence begins with the onset of puberty and ends with its completion. T or F?

2. Early maturing boys tend to experience more clear-cut advantages than do early maturing girls. T or F?

3. According to David Elkind, the traditional markers of adolescence and adulthood have been blurred. T or F?

4. The imaginary audience refers to conformity pressures that adolescents believe adults apply to them. T or F?

5. The establishment phase of career development is a time during which an initial search for career possibilities is made. T or F?

6. Many people go through a _____ stage and a _____ stage before they become more realistic about choosing a career.

7. The best single predictor of what occupations college students will enter is their IQ scores. T or F?

Critical Thinking

8. Elkind suggests that many adolescents are "hurried into adulthood." Yet, many young people live at home longer than ever before (often into their early 20s). Does this contradict Elkind's thesis?

Answers:

1. F 2. T 3. T 4. F 5. F 6. fantasy, tentative 7. F 8. Not necessarily. Prolonged dependence on parents appears to be based on economic pressures, not on an extension of adolescent social status.

Challenges of Adulthood—Charting Life's Ups and Downs

After a "settling down" period somewhere in the 20s, adult development is uniform and uninteresting, right? Wrong! A fairly predictable series of challenges is associated with development from adolescence to old age.

What personality changes and psychological developments can a person look forward to in adulthood?

Further study has added important detail to the events discussed by Erikson. One informative account is based on clinical work by Roger Gould, a psychiatrist interested in adult personality. Gould's research (1975) reveals that common patterns for North American adults are as follows.

Ages 16–18: Escape from Dominance
Ages 16 to 18 are marked by a struggle to escape from parental dominance. Efforts to do so cause considerable anxiety about the future and conflicts about continuing dependence on parents.

Ages 18–22: Leaving the Family
The majority of people break away from their families in their early 20s. Leaving home is usually associated with building new friendships with other adults. These friends serve as substitutes for the family and as allies in the process of breaking ties.

Ages 22–28: Building a Workable Life
The trend in the mid-20s is to seek mastery of the real world. Two dominant activities are striving for accomplishment (seeking competence) and reaching out to others. Note that the second activity corresponds to Erikson's emphasis on seeking intimacy at this time. Married couples in this age group tend to place a high value on "togetherness."

Ages 29–34: Crisis of Questions
Around the age of 30 many people experience a minor life crisis. The heart of this crisis is a serious questioning of what life is all about. Assurance about previous choices and values tends to waver. Unsettled by these developments, the person actively searches for a style of living that will bring meaning to the second half of life. Marriages are particularly vulnerable during this time of dissatisfaction. Extramarital affairs and divorces are common symptoms of the "crisis of questions."

Ages 35–43: Crisis of Urgency
People of ages 35 to 43 are typically beginning to become more aware of the reality of death. Having a limited number of years to live begins to exert pressure on the individual. Intensified attempts are made to succeed at a career or to achieve one's life goals. Generativity, in the form of nurturing, teaching, or serving others, helps alleviate many of the anxieties of this stage.

Ages 43–50: Attaining Stability
The urgency of the previous stage gives way to a calmer acceptance of one's fate in the late 40s. The predominant feeling is that the die is cast and that former decisions can be lived with. Those who have families begin to appreciate their children as individuals and ease up on their tendency to extend their own goals to their children's behavior.

Age 50 and Up: Mellowing
After age 50 a noticeable mellowing occurs. Emphasis is placed on sharing day-to-day joys and sorrows. There is less concern with glamour, wealth, accomplishment, and abstract goals. Many of the tensions of earlier years give way to a desire to savor life and its small

pleasures. (A recent study of typical life goals and concerns at various ages parallels many of the points made by Gould. See Table 5–3 ■.)

Where does the mid-life crisis fit in?

A Mid-life Crisis?

Difficulty at the midpoint of life is far from universal. Many people thrive during this period and have no special problems. However, psychologist Daniel Levinson did an in-depth study of adults and learned what a "mid-life crisis" looks like if one does occur. Levinson (1978, 1986) identified five periods during adulthood when people typically make major transitions (Table 5–4 ■). A **transition period** *ends one life pattern and opens the door to new possibilities* (Levinson, 1986). At such times, people address concerns about themselves, their work, and their relationships.

Levinson's first study focused on the lives of men. As they approached the mid-life transition (between the ages of 37 and 41), most men went through a period of instability, anxiety, and change. (Notice that this corresponds closely to Gould's crisis-of-urgency period.) In a later study, Levinson found that most of what he learned about men's lives also applies to women (Levinson & Levinson, 1996).

Of the men Levinson studied, roughly half defined the mid-life period as a "last chance" to achieve their goals. Such goals were often stated as a key event, such as reaching a certain income, or becoming a supervisor, a full professor, a shop steward, and so forth. For these individuals the mid-life period was stressful, but manageable.

A smaller percentage of men experienced a serious mid-life decline. Often, this pattern was based on having chosen a dead-end job or lifestyle. In some cases it meant that subjects had achieved material success but felt that what they were doing was pointless.

In a third pattern, a few hardy individuals appeared to "break out" of a seriously flawed life structure. For them, a decision to "start over" was typically followed by 8 to 10 years of rebuilding.

In what ways does the mid-life transition differ for women?

Compared with men, Levinson found that women were less likely to enter adulthood with clearly formulated "goals." As a result, they were less likely to define "success" in terms of some key event. Rather than focusing on external goals, changes in personal identity tended to define the mid-life transition for women. For example, a woman might become more self-reliant and independent—qualities she may have regarded as "masculine" earlier in life (Levinson & Levinson, 1996).

In summary, it can be seen that the mid-life crisis, if it takes place at all, can be both a danger and an opportunity. Ideally the mid-life transition is a time of reworking old identities, of achieving long-sought goals, of finding one's own truths, and of preparing for later maturity and aging. It is important to emphasize again, however, that many lives differ greatly from the generalized summaries given here. Adult development is complex and each person's path is unique. At the very least, however, we can say that both men and women repeatedly move through cycles of stability and transition in their adult lives (Ornstein & Isabella, 1990).

Using Psychology

Making Career Decisions

Why do adults always ask children what they want to be when they grow up?
Because they're looking for good ideas.

Making career transitions is one of the major challenges of adulthood. One way to improve career decisions is to examine how you approach them. Psychologist Irving Janis and Dan Wheeler (1978) have described how people typically deal with work dilemmas, especially those that lead to a major change in jobs or careers. Their analysis suggests that there are four basic coping styles. See if you recognize yourself in any of the following descriptions.

Table 5–3 ■ Typical Life Goals and Concerns		
	Typical Goals are Related to:	**Typical Concerns are Related to:**
Young adults	Education and family	Relationships and friends
Middle-aged	Children's lives and personal property	Occupational worries
Elderly	Good health, retirement, leisure, community	Health fears

Nurmi, 1992.

The Vigilant Style This style is the most effective of the four. It describes individuals who evaluate information objectively and make decisions with a clear understanding of the alternatives. Persons using this style make mental "balance sheets" to weigh possible gains and losses before taking action.

The Complacent Style Persons of this type drift along with a nonchalant attitude toward job decisions. They tend to let chance direct their careers and to take whatever comes along without really making plans.

The Defensive-Avoidant Style These people are fully aware of the risks and opportunities presented by career choices and dilemmas. However, they are uncomfortable making decisions. This leads them to procrastinate, rationalize, and make excuses for their inaction and indecision.

The Hypervigilant Style People with this style more or less panic when forced to make career decisions. They may collect hundreds of job announcements and brochures, but they become so frantic that making logical decisions is nearly impossible.

These coping styles may seem exaggerated, but they are easy to observe when people are forced to change jobs or make major alterations in career plans. To relate

Table 5–4 ■ Three Views of Developmental Challenges		
Erikson	**Gould**	**Levinson**
CHILDHOOD		
Trust/mistrust (1)		
Autonomy/shame, doubt (1–3)		
Initiative/guilt (3–5)		
Industry/inferiority (6–12)		
ADOLESCENCE		
Identity/confusion (12–18)	Escape from dominance (16–18)	Early adulthood transition (17–22)
EARLY ADULTHOOD		
Intimacy/isolation	Leaving the family (18–22)	Early adulthood transition (17–22)
	Building a workable life (22–28)	
	Crisis of questions (29–34)	Age 30 transition (28–33)
MIDDLE ADULTHOOD		
Generativity/self-absorption	Crisis of urgency (35–43)	
	Attaining stability (43–50)	Midlife transition (40–45)
	Mellowing (50+)	Age 50 transition (50–55)
LATE ADULTHOOD		
		Late adult transition (60–65)
OLD AGE		
Integrity/despair		

them to yourself, think about how you have handled vocational decisions to date, or decisions about your college career. Of the four, Janis and Wheeler consider only the vigilant style to be constructive. With this insight, you may be able to improve the quality of your career decisions.

Middle Age

When individuals reach their 40s and 50s, declining vigor, strength, and youthfulness make it clear that more than half their years are gone. At the same time, greater stability comes from letting go of the "impossible dream." That is, there is an increased attempt to be satisfied with the direction one's life has taken and to accept that hoped-for life goals may no longer be possible.

For most women during this era, menopause represents the first real encounter with growing "old" (Kirk, 1995). At **menopause,** which occurs at an average age of 51, *monthly menstruation ends,* and a woman is no longer able to bear children. At the same time, the level of the hormone estrogen drops—sometimes causing changes in mood or appearance. Menopause also can cause physical symptoms, such as "hot flashes" (a sudden uncomfortable sensation of heat) or night sweats. Many of the small discomforts of menopause appear to be related to a disruption of bodily rhythms. They are, in other words, a little like suffering from jet lag (Gannon, 1993).

A few women find menopause as difficult to adjust to as adolescence, and some experience anxiety, irritability, or depression at this time. Most women, however, are neutral about the loss of reproductive ability. Many, in fact, express relief at being freed from concerns about pregnancy, birth control, and menstruation. All considered, the vast majority of women easily take "the pause" in stride, with no major emotional problems (Matthews et al., 1990).

Do men go through similar changes?

Males do not undergo any physical change that is directly comparable to menopause. With aging, the production of the male hormone testosterone gradually lessens. However, men remain fertile at this time. On the other hand, aging males may be affected by changes in appearance and physical vigor. Some 40- to 60-year-old males do appear to pass through a **climacteric** (kly-MAK-ter-ik: *"change of life"*). But their symptoms (depression, anxiety, irritability) are probably psychological in origin.

Well-being at Mid-life The pitfalls of adulthood are all too familiar: marital discord, divorce, career difficulties, unemployment, health problems, financial pressures, legal conflicts, and personal tragedies—to name but a few. How do people maintain a state of well-being as they run the gauntlet of modern life?

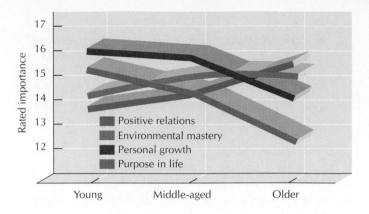

Figure 5–4 ◆ Feelings of personal growth and that one has a purpose in life tend to decline with increasing age. However, positive relations with other people and mastery of the environment tend to increase. Thus, the basis for a continued sense of well-being makes an interesting shift between young adulthood and old age. (Graph courtesy of Dr. Carol Ryff.)

Psychologist Carol Ryff (1995) has proposed that well-being during adulthood consists of six elements:

- Self-acceptance
- Positive relations with others
- Autonomy (personal freedom)
- Environmental mastery
- A purpose in life
- Continued personal growth

Based on a national survey, Ryff found that personal growth and having a sense of purpose in life tend to decline with increasing age. However, these declines are offset by increases in two other areas (Fig. 5–4 ◆). As people age, positive relations with others tend to increase, as does mastery of the complex demands of life (Ryff & Keyes, 1995).

Thus, sharing life's joys and sorrows with others, coupled with a better understanding of how the world works, can help carry people through the mid-life period and into their later years.

After the late 50s, the problems an individual faces in maintaining a healthy and meaningful life are complicated by the inevitable process of aging. How unique are the problems of older people, and how severely do they challenge the need to maintain integrity and personal comfort? We will look at some answers in the next section.

Aging—Will You Still Need Me When I'm 64?

Some years ago, students at Long Beach City College in California elected Pearl Taylor their spring festival queen. Ms. Taylor had everything necessary to win: looks, intelligence, personality, and campus-wide popularity. At about the same time, citizens of Raleigh, North Carolina, elected Isabella Cannon as their mayor.

What's so remarkable about these events?

Not too much really, except that Pearl was 90 years old when elected, and Isabella was 73. Both are part of the graying of America. Currently, some 35 million North Americans are over the age of 65. By the year 2020, some 60 million persons in the U.S. and Canada, or *1 out of every 5*, will be 65 years of age or older (Fig. 5–5 ◆). These figures make the elderly the fastest-growing segment of society. Understandably, psychologists have become increasingly interested in aging. You should be too. If you are now in your 20s, you will be part of the "grandparent boom" in 2020 (Taeuber, 1993).

What is life like for the aged?

There are large variations in aging. Most of us have known elderly persons at both extremes: those who are active, healthy, satisfied, lucid, and alert; and those who are confused, child-like, dependent, or senile. Despite such variations, some generalizations can be made.

The Course of Aging

Biological aging refers to *age-related changes in physiological functioning.* Aging is a gradual process that begins quite early in life. Peak functioning in most physical capacities reaches a maximum by about 25 to 30 years of age (Fig. 5–6 ◆). Thereafter, gradual declines occur in muscular strength, flexibility, circulatory efficiency, speed of response, sensory acuity, and other functions (Birren & Fisher, 1995b). Given the natural course of aging, it is extremely unlikely that a 50-year-old, or even a 40-year-old, will ever hold the world record for the 100 meter dash (Schulz & Heckhausen, 1996).

So people are "over the hill" by 30?

Figure 5–5 ◆ Longer life expectancy will produce an unprecedented increase in the percentage of the population over age 65. The "boom" is expected to start at the turn of the century and peak by about the year 2030 (Taeuber, 1993).

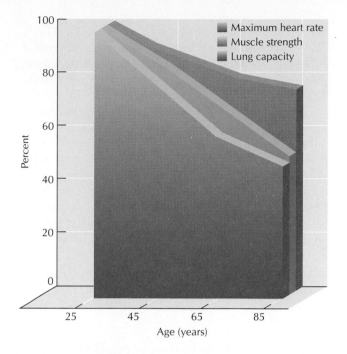

Figure 5–6 ◆ Physical aging, which is biologically programmed, progresses steadily from early adulthood onward. Regular exercise, good health practices, and a positive attitude can help minimize the impact of physical aging.

Hardly! Prime abilities come at different ages for different activities. Peak performances for professional football and baseball players usually occur in the mid-20s; for professional bowlers, the mid-30s; for artists and musicians, the 50s; and for politicians, philosophers, business or industrial leaders, and others, the early 60s (Fig. 5–7 ◆).

For those who are still young, physical aging may be the greatest threat of old age. However, it is wrong to believe that most elderly people are sickly, infirm, or senile. Only about 5 percent of those over 65 years old are in nursing homes. In fact, the percentage of elderly who are chronically disabled has declined significantly in the last 10 years (Manton & Stallard, 1991). As for the possibility of a mental slide, physician Alex Comfort comments, "The human brain does not shrink, wilt, perish, or deteriorate with age. It normally continues to function well through as many as 9 decades."

the maximum human life span place it around 110 to 120 years. The oldest documented age ever achieved is 120 years, by Shigechiyo Izumi, a Japanese stevedore. Among the more than 5 billion persons currently living, only 2 or 3 will reach the age of 115.

For most people, **life expectancy** (*the actual number of years the average person lives*) is shorter than the maximum life span. In the 1800s the average life expectancy was 36 years. Now, average life expectancy at birth for American males is 73 years, and for females it is 81 years. With improved health care, life expectancy should move even closer to the maximum life span.

At present there is no known way to extend the maximum human life span. On the other hand, there is every reason to believe that life expectancy can be increased. If you would personally like to add to a new, higher average, here are some deceptively simple rules for living a long life (Coni et al., 1984):

1. Do not smoke.

2. Use alcohol in moderation or not at all.

3. Avoid becoming overweight.

4. If you suffer from high blood pressure, have it treated.

5. Remain socially and economically active in retirement.

6. Exercise regularly throughout life.

To this we can add: Get married (married persons live longer), learn to manage stress, and choose long-lived parents!

Gerontologists (jer-ON-TOL-o-jists: *those who study aging*), estimate that only 25 percent of the disability of old people is medical. The remaining 75 percent is social, political, and cultural. This view is backed up by intelligence test scores, which decline little with aging. Although it is true that **fluid abilities** (*those requiring speed or rapid learning*) may diminish, many **crystallized abilities** (*learned knowledge and skills*), such as vocabulary and stored-up facts, actually improve—at least into the 60s (Schaie, 1994). (See Figure 5–8 ◆.)

Many elderly persons are at least as mentally able as the average young adult. On intellectual tests, top scorers over the age of 65 match the average for men under 35. What sets these silver-haired stars apart? Typically they are people who have continued to work and remain intellectually active (Weintraub et al., 1994). Gerontologist Warner Schaie (1994) found that you are most likely to stay mentally sharp in old age if:

1. You remain healthy.

2. You live in a favorable environment (you are educated, have a stimulating occupation, above-average income, and an intact family).

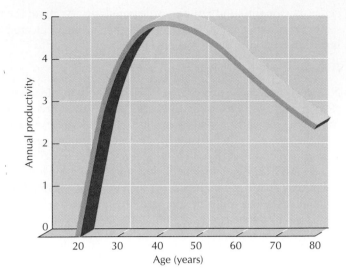

Figure 5–7 ◆ At what point during life are people most productive? On average, when do people make their greatest contributions to fields such as science, literature, philosophy, music, and the visual arts? No matter how achievement is tallied, productivity tends to rise rapidly to a single peak that is followed by a slow decline. The graph you see here is typical of contributions to the field of psychology. Fields such as poetry, pure math, and theoretical physics have earlier peaks, around the early 30s or even the late 20s. Other fields, such as novel writing, history, philosophy, medicine, and scholarship are marked by peaks in the late 40s, 50s, or even 60s. (After Simonton, 1988.)

Comedian George Burns continued an active career as an entertainer well into his 90s. Aging does not inevitably bring an end to creative work. Many artists, writers, composers, poets, and scientists have continued to make contributions to society during the eighth and ninth decades of their lives.

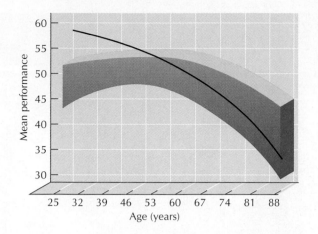

Figure 5-8 ◆ Average performance at various ages for verbal, numeric, spatial, and reasoning abilities all fall within the blue area of this graph. Notice that in general, mental abilities show modest gains from young adulthood to early middle age. After that, they begin a slow decline. Notice, too, that most abilities at age 70 return to about the same levels found at age 25. Only after age 80 do declines become large enough to make a practical difference in mental abilities. One exception is perceptual speed (black line). This fluid ability declines steadily after age 25. (Adapted from Schaie, 1994.)

3. You are involved in intellectually stimulating activities (reading, travel, cultural events, continuing education, clubs, professional associations).

4. You have a flexible personality.

5. You are married to a smart spouse.

6. You maintain your perceptual processing speed.

7. You were satisfied with your accomplishments in mid-life.

In general, what kind of person adjusts most successfully to aging?

Activity and Disengagement   Two main theories have been proposed to explain successful adjustment to aging. **Disengagement theory** *assumes that it is normal and desirable for people to withdraw from society as they age* (Cumming & Henry, 1961). According to this theory, the elderly welcome disengagement since it relieves them of roles and responsibilities they are less able to fulfill. Likewise, society benefits from disengagement, as younger persons with new energy and skills fill positions vacated by aging individuals.

Certainly we have all known people who disengaged from society as they grew older. Nevertheless, disengagement theory seems to describe successful aging as a retreat. While disengagement may be common, it is not necessarily ideal (Clair, Karp, & Yoels, 1994).

What does the second theory say?

The second theory of optimal aging is a sort of "use-it-or-lose-it" view. **Activity theory** *assumes that activity is the essence of life for people of all ages.* Activity theory predicts that people who remain active physically, mentally, and socially will adjust better to aging (Havighurst, 1961).

Proponents of activity theory believe that aging persons should maintain the activities of their earlier years for as long as possible. If a person is forced to give up particular roles or activities, they should be replaced with others. That way, the aging person is able to maintain a better self-image, greater satisfaction, and more social support—resulting in more successful aging.

Which theory is correct?

The majority of studies support the *activity theory*, although there have been exceptions (Clair, Karp, & Yoels, 1994). At the same time, some people do seek disengagement, so neither theory is absolutely "correct." Actually, successful aging probably requires a combination of continued activity and selective disengagement.

Learning to compensate for age-related changes is one of the keys to remaining active and happy in old age. Another is spending as much time as possible doing the things one finds meaningful (Brandstadter et al., 1993; Glass et al., 1995; Horn & Meer, 1987). In general, people age best when they are able to maintain *control* of their lives (Schulz & Heckhausen, 1996).

Ageism   You have almost certainly encountered ageism in one way or another. **Ageism,** which refers to *discrimination or prejudice based on age,* can oppress the young as well as the old. For instance, a person applying for a job may just as well be told, "You're too young," as "You're too old." In some societies ageism is based on respect for the elderly. In Japan, for instance, aging is seen as positive, and greater age brings more status and respect (Kimmel, 1988). In most Western nations, however, ageism tends to have a negative impact on older individuals. Usually, it is expressed as a rejection of the elderly. As Alex Comfort points out, the concept of "oldness" is often used to expel people from useful work: Too often, retirement is just another name for dismissal and unemployment.

Stereotyping is a major facet of ageism. Popular stereotypes of the "dirty old man," "meddling old woman," "senile old fool," and the like, help perpetuate the myths underlying ageism. Contrast such images to those associated with youthfulness: The young are perceived as fresh, whole, attractive, energetic, active, emerging, and appealing. Yet, even positive stereotypes can be a problem. For example, if older people are perceived as financially well off, wise, or experienced, it can blind others to the real problems of the elderly (Gatz & Pearson, 1988). The important point is that age-based stereotypes are often wrong. A tremendous diversity exists among the elderly—ranging from the infirm and senile, to aerobic-dancing grandmothers.

What can be done about ageism?

Social centers and exercise programs for senior citizens are a direct expression of the benefits predicted by activity theory. Remaining active may also give older persons a feeling of *control* over their lives. As we will discuss further in Chapter 14, feelings of control contribute to mental and physical well-being.

Countering Myths about Aging

One of the best ways to combat ageism is to counter stereotypes with facts. For example, studies show that in many occupations older workers perform better at jobs requiring *both* speed and skill (Giniger et al., 1983). Gradual slowing with age is a reality. But often, workers can compensate for it with experience, skill, or expertise (Schaie, 1988). One study, for instance, showed that older typists responded slower on reaction-time tests than younger typists. Nevertheless, there was no difference in the actual typing speeds of younger and older typists (Salthouse, 1987). Rather than basing retirement on a person's age, it would make more sense, perhaps, to base it on job performance (Birren & Fisher, 1995a).

Taking a broader view, Bernice Neugarten (1971) examined the lives of 200 people between the ages of 70 and 79. Neugarten found that 75 percent of these people were satisfied with their lives after retirement. Similarly, another study found that only 30 percent of retirees find retirement stressful (Bosse et al., 1991). Neugarten's findings also refuted other myths about aging.

1. Old persons generally do not become isolated and neglected by their families. Most *prefer* to live apart from their children.

2. Old persons are rarely placed in mental hospitals by uncaring children.

3. Old persons who live alone are not necessarily lonely or desolate.

4. Few elderly persons ever show signs of senility or mental decay, and few ever become mentally ill.

In the United States, commercial airline pilots are required to retire at age 60. However, in the 35 years since this age was set, many changes have taken place in life expectancy and the nature of flying. There is no reason why a person who is physically healthy cannot continue flying beyond age 60. Actual job performance is probably the best measure of a pilot's ability to continue working (Birren & Fisher, 1995b). The same is true of most jobs.

In short, most of the elderly studied by Neugarten were integrated, active, and psychologically healthy.

Enlightened views of aging call for an end to the forced obsolescence of the elderly. As a group, older people represent a valuable source of skill, knowledge, and energy that we can't afford to cast aside. As we face the challenges of this planet's uncertain future, we need all the help we can get!

Death and Dying— The Curtain Falls

DEAR ABBY: Do you think about dying much? (*signed*) CURIOUS

DEAR CURIOUS: No, it's the last thing I want to do.

"I'm not afraid of dying. I just don't want to be there when it happens." Woody Allen

"Why not? Why not?" Timothy Leary (his last words before dying)

"To die well is no less an accomplishment than to live well." Sogyal Rinpoche

Death is a topic of importance to us all. The statistics on death are very convincing: One out of one dies. In spite of this, there tends to be a conspiracy of silence surrounding death. As a result, most of us are poorly informed about a process that is as basic as birth.

We have seen in this chapter that it is valuable to understand major trends in the course of development. With this in mind, let us now explore emotional responses to death, the inevitable conclusion of every life.

Fears of Death

Fears of death are not so extensive as might be supposed. In a poll of adults, only about 4 percent directly feared their own death (Kastenbaum & Aisenberg, 1972). It might seem that as people grow older they would fear death more. However, older persons actually have fewer death fears than younger people. Older people more often fear the *circumstances* of dying, such as pain or helplessness, rather than death itself (Thorson & Powell, 1990).

These findings seem to indicate a general lack of death fears, but they may actually reflect a widespread denial of death. Notice how denial is apparent in the language used to talk about death: Often we speak of a dead person as having "passed away," "expired," "gone to God," or "gone to rest" (Morgan, 1995).

Many people have little direct experience with death until they, themselves, are fairly old (Morgan, 1995). The average person's exposure to death consists of the artificial and unrealistic portrayals of death on TV. By the time the

Death may be inevitable, but it can be faced with dignity and, sometimes, even humor. Mel Blanc's famous sign-off, "That's all folks," is engraved on a marble headstone over his grave. Blanc was the voice of Bugs Bunny, Porky Pig, and many other cartoon characters.

average person is 17 years old, she or he will have witnessed roughly 18,000 TV deaths. With few exceptions these will have been *homicides*, not deaths due to illness or aging.

Reactions to Impending Death

A more direct account of emotional responses to death comes from the work of Elizabeth Kübler-Ross (1975). Kübler-Ross is a **thanatologist** (THAN-ah-TOL-oh-jist: *one who studies death*). Over the years she has spent hundreds of hours at the bedsides of the terminally ill, where she has observed emotional reactions to impending death. Five basic reactions are described here.

1. Denial and isolation. A typical first reaction is to *deny death's reality and isolate oneself from information* confirming that death is really going to occur. Initially the person may be sure that "It's all a mistake." "Surely," he or she thinks, "the lab reports have been mixed up or the doctor made an error." This sort of denial may proceed to attempts to avoid any reminder of the situation.

2. Anger. Many dying individuals *feel anger and ask, "Why me?"* As they face the ultimate threat of having life torn away, their anger may spill over into rage toward the living. Even good friends may temporarily evoke anger because their health is envied.

3. Bargaining. In another common reaction, the terminally ill *bargain with themselves or with God*. The dying person thinks, "Just let me live a little longer and I'll do anything to earn it." Individuals may bargain for time by trying to be "good" ("I'll never smoke again"), by righting past wrongs, or by praying that if they are granted more time they will dedicate themselves to their religion.

4. Depression. As death draws near and the person begins to recognize it cannot be prevented, *feelings of futility, exhaustion, and deep depression may set in*. The person realizes she or he will be separated from friends, loved ones, and the familiar routines of life, and this causes a profound sadness.

5. Acceptance. If death is not sudden, many people manage to *come to terms with dying and accept it calmly*. The person who accepts death is neither happy nor sad, but at peace with the inevitable. Acceptance usually signals that the struggle with death has been resolved. The need to talk about death ends, and silent companionship from others is frequently all the person desires.

Not all terminally ill persons display all these reactions, nor do they always occur in this order. Individual styles of dying vary greatly, according to emotional maturity, religious belief, age, education, the attitudes of relatives, and so forth. Generally, there does tend to be a movement from initial shock, denial, and anger toward eventual acceptance of the situation. However, some people who seem to have accepted death may die angry and raging against the inevitable. Conversely, the angry fighter may let go of the struggle and die peacefully. In general, one's approach to dying will mirror his or her style of living (DeSpelder & Strickland, 1995).

It is best not to think of Kübler-Ross' list as a fixed series of stages to go through in order. It is an even bigger mistake to assume that someone who does not show all the listed emotional reactions is somehow deviant or immature (Shneidman, 1987). Rather, the list describes typical reactions to impending death. Note, as well, that many of the same reactions accompany any major loss, be it divorce, loss of a home due to fire, death of a pet, or loss of a job.

How can I make use of this information?

First, it can help both the dying and survivors to recognize and cope with periods of depression, anger, denial, and bargaining. Second, it helps to realize that close friends or relatives may feel many of the same emotions before or after a person's death because they, too, are facing a loss.

Perhaps the most important thing to recognize is that the dying person needs to share feelings with others and to discuss death openly. Too often, dying persons feel isolated and separated from others by the wall of silence erected by doctors, nurses, and family members. Adults tend to "freeze up" with someone who is dying, saying such things as, "I don't know how to deal with this."

Understanding what the dying person is going through may make it easier for you to offer support at this important time. A simple willingness to be with the person and to honestly share his or her feelings can help bring dignity, acceptance, and meaning to death.

Emotional reactions to impending death tell us little about what it is actually like to die. As you will soon discover, however, many people have "died" and then lived to tell about it. Let's see what we can learn from their very close encounters with death.

Near-Death Experiences— Back from the Brink

The emergency room doctors work feverishly over a heart attack victim. "I think we've lost him," says one of the doctors. The patient, who appears to have died, hears the doctor's words, then a buzzing sound. From somewhere above, he sees his own lifeless body on the table. Then he enters a dark tunnel and passes into an area of bright light. There, he is met by a "being of light" who shows him a rapid playback of his entire life. At some point he reaches a barrier. He is completely at peace and feels engulfed by love, but he knows he must go back. Suddenly, he is in his body again. One of the doctors exclaims, "Look, his heart's beating!" The patient recovers. For the rest of his life, he is profoundly affected by his journey to the threshold of death and back.

The preceding description contains all the core elements of a **near-death experience (NDE)** (*a pattern of experiences that may occur when a person is clinically dead and then resuscitated*). During an NDE, people typically experience all or most of the following: a feeling of separation from their body, entering darkness or a tunnel, seeing a light, entering the light, a life review, feeling at peace.

Many people regard NDEs as spiritual experiences that seem to verify the existence of an afterlife. In contrast, medical explanations attribute NDEs to the physiological reactions of an oxygen-starved brain (Fig. 5–9 ◆). Indeed, many elements of NDEs can be produced by other conditions, such as hallucinogenic drugs, migraine headaches, general anesthetics, extreme fatigue, high fever, or just falling asleep.

While debate about the meaning of NDEs continues, one thing is certain: Near-death experiences can profoundly change personality and life goals. Many near-death survivors claim that they are no longer motivated by greed, competition, or material success. Instead, they become more concerned about the needs of other people.

There is a degree of comfort in knowing that people who have "died" and lived to tell about it were

Figure 5–9 ◆ Visual sensations in the form of a tunnel of light or a spiral can be induced by many conditions other than near-death experiences. Such patterns appear to be related to activity in the visual cortex of the brain—especially those that occur when the brain is deprived of oxygen (Blackmore, 1993).

not frightened or in pain. Beyond that, perhaps we can learn something from such close encounters with death. As many near-death survivors have learned, death can be an excellent yardstick for measuring what is really important in life. (Sources: Blackmore, 1991b, 1993; Kellehear, 1993; MacHovec, 1994; Moody, 1975; Ring, 1980.)

Bereavement and Grief

Typically, a period of grief follows **bereavement** (*the loss of a friend or relative to death*). **Grief** (*intense sorrow and distress*) is a natural and normal reaction as survivors adjust to their loss. Bereavement can make a person feel vulnerable or worthless. It typically changes one's views of the world and the future. Understandably, there's a lot to work through emotionally when you lose someone you love (Gluhoski, 1995).

Grief tends to follow a predictable pattern (Parkes, 1979; Schulz, 1978). Usually, grief begins with a period of **shock** *or emotional numbness.* For a brief time the bereaved remain in a dazed state in which they may show little emotion. Most find it extremely difficult to accept the reality of their loss. This phase usually ends by the time of the funeral, which unleashes tears and bottled-up feelings of despair.

Initial shock is followed by sharp **pangs of grief.** These are *episodes of painful yearning for the dead person* and, sometimes, anguished outbursts of anger. During this period the wish to have the dead person back is intense. Often,

As cultural rituals, funerals and memorial services are rites of separation and leave-taking. Funerals encourage a release of emotion and provide a sense of closure for survivors, who must come to terms with the death of a loved one (Morgan, 1995).

From Birth to Death: Life-Span Development | **155**

mourners continue to think of the dead person as alive. They may hear his or her voice and see the deceased vividly in dreams. For some time, agitated distress alternates with silent despair, and suffering is acute.

The first powerful reactions of grief gradually give way to weeks or months of **apathy** (*listlessness*), **dejection** (*demoralization*), and **depression** (*deep despondency*). The person faces a new emotional landscape with a large gap that cannot be filled. Life seems to lose much of its meaning, and a sense of futility dominates. The mourner is usually able to resume work or other activities after 2 or 3 weeks. However, insomnia, loss of energy and appetite, and similar signs of depression may continue.

Little by little, the bereaved person accepts what cannot be changed and makes a new beginning. Pangs of grief may still occur, but they are less severe and less frequent. Memories of the dead person, though still painful, now include positive images and nostalgic pleasure. At this point, the person can be said to be moving toward **resolution** (*acceptance and rebuilding*). For many people, the pain of grieving will have eased considerably by the end of about one year (Lindstrom, 1995). However, it is not unusual for 2 to 3 years to pass before grief is fully resolved. At a lower level of intensity, mourning the loss of someone you love can continue indefinitely (Rando, 1995).

As was true of approaching death, individual reactions to grief vary considerably. The amount of pain a person feels depends on his or her personality, relationship to the deceased, the nature of the death (Was it natural, a homicide, suicide, peaceful, agonized?), and the bereaved person's social situation—especially the amount of support she or he receives from others (Rando, 1995).

Is it true that suppressing grief causes more problems later?

It has long been assumed that suppressing grief may lead to more severe and lasting depression. However, there is little evidence to support this idea. A lack of intense grief does not usually predict later problems (Bonanno et al., 1995). Bereaved persons should work through their grief at their own pace and in their own way—without worrying about whether they are grieving too much or too little. Time doesn't heal all wounds, but with the passage of time the pain of loss does lessen (Reif, Patton, & Gold, 1995).

Grief allows survivors to discharge their anguish, but it may not prepare them to go on living. Typically they must also do **grief work,** in which they *actively adapt to their loss and integrate changes into their lives* (Rando, 1995). Some suggestions for coping with grief follow.

Coping with Grief

- Acknowledge and accept that the person is gone.
- Face the loss directly and do not isolate yourself.
- Discuss your feelings with relatives and friends.
- Do not block out your feelings with drugs or alcohol.
- Allow grief to progress naturally; neither hurry nor suppress it.
- Honor the memory of the deceased, but accept the need to rebuild your life. (Coni et al., 1984; Rando, 1995)

A Look Ahead   The subject of death brings us full circle in the cycle of life. In the upcoming Applications section, we will return to the topic of parenting, a process that deeply links the lives of adults and children. But first, a word from your conscience: It's time for a Learning Check.

Learning Check	Critical Thinking

Check your comprehension with these questions.

1. Building a workable life tends to be the dominant activity during which age range?
   a. 18–22   **b.** 22–28   **c.** 29–34   **d.** 35–43

2. Levinson's description of the "mid-life crisis" corresponds roughly to Gould's
   a. escape from dominance   **b.** crisis of questions   **c.** crisis of urgency
   d. settling-down period

3. The vigilant style of making career choices is characterized by panic and illogical decisions. T or F?

4. The average male experiences menopause between the ages of 45 and 50. T or F?

5. Many indications of biological aging start to become evident as early as the mid-20s. T or F?

6. An expert on the problems of aging is called a _____ .

7. The activity theory of optimal aging holds that aging individuals should restrict their activities and withdraw from former community activities. T or F?

8. After age 65, a large proportion of older people show significant signs of senility and most require special care. T or F?

9. In the reaction that Kübler-Ross describes as bargaining, the dying individual asks, "Why me?" T or F?

10. A dazed state of shock or numbness is typical of the first phase of grief. T or F?

11. Most evidence supports the idea that suppressing grief leads to later problems, such as severe depression. T or F?

12. Why might you reasonably question Gould's and Levinson's accounts of adult development?

Answers:

1. b 2. c 3. f 4. F 5. T 6. gerontologist 7. F 8. F 9. F 10. T 11. F 12. As mentioned, Levinson's studies only involved men. Also, both Gould and Levinson may be describing typical patterns of adult development in western societies. It is doubtful that these patterns apply equally well to all cultures.

*R*aising children draws many of the problems of development into a single arena. When parenting is effective, both adult and child benefit. When parents fail to give their children a good start in life, everybody suffers—the child, the parents, and society as a whole. In addition to the skills needed for achievement, capable parents give children a capacity for love, joy, responsibility, and fulfillment.

Most people discipline their children in the same way they were disciplined. Unfortunately, this means that many parents make the same mistakes their parents did (Covell, Grusec, & King, 1995).

What can parents do to promote healthy development in their children?

Two key ingredients of effective parenting are communication and discipline. In each area, parents can set an example that goes beyond merely dispensing "dos" and "don'ts."

Rearing Children

No psychologist would deny that love is essential for healthy development, but **discipline** (*guidance regarding acceptable behavior*) can be equally important. Parents with unmanageable, delinquent, or unhappy children often can honestly claim that they give them lots of love. Yet when parents fail to provide guidelines for behavior, children become antisocial, aggressive, and insecure. As noted earlier in this chapter, overly permissive parents—those who allow themselves to be dominated or manipulated—create lifelong patterns of self-serving behavior in their children.

Does this mean that discipline should be strict and unbending?

No. Recall that authoritarian parenting also has undesirable effects on children. Families are not military boot camps. Children are no more comfortable with autocratic commands than adults are. As stated before, effective discipline is fair but loving, authoritative yet sensitive. The goal is to socialize a child without destroying the bond of love and trust between parent and child. One 22-year-long study found that children whose parents are critical, harsh, or authoritarian often become self-absorbed adults. They also have a higher than average record of violence and substance abuse (Dubow et al., 1987; Weiss et al., 1992).

How can a balance be maintained?

Consistency Discipline should give children freedom to express their deepest feelings through speech and actions.

However, this does not mean freedom to do entirely as one pleases. It means that the child can move freely within well-defined guidelines for acceptable behavior. Of course, individual parents may choose limits that are more "strict" or less "strict." But this choice is less important than **consistency** (*maintaining stable rules of conduct*). Consistent discipline gives a child a sense of security and stability. Inconsistency makes the child's world seem unpredictable.

What does consistency in child management mean in practice?

To illustrate the errors that parents often make, let's consider some examples of *inconsistency* (Fontenelle, 1989). The following are mistakes to avoid.

- Saying one thing and doing something else. You tell the child, "Bart, if you don't eat your Brussels sprouts you can't have any dessert." Then you feel guilty and offer him some dessert.

- Making statements you don't mean. "If you don't quiet down I'm going to stop the car and make you walk home."

- Overstating consequences. "Look what you did to the flower bed. You can't ever ride your bike again."

- Changing *no* to *yes*, especially to quiet a nagging child. A good example is the parent who first refuses to buy the child a toy, and later gives in and buys it.

- Not checking to see if the child has actually done something you requested, such as picking up clothes or making a bed.

- Contradicting the rules your spouse has set for the child. Parents need to agree on child discipline and not undermine each other's efforts.

- Not meaning what you say the first time. Children quickly learn how many times they can be warned before they are actually about to be punished.

- Responding differently to the same misbehavior. One day a child is sent to his room for fighting with his sister. The next day the fighting is overlooked.

Random discipline makes children feel angry and confused because they cannot control the consequences of their own behavior. Inconsistency also gives children the message: "Don't believe what I say because I usually don't mean it."

Effects of Child Discipline

Consistent or not, parents tend to base discipline on one or more of the following techniques: power assertion, withdrawal of love, or child management (Coopersmith, 1968; Hoffman, 1977).

Power assertion refers to *physical punishment or a show of force* in which parents take away toys or privileges. As an alternative, some parents use **withdrawal of love** (*withholding affection*) by refusing to speak to a child, by threatening to leave, by rejecting the child, or by otherwise acting as if the child is temporarily unlovable. **Management techniques** *combine praise, recognition, approval, rules, reasoning,* and the like to encourage desirable behavior. Each of these approaches can effectively control a child's behavior, but their side effects differ considerably.

What are the side effects?

Power-oriented techniques—particularly harsh or severe physical punishment—are associated with fear, hatred of parents, and a lack of spontaneity and warmth. Severely punished children also tend to be defiant, rebellious, and aggressive (Patterson, 1982). Sadly, power assertion remains the most frequently used type of discipline (Papps et al., 1995).

Withdrawal of love produces children who tend to be self-disciplined. We might say that such children have developed a good conscience. Often, they are described as "model" children or as unusually "good." But as a side effect, they are also frequently anxious, insecure, and dependent on adults for approval.

Management techniques also have limitations. Most important is the need to carefully adjust them to a child's level of understanding. Younger children may not always see the connection between rules, explanations, and their own behavior. In spite of this limitation, management techniques receive a big plus in another area. Psychologist Stanley Coopersmith (1968) found a direct connection between parental styles of discipline and a child's *self-esteem.*

Question: What is self-esteem?

Self-Esteem   The term **self-esteem** refers to *regarding oneself as a worthwhile person.* High self-esteem is essential for emotional health. Individuals with low self-esteem place a low value on themselves as people.

In direct studies of children, Coopersmith found that low self-esteem is related to physical punishment and the withholding of love. High self-esteem, in contrast, was related to management techniques that emphasized clear and consistent discipline, high parental interest, and concern for the child. Thus it seems best for parents to minimize physical punishment and to avoid unnecessary withdrawal of love. Children who feel that their parents support them emotionally tend to have high self-esteem (Nielsen & Metha, 1994).

Are you saying that physical punishment and withdrawal of love should not be used?

Guidelines for Parents   Effective parents use each of the three major types of discipline at one time or another, and each has its place. Coopersmith's findings simply suggest that physical punishment and withdrawal of love should be used with caution. In using these two forms of punishment, parents should observe the following guidelines (also see Chapter 9).

1. Parents should separate disapproval of the act from disapproval of the child. Instead of saying, "I'm going to punish you because *you are bad,*" say, "I'm upset about *what you did.*"

2. State specifically what misbehavior you are punishing. Explain why you have set limits on this kind of conduct.

3. Punishment should never be harsh or injurious to a child. Don't physically punish a child while you are angry. Also remember that giving a child the message "I don't love you right now" can be more painful and damaging than any spanking.

4. Punishment is most effective when it is administered immediately. This statement is especially true for younger children.

5. Spanking and other forms of physical punishment are not particularly effective for children under age 2. The child will only be confused and frightened. Spankings also become less effective after age 5 because they tend to humiliate the child and breed resentment.

6. Many psychologists believe that children should never be physically punished. If you do choose to use physical punishment, reserve it for situations that pose an immediate danger to the younger child; for example, when a child runs into the street.

7. Remember, too, that it is usually more effective to reinforce children when they are being good than it is to punish them for misbehavior.

After age 5, management techniques are the most effective form of discipline, especially techniques that emphasize communication. It is not possible here to discuss all of the methods used by effective parents. Instead, we will focus on several principles that apply broadly to parenting.

Effective Parenting

Parenting experts Don Dinkmeyer and Gary McKay (1989) believe that there are four basic ingredients of a positive parent-child relationship.

CALVIN AND HOBBES COPYRIGHT 1986 WATTERSON. REPRINTED WITH PERMISSION OF UNIVERSAL PRESS SYNDICATE. ALL RIGHTS RESERVED.

■ **Mutual respect.** Effective parents try to avoid nagging, hitting, debating, and talking down to their children. They also avoid doing things for their children that children can do for themselves. (Constantly stripping children of opportunities to learn and take responsibility prevents them from becoming independent and developing self-esteem.)

■ **Shared enjoyment.** Some time each day, effective parents spend time with their children, doing something that both the parent and child enjoy.

■ **Love.** This goes almost without saying, but many parents assume their children know that they are loved. It is important to communicate your caring by words and by actions such as hugging.

■ **Encouragement.** Children who receive frequent encouragement come to believe in themselves. In authoritarian households the child's sense of worth comes from getting rewards and avoiding punishments from powerful parents. Effective parents don't just praise their children for "winning," for "success," or for "good" behavior. They encourage their children by recognizing *progress and attempts to improve.*

In practice, encouragement means:

■ Valuing and accepting children.

■ Pointing out positive aspects of a child's behavior.

■ Showing faith in children; letting them try things on their own.

■ Giving recognition for effort and improvement.

■ Showing appreciation for the child's contributions to the family.

Communication between Parents and Children

Creative communication is the core of successful child management (Bath, 1996). Child expert Haim Ginott (1965) believed that making a distinction between feelings and behavior is the key to clear communication. Since children (and parents, too) do not choose how they will feel, it is important to allow free expression of feelings.

Accepting Feelings The child who learns to regard some feelings as "bad," or unacceptable, is being asked to deny a very real part of his or her experience. Ginott encouraged parents to teach their children that all feelings are appropriate; it is only actions that are subject to disapproval. Many parents are unaware of just how often they block communication about their children's feelings. Consider this typical conversation excerpted from Ginott's book (1965):

Son: I am stupid, and I know it. Look at my grades in school.

Father: You just have to work harder.

Son: I already work harder and it doesn't help. I have no brains.

Father: You are smart, I know.

Son: I am stupid, I know.

Father: (loudly) You are not stupid!

Son: Yes, I am!

Father: You are not stupid. Stupid!

By debating with the child, the father misses the point that his son *feels* stupid. It would be far more helpful for the father to encourage the boy to talk about his feelings.

How could he do that?

He might say, "You really feel that you are not as smart as others, don't you? Do you feel this way often? Are you feeling bad at school?" In this way, the child is given a chance to express his emotions and be understood. The father might conclude the conversation by saying, "Look, son, in my eyes you are a fine person. But I understand how you feel. Everyone feels stupid at times."

Encouragement   Again, it is valuable to remember that supportive parents encourage their children. In terms of communication, encouragement sounds like this (Dinkmeyer & McKay, 1989):

"It looks like you enjoyed that."

"I have confidence in you, you'll make it."

"It was thoughtful of you to _____ ."

"Thanks. That helped a lot."

"You really worked hard on that."

"You're improving. Look at the progress you've made."

I-Messages   Communication with a child can also be the basis of effective discipline. Thomas Gordon (1970), a child psychologist who has developed a program called Parent Effectiveness Training (PET), offers a useful suggestion. Gordon believes that parents should send *I-messages* to their children, rather than *you-messages*.

What's the difference?

You-messages take the form of threats, name-calling, accusing, bossing, lecturing, or analyzing. Generally, you-messages tell children what's "wrong" with them.

An **I-message** *tells children what effect their behavior had on you*. To illustrate the difference, consider this example. After a hard day's work, Susan wants to sit down and rest awhile. She begins to relax with a newspaper when her 5-year-old daughter starts banging loudly on a toy drum. Most parents would respond with a you-message:

"You go play outside this instant." (bossing)

"Don't ever make such a racket when someone is reading." (lecturing)

"You're really pushing it today, aren't you?" (accusing)

"You're a spoiled brat." (name-calling)

"You're going to get a spanking!" (threatening)

Gordon suggests sending an I-message such as, "I am very tired, and I would like to read. I feel upset and can't read with so much noise." This forces the child to accept responsibility for the effects of her actions.

To summarize, an I-message states the behavior to which you object. It then clearly tells the child the consequence of his or her behavior and how that makes you feel. Here's a "fill-in-the-blanks" I-message: "When you (state the child's behavior), I feel (state your feelings) because (state the consequences of the child's behavior)."

For example, "When you go to Jenny's without telling me, I worry that something might have happened to you because I don't know where you are" (Dinkmeyer & McKay, 1989).

Natural and Logical Consequences   Sometimes events automatically discourage misbehavior. For example, the child who refuses to eat dinner will get uncomfortably hungry. A child who throws a temper tantrum may gain nothing but a sore throat and a headache if the tantrum is ignored (Fontenelle, 1989). In such instances, a child's actions have **natural consequences** (*intrinsic effects*). In situations that don't produce natural consequences, parents can set up **logical consequences** (*rational and reasonable effects*). For example, a parent might say, "We'll go to the zoo when you've picked up all these toys," or "You can play with your dolls as soon as you've taken your bath," or "You two can stop arguing or leave the table until you're ready to join us."

The concept of logical, parent-defined consequences can be combined with I-messages to handle many day-to-day instances of misbehavior. The key idea is to use an I-message to set up consequences and then give the child a choice to make: "Michelle, we're trying to watch TV. You may settle down and watch with us or go play elsewhere. You decide which you'd rather do" (Dinkmeyer & McKay, 1989).

How could Susan have dealt with her 5-year-old—the one who was banging on a drum?

A response that combines an I-message with logical consequences would be, "I would like for you to stop banging on that drum; otherwise, please take it outside." If the child continues to bang on the drum inside the house, then she has caused the toy to be put away. If she takes it outside, she has made a decision to play with the drum in a way that respects her mother's wishes. In this way, both parent and child have been allowed to maintain a sense of self-respect and a needless clash has been averted.

After you have stated consequences and let the child decide, be sure to respect the child's choice. If the child repeats the misbehavior, you can let the consequences remain in effect longer. But later, give the child another chance to cooperate.

With all child management techniques, remember to be firm, kind, consistent, respectful, and encouraging. And most of all, try every day to live the message you wish to communicate.

Learning Check

1. Effective discipline gives children freedom within a structure of consistent and well-defined limits. T or F?

2. Coopersmith found that high self-esteem in childhood is related to discipline based on either management techniques or withdrawal of love. T or F?

3. Spankings and other physical punishments are most effective for children under the age of 2. T or F?

4. Authoritarian parents view children as having few rights but many responsibilities. T or F?

5. I-messages are a gentle way of accusing a child of misbehavior. T or F?

6. In situations where natural consequences are unavailable or do not discourage misbehavior, parents should define logical consequences for a child. T or F?

Critical Thinking

7. From the standpoint of learning, why is consistency in child discipline so important?

Answers:

1. T 2. F 3. F 4. T 5. F 6. T 7. Because much learning is based on the consequences that follow responses. In addition to fostering clear communication, consistent rewards and punishments shape the behavior patterns that children learn.

*I*n 1967, Mr. Bedford, a psychology professor from Glendale, California, died at the age of 73. His body was immediately frozen—submerged in liquid nitrogen—making him the first person in the United States to try to cheat death by cryonic suspension. Mr. Bedford's story is only one indication of changing attitudes toward dying.

For some, death is a sudden tragedy. For others, it is a long-wished-for release. Whatever the case, death—the last phase of life—is something we all must face. It therefore behooves each of us to know something about death. In this section we will add to our earlier discussion of death by considering four departures from traditional approaches to dying. These are the hospice movement, passive euthanasia, active euthanasia, and cryonics.

Hospice

At the beginning of this century most people died at home. Today, more than 70 percent of all deaths in the U.S. and Canada take place outside the home, most often in a hospital or nursing home. Just as some people have begun to question traditional funeral practices (embalming, viewing, elaborate and expensive caskets and ceremonies), many now question treatment of the terminally ill. Too often, dying persons are isolated, frightened, in pain, and stripped of control over their final days of life. The hospice concept was created to counter this situation.

A **hospice** *provides supportive care for the terminally ill.* Hospices may be housed in medical centers or they may combine temporary in-patient care with care at home. Hospice care neither hastens nor postpones death. The goal is to improve the quality of life in the person's final days. The first hospice was created in recognition of dying individuals' needs to be included, to know that someone still cares, to maintain control over their lives, and to have a say in their own death. In operation, the first hospices presented a striking contrast to the grim wards for the terminally ill found in many hospitals (Lattanzi-Licht & Connor, 1995).

How is a hospice different?

First, there are lots of people present. A hospice offers support, counseling, guidance, and companionship from volunteers, other patients, staff, clergy, and visitors. Friendship and kindness are expressed toward patients so that when the time comes to die, they know they will be remembered with respect and love. This support from others is a major factor in how well people cope with dying (Dobratz, 1995).

Second, the atmosphere differs markedly from that of a traditional hospital. A hospice attempts to provide pleasant surroundings, an atmosphere of intentional informality, and a sense of continued living for patients. Unlimited around-the-clock visits are permitted by relatives, friends, children, and even pets. Patients receive constant attention, play games, make day trips, have pre-dinner cocktails if they choose, enjoy entertainment, and visit with volunteers. In short, life goes on for them.

A third aspect of hospice care is the freedom of choice allowed to patients. Patients decide about their own diets, activities, and whether they want to continue medical care. Patients can also choose freedom from intolerable pain. This is usually achieved by giving drugs, such as morphine, in dosages that relieve pain without making the person groggy (Larson, 1990).

Many communities in the United States now have hospice programs or free-standing hospice facilities. In either case, treatment for the terminally ill has drastically improved. Even tradi-

tional hospitals are doing a better job—largely as a result of pioneering efforts in the hospice movement.

A Right to Die?

The "right to die" concept might be better stated as a right to live in peace and comfort until death. Much of the interest in this issue began with the Karen Ann Quinlan case. In 1975 Karen lapsed into a coma after suffering an overdose of drugs and alcohol. After doctors said she would never recover, Karen's parents began a legal fight to turn off the respirator and other devices being used to prolong her life. In 1976 the New Jersey Supreme Court issued a landmark decision giving permission to the parents to order removal of Karen's life-support equipment. Despite the doctors' prediction, Karen continued to live for another 10 years. She died in 1985 at the age of 31.

Is there a right to die? Doctors and other medical personnel are legally and morally bound to prolong and preserve life. Likewise, in most states relatives and guardians cannot legally give permission to remove life-supporting equipment. One way out of this dilemma that is gaining support is the **living will** (*a declaration that a person's life should not be artificially prolonged*). The intent of a living will is to free the terminally ill from a slow and cruel death, allowing death with dignity. The will is made out when the person is still healthy, and states that, in the event of terminal illness (as diagnosed by two or more doctors), the person does not want to have life sustained by medical machines or heroic measures.

A living will is not yet binding in most states, but it does make clear the wishes of terminally ill persons who can't speak for themselves. The following excerpt is from one widely used living will.

A Living Will

If at such a time the situation should arise in which there is no reasonable expectation of my recovery from extreme physical or mental disability, I direct that I be allowed to die and not be kept alive by medications, artificial means or "heroic measures." I do, however, ask that medication be mercifully administered to me to alleviate suffering even though this may shorten my remaining life. (Reprinted with permission from Concern for Dying, 250 West 57th Street, New York, NY, 10017.)

To make sure your living will is effective you should do the following: Use a form that is recognized by your state's laws. Obtain signatures of the required number of witnesses, preferably non-relatives. Ask your doctor whether she or he will honor your wishes. If so, give your physician a copy of your living will. Give copies of your living will to several close friends and relatives. Periodically review your living will and revise it if necessary.

Euthanasia

The right to die won for Karen Quinlan by her parents may be thought of as **passive euthanasia** (YOU-tha-NAY-zyah), in which *death is allowed to occur but is not actively caused*. In **active euthanasia,** or "physician assisted suicide," *steps would be taken at a patient's request to deliberately hasten death,* perhaps by administering drugs that induce death painlessly. Both forms of euthanasia present ethical dilemmas for physicians, who are trained to keep patients alive. On the other hand, doctors are sworn to *humane* treatment. With the second point in mind, proponents of euthanasia believe that it is a basic human right to die with dignity and a minimum of discomfort (Markson, 1995).

To a degree, passive euthanasia is already practiced in North America. However, it is done quietly here, without legal protection for doctors. In the Netherlands and parts of Australia, doctors are allowed to help patients die, as long as certain safeguards are followed. The patient has to be terminally ill, in pain, mentally competent, and must repeatedly express a wish to die (Shapiro & Bowermaster, 1994). Should active euthanasia ever become legal in other countries (many people find the idea totally unacceptable), it might also become possible for next of kin to request euthanasia for an incapacitated individual.

There are several arguments against euthanasia. The case of Karen Delahanty of Avon, Connecticut, provides a good starting point. After a head-on automobile accident, Karen entered a coma from which doctors predicted she would never recover. One year later she miraculously regained consciousness. What if euthanasia had been carried out?

Other questions that arise, in addition to unexpected recovery, include: What guarantee is there that the choice of euthanasia would be made freely and without pressure (Hendin, 1995)? Would the infirm feel that it is their "duty" to die, to avoid being a burden to families? Can family members be trusted to make a correct decision? Would they feel guilt afterward? What about the medical personnel involved; how would they respond emotionally to "mercy killing"? (Shapiro & Bowermaster, 1994). No doubt you can think of other objections.

Cryonics

To complete our brief sampling of new approaches to death, let's return to cryonics. **Cryonic suspension** *involves freezing a person's body (or head) immediately after death*. The idea is to keep the person frozen until medical science perfects ways to thaw, restore, and revive the person. Those who have been placed in cryonic suspension obviously are gambling that if they are revived, a cure will exist for whatever killed them.

In the United States, public debate about euthanasia has focused on Dr. Jack Kevorkian, a retired pathologist. Dr. Kevorkian has been charged with murder for assisting several suicides. To date, he hasn't been convicted, but the legal debate continues. It is perhaps unfortunate that Dr. Kevorkian is in the spotlight since some of the people he has "helped die" were not terminally ill. In the Netherlands, euthanasia is not permitted in such cases. Only hopelessly terminal patients, who are suffering dire physical and emotional pain, are candidates for legal, doctor-assisted euthanasia.

Does freezing actually work?

Cryonic suspension must be viewed as a symbolic attempt to cheat death or perhaps as an emotional hedge against the finality of death. At this point, cryonic suspension is impractical because freezing does serious damage to the body. The ice crystals formed by freezing and unfreezing the human brain would almost surely turn it to mush—wiping out most or all of the memories stored there. If persons frozen at death were ever successfully revived, they would have no identity, and perhaps no understanding of where they were or why they were there. Such persons would, in most cases, be quite old. (To date, most frozen individuals have been middle-aged or older.) Even the most optimistic supporters of cryonic suspension admit that there is currently no way to preserve bodies so that their organs will resume functioning when they are thawed (Darwin & Wowk, 1992).

Another problem is the great expense of maintaining cryonic capsules for many years. (LSD guru Tim Leary arranged to have his head frozen—he couldn't afford the whole-body treatment.) And in California (where else?), a case has already surfaced where careless operators of a cryonics service allowed a number of bodies to defrost.

Whereas it is true that for a few pioneering souls there is clearly "ice after death," immortality, it would seem, does not yet fall within the province of technology (Shermer, 1992).

Learning Check

1. The goal of a hospice is to freeze persons who have died of diseases that might one day become curable. T or F?

2. In passive euthanasia, death is allowed to occur but is not actively induced. T or F?

3. Cryonic suspension is a type of passive euthanasia. T or F?

4. Active euthanasia is now legal in most countries, providing that the terminally ill patient has signed a living will. T or F?

Critical Thinking

5. Which of the emotional reactions to impending death (described earlier) relates most directly to cryonic suspension?

Answers:

1. F 2. T 3. F 4. F 5. A good case can be made for the idea that people seeking cryonic suspension are still bargaining: "Just let me live a little longer and I'll do anything to earn it."

Chapter Summary

What are the typical tasks and dilemmas through the life span?

◆ According to Erikson, each life stage provokes a specific **psychosocial dilemma.** In order of occurrence, these are: *trust versus mistrust, autonomy versus shame and doubt, initiative versus guilt, industry versus inferiority, identity versus role confusion, intimacy versus isolation, generativity versus stagnation,* and *integrity versus despair.*

◆ In addition to the dilemmas identified by Erikson, we recognize that each **life stage** requires successful mastery of certain **developmental tasks.**

What is the nature of effective parenting?

◆ Three major parental styles are **authoritarian, permissive,** and **authoritative** (effective). When judged by its effects on children, authoritative parenting appears to benefit children the most.

What are some of the more serious childhood problems?

◆ Few children grow up without experiencing some of the normal problems of childhood, including **negativism, clinging, specific fears, sleep disturbances, general dissatisfaction, regression, sibling rivalry,** and **rebellion.**

◆ Major areas of difficulty in childhood are *toilet training* (including **enuresis** and **encopresis**); *feeding disturbances,* such as **overeating, anorexia nervosa** (self-starvation), and **pica** (eating non-food substances); *speech disturbances* (**delayed speech, stuttering**); **learning disorders,** including **dyslexia; attention-deficit hyperactivity disorder;** and other problems.

◆ **Childhood autism** is representative of some of the more severe problems that can occur. Some cases of autism are being treated successfully with **behavior modification.**

◆ **Child abuse** is a major problem for which few solutions currently exist. Roughly 30 percent of all abused children become abusive adults. Emotional support and therapy appear to help break the cycle of abuse.

Why is adolescent development especially challenging?

◆ **Adolescence** is a culturally defined social status. **Puberty** is a biological event.

◆ *Early maturation* is beneficial mostly for boys; its effects are mixed for girls. One danger of early maturation is *premature identity formation.*

◆ Adolescent **identity formation** is accelerated by cognitive development and influenced by parents and **peer groups.**

How do people select careers for themselves?

◆ Four broad periods in **career development** are the **exploration phase,** the **establishment phase,** the **mid-career phase,** and the **later career phase.**

◆ The exploration phase can be further divided into a **fantasy stage,** a **tentative stage,** and a **realistic stage.**

◆ **Vocational counseling** can greatly aid career decision making.

What happens psychologically during adulthood?

◆ Certain relatively consistent events mark **adult development** in western societies. These range from escaping parental dominance in the late teens to a noticeable acceptance of one's lot in life during the 50s.

◆ A *mid-life crisis* affects some people in the 37–41 age range, but this is by no means universal. Even if no crisis occurs, people tend to move through repeated cycles of stability and transition throughout adulthood.

◆ Adjustment to later middle age can be complicated for women by **menopause.** To a lesser degree, some men may experience a psychologically based **climacteric.**

◆ Well-being during adulthood consists of six elements: self-acceptance, positive relations with others, autonomy, environmental mastery, having a purpose in life, and continued personal growth.

What are some of the psychological challenges of aging?

◆ Both the *number* and *proportion* of older people in the population has grown.

◆ **Biological aging** begins between 25 and 30, but peak performance in specific pursuits may come at various points throughout life.

◆ Intellectual declines associated with aging are limited, at least through one's 70s. This is especially true of individuals who remain mentally active.

◆ **Gerontologists** have proposed two major theories of successful aging. The **disengagement theory** holds that withdrawal from society is necessary and desirable in old age. The **activity theory** counters that optimal adjustment to aging is tied to continuing activity and involvement. There is an element of truth to each, but the activity theory applies to more people.

◆ **Ageism** refers to prejudice, discrimination, and stereotyping on the basis of age. It affects people of all ages, but is especially damaging to older people. Most ageism is based on stereotypes, myths, and misinformation.

What are typical emotional and psychological reactions to death and bereavement?

◆ Typical emotional reactions to impending death are **denial, anger, bargaining, depression,** and **acceptance.**

- **Near-death experiences** frequently result in significant changes in personality, values, and life goals.
- **Bereavement** also brings forth a typical series of **grief** reactions, ranging from shock to final acceptance.

How do effective parents discipline their children?

- Effective parental discipline tends to emphasize **child management techniques** (especially communication), rather than **power assertion** or **withdrawal of love.**
- Responsibility, mutual respect, consistency, love, encouragement, and clear communication are features of effective parenting.
- Much misbehavior can be managed by use of **I-messages** and the application of **natural** and **logical consequences.**

In what ways are attitudes toward death changing?

- New approaches to death include the **hospice** movement, **living wills,** and **cryonic suspension.**
- A continuing controversy concerns the ethics of **passive euthanasia** and **active euthanasia.**

Where to Write for Information

- **Anorexia Nervosa** National Association of Anorexia Nervosa and Associated Disorders, Box 271, Highland Park, Illinois 60035.
- **Autism** The National Society for Autistic Children, 101 Richmond St., Huntington, West Virginia, 25701; or, Autism Society of America, Suite C1017, 1234 Massachusetts Ave., NW, Washington, D.C., 20005.
- **Child Abuse** Parents Anonymous, call toll free, (800) 421-0353 to find local chapters or call the National Child Abuse Hot Line, toll free, (800) 422-4453.
- **Hospice** The National Hospice Organization, 1901 North Ft. Meyer Drive, Arlington, Virginia, 22180.
- **Hyperactivity** Department of Health, Education, and Welfare, Office of the Secretary, Secretary's Committee on Mental Retardation, Washington, D.C., 20201.
- **Learning Disorders** National Association for Children with Learning Disabilities, 5225 Grace St., Pittsburgh, Pennsylvania, 15236.
- **Living Will** Concern for Dying, 250 West 57th St., New York, New York, 10019.

6

Sensation and Reality

Preview

Sensation—A Window on the World

At this very moment you are bathed in a swirling kaleidoscope of light, heat, pressure, vibrations, molecules, radiation, mechanical forces, and other physical energies. Without the senses, all of this would seem like a void of darkness and silence. The next time you drink in the beauty of a sunset, a flower, or a friend, remember this: Sensation makes it all possible.

It is apparent that the world as we know it is created from sensory impressions. Less obvious is that what passes for "reality" is shaped by the senses. Our sensory organs can detect only a limited range of physical energies. Thus, events go unrecorded when the senses are not attuned to them. We have, for instance, no receptors for atomic radiation, X-rays, or microwaves. For this reason, it is possible to be injured by each of these energies, without knowing it.

Yellow Is Amazing but Red Is Best   What would the world be like if new senses could be added—if we could "see" gamma rays, "hear" changes in barometric pressure, or "taste" light? We can only guess. It is far easier to imagine losing or regaining a sensory system. Consider the words of Bob Edens, who had his sight restored at age 51 after being blind since birth:

> I never would have dreamed that yellow is so . . . so yellow. I don't have the words, I'm amazed by yellow. But red is my favorite color. I just can't believe red. I can't wait to get up each day to see what I can see. And at night I look at the stars in the sky and the flashing lights. You could never know how wonderful everything is. I saw some bees the other day, and they were magnificent. I saw a truck drive by in the rain and throw a spray in the air. It was marvelous. And did I mention, I saw a falling leaf just drifting through the air?

If you are ever tempted to take everyday sensory impressions for granted, remember Bob Edens. As his words show, sensation is our window on the world. All our meaningful behavior, our awareness of physical reality, and our ideas about the universe ultimately spring from the senses. It may be no exaggeration then, to claim that our topic for this chapter is quite . . . "sensational."

Chapter Survey

Theme: Sensory systems link us to the external world and shape the flow of information to the brain.

General Properties of Sensory Systems—What You See Is What You Get

We begin with a paradox. On one hand, we have the magnificent power of the senses. In one instant you can view a star light-years away, and in the next, you can peer into the microscopic universe of a dewdrop. Yet vision is also narrowly limited in sensitivity. Like all senses, vision acts as a **data reduction system** (*a system that selects, analyzes, and condenses incoming information*). As you will see, each of our senses routinely "boils down" floods of information into a stream of useful data.

Sensory selection is illustrated by the fact that "light" is only a small slice of a broad range of energies. In addition to visible light, the **electromagnetic spectrum** (*entire spread of electromagnetic wavelengths*), includes infrared and ultraviolet light, radio waves, television broadcasts, gamma rays, and other energies (see Fig. 6–3). If our eyes were not limited to light sensitivity, "seeing" would be like getting hundreds of different "channels" at once. The confusion would be overwhelming. Obviously, *selection* of information is important.

How are selection and data reduction accomplished?

Some selection occurs simply because sensory receptors are biological *transducers*. A **transducer** *is a device that converts one kind of energy into another.* For example, an electric guitar converts string vibrations into electrical signals, which are amplified and fed into a speaker. Pluck a string and the speaker will blast out sound. However, if you shine a light on

the string, or pour cold water on it, the speaker will remain silent. (The owner of the guitar, however, may get quite loud at this point!) Similarly, each sensory organ is most sensitive to a select range of energy, which it most easily translates into nerve impulses.

As they transduce information, many senses *analyze* the environment before sending messages to the brain. **Sensory analysis** *is the separation of sensory information into important features.* **Perceptual features,** in turn, *are basic elements of a stimulus pattern,* such as lines, shapes, edges, spots, or colors (Fig. 6-1 ◆). The neural circuits of many sensory systems act as **feature detectors** (*the system is highly attuned to specific stimulus patterns*). Frog eyes, for example, are especially sensitive to small, dark, moving spots. Researcher Jerome Lettvin (1961) calls this sensitivity a "bug detector." It seems that the frog's eyes are "wired" to detect bugs flying nearby. But the insect (spot) must be moving. A frog may starve to death surrounded by dead flies.

After sensory systems have accomplished selection and analysis, they must *code* information. **Sensory coding** *refers to converting important features of the world into neural messages understood by the brain* (Hubel & Wiesel, 1979). To see coding at work, try this simple demonstration:

> Close your eyes for a moment. Then take your fingertips and press firmly on your eyelids. Apply enough pressure to "squash" your eyes slightly. Do this for about 30 seconds and observe what happens. (Readers with eye problems or contact lenses should not try this.)

If you followed the instructions, you probably saw stars, checkerboards, and flashes of color called **phosphenes** (FOSS-feens: *visual sensations caused by mechanical excitation of the retina*). The reason for this is that the eye's receptor cells,

Figure 6–1 ◆ Notice how eye-catching the single vertical line is among a group of slanted lines. This visual effect is known as pop-out. Pop-out occurs because the visual system is highly sensitive to elementary visual features, such as colors, shapes, and lines. Identification of such features appears to take place very early in the processing of visual information. (Adapted from Ramachandran, 1992b.)

which normally respond to light, are also somewhat sensitive to pressure. Notice though, that the eye is only prepared to code stimulation—including pressure—into *visual features*. As a result, you experience *light sensations*, not pressure. Also important in producing this effect is *localization of function* in the brain.

What does localization of function mean?

Localization of function *means that the type of sensation you experience depends on the area of the brain that is activated.* Some brain areas receive visual information; others receive audi-

tory information; still others receive taste, touch, and so forth. Knowing which brain areas are active would tell us, in general, what kinds of sensations you are feeling.

Localization may someday make it possible to artificially stimulate specific regions of the brain to restore sight, hearing, or other senses. Researchers have already used a miniature television camera to create electrical signals which are applied to the visual cortex of the brain (Bak et al., 1990; Zimmer, 1993). (See Figure 6–2 ◆.) Unfortunately, artificial vision of this type still faces major hurdles. However, artificial hearing is proving more workable—as we will see later.

It is fascinating to realize that experiences such as "seeing" and "hearing" ultimately take place in the brain, not in the eye or ear. Each sense organ is merely the first link in a long chain of events that ends in the brain. Much as we may be tempted to think so, our sensory systems do not operate like cameras or tape recorders, sending back "pictures" of the world. Rather, they collect, transduce, analyze, code, and transmit an unending flow of data to an active, information-hungry "biocomputer." This *incoming flow of information* is what we refer to as **sensation.** (When the brain organizes sensations into meaningful patterns, we speak of *perception*, which is the topic of Chapter 7.) In a moment we will see how each of the senses operates. But first, let's explore a little more. How sensitive are we to our "sensational" world?

Psychophysics—Life at the Limit

What is the quietest sound that can be heard? The weakest light that can be seen? The lightest touch that can be felt?

Figure 6–2 ◆ Artist's concept of an artificial visual system. Cameras mounted on a pair of glasses would transmit electrical signals to a grid of tiny electrodes placed in the visual areas of the brain (shown in cutaway view). One woman who had an experimental implant of this type in 1992 could "see" 34 dots of light, which were used to form crude letters (Bak et al., 1990). A larger number of dots could make reading and the perception of large objects, such as furniture and doorways, possible (Zimmer, 1993). A major barrier to such systems is the brain's tendency to reject implanted electrodes.

Visual cortex

Electrodes

Actual image

Cameras

Perceived image

The sense organs are our link to reality. What are their limits? An approach called *psychophysics* provides some answers. In **psychophysics,** *physical changes in stimuli are measured and related to psychological sensations,* such as loudness, brightness, or taste. A basic question psychophysics asks is, *What is the absolute minimum amount of energy necessary for a sensation to occur?* The answer defines the **absolute threshold** for a sensory system.

Testing for absolute thresholds shows just how sensitive we are. For example, it only takes 3 photons of light striking the retina of the eye to produce a sensation. A **photon** (FOE-tahn: *one quantum of energy*) is the smallest possible "package" of light. Responding to 3 photons is the equivalent of seeing a candle flame 30 miles away! Table 6–1 ■ gives the approximate absolute thresholds for the five major senses.

Some sensory systems have upper limits as well as lower ones. For example, when the ears are tested for pitch (higher and lower tones), we find that humans can hear sounds down to 20 **hertz** (*vibrations per second*) and up to about 20,000 hertz. This is an impressive range—from the lowest rumble of a pipe organ to the highest squeak of a stereo "tweeter." On the lower end, the threshold is as low as practical. If the ears could respond to tones below 20 hertz, you would hear the movements of your own muscles. Imagine how disturbing it would be to hear your body creak and groan like an old ship each time you move.

The 20,000 hertz upper threshold for human hearing, on the other hand, could easily be higher. Dogs, bats, cats, and other animals can hear sounds well above this limit. That's why a "silent" dog whistle (which may make sounds as high as 40,000 to 50,000 hertz) can be heard by dogs, but not by humans. For dogs, the sound exists. For humans it is beyond awareness. It's easy to see how thresholds define the limits of the sensory world in which we live. (If you want to buy a stereo system for your dog, you will have a hard time finding one that reproduces sounds above 20,000 hertz!)

Table 6–1 ■ Absolute Thresholds	
Sensory Modality	**Absolute Threshold**
Vision	Candle flame seen at 30 miles on a clear dark night
Hearing	Tick of a watch under quiet conditions at 20 feet
Taste	1 teaspoon of sugar in 2 gallons of water
Smell	1 drop of perfume diffused into a three-room apartment
Touch	A bee's wing falling on your cheek from 1 centimeter above

From Galanter, 1962.

Perceptual Defense and Subliminal Perception

Wouldn't the absolute threshold be different for different people?

Not only do absolute thresholds vary from person to person, they also vary from time to time for a single person. The type of stimulus, the state of one's nervous system, and the costs of false "detections" all make a difference. Emotional factors are also important. Unpleasant stimuli, for example, may *raise* the threshold for recognition. This *resistance to perceiving threatening or disturbing stimuli* is called **perceptual defense.** It was first revealed in experiments on the perception of "dirty" and "clean" words (McGinnies, 1949). So-called dirty words such as *whore, rape, bitch,* and *penis* were briefly flashed on a screen. Such words took longer to recognize than did "clean" words such as *wharf, rope, batch,* and *pencil.*

Couldn't it be that people wanted to be really sure they had seen a word like penis *before saying it?*

Yes. For many years, psychologists worried about this and other flaws in the original experiment. But researchers continue to find evidence that perceptual defense does occur. For example, new mothers who are emotionally depressed take longer than non-depressed women to recognize pictures related to pregnancy, birth, and babies (David et al., 1990). Apparently, we process information on more than one level and resist information that causes anxiety, discomfort, or embarrassment (Mogg et al., 1993).

Is that "subliminal" perception?

Basically, yes. Anytime information is processed below the normal **limen** (LIE-men: *threshold or limit*) for awareness, it is *subliminal.* **Subliminal perception** was demonstrated by a recent study in which college students saw photographs of a person flashed on a screen. Each time before the face appeared, it was preceded by a subliminal image. Some of these images (such as cute kittens) were chosen to make viewers feel good. Others (a face on fire) made them feel bad. All of the emotional images were flashed too briefly to be recognized. Nevertheless, they altered the impressions students formed of the target person (Krosnick et al., 1992).

Could that be applied to advertising?

Subliminal Persuasion? The urge to manipulate shoppers must be strong, since many businesses have tried subliminal advertising over the years. But do subliminal sales pitches actually work? Let's see.

In a famous, early attempt at subliminal advertising, a New Jersey theater flashed the words *Eat popcorn* and *Drink Coca-Cola* on the screen for 1/3000 second every 5 seconds during movies. Because the words were presented so briefly, they were below the normal threshold for awareness. During the 6 weeks the messages ran, the firm claimed an increase of 57 percent in popcorn sales and an 18 percent increase in Coca-Cola sales.

In the furor that followed this "experiment," some states rushed to pass laws against the "invisible sell." However, they really had nothing to fear. Psychologists immediately pointed out that the "Eat popcorn/drink Coke" "experiment" was seriously flawed. The original "experiment" didn't take into account other conditions that might increase sales. These included temperature, the time of year, the films shown, the type of audience, snack bar displays, and so forth.

Some years later, subliminal persuasion suffered an even bigger blow: The advertising expert who supposedly performed the "Eat popcorn/drink Coke" experiment admitted that he faked the whole thing. By lying about his ability to control audiences, he had hoped to gain customers for his marketing business (Pratkanis, 1992). Today, after many careful experiments, we can conclude that subliminal advertising is largely ineffective (Moore, 1992; Smith & Rogers, 1994; Trappey, 1996).

To summarize, there is evidence that subliminal perception occurs. However, well-controlled experiments have shown that subliminal stimuli are basically *weak* stimuli. There is little evidence that subliminal messages can persuade us or greatly influence our behavior (Trappey, 1996). Advertisers are better off using the loudest, clearest, most attention-demanding stimuli available—as most do (Smith & Rogers, 1994).

Despite the evidence, some advertisers still use subliminal messages. Maybe *they* haven't gotten the message. Similar conclusions apply to the so-called "subliminal tapes" and computer software offered by mail-order promoters: There is no scientific evidence that they work (Merikle & Skanes, 1992; Mitchell, 1995; Moore, 1995). The next highlight discusses a related controversy.

Focus on a Controversy

Rock Music—Subliminal Messages or Subliminal Myths?

In another uproar over subliminal perception, critics heatedly charged that spoken messages recorded backward ("backmasking") in rock music are perceived unconsciously by listeners.

Psychologists John Vokey and Don Read (1985) point out that religious leaders, journalists, and lawmakers merely *assumed* that if subliminal messages exist in records, they must affect listeners. But do they? Vokey and Read decided to find out.

Vokey and Read recorded a variety of sentences backward, including selections from Lewis Carroll's *Jabberwocky* and the 23rd Psalm of the Bible. In tests using the backward sentences, Vokey and Read found no evidence that listeners consciously or unconsciously

recognized their meaning. Other studies have shown that backward messages have no influence whatsoever on behavior (Begg et al., 1993; Swart & Morgan, 1992).

Undoubtedly, a few misguided musicians have placed backward messages in their recordings—some of which are highly offensive. However, Vokey and Read's research shows that subliminal messages in music offer no threat to listeners. Musicians who have played this game are just fooling themselves.

Difference Thresholds

Psychophysics also involves the study of **difference thresholds.** Here we are asking, *How much must a stimulus change (increase or decrease) before it becomes just noticeably different?* The study of **just noticeable differences** (**JNDs**) led to one of psychology's first natural "laws." Called **Weber's law** (VAY-bears), it can be roughly stated as follows: *The amount of change needed to produce a JND is a constant proportion of the original stimulus intensity.*

What does that mean in practice?

Let's take an example. Pretend that you are sitting in a room in which there are 10 candles burning. Ten candles is the original stimulus intensity. Let's say that we begin lighting candles until the room becomes just noticeably brighter. If this takes 3 more candles, how many more candles will we have to light in a room in which 20 candles are burning, in order to cause a just noticeable increase in brightness? Your first guess may be 3, but remember, the JND is a *proportion.* We will have to light 6 candles if we start with 20; 9 if we start with 30; and 12 if we start with 40. Table 6–2 ■ lists Weber's proportions for some common judgments.

Notice the big difference in auditory sensitivity (pitch and loudness) compared to taste. Very small changes in hearing are easy to detect. A voice or a musical instrument that is off pitch 1/3 of 1 percent will be noticeable. For taste, we find that a 20 percent change is necessary to produce a JND. If a cup of coffee has 5 teaspoons of sugar in it, 1 more (1/5 of 5) will have to be added before there is a noticeable increase in sweetness. It takes a lot of cooks to spoil the broth.

Weber's law is really just an approximation because it applies mainly to stimuli in the mid-range. For other than

Table 6–2 ■	Weber's Proportions for Common Judgments
Pitch	1/333 (1/3 of 1 percent)
Weight	1/50
Loudness	1/10
Taste	1/5

pure sensory judgments, it is even more approximate. In spite of this, there is a lesson to be learned from it. Consider judgments of money, for instance. If you discovered that you had been overcharged $10 on the purchase of a shirt, would you return to demand your money? If you discovered that you had been overcharged $10 on the purchase of an automobile, would you return to demand your money? If your answer to the first question is yes, then rationally your answer to the second should be yes, too. It may not be, however, since the larger base price of a car makes $10 seem a very small difference.

It's now time to examine each of the senses in more detail. In the next section, we will begin with vision, which is perhaps the most magnificent sensory system of all.

| **Learning Check** | **Critical Thinking** |

Before you read more, it might be a good idea to stop for a quick check on some of the ideas we have covered.

1. Sensory receptors are biological _____ , or devices for converting one type of energy to another.

2. Lettvin found that a frog's eyes are especially sensitive to phosphenes. T or F?

3. Important features of the environment are transmitted to the brain through a process known as
    a. phosphenation   **b.** coding   **c.** detection   **d.** programming

4. The minimum amount of stimulation necessary for a sensation to occur defines the _____ _____ .

5. A stimulus that causes discomfort or embarrassment may have to be viewed longer before it is perceived because of _____ _____ .

6. Subliminal stimuli have been shown to have a powerful effect on the behavior of viewers, especially when embedded in movies. T or F?

7. William James once said, "If a master surgeon were to cross the auditory and optic nerves, we would hear lightning and see thunder." What did James mean?

8. When promoters of self-help "subliminal tapes" are challenged to provide evidence that their products work, what study do you think they most often cite?

Answers:

1. transducers 2. F 3. b 4. absolute threshold 5. perceptual defense 6. F 7. James was referring to localization of function: If a lightning flash caused re-routed messages from the eyes to activate auditory areas of the brain, we would experience a sound sensation. Likewise, if the ears transduced a thunder-clap, and sent impulses to the visual area, a sensation of light would occur. 8. Good guess! That's right, it's the faked "Eat popcorn/drink Coke" study (Pratkanis, 1992).

Vision—Catching Some Rays

For most people loss of vision is the single most devastating sensory disability. Because of its great importance, we will explore vision in more detail than the other senses. Let's begin with the basic dimensions of light and vision.

Dimensions of Vision   Recall that the room in which you are sitting is filled with electromagnetic radiation, including light and other energies. Light of various wavelengths makes up the **visible spectrum** (*electromagnetic energies to which the eyes respond*). The spectrum starts at wavelengths of 400 **nanometers** (nan-OM-et-er: *one billionth of a meter*). Wavelengths at this end of the spectrum produce sensations of purple or violet. Longer wavelengths produce blue, green, yellow, and orange, until we reach red, with a wavelength of 700 nanometers (Fig. 6–3 ◆).

The formal term for color is **hue,** which refers to *the basic color categories* of red, orange, yellow, green, blue, indigo, and violet. As we have seen, various hues (or color sensations) correspond to light's *wavelength*. White light, in contrast, is made up of a mixture of wavelengths from all over the color spectrum. Hues (colors) produced by a *narrow band of wavelengths* are said to be very **saturated,** or "pure." (An intense "fire-engine" red is more saturated than a muddy "brick" red.) A third dimension of vision, **brightness,** corresponds roughly to *the physical amplitude of light waves*. Waves of greater amplitude are "taller," carry more energy, and cause colors to appear *brighter or more intense*. For example, the same "brick" red would look bright under intense, high-energy illumination and drab under dim light.

Structure of the Eye

Is it true that the eye is like a camera?

By pushing the issue a bit, the eye could be used as a camera. When the light-sensitive back surface of the eye is bathed in alum solution, the last image to strike it will appear like a tiny photograph. This fact might make for a great murder mystery, but it's not much of a way to take a photograph. In

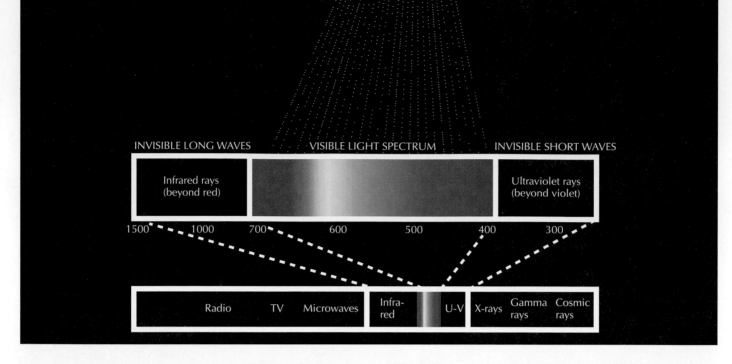

INVISIBLE LONG WAVES | VISIBLE LIGHT SPECTRUM | INVISIBLE SHORT WAVES

Infrared rays (beyond red)

Ultraviolet rays (beyond violet)

1500   1000   700   600   500   400   300

Radio   TV   Microwaves   Infra-red   U-V   X-rays   Gamma rays   Cosmic rays

Figure 6–3 ◆ The visible spectrum.

any case, several basic elements of eyes and cameras are similar. Both have a *transparent structure* called a **lens** that *focuses images* on a light-sensitive layer at the back of a closed space. In a camera, this layer is the film. In the eye, it is a layer of **photoreceptors** (*light-sensitive cells*). These cells are part of the **retina,** *a receiving area for images* that is about the size and thickness of a postage stamp (Fig. 6–4 ◆).

3A PsychNow!

How does the eye focus?

Focusing The front of the eye is covered by *a clear membrane* called the **cornea.** The curvature of this transparent "window" bends light rays inward. Additional

focusing of light rays occurs in the lens. The lens, which is elastic, is stretched or thickened by a series of muscles, so that more or less additional bending of light occurs. This *bending, fattening, and stretching of the lens* is called **accommodation.** In cameras, focusing is done more simply—by changing the distance between the lens and the film.

Visual Problems The shape of the eye also affects focusing. If the eye is too short, nearby objects cannot be focused, but distant objects are clear. This is called **hyperopia** (HI-per-OPE-ee-ah: *farsightedness*). If the eyeball is too long, the image falls short of the retina, and distant objects cannot be focused. This condition results in **myopia**

Figure 6–4 ◆ The human eye, a simplified view.

Ciliary muscle
Aqueous humor
Iris
Pupillary opening
Cornea
Lens
Fovea
Blind spot
Optic nerve
Retinal arteries and veins
Retina

Point of focus

Distant point

Near point

Misshapen cornea

Misshapen lens

Part of image is focused; part is not

Concave lens

Convex lens

Non-symmetrical lens

(a) Nearsighted Eye

(b) Farsighted Eye

(c) Astigmatic Eye

Figure 6–5 ◆ Visual defects and corrective lenses: **(a)** A myopic (longer than usual) eye. The concave lens spreads light rays just enough to increase the eye's focal length. **(b)** A hyperopic (shorter than usual) eye. The convex lens increases refraction (bending), returning the point of focus to the retina. **(c)** An astigmatic (lens or cornea not symmetrical) eye. In astigmatism, parts of vision are sharp and parts are unfocused. Lenses to correct astigmatism are non-symmetrical.

(my-OPE-ee-ah: *nearsightedness*). When the cornea or the lens is misshapen, part of the visual field will be focused and part will be fuzzy. In this case, the eye *has more than one focal point*, a problem called **astigmatism** (ah-STIG-mah-tiz-em). All three visual defects can be corrected by placing glasses or contact lenses in front of the eye. These added lenses change the path of incoming light to restore crisp focusing (Fig. 6–5 ◆).

As people age, the lens becomes less flexible and less able to accommodate. Since the lens must do its greatest bending to focus nearby objects, the result is **presbyopia** (prez-bee-OPE-ee-ah: *old vision, or farsightedness due to aging*). Perhaps you have seen a grandparent or older friend reading a newspaper at arm's length because of presbyopia. Also, if you now wear glasses for nearsightedness, you may need bifocals as you age. Bifocal lenses correct near vision *and* distance vision.

Light Control There is one more major similarity between the eye and a camera. In front of the lens in both is a mechanism to control the amount of light entering. This mechanism in a camera is the diaphragm; in the eye it is the *iris* (Fig. 6–6 ◆). The **iris** is *a colored circular muscle that expands and contracts*. As it does so, it changes the size of the **pupil** (*the opening at the center of the eye*).

The iris is quite important for normal vision. The retina can adapt to changing light conditions, but only very slowly. By making rapid adjustments, the iris allows us to move quickly from darkness to bright sunlight, or the reverse. In dim light the pupils **dilate** (*enlarge*), and in bright light they **constrict** (*narrow*). At the largest opening of the iris, the pupil is 17 times larger than at the smallest. Were it not for this, you would be blinded for quite some time upon walking into a darkened room.

Rods and Cones At this point, our eye-camera comparison breaks down. From the retina on, vision becomes a complex system for analyzing patterns of light. Besides, the eye would make a very strange camera. First of all, the eye has two types of "film," consisting of receptor cells called *rods* and *cones*. The **cones**, numbering about 6.5 million in each eye, *work best in bright light. They also produce color sensations and pick up fine details.* In contrast, the **rods**, numbering about 100 million, *are unable to detect colors.* Pure rod vision is black and white. However, the rods are *much more sensitive to light than the cones are.* The rods therefore allow us to see in very dim light.

Compared to the film in a camera, the visual receptors are backward. The rods and cones point toward the *back* of the eye, away from incoming light (Fig. 6–7 ◆). In addition, the eye is constantly in motion. This would be disastrous for a camera, but as we shall see later, it is essential for normal vision. Finally, the "film" (retina) has a hole in it: Each eye has a **blind spot** *because there are no receptors where the optic nerve leaves the eye* (Fig. 6–8a ◆).

The blind spot shows again that vision depends greatly on the brain. If you close one eye, part of the scene ahead will fall on the blind spot of your open eye. Why isn't

Figure 6–6 ◆ The diaphragm and iris.

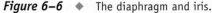

Figure 6–7 ◆ Anatomy of the retina, the light-sensitive element of the eye. The retina lies behind the vitreous humor, which is the jelly-like substance that fills the eyeball. Note that light does not fall directly on the rods and cones. It must first pass through the outer layers of the retina, made up of additional nerve cells. Only about one half of the light falling on the front of the eye reaches the rods and cones—testimony to the eye's amazing light sensitivity. The rods and cones are much smaller than implied here. The smallest receptors are 1 micron (one millionth of a meter) wide. The lower left photograph shows rods and cones as seen through an electron microscope. In the photograph the cones are colored green and the rods blue.

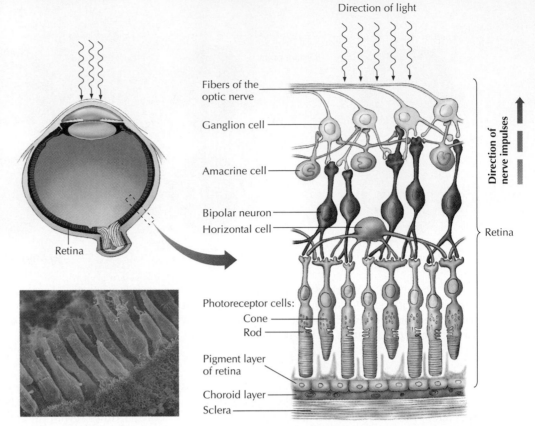

there a gap in your vision? The answer is that the visual cortex of the brain actively extends patterns into the gap from surrounding areas (Fig. 6–8b ◆). According to folklore, King Charles II of England used this feature of the blind spot to amuse himself. Whenever he became bored, Charles II closed one eye and visually "beheaded" members of his court (Ramachandran, 1992a, 1992b).

Research Classic

How the Brain Sees the World

Early ideas of vision often assumed an almost movie-like projection of "pictures" to the brain. But this

Figure 6–8 ◆ Experiencing the blind spot. **(a)** With your right eye closed, stare at the upper right cross. Hold the book about 1 foot from your eye and slowly move it back and forth. You should be able to locate a position that causes the black spot to disappear. When it does, it has fallen on the blind spot. With a little practice you can learn to make people or objects you dislike disappear too! **(b)** Repeat the procedure described, but stare at the lower cross. When the white space falls on the blind spot, the black lines will appear to be continuous. This may help you understand why you do not usually experience a blind spot in your visual field.

(a)

(b)

Figure 6–9 ◆ **(a)** A "typical" brain cell responds to only a small area of the total field of vision. The bar graph **(b)** illustrates how a brain cell may act as a feature detector. Notice how the cell primarily responds to just one type of stimulus. (Adapted from Hubel, 1979.)

mistaken notion immediately raises the question, Who's watching the movie? Thanks to the Nobel Prize-winning work of biopsychologists David Hubel and Torsten Wiesel, we now know that vision acts more like a computer than like a television or movie camera.

Hubel and Wiesel directly recorded the activities of single cells in the visual cortex of the brain. As they did, they noted the area of the retina to which each cell responded. Then they shone lights of various sizes and shapes on the retina and recorded how often the corresponding brain cell fired nerve impulses (Fig. 6–9 ◆).

The results were fascinating. Many brain cells responded only to lines of a certain width or orientation. These same cells didn't get the least bit "excited" over a dot of light or overall illumination. Other cells responded only to lines at certain angles, or lines of certain lengths, or lines moving in a particular direction (Hubel, 1979b; Hubel & Wiesel, 1979).

The upshot of such findings is that cells in the brain, like the frog's retina described earlier, act as feature detectors. The brain seems to first analyze incoming information into lines, angles, shading, movement, and other basic features. Then, other brain areas combine these features into meaningful visual experiences. (This concept is discussed further in Chapter 7.) Reading the letters on this page is a direct result of such feature analysis. Given the size of the task, it's little wonder that as much as 30 percent of the human brain may be involved in vision.

Visual Acuity Let's return now to the rods and cones. Differences in these receptors also affect **visual acuity,** *or sharpness.* The cones lie mainly at the center of the eye. In fact, the **fovea** (FOE-vee-ah: *a small cup-shaped area in the middle of the retina*) contains only cones—about 50,000 of them. If you look at your thumbnail at arm's length, its image just about covers the fovea. Like a newspaper photograph made of many small dots, the tightly packed cones of the fovea produce the greatest visual acuity. In

other words, vision is sharpest when an image falls on the fovea. Acuity steadily decreases as images are moved to the edge of the retina. Note that visual acuity is based on the optics of the eye. Sharpness cannot be improved by eye exercises or commercial "vision training" courses (Long, 1994).

Figure 6–10 ◆ describes a widely used rating system for acuity. If vision can be corrected to no better than 20/200 acuity, a person is considered legally blind. With 20/200 vision, the world is seen as nothing but a blur.

What is the purpose of the rest of the retina?

Peripheral Vision Areas outside the fovea also get light, creating a large region of **peripheral** (*side*) **vision.** The rods are most numerous about 20 degrees from the center of

(a) **(b)** **(c)**

Figure 6–10 ◆ Tests of visual acuity. Here are some common tests of visual acuity. In **(a)**, sharpness is indicated by the smallest grating still seen as individual lines. The Snellen chart **(b)** requires that you read rows of letters of diminishing size until you can no longer distinguish them. The Landolt rings **(c)** require no familiarity with letters. All that is required is a report of which side has a break in it. Normal acuity is designated as 20/20 vision: At 20 feet in distance, you can distinguish what the average person can see at 20 feet. If your vision is 20/40, you can only see at 20 feet what the average person can see at 40 feet. If your vision is 20/200, you need glasses! Vision that is 20/12 would mean that you can see at 20 feet what the average person must be 8 feet nearer to see, indicating better than average acuity. American astronaut Gordon Cooper, who claimed to see railroad lines in northern India from 100 miles above, had 20/12 acuity.

the retina, so much peripheral vision is rod vision. Fortunately, the rods are quite sensitive to *movement*. Thus, while the eye gives its best acuity to the center of vision, it maintains a radar-like scan for movement in side vision. Seeing "out of the corner of the eye" is important for sports, driving, and walking down dark alleys. People who suffer from **tunnel vision** (*a loss of peripheral vision*) feel as if they are wearing blinders. Tunnel vision can also occur temporarily when we are overloaded by a task. For example, if you were playing a demanding video game you might be excused for not noticing that a friend had walked up beside you (Williams, 1995).

Sailors, pilots, astronomers, and military spotters have long made use of an interesting fact about peripheral vision. Although the rods give poor acuity, they are many times more responsive to light than the cones are. Since most rods are 20 degrees to each side of the fovea, the best night vision is obtained by looking *next to* an object you wish to see. Test this yourself some night by looking at, and next to, a very dim star.

Color Vision—There's More to It Than Meets the Eye

What would you say is the brightest color? Red? Yellow? Blue? Actually, there are two answers to this question, one for the rods and one for the cones. The rods and cones differ in *maximal color sensitivity*, a difference that has practical importance. The cones are most sensitive to the *yellowish-green* region of the spectrum. In other words, if all colors are tested in daylight (with each reflecting the same total amount of light) then yellowish green appears *brightest*. The increased use of yellow fire trucks and the Day-Glo yellow vests worn by roadside work crews reflect this fact.

To what color are the rods most sensitive?

Remember that the rods do not produce color sensations. If very dim colored lights are used, no color will be seen. Even so, one light will appear brighter than the others. When tested this way, the rods are most sensitive to *blue-green* lights. Thus, at night or in dim light, when rod vision prevails, the brightest-colored light will be one that is blue or blue-green. For this reason, police and highway patrol cars in many states now have blue emergency lights for night work. Also, you may have wondered why the taxiway lights at airports are blue. It seems like a poor choice, but blue is actually highly visible to pilots.

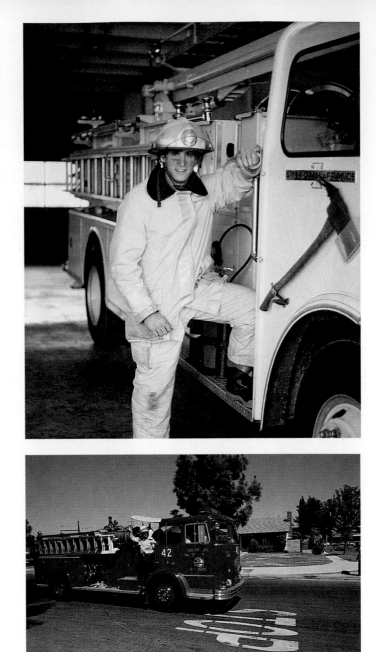

Yellow-green fire trucks are far more visible in daylight because their color matches the cones' sensitivity peak. However, many cities continue to prefer red trucks because of tradition.

Color Theories

How do the cones produce color sensations?

No short answer can do justice to the complexities of color vision, but briefly, here is the best current explanation. The **trichromatic theory** (TRY-kro-MAT-ik) of color vision holds that there are *three types of cones, each most sensitive to either red, green, or blue.* Other colors are assumed to result from combinations of these three, whereas black and white sensations are produced by the rods.

Figure 6–11 ◆ Negative afterimages. Stare at the dot near the middle of the flag for at least 30 seconds. Then look immediately at a plain sheet of white paper or a white wall. You will see the American flag in its normal colors. Reduced sensitivity to yellow, green, and black in the visual system, caused by prolonged staring, results in the appearance of complementary colors. Project the afterimage of the flag on other colored surfaces to get additional effects.

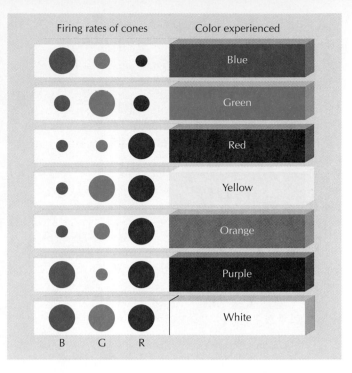

Figure 6–12 ◆ Firing rates of blue, green, and red cones in response to different colors. The larger the colored circle, the higher the firing rates. Colors are coded by activity in all three types of cones in the normal eye. (Adapted from Goldstein, 1989.)

A basic problem with the trichromatic theory is that four colors seem psychologically primary: red, green, blue, and yellow. Also, why is it impossible to have a reddish green or a yellowish blue? A second view, known as the **opponent-process theory,** *states that vision analyzes colors into "either-or" messages.* It is assumed that the visual system can produce messages for either red or green, yellow or blue, black or white. Coding one color in a pair (red, for instance) seems to block the opposite message (green), so a reddish green is impossible, but a yellowish red (orange) can occur.

According to opponent-process theory, fatigue caused by making one response produces an *afterimage* of the opposite color as the system recovers. **Afterimages** *are visual sensations that persist after a stimulus is removed.* To see an afterimage of the type predicted by opponent-process theory, look at Figure 6–11 ◆ and follow the instructions given there.

Which color theory is correct?

Both! The three-color theory applies to the retina, where three types of **visual pigments** (*light-sensitive chemicals*) have been found. As predicted, each pigment is most sensitive to a different wavelength of light. The three peaks of sensitivity fall in roughly the red, green, and blue regions. As a result, the three types of cones fire nerve impulses at different rates when various colors are viewed (Fig. 6–12 ◆). In further support of the three-color theory, researchers have confirmed that each cone contains only one pigment and that each pigment is controlled by its own gene (Nathans et al., 1986).

In contrast, the opponent-process theory seems to explain events recorded in optic pathways *after* information leaves the eye. So both theories are "correct." One explains what happens in the eye itself. The other explains how visual information is analyzed on its way to the brain. Together they explain color vision.

Color Blindness and Color Weakness

Do you know anyone who regularly draws hoots of laughter by wearing clothes of wildly clashing colors? Or someone who sheepishly tries to avoid saying what color an object is? If so, you probably know someone who is color-blind.

What is it like to be color-blind? What causes color blindness?

A person who is **color-blind** *cannot perceive colors.* It is as if the world is a black and white movie. How do we know? In a few rare cases, people have been color-blind in only one eye and can compare (Hsia & Graham, 1965). Two colors of equal brightness look exactly alike to the color-blind individual. The color-blind person either lacks cones or has cones that do not function normally.

Total color blindness is rare. In **color weakness,** *the person is unable to distinguish some colors.* Partial color blindness of this type is more common. Approximately 8 percent of the male population (but less than 1 percent of women) are red-green color-blind. (Another form of color weakness, involving yellow and blue, is extremely rare.)

Color blindness is caused by changes in the genes that control red, green, and blue pigments in the cones (Nathans et al., 1986). Red-green color blindness is a recessive, sex-linked trait. That means it is carried on the *X*, or female

(a)   (b)   (c)

Figure 6–13 ◆ Color blindness and color weakness. **(a)** Photograph illustrates normal color vision. **(b)** Photograph is printed in blue and yellow and gives an impression of what a red-green color-blind person sees. **(c)** Photograph simulates total color blindness. If you are totally color-blind, all three photos will look nearly identical.

chromosome. Women have two *X* chromosomes, so if they receive only one defective color gene, they still have normal vision. Color-blind men, however, have only one *X* chromosome, so they can inherit the defect from their mothers (who are usually not color-blind themselves). The red-green color-blind individual sees both reds and greens as the same color, usually a yellowish brown (see Fig. 6–13 ◆).

Then how can color-blind individuals drive? Don't they have trouble with traffic lights?

Red-green color-blind individuals have normal vision for yellow and blue, so their main problem is telling red lights from green. In practice, this is not difficult. In the United States and Canada, the red light is always on top, and the green light is brighter than the red. Also, to help remedy this problem, most modern traffic signals have a "red" light that has a background of yellow light mixed with it, and a "green" light that is really blue-green.

How can a person tell if she or he is color-blind?

The **Ishihara test** *is a common measure of color blindness and weakness.* In the test, numbers and other designs made of dots are placed on a background also made of dots. The background and the numbers are of different colors (red and green, for example). A person who is color-blind sees only a jumble of dots. The person with normal color vision can detect the presence of the numbers or designs. Figure 6–14 ◆ is a replica of the Ishihara test. You should not consider Figure 6–14 a true test of color vision, but it may give you some idea of whether or not you are color-blind. The real test is highly accurate (Birch & McKeever, 1993).

Dark Adaptation—Let There Be Light!

What happens to the eyes when they adapt to a dark room?

Dark adaptation *is the dramatic increase in retinal sensitivity to light* that occurs after entering the dark. Consider walking into a theater. If you enter from a brightly lighted lobby, you practically need to be led to your seat. After a short time, however, you can see the entire room in detail (including the couple kissing over in the corner). Studies of dark adaptation show that it takes about 30 to 35 minutes of complete darkness to reach maximum visual sensitivity (Fig. 6–15 ◆). When dark adaptation is complete, the eye can detect lights 10,000 times weaker than those to which it was originally sensitive.

What causes dark adaptation?

Like the cones, the rods contain a light-sensitive visual pigment. When struck by light, visual pigments *bleach,* or break down chemically. (The afterimages caused by flashbulbs are a direct result of this bleaching.) To restore light sensitivity, the visual pigments must recombine, which takes time. Night vision is due mainly to an increase in **rhodopsin** (row-DOP-sin), *the rod pigment.* When completely dark adapted, the human eye is almost as sensitive to light as the eye of an owl.

Before artificial lighting, gradual adaptation at sunset posed few problems. Now we are often caught in temporary

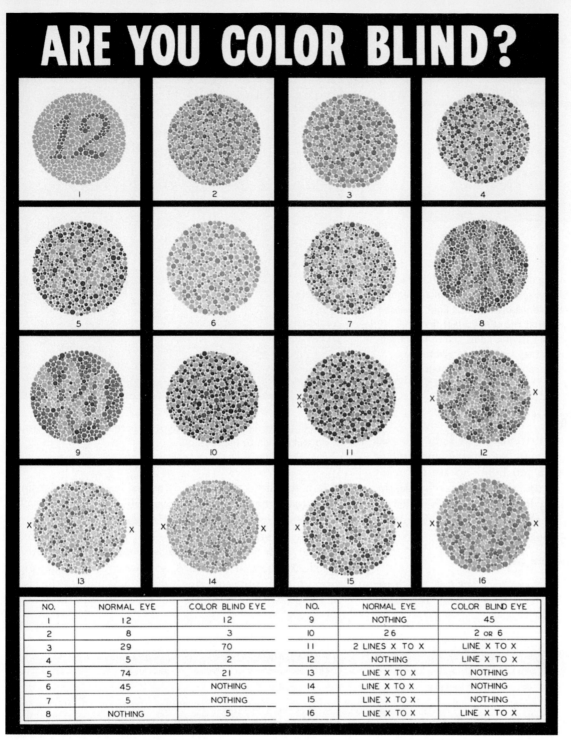

ARE YOU COLOR BLIND?

NO.	NORMAL EYE	COLOR BLIND EYE	NO.	NORMAL EYE	COLOR BLIND EYE
1	12	12	9	NOTHING	45
2	8	3	10	26	2 OR 6
3	29	70	11	2 LINES X TO X	LINE X TO X
4	5	2	12	NOTHING	LINE X TO X
5	74	21	13	LINE X TO X	NOTHING
6	45	NOTHING	14	LINE X TO X	NOTHING
7	5	NOTHING	15	LINE X TO X	NOTHING
8	NOTHING	5	16	LINE X TO X	LINE X TO X

Figure 6–14 ◆
Replica of the Ishihara test for color blindness.

semi-blindness. Usually this isn't dangerous, but it can be. Even though dark adaptation takes a long time, it can be wiped out by just a few seconds of viewing bright light. Try this demonstration:

See (and Don't See) for Yourself

Spend 15 or 20 minutes in a darkened room. At the end of this time, you should be able to see clearly. Now, close your left eye and cover it tightly with your hand. Turn on a bright light for 1 or 2 seconds and look at it with your right eye. With the light off again, compare the vision in your two eyes, first opening one and then the other. You will be completely blinded in your right eye.

This experience should convince you to avoid looking at the headlights of approaching cars during night driving. Under normal conditions, glare recovery takes about 20 seconds, plenty of time for an accident. After a few drinks, it may take 30 to 50 percent longer, because alcohol dilates the pupils, allowing more light to enter. Note, too, that dark adaptation occurs more slowly as we grow older. This is one reason why injuries caused by falling in the dark become more common among the elderly (McMurdo & Gaskell, 1991).

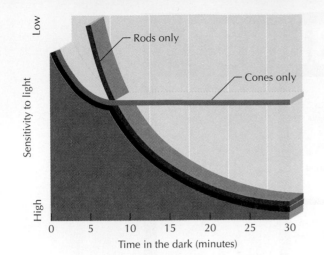

Figure 6-15 ◆ Typical course of dark adaptation. The black line shows how the threshold for vision lowers as a person spends time in the dark. (A lower threshold means that less light is needed for vision.) The green line shows that the cones adapt first, but they soon cease adding to light sensitivity. Rods, shown by the red line, adapt more slowly. However, they continue to add to improved night vision long after the cones are fully adapted.

Is there any way to speed up dark adaptation?

The rods are *insensitive* to extremely red light. To take advantage of this lack of sensitivity, submarines and airplane cockpits are illuminated with red light. So are the ready rooms for fighter pilots and ground crews. In each case, this allows people to move quickly into the dark without having to adapt. Because the red light doesn't stimulate the rods, it is as if they had already spent time in the dark.

Can eating carrots really improve vision?

One *chemical "ingredient" of rhodopsin* is **retinal,** which the body makes from vitamin A. (Retinal is also called **retinene.**)

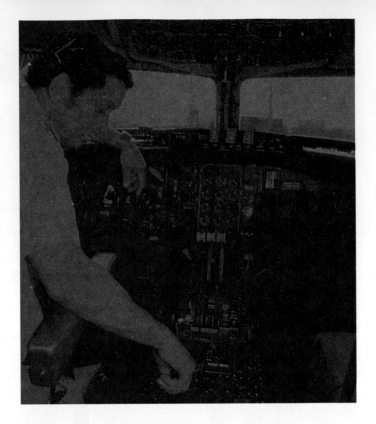

Red light allows dark adaptation to occur because it provides little or no stimulation to the rods.

When too little vitamin A is available, less rhodopsin is produced. Thus, a person lacking vitamin A may develop *night blindness.* In **night blindness,** the person can see normally in bright light while using the cones, but becomes *blind at night when the rods must function.* Carrots are an excellent source of vitamin A, so they could improve night vision for someone suffering a deficiency, but not the vision of anyone with an adequate diet (Carlson, 1994).

Learning Check　　　　　　　　　　　　　　　　　　　　**Critical Thinking**

After such an extended discussion of vision you may find it helpful to review the following questions.

1. The _____ _____ is made up of electromagnetic radiation with wavelengths between 400 and 700 nanometers.

2. Match:
   ____ Myopia　　　　　**A.** Farsightedness
   ____ Hyperopia　　　　**B.** Elongated eye
   ____ Presbyopia　　　　**C.** Farsightedness due to aging
   ____ Astigmatism　　　　**D.** Lack of cones in fovea
   　　　　　　　　　　　　E. Misshapen cornea or lens

3. In dim light, vision depends mainly on the _____ . In brighter light, color and fine detail are produced by the _____ .

4. The fovea has the greatest visual acuity due to the large concentration of rods found there. T or F?

5. Hubel and Wiesel found that cells in the visual cortex of the brain function as _____ _____ .

6. The term 20/20 vision means that a person can see at 20 feet what can normally be seen from 20 feet. T or F?

7. When using the cones, the most visible color is
   a. reddish orange   **b.** blue-green   **c.** yellow-orange   **d.** yellowish green

8. The eyes become more sensitive to light at night because of a process known as
   _____ _____ .

9. Sensory transduction in the eye takes place first in the cornea, then in the lens, then in the retina. T or F?

Answers:

1. visible spectrum   2. B, A, C, E   3. rods, cones   4. F   5. feature detectors   6. T   7. d   8. dark adaptation   9. False. The cornea and lens bend and focus light rays, but they do not change light to another form of energy. No change in the type of energy takes place until the retina converts light to nerve impulses.

Hearing—Good Vibrations

Rock, classical, jazz, rap, country, pop—whatever your musical taste, you have probably been moved or soothed by the riches of sound. Hearing also provides the brain with a wealth of information not available through the other senses, such as the approach of an unseen car or the information imparted by spoken language. Hearing collects information from all around the body. Vision, in all its glory, is limited to stimuli in front of the eyes (unless, of course, your "shades" have rear-view mirrors attached).

What is the stimulus for hearing?

If you throw a stone into a quiet pond, a circle of waves will spread in all directions. In much the same way, sound travels as a series of invisible waves of **compression** (*peaks*) and **rarefaction** (RARE-eh-fak-shun: *valleys*) in the air. Any vibrating object—a tuning fork, the string of a musical instrument, or the vocal cords—will produce **sound waves** (*rhythmic movement of air molecules*). Other materials, such as fluids or solids, will also carry sound. But sound does not travel in a vacuum. Movies that show characters reacting to the "roar" of alien starships or to titanic battles in deep space are in error.

The **frequency** of sound waves (*the number of waves per second*) corresponds to the perceived **pitch** (*higher or lower tone*) of a sound. The **amplitude** or *physical "height," of a sound wave* tells how much energy it contains. Psychologically, amplitude corresponds to sensed **loudness** (*sound intensity*) (Fig. 6–16 ◆).

How are sounds converted to nerve impulses?

What we call the "ear" is only the **pinna** (PIN-ah: *the visible, external part of the ear*). In addition to being a good place to hang earrings or balance pencils, the pinna acts like a funnel to concentrate sounds. After they are guided into the ear, sound waves collide with the **tympanic membrane** (*eardrum*), which is like a tight drumhead within the ear canal.

The sound waves set the eardrum in motion. This, in turn, causes *three small bones* (the **auditory ossicles**) (OSS-ih-kuls) to vibrate (Fig. 6–17 ◆). The ossicles are the malleus (MAL-ee-us), incus, and stapes (STAY-peas). Their common names are the hammer, anvil, and stirrup. The ossicles link the eardrum with the **cochlea** (KOCK-lee-ah: *a snail-shaped organ that makes up the inner ear*). The stapes is attached to a *membrane on the cochlea* called the **oval window.** As the oval window moves back and forth, it makes waves in a fluid inside the cochlea.

The cochlea is really the organ of hearing, since it is here that tiny **hair cells** *detect waves in the fluid*. The hair cells are part of a structure called the **organ of Corti** (KOR-tee), *which makes up the center part of the cochlea* (Fig. 6–18 ◆). A set of **stereocilia** (STER-ee-oh-SIL-ih-ah) or *"bristles" atop each hair cell* brush against the tectorial membrane when waves ripple through the fluid surrounding the organ of Corti. As the stereocilia are bent, nerve impulses are triggered, which then flow to the brain.

How are higher and lower sounds detected?

The **frequency theory** of hearing states that *as pitch rises, nerve impulses of the same frequency are fed into the auditory nerve.* That is, an 800 hertz tone produces 800 nerve

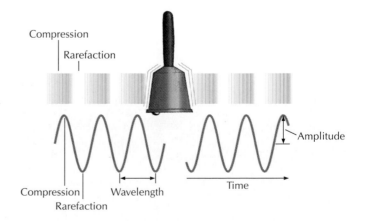

Figure 6–16 ◆ Waves of compression in the air, or vibrations, are the stimulus for hearing. The frequency of sound waves determines their pitch. The amplitude determines loudness.

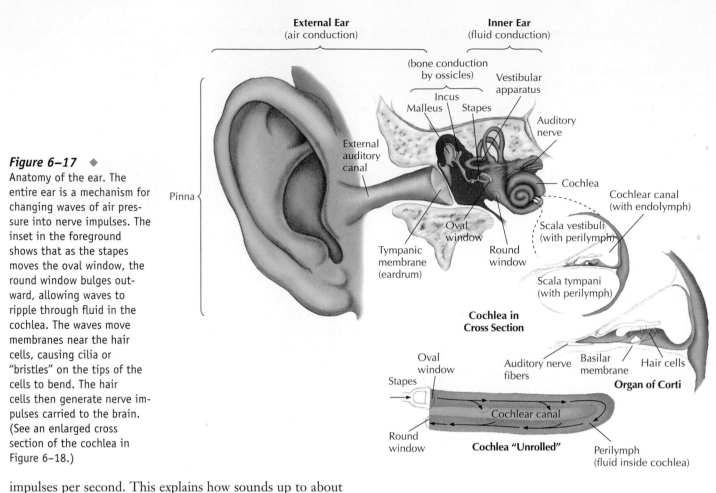

External Ear
(air conduction)

Inner Ear
(fluid conduction)

(bone conduction
by ossicles)

Vestibular
apparatus

Incus

Malleus   Stapes

Auditory
nerve

Pinna

External
auditory
canal

Cochlea

Cochlear canal
(with endolymph)

Scala vestibuli
(with perilymph)

Oval
window

Tympanic
membrane
(eardrum)

Round
window

Scala tympani
(with perilymph)

**Cochlea in
Cross Section**

Oval
window

Stapes

Round
window

Auditory nerve
fibers

Basilar
membrane

Hair cells

Organ of Corti

Cochlear canal

Cochlea "Unrolled"

Perilymph
(fluid inside cochlea)

Figure 6–17 ◆
Anatomy of the ear. The entire ear is a mechanism for changing waves of air pressure into nerve impulses. The inset in the foreground shows that as the stapes moves the oval window, the round window bulges outward, allowing waves to ripple through fluid in the cochlea. The waves move membranes near the hair cells, causing cilia or "bristles" on the tips of the cells to bend. The hair cells then generate nerve impulses carried to the brain. (See an enlarged cross section of the cochlea in Figure 6–18.)

impulses per second. This explains how sounds up to about 4,000 hertz reach the brain. But higher tones require a different explanation. **Place theory** *states that higher and lower tones excite specific areas of the cochlea.* High tones register most strongly at the base of the cochlea (near the oval window). Lower tones, on the other hand, mostly move hair cells near the outer tip of the cochlea (Fig. 6–19 ◆). Pitch is therefore signaled by the area of the cochlea most strongly

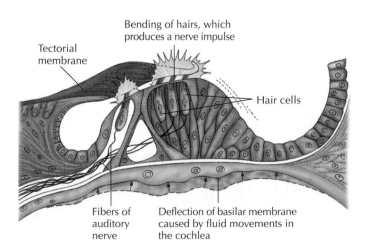

Tectorial
membrane

Bending of hairs, which
produces a nerve impulse

Hair cells

Fibers of
auditory
nerve

Deflection of basilar membrane
caused by fluid movements in
the cochlea

Figure 6–18 ◆ A closer view of the hair cells shows how movement of fluid in the cochlea causes the bristling "hairs" or cilia to bend, generating a nerve impulse.

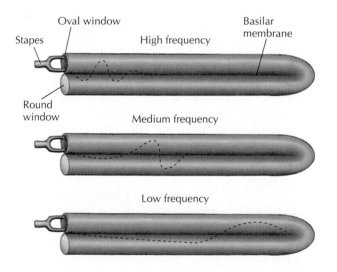

Oval window

Stapes

Round
window

High frequency

Basilar
membrane

Medium frequency

Low frequency

Figure 6–19 ◆ Here we see a simplified side view of the cochlea "unrolled." Remember that the basilar membrane is the elastic "roof" of the lower chamber of the cochlea. The organ of Corti, with its sensitive hair cells, rests atop the basilar membrane. The colored line shows where waves in the cochlear fluid cause the greatest deflection of the basilar membrane. (The amount of movement is exaggerated in the drawing.) Hair cells respond most in the area of greatest movement, which helps identify sound frequency.

activated. Place theory also explains why hunters sometimes lose hearing in a narrow pitch range. "Hunter's notch," as it is called, occurs when hair cells are damaged in the area activated by the pitch of gunfire.

What causes other types of deafness?

Deafness There are three principal types of deafness. **Conduction deafness** *occurs when there is poor transfer of sounds from the eardrum to the inner ear.* For example, the eardrums or ossicles may be damaged or immobilized by disease or injury. In many cases, conduction deafness can be overcome by a hearing aid, which makes sounds louder and clearer.

Nerve deafness *results from damage to the hair cells or auditory nerve.* Hearing aids are of no help in this case, because auditory messages are blocked from reaching the brain. However, a new artificial hearing system is making it possible for some persons with nerve deafness to break through the wall of silence.

Using Psychology

Artificial Hearing

In many cases of "nerve" deafness, the nerve is actually intact. This finding has spurred development of **cochlear implants** *that bypass hair cells and stimulate the auditory nerves directly* (Fig. 6–20 ◆).

Figure 6–20 ◆ A cochlear implant, or "artificial ear."

As you can see, wires from a microphone carry electrical signals to an external coil. A matching coil under the skin picks up the signals and carries them to one or more areas of the cochlea. Early implants allowed patients to hear only low-frequency sounds, such as a dog's bark or the horn of a speeding car. Newer multi-channel models make use of place theory to separate higher and lower tones. This has allowed some formerly deaf persons to hear human voices and other higher frequency sounds. About 60 percent of all multi-channel implant patients can understand some spoken words and some children learn to speak (Cohen et al, 1993; Tye-Murray et al., 1995).

At present, artificial hearing remains crude. All but the most successful implant patients describe the sound as "like a radio that isn't quite tuned in." In fact, 30 percent of all adults who have tried implants have given up on them. But the implants are improving. And even now it is hard to argue with enthusiasts like Kristen Cloud. Shortly after Kristen received an implant, she was able to hear a siren and avoid being struck by a speeding car (Williams, 1984). She says simply, "The implant saved my life."

A particular type of nerve deafness is of special interest, because many jobs, hobbies, and pastimes can cause it. **Stimulation deafness** *occurs when very loud sounds damage hair cells in the cochlea* (as in hunter's notch). Each of us starts life with about 32,000 hair cells (Fig. 6–21 ◆). However, we begin losing them the moment we are born. By age 65 more than 40 percent are gone.

If you work in a noisy environment or enjoy loud music, motorcycling, snowmobiling, hunting, or similar pursuits, you may be risking stimulation deafness. The hair cells, which are about as thick as a cobweb, are very fragile and easily damaged. Once dead, they are never replaced: When you abuse them you lose them.

How loud must a sound be to be hazardous?

The danger of hearing loss depends on both the loudness of sound and how long you are exposed to it. Daily exposure to 85 decibels or more may cause permanent hearing loss. Even short periods at 120 decibels (a rock concert) may cause a **temporary threshold shift** (*a partial, transitory loss of hearing*). Brief exposure to 150 decibels (a jet airplane nearby) can cause permanent deafness.

You might find it interesting to check the decibel ratings of some of your activities in Figure 6–22 ◆ as a way of estimating hearing risk. Don't be fooled by the numbers, though. Decibels are plotted on a logarithmic scale (like earthquake intensity!). Every 20 decibels increases the amount of energy in a sound by a factor of 10. In other words, a rock concert at 120 decibels is not just twice as powerful as a normal voice at 60 decibels. It is actually 1,000 times stronger.

Music, as well as noise, can do damage. People who sit directly in front of the speaker columns at highly amplified musical concerts run considerable risk of hearing loss.

Figure 6–21 ◆ A highly magnified electron microscope photo of the cilia (orange bristles) found on the top of human hair cells. (Colors are artificial.)

Dancing or aerobic exercise heightens the risk by diverting blood flow from the inner ear to the extremities. Rock musicians Neil Young and David Lee Roth have been sued by fans who claim their hearing was damaged at concerts. Walkman-style stereo headphones also present a danger. Many can reach 115 decibels or more. If you can hear the sound from the headset on the person standing next to you, the volume is probably damaging the user's ears. "Boom box" car stereos present similar dangers.

If **tinnitus** (tin-NYE-tus: *a ringing or buzzing sensation*) follows exposure to loud sounds, chances are that hair cells have been damaged. Almost everyone has tinnitus at times, especially with increasing age. But after repeated sounds that produce this warning, you can expect to become permanently hard-of-hearing. A recent study of people who regularly go to amplified concerts found that 44 percent had tinnitus and most had some hearing loss (Meyer-Bisch, 1996).

Figure 6–22 ◆ The loudness of sound is measured in decibels. Zero decibels is the faintest sound most people can hear. Sound in the range of 110 decibels is uncomfortably loud. Prolonged exposure to sounds above 85 decibels may damage the inner ear. Rock music, which may rate 120 decibels, is known to have caused hearing loss in musicians and may affect audiences as well. Sounds of 130 decibels pose an immediate danger to hearing.

The next time you are exposed to a very loud sound, remember Figure 6–22 and take precautions against damage. (Remember, too, that for temporary ear protection, fingers are always handy.)

Smell and Taste—The Nose Knows When the Tongue Can't Tell

Unless you are a wine taster, a perfume blender, a chef, or a gourmet, you may think of **olfaction** (*smell*) and **gustation** (*taste*) as least important among the senses. Certainly a person could survive without these two **chemical senses** (*receptors that respond to chemical molecules*). Just the same, the chemical senses occasionally prevent poisonings and they add pleasure to our lives. Let's see how they operate.

The Sense of Smell

The receptors for smell respond primarily to gaseous molecules carried in the air. As air enters the nose, it passes over roughly 5 million nerve fibers embedded in the lining of the upper nasal passages. Airborne molecules passing over the exposed fibers trigger nerve signals that are sent to the brain (Fig. 6–23 ◆).

How are different odors produced?

This is still something of a mystery. One hint comes from the fact that it is possible to develop a sort of "smell blindness" for a single odor. This **anosmia** (an-NOSE-me-ah: *loss of smell*) suggests that olfactory nerve fibers have specific receptors for different odors. Indeed, scientists have noticed that molecules having a particular odor are quite similar in shape. Specific shapes have been identified for the following odors: *floral* (flower-like), *camphoric* (camphor-like), *musky* (Have you ever smelled a sweaty musk ox?), *minty* (mint-like), and *etherish* (like ether or cleaning fluid). This does not mean, however, that there are five different olfactory receptors, like the three types of cones in vision. At least 1,000 types of receptors for smell exist.

Each olfactory receptor is sensitive to only part of a molecule's structure. As they react to portions of various molecules, olfactory receptors send messages to the brain. These messages tell the brain, in effect, "The following types of molecules have been detected." The brain then uses distinctive patterns of messages to recognize the "molecular fingerprints" that identify a particular scent (Axel, 1995). (See Figure 6–24 ◆.)

It is currently believed that there are different shaped "holes," or "pockets," on the odor receptors. Like a piece fits in a puzzle, *chemicals produce odors when part of a molecule matches* a hole of the same shape. This is called the **lock and key theory.** Scents are also identified, in part, by the *location* of receptors in the nose activated by an odor. And finally, the *number of activated receptors* tells the brain how strong an odor is (Freeman, 1991).

A large-scale test found that 1.2 percent of the population cannot smell at all (Gilbert & Wysocki, 1987). People with total anosmia typically find that olfaction is not such a minor sense after all. One anosmic individual, for instance, failed to notice that his apartment building was on fire. He was awakened just in time by neighbors, not by the smell of smoke (Monmaney, 1987). Even in everyday terms, anosmia can be a real loss. Many anosmics are unable to cook, and they may be poisoned by spoiled food.

What causes anosmia?

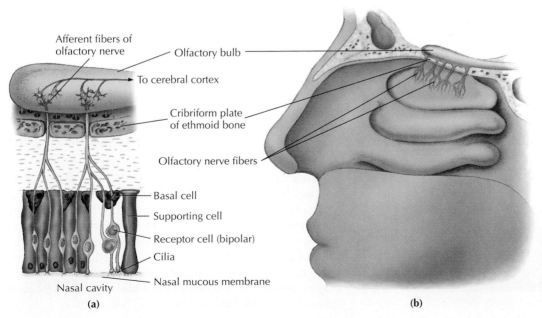

Figure 6–23 ◆ Receptors for the sense of smell (olfaction). Olfactory nerve fibers respond to gaseous molecules. Receptor cells are shown in cross section at left of part **(a)**.

Afferent fibers of olfactory nerve
Olfactory bulb
To cerebral cortex
Cribriform plate of ethmoid bone
Olfactory nerve fibers
Basal cell
Supporting cell
Receptor cell (bipolar)
Cilia
Nasal mucous membrane
Nasal cavity
(a)

(b)

Figure 6-24 ◆ This extreme close-up of an olfactory receptor cell shows the thread-like fibers that project into the air flow inside the nose. Receptor proteins on the surface of the fibers are sensitive to different airborne molecules. Nerve impulses are triggered when gaseous molecules match the structure of specific proteins in a lock-and-key fashion.

Risks include infections, allergies, and blows to the head (which may tear the olfactory nerves). Exposure to chemicals such as ammonia, photo-developing chemicals, and hairdressing potions can also cause anosmia. If you value your sense of smell, be careful what you breathe.

Could the nose be the home of another, poorly understood chemical sense? Let's investigate.

The **vomeronasal organ** (**VNO**) (voh-MARE-oh-NAZE-ul) *is the sense organ for pheromones.* Until recently, humans were assumed to have only a vestigial VNO or none at all. Now, however, scientists believe they have located the VNO in humans.

The suspected human vomeronasal organ looks like a small pit inside the nose (one on each side of the septum). These pits are lined with nerve cells and respond to chemicals that are suspected pheromones.

What would a pheromone smell like?

Pheromones are not smelled, felt, seen, tasted, or heard. In humans, pheromones would most likely produce vague feelings, such as well-being, attraction, aversion, unease, or anxiety. When people say that their relationships are influenced by good or bad "chemistry," there may be some truth to it. Pheromones could add to the intoxicating feelings of romantic attraction or the sourness of instant dislike. (Men shouldn't expect "Boar's Breath" cologne to be offered anytime soon, however.)

Evidence for the existence of human pheromones remains preliminary and controversial. Nevertheless, the possibilities are intriguing. For instance, human pheromones may explain why the menstrual cycles of women who live together tend to become synchronized. It's also possible that pheromones may one day be used to decrease anxiety, curb hunger, or relieve premenstrual discomforts. Only further study will tell if searching for a sixth sense makes sense. (Sources: Monti-Bloch et al., 1994; Stensaas et al., 1991; Weller & Weller, 1995.)

Taste

There are at least four basic taste sensations: *sweet, salt, sour,* and *bitter.* We are most sensitive to bitter, less sensitive to sour, even less sensitive to salt, and least sensitive to sweet. This order may have helped prevent poisonings when most humans foraged for food, because bitter and sour foods are more likely to be inedible (McLaughlin & Margolskee, 1994).

If there are only four tastes, how can there be so many different flavors?

Flavors seem more varied than suggested by the four taste qualities because we tend to include sensations of texture, temperature, smell, and even pain ("hot" chili peppers) along with taste. Smell is particularly important in determining flavor. Small bits of apple, potato, and onion "taste" almost exactly alike when the nose is plugged. So do gourmet jelly beans! It is probably no exaggeration to say that subjective flavor is one half smell. This is why food loses its "taste" when you have a cold.

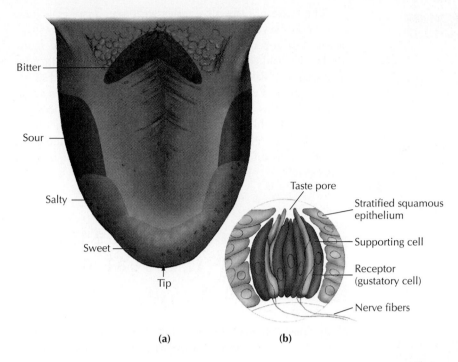

Bitter

Sour

Salty

Sweet

Tip

(a)

Taste pore

Stratified squamous epithelium

Supporting cell

Receptor (gustatory cell)

Nerve fibers

(b)

Figure 6–25 ◆ Receptors for taste: **(a)** Position of receptors (taste buds) especially sensitive to four taste qualities. **(b)** Detail of a taste bud within the tongue. The buds also occur in other parts of the digestive system.

Taste buds (*taste-receptor cells*) are mainly located on the top side of the tongue. However, a few are found elsewhere inside the mouth (Fig. 6–25 ◆). As food is chewed, it dissolves and enters the taste buds, where it sets off nerve impulses to the brain. Taste receptors are not equally distributed. Look at Figure 6–25 and you will see that some areas of the tongue are more sensitive to certain tastes than others.

Much like smell, sweet and bitter tastes appear to be based on a lock-and-key match between molecules and intricately shaped receptors. Saltiness and sourness, however, are triggered by a direct flow of charged atoms into the tips of taste cells.

Many chemical salts taste salty. Sour tastes are triggered by acids. However, chemical compounds that taste sweet can take many forms. Those that taste bitter vary even more. (See Table 6–3 ■.) Again, our broad sensitivity to bitter chemicals is probably related to survival in a world filled with bitter-tasting toxins (McLaughlin & Margolskee, 1994).

People seem to have very different tastes. Why is that?

Some differences are genetic. The chemical phenylthiocarbamine (FEEN-il-thi-oh-CAR-bah-meen), or PTC, tastes bitter to about 70 percent of those tested and has no taste for the other 30 percent. More generally, taste sensitivity is related to how many taste buds you have on your tongue. Some people have as few as 500 taste buds, while others have as many as 10,000. Those with many taste buds are "supertasters" who need only half as much sugar in their coffee to make it sweet (Pennisi, 1992).

Table 6–3   ■   **Taste Intensity of Various Substances**

Salty substances	Saltiness*
sodium chloride (table salt)	100 percent
sodium bromide	40 percent
potassium chloride	60 percent
sodium fluoride	200 percent
ammonium chloride	250 percent
Sour substances	**Sourness***
hydrochloric acid	100 percent
citric acid	46 percent
malic acid	60 percent
lactic acid	85 percent
formic acid	110 percent
Sweet substances	**Sweetness***
sucrose (common sugar)	100 percent
glucose	80 percent
fructose	170 percent
aspartame	1500 percent
saccharin	6750 percent
Bitter substances	**Bitterness***
quinine	100 percent
caffeine	40 percent
nicotine	130 percent
strychnine	310 percent
denatonium	10,000 percent

*Relative to reference substance (shown as 100 percent)
(Adapted from McLaughlin & Margolskee, 1994.)

Are You a Supertaster?

Spicy foods? Some like it hot. Others breathe fire if a dish contains a tiny bit too much pepper. And what about sweets? One person's sumptuous delight is another's cloying goo. Clearly, all tongues are not created equal. To learn a little more about taste sensitivity, try the following tests, devised by Linda Bartoshuk and Laurie Lucchina of Yale University.

Sweet Place one-half cup of sugar in a measuring cup and add enough water to make one cup of solution. Rinse your mouth with plain water. Use a cotton swab dipped in the sugar solution to coat the front half of your tongue, including the tip. Wait a few seconds and rate the sensation of sweetness according to the taste scale.

Taste Scale

Barely detectable — Weak — Moderate — Strong — Very strong — Strongest imaginable sensation

0 10 20 30 40 50 60 70 80 90 100

Spicy Add one teaspoon of Tabasco sauce to one cup of water. Coat one-half inch of your tongue, starting at the tip. Keep your tongue outside of your mouth until the burning sensation peaks. Rate the sensation of "heat" you feel on the scale.

Results Table 6–4 ■ shows typical ratings for non-tasters and supertasters. Most people, of course, fall in between these extremes.

Table 6–4 ■ Average Taste Test Ratings		
	Non-taster	**Supertaster**
Sweet	32	56
Spicy	31	64

Supertasters tend to have stronger tastes for sweet, bitter, and irritants such as alcohol and capsaicin (the chemical that makes chilies hot). Women are more often supertasters. Non-tasters tend to prefer sweets and fatty foods, which may be why supertasters tend to be slimmer than non-tasters. (Sources: Bartoshuk, Duffy, & Miller, 1994; Brownlee, 1997)

The sense of taste also varies with age. Taste cells have a life of only several days. With aging, cell replacement slows down, so the sense of taste diminishes. That's why many foods you disliked in childhood may seem appetizing now. Children who will not eat broccoli, spinach, liver, and so on, may be having a very different taste experience than an adult. Aside from this fact, however, most taste preferences are acquired. Would you eat the coagulated secretion of the modified skin glands of a cow after it had undergone bacterial decomposition? If you would, you are a *cheese fancier!*

The Somesthetic Senses— Flying by the Seat of Your Pants

A gymnast "flying" through a routine on the uneven bars may rely as much on the **somesthetic senses** as on vision (*soma* means "body," *esthetic* means "feel"). Even the most routine activities, such as walking, running, or passing a sobriety test, would be impossible without somesthetic information from the body.

What are the somesthetic senses?

Somesthetic sensitivity includes the **skin senses** (*touch*), the **kinesthetic senses** (*receptors in muscles and joints that detect body position and movement*), and the **vestibular senses** (*receptors for balance, gravity, and acceleration*). (The vestibular senses also contribute to motion sickness, as discussed in this chapter's Exploration.) Because of their importance, let us focus on the skin senses.

Skin receptors produce at least five different sensations: *light touch, pressure, pain, cold, and warmth.* Receptors with particular shapes appear to specialize somewhat in various sensations (Fig. 6–26 ◆). However, the surface of the eye, which only has free nerve endings, can produce all five sensations (Carlson, 1994). Altogether, the skin has about 200,000 nerve endings for temperature, 500,000 for touch and pressure, and 3 million for pain.

Does the number of receptors in an area of skin relate to its sensitivity?

Yes. Your skin could be "mapped" by applying heat, cold, touch, pressure, or pain to points all over your body. Such testing would show that the number of skin receptors varies, and that sensitivity generally matches the number of receptors in a given area. As a rough-and-ready illustration, try this two-point touch test:

> The density of touch receptors on various body areas can be checked by having a friend apply two pencil points to the skin with varying distances between them. Without looking, you should respond "one" or "two" each time. Record the distance between the pencils each time you feel two points.

Outer layer
of skin

Merkel's disks

Free nerve
endings

Meissner's
corpuscle

Krause's
end-bulb

Nerve endings
around hair follicle

Pacinian
corpuscle

Figure 6–26 ◆ The skin senses include touch, pressure, pain, cold, and warmth. This drawing shows different forms the skin receptors can take. Other shapes were once recognized, but most turned out to be variations of the shapes shown here. The only clearly specialized receptor is the Pacinian corpuscle, which is highly sensitive to pressure. Free nerve endings are receptors for pain and any of the other sensations. For reasons that are not clear, cold is sensed near the surface of the skin, and warmth is sensed deeper (Carlson, 1994).

You should find that two points are recognizable when they are 1/10 inch apart on the fingertips, 1/4 inch on the nose, and 3 inches at the middle of the back. Generally speaking, important areas such as the lips, tongue, face, hands, and genitals have a higher density of receptors.

There are many more pain receptors than other kinds. Why is pain so heavily represented, and does the concentration of pain receptors also vary?

Like the other skin senses, pain receptors vary in their distribution. An average of about 232 pain points per square centimeter are found behind the knee, 184 per centimeter on the buttocks (an area preferred by many parents for spankings), 60 on the pad of the thumb, and 44 on the tip of the nose. (Is it better then, to be pinched on the nose than behind the knee? It depends on what you like!)

Pain fibers are also found in the internal organs. Stimulation of these fibers causes **visceral pain.** Curiously, visceral pain is often felt on the surface of the body, *at a site some distance from the point of origin* (Chiras, 1991). Experiences of this type are called **referred pain** (Fig. 6–27 ◆). For example, a person having a heart attack may feel pain in the left shoulder, arm, or even the little finger.

Pain from the skin, muscles, joints, and tendons is known as **somatic** (*bodily*) **pain.** Somatic pain carried by *large nerve fibers* is sharp, bright, fast, and seems to come from specific body areas. This is the body's **warning system.** Give yourself a small jab with a pin and you will feel this type of pain. As you do this, notice that warning pain quickly disappears. Much as we may dislike warning pain, it is *usually a signal that the body has been, or is about to be, damaged.* Without warning pain, we would be unable to detect or prevent injury. Children who are born with a rare inherited insensitivity to pain repeatedly burn themselves, break bones, bite their tongues, and become ill without knowing it (Larner et al., 1994).

A second type of somatic pain is carried by *small nerve*

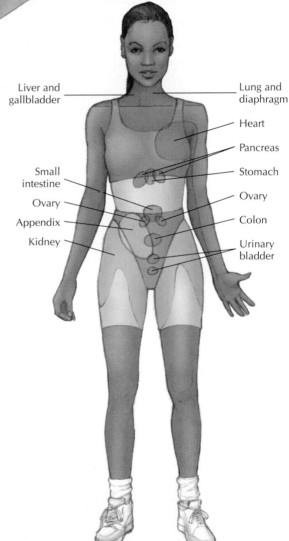

Liver and
gallbladder

Lung and
diaphragm

Heart

Pancreas

Small
intestine

Stomach

Ovary

Ovary

Appendix

Colon

Kidney

Urinary
bladder

Figure 6–27 ◆ Visceral pain often seems to come from the surface of the body, even though its true origin is internal. Referred pain is believed to result from the fact that pain fibers from internal organs enter the spinal cord at the same location as sensory fibers from the skin. Apparently, the brain misinterprets the visceral pain messages as impulses from the body's surface (Chiras, 1991).

fibers. This type is slower, nagging, aching, widespread, and very unpleasant. It gets worse if the pain stimulus is repeated. This is the body's **reminding system.** *It reminds the brain that the body has been injured.* A sad thing about the reminding system is that it often causes agony even when the reminder is useless, as in terminal cancer, or when pain continues after an injury has healed. Later in the chapter we will return to pain to learn how it can be controlled. If you got carried away with the pin demonstration, maybe you should read ahead now!

Before we leave the topic, here's another aspect of touch you might find interesting.

Dynamic Touch

A carpenter swings a hammer with practiced precision. A juggler fluidly tosses and catches five balls. An ice hockey player embeds his stick in an opposing player's helmet. In sports and everyday life, touch is rarely static. Most skilled performances rely on **dynamic touch,** *which combines sensations from skin receptors with kinesthetic information from the muscles and tendons.*

Figure 6–28 ◆ Hold a variety of elongated objects upright between your fingertips. Close your eyes and move each object about. Your ability to estimate the size, length, shape, and orientation of each object will be quite accurate. (After Turvey, 1996.)

Recent studies have shown that dynamic touch provides surprisingly detailed information about objects, such as their size and shape. (See Figure 6–28 ◆.)

How are we able to make such judgments? Psychologist M. T. Turvey has found that most bodily motions form an arc or a combination of arcs. Dynamic touch is largely a matter of sensing the *inertia* of objects as they move through these arcs.

The fact that dynamic touch is a reliable source of information is what makes it possible for us to use a wide range of tools, utensils, and objects as if they were extensions of our bodies (Turvey, 1996).

Adaptation, Attention, and Gating—Tuning In and Tuning Out

Each of the senses we have described is continuously active. Even so, many sensory events never reach awareness. One reason for this is *sensory adaptation,* a second is *selective attention,* and a third is *sensory gating.* Let's see how information is filtered by these processes.

Sensory Adaptation Think about walking into a house where fried fish, sauerkraut, and head cheese were prepared for dinner. (Some dinner!) You would probably pass out at the door, yet people who had been in the house for some time would be unaware of the food odors. Why? Because **sensory adaptation** (*decreased response to a constant or unchanging stimulus*) would occur.

Fortunately, the olfactory (smell) receptors are among the most quickly adapting. When exposed to a constant odor, they send fewer and fewer nerve impulses to the brain until the odor is no longer noticed. Adaptation to sensations of pressure from a wristwatch, waistband, ring, or glasses is based on the same principle. Sensory receptors generally respond best to *changes* in stimulation. As David Hubel says, "We need above all to know about changes; no one wants or needs to be reminded 16 hours a day that his shoes are on" (Hubel, 1979a).

If change is necessary to prevent sensory adaptation, why doesn't vision undergo adaptation like the sense of smell does? If you stare at something, it certainly doesn't go away.

The rods and cones, like other receptor cells, would respond less to a constant stimulus were it not for the fact that the eye normally makes thousands of tiny movements every minute. These movements are caused by **physiological nystagmus** (nis-TAG-mus: *involuntary tremors of the eye muscles*). Although they are too small to be seen, these movements shift visual images from one receptor cell to another.

Constant shifting of the eyes ensures that images always fall on fresh, unfatigued receptors. Evidence for this comes from experiments in which subjects are fitted with a special contact lens that has a miniature slide projector attached to

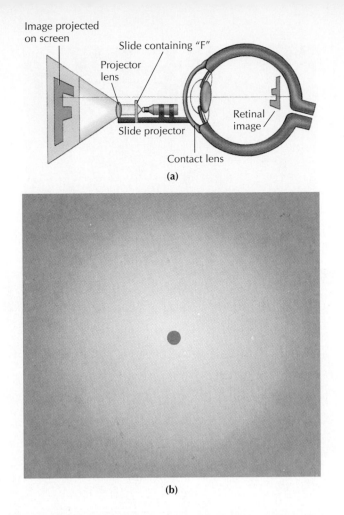

(a)

(b)

Figure 6–29 ◆ Stabilized images. **(a)** Miniature slide projector attached to a contact lens moves each time the eye moves. As a result, the projected image disappears in a few seconds because it does not move on the retina. **(b)** A similar effect occurs when changes in brightness do not define a distinct edge. In this case, eye movements cannot prevent adaptation. Therefore, if you stare at the dot, the lighter area will disappear. (After Cornsweet, 1970.)

it (Fig. 6–29a ◆). Since the projector follows the exact movements of the eye, an image can be stabilized on the retina. When this is done, projected geometric designs fade from view within a few seconds (Pritchard, 1961). You can get the same effect by staring at Figure 6–29b ◆. Since the lighter circle does not form a distinct edge, the retina adapts to the brightness difference and the circle gradually disappears.

Selective Attention The so-called "seat-of-your-pants phenomenon" also relates to the functioning of sensory systems. As you sit reading this chapter, receptors for touch and pressure in the seat of your pants are sending nerve impulses to your brain. Even though these sensations have been present all along, you were probably not aware of them until just now. The seat-of-your-pants phenomenon is an example of **selective attention** (*voluntarily focusing on a specific sensory input*). We are able to "tune in on" any of the many sensory messages bombarding us while excluding

others. Another familiar example of this is the "cocktail party effect." When you are in a group of people, surrounded by voices, you can still select and attend to the voice of the person you are facing. Or if that person gets dull, you can eavesdrop on conversations all over the room. (Be sure to smile and nod your head occasionally!) The cocktail party effect is quite powerful. If you are listening to one person, another person nearby can talk *backward* and you will not notice their strange speech (Wood & Cowan, 1995).

What makes that possible?

Selective attention appears to be based on the ability of various brain structures to select and divert incoming sensory messages (Mangun, 1995). But what about messages that haven't reached the brain? Is it possible that some are blocked while others are allowed to pass? Evidence suggests there are *sensory gates* that control the flow of incoming nerve impulses in just this way. In particular, **sensory gating** *refers to facilitating or blocking sensory messages in the spinal cord* (Melzack, 1993).

Sensory Gating of Pain A fascinating example of sensory gating is provided by Ronald Melzack and Patrick Wall, who study "pain gates" in the spinal cord (Melzack & Wall, 1983). Melzack and Wall noticed, as you may have, that one type of pain will sometimes cancel another. Their **gate control theory** *suggests that pain messages from different nerve fibers pass through the same neural "gate" in the spinal cord.* If the gate is "closed" by one pain message, other messages may not be able to pass through.

How is the gate closed?

Messages carried by large, fast nerve fibers seem to close the spinal pain gate directly. Doing so can prevent slower, "reminding system" pain from reaching the brain. Pain clinics use this effect by applying a mild electrical current to the skin. Such stimulation, felt only as a mild tingling, can greatly reduce more agonizing pain (Long, 1991).

Messages from small, slow fibers seem to take a different route. After going through the pain gate, they pass on to a "central biasing system" in the brain. Under some circumstances, the brain then sends a message back down the spinal cord, closing the pain gates. (See Figure 6–30 ◆.) Melzack and Wall believe that gate control theory explains the painkilling effects of *acupuncture*.

Acupuncture *is the Chinese medical art of relieving pain and illness by inserting thin needles into the body.* As the acupuncturist's needles are twirled, heated, or electrified, they activate small pain fibers. These relay through the biasing system to close the gates to intense or chronic pain (Melzack & Wall, 1983). Controlled studies have shown that acupuncture produces short-term pain relief for 50–80 percent of patients tested (Ernst, 1994; Murray, 1995).

Acupuncture has an interesting side effect not predicted by sensory gating. People given acupuncture often report feelings of light-headedness, relaxation, or euphoria. How are these feelings explained? The answer seems to lie in the

Figure 6–30 ◆ Diagram of a sensory gate for pain. A series of pain impulses going through the gate may prevent other pain messages from passing through. Or pain messages may relay through a "central biasing mechanism" that exerts control over the gate, closing it to other impulses.

body's ability to produce opiate-like chemicals. To combat pain, the brain causes the pituitary gland to release a *painkilling chemical* called **beta-endorphin** (BAY-tah-en-DOR-fin: from *endo*, "within" and *orphin*, "opiate"). Chemically, beta-endorphin is quite similar to morphine.

Receptor sites for endorphins are found in large numbers in the limbic system and other brain areas associated with pleasure, pain, and emotion. Both acupuncture and electrical stimulation cause a build-up of endorphins in the brain. In other words, the nervous system makes its own "drugs" to block pain. Actually, this ties in nicely with the idea of pain gates. The central biasing system, which closes pain gates in the spinal cord, is highly sensitive to morphine and other opiate painkillers (Melzack & Wall, 1983).

The discovery of endorphins and their painkilling effect has caused quite a stir in psychology. At long last it may be possible to explain a number of puzzling phenomena. For example, the painkilling effect of placebos (fake pills or injections) appears to be based on a rise in beta-endorphin levels (Lipman et al., 1990). A release of endorphins also appears to underlie "runner's high," masochism, acupuncture, and the euphoria sometimes associated with childbirth and painful initiation rites. In each instance there is reason to believe that pain and stress cause the release of endorphins. These in turn induce feelings of pleasure or euphoria similar to morphine intoxication (Kruger & Liebeskind, 1984; Ulett, 1992).

The "high" often felt by long-distance runners serves as a good example of the endorphin effect. In one experiment, subjects were tested for pain tolerance. After running 1 mile, each was tested again. In the second test, all could withstand

(top) An acupuncturist's chart. (bottom) Thin stainless steel needles are inserted into areas defined by the chart. Modern research has begun to explain the painkilling effects of acupuncture (see text). Acupuncture's claimed ability to cure diseases is more debatable.

pain about 70 percent longer than before. The runners were then given naloxone, a drug that blocks the effects of endorphins. Following another 1-mile run the subjects were tested again. This time they had lost their earlier protection from pain (Haier et al., 1981). People who say they are "addicted" to running may be closer to the truth than they realize. And more important, we may at last have an explanation for those hardy souls who take hot saunas followed by cold showers!

A Look Ahead The severity of pain is also affected by a variety of psychological factors. Since you may not want to try acupuncture or electrical stimulation to control everyday pain, the following Applications describes several practical ways to reduce pain. After that, we will explore the sense of balance—and motion sickness. Before we turn to these topics, here's a Learning Check.

Learning Check

1. Which of the following is not important for the transduction of sound?
   a. pinna   **b.** ossicles   **c.** phosphenes   **d.** oval window   **e.** hair cells

2. Daily exposure to sounds with a loudness of _____ decibels may cause permanent hearing loss.

3. Cochlear implants have been used primarily to overcome
   a. conduction deafness   **b.** stimulation deafness   **c.** nerve deafness   **d.** tinnitus

4. Olfaction appears to be at least partially explained by the _____ _____ _____ theory of molecule shapes and receptor sites.

5. From the standpoint of survival, we are fortunate that bitter tastes register primarily on the tip of the tongue. T or F?

6. Which of the following is a somesthetic sense?
   a. gustation   **b.** olfaction   **c.** rarefaction   **d.** kinesthesis

7. Warning pain is carried by _____ nerve fibers.

8. Sensory adaptation refers to an increase in sensory response that accompanies a constant or unchanging stimulus. T or F?

9. The brain-centered ability to influence what sensations we will receive is called
   a. sensory gating   **b.** central adaptation   **c.** selective attention   **d.** sensory biasing

10. The painkilling effects of acupuncture appear to result from _____ _____ and the release of beta-endorphin.

Critical Thinking

11. What precautions would you need to take to test claims that acupuncture reduces pain?

Answers:

1. c   2. 85   3. c   4. lock and key   5. F   6. d   7. large   8. F   9. c   10. sensory gating   11. At the very least, you would have to control for the placebo effect by giving fake acupuncture to control group members. However, true double-blind studies of acupuncture are difficult to do. Acupuncturists know if they are giving a placebo treatment or the real thing, which means they might unconsciously influence subjects.

Applications

Controlling Pain—This Won't Hurt a Bit

There are many indications that pain may be controlled psychologically. In India, fakirs pierce their cheeks with needles or sit on beds of spikes. In other cultures, people endure tattooing, stretching, cutting, burning, and the like, with little apparent pain. How is such insensitivity achieved? There is no evidence that these people lack normal pain responses. Very likely the answer lies in four factors that can be used by anyone to alter the amount of pain felt in a particular situation. These are: (1) **anxiety,** (2) **control,** (3) **attention,** and (4) **interpretation.**

Anxiety The basic sensory message of pain can be separated from emotional reactions to it. Fear or high levels of anxiety almost always increase pain. A dramatic reversal of this effect is the surprising lack of pain displayed by soldiers wounded in battle. Being excused from further combat apparently produces a flood of relief. This emotional state leaves many soldiers insensitive to wounds that would agonize a civilian (Melzack & Wall, 1983).

Control A moment's reflection should convince you that the most upsetting pain is that over which you have no control. Loss of control seems to increase pain by increasing anxiety and emotional distress. People who are allowed to regulate, avoid, or control a painful stimulus suffer less. In general, the more control one *feels* over a painful stimulus, the less pain experienced (Kruger & Liebeskind, 1984; Wells, 1994).

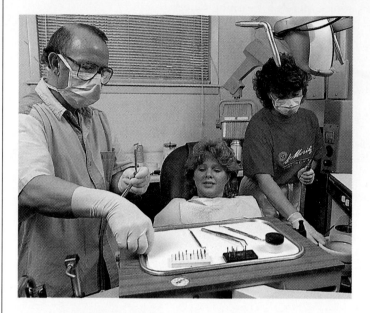

Pain is a complex experience. In addition to producing a physical sensation, pain messages activate areas of the brain associated with emotion. If you are fearful or anxious, the emotional part of pain will be magnified, and you will feel more intense pain. Reducing fear and anxiety is one of several things you can do to diminish pain.

Attention   Distraction can also radically reduce pain. Pain, even though it is highly persistent, can be selectively "tuned out" (at least partially), just like any other sensation. Subjects in one experiment who were exposed to intense pain experienced the greatest relief when they were distracted by the task of reading letters aloud (Dubreuil, Endler, & Spanos, 1988).

In another experiment, pain was lessened when subjects concentrated on trying to name all their high school courses and teachers (Ahles et al., 1983). For the same reason, you may have temporarily forgotten about a toothache or similar pain while absorbed in a movie or book. Concentrating on pleasant, soothing images can be especially helpful (Fernandez & Turk, 1989). Instead of listening to the whirr of a dentist's drill, for example, you might imagine that you are lying in the sun at a beach, listening to the roar of the surf. At home, music can be a good distractor from chronic pain (Good, 1995; Michel & Chesky, 1995).

Interpretation   The meaning or interpretation given a painful stimulus also affects pain (Keefe, 1982). For example, if you give a child a swat on the behind while playing, you'll probably get a burst of laughter. Yet the same swat given as punishment may bring tears (Bresler & Trubo, 1979). The effects of interpretation have also been demonstrated in the lab (Devine & Spanos, 1990). For example, in one experiment it was found that thinking of pain as pleasurable

(denying the pain) greatly increased pain tolerance (Neufeld, 1970).

Coping with Pain

How can these facts be applied?

In a sense, they have already been applied to childbirth. **Prepared childbirth training,** *which promotes birth with a minimum of drugs or painkillers,* uses all four factors. To prepare for natural childbirth, the expectant mother learns in great detail what to anticipate at each stage of labor. This greatly relieves her fears and anxieties. During labor, she attends to sensations that mark her progress and she adjusts her breathing accordingly. Her attention is shifted to sensations other than pain, resulting in less discomfort (Leventhal et al., 1989). Also, her positive attitude is maintained by use of the term *contractions* rather than *labor pains*. Finally, because of her months of preparation and her active participation, she feels *in control* of the situation.

Natural childbirth techniques reduce pain by an average of about 30 percent. Many women find this reduction quite helpful. However, it is important to remember that labor can produce very severe pain. A woman should not feel guilty if she needs painkillers during labor. Many women who have had prepared childbirth training still end up asking for an epidural block (Melzack, 1984).

With more moderate pain, reduced anxiety, redirected attention, and added control can make quite a difference. In any situation where pain can be anticipated (a trip to the doctor, dentist, and so on), lowered anxiety may be achieved by making sure that you are *fully informed.* Be sure that everything that will happen or could happen to you is explained. Also, be sure to fully discuss any fears you have. If you are physically tense, the use of relaxation exercises can help lower your level of arousal. Relaxation methods involve tensing and then releasing muscles in various parts of the body. A typical technique is described in detail in the Applications section of Chapter 19. (The desensitization procedure described there may also help reduce anxiety.)

Distraction and Reinterpretation   Some dentists are now equipped to help you shift attention away from pain. Patients are actively distracted with video games and headphones carrying music. In other situations, focusing on some external object may help you shift attention away from pain. Pick a tree outside a window, a design on the wall, or some other stimulus and examine it in great detail. Prior practice in meditation can be a tremendous aid to such attention shifts. (Meditation techniques are described in Chapter 14.) Research suggests that distraction of this type works best for mild or brief pain. For chronic or strong pain, reinterpretation is more effective (McCaul & Malott, 1984).

Is there any way to increase control over a painful stimulus?

Counterirritation   Practically speaking, the choices may be limited. You may be able to arrange a signal with a doctor or dentist that will give you control over whether a painful procedure will continue. A second possibility is more unusual. Ronald Melzack's gate control theory of pain suggests that sending *mild* pain messages to the spinal cord and brain may effectively close the neurological gates to more severe or unpredictable pain. Medical texts have long recognized this effect. Physicians have found that intense surface stimulation of the skin can control pain from other parts of the body. *Likewise, a brief, mildly painful stimulus can relieve more severe pain.* Such procedures, known as **counterirritation,** are evident in some of the oldest techniques used to control pain: applying ice packs, hot-water bottles, mustard packs, vibration, or massage to other parts of the body (Kakigi et al., 1993; Melzack, 1974).

These facts suggest a way to minimize pain that is based on increased control, counterirritation, and the release of endorphins. If you pinch yourself, you can easily *create and endure* pain equal to that produced by many medical procedures (receiving an injection, having a tooth drilled, and so on). The pain doesn't seem too bad because you have control over it, and it is predictable.

This fact can be used to *mask* one pain with a second painful stimulus that is under your control. For instance, if you are having a tooth filled, try pinching yourself or digging a fingernail into a knuckle while the dentist is working. Focus your attention on the pain you are creating, and increase its intensity anytime the dentist's work becomes more painful. This suggestion may not work for you, but casual observation suggests that it can be a useful technique for controlling pain in some circumstances. Generations of children have used it to take the edge off a spanking.

Learning Check

1. Like heightened anxiety, increased control tends to increase subjective pain. T or F?

2. In one experiment, subjects given the task of reading letters aloud experienced less pain than subjects who paid attention to the pain stimulus. T or F?

3. Imagining a pleasant experience can be an effective way of reducing pain in some situations. T or F?

4. The concept of counterirritation holds that relaxation and desensitization are key elements of pain control. T or F?

Critical Thinking

5. What measures would you take to ensure that an experiment involving pain is ethical?

Answers:
1. F 2. T 3. T 4. F 5. Experiments that cause pain must be handled with care and sensitivity. Participation must be voluntary; the source of pain must be non-injurious; and subjects must be allowed to quit at any time.

Exploration

Sensation in Space—Adapting to an Alien Environment

On television, astronauts are often shown playfully enjoying the acrobatics made possible by weightlessness. But adapting to life in space is not as easy or pleasant as such images imply. Indeed, if you were to ride into space, it is about 70 percent likely that your first experience in orbit would be throwing up (Davis et al., 1988). Over one half of all astronauts have suffered from **space adaptation syndrome,** or *"space sickness."*

Is space sickness like sea sickness?

Space Sickness   Space sickness is a type of motion sickness. Like sea sickness, car sickness, and air sickness, its first signs are dizziness and mild disorientation.

However, space sickness usually does not produce the pallor, "cold sweating," and nausea so common on earth. In most types of motion sickness, these signs warn that vomiting is about to occur. But in space, vomiting is usually sudden and unexpected. Seeing another astronaut drift by upside down or viewing the earth at an odd angle is often all it takes to trigger repeated vomiting. Space sickness is especially intense because weightlessness drastically alters sensations the brain receives from the head, muscles, and joints (Lackner & DiZio, 1993).

The Vestibular System

What causes motion sickness?

Motion sickness is directly related to the vestibular system (Fig. 6–31 ◆). Fluid-filled sacs called **otolith organs** (OH-toe-lith) *are sensitive to movement, acceleration, and gravity.* The otolith organs contain tiny crystals in a soft, gelatin-like mass. The tug of gravity or rapid head movements can cause the mass to shift. This, in turn, stimulates hair-like receptor cells, allowing us to sense gravity and movement through space.

Three fluid-filled tubes called the **semicircular canals** *are the sensory organs for balance.* If you could climb inside these tubes, you would find that head movements cause the fluid to swirl about. As the fluid moves, it bends a small "flap," or "float," called the **crista,**

Figure 6–31 ◆
The vestibular system. (See text for explanation.)

Weightlessness presents astronauts with a real challenge in sensory adaptation.

that detects movement in the semicircular canals. A crista can be found within each **ampulla** (am-PULL-ah), *a wider part of the canal.* The bending of each crista again stimulates hair cells and signals head rotation.

Motion Sickness   The most widely accepted explanation of motion sickness is the **sensory conflict theory.** According to this theory, dizziness and nausea occur when *sensations from the vestibular system fail to match information received from the eyes and body* (Warwick-Evans & Beaumont, 1995).

You can create an example of sensory conflict by turning around repeatedly until you become dizzy. Doing so sets the fluid spinning in the semicircular canals. When you stop, the fluid continues to swirl about, so the brain thinks your head is still moving. This causes the eyes to move involuntarily and makes the world seem like it is still spinning.

On solid ground, information from the vestibular system, vision, and kinesthesis usually matches. However, in a heaving, pitching boat, car, or airplane, a serious mismatch can occur—causing disorientation and heaving of another kind.

Why would sensory conflict cause nausea?

According to the most popular theory, you can blame (or thank) evolution. Many poisons disturb the coordination of messages from the vestibular system, vision, and the body. Therefore, we may have evolved so that we react to sensory conflict by vomiting to expel poison. The value of this reaction, however, may be of little comfort to anyone who has ever been "green" and miserable with motion sickness.

In space, sensory conflict can be especially intense. During weightlessness, merely pulling on one's shoes can result in a backward somersault. Under such conditions, the otolith organs send unexpected signals to the brain, and head movements are no longer confirmed by the semicircular canals. Few of the messages the brain receives from the vestibular system and kinesthetic receptors agree with a lifetime of past experience (Yardley, 1992).

How long does it take to adapt to weightlessness?

Space sickness usually disappears in 2 or 3 days. Recent research suggests that

Many people become nauseated the first time they experience virtual reality. Why? Because virtual reality also creates a sensory conflict: Computer-generated visual images change as if the viewer's body is in motion, but the vestibular system tells viewers that they are standing still. The result? The scenery may not be real but the nausea is.

this adaptation occurs because astronauts shift to using visual cues instead of vestibular information. Later, this same shift can cause "earth sickness." Immediately after returning to earth (especially after very long missions), some astronauts have experienced dizziness and nausea. All had considerable difficulty in standing with their eyes closed for the first day or two (Von Baumgarten et al., 1984).

How to Minimize Motion Sickness

Researchers trying to prevent space sickness have learned a great deal about what helps and what doesn't. The following points may be of some aid to you here on earth (Jackson, 1994).

- Medical treatment for space sickness has concentrated on drugs. The most successful so far is scopolamine, which is available by prescription. Nonprescription "sea sickness" pills also offer some protection. Alcohol and other intoxicating drugs, however, usually make motion sickness worse.

- Soviet cosmonauts have had some success with a system that limits head movements for the first 2 days in space. In a boat, car, or airplane, it helps to

move your head as little as possible (Jackson, 1994). You may even want to place a towel around your neck to restrict head movement. (If it doesn't help, you may soon find another use for it.)

- To minimize sensory conflict, stay out of the cabin on boats. In cars and airplanes, try closing your eyes. Or as an alternative, fixate your eyes on an unmoving point (such as the horizon) or look above the horizon at the unmoving sky (Stern et al., 1990).

- If possible, you should lie down. The otoliths are less sensitive to vertical movements when you are horizontal, and your head will move less.

- Anxiety intensifies motion sickness. Some of the astronauts have had success at learning to focus their attention on pleasant, distracting thoughts or calming images. If you do the same, be sure to also breathe slowly and deeply. Breathing can, in fact, be a good focus for attention (Jackson, 1994; Nicogossian & Parker, 1982).

- Relaxation helps minimize motion sickness. You may find it valuable to learn relaxation exercises that you can use when needed (Jackson, 1994). (Relaxation methods are described in Chapter 19 of this book.)

Space sickness is only one of the behavioral challenges of space travel. In fact, the long-term effects of space flight are still largely unknown. Although space missions seem relatively routine, astronauts remain true pioneers in a strange and alien sensory environment.

Learning Check

1. At least 170 out of every 200 astronauts have suffered from space sickness. T or F?

2. Head movements are detected primarily in the semicircular canals, gravity by the otolith organs. T or F?

3. Sensory conflict theory appears to explain space sickness, but it does not seem to apply to other types of motion sickness. T or F?

4. The drug amphetamine has been used successfully to prevent motion sickness. T or F?

Critical Thinking

5. Drivers are less likely to become car-sick than passengers are. Why do you think drivers and passengers differ in susceptibility to motion sickness?

Answers:

1. F 2. T 3. F 4. F 5. Drivers experience less sensory conflict because they control the car's motion. This allows them to anticipate the car's movements and to coordinate their head and eye movements with those of the car.

Chapter Summary

In general, how do sensory systems function?

◆ Sensory organs **transduce** physical energies into nerve impulses.

◆ Because of **selectivity,** limited **sensitivity, feature detection,** and **coding** patterns, the senses act as **data reduction systems.**

◆ Sensory response can be partially understood in terms of **localization of function** in the brain.

What are the limits of our sensory sensitivity?

◆ The minimum amount of physical energy necessary to produce a sensation defines the **absolute threshold.** The amount of change necessary to produce a **just noticeable difference** in a stimulus defines a **difference threshold.** The study of thresholds and related topics is called **psychophysics.**

◆ Threatening or anxiety-provoking stimuli may raise the threshold for recognition, an effect called **perceptual defense.**

◆ Any stimulus below the level of conscious awareness is said to be **subliminal.** There is evidence that **subliminal perception** occurs, but subliminal advertising is largely ineffective.

How is vision accomplished?

◆ The **visible spectrum** consists of electromagnetic radiation in a narrow range.

◆ The eye is in some ways like a camera, but ultimately, it is a **visual system,** not a photographic one. Individual cells in the visual cortex of the brain act as **feature detectors** to analyze visual information.

◆ Four common visual defects, correctable with glasses, are **myopia** (nearsightedness), **hyperopia** (farsightedness), **presbyopia** (loss of accommodation), and **astigmatism.**

◆ The **rods** and **cones** are **photoreceptors** making up the **retina** of the eye. The rods specialize in night vision, black and white reception, and motion detection. The cones, found exclusively in the **fovea** and otherwise toward the middle of the eye, specialize in color vision, **acuity** (perception of fine detail), and daylight vision. Much **peripheral vision** is supplied by the rods.

How do we perceive colors?

◆ The rods and cones differ in color sensitivity. *Yellowish green* is brightest for cones; *blue-green* for the rods (although they will see it as colorless). Color vision is explained by the **trichromatic theory** in the retina and by the **opponent-process theory** in the visual system beyond the eyes.

◆ Total **color blindness** is rare, but 8 percent of males and 1 percent of females are red-green color-blind or color-weak. Color blindness is a **sex-linked trait** carried on the X chromosome. The **Ishihara test** is used to detect color blindness.

◆ **Dark adaptation,** an increase in sensitivity to light, is caused by increased concentration of visual pigments in both the rods and the cones, but mainly by **rhodopsin** recombining in the rods. Vitamin A deficiencies may cause **night blindness.**

What makes hearing possible?

◆ **Sound waves** are the stimulus for hearing. They are transduced by the **eardrum, auditory ossicles, oval window, cochlea,** and ultimately, the **hair cells.**

◆ The **frequency theory** and **place theory** of hearing together explain how pitch is sensed.

◆ Three basic types of deafness are **nerve deafness, conduction deafness,** and **stimulation deafness.**

How do the chemical senses operate?

◆ **Olfaction** (smell) and **gustation** (taste) are **chemical senses** responsive to airborne or liquefied molecules. It is also suspected that humans are sensitive to **pheromones,** although the evidence for this sense remains preliminary.

◆ The **lock and key** theory partially explains smell. In addition, the location of the olfactory receptors in the nose helps identify various scents.

◆ Specific areas on the tongue are more responsive to sweet, salty, sour, and bitter tastes. Taste also appears to be based in part on lock-and-key coding of molecule shapes.

What are the somesthetic senses and why are they important?

◆ The **somesthetic senses** include the **skin senses, vestibular senses,** and **kinesthetic senses** (receptors that detect muscle and joint positioning).

◆ The skin senses include **touch, pressure, pain, cold,** and **warmth.** Sensitivity to each is related to the number of receptors found in an area of skin.

◆ Distinctions can be made among various types of pain, including **visceral pain, somatic pain, referred pain, warning system pain,** and **reminding system pain.**

Why are we more aware of some sensations than others?

◆ Incoming sensations are affected by **sensory adaptation** (a reduction in the number of nerve impulses sent), by **selective attention** (selection and diversion of messages in the brain), and by **sensory gating** (blocking or alteration of messages flowing toward the brain).

◆ Selective gating of pain messages apparently takes place in the spinal cord. **Gate control theory** proposes an explanation for many pain phenomena.

How can pain be reduced in everyday situations?

◆ Pain is greatly affected by **anxiety, attention, control** over the stimulus, the **interpretation** placed on an experience, and by **counterirritation**. Pain can therefore be reduced by controlling these factors.

How is balance related to motion sickness?

◆ Various forms of **motion sickness** are related to messages received from the **vestibular system,** which senses gravity and movement.

◆ According to **sensory conflict theory,** motion sickness is caused by a mismatch of visual, kinesthetic, and vestibular sensations. Motion sickness can be avoided by minimizing sensory conflict.

7

Perceiving the World

Preview

Murder!

The following is a true account. Only the degree of exaggeration has been changed for educational purposes.

I was in a supermarket when a girl suddenly came running around a corner. She looked back and screamed, "Stop! Stop! You're killing him! You're killing my father!" Naturally I was interested! As I quickly retraced her path, I was greeted by a grisly scene. A man was stretched out on the floor with another man on top of him. The guy on top was huge. At 6 feet 6 inches tall and 300 pounds, he looked only half human. He had his victim by the throat and was beating his head against the floor. There was blood everywhere. I decided to do the right thing. I ran.

By the time the store manager and I returned to the "scene of the crime," the police were just arriving. It took quite a while to sort things out, but here is what happened: The "guy on the bottom" had passed out and hit his head. That caused the cut (actually quite minor) which explained the "blood everywhere." The "guy on top" saw the first man fall and was trying to prevent him from further injuring himself. He was also loosening the man's collar.

If I had never returned, I would have sworn in court that I had seen a murder. The girl's words completely dictated my own perceptions. This perhaps is understandable. But what I will never forget is the shock I felt when I met the "murderer"—the man I had seen a few moments before, in broad daylight, as a huge, vicious, horrible-looking creature. The man was not a stranger. He was a neighbor of mine. I had seen him dozens of times before. I know him by name. He is a rather small man.

In the last chapter we discussed sensation, the process of bringing information into the nervous system. This chapter is about **perception,** *or how we assemble sensations into meaningful patterns.* As we perceive events, the brain actively selects, organizes, and integrates sensory information into a "picture" or model of the world. These mental processes are so automatic, it may take drastic misperceptions to call attention to them. Perception creates faces, melodies, works of art, illusions, and on occasion, "murders" out of the raw material of sensation. Let's see how this takes place.

Chapter Survey

Theme: Perception is an active process; perceptual impressions are not always accurate models of events.

Key Questions:	Key Topics to Watch for:
What are perceptual constancies, and what is their role in perception?	Shape, size, and brightness constancy
What basic principles do we use to group sensations into meaningful patterns?	Gestalt principles of perceptual organization
How is it possible to see depth and judge distance?	Stereoscopic vision Physical and pictorial depth cues
What effect does learning have on perception?	Perceptual habits Adaptation level Perceptual illusions
How are perceptions altered by attention, motives, values, and expectations?	Selective attention and divided attention Habituation and the OR Perceptual set
How reliable are eyewitness reports?	Perception and objectivity Enhancing perceptual accuracy
Is extrasensory perception possible?	Parapsychology A critique of psi research Stage ESP

Perceptual Constancies—Taming an Unruly World

What would it be like to have your vision restored after a lifetime of blindness? In reality, a first look at the world can be disappointing. A newly sighted person must *learn* to identify objects, to read clocks, numbers, and letters, and to judge sizes and distances (Senden, 1960). Indeed, learning to "see" can be quite frustrating.

Richard Gregory (1990) describes the experiences of Mr. S. B., a 52-year-old cataract patient who had been blind since birth. After an operation restored his sight, Mr. S. B. struggled to use his vision. At first, he could only judge distance in familiar situations. One day he was found crawling out of a hospital window to get a closer look at traffic on the street. It's easy to understand his curiosity, but he had to be restrained. His room was on the fourth floor!

Why would Mr. S. B. try to crawl out of a fourth-story window? Couldn't he at least tell distance from the size of the cars?

No, because using size to judge distance requires familiarity with the appearance of objects. Try holding your left hand a few inches in front of your eyes and your right hand at arm's length. The image of your right hand should be about half the size of your left hand. Still, because you have viewed your hands from different distances countless times, you know your right hand did not suddenly shrink. This is called **size constancy:** *The perceived size of an object remains the same,*

Visual perception involves finding meaningful patterns in complex stimuli. If you look closely at this painting by the artist Yvaral, you will see that it is entirely made up of small, featureless squares. An infant or newly sighted person would see only a jumble of meaningless colors. But because the squares form a familiar pattern, you should easily see Marilyn Monroe's face. (Or is that Madonna?) ("Marilyn Numerise," 1990, courtesy Circle Gallery.)

despite changes in the size of the image it casts on the retina. Even newborn babies show some evidence of size constancy (Slater, Mattock, & Brown, 1990).

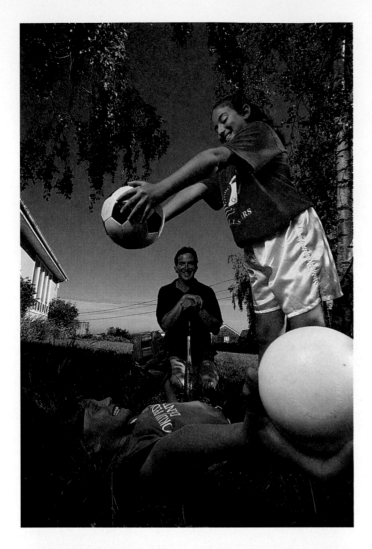

Almost everyone's family album has at least one photo like this. Extreme viewing angles can make maintaining size constancy difficult, even for familiar objects.

To perceive your hand accurately, you had to draw on past experience. Some perceptions are so basic they seem to be **native** (*inborn*). An example is the ability to see a line on a piece of paper. However, much perception is **empirical** (*based on prior experience*). For instance, Colin Turnbull (1961) tells of the time he took a Pygmy from the dense rain forests of Africa to the vast African plains. The Pygmy had never before seen objects at a great distance. Hence, the first time he saw a herd of buffalo in the distance, he thought it was a swarm of insects. Imagine his confusion when he was driven toward the animals. He concluded that he was being fooled by witchcraft because the "insects" seemed to grow into buffalo before his eyes.

Perhaps you have also experienced the failure of size constancy in unfamiliar situations. When viewed from aloft, while flying in an airplane, houses, cars, and people no longer seem normal in size; instead, they begin to look like toys. Thus, we can summarize that size constancy, while being innate, is also molded by experience.

Shape constancy is another interesting effect: *The perceived shape of an object is unaffected by changes in the shape of its retinal image.* You can demonstrate shape constancy by looking at this page from directly overhead and then from an angle. Obviously, the page is rectangular, but most of the time the image that reaches your eye is distorted. Even though the book's image changes, your perception of its shape remains constant. (For additional examples, see Figure 7–1 ◆.) In a movie theater, preserving shape constancy is difficult if you sit in the front row or near the front and to the side. Nevertheless, most people are able to tolerate a fair amount of shape distortion, as long as all objects on the screen are similarly deformed (Cutting, 1987). On the highway, alcohol intoxication impairs size and shape constancy, adding to the accident rate among drunk drivers (Farrimond, 1990).

Figure 7–1 ◆ Shape constancy. **(a)** When a door is open its image actually forms a trapezoid. Shape constancy is indicated by the fact that it is still perceived as a rectangle. **(b)** With great effort you may be able to see this design as a collection of flat shapes. However, if you maintain shape constancy the distorted squares strongly suggest the surface of a sphere. (From Spherescapes-1 by Scott Walter and Kevin McMahon, 1983.)

(a) (b)

Let's say that you are outside in bright sunlight. Beside you is a friend wearing a gray skirt and a white blouse. Suddenly a cloud shades the sun. It might seem that the blouse would grow dimmer, but it still appears to be bright white. This happens because the blouse continues to reflect a larger *proportion* of light than nearby objects. **Brightness constancy** refers to the fact that *the apparent brightness of an object stays the same under changing light conditions.* However, this holds true only if the blouse and surrounding objects are all illuminated by the same amount of light. You could make an area on your friend's gray skirt look whiter than the shaded blouse by shining a bright spotlight on the skirt.

To summarize, the energy patterns reaching our senses are constantly changing, even when they come from the same object. Size, shape, and brightness constancy rescue us from a confusing world in which objects would seem to shrink and grow, change shape as if made of rubber, and light up or fade like neon lamps. Gaining these constancies was only one of the hurdles Mr. S. B. faced in learning to see. In the next section, we will consider some others.

Figure 7–2 ◆ A reversible figure-ground design. Do you see two faces in profile, or a wineglass?

Perceptual Grouping— Getting It All Together

William James said, "To the infant the world is just a big, blooming, buzzing confusion." Like an infant, Mr. S. B. had to find meaning in his visual sensations. He was soon able to tell time from a large wall clock and to read block letters he had known only from touch. At a zoo, he recognized an elephant from descriptions he had heard. However, hand-writing meant nothing to him for more than a year after he regained sight, and many objects were meaningless until he touched them. Thus, while Mr. S. B. had visual *sensations*, his ability to *perceive* remained limited.

How are sensations organized into meaningful perceptions?

Figure and Ground The simplest organization involves *grouping some sensations into an object, or figure, that stands out on a plainer background.* **Figure-ground organization** is probably inborn, since it is the first perceptual ability to appear after cataract patients regain sight. In the brain, cells that receive visual information respond more actively to seeing figures than to seeing backgrounds (Lamme, 1995).

In normal figure-ground perception, only one figure is seen. In **reversible figures,** however, *figure and ground can be switched.* In Figure 7–2 ◆ it is equally possible to see either a wineglass figure on a dark background or two face profiles on a light background. As you shift from one pattern to the other, you should get a clear sense of what figure-ground organization means.

Gestalt Principles

What causes the formation of a figure?

The Gestalt psychologists (see Chapter 1) studied this question in detail. Even if you were seeing for the first time, they concluded, a number of factors would bring some order to your perceptions (Fig. 7–3 ◆).

1. **Nearness.** Stimuli that are near each other tend to be grouped together (see Fig. 7–3a). Thus, if three people stand near each other and a fourth person stands 10 feet away, the adjacent three will be seen as a group and the distant person as an outsider.

2. **Similarity.** "Birds of a feather flock together," and stimuli that are similar in size, shape, color, or form tend to be grouped together (see Fig. 7–3b). Picture two bands marching side by side. If their uniforms are different colors, the bands will be seen as two separate groups, not as one large group.

3. **Continuation, or continuity.** Perceptions tend toward simplicity and continuity. In Figure 7–3c it is easier to visualize a wavy line on a squared-off line than it is to see a complex row of shapes.

4. **Closure.** Closure refers to the tendency to *complete* a figure, so that it has a consistent overall form. Each of the drawings in Figure 7–3d has one or more gaps, yet each is perceived as a recognizable figure. The "shapes" that appear in the two right drawings in Figure 7–3d are **illusory figures** (*implied shapes that are not actually bounded by an edge or an outline*). Even young children see these shapes, despite knowing that they are "not really there." Illusory figures reveal that our tendency to form shapes—even with minimal cues—is powerful.

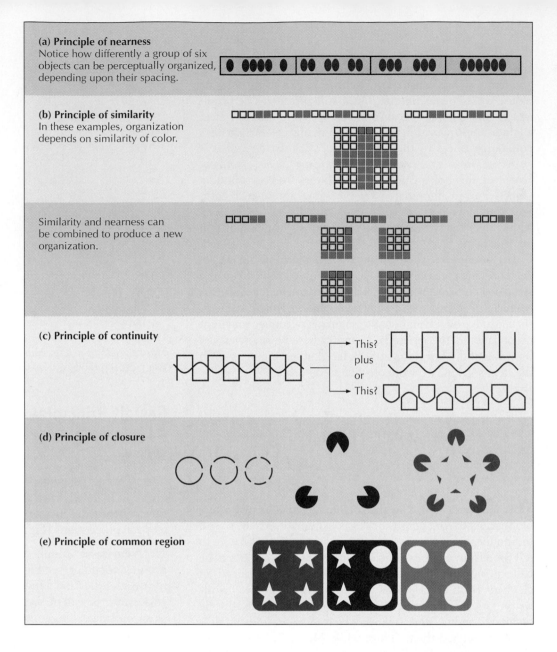

(a) Principle of nearness
Notice how differently a group of six objects can be perceptually organized, depending upon their spacing.

(b) Principle of similarity
In these examples, organization depends on similarity of color.

Similarity and nearness can be combined to produce a new organization.

(c) Principle of continuity

This?
plus
or
This?

(d) Principle of closure

(e) Principle of common region

Figure 7–3 ◆ Perceptual grouping illustrations.

5. Contiguity. A principle that can't be shown in Fig. 7–3 is contiguity, or nearness in time *and* space. Contiguity is often responsible for the perception that one thing has *caused* another (Michotte, 1963). A psychologist friend of the author's demonstrates this principle in class by knocking on his head with one hand while knocking on a wooden table (out of sight) with the other. The knocking sound is perfectly timed with the movements of his visible hand. This leads to the irresistible perception that his head is made of wood.

In addition to these classical principles, psychologist Stephen Palmer recently demonstrated one more way in which we organize perceptions (Palmer, 1992).

6. Common region. As you can see in Figure 7–3e, stimuli that are found within a common region or area tend to be seen as a group. On the basis of similarity and nearness, the stars in Figure 7–3e should be one group and the dots another. However, the colored backgrounds define regions that create three groups of objects (four stars, two stars plus two dots, and four dots). Perhaps the principle of common region explains why we tend to mentally group together people from a particular country, state, province, or geographic region.

The principles that guide perceptual organization have many practical applications, as discussed in the following highlight.

Designing for Human Use

Machines are of little value unless humans can operate them. A pocket calculator that is difficult to handle might just as well be a paperweight. An automobile design that blocks large areas of the driver's vision

Standard Indicators

Left roll   Right roll

Improved Indicators

Left roll   Right roll

(a)   (b)   (c)

Figure 7–4 ◆ Human factors engineering. **(a)** Early roll indicators in airplanes were perceptually confusing and difficult to read (top). Improved displays are clear even to non-pilots. Which would you prefer if you were flying an airplane in heavy fog? **(b)** Even on a stove, the placement of controls is important. During simulated emergencies, people made no errors in reaching for the controls on the top stove. In contrast, they erred 38 percent of the time with the bottom arrangement (Chapanis & Lindenbaum, 1959). **(c)** Sometimes the shape of a control is used to indicate its function, so as to discourage errors. For example, the left control might be used to engage and disengage the gears of an industrial machine, whereas the right control might operate the landing flaps on an airplane.

could be deadly. To adapt machines for human use, the **engineering psychologist** (*human factors engineer*) must make them *compatible* with our sensory and motor capacities (Howell, 1993). For example, *displays* must be easy to perceive, *controls* must be easy to use, and the tendency to make errors must be minimized (Fig. 7–4 ◆). (A **display** *is any dial, screen, light, or other device used to provide information about a machine's activity to a human operator. A* **control** *is any knob, handle, button, lever, or other device used to alter the activity of a machine.*)

Many of the machines we rely on each day were designed, in part, by human factors engineers. Some familiar examples include push-button telephones, "user-friendly" computers, home appliances, cameras, airplane controls, and traffic signals.

Psychologist Donald Norman (1994) refers to effective human factors engineering as **natural design.** Effective design *makes use of perceptual signals that people understand naturally, without needing to learn them.* An example of natural design is the row of vertical buttons in elevators. The buttons mimic the layout of the floors. This is simple, natural, and clear. Effective design also provides clear **feedback** (*information about the effect of making a response*). The audible click designed into many computer keyboards is a good example. As Norman points out, the "human error" cited as the cause of many accidents and disasters often misses the real culprit: poor design.

Clearly, the Gestalt principles shape our day-to-day perceptions. Learning and past experience also greatly affect perceptual organization. Contrast Mr. S. B.'s immediate ability to recognize letters to his inability to read handwriting. Also, take a moment and look for the camouflaged

animal pictured in Figure 7–5 ◆. (**Camouflage** *patterns break up figure-ground organization*). If you had never seen similar animals before, could you have located this one? Mr. S. B. would have been at a total loss to find meaning in such a picture.

In a way, we are all detectives, seeking patterns in what we see. In this sense, a meaningful pattern represents a **perceptual hypothesis,** *or initial guess about how to organize sensations.* Have you ever seen a "friend" in the distance, only to have the friend turn into a stranger as you drew closer? Pre-existing ideas and expectations *actively* guide our interpretation of sensations in many situations (Coren, Ward, & Enns, 1994).

The active nature of perception is perhaps most apparent for **ambiguous stimuli** (*patterns allowing more than one*

Figure 7–5 ◆ A challenging example of perceptual organization. Once the camouflaged insect (known as a giant walking-stick) becomes visible, it is almost impossible to view the picture again without seeing the insect.

Figure 7–6 ◆ Necker's cube. Visualize the top cube as a wire box. If you stare at the cube, its organization will change. Sometimes it will seem to project upward, like the lower left cube; other times it will project downward. The difference lies in how the brain interprets the same information.

interpretation). If you look at a cloud, you may discover dozens of ways to organize its contours into fanciful shapes and scenes. Even clearly defined stimuli may permit more than one interpretation. Stare at the design in Figure 7–6 ◆ if you doubt that perception is an active process. In some instances, a stimulus may offer such conflicting information that perceptual organization becomes impossible. For example, the tendency to make a three-dimensional object out of a drawing is frustrated by the "three-pronged widget" (Fig. 7–7 ◆), an **impossible figure**. *Such patterns cannot be organized into stable, consistent, or meaningful perceptions.*

Is the ability to understand drawings learned?

Figure 7–7 ◆ An impossible figure—the "three-pronged widget."

Figure 7–8 ◆ Stimuli similar to those used by Kennedy (1983) to study the kinds of information universally recognized in drawings. (See text for explanation.)

Humans almost always appear to understand lines that represent the *edges of surfaces.* We also have no problem with a single line used to depict the *parallel edges* of a narrow object, such as a rope. One thing that we *do not* easily recognize is lines showing color boundaries on the surface of an object (Kennedy, 1983).

To illustrate the last point, let's pay a brief visit to the Songe, a small tribe in Papua New Guinea. Before they were tested, the Songe had never made or seen line drawings—not even doodles scratched on the ground. As a test, the Songe were shown drawings like those in Figure 7–8 ◆. When this was done, they easily recognized the hand and the parrot from simple outlines. But lines showing color boundaries confused them. The half-moons on the fingernails, for example, made them think that the nails had been damaged and new ones were growing in. Similarly, they thought that the parrot must have been cut repeatedly. This was true even though the lines in the drawing match color markings of parrots found in Songe territory (Kennedy, 1983).

One of the most amazing feats of perceptual organization deserves a separate discussion. In the next section we will explore our capacity to create three-dimensional space from flat retinal images. In the meantime, don't let your attention go flat: Here's a Learning Check.

Learning Check   **Critical Thinking**

Try these questions before reading more.

1. Which among the following are subject to basic perceptual constancy?
   a. figure-ground organization **b.** size **c.** ambiguity **d.** brightness
   e. continuity **f.** closure **g.** shape **h.** nearness

2. The first and most basic perceptual organization to emerge when sight is restored to a blind person is:
   a. continuity **b.** nearness constancy **c.** recognition of numbers and letters **d.** figure-ground

3. At times, meaningful perceptual organization represents a _____ , or "guess," held until the evidence contradicts it.

4. The design known as Necker's cube is a good example of an impossible figure. T or F?

5. There is evidence that humans universally recognize line drawings depicting the edges of _____ and narrow parallel lines.

6. An important element of engineering psychology is making _____ and _____ compatible with human perceptual capacities. This is often best accomplished through _____ design.

7. People who have taken psychedelic drugs, such as LSD or mescaline often report that the objects and people they see appear to be changing in size, shape, and brightness. This suggests that such drugs disrupt what perceptual process?

Depth Perception— What If the World Were Flat?

Depth perception *is the ability to see three-dimensional space and to accurately judge distances.* Without depth perception, you would be unable to drive a car or ride a bicycle, play catch, shoot baskets, thread a needle, or simply navigate around a room. The world would look like a flat surface.

Mr. S. B. had trouble with depth perception after his sight was restored. Is depth perception learned?

Some psychologists (nativists) hold that depth perception is inborn. Others (the empiricists) view it as learned. Most likely, depth perception is partly learned and partly innate. Some evidence on the issue comes from work with the **visual cliff,** *an apparatus that looks like the edge of an elevated platform.*

Basically, a visual cliff is a glass-topped table (Fig. 7–9 ◆). On one side a checkered surface lies directly beneath the glass. On the other side, the checkered surface is 4 feet below. This makes the glass look like a tabletop on one side and a cliff, or drop-off, on the other.

To test for depth perception, 6- to 14-month-old infants were placed in the middle of the visual cliff. This gave them a choice of crawling to the shallow side or the deep side. (The glass prevented them from doing any "skydiving" if they chose the deep side.) Most infants chose the shallow side. In fact, most refused the deep side even when their mothers tried to call them toward it (Gibson & Walk, 1960).

If the infants were at least 6 months old when they were tested, isn't it possible that they learned to perceive depth?

Yes, it is. However, other tests have shown that human depth perception consistently emerges at about 4 months of age (Aslin & Smith, 1988). For example, psychologist Jane Gwiazda fitted infants with goggles that make some designs

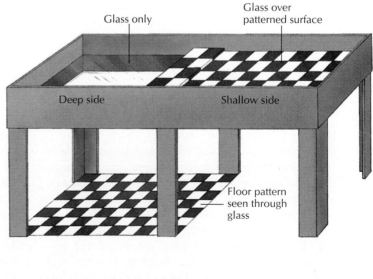

Figure 7–9 ◆ Human infants and newborn animals refuse to go over the edge of the visual cliff.

stand out three-dimensionally while others remain flat. By watching head movements, Gwiazda could tell when babies first became aware of "3-D" designs. As in other tests, this occurred at age 4 months. The nearly universal emergence of depth perception at this time suggests that it depends more on brain development than on individual learning. It is very likely that at least a basic level of depth perception is innate.

Then why do some babies crawl off tables or beds?

As soon as infants become active crawlers, they refuse to cross the deep side of the visual cliff (Campos et al., 1978). But even babies who perceive depth may not be able to catch themselves if they slip. A lack of coordination—not an inability to see depth—probably explains most "crash landings" after about 4 months of age.

How do adults perceive depth?

A number of *depth cues* combine to produce our experience of three-dimensional space. **Depth cues** *are features of the environment and messages from the body that supply information about distance and space.* Some cues will work with just *one eye* (**monocular cues**), while others require *two eyes* (**binocular cues**).

Muscular Cues
As their name implies, muscular cues come from within the body. One such cue is **accommodation,** *the bending of the lens that occurs when the eye focuses on nearby objects.* Accommodation is a monocular cue. Sensations from muscles attached to each lens are channeled back to the brain. Changes in these sensations help us judge distances within about 4 feet of the eyes. Beyond 4 feet, accommodation has limited value. (It does, however, contribute to an interesting illusion described later under the heading "The Moon Illusion.") Obviously, accommodation is more important to a watchmaker or a person trying to thread a needle than it is to a basketball player or someone driving an automobile.

A second bodily source of information about depth is **convergence,** a binocular cue. When you look at a distant object, the lines of vision from your eyes are parallel. However, when you look at something 50 feet or less in distance, *your eyes must converge (turn in) to focus the object* (Fig. 7–10 ◆).

You are probably not aware of it, but whenever you estimate a distance under 50 feet (as when you approach a stop sign, play catch, or zap flies with your personal laser), you are using convergence. How? Again there is a relationship between muscle sensations and distance. Convergence is controlled by a group of muscles attached to the eyeball. These muscles feed information on eye position to the brain to help it judge distance. You can feel convergence by exaggerating it: Focus on your fingertip and bring it toward your eyes until they almost cross. At that point you can feel the sensations from the muscles that control eye movement.

Figure 7–10 ◆ The eyes must converge, or turn in toward the nose, to focus close objects.

Stereoscopic Vision
The most basic source of depth perception is **retinal disparity** (*a discrepancy in the images that reach the right and left eyes*). Retinal disparity, which is a binocular cue, is based on the fact that the eyes are about 2.5 inches apart. Because of this, each eye receives a slightly different view of the world. When the two images are fused into one overall image, **stereoscopic vision** (*three-dimensional sight*) occurs. The result is a powerful sensation of depth (Fig. 7–11 ◆).

Retinal disparity can be used to produce 3-D movies by filming with two cameras separated by several inches. Later, both images are simultaneously projected on a screen. Audience members wear glasses that filter out one of the images to each eye. Since each eye gets a separate image, normal stereoscopic vision is duplicated. Try the following demonstration of retinal disparity and fusion.

Totally Tubular

Roll a piece of paper into a tube. Close your left eye. Hold the tube to your right eye like a telescope. Look through the tube at some object in the distance. Place your left hand against the tube halfway down its length and in front of your left eye. Now open your left eye. You should see a "hole" in your hand. You couldn't expect a professional photographer to do a better job of blending the two images than your brain and visual system does automatically.

How does retinal disparity produce depth?

Perceiving depth is more than a simple blending of two "pictures" of the world. In Figure 7–11c you will find two **random dot stereograms** (*patterns of dots that produce an illusion of depth*). Notice that they contain no objects, lines, or edges. Just the same, when the stereograms are properly viewed (one to each eye), a center area seems to float above the background. Researcher Bela Julesz believes such designs show that the brain is very sensitive to any *mismatch* of information from the eyes. In Figure 7–11c, depth comes from shifting dots in the center of one square so they do not match dots in the other square (Julesz, 1971; Ross, 1976). (Also see Figure 7–12 ◆.)

To a large extent, three-dimensional space is woven from countless tiny differences between what the right and left eyes see. Direct studies of the brain have shown that visual

Stereoscopic: optic nerve
transmissions from each eye are
relayed to both sides of brain

Binocular: both eyes
have overlapping
fields of vision

Allows depth perception
with accurate distance
estimation

(a)

(b) (c)

Figure 7–11 ◆ **(a)** Stereoscopic vision. **(b)** The photographs show what the right and left eyes would see when viewing a plant. Hold a file card or small piece of paper (4 or 5 inches tall) vertically between the two photos. Place the bridge of your nose on the card so that each eye sees only one photo. Relax your eyes so that they sight along parallel lines, as if looking at something in the distance. Then try to fuse the leaves into one image. The third dimension appears like magic. **(c)** Now do the same with the random dot stereogram, but with your eyes 8 or 10 inches from the page. With luck you will see a diamond shape hovering over the background. (See text for explanation.) Most readers will not be able to get the effect without using a prism to perfectly fuse the right and left dot squares. (Julesz, 1971; reprinted by permission of the University of Chicago Press.)

Figure 7–12 ◆ This popular style of computer-generated art creates a 3-D illusion by superimposing two random dot patterns. Mismatches between the two patterns create a sensation of depth. To get the 3-D effect, hold the stereogram about 6 to 8 inches from the end of your nose. Relax your eyes and look *through* the art, as if you were focusing on something in the distance. If you're patient, you may see a 3-D maze. (Stereogram © Anything Enterprises, 1994.)

areas do, in fact, contain cells that detect disparities (Ohzawa, DeAngelis, & Freeman, 1990).

If disparity is so important, can a person with one eye perceive depth?

A one-eyed person lacks convergence and retinal disparity, and accommodation is helpful mainly for judging short distances. That means a person with only one eye will have limited depth perception. Try driving a car or riding a bicycle with one eye closed. You will find yourself braking too soon or too late, and you will have difficulty estimating your speed. ("But officer, my psychology text said to. . . .") Despite this, you will be able to drive, although it will be more difficult than usual. A person with one eye can even successfully land an airplane—a task that depends strongly on depth perception. Overall, however, stereoscopic vision is ten times better for judging depth than perception based on just one eye (Rosenberg, 1994).

It is tempting to assume that higher animals perceive depth much as we do. While this is sometimes true, there are many exceptions. Let's explore some examples of how a "bird's-eye" view of the world might differ from our own.

A Closer Look

Stereoscopic Vision—A Bird's-Eye View

Harness yourself to a hang glider, step off a cliff, and soar. No matter how exhilarating, your flight still wouldn't provide a true "bird's-eye" view. Scientist Jerry Waldvogel has found that many birds see the world in ways that would seem strange to a human. For example, pigeons, ducks, and hummingbirds can see ultraviolet light, which adds an extra color to their visual palette. Homing pigeons and many migrating birds perceive polarized light, which aids them in navigation.

It might seem that birds would have acute stereoscopic vision, and some do. But most birds are prey for other animals. When you spend life as a potential meal, it's important to detect approaching predators. Accordingly, nature has given many birds an unusually wide field of view (Fig. 7–13b ◆). An extreme case is the American woodcock, a bird that can survey a 360 degree panorama without moving its eyes or head. The trade-off for this wide-angle view is a very limited area of binocular vision (Fig. 7–13c ◆). But to the woodcock, an ability to spot hungry predators is probably more valuable than depth perception.

What does the world look like to a woodcock? You can put away the hang glider: Computer scientist Ping-Kang Hsiung (1990) used optical ray-tracing to simulate the woodcock's view (Fig. 7–13e ◆, 7–13f ◆). As you can see in Figure 7–13, even a pretty foxy predator would have trouble sneaking up on a woodcock.

Most variations in vision have a purpose. Scientists theorize that human depth perception is an evolutionary holdover—from life in the tree-tops. The superb depth perception that helped our distant ancestors swing from branch to branch now helps us swing at a softball or avoid erratic drivers in traffic. Perhaps it's too bad that a little of the woodcock's wide-angle vision didn't get thrown in as well. (Source: Waldvogel, 1990.)

Pictorial Cues for Depth—A Deep Topic

A good movie, painting, or photograph can create a convincing sense of depth where none exists. And, as noted, a one-eyed person can learn to gauge depth with some success.

How is the illusion of depth created on a two-dimensional surface, and how is it possible to judge depth with one eye?

The answers lie in the *pictorial depth cues*, all of which are monocular (they will work with just one eye). **Pictorial depth cues** *are features found in paintings, drawings, and photographs that impart information about space, depth, and distance.* To understand how these cues work, imagine that you are looking outdoors through a window. If you trace everything you see through the window onto the glass, you will have an excellent drawing, with convincing depth. If you then analyze what is on the glass you will find the following features.

Pictorial Depth Cues

1. **Linear perspective.** This cue is based on the apparent convergence of parallel lines in the environment. If you stand between two railroad tracks, they appear to meet near the horizon. Since you know they are parallel, their convergence implies great distance (Fig. 7–14a ◆).

2. **Relative size.** If an artist wishes to depict two objects of the same size at different distances, the artist makes the more distant object smaller (Fig. 7–14b ◆). Films such as *Star Wars* and *Independence Day* created sensational illusions of depth by rapidly changing the image size of planets, space stations, and starships. (Also see Figure 7–15 ◆.)

3. **Height in the picture plane.** Objects that are placed higher (closer to the horizon line) in a drawing tend to be perceived as more distant. In the upper frame of Figure

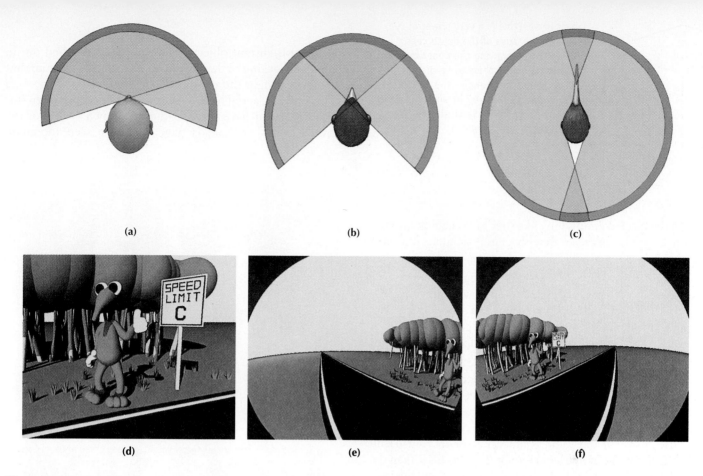

Figure 7–13 ◆ **(a)** When viewed from above the head, a human's field of view for the right and left eyes contains a large area of overlapping, stereoscopic vision (darker shading). **(b)** The barn swallow's vision, like that of many birds, covers a much wider field of view than ours. Although the swallow's area of binocular vision is smaller than a human's, the swallow has sharper peripheral vision. **(c)** A bird called the American woodcock can see all the way around its head. Binocular vision is limited to a narrow band, but an extremely wide field of view helps the woodcock detect predators. (Adapted from Waldvogel, 1990.) **(d)** This image, created by Ping-Kang Hsiung (1990), shows how an imaginary scene would look to a person standing across the road from a rather strange hitchhiker. **(e) (f)** This is what a woodcock's left and right eyes would see if the bird were at the same point as the human in view *d*. (Computer graphics courtesy of Dr. Hsiung.)

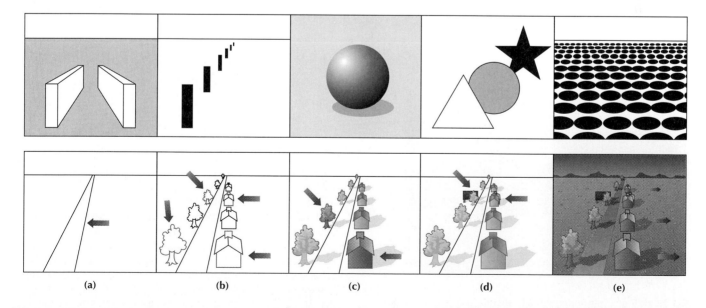

Figure 7–14 ◆ **(a)** Linear perspective. **(b)** Relative size. **(c)** Light and shadow. **(d)** Overlap. **(e)** Texture gradients. Drawings in the top row show fairly "pure" examples of each of the pictorial depth cues. In the bottom row, the pictorial depth cues are used to assemble a more realistic scene.

Linear perspective is a very powerful cue for depth. Because of the depth cues implied in this drawing the upper cross on the vertical line appears to be diagonal. It is actually a right angle. The lower cross, which appears to be a right angle, is actually diagonal to the vertical line. (After Enns & Coren, 1995.)

7–14b the black columns look like they are receding into the distance partly because they become smaller, but also because they move higher in the drawing.

4. **Light and shadow.** Most objects are lighted in ways that create clear patterns of light and shadow. Copying such patterns of light and shadow can give a two-dimensional design a three-dimensional appearance (Fig. 7–14c ◆). (Also, look ahead to Figure 7–16 ◆ for more information on light and shadow.)

5. **Overlap.** Overlap (also known as **interposition**) is a depth cue that occurs when one object partially blocks another object. Hold your hands up and have a friend try to tell from across the room which is nearer. Relative size will give the answer if one hand is much nearer to your friend than the other. But if one hand is only slightly closer than the other, your friend may have difficulty—until you slide one hand in front of the other. Overlap then removes any doubt (Fig. 7–14d ◆).

6. **Texture gradients.** Changes in texture also contribute to depth perception. If you stand in the middle of a cobblestone street, the street will look coarse near your feet. However, its texture will get smaller and finer if you look into the distance (Fig. 7–14e ◆).

7. **Aerial perspective.** Smog, fog, dust, and haze add to the apparent distance of an object. Because of aerial perspective, distant objects tend to be hazy, washed out in color, and lacking in detail. This is true even in clear air, but it is increasingly the case in our mechanized society. As a matter of fact, aerial haze is often most noticeable when it is missing. If you have traveled the wide-open spaces of the United States or Canada, you may have seen mountain

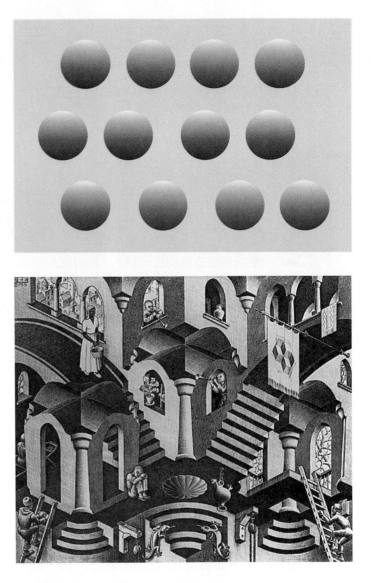

Figure 7–16 ◆ *(Top)* We typically make two assumptions when using light and shadow to judge depth in a picture or drawing. First, we usually assume that light comes mainly from one direction. Second, we tend to assume that the source of light is above pictured objects. Squint a little to blur the image you see here. You should perceive a collection of globes projecting outward. If you turn this page upside-down, the globes should become cavities. (After Ramachandran, 1995.) *(Bottom)* The famed Dutch artist M. C. Escher violated both assumptions about light to create the dramatic illusions of depth found in his 1955 lithograph *Convex and Concave*. In this print, light appears to come from all sides of the scene. (Courtesy of the Collection Haags Gemeente Museusm, The Hague. © 1994 M. C. Escher/Cordon Art, Baarn, The Netherlands. All rights reserved.)

Figure 7–15 ◆ On a dry lake bed, relative size is just about the only depth cue available for judging the camera's distance from this vintage aircraft. What do you estimate the distance to be? For the answer, look ahead to Figure 7–20 ◆.

ranges that seemed to be only a few miles away. You may have then been shocked to find that you were actually viewing them through 50 miles of crystal-clear air.

8. Relative motion. Relative motion, also known as **motion parallax** (PAIR-ah-lax), can be seen by looking out a window and moving your head from side to side. Notice that nearby objects appear to move a sizable distance as your head moves. In comparison, trees, houses, and telephone poles at a greater distance appear to move slightly in relation to the background. Distant objects like hills, mountains, or clouds don't seem to move at all.

When combined, pictorial cues can create a powerful illusion of depth. (Also, see Table 7–1 ■ for a summary of all the depth cues we have discussed.)

Is motion parallax really a pictorial cue?

Strictly speaking it is not, except in movies, television, or animated cartoons. However, when parallax is present, depth is almost always perceived. Much of the apparent depth of a good movie comes from relative motion captured by the camera. People who can only see with one eye depend heavily on motion parallax. Typically, they make frequent head movements to exaggerate parallax and improve depth perception. In fact, we all use head movements at times to more accurately judge the distance of objects (Enright, 1996).

Figure 7–17 ◆ illustrates an interesting feature of motion parallax. Imagine that you are in a bus and watching the passing scenery with your gaze at a right angle to the road. Under these conditions, nearby objects will appear to rush *backward*. Those farther away, such as distant mountains, will seem to move very little or not at all. Objects that are more remote, such as the sun or moon, will appear to move in the *same* direction you are traveling. (That's why the moon appears to "follow" you when you take a stroll at night.) To re-create motion parallax in cartoons, animators draw scenes

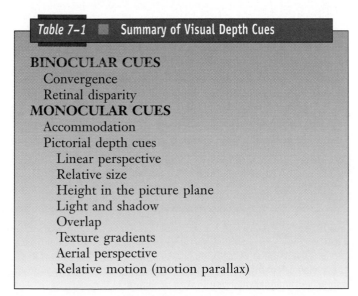

Table 7–1 ■ **Summary of Visual Depth Cues**

BINOCULAR CUES
  Convergence
  Retinal disparity
MONOCULAR CUES
  Accommodation
  Pictorial depth cues
    Linear perspective
    Relative size
    Height in the picture plane
    Light and shadow
    Overlap
    Texture gradients
    Aerial perspective
    Relative motion (motion parallax)

◀■ Direction of travel

Figure 7–17 ◆ The apparent motion of objects viewed during travel depends on their distance from the observer. Apparent motion can also be influenced by an observer's point of fixation. At middle distances, objects closer than the point of fixation appear to move backward; those beyond the point of fixation appear to move forward. Objects at great distances, such as the sun or moon, always appear to move forward.

in several layers, each of which is moved appropriately during filming.

Are pictorial depth cues universal, like the understanding of basic drawings noted earlier?

Not entirely. Some cultures use only selected pictorial cues to represent depth. People in these cultures may not easily recognize other cues (Deregowski, 1972). For example, researcher William Hudson tested members of remote tribes who do not use relative size to show depth in drawings. These people perceive simplified drawings as flat designs. As you can see in Figure 7–18 ◆, they do not assume, as we do, that a larger image means that an object is closer. Of course, members of non-Western cultures can learn to interpret drawings of depth if they are given a chance to practice (Mshelia & Lapidus, 1990).

How do the depth perception cues relate to daily experience?

The Moon Illusion We constantly use both pictorial cues and bodily cues to sense depth and judge distances. Cues of both types combine to produce an intriguing perceptual effect called the **moon illusion** (*perceiving the moon as larger when it is low in the sky*). When the moon is on the horizon, it tends to look as large as a silver dollar. When it is directly overhead, it looks like a dime, very much smaller than it did earlier the same evening. Contrary to what some people believe, the moon's image is not magnified by the atmosphere. If you take a photograph of the moon and measure its image, you will find that it is not larger when it is near the horizon. But the moon *looks* nearly twice as large when it's low in the sky (Plug & Ross, 1994). This occurs, in part, because the moon's *apparent distance* is greater when

Figure 7–18 ◆ A Hudson test picture. Two-dimensional perceivers assume the hunter is trying to spear the distant elephant rather than the nearby antelope. Some acquaintance with conventions for representing depth in pictures and photographs seems necessary. (From "Pictorial Perception and Culture" by J. B. Deregowski. © 1972 by Scientific American, Inc. All rights reserved.)

it is near the horizon than when it is overhead (Kaufman & Rock, 1989).

But if it seems farther away, shouldn't it look smaller?

No. When the moon is overhead, few depth cues surround it. In contrast, when you see the moon on the horizon, it is behind houses, trees, telephone poles, and mountains. These objects add numerous depth cues, which cause the horizon to seem more distant than the sky overhead. The moon illusion is so powerful that it can occur in photographs if they contain depth cues (Coren & Aks, 1990).

To better understand the moon illusion, picture two balloons, one 10 feet away and the second 20 feet away. Suppose the more distant balloon is inflated until its image matches the image of the nearer balloon. How do we know the more distant balloon is larger? Because its image is the same size as a balloon that is closer. Similarly, the moon makes the same-size image on the horizon as it does overhead. However, the horizon seems more distant because more depth cues are present. As a result, the horizon moon must be perceived as larger (Rock & Kaufman, 1962). (See Figure 7–19 ◆.)

This explanation is known as the **apparent distance hypothesis** (*the horizon seems more distant than the night sky*). You can test it by removing depth cues while looking at a horizon moon. Try looking at the moon through a rolled-up paper tube, or make your hands into a "telescope" and look at the next large moon you see. It will immediately appear to shrink when viewed without depth cues (Plug & Ross, 1994).

How exactly does apparent distance change the moon's perceived size?

Researchers have discovered that the moon illusion is directly related to changes in accommodation (Iavecchia et al., 1983; Roscoe, 1985). Extra depth cues near the horizon cause the eyes to focus on a more distant point than they do when you look overhead. Such changes in accommodation appear to provide the brain with a "yardstick" for judging the size of images, including that of the moon.

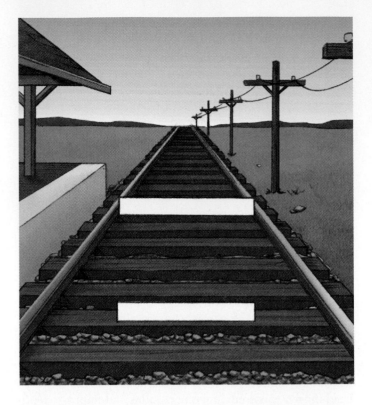

Figure 7–19 ◆ The Ponzo illusion may help you understand the moon illusion. Picture the two white bars as resting on the railroad tracks. In the drawing, the upper bar is the same length as the lower bar. However, because the upper bar appears to be farther away than the lower bar, we perceive it as longer. The same logic applies to the moon illusion.

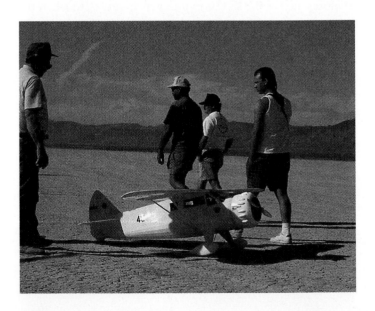

Figure 7–20 ◆ Before you can use familiar size to judge distance, objects must actually be the size you assume they are. Either these men are giants, or the model airplane was closer than you may have thought when you looked at Figure 7–15.

If you have difficulty with any of these questions, skim back over the previous material.

1. The visual cliff is used to test for infant sensitivity to linear perspective. T or F?

2. Write an M or a B after each of the following to indicate if it is a monocular or binocular depth cue. accommodation _____ convergence _____ retinal disparity _____ linear perspective _____ motion parallax _____ overlap _____ relative size _____ height in plane _____

3. Which of the depth cues listed in question 2 are based on muscular feedback? _____ .

4. Interpretation of pictorial depth cues requires no prior experience. T or F?

5. The moon's image is greatly magnified by the atmosphere near the horizon. T or F?

6. What hearing ability would you say is most closely related to stereoscopic vision?

Answers:

1. F 2. accommodation (M), convergence (B), retinal disparity (B), linear perspective (M), motion parallax (M), overlap (M), relative size (M), height in plane (M) 3. accommodation or convergence 4. F 5. F 6. If you close your eyes, you can usually tell the direction and perhaps the location of a sound source, such as a hand-clap. Locating sounds in space is heavily dependent on having two ears, just as stereoscopic vision depends on having two eyes.

Perceptual Learning— What If the World Were Upside Down?

England is one of a few countries in the world where people drive on the left side of the road. In view of this reversal, it is not unusual for visitors to step off curbs in front of cars—after carefully looking for traffic in the *wrong* direction. This problem is so common, in fact, that crosswalks near tourist attractions in London are stenciled with the words, "Look right"! As this example suggests, learning has a powerful impact on perception, something we have already seen in other ways.

How does learning affect perception?

Perceptual Habits　　One way learning affects perception is through **perceptual habits** (*ingrained patterns of organization and attention*). Stop for a moment and look at Figure 7–21 ◆. The left face looks somewhat unusual, to be sure. But the distortion seems mild—until the page is turned upside down. Viewed normally, the face looks quite grotesque. Why is there a difference? Apparently, most people have little experience with upside-down faces. Perceptual learning, therefore, has less impact on our perceptions of an upside-down face. With a face in the normal position, you know what to expect and where to look. Also, you tend to see the entire face as a recognizable pattern. When a face is inverted, we are forced to perceive its individual features separately (Bartlett & Searcy, 1993).

Before we continue, read aloud the short phrase in Figure 7–22 ◆. Did you read "Paris in the spring"? If so, look again. The word *the* appears twice in the phrase. Because of past experience with the English language, good readers often overlook the repeated word. Again, the effects of perceptual learning are apparent.

Figure 7–21 ◆ The effects of prior experience on perception. The doctored face looks far worse when viewed right side up, because it can be related to past experience.

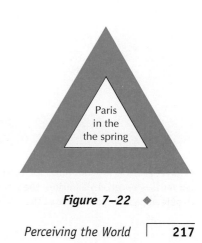

Paris in the the spring

Figure 7–22 ◆

Magicians rely on perceptual habits when they use sleight of hand to distract observers while performing tricks. Another kind of "magic" is related to consistency in the environment. It is usually safe to assume that a room is shaped roughly like a box. This need not be true, however. An **Ames room** (named for the man who designed it) *is a lopsided space that appears square when viewed from a certain point* (Fig. 7–23 ◆). This illusion is achieved by carefully distorting the proportions of the walls, floor, ceiling, and windows.

An Ames room presents a unique problem for the perceptual habits of an observer. Since the left corner of the Ames room is farther from a viewer than the right, a person standing in that corner looks very small; one standing in the nearer, shorter right corner looks very large. If a person walks from the left corner of the room to the right, observers are faced with a conflict. They can maintain shape constancy by perceiving the room as square, or they can maintain size constancy by refusing to see the person "grow." Most people choose shape constancy and see people "shrink" and "grow" before their eyes.

As mentioned in the previous chapter, the brain is especially sensitive to **perceptual features** *such as lines, shapes, edges, spots, and colors.* At least some of this sensitivity appears to be learned. Colin Blakemore and Graham Cooper of Cambridge University raised kittens in a room with only vertical stripes on the walls. Another set of kittens saw only horizontal stripes. When returned to normal environments, the "horizontal" cats could easily jump onto a chair, but when walking on the floor, they bumped into chair legs. "Vertical" cats, on the other hand, easily avoided chair legs, but they missed when trying to jump to horizontal surfaces. The cats raised with vertical stripes were "blind" to horizontal lines, and the "horizontal" cats acted as if vertical lines were invisible. Other experiments show that there is an actual decrease in brain cells tuned to the missing features (Grobstein & Chow, 1975).

Would it be possible, then, for an adult to adapt to a completely new perceptual world?

Inverted Vision An answer comes from an experiment in which a person wore goggles that turned the world upside down and reversed objects from right to left. At first, even the simplest tasks—walking, eating, and so forth—were incredibly difficult. Imagine trying to reach for a door handle and watching your hand shoot off in the wrong direction.

Participants in the experiment also reported that head movements made the world swing violently through space, causing severe headaches and nausea. Yet, after several days they began to adapt to inverted vision. Their success, while not complete, was impressive.

Did everything turn upright again for the humans?

No. While they wore the goggles, their visual images remained upside down. But in time they learned to perform most routine activities, and their inverted world began to seem relatively normal. In later experiments, some people wearing inverting lenses were able to successfully drive cars. One person even flew an airplane (Kohler, 1962). These feats

Figure 7–23 ◆ The Ames room. From the front, the room looks normal; actually, the right-hand corner is very short, and the left-hand corner is very tall. In addition, the left side of the room slants away from viewers. The diagram shows the shape of the room and reveals why people appear to get bigger as they cross the room toward the nearer, shorter right corner.

Inverted vision. Adaptation to complete inversion of the visual world is possible, but challenging.

Even small distortions of the visual world may necessitate perceptual learning. For example, the apparent size, distance, and curvature of objects is distorted underwater. Experiments confirm that professional divers gradually correct for these distortions as they gain experience with them (Vernoy, 1989).

are like driving or flying upside down, with right and left reversed. Some ride!

Interacting with a new visual world through **active movement** (*self-generated action*) seems to be a key to rapid adaptation. In one experiment, people wore glasses that grossly distorted vision. Those who walked on their own adapted more quickly than persons pushed around in a wheeled cart (Held, 1971). Why does movement help? Probably because commands sent to the muscles can be related to sensory feedback. Remaining immobile would be like watching a weird movie over which you have no control. There would be little reason for any perceptual learning to occur.

Who's Flying this Thing?

Two people sit in the cockpit of an airplane. One is piloting the plane; the other watches intently through the windshield. Suddenly the plane enters a dark cloud and everything goes black. While it is inside the cloud, the plane is pushed off course by a gust of wind. When the plane emerges into the sunlight, who will be better able to tell that it changed course, the pilot or the passenger?

In a recent experiment, the conditions just described were created with a computerized flight simulator (see Fig. 7–24 ◆). In general, "pilots" were better than "passengers" at detecting unexpected changes in the plane's path (Larish & Andersen, 1995).

Why should this be the case? It appears that controlling the plane helped pilots to *actively* extract information from the environment. Couch potatoes take note: The human perceptual system appears to

function best during active interactions with our surroundings. We can't all be pilots, but it is probably better to participate than to spectate, whenever possible.

Adaptation Level   The external *context* in which a stimulus is judged is an important factor affecting perception. **Context** *refers to information surrounding a stimulus.* For example, a man 6 feet in height will look "tall" when surrounded by others of average height, and "short" among a group of professional basketball players. In Figure 7–25 ◆, the center circle is the same size in both designs. But like the man in different company, context alters the circle's apparent size. The importance of context is also shown by Figure 7–26 ◆. What do you see in the middle? If you read across, context causes it to be organized as a 13. Reading down makes it a B.

In addition to external contexts, we all have personal **frames of reference** (*internal standards for judging stimuli*). If you were asked to lift a 10-pound weight, would you label it light, medium, or heavy? The answer to this question depends on your **adaptation level** (*the "medium point" of your personal frame of reference*). Each person's adaptation level is constantly modified by experience (Helson, 1964). If most of the weights you lift in day-to-day

Figure 7–24 ◆ As one person "flew" an airplane on a flight simulator a second saw the same aerial views, but did not control the plane's movements. After a short blackout both observers saw a view that was either a correct extension of the plane's previous path, or a different view.

Figure 7–26 ◆ Context alters the meaning of the middle figure.

Figure 7–25 ◆ Are the center dots in both figures the same size?

life *average* around 10 pounds, you will call a 10-pound weight medium. If you are a watchmaker and spend your days lifting tiny watch parts, you will probably call a

10-pound weight heavy. If you work as a furniture mover, your adaptation level will exceed 10 pounds, and you will call a 10-pound weight light. (If you are an aging rock star, you will no doubt call everything "heavy," man.)

Illusions Perceptual learning is responsible for a number of *illusions*. In an **illusion,** *length, position, motion, curvature, or direction is consistently misjudged* (Gillam, 1980). Note that illusions distort stimuli that actually exist. In a **hallucination,** *people perceive objects or events that have no external reality.* For example, they hear voices that are not there. If you think you see a 3-foot-tall butterfly, you can confirm you are hallucinating by trying to touch its wings. To detect an illusion, it is often necessary to measure a drawing or apply a straight-edge to it.

Illusions are a fascinating challenge to our understanding of perception. On occasion, they also have practical uses. An illusion called *stroboscopic movement* (strobe-oh-SKOP-ik) puts the "motion" in motion pictures. **Stroboscopic movement** *refers to the illusory movement perceived when an object is shown in rapidly changing positions.* The strobe lights sometimes used on dance floors reverse this illusion. Each time the strobe flashes, it "freezes" dancers in particular positions. However, if the light flashes fast enough, normal motion is seen. In a similar way, movies project a rapid series of "snapshots," so the gaps in motion are imperceptible.

(a) Which of the horizontal lines is longer?

(b) Is the diagonal a single straight line? Check it with a ruler.

(c) Is this a drawing of a staircase descending from upper left to lower right . . . or is it the view of the underneath of a staircase from lower right to upper left?

(d) Are these lines parallel? Cover some of the slash marks to see.

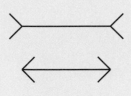

(e) Which line is longer, horizontal or vertical?

(f) Notice how the background distorts the square.

(g) Which quadrilateral is larger?

(h) Which column is shortest? Which is longest?

Figure 7–27 ◆ Some interesting perceptual illusions.

Can other illusions be explained?

Not in all cases, or to everyone's satisfaction. Generally speaking, size and shape constancy, habitual eye movements, continuity, and perceptual habits combine in various ways to produce the illusions in Figure 7–27 ◆. Rather than attempt to explain all of the pictured illusions, let's focus on one deceptively simple example.

Consider the drawing in Figure 7–27a ◆. This is the familiar **Müller-Lyer illusion** (MUE-ler-LIE-er) *in which the horizontal line with arrowheads appears shorter than the line with V's.* A quick measurement will show that they are the same length. How can we explain this illusion? Evidence suggests it is based on a lifetime of experience with the edges and corners of rooms and buildings. Richard Gregory (1990) believes you see the horizontal line with the V's as if it were the corner of a room viewed from inside (Fig. 7–28 ◆). The line with arrowheads, on the other hand, suggests the corner of a room or building seen from outside. In other words, cues that suggest a 3-D space alter our perception of a two-dimensional design (Enns, & Coren, 1995).

Earlier, to explain the moon illusion, we said that if two objects make images of the same size, the more distant object must be larger. This is known formally as **size-distance invariance** (*the size of an object's image is precisely related to its distance from the eyes*). Gregory believes the same concept explains the Müller-Lyer illusion. If the V-tipped line looks farther away than the arrowhead-tipped line, then you must

compensate by seeing the V-tipped line as longer. This explanation of the Müller-Lyer illusion presumes that you have had years of experience with straight lines, sharp edges, and corners—a pretty safe assumption in our culture.

Is there any way to show that past experience causes the illusion?

If we could test someone who saw only curves and wavy lines as a child, we would know if experience with a "square" culture is important. Fortunately, a group of people in South Africa, the Zulus, live in a "round" culture. In their daily lives, Zulus rarely encounter a straight line: Their huts are shaped like rounded mounds and arranged in a circle, tools and toys are curved, and there are no straight roads or square buildings.

What happens if a Zulu looks at the Müller-Lyer design?

The typical Zulu does not experience the illusion. At most, she or he sees the V-shaped line as *slightly* longer than the other (Gregory, 1990). This seems to confirm the importance of past experience and perceptual habits in determining our view of the world. But, like many topics in psychology, room for debate remains. The Müller-Lyer illusion also seems to be partly based on directly misperceiving the location of the ends of the lines (Morgan, Hole, & Glennerster, 1990). Thus, it could be that both apparent size and direct misperception causes the illusion.

Figure 7–28 ◆ Why does line **(b)** in the Müller-Lyer illusion look longer than line **(a)**? Probably because it looks more like a distant corner than a nearer one. Since the vertical lines form images of the same length, the more "distant" line must be perceived as larger. As you can see in the drawing on the right, additional depth cues accentuate the Müller-Lyer illusion. (After Enns & Coren, 1995.)

Learning Check

1. Perceptual habits may become so ingrained that they lead us to misperceive a stimulus. T or F?

2. Perceptual learning seems to program the brain for sensitivity to important _____ of the environment.

3. The Ames room is used to test for adaptation to inverted vision. T or F?

4. An important factor in adaptation to inverted vision is
   a. learning new categories **b.** active movement **c.** overcoming illusions **d.** the horizontal-vertical invariance

5. Size-distance relationships appear to underlie which two illusions? _____ and _____

6. An adaptation level represents a personal "medium point," or internal _____ _____

Critical Thinking

7. What size object do you think you would have to hold at arm's length to cover up a full moon?

Answers:

1. T 2. features 3. F 4. b 5. moon illusion and Müller-Lyer illusion 6. frame of reference 7. The most popular answers range from a quarter to a softball. Actually, a pea held in the outstretched hand will cover a full moon (Kunkel, 1993). If you listed an object larger than a pea, be aware that perceptions, no matter how accurate they seem, may distort reality.

Motives and Perception—May I Have Your . . . Attention!

You are surrounded by sights, sounds, odors, tastes, and touch sensations. Which are you aware of? The first stage of perception is attention, the selection of incoming messages (Fig. 7–29 ◆). There is little doubt about the importance of attention. Think, for instance, about an airline pilot who fails to notice that the flaps are not down before a landing. This error caused a major air disaster at Detroit's airport in 1987.

Attention As you may recall from Chapter 6, **selective attention** *refers to the fact that we give some messages priority and put others on hold* (Johnston & Dark, 1986). Psycholo-

Figure 7–29 ◆ The attentional "spotlight" can be widened or narrowed. If you focus on local details in this drawing you will see the letter *A* repeated 13 times. If you broaden your field of attention to encompass the overall pattern, you will see the letter *H*. (After Lamb & Yund, 1996.)

gists have found it helpful to think of selective attention as a sort of *bottleneck*, or narrowing in the information channel linking the senses to perception. When one message enters the bottleneck, it seems to prevent others from passing through. This may be why it is very difficult to listen to two people speaking at once. Typically, you can "tune in" one person or the other, but not both (Reed, 1996).

Have you ever felt overloaded when trying to do several things at once? **Divided attention** arises when you must *divide your mental effort among tasks, each of which requires more or less attention.* Divided attention is related to our limited *capacity* for storing and thinking about information. For example, when people first learn to drive, almost all of their attention is needed to steer, brake, shift, and so forth. However, as a skill becomes more automatic, it requires less attention. In driving, greater skill frees mental capacity for other things, such as tuning the car's radio or carrying on a conversation (Desimone & Duncan, 1995).

Are some stimuli more attention getting than others?

Yes. Very *intense* stimuli usually command attention. Stimuli that are brighter, louder, or larger tend to capture attention: A gunshot in a library would be hard to ignore. Big, bright cars probably get more tickets than small, dull ones. Loud, irritating comedian Don Rickles has made a career out of the first principle of attention.

Repetitious stimuli, repetitious stimuli, repetitious stimuli, repetitious stimuli, repetitious stimuli, repetitious stimuli are also attention getting. A dripping faucet at night makes little noise by normal standards, but because of repetition, it may become as attention getting as a single sound many times louder. This effect is used repeatedly, so to speak, in television and radio commercials.

ATTENTION IS ALSO **FREQUENTLY** RELATED TO contrast OR *change* IN STIMULATION. The contrasting type styles in the preceding sentence draw attention because they are *unexpected*. Norman Mackworth and Geoffrey Loftus (1978) found that people who look at drawings like Figure 7–30 ◆ focus first and longest on unexpected objects (the octopus, in this case). Change, contrast, and incongruity are perhaps the most basic sources of attention. We quickly **habituate** (*respond less*) to predictable and unchanging stimuli. Notice that repetition without variation leads to habituation. Repetition is attention getting when it is irritating or annoying. A dripping faucet varies in timing just enough to gain attention. In contrast, we quickly habituate to the steady tick of a clock.

How does habituation differ from sensory adaptation?

Habituation As described in Chapter 6, *adaptation* decreases the actual number of sensory messages sent to the brain. When messages do reach the brain, the body makes a sort of "What is it?" reaction, known as an *orientation response*. An **orientation response (OR)** *prepares us to receive information from a stimulus:* the pupils enlarge, brain-wave patterns shift, breathing stops briefly, blood flow to the head

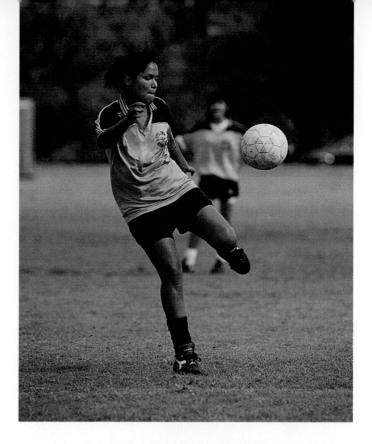

In many sports, experts are much better than beginners at paying attention to key information. Compared with novices, experts scan actions and events more quickly and they focus on only the most meaningful information. This allows experts to make decisions and react more quickly (Bard, Fleury, & Goulet, 1994).

increases, and we turn toward the stimulus. Have you ever seen someone do a double take? If so, you have observed an orientation response.

Now, think about what happens when you buy a new CD. At first the music holds your attention all the way through.

Figure 7–30 ◆ One of the drawings used by Mackworth and Loftus (1978) to investigate attention. Observers attend to unexpected objects longer than they do to expected objects. In this drawing, observers looked longer at the octopus than they did at a tractor placed in the same spot. What do you think would happen if a tractor were shown upside down or on the roof of the barn?

But when the CD becomes "old," all the songs may play without your really attending to them. When a stimulus is repeated *without change*, the OR habituates, or decreases.

Interestingly, creative people habituate *more slowly* than average. We might expect that they would rapidly become bored with a repeated stimulus. Instead, it seems that creative people actively attend to stimuli, even those that are repeated (Colin, Moore, & West, 1996).

As we have noted, the perceptual system is impressed most by dramatic changes. Humans evolved to detect sharp changes and distinctive events, such as the sudden appearance of a lion, a potential mate, or sources of food. We are far less able to detect gradual changes.

Robert Ornstein, a biopsychologist, and Paul Ehrlich, a population biologist, believe perceptual capacities that aided survival when most humans were hunters and gatherers can now be a handicap. Many of the threats facing civilization develop very slowly. As examples, they cite the accumulation of tens of thousands of nuclear warheads, degradation of the environment, global deforestation, the slow build-up of the greenhouse effect, gradual depletion of the ozone layer, and run-away human population growth.

Ornstein and Ehrlich relate the large-scale threats we face to what they call the "boiled frog syndrome." Frogs placed in a pan of water that is slowly heated cannot detect the gradual rise in temperature. They will sit still until they die.

Like the doomed frogs, many people seem unable to detect gradual but deadly trends in modern civilization. To avoid disasters, it may take a conscious effort by large numbers of people to see the "big picture" and reverse lethal but easily overlooked patterns (Ornstein & Ehrlich, 1989).

Motives Motives also play a role in attention. If you are riding in a car and become hungry, you will notice restaurants and billboards picturing food. If you are running low on gas, your attention will shift to gas stations. Advertisers, of course, know that their pitch will be more effective if it gets your attention. Ads are therefore loud, repetitious, and intentionally irritating. They are also designed to take advantage of two motives that are widespread in our society: *anxiety* and *sex*.

Everything from mouthwash to automobile tires is merchandised by using sex to gain attention. For instance, an ad for Triple Sec liqueur ran under the heading "Sec's

Appeal." Another liquor ad shows a woman in a seductive velvet dress and says, "Feel the velvet." And what could be more obvious than ads for designer jeans that feature a shapely posterior pointed at the camera? Other ads combine sex with anxiety. Mouthwash, deodorant, soaps, toothpaste, and countless other articles are pushed in ads that play on desires to be attractive, to have "sex appeal," or to avoid embarrassment. Is it really so terrible to have "morning breath," a ring around your collar, or to perspire at times?

In addition to directing attention, motives may alter what is perceived:

> As part of a supposed study of "the dating practices of college students," male volunteers were shown a picture of a female student and asked to give a first impression of how attractive she was. Before making these ratings, each person read one of two short written passages: One was sexually arousing and the other was not. The important finding was that men who read the more arousing passage rated the female as more attractive. (Stephan et al., 1971)

This result may come as no surprise if you have ever been infatuated with someone and then fallen out of love. A person who once seemed highly attractive may look quite different when your feelings change.

An emotional stimulus can shift attention away from other information. In an experiment, members of a Jewish organization watched as pictures like Figure 7–31 ◆ were flashed on a screen for a split second. People were less likely to recognize symbols around the drawing's edge when the center item was an emotional symbol like the swastika (Erdelyi & Appelbaum, 1973). This effect probably explains why fans of opposing sports teams often act as if they had seen two completely different games.

Figure 7–31 ◆ Emotionally significant stimuli influence attention (Erdelyi & Appelbaum, 1973, p. 50. Reprinted by permission.)

Perceptual Expectancies—On Your Mark, Get Set

On a piece of paper, draw a circle about 3 inches in diameter. Inside the circle, above and to the left of center, make a large black dot, about one-half inch in diameter. Make another dot inside the circle above and to the right of center. Now, still inside the circle, draw an arc, curved upward and about 2 inches long just below the center of the circle. If you followed these instructions, your reaction might now be, "Oh! Why didn't you just say to draw a happy face?"

Like the happy face drawing, perception seems to proceed in two major ways. In **bottom-up processing**, *we analyze information starting at the "bottom" with small sensory units (features) and build upward to a complete perception.* The reverse also seems to occur. In **top-down processing** *pre-existing knowledge is used to rapidly organize features into a meaningful whole.* Bottom-up processing is like putting together a picture puzzle you've never seen before: you must assemble small pieces until a recognizable pattern appears. Top-down processing is like putting together a puzzle you have solved many times: After only a few pieces are in place you begin to see outlines of the final picture.

Figure 7–32 ◆ This painting by abstract artist Al Held is 9 feet by 9 feet. If you process the painting "bottom-up," all you will see is two small dark geometric shapes. Would you like to try some top-down processing? Knowing the painting's title will allow you to apply your knowledge and see the painting in an entirely different way. The title? It's *The Big N*. Can you see it now? (Courtesy The Museum of Modern Art, New York.)

Both types of processing are illustrated by Figure 7–32 ◆. Also, return to Figure 7–5, the giant walkingstick. The first time you saw the photo you probably processed it bottom-up, picking out features until the insect was recognizable. This time, because of top-down processing, you should see the insect instantly. Another good example of top-down processing is found in perceptual expectancies.

Perceptual Set

What is a perceptual expectancy?

A runner in the starting blocks at a track meet is *set* to respond in a certain way. Likewise, past experience, motives, context, or suggestions may create a **perceptual expectancy** (or **set**) *that prepares you to perceive in a certain way.* If a car backfires, runners at a track meet may jump the gun. As a matter of fact, we all frequently jump the gun when perceiving. In essence, an expectancy is a perceptual hypothesis we are *very likely* to apply to a stimulus—even if applying it is inappropriate.

Perceptual sets often lead us to see what we *expect* to see. For example, let's say you are driving across the desert. You are very low on gas. Finally, you see a sign approaching. On it are the words FUEL AHEAD. You relax, knowing you will not be stranded. But as you draw nearer, the words on the sign become FOOD AHEAD. Most people have had similar experiences in which expectations altered their perceptions. To observe perceptual expectancies firsthand, perform the experiment described in Figure 7–33 ◆.

Perceptual expectancies are frequently created by *suggestion.* This is especially true of perceiving other people. For example, a psychology professor once arranged for a guest lecturer to teach his class. Half the students in the class were given a page of notes that described the lecturer as a "rather *cold* person, industrious, critical, practical, and determined." The other students got notes describing him as a "rather *warm* person, industrious, critical, practical, and determined" (Kelley, 1950; italics added). Students who received the "cold" description perceived the lecturer as unhappy and irritable and didn't volunteer in class discussion. Those who got the "warm" description saw the lecturer as happy and good natured, and they actively took part in discussion with him.

Categories   Have you ever seen playing cards with a *red* ace of spades or a *black* four of hearts? Psychologist Jerome Bruner used a **tachistoscope** (tack-ISS-toh-scope: *a device for displaying images for very brief periods*) to flash pictures of cards on a screen. He found that observers misperceived cards that did not fit their knowledge and expectations. For instance, a *red* six of spades would be misperceived as a normal six of hearts (Bruner & Postman, 1949). Bruner believes that learning builds up **perceptual categories** (*classes, types, or groups*). Experiences are then "sorted" into

View I   View II   View III

Figure 7–33 ◆ "Young woman/old woman" illustrations. As an interesting demonstration of perceptual expectancy, show some of your friends view I and some view II (cover all other views). Next show your friends view III and ask them what they see. Those who saw view I should see the old woman in view III; those who saw view II should see the young woman in view III. Can you see both? (After Leeper, 1935.)

these categories. Since observers had no category for a red six of spades, they saw it as a six of hearts. Categories such as "punk," "mental patient," "queer," "honky," "bitch," and so on, are particularly likely to distort perceptions.

Those are extremes. Does it really make that much difference what you call someone or something?

Perceptual categories, especially those defined by labels, do make a difference. This is especially true in perceiving people, where even trained observers may be influenced. For example, in one study, psychotherapists were shown a videotaped interview. Half of the therapists were told that the man being interviewed was applying for a job. The rest were told that the man was a mental patient. Therapists who

thought the man was a job applicant perceived him as "realistic," "sincere," and "pleasant." Those who thought he was a patient perceived him as "defensive," "dependent," and "impulsive" (Langer & Abelson, 1974).

A Look Ahead   In this chapter we have moved from basic perceptions of form to the complexities of perceiving people and events. In the Applications section, we will continue this progression with a look at objectivity and eyewitness testimony. After that, an Exploration addresses an interesting question: Is there any evidence that extrasensory perception exists? Before we continue, here's a Learning Check.

Learning Check

1. Selective attention is promoted by all but one of the following. Which does not fit?
   a. habituation   **b.** contrast   **c.** change   **d.** intensity

2. The occurrence of an orientation response shows that habituation is complete. T or F?

3. Changes in brain waves and increased blood flow to the head are part of an OR. T or F?

4. Research shows that heightened sexual arousal can cause a person to perceive members of the opposite sex as more physically attractive. T or F?

5. In top-down processing of information, individual features are analyzed and assembled into a meaningful whole. T or F?

6. When a person is prepared to perceive events in a particular way, it is said that a perceptual expectancy or _____ exists.

7. Perceptual expectancies are greatly influenced by the existence of mental categories and labels. T or F?

Critical Thinking

8. Cigarette advertisements in the United States are required to carry a warning label about the health risks of smoking. How have tobacco companies made these labels less visible?

Answers:

1. a 2. F 3. T 4. T 5. F 6. set 7. T 8. Advertisers place health warnings in the corners of ads, where they attract the least possible attention. Also, the labels are often placed on "busy" backgrounds so that they are partially camouflaged. Finally, the main images in ads are designed to strongly attract attention. This further distracts readers from seeing the warnings.

*H*ave you ever seen the sun set? You may think you have. Yet, in reality, we know the sun does not "set." Instead, our viewing angle changes as the earth turns, until the sun is obscured by the horizon. Want to try the alternative? This evening, stand facing the west. With practice, you can learn to feel yourself being swept backward on the rotating surface of the earth as you watch an unmoving sun recede in the distance (Fuller, 1969).

This radical shift in perspective illustrates the limitations of "objective" observation. Like most experiences, seeing a "sunset" is a **perceptual reconstruction** (*mental model*) of an external event. As we have seen, perception reflects the needs, expectations, attitudes, values, and beliefs of the perceiver. In this light, the phrase "seeing is believing" must be modified. Clearly, we see what we believe, as well as believe what we see.

In some cases, subjective perception nurtures the personal vision valued in art, music, poetry, and scientific innovation. Often, however, it is a real liability.

Eyewitness　In the courtroom, eyewitness testimony can be a key to proving guilt or innocence. The claim, "I saw it with my own eyes," carries a lot of weight with a jury. But to put it bluntly, eyewitness testimony is frequently wrong. Juries are most swayed by witnesses who are certain that their testimony is accurate. Yet, in fact, a person's confidence in his or her testimony has almost no bearing on its accuracy (Wells, 1993)! In addition, being questioned tends to make witnesses more confident about what they saw, even if they are wrong. Thus, police questioning can actually degrade the value of the testimony witnesses give later, in court (Shaw, 1996).

Psychologists are gradually convincing lawyers, judges, and police officers of the fallibility of eyewitness testimony. Even so, thousands of people have been wrongfully convicted (Loftus, 1993). In one typical court case, a police officer testified that he saw the defendant shoot the victim as both stood in a doorway 120 feet away. Measurements made by a psychologist showed that at that distance, light from the dimly lit doorway was extremely weak—less than a fifth of that from a candle. To further show that identification was improbable, a juror stood in the doorway under identical lighting conditions. None of the other jurors could identify him. The defendant was acquitted (Buckhout, 1974).

Unfortunately, perception rarely provides an "instant replay" of events. Even in broad daylight, eyewitness testimony is untrustworthy. After a horrible DC-10 airliner crash in Chicago in 1979, 84 pilots who saw the accident were interviewed. Forty-two said the DC-10's landing gear

was up, and 42 said it was down! As one investigator commented, the best witness may be a "kid under 12 years old who doesn't have his parents around." Adults, it seems, are easily swayed by their expectations.

Impressions formed when a person is surprised, threatened, or under stress are especially prone to distortion. That's why witnesses to crimes so often disagree. As a dramatic demonstration of this problem, a college professor was attacked by an actor in a staged assault. Immediately after the event, 141 witnesses were questioned in detail. Their descriptions were then compared to a videotape made of the staged "crime." The total accuracy score for the group (on features such as appearance, age, weight, and height of the assailant) was only *25 percent* of the maximum possible (Buckhout, 1974).

Wouldn't the victim of a crime remember more than a mere witness?

A revealing study found that eyewitness accuracy is virtually the same for witnessing a crime (seeing a pocket calculator stolen) as it is for being a victim (seeing one's own watch stolen) (Hosch & Cooper, 1982). Jurors who place more weight on the testimony of victims may be making a serious mistake. Also, it is worth repeating that witnesses who are confident in their testimony are no more likely to be accurate than those who have doubts (Smith, Kassin, & Ellsworth, 1989).

In many crimes, victims fall prey to the phenomenon of **weapon focus.** Understandably, victims often *fix their entire attention on the knife, gun, or other weapon* used by an attacker. In doing so, they fail to perceive details of appearance, dress, or other clues to identity (Steblay, 1992).

Additional factors affecting eyewitnesses are summarized in Table 7–2 ■. (Inaccuracies in memory also affect eyewitness testimony; see Chapter 10 for more information.)

Implications　How often are everyday perceptions as inaccurate or distorted as those of an emotional eyewitness? The answer we have been moving toward is, very frequently. Bearing this in mind may help you be more tolerant of the views of others and more cautious about your own objectivity. It may also encourage more frequent *reality testing* on your part.

What do you mean by reality testing?

Reality Testing　In any situation having an element of doubt or uncertainty, **reality testing** *involves obtaining additional information to check your perceptions.* Even simple designs like

Table 7–2   ■   Factors Affecting the Accuracy of Eyewitness Perceptions

Sources of Error	Summary of Findings
1. Stress	Very high levels of stress impair the accuracy of eyewitness perceptions.
2. Weapon focus	The presence of a weapon impairs an eyewitness' ability to accurately identify the culprit's face.
3. Exposure time	The less time an eyewitness has to observe an event, the less accurately she or he will perceive and remember it.
4. Accuracy-confidence	An eyewitness' confidence is not a good predictor of his or her accuracy.
5. Cross-racial perceptions	Eyewitnesses are better at identifying members of their own race than they are at identifying people of other races.
6. Post-event information	Eyewitness testimony about an event often reflects not only what was actually seen but also information obtained later on.
7. Color perception	Judgments of color made under monochromatic light (such as an orange street light) are highly unreliable.
8. Wording of questions	An eyewitness' testimony about an event can be affected by how the questions put to that witness are worded.
9. Unconscious transference	Eyewitnesses sometimes identify as a culprit someone they have seen in another situation or context.
10. Trained observers	Police officers and other trained observers are no more accurate as eyewitnesses than the average person.
11. Time estimation	Eyewitnesses tend to overestimate the duration of events.
12. Attitudes, expectations	An eyewitness' perception and memory for an event may be affected by his or her attitudes and expectations.

Adapted from Kassin, Ellsworth, & Smith, 1989.

those in Figure 7–34 ◆ are easily misperceived. One of the designs in the drawing is a continuous line; the other is not. Most people cannot see this difference spontaneously. Instead, they must carefully trace and compare the two designs as a check on pure perception (Julesz, 1975).

Figure 7–34   ◆   The limits of pure perception. Even simple designs are easily misperceived. The drawing on the left is a continuous line; the one on the right is not. Most people cannot see this difference without carefully tracing the lines. (Adapted from patterns devised by Marvin Minsky and Seymour Papert.)

Psychologist Sidney Jourard once offered a more pertinent example of reality testing. One of Jourard's students believed her roommate was stealing from her. The student gradually became convinced of her roommate's guilt, but said nothing. As her distrust and anger grew, their relationship turned cold and distant. Finally, at Jourard's urging, she confronted her roommate. The roommate cleared herself immediately and expressed relief when the puzzling change in their relationship was explained (Jourard, 1974). With their friendship reestablished, the true culprit was soon caught. (The cleaning woman did it!)

If you have ever concluded that someone was angry, upset, or unfriendly without checking the accuracy of your perceptions, you have fallen into a subtle trap. Personal objectivity is an elusive quality, requiring frequent reality testing to maintain. At the very least, it pays to ask a person what she or he is feeling when you are in doubt. Clearly, most of us could learn to be better "eyewitnesses" to daily events.

Do some people perceive things more accurately than others?

Perceptual Awareness Humanistic psychologist Abraham Maslow (1969) believed that some people perceive themselves and others with unusual accuracy. Maslow characterized these people as especially alive, open, aware, and mentally healthy. He found that their perceptual styles were marked by immersion in the present, a lack of self-consciousness, freedom from selecting, criticizing, or evaluating, and a general "surrender" to experience. The kind of perception Maslow described is like that of a mother with her newborn infant, a child at Christmas, or two people in love.

Other researchers have tested Zen masters for habituation to repeated stimuli. The results indicate that Zen masters fail to show the expected habituation (Kasamatsu & Hirai, 1966). This finding lends some credibility to claims that Zen masters perceive a tree as vividly after seeing it 500 times as they did the first time.

Attention Whereas the average person has not reached perceptual restriction of the "if you've seen one tree, you've seen them all" variety, the fact remains that most of us tend to look at a tree and classify it into the perceptual category of "trees in general" without really appreciating the miracle standing before us. How, then, can we bring about **dishabituation** (*a reversal of habituation*) on a day-to-day basis? Does perceptual clarity require years of meditative discipline, like that of a Zen master? Fortunately, a more immediate avenue is available. The deceptively simple key to dishabituation is: Pay attention.

The following quote summarizes the importance of attention:

> One day a man of the people said to Zen Master Ikkyu: "Master, will you please write for me some maxims of the highest wisdom?"
>
> Ikkyu immediately took his brush and wrote the word "Attention."
>
> "Is that all?" asked the man. "Will you not add something more?"
>
> Ikkyu then wrote twice running: "Attention. Attention."
>
> "Well," remarked the man rather irritably, "I really don't see much depth or subtlety in what you have just written."
>
> Then Ikkyu wrote the same word three times running: "Attention. Attention. Attention." Half angered, the man demanded, "What does that word 'Attention' mean anyway?"
>
> And Ikkyu answered gently: "Attention means attention." (Kapleau, 1966)

To this we can add only one thought, provided by the words of poet William Blake: "If the doors of perception were cleansed, man would see everything as it is, infinite."

Becoming a Better "Eyewitness" to Life

Here's a summary of ideas from this chapter to help you maintain and enhance perceptual accuracy.

1. *Remember that perceptions are reconstructions of reality.* Learn to regularly question your own perceptions. Are they accurate? Could another interpretation fit the facts? What assumptions are you making? Could they be false? How might your assumptions be distorting your perceptions?

2. *Break perceptual habits and interrupt habituation.* Each day, try to do some activities in new ways. For example, take different routes when you travel to work or school. Do routines, such as brushing your teeth or combing your hair, with your non-preferred hand. Try to look at friends and family members as if they are persons you just met for the first time.

3. *Shift adaptation levels and broaden frames of reference by seeking out-of-the-ordinary experiences.* The possibilities here range from trying foods you don't normally eat, to reading opinions very different from your own. Experiences ranging from a quiet walk in the woods to a trip to an amusement park may be perceptually refreshing.

4. *Beware of perceptual sets.* Anytime you pigeonhole people, objects, or events, there is a danger that your perceptions will be distorted by expectations or pre-existing categories. Be especially wary of labels and stereotypes. Try to see people as individuals and events as unique, one-time occurrences.

5. *Be aware of the ways in which motives and emotions influence perceptions.* It is difficult to avoid being swayed by your own interests, needs, desires, and emotions. But be aware of this trap and actively try to see the world through the eyes of others. Taking the other person's perspective is especially valuable in disputes or arguments. Ask yourself, "How does this look to her or him?"

6. *Make a habit of engaging in reality testing.* Actively look for additional evidence to check the accuracy of your perceptions. Ask questions, seek clarifications, and find alternate channels of information. Remember that perception is not automatically accurate. You could be wrong—we all are frequently.

7. *Pay attention.* Make a conscious effort to pay attention to other people and your surroundings. Don't drift through life in a haze. Listen to others with full concentration. Watch their facial expressions. Make eye contact. Try to get in the habit of approaching perception like you are going to have to testify later about what you saw and heard.

Learning Check

1. Most perceptions can be described as active reconstructions of external reality. T or F?

2. Inaccuracies in eyewitness perceptions obviously occur in "real life," but they cannot be reproduced in psychology experiments. T or F?

3. Accuracy scores for facts provided by witnesses to staged crimes may be as low as 25 percent correct. T or F?

4. Victims of crimes are more accurate eyewitnesses than are impartial observers. T or F?

5. *Reality testing* is another term for dishabituation. T or F?

Critical Thinking

6. Return for a moment to the incident described in the Chapter Preview. What perceptual factors were involved in the first version of the "murder"? How did the girl affect what was seen?

Answers:

1. T 2. F 3. T 4. F 5. F 6. The girl's misperception, communicated so forcefully to other eyewitnesses, created a powerful expectancy that influenced what they perceived. Also, the stressful or emotional nature of the incident encouraged misperception.

Exploration

Extrasensory Perception—Do You Believe in Magic?

*I*n a quiet laboratory, Uri Geller, a self-proclaimed "psychic," has agreed to demonstrate his claimed paranormal abilities. In the course of testing, Geller was supposedly able to select, from a row of 10 film canisters, the one that contained an object, correctly guess the number that would come up on a die shaken in a closed box 8 out of 8 times, and reproduce drawings sealed in opaque envelopes.

Was Geller cheating, or was he using some ability beyond normal perception?

There is little doubt that Geller was cheating (Randi, 1980). But how? The answer lies in a discussion of **extrasensory perception (ESP)**—*the purported ability to perceive events in ways that cannot be explained by known sensory capacities.*

Parapsychology

Parapsychology *is the study of ESP and other* **psi phenomena** (*events that seem to defy accepted scientific laws*). (Psi is pronounced like sigh.) Parapsychologists seek answers to the questions raised by three basic forms that ESP could take. These are:

1. **Clairvoyance.** The purported ability to perceive events or gain information in ways that appear unaffected by distance or normal physical barriers.

2. **Telepathy.** Extrasensory perception of another person's thoughts, or more simply, the purported ability to read someone else's mind.

3. **Precognition.** The purported ability to perceive or accurately predict future events. Precognition may take the form of *prophetic dreams* that foretell the future.

While we are at it, we might as well toss in another purported psi ability:

4. **Psychokinesis.** The purported ability to exert influence over inanimate objects by willpower ("mind over matter"). (Psychokinesis cannot be classed as a type of ESP, but it is frequently studied by parapsychologists.)

Have parapsychologists confirmed the existence of ESP and other psi abilities?

Psychologists as a group are highly skeptical about psi abilities. But the general public remains split on the issue. A national poll found that 49 percent of all American adults believe in ESP (Gallup & Newport, 1991). If you doubt ESP, then you should know that some experiments seem to hint that it may exist. If you are among those who believe in ESP, then you should know why the scientific community doubts many of these experiments!

Coincidence Anyone who has ever had an apparent clairvoyant or telepathic experience may find it hard to question the existence of ESP. Yet, the difficulty of excluding *coincidence* makes natural ESP occurrences less conclusive than they might seem. Consider a typical psychic experience: During the middle of the night, a woman away for a weekend visit suddenly had a strong impulse to return home. When she arrived she found the house on fire with her husband asleep inside (Rhine, 1953).

An experience like this is striking, but it does not confirm the existence of ESP. If, by coincidence, a hunch turns out to be correct, it may be *reinterpreted* as precognition or clairvoyance (Marks & Kammann, 1979). If it is not confirmed, it will simply be forgotten. Most people don't realize it, but such coincidences

occur quite often. In fact, we should *expect* them, not consider them strange or mysterious (Alcock, 1990). Believers in ESP are especially prone to misjudge seemingly unusual events. That's because believers tend to falsely see cause-and-effect links in everyday coincidences (Brugger, Landis, & Regard, 1990).

The formal study of psi events owes much to the late J. B. Rhine. Rhine established the first parapsychological laboratory at Duke University and spent the rest of his life trying to document ESP. To avoid the problems of "natural"

psi events, Rhine tried to study ESP more objectively. Many of his experiments made use of the **Zener cards** (*a deck of 25 cards, each bearing one of five symbols*) (Fig. 7–35 ◆). In a typical clairvoyance test, people tried to guess the symbols on the cards as they were turned up from a shuffled deck. Pure guessing in this test will produce an average score of 5 "hits" out of 25 cards.

Unfortunately, some of Rhine's most dramatic early experiments used badly printed Zener cards that allowed the symbols to show faintly on the back. It is also very easy to cheat, by marking cards with a fingernail or by noting marks on the cards caused by normal use. Even if this were not the case, there is evidence that early experimenters sometimes unconsciously gave people cues about the cards with their eyes, facial gestures, or lip movements. In short, none of the early studies in parapsychology were done in a way that eliminated the possibility of fraud or "leakage" of helpful information (Alcock, 1990).

Modern parapsychologists are now well aware of the need for double-blind experiments, security and accuracy in record keeping, meticulous control, and

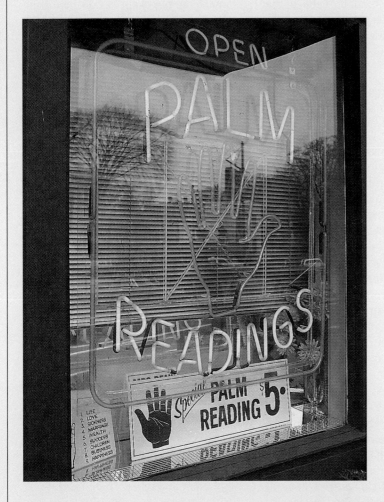

Most so-called psychics are simply keen observers. The "psychic" begins a "reading" by making general statements about a person. The "psychic" then plays "hot and cold" by attending to the person's facial expressions, body language, or tone of voice. When the "psychic" is "hot" (on the right track) the "psychic" continues to make similar statements about the person. If the person's reactions signal that the "psychic" is "cold" the psychic drops that topic or line of thought and tries another (Schouten, 1994).

Figure 7–35 ◆ ESP cards used by J. B. Rhine, an early experimenter in parapsychology.

repeatability of experiments. In the last 10 years, hundreds of experiments have been reported in parapsychological journals. Many of them seem to support the existence of psi abilities.

Then why do most psychologists remain skeptical about psi abilities?

For one thing, fraud continues to plague the field. Walter J. Levy, who was former director of Rhine's laboratory, was caught faking records. So have some others who got positive results. Even honest scientists have been fooled by various frauds and cheats, so there is reason to remain skeptical and on guard. The greatest danger may lie in errors by sincere, but self-deceiving, investigators (Hyman, 1989). It is remarkable, for instance, that many parapsychologists chose to ignore a famous "psychic's" habit of peeking at ESP cards during testing (Cox, 1994). As one critic put it, positive ESP results usually mean "Error Some Place" (Marks, 1990). The more closely psi experiments are examined, the more likely it is that claimed successes will evaporate (Alcock, 1990; Hyman, 1996b).

Statistics and Chance A major criticism of psi research has to do with inconsistency. For every study with positive results, there are others that fail (Hansel, 1980; Hyman, 1996b). It is rare—in fact, almost unheard of—for a person to maintain psi ability over any sustained period of time (Jahn, 1982). ESP researchers consider this "decline effect" an indication that parapsychological skills are very fragile and unpredictable (Rhine, 1977). But critics argue that a person who only temporarily scores above chance has just received credit for a **run of luck** (*a statistically unusual outcome that could occur by chance alone*). When the run is over, it is not fair to assume that ESP is temporarily gone. We must count *all* attempts.

To understand the run-of-luck criticism, consider an example. Say that you flip a coin 100 times and record the results. You then flip another coin 100 times, again recording the results. The two lists are compared. For any 10 pairs of flips, we would expect heads or tails to match 5 times. Let's say that you go through the list and find a set of 10 pairs where 9 out of 10 matched. This is far above chance expectation. But does it mean that the first coin "knew" what was going to come up on the second coin? The idea is obviously silly.

Now, what if a person guesses 100 times what will come up on a coin. Again, we might find a set of 10 guesses that matches the results of flipping the coin. Does this mean that the person, for a time, had precognition—then lost it? Parapsychologists tend to believe the answer is yes. Skeptics assume that nothing more than random matching occurred, as in the two-coin example.

Research Methods

Unfortunately, many of the most spectacular findings in parapsychology simply cannot be **replicated** (*reproduced or repeated*) (Hyman, 1996a). Even the same researchers using the same experimental subjects typically can't get similar results every time (Schick & Vaughn, 1995). More importantly, improved research methods usually result in fewer positive results (Hyman, 1996b).

Recently, parapsychologist Charles Honorton conducted some interesting studies of ESP. Participants in Honorton's experiments had ping-pong balls (cut in half) taped over their eyes and they heard "white noise" (a hissing sound) played through headphones. The intent of these measures was to create a **ganzfeld,** *or perceptual "blank screen."* After about 15 minutes, Honorton's subjects began to have vivid mental images. At that time, a "sender" in another room tried to mentally transmit images to the subject. Honorton claims that some of his participants received impressions of the images and thereby demonstrated ESP (Honorton & Bem, 1994). But as psychologist Ray Hyman points out, it can take years of close scrutiny before the flaws in a particular parapsychology experiment come to light. Hyman regards Honorton's experiments as inconclusive unless they are replicated by other scientists (Hyman, 1996b). It will be interesting to see if other studies follow parapsychology's long pattern of unrepeatable results.

Believers in ESP, such as ex-astronaut Edgar Mitchell, claim that failures to find ESP may occur for another reason. According to Mitchell, "The scientist has to recognize that his own mental processes may influence the phenomenon he's observing. If he's really a total skeptic, the scientist may well turn off the psychic subject." This may sound convincing, but skeptics consider it unfair. With Mitchell's argument in effect, anyone attempting an objective experiment can only get two results: He or she may find evidence of ESP or be accused of having suppressed it. This makes it impossible to disprove ESP to believers, even if it truly does not exist.

Reinterpretation is also a problem in psi experiments. For example, Mitchell claimed he did a successful telepathy experiment from space. Yet news accounts never mentioned that on some trials Mitchell's "receivers" scored above chance, while on others they scored *below* chance. The second outcome, Mitchell decided, was also a "success" because it represented intentional "psi missing." But, as skeptics have noted, if both high scores and low scores count as successes, how can you lose?

Of course, in many ESP tests the outcome is beyond debate. For instance, English "psychic" Chris Robinson, who claims to have precognitive dreams, was tested recently. The result? His performance did not exceed what would be expected on the basis of chance (Blackmore, 1995). It's interesting that Mr. Robinson didn't foresee his own impending failure and refuse to be tested!

Stage ESP

Skeptics and serious researchers in ESP both agree on one point. If psychic phenomena do occur, they cannot be controlled well enough to be used by entertainers. **Stage ESP** *simulates ESP for the purpose of entertainment.* Like stage magic, it is based on a combination of sleight of hand, deception, and patented gadgets (Fig. 7–36 ◆). A case in point is Uri Geller, a former nightclub magician who "astounded" audiences—and some scientists—with apparent telepathy, psychokinesis, and precognition.

Geller's performance on tests was described earlier. Not mentioned is what psychologist Ray Hyman calls the "incredible sloppiness" of these tests. One example is Geller's reproductions of sealed drawings. These, it turns out, were done in a room next to the one where the drawings were made. Original reports of Geller's alleged "ability" failed to mention that there was a hole in the wall between the two rooms, through which Geller might have heard discussions of the pictures being drawn. Also unreported was the fact that Geller's friend Shipi Stang was present at every test. Geller's manager has since testified that Stang frequently acted as Geller's accomplice in trickery (Alcock, 1990). Is it a coincidence that when a picture of a rocket ship was drawn, Stang hummed

the theme music from the motion picture *2001: A Space Odyssey?* A similar lack of control pervaded every other test. In the "die in the box" tests, for instance, Geller was allowed to hold the box, shake it, and have the honor of opening it (Randi, 1980; Wilhelm, 1976). Why weren't such pertinent details reported?

Sensational and uncritical reporting of apparent paranormal events is widespread. Hundreds of books, articles, and television programs are produced each year by people who have become wealthy promoting unsupported claims. If a person did have psychic powers, he or she would not have to make a living by entertaining, giving demonstrations, or making personal appearances. A quick trip to a casino would allow the person to retire for life.

Conclusion   After close to 130 years of investigation, it is still impossible to say conclusively whether psi events occur. As we have seen, a close look at psi experiments often reveals serious problems of evidence, procedure, and scientific rigor (Alcock, 1990; Hyman, 1996b; Marks & Kammann, 1979; Swets et al., 1988). It is also interesting to note that a survey of leading parapsychologists and skeptics

found that almost all in both camps said their belief in psi had decreased (Blackmore, 1989). Yet, being a skeptic does not mean a person is against something. It means that you are unconvinced. The purpose of this discussion, then, has been to counter the *uncritical* acceptance of psi events that is rampant in the media.

What would it take to scientifically demonstrate the existence of ESP?

Quite simply, a set of instructions that would allow any competent, unbiased observer to produce a psi event under standardized conditions that rule out any possibility of fraud (Schick & Vaughn, 1995). Undoubtedly, some intrepid researchers will continue their attempts to supply just that. Others remain skeptics and consider 130 years of inconclusive efforts reason enough to abandon the concept of ESP (Marks, 1990; Swets et al., 1988). At the least, it seems essential to be carefully skeptical of evidence reported in the popular press or by researchers who are uncritical "true believers." (But then, you already knew I was going to say that, didn't you!)

(a)   (b)   (c)

Figure 7–36 ◆ Fake psychokinesis. **(a)** The performer shows an observer several straight keys. While doing so, he bends one of the keys by placing its tip in the slot of another key. Normally, this is done out of sight, behind the "psychic's" hand. It is clearly shown here so you can see how the deception occurs. **(b)** Next, the "psychic" places the two keys in the observer's hand and closes it. By skillful manipulation, the observer has been kept from seeing the bent key. The performer then "concentrates" on the keys to "bend them with psychic energy." **(c)** The bent key is revealed to the observer. "Miracle" accomplished! (Adapted from Randi, 1983.)

Learning Check

1. Four purported psi events investigated by parapsychologists are clairvoyance, telepathy, precognition, and _____ .

2. The _____ cards were used by J. B. Rhine in early tests of ESP.

3. Natural, or "real life," occurrences are regarded as the best evidence for the existence of ESP. T or F?

4. Skeptics attribute positive results in psi experiments to statistical runs of luck. T or F?

5. Replication rates are very high for ESP experiments. T or F?

Critical Thinking

6. A "psychic" on television offers to fix broken watches for viewers. Moments later, dozens of viewers call the station to say that their watches miraculously started running again. What have they overlooked?

Answers:

1. psychokinesis 2. Zener 3. F
4. T 5. F 6. When psychologists handled watches awaiting repair at a store, 57 percent began running again, with no help from a "psychic." Believing the "psychic's" claim also overlooks the impact of big numbers: If the show reached a large audience, at least a few "broken" watches would start working merely by chance.

Chapter Summary

What are perceptual constancies, and what is their role in perception?

◆ **Perception** is the process of assembling sensations into a usable mental representation of the world.

◆ In vision, the image projected on the retina is constantly changing, but the external world appears stable and undistorted because of **size, shape,** and **brightness constancy.**

What basic principles do we use to group sensations into meaningful patterns?

◆ The most basic organization of sensations is a division into **figure and ground** (object and background).

◆ A number of factors contribute to the organization of sensations. These are **nearness, similarity, continuity, closure, contiguity, common region,** and combinations of the preceding. Basic elements of line drawings appear to be universally recognized.

◆ A perceptual organization may be thought of as a **hypothesis** held until evidence contradicts it. Perceptual organization shifts for **ambiguous stimuli. Impossible figures** resist stable organization altogether.

How is it possible to see depth and judge distance?

◆ **Depth perception** (the ability to perceive three-dimensional space and judge distances) is present in basic form soon after birth (as shown by testing with the **visual cliff** and other methods).

◆ Depth perception depends on the **muscular cues** of **accommodation** (bending of the lens) and **convergence** (inward movement of the eyes). **Stereoscopic vision** is created mainly by **retinal disparity** and the resulting overlap and **mismatch** of visual sensations.

◆ A number of **pictorial cues** also underlie depth perception. These are **linear perspective, relative size, height in the picture plane, light and shadow, overlap, texture gradients, aerial haze,** and **relative motion** (motion parallax). All are monocular depth cues (only one eye is needed to make use of them).

◆ The **moon illusion** is at least partially explained by the **apparent distance hypothesis,** which emphasizes the greater number of depth cues present when the moon is on the horizon. Changes in accommodation also contribute to the moon illusion.

What effect does learning have on perception?

◆ Organizing and interpreting sensations is greatly influenced by **perceptual habits.** Studies of **inverted vision** show that even the most basic organization is subject to a degree of change. **Active movement** speeds adaptation to a new perceptual environment.

- Perceptual judgments are not made in a vacuum. They are almost always related to **context,** or to an internal **frame of reference** called the **adaptation level.**
- One of the most familiar of all illusions, the **Müller-Lyer illusion,** seems to be related to perceptual learning, linear perspective, **size-distance invariance** relationships, and mislocating the end-points of the figure.

How are perceptions altered by attention, motives, values, and expectations?

- **Attention** is **selective,** and it may be **divided** among various activities. Attention is closely related to **stimulus intensity, repetition, contrast, change,** and **incongruity.**
- Attention is accompanied by an **orientation response.** When a stimulus is repeated without change, the orientation response undergoes **habituation.**
- Personal **motives** and **values** often alter perceptions by changing the evaluation of what is seen or by altering attention to specific details.
- Perceptions may be based on **top-down** or **bottom-up processing** of information.
- Attention, prior experience, suggestion, and motives combine in various ways to create **perceptual sets,** or

expectancies. These prepare a person to perceive or misperceive in a particular way.

How reliable are eyewitness reports?

- Perception is an active **reconstruction** of events. This is one reason why **eyewitness testimony** is surprisingly unreliable. Eyewitness accuracy is further damaged by **weapon focus,** and a number of similar factors.
- Perceptual accuracy is enhanced by **reality testing, dishabituation,** and conscious efforts to **pay attention.** It is also valuable to break perceptual habits, to broaden frames of reference, to beware of perceptual sets, and to be aware of the ways in which motives and emotions influence perceptions.

Is extrasensory perception possible?

- **Parapsychology** is the study of purported **psi phenomena,** including **clairvoyance, telepathy, precognition,** and **psychokinesis.**
- Research in parapsychology remains controversial owing to a variety of problems and shortcomings. The bulk of the evidence to date is against the existence of ESP. **Stage ESP** is based on deception and tricks.

8

States of Consciousness

Preview

Living Nightmares

In New York's Times Square, a strange spectacle unfolds: To raise money for charity, disc jockey Peter Tripp has agreed to go without sleep for 200 hours. All too soon Tripp's fight to stay awake turns brutal. After 100 hours, he begins to have visual hallucinations: He sees cobwebs in his shoes and watches in terror as a tweed coat becomes a suit of "furry worms." When Tripp goes to a hotel to change clothes, a dresser drawer seems to burst into flames.

After 170 hours, Tripp's agony is almost unbearable. He struggles with the simplest thought, reasoning, and memory problems. His brain-wave patterns look like those of sleep, and he is no longer sure who he is. By the end of 200 hours, Tripp is unable to distinguish between his waking nightmares, hallucinations, and reality (Luce, 1965).

The Womb Tank We shift now to a scene far removed from Peter Tripp's ordeal. Some years ago, physician John Lilly pioneered the use of an unusual *sensory deprivation* environment. Subjects in Lilly's experiments wore darkened goggles and floated naked in a tank of body-temperature water (Lilly, 1972). As they drifted weightlessly in this "womb-like" environment, subjects were cut off from smell, touch, vision, hearing, and taste sensations.

What effect does sensory deprivation have?

Under such conditions, people often lose track of time and find it hard to concentrate. Some also undergo strange alterations in consciousness. For example, one person screamed in panic, "There is an animal having a long slender body with many legs. It's on the screen, crawling in back of me!"

As you can see, both sleep loss and sensory deprivation have a major impact on *consciousness*. In the discussion of consciousness that follows, we will begin with the familiar realms of sleep and dreaming and then move to points beyond.

States of Consciousness—The Many Faces of Awareness

To be conscious means to be aware. **Consciousness** *consists of all the sensations, perceptions, memories, and feelings you are aware of at any instant* (Farthing, 1992). As William James noted, consciousness is an ever-changing "stream," or flow of awareness. We spend most of our lives in **waking consciousness,** *a normal state of clear, organized alertness.* In ordinary waking consciousness we perceive times, places, and events as real, meaningful, and familiar. But as James also noted, states of consciousness related to fatigue, delirium, hypnosis, drugs, and ecstasy differ markedly from "normal" awareness. Everyone experiences at least some altered states, such as sleep, dreaming, and daydreaming. In everyday life, changes in consciousness may accompany long-distance running, listening to music, making love, or other circumstances.

It's clear that there are many altered states of consciousness. How are they distinguished from normal awareness?

Altered States of Consciousness During an **altered state of consciousness** (ASC) *distinct changes occur in the quality and pattern of mental activity.* Typically there are shifts in perceptions, emotions, memory, time sense, thinking, feelings of self-control, and suggestibility (Tart, 1986). Definitions aside, most people know when they have experienced an ASC.

Are there other causes of ASCs?

The list of causes is nearly endless. In addition to those already mentioned, we could add: sensory overload (for example, a light show, Mardi Gras crowd, or mosh pit), monotonous stimulation (meditation and "highway hypnotism" on long drives are good examples), unusual physical conditions (high fever, hyperventilation, dehydration, sleep loss, near-death experiences), sensory deprivation, and many other possibilities. As the following highlight points out, altered states of awareness may have important cultural significance.

Cultural Diversity

States of Consciousness in Other Cultures

Throughout history people have sought ways to alter consciousness. A dramatic example is the sweat lodge ritual of the Sioux Indians. During the ritual, several men sit in total darkness inside a small chamber heated by a bed of coals. Cedar smoke, bursts of steam, and the aroma of sage fill the air. The men chant rhythmically. The heat builds. At last they can stand it no more. The door is thrown open. Cooling night breezes rush in. And then? The cycle begins again—often to be repeated four or five times more. Among the Sioux this ritual is viewed as a cleansing of mind and body. When it is especially intense, it brings altered awareness and personal revelation.

Some people seek altered states primarily for pleasure, as is often true of drug intoxication. Yet as the Sioux illustrate, many cultures regard changes in consciousness as pathways to enlightenment. Almost every known religion has accepted at least some altered states as a source of mystical experience. Accepted avenues have ranged from fasting, meditation, prayer, isolation, sleep loss, whirling, and chanting, to self-inflicted pain and psychedelic substances. Often, altered awareness is a part of rituals that help build tribal bonds within a community.

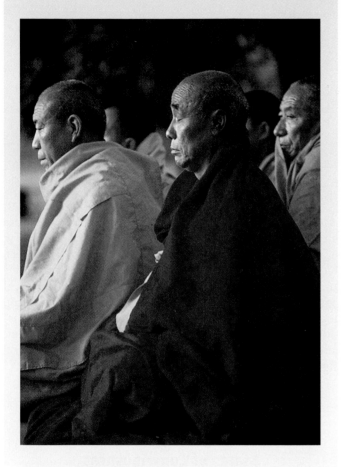

In many cultures, rituals of healing, prayer, purification, or personal transformation are accompanied by altered states of consciousness.

In short, all cultures recognize and accept some alterations of consciousness. However, the meanings given various states vary greatly—from signs of "madness" and "possession" by spirits, to life-enhancing breakthroughs. Thus, cultural conditioning greatly affects what altered states each of us recognizes, seeks, considers normal, and attains (Ward, 1989).

In this chapter we will focus on sleep, dreaming, hypnosis, stimulus deprivation, and the effects of drugs (psychoactive chemicals). To get right to the questions raised by the Chapter Preview, let's begin with the familiar altered states of sleep and dreaming.

Sleep—A Nice Place to Visit

Each of us will spend some 25 years of life in a strange state of semi-consciousness called sleep. Contrary to common belief, people are not totally unresponsive during sleep. Studies show that you are more likely to awaken if you hear your own name spoken, instead of another. Likewise, a sleeping mother may ignore a jet thundering overhead, but wake at the slightest whimper of her child. Some people can even do simple tasks while asleep. In one experiment, people learned to avoid an electric shock by touching a switch each time a tone sounded. Eventually, they could do it without waking. (This is much like the basic survival skill of turning off your alarm clock without waking.) Of course, sleep does impose limitations. There is no evidence, for instance, that a person can learn math, a foreign language, or other complex skills while asleep—especially when the snooze takes place in class (Druckman & Bjork, 1994; Wood et al., 1992).

Because of its many contradictions, sleep has always aroused curiosity. What do we know about this daily retreat from the world?

The Need for Sleep

How strong is the need for sleep?

Sleep expert Wilse Webb calls sleep a "gentle tyrant." Webb regards sleep as an **innate biological rhythm** (*natural bodily cycle*). As such, sleep can never be entirely sidestepped (Webb, 1994). But if flexibility is needed, sleep will give way temporarily, especially at times of great danger. As one comic put it, "The lion and the lamb shall lie down together, but the lamb will not be very sleepy." You could choose, then, to stay awake for an extended period. But there are limits. A rare disease that prevents sleep always ends the same way: The patient falls into a stupor, followed by coma, followed by death (Oliwenstein, 1993).

In one set of experiments, animals were placed on treadmills over a pool of water. Needless to say, they didn't find it easy to sleep. Even so, sleep won out. The animals soon began to drift into repeated microsleeps (Goleman, 1982). A **microsleep** *is a brief shift of brain activity to patterns normally recorded during sleep.* Microsleeps also occur in humans: When you drive, it is well worth remembering that a microsleep can lead to a macro-accident. Even a driver whose eyes are open can be asleep for a few seconds. By the way, if you are fighting to stay awake while driving, stopping for a brief nap is more effective than just taking a break. Coffee helps too (Horne & Reyner, 1996).

How long could a person go without sleep?

Sleep Deprivation   With few exceptions, 4 days or more without sleep becomes hell for anyone, but longer sleepless periods are possible. The world record for staying awake is held by Randy Gardner—who at age 17 went 268 hours (11 days) without sleep. Surprisingly, Randy needed only 14 hours of sleep to recover (Dement, 1972). It is usually not necessary to completely replace lost sleep. As Randy found, most symptoms of **sleep deprivation** (*sleep loss*) are reversed by a single night's rest.

What are the costs of sleep loss? Age and personality make a big difference. Randy Gardner remained clear-headed to the end of his vigil. In contrast, Peter Tripp's behavior became quite bizarre. In general, there is little impairment on complex mental tasks after 2 or 3 days without sleep. But most people do decline in their ability to pay attention, remain vigilant, and follow simple routine (Mikulincer et al., 1989).

Sleep loss doesn't have to be total to take a toll. For example, players in a marathon, week-long tennis match averaged about 3 hours of sleep per night. After the match, the players' scores had declined on tests of perceptual-motor coordination and memory (Edinger et al., 1990). (Maybe they kept playing because they couldn't remember who was ahead?)

If you were mildly deprived of sleep you would probably be able to rouse yourself for more complex or challenging tasks. What usually suffers most is low-level, boring, self-motivated tasks. As Wilse Webb says, "It's not your thinking or memory that goes, it's your will to continue; you would prefer to be asleep." For a driver, pilot, or machine operator, this may be enough to spell disaster.

Greater sleep loss sometimes causes a temporary **sleep-deprivation psychosis** like Peter Tripp suffered. *Confusion, disorientation, delusions, and hallucinations are typical of this reaction.* Hallucinations may be visual, like Tripp's "coat of furry worms," or tactile, such as feeling cobwebs on the face. Fortunately, such "crazy" behavior is not common. Hallucinations and delusions are rarely evident before 60 hours of continuous wakefulness. The most typical reactions to sleep loss are trembling hands, drooping eyelids, inattention, staring, increased pain sensitivity, and general discomfort (Naitoh et al., 1989).

Sleep Patterns

Sleep was described as an innate biological rhythm. What does that mean?

Daily *sleep and waking periods* create a variety of **sleep patterns.** These **rhythms of sleep and waking** are so steady that they continue for many days, even when clocks and light-dark cycles are removed. However, under such conditions, humans eventually shift to a sleep-waking cycle that averages *25 hours*, not 24. This finding suggests that external time markers, especially light and dark, help tie our sleep rhythms to a normal 24-hour day (Fig. 8–1 ◆). Otherwise, many of us would drift into our own unusual sleep cycles.

What is the normal range of sleep?

According to medical records there is a man in England who gets by on only an hour of sleep each night—and feels

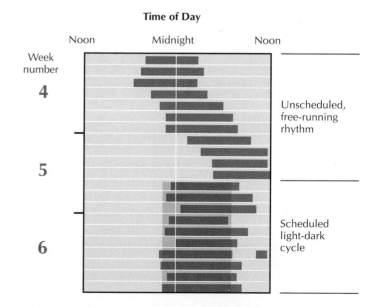

Figure 8–1   ◆   Sleep rhythms. Bars show periods of sleep during the fourth, fifth, and sixth weeks of an experiment with a human subject. During unscheduled periods, the subject was allowed to select times of sleep and lighting. The result was a sleep rhythm of about 25 hours. Notice how this free-running rhythm began to advance around the clock. When periods of darkness were scheduled (colored area), the rhythm quickly resynchronized with 24-hour days. (Adapted from Czeisler, 1981.)

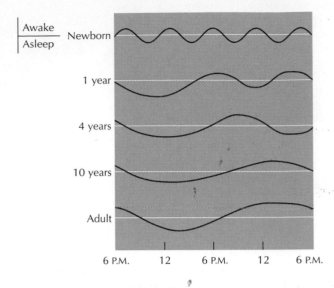

Figure 8–2 ◆ Development of sleep patterns. Short cycles of sleep and waking gradually become the night-day cycle of an adult. While most adults don't take naps, midafternoon sleepiness is a natural part of the sleep cycle. (After Williams et al., 1964.)

perfectly fine. However, this is rare. Only 8 percent of the population are **short sleepers,** *averaging 5 hours of sleep or less per night.* On the other end of the scale we find **long sleepers,** *who doze 9 hours or more* (and tend to be daytime worriers) (McCann & Stewin, 1988). The majority of us sleep on a familiar 7- to 8-hour-per-night schedule. It is quite normal, however, to sleep as little as 5 hours per night or as much as 11. Urging everyone to sleep 8 hours would be like advising everyone to wear medium-size shoes.

Do elderly people need more sleep?

They may need it, but they seldom get it. As people age they usually sleep less. People over the age of 50 average only 6 hours of sleep a night. In contrast, infants spend up to 20 hours a day sleeping, usually in 2- to 4-hour cycles. As they mature, most children go through a "nap" stage and eventually settle into a steady cycle of sleeping once a day (Fig. 8–2 ◆). Some people, of course, maintain the afternoon "siesta" as an adult pattern. Perhaps we all should. Experts now regard midafternoon sleepiness as a natural part of the sleep cycle. Brief, well-timed naps, therefore, may be the key to maintaining alertness in people like truck drivers and hospital interns, who often must fight drowsiness (Aschoff, 1994; Goleman, 1989).

It is very tempting to try to reduce sleep time. However, people on *shortened* cycles—for example, 3 hours of sleep to 6 hours awake—often can't get to sleep when the cycle calls for it. The underlying sleep rhythm simply won't cooperate. That's why astronauts continue to sleep on their normal earth schedule while in space. Adapting to *longer* than normal days is more promising. Such days can be tailored to match natural sleep patterns, which have a ratio of *2 to 1* between time awake and time asleep. One study showed that 28-hour "days" work for some people. Unfortunately, subjects did

poorly on longer, 38-hour cycles (24 hours awake and 12 hours asleep). Most people couldn't use the entire 12-hour sleep period, so they repeatedly lost sleep. As with sleep needs, we see again that sleep is a "gentle tyrant." Sleep patterns may be bent and stretched, but they rarely yield entirely to human whims (Akerstedt et al., 1993).

Stages of Sleep—The Nightly Roller-Coaster Ride

What causes sleep?

Early sleep experts thought that some substance in the bloodstream must cause sleep. But studies of Siamese twins (individuals whose bodies are joined at birth) show that this is false. One twin can frequently be observed sleeping while the second is awake (Fig. 8–3 ◆). During waking hours, a **sleep hormone** (*sleep-promoting chemical*) collects in the brain and spinal cord, *not* in the blood. If this sleep hormone is extracted from one animal and injected into another, the second animal will quickly fall asleep and sleep deeply for many hours (Cravatt et al., 1995). Notice, however, that this explanation is incomplete. For example, how do we explain why well-rested students may have to fight to stay awake during a boring lecture?

Whether you are awake or asleep depends on the *balance* between opposed sleep and waking systems in the brain. One system consists of circuits and transmitter chemicals that promote sleep. The second is a network of brain cells that respond to other chemicals and inhibit sleep. The two systems seesaw back and forth, switching the brain from

Figure 8–3 ◆ These Siamese twins share the same blood supply, yet one sleeps while the other is awake. (Photo by Yale Joel, Life Magazine. © 1954 Time, Inc.)

sleep to wakefulness and back again. The brain does not "shut down" during sleep. Rather, the brain changes the *pattern* of its activity. The total *amount* of activity remains fairly constant (Steriade & McCarley, 1990).

What happens when you fall asleep?

Stages of Sleep

The changes that come with sleep can be measured with an **electroencephalograph** (eh-LEK-tro-en-SEF-uh-lo-graf), or *brain-wave machine*, commonly called an **EEG**. The brain gives off tiny electrical signals that can be amplified and recorded (see the Exploration in Chapter 3 for more information). When you are awake and alert, the EEG reveals a pattern of *small fast waves* called **beta** (Fig. 8–4 ◆). Immediately before sleep the EEG record shifts to a pattern of *larger and slower waves* called **alpha.** (Alpha waves also occur when a person is relaxed and thoughts are allowed to drift.) As the eyes close, breathing becomes slow and regular, the pulse rate slows, and body temperature drops. Soon after, four separate **sleep stages** can be identified, based on *a combination of brain-wave patterns and behavioral changes*.

Stage 1 As you lose consciousness and enter **light sleep** (*stage 1 sleep*), your heart rate slows even more. Breathing becomes more irregular; the muscles of your body relax. This may trigger a *reflex muscle contraction throughout the body* called a **hypnic jerk** (HIP-nik: sleep). (This is quite normal, so have no fear about admitting to your friends that you fell asleep with a hypnic jerk.)

In **stage 1 sleep** *the EEG is made up mainly of small, irregular waves with some alpha.* Persons awakened at this time may or may not say they were asleep.

Stage 2 As sleep deepens, body temperature drops further. Also, the EEG begins to include **sleep spindles**, which are *short bursts of distinctive brain-wave activity.* Spindles seem to mark the true boundary of sleep. Within 4 minutes after spindles appear, most people who are awakened say they were asleep (Bonnet & Moore, 1982).

Stage 3 In stage 3, a new brain wave called *delta* begins to appear. **Delta waves** *are very large and slow.* Their presence signals deeper sleep and a further loss of consciousness.

Stage 4 Deep sleep (*the deepest level of normal sleep*) is reached after about an hour. In stage 4, brain waves become almost pure delta, and the sleeper is in a state of oblivion. If you make a loud noise during stage 4, the sleeper will awaken in confusion and may not remember the noise.

After spending some time in stage 4, the sleeper returns (through stages 3 and 2) to stage 1. Further shifts between deeper and lighter sleep occur throughout the night (Fig. 8–5 ◆).

Two Basic States of Sleep

If you watch a person who is asleep, you will soon notice that the *sleeper's eyes occasionally move* under the eyelids. These **rapid eye movements** (or **REMs**) are strongly associated with dreaming (Fig. 8–5). Roughly 85 percent of the time, people awakened during REMs report vivid dreams. In addition to rapid eye movements, **REM sleep** *is marked by a return to stage 1 EEG patterns.* REM sleep is easy to observe in pets, such as dogs and cats. Watch for eye and facial movements and for irregular breathing. (You can forget about your pet iguana, though. Reptiles show no signs of REM sleep.)

(a)

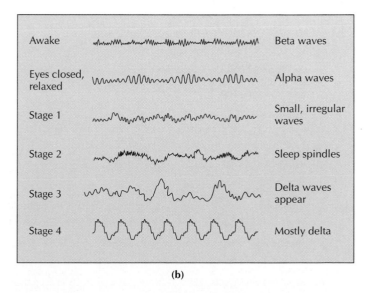

Awake		Beta waves
Eyes closed, relaxed		Alpha waves
Stage 1		Small, irregular waves
Stage 2		Sleep spindles
Stage 3		Delta waves appear
Stage 4		Mostly delta

(b)

Figure 8–4 ◆ **(a)** Photograph of an EEG recording session. The man in the background is asleep. **(b)** Changes in brain-wave patterns associated with various stages of sleep. Actually, most wave types are present at all times, but they occur more or less frequently in various sleep stages.

Figure 8–5 ◆ **(a)** Average proportion of time adults spend daily in REM sleep and NREM sleep. REM periods add up to about 20 percent of total sleep time. **(b)** Typical changes in stages of sleep during the night. Notice that dreams mostly coincide with REM periods.

REM and NREM Sleep   The two most basic states of sleep now appear to be REM sleep with its associated dreaming and **non-REM (NREM) sleep,** *which occurs during stages 2, 3, and 4* (Hobson & Stickgold, 1994). NREM sleep is dream free about 90 percent of the time. Dreams during REM sleep are usually longer, clearer, more detailed, more bizarre, and more "dream-like" than thoughts and images that occur in NREM sleep (Foulkes & Schmidt, 1983). Your first period of stage 1 sleep is usually free of REMs and dreams. Stage 1 sleep during the rest of the night is usually accompanied by rapid eye movements.

NREM sleep seems to help us recover from fatigue built up during the day. It increases with exercise or physical exertion (Horne & Staff, 1983). In comparison, added daytime stress tends to increase REM sleep. REM sleep totals only about 90 minutes per night (about the same as a feature movie). Yet, its link with dreaming makes it as important as NREM sleep. REM sleep may rise dramatically when there is a death in the family, trouble at work, a marital conflict, or other emotionally-charged events.

What happens to the body when a person dreams?

REM Sleep and Dreaming   REM sleep is a time of high emotion. The heart beats irregularly. Blood pressure and breathing waver. Both males and females appear to be sexually aroused: Males usually have an erection, and genital blood flow increases in women. This occurs for all REM sleep, so it is not strictly related to erotic dreams (Shafton, 1995).

During REM sleep your body becomes quite still, as if you were paralyzed. Imagine for a moment the results of acting out some of your recent dreams. Very likely, REM-sleep paralysis prevents some hilarious— and dangerous—nighttime escapades. When it fails, some people thrash violently, leap out of bed, and may attack their bed partners. A *failure of normal muscle paralysis during REM sleep* is called **REM behavior disorder**. One patient suffering from the disorder tied himself to his bed every night. That way, he couldn't jump up and crash into furniture or walls (Shafton, 1995).

In a moment we will survey some additional sleep problems—if you are still awake. First, here are a few questions to check your memory of our discussion so far.

Learning Check	Critical Thinking
1. Altered states of consciousness are defined mainly by changes in patterns of alertness. T or F?	8. Why might it be better for the unscheduled human sleep-waking cycle to average more than 24 hours, instead of less?
2. A momentary shift in brain activity to a pattern characteristic of sleep is referred to as **a.** delta sleep **b.** light sleep **c.** microsleep **d.** deprivation sleep	
3. Delusions and hallucinations typically continue for several days after a sleep-deprived individual returns to normal sleep. T or F?	
4. Older adults, and particularly the elderly, sleep more than children do because the elderly are more easily fatigued. T or F?	**Answers:**
5. Most studies of sleep patterns show a consistent ratio of 2 to 1 between time awake and time asleep. T or F?	ery day to adjust. hours, we all might have to "stretch" every day to adjust.
6. Rapid eye movements (REMs) indicate that a person is in deep sleep. T or F?	If the bodily cycle were shorter than 24 can then retard the bodily cycle slightly to synchronize it with light-dark cycles. "slack" in the cycle. External time markers
7. Alpha waves are to presleep drowsiness as _____ _____ are to stage 4 sleep.	that the 25-hour average leaves a little **7.** delta waves **8.** Sleep experts theorize 1. F 2. c 3. F 4. F 5. T 6. F

Sleep Disturbances— Showing Nightly: Sleep Wars!

Sleep clinics treat thousands of people each year who suffer from sleep disorders or complaints. (See Table 8–1 ■.) Let's see what has been learned about a few of the most common problems.

Sleepwalking and Sleeptalking

Sleepwalking is eerie and fascinating. **Somnambulists** (som-NAM-bue-lists: *those who sleepwalk*) avoid obstacles, descend stairways, climb trees, and on rare occasions may step out of windows or in front of automobiles. The sleepwalker's eyes are usually open, but a blank face, a lack of recognition, and shuffling feet show that the person is still asleep. Parents who are sleepwalkers or sleeptalkers tend to have children with the same problems. This suggests that these disturbances are partially hereditary (Abe et al., 1984). A parent who finds a child sleepwalking should gently guide the child back to bed. Awakening a sleepwalker does no harm, but it is not necessary.

Does sleepwalking occur during dreaming?

It might seem that sleepwalkers are acting out dreams. But remember that people are normally immobilized during REM sleep. EEG studies have shown that somnambulism occurs during NREM stages 3 and 4. Sleeptalking also occurs mostly in *NREM stages of sleep*. A link with the deeper stages of sleep seems to explain why sleeptalking makes little sense and why sleepwalkers are confused and remember little when awakened (DSM-IV, 1994).

Nightmares and Night Terrors

Stage 4 sleep is also the realm of *night terrors*. These severely frightening episodes are quite different from ordinary, garden-variety nightmares (Table 8–2 ■). A **nightmare** is simply *a bad dream that takes place during REM sleep*. Nightmares are usually brief and easily remembered. For most people, nightmares occur, on average, about twice a month (Wood & Bootzin, 1990).

During stage 4 **night terrors**, *a person suffers total panic and may hallucinate frightening dream images into the bedroom.* An attack may last 15 or 20 minutes. When it is over, the person awakens drenched in sweat, but only vaguely remembers the terror. Since night terrors occur during NREM sleep (when the body is not immobilized), victims may sit up, scream, get out of bed, or run around the room. Night terrors are most common in childhood, but they

Table 8–1 ■ Sleep Disturbances –Things That Go Wrong in the Night

Hypersomnia Excessive daytime sleepiness. This can result from depression, insomnia, narcolepsy, sleep apnea, sleep drunkenness, periodic limb movements, drug abuse, and other problems.

Insomnia Difficulty in getting to sleep or staying asleep; also, not feeling rested after sleeping.

Narcolepsy Sudden, irresistible, daytime sleep attacks that may last anywhere from a few minutes to a half hour. Victims may fall asleep while standing, talking, or even driving.

Nightmare disorder Vivid, recurrent nightmares that significantly disturb sleep.

Periodic limb movement syndrome Muscle twitches (primarily affecting the legs) which occur every 20 to 40 seconds and severely disturb sleep.

REM behavior disorder A failure of normal muscle paralysis, leading to violent actions during REM sleep.

Restless legs syndrome An irresistible urge to move the legs in order to relieve sensations of creeping, tingling, prickling, aching, or tension.

Sleep apnea During sleep, breathing stops for 20 seconds or more until the person wakes a little, gulps in air, and settles back to sleep; this cycle may be repeated hundreds of times per night.

Sleep drunkenness A slow transition to clear consciousness after awakening; sometimes associated with irritable or aggressive behavior.

Sleep terror disorder The repeated occurrence of night terrors that significantly disturb sleep.

Sleep-wake schedule disorder A mismatch between the sleep-wake schedule demanded by a person's bodily rhythm and that demanded by the environment.

Sleepwalking disorder Repeated incidents of leaving bed and walking about while asleep.

Bond & Wooten, 1996; DSM-IV, 1994; Hauri & Linde, 1990.

continue to plague some adults throughout their lives (DSM-IV, 1994).

Before we move on to a new topic, here's a suggestion for eliminating nightmares.

Using Psychology

How to Eliminate a Nightmare

A bad nightmare can be worse than any horror movie. You can leave a theater, but often we remain trapped in

	Nightmare	Night Terror
Table 8-2 ■ Was It a Nightmare or a Night Terror?		
Stage of sleep	■ REM	■ NREM
Activity	■ Slight or no movement	■ Violent body movement, sits up, cries out, may run
Emotion	■ Fear or anxiety	■ Terror and disorganizing panic
Mental state when awakened	■ Coherent, can be calmed	■ Incoherent, disoriented, cannot be calmed, may be hallucinating
Physiological changes	■ No perspiration	■ Perspires heavily
Recall	■ Dream activity usually remembered	■ Amnesia for episode

Adapted from Woods & Greenhouse, 1974.

our most terrifying dreams. Yet bad as they may be, most nightmares can be banished by following three simple steps. First, write down your nightmare, describing it in detail. Next, change the dream any way you wish, being sure to spell out the details of the new dream. The third step is **imagery rehearsal,** in which you *mentally rehearse the changed dream before you fall asleep again* (Krakow & Neidhardt, 1992).

Imagery rehearsal may work because it makes upsetting dreams familiar while a person is awake and feeling safe. Or perhaps it mentally "reprograms" future dream content. In any case, the technique has proved helpful for many people (Krakow et al., 1995).

Narcolepsy

One of the most dramatic sleep problems is **narcolepsy** (NAR-koe-lep-see) or sudden, irresistible *sleep attacks.* These last anywhere from a few minutes to a half hour. Victims may fall asleep while standing, talking, or even driving. Emotional excitement, especially laughter, commonly triggers narcolepsy. (Tell a good joke and a narcoleptic may fall asleep.) Over half of all victims also suffer from **cataplexy** (CAT-uh-plex-see), *a sudden temporary paralysis of the muscles,* leading to complete body collapse. It is easy to understand why narcolepsy can devastate careers and relationships (Broughton & Broughton, 1994).

Sudden paralysis sounds like what happens during dreaming. Does that suggest a connection between narcolepsy and REM sleep?

Yes. When monitored on an EEG, narcoleptics tend to fall directly into REM sleep. Thus, the narcoleptic's sleep attacks and paralysis seem to occur when REM sleep intrudes into the waking state (Siegel et al., 1991).

Fortunately, narcolepsy is rare. It tends to run in families, which suggests that it is hereditary. This has been confirmed by breeding several generations of narcoleptic dogs. (These

dogs, by the way, are simply outstanding at learning the trick "Roll over and play dead.") There is no known cure for narcolepsy, but stimulant drugs may cut down the frequency of attacks. Scheduling a long nap each day also helps narcoleptics manage their sleep attacks (Mullington & Broughton, 1993).

Insomnia

While some people sleep when they don't want to, many more have trouble getting enough sleep. About 30 percent of all adults report some degree of insomnia. Roughly 9 percent have a serious or chronic problem. **Insomnia** *includes difficulty in going to sleep, frequent nighttime awakenings, waking too early, or a combination of these problems* (Bond & Wooten, 1996).

The citizens of North America will spend well over one-half billion dollars this year on sleeping pills. There is real irony in this expense. Non-prescription sleeping pills such as *Sominex, Nytol,* and *Sleep-eze* have little or no sleep-inducing effect. Even worse are most prescription sedatives. These drugs (usually barbiturates) decrease both stage 4 sleep and REM sleep, drastically lowering sleep quality. In addition, the initial dosage quits working because a drug tolerance builds rapidly. Many users become "sleeping-pill junkies" who need an ever-greater number of pills to get to sleep. The end result is **drug-dependency insomnia** (*sleeplessness caused by withdrawal from sleeping pills*). Victims of this problem must be painstakingly weaned from their sleep medicines. Otherwise, terrible nightmares and "rebound insomnia" may drive them back to drug use.

If sleeping pills are a poor way to treat insomnia, what can be done?

Actually, a drug called triazolam (try-AS-o-lam) appears to help in some cases of insomnia. However, even triazolam has drawbacks, and it too can cause rebound insomnia on the first few nights after it is withdrawn. Rather than using drugs, it is often far better to learn behavioral techniques to treat insomnia (Jacobs et al., 1993).

Types and Causes of Insomnia Worry, stress, and excitement often cause **temporary insomnia** (*a brief period of sleeplessness*) and a self-defeating cycle. First, heightened arousal blocks sleep. Then, frustration and anger cause more arousal, which further delays sleep. Delayed sleep causes more frustration, and so on. A good way to beat this cycle is to avoid fighting it. It is usually best to get up and do something useful or satisfying when you have difficulty sleeping. (Reading a textbook might be a good choice of useful activities.)

The restlessness that some insomniacs suffer is caused by hunger. This can be prevented by having a small snack before retiring. Also, scientists have discovered that **tryptophan** (TRIP-tuh-fan: *an amino acid*) can promote sleep. Interestingly, tryptophan is found in a glass of milk. So grandma was right after all! But she apparently didn't know that an egg-tuna-cottage cheese-soybean-cashew-chicken-turkey-banana sandwich would be even better for inducing sleep. All of the listed foods are also high in tryptophan.

What about more serious cases of insomnia?

Chronic insomnia exists if sleeping problems last for *more than 3 weeks.* Treatment for chronic insomnia usually begins with a careful analysis of a patient's sleep history. Possible reasons for insomnia, such as depression, anxiety, medical problems, lifestyle, stress, and sleep habits are carefully assessed (Bond & Wooten, 1996).

The first thing anyone suffering from insomnia should do is to consume less caffeine, alcohol, and tobacco. Some insomniacs benefit from relaxation training to lower arousal before sleep. (See the Applications section in Chapter 19 for more information about relaxation.) *Stimulus control* strategies also help. **Stimulus control** *refers to linking a response with specific stimuli.* For example, patients are told to strictly avoid doing anything but sleeping when they are in bed. They are not to study, eat, watch TV, read, pay the bills, or even think in bed. In this way, only sleeping becomes associated with retiring (Hauri & Linde, 1990).

One of the best ways to combat insomnia is also the simplest. Many insomniacs have scattered sleep habits. For these people, adopting a regular schedule helps establish a firm body rhythm, greatly improving sleep. Patients are told to get up and go to sleep at the same time each day, including weekends. (Many people disturb their sleep rhythms by staying up late on weekends.) These and other ways of combating insomnia are summarized in the next highlight.

restriction and stimulus control are the most effective (Lacks & Morin, 1992).

Stimulants Avoid stimulants such as coffee and cigarettes. Remember too that alcohol, while not a stimulant, impairs sleep quality.

Worries Schedule time in the early evening to write down worries or concerns. Plan what you will do about them the next day. Then put them out of mind until morning.

Relaxation Learn a physical or mental strategy for relaxing, such as progressive muscle relaxation (see Chapter 19), meditation (see Chapter 14), or blotting out worries with calming images. Strenuous exercise during the day promotes sleep, but it is usually too stimulating in the evening. Very light evening exercise may be helpful, however (Jacobs et al., 1993).

Sleep Restriction Even if you miss an entire night's sleep, do not sleep late in the morning, nap more than an hour, sleep during the evening, or go to bed early the following night. Try to restrict sleep to your normal bedtime hours. That way, you will avoid fragmenting your sleep rhythms (Lacks & Morin, 1992).

Stimulus Control Link only sleep with your bedroom so that it does not trigger worrying: (1) Go to bed only when you are feeling sleepy. (2) Awaken at the same time each morning. (3) Avoid non-sleep activities in bed. (4) Always leave the bedroom if sleep has not occurred within 10 minutes. (5) Do something else when you are upset about not being able to sleep (Lacks & Morin, 1992).

Paradoxical Intention To remove the pressures of trying to get to sleep, try instead to keep your eyes open (in the dark) and stay awake as long as possible (Horvath & Goheen, 1990). This allows sleep to overtake you unexpectedly and lowers performance anxiety. Never try to go to sleep. Arrange to let it happen.

Sleep Apnea

Some sage once said, "Laugh and the whole world laughs with you; snore and you sleep alone." Nightly "wood sawing" is often harmless, but it can signal a serious problem. A person who snores loudly, with short silences and loud gasps or snorts, may suffer from *apnea* (AP-nee-ah: interrupted breathing). In **sleep apnea,** *breathing stops for periods of 20 seconds to 2 minutes.* As the need for oxygen becomes intense, the person wakes a little and gulps in air. She or he then settles back to sleep. But soon, breathing stops again. This cycle is repeated hundreds of times a night. As you might guess, apnea victims complain of **hypersomnia** (hi-per-SOM-nee-ah: *excessive daytime sleepiness*) (DSM-IV, 1994).

What causes sleep apnea?

Some cases occur because the brain stops sending signals to the diaphragm to maintain breathing. Another cause is blockage of the upper air passages. In either case the person can breathe normally during the day, so he or she may be unaware of the problem. Apnea should be suspected any time a person snores loudly. In addition to the misery it causes, apnea seriously endangers health. Persons who suspect they are apneic should seek treatment at a sleep clinic. The most effective treatments are weight loss, surgery for breathing obstructions, and use of a CPAP (Continuous Positive Airway Pressure) mask to aid breathing during sleep (Koenig, 1996).

SIDS   Sleep apnea is especially dangerous in infancy, when it is suspected as one cause of sudden infant death syndrome (SIDS), *or "crib death."* SIDS is the most frequent cause of death for infants under 1 year of age. Each year 1 out of every 500 babies is a victim of SIDS. In the "typical" crib death, a slightly premature or small baby with some signs of a cold or cough is bundled up and put to bed. A short time later, parents return and find the child is dead.

Some cases of SIDS are caused by apnea due to immature breathing centers in the brainstem (Thoman et al., 1988). In other instances it appears that direct blockage of the nose is responsible. A few babies remain passive when breathing is blocked, raising the risk of crib death (Lipsett, 1980).

Secondhand smoke may pose an even higher risk. Babies are 3 times more likely to die of SIDS if they are in the same house with adults who smoke (Klonoff-Cohen et al., 1995).

Babies at risk for SIDS must be carefully watched for the first 6 months of life. To aid parents in this task, a special monitor may be used that sounds an alarm when breathing or pulse becomes weak (Fig. 8–6 ◆). The list that follows gives some danger signals for SIDS (Einspieler et al., 1988). Be aware, however, that SIDS can also strike babies who show none of these signs.

Some Warning Signs for SIDS

- The mother is a teenager.
- The baby is premature.
- The baby has a shrill, high-pitched cry.
- The baby engages in "snoring," breath-holding, or frequent awakening at night.
- The baby breathes mainly through an open mouth.
- The baby remains passive when its face rolls into a pillow or blanket and moves little during sleep.
- Parents or other adults in the home are smokers.

"Back to Sleep"

Pop quiz: Should babies be placed face down or face up in bed? Another major risk factor for SIDS is the position in which babies sleep. Doctors used to advise parents to place infants face down in bed. Now, experts believe that healthy infants are better off sleeping on their backs or sides. (Premature babies, those with respiratory problems, and those who often vomit may still need to sleep face down. Ask a pediatrician for guidance.) Since this advice was first

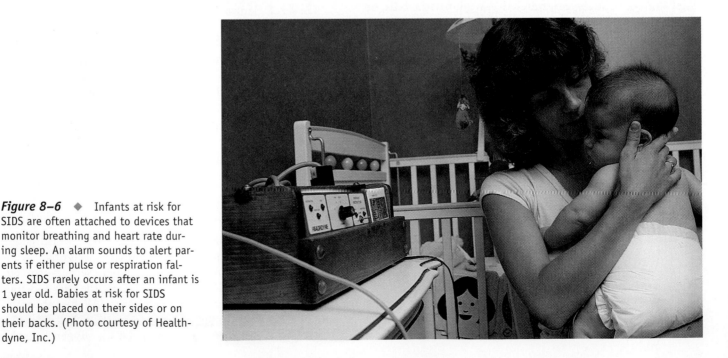

Figure 8–6 ◆ Infants at risk for SIDS are often attached to devices that monitor breathing and heart rate during sleep. An alarm sounds to alert parents if either pulse or respiration falters. SIDS rarely occurs after an infant is 1 year old. Babies at risk for SIDS should be placed on their sides or on their backs. (Photo courtesy of Healthdyne, Inc.)

publicized, there has been a 50 percent drop in SIDS deaths. Remember, "*back* to sleep" is the safest position for most infants (Willinger et al., 1994).

Dreams—A Separate Reality?

When researchers Nathaniel Kleitman and Eugene Aserinsky discovered REM sleep in 1952, they ushered in a "Golden Era" of dream inquiry. To conclude our discussion of sleep, let's consider some age-old questions about dreaming.

Does everyone dream? Do dreams occur in an instant?

Most people dream four or five times a night, but not all people remember their dreams. "Non-dreamers" are often shocked by their dreams when first awakened during REM sleep. Dreams are usually spaced about 90 minutes apart. The first dream lasts only about 10 minutes; the last averages 30 minutes and may run as long as 50. Dreams, therefore, occur in real time, not as a "flash" (Shafton, 1995).

How important is dream sleep? Is it essential for normal functioning?

REM Sleep Deprivation To answer these questions, sleep expert William Dement awakened volunteers each time they entered REM sleep. People kept from dreaming several nights in a row showed an increased tendency to dream. By the fifth night, many had to be awakened 20 or 30 times to prevent REM sleep. Finally, the volunteers were allowed to sleep undisturbed. During the next night, they *dreamed extra amounts.* This effect is called a **REM rebound.** It explains why alcoholics often have horrible nightmares after they quit drinking. Alcohol suppresses REM sleep and sets up a powerful rebound effect when it is withdrawn. It's worth remembering that while alcohol and other depressant drugs may help a person go to sleep, they often greatly reduce sleep quality.

While they were deprived of dream sleep, Dement's volunteers complained of daytime anxiety, poor memory, and lapses in concentration. For a time, it looked like people deprived of dreaming might go crazy. But sleep experts now refer to this idea as the "REM myth." Later experiments showed that missing *any* sleep stage can cause a rebound for that stage. In general, daytime disturbances are related to the *total amount* of sleep lost, not the *type* of sleep lost (Glovinsky et al., 1990).

Functions of REM Sleep What, then, is the purpose of REM sleep? Early in life, dreaming may stimulate the developing brain. Newborn babies spend about 50 percent of their sleeping time in REM sleep. This amounts to a hearty 8 or 9 hours a day of dream time. In adulthood, REM sleep

Dr. John Herman of the University of Texas may look like he just stepped out of the movie *Star Wars,* but he is actually involved in dream research. Dr. Herman is wearing goggles that electronically monitor eye movements during sleep. Use of such devices has greatly extended our understanding of dreaming.

may serve other purposes. Dreams may prevent sensory deprivation during sleep and aid the processing of emotional events. REM sleep also seems to help sort and integrate memories formed during the day. Although we have much to learn, it seems clear that REM sleep and dreaming are valuable for keeping the brain in good working order.

Research Frontier

REM Sleep and Memory

No one has to remember to dream. But do we dream to remember? In one study, college students did two mental tasks, one easy and the other difficult. For the easy task, students merely memorized a list of paired words. The difficult task was a logic game that required some tricky mental gymnastics. Later, students spent the night in a sleep lab. Some were awakened each time they entered REM sleep. Others were awakened only during NREM periods. A third group was kept awake all night. The lucky fourth group was allowed to sleep undisturbed.

The following day, all four groups performed equally well on the easy memory task. But on the hard task, those who lost REM sleep did much worse than the other groups (Chollar, 1989). To succeed at the logic game, students had to create new *mental strategies* and remember what worked.

In summary, REM sleep seems to aid the development of memories and strategies that help us cope with the world (Hennevin et al., 1995; Smith, 1995). Dreaming may also help *remove* useless memories before they are stored (Crick & Mitchison, 1995). Speaking very loosely, it's as if the dreaming brain were reviewing messages left on a telephone answering machine, in order to decide which are worth keeping.

Dream Worlds

Calvin Hall, a noted authority on dreaming, collected and analyzed over 10,000 dreams (Hall, 1966; Hall et al., 1982). Hall found that most dreams reflect everyday events. The favorite dream setting is familiar rooms in a house. Action usually takes place between the dreamer and two or three other emotionally important people—friends, enemies, parents, or employers. Dream actions are mostly familiar: running, jumping, riding, sitting, talking, and watching. About half of the recorded dreams had sexual elements. Dreams of flying, floating, and falling occur less frequently. Researchers have also found that if you're dreaming more now, you may be enjoying it less. Unpleasant emotions such as anxiety, fear, anger, and sadness are more frequent in dreams than pleasant emotions (Merritt et al., 1994).

Dream Theories

How meaningful are dreams?

Most theorists agree that dreams reflect our waking thoughts, fantasies, and emotions (Cartwright & Lamberg, 1992; Winget & Kramer, 1979). Thus, a better question might be, How deep should we dig in interpreting dreams? Some theorists believe that dreams have deeply hidden meanings. Others regard dreams as meaningless. Let's examine both views.

Psychodynamic Dream Theory Sigmund Freud's book *The Interpretation of Dreams* (1900) opened a whole new psychological world. After analyzing his own dreams, Freud concluded that many dreams represent **wish fulfillment** (*an expression of unconscious desires*). Thus, a student who is angry at a teacher may dream of embarrassing the teacher in class;

a lonely person may dream of romance; or a hungry child may dream of food.

Freud's **psychodynamic theory** of dreaming *emphasizes internal conflicts and unconscious forces*. While many of Freud's ideas are attractive, there is evidence against them. For example, volunteers in a study of starvation showed no particular increase in dreams about food and eating (Keys, 1950). Freud's response, no doubt, would have been that dreams rarely express needs so directly. One of Freud's key insights is that ideas in dreams are expressed as *images* or pictures, rather than in words (Globus, 1987).

Freud believed that dreams express unconscious desires and conflicts as disguised **dream symbols** (*images that have deeper symbolic meaning*). For instance, death might be symbolized by a journey, children by small animals, or sexual intercourse by horseback riding or dancing. Similarly, a woman sexually attracted to her best friend's husband might dream of stealing her friend's wedding ring and placing it on her own hand, an indirect symbol of her true desires. (For a discussion of dream analysis in psychotherapy, see Chapter 19.)

Do all dreams have hidden meanings?

Probably not. Even Freud realized that some dreams are trivial or unimportant "day residues," or carryovers from ordinary waking events. Also, you may be relieved to learn that Freud's is not the only approach to dream interpretation.

The Activation-Synthesis Hypothesis At the other end of the scale from Freud stands a radically different view of dreaming. Scientists Allan Hobson and Robert McCarley believe that dreams are made in this way: During REM sleep, brain cells are activated that normally control eye movements, balance, and actions. However, messages from the cells are blocked from reaching the body, so no movement occurs. But the cells continue to tell higher brain areas of their activities. Struggling to interpret this information, the brain searches through stored memories and manufactures a dream. Hobson and McCarley call this explanation of dreaming the **activation-synthesis hypothesis.** Hobson (1988) explains that *"the brain is turned on (activated) during sleep and then generates and integrates (synthesizes) its own sensory and motor information."*

How does this help explain dream content?

Let's use the classic chase dream as an example. In such dreams we feel we are running from danger or a pursuer, but not going anywhere. Hobson and McCarley suggest that in such dreams the brain is being told that the body is running. However, it gets no feedback from the motionless body to confirm it. As it tries to make sense of this information, the brain creates a chase drama. From this perspective, dreams have no "latent" or hidden meanings. They are merely a different type of thinking that occurs during sleep (Hobson, 1988; Porte & Hobson, 1996).

The activation-synthesis hypothesis certainly seems to

account for some dream experiences. For instance, it may explain why bizarre images are twice as common in dreams as they are in daytime fantasies (Williams et al., 1992). Nevertheless, many psychologists continue to believe that dreams have deeper meaning (Cartwright & Lamberg, 1992; Globus, 1987; Shafton, 1995).

There seems little doubt that dreams can make a difference in our lives: Veteran sleep researcher William Dement once dreamed that he had lung cancer. In the dream a doctor told Dement he would die soon. At the time,

Dement was smoking two packs of cigarettes a day. He says, "I will never forget the surprise, joy, and exquisite relief of waking up. I felt reborn." Dement quit smoking the following day (Hales, 1980).

It was once assumed that dreams can only be interpreted by trained professionals. Now, there is greater acceptance of the personal nature of dream meanings. As a result, many psychologists urge people to collect and interpret their own dreams. Later in this chapter, the Applications section offers some practical suggestions for doing just that.

Learning Check | **Critical Thinking**

1. Night terrors, sleepwalking, and sleeptalking all occur during stage 1, NREM sleep. T or F?

2. Narcolepsy and cataplexy are both associated with _____ sleep.

3. Sleep _____ is suspected as one cause of SIDS.

4. Which of the following is *not* a behavioral remedy for insomnia?
   a. daily hypersomnia   **b.** stimulus control   **c.** progressive relaxation
   d. paradoxical intention

5. The favored setting for dreams is
   a. work   **b.** school   **c.** outdoors or unfamiliar places   **d.** familiar rooms

6. Unpleasant emotions such as fear, anger, and sadness are more frequent in dreams than pleasant emotions. T or F?

7. According to the activation-synthesis model of dreaming, dreams are constructed from _____ to explain messages received from nerve cells controlling eye movement, balance, and bodily activity.

8. REM sleep seems to contribute to learning, especially to the formation of memories associated with _____ that aid survival or coping.

9. Even without being told that somnambulism is an NREM event, you could have predicted that sleepwalking doesn't occur during dreaming. Why?

Answers:
1. F 2. REM 3. apnea 4. a 5. d 6. T 7. memories 8. strategies 9. Because people are immobilized during REM sleep and REM sleep is strongly associated with dreaming. This makes it unlikely that sleepwalkers are acting out dreams.

Hypnosis—Look into My Eyes

"**Y**our body is becoming heavy. Your eyes are so tired you can barely keep them open. You feel warm and relaxed and very heavy. You are so tired you can't move. Relax. Let go. Relax. Close your eyes and relax." These are the last words a textbook should ever say to you, and the first a professional hypnotist might say.

Hypnosis, like dreaming, has an aura of mystery surrounding it. Actually, hypnosis is not nearly so mysterious as it might seem. **Hypnosis** *is an altered state of consciousness, characterized by narrowed attention and an increased openness to suggestion.* Not all psychologists agree with this definition. Some regard hypnosis as no more than a blend of conformity, relaxation, imagination, obedience, suggestion, and role-playing (Kirsch & Lynn, 1995; Spanos, 1990). Either way, the point is that hypnosis can be explained by normal psychological principles. It is not "magical."

Interest in hypnosis began in the 1700s with Franz Mesmer, whose name is the basis for the term **mesmerize** (*to hypnotize*). Mesmer, an Austrian physician, believed that he could cure diseases by passing magnets over the body. Mesmer's mysterious "treatments" are related to hypnosis because he relied heavily on the power of suggestion. For a time, mesmerism enjoyed quite a following. In the end, however, Mesmer's theories of "animal magnetism" were rejected and he was branded a quack and a fraud.

The term *hypnosis* was coined by an English surgeon named James Braid. The Greek word *hypnos* means "sleep," and Braid used it to describe the hypnotic state. Today we know that hypnosis is *not* sleep. Confusion about this point remains because some hypnotists give the suggestion, "Sleep, sleep." However, EEG records made during hypnosis differ from those seen when a person is asleep (Graffin, Ray, & Lundy, 1995).

Can anyone be hypnotized?

Hypnotic Susceptibility Approximately 8 people out of 10 can be hypnotized, but only 4 out of 10 will be good hypnotic subjects. People who are imaginative, prone to fantasy, and who easily become absorbed in tasks are often highly responsive to hypnosis (Crawford et al., 1993; Silva & Kirsch, 1992). But people who lack these traits may also be hypnotized. If you are willing to be hypnotized, chances are good that you could be. Hypnosis depends more on the efforts and abilities of the hypnotized person than the skills of the hypnotist (Kirsch & Lynn, 1995).

Hypnotic susceptibility *is one's capacity to become hypnotized.* It can be measured by making a series of suggestions and counting the number to which a person responds. A typical hypnotic test is the *Stanford Hypnotic Susceptibility Scale* shown in Table 8–3 ■. (Also see Fig. 8–7 ◆.) Notice that the scale ranges from easy to more difficult tasks. If you were to score high on the scale today, you probably would do the same years from now. Hypnotizability is very stable over time (Piccione et al., 1989).

How is hypnosis done? Could I be hypnotized against my will?

Figure 8–7 ◆ In one test of hypnotizability, subjects attempt to pull their hands apart after hearing suggestions that their fingers are "locked" together.

Table 8–3 ■	Stanford Hypnotic Susceptibility Scale
Suggested Behavior	**Criterion of Passing**
1. Postural sway	Falls without forcing
2. Eye closure	Closes eyes without forcing
3. Hand lowering (left)	Lowers at least 6 inches by end of 10 seconds
4. Immobilization (right arm)	Arm rises less than 1 inch in 10 seconds
5. Finger lock	Incomplete separation of fingers at end of 10 seconds
6. Arm rigidity (left arm)	Less than 2 inches of arm bending in 10 seconds
7. Hands moving together	Hands at least as close as 6 inches after 10 seconds
8. Verbal inhibition (name)	Name unspoken in 10 seconds
9. Hallucination (fly)	Any movement, grimacing, acknowlegment of effect
10. Eye catalepsy	Eyes remain closed at end of 10 seconds
11. Posthypnotic (changes chairs)	Any partial movement response
12. Amnesia test	Three or fewer items recalled

Adapted from Weitzenhoffer & Hilgard, 1959.

Inducing Hypnosis There are as many different hypnotic routines as there are hypnotists. Still, all techniques encourage a person (1) to focus attention on what is being said, (2) to relax and feel tired, (3) to "let go" and accept suggestions easily, and (4) to use vivid imagination (Druckman & Bjork, 1994).

A person who is deeply hypnotized may relax "reality testing" so that normal "willpower," or self-control, is reduced. Nevertheless, most people will not act out hypnotic suggestions that they consider immoral or repulsive (such as disrobing in public or harming someone). Note, too, that a person must cooperate to become hypnotized. Many theorists believe that all hypnosis is really **self-hypnosis** (*autosuggestion*). In other words, the hypnotist acts as a guide to help another person follow a series of suggestions that alter sensations, perceptions, thoughts, feelings, and behaviors (Druckman & Bjork, 1994; Kirsch & Lynn, 1995).

What does it feel like to be hypnotized?

You might be surprised at some of your actions during hypnosis. You also might have mild feelings of floating, sinking, anesthesia, or separation from your body. Personal experiences vary widely. However, hypnotized people generally remain in control of their behavior and aware of what is going on (Kirsch & Lynn, 1995).

A key element in hypnosis is the **basic suggestion effect** (*a tendency of hypnotized persons to carry out suggested actions as if they were involuntary*). Hypnotized persons feel like their actions and experiences are *automatic*—they seem to happen without effort (Kihlstrom, 1985). Here is how one person described his hypnotic session:

> I felt lethargic, my eyes going out of focus and wanting to close. My hands felt real light. . . . I felt I was sinking deeper into the chair. . . . I felt like I wanted to relax more and more. . . . My responses were more automatic. I didn't have to *wish* to do things so much or *want* to do them. . . . I just did them. . . . I felt floating . . . very close to sleep (Hilgard, 1968).

Hypnosis may also cause a *dissociation* or "split" in awareness. To illustrate, researcher Ernest Hilgard asks hypnotized subjects to plunge one hand into a painful bath of ice water. Subjects told to feel no pain say they feel none. The same subjects are then asked if there is any part of their mind that does feel pain. With their free hand, many write, "It hurts," or "Stop it, you're hurting me," while they continue to act pain-free (Hilgard, 1977, 1978). One part of the hypnotized person says there is no pain and acts as if there is none. Another part, which Hilgard calls the *hidden observer*, is aware of the pain but remains in the background. The **hidden observer** *is a detached part of the hypnotized person's awareness that silently observes events.*

What can (and cannot) be achieved with hypnosis?

Effects of Hypnosis   Many abilities have been tested for responsiveness to hypnosis. In some cases, the evidence is incomplete or conflicting. Even so, the following conclusions seem justified (Druckman & Bjork, 1994; Kihlstrom, 1985; Kirsch & Lynn, 1995):

1.   Superhuman acts of strength. Hypnosis has no more effect on physical strength than instructions that encourage a person to make his or her best effort.

2.   Memory. There is some evidence that hypnosis can enhance memory. However, it frequently increases the number of false memories as well. For this reason, many states now bar persons who have been hypnotized from testifying in court. (See Chapter 10 for more information.)

3.   Amnesia. A person told not to remember something heard during hypnosis may claim not to remember. In some instances this may be nothing more than a deliberate attempt to avoid thinking about specific ideas. However, a recent study concluded that brief memory loss of this type actually does occur (Bowers & Woody, 1996).

4.   Pain relief. Hypnosis can relieve pain (Holroyd, 1996). Therefore, it can be especially useful in situations where chemical painkillers cannot be used or are ineffective. One such situation is control of phantom limb pain. (Phantom limb pains are recurring pains that amputees sometimes feel coming from the missing limb.)

5.   Age regression. Given the proper suggestions, some hypnotized people appear to "regress" to childhood. However, most theorists now believe that "age-regressed" subjects are only acting out a suggested role.

6.   Sensory changes. Hypnotic suggestions concerning sensations are among the most effective. Given the proper instructions, a person can be made to smell a small bottle of ammonia and respond as if it were a wonderful perfume. It is also possible to alter color vision, hearing sensitivity, time sense, perception of illusions, and many other sensory responses.

Hypnosis is a valuable tool for inducing relaxation, controlling pain, and enhancing psychotherapy (Kirsch, Montgomery, & Sapirstein, 1995). In general, hypnosis is better at changing subjective experience than it is at modifying behaviors such as smoking or overeating. Hypnotic effects are useful, but seldom amazing (Druckman & Bjork, 1994; Gibson & Heap, 1991).

Stage Hypnosis

On stage the hypnotist intones, "When I count to three, you will imagine that you are on a train to Disneyland, and growing younger and younger as the train approaches." Responding to these suggestions, grown men and women begin to giggle and squirm like children on their way to a circus.

How do stage entertainers use hypnosis to get people to do strange things?

They don't. Little or no hypnosis is needed to do a good hypnosis act. **Stage hypnosis** *is often merely a simulation of hypnotic effects.* T. X. Barber, an authority on hypnosis, says that stage hypnotists make use of several features of the stage setting to perform their act (Barber, 1970).

1.   Waking suggestibility. We are all more or less open to suggestion, but on stage people are unusually cooperative because they don't want to "spoil the act." As a result, they will readily follow almost any instruction given by the entertainer.

2.   Selection of responsive subjects. Participants in stage hypnotism (all *volunteers*) are first "hypnotized" as a group. Thus, anyone who doesn't yield to instructions is eliminated.

3.   The hypnosis label disinhibits. Once a person has been labeled "hypnotized," she or he can sing, dance, act silly, or whatever, without fear or embarrassment. On stage, being "hypnotized" takes away personal responsibility for one's actions.

4.   The hypnotist as a "director." After volunteers loosen up and respond to a few suggestions, they find that they are suddenly the stars of the show. Audience response to the antics on stage brings out the "ham" in many people. All the "hypnotist" needs to do is direct the action.

5.   The stage hypnotist uses tricks. Stage hypnosis is about 50 percent taking advantage of the situation and 50 percent deception. Here is a common deception: One of the more impressive stage tricks is to rigidly suspend a person between two chairs. This is astounding only because the

Figure 8–8 ◆ Arrange three chairs as shown. Have someone recline as shown. Ask him to lift slightly while you remove the middle chair. Accept the applause gracefully! (Concerning hypnosis and similar phenomena, the moral, of course, is "Suspend judgment until you have something solid to stand on.")

audience does not question it. Anyone can do it, as is shown in the photographs and instructions in Figure 8–8 ◆. Try it!

To summarize, hypnosis is real, and it can significantly alter private experience. Hypnosis is a useful tool that has been applied in a variety of settings. The TV or nightclub stage, however, is not one of these settings. Stage "hypnotists" entertain; they rarely hypnotize.

Sensory Deprivation— Life on a Sensory Diet

Throughout history, *sensory deprivation* has been one of the most widely used means of altering consciousness. **Sensory deprivation (SD)** *refers to any major reduction in external stimulation.*

What happens when stimulation is greatly reduced?

A hint comes from reports by prisoners in solitary confinement, arctic explorers, high-altitude pilots, long-distance truck drivers, and radar operators. When faced with limited or monotonous stimulation, these people have at times had bizarre sensations, dangerous lapses in attention, and wildly distorted perceptions. To find out why, D. O. Hebb paid volunteers to undergo sensory deprivation under controlled conditions.

Subjects spent several days lying on their backs in a small cubicle. To prevent vision, they wore darkened goggles. Gloves and cardboard cuffs restricted touch. In the background, a constant hissing noise masked all other sounds. Do these conditions sound interesting? If you were placed in similar circumstances, you might be in for a surprise. Few subjects could take more than 2 or 3 days of sensory

deprivation without "pushing the panic button" (Heron, 1957).

Disruptive Effects

What sort of changes take place during sensory deprivation?

As mentioned in the Chapter Preview, a person may misjudge time and have trouble concentrating. After emerging from sensory deprivation, some people experience color distortions, heightened visual illusions, slower reactions, and a brief warping of visual lines and spaces. Volunteers in some early studies also reported strange and vivid images.

Spurred by such reports, researchers soon created an ingenious array of sensory deprivation environments, and volunteers seeking a drugless high flocked to experiments. Most were disappointed, however. We now know that true hallucinations are rare during sensory deprivation (Zubek, 1969). The fanciful, dream-like visions that sometimes occur are more likely to be **hypnogogic images** (hip-no-GAH-jik) (*images like those that occur just before sleep*). These images may be vivid and surprising, but they are rarely mistaken for real objects. Hypnogogic images are apparently linked to an increase in the number of *theta waves* produced by the brain. These brain waves, in the 4- to 7-cycle-per-second range, are usually recorded just before sleep. Sensory deprivation also increases their occurrence (Taylor, 1983).

Benefits of Sensory Restriction

In recent years, psychologists have begun to explore the possible benefits of sensory deprivation. Much of this work has involved sensory restriction in small isolation tanks like the one pictured in Figure 8–9 ◆.

French artist René Magritte drew on hypnagogic imagery as an inspiration for his work (McKellar, 1995). Vivid hypnogogic images that occur during sensory deprivation can contribute to other creative pursuits as well.

How could sensory deprivation be beneficial?

Sensory Enhancement One of the most consistent after-effects of sensory deprivation is increased sensory acuity.

Figure 8–9 ◆ A sensory isolation chamber. Small flotation tanks like the one pictured have been used by psychologists to study the effects of mild sensory deprivation. Subjects float in darkness and silence. The shallow body-temperature water contains hundreds of pounds of Epsom salts, so that subjects float near the surface. Mild sensory deprivation produces deep relaxation.

That is, vision, hearing, touch, and taste are temporarily more sensitive. Some people report using this after-effect to aid creative thinking (Hutchison, 1984). At the very least, it seems that wearing earplugs for a day might be an interesting prelude to hearing a musical concert!

Relaxation As we already noted, most people find prolonged sensory deprivation stressful and uncomfortable. Yet, oddly, brief periods of restricted sensation are very relaxing for most people (Forgays & Belinson, 1986; Suedfeld, 1980). An hour or two spent in a flotation tank, for instance, causes a large drop in blood pressure, muscle tension, and other signs of stress. Of course, it could be argued that a warm bath has the same effect. But evidence suggests that brief sensory deprivation is one of the surest ways to induce deep relaxation.

Changing Habits Psychologist Peter Suedfeld has found that sensory deprivation can help people quit smoking or lose weight. Suedfeld calls his technique **REST**, for *Restricted Environmental Stimulation Therapy*. In one study, Suedfeld tested the effects of standard anti-smoking messages. These were then compared to the effects of the same messages combined with sensory deprivation. He found that roughly equal numbers of people succeeded in stopping smoking with either treatment. But 3 months later, members of the REST group were smoking 40 percent less than the others (Suedfeld, 1980). Another study found similar benefits for people in a weight-loss program based on sensory deprivation (Borrie & Suedfeld, 1980).

How does sensory deprivation help?

Tape-recorded suggestions to eat less or stop smoking are played for clients while they are isolated in a flotation tank. Suedfeld speculates that deep relaxation makes a person less likely to argue against, or otherwise resist suggestions. Also, some mental confusion usually accompanies sensory deprivation. This, he believes, helps unfreeze or "loosen" belief systems. Unfreezing, in other words, may make it easier to bring about lasting changes in beliefs that maintain bad habits.

Prospect After years of being viewed only as a disruptive state, sensory deprivation may yet prove to have other benefits. For example, REST also shows promise as a way to stimulate creative thinking (Harrison & Newirth, 1990; Suedfeld et al., 1987). Other researchers have reported that REST sessions can enhance performance in skilled sports, such as gymnastics, tennis, basketball, darts, and marksmanship (Druckman & Bjork, 1994). At the very least, further study of sensory deprivation should add to our understanding of brainwashing, isolation at remote weather outposts, the after-effects of eye surgery, and the problems of extended space flight. Clearly, there is much yet to be learned from studying "nothingness."

See if you can answer these questions before reading on.

1. The term *hypnotism* was coined by a British surgeon named
   a. Franz Mesmer   **b.** James Stanford   **c.** T. A. Kreskin   **d.** James Braid

2. Only 4 out of 10 people can be hypnotized. T or F?

3. Which of the following can most definitely be achieved with hypnosis?
   a. unusual strength   **b.** pain relief   **c.** improved memory   **d.** sleep-like brain waves

4. Which of the following is not a disruptive effect observed during or immediately after sensory deprivation?
   a. impaired time sense   **b.** difficulty concentrating   **c.** elevated blood pressure
   d. heightened visual illusions

5. Vivid images during sensory deprivation usually can be best described as
   a. daydreams   **b.** hypnogogic   **c.** hallucinations   **d.** hypodynamic

6. Prolonged periods of sensory deprivation lower anxiety and induce deep relaxation. T or F?

7. What kind of control group would you need in order to identify the true effects of hypnosis?

Answers:
7. Most experiments on hypnosis include a control group in which people are asked to simulate being hypnotized. Without such controls, the tendency of subjects to cooperate with experimenters makes it difficult to identify true hypnotic effects.
1. d   2. F   3. b   4. c   5. b   6. F

Drug-Altered Consciousness—The High and Low of It

Alcohol, heroin, amphetamines, barbiturates, marijuana, cocaine, LSD, caffeine, nicotine. . . . The list of mind-altering drugs—legal and illegal—is extensive. The surest way to alter human consciousness is to administer a **psychoactive drug** (*a substance capable of altering attention, judgment, memory, time sense, self-control, emotion, or perception*) (Julien, 1995).

Facts about Drugs

Most psychoactive drugs can be placed on a scale ranging from *stimulation* to *depression*. A **stimulant** *is a substance that increases activity in the body and nervous system.* A **depressant** *does the reverse.* Figure 8–10 ◆ shows various drugs and their approximate effects on the central nervous system. A more complete summary of frequently abused psychoactive drugs is given in Table 8–4 ■.

Drug dependence falls into two broad categories. When a person compulsively uses a drug to maintain bodily comfort, a **physical dependence** (*addiction*) exists. Physical dependence occurs most often with drugs that cause **withdrawal symptoms** (*physical illness that follows removal of a drug*). Withdrawal from drugs such as alcohol, barbiturates, and opiates can be extremely unpleasant. Quitting opiates, for example, causes violent flu-like symptoms of nausea, vomiting, diarrhea, chills, sweating, and cramps (Feldman & Meyer, 1996). Addiction is often accompanied by a **drug tolerance** (*reduced response to a drug*). This leads users to take larger and larger doses to get the desired effect.

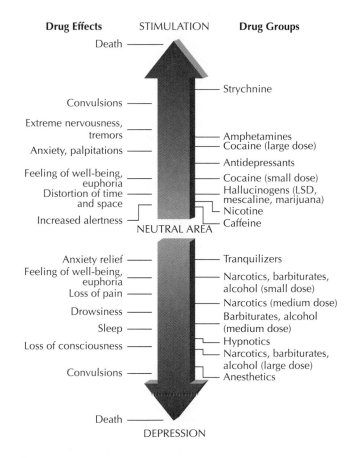

Drug Effects — STIMULATION — **Drug Groups**

- Death
- Strychnine
- Convulsions
- Extreme nervousness, tremors
- Amphetamines
- Cocaine (large dose)
- Anxiety, palpitations
- Antidepressants
- Feeling of well-being, euphoria
- Cocaine (small dose)
- Distortion of time and space
- Hallucinogens (LSD, mescaline, marijuana)
- Nicotine
- Increased alertness
- Caffeine
- NEUTRAL AREA
- Anxiety relief — Tranquilizers
- Feeling of well-being, euphoria — Narcotics, barbiturates, alcohol (small dose)
- Loss of pain — Narcotics (medium dose)
- Drowsiness — Barbiturates, alcohol (medium dose)
- Sleep — Hypnotics
- Loss of consciousness — Narcotics, barbiturates, alcohol (large dose)
- Convulsions — Anesthetics
- Death
- DEPRESSION

Figure 8–10 ◆ Spectrum and continuum of drug action. Many drugs can be rated on a stimulation-depression scale according to their effects on the central nervous system. Although LSD, mescaline, and marijuana are listed here, the stimulation-depression scale is less relevant to these drugs. The principal characteristic of such hallucinogens is their mind-altering quality.

When a person develops a **psychological dependence,** he or she feels that a drug is *necessary to maintain emotional or psychological well-being.* Usually, this is based on an intense craving for the drug and its rewarding qualities (Feldman & Meyer, 1996). Make no mistake, however: Psychological dependence may affect a drug user as powerfully as physical addiction does. That's why some psychologists prefer to define addiction more broadly as any compulsive habit pattern. By this definition, a person who has lost control over his or her drug use, for whatever reason, is addicted (Marlatt et al., 1988).

Note in Table 8–4 that the drugs most likely to lead to physical dependence are alcohol, amphetamines, barbiturates, cocaine, codeine, heroin, methadone, morphine, and tobacco (nicotine). Using *any* of the drugs listed in Table 8–4 can result in psychological dependence. Note too that people who take drugs intravenously are at high risk for developing AIDS (see Chapter 15).

Patterns of Abuse   Some drugs, of course, have a higher potential for abuse than others. Heroin is certainly more dangerous than caffeine. However, this is only one side of the picture. It can be as useful to classify drug-taking *behavior* as it is to rate drugs. For example, some people remain social drinkers for life, whereas others become alcoholics within weeks of taking their first drink. In this sense, drug use can be classified as **experimental** (*short-term use based on curiosity*), **social-recreational** (*occasional social use for pleasure or relaxation*), **situational** (*use to cope with a specific problem, such as needing to stay awake*), **intensive** (*daily use with elements of dependence*), or **compulsive** (*intense use and extreme dependence*). The last three categories of drug taking tend to be damaging no matter what drug is used. The discussion that follows focuses on the drugs most often abused by college students.

Uppers—Amphetamines, Cocaine, Caffeine, Nicotine

Amphetamines form a large group of *synthetic stimulants,* such as Dexedrine, Methedrine, and Benzedrine. Amphetamines were once widely prescribed to aid weight loss or to combat mild depression. Both practices are now frowned on because too many patients became dependent on their legal amphetamines. The only fully legitimate medical uses of amphetamines are to treat narcolepsy, childhood hyperactivity, and overdoses of depressant drugs. Illicit use of amphetamines is widespread among individuals seeking an easy way to stay awake and by those who think drugs can improve mental or physical performance.

Amphetamines rapidly produce a drug tolerance. Most abusers who begin with 1 or 2 pills a day progress to taking dozens to get the same effect. Eventually, some users switch to injecting Methedrine ("speed") directly into the bloodstream. True speed freaks typically go on binges lasting several days, after which they "crash" from lack of sleep and food.

How dangerous are amphetamines?

Abuse   Amphetamines pose many dangers. To stay high, the abuser must take more and more as the body's tolerance grows. Higher doses can cause nausea, vomiting, high blood pressure, fatal heart arrhythmias, and crippling strokes. Also, it is important to realize that amphetamines speed the use of bodily resources; they do not magically supply energy.

The after-effects of an amphetamine binge can be dangerous and unpleasant. Possible effects include fatigue, depression, terrifying nightmares, confusion, uncontrolled irritability, and aggression. Repeatedly overextending the body with stimulants may lead to self-starvation, sores and non-healing ulcers, brittle fingernails, tooth grinding, chronic chest infections, liver disease, high blood pressure, and brain hemorrhage.

Amphetamines can also cause a *loss of contact with reality* known as **amphetamine psychosis.** Affected users feel threatened and suffer from paranoid delusions that someone is out to get them. Acting on these delusions, the speed freak may become violent, resulting in self-injury or injury to others (Kratofil, Baberg, & Dimsdale, 1996).

A potent new smokable form of crystal methamphetamine has recently added to the problem of stimulant abuse. The drug, known as "ice" on the street, is highly addictive. Like "crack," the smokable form of cocaine, it produces an intense high without the use of needles. Also like crack (discussed in a moment), crystal methamphetamine leads very rapidly to compulsive abuse and severe drug dependence.

Designer Drugs—Agony or Ecstasy?

Small variations in the structure of a drug can change its effects. For example, the drug MDMA ("ecstasy") is chemically similar to amphetamine. But in addition to producing a rush of energy, users say it makes them feel closer to others and heightens their sensory experiences.

MDMA is a "designer drug," a chemically engineered variation of an existing drug. Many designer drugs were first created in clandestine labs to circumvent drug laws. Because designer drugs are not tested for safety, some have extremely toxic effects. One notorious drug damaged the brain in a way that left hundreds of users suffering from severe Parkinson's disease.

Table 8-4 ■ Comparison of Psychoactive Drugs

Name	Classification	Medical Use	Usual Dose	Duration of Effect
Alcohol	Sedative-hypnotic	Solvent, antiseptic	Varies	1–4 hours
Amphetamines	Stimulant	Relief of mild depression, control of appetite and narcolepsy	2.5–5 milligrams	4 hours
Barbiturates	Sedative-hypnotic	Sedation, relief of high blood pressure, hyperthyroidism	50–100 milligrams	4 hours
Benzodiazepines	Anxiolytic	Tranquilizer	2–100 milligrams	1–8 hours
Caffeine	Stimulant	Counteract depressant drugs, treatment of migraine headaches	Varies	Varies
Cocaine	Stimulant, local anesthetic	Local anesthesia	Varies	Varied, brief periods
Codeine	Narcotic	Ease pain and coughing	30 milligrams	4 hours
Heroin	Narcotic	Pain relief	Varies	4 hours
LSD	Hallucinogen	Experimental study of mental function, alcoholism	100–500 milligrams	10 hours
Marijuana (THC)	Relaxant, euphoriant; in high doses, hallucinogen	Treatment of glaucoma	1–2 cigarettes	4 hours
Mescaline	Hallucinogen	None	350 micrograms	12 hours
Methadone	Narcotic	Pain relief	10 milligrams	4–6 hours
Morphine	Narcotic	Pain relief	15 milligrams	6 hours
PCP	Anesthetic	None	2–10 milligrams	4–6 hours, plus 12-hour recovery
Psilocybin	Hallucinogen	None	25 milligrams	6–8 hours
Tobacco (nicotine)	Stimulant	Emetic (nicotine)	Varies	Varies

Question marks indicate conflict of opinion. It should be noted that illicit drugs are frequently adulterated and thus pose unknown hazards to the user.

Table 8–4 ■ Comparison of Psychoactive Drugs (continued)

Effects Sought	Long-Term Symptoms	Physical Dependence Potential	Psychological Dependence Potential	Organic Damage Potential
Sense alteration, anxiety reduction, sociability	Cirrhosis, toxic psychosis, neurologic damage, addiction	Yes	Yes	Yes
Alertness, activeness	Loss of appetite, delusions, hallucinations, toxic psychosis	Yes	Yes	Yes
Anxiety reduction, euphoria	Addiction with severe withdrawal symptoms, possible convulsions, toxic psychosis	Yes	Yes	Yes
Anxiety relief	Irritability, confusion, depression, sleep disorders	Probably	Yes	No
Wakefulness, alertness	Insomnia, heart arrhythmias, high blood pressure	No?	Yes	Yes
Excitation, talkativeness	Depression, convulsions	Yes	Yes	Yes
Euphoria, prevent withdrawal discomfort	Addiction, constipation, loss of appetite	Yes	Yes	No
Euphoria, prevent withdrawal discomfort	Addiction, constipation, loss of appetite	Yes	Yes	No*
Insightful experiences, exhilaration, distortion of senses	May intensify existing psychosis, panic reactions	No	No?	No?
Relaxation; increased euphoria, perceptions, sociability	Possible lung cancer, other health risks	No	Yes	Yes
Insightful experiences, exhiliration, distortion of senses	May intensity existing psychosis, panic reactions	No	No?	No?
Prevent withdrawal discomfort	Addiction, constipation, loss of appetite	Yes	Yes	No
Euphoria, prevent withdrawal discomfort	Addiction, constipation, loss of appetite	Yes	Yes	No*
Euphoria	Unpredictable behavior, suspicion, hostility, psychosis	Debated	Yes	Yes
Insightful experiences, exhilaration, distortion of senses	May intensify existing psychosis, panic reactions	No	No?	No?
Alertness, calmness, sociability	Emphysema, lung cancer, mouth and throat cancer, cardiovascular damage, loss of appetite	Yes	Yes	Yes

*Persons who inject drugs under non-sterile conditions run a high risk of contracting AIDS, hepatitis, abscesses, or circulatory disorders.

The risk posed by MDMA remains unclear. In England, a number of deaths have been traced to the use of MDMA at "rave" parties. However, these deaths were caused by heat exhaustion, not by drug poisoning. MDMA raises body temperature, which can be fatal when combined with all-night dancing in an over-heated club.

MDMA sometimes causes severe liver damage, which can also be fatal. Aside from these documented risks, the long-term effects of MDMA are unknown. It may take another 10 to 20 years before MDMA's impact on the health of users emerges. Of more immediate concern is the fact that many of the street drugs sold as "ecstasy" are impure and adulterated with other substances. Like other designer drugs, MDMA may ultimately prove to be a costly trip into the unknown (Abbott & Concar, 1992; McKim, 1997).

Cocaine

Cocaine is a powerful *central nervous system stimulant* extracted from the leaves of the coca plant. Cocaine produces feelings of alertness, euphoria, well-being, power, boundless energy, and pleasure (Gawin, 1991).

Cocaine has a long history of use and misuse. At the turn of the century, dozens of non-prescription potions and cure-alls contained cocaine. It was during this time that Coca-Cola was indeed the "real thing." From 1886 until 1906, when the Pure Food and Drug Act was passed, Coca-Cola contained cocaine (which has since been replaced with caffeine). Today, cocaine is one of the most widely abused drugs (Gawin, 1991). Among college students cocaine use has increased fourfold, compared to 15 years ago.

How does cocaine differ from amphetamines?

The two are very much alike in their effects on the central nervous system. The main difference is that amphetamine lasts several hours; cocaine is quickly metabolized, so its effects last only about 15 to 30 minutes (Woods et al., 1987).

How dangerous is cocaine?

Abuse Cocaine is one of the most dangerous drugs of abuse. Even casual or first-time users run a risk because cocaine can cause convulsions, heart attack, or a stroke (Cregler & Mark, 1985; Lacayo, 1995). The highly publicized death of All-American basketball star Len Bias is a case in point. The most tragic cocaine victims are children who were exposed to the drug before birth. Just one hit of cocaine taken by a pregnant woman can cause defects in her fetus. At birth, "crack babies" are very excitable and jittery if their mothers recently used cocaine. Otherwise, they are sluggish and depressed. By the time cocaine babies start school, they often suffer from tremors, hyperactivity, listlessness, slowed language learning, and disorganized thinking (Lester et al., 1991; Mayes et al., 1996; Phillips et al., 1996). Many will never be normal.

When rats and monkeys are given free access to cocaine, they find it irresistible. Many, in fact, end up dying of convulsions from self-administered overdoses of the drug. Cocaine increases activity in brain pathways sensitive to the *chemical messengers* **dopamine** (DOPE-ah-meen) and **noradrenaline** (nor-ah-DREN-ah-lin). Noradrenaline arouses the brain, and added dopamine produces a "rush" of pleasure. This combination is so powerfully rewarding that cocaine users run a high risk of becoming compulsive abusers.

A person who stops using cocaine does not suffer the physical withdrawal symptoms typical of drugs such as heroin. But cocaine has its own withdrawal pattern and can be just as addicting. First, there is a jarring "crash" of mood and energy following a cocaine binge. Within a few days, the person enters a long period of fatigue, anxiety, paranoia, boredom, and **anhedonia** (an-he-DAWN-ee-ah: *an inability*

Cocaine was the main ingredient in many non-prescription elixirs before the turn of the century. Today cocaine is recognized as a powerful and dangerous drug. Its high potential for abuse has damaged the lives of countless users.

The future looked bright in 1986 when college basketball star Len Bias was chosen to play for the Boston Celtics. Thrilled by his hard-earned achievement, and perhaps feeling invincible, Bias tried cocaine, probably for the first time. Hours later his dream perished. Bias was dead from cardiac arrest at age 22.

to feel pleasure). This occurs because the brain adapts to cocaine abuse in ways that upset its chemical balance, causing depression when cocaine is withdrawn (Hurley, 1989).

During withdrawal, cravings for cocaine are intense: The person feels wretched and vividly remembers the intense pleasure of previous cocaine highs. The urge to use cocaine grows overwhelming. So, while cocaine does not fit the classic pattern of physical addiction, there is little doubt about its potential for compulsive abuse. Even a person who gets through withdrawal may crave cocaine months or years later (Withers et al., 1995).

Many authorities estimate that if cocaine were cheaper, 9 out of 10 users would progress to compulsive abuse. In fact, rock cocaine (or "crack"), which is cheaper, produces very high abuse rates among those who try it. Here are some increasingly serious signs of cocaine abuse (Pursch, 1983).

- **Compulsive use.** If cocaine is available—say, at a party—you will undoubtedly use it. You can't say no to it.

- **Loss of control.** Once you have had some cocaine, you will keep using it until you are exhausted or the cocaine is gone.

- **Disregarding consequences.** You don't care if the rent gets paid, your job is endangered, your lover disapproves, or your health is affected, you'll use cocaine anyway.

It is becoming clear that cocaine's capacity for abuse and social damage rivals or exceeds that of such unglamorous drugs as opium and heroin. Anyone who thinks he or she may be developing a cocaine problem should seek advice at a drug clinic or a Cocaine Anonymous meeting. From 30 to 90 percent of cocaine abusers who remain in treatment

programs succeed in breaking their coke addiction (Gawin, 1991).

Caffeine

Caffeine is the most frequently used psychoactive drug in North America. **Caffeine** *stimulates the brain by blocking chemicals that normally inhibit or slow nerve activity* (Julien, 1995). Its effects become apparent with doses as small as 50 milligrams (the amount found in about one-half cup of brewed coffee). Physically, caffeine causes sweating, talkativeness, tinnitus (ringing in the ears), and hand tremors (Hughes et al., 1991). Psychologically, caffeine suppresses fatigue or drowsiness and increases feelings of alertness. Some people have a hard time starting a day without it.

How much caffeine did you consume today? It is common to think of coffee as the major source of caffeine, but there are many others. Caffeine is found in tea, many soft drinks (especially colas), chocolate, and cocoa. Over 2,000 non-prescription drugs also contain caffeine, including stay-awake pills, cold remedies, and many name-brand aspirin products. Table 8–5 ■ gives the approximate caffeine content of several foods.

Are there any serious drawbacks to using caffeine?

Abuse Serious abuse may result in an *unhealthy dependence on caffeine* known as **caffeinism.** Insomnia, irritability, loss of appetite, chills, racing heart, and elevated body temperature are all signs of caffeinism. It is not uncommon to find that individuals with these symptoms are drinking 15 or 20 cups of coffee a day. Even in the absence of caffeinism, there are some caffeine-related health risks. Caffeine encourages the development of breast cysts in women, and it contributes to bladder cancer, heart problems, and high blood pressure. Health authorities urge pregnant women to give up caffeine entirely because of a suspected link between caffeine and birth defects. Also, caffeine can double or triple the risk of miscarriages (Grady, 1986; Infante-Rivard et al., 1993).

Table 8–5 ■ Average Caffeine Content of Various Foods
Instant coffee (5 ounces), 64 milligrams
Percolated coffee (5 ounces), 108 milligrams
Drip coffee (5 ounces), 145 milligrams
Decaf. coffee (5 ounces), 3 milligrams
Black tea (5 ounces), 42 milligrams
Canned iced tea (17 ounces), 30 milligrams
Cocoa drink (6 ounces), 8 milligrams
Chocolate drink (8 ounces), 14 milligrams
Sweet chocolate (1 ounce), 20 milligrams
Colas (12 ounces), 50 milligrams
Soft drinks (12 ounces), 0–52 milligrams

It is customary to think of caffeine as a non-drug. However, as few as 2.5 cups of coffee a day (or the equivalent) can be a problem. People who consume even such modest amounts of caffeine may experience anxiety, depression, fatigue, headaches, and flu-like symptoms during withdrawal (Silverman et al., 1992). At work, that means coffee drinkers deprived of caffeine are less able to do their jobs (Streufert et al., 1995). It is wise to remember that caffeine *is* a drug and use it in moderation.

Nicotine

Nicotine *is a natural stimulant found mainly in tobacco.* Next to caffeine, it is the most widely used psychoactive drug (Julien, 1995).

How does nicotine compare with other stimulants?

Nicotine is a potent drug. It is so toxic that it is sometimes used as an insecticide! In large doses it causes stomach pain, vomiting and diarrhea, cold sweats, dizziness, confusion, and muscle tremors. In very large doses, nicotine may cause convulsions, respiratory failure, and death. For a non-smoker, 50 to 75 milligrams of nicotine taken in a single dose could be lethal. (Chain-smoking about 17 to 25 cigarettes will produce this dosage.)

Most first-time smokers get sick on one or two cigarettes. In contrast, a heavy smoker may inhale 40 cigarettes a day without feeling ill. This difference indicates that regular smokers build a tolerance for nicotine (Perkins, 1995; Stolerman & Jarvis, 1995).

Is it true that nicotine can be addicting?

Abuse   A vast array of evidence confirms that nicotine is addictive (Henningfield & Heishman, 1995). For many smokers, withdrawal from nicotine causes headaches, sweating, cramps, insomnia, digestive upset, irritability, and a sharp craving for cigarettes. These symptoms may last from 2 to 6 weeks and may be worse than heroin withdrawal. Indeed, relapse patterns are nearly identical for alcoholics, heroin addicts, cocaine abusers, and smokers who try to quit (Koop, 1988a; Stolerman & Jarvis, 1995). Eight out of 10 people who quit smoking relapse within one year (Jarvik, 1995).

How serious are the health risks of smoking?

Impact on Health   A burning cigarette releases more than 6,800 different chemicals. Many of these are potent **carcinogens** (car-SIN-oh-jins: *cancer-causing substances*). In addition, nicotine itself may be cancer causing. Lung cancer and other cancers caused by smoking are now considered the single most preventable cause of death in Canada and the United States. Among men, 97 percent of lung cancer deaths are caused by smoking. For women, 74 percent of all lung cancers are due to smoking, a rate that has risen sharply in recent years. Altogether, smoking is responsible for about

THE FAR SIDE, BY GARY LARSON © 1982 CHRONICLE FEATURES

Chronicle Features, 1982

The real reason dinosaurs became extinct

Actress Lilly Tomlin took up smoking for a role in the movie *Shadows and Fog* and developed a 4-pack-a-day habit. As Tomlin's experience shows, the best way to avoid developing a nicotine addiction is to not begin smoking in the first place.

one third of all cancer deaths. Skeptics take note: Wayne McLaren, who portrayed the rugged "Marlboro Man" in cigarette ads, died of lung cancer at age 51. Here are some sobering facts about smoking:

Smoking Facts

- Every cigarette reduces a smoker's life expectancy by 7 minutes.
- Smoking is the number one cause of deaths in the United States and Canada—more than the number of deaths from alcohol, drugs, car accidents, and AIDS combined.
- In the United States alone, smoking-related costs total $50 billion a year. Taxpayers pick up the bill for 43 percent of this total.
- Forty percent of all smokers who develop throat cancer try smoking again.
- Each year, only 1 out of 5 smokers who tries to quit smoking succeeds.
- Some tobacco companies manipulate nicotine levels in their cigarettes to keep smokers addicted.
- Daily exposure to secondhand smoke at home or work causes a 24 to 39 percent increase in cancer risk to non-smokers.

If you think smoking is harmless, or that there's no connection between smoking and cancer, you're kidding yourself. The scientific link between tobacco smoking and cancer is as firmly established as any cause of human disease can possibly be (Reif, 1981). By the way, urban cowboys and Skol bandits, similar conclusions apply to chewing tobacco and snuff. Users of smokeless tobacco run a 4 to 6 times higher risk of developing oral cancer. Smokeless tobacco also causes shrinkage of the gums, contributes to heart disease, and is as addicting as cigarettes (Christian & McDonald, 1987; Foreyt, 1987b).

Smokers don't just risk their own health, they also endanger those who live and work nearby. Secondary smoke causes 20 percent of all lung cancers. Non-smoking women who are married to smokers suffer a 30 percent increase in their risk of developing lung cancer. It is particularly irresponsible of smokers to expose young children to secondhand smoke (Abramson, 1993).

Dynamics of Smoking   Smokers, unless they have a death wish, must be getting something out their habit. Most claim that smoking helps them concentrate, feel sociable, or calm down. But psychologist Stanley Schachter asserts, "The heavy smoker gets nothing out of smoking. He smokes only to prevent withdrawal." Schachter has shown that smoking does not improve the mood or the performance of heavy smokers compared to non-smokers. On the other hand, heavy smokers who are *deprived* of nicotine feel worse and perform worse than non-smokers (Foulds et al., 1996).

Schachter has also shown that heavy smokers adjust their smoking to keep bodily levels of nicotine constant. Thus, when smokers are given lighter cigarettes, they smoke more. Also, if they are under stress (which speeds the removal of nicotine from the body), they smoke more. The link between stress and nicotine probably explains why students smoke more during stressful periods such as final exams, or at parties, which are also stressful.

Is it better for a person to quit smoking abruptly or taper down gradually?

Quitting Smoking   For many years, smokers were advised to quit cold turkey. The current view is that quitting all at once isn't as effective as tapering off. Going cold turkey

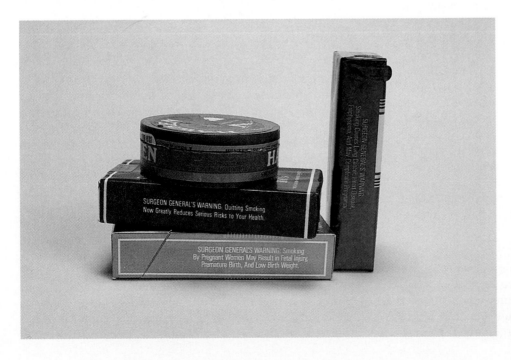

A recent study found that 5th–12th graders who smoke are less likely than non-smokers to believe the health warning labels on cigarette packs (Cecil, Evans, & Stanley, 1996). Smokers in general are less likely to believe that smoking poses a serious risk to health.

makes quitting an all-or-nothing proposition. Smokers who smoke even one cigarette after "quitting forever" tend to feel they've failed. Many figure they might just as well resume smoking. Those who quit gradually accept that success may take many attempts, spread over several months.

The following highlight summarizes several helpful strategies for quitting smoking.

New Strategies to Stop Smoking

If you smoke and would like to quit, here are some basic steps you can take: (1) Delay having a first cigarette in the morning. Then try to delay a little longer each day. (2) Gradually reduce the total number of cigarettes you smoke each day. (3) Quit completely, but for just one week. Then quit again, a week at a time, for as many times as necessary to make it stick (Pierce, 1991).

A recent study suggests that you will be most successful at strategy number 2 if you *schedule* a gradual reduction in smoking. To begin, count the number of cigarettes you smoke per day. For the first week your goal will be to smoke only two thirds of that "baseline" number each day. In addition, you should divide the 16 waking hours in each day by the number of cigarettes you will smoke that day. For example, if you plan to smoke 16 cigarettes per day, then you only get to smoke one per hour. When a scheduled "smoking time" arrives, smoke only for 5 minutes, whether you finish the cigarette or not. Don't smoke any "missed" cigarettes later.

During the second week, you should smoke only one third as many cigarettes as you did during your baseline. Again, divide each 16-hour day by the number of cigarettes, so you can plan how much time to allow between smoking periods.

During week three, reduce your cigarette allowance to 20 percent of the original baseline number.

In the fourth week, stop smoking entirely.

Gradually stretching the time periods between cigarettes is a key part of this program. Scheduled smoking apparently helps people learn to cope with the urge to smoke. As a result, people using this method are more likely to succeed. Also, they more often remain permanent non-smokers than people using other approaches (Cincirpini et al., 1995).

Whatever approach is taken, quitting smoking is not easy. It does help, though, if you get a spouse or partner to support your effort (Cohen & Lichtenstein, 1990). Also, as we have noted, anyone trying to quit should be prepared to make several attempts before succeeding (Brownell et

al., 1986). But the good news is tens of millions of people have quit.

Downers—Sedatives, Tranquilizers, and Alcohol

How do downers differ from the stimulant drugs?

The most widely used downers, or depressant drugs, are *alcohol*, *barbiturates*, and *benzodiazepine* (ben-zoe-die-AZ-eh-peen) *tranquilizers*. These drugs are much alike in their effects. In fact, barbiturates and tranquilizers are sometimes referred to as "solid alcohol." Let's examine the properties of each.

Barbiturates

Barbiturates *are sedative drugs that depress brain activity.* Medically, they are used to calm patients or to induce sleep. In mild doses, barbiturates have an effect similar to alcohol intoxication. Higher doses can cause severe mental confusion or even psychotic symptoms (a loss of contact with reality). Overdoses can easily cause coma or death. Barbiturates are often taken in excess amounts because a first dose may be followed by others as the user becomes uninhibited or forgetful. Over the years, Marilyn Monroe, Judy Garland, and a number of other well-known personalities have died of barbiturate overdoses. An overdose first causes unconsciousness. Then it severely depresses brain centers controlling heartbeat and breathing, resulting in death (McKim, 1997).

Tranquilizers

A **tranquilizer** is a drug that *lowers anxiety and reduces tension.* Doctors prescribe benzodiazepine tranquilizers to alleviate nervousness and stress. Valium is the best-known drug in this family; others are Xanax, Halcion, and Librium. Even at normal doses these drugs can cause drowsiness, shakiness, and confusion. When used at too high a dose or for too long a time, benzodiazepines have strong addictive potential (McKim, 1997).

Recently, a drug sold under the trade name Rohypnol (ro-HIP-nol) has added to the problem of tranquilizer abuse. This drug, which is related to Valium, is cheap and potent. It lowers inhibitions and produces relaxation or intoxication. Large doses induce short-term amnesia and sleep. "Roofies," as they are known on the street, have been used to spike drinks, which are given to the unwary. Drugged victims are then sexually assaulted or raped while they are unconscious (Navarro, 1995).

Abuse The most frequently abused barbiturates are Seconal and Tuinal. These drugs act quickly and the rush of intoxication only lasts from 2 to 4 hours. Repeated use of any barbiturate can cause physical dependence. Some abusers suffer severe emotional depression that may end in suicide. Similarly, when tranquilizers are used at too high a dose or for too long a time, addiction may occur. Many people have learned the hard way that their legally prescribed tranquilizers are as dangerous as many illicit drugs (McKim, 1997).

Combining barbiturates or tranquilizers with alcohol is extremely risky. When mixed, the effects of both drugs are multiplied by a **drug interaction** (*one drug enhances the effect of another*). This combination is responsible for many hundreds of fatal drug overdoses every year. All too often, depressants are gulped down with alcohol or added to a spiked punch bowl. This is the combination that left a young woman named Karen Ann Quinlan in a coma that lasted 10 years, ending with her death. It is no exaggeration to restate that mixing depressants with alcohol can be fatal.

Alcohol

Alcohol *is the common name for ethyl alcohol*, the intoxicating element in fermented and distilled liquors. Contrary to popular belief, alcohol is not a stimulant. Lively behavior at drinking parties is actually due to the fact that alcohol is a central nervous system *depressant*. As Figure 8–11 ◆ shows, small amounts of alcohol reduce inhibitions and produce feelings of relaxation and euphoria. Larger amounts cause ever-greater impairment of the brain until the drinker loses consciousness. Alcohol is also not an aphrodisiac. It usually

Alcohol Consumed	Neural Representation	Behavioral Effect
2 ounces 90 proof whiskey .05% blood alcohol		Affects higher nervous centers; drinker loses inhibitions, forgoes conventions and courtesies, relaxes
6 ounces 90 proof whiskey .15% blood alcohol		Affects deeper motor areas; drinker staggers, has slurred speech, is overconfident, acts on impulse
10 ounces 90 proof whiskey .25% blood alcohol		Affects emotional centers of midbrain; drinker has impaired motor reactions and unsteady gait; sensations are distorted; drinker tends to see double, to fall asleep
16 ounces 90 proof whiskey .4% blood alcohol		Affects sensory area of cerebellum; senses are dulled; drinker is in stupor
24 ounces 90 proof whiskey .6% blood alcohol		Affects perceptual areas; drinker loses consciousness; only functions of breathing and heartbeat remain
32 ounces 90 proof whiskey .8% blood alcohol		Affects entire brain; heartbeat and respiration stop; **death**

Figure 8–11 ◆ The behavioral effects of alcohol are related to blood alcohol content and the resulting suppression of higher mental function. Arrows indicate the typical threshold for legal intoxication in the United States. (From Jozef Cohen, *Eyewitness Series in Psychology*, p. 44. Copyright © by Rand McNally and Company. Reprinted by permission.)

impairs sexual performance, particularly in males. As William Shakespeare observed long ago, drink "provokes the desire, but it takes away the performance."

Some people become aggressive and want to argue or fight when they are drunk. Others become relaxed and friendly. How can the same drug have such different effects?

When a person is drunk, *thinking and perception become dulled or shortsighted*, a condition that has been called **alcohol myopia** (my-OH-pea-ah). Only the most obvious and immediate stimuli catch a drinker's attention. Worries and "second thoughts" that would normally restrain behavior are banished from the drinker's mind. That's why many behaviors become more extreme when a person is drunk. Alcohol also reduces anxiety and temporarily makes people feel better about themselves (Steele & Josephs, 1990). It's easy to see why it is such a seductive drug.

Abuse Alcohol, the world's favorite depressant, breeds our biggest drug problem. Over 180 million people in the U.S. and Canada use alcohol, and an estimated 25 million have serious drinking problems. A particularly alarming trend is the high level of alcohol abuse among adolescents and young adults. One survey of college students found that 17 percent (more than 1 out of 6) are heavy drinkers. For college males, the figure was 25 percent, or 1 out of 4 male students (Olmstead, 1983).

Children of alcoholics must be very cautious about drinking. As adults, these people have an elevated risk of becoming alcohol abusers (Blane, 1988). Women also face special risks. For one thing, alcohol is absorbed faster and metabolized more slowly by women's bodies. As a result, women get intoxicated from less alcohol than men do. Women who drink are also more prone to liver disease, osteoporosis, and depression. As few as 3 drinks a week may increase a woman's risk of breast cancer by 50 percent. In addition, women who abuse alcohol are more likely to face social rejection and stigma than men who drink similar amounts (Gomberg, 1993).

What are the signs of alcohol abuse?

Recognizing Problem Drinking Because alcohol abuse is such a common problem, it is important to recognize the danger signals of growing dependency. The progression from a social drinker to an alcohol abuser to an alcoholic is often subtle. Jellinek (1960) gives these typical steps in the development of a drinking problem.

1. **Initial phase.** At first, the social drinker begins to turn more often to alcohol to relieve tension or to feel good. Four danger signals in this period that signal excessive dependence on alcohol are:

   Increasing consumption. The individual drinks more and more and may begin to worry about his or her drinking.

   Morning drinking. Morning drinking is a dangerous sign, particularly when it is used to combat a hangover or to "get through the day."

   Regretted behavior. The person engages in extreme behavior while drunk that leaves her or him feeling guilty or embarrassed.

   Blackouts. Abusive drinking may be revealed by an inability to remember what happened during intoxication.

2. **Crucial phase.** A crucial turning point comes as the person begins to lose control over drinking. At this stage, there is still some control over when and where a first drink is taken. But one drink starts a chain reaction leading to a second and a third, and so on.

3. **Chronic phase.** At this point, the person is alcohol dependent. Victims drink compulsively and continuously. They rarely eat, they become intoxicated from far less alcohol than before, and they crave alcohol when deprived of it. Work, family ties, and social life all deteriorate. The person's self-drugging is usually so compulsive that when given a choice, the bottle comes before friends, relatives, employment, and self-esteem. The person is an addict.

To add to this summary, the next highlight may help you form a clearer picture of the development of a drinking problem.

A Closer Look

The Development of a Drinking Problem

Early Warnings

You are beginning to feel guilty about your drinking.

You drink more than you used to and tend to gulp your drinks.

You try to have a few extra drinks before or after drinking with others.

You have begun to drink at certain times or to get through certain situations.

You drink to relieve feelings of boredom, depression, anxiety, or inadequacy.

You are sensitive when others mention your drinking.

You have had memory blackouts or have passed out while drinking.

Signals Not To Be Ignored

There are times when you need a drink.

You drink in the morning to overcome a hangover.

You promise to drink less and are lying about your drinking.

You often regret what you have said or done while drinking.

You have begun to drink alone.

You have weekend drinking bouts and Monday hangovers.

You have lost time at work or school because of drinking.

You are noticeably drunk on important occasions.

Your relationship to family and friends has changed because of your drinking.

Moderated Drinking Many social-recreational drinkers could do a far better job of managing their use of alcohol. Almost everyone has been to a party spoiled by someone who drank too much too fast. Those who avoid overdrinking have a better time, and so do their friends. But how do you avoid drinking too much? After all, as one wit once observed, "The conscience dissolves in alcohol." Psychologists Roger Vogler and Wayne Bartz (1982, 1992) provide a partial answer.

Vogler and Bartz observe that drinking makes you feel good while blood alcohol is rising and remains below a level of about 0.05. In this range, people feel relaxed, euphoric, and sociable. At higher levels they go from moderately intoxicated to thoroughly drunk. Later, as blood alcohol begins to fall, those who overdrink become sick and miserable. Table 8–6 ■ shows the approximate amount per hour that can be consumed without exceeding the 0.05 blood alcohol level. (Even at this level, driving may be affected.) By pacing themselves, those who choose to drink can remain comfortable, pleasant, and coherent during a long party or other social event. In short, if you drink, it might be wise to learn your "magic" number from Table 8–6.

Table 8–6 ■ Drinking in Moderation		
Your Weight (Pounds)	**Approximate Number of Drinks per Hour to Stay Below 0.05 Blood Alcohol***	
	Male	*Female*
100	0.75	0.60
120	1.00	0.75
140	1.25	0.90
160	1.30	1.00
180	1.50	1.10
200	1.60	1.20
220	1.80	1.35

One drink = 12 ounces beer, 4 ounces wine, 2.5 ounces brandy, or 1.25 ounces 80 proof liquor.
*Table entries are approximate, owing to the individual differences in metabolism, recency of meals, and other factors. Estimates are from tables prepared by Vogler and Bartz (1982, 1992).

It takes skill to regulate drinking in social situations, where the temptation to drink can be strong. If you choose to drink, here are some guidelines that may be helpful. (Adapted from Vogler & Bartz, 1992.)

Paced Drinking

1. Think about your drinking beforehand and plan how you will manage it.
2. Drink slowly, eat while drinking, and make every other drink (or more) a non-alcoholic beverage.
3. Limit drinking primarily to the first hour of a social event or party. Pace your drinking using the information from Table 8–6.
4. Practice how you will politely but firmly refuse drinks.
5. Learn how to relax, meet people, and socialize without relying on alcohol.

Treatment Treatment for alcohol dependence begins by sobering up the person and cutting off the supply. This phase is referred to as **detoxification** (*literally, "to remove poison"*). It frequently produces all the symptoms of drug withdrawal and can be extremely unpleasant for the alcoholic. The next step is to try to restore the person's health. Heavy abuse of alcohol usually causes severe damage to body organs and the nervous system. Food, vitamins, and medical care cannot fully reverse the damage, but a reasonable state of health may be obtained. When alcoholics have "dried out" and their health has been restored, they may be treated with tranquilizers, antidepressants, or psychotherapy. Unfortunately, the success of these procedures has been limited.

One mutual-help approach that has been fairly successful is Alcoholics Anonymous (AA). AA acts on the premise that it takes a former alcoholic to understand and help a current alcoholic. Participants at AA meetings admit that they have a problem, share feelings, and resolve to stay "dry" one day at a time. Other group members provide support for those struggling to end dependency. (Cocaine Anonymous and Narcotics Anonymous use the same approach.)

Eighty-one percent of those who remain in AA over 1 year get through the following year without a drink (Sexias, 1981). However, AA's success rate may simply reflect the fact that members participate voluntarily, meaning they have admitted that they have a serious problem (McLatchie & Lomp, 1988). Sadly, it seems that alcohol abusers will often not face their problems until they have "hit rock bottom." If they are willing, though, AA presents a practical approach to the problem.

Two newer groups offer a rational, non-spiritual approach to alcohol abuse that better fits the needs of some people. These are Rational Recovery and Secular Organizations for Sobriety (SOS). Other alternatives to AA include medical treatment, group therapy, and individual psychotherapy (Institute of Medicine, 1990). There is a strong tendency for abusive drinkers to deny that they have a problem. Nevertheless, the sooner they seek help the better.

Marijuana—What's in the Pot?

If you pick any three citizens at random, one will have tried marijuana at least once. More than 20 million people in Canada and the U.S. may be regular users, which puts marijuana in a league with tobacco and alcohol. *Marijuana and hashish are derived from the hemp plant Cannabis sativa.* **Marijuana** *consists of the leaves and flowers of the hemp plant.* **Hashish** *is a resinous material scraped from Cannabis leaves.* The main *active chemical in marijuana* is **tetrahydrocannabinol** (tet-rah-hydro-cah-NAB-ih-nol) or **THC,** for short. THC is a mild **hallucinogen** (hal-LU-sin-oh-jin: *a substance that alters sensory impressions*).

Hallucinogens   The drug LSD (lysergic acid diethylamide) is perhaps the best-known hallucinogen. Even when taken in tiny amounts, LSD can produce hallucinations and psychotic-like disturbances in thinking and perception. Two other common hallucinogens are mescaline (peyote) and psilocybin ("magic mushrooms"). Incidentally, the drug PCP (phencyclidine) can have hallucinogenic effects. However, PCP, which is an anesthetic, also has stimulant and depressant effects. This potent combination can cause extreme agitation, disorientation, violence—and too often, tragedy. All of the hallucinogens, including marijuana, typically affect neurotransmitter systems that carry messages between brain cells (Julien, 1995).

Artists have tried at times to capture the effects of hallucinogens. Here, the artist depicts visual experiences he had while under the influence of LSD.

Marijuana   Marijuana's typical psychological effects include a sense of euphoria or well-being, relaxation, altered time sense, and perceptual distortions. At high dosages, however, paranoia, hallucinations, and delusions can occur (Palfai & Jankiewicz, 1991). All considered, marijuana intoxication is relatively subtle by comparison to drugs such as LSD or alcohol (Kelly et al., 1990). Nevertheless, it is well established that driving a car or operating machinery while high on marijuana can be extremely hazardous. As a matter of fact, driving under the influence of any intoxicating drug is dangerous.

No overdose deaths have been reported from marijuana. However, marijuana cannot be considered harmless. Particularly worrisome is the fact that THC accumulates in the body's fatty tissues, especially in the brain and reproductive organs. Even if a person smokes marijuana just once a week, the body is never entirely free of THC. Scientists recently located a specific receptor site on the surface of brain cells where THC binds to produce its effects (Fig. 8–12 ◆). These receptor sites are found in large numbers in the cerebral cortex, which is the seat of human consciousness (Matsuda et al., 1990).

Does marijuana produce physical dependence?

Studies of long-term heavy users of marijuana in Jamaica, Greece, and Costa Rica failed to find any physical dependence (Carter, 1980; Rubin & Comitas, 1975; Stefanis et al., 1977). Marijuana's potential for abuse lies primarily in the realm of psychological dependence, not addiction.

There have been very alarming reports in the press about the dangers of marijuana. Are they accurate?

Dangers of Marijuana Use   As one pharmacologist put it, "Those reading only *Good Housekeeping* would have to believe that marijuana is considerably more dangerous than the black plague." Unfortunately, an evaluation of marijuana's risks has been clouded by emotional debate. Let's see if we can make a realistic appraisal.

In the past it was widely reported that marijuana causes brain damage, genetic damage, and a loss of motivation. Each of these charges can be criticized for being based on poorly done or inconclusive research. However, that doesn't mean that marijuana gets a clean bill of health. For about a day after a person smokes marijuana, his or her attention, coordination, and short-term memory are affected (Pope, Gruber, & Yurgelun-Todd, 1995). Long-term marijuana users tend to show small but persistent impairments of learning, memory, attention, and thinking abilities. These changes, while subtle, can be a serious problem for frequent users (Pope & Yurgelun-Todd, 1996; Solowij, Michie, & Fox, 1995).

Health Risks   After many years of conflicting information, some of marijuana's health hazards are also being clarified.

Figure 8–12 ◆ This thin slice of a rat's brain has been washed with a radioactive THC-like drug. Yellowish areas show where the brain is rich in THC receptors. In addition to the cortex, or outer layer of the brain, THC receptors are found in abundance in areas involved in the control of coordinated movement. Naturally occurring chemicals similar to THC may help the brain cope with pain and stress. However, when THC is used as a drug, high doses can cause paranoia, hallucinations, and dizziness (Fackelmann, 1993).

Marijuana's long-term effects include the following health risks.

1. In regular users, marijuana causes chronic bronchitis and pre-cancerous changes in lung cells. At present no direct link between marijuana and lung cancer has been proved, but it is suspected. Marijuana smoke contains 50 percent more cancer-causing hydrocarbons than does tobacco smoke. Some doctors estimate that smoking several "joints" a week is the equivalent of smoking a dozen cigarettes a day. Other researchers have found that "smokers of only a few joints a day have as much microscopic damage to the cells lining the airways as smokers of more than a pack of cigarettes a day" (Tashkin et al., 1988).

2. Marijuana temporarily lowers sperm production in males, and users produce more abnormal sperm. This could be a problem for a man who is marginally fertile and wants to have a family (Palfai & Jankiewicz, 1991).

3. In experiments with female monkeys, THC causes abnormal menstrual cycles and disrupts ovulation. Other animal studies show that THC causes a higher rate of miscarriages and that it can reach the developing fetus. As is true for so many other drugs, it appears that marijuana should be avoided during pregnancy.

4. THC can suppress the body's immune system, possibly increasing the risk of disease (Turkington, 1986).

5. In animals, marijuana causes genetic damage within cells of the body. It is not known to what extent this happens in humans, but it does suggest that marijuana can be detrimental to health (Zimmerman & Zimmerman, 1990).

6. Activity levels in the cerebellum are lower than normal in marijuana abusers. This may explain why chronic

An outdated anti-marijuana poster demonstrates the kind of misinformation that has long been attached to this drug. Research is beginning to sort out what risks are associated with continued use of marijuana.

marijuana users tend to show some loss of coordination (Volkow et al., 1996).

When the preceding findings are compared with the studies of veteran marijuana users, it is clear that no one can say with certainty that marijuana is extremely harmful or completely safe. Although much is still unknown, marijuana appears to be in a class with two other potent drugs—tobacco and alcohol. Only future research will tell for sure "what's in the pot."

A Look Ahead Of the many states of consciousness we have discussed, dreaming remains one of the most familiar—and the most surprising. Are there lessons to be learned from dreams? What personal insights lie hidden in the ebb and flow of dream images? The following Applications section probes such questions. After that, in the Exploration, we will conclude by wrestling with the questions, Why do people abuse drugs? and What can be done about it?

Learning Check

1. Which of the drugs listed below are known to cause a physical dependence?
   a. heroin   **b.** morphine   **c.** codeine   **d.** methadone   **e.** barbiturates
   f. alcohol   **g.** caffeine   **h.** amphetamines   **i.** cocaine   **j.** nicotine

2. Amphetamine psychosis is similar to extreme _____ , in which the individual feels threatened and suffers from delusions.

3. Cocaine is very similar to which of the following in its effects on the central nervous system?
   a. Seconal   **b.** codeine   **c.** Cannabis   **d.** amphetamine

4. The combination of _____ or _____ and alcohol can be fatal.

5. One drink starts a chain reaction leading to a second and a third in the crucial phase of problem drinking. T or F?

6. In terms of sheer numbers, this country's biggest drug problem centers on abuse of
   a. marijuana   **b.** alcohol   **c.** tobacco   **d.** heroin

7. Most experts now acknowledge that marijuana is physically addicting. T or F?

Critical Thinking

8. The United States government, which helps fund anti-smoking campaigns and smoking-related health research, also continues to subsidize tobacco growers. Can you explain this contradiction?

Answers:

1. All but g   2. paranoia   3. d   4. barbiturates or tranquilizers   5. T   6. b   7. F   8. Neither can I.

---

*A*t one time or another almost everyone has had a dream that seemed to have deep meaning. In view of this, it seems appropriate to return to dreaming. Let's start with Freud's approach to dream interpretation.

Interpreting Your Dreams

To unlock dreams, Freud identified four **dream processes,** or mental filters, *that disguise the meanings of dreams.* The first is **condensation,** *in which several people, objects, or events are combined into a single dream image.* A dream character that looks like a teacher, acts like your father, talks like your mother, and is dressed like your employer might be a condensation of authority figures in your life.

Displacement is a second way of disguising dream content. Displacement may cause important emotions or actions of a dream to be *redirected toward safe or seemingly unimportant images.* Thus, a student angry at his parents might dream of accidentally wrecking their car instead of directly attacking them.

A third dream process is **symbolization.** As mentioned earlier, Freud believed that dreams are often expressed in *images that are symbolic rather than literal.* That's why it helps to ask what feelings or ideas a dream image might symbolize. Let's say, for example, that a student dreams of coming to class naked. A literal interpretation would be that the student is an exhibitionist! A more likely symbolic meaning is that the student feels vulnerable or unprepared in the class.

Secondary elaboration is the fourth method by which dream meanings are disguised. **Secondary elaboration** *is the tendency to make a dream more logical, and to add details when remembering it.* The fresher a dream memory is, the more useful it is likely to be.

Looking for condensation, displacement, symbolization, and secondary elaboration may help you unlock your dreams. But there are other ways to proceed. Dream theorist Calvin Hall (1974) preferred to think of dreams as plays and the dreamer as a playwright. Hall admitted that dream images and ideas tend to be more primitive than waking thoughts. Nevertheless, much can be learned by simply considering the **setting, cast of characters, plot,** and **emotions** portrayed in a dream.

Another dream researcher, Rosalind Cartwright, suggests that dreams are primarily "feeling statements." According to her, the overall **emotional tone** (*underlying mood*) of a dream is a major clue to its meaning. Is the dream comical, threatening, joyous, or depressing? Were you lonely, jealous, frightened, in love, or angry? Cartwright encourages use of everyday dream life as a source of personal enrichment and personal growth (Cartwright & Lamberg, 1992).

In many ways, dreams can be thought of as a message *from* yourself *to* yourself. Thus, the way to understand dreams is to remember them, write them down, look for the messages they contain, and become deeply acquainted with *your* own symbol system. Here's how.

How to Catch a Dream

1. Before retiring, plan to remember your dreams. Keep a pen and paper or a tape recorder beside your bed.

2. If possible, arrange to awaken gradually without an alarm. Natural awakening almost always follows soon after a REM period.

3. If you rarely remember your dreams, you may want to set an alarm clock to go off an hour before you usually awaken. Although less desirable than awakening naturally, this may let you catch a dream.

4. Upon awakening, lie still and review the dream images with your eyes closed. Try to recall as many details as possible.

5. If you can, make your first dream record (whether by writing or by tape) with your eyes closed. Opening your eyes will disrupt dream recall.

6. Review the dream again and record as many additional details as you can remember. Dream memories disappear quickly. Be sure to describe feelings as well as the plot, characters, and actions of the dream.

7. Put your dreams into a permanent dream diary. Keep dreams in chronological order and review them periodically. This procedure will reveal recurrent themes, conflicts, and emotions. It almost always produces valuable insights.

8. Remember, a number of drugs suppress dreaming (see Table 8–7 ■)

Dream images may contain symbolic messages, as well as literal meanings. If you find yourself wearing a mask in a dream, for instance, it could relate to important roles that you play at school, work, or home. It could also mean that you want to hide or that you are looking forward to a costume party. To accurately interpret a dream it is important to learn your own "vocabulary" of dream images and meanings. Keeping a dream diary is the first step toward gaining valuable insights.

Table 8–7 ■ Effects of Selected Drugs on Dreaming	
Drug	**Effect on REM Sleep**
Alcohol	Decrease
Amphetamines	Decrease
Barbiturates	Decrease
Caffeine	None
Cocaine	Decrease
LSD	Slight increase
Marijuana	Slight decrease or no effect
Opiates	Decrease
Valium	Decrease

Dream Work   Because each dream has several possible meanings or levels of meaning, there is no fixed way to work with it. Telling the dream to others and discussing its meaning can be a good start. Describing it may help you relive some of the feelings in the dream, Also, family members or friends may be able to offer interpretations to which you would be blind. Watch for verbal or visual puns and other playful elements in dreams. If, for example, you dream that you are in a wrestling match and your arm is pinned behind your back, it may mean that you feel someone is "twisting your arm" in real life.

The meaning of most dreams will yield to a little detective work. Rosalind Cartwright suggests asking a series of questions about dreams you would like to understand (Cartwright and Lamberg, 1992).

Probing Dreams

1. Who was in the dream? Do you recognize any of the characters?
2. What was happening? Were you active in the dream or watching it transpire? Did someone else do something to you?
3. Where did the action of the dream take place? Have you seen the setting or any part of it in real life, or was it a fantasy scene?
4. What was the time frame? What was your age in the dream?
5. Who is responsible for what happened in the dream?
6. Who are you in your dreams? Are you someone you would like to be or someone you'd rather not be?

If you still have trouble seeing the meaning of a dream, you may find it helpful to use a technique developed by Fritz Perls. Perls, the originator of Gestalt therapy, considered most dreams a special message about what's missing in our lives, what we avoid doing, or feelings that need to be "re-owned." Perls felt that dreams are a way of filling in gaps in personal experience (Perls, 1969).

An approach that Perls found helpful is to "take the part of" or "speak for" each of the characters and objects in the dream. In other words, if you dream about a strange man standing behind a doorway, you would speak aloud to the man, then answer for him. To use Perls' method, you would even speak for the door, perhaps saying something like, "I am a barrier. I keep you safe, but I also keep you locked inside. The stranger has something to tell you. You must risk opening me to learn it."

A particularly interesting dream exercise is to continue a dream as waking fantasy so that it may be concluded or carried on to a more meaningful ending. As the world of dreams and your personal dream language become more familiar, you will doubtless find many answers, paradoxes, intuitions, and insights into your own behavior.

Using Your Dreams

Creative people tend to remember more dreams (Schredl, 1995). It could be that such people just pay more attention to their dreams. But dream theorist Gordon Globus (1987) believes that dreams make a major contribution to creativity. Globus points out that some of our most creative moments take place during dreaming. Even unimaginative people may create amazing worlds each night in their dreams. For many of us, this rich ability to create is lost in the daily rush of sensory input. How might we tap the creative power of dreams that is so easily lost during waking?

Dreams and Creativity   History is full of cases where dreams have been a pathway to creativity and discovery. A striking example is provided by Dr. Otto Loewi, a pharmacologist and winner of a Nobel Prize. Loewi had spent years studying the chemical transmission of nerve impulses. A tremendous breakthrough in his research came when he dreamed of an experiment three nights in a row. The first two nights he woke up and scribbled the experiment on a pad. But the next morning, he couldn't tell what the notes meant. On the third night, he got up after having the dream. This time, instead of making notes he went straight to his laboratory and performed the crucial experiment. Loewi later said that if the experiment had occurred to him while awake he would have rejected it.

Loewi's experience gives some insight into using dreams to produce creative solutions. Inhibitions are reduced during dreaming, which may be especially useful in solving problems that require a fresh point of view.

Being able to take advantage of dreams for problem solving is improved if you "set" yourself before retiring. Before you go to bed, try to think intently about a problem you wish to solve. Steep yourself in the problem by stating it clearly and reviewing all relevant information. Then use the suggestions listed in the previous section to catch your dreams. While this method is not guaranteed to produce a novel solution or a new insight, it is certain to be an adventure. About half of a group of college students using the method for one week recalled a dream that helped them solve a personal problem (Barrett, 1993).

Lucid Dreaming   If you would like to press further into the territory of dreams, you may want to learn lucid dreaming. During a **lucid dream** *a person feels as if she or he is fully awake within the dream world and capable of normal thought and action.* If you ask yourself, "Could this be a dream?" and answer "Yes," you are having a lucid dream (Blackmore, 1991a).

Stephen La Berge and his colleagues at the Stanford University Sleep Research Center have used a unique approach to show that lucid dreams are real and that they occur during REM sleep. In the sleep lab, lucid dreamers agree to make prearranged signals when they become aware they are dreaming. One such signal is to look up abruptly in a dream, causing a distinct upward eye movement. Another signal is to clench the right and left fists (in the dream) in a prearranged pattern. Such signals show very clearly that lucid dreaming and voluntary action in dreams is possible (La Berge, 1981, 1985; La Berge et al., 1981; Moss, 1989).

How would a person go about learning to have lucid dreams?

La Berge found he could greatly increase lucid dreaming by following this simple routine: When you awaken spontaneously from a dream, take a few minutes to try to memorize it. Next, engage in 10 to 15 minutes of reading or any other activity that requires you to be fully awake. Then while returning to sleep, say to yourself, "Next time I'm dreaming, I want to remember I'm dreaming." Finally, visualize yourself lying in bed asleep while in the dream you just rehearsed. At the same time, picture yourself realizing that you are dreaming. Follow this routine each time you awaken (substitute a dream memory from another occasion if you don't awaken from a dream). Researchers recently found that stimulation from the vestibular system also tends to increase

lucidity. Thus, sleeping in a hammock or on a waterbed might increase the number of lucid dreams you have (Leslie & Ogilvie, 1996).

Why would anyone want to have more lucid dreams?

Researchers are interested in lucid dreams because they provide a tool for understanding dreaming. Using subjects who can signal while they are dreaming makes it possible to explore dreams with firsthand data from the dreamer's world itself (La Berge, 1985).

On a more personal level, lucid dreaming can convert dreams into a nightly "workshop" for emotional growth. Consider, for example, a recently divorced woman who kept dreaming that she was being swallowed by a giant wave. Rosalind Cartwright asked the woman to try swimming the next time the wave engulfed her. She did, with great determination, and the nightmare lost its terror. More importantly, her revised dream made her feel that she could cope with life again. For reasons such as this, people who have lucid dreams tend to feel a sense of emotional well-being (Wolpin et al., 1992). So, day or night, don't be afraid to dream a little.

Learning Check

1. In secondary elaboration, one dream character stands for several others. T or F?

2. Calvin Hall's approach to dream interpretation emphasizes the setting, cast, plot, and emotions portrayed in a dream. T or F?

3. Rosalind Cartwright stresses that dreaming is a relatively mechanical process having little personal meaning. T or F?

4. Both alcohol and LSD cause a slight increase in dreaming. T or F?

5. "Taking the part of" or "speaking for" dream elements is a dream interpretation technique originated by Fritz Perls. T or F?

6. Recent research shows that lucid dreaming occurs primarily during NREM sleep or micro-awakenings. T or F?

Critical Thinking

7. If you were dreaming right now, how could you prove it?

Answers:

1. F 2. T 3. F 4. F 5. T 6. F 7. In waking consciousness, our actions have consequences that produce immediate sensory feedback. Dreams lack such external feedback (Tart, 1986). Thus, trying to walk through a wall or doing similar tests would reveal if you were dreaming.

Why do people use drugs?

People take drugs for reasons ranging from curiosity, to wanting to belong to a group, to an escape from feelings of inadequacy. The best predictors of adolescent drug use and abuse are peer drug use, parental drug use, delinquency, parental maladjustment, poor self-esteem, social non-conformity, and stressful life changes (Marlatt et al., 1988).

How early do danger signs for drug use appear? A recent study followed 1,000 boys in French-Canadian schools for over a decade, starting in kindergarten. Investigators found that 5 to 10 percent of the kindergartners tended to act without thinking, showed little caution, and were anxious to experiment. Years later, in childhood and early adolescence, these boys were significantly more likely to begin smoking, get drunk, and use drugs (Masse & Tremblay, 1997).

For many young people, drug abuse is just one part of a general pattern of problem behavior. Another study found that adolescents who abuse drugs tend to be maladjusted, alienated, impulsive, and emotionally distressed. The study makes it clear that drug abuse is a symptom, rather than a cause, of personal and social maladjustment (Shedler & Block, 1990).

The Dynamics of Drug Abuse Many abusers turn to drugs in a self-defeating attempt to cope with life. All of the frequently abused drugs produce immediate feelings of pleasure. The negative consequences follow much later. This combination of immediate pleasure and delayed punishment allows abusers to feel good on demand. In time, of course, most of the pleasure goes out of drug abuse, and the abuser's problems get worse. But if an abuser merely feels *better* (however briefly) after taking a drug, drug taking can become compulsive (Barrett, 1985).

Drug Expectancies Closely related to a drug's actual effects are users' beliefs and expectations about drugs (Stacy et al., 1996). Patterns of drinking alcohol offer a good example of how expectations promote abuse. In one study, drinkers were asked about alcohol's effects on good feelings, sexual performance, social and physical pleasure, self-assertion, relaxation, and feelings of power. Heavy drinkers expect far more positive effects and fewer negative consequences from drinking alcohol than light drinkers do (Brown, Goldman, & Christiansen, 1985). Children who learn such expectancies are likely to become problem drinkers (Christiansen et al., 1989). The three most dangerous beliefs are:

- Alcohol makes experiences more positive.
- Alcohol facilitates social behavior.
- Alcohol improves thinking and physical performance.

Cultural Values There is a widespread tendency to think of drugs as a magic way to produce good feelings by avoiding, minimizing, or escaping negative situations. Some observers believe that drug use is so deeply ingrained that "we are addicted to addiction. This is to say that, with few exceptions we subscribe to the premise that life cannot be lived without drugs." We are so used to having our own way that we have come to believe "we should be able to will ourselves to be calm, cheerful, thin, industrious, creative—and moreover, to have a good night's sleep." Some critics believe that the medical profession, well meaning but misguided, unnecessarily encourages legal drug use. Indeed, one psychologist observed:

> Depression, social inadequacy, anxiety, apathy, marital discord, children's misbehavior, and other psychological and social problems of living are now being redefined as medical problems, to be solved by physicians with prescription pads. (Rogers, 1971)

Perhaps we all can be partially excused for placing undue faith in drugs. Doctors and the general public are the target of multimillion-dollar advertising campaigns aimed at encouraging drug use. Even the lowly aspirin is pushed as a means of relieving "nervous tension." Advertisements directed at physicians encourage overuse of drugs even more blatantly. An ad pictures a distraught mother with a child and asks, "Her kind of pressures last all day . . . shouldn't her tranquilizer?" Another reads:

> School, the dark, separation, dental visits, monsters. The everyday anxiety of children sometimes gets out of hand. A child can usually deal with his anxieties. But sometimes the anxieties overpower the child. Then he needs your help. Your help may include Vistaril.

Drugs have legitimate uses and have alleviated much suffering. The problem is that drugs strong enough to ease pain, induce sleep, end depression, or otherwise alter consciousness have a high potential for abuse. Rather than sounding the alarm about illicit drug use, politicians and public health officials need to pay more attention to the far more widespread abuse of legally prescribed drugs (MacCoun, 1993).

Drug abuse in Western nations has reached epidemic proportions in recent years. Problems once restricted to drug-related subcultures and the urban poor are now seen regularly among high school and college students and among the vast middle classes.

What, if anything, should be done about drug abuse?

Prevention Traditional approaches have emphasized limiting drug supplies, strict law enforcement, and legal penalties. Limiting supplies has been relatively successful in the case of some drugs. But

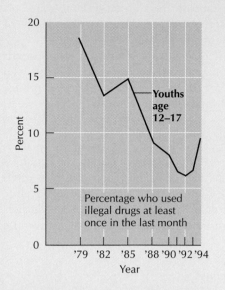

In the United States, drug use among youths has been on the rise again in recent years. (Source: Department of Health and Human Services, National Household Survey on Drug Abuse.)

drug abuse and the legality are two separate issues. This distinction becomes clear when it is recognized that one of the most potent, destructive, and potentially dangerous drugs available is alcohol. By the government's own standards, alcohol should be at the top of the list of controlled substances. Yet it is legal.

Facts such as these have led some observers to conclude that anyone who seeks drug-induced consciousness alteration will find a drug, legal or illegal, to achieve it. Psychiatrist Thomas Szasz

(1983) believes that it is futile for the government to attempt to "legislate morality" by regulating what drugs a person chooses to take. Szasz suggests that current drug regulations have an effect similar to the prohibition of alcohol in the United States in the 1920s. That is, they encourage a black market, organized crime, disrespect for the law, and occasional poisonings from adulterated drugs. As Szasz points out, "tobacco is not legally considered a drug, marijuana is, gin is not, but Valium is. . . ."

After an extensive review of research on drugs, drug abuse, and drug laws, the magazine *Consumer Reports* drew the same conclusion and added this recommendation (Brecher, 1972):

> Stop misclassifying drugs. Our current legal classification system treats alcohol and nicotine—two of the most harmful drugs—essentially as non-drugs, while marijuana is equated with heroin—a shocking and harmful bit of foolishness. Cocaine is still listed as a narcotic when it is clearly a stimulant. A scientifically based legal system must replace the current politically based one.

Think About It   Whereas it is true that drug *use* is essentially a "victimless crime," the fact remains that *abuse* of drugs—legal or illegal—represents a serious loss to society.

The point of view expressed by Szasz is obviously controversial. Many in fact, believe that the answer to drug problems

is to be found in stricter penalties and law enforcement. And yet, a sober look at drug abuse makes it clear that some psychoactive drugs are almost always available. In general, we tend to overlook the frequent abuse of legal drugs such as tranquilizers or alcohol and overestimate the misuse of illegal drugs (MacCoun, 1993).

Although billions of dollars have been spent on drug enforcement, there has been an increase in the overall level of drug use. On the other hand, there has been no increase in marijuana use in states that have relaxed penalties for its possession to a fine (Thies & Register, 1993).

In the Dutch city of Amsterdam, drug addiction is treated as a medical problem rather than a criminal offense. Methadone is freely available to heroin addicts and little effort is made to prevent the use of "soft drugs" such as marijuana. Contrary to what critics predicted, the proportion of younger addicts in Amsterdam has fallen during the last decade. The overall addict population has dropped by a third. The rate in other European countries is twice as high; in the U.S. it is six times higher.

Given such facts, some experts believe that prevention through education and early intervention—rather than tougher enforcement—is the answer to drug problems (MacCoun, 1993). What do you think?

Learning Check

1. Advertising campaigns directed at physicians tend to overstate the need for treating behavioral problems with drugs. T or F?

2. Heavy drinkers of alcohol learn from experience to expect more negative consequences from alcohol's effects. T or F?

3. Thomas Szasz believes that it is time for the government to take a lead in "legislating morality" with regard to drug use. T or F?

4. Current laws in the United States have been accused of misclassifying some drugs. T or F?

5. The immediate reinforcing effects of drugs and the delayed negative consequences are believed to play a major role in drug abuse. T or F?

Critical Thinking

6. Why do you think there is such a contrast between the laws regulating marijuana and those regulating alcohol and tobacco?

Answers:

1. T 2. F 3. F 4. T 5. T 6. Drug laws in Western societies reflect cultural values and historical patterns of use. Inconsistencies in the law can often cannot be justified on the basis of pharmacology, health risks, or abuse potential.

Chapter Summary

What is an altered state of consciousness?

◆ States of awareness that differ from normal, alert, **waking consciousness** are called **altered states of consciousness** (ASCs). Altered states are especially associated with sleep and dreaming, hypnosis, sensory deprivation, and psychoactive drugs.

◆ Cultural conditioning greatly affects what altered states a person recognizes, seeks, considers normal, and attains.

What are the effects of sleep loss and changes in sleep patterns?

◆ Sleep is an **innate biological rhythm** essential for survival. Higher animals and people deprived of sleep experience involuntary **microsleeps.**

◆ Moderate sleep loss mainly affects vigilance and performance on routine or boring tasks. Extended sleep loss can (somewhat rarely) produce a temporary **sleep-deprivation psychosis.**

◆ **Sleep patterns** show some flexibility, but 7 to 8 hours remains average. The amount of daily sleep decreases steadily from birth to old age. Once-a-day **sleep patterns,** with a 2-to-1 ratio of waking and sleep, are most efficient for most people.

Are there different stages of sleep?

◆ Sleep occurs in four **stages.** Stage 1 is **light sleep,** and stage 4 is **deep sleep.** The sleeper alternates between stages 1 and 4 (passing through stages 2 and 3) several times each night.

How does dream sleep differ from dreamless sleep?

◆ There are two basic sleep states, **rapid eye movement (REM)** sleep and **non-REM (NREM)** sleep. REM sleep is much more strongly associated with dreaming than non-REM sleep is.

◆ Dreaming and REMs occur mainly during stage 1. Dreaming is accompanied by emotional arousal but relaxation of the skeletal muscles.

◆ People deprived of dream sleep show a **REM rebound** when allowed to sleep without interruption. However, total sleep loss seems to be more important than loss of a single stage.

◆ In addition to several other possible functions, REM sleep appears to aid the processing of memories.

What are the causes of sleep disorders and unusual sleep events?

◆ **Sleepwalking** and **sleeptalking** occur during NREM sleep. **Night terrors** occur in NREM sleep, whereas **nightmares** occur in REM sleep. **Narcolepsy** (sleep attacks) and **cataplexy** are caused by a sudden shift to stage 1 REM patterns during normal waking hours.

◆ **Sleep apnea** (interrupted breathing) is one source of insomnia and daytime **hypersomnia** (sleepiness).

◆ Apnea is suspected as one cause of **sudden infant death syndrome** (SIDS). Exposure to secondhand smoke is a major risk factor for SIDS. With only a few exceptions, healthy infants should sleep face up or on their sides.

Can insomnia be prevented?

◆ Insomnia may be temporary or chronic. When it is treated through the use of drugs, sleep quality is often lowered and **drug-dependency insomnia** may develop. **Behavioral approaches** to managing insomnia, such as **sleep restriction** and **stimulus control,** are quite effective.

Do dreams have meaning?

◆ Most **dream content** is about familiar settings, people, and actions. Dreams more often involve negative emotions than positive emotions.

◆ The Freudian, or **psychodynamic,** view is that dreams express unconscious wishes, frequently hidden by **dream symbols.** Many theorists have questioned Freud's view of dreams. For example, the **activation-synthesis model** portrays dreaming as a physiological process.

How is hypnosis done, and what are its limitations?

◆ **Hypnosis** is an altered state characterized by narrowed attention and increased suggestibility. (Not all psychologists agree that hypnotic effects require an alteration of consciousness.)

◆ Hypnosis appears capable of producing relaxation, controlling pain, and altering perceptions. **Stage hypnotism** takes advantage of typical stage behavior and uses deception to simulate hypnosis.

How does sensory deprivation affect consciousness?

◆ Extreme or unusual stimulus conditions often induce altered states of consciousness. A prime example is **sensory deprivation.**

◆ Prolonged sensory deprivation is stressful and disruptive. However, brief sensory deprivation can enhance sensitivity and relaxation. Sensory deprivation also appears to aid the breaking of long-standing habits and promotes creative thinking.

What are the effects of the more commonly used psychoactive drugs?

◆ A **psychoactive drug** is a substance that affects the brain in ways that alter consciousness. Most psychoactive drugs can be placed on a scale ranging from **stimulation** to **depression.**

- Drugs may cause a **physical dependence** (addiction) or a **psychological dependence,** or both. The physically addicting drugs are heroin, morphine, codeine, methadone, barbiturates, alcohol, amphetamines, tobacco, and cocaine. All psychoactive drugs can lead to psychological dependence.

- Drug use can be classified as **experimental, recreational, situational, intensive,** and **compulsive.** Drug abuse is most often associated with the last three.

- **Stimulant drugs** are readily abused because of the period of depression that often follows stimulation. The greatest risks are associated with **amphetamines, cocaine,** and **nicotine,** but even **caffeine** can be a problem. Nicotine includes the added risk of lung cancer, heart disease, and other health problems.

- **Barbiturates** and **tranquilizers** are depressant drugs whose action is similar to that of alcohol. The overdose level for barbiturates is close to the intoxication dosage, making them dangerous drugs. Mixing barbiturates or tranquilizers and alcohol may result in a fatal **drug interaction.**

- **Alcohol** is the most heavily abused drug in common use today. The development of a drinking problem is usually marked by an **initial phase** of increasing consumption, a **crucial phase,** in which a single drink can set off a chain reaction, and a **chronic phase,** in which a person lives to drink and drinks to live.

- **Marijuana** is subject to an abuse pattern similar to alcohol. Studies have linked chronic marijuana use with lung cancer, various mental impairments, and other health problems.

How can dreams be used to promote personal understanding?

- Dreams may be used to promote self-understanding. Freud held that the meaning of dreams is hidden by **condensation, displacement, symbolization,** and **secondary elaboration.**

- Hall emphasizes the **setting, cast, plot,** and **emotions** of a dream. Cartwright's view of dreams as **feeling statements** and Perls' technique of speaking for dream elements are also helpful. Dreams may be used for **creative problem solving,** especially when dream control is achieved through **lucid dreaming.**

Why is drug abuse so widespread?

- Drug abuse is related to a variety of factors, especially personal and social maladjustment, attempts to cope, the immediate reinforcing qualities of psychoactive drugs, peer group influences, and expectations about the value and effects of drugs.

- Proposed remedies for drug abuse have ranged from severe punishment to legalization. The search for a solution continues.

Conditioning and Learning

Preview

What Did You Learn in School Today?

When your aging author was in college, students discovered an interesting "game" that could be played with the plumbing in the dorms. When a toilet was flushed while someone was taking a shower, the cold water pressure suddenly dropped. This caused the shower to become scalding hot. Naturally, the shower victim screamed in terror and his reflexes caused him to leap back in pain. Soon we discovered that if we flushed *all* the toilets at once, the effects were multiplied many times over!

The sound of a flushing toilet has to be one of the world's most uninspiring stimuli. But for a time, a whole flock of college students twitched involuntarily whenever they heard a toilet flush. Their reactions to this formerly neutral stimulus were the result of *classical conditioning,* a special type of learning. Details about classical conditioning are explored in this chapter.

Now consider another learning situation: Let's say that you are at school and that you feel like you are "starving to death." Locating a vending machine, you deposit your last two quarters to buy a candy bar. You press the button, and . . . nothing happens. Being civilized and in complete control, you press the other buttons, try the coin return, and look for an attendant. Still nothing. Your stomach growls. Being no longer either civilized or self-controlled, you give the machine a little kick (just to let it know how you feel). Then, as you turn away, the machine begins to whirr and out pops a candy bar plus 25 cents change. Once this happens, chances are good that you will repeat the "kicking response" in the future. If it pays off several times more, kicking vending machines may become a regular feature of your behavior. In this case, learning is based on *operant conditioning* (also called *instrumental learning*).

Classical and operant conditioning underlie much human learning. In fact, conditioning reaches into every corner of our lives. You should certainly find it useful to learn more about it. Are you ready to learn more about learning? If so, read on! This chapter explores conditioning and other basic forms of learning.

Chapter Survey

Theme: The principles of learning can be used to understand and manage behavior.

Key Questions:

Key Topics to Watch for:

Key Questions	Key Topics to Watch for
What is learning?	A definition of learning Antecedents and consequences Two types of conditioning
How does classical conditioning occur?	Elements of classical conditioning Conditioning procedures and phenomena
Does conditioning affect emotions?	Conditioned emotional responses Vicarious conditioning
How does operant conditioning occur?	Elements of operant conditioning Conditioning procedures and phenomena
Are there different kinds of operant reinforcement?	Types of operant reinforcers
How are we influenced by patterns of reward?	Schedules of reinforcement Stimulus control
What does punishment do to behavior	Types of punishment Side effects of punishment Effective use of punishment
What is cognitive learning?	Cognitive maps, latent learning, discovery learning
Does learning occur by imitation?	Observational learning and modeling
How does conditioning apply to practical problems?	Behavioral self-management Self-regulated learning
How does biology influence learning?	Biological constraints on learning

What Is Learning—Does Practice Make Perfect?

Most of our daily activities are either wholly learned or affected by learning. Imagine what you would be like if you suddenly forgot everything you had ever learned. What could you do? You would be unable to read, write, or speak. You couldn't feed yourself, find your way home, drive a car, play the bassoon, or "party." Needless to say, you would be totally incapacitated. (Dull, too!)

Learning is obviously important. What's a formal definition of learning?

Learning is a *relatively permanent change in behavior due to experience*. Notice that this definition excludes temporary changes caused by motivation, fatigue, maturation, disease, injury, or drugs. Each of these can alter behavior, but none qualifies as learning.

Isn't learning the result of practice?

It depends on what you mean by practice. Merely repeating a response will not always produce learning. *Reinforcement* is the key to learning in both classical and operant conditioning. **Reinforcement** *refers to any event which increases the probability that a response will occur again.* A **response** *is any identifiable behavior.* Responses may be observable actions, such as blinking, eating a piece of candy, or turning a door handle; or, they may be internal, such as changes in heart rate.

If I want to teach a dog a trick, I could reinforce correct responses by giving the dog some food each time it sits up. Similarly, you could teach a child to be neat by praising her for picking up her toys. Learning can also occur in ways quite different than these examples imply. For instance, if a girl gets stung by a bee, she may learn to fear bees. In this case, the girl's fear is reinforced by the pain she feels immediately after seeing the bee. Later in this chapter we will see how such varied experiences lead to learning.

Antecedents and Consequences Unlocking the secrets of learning begins with noting what happens before and after a response. *Events that precede a response* are called **antecedents.** *Effects that follow a response* are **consequences.** Paying careful attention to the "before and after" of learning is a key to understanding it.

Classical Conditioning

Classical conditioning is based on what happens before a response. We begin with a stimulus that reliably triggers a response. Imagine, for example, that a puff of air (the stimulus) is aimed at your eye. The air puff will make you blink (a response) every time. The eye-blink is a **reflex**

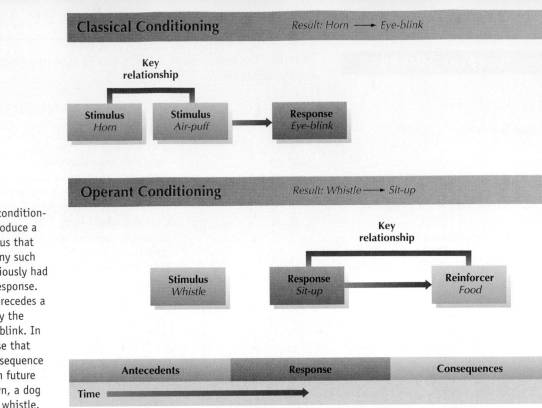

Figure 9–1 ◆ In classical conditioning, a stimulus that does not produce a response is paired with a stimulus that does elicit a response. After many such pairings, the stimulus that previously had no effect begins to produce a response. In the example shown, a horn precedes a puff of air to the eye. Eventually the horn alone will produce an eye-blink. In operant conditioning, a response that is followed by a reinforcing consequence becomes more likely to occur on future occasions. In the example shown, a dog learns to sit up when it hears a whistle.

(*automatic, non-learned response*). Now, assume that we sound a horn (another stimulus) just before each puff of air hits your eye. If the horn and the air puff occur together many times, what happens? Soon, the horn alone will make you blink. How do we know that learning has occurred? Because before you were conditioned, the horn didn't make you blink. Similarly, if your mouth waters each time you eat a cookie, you may learn to salivate when you merely *see* a cookie, a picture of cookies, a cookie jar, or other stimuli that have preceded salivation.

In **classical conditioning**, *antecedent events become associated with one another*: A stimulus that does not produce a response is linked with one that does (a horn is associated with a puff of air to the eye, for example). Learning is evident when the new stimulus also begins to elicit (bring forth) responses (Fig. 9–1 ◆).

Operant Conditioning

In **operant conditioning**, *learning is based on the consequences of responding*. Each time a response is made, it may be followed by a reinforcer (such as food). Or by punishment. Or by nothing. These results determine whether a response is likely to be made again (Fig. 9–1). For example, if you wear a particular shirt or blouse and get lots of compliments (reinforcement), you are likely to wear it more often. If people snicker, insult you, call the police, or scream (punishment), you will probably wear it less often.

Now that you have an idea of what happens in the two basic kinds of learning, let's look at classical conditioning in more detail.

Classical Conditioning—Does the Name Pavlov Ring a Bell?

How was classical conditioning discovered?

At the beginning of the 20th century, something happened in the lab of *Russian physiologist* **Ivan Pavlov** that brought him lasting fame. The event seems so trivial that a lesser man might have ignored it: Pavlov's subjects drooled at him.

Actually, Pavlov was studying digestion. To observe salivation, he placed meat powder or some tidbit on a dog's tongue. After doing this many times, Pavlov noticed that his dogs were salivating *before* the food reached their mouths. Later, the dogs even began to salivate when they saw Pavlov enter the room. Was this misplaced affection? Pavlov knew better. Salivation is normally a reflex. For the animals to salivate at the mere sight of food, some type of learning had to have occurred. Pavlov called it *conditioning* (Fig. 9–2 ◆). Because of its importance in psychology's history, it is now called **classical conditioning** (also known as **Pavlovian conditioning** or **respondent conditioning**).

How did Pavlov study conditioning?

Pavlov's Experiment After Pavlov observed that meat powder made his dogs salivate, he began his classic experiments (Fig. 9–2). To begin, he rang a bell. At first, the bell was a **neutral stimulus** (*it did not evoke a response*).

Figure 9–2 ◆ Pavlov's conditioning apparatus. In Pavlov's early experiments, a tube carried saliva from the dog's mouth to a lever that activated a recording device (far left). The placing of a dish of food in front of the dog was paired with various other stimuli for conditioning.

Immediately after Pavlov rang the bell, he placed meat powder on the dog's tongue, which caused reflex salivation. This sequence was repeated many times: bell, meat powder, salivation; bell, meat powder, salivation. Eventually (as conditioning took place), the dogs began to salivate when they heard the bell (Fig. 9–3 ◆). By association, the bell, which before had no effect, began to evoke the same response as food. This was shown by sometimes ringing the bell alone. Pavlov then observed that the dog salivated, even when no food was present.

Psychologists use several terms to describe these events. The bell in Pavlov's experiment starts out as a **neutral stimulus (NS)** (*a stimulus that does not evoke a response*). In time, the bell becomes a **conditioned stimulus (CS)** (*a stimulus that, because of learning, will evoke a response*). The meat powder is an **unconditioned stimulus (US)** (*a stimulus innately capable of eliciting a response*). Notice that the dog did not have to learn to respond to the US. Unconditioned stimuli typically produce reflexive responses or involuntary emotional reactions.

Since a reflex is "built in," it is called an **unconditioned** (*non-learned*) **response (UR)**. In Pavlov's study, salivation is the UR. When the bell alone will cause salivation, the response it evokes can no longer be called an unlearned reflex. Instead, salivation has become a **conditioned** (*learned*) **response (CR)** (see Fig. 9–3). Table 9–1 ■ summarizes the important elements of classical conditioning.

Are all these terms really necessary?

In a word, yes, because they help us recognize similarities in various instances of classical conditioning. Let's summarize the terms using an earlier example:

Before Conditioning	Example
US → UR	Puff of air → eye blink
NS → no effect	Horn → no effect
After Conditioning	**Example**
CS → CR	Horn → eye blink

Now, let's see if we can apply the terms to explain the

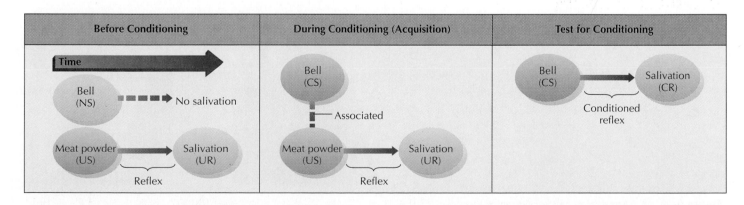

Before Conditioning	During Conditioning (Acquisition)	Test for Conditioning
Time → Bell (NS) - - -> No salivation Meat powder (US) → Salivation (UR) Reflex	Bell (CS) —Associated Meat powder (US) → Salivation (UR) Reflex	Bell (CS) → Salivation (CR) Conditioned reflex

Figure 9–3 ◆ The classical conditioning procedure.

Table 9–1 ■ Elements of Classical Conditioning

Element	Symbol	Description	Example
Neutral stimulus	NS	A stimulus that does not evoke a response	Bell
Unconditioned stimulus	US	A stimulus innately capable of eliciting a response	Meat powder
Conditioned stimulus	CS	A stimulus that evokes a response because it has been repeatedly paired with an unconditioned stimulus	Bell
Unconditioned response	UR	An innate reflex response elicited by an unconditioned stimulus	Reflex salivation
Conditioned response	CR	A learned response elicited by a conditioned stimulus	Salivation

effects of the shower and flushing toilet described in the chapter Preview. The unconditioned, or non-learned, response was a reflex jump from the hot water. The unconditioned stimulus was the hot water. The conditioned stimulus was the sound of a flushing toilet. That is, the flushing sound was at first neutral. But through conditioning, it became capable of eliciting a response.

Principles of Classical Conditioning—Teach Your Little Brother to Salivate

To observe conditioning, you could ring a bell, squirt lemon juice into a child's mouth, and condition salivation to the bell. The child's reactions might then be used to explore other aspects of classical conditioning.

Acquisition

During **acquisition**, *or training*, a conditioned response must

be reinforced (strengthened) (Fig. 9–4 ◆). Classical conditioning is **reinforced** *when the CS is followed by, or paired with, an unconditioned stimulus.* For our child, the bell is the CS; salivating is the UR; and the sour lemon juice is an unconditioned stimulus. To reinforce salivating to the bell, we must link the bell with the lemon juice. Conditioning will be most rapid if the US (lemon juice) follows *immediately* after the CS (the bell). With most reflexes, the optimal delay between CS and US is from one-half second to about 5 seconds (Schwartz & Robbins, 1995).

Higher Order Conditioning   Once a response is learned, it can bring about **higher order conditioning.** In this case, *a well-learned CS is used to reinforce further learning.* That is, the CS has become strong enough to be used like an unconditioned stimulus. Let's illustrate again with our salivating child.

As a result of earlier learning, the bell now makes the boy salivate. (No lemon juice is needed.) To go a step further, you could clap your hands and then ring the bell. (Again, no lemon juice would be used.) Through higher order conditioning, the child would soon learn to salivate when you clapped your hands (Fig. 9–5 ◆). (This little trick could be a real hit with friends and neighbors.)

Figure 9–4 ◆ Acquisition and extinction of a conditioned response. (After Pavlov, 1927.)

Figure 9–5 ◆ Higher order conditioning takes place when a well-learned conditioned stimulus is used as if it were an unconditioned stimulus. In this example, a child is first conditioned to salivate to the sound of a bell. In time, the bell will elicit salivation. At that point, you could clap your hands and then ring the bell. Soon, after repeating the procedure, the child would learn to salivate when you clapped your hands.

Higher order conditioning extends learning one or more steps beyond the original conditioned stimulus. Many advertisers use this effect by pairing images that evoke good feelings (such as people smiling and having fun) with pictures of merchandise. Obviously, they hope that you will learn, by association, to feel good when you see their products.

Expectancies

How does classical conditioning occur? Many psychologists believe it takes place as we process information that might aid survival. According to this **informational view,** classical conditioning occurs *as we detect associations among events.* Doing so creates new mental **expectancies,** *or expectations about how events are related.*

How does classical conditioning alter expectancies?

Notice that the conditioned stimulus reliably precedes the unconditioned stimulus. Because it does, the CS *predicts* the US (Rescorla, 1987). During conditioning, the brain learns to *expect* that the US will follow the CS. As a result, the brain prepares the body to respond to the US. Here's an example: When you are about to get a shot with a hypodermic needle, your muscles tighten and there is a catch in your breathing. Why? Because your body is preparing for pain. You have learned to expect that getting poked with a needle will hurt.

This expectancy, which was acquired during classical conditioning, changes your behavior.

Extinction and Spontaneous Recovery

After conditioning has occurred, what would happen if the US no longer followed the CS?

If the US never again follows the CS, conditioning will *extinguish.* Let's return to the example of the boy and the bell. If you ring the bell many times and do not follow it with lemon juice, the boy's expectancy that "bell precedes lemon juice" weakens. As it does, his tendency to salivate when he hears the bell will diminish. Thus, we see that *classical conditioning can be weakened by removing reinforcement* (see Fig. 9–4). This process is called **extinction.**

If conditioning takes a while to build up, shouldn't it take time to reverse?

Yes. In fact, several extinction sessions may be necessary to completely reverse conditioning. If the bell is rung until the child quits responding, it might seem that extinction is complete. However, the boy will probably respond to the bell again on the following day, at least at first. *The reappearance of a response following apparent extinction* is called **spontaneous recovery.** It explains why people who have had terrifying automobile accidents may need many slow, calm rides before their fears are completely extinguished.

Generalization

Once a person or an animal has been conditioned, *other stimuli similar to the CS may also trigger a response.* This effect is called **stimulus generalization.** For example, we might find that our conditioned child salivates to the sound of a ringing telephone or doorbell, even though they were never used as conditioning stimuli.

It is easy to see the value of stimulus generalization. Consider the child who burns her finger while playing with matches. Learning principles predict that the sight of a lighted match will become a conditioned stimulus for fear. But will the child fear only matches? Because of stimulus generalization, she should also show a healthy fear of flames from lighters, fireplaces, stoves, and so forth. It's fortunate that generalization extends learning to related situations. Were it not for this, we would all be far less adaptable.

As you may have guessed, stimulus generalization does have limits. Responding tapers down as stimuli become less like the original CS (Siegel et al., 1968). In other words, if you condition a person to blink each time you play a particular note on a piano, blinking will decline as you play higher or lower notes. If the notes are *much* higher or lower, the person will not respond at all (Fig. 9–6 ◆).

Figure 9–6 ◆ **(a)** Stimulus generalization. Stimuli similar to the CS also elicit a response. **(b)** This cat has learned to salivate when it sees a cat food box. Because of stimulus generalization, it also salivates when shown a similar-looking detergent box.

Discrimination

Let's consider one more idea with our salivating child (who by now must be ready to hide in the closet). Suppose the child is again conditioned with a bell as the CS. As an experiment, we occasionally sound a buzzer instead of the bell, but never follow it with the US (lemon juice). At first, the buzzer produces salivation (because of generalization). But after hearing the buzzer several times more, the child will stop responding to it. The child has now learned to *discriminate*, or respond differently, to the bell and the buzzer. In essence, the child's generalized response to the buzzer has extinguished.

Stimulus discrimination *is the ability to respond differently to varied stimuli.* As an example, you might remember the feelings of anxiety or fear you had as a child when your mother's or father's voice changed to its you're-about-to-get-swatted tone. (Or the dreaded, "Give-me-that-Game-Boy" tone.) Most children quickly learn to discriminate voice tones associated with pain from those associated with praise or affection.

Classical Conditioning in Humans—An Emotional Topic

How much human learning is based on classical conditioning?

In its simplest form, classical conditioning depends on

reflex responses. As mentioned earlier, a reflex is a dependable, inborn stimulus-and-response connection. For example, pain causes reflex withdrawal of various parts of the body. The pupil of the eye reflexively narrows in response to bright lights. Various foods cause salivation. It is entirely possible for humans to associate any of these—or other—reflex responses with a new stimulus. At the very least, you have probably noticed how your mouth waters when you see or smell a bakery. You may even have salivated to pictures of food (a picture of a lemon is great for this).

Conditioned Emotional Responses

Of larger importance, perhaps, are the more subtle ways that conditioning affects us. In addition to simple reflexes, more complex *emotional*, or "gut," responses may be conditioned to new stimuli. For instance, if your face reddened as part of your emotional reaction to being punished as a child, you may blush now when you are embarrassed or ashamed. Or think about the effects of associating pain with a dentist's office during your first visit. On later visits, did your heart pound and your palms sweat *before* the dentist began?

Many *involuntary*, autonomic nervous system responses ("fight-or-flight" reflexes) are linked with new stimuli and situations by classical conditioning (Mazurski et al., 1993). Of course, this also applies to animals. One of the most common mistakes people make with pets (especially dogs) is hitting them if they do not come when called. Calling the animal then becomes a conditioned stimulus for fear and withdrawal. No wonder the pet

(a)

(b)

(c)

(d)

Figure 9–7 ◆ Hypothetical example of a CER becoming a phobia. Child approaches dog **(a)** and is frightened by it **(b)**. Fear generalizes to other household pets **(c)** and later to virtually all furry animals **(d)**.

disobeys when called on future occasions. Parents who belittle, scream at, or physically abuse their children make the same mistake.

Learned Fears Phobias (FOE-bee-ahs) are another example of emotional conditioning. A **phobia** *is a fear that persists even when no realistic danger exists.* Persons with fears of animals, water, heights, thunder, fire, bugs, elevators, or whatever, can often trace their fears to a time when they were frightened, injured, upset, or in pain while exposed to the feared object or stimulus. Reactions of this type are called **conditioned emotional responses (CERs).** A CER is *a learned emotional reaction to a previously neutral stimulus.* CERs may be broadened into phobias by stimulus generalization (Fig. 9–7 ◆). In fact, a therapy called **desensitization** is now widely used to *extinguish* fears, anxieties, and phobias. This is done by *gradually exposing the phobic person to feared stimuli* while she or he tries to remain calm and relaxed. (Desensitization is described in detail in Chapter 19.)

Undoubtedly, we acquire many of our likes, dislikes, and fears as conditioned emotional responses. For example, in one study, college students developed CERs when colored geometric shapes were paired with the theme music from the movie *Star Wars.* The colored shapes were the CS and the music, which presumably made the students feel good, was the US. When tested later, the students gave higher ratings to shapes paired with the pleasant music than to shapes associated with silence (Bierly et al., 1985). As noted before, advertisers try to achieve the same effect by pairing products with pleasant images and music. So do many students on a first date.

Vicarious, or Secondhand, Conditioning

Conditioned emotional responses can also be learned indirectly, which adds to their impact on us. For example, people will learn to respond emotionally to a signal light if they merely see another person get an electric shock when the light comes on. Even though subjects are never shocked, they develop a CER to the light just the same (Bandura & Rosenthal, 1966). Children who learn to fear thunder by watching their parents react to it have undergone similar conditioning.

Vicarious classical conditioning occurs when *we observe another person's emotional reactions to a stimulus. In doing so, we learn to respond to it emotionally ourselves.* Such "secondhand" learning probably affects feelings in many situations. For example, "horror" movies probably add to fears of snakes, caves, spiders, heights, and other terrors. If movies can affect us, we might expect the emotions of parents, friends, and relatives to have even more impact. How, for instance, does a city child learn to fear snakes and respond emotionally to mere pictures of them? Being told that "snakes are dangerous" may not explain the child's *emotional* response. More likely, the child has observed others reacting fearfully to the word *snake* or to snake images on television (Ollendick & King, 1991).

The emotional attitudes we develop toward foods, political parties, ethnic groups, escalators—whatever—are probably not only conditioned by direct experience, but vicariously as well. Parents may do well to look in a mirror if they wonder how or where a child has "picked up" a particular fear or emotional attitude.

Be sure you can answer these questions before continuing.

1. In learning, antecedents are the effects that follow the making of a response. T or F?

2. Classical conditioning, studied by the Russian physiologist ~~Pavlov~~ , is also referred to as ~~Pavlovian~~ conditioning.

3. Classical conditioning is strengthened or reinforced when the _____ follows the _____ .

   a. CS, US   **b.** US, CS   **c.** UR, CR   **d.** CS, CR

4. The informational view says that classical conditioning is based on changes in mental ~~expectancies~~ about the CS and US.

5. Training that inhibits (or weakens) a conditioned response is called ~~extinction~~ .

6. When a conditioned stimulus is used to reinforce the learning of a second conditioned stimulus, higher order conditioning has occurred. T or F?

7. Psychologists theorize that many phobias begin when a CER generalizes to other, similar situations. T or F?

8. Conditioning brought about by observing pain, joy, or fear in others is called ~~vicarious~~ conditioning.

9. Lately you have been getting a shock of static electricity every time you touch a door handle. Now there is a hesitation in your door-opening movements. Can you analyze this situation in terms of classical conditioning?

Answers:

1. F 2. Pavlov, respondent 3. b 4. expectancies 5. extinction 6. T 7. T 8. vicarious 9. Door handles have become conditioned stimuli that elicit the reflex withdrawal and muscle tensing that normally follows getting a shock. This conditioned response has also generalized to other handles.

Operant Conditioning— Can Pigeons Play Ping-Pong?

As stated earlier, in **operant conditioning** *we learn to associate responses with their consequences.* The basic principle of operant conditioning (or instrumental learning) is simple: Acts that are reinforced tend to be repeated. Pioneer learning theorist Edward L. Thorndike called this the **law of effect** (*the probability of a response is determined by the effect that it has*). According to Thorndike, *learning is strengthened each time a response is followed by a satisfying state of affairs.* Think of the earlier example of the vending machine. Because kicking the machine had the effect of producing food and money, the odds of repeating the "kicking response" increased.

5B
PsychNow!

As we have seen, classical conditioning tends to be passive and involuntary. It simply "happens to" the learner when a US closely follows a CS. In operant conditioning, the learner actively "operates on" the environment. Thus, operant conditioning refers mainly to learning *voluntary* responses. For example, waving your hand in class to get a teacher's attention is a learned operant response. It is reinforced by gaining the teacher's attention. (See Table 9–2 ■ for a further comparison of classical and operant conditioning.)

The idea that reward affects learning is certainly nothing new to parents (and other trainers of small animals). However, parents, as well as teachers, politicians, supervisors, and even you, may use reward in ways that are haphazard, inexact, or misguided. A case in point is the term *reward.* To be correct, it is better to say *reinforcer.* Why? Because rewards do not always increase responding. If you try to give licorice candy to a child as a reward for good behavior, it will work only if the child likes licorice. What is reinforcing for one person may not be for another. As a practical rule of thumb, psychologists define an **operant reinforcer** *as any event that follows a response and increases its probability* (Fig. 9–8 ◆).

Acquiring an Operant Response

Most laboratory studies of instrumental learning take place in a **conditioning chamber,** *an apparatus designed for the study of operant conditioning in animals.* This device is also sometimes called a Skinner box, after B. F. Skinner, who invented it (Fig. 9–9 ◆). A look into a typical Skinner box will clarify the process of operant conditioning.

The Adventures of Mickey Rat

A hungry rat is placed in a small cage-like chamber. The walls are bare except for a metal lever and a tray into which food pellets can be dispensed (see Fig. 9–9).

Frankly, there's not much to do in a Skinner box. This increases the chances that our subject will make the response we want to reinforce, which is pressing the bar. Hunger also ensures that the animal will be motivated to seek food and to actively *emit,* or freely give off, a variety of responses. Now let's take another look at our subject.

Table 9–2 ■ Comparison of Classical and Operant Conditioning

	Classical Conditioning	Operant Conditioning
Nature of response	Involuntary, reflex	Spontaneous, voluntary
Reinforcement	Occurs *before* response (conditioned stimulus paired with unconditioned stimulus)	Occurs *after* response (response is followed by reinforcing stimulus or event)
Role of learner	Passive (response is *elicited* by US)	Active (response is *emitted*)
Nature of learning	Neutral stimulus becomes a CS through association with a US	Probability of making a response is altered by consequences that follow it
Learned expectancy	US will follow CS	Response will have a specific effect

Further Adventures of Mickey Rat

For a while our subject walks around, grooms, sniffs at the corners, or stands on his hind legs—all typical rat behaviors. Then it happens. He places his paw on the lever to get a better view of the top of the cage. *Click!* The lever depresses, and a food pellet drops into the tray. The rat walks to the tray, eats the pellet, then grooms himself. Up and exploring the cage again, he leans on the lever. *Click!* After a trip to the food tray, he returns to the bar and sniffs it, then puts his foot on it. *Click!* Soon the rat settles into a smooth pattern of frequent bar pressing.

Notice that the rat did not acquire a new skill in this situation. He was already able to depress the bar. Reward only alters how *frequently* he presses the bar. In operant conditioning, reinforcement is used to alter the frequency of responses, or to mold them into new patterns.

Information Like classical conditioning, operant learning is based on information and expectancies. In operant conditioning, *we learn to expect that a certain response will have*

Figure 9–8 ◆ Assume that a child who is learning to talk points to her favorite doll and says either "doll," "duh," or "dat" when she wants it. Day 1 shows the number of times the child uses each word to ask for the doll (each block represents one request). At first, she uses all three words interchangeably. To hasten learning, her parents decide to give her the doll only when she names it correctly. Notice how the child's behavior shifts as operant reinforcement is applied. By Day 20, saying "doll" has become the most probable response.

Figure 9–9 ◆ The Skinner box. This simple device, invented by B. F. Skinner, allows careful study of operant conditioning. When the rat presses the bar, a pellet of food or a drop of water is automatically released. (Photographs of Skinner boxes appear in Chapters 1 & 2.)

Figure 9–10 ◆ Reinforcement and human behavior. The percentage of times that a severely disturbed child said "Please" when he wanted an object was increased dramatically by reinforcing him for making a polite request. Reinforcement produced similar improvements in saying "Thank you" and "You're welcome," and the boy applied these terms in new situations as well. (Adapted from Matson et al., 1990.)

a certain effect at certain times (Bolles, 1979). From this point of view, a reinforcer tells a person or an animal that a response was "right" and worth repeating.

A good example of how operant reinforcement can change behavior is shown in Figure 9–10 ◆. The results are from an effort to teach a severely disturbed nine-year-old child to say "Please," "Thank you," and "You're welcome." As you can see, during the initial, baseline period, the child rarely used the word *please*. Typically, he just grabbed objects he desired and became angry if he couldn't have them. However, when he was reinforced for saying "Please," he soon learned to use the word nearly every time he wanted something. When the child said "Please" he was reinforced in three ways: he received the object he requested (a crayon, for example); he was given a small food treat, such as a piece of candy, popcorn, or a grape; and he was praised for his good behavior (Matson et al., 1990).

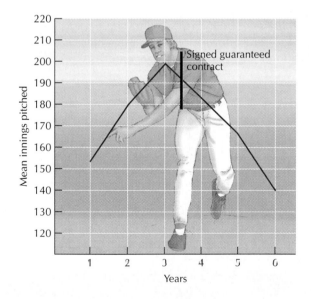

Figure 9–11 ◆ Mean number of innings pitched by major league baseball players before and after signing long-term guaranteed contracts. The performance of 38 pitchers who signed multi-year contracts for large salaries is shown. When salary was no longer contingent on good performance, there was a rapid decline in innings pitched and in the number of wins. During the same 6-year period, the performance of pitchers on 1-year contracts remained fairly steady. (Data from O'Brien et al., 1981.)

Contingent Reinforcement Operant reinforcement works best when it is **response contingent** (kon-TEN-jent). That is, *it must be given only after a desired response has occurred.* If the child in the preceding study had received reinforcers haphazardly, his behavior wouldn't have changed at all. In situations ranging from studying, to working hard on the job, contingent reinforcement also affects the *performance* of responses (Fig. 9–11 ◆). The following highlight discusses an interesting application of this principle.

Using Psychology

Life in an Operant Community

In 1948, B. F. Skinner published *Walden Two*, a utopian novel about a model community based on behavioral engineering. Would such a community work? On a small scale, the answer appears to be yes. One such operant community organized at the University of Kansas was quite successful. College students took part in an Experimental Living Project in which 30 men and women shared a large house (Miller, 1976). In this "community," work, leadership, and self-government were tied directly to behavioral principles.

Work sharing provides a good example of the project's operant approach. Basic jobs such as preparing food and cleaning were divided into approximately 100 tasks. Each task was described in terms of its expected end result. Residents performed all of the tasks themselves, and one community member checked daily to see that each job was completed. (This role was rotated.) To maintain job performance, credits were assigned for each of the tasks. At the end of the month, residents who had collected 400 credits got a sizable rent reduction.

This system was very effective in maintaining day-to-day work habits. As anyone who has shared living quarters knows, good intentions are no guarantee that the chores will get done. More importantly, residents rated the project as superior to dormitory living and similar alternatives. Most were highly satisfied with the system (Miller, 1976). The Experimental Living Project is a good example of the possibilities of applying conditioning principles to human behavior.

The Timing of Reinforcement

Operant reinforcement is more effective if it rapidly follows a correct response. For rats in a Skinner box, very little learning occurs when the delay between bar pressing and receiving food reaches 50 seconds. If the food reward is delayed more than about 90 seconds, no learning occurs (Perin, 1943) (Fig. 9–12 ◆). In general, you will be most successful if you present a reinforcer *immediately* after a response you wish to change. Thus, a child who is helpful or courteous should be praised immediately for her good behavior.

Let's say I work hard all semester in a class to get an A grade. Wouldn't the delay in reinforcement keep me from learning anything?

No, for several reasons. First, as a human you can anticipate future reward. Second, you get reinforced by quiz and test grades all through the semester. Third, a single reinforcer can often maintain a long **response chain** (*a linked series of actions that lead to reinforcement*). A simplified example of response chaining is provided by Barnabus, a rat trained by psychologists at Brown University.

The Great Barnabus

By carefully working from the last response to the first, Barnabus was trained to make an ever-longer chain of responses to obtain a single food pellet. When in top form, Barnabus was

Figure 9–12 ◆ The effect of delay of reinforcement. Notice how rapidly the learning score drops when reward is delayed. Animals learning to press a bar in a Skinner box showed no signs of learning if food reward followed a bar press by more than 100 seconds. (Perin, 1943.)

able to climb a spiral staircase, cross a narrow bridge, climb a ladder, pull a toy car with a chain, get into the car, pedal it to a second staircase, climb the staircase, wriggle through a tube, climb onto an elevator and descend to a platform, press a lever to receive a food pellet, and . . . start over! (Pierrel & Sherman, 1963.)

Many of the things we do every day involve similar response chains. The long series of events necessary to prepare a meal, for instance, is rewarded by the final eating. A violin maker may spend three months carrying out thousands of steps for the final reward of hearing the first note from an instrument. Dialing a telephone is a short but familiar response chain.

Superstitious Behavior   Reinforcers affect not only the response they follow, but also other responses that occur shortly before. This helps account for the learning of many human superstitions. If a golfer taps her club on the ground three times and then hits an unusually fine shot, the successful shot reinforces not only the correct swing but also the three taps. During operant training, animals often develop similar unnecessary responses. If a rat scratches its ear just before its first bar press, it may continue to scratch before every bar press. A bar press is all that is needed to produce food, but the animal may continue to "superstitiously" scratch its ear, as if this were necessary.

Superstitious behaviors *are repeated because they appear to produce reinforcement*, even though they are actually unnecessary. If you get the large half of a wishbone and have good fortune soon after, you may credit your luck to the wishbone. If you walk under a ladder and then break a leg, you may avoid ladders in the future. Each time you avoid a ladder and nothing bad happens, your superstitious action is reinforced. Belief in magic can also be explained along such lines. Rituals to bring rain, ward off illness, or produce abundant crops very likely earned the faith of participants by occasionally appearing to succeed. Besides, better safe than sorry!

Shaping

How is it possible to reinforce responses that rarely occur? Even in a barren Skinner box, it might be a long time before a rat accidentally pressed the bar and ate a food pellet. We might wait forever for more complicated responses to occur. For example, you would have to wait a long time for a duck to accidentally walk out of its cage, turn on a light, play a toy piano, turn off the light, and walk back to its cage. If this is what you wanted to reward, you would never get the chance.

Then how are the animals on TV and at amusement parks taught to perform complicated tricks?

The answer lies in **shaping,** *which is the gradual molding of responses to a desired pattern.* Let's look again at our subject, Mickey Rat.

Mickey Rat Shapes Up

Assume that the rat has not yet learned to press the bar. He also shows no signs of interest in the bar. Instead of waiting for the first accidental bar press, we can shape his behavior. At first, we settle for just getting him to face the bar. Any time he turns toward the bar, he is reinforced with a bit of food. Soon Mickey spends much of his time facing the bar. Next, we reinforce him every time he takes a step toward the bar. When he turns toward the bar, then walks away, nothing happens. But when he faces the bar and takes a step forward, *click!* His responses are being shaped.

By changing the rules about what makes a successful response, we can gradually train the rat to approach the bar and press it. We can reward responses that come closer and closer to the final desired pattern until it occurs. The principle of shaping, then, is that **successive approximations** (*ever-closer matches*) to the desired response are reinforced. B. F. Skinner once taught two pigeons to play Ping-Pong in this way (Fig. 9–13 ◆). Shaping applies to humans, too. Let's say that you want to study more, clean the house more often, or exercise more. Success in each case would be aided if you set a series of gradual, daily goals and rewarded yourself for each small step in the right direction (Watson & Tharp, 1996).

Operant Extinction

Would a rat's bar pressing stop if food delivery ended? Yes, but not immediately. *If a learned response is not reinforced, it gradually drops out of behavior,* a process called **operant extinction.** Just as acquiring an operant response takes time, so does extinction. For example, if a particular TV program repeatedly bores you, watching the program will probably extinguish over time.

Even after extinction seems complete, the previously reinforced response may return. If a rat is removed from a Skinner box after extinction and given a short rest, the rat will press the bar again when returned to the Skinner box.

Figure 9–13 ◆ Operant conditioning principles were used to train these pigeons to play Ping-Pong.

Similarly, a few weeks after they give up on buying state lottery tickets, many people are tempted to try again.

Does extinction take as long the second time?

If reinforcement is still withheld, a rat's bar pressing will extinguish again, usually more quickly. The brief return of an operant response after extinction is another example of *spontaneous recovery* (mentioned earlier regarding classical conditioning). Spontaneous recovery seems to be very adaptive. After a rest period, the rat responds again in a situation that produced food in the past: "Just checking to see if the rules have changed!"

Reinforcement and extinction are often combined to change behavior. For example, attention and approval from parents are very powerful reinforcers for children. As a result, parents often unknowingly reinforce **negative attention seeking** (*misbehavior used to gain attention*). Generally, children are *ignored* when they are playing quietly. Instead, they get attention as they become louder and louder, when they yell "Hey, Mom!" at the top of their lungs, when they throw tantrums, show off, or break something. Granted, the attention they get is often a scolding, but it is still attention, and it still reinforces negative attention seeking. Parents report dramatic improvements when they *ignore* their children's disruptive behavior and praise or attend to a child who is quiet or playing constructively.

Negative Reinforcement

Until now, we have stressed **positive reinforcement,** which occurs when *a pleasant or desired event follows a response.* But how else could operant learning be reinforced? The time has come to consider the "flip side" of operant conditioning: **Negative reinforcement** *occurs when making a response removes an unpleasant event.* Like positive reinforcement, negative reinforcement also increases responding. However, it does so by *ending discomfort.*

Let's say that you have a headache and take an aspirin. Your aspirin taking will be negatively reinforced if the headache stops. Likewise, a rat could be taught to press a bar to get food (positive reinforcement); or the rat could be given a continuous mild shock that is turned off by a bar press (negative reinforcement). Either way, bar pressing would increase. Why? Because it leads to a desired state of affairs (food or an end to pain). Often, positive and negative reinforcement combine. If you are uncomfortably hungry, eating a meal is reinforced by the good tasting food (positive reinforcement) and by an end to nagging hunger (negative reinforcement).

Punishment

Many people mistake negative reinforcement for punishment. However, **punishment** *is any event following a response that decreases its likelihood of occurring again.* As noted, negative reinforcement *increases* responding. The difference can be seen in a hypothetical example. Let's say you live in an apartment and your neighbor's stereo is blasting so loudly that your ears hurt. If you pound on the wall and the volume suddenly drops (negative reinforcement), future wall pounding will be more likely. But if you pound on the wall and the volume increases (punishment), or if the neighbor comes over and pounds on you (more punishment), wall pounding becomes less likely.

As another example, consider a drug addict undergoing withdrawal. Taking the drug will temporarily end painful withdrawal symptoms. Drug taking is therefore negatively reinforced. If, on the other hand, the drug made the pain worse (punishment), the addict would quickly stop taking it.

Isn't it also punishing to have privileges, money, or other positive things taken away for making a particular response?

Yes. Punishment also occurs when *a reinforcer or positive state of affairs is removed*, such as losing privileges. This second type of punishment is called **response cost** (Cautela & Kearney, 1986). Parents who "ground" their teenage children for misbehavior are applying response cost. Parking tickets and other fines are also based on response cost. For your convenience, Table 9–3 ■ summarizes four basic consequences of making a response.

Operant Reinforcers— What's Your Pleasure?

For humans, an effective operant reinforcer may be anything from an M&M candy to a pat on the back. In categorizing such reinforcers, useful distinctions can be made between *primary reinforcers, secondary reinforcers,* and *feedback.* Operant reinforcers of all types have a large impact on our lives. Let's examine them in more detail.

Primary Reinforcers

Primary reinforcers *are natural, or unlearned.* As a result, primary reinforcers are almost universally effective for a particular species. They are usually rooted in biology and produce comfort, end discomfort, or fill an immediate physical need. Food, water, and sex are obvious primary reinforcers. Every time you open the refrigerator, walk to a drinking fountain, turn up the heat, or make a trip to an ice cream parlor, your actions reflect primary reinforcement.

In addition to obvious examples, there are other less natural primary reinforcers. One of the most unusual (and powerful) is **intra-cranial stimulation (ICS).** ICS involves *direct activation of "pleasure centers" in the brain* (Olds & Fobes, 1981) (Fig. 9–14 ◆).

Wiring a Rat for Pleasure

Use of brain stimulation for reward requires the permanent implantation of tiny electrodes in specific areas of the brain. A rat "wired for pleasure" can be trained to press the bar in a Skinner box to deliver electrical stimulation to its own brain. Some rats will press the bar thousands of times per hour to obtain brain stimulation. After 15 or 20 hours of constant pressing, animals sometimes collapse from exhaustion. When they revive, they begin pressing again. If the reward circuit is not turned off, an animal will ignore food, water, and sex in favor of bar pressing.

Many natural primary reinforcers activate the same pleasure pathways in the brain that make ICS so powerful. One shudders to think what might happen if brain implants were easy and practical to do. (They are not.) Every company from *Playboy* to General Motors would have a device on the

Table 9–3 ■ Behavioral Effects of Various Consequences			
	Consequences of Making a Response	**Example**	**Effect on Response Probability**
Positive reinforcement	Positive event begins	Food given	Increase
Negative reinforcement	Negative event ends	Pain stops	Increase
Punishment	Negative event begins	Pain begins	Decrease
Punishment (response cost)	Positive event ends	Food removed	Decrease
Non-reinforcement	Nothing	—	Decrease

Figure 9–14 ◆ In the apparatus shown in **(a)**, the rat can press a bar to deliver mild electric stimulation to a "pleasure center" in the brain. Humans also have been "wired" for brain stimulation, as shown in **(b)**. However, in humans, this has been done only as an experimental way to restrain uncontrollable outbursts of violence. Implants have not been done merely to produce pleasure. (See Chapter 3 for more information on ICS.)

(a)

(b)

market, and we would have to keep a closer watch on politicians than usual!

Secondary Reinforcers

In some traditional societies, learning is still strongly tied to food, water, and other primary reinforcers. Most of us, however, respond to a much broader range of rewards and reinforcers. Money, praise, attention, approval, success, affection, grades, and similar rewards, all serve as *learned* or **secondary reinforcers.**

How does a secondary reinforcer gain its ability to promote learning?

Some secondary reinforcers are simply associated with a primary reinforcer. This can be shown in the following way.

The Push-Button Rat

A rat caged in a Skinner box has learned through operant conditioning to press the bar for food pellets. Each rewarded bar press is also followed by a brief auditory tone. After a period of training in which bar pressing, food, and the tone are associated, the rat is moved to a new cage. This cage has no bar, but it does have a button mounted on the wall. If the rat pushes the button, the tone sounds, but no food is delivered. Even though no primary reinforcement (food) is given, the rat learns to press the button to turn on the tone. Because it was associated with food, the tone has become a secondary reinforcer.

Tokens Secondary reinforcers that can be *exchanged* for primary reinforcers gain their value more directly. Printed money obviously has little or no value of its own. You can't eat it, drink it, or sleep with it. However, it can be exchanged for food, water, lodging, and other necessities.

In a series of classic experiments, chimpanzees were taught to work for *tokens*. A **token reinforcer** *is a tangible*

secondary reinforcer such as money, gold stars, poker chips, and the like. Chimps were first trained to put poker chips into a "Chimp-O-Mat" vending machine that dispensed a few grapes or raisins for each chip. Once the animals had learned to exchange tokens for food, they would learn new tasks to earn the chips. Value of the tokens was maintained by occasionally allowing the chimps to use the "Chimp-O-Mat" (Fig. 9–15 ◆) (Wolfe, 1936; Cowles, 1937).

One problem with primary reinforcers is that people and animals receiving them may quickly *satiate* (SAY-she-ate). (To be satiated means to be fully satisfied or to have reduced desire.) If, for example, you want to use candy to reinforce a retarded child for correctly naming things, the child might

Figure 9–15 ◆ Poker chips normally have little or no value for chimpanzees, but this chimp will work hard to earn them once he learns that the "Chimp-O-Mat" will dispense food in exchange for them.

only be interested while hungry. A major advantage of tokens is that they do not lose reinforcing value as quickly as primary reinforcers do. That's why tokens have been useful in work with troubled children, adolescents, and adults in special programs, as well as in educating the mentally retarded (Fig. 9–16 ◆).

Tokens are even used at times in ordinary elementary school classrooms. In each case the goal is to provide an immediate reward for learning. Typically, tokens may be exchanged for food, desired goods, special privileges, or trips to movies, amusement parks, and so forth. (See Chapter 19 for more information on the use of tokens in therapy.)

Many parents have found that tokens greatly reduce discipline problems with younger children. For example, children can earn points or gold stars during the week for good behavior. If they earn enough tokens they are allowed on Sunday to choose one item out of a "grab bag" of small treats.

Social Reinforcers   As we have noted, *learned desires for attention and approval from other people* (**social reinforcers**) often influence human behavior. This fact can be used in a classic, if somewhat mischievous, demonstration of the effects of secondary reinforcement.

Figure 9–16   ◆   Reinforcement in a token economy. This graph shows the effects of using tokens to reward socially desirable behavior in a mental hospital ward. Desirable behavior was defined as cleaning, bed making, attending therapy sessions, and so forth. Tokens earned could be exchanged for basic amenities such as meals, snacks, coffee, game-room privileges, or weekend passes. The graph shows more than 24 hours per day because it represents the total number of hours of desirable behavior performed by all patients in the ward. (Adapted from Ayllon & Azrin, 1965.)

Shaping a Teacher

For this demonstration, approximately one half (or more) of the students in a classroom must participate. First, a target behavior should be selected. This should be something like "lecturing from the right side of the room." (Keep it simple, in case your teacher is a slow learner.) Begin training in this way: Each time the instructor turns toward the right side of the room or takes a step in that direction, participating students should look *really* interested. Also, smile, ask questions, lean forward, and make eye contact. If the teacher turns to the left or takes a step in that direction, participating students should lean back, yawn, check out their split ends, close their eyes, or generally look bored. Soon, without being aware of why, the instructor should be spending most of his or her time each class period lecturing from the right side of the classroom.

This trick has been a favorite of psychology graduate students for decades. For a time, one of my professors delivered all of his lectures from the right side of the room while toying with the cords from the venetian blinds. (We added the cords the second week!) The point to remember from this example is that attention and approval can change the behavior of children, family members, friends, roommates, and co-workers. Be aware of what you are reinforcing.

Feedback

His eyes, driven and blazing, dart from side to side. His left hand twitches, dances, rises, and strikes, hitting its target again and again. At the same time, his right hand furiously spins in circular motions. Does this describe some strange neurological disorder? Actually, it depicts 10-year-old Mark as he plays his favorite video game, an animated skateboarding adventure!

How did Mark learn the complex movements needed to excel at this unusual task? After all, he was not rewarded with food or money for correct responses. The answer lies in the fact that Mark's favorite video game provides two key elements that underlie learning: *a responsive environment* and *information*.

Whenever you move one of the controls on a video game, the machine responds instantly with sounds, animated actions, and a higher or lower score. The machine's responsiveness and the information flow it provides can be very motivating if you want to win or master a game. The same principle applies to many other learning situations: If you are trying to learn to use a computer, to play a musical instrument, to cook, or to solve math problems, reinforcement comes from knowing that you succeeded at getting a desired result.

The adaptive value of information helps explain why much human learning occurs without obvious reinforcement by food, water, and the like. Humans readily learn responses that merely have a desired effect or that bring a goal closer. Let's explore this idea further.

Knowledge of Results Imagine that you are asked to throw darts at a target. Each dart must pass over a screen that prevents you from telling if you hit the target. If you threw 1,000 darts this way, we would expect little improvement in your performance, because no *feedback* is provided. **Feedback** (*information about the effect a response had*) is particularly important in human learning. Recall, for instance, that Mark's video game did not explicitly reward him for correct responses. Yet, because it provided feedback, rapid learning took place.

The value of *informational feedback* (also called **knowledge of results**, or **KR**) is one of the most useful lessons to be gained from studies of learning. Increased feedback almost always improves learning and performance (Lee & Carnahan, 1990).

How can feedback be applied?

There are many methods already in wide use. If you want to learn to play a musical instrument, to sing, to speak a second language, or to deliver a speech, tape-recorded feedback can be very helpful. In sports, videotapes are used to improve everything from tennis serves to pick-off moves in baseball. If you would like to make a similar use of feedback, it's worth knowing that taped replays are most helpful when a skilled coach directs attention to key details (Salmoni et al., 1984).

Learning Aids

As we have noted, learning is based on information. In recent years, operant learning and feedback have been combined in two interesting ways. These are programmed instruction and computer-assisted instruction.

How do these techniques make use of feedback?

Feedback is most effective when it is *frequent, immediate,* and *detailed.* **Programmed instruction** teaches students in a format that *presents information in small amounts, gives immediate practice, and provides continuous feedback* to learners. Frequent feedback keeps learners from practicing errors. It also has the advantage of letting students work at their own pace. (A small sample of programmed instruction is shown in Figure 9–17 ◆ so that you can see what the format looks like.)

In **computer-assisted instruction (CAI)**, *learning is aided by computer-presented information and exercises.* Typically, the computer displays lessons on a screen, and students type their answers. In addition to giving immediate feedback, the computer can analyze each answer. This allows use of a **branching program** *that supplies extra information and asks extra questions based on the errors made.* The newest CAI programs, which use artificial intelligence (see Chapter 11), can even give hints about why an answer was wrong and what is needed to correct it (Fath, Mitchell, & Govindaraj, 1990).

Although the final level of skill or knowledge is no higher than that gained by conventional methods, CAI can save much time and effort. People often do better with feedback from a computer because they don't feel they are being watched and evaluated by a teacher (Schneider & Shugar, 1990). This allows students to freely make mistakes and learn from them.

The simplest computerized instruction consists of self-paced **drill and practice.** In this format, *students answer questions similar to those in printed workbooks, but they instantly get correct answers.* In addition, the computer can give extra KR, such as how fast you worked, your percentage correct, or how your work compared with previous scores (Lepper, 1985).

Figure 9–17 ◆ To sample a programmed instruction format, try covering the terms on the left with a piece of paper. As you fill in the blanks, uncover one new term for each response. In this way, your correct (or incorrect) responses will be followed by immediate feedback. (Actually, this is a somewhat simplified example. In true programmed instruction, new ideas are presented along with opportunities to practice them.)

Types of Conditioning

Terms	
classical *reflex* *voluntary*	Much _____ conditioning involves involuntary _____ responses. In contrast, operant conditioning affects spontaneous, or _____ , responses.
response *CS*	Reinforcement occurs before the _____ in classical conditioning as the _____ is paired with the US.
reinforcement *after* *reinforcer*	In operant conditioning, _____ occurs _____ the response. In this case, the response is followed by a _____.
passive *elicited*	In classical conditioning, the learner is _____ because responses are _____ by the US.
learner *emits*	In operant conditioning, the _____ actively _____ responses that are affected by reinforcement.

Figure 9–18 ◆ Computer-assisted instruction. The screen on the left shows a typical drill-and-practice math problem, in which students must find the hypotenuse of a triangle. The center screen presents the same problem as an instructional game to increase interest and motivation. In the game, a child is asked to set the proper distance on a ray gun in the hovering space ship to "vaporize" an attacker. The screen on the right depicts an educational simulation. Here, students place a "probe" at various spots in a human brain. They then "stimulate," "destroy," or "restore" areas. As each area is altered, it is named on the screen, and the effects on behavior are described. This allows students to explore basic brain functions on their own.

Higher level CAI programs include *instructional games* and *educational simulations*. **Instructional games** *use stories, competition with a partner, sound effects, and game-like graphics to increase interest and motivation* (Fig. 9–18 ◆.) In **educational simulations,** *students explore an imaginary situation or "microworld" that simulates real-world problems.* By seeing the effects of their choices, students discover basic principles of physics, biology, psychology, or other subjects (Lepper, 1985).

Recently, interactive videodiscs have added a new dimension to CAI. **Interactive videodisc instruction** (*multimedia-based learning*) provides a stimulating mixture of text, still photos, motion video, and sound, as well as built-in feedback and coaching (Tannenbaum & Yukl, 1992). (Appendix B describes two CD-ROM learning programs available to supplement this text.)

Psychologists are only now beginning to fully explore the value and limits of computer-assisted instruction. Nevertheless, it seems likely that their efforts will improve not only education, but our understanding of human learning as well.

Let's pause now for a Learning Check so you can get some feedback on your mastery of the preceding ideas.

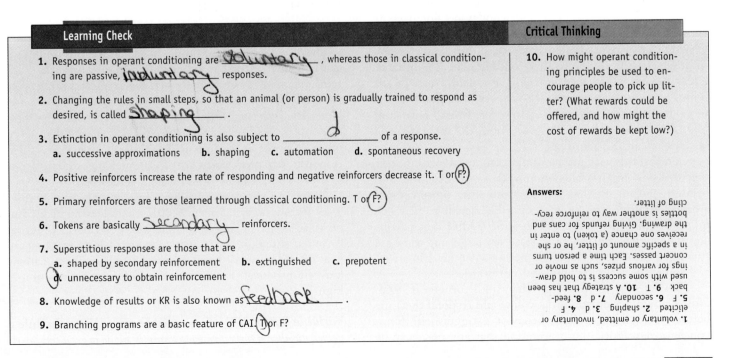

Learning Check

1. Responses in operant conditioning are _Voluntary_, whereas those in classical conditioning are passive, _involuntary_ responses.

2. Changing the rules in small steps, so that an animal (or person) is gradually trained to respond as desired, is called _Shaping_.

3. Extinction in operant conditioning is also subject to ___d___ of a response.
   a. successive approximations   b. shaping   c. automation   d. spontaneous recovery

4. Positive reinforcers increase the rate of responding and negative reinforcers decrease it. T or F?

5. Primary reinforcers are those learned through classical conditioning. T or F?

6. Tokens are basically _Secondary_ reinforcers.

7. Superstitious responses are those that are
   a. shaped by secondary reinforcement   b. extinguished   c. prepotent
   d. unnecessary to obtain reinforcement

8. Knowledge of results or KR is also known as _feedback_.

9. Branching programs are a basic feature of CAI. T or F?

Critical Thinking

10. How might operant conditioning principles be used to encourage people to pick up litter? (What rewards could be offered, and how might the cost of rewards be kept low?)

Answers:

1. voluntary or emitted, involuntary or elicited 2. shaping 3. d 4. F 5. F 6. secondary 7. d 8. feedback 9. T 10. A strategy that has been used with some success is to hold drawings for various prizes, such as movie or concert passes. Each time a person turns in a specific amount of litter, he or she receives one chance (a token) to enter in the drawing. Giving refunds for cans and bottles is another way to reinforce recycling of litter.

Partial Reinforcement— Las Vegas, a Human Skinner Box?

SERENDIPITY (*n*): to discover one thing while looking for another

B. F. Skinner, so the story goes, was studying operant conditioning when he ran short of food pellets. In order to continue, he arranged for a pellet to reward every other response. Thus began the formal study of **schedules of reinforcement** (*plans for determining which responses will be reinforced*). Until now, we have treated operant reinforcement as if it were continuous. **Continuous reinforcement** means that *a reinforcer follows every correct response*. This is fine for the lab, but it has little to do with the real world. Most of our responses are more inconsistently rewarded. In daily life, learning is usually based on **partial reinforcement**, *in which reinforcers do not follow every response.*

Partial reinforcement may be given in several patterns, each of which affects responding. In addition to these specific effects (to be explored in a moment), there is a general effect: *Responses acquired by partial reinforcement are highly resistant to extinction.* For some obscure reason, lost in the lore of psychology, this is called the **partial reinforcement effect.**

How does getting reinforced part of the time make a habit stronger?

If you have ever visited Las Vegas or a similar gambling mecca, you have probably been amused by row after row of people pulling slot machine handles. To gain insight into partial reinforcement effects, imagine that you are making your first visit to Las Vegas. You put a dollar in a slot machine and pull the handle. Ten dollars spills into the tray. Using one of your newly won dollars, you pull the handle again. Another payoff! Let's say this continues for 15 minutes. Every pull is followed by a payoff. Suddenly each pull is followed by nothing. Obviously, you would respond several times more before giving up. However, when continuous reinforcement is followed by extinction, the message soon becomes clear: No more payoffs.

Contrast this with partial reinforcement. Again, imagine that this is your first encounter with a slot machine. You begin by putting a dollar in the machine five times without a payoff. You are just about to quit, but decide to play one more. Bingo! The machine returns $20. After this, payoffs continue on a partial schedule; some are large, and some are small. All are unpredictable. Sometimes you hit 2 in a row, and sometimes 20 or 30 pulls go unrewarded.

Now let's say the payoff mechanism is turned off again. How many times do you think you would respond this time before your handle-pulling behavior extinguished? Since you have developed the expectation that any play may be

The one-armed bandit (slot machine) is a dispenser of partial reinforcement.

"the one," it will be hard to resist just one more play . . . and one more . . . and one more. Also, since partial reinforcement includes long periods of non-reward, it will be harder to discriminate between periods of reinforcement and extinction. It is no exaggeration to say that the partial reinforcement effect has left many people penniless. Even psychologists visiting Las Vegas often get "cleaned out"—and they should know better!

Schedules of Partial Reinforcement

The patterns in which partial reinforcement could be given are limitless. Let's consider the four most basic possibilities, which have some interesting effects on us.

Fixed Ratio (FR)   What would happen if a reinforcer only followed every other response? Or what if we followed every third, fourth, fifth, or other number of responses with reinforcement? Each of these patterns is a **fixed ratio (FR) schedule** (*a set number of correct responses must be made to obtain a reinforcer*). Notice that in an FR schedule the ratio of reinforcers to responses is fixed: FR-2 means that every other response is rewarded; FR-3 means that every third response is reinforced; in an FR-10 schedule, exactly 1 out of every 10 responses would yield a reinforcer.

Fixed ratio schedules produce *very high response rates* (Fig. 9–19 ◆). A hungry rat on an FR-10 schedule will quickly run off 10 responses, pause to eat, and will then run off 10 more. A similar situation occurs when factory or farm workers are paid on a piecework basis. When a fixed number of items must be produced for a set amount of pay, work output is high.

Variable Ratio (VR)   In a **variable ratio (VR) schedule** *a varied number of correct responses must be made to get a reinforcer.*

Figure 9–19 ◆ Typical response patterns for reinforcement schedules. Results such as these are obtained when a cumulative recorder is connected to a Skinner box. The device consists of a moving strip of paper and a mechanical pen that jumps upward each time a response is made. Rapid responding causes the pen to draw a steep line; a horizontal line indicates no response. Small tick marks on the lines show when a reinforcer was given.

Instead of reinforcing, for example, every fourth response (FR-4), a person or animal on a VR-4 schedule gets rewarded *on the average* every fourth response. Sometimes a response must be made 2 times to obtain a reinforcer, sometimes it's 5 times, sometimes 4, and so on. The actual number of required responses varies, but it averages out to 4 (in this example). Variable ratio schedules also produce high response rates.

VR schedules seem less predictable than FR. Does that have any effect on extinction?

Yes. Since reinforcement is less predictable, VR schedules tend to produce greater resistance to extinction than fixed ratio schedules. Playing a slot machine is an example of behavior maintained by a variable ratio schedule. Another would be a child asking for a "treat" at the supermarket. The number of times the child must ask before getting reinforced varies, so the child becomes quite persistent. Golf, tennis, and many other sports are also reinforced on a variable ratio basis: An average of perhaps one good shot in 5 or 10 may be all that's needed to create a sports fanatic.

Fixed Interval (FI) In another pattern, reinforcement is given only when a correct response is made after a fixed amount of time has passed. This time interval is measured from the last reinforced response. Responses made during the time interval are not reinforced. In a **fixed interval (FI) schedule** *the first correct response made after the time period has passed is reinforced.* Thus, a rat on an FI-30-second schedule has to wait 30 seconds after the last reinforced response before a bar press will pay off again. The rat can press the bar as often as it wants during the interval, but it will not be rewarded.

Fixed interval schedules produce *moderate response rates*. These are marked by spurts of activity mixed with periods of inactivity. Animals working on an FI schedule seem to develop a keen sense of the passage of time. For example:

Mickey Rat Takes a Break

Mickey Rat, trained on an FI-60-second schedule, has just been reinforced for a bar press. What does he do? He saunters around the cage, grooms himself, hums, whistles, reads magazines, and polishes his nails. After 50 seconds, he walks to the bar and gives it a press—just testing. After 55 seconds, he gives it two or three presses, but there's still no payoff. Fifty-eight seconds, and he settles down to rapid pressing, 59 seconds, 60 seconds, and he hits the reinforced press. After one or two more presses (unrewarded), he wanders off again for the next interval.

Is getting paid weekly an FI schedule?

Pure examples of fixed interval schedules are rare, but getting paid each week at work does come close. Notice, however, that most people do not work faster just before payday, as an FI schedule predicts. A closer parallel would be having a report due every 2 weeks for a class. Right after turning in a paper, your work would probably drop to zero for a week or more. Then, as the next due date draws near, a work frenzy occurs. Another fixed interval example is checking a Thanksgiving turkey in the oven. Typically, the frequency of checking increases as the time for the turkey to be done draws near (Schwartz & Robbins, 1995).

Variable Interval (VI) Variable interval (VI) schedules are a variation on fixed intervals. Here, reinforcement is given for *the first correct response made after a varied amount of time.* On a VI-30-second schedule, reinforcement is available after an interval that *averages* 30 seconds.

VI schedules produce *slow, steady rates* of response and tremendous resistance to extinction. When you dial a phone number and get a busy signal, reward (getting through) is on a VI schedule. You may have to wait 30 seconds or 30 minutes. If you are like most people, you will doggedly dial over and over again until you get a connection. Success in fishing is also on a VI schedule—which may explain the bulldog tenacity of many anglers (Schwartz & Robbins, 1995).

Stimulus Control—Red Light, Green Light

When you are driving, your behavior at intersections is controlled by the red or green light. In similar fashion, many of the stimuli we encounter each day act like stop or go signals that guide our behavior. This is called **stimulus control.** To state the idea more formally, *stimuli that* *consistently precede a rewarded response tend to influence when and where the response will occur.* Notice how this works with our friend Mickey Rat.

Lights Out for Mickey Rat

While learning the bar-pressing response, Mickey has been in a Skinner box illuminated by a bright light. During several training sessions, the light is alternately turned on and off. When the light is on, a bar press will produce food. When the light is off, bar pressing goes unrewarded. We soon observe that the rat presses vigorously when the light is on and ignores the bar when the light is off.

In this example, the light signals what consequences will follow if a response is made. Evidence for stimulus control could be shown by turning the food delivery *on* when the light is *off.* A well-trained animal might never discover that the rules had changed. A similar example of stimulus control would be a child learning to ask for candy when her mother is in a good mood, but not asking at other times.

Generalization Two important aspects of stimulus control are *generalization* and *discrimination.* Let's return to the example of the vending machine (from the Chapter Preview) to illustrate these concepts. First, generalization.

Is generalization the same in operant conditioning as it is in classical conditioning?

Basically, yes. **Operant stimulus generalization** *is the tendency to respond to stimuli similar to those which preceded operant reinforcement.* Thus, responses followed by reinforcement tend to be made again when similar antecedents are present. Assume, for instance, that you have been reliably rewarded for kicking one particular vending machine. Your kicking response tends to occur in the presence of that machine. It has come under stimulus control. Now let's say that there are three other machines on campus identical to the one that pays off. Because they are similar, your kicking response will very likely transfer to them. If each of these machines also pays off when kicked, your kicking response may *generalize* to other machines only mildly similar to the original. Similar generalization explains why children may temporarily call all men *daddy*—much to the embarrassment of their parents.

Discrimination Meanwhile, back at the vending machine. . . . As stated earlier, to discriminate means to respond differently to varied stimuli. Because one vending machine reinforced your kicking response, you began kicking other identical machines (generalization). Because these also paid off, you began kicking similar machines (more generalization). If kicking these new machines has no effect, the kicking response that generalized to them will extinguish because of non-reinforcement. Thus, your response to machines of a particular size and color is consistently rewarded, whereas the same response to different machines is extinguished. Through **operant stimulus discrimination** you have

Stimulus control. Operant shaping was used to teach this whale to "bow" to an audience. Fish were used as reinforcers. Notice the trainer's hand signal, which serves as a discriminative stimulus to control the performance.

learned to *differentiate between antecedent stimuli that signal reward and non-reward.* As a result, your response pattern will shift to match these **discriminative stimuli** (*stimuli that precede rewarded and non-rewarded responses*).

A discriminative stimulus that most drivers are familiar with is a police car on the freeway. This stimulus is a clear signal that a specific set of reinforcement contingencies applies. As you have probably observed, the presence of a police car brings about rapid reductions in driving speed, lane changes, tail-gating, and, in Los Angeles, gun battles.

Stimulus discrimination is also aptly illustrated by the "sniffer" dogs used at airports and border stations to locate drugs and explosives. Operant discrimination training is used to teach these dogs to recognize contraband. During training, the dogs are reinforced only for approaching containers baited with drugs or explosives.

Stimulus discrimination clearly has a tremendous impact on human behavior. Learning to recognize different automobile brands, birds, animals, wines, types of music, and even the answers on psychology tests all depends, in part, on operant discrimination learning. The following close-up provides a further look at how discriminations are formed.

A Closer Look

Stimulus Control—The Cat's Meow

The role of discriminative stimuli may be clarified by an interesting feat achieved by Jack, a psychologist friend of the author's. Jack decided to teach his cat to say its name. Here is how he proceeded. First he gave the cat a pat on the back. If the cat meowed in a way that sounded anything like its name, Jack immediately gave the cat a small amount of food. If the cat made this unusual meow at other times, it received nothing. This process was repeated many times each day.

By gradual shaping, the cat's meow was made to sound very much like its name. Also, this peculiar meow came under stimulus control: When it received a pat on the back, the cat said its name; without the pat, it remained silent or meowed normally. Psychologists symbolize a stimulus that precedes reinforced responses as an S+. Discriminative stimuli that precede unrewarded responses are symbolized as S– (Schwartz & Robbins, 1995). Thus, the accompanying diagram summarizes the cat's training.

I should add at this point that I was unaware that Jack had a new cat or that he had trained it. I went to visit him one night and met the cat on the front steps. I gave the cat a pat on the back and said, "Hi kitty, what's your name?" Imagine my surprise when the cat immediately replied, "Ralph"!

Antecedent	Response	Consequence
S+ →	"Ralph" →	Food
S– →	"Ralph" →	Nothing
S+ →	"Meow" →	Nothing

Learning Check

1. Two aspects of stimulus control are *generalization* and ~~stimulus~~ *discrimination*

2. Responding tends to occur in the presence of discriminative stimuli associated with reinforcement and tends not to occur in the presence of discriminative stimuli associated with non-reinforcement. (T) or F?

3. Stimulus generalization refers to making an operant response in the presence of stimuli similar to those that preceded reinforcement. (T) or F?

4. When a reward follows every response, it is called
   (a.) continuous reinforcement   b. fixed reinforcement   c. ratio reinforcement
   d. controlled reinforcement

5. Partial reinforcement tends to produce slower responding and reduced resistance to extinction. T or (F?)

6. The schedule of reinforcement associated with playing slot machines and other types of gambling is
   a. fixed ratio   (b.) variable ratio   c. fixed interval   d. variable interval

Critical Thinking

7. How could you use conditioning principles to teach a dog or a cat to come when called?

Answers:

1. generalization and discrimination 2. T 3. T 4. a 5. F 6. b 7. An excellent way to train a pet is to come when you call is to give a distinctive call or whistle each time you feed the animal. This makes the signal a secondary reinforcer and a discriminative stimulus for reward (food). Of course, it also helps to directly reinforce an animal with praise, petting, or food for coming when called.

Punishment—Putting the Brakes on Behavior

For better or worse, punishment is one of the more popular ways to control behavior. Spankings, reprimands, loss of privileges, fines, jail sentences, firings, failing grades, and the like are commonplace. Clearly, the story of learning is unfinished without a return to the topic of punishment. Recall that **punishment** *lowers the probability that a response will occur again.* To be most effective, punishment must be given *contingently* (only after an undesired response occurs).

Punishers, like reinforcers, are best defined by observing their effects on behavior. A **punisher** *is any consequence that reduces the frequency of a target behavior.* It is not always possible to know ahead of time what will act as a punisher for a particular individual. For example, when Jason's mother reprimanded him for throwing toys, he stopped doing it. In this instance, the reprimand was a punisher. However, Chris is starved for attention of any kind from his parents, who both work. For Chris, a reprimand, or even a spanking, might actually reinforce toy throwing. Remember, too, that a punisher can be either the onset of an unpleasant event, or the removal of a positive state of affairs (response cost).

Variables Affecting Punishment

How effective is punishment?

Many people assume that punishment stops undesired behavior. Is this always true? Psychologists have learned that the effectiveness of punishers depends greatly on their *timing, consistency,* and *intensity.* Punishment suppresses behavior best when it occurs as the response is being made,

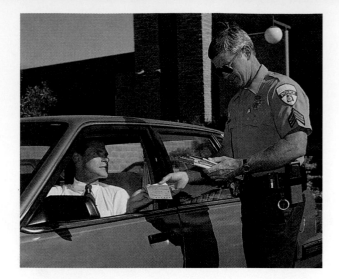

Punishers are consequences that lower the probability that a response will be made again. Receiving a traffic citation is directly punishing because the driver is delayed and reprimanded. Paying a fine and higher insurance rates add to the punishment, in the form of response cost.

or *immediately* afterward (timing), and when it is given *each time* a response occurs (consistency). Thus, you could effectively (and humanely) punish a dog that barks incessantly by spraying water on its nose each time it barks. Ten to 15 such treatments are usually enough to greatly reduce barking. This would not be the case if you applied punishment haphazardly or long after the barking stopped. If you discover that your dog dug up a tree and ate it while you were gone, punishing the dog hours later will do little good. Likewise, the commonly heard childhood threat, "Wait 'til your father comes home, then you'll be sorry," does more to make father an ogre than it does to effectively punish an undesirable response.

Severe punishment (*an intensely aversive or unpleasant stimulus*) can be extremely effective in stopping behavior. If 3-year-old Beavis sticks his finger in a light socket and gets a shock, that may be the last time he *ever* tries it. More often, however, punishment only temporarily *suppresses* a response. If the response is still reinforced, punishment may be particularly ineffective. Responses suppressed by **mild punishment** *usually reappear later*. If 7-year-old Alissa sneaks a snack from the refrigerator before dinner and is punished for it, she may pass up snacks for a short time. But since snack sneaking was also rewarded by the sneaked snack, she will probably try sneaky snacking again, sometime later (the sneaky little devil).

This fact was demonstrated experimentally by slapping rats on the paw as they were bar pressing in a Skinner box. Two groups of well-trained rats were placed on extinction. One group was punished with a slap for each bar press, while the other group was not. It might be expected that the slap would cause bar pressing to extinguish more quickly. Yet, this was not the case, as you can see in Figure 9–20 ◆. Punishment temporarily slowed responding, but it did not cause more rapid extinction. Slapping the paws of rats or

Figure 9–20 ◆ The effect of punishment on extinction. Immediately after punishment, the rate of bar pressing is suppressed, but by the end of the second day, the effects of punishment have disappeared. (After B. F. Skinner, *The Behavior of Organisms*. © 1938. D. Appleton-Century Co., Inc. Reprinted by permission of Prentice-Hall, Inc.)

children has little permanent effect on a reinforced response. It is worth stating again, however, that intense punishment may permanently suppress responding, even for actions as basic as eating. Animals severely punished while eating may never eat again (Bertsch, 1976).

Then should punishment be used to control behavior?

Using Punishment Wisely

Parents, teachers, animal trainers, and the like have three basic tools to control simple learning: (1) *Reinforcement* strengthens responses; (2) *non-reinforcement* causes responses to extinguish; (3) *punishment* suppresses responses. (Consult Figure 9–21 ◆ to refresh your memory about the different types of reinforcement and punishment.) These tools work best in combination. (Of course, behavioral methods are only one element of effective child management. The Applications section in Chapter 5 describes other techniques.)

If punishment is used at all, it should always be mild. But remember that mild punishment will be ineffective if reinforcers are still available in the situation. That's why it is best to also reward an alternate, desired response. For example, a child who has a habit of taking toys from her sister should not just be reprimanded for it. She should also be praised for cooperative play and sharing her toys with others. Punishment tells a person or an animal that a response was "wrong." However, it does not say what the "right" response is, so it *does not teach new behaviors*. If reinforcement is missing from the formula, punishment becomes less effective.

In a situation that poses immediate danger, such as when a child reaches for something hot or a dog runs into the street, mild punishment may prevent disaster. Punishment in such cases works best when it produces actions *incompatible* with the response you want to suppress. Let's say a child reaches toward a stove burner. Would a swat

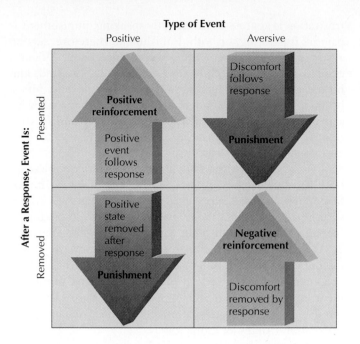

Type of Event

Positive | Aversive

After a Response, Event Is: Presented / Removed

Positive reinforcement — Positive event follows response

Punishment — Discomfort follows response

Punishment — Positive state removed after response

Negative reinforcement — Discomfort removed by response

Figure 9–21 ◆ Types of reinforcement and punishment. The impact of an event depends on whether it is presented or removed after a response is made. Each square defines one possibility: Arrows pointing upward indicate that responding is increased; downward-pointing arrows indicate that responding is decreased. (Adapted from Kazdin, 1975.)

on the bottom serve as an effective punisher? Probably so. It would be better, however, to slap the child's outstretched hand so it will be *withdrawn* from the source of danger. The next highlight provides some additional tips on using punishment.

If You Must Punish, Here's How

There are times when punishment may be necessary to manage the behavior of an animal, child, or even another adult. If you feel that you must punish, here are some tips to keep in mind.

1. *Don't use punishment at all if you can discourage misbehavior in other ways.* Make liberal use of positive reinforcement, especially praise, to encourage good behavior. Also, try extinction first: See what happens if you ignore a problem behavior; or shift attention to a desirable activity and then reinforce it with praise.

2. *Apply punishment during, or immediately after, misbehavior.* Of course, immediate punishment is not always possible. With older children and adults, you can bridge the delay by clearly stating what act you are punishing. If you cannot punish an animal *immediately*, wait for the next instance of misbehavior.

3. *Use the minimum punishment necessary to suppress misbehavior.* Often, a verbal rebuke or a scolding is enough. Avoid harsh physical punishment. (Never slap a child's face, for instance.) Taking away privileges or other positive reinforcers (response cost) is usually best for older children and adults. Frequent punishment may lose its effectiveness, and harsh or excessive punishment has serious negative side effects (discussed in a moment).

4. *Be consistent.* Be very clear about what you regard as misbehavior. Punish every time the misbehavior occurs. Don't punish for something one day and ignore it the next. If you are usually willing to give a child three chances, don't change the rule and explode without warning after a first offense. Both parents should try to punish their children for the same things and in the same way.

5. *Expect anger from a punished person.* Briefly acknowledge this anger, but be careful not to reinforce it. Be willing to admit your mistake if you wrongfully punish someone or if you punished too severely.

6. *Punish with kindness and respect.* Allow the punished person to retain self-respect. For instance, do not punish a person in front of others, if at all possible. A strong, trusting relationship tends to minimize behavior problems. Ideally, others should *want* to behave well to get your praise, not because they fear punishment.

Side Effects of Punishment

What are the drawbacks of using punishment?

The basic problem with punishment is that it is usually **aversive** (*painful or uncomfortable*). As a result, people and situations associated with punishment tend, through classical conditioning, to become feared, resented, or disliked. This association, perhaps, is why children so often choose school windows to break when other targets are available. The aversive nature of punishment makes it especially poor to use when teaching children to eat politely or in toilet training.

Escape and Avoidance A second major problem is that aversive stimuli usually encourage *escape* and *avoidance learning*. In **escape learning** *we learn to make a response in order to end an aversive stimulus.* Escape learning simply reflects the operation of negative reinforcement, as the following example shows.

> A dog is placed in a two-compartment cage called a shuttle box. If the dog is shocked while in one of the compartments, it will quickly learn to jump to the other compartment to *escape* the shock. If a buzzer is sounded 10 seconds before each shock begins, the dog will soon learn to associate the buzzer with

shock. It will then *avoid* pain by jumping *before* the shock begins. (Solomon & Wynne, 1953)

Avoidance learning appears to involve *both* classical and operant conditioning (Levis, 1989). In a shuttle box a dog first learns, through classical conditioning, to fear the buzzer. (The buzzer is a CS, which is followed by shock, a US for pain and fear.) Each time the buzzer sounds, the dog becomes fearful. But, by jumping to the "safe" compartment the dog can end the unpleasant fear it feels. Therefore, learning to jump *before* the onset of the shock is negatively reinforced by fear reduction. This is the operant part of avoidance learning.

Once avoidance is learned it is very persistent. The electric shock in a shuttle box can be turned off, yet the dog will continue to leap from the compartment each time the buzzer sounds. This fact is rather puzzling: If the buzzer is never followed by shock, why doesn't fear of the buzzer extinguish? The dog, it seems, has learned to *expect* that the buzzer will be followed by shock. If the dog leaves before the shock would normally occur, it gets no new information to change the expectancy (Schwartz & Robbins, 1995).

Escape and avoidance learning are a regular part of daily experience. For example, if you work with a loud and obnoxious person, you may at first escape from conversations with him to obtain relief. Later you may dodge him altogether. This is an example of **avoidance learning** (*making a response in order to postpone or prevent discomfort*). Each time you sidestep him, your avoidance is again reinforced by a sense of relief. In many situations involving frequent punishment, similar desires to escape and avoid are activated. For example, children who run away from punishing parents (escape) may soon learn to lie about their behavior (avoidance) or to spend as much time away from home as possible (also an avoidance response).

Aggression A third problem with punishment is that it can greatly increase *aggression*. Researchers have shown that animals consistently react to pain by attacking whomever or whatever else is around (Azrin et al., 1965). A common example of this effect is the faithful dog that nips its owner during a painful procedure at the veterinarian's office.

We also know that one of the most common responses to frustration is aggression. Generally speaking, punishment is painful, frustrating, or both. Punishment, therefore, sets up a powerful environment for learning aggression. When a child is spanked, the child may feel angry, frustrated, and hostile. What if the child then goes outside and hits a brother, sister, or a neighbor? The danger is that aggressive acts may feel good because they release anger and frustration. If so, aggression has been rewarded and will tend to occur again in other frustrating situations.

One classic study found that overly aggressive adolescent boys had been severely punished for aggression at home. Since aggression was suppressed at home, parents were often surprised to learn that their "good boys" were in trouble at school for fighting and other forms of aggression (Bandura & Walters, 1959). A more recent study of classroom discipline problems found that physical punishment, yelling, and humiliation are generally ineffective. Positive reinforcement, in the form of praise, approval, and reward, is much more likely to quell classroom disruptions, defiance, and inattention (Tulley & Chiu, 1995).

Should You Punish or Not? To summarize, the most common error in using punishment is to rely on it alone for training or discipline. The overall emotional adjustment of a child or pet disciplined mainly by reward is usually superior to one disciplined mainly by punishment. Frequent punishment makes a person or an animal unhappy, confused, anxious, aggressive, and fearful of the source of punishment. Children who are punished often by parents or teachers learn to dislike parents and teachers. They also tend to dislike and avoid activities associated with punishment (schoolwork or household chores, for instance).

Parents and teachers should be aware that using punishment can be "habit forming." When children are being noisy, messy, disrespectful, or otherwise misbehaving, the temptation to punish can be strong. The trouble is that punishment often works. When it does, a sudden end to the adult's irritation acts as a negative reinforcer. This encourages the adult to use punishment more often in the future (Alberto & Troutman, 1995). Immediate silence may be "golden," but its cost can be very high in terms of a child's emotional health.

Learning Check	Critical Thinking

1. Negative reinforcement increases responding; punishment suppresses responding. T or F?

2. Three factors that greatly influence the effects of punishment are timing, consistency, and _intensity_.

3. Mild punishment tends to only temporarily _____ a response that is also reinforced.
   a. enhance   **b.** aggravate   **c.** replace   **d.** suppress

4. Three undesired side effects of punishment are: (1) conditioning of fear and resentment, (2) encouragement of aggression, and (3) the learning of escape or _avoidance_ responses.

5. Using punishment can be "habit forming" because putting a stop to someone else's irritating behavior can ~~negatively~~ ~~reinforce~~ the person who applies the punishment.

6. Using the concept of partial reinforcement, can you explain why inconsistent punishment is especially ineffective?

Answers:

1. T 2. intensity 3. d 4. avoidance 5. negatively reinforce 6. An inconsistently punished response will continue to be reinforced on a partial schedule, which makes it even more resistant to extinction.

Cognitive Learning— Beyond Conditioning

Is all learning just a connection between stimuli and responses?

Some learning can be thought of this way. But, as we have seen, even basic conditioning has "mental" elements. As a human, you can anticipate future reward or punishment and react accordingly. (You may wonder why this doesn't seem to work when a doctor or dentist says, "This won't hurt a bit." Here's why: They lie!) There is no doubt that human learning includes a large *cognitive*, or mental, dimension. As humans, we are greatly affected by information, expectations, perceptions, mental images, and the like.

Loosely speaking, **cognitive learning** *refers to understanding, knowing, anticipating, or otherwise making use of information-rich higher mental processes.* Cognitive learning extends beyond basic conditioning into the realms of memory, thinking, problem solving, and language. Since these topics are covered in later chapters, our discussion here is limited to a first look at learning beyond conditioning.

Cognitive Maps How do you navigate around the town you live in? Is it fair to assume that you have simply learned to make a series of right and left turns to get from one point to another? It is far more likely that you have an overall mental picture of how the town is laid out. This *cognitive map* acts as a guide even when you must detour or take a new route. A **cognitive map** is an *internal representation of an area, such as a maze, city, or campus.* Even the lowly rat—not exactly a mental giant—learns *where* food is found in a maze, not just which turns to make to reach the food (Tolman et al., 1946). In a sense, cognitive maps also apply to other kinds of knowledge. For instance, it could be said that you have been developing a "map" of psychology while reading this book. This may be why students sometimes find it helpful to draw pictures or diagrams of how they envision concepts fitting together.

Latent Learning Cognitive learning is also revealed by

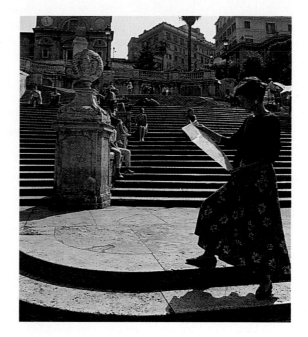

It's easy to get lost when visiting a new city if you don't have a cognitive map of the area. Printed maps help, but they may still leave you puzzled until you begin to form a mental representation of major landmarks and directions.

latent (hidden) learning. **Latent learning** *occurs without obvious reinforcement and remains hidden until reinforcement is provided.* Here's an example provided by a classic animal study: Two groups of rats are allowed to explore a maze. The animals in one group find food at the far end of the maze. Soon, they learn to rapidly make their way through the maze when released. Rats in the second group are unrewarded and show no signs of learning. But later, when the "uneducated" rats are given food, they run the maze as quickly as the rewarded group (Tolman & Honzik, 1930). Although there was no outward sign of it, the unrewarded animals had learned their way around the maze. Their learning, therefore, remained latent at first (Fig. 9–22 ◆).

How did they learn if there was no reinforcement?

Apparently, satisfying curiosity can be enough to reward learning (Harlow & Harlow, 1962). In humans, latent

Conditioning and Learning   **301**

© ED ARNO/SCIENCE 80

(a)

(b)

Figure 9-22 ◆ Latent learning. **(a)** The maze used by Tolman and Honzik to demonstrate latent learning by rats. **(b)** Results of the experiment. Notice the rapid improvement in performance that occurred when food was made available to the previously unreinforced animals. This indicates that learning had occurred, but that it remained hidden or unexpressed. (Adapted from Tolman & Honzik, 1930.)

learning is probably related to higher level abilities, such as anticipating future reward. For example, if you give an attractive classmate a ride home, you may make mental notes about how to get to his or her house, even if a date is only a remote future possibility.

Discovery Learning   Much of what is meant by cognitive learning is summarized by the word *understanding*. Each of us has, at times, learned ideas by **rote** (*repetition and memorization*). Although rote learning is efficient, many psychologists believe that learning is more lasting and flexible when people *discover* facts and principles on their

own (Lepper, 1985). In **discovery learning,** skills are gained by *insight and understanding* instead of by rote.

As long as learning occurs, what difference does it make?

Figure 9–23 ◆ illustrates the difference. Two groups of students were taught to calculate the area of a parallelogram. Some were encouraged to see that a "piece" of a parallelogram could be "moved" to create a rectangle. Later, they were better able to solve unusual problems than were students who simply memorized a rule (Wertheimer, 1959). As this suggests, discovery learning tends to produce better understanding of new problems and situations (Lepper,

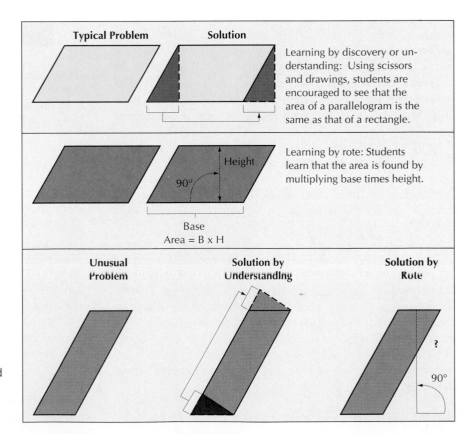

Figure 9–23 ◆ Learning by understanding and by rote. For some types of learning, understanding may be superior, although both types of learning are useful. (After Wertheimer, 1959.)

1985). Discovery learning is particularly valuable if a person has to try new strategies or discover new solutions to problems during learning (McDaniel & Schlager, 1990). In sum, it seems worthwhile to take extra steps to foster insight and deeper understanding, even if learning by discovery takes longer.

Modeling—Do as I Do, Not as I Say

The class watches intently as a skilled potter pulls a spinning ball of clay into the form of a vase. There is little doubt that many skills are learned by what Albert Bandura (1971) calls *observational learning*, or *modeling*. **Observational learning** is achieved by *watching and imitating the actions of another person or by noting the consequences of the person's actions*. In other words, modeling is any process in which information is imparted by example, before direct practice is allowed (Rosenthal & Steffek, 1991).

The value of learning by observation is obvious: Imagine trying to *tell* someone how to tie a shoe, do a dance step, crochet, or play a guitar. Bandura believes that anything that can be learned from direct experience can be learned by observation. Often, this allows a person to skip the tedious trial-and-error stage of learning.

It seems obvious that we learn by observation, but how does it occur?

Observational Learning

By observing a **model** (*someone who serves as an example*), a person may (1) learn new responses, (2) learn to carry out or avoid previously learned responses (depending on what happens to the model for doing the same thing), or (3) learn a general rule that can be applied to various situations.

For observational learning to occur, several things must take place. First, the learner must pay *attention* to the model and *remember* what was done. (A beginning auto mechanic might be interested enough to watch an entire tune-up, but unable to remember all the steps.) Next, the learner must be able to *reproduce* the modeled behavior. (Sometimes this is a matter of practice, but it may be that the learner will never be able to perform the behavior. I may admire the feats of world-class gymnasts, but with no amount of practice could I ever reproduce them.) If a model is *successful* at a task or *rewarded* for a response, the learner is more likely to imitate the behavior. In general, models who are attractive, rewarding, admired, or high in status also tend to be imitated (Bandura & Walters, 1963b). Finally, once a new response is tried, *normal reinforcement determines if it will be repeated thereafter.* (Notice the similarity here to latent learning, described earlier.)

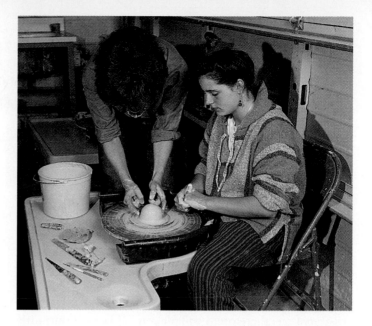

Observational learning often imparts large amounts of information that would be difficult to obtain by reading instructions or memorizing rules.

Imitating Models Modeling has a powerful effect on behavior. In a classic experiment, children watched an adult attack a large blowup "Bo-Bo the Clown" doll. Some children saw an adult sit on the doll, punch it, hit it with a hammer, and kick it around the room. Others saw a color movie of these actions. A third group saw a cartoon version of the aggression. Later, the children were frustrated (by having some attractive toys taken away from them) and then allowed to play with the Bo-Bo doll. Most imitated the attack they had seen the adult perform (Fig. 9–24 ◆). Some even added new aggressive acts of their own! Interestingly, the cartoon was only slightly less effective in encouraging aggression than either the live adult model or the filmed model (Bandura et al., 1963).

Then do children blindly imitate adults?

No. Remember that observational learning equips a person to duplicate a response, but whether it is actually imitated depends on whether the model was rewarded or punished. Nevertheless, research shows that when parents tell a child to do one thing, but model a completely different response, children tend to imitate what the parents *do*, and *not* what they *say* (Bryan & Walbek, 1970). Thus, through modeling, children learn not only attitudes, gestures, emotions, and personality traits, but fears, anxieties, and bad habits as well. For example, the children of smokers are much more likely to try smoking than children from smoke-free homes (Rowe et al., 1996).

Now, consider a typical situation. Little Shawn-Erin-Ringo-Jeremy Jones has just been interrupted at play by his younger brother, Mildew. Angry and frustrated, he screams at Mildew. This behavior interrupts his father's TV watching. Father promptly spanks little Shawn-Erin-Ringo-Jeremy, saying, "This will teach you to hit your little

Figure 9–24 ◆ A nursery school child imitates the aggressive behavior of an adult model he has just seen in a movie. (Photos courtesy of Albert Bandura.)

brother." And it will. Because of modeling effects, it is unrealistic to expect a child to "Do as I say, not as I do." The message the father has given the child is clear: "You have frustrated me; therefore, I will hit you." The next time little Shawn-Erin-Ringo-Jeremy is frustrated, it will be no surprise if he imitates his father and hits his brother.

Modeling and Television

Does television promote observational learning?

The impact of TV can be found in these figures: By the time the average person has graduated from high school, she or he will have viewed some 15,000 hours of TV, compared with only 11,000 hours spent in the classroom. In that time, such viewers will have seen some 18,000 murders and countless acts of robbery, arson, bombing, torture, and

Televised violence may promote observational learning of aggression. In addition to providing poor behavioral models, constant exposure to aggressive imagery can lower viewers' emotional sensitivity to violence.

beatings. It's true that TV programming has improved somewhat during the last decade. Overall, however, violent acts, dynamite blasts, gun battles, high-speed car wrecks, stereotypes, and sexism still prevail (Kubey & Csikszentmihaly, 1990). Children watching Saturday morning cartoons see a chilling 26 or more violent acts each hour (Pogatchnik, 1990). Teenage mutant ninja turtles, indeed!

Life after TV What effect does the North American penchant for TV watching have on behavior? To answer this question, a team of researchers located a town in northwestern Canada that did not receive TV broadcasts. Discovering that the town was about to get TV, the team seized a rare opportunity. Tannis Williams and her colleagues carefully tested residents of the town just before TV arrived and again 2 years later. This natural experiment revealed that after the tube came to town:

- Reading development among children declined (Corteen & Williams, 1986).
- Children's scores on tests of creativity dropped (Harrison & Williams, 1986).
- Children's perceptions of sex roles became more stereotyped (Kimball, 1986).
- There was a significant increase in both verbal and physical aggression (Fig. 9–25 ◆). This occurred for both boys and girls, and it applied equally to children who were high or low in aggression before they began watching TV (Joy et al., 1986).

Televised Aggression The last finding comes as no surprise. At this point, hundreds of studies, involving well over 10,000 children, have been completed. The vast majority point to the same conclusion: "If large groups of children watch a great deal of televised violence, they will be more prone to behave aggressively" (Heath, Bresolin, & Rinaldi, 1989; Joy et al., 1986; Levinger, 1986; National Institute of Mental Health, 1982). In other words, not all children will become more aggressive, but many will. Incidentally, the same conclusion applies to violent video games (Schutte et al., 1988).

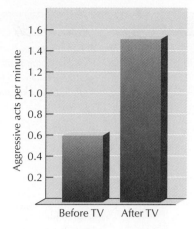

Figure 9–25 ◆ This graph shows the average number of aggressive acts per minute before and after television broadcasts were introduced into a Canadian town. The increase in aggression after television watching began was significant. Two other towns that already had television were used for comparison. Neither showed significant increases in aggression during the same time period. (Data compiled from Joy et al., 1986.)

Is it fair to say, then, that televised violence causes aggression in viewers, especially children?

Fortunately, that would be an exaggeration. Televised violence can make aggression more *likely*, but it does not invariably "cause" it to occur (Freedman, 1984; Levinger, 1986). Many other factors affect the chances that hostile thoughts will be turned into actions (Berkowitz, 1984). Among children, one such factor is the extent to which a child *identifies* with aggressive characters (Huesmann et al., 1983). That's why it is so sad to find TV *heroes* behaving aggressively, as well as villains.

A recent study investigated the effects on aggressive behavior of a popular children's TV program, *The Mighty Morphin Power Rangers*. In each episode, the "Power Rangers" "morph" into super-heroes who use karate and other violent actions to conquer monsters. The study found that after watching an episode of the Power Rangers, a group of 7-year-old children committed 7 times more aggressive acts than a control group that did not watch the program. The aggressive children hit, kicked, and karate-chopped their peers, often directly imitating the "Power Rangers" (Boyatzis, Matillo, & Nesbitt, 1995).

Youngsters who believe that aggression is an acceptable way to solve problems, who believe that TV portrayals of violence are realistic, and who identify with TV characters are most likely to copy televised aggression (Eron, 1986). In view of such findings, it is understandable that Canada, Norway, and Switzerland have restricted the amount of permissible violence on television (Levinger, 1986). Should all countries do the same?

A Look Ahead Conditioning principles are often derived from animal experiments. However, it should be apparent that the same principles apply to human behavior. Perhaps the best way to appreciate this fact is to observe how reinforcement affects your own behavior. With this in mind, the upcoming Applications section proposes a personal experiment in operant conditioning. We'll also consider steps you can take to better manage your learning at school. Don't miss this coming attraction!

TV heroes can act as powerful models for observational learning of aggression.

Learning Check

1. An internal representation of relationships is referred to as a *cognitive map* .

2. Learning that suddenly appears when a reward or incentive for performance is given is called
   a. discovery learning   **b.** latent learning   c. rote learning   d. reminiscence

3. Psychologists use the term *modeling* to describe observational learning.

4. If a model is successful, rewarded, attractive, or high in status, his or her behavior is
   a. difficult to reproduce   b. less likely to be attended to   **c.** more likely to be imitated
   d. subject to positive transfer

5. Children who observed a live adult behave aggressively became more aggressive; those who observed movie and cartoon aggression did not. T or **F?**

6. Children are most likely to imitate TV characters with whom they identify, but this applies primarily to characters who are non-violent. T or **F?**

7. Psychological research indicates that televised violence causes aggressive behavior in children. T or **F?**

Critical Thinking

8. Children who watch many aggressive programs on television tend to be more aggressive than average. Why doesn't this observation prove that televised aggression causes aggressive behavior?

Answers:
1. cognitive map 2. b 3. modeling 4. c 5. F 6. F 7. F 8. Because the observation is based on a correlation. Children who are already aggressive may choose to watch more aggressive programs, rather than being made aggressive by them. It took experimental studies to verify that televised aggression promotes aggression by viewers.

Applications
Behavioral Self-Management

This discussion could be the start of one of the most personal "Applications" in this book. There is now little doubt that self-administered reward affects behavior (Watson & Tharp, 1996). Many people have learned to successfully use reinforcement to alter or manage their own behavior. At the very least, trying self-management can make you more aware of your behavior and what controls it.

This, then, is an invitation to carry out a self-management project of your own. Would you like to increase the number of hours you spend studying each week? Would you like to exercise more, attend more classes, concentrate longer, or read more books? All these activities and many others can be improved by following the rules described here.

Self-Managed Behavior—A Rewarding Project

Managing your own behavior can be achieved by adapting the principles of operant conditioning for personal use.

1. **Choose a target behavior.** Identify the activity you want to change.

2. **Record a baseline.** Record how much time you currently spend performing the target activity, or count the number of desired or undesired responses you make each day.

3. **Establish goals.** Your goals may be stated as increases or decreases in a target behavior. Remember the principle of shaping and set realistic goals for gradual improvement on each successive week. Also, set daily goals that add up to the weekly goal.

4. **Choose reinforcers.** If you meet your daily goal, what reward will you allow yourself? Daily rewards might be watching television, eating a candy bar, socializing with friends, playing a musical instrument, or whatever you enjoy. Also establish a weekly reward. If you reach your weekly goal, what reward will you allow yourself? A movie? A dinner out? A weekend hike?

5. **Record your progress.** Keep accurate records of the amount of time spent each day on the desired activity or the number of times you make the desired response.

6. **Reward successes.** If you meet your daily goal, collect your reward. If you fall short, be honest with yourself and skip the reward. Do the same for your weekly goal.

7. **Adjust your plan as you learn more about your behavior.** Overall progress will reinforce your attempts at self-management.

Discovering what will serve as a reinforcer can sometimes be tricky. Praise, candy, or a pat on the back may be reinforcing for one person but not for another. One way out of this dilemma is to apply the **Premack principle.** The idea, advanced by David Premack (1965), is that *any frequent (or* "prepotent") response can be used to reinforce an infrequent response. Let's say you love music and listen to it frequently. In contrast, you hate to take out the trash and rarely do it. If this is the case, listening to music can be used to reinforce taking out the trash. By requiring yourself to take out the trash before turning on music, you will boost the infrequent response. Remember that anything you do frequently (watching television, talking with friends, listening to music) can serve as a reinforcer.

Here is a sample of one student's plan for getting more aerobic exercise by walking, swimming, and biking:

1. *Target behavior:* Number of hours spent exercising each week.

2. *Recorded baseline:* An average of 17 minutes per day, for a weekly total of 2 hours.

3. *Goal for the first week:* Increase exercise time to 25 minutes per day; weekly goal of 3 hours total exercise time.
   Goal for second week: Increase to 35 minutes per day and 4 hours per week.
   Goal for third week: Increase to 45 minutes per day and 5 hours per week.
   Ultimate goal: To reach and maintain 1 hour per day, 7 hours per week of aerobic exercise.

4. *Daily reward for reaching goal:* One half hour of guitar playing in the evening; no playing if the goal is not met. Weekly reward for reaching goal: going to a movie or buying a compact disc.

Self-Recording   Even if you find it difficult to give and withhold the rewards in your program, you are likely to succeed. Simply knowing that you are reaching a desired goal can be reward enough. The key to any self-management program, therefore, is **self-recording** (*keeping records of response frequencies*). The concept is demonstrated by students in a psychology course. Some students recorded their study time and graphed their daily and weekly study behavior. Even though no extra rewards were offered, these students earned better grades than others who were not required to keep records (Johnson & White, 1971).

As discussed earlier, utilizing *feedback* is one of the most direct of all approaches to changing personal behavior. Feedback can help you decrease bad habits as well as increase desirable responses. Keep track of the number of times daily that you arrive late to class, smoke a cigarette, watch an hour of TV, drink a cup of coffee, bite your fingernails, swear, or whatever you are interested in changing. A simple tally on a piece of paper will do, or you can get a small mechanical counter like those used to keep golf scores or count calories. Record keeping alone helps break patterns, and the feedback can be motivating as you begin to make progress.

Good Ways to Break Bad Habits

How can I use learning principles to break a bad habit?

By using the methods we have discussed, you can reinforce yourself for *decreasing* unwanted behaviors, such as swearing, nail biting, criticizing others, smoking, drinking coffee, excess TV watching, or any other behavior you choose to target. However, breaking bad habits may require some additional techniques. Here are four strategies to help you change bad habits.

Alternate Responses   A good strategy for change is to try to get the same reinforcement with a new response.

Example: Marta often tells jokes at the expense of others. Her friends sometimes feel hurt by her sharp-edged humor. Marta senses this and wants to change. What can she do? Usually, Marta's joke telling is reinforced by attention and approval. She could just as easily get the same reinforcement by giving other people praise or compliments. Making a change in her behavior should be easy because she will continue to receive the reinforcement she seeks.

Extinction   Try to discover what is reinforcing an unwanted response and remove, avoid, or delay the reinforcement (Ferster et al., 1962).

Example: Tiffany has developed a habit of taking longer and longer "breaks" to watch TV when she should be studying. Obviously, TV watching is reinforcing her break taking. To improve her study habits, Tiffany could delay reinforcement by studying at the library or some other location a good distance from her TV.

Response Chains   Break up response chains that precede an undesired behavior. The key idea is to scramble the chain of events that leads to an undesired response (Watson & Tharp, 1996).

Example: Almost every night Steve comes home from work, turns on the TV, and eats a whole bag of cookies or chips. He then takes a shower and changes clothes. By dinner time he has lost his appetite. Steve realizes he is substituting junk food for dinner. Steve could solve the problem by breaking the response chain that precedes dinner. For instance, he could shower immediately when he gets home or he could avoid turning on the television until after dinner.

Cues and Antecedents   Try to avoid, narrow down, or remove stimuli that elicit the bad habit.

Example: Raul wants to cut down on smoking. He has taken many smoking cues out of his surroundings by removing ashtrays, matches, and extra cigarettes from his house, car, and office. Raul should try narrowing antecedent stimuli even more. He could begin by smoking only in the lounge at work, never in his office or in his car. He could then limit his smoking to home. Then to only one room at home. Then to one chair at home. If he succeeds in getting this far, he may want to limit his smoking to only one unpleasant place, such as a bathroom, basement, or garage (Goldiamond, 1971).

Contracting

If you try the techniques described here and have difficulty sticking with them, you may want to try *behavioral contracting*. In a **behavioral contract,** *you state a specific problem behavior you want to control, or a goal you want to achieve. Also state the rewards you will receive, privileges you will forfeit, or punishments you must accept.* The contract should be typed and signed by you and a person you trust.

A behavioral contract can be quite motivating, especially when mild punishment is part of the agreement. Here's an example: A student working on his Ph.D. had completed all requirements but his dissertation, yet for 2 years he had not written a single page. A contract was drawn up in which he agreed to meet weekly deadlines on the number of pages he would complete. To make sure he would meet the deadlines, he wrote postdated checks. These were to be forfeited if he failed to reach his weekly goal. The checks were made out to organizations he despised (the Ku Klux Klan and American Nazi Party). From the time he signed the contract until he finished his degree, the student's work output was greatly improved (Nurnberger and Zimmerman, 1970).

Effective learning at school poses a special set of challenges. The next section describes some additional steps you can take to increase your chances of success.

Self-Regulated Learning—Academic All-Stars

Think for a moment about a topic that you are highly interested in, such as music, sports, fashion, automobiles, cooking, politics, or movies. Whatever the topic may be, you have probably learned a large amount of information about it—painlessly. How could you make your college work more like such voluntary learning? An approach known as *self-regulated learning* might be a good start. **Self-regulated learning** *is active, self-guided learning.* The strategies described here can be used to change passive studying into more active, goal-oriented learning (Zimmerman, 1996).

1. *Set specific, objective learning goals.* Try to begin each learning session with specific goals in mind. What knowledge or skills are you trying to master? What do you hope to accomplish? (Schunk, 1990)

2. *Plan a learning strategy.* How will you accomplish your goals? Make daily, weekly, and monthly plans for learning. Then put them into action.

3. *Be your own teacher.* Effective learners silently give themselves guidance and ask themselves questions. For example, when you are reading, you might ask yourself at the end of each paragraph, "What is the main idea here? What do I remember? What don't I understand? What do I need to review? What should I do next?"

4. *Monitor your progress.* Self-regulated learning depends on feedback. Exceptional learners keep records of their progress toward learning goals (pages read, hours of studying, assignments completed, and so forth). They quiz themselves, use study guides, and find other ways to check their understanding while learning.

5. *Use self-reinforcement.* When you meet your daily, weekly, or monthly performance standards, reward your efforts in some way. Be aware that self-praise also rewards learning. Being able to say "Hey, I did it!," or "Good work!" and know that you deserve it can be very reinforcing. In the long run, success, feelings of accomplishment, and personal satisfaction provide the real payoffs for self-regulated learning.

6. *Evaluate your progress and goals.* It is a good idea to frequently evaluate your performance records and goals. Are there specific areas of your work that need improvement? If you are not making good progress toward long-range goals, do you need to revise your short-term targets?

7. *Take corrective action.* If you fall short of your goals you may need to adjust how you budget your time. You may also need to change your learning environment, to deal with distractions such as watching TV, daydreaming, talking to friends, or testing the structural integrity of the walls with your stereo system.

If you discover that you lack necessary knowledge or skills, ask for help, take advantage of tutoring programs, or look for sources of information beyond your courses and textbooks. Knowing how to regulate and control learning can be a key to life-long enrichment and personal empowerment.

Getting Help

Attempting to manage or alter your own behavior may be more difficult than it sounds. If you feel you need more information, consult either of the books listed below. You will also find helpful advice in the Applications section of Chapter 19. If you do try a self-modification project or self-regulated learning, but find it impossible to reach your goals, be aware that professional advice is available.

Where to Obtain More Information:

Watson, D. L. and Tharp, R. G. *Self-directed behavior.* Pacific Grove, CA: Brooks/Cole, 1996.

Williams, R. L. and Long, J. D. *Toward a self-managed life style.* Boston, MA: Houghton Mifflin, 1991.

Learning Check

1. After a target behavior has been selected for reinforcement, it's a good idea to record a baseline so you can set realistic goals for change. T or F?

2. Self-recording, even without the use of extra rewards, can bring about desired changes in target behaviors. T or F?

3. The Premack principle states that behavioral contracting can be used to reinforce changes in behavior. T or F?

4. A self-management plan should make use of the principle of shaping by setting a graduated series of goals. T or F?

5. A key aspect of self-_____ learning is feedback, which means your should find ways to _____ your progress.

6. Self-instruction refers to the process of comparing short-term performance to long-term goals. T or F?

Critical Thinking

7. How does setting daily goals in a behavioral self-management program help maximize the effects of reinforcement?

Answers:

1. T 2. T 3. F 4. T 5. regulated, monitor 6. F 7. Daily performance goals and rewards reduce the delay of reinforcement, which maximizes its impact.

Exploration

Biological Constraints on Learning—Snakes, Spiders, and the Reluctant Raccoon

The weaverbird is a curious creature that ties a special grass knot to hold its nest together. How does it learn to make the knot? It doesn't! Weaverbirds raised in total isolation for several generations still tie the knot the first time they build a nest.

Knot tying in the weaverbird is a **fixed action pattern (FAP).** A FAP is *an instinctual chain of movements found in almost all members of a species.* Like other **innate** (*inborn*) **behaviors,** fixed action patterns help animals meet major needs in their lives (picture a cat's face-washing routine, for instance). More complicated behaviors, like the maternal instinct in lower animals, combine both fixed action patterns and various reflexes.

Do humans have instincts?

Humans do not have instincts as most psychologists define them. To qualify as instinctual, a behavior must be innate, complex, and "species specific." **Species-specific behaviors** are those that occur *with little variation in almost all members of a species.* Species-specific behaviors appear to be "wired into" the nervous system. Other than reflexes, no human behaviors are so rigidly programmed. However, that doesn't mean that human learning isn't affected by innate behavior.

All species, including humans, engage in a large number of **species-typical behaviors** (*actions that are typical of a species, but not automatic*). For example, pigeons typically peck at things when they are hungry. If you want to train a pigeon to peck a button to receive food, the pigeon will learn quickly. Likewise, if you want to teach a pigeon to flap its wings to escape an electric shock, learning will be rapid. But, just try to teach a pigeon to flap its wings to receive food or to peck a button to turn off a shock to its feet. In both cases little or no learning will take place.

Such observations suggest that there are **biological constraints,** *or limits to learning*—especially among animals. Some associations between stimuli and responses or between responses and consequences are easily learned. Others can be acquired only with great difficulty. For example, many people find it very difficult to do the following: Move the tip of your right foot in a *clockwise* circle on the floor; at the same time, hold your right hand out at waist level and move it in a *counterclockwise* circle, parallel to the floor. Even for a substantial reward, you might find it hard to learn these biologically atypical movements. Perhaps we appreciate gifted musicians and athletes, in part, because they succeed at learning responses that are biologically constrained.

Biological constraints affect both classical conditioning and operant conditioning, as shown by the examples that follow.

Conditioned Fears

Through classical conditioning, it is possible to learn to fear or dislike just about anything. Is it possible, however, that some fears are easier to learn than others (Fig. 9–26 ◆)? Martin Seligman's (1972b) **prepared fear theory** holds that it is. Seligman believes that we are *prepared by evolution to readily develop fears to certain stimuli,* such as snakes and spiders. Other common objects are more likely to cause pain or harm (a hammer, electric fan, light socket, or skis, for example). Even so, phobias are less likely to develop for such objects than for spiders or snakes. Seligman also believes that our readiness to learn such fears makes them highly resistant to extinction.

Why should fears of "crawly things" be easier to acquire? According to Seligman's theory, such stimuli posed dangers earlier in human history. Through natural selection, they have become highly effective conditioning stimuli. Experiments in which fear was conditioned to images of spiders, snakes, neutral shapes, and electrical plugs offer some support for Seligman's theory (Hugdahl & Karker, 1981). Maybe with further evolution, humans will develop proper fears of light sockets and skis, too!

The Reluctant Raccoon

B. F. Skinner's success in shaping pigeons to play Ping-Pong was aided by the fact that pigeons naturally peck objects. At one time, psychologists assumed that almost any voluntary response could be taught by operant conditioning. However, it has become clear that operant responses are also subject to biological constraints. For example, two noted psychologists, Keller and Marion Breland, went into business training animals for television shows, zoo displays, and amusement parks. Along with their successes came some revealing failures (Bailey & Bailey, 1993).

In one instance, the Brelands tried to condition a raccoon to put coins in a piggy bank for an advertisement. Instead, the raccoon repeatedly rubbed the coins together in a miserly looking fashion (Breland & Breland, 1961). No amount of reinforcement would change this behavior. The Brelands ran into similar snags with other animals. In each case an innate behavior pattern hindered learning. They called this problem **in-stinctive drift:** *Learned responses tend to "drift" toward innate ones.* The "miserly" behavior of the raccoon was simply an innate food-washing response. In view of such observations, it is wise to remember that the laws of learning operate within a framework of biological limits and possibilities.

Think about It

An advantage of biologically programmed behavior is that it prepares animals and humans to survive in their natural environments. A disadvantage is that evolution is slow. Natural selection prepares a species only for a future which resembles the biological past (Skinner, 1990).

Under normal circumstances, animals are superbly adapted to their surroundings. But throw them a curve by changing the environment in unexpected ways and their behavior may suddenly look very "stupid." For example, if a spider begins spinning a cocoon and its silk glands are removed, it will continue to make all 6400 spinning movements to complete the job. Then it will lay eggs in the non-existent cocoon. We are indeed fortunate that an overriding feature that emerged in human evolution is our capacity to learn.

Figure 9–26 ◆ Which of these stimuli do you think would make a better conditioned stimulus for learned fear? Why did you choose as you did? Fear-relevant stimuli are much more effective conditioned stimuli for learned fears (Ohman & Soares, 1993).

Learning Check	Critical Thinking

Learning Check

1. An instinctual chain of responses found in nearly all members of a species is called a _____ _____ _____ .

2. Biological constraints on learning reflect underlying potentials and limitations imposed by prior conditioning. T or F?

3. A child rapidly learned to fear a neighbor's dog that knocked her down, growled, and showed its teeth. Yet, the same child seems to have no fear of the cars passing by her house. This difference may be explained by _____ _____ theory.

4. Instinctive drift can be said to have occurred any time an unlearned stimulus triggers a reflex. T or F?

Critical Thinking

5. Biologically based patterns of behavior evolve very slowly. Changes based on learning occur very quickly. Can you identify a dimension of human behavior that helps bridge this gap?

Answers:

1. fixed action pattern 2. F 3. prepared fear 4. F 5. B. F. Skinner argued that cultures evolve far more quickly than organisms do. Cultures, therefore, help humans survive and adapt by passing on time-tested behavior patterns.

Chapter Summary

What is learning?

◆ Learning is a relatively permanent change in behavior due to experience. Learning resulting from conditioning depends on **reinforcement.** Reinforcement increases the probability that a particular response will occur.

◆ **Classical,** or **respondent,** conditioning and **instrumental,** or **operant,** conditioning are two basic types of learning.

◆ In classical conditioning, a previously neutral stimulus begins to elicit a response through **association** with another stimulus.

◆ In operant conditioning, the frequency and pattern of voluntary responses are altered by their **consequences.**

How does classical conditioning occur?

◆ Classical conditioning, studied by **Pavlov,** occurs when a **neutral stimulus** (NS) is associated with an **unconditioned stimulus** (US).

◆ The US causes a reflex called the **unconditioned response** (UR). If the NS is consistently paired with the US, it becomes a **conditioned stimulus** (CS) capable of producing a response by itself. This response is a **conditioned** (learned) **response** (CR).

◆ When the conditioned stimulus is followed by the unconditioned stimulus, conditioning is **reinforced** (strengthened).

◆ From an **informational view,** conditioning creates **expectancies,** which alter response patterns. In classical conditioning, the CS creates an expectancy that the US will follow.

◆ **Higher order** conditioning occurs when a well-learned conditioned stimulus is used as if it were an unconditioned stimulus, bringing about further learning.

◆ When the CS is repeatedly presented alone, conditioning is **extinguished** (weakened or inhibited). After extinction seems to be complete, a rest period may lead to the temporary reappearance of a conditioned response. This is called **spontaneous recovery.**

◆ Through **stimulus generalization,** stimuli similar to the conditioned stimulus will also produce a response. Generalization gives way to **stimulus discrimination** when an organism learns to respond to one stimulus, but not to similar stimuli.

Does conditioning affect emotions?

◆ Conditioning applies to visceral or emotional responses as well as simple reflexes. As a result, **conditioned emotional responses** (CERs) also occur.

◆ Irrational fears called **phobias** may be CERs. Conditioning of emotional responses can occur **vicariously** (secondhand) as well as directly.

How does operant conditioning occur?

◆ Operant conditioning occurs when a voluntary action is followed by a **reinforcer.** Reinforcement in operant conditioning increases the frequency or probability of a response. This result is based on the **law of effect.**

◆ Complex operant responses can be taught by reinforcing **successive approximations** to a final desired response.

This is called **shaping.** It is particularly useful in training animals.

♦ If an operant response is not reinforced, it may **extinguish** (disappear). But after extinction seems complete, it may temporarily reappear (**spontaneous recovery**).

Are there different kinds of operant reinforcement?

♦ In **positive reinforcement,** reward or a pleasant event follows a response. In **negative reinforcement,** a response that ends discomfort becomes more likely.

♦ **Primary reinforcers** are "natural," physiologically based rewards. **Intra-cranial stimulation** of "pleasure centers" in the brain can also serve as a primary reinforcer.

♦ **Secondary reinforcers** are learned. They typically gain their reinforcing value by direct association with primary reinforcers or because they can be exchanged for primary reinforcers. **Tokens** and money gain their reinforcing value in this way.

♦ **Feedback,** or **knowledge of results,** aids learning and improves performance. It is most effective when it is **immediate, detailed,** and **frequent.**

♦ **Programmed instruction** breaks learning into a series of small steps and provides immediate feedback. **Computer-assisted instruction (CAI)** does the same, but has the added advantage of providing alternate exercises and information when needed. Four variations of CAI are **drill and practice, instructional games, educational simulations,** and **interactive videodisc instruction.**

How are we influenced by patterns of reward?

♦ **Delay** of reinforcement greatly reduces its effectiveness, but long **chains** of responses may be built up so that a single reinforcer maintains many responses.

♦ **Superstitious behaviors** often become part of response chains because they *appear* to be associated with reinforcement.

♦ Reward or reinforcement may be given **continuously** (after every response), or on a **schedule of partial reinforcement.** Partial reinforcement produces greater resistance to extinction.

♦ The four most basic schedules of reinforcement are **fixed ratio, variable ratio, fixed interval,** and **variable interval.** Each produces a distinct pattern of responding.

♦ Stimuli that precede a reinforced response tend to control the response on future occasions (**stimulus control**). Two aspects of stimulus control are **generalization** and **discrimination.**

♦ In generalization, an operant response tends to occur when stimuli similar to those preceding reinforcement are present.

♦ In discrimination, responses are given in the presence of **discriminative stimuli** associated with reinforcement **(S+)** and withheld in the presence of stimuli associated with non-reinforcement **(S−).**

What does punishment do to behavior?

♦ Punishment decreases responding. Punishment occurs when a response is followed by the onset of an aversive event or by the removal of a positive event (**response cost**).

♦ Punishment is most effective when it is **immediate, consistent,** and **intense. Mild punishment** tends only to temporarily suppress responses that are also reinforced or were acquired by reinforcement.

♦ The undesirable side effects of punishment include the **conditioning of fear** to punishing agents and situations associated with punishment; the learning of **escape** and **avoidance responses;** and the encouragement of **aggression.**

What is cognitive learning?

♦ Cognitive learning involves higher mental processes, such as understanding, knowing, or anticipating. Even in relatively simple learning situations, animals and people seem to form **cognitive maps** (internal representations of relationships).

♦ In **latent learning,** learning remains hidden or unseen until a reward or incentive for performance is offered.

♦ **Discovery learning** emphasizes insight and understanding, in contrast to **rote learning.**

Does learning occur by imitation?

♦ Much human learning is achieved through observation, or modeling. **Observational learning** is influenced by the personal characteristics of the **model** and the success or failure of the model's behavior. Studies have shown that aggression is readily learned and released by modeling.

♦ Television characters can act as powerful models for observational learning. Televised violence increases the likelihood of aggression by viewers.

How does conditioning apply to practical problems?

♦ Operant principles can be readily applied to manage behavior in everyday settings. When managing one's own behavior, **self-reinforcement, self-recording, feedback,** and **behavioral contracting** are all helpful.

♦ Four strategies that can help change bad habits are reinforcing alternate responses, promoting extinction, breaking response chains, and avoiding antecedent cues

♦ In school, **self-regulated learners** typically do all of the following: They set learning goals, plan learning strategies, use self-instruction, monitor their progress, evaluate themselves, reinforce successes, and take corrective action when required.

How does biology influence learning?

♦ Many animals are born with **innate** behavior patterns far more complex than **reflexes.** These are organized into **fixed action patterns** (FAPs), which are stereotyped, **species-specific** behaviors.

◆ Learning in animals is limited at times by various **biological constraints** and **species-typical** behaviors.

◆ According to **prepared fear theory,** some stimuli are especially effective conditioned stimuli.

◆ Many responses are subject to **instinctive drift** in operant conditioning. Human learning is subtly influenced by many such biological potentials and limits.

10

Memory

Preview

"What the Hell's Going on Here?"

It's February, and Steven Kubacki is cross-country skiing on the ice of Lake Michigan. He stops for a moment, pausing to enjoy the winter solitude. It's cold; colder in fact than he had realized. Steven decides to turn back. In a few minutes comes a new realization: He is lost. Wandering on the ice, he grows numb and very, very tired.

Put yourself in Steven Kubacki's shoes, and you will appreciate the shock of what happened next. Steven clearly recalls wandering lost and alone on the ice. Immediately after that, he remembers waking up in a field. But as he looked around, Steven knew something was wrong. It was spring! The backpack beside him contained running shoes, swimming goggles, and a pair of glasses—all unfamiliar. As he looked at his clothing—also unfamiliar—Steven thought to himself, "What the hell's going on here?" Fourteen months had passed since he left to go skiing (Loftus, 1980). How did he get to the field? Where did the strange gear come from? Steven couldn't say. He had lost over a year of his life to total amnesia.

As Steven Kubacki's amnesia vividly shows, life without memory would be meaningless. Imagine the terror and confusion of having all of your memories wiped out. You would have no identity, no knowledge, no life history, no recognition of friends or family. Your past would be a total blank. In a very real sense, we are our memories.

This chapter discusses memory and forgetting. By reading it you'll almost certainly discover ways to improve your memory.

Chapter Survey

Theme: Memory is not like a tape recorder or a video camera: Memories change as they are stored and retrieved.

Key Questions:

Is there more than one type of memory?

Key Topics to Watch for:

Sensory memory
Short-term memory
Long-term memory

What are the features of each type of memory?	Characteristics of short- and long-term memories

Is there more than one type of long-term memory?	Declarative memory
	Procedural memory

How is memory measured?	Recall, recognition, and relearning
	Implicit memory and priming

What are "photographic" memories?	Eidetic imagery
	Exceptional memory

What causes forgetting?	The curve of forgetting
	Theories of forgetting

How accurate are everyday memories?	Repression and suppression

What happens in the brain when memories are formed?	Engrams and memory consolidation

How can memory be improved?	Strategies for enhancing memory
	Mnemonic techniques

What is the "recovered-memory" debate?	Repressed memories of childhood sexual abuse

Stages of Memory—Do You Have a Mind Like a Steel Trap? Or a Sieve?

"**A** dusty storehouse of facts." That's how many people think of memory. In reality, **memory** is an *active system that receives, stores, organizes, alters, and recovers information* (Baddeley, 1990, 1996). In some ways memory acts like a computer (Fig. 10–1 ◆). Incoming information is first **encoded,** *or changed into a usable form.* This step is like typing data into a computer. Next, information is **stored,** *or held in the system.* (As we will see in a moment, human memory can be pictured as three separate storage systems.) Finally, memories must be **retrieved,** *or taken out of storage,* to be useful. If you're going to remember all of the 9,856 new terms that will appear on your next psychology exam, you must successfully encode, store, and retrieve them.

What are the three separate memory systems just mentioned?

Psychologists have identified three stages of memory. To be stored for a long time, information must pass through all three (Fig. 10–2 ◆).

Sensory Memory

Let's say a friend asks you to pick up several things at a market. How do you remember them? Incoming information first enters **sensory memory,** *which holds an exact copy of*

Figure 10–1 ◆ In some ways, a computer acts like a mechanical memory system. Both systems process information, and both allow encoding, storage, and retrieval of data.

what is seen or heard, for a few seconds or less. For instance, look at an object and then close your eyes. An **icon** (EYE-kon), or fleeting *mental image,* will persist for about one-half second. Without sensory memory, a movie would look like a flickering series of still pictures. Similarly, information you hear is held in sensory memory as an *echo* for up to 2 seconds (Schweickert, 1993). (An **echo** *is a brief continuation of activity*

Figure 10–2 ◆ Remembering is thought to involve at least three steps. Incoming information is first held for a second or two by sensory memory. Information selected by attention is then transferred to temporary storage in short-term memory. If new information is not rapidly encoded, or rehearsed, it is forgotten. If it is transferred to long-term memory, it becomes relatively permanent, although retrieving it may be a problem. The preceding is a useful, but highly simplified, *model* of memory; it may not be literally true of what happens in the brain (Eysenck & Keane, 1995).

in the auditory system.)

Let's say your attention wanders as your friend names the last item on her shopping list. Without thinking you ask, "What did you say?" But before she can answer, you realize you already know what the last item is. This ability to mentally "play back" what someone else just said is based on echoic memory (Eysenck & Keane, 1995).

In general, sensory memory holds information just long enough to transfer it to the second memory system.

Short-Term Memory

Not everything we see or hear is kept in memory. A radio is playing in the background as your friend reads her shopping list. Do you remember what the announcer says too? Probably not, because **selective attention** (*focusing on a selected portion of sensory input*) controls what information moves on to *short-term memory*. **Short-term memory (STM)** *holds small amounts of information for relatively brief periods*. By paying attention to your friend, you will place the shopping list in short-term memory (while you ignore the voice on the radio saying, "Buy Burpo Butter").

How are short-term memories encoded?

Short-term memories can be stored as images. But more often they are stored **phonetically** (*by sound*), especially in recalling words and letters (Anderson, 1995). If you are introduced to Tim at a party and you forget his name, you are more likely to call him by a name that *sounds like* Tim (Jim, Kim, or Slim, for instance) than a name that sounds different, such as Bob or Mike. Your friend with the shopping list may be lucky if you don't bring home peas instead of cheese and soap instead of soup!

Short-term memory acts as a *temporary* storehouse for *small amounts* of information. Unless the information is important, it is quickly "dumped" from STM and forever lost. Short-term memory prevents our minds from collecting useless names, dates, telephone numbers, and other trivia. At the same time, it provides an area of **working memory** *where*

we do much of our thinking. Dialing a phone number, doing mental arithmetic, remembering a shopping list, and the like, all rely on STM.

As you may have noticed when dialing a telephone, STM is very sensitive to *interruption*, or *interference*. You've probably had this happen with STM: You look up a number and walk to the phone repeating it to yourself. You dial the number and get a busy signal. Returning a few minutes later, you find that you must look up the number again. This time as you are about to dial, someone asks you a question. You answer, turn to the phone, and find that you have forgotten the number. Notice again that only a small amount of information can be processed in working memory. It is very difficult to carry out more than one task at a time in STM (Anderson, Reder, & Lebiere, 1996).

If short-term memory is brief, easily interrupted, and limited in "size," how do we remember for greater lengths of time?

Long-Term Memory

Information that is important or *meaningful* is transferred to the third memory system, called *long-term memory*. In contrast to STM, **long-term memory (LTM)** *acts as a permanent storehouse for meaningful information*. LTM contains everything you know about the world—from aardvark to zucchini, math to Monopoly, facts to fantasy. And yet, there appears to be no danger of running out of room. LTM has a nearly limitless storage capacity. In fact, the more you know, the easier it becomes to add new information to memory. This is the reverse of what we would expect if LTM could be "filled up" (Eysenck & Keane, 1995). It is also one of many powerful reasons for getting an education.

Are long-term memories also encoded as sounds?

No. Information in LTM is stored on the basis of *meaning* and importance, not by sound. If you make an error in LTM, it will probably be related to meaning. For example, if you are trying to recall the word *barn* from a memorized list, you are more likely to mistakenly say *shed* or *farm* than *born*.

When new information enters STM, it is related to

knowledge stored in LTM. This gives the new information meaning and makes it easier to remember. As an example, try to memorize this story:

> With hocked gems financing him, our hero bravely defied all scornful laughter. "Your eyes deceive," he had said, "An egg, not a table, correctly typifies this unexplored planet." Now three sturdy sisters sought proof. Forging along, days became weeks as many doubters spread fearful rumors about the edge. At last from nowhere welcome winged creatures appeared, signifying momentous success. (Adapted from Dooling & Lachman, 1971)

This odd story emphasizes the impact that meaning has on memory. People given the title of the story were able to remember it far better than those not given a title. See if the title helps you as much as it did them. The title is "Columbus Discovers America."

Dual Memory Most of our daily memory chores are handled by STM and LTM. To summarize their connection, picture short-term memory as a small desk at the front of a huge warehouse full of filing cabinets (LTM). As information enters the warehouse, it is first placed on the desk. Since the desk is small, it must be quickly cleared off to make room for new information. Some items are simply tossed away because they are unimportant. Meaningful or important information is placed in the permanent files (long-term memory).

When we want to use knowledge from LTM to answer a question, the information is returned to STM. Or, in our analogy, a folder is taken out of the files (LTM) and moved to the desk (STM), where it can be used. Computer users may prefer to think of STM as being like RAM and LTM as being like a hard disk. However, in the human brain it is unlikely that short- and long-term memories are simply stored at different locations. STM and LTM are more likely different stages in the storage of information (Best, 1995).

Now that you have a general picture of STM and LTM it is time to explore both in more detail. The discussions that follow should add to your understanding.

Short-Term Memory—Do You Know the Magic Number?

How much information can be held in short-term memory?

For an answer, read the following numbers once. Then close the book and write as many as you can in the correct order.

> 8 5 1 7 4 9 3

This is called the **digit-span test.** It is a *measure of attention and short-term memory.* If you were able to correctly repeat 7 digits, you have an average short-term memory. Now try to memorize the following list, reading it only once.

> 7 1 8 3 5 4 2 9 1 6 3 4

This series was probably beyond your short-term memory capacity. Psychologist George Miller found that short-term memory is limited to what he calls the "magic number" 7 **information bits** (Miller, 1956). A bit is a *single meaningful "piece" of information*—such as a digit. It is as if short-term memory has 7 "slots" or "bins" into which separate items can be placed. Actually, 7 bits is the average *upper limit* for short-term memory. For some types of information, 5 bits is more typical (Barsalou, 1992).

When all of the "slots" in STM are filled, there is no room for new information. Picture how this works at a party: Let's say your hostess begins introducing everyone who is there, "Ted, Barbara, Donna, Roseanna, Wayne, Shawn, Linda...." "Stop," you think to yourself. But she continues, "Eddie, Jay, Gordon, Frank, Marietta, Dan, Patty, Glen,

Ricky." The hostess leaves, satisfied that you have met everyone. And you spend the evening talking with Ted, Barbara, and Ricky, the only people whose names you remember!

Recoding

Before we continue, try your short-term memory again, this time on letters. Read the following letters once, then look away and try to write them in the proper order.

> T V I   B M U S   N Y   M C A

Notice that there are 12 letters, or "bits" of information. This should be beyond the 7-item limit of STM. However, since the letters are presented as four groups, or *chunks* of information, many students are able to memorize them. **Information chunks** *are made up of bits grouped into larger units.*

How does chunking help?

Chunking **recodes** (*modifies or reorganizes*) information into units that are already in LTM. For example, you may have noticed that NY is the abbreviation for New York. If so, the two bits N and Y became one chunk. In an experiment that used lists like this one, people remembered best when the letters were read as familiar meaningful chunks: TV, IBM, USN, YMCA (Bower & Springston, 1970). If you recoded the letters this way, you undoubtedly remembered the entire list.

Chunking suggests that STM holds about 5 to 7 of whatever units we are using. A single chunk could be made up of numbers, letters, words, phrases, or familiar sentences (Barsalou, 1992). Picture STM as a small desk again. Through chunking, we combine several items into one "stack" of information. This allows us to place 7 stacks on the desk, where before there was only room for 7 separate items.

How long do short-term memories last?

Rehearsal

Short-term memories appear to weaken and disappear very rapidly. However, a short-term memory can be prolonged *by silently repeating it until it is needed,* a process called **maintenance rehearsal.** You have probably remembered an address or telephone number this way. The more times a short-term memory is rehearsed, the greater its chances of being stored in LTM (Barsalou, 1992).

What if rehearsal is prevented, so a memory cannot be recycled or moved to LTM? Without maintenance rehearsal, STM is incredibly short.

In one experiment, subjects heard meaningless syllables like XAR followed by a number like 67. As soon as subjects heard the number, they began counting backward by threes (to prevent them from repeating the syllable). After only 18 seconds of delay, memory scores fell to zero. (Peterson & Peterson, 1959)

After *18 seconds* without rehearsal, the short-term memories were gone forever! Keep this in mind when you get only one chance to hear information you want to remember. For example, if you are introduced to someone, and the name slips out of STM, there is no way to retrieve it. It is gone forever. To escape this awkward situation you might try saying something like, "I'm curious, how do you spell your name?" Unfortunately, the response is often an icy reply like, "B-O-B S-M-I-T-H, it's really not too difficult." To avoid embarrassment, pay careful attention to the name, repeat it to yourself several times, and try to use it in the next sentence or two—before you lose it.

Maintenance rehearsal primarily keeps memories alive in STM. It is not a very good way to transfer information to long-term memory. **Elaborative rehearsal,** *which enhances the meaningfulness of information,* is far more effective. In other words, rehearsal works best when you link new information to existing memories and knowledge (Barsalou, 1992). That's why passively reading a textbook is a poor way to study. If you don't elaborate, digest, extend, and think about information, you won't remember much later.

Long-Term Memory—Where the Past Lives

An electrode was placed at location number 11 on the patient's brain. She immediately said, "Yes, sir, I think I heard a mother calling her little boy somewhere. It seemed to be something happening years ago. It was somebody in the neighborhood where I live." A short time later the electrode was applied to the same spot. Again the patient said, "Yes, I hear the same familiar sounds, it seems to be a woman calling, the same lady" (Penfield, 1958). These statements were made by a woman undergoing brain surgery for epilepsy. Only local anesthetics were used (there are no pain receptors in the brain), so the patient was awake as her brain was electrically stimulated (Fig. 10–3 ◆). When activated, some brain areas seemed to produce vivid memories of long-forgotten events.

Does that mean every experience a person has ever had is recorded in memory?

Permanence Results like those described led neurosurgeon Wilder Penfield to claim that the brain records the past like a "continuous strip of movie film, complete with sound track" (Penfield, 1957). But as you now know, this is an exaggeration. Many events never get past short-term

Figure 10–3 ◆ Exposed cerebral cortex of a patient undergoing brain surgery. Numbers represent points that reportedly produced "memories" when electrically stimulated. A critical evaluation of such reports suggests that they are more like dreams than memories. This fact raises questions about claims that long-term memories are permanent. (From Wilder Penfield, *The Excitable Cortex in Conscious Man,* 1958. Courtesy of the author and Charles C Thomas, Publisher, Springfield, Illinois.)

memory. More importantly, in only about 3 percent of cases does brain stimulation produce memory-like experiences. Most reports resemble dreams more than memories, and many are clearly fictional. Memory experts Elizabeth and

Geoffrey Loftus carefully examined Penfield's work, as well as research on "truth serums" and hypnosis. They concluded that there is little evidence that long-term memories are absolutely permanent (Loftus & Loftus, 1980). It is probably more accurate to say that long-term memories are *relatively* permanent, or long lasting (Barsalou, 1992).

Constructing Memories

There is another reason to doubt Penfield's claim. As new long-term memories are formed, older memories are often updated, changed, lost, or *revised* (Baddeley, 1990, 1996). To illustrate this point, Elizabeth Loftus and John Palmer (1974) showed people a filmed automobile accident. Afterward, some participants were asked

Eyewitness memories are notoriously inaccurate. By the time witnesses are asked to testify in court, information they learned after an incident may blend into their original memories.

to estimate how fast the cars were going when they "smashed" into each other. For others the words "bumped," "contacted," or "hit" replaced "smashed." One week later, each person was asked, "Did you see any broken glass?" Those asked earlier about the cars that "smashed" into each other were more likely to say yes. (No broken glass was shown in the film.) The new information ("smashed") was included in memories and altered them.

Revised memories often change in ways that enhance one's self-image. (As long as you're altering memories you might as well make yourself look good.) For example, college students were recently asked to remember their high-school grades. As a group they were 90 percent accurate in remembering A grades. However, only 30 percent of D grades were accurately recalled (Bahrick, Hall, & Berger, 1996).

Try It Yourself

Old or New?

Now, without looking back to the list of words you read a few minutes ago, see if you can tell which of the following are "old" words (items from the list you read) and which are "new" words (items that weren't on the list). Mark each of the following words as old or new:

    sofa

    sleep

    lamp

    kitchen

Updating memories is called **constructive processing.** Research shows that gaps in memory, which are common, may be filled in by logic, guessing, or new information (Loftus, 1977, 1980). Indeed, it is possible to have "memories" for things that never happened (such as remembering broken glass at an accident when there was none). People in Elizabeth Loftus' experiments who had these **pseudo-memories** (*false memories*) were often quite upset to learn they had given false "testimony" (Loftus & Ketcham, 1991).

Try It Yourself

And Now, the Results

Return now and look at the labels you wrote on the "old or new" word list. If you answered as most people do, this exercise may help you appreciate how often we

have false memories. All of the listed words are "new." None was on the original list!

If you thought you "remembered" that sleep was on the original list, you had a false memory. The word *sleep* is associated with most of the words on the original list, which creates a strong impression that you saw it before (Roediger & McDermott, 1995).

The updating of long-term memories is a common problem in police work. For example, a witness may select a photo of a suspect from police files or see a photo in the news. Later, the witness identifies the suspect in person (in a lineup or in court). Did the witness really remember the suspect from the scene of the crime? Or was it from the more recently seen photograph? Even an innocent person may be "remembered" as the criminal. It is quite possible for a photo to update or *blend* with the original memory. Many tragic cases of mistaken identity have occurred in this way.

Couldn't hypnosis be used to avoid such problems?

News stories often give the impression that it can. Is this true? The next highlight examines this intriguing question.

Focus on a Controversy

Hypnosis, Imagination, and Memory

In 1976, near Chowchilla, California, 26 children were abducted from a school bus and held captive for ransom. Under hypnosis, the bus driver recalled the license plate number of the kidnappers' van. This memory helped break the case and led to the children's rescue. Such successes seem to imply that hypnosis can improve memory. But does it? Read on, and judge for yourself.

Research has shown that a hypnotized person is more likely than normal to use imagination to fill in gaps in memory. Also, when hypnotized persons are given false information, they tend to weave it into their memories (Sheehan & Statham, 1989). Even when a memory is completely false, the hypnotized person's confidence in it can be unshakable (Laurence & Perry, 1983). Most telling of all is the fact that hypnosis increases false memories more than it does true ones. Eighty percent of the new memories produced by hypnotized subjects in one experiment were *incorrect* (Dywan & Bowers, 1983).

Overall, it can be concluded that hypnosis does not greatly improve memory (Kassin et al., 1989; Murray-Smith, 1990). It is true that hypnosis sometimes uncovers more information (Watkins, 1989). However, when it does there is no sure way to tell which memories are true and which are false (Perry et al., 1996). Clearly, hypnosis is not the "magic bullet" against forgetting that some police investigators hoped it would be.

To summarize, forming and using memories is an active, creative, highly personal process. Our memories are colored by emotions, judgments, and quirks of personality. If you and a friend were lashed together, and you went through life side-by-side, you would still have different memories. What we remember depends on what we pay attention to, what we regard as meaningful or important, and what we feel strongly about (Schacter, 1996).

Organization

Long-term memory stores a seemingly infinite amount of information in a lifetime. How is it possible to quickly find specific memories? The answer is that each person's "memory index" is highly organized.

Do you mean that information is arranged alphabetically, as in a dictionary?

Not a chance! If I ask you to name a black and white animal that lives on ice, is related to a chicken, and cannot fly, you don't have to go from aardvark to zebra to find the answer. You will probably only think of black and white birds living in the Antarctic. Which of these cannot fly? *Voila*, the answer is penguin.

The arrangement of information in LTM may be based on rules, images, categories, symbols, similarity, formal meaning, or personal meaning (Baddeley, 1990, 1996). In recent years, psychologists have begun to develop a picture of the *structure*, or arrangement, of memories. **Memory structure** *is the pattern of associations among items of information stored in memory*. One example will serve to illustrate this research.

You are given the following two statements, to which you must answer yes or no: *A canary is an animal. A canary is a bird.* Which do you answer more quickly? Collins and Quillian (1969) found that *A canary is a bird* produced a faster yes than *A canary is an animal.* Why should this be so? Many psychologists believe that a **network model** of memory explains why. According to them, *LTM is organized as a network of linked ideas* (Fig. 10–4 ◆). When ideas are "farther" apart, it takes a longer chain of associations to connect them. The more two items are separated, the longer it takes to answer. In terms of information links, *canary* is probably "close" to *bird* in your "memory files." *Animal* and *canary* are farther apart. Remember though, this has nothing to do with alphabetical order. We are talking about organization based on linked meanings.

Redintegrative Memories Networks of associated memories may help explain a common experience: Imagine finding a picture taken on your sixth birthday or tenth Christmas. As you look at the photo, one memory leads to another, which leads to another, and another. Soon you have unleashed a flood of seemingly forgotten details. This process is called *redintegration* (ruh-DIN-tuh-GRAY-shun).

Redintegrative memories *seem to spread through the "branches" of memory networks.* Many people find that such memories are also touched off by distinctive odors out of the past—from a farm visited in childhood, Grandma's kitchen, the seashore, a doctor's office, the perfume or after-shave of a former lover, and so on. The key idea in redintegration is that one memory serves as a cue to trigger another. As a result, an entire past experience may be reconstructed from one small recollection.

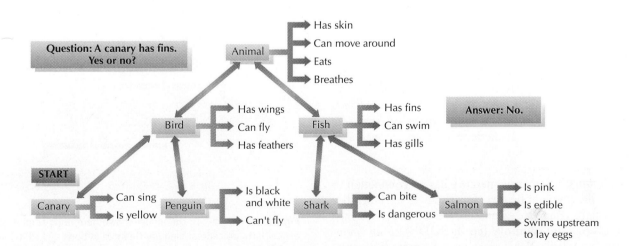

Figure 10–4 ◆ A hypothetical network of facts about animals shows what is meant by the structure of memory. Small networks of ideas such as this are probably organized into larger and larger units and higher levels of meaning. (Adapted from Collins & Quillian, 1969.)

Types of Long-Term Memory

How many types of long-term memory are there?

As we have seen, *memory* is an umbrella term that includes both short-term and long-term memory. Beyond this, it is becoming clear that more than one type of long-term memory exists. Let's probe a little further into the mysteries of memory.

Skill Memory and Fact Memory

A curious thing happens to many people who develop amnesia. Amnesic patients may be unable to learn a telephone number, an address, or a person's name. And yet, the same patients may learn to solve complex puzzles in the same amount of time as normal subjects (Squire & Zola-Morgan, 1988) (Fig. 10–5 ◆). These and other observations have led many psychologists to conclude that long-term memories fall into at least two categories. One of these might be called *procedural memory* (or skill memory). The other is *declarative memory* (also sometimes called fact memory).

Procedural memory *includes basic conditioned responses and learned actions* like those involved in typing, solving a puzzle, or swinging a golf club. Memories such as these can be fully expressed only as actions (or "know-how"). It is likely that skill memories register in "lower" brain areas, especially the cerebellum (Squire et al., 1993). They represent the more basic "automatic" elements of conditioning, learning, and memory (Thompson, 1991).

Declarative memory *involves remembering specific factual information*, such as names, faces, words, dates, and ideas. Declarative memories are expressed as words or symbols. For example, knowing that Steven Spielberg directed both *Close Encounters of the Third Kind* and *Jurassic Park* is a declarative memory. This is the type of memory that a person with amnesia lacks and that most of us take for granted. Some psychologists believe that declarative memory can be further divided into two other types, called *semantic* and *episodic memory* (Nyberg & Tulving, 1996).

Semantic Memory

Most of our basic *factual knowledge* about the world is almost totally immune to forgetting. The names of objects, the days of the week or months of the year, simple math skills, the seasons, words and language, and other general facts are all quite lasting. Such *impersonal facts make up a part of LTM called* **semantic memory.** Semantic memory serves as a mental dictionary or encyclopedia of basic knowledge.

Episodic Memory

Semantic memory has no connection to times or places. It would be rare, for instance, to remember when and where you first learned the names of the seasons. In contrast, **episodic memory** (ep-ih-SOD-ik) *is an "autobiographical" record of personal experiences.* It stores life events (or "episodes") day after day, year after year. Can you remember your seventh birthday? Your first date? An

Figure 10–5 ◆ The tower puzzle. In this puzzle, all the colored disks must be moved to another post, without ever placing a larger disk on a smaller one. Only one disk may be moved at a time, and a disk must always be moved from one post to another (it cannot be held aside). An amnesic patient learned to solve the puzzle in 31 moves, the minimum possible. Even so, each time he began, he protested that he did not remember ever solving the puzzle before and that he did not know how to begin. Evidence like this suggests that memories for skills are distinct from memories for facts.

accident you witnessed? The first day of college? What you had for breakfast 3 days ago? All are episodic memories.

Are episodic memories as lasting as semantic memories?

In general, episodic memories are more easily forgotten than semantic memories. This is because new information constantly pours into episodic memory. Stop for a moment and remember what you did last summer. That was an episodic memory. Notice that you now remember that you just remembered something. You have a new episodic memory in which you remember that you remembered while reading this text! It's easy to see how much we ask of our memory system.

Figure 10–6 ◆ In the model shown here, long-term memory is divided into procedural memory (learned actions and skills) and declarative memory (stored facts). Declarative memories can be either semantic (impersonal knowledge) or episodic (personal experiences associated with specific times and places).

How Many Types of Memory? In answer to the question posed at the beginning of this section, it is very likely that three kinds of long-term memories exist: procedural, semantic, and episodic (Mitchell, 1989; Squire et al., 1993) (Fig. 10–6 ◆). However, the relationship among them is still actively debated. While the debate continues—and other types may be discovered in the future—it appears that some pieces of the puzzle called memory are falling into place.

Learning Check

1. The digit-span test is commonly used to measure LTM. T or F?

2. There is evidence that STM lasts about 18 seconds, without rehearsal. T or F?

3. Information is best transferred from STM to LTM when a person engages in
   a. maintenance chunking   **b.** maintenance recoding   **c.** elaborative networking
   d. elaborative rehearsal

4. Constructive processing is often responsible for creating pseudo-memories. T or F?

5. Electrical stimulation of the brain has shown conclusively that all memories are stored permanently, but not all memories can be retrieved. T or F?

6. Memories elicited under hypnosis are more vivid, complete, and reliable than normal. T or F?

7. _Networks_ of related information are an example of the structure or organization found in LTM.

8. Procedural memories are stored in STM, whereas declarative memories are stored in LTM. T or F?

9. Episodic memories are almost totally immune to forgetting. T or F?

Critical Thinking

10. Telephone companies are aware of the limitations of short-term memory. In what way is this evident?

Answers:
1. F 2. T 3. d 4. T 5. F 6. F 7. Networks 8. F 9. F 10. Local numbers are broken into a 3-digit chunk and a 4-digit chunk. Long-distance numbers consist of a 3-digit chunk (the area code) plus a 3-digit chunk and a 4-digit chunk. If telephone numbers weren't recoded this way, a long-distance number would be 10 single digits—too many for most people's short-term memory.

Measuring Memory—The Answer Is on the Tip of My Tongue

You either remember something or you don't, right? Wrong. A moment of thought should convince you that partial memories are commonplace. For instance, have you ever recognized someone you only saw once before—someone you thought you had completely forgotten? If so, you have used a form of partial memory called *recognition*. Partial memory is also demonstrated by the **tip-of-the-tongue (TOT) state.** *This is the feeling that a memory is available, but not quite retrievable.* It is as if an answer or a memory is just out of reach—on the "tip of your tongue." In a recent study, people listened to theme music from popular TV shows and tried to name the program the tune came from. This produced TOT experiences for about 1 out of 5 tunes (Riefer, Keveri, & Kramer, 1995).

Here are some definitions that may induce the TOT state. See if you can name the defined word.

What's on the Tip of Your Tongue?

1. A person who collects and studies postage stamps.
2. A decorative loop of fabric on the shoulder of a coat or dress.
3. A tobacco pipe with a large flared bowl made from a gourd.
4. The dark, dense rock of a lava flow.
5. Thin plant strips pressed together to make a writing material used in ancient Egypt.
6. A small fish that attaches itself to a shark.

Answers are at the bottom of this page.*

In one TOT study, university students read the definitions of words such as *sextant, sampan,* and *ambergris.* Students who "drew a blank" and couldn't name a defined word were asked to give whatever other information they could about it. Often, they could accurately guess the first and last letter and even the number of syllables of the word they were seeking. They also gave words that sounded like or meant the same thing as the defined word (Brown & McNeill, 1966). Did any of these signs of the TOT state occur as you read the definitions above?

Closely related to the TOT state is the fact that *people can often tell beforehand if they are likely to remember something.* This condition is called the **feeling of knowing** (Nelson, 1987). Feeling-of-knowing reactions are easy to observe on television game shows, where they occur just before contestants are allowed to answer.

Because memory is not an all-or-nothing event, there are several ways of measuring it. Three commonly used **memory tasks** (*tests of memory*) are *recall, recognition,* and *relearning.* Let's see how they differ.

---

1. philatelist 2. epaulet 3. calabash 4. basalt 5. papyrus 6. remora.

Recall

What is the name of the first song on your favorite compact disc? Who won the World Series last year? Who wrote *Hamlet?* If you can answer these questions you are demonstrating recall. To **recall** *means to supply or reproduce facts or information.* Tests of recall often require *verbatim* (word-for-word) memory. If you study a poem or a speech until you can recite it without looking, you are recalling it. If you complete a fill-in-the-blank question, you are using recall. When you take an *essay* exam and provide facts and ideas without prompting you are also using recall, even though you didn't learn your essay verbatim. Essay tests tend to be difficult because they offer few cues to aid memory.

The order in which information is memorized has an interesting effect on recall. To experience it, try to memorize the following list, reading it only once:

> bread, apples, soda, ham, cookies,
> rice, lettuce, beets, mustard, cheese,
> oranges, ice cream, crackers, flour, eggs

If you are like most people, you will have the most difficulty recalling items from the middle of the list. Figure 10–7 ◆ shows the results of a similar test. Notice that *the greatest number of errors is found for middle items of an ordered list.* This is the **serial position effect.** The last items on a list are remembered best because they are still in STM. The first items are also remembered because they entered an "empty" short-term memory where they could be rehearsed and moved to long-term memory (Medin & Ross, 1992). The middle items are neither held in short-term memory nor moved to long-term memory, so they are often lost.

Figure 10–7 ◆ The serial position effect. The graph shows the percentage of subjects correctly recalling each item in a 15-item list. Recall is best for the first and last items. (Data from Craik, 1970.)

Recognition

Try to write down everything you can remember from a class you took last year and you might conclude that you learned very little. However, a more sensitive test based on recognition could be used. In **recognition memory,** *previously learned material is correctly identified.* For instance, you could be given a *multiple-choice test* on facts and ideas from the course. Since multiple-choice tests only require you to recognize the correct answer, we would probably find evidence of considerable learning.

Recognition memory can be amazingly accurate for pictures, photographs, or other visual input. One investigator showed people 2,560 photographs at a rate of one every 10 seconds. Each person was then shown 280 pairs of photographs. One in each pair was from the first set of photos and the other was similar but new. Subjects could tell with 85 to 95 percent accuracy which photograph they had seen before (Haber, 1970). This finding may explain why people so often say, "I may forget a name, but I never forget a face."

Recognition is usually superior to recall. That's why police departments use photographs or a lineup to identify criminal suspects. Witnesses who disagree in their recall of a suspect's height, weight, age, or eye color often agree completely when recognition is all that is required.

Is recognition always superior?

It depends greatly on the kind of **distractors** used. *These are false items included with an item to be recognized.* If distractors are very similar to the correct item, memory may be poor. A reverse problem sometimes occurs when only one choice looks like it could be correct. This can produce a **false positive,** *or false sense of recognition.* For example, there have been instances in which witnesses described a criminal as black, tall, or young. Then a lineup was held in which a suspect was the only African American among whites, the only tall suspect, or the only young person. In such cases a false identification is very likely. A better method is to have all the distractors look like the description witnesses gave. This reduces false positives and increases accurate identifications (Wells et al., 1993). The worst situation occurs when only one person is presented as a suspect. In that case, false identifications of look-alike innocent persons are a real danger (Yarmey, Yarmey, & Yarmey, 1996).

Relearning

In a classic experiment on memory, a psychologist read a short passage in Greek to his son. This was done daily when the boy was between 15 months and 3 years of age. At age 8, the boy was asked if he remembered the Greek passage. He showed no evidence of recall. He was then given selections from the passage he heard and selections from other Greek passages. Could he recognize the one

Police lineups make use of the sensitivity of recognition memory.

he heard as an infant? "It's all Greek to me!" he said, indicating no recognition (and drawing a frown from everyone in the room).

Had the psychologist stopped, he might have concluded that no memory of the Greek remained. However, the child was then asked to memorize the original quotation and others of equal difficulty. This time his earlier learning became evident. The boy memorized the passage he had heard in childhood 25 percent faster than the others (Burtt, 1941). As this experiment suggests, **relearning** *is typically the most sensitive measure of memory.*

When a person is tested by relearning, how do we know a memory still exists? As with the boy described, relearning is measured by a **savings score** (*the amount of time saved when relearning information*). Let's say it takes you 1 hour to memorize all the names in a telephone book. (It's a small town.) Two years later you relearn them in 45 minutes. Because you "saved" 15 minutes, your savings score would be 25 percent (15 divided by 60 times 100). Savings of this type are a good reason for studying a wide range of subjects. It may seem that time spent learning algebra, history, or a foreign language is wasted because so much is lost within a year or two. But if you ever need such information, you will find you can relearn it in far less time.

Implicit Memory

Psychologists have discovered that many memories remain outside of conscious awareness. For example, if you know how to type, it is apparent that you know where the letters are on the keyboard. But how many typists could correctly label blank keys in a drawing of a typewriter? Many people find that they cannot directly remember such information, even though they "know" it.

Who were the last three presidents of the United States? What did you have for breakfast today? What is the title of Michael Jackson's best-selling album? Explicit memory is used in answering each of these questions. **Explicit memories** *are past experiences that are consciously brought to mind.* Recall, recognition, and the tests you take in school rely on explicit memories. In contrast, **implicit memories** *lie outside of awareness* (Roediger, 1990). That is, we are not aware that a memory or record of past experience exists. Nevertheless, implicit memories—such as unconsciously knowing where the letters are on a typewriter—greatly influence our behavior (Bower, 1990; Schacter, 1996).

How is it possible to show that a memory exists if it lies outside of awareness?

Priming Psychologists first noticed implicit memory while studying memory loss caused by brain injuries. Let's say, for example, that a patient is shown a list of common words, such as *chair, tree, lamp, table,* and so on. A few minutes later, the patient is asked to recall words from the list. Sadly, he has no memory of the words.

Now, instead of asking the patient to explicitly recall the list, we could "prime" his memory by giving him the first two letters of each word. "We'd like you to say a word that begins with these letters," we tell him. "Just say whatever comes to mind." Of course, many words could be made from each pair of letters. For example, the first item (from chair) would be the letters CH. The patient could say "child," "chalk," "chain," "check," or many other words. Instead, he says "chair," a word from the original list. The patient is not aware that he is remembering the list, but as he gives a word for each letter pair, almost all are from the list. Apparently, the letters **primed** (*activated*) hidden memories, which then influenced his answers.

Similar effects have been found for people with normal memories. As the preceding example implies, implicit memories are often revealed by giving a person limited cues, such as the first letter of words or partial drawings of objects. Typically, the person believes that he or she is just saying whatever comes to mind. Nevertheless, information previously seen or heard affects his or her answers (Roediger, 1990). Some nutritionists like to say, "You are what you eat." In the realm of memory it appears that we are what we experience—to a far greater degree than once realized.

Exceptional Memory— Wizards of Recall

Can you remember how many doors there are in your house or apartment? To answer a question like this, many people

Figure 10–8 ◆ **(a)** "Treasure map" similar to the one used by Kosslyn, Ball, and Reiser (1978) to study images in memory. **(b)** This graph shows how long it took subjects to move a visualized spot various distances on their mental images of the map. (See text for explanation.)

(a)

(b)

form **internal images** (*mental pictures*) of each room and count the doorways they visualize. As this example implies, many memories are stored as mental images (Dewhurst & Conway, 1994).

Stephen Kosslyn, Thomas Ball, and Brian Reiser (1978) found an interesting way to show that memories do exist as images. Participants first memorized a sort of treasure map similar to the one shown in Figure 10–8a ◆. They were then asked to picture a black dot moving from one object, such as one of the trees, to another, such as the hut at the top of the island. Did people really form an image to do this task? It seems they did. As shown in Figure 10–8b ◆, the time it took to "move" the dot was directly related to actual distances on the map.

Is that an example of photographic memory?

In some ways, internal memory images do have "photographic" qualities. However, the term *photographic memory* is more often used to describe a type of memory called eidetic imagery.

Eidetic Imagery

Eidetic (eye-DET-ik) **imagery** occurs when a person has *visual images clear enough to be "scanned" or retained for at least 30 seconds.* Internal memory images can be "viewed" mentally with the eyes closed. In contrast, eidetic images are "projected" out in front of a person. That is, they are best "seen" on a plain surface, such as a blank piece of paper. In this respect eidetic images are somewhat like the after-images you might have after looking at a flashbulb or a brightly lit neon sign (Kunzendorf, 1989).

Eidetic memory occurs most often in childhood, with about 8 children out of 100 having eidetic images. In one series of tests, children were shown a picture from *Alice in Wonderland* (Fig. 10–9 ◆). To test your eidetic imagery, look at the picture and read the instructions there.

Now, let's see how much you remember. Can you say (without looking again) which of Alice's apron strings is longer? Are the cat's front paws crossed? How many stripes are on the cat's tail? After the picture was removed from

view, one 10-year-old boy was asked what he saw. He replied, "I see the tree, gray tree with three limbs. I see the cat with stripes around its tail." Asked to count the stripes, the boy replied, "There are about 16" (a correct count!). The boy then went on to describe the remainder of the picture in striking detail (Haber, 1969).

Figure 10–9 ◆ A test picture like that used to identify children with eidetic imagery. To test your eidetic imagery, look at the picture for 30 seconds. Then look at a blank surface and try to "project" the picture onto it. If you have good eidetic imagery, you will be able to see the picture in detail. Return now to the text and try to answer the questions there. (Redrawn from an illustration in Lewis Carroll's *Alice in Wonderland*.)

Don't be disappointed if you didn't do too well when you tried your eidetic skills. Most eidetic imagery disappears during adolescence and becomes quite rare by adulthood (Kunzendorf, 1989). Actually, this change may not be too much of a loss. The majority of eidetic memorizers have no better long-term memory than average.

Exceptional Memory

Let's return now to the concept of internal memory images. In rare instances, such images may be so vivid that it is reasonable to say that a person has "photographic memory." A notable example was reported by Aleksandr Luria (1968) in his book, *The Mind of a Mnemonist*. Luria studied a man he called Mr. S who had practically unlimited memory for visual images. Mr. S could remember almost everything that ever happened to him with incredible accuracy. Luria tried to test Mr. S's memory by using longer and longer lists of words or numbers. However, he soon discovered that no matter how long the list, Mr. S was able to recall it without error. Mr. S could memorize, with equal ease, strings of digits, meaningless consonants, mathematical formulas, and poems in foreign languages. His memory was so powerful that he had to devise ways to *forget*—such as writing information on a piece of paper and then burning it.

As fantastic as it might sound to a struggling student, Mr. S's memory caused him great difficulty. He remembered so much that he couldn't separate important facts from trivia. For instance, if you asked him to read this chapter he might remember every word. However, he might also recall all the images each word made him think of and all the sights, sounds, and feelings that occurred as he was reading. Therefore, finding the answer for a specific question, writing a logical essay, or even understanding a single sentence was very difficult for him.

Few people in history have possessed memory abilities like Mr. S's. However, you probably know at least one person who has an especially good memory. Is superior memory a biological gift? Or do excellent memorizers merely make better-than-average use of normal memory capacities? Let's investigate further.

Learned Strategies   At first, a student volunteer we will call Steve could remember 7 digits—a typical score for a college student. Could he improve with practice? For 20 months Steve practiced memorizing ever-longer lists of digits. Ultimately, he was able to memorize around 80 digits, like this sample:

92842048050842268953990190252912807999970
660657471731060108058526972602635733235

How did Steve reach such lofty heights of memory? Basically, he worked by chunking digits into meaningful groups containing 3 or 4 digits each. Steve's avid interest in

REPRINTED BY PERMISSION: TRIBUNE MEDIA SERVICES

long-distance running helped greatly. To him, the first three digits above represented 9 minutes and 28 seconds, a good time for a 2-mile run. When running times wouldn't work, Steve used other associations, such as ages or dates, to chunk digits (Ericsson & Chase, 1982). It seems apparent that Steve's success was based on learned strategies. Indeed, by using similar memory systems, other people have trained themselves to equal Steve's feat (Bellezza, Six, & Phillips, 1992).

Psychologist Anders Ericsson believes that Steve's performance shows that exceptional memory is merely a learned extension of normal memory. As further evidence, he notes that Steve's short-term memory did not improve during months of practice. For example, Steve could still memorize only 7 consonants.

Steve's phenomenal memory for numbers grew as he figured out new ways to encode digits. Each new strategy helped him to better store digits in LTM.

Researchers studying Rajan Mahadevan have drawn similar conclusions about his spectacular memory for long strings of digits. In 1981 Rajan earned a place in the *Guinness Book of World Records* by reciting the first 31,811 digits of *pi*! Yet, like Steve, Rajan's memory for most other types of information is average. His exceptional memory seems to be based on highly practiced strategies for encoding and storing digits (Thompson et al., 1993).

Steve and Rajan began with normal memory for digits. Both extended their memory abilities by diligent practice. Clearly, exceptional memory can be learned. However, we still have to wonder, do some people have naturally superior memories?

Memory Champions   In 1991 the first World Memory Championship was held in London. There, a variety of mental athletes competed to see who had the best memory. To remain in the running, each contestant had to rapidly memorize daunting amounts of information, such as long lists of unrelated words and numbers. Psychologists John Wilding and Elizabeth Valentine saw an opportunity to study exceptional memory and persuaded the contestants to take part in further testing. Each person was given a series of additional memory tests. These ranged from ordinary (recall a story), to challenging (recall the telephone numbers of 6 different people), to diabolical (recall 48 numerals arranged in rows and columns; recognize 14 previously seen pictures of snowflakes among 70 new photos) (Wilding & Valentine, 1994a).

```
8 7 3 7 9 2 6 8
2 0 1 1 7 4 9 5
0 1 7 5 8 7 8 3
1 9 4 7 6 0 6 9
3 6 1 6 8 1 5 4
4 5 2 4 0 2 9 7
```

This number matrix is similar to the ones contestants in the World Memory Championship had to memorize. To be scored as correct, digits had to be recalled in their proper positions (Wilding & Valentine, 1994a).

Wilding and Valentine found that exceptional memorizers:

- Use memory strategies and techniques
- Have specialized interests and knowledge that make certain types of information easier to encode and recall

- Have naturally superior memory abilities, often including vivid mental images

The first two points confirm what we learned from Steve's acquired memory ability. Many of the contestants, for example, actively used memory strategies called *mnemonics* (nee-MON-iks). (Mnemonics are explained in this chapter's Applications.) Specialized interests and knowledge also helped for some tasks. For example, one contestant, who is a mathematician, was exceedingly good at memorizing numbers (Wilding & Valentine, 1994a).

Several of the memory contestants were able to excel on tasks that prevented the use of learned strategies and techniques. This observation implies that superior memory ability can be a "gift" as well as a learned skill. Wilding and Valentine conclude that exceptional memory may be based on either natural ability or learned strategies. Usually it requires both. In fact, most super memorizers use strategies to augment their natural talents, whenever possible. As mentioned earlier, some of these strategies are described in this chapter's Applications. Please do remember to read it.

Learning Check

Unless you have a memory like Mr. S's, it might be a good idea to see if you can answer these questions before reading on.

1. Four techniques for measuring or demonstrating memory are
   recall   recognition
   relearning   priming

2. Multiple-choice tests primarily require *recognition* memory.

3. Essay tests require *recall* of facts or ideas.

4. As a measure of memory, a savings score is associated with
   a. recognition   **b.** eidetic images   **c.** relearning   **d.** reconstruction

5. Tests of *implicit* memory are designed to reveal the influences of information that is stored, but which remains unconscious.

6. Children with eidetic imagery typically have no better than average long-term memory. T or F?

7. In order to perform well on tests of memory, one must be born with naturally superior memory abilities. T or F?

Critical Thinking

8. Mr. S had great difficulty remembering faces. Can you guess why?

Answers:

1. recall, recognition, relearning, priming 2. recognition 3. recall 4. c 5. implicit 6. T 7. F 8. Mr. S's memory was so specific that faces seemed different and unfamiliar if he saw them from a new angle or if a face had a different expression on it than when Mr. S last saw it.

Forgetting—Why We, Uh, Let's See; Why We, Uh . . . Forget!

Why are some memories lost so quickly? For example, why is it hard to remember information a week or two after taking a test in class?

Most forgetting tends to occur immediately after memorization. In a famous set of experiments, *memory researcher*

Herman Ebbinghaus (1885) tested his own memory at various times after learning. Ebbinghaus wanted to be sure he would not be swayed by prior learning, so he memorized **nonsense syllables.** These are *meaningless three-letter words* such as GEX, CEF, and WOL. The importance of using meaningless words is shown by the fact that VEL, FAB, and DUZ are no longer used on memory tests. Subjects who recognize these words as detergent names find them very easy to remember.

By waiting various lengths of time before testing himself, Ebbinghaus plotted a **curve of forgetting.** *This graph shows the amount of information remembered after varying lengths of*

Figure 10–10 ◆ The curve of forgetting. This graph shows the amount remembered (measured by relearning) after varying lengths of time. Notice how rapidly forgetting occurs. The material learned was nonsense syllables. Forgetting curves for meaningful information also show early losses followed by a long gradual decline, but overall, forgetting occurs much more slowly. (After Ebbinghaus, 1885.)

time (Fig. 10–10 ◆). Because Ebbinghaus took great care in his work, his findings remain valid today. Notice that forgetting is rapid at first and is then followed by a slow decline.

As a student, you should note that forgetting is minimized when there is little delay between review and taking a test. However, don't take this as a reason for cramming. The error most students make is to cram *only*. If you cram, you don't have to remember for very long, but you may not learn enough in the first place. If you use short, daily study sessions and, in addition, review intensely before a test, you will get the benefit of good preparation and a minimum time lapse.

The Ebbinghaus curve shows less than 30 percent remembered after only 2 days have passed. Is forgetting really that rapid?

No, not always. Meaningful information is not lost nearly as quickly as nonsense syllables. For example, it took students who completed a university psychology course about 3 years to forget 30 percent of the facts they had learned. After that, little more forgetting occurred (Conway et al., 1992). In fact,

as learning grows stronger, some knowledge may become nearly permanent (Bahrick, 1984). Semantic memories and implicit memories (both mentioned earlier) appear to be very lasting (Bower, 1990).

"I'll never forget old, old . . . oh, what's his name?" Forgetting is both frustrating and embarrassing. Why *do* we forget? The Ebbinghaus curve gives a general picture of forgetting, but it doesn't explain it. For explanations we must search further.

Encoding Failure

Whose head is on a U.S. penny? Which way is it facing? What is written at the top of a penny? Can you accurately draw and label a penny? In an interesting experiment, Raymond Nickerson and Marilyn Adams (1979) asked a large group of students to draw a penny. Few could. Well, then, could the students at least recognize a drawing of a real penny among fakes? (See Figure 10–11 ◆.) Again, few could.

The most obvious reason for forgetting is also the most commonly overlooked. In many cases we "forget" because of **encoding failure.** That is, *a memory was never formed in the first place.* Obviously, few of us ever encode the details of a penny. If you are bothered by frequent forgetting, it is wise to ask yourself, "Have I been storing the information in the first place?" When 140 college professors were asked what strategies they use to improve their memory, the most frequently recommended technique was to *write things down* (Park, et al., 1990). Making notes ensures that information will not be lost from short-term memory before you can review it and store it more permanently.

Decay

One view of forgetting holds that **memory traces** (*changes in nerve cells or brain activity*) **decay** (*fade or weaken*) over time. Decay appears to be a factor in the loss of sensory memories. Such fading also applies to short-term memory. Information

Figure 10–11 ◆ Some of the distractor items used in a study of recognition memory and encoding failure. Penny **(a)** is correct but was seldom recognized. Pennies **(g)** and **(j)** were popular wrong answers. (Adapted from Nickerson & Adams, 1979.)

stored in STM seems to initiate a brief flurry of activity in the brain that quickly dies out. Short-term memory therefore operates like a "leaky bucket": New information constantly pours in, but it rapidly fades away and is replaced by still newer information.

Disuse Is it possible that the decay of memory traces also explains long-term forgetting? That is, could long-term memory traces fade from **disuse** (*infrequent retrieval*) and eventually become so weak they cannot be retrieved? As tempting as this theory may be, there are reasons to doubt it. One reason already mentioned is the recovery of seemingly forgotten memories through redintegration, relearning, and priming. Another is that disuse fails to explain why some unused memories fade, while others are carried for life. A third contradiction will be recognized by anyone who has spent time with the elderly. People growing senile may become so forgetful that they can't remember what happened a week ago. Yet at the same time your Uncle Oscar's recent memories are fading, he may have vivid memories of trivial and long-forgotten events from the past. "Why, I remember it as clearly as if it were yesterday," he will say, forgetting that the story he is about to tell is one he told earlier the same day. In short, disuse alone does not adequately explain long-term forgetting.

If decay and disuse don't fully explain forgetting, what does?

There are several additional possibilities. Let's briefly consider each.

Cue-Dependent Forgetting

Often, memories appear to be *available*, but not accessible. An example is having an answer on the "tip of your tongue." You know the answer is there, but it remains just "out of reach." This situation indicates that many memories are "forgotten" because **memory cues** (*stimuli associated with a memory*) present at the time of learning are absent when the time comes to retrieve information. For example, if you were asked, "What were you doing on Monday afternoon of the third week in September 2 years ago?" your reply might be, "Come on. How should I know?" However, if you were reminded, "That was the day the courthouse burned," or "That was the day Mary had her automobile accident," you might remember immediately. The presence of such cues almost always enhances memory. In theory, memory will be best if you study in the same room where you will be tested. Since this is often impossible, try to visualize the room where you will be tested, while you are studying. Doing so can enhance memory later (Jerabek & Standing, 1992).

State-Dependent Learning Nearly everyone has heard the story about the drunk who misplaced his wallet and had to get drunk again to find it. Although this tale is often told as a joke, it is not too farfetched. *The bodily state that exists*

External cues like those found in a photograph, a scrapbook, or during a walk through an old neighborhood often aid recall of seemingly lost memories. For many veterans, finding a familiar name engraved in the Vietnam Veterans Memorial unleashes a flood of memories.

during learning can be a strong cue for later memory, an effect known as **state-dependent learning** (Overton, 1985). Being very thirsty, for instance, might make you remember events that took place on another occasion when you were thirsty. Because of such effects, information learned under the influence of a drug is best remembered when the drugged state occurs again.

A similar effect may apply to emotional states. For instance, Gordon Bower (1981) found that people who learned a list of words while in a happy mood recalled them better when they were again happy. People who learned while they felt sad remembered best when they were sad (Fig. 10–12 ◆). Similarly, if you are in a happy mood you are more likely to remember recent happy events (Salovey & Singer, 1989). If you are in a bad mood you will tend to have

Figure 10–12 ◆ The effect of mood on memory. Subjects best remembered a list of words when their mood during testing was the same as their mood was when they learned the list. (Adapted from Bower, 1981.)

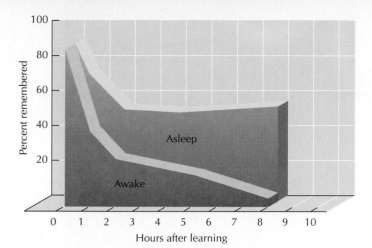

Figure 10–13 ◆ The amount of forgetting after a period of sleep or of being awake. Notice that sleep causes less memory loss than activity that occurs while one is awake. (After Jenkins & Dallenbach, 1924.)

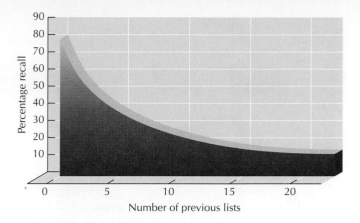

Figure 10–14 ◆ Effects of interference on memory. A graph of the approximate relationship between percentage recalled and number of different word lists memorized. (Adapted from Underwood, 1957.)

unpleasant memories (Eich et al., 1990). Such links between emotional cues and memory could explain why couples who quarrel often end up remembering—and rehashing—old arguments.

Interference

Further understanding of forgetting comes from a classic experiment in which college students learned lists of nonsense syllables. After studying, students in one group slept for 8 hours and were then tested for memory of the lists. A second group remained awake for 8 hours and went about business as usual. When members of the second group were tested, they remembered *less* than the group that slept (Fig. 10–13 ◆). This difference is based on the fact that new learning can *interfere* with previous learning. **Interference** *refers to the tendency for new memories to impair retrieval of older memories (and the reverse).* It seems to apply to both short-term and long-term memory.

It is not completely clear if new memories alter existing memory traces or if they make it harder to "locate" (retrieve) earlier memories. In any case, there is no doubt that interference is a major cause of forgetting (Johnson & Hasher, 1987). College students who memorized 20 lists of words (one list each day) were able to recall only 15 percent of the last list. Students who learned only one list remembered 80 percent (Underwood, 1957) (Fig. 10–14 ◆).

Order Effects The sleeping college students remembered more because *retroactive* (RET-ro-AK-tiv) *interference* was held to a minimum. **Retroactive interference** *refers to the tendency for new learning to inhibit retrieval of old learning.* Avoiding new learning prevents retroactive interference. This fact doesn't exactly mean you should hide in a closet after you study for an exam. However, you should avoid

studying other subjects until the exam. Sleeping after study can help you retain memories, and reading, writing, or even watching TV may cause interference.

Retroactive interference is easily demonstrated in the laboratory by this arrangement:

Experimental group:	Learn A	Learn B	Test A
Control group:	Learn A	Rest	Test A

Imagine yourself as a member of the experimental group. In task A, you learn a list of telephone numbers. In task B, you learn a list of Social Security numbers. How do you do on a test of task A (the telephone numbers)? If you do not remember as much as the control group that learns *only* task A, then retroactive interference has occurred. The second thing learned has interfered with memory of the first thing

How could anyone lose something as large as a car? If you park your car in a different place every day you may have experienced forgetting caused by interference. Today's memory about your car's location is easily confused with memories from yesterday, and the day before, and the day before that.

Retroactive — Learn A — Learn B — Memory loss for A | New learning interferes with old memory

Interference

Proactive — Learn A — Learn B — Memory loss for B | Old learning interferes with new memory

Interference

Order of Events ➡

Figure 10–15 ◆ Retroactive and proactive interference. The order of learning and testing shows whether interference is retroactive (backward) or proactive (forward).

learned; the interference went "backward," or was "retroactive" (Fig. 10–15 ◆).

Proactive (pro-AK-tiv) *interference* is a second basic source of forgetting. **Proactive interference** *occurs when prior learning inhibits recall of later learning.* A test for proactive interference would take this form:

| Experimental group: | Learn A | Learn B | Test B |
| Control group: | Rest | Learn B | Test B |

If the experimental group remembers less than the control group on a test of task B, then learning task A has interfered with memory of task B.

Then proactive interference goes "forward"?

Yes. For instance, if you cram for a psychology exam and then later the same night cram for a history exam, your memory for the second subject studied (history) will be less accurate than if you had studied only history. (Because of retroactive interference, your memory for psychology would probably also suffer.) The greater the similarity in the two subjects studied, the more interference takes place. The moral, of course, is don't procrastinate in preparing for exams.

The interference effects we have described apply primarily to memories of verbal information, such as the contents of this chapter. When you are learning a skill, similarity can sometimes be beneficial, rather than disruptive. The next section explains how this occurs.

Transfer of Training

Two people begin taking mandolin lessons. One already plays the violin. The other is a trumpet player. All other things being equal, which person will initially do better in learning the mandolin? If you chose the violin player you have an intuitive grasp of what *positive transfer* is. (The strings on a mandolin are tuned the same as a violin.) **Positive transfer** is said to have taken place when *mastery of one task aids mastery of a second task.* Another example would be

learning to balance and turn on a bicycle before learning to ride a motorcycle or motor scooter. Likewise, surfing and skateboarding skills transfer to snowboarding.

Is there such a thing as negative transfer?

There is indeed. In **negative transfer,** *skills developed in one situation conflict with those required to master a new task.* Learning to back a car with a trailer attached is a good example. Normally, when you are backing a car, the steering wheel is turned in the direction you want to go, the same as when moving forward. However, with a trailer attached, the steering wheel must be turned opposite from the direction you want the trailer to go. This situation results in negative transfer, and often creates comical scenes at campgrounds and boat launching ramps.

On a more serious note, many tragic crashes caused by negative transfer finally led to greater standardization of airplane cockpits. Fortunately, negative transfer is usually brief, and it occurs less often than positive transfer (Drowatzky, 1975). Negative transfer is most likely to occur when a new response must be made to an old stimulus. If you have ever encountered a pull-type handle on a door that must be pushed open, you will appreciate this point.

Repression

Take a moment from reading and scan over the events of the last few years of your life. What kinds of things most easily come to mind? Many people find that they tend to remember happy, positive events better than disappointments and irritations (Linton, 1979). A clinical psychologist would call this tendency **repression,** *or motivated forgetting.* Through repression, painful, threatening, or embarrassing memories are held out of consciousness by forces within one's personality.

The forgetting of past failures, upsetting childhood events, the names of people you dislike, or appointments you don't want to keep may reveal repression. People prone to repression tend to be hyper-sensitive to emotional events. As a result, they use repression to protect themselves from threatening situations (Mendolia, Moore, & Tesser, 1996).

Adults who were sexually abused as children may repress all memory of their mistreatment. Some are startled when

Figure 10–16 ◆ In what appeared to be an extreme case of repression, Eileen Franklin testified in court in 1990 that her father, George Franklin, abducted, raped, and killed 8-year-old Susan Nason in 1969. Eileen testified that the memory surfaced one day as she looked into the eyes of her own young daughter. Her father was convicted solely on the basis of her "repressed" memory. However, in 1996, the conviction was overturned when DNA tests cleared her father of a second murder she also accused him of committing. As the Franklin case illustrates, trying to separate true memories from fantasies has become a major headache for psychologists and the courts.

their repressed memories are brought to the surface by psychotherapy or other events. However, as discussed in Figure 10–16 ◆, caution is required anytime accusations are made on the basis of seemingly repressed memories. (This chapter's Exploration discusses some important additional cautions about the "recovery" of repressed memories.)

If I try to forget a test I have failed, am I repressing it?

No. Repression can be distinguished from **suppression**, *an active, conscious attempt to put something out of mind.* By not thinking about the test, you have merely suppressed a memory. If you choose to, you can remember the test. Clinicians consider true repression an *unconscious* event. When a memory is repressed we are unaware that forgetting has even occurred. (See Chapter 14 for more information on repression.)

Psychologists Kenneth Bowers and Peter Farvolden believe that repression is a form of avoidance. If you have experienced a painful emotional event, you will probably avoid all thoughts associated with it. This tends to keep cues out of mind that could trigger a painful memory (Bowers & Farvolden, 1996).

Flashbulb Memories

Why are some traumatic events vividly remembered while others are repressed? Psychologists use the term **flashbulb**

memories to describe *images that seem to be frozen in memory* at times of personal tragedy, accident, or other *emotionally significant events.* Depending on your age, you may have a "flashbulb" memory for the Pearl Harbor attack, the assassinations of John F. Kennedy and Martin Luther King, Jr., or the *Challenger* space shuttle disaster. Flashbulb memories are most often formed when an event is surprising, important, or emotional (Rubin, 1985). They are frequently associated with public tragedies, but memories of positive events may also have "flashbulb" clarity.

Flashbulb memories seem to be very detailed. Often, they focus primarily on how you reacted to the event. Table 10–1 ■ lists some memories that had "flashbulb" clarity for at least 50 percent of a group of college students. How vivid are the memories they trigger for you? (Note again that both positive and negative events are listed.)

The term *flashbulb memories* was first used to describe recall that seemed to be unusually vivid and permanent. It

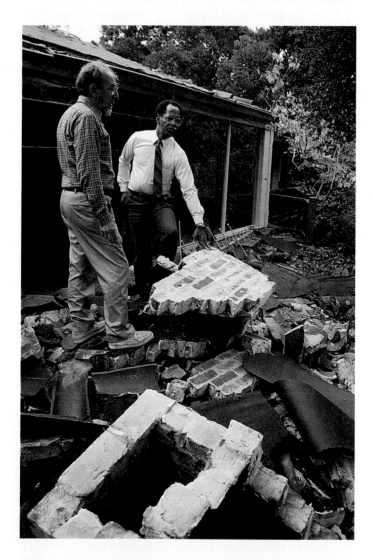

People who survive earthquakes almost always have flashbulb memories of the event. Typically, people vividly remember where they were when the quake started, what they thought as it was occurring, and how they reacted to it.

For a flashbulb memory to form we must be surprised and/or the event must be perceived as important. Eighty-six percent of college students tested in England had flashbulb memories of former British Prime Minister Margaret Thatcher's unexpected resignation. Only 26 percent of students in the United States and Denmark did (Conway et al., 1994).

	Table 10–1 ■ **Bright Flashes of Memory**

Memory Cue	Percentage of Students with Flashbulb Memories
A car accident you were in or witnessed	85
When you first met your college roommate	82
The night of your high school graduation	81
The night of your senior prom (if you went or not)	78
An early romantic experience	77
A time you had to speak in front of an audience	72
When you first got your college admissions letter	65
Your first date—the moment you met him/her	57
When President Reagan was shot in Washington	52

From Rubin, 1985.

has become clear, however, that flashbulb memories are not always accurate (Harsch & Neisser, 1989). More than anything else, what sets flashbulb memories apart is that we tend to place great *confidence* in them—even when they are wrong (Weaver, 1993). Perhaps that's because such memories act as prominent landmarks in our lives. We usually review emotionally charged events over and over and tell others about them. Also, public events such as wars, earthquakes, and assassinations reappear many times in the news, which highlights them in memory (Wright, 1993).

Memory Formation— Some "Shocking" Findings

One possibility overlooked in our discussion of forgetting is that memories may be lost as they are being formed. For example, a head injury may cause a "gap" in memories preceding the accident. **Retrograde amnesia,** as this is called, *involves forgetting events that occurred before an injury or trauma.* (In contrast, **anterograde amnesia** *involves forgetting events that follow an injury or trauma.*)

Consolidation

Retrograde amnesia can be understood if we assume that it takes a certain amount of time to move information from short-term to long-term memory. *The forming of a long-term memory is called* **consolidation** (Squire et al., 1993). You can think of consolidation as being somewhat like writing your

name in wet concrete. Once the concrete is set, the information (your name) is fairly lasting, but while it is setting, it can be wiped out (amnesia) or scribbled over (interference).

Consider a classic experiment on consolidation, in which a rat is placed on a small platform. The rat steps down to the floor and receives a painful electric shock. After one shock, the rat can be returned to the platform repeatedly, but it will not step down. Obviously, the rat remembers the shock. Would it remember if consolidation were disturbed?

Interestingly, one way to prevent consolidation is to give a different kind of shock called **electroconvulsive shock (ECS)** (Jarvik, 1964). ECS is *a mild electric shock to the brain.* It does not harm the animal, but it does destroy any memory that is being formed. If each painful shock (the one the animal remembers) is followed by ECS (which wipes out memories during consolidation), the rat will step down over and over. Each time, ECS will erase the memory of the painful shock. (ECS has been employed as a psychiatric treatment for severe depression in humans. Used in this way, electroshock therapy also causes memory loss. See Chapter 19 for details.)

What would happen if ECS were given several hours after the learning?

Recent memories are more easily disrupted than older memories (Gold, 1987). If enough time is allowed to pass between learning and ECS, the memory is unaffected. Apparently, consolidation is already completed. This is why people with mild head injuries usually only lose memories from just before the accident, while older memories remain intact (Baddeley, 1990). Likewise, you would forget more if you studied, stayed awake 8 hours, and then slept 8 hours than you would if you studied, slept 8 hours, and were then awake for 8 hours (Nesca & Koulack, 1994). Both cases involve the passage of 16 hours. However, in the second instance forgetting is reduced because more consolidation takes place before interference begins.

Can memory be improved with drugs?

Drugs and Memory   The possibility of chemically improving memory has long intrigued psychologists. We have known for some time that various stimulating drugs speed up consolidation if they are given just after learning (McGaugh, 1983). Note, however, that this only reduces the time during which interference can take place; it does not magically improve memory. Also, the drugs involved (metrazol, strychnine, nicotine, caffeine, and amphetamine) must be given in carefully controlled dosages. If the dosage is too high by even a small amount, memory will be *disrupted*.

What effect does alcohol have on memory?

Memory losses are common when a person overindulges in alcohol. This may be due, in part, to state-dependent learning. At higher levels of intoxication, alcohol seems to directly impair encoding and consolidation of memories. A person suffering an alcohol blackout may lose anywhere from a few minutes to several hours of memory (Goodwin, 1995). Research makes it clear that studying while drunk is an excellent way to *lower* test scores (Birnbaum et al., 1978). Even intoxicated eyewitnesses to crimes, which are usually memorable events, suffer impaired memory for what they saw (Yuille & Tollestrup, 1990).

What part of the brain causes consolidation?

From STM to LTM

Actually, many areas of the brain are responsible for memory, but the **hippocampus** is particularly important. This structure, buried deep within the brain, seems to act as a sort of *"switching station"* between short-term and long-term memory. The hippocampus is essential for memories of facts and information, rather than for skills and habits (Squire, 1992).

Humans who have had hippocampal damage show a striking inability to store new memories (Bigler et al., 1996). A patient described by Brenda Milner is typical. Two years after an operation damaged his hippocampus, a 29-year-old patient continued to give his age as 27, and reported that it seemed that the operation had just taken place (Milner, 1965). His memory of events before the operation remained clear, but he found forming new long-term memories almost impossible. (He suffered, in other words, from anterograde amnesia.) When his parents moved to a new house a few blocks away on the same street, he could not remember the new address. Month after month, he read the same magazines over and over again without finding them familiar. If you were to meet this man, he would seem fairly normal, since he still has short-term memory. But if you were to leave the room and return 15 minutes later, he would act as if he had never seen you before. Years ago his favorite uncle died, but he suffers the same grief anew each time he is told of the death. Lacking the ability to form new lasting memories, he lives eternally in the present (Hilts, 1995).

The Brain and Memory   Somewhere within the 3-pound mass of the human brain lies all we know: ZIP codes, faces of loved ones, history, favorite melodies, the taste of an apple, and much, much more. Where is this information? Karl Lashley, a pioneering brain researcher, set out in the 1920s to find an **engram,** *or memory trace*. Lashley taught animals to run mazes and then removed parts of their brains to see how memory of the maze changed. After 30 years he had to concede defeat: Engrams are not located in any one area of the brain. It mattered little which part of the brain's cortex he removed. Only the *amount* removed correlated to memory loss. This conclusion may remain true for specific memories. However, some areas of the cerebral cortex *are* more important to memory than others (Tulving, 1989). Figure 10–17 ◆ explains why.

Then how are memories recorded in the brain?

Figure 10–17   ◆   Patterns of blood flow in the cerebral cortex (wrinkled outer layer of the brain) change as areas become more or less active. Thus, blood flow can be used to draw "maps" of brain activity. This drawing, which views the brain from the top, shows the results of measuring cerebral blood flow while people were thinking about a semantic memory **(a)** or an episodic memory **(b)**. In the map, green indicates areas that are more active during semantic thinking. Reds show areas of greater activity during episodic thinking. The brain on the right shows the difference in activity between views **(a)** and **(b)**. The resulting pattern suggests that the front of the cortex is related to episodic memory. Back areas are more associated with semantic memory (Tulving, 1989).

(a)   (b)   (c)

Scientists studying simple animals are beginning to identify the exact ways in which individual nerve cells record information. There is now much evidence that learning alters the electrical activity, structure, and chemistry of the brain (McGaugh, 1983). For example, Eric Kandel and his colleagues have studied learning in the marine snail *Aplysia* (Fig. 10–18 ◆). Kandel has found that learning in *Aplysia* (ah-PLEEZ-yah) occurs when certain nerve cells in a circuit alter the amount of transmitter chemicals they release (Kandel, 1976). Such changes determine which circuits get stronger and which become weaker. It has also been shown that an increase in receptor sites for transmitter chemicals occurs during learning (Lynch & Baudry, 1984).

On the basis of such breakthroughs, scientists are now studying a bewildering array of chemicals and brain processes that affect memory. If this research succeeds, it may be possible to help the millions of persons who suffer from memory impairment. Will researchers ever produce a "memory pill" for those with normal memory? Some

Figure 10–18 ◆ An *Aplysia*. The relatively simple nervous system of this sea animal allows scientists to study memory as it occurs in single nerve cells.

neuroscientists are confident that memory can be and will be artificially enhanced. At present, however, the possibility of something like a "physics pill" or a "math pill" seems especially remote.

Learning Check

1. According to the Ebbinghaus curve of forgetting, we forget slowly at first and then a rapid decline occurs. T or F?

2. Which explanation seems to account for the loss of short-term memories?
   a. decay   **b.** disuse   **c.** repression   **d.** interference

3. When memories are available but not accessible, forgetting may be cue dependent. T or F?

4. When learning one thing makes it more difficult to recall another, forgetting may be caused by interference .

5. You are asked to memorize long lists of telephone numbers. You learn a new list each day for 10 days. When tested on list 3, you remember less than a person who only learned the first three lists. Your larger memory loss is probably caused by
   a. disuse   **b.** retroactive interference   **c.** regression   **d.** proactive interference

6. Negative transfer is said to occur when skills learned in one situation conflict with those required to master a new task.

7. Repression is thought of as a type of motivated forgetting. T or F?

8. Retrograde amnesia results when consolidation is speeded up. T or F?

9. Researchers have clearly established that engrams are stored in the hippocampus. T or F?

Critical Thinking

10. You must study French, Spanish, psychology, and biology in one evening. What do you think would be the best order in which to study these subjects so as to minimize interference?

Answers:

1. F   2. a and d   3. T   4. interference   5. b   6. Negative transfer   7. T   8. F   9. F   10. Any order that separates French from Spanish and psychology from biology would work (for instance: French, psychology, Spanish, biology).

Improving Memory— Keys to the Memory Bank

While we're waiting around for the development of a memory pill, let's focus on some ways of improving your memory skills right now.

Knowledge of Results Learning proceeds best when *feedback*, or **knowledge of results,** allows you to check your progress. Feedback can help you identify ideas that need extra practice. In addition, knowing that you have remembered or answered correctly is rewarding. A prime way to provide feedback for yourself while studying is *recitation*.

Recitation If you are going to remember something, eventually you will have to retrieve it. **Recitation** *refers to* *summarizing aloud while you are learning.* Recitation forces you to practice retrieving information. When you are reading a text, you should stop frequently and try to remember what you have just read by restating it in your own words. In one experiment, the best memory score was earned by a group of students who spent 80 percent of their time reciting and only 20 percent reading (Gates, 1958). Maybe students who talk to themselves aren't crazy after all.

Rehearsal The more you **rehearse** (*mentally review*) information as you read, the better you will remember it (Muth et al., 1988). But remember that maintenance rehearsal alone is not very effective. Elaborative rehearsal, in which you look for meanings and connections to existing knowledge, is far better. It's also helpful to frequently ask yourself "why" questions as you read (McDaniel & Donnelly, 1996). Thinking about facts helps link them together in memory. To learn college-level information well, you must make active use of rehearsal strategies (Nist, Sharman, & Holschuh, 1996).

Selection The Dutch scholar Erasmus said that a good memory should be like a fishnet: It should keep all the big fish and let the little ones escape. If you boil down the paragraphs in most textbooks to one or two important terms or ideas, your memory chores will be more manageable. Practice very selective marking in your texts and use marginal notes to further summarize ideas. Most students mark their texts too much instead of too little. If everything is underlined, you haven't been selective. And, very likely, you didn't pay much attention to what you read in the first place (Peterson, 1992).

Organization Assume that you must memorize the following list of words: *north, man, red, spring, woman, east, autumn, yellow, summer, boy, blue, west, winter, girl, green, south.* This rather difficult list could be reorganized into *chunks* as follows: *north-east-south-west, spring-summer-autumn-winter, red-yellow-green-blue, man-woman-boy-girl.* This simple reordering made the second list much easier to learn when college students were tested on both lists (Deese & Hulse, 1967). Organizing class notes and summarizing chapters can be helpful when studying (Dickinson & O'Connell, 1990). It may even be helpful to summarize your summaries, so that the overall network of ideas becomes clearer and simpler. One of the big advantages of categorizing and organizing information is that it helps reduce interference (Bower et al., 1996).

Whole versus Part Learning If you have to memorize a speech, is it better to try to learn it from beginning to end? Or in smaller parts like paragraphs? Generally it is better to *practice whole packages of information* rather than smaller parts (**whole learning**). This is especially true for fairly short, organized information. An exception is that learning parts may be better for extremely long, complicated information. In **part learning,** *subparts of a larger body of information are*

studied (such as sections of a textbook chapter). To decide which approach to use, remember to study the *largest meaningful amount of information* possible at one time.

For very long or complex material, try the **progressive part method,** *by breaking a learning task into a series of short sections.* At first, you study part A until it is mastered. Next, you study parts A and B; then A, B, and C; and so forth. This is a good way to learn the lines of a play, a long piece of music, or a poem (Ash & Holding, 1990). After the material is learned, you should also practice it by starting at points other than A (at C, D, or B, for example). This helps prevent getting "lost" or going blank in the middle of a performance.

Serial Position Whenever you must learn something in *order,* be aware of the **serial position effect.** As you will recall, this is *the tendency to make the most errors in remembering the middle of a list.* If you are introduced to a long line of people, the names you are likely to forget will be those in the middle, so you should make an extra effort to attend to them. You should also give extra practice to the middle of a list, poem, or speech. Try to break long lists of information into short sub-lists, and make the middle sub-lists the shortest of all.

Cues The best **memory cues** (*stimuli that aid retrieval*) are those that were present during encoding (Reed, 1996). For example, students in one study had the daunting task of trying to recall a list of 600 words. As they read the list (which they did not know they would be tested on), the students gave three other words closely related in meaning to each listed word. In a test given later, the words each student supplied were used as cues to jog his or her memory. The students recalled an astounding 90 percent of the original word list (Mantyla, 1986). Now read the following sentence:

The fish bit the swimmer.

If you were tested a week from now, you would be more likely to recall the sentence if you were given a memory cue. And, surprisingly, the word *shark* would work better as a reminder than *fish* would. The reason for this is that most people think of a shark when they read the sentence. As a result, shark becomes a potent memory cue (Schacter, 1996).

The preceding examples show, once again, that it often helps to *elaborate* information as you learn. When you study, try to use new names, ideas, or terms in several sentences. Also, form images that include the new information, and relate it to knowledge you already have (Pressley et al., 1988). Your goal should be to knit meaningful cues into your memory code to help you retrieve information when you need it.

Overlearning Numerous studies have shown that memory is greatly improved when you **overlearn.** That is, when *study is continued beyond bare mastery.* After you have learned material well enough to remember it once without error, you should continue studying. Overlearning is your best insurance against going blank on a test because of nervousness.

Spaced Practice To keep boredom and fatigue to a minimum, try *alternating short study sessions with brief rest periods*. This pattern, called **spaced practice**, is generally superior to **massed practice**, *in which little or no rest is given between learning sessions* (Naveh-Benjamin, 1990). By improving attention and consolidation, three 20-minute study sessions can produce more learning than one hour of continuous study.

Perhaps the best way to make use of spaced practice is to *schedule* your time. If most students were to keep a totally honest record of their weekly activities, they would probably find that they had spent very few hours really studying. To make an effective schedule, designate times during the week before, after, and between classes when you will study particular subjects. Then treat these times just as if they were classes you had to attend.

Sleep Remember that sleeping after study reduces interference. Since you obviously can't sleep after every study session or study everything just before you sleep, your study schedule (see Spaced Practice) should include ample breaks between subjects. Using your breaks and free time in a schedule is as important as living up to your study periods.

Review If you have spaced your practice and overlearned, review will be like icing on your study cake. Reviewing shortly before an exam cuts down the time during which you must remember details that may be important for the test. When reviewing, hold the amount of new information you try to memorize to a minimum. It may be realistic to take what you have actually learned and add a little more to it at the last minute by cramming. But remember that more than a little new learning may interfere with what you already know.

Using a Strategy to Aid Recall Successful recall is usually the result of a planned *search* of memory (Reed, 1996). For example, one study found that students were most likely to recall names that eluded them if they made use of partial information (Reed & Bruce, 1982). The students were trying to answer questions such as, "He is best remembered as the scarecrow in the Judy Garland movie *The Wizard of Oz.*" (The answer is Ray Bolger.) Partial information that helped students remember included impressions about the length of the name, letter sounds within the name, similar names, and related information (such as the names of other characters in the movie). A similar helpful strategy is to go through the alphabet, trying each letter as the first sound of a name or word you are seeking.

Using a variety of cues, even partial ones, opens more paths to a memory. The next highlight gives further hints for recapturing context and jogging memories.

Memory Detectives

You may not think of yourself as a "memory detective," but active probing often helps improve recall. A case in point is the **cognitive interview**, *a technique used to jog the memory of eyewitnesses*. The cognitive interview was created by R. Edward Geiselman and Ron Fisher to help police detectives. When used properly, it produces 35 percent more correct information than standard questioning (Geiselman et al., 1986). This improvement comes without adding to the number of false memories elicited, as occurs with hypnosis (Chapman & Perry, 1995).

Some police detectives, following the advice of psychologists, recreate crime scenes to help witnesses remember what they saw. Typically, people return to the scene at the time of day the crime occurred. They are also asked to wear the same clothing they wore and go through the same motions as they did before the crime. With so many memory cues available, witnesses sometimes remember key items of information they hadn't recalled before.

By following four simple steps, you can apply cognitive principles to your own memory. The next time you are searching for a "lost" memory—one that you know is in there somewhere—try the following search strategies.

1. Say or write down *everything* you can remember that relates to the information you are seeking. Don't worry about how trivial any of it seems; each bit of information you remember can serve as a cue to bring back others.

2. Try to recall events or information in different orders. Let your memories flow out backward or out of order, or start with whatever impressed you the most.

3. Recall from different viewpoints. Review events by mentally standing in a different place. Or try to view information as another person would remember it. When taking a test, for instance, ask yourself what other students or your professor would remember about the topic.

4. Mentally put yourself back in the situation where you learned the information. Try to mentally re-create the learning environment or relive the event. As you do, include sounds, smells, details of weather, nearby objects, other people present, what you said or thought, and how you felt as you learned the information (Fisher & Geiselman, 1987).

These strategies help re-create the context in which information was learned, and they provide multiple memory cues. If you think of remembering as a sort of "treasure hunt," you might even learn to enjoy the detective work.

A Look Ahead Psychologists still have much to learn about the nature of memory and how to improve it. For now, one thing stands out clearly: People who have good memories excel at organizing information and making it meaningful. With this in mind, the Applications for this chapter tells how you can combine organization and meaning into a powerful method for improving memory. In the Explorations section, we will examine the bitter controversy concerning the purported recovery of long-repressed memories of childhood sexual abuse.

Learning Check

1. To improve memory, it is reasonable to spend as much or more time reciting as reading. T or F?

2. Organizing information while studying has little effect on memory because long-term memory is already highly organized. T or F?

3. The progressive part method of study is best suited to long and complex learning tasks. T or F?

4. Sleeping immediately after studying is highly disruptive to the consolidation of memories. T or F?

5. As new information is encoded and rehearsed it is helpful to elaborate on its meaning and connect it to other information. T or F?

Critical Thinking

6. What advantages would there be to taking notes as you read a textbook, as opposed to underlining words in the text?

Answers:

1. T 2. F 3. T 4. F 5. T 6. Note-taking is a form of recitation, it encourages elaborative rehearsal, it facilitates the organization and selection of important ideas, and your notes can be used for review.

Applications
Mnemonics—Memory Magic

Some stage performers use memory as part of their acts. Do they have eidetic imagery?

Various "memory experts" entertain by memorizing the names of everyone at a banquet, the order of all the cards in a deck, long lists of words, or other seemingly impossible amounts of information. Such feats may seem like magic, but if they are, you can have a magic memory too. These tricks are performed through the use of *mnemonics* (nee-MON-iks) (Wilding & Valentine, 1994b). A **mnemonic** *is any kind of memory system or aid.* In some cases, mnemonic strategies increase recall tenfold (Patten, 1990).

Some mnemonic systems are so common that almost everyone knows them. If you are trying to remember how many days there are in a month, you may find the answer by reciting, "Thirty days hath September. . . ." Physics teachers often help students remember the colors of the spectrum by giving them the mnemonic "Roy G. Biv": **R**ed, **O**range, **Y**ellow, **G**reen, **B**lue, **I**ndigo, **V**iolet. The budding sailor who has trouble telling port from starboard may remember that port and left both have four letters or may remind herself, "I *left* port." And what beginning musician hasn't remembered the notes represented by the lines and spaces of the musical staff by learning "F-A-C-E" and "**E**very **G**ood **B**oy **D**oes **F**ine"?

Mnemonic techniques are ways to avoid *rote* learning (learning by simple repetition). The superiority of mnemonic learning as opposed to rote learning has been demonstrated many times. For example, Bower (1973) asked college students to study 5 different lists of 20 unrelated words. At the end of a short study session, subjects tried to recall all 100 items. People using mnemonics remembered an average of 72 items, whereas members of a control group using rote learning remembered an average of 28.

Stage performers rarely have naturally superior memories. Instead, they make extensive use of memory systems to perform their feats (Wilding & Valentine, 1994b). Few of these systems are of practical value to you as a student, but the principles underlying mnemonics are. By practicing mnemonics you should be able to greatly improve your memory with little effort (Dretzke & Levin, 1996).

Here, then, are the basic principles of mnemonics.

1. **Use mental pictures.** Visual pictures, or images, are generally easier to remember than words. Turning information into mental pictures is therefore very helpful (Kroll et al., 1986).

2. **Make things meaningful.** Transferring information from short-term to long-term memory is aided by making it meaningful. If you encounter technical terms that have little or no immediate meaning for you, *give* them meaning, even if you have to stretch the term to do so. (This point is clarified by the examples following this list.)

3. **Make information familiar.** Connect it to what you already know. Another way to get information into long-term memory is to connect it to information already stored there. If some facts or ideas in a chapter seem to stay in your memory easily, associate other more difficult facts with them.

4. **Form bizarre, unusual, or exaggerated mental associations.** Forming images that make sense is better in most situations. However, when associating two ideas, terms, or especially mental images, you may find that the more outrageous and exaggerated the association, the more likely you are to remember (Lang, 1995). Bizarre images make stored information more *distinctive* and therefore easier to retrieve (Worthen & Marshall, 1996).

   Bizarre images mainly help improve immediate memory and they work best for fairly simple information (Robinson-Riegler & McDaniel, 1994). Nevertheless, they can be a first step toward learning.

A sampling of typical applications of mnemonics should make these four points clearer to you.

Example 1 Let's say you have 30 new vocabulary words to memorize in Spanish. You can proceed by rote memorization (repeat them over and over until you begin to get them), or you can learn them with little effort by using the *keyword method* (Pressley, 1987). In the **keyword method** *a familiar word or image is used to link two other words or items.* To remember that the word *pajaro* (pronounced PAH-hah-ro)

Mnemonics can be an aid in preparing for tests. However, because mnemonics help most in the initial stages of storing information, it is important to follow through with other learning strategies.

means bird, you can link it to a "key" word in English: *Pajaro* (to me) sounds like "parked car-o." Therefore, to remember that *pajaro* means bird, I will visualize a parked car jam-packed full of birds. I will try to make this image as vivid and exaggerated as possible, with birds flapping and chirping and feathers flying everywhere. Similarly, for the word *carta* (which means "letter"), I will imagine a shopping *cart* filled with postal letters.

If you link similar keywords and images for the rest of the list, you may not remember them all, but you will get most without any more practice. As a matter of fact, if you have formed the *pajaro* and *carta* images just now, it is going to be almost impossible for you to ever see these words again without remembering what they mean. The keyword method is also superior when you want to work "backward" from an English word to a foreign vocabulary word (Hogben & Lawson, 1992).

What if I think that pajaro *means "parked car" when I take my Spanish test?*

This is why you should form one or two extra images so that the important feature (bird, in this case) is repeated.

Example 2 Let's say you have to learn the names of all the bones and muscles in the human body for biology. You are trying to remember that the jawbone is the *mandible*. This one is easy because you can associate it to a *man nibbling*, or

Exaggerated mental images can link two words or ideas in ways that aid memory. Here, the keyword method is used to link the English word *letter* with the Spanish word *carta*.

maybe you can picture a *man dribbling* a basketball with his jaw (make this image as ridiculous as possible). If the muscle name *latissimus dorsi* gives you trouble, familiarize it by turning it into *"the ladder misses the door, sigh."* Then picture a ladder glued to your back where the muscle is found. Picture the ladder leading up to a small door at your shoulder. Picture the ladder missing the door. Picture the ladder sighing like an animated character in a cartoon.

This seems like more to remember, not less; and it seems like it would cause you to misspell things.

Mnemonics are not a complete substitute for normal memory; they are an aid to normal memory. Mnemonics are not likely to be helpful unless you make extensive use of *images*. Your mental pictures will come back to you easily. As for misspellings, mnemonics can be thought of as a built-in hint in your memory. Often, when taking a test, you will find that the slightest hint is all you need to remember correctly. A mnemonic image is like having someone leaning over your shoulder who says, "Psst, the name of that muscle sounds like 'ladder misses the door, sigh.' " If misspelling continues to be a problem, try to create memory aids for spelling, too.

Here are two more examples to help you appreciate the flexibility of a mnemonic approach to studying.

Example 3   Your art history teacher expects you to be able to name the artist when you are shown slides as part of exams. You have seen many of the slides only once before in class. How will you remember them? As the slides are shown in class, make each artist's name into an object or image. Then picture the object *in* the paintings done by the artist. For example, you can picture Van Gogh as a *van* (automobile) *going* through the middle of each Van Gogh painting. Picture the van running over things and knocking things over. Or, if you remember that Van Gogh cut off his ear, picture a giant bloody ear in each of his paintings.

Example 4   If you have trouble remembering history, try to avoid thinking of it as something from the dim past. Picture each historical personality as a person you know right now (a friend, teacher, parent, and so on). Then picture these people doing whatever the historical figures did. Also, try visualizing battles or other events as if they were happening in your town or make parks and schools into countries. Use your imagination.

How can mnemonics be used to remember things in order?

Here are three techniques that are helpful.

1.   Form a chain. To remember lists of ideas, objects, or words in order, try forming an exaggerated association (mental image) connecting the first item to the second, then the second to the third, and so on. To remember the following short list in order—*elephant, doorknob, string, watch, rifle, oranges*—picture a full-sized *elephant* balanced on a *doorknob* playing with a *string* tied to him. Picture a *watch* tied to the string, and a *rifle* shooting *oranges* at the watch. This technique can be used quite successfully for lists of 20 or more items. In a recent test, people who used a linking mnemonic did much better at remembering lists of 15 and 22 errands (Higbee et al., 1990). Try it next time you go shopping and leave your list at home.

2.   Take a mental walk. Ancient Greek orators had an interesting way to remember ideas in order when giving a speech. Their method was to take a mental walk along a familiar path. As they did, they associated topics with the images of statues found along the walk. You can do the same thing by "placing" objects or ideas along the way as you mentally take a familiar walk.

3.   Use a system. Many times, the first letters or syllables of words or ideas can be formed into another word that will serve as a reminder of order. "Roy G. Biv" is an example. As an alternative, learn the following: 1 is a bun, 2 is a shoe, 3 is a tree, 4 is a door, 5 is a hive, 6 is sticks, 7 is heaven, 8 is a gate, 9 is a line, 10 is a hen. To remember a list in order, form an image associating bun with the first item on your list. For example, if the first item is *frog*, picture a "frog-burger" on a bun to remember it. Then, associate shoe with the second item, and so on.

If you have never used mnemonics, you may still be skeptical, but give this approach a fair trial. Most people find they can greatly extend their memory through the use of mnemonics. For example, college students who used the keyword method to learn medical terms scored significantly higher than those using conventional memory (Troutt-Ervin, 1990). But remember, mnemonics only supplement the memory tips given earlier. They tend to be most effective for short-term memory (Krinsky & Krinsky, 1996). At some point you will need to work on making your learning more permanent. Like most things worthwhile, remembering takes effort.

Learning Check

1. Memory systems and aids are referred to as _____ .

2. Which of the following is least likely to improve memory?
   a. using exaggerated mental images
   b. forming a chain of associations
   c. turning visual information into verbal information
   d. associating new information to information that is already known or familiar

3. Picturing your knee moaning as it tries to remember something could serve as a mnemonic for the term mnemonic. T or F?

4. Bower's 1973 study showed that, in general, mnemonics only improve memory for related words or ideas. T or F?

Critical Thinking

5. How could you use mnemonics to make the nonsense syllables LAZ, CEF, and WOL easier to remember?

Answers:
5. How about, the "LAZy CHEF is a WOLf"?
1. mnemonics 2. c 3. T 4. F

Exploration

The Recovered-Memory/False-Memory Debate

The idea that early traumatic memories are often deeply repressed has gained wide acceptance. Perhaps too wide. "Recovered" memories of childhood sexual abuse are surfacing by the thousands in therapists' offices, incest recovery groups, celebrity confessions, TV talk shows, and courtrooms.

How valid are memories of sexual abuse that return to awareness long after childhood?

Psychologists are currently debating this question. To grasp the nature of their debate, consider the following sketches.

Laura's Story Laura visits a psychotherapist for help with depression and marital difficulties. The therapist tells Laura that her symptoms suggest she was sexually abused as a child. At first, Laura insists that she doesn't remember any abuse. But with the therapist's guidance, Laura begins to bring disturbing memory fragments to the surface. Eventually, in a horrifying rush of flashbacks, Laura remembers her father raping her.

Through hypnosis, dream analysis, guided visualization, and an incest survivors group, Laura recovers other lost memories of childhood sexual abuse. In doing so, she takes the first painful steps toward healing the long-hidden cause of her problems.

Kathy's Story Kathy seeks help from a psychotherapist for depression and marital difficulties. Unbeknownst to her, Kathy has blundered into a "memory mill" run by an incompetent therapist who believes that sexual abuse is the root of nearly all problems. During the very first session, the therapist tells Kathy that she was sexually abused as a child. Kathy resists this idea, saying that she has no memory of any abuse. But gradually, as she submits to hypnosis, dream analysis, guided visualization, and participation in an incest survivors group, Kathy begins to have detailed memories of childhood abuse.

Kathy's "recovered memories" are actually pure fantasy, spawned by her therapist's suggestions. Nevertheless, she believes them completely. Kathy accuses her father of sexual abuse and breaks all ties with him. Kathy's father loses his job and her family is shattered. Yet, there is no way of proving Kathy's memories are false.

Recovered Memories?

Laura's and Kathy's stories represent two extremes of the recovered-memory debate. Advocates of recovered-memory therapy view it as an antidote for the long-buried pain of childhood incest and sexual abuse. Critics see it as a nightmare of malpractice that can create false memories and destroy families. Let's examine some points of the debate.

Point   Many adults who suffer from depression, low self-esteem, sexual problems, and other complaints, have documented histories of sexual abuse. Recovered-memory therapists think it is reasonable to suspect hidden abuse when a person like Laura or Kathy has similar problems.

Counterpoint   Critics believe that the purported symptoms of hidden abuse are dubious at best. For example, signs of abuse listed in one pop-psychology book include "too much or too little trust of others, high risk-taking or an inability to take risks, too much interest in sex or too little." On the basis of such vague symptoms, and others like them, almost anyone could be suspected of harboring hidden memories of abuse.

Point   Most victims of childhood sexual abuse vividly remember having been molested. That's why skeptics doubt that many victims repress the experience. Childhood memories of other atrocities, such as seeing a family member killed, are usually carried for life. The problem for most victims of abuse is that they can't forget what happened to them, not that they don't remember it.

Counterpoint   Proponents of recovered memory theorize that sexual abuse is a special case, because the abuse is repeated and extremely threatening. To cope with ongoing abuse the child must repress it, they say.

Reply   Critics reply that children who survived the Holocaust in Nazi concentration camps vividly remember the experience. Again, their problem is an inability to forget repeated atrocities, not a failure to remember.

Point   From 10 to 60 percent of early sexual abuse victims say that there was a time in their lives when they "forgot" about having been abused.

Counterpoint   Estimates of repression rates are probably inflated. Books, survivors groups, celebrity testimonials, and media coverage have led many people to believe that "recovered" memories are common.

Point   Memory experts argue that countless studies have shown that everyday memories are unreliable and easily altered. A patient guided by an incompetent therapist might confuse dreams with memories, unconsciously transforming fantasies and old resentments into a forgotten molestation.

Counterpoint   Defenders of recovered-memory therapy reply that only minor details of memory are altered in lab experiments. They believe that personally important or traumatic memories cannot be created through suggestion.

Reply   In fact, memory researcher Elizabeth Loftus has shown that false memories are easy to create. Loftus arranged for older relatives to tell college students false stories about how the students got lost in a shopping mall as children. When they were later asked to recall further details, 1 out of 4 students described elaborate memories of the fictitious incidents.

Loftus also cites a study of children who were not at their elementary school when a sniper shot at youngsters on the playground. Despite being absent, many of the children later reported intricate memories of the event.

Point   Suggestion and fantasy are major elements of most of the techniques used to recover repressed memories, such as hypnosis and guided visualization. A person seeking an explanation for his or her suffering may be especially susceptible to suggestion. Certainly, some memories that are brought to awareness by suggestion are genuine. However, there is no way to distinguish real memories from false memories.

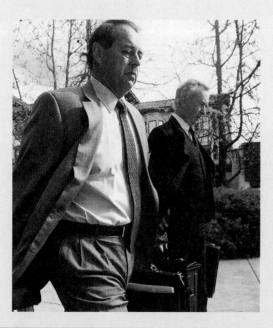

Gary Ramona lost his marriage and his $400,000-a-year job as a business executive when his 19-year-old daughter Holly alleged that he molested her throughout her childhood. Ramona sued Holly's therapists, claiming that they had been irresponsible. To prove to Holly that her memories were true, the therapists gave her the drug sodium amytal, and told her that it was a "truth drug." (Sodium amytal is a hypnotic drug that induces a twilight state of consciousness. People do not automatically tell the truth while under its influence.) After reviewing the evidence for 2 months, a jury awarded Gary Ramona $500,000 in damages.

Counterpoint Defenders of recovered memories state that therapists rarely wield enough power or influence over patients to impose false memories on them. They believe that false complaints are rare. Most survivors unfairly blame themselves, not their abusers.

Point Psychologist Margaret Singer has interviewed 50 people who once believed they had recovered repressed memories of abuse but now think they were mistaken. All say that their therapists were far more sure than they were that their parents had molested them. Thousands of recovered-memory patients have now retracted their accusations. Some have joined their families in suing the therapists and clinics they claim led them astray.

Counterpoint Recovered-memory advocates believe that those who recant may *prefer* to believe their troubling memories are not true. Accusations of incest and sexual abuse cause great pain and are followed by many pressures to recant.

Reply Skeptics reply that there are equally strong pressures to not retract an accusation. Once a charge of sexual abuse has been made public it is very difficult for an accuser to admit she or he was wrong. Researchers have identified many instances in which "recovered" traumatic memories were shown to be absolutely false.

Summary

As you can see, persuasive arguments exist on both sides of the recovered-memory debate. There is evidence that memories of sexual abuse are sometimes repressed, or at least suppressed for periods of time. Likewise, there is little doubt that some "recovered" memories are pure fantasy. Clearly there is a need to strike a balance between uncovering and treating real repressed trauma and doing damage by fabricating memories.

What can therapists do to help protect their clients from creating false memories?

Suggestions for Therapists

1. Mental health professionals should re-evaluate their work. Therapists who too readily assume that problems must be caused by childhood sexual abuse are probably harming some of their clients.

2. Therapists must not push clients to find "hidden" memories. If a therapist strongly suspects hidden trauma, she or he might ask a client to jog memories in some neutral way, such as by reviewing old family photographs. But this should be done without suggesting what kind of memories the person will find.

3. Therapists should be extremely cautious about using techniques that can foster false memories. Clients should be warned that such techniques may cause them to misinterpret dreams or fantasies as genuine memories.

4. Therapists should not encourage clients to join incest survivors groups until they are reasonably certain that sex abuse actually happened. The shared recollections of group members can be highly persuasive and may promote false memories.

5. Therapists should maintain a healthy skepticism regarding recovered memories. "Memories" of sexual abuse may be symbolic, rather than literally true. For instance, they may reveal that a client felt emotionally "raped" in childhood, not that the person was actually molested. In the absence of firm supporting evidence, there is no way to tell if a memory is real or not.

What can individuals who suspect they were sexually abused do to avoid making false accusations?

Suggestions for Consumers

1. If you think you may have been sexually abused but aren't sure, consult an experienced psychotherapist. (See the Applications section of Chapter 19 for information on finding a competent therapist.) Never put yourself in the hands of a self-described "recovered-memory therapist."

2. Be wary of any therapist who tells you within the first few sessions that you were probably sexually abused as a child.

3. If a therapist pressures you to believe that you were sexually abused, discuss your concerns with the therapist. If the pressure continues, report the experience to the therapist's professional association and consider changing therapists.

4. Beware of anyone who treats failure to recall abuse as evidence of abuse. One popular book on abuse states that "If you think you were abused and your life shows the symptoms, then you were," and "If you don't remember your abuse, you are not alone. Many women don't have memories . . . this doesn't mean they weren't abused." Both are dangerously misleading ideas.

5. Maintain a healthy skepticism regarding recovered memories. Remember, unless a memory can be independently confirmed, there is no way to tell if it is real or not real.

6. Before making accusations of abuse against anyone, seek confirming evidence. If none is available, consider consulting another therapist before acting on your memories. In the absence of firm evidence you should be cautious about accusing anyone based on recovered memories alone.

The saddest aspect of the epidemic of false claims about childhood abuse is that it has helped deaden public sensitivity to actual abuse. Childhood sexual abuse is widespread. Awareness of its existence must not be repressed.

Sources: Byrd, 1994; Gold et al., 1994; Hembrooke & Ceci, 1995; Loftus, 1994; Loftus, Feldman, & Dashiell, 1995; Pendergast, 1995; Porter & Lane, 1996; Reisner, 1996; Schacter, 1996; Terr, 1991; Whitfield, 1995.

Learning Check	**Critical Thinking**

1. Hypnosis, dream analysis, and guided verbalization are methods that are commonly used to "recover" repressed memories. T or F?

2. A reasonable conclusion to be drawn from the recovered-memory debate is that creating false memories is so rare as to be nearly impossible. T or F?

3. Like sexual abuse, memories of other types of severe trauma in childhood are almost always repressed. T or F?

4. Advocates of recovered-memory therapy believe that lab studies which show that memories can be altered by suggestion do not apply to childhood memories of sexual abuse. T or F?

5. People who have renounced their "recovered" memories generally admit that they were guilty of persuading skeptical therapists that their memories were real. T or F?

6. If you think you were abused and your life shows the symptoms, then you were. T or F?

7. Why does the use of hypnosis to unlock repressed memories limit the credibility of any "memories" that may be "recovered"?

Answers:

7. As stated earlier in this chapter, hypnosis tends to increase the occurrence of false memories. Also, people often have unshakable confidence in false memories that are retrieved under hypnosis.

1. F   2. F   3. F   4. T   5. F   6. F

Chapter Summary

Is there more than one type of memory?

◆ **Memory** is an active system that **encodes, stores,** and **retrieves** information.

◆ Humans appear to have three interrelated memory systems. These are **sensory memory, short-term memory** (STM, also called **working memory**), and **long-term memory** (LTM).

What are the features of each type of memory?

◆ Sensory memory is exact, but very brief. Through **selective attention,** some information is transferred to STM.

◆ STM has a capacity of about **seven bits** of information, but this can be extended by **chunking,** or **recoding.** Short-term memories are brief and very sensitive to **interruption,** or **interference**; however, they can be prolonged by **maintenance rehearsal.**

◆ LTM functions as a general storehouse of information, especially *meaningful* information. **Elaborative rehearsal** helps transfer information from STM to LTM. Long-term memories are *relatively permanent*, or lasting. LTM seems to have an almost *unlimited* storage capacity.

◆ LTM is subject to **constructive processing,** or ongoing revision and updating. LTM is highly *organized* to allow retrieval of needed information. The pattern, or **structure,** of memory **networks** is the subject of current memory research.

◆ **Redintegrative memories** are *reconstructed* as each memory provides a cue for the next memory.

Is there more than one type of long-term memory?

◆ Within long-term memory, **declarative memories** for facts seem to differ from **procedural memories** for skills. Declarative memories may be further categorized as **semantic memories** or **episodic memories.** The properties and relationships among types of memory are currently being debated.

How is memory measured?

◆ The **tip-of-the-tongue state** shows that memory is not an all-or-nothing event. Memories may therefore be revealed by **recall, recognition,** or **relearning.**

◆ In recall, memory proceeds without *specific cues*, as in an *essay* exam. Recall of listed information often reveals a **serial position effect** (middle items on the list are most subject to errors). A common test of recognition is the *multiple-choice* question. In relearning, "forgotten" material is learned again, and memory is indicated by a **savings score.**

◆ Recall, recognition, and relearning mainly measure **explicit memories.** Other techniques, such as **priming,** are necessary to reveal the existence of **implicit memories.**

What are "photographic" memories?

◆ **Eidetic imagery** (photographic memory) occurs when a person is able to project an image onto a blank surface. Such images allow brief, nearly complete recall by some children. Eidetic imagery is rarely found in adults. However, many adults have **internal memory images,** which can be very vivid.

◆ **Exceptional memory** can be learned by finding ways to directly store information in LTM. Learning has no effect on the limits of STM. Some people may have exceptional memories that exceed what can be achieved through learning.

What causes forgetting?

◆ Forgetting and memory were extensively studied by **Herman Ebbinghaus,** whose **curve of forgetting** shows that forgetting is typically most rapid immediately after learning. While the shape of the curve remains the same, forgetting is much slower for meaningful information.

◆ **Failure to encode** information is a common cause of "forgetting." Forgetting in sensory memory and STM probably reflects **decay** of **memory traces** in the nervous system. Decay or **disuse** of memories may also account for some LTM loss, but most forgetting cannot be explained this way.

◆ Often, forgetting is **cue dependent.** The power of cues to trigger memories is revealed by **state-dependent learning** and the link between moods and memory.

◆ Much forgetting in both STM and LTM can be attributed to **interference** of memories with one another. When recent learning interferes with retrieval of prior learning, **retroactive interference** has occurred. If old memories interfere with new memories, **proactive interference** has occurred. Depending on the relationship between prior learning and a new task, skills may show **positive transfer** or **negative transfer** (carryover to a new situation).

How accurate are everyday memories?

◆ **Repression** is the forgetting of painful, embarrassing, or traumatic memories. Repression is thought to be unconscious, in contrast to **suppression,** which is a conscious attempt to avoid thinking about something.

What happens in the brain when memories are formed?

◆ **Retrograde amnesia** and the effects of electroconvulsive shock (ECS) may be explained by the concept of **consolidation.** Consolidation theory holds that **engrams** (permanent memory traces) are formed during a critical period after learning. Until they are consolidated, long-term memories are easily destroyed.

◆ The **hippocampus** is a brain area that has been linked with consolidation of memories.

◆ The search within the brain for engrams has now settled on changes in individual nerve cells. The best-documented changes are alterations in the amounts of **transmitter chemicals** released by the cells and the number of **receptor sites** on each cell.

How can memory be improved?

◆ Memory can be improved by using **feedback, recitation,** and **rehearsal,** by **selecting** and **organizing** information, and by using the **progressive part method, spaced practice, overlearning,** and active **search strategies.** Effects of **serial position, sleep, review, cues,** and **elaboration** should also be kept in mind when studying or memorizing.

◆ **Mnemonic systems** use mental images and unusual associations to link new information with familiar memories already stored in LTM. Such strategies give information personal meaning and make it easier to recall.

What is the "recovered-memory" debate?

◆ Experts are currently debating the validity of childhood memories of abuse that reappear after apparently being repressed for decades.

◆ Independent evidence has verified that some recovered memories are true. However, others have been shown to be false.

◆ In the absence of confirming or disconfirming evidence, there is currently no way to separate true memories from fantasies. Caution is advised for all concerned with attempts to retrieve supposedly hidden memories.

Cognition and Creativity

Preview

The Monster

Garry was in trouble. It was the last game of a six-game chess match, and Garry was losing. If he blew the match, he would forfeit $300,000 in prize money. Usually, Garry's fierce attacks and unexpected moves threw opponents off balance. But this time, his challenger seemed unfazed. Today, Garry had met his match. Silently, he watched as Deep Blue made its final move, winning game 6.

Deep Blue is the world's most powerful chess computer. World chess champion Garry Kasparov calls it—with all due respect—"the monster." Deep Blue can calculate 200 million moves a second. That's enough power to check billions of future chess positions before each move.

Deep Blue was the first computer to defeat a world champion in an actual tournament game. Kasparov's ultimate defeat by Deep Blue in 1997 marked the first time he had lost a tournament to any opponent since becoming champion in 1985.

It might seem that Deep Blue's victory diminishes human thinking capacity. On the contrary, it shows just how powerful the human intellect can be. It took 500 microprocessors working together, plus countless hours of programming, to match Kasparov's thinking abilities in the limited arena of a chess match. Moreover, Deep Blue will never be capable of writing a novel, composing rap music, or investigating the origins of consciousness. No matter how powerful computers may become, adaptability, reasoning, and creative thinking remain human strengths. Indeed, it was human thinking that led to the invention of computers in the first place.

We know how computers "think" because we created them. But how do we explain a chess master's creativity and problem-solving ability? Or yours? Thinking, problem solving, and creativity are the challenging topics of this chapter.

Theme: Thinking, problem solving, language, and creativity are the origins of intelligent behavior.

Key Questions	Key Topics to Watch for:
What is the nature of thought?	Internal representations Basic units of thought
In what ways are images related to thinking?	Mental imagery Properties of mental images
How are concepts learned? Are there different kinds of concepts?	Concept formation Types of concepts Connotative and denotative meaning
What is the role of language in thinking?	Semantics, grammar, and syntax Theories of language
Can animals be taught to use language?	Animal communication
What do we know about problem solving?	Types of problem solving Heurisitics Insight and fixations
What is artificial intelligence?	Computer simulations and expert systems Novices and experts
What is the nature of creative thinking?	Divergent thinking Stages of creative thought Tests of creativity The creative personality
How accurate is intuition?	Intuitive thinking errors
What can be done to improve thinking and promote creativity?	Steps to better thinking Enhancing creativity
Do animals think?	Animal intelligence

What Is Thinking?—It's All in Your Head!

Thinking takes many forms, including daydreaming, problem solving, and reasoning (to name but a few). Stated more formally, thinking, or **cognition**, *refers to mentally processing information* (images, concepts, words, rules, and symbols). Studying thinking is similar to figuring out how a computer works by asking, "I wonder what would happen if I did this?" But in **cognitive psychology** (*the study of human information processing*) the "computer" is the brain, and thinking is the "programming" we seek to understand.

Although an ability to think is not limited to humans, imagine trying to teach an animal to match the feats of Shakuntala Devi, who holds the "world record" for mental calculation. Devi once multiplied two 13-digit numbers (7,686,369,774,870 times 2,465,099,745,779) in her head, giving the answer in 28 seconds (Morain, 1988). (That's 18,947,668,177,995,426,773,730 if you haven't already figured it out yourself.)

Some Basic Units of Thought

At its most basic, thinking is an **internal representation** (*mental expression*) of a problem or situation. (Picture a chess player who mentally tries out several moves before actually touching a chess piece.) The power of being able to represent problems internally is dramatically illustrated by Chess Grand Master Miguel Najdorf, who once simultaneously played 45 chess games, while *blindfolded*.

How did Najdorf perform his feat? Like most people, he used the following basic units of thought: (1) *images*, (2) *concepts*, and (3) *language*, or *symbols*. The three basic units can be defined in this way:

- **Image:** *Most often, a mental representation that has picture-like qualities; a visual likeness or icon.*

- **Concept:** *A generalized idea representing a class of related objects or events.*

- **Language:** *Words or symbols, and rules for combining them, which are used for thinking and communication.*

Complex thinking may require all three representations. Indeed, in some situations people need all the help they can

The power of thought is beautifully expressed by Stephen W. Hawking, a theoretical physicist and one of the best-known scientific minds of modern times. Now in his late 40s, Hawking has suffered since age 13 from amyotrophic lateral sclerosis, a disabling condition also known as Lou Gehrig's disease. Today, he can only control his left hand, and he cannot speak. Nevertheless, his brain remains fiercely active. With courage and determination, he has used his intellect to advance our understanding of the universe.

get. To accomplish their mental feats, blindfolded chess players rely on visual images, kinesthetic (muscular) images involving "lines of force," concepts ("Game 2 is an English opening"), and the special notational system, or "language," of chess.

In a moment we will explore the units of thought identified here. Be aware, however, that thinking involves attention, pattern recognition, memory, decision making, intuition, knowledge, and more. This chapter is only a sample of what cognitive psychologists study.

Mental Imagery—Does a Frog Have Lips?

Ninety-seven percent of all people have visual images and 92 percent have auditory images. Over 50 percent have imagery that includes movement, touch, taste, smell, and pain. When we speak of images, we usually think of mental "pictures" (Kosslyn, 1990). But as you can see, images may involve the other senses as well. Your image of a bakery, for example, may include its delicious odor, as well as its appearance.

Some people have a rare form of imagery called **synesthesia** (sin-es-THEE-zyah). For these individuals, *images cross normal sensory barriers* (Cytowic, 1993). For instance, a synesthetic individual listening to music may experience a burst of colors or tastes, as well as sound sensations. Despite such variations, it is generally accepted that most people use images to think, remember, and solve problems (Kosslyn, 1990). Table 11–1 ■ lists the most common uses for mental images.

Properties of Mental Images

Stephen Kosslyn and other researchers have discovered that mental images are not flat, like photographs. To sample Kosslyn's work, think about the following question: Does a frog have lips and a stubby tail? Unless you often kiss frogs, you will probably tackle this question by using mental images. To answer, most people picture a frog, "look" at its mouth, and then *mentally rotate* the frog to check its tail (Kosslyn, 1983). (**Mental rotation** *is the ability to change the position of an image in mental space*).

It can be seen that mental images of objects can be moved about as needed (Fig. 11–1 ◆). As our first highlight explains, images of entire three-dimensional spaces may be created just from descriptions, like those in a novel.

Table 11–1 ■ Common Uses of Mental Images

Mental images are most frequently used for the following purposes:
- **To make a decision or solve a problem.**
  Examples: Choosing what clothes to wear; figuring out how to arrange furniture in a room.
- **To help understand a verbal description.**
  Examples: Mentally picturing what a person is talking about; picturing a scene described in a novel.
- **To change feelings.**
  Examples: Thinking of pleasant images to get out of a bad mood; imagining oneself as thin to help stay on a diet.
- **To help explain or describe something.**
  Example: Visualizing a scene at a party to describe it to a friend.
- **To improve a skill or to prepare for some action.**
  Examples: Using images to improve a swimming stroke; mentally rehearsing how you will ask for a raise.
- **To aid memory.**
  Example: Picturing Mr. Cook wearing a chef's hat, so you can remember his name.

Kosslyn et al., 1990.

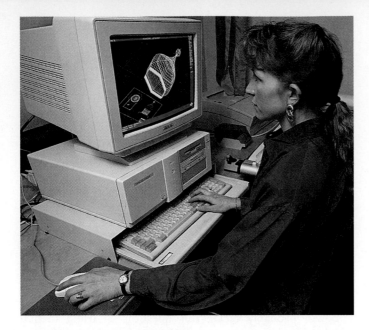

An ability to mentally rotate objects is very valuable for people who work in industrial design and drafting.

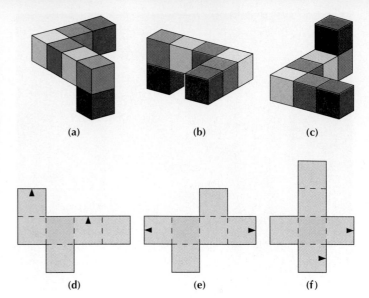

Figure 11–1 ◆ Imagery in thinking. (*Top*) Subjects were shown a drawing similar to **(a)** and drawings of how **(a)** would look in other positions, such as **(b)** and **(c)**. Subjects could recognize **(a)** after it had been "rotated" from its original position. However, the more **(a)** was rotated in space, the longer it took to recognize it. This result suggests that subjects actually formed a three-dimensional image of **(a)** and rotated the image to see if it matched. (Shepard, 1975.) (*Bottom*) Try your ability to manipulate mental images: Each of these shapes can be folded to make a cube; in which do the arrows meet? (After Kosslyn, 1985.)

3-D Images—Now Showing in Imaginations Everywhere

Detective Psyche slowly pushed open the window and stepped into the dingy room. On the opposite wall, above a rumpled bed, a mirror reflected her image, startling her. "This is creepy," she thought. Psyche's eyes drifted from the mirror to the floor at her right. Was that someone's shadow spilling under the closed door?

When you read a description of a scene, how do you remember the locations of objects? Psychologists Nancy Franklin and Barbara Tversky (1990) believe that we don't merely remember words, such as "mirror above bed." Typically, we form a spatial image of how objects are arranged.

To explore imagery, Franklin and Tversky had people read descriptions of various environments. Five objects were located in each scene. In a barn scene, for example, the objects were a saddle, a rake, a pail, a lantern, and shears. Participants imagined themselves in each setting and were quizzed about the locations of objects. Periodically, they were asked to change position in the imagined scene ("Turn 90 degrees to the right" or "Face the pail"). Everyone who was tested used imagery to locate the objects. Most, in fact, reported that they mentally "turned" and "looked at" objects to answer questions about them.

Subjects were quickest at locating objects above or below themselves. Finding objects placed to the right or left was the most difficult. This insight into how we construct mental images may aid the design of such things as airplane cockpits or nuclear power plant controls. To minimize confusion about the location of controls it is better to concentrate on the up-down dimension instead of right-left positioning.

What happens in the brain when a person has visual images?

"Reverse Vision" Seeing something in your "mind's eye" is closely related to seeing real objects. Information from the eyes normally activates the brain's primary visual area, creating an image (Fig. 11–2 ◆). Other brain areas then help us recognize the image by relating it to stored knowledge. When you form a mental image, the system works in reverse. A stimulus, such as an odor, a song, or a question, activates memories in higher brain areas. These areas send signals back to the visual cortex, where once again, an image is created (Farah, 1988; Farah et al., 1989; Kosslyn, Thompson, & Alpert, 1995).

How are images used to solve problems?

Using Mental Images **Stored images** can be *retrieved from memory* to apply prior experience to problem solving. If you were asked, "How many uses can you think of for an old automobile tire?" you might begin by picturing uses you have already seen. To generate more original solutions, *created* images may be used. A **created image** *is assembled or invented rather than simply remembered*. Thus, an artist may

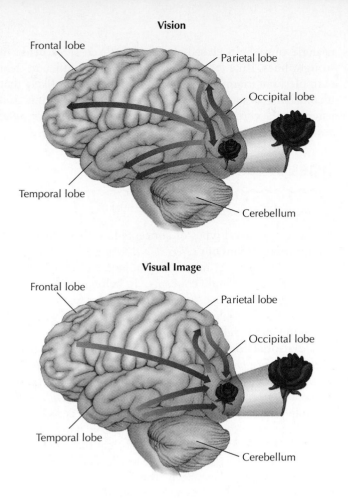

Vision

Frontal lobe

Parietal lobe

Occipital lobe

Temporal lobe

Cerebellum

Visual Image

Frontal lobe

Parietal lobe

Occipital lobe

Temporal lobe

Cerebellum

Figure 11–2 ◆ When you see a flower, its image is represented by activity in the primary visual area of the cortex, at the back of the brain. Information about the flower is also relayed to other brain areas. If you form a mental image of a flower, information follows a reverse path. The result, once again, is activation of the primary visual area.

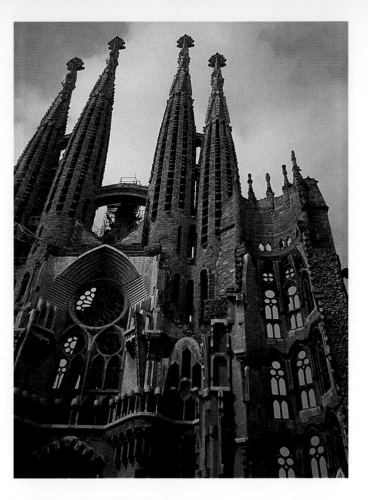

The Church of the Sacred Family in Barcelona, Spain, was designed by Antonio Gaudi. Could a person lacking mental imagery design such a masterpiece? Three people out of 100 find it impossible to produce mental images and 3 out of 100 have very strong imagery. Most artists, architects, designers, sculptors, and filmmakers have excellent visual imagery.

completely picture a proposed sculpture before beginning work. People who have good imaging abilities tend to score higher on tests of creativity (Campos & Gonzalez, 1995). In fact, some of history's most original intellects relied heavily on imagery. Examples include Albert Einstein, Thomas Edison, Lewis Carroll, and Winston Churchill (West, 1991).

Does the "size" of a mental image affect thinking? To find out, first picture a cat sitting beside a housefly. Now try to "zoom in" on the cat's ears so you see them clearly. Next, picture a rabbit sitting beside an elephant. How quickly can you "see" the rabbit's front feet? Did it take longer than picturing the cat's ears?

When a rabbit is pictured with an elephant, the rabbit's image must be small because the elephant is large. Using such tasks, Stephen Kosslyn found that the smaller an image is, the harder it is to "see" its details. To put this finding to use, try forming oversized images of things you want to think about. For example, to understand electricity, picture the wires as large pipes with electrons the size of golf balls moving through them; to understand the human ear, explore it (in your mind's eye) like a large cave; and so forth.

Kinesthetic Imagery

How do muscular responses relate to thinking?

In a sense, we think with our bodies as well as our heads. Information can be represented in **kinesthetic images** *created from produced, remembered, or imagined muscular sensations* (Oyama & Ichikawa, 1990). People who "talk" with their hands are using gestures to help themselves think, as well as to communicate.

Much information is contained in **kinesthetic sensations** (*feelings from the muscles and joints*). As a person talks, these sensations help structure the flow of ideas. If you try to tell a friend how to knead bread dough, you may find it impossible to resist moving your hands in the proper motion. Or, try answering this question: Which direction must you turn the hot-water handle in your kitchen to shut the water off? Most people haven't simply memorized the words "Turn it clockwise," or "Turn it counterclockwise." Instead you will probably "turn" the faucet in your imagination before answering. You may even find yourself making the required hand motions before you answer.

Kinesthetic images are especially important in music, sports, dance, martial arts, and other movement-oriented skills. People with good kinesthetic imagery learn such skills faster than those with poor imagery (Glisky, Williams, & Kihlstrom, 1996).

Most thinking is accompanied by muscular tension and *micromovements* throughout the body. **Micromovements** *are tiny, nearly imperceptible motions of the muscles.* For example, a burst of activity can be detected in the muscles of a person's unmoving arm when she or he imagines lifting a weight (Bakker, Boschker, & Chung, 1996). Such micromovements are an outward expression of the brain activity that accompanies kinesthetic images (Parsons et al., 1995).

If you would like to demonstrate the link between muscular activity and thinking, ask a friend who was in a sports event to describe what occurred. Along with a description, you will probably get an "instant replay" of the high points!

Concepts—I'm Positive, It's a Whatchamacallit

A **concept** *is an idea that represents a class of objects or events.* Concepts are powerful tools because they allow us to think more *abstractly*, free from distracting details.

How are concepts learned?

Concept formation *is the process of classifying information into meaningful categories.* At its most basic, concept formation is based on experience with **positive** and **negative instances** (*examples that belong, or do not belong, to the concept class*).

Concept formation is not as simple as it might seem. Imagine a child learning the concept of *dog.*

Dog Daze

A child and her father go for a walk. At a neighbor's house, they see a medium-sized dog. The father says, "See the dog." As they pass the next yard, the child sees a cat and says, "Dog!" Her father corrects her, "No, that's a *cat.*" The child now thinks, "Aha, dogs are large and cats are small." In the next yard, she sees a Pekingese and says, "Cat!" "No, that's a dog," replies her father.

The child's confusion is understandable. At first she might even mistake a Pekingese for a dust mop. However, with more positive and negative instances, the child will eventually recognize everything from Great Danes to Chihuahuas as examples of the same category—dogs.

As adults, we more often acquire concepts by learning or forming *rules.* A **conceptual rule** *is a guideline for deciding if an object or event belongs to a concept class.* For example, a

triangle must be a closed shape with three sides made of straight lines. Rule learning is generally more efficient than examples, but examples remain important. It is unlikely that memorizing a series of rules would allow an uninitiated listener to accurately categorize *punk, hip hop, fusion, salsa, heavy metal, grunge rock,* and *rap* music.

Types of Concepts

Are there different kinds of concepts?

Yes, several general types of concepts have been identified. A **conjunctive concept** *refers to a class of objects having more than one feature in common.* Conjunctive concepts are sometimes called "and" concepts: To belong to the concept class, an item must have "this feature *and* this feature *and* this feature." For example, a *motorcycle* must have two wheels *and* an engine *and* handlebars.

Relational concepts classify objects on the basis of *their relationship to something else,* or by *the relationship between features of an object.* All of the following are relational concepts: *larger, above, left, north,* and *upside down.* Another example is *sister,* which is defined as "a female considered in her relation to another person having the same parents."

Disjunctive concepts refer to objects that have *at least one of several possible features.* These are "either-or concepts." To belong, an item must have "this feature *or* that feature *or* another feature." For example, in the game of baseball, a *strike* is *either* a swing and a miss *or* a pitch down the middle *or* a foul ball. The either-or quality of disjunctive concepts makes them difficult to learn.

Prototypes When you think of the concept *bird,* do you make a mental list of features that birds have? Probably not. In addition to rules and features, we frequently use **prototypes,** *or ideal models,* to identify concepts (Rosch, 1977; Smith, 1989). A robin, for instance, is a model bird, whereas an ostrich is not. What this tells us is that not all examples of a concept are equally representative. For instance, which of the drawings in Figure 11–3 ◆ best represents a cup? At some point, a cup that is made taller or wider becomes a vase or a bowl. How do we know when the

Figure 11–3 ◆ When does a cup become a bowl or a vase? Deciding if an object belongs to a conceptual class is aided by relating it to a prototype, or ideal example. Subjects in one experiment chose number 5 as the "best" cup. (After Labov, 1973.)

line is crossed? Probably, we mentally compare objects to an "ideal" cup, like number 5. The upshot is that identifying concepts is difficult when we cannot come up with a prototype relevant to what we see. What, for example, are the objects shown in Figure 11–4 ◆?

Connotative Meaning   Generally speaking, concepts have two types of meaning. The **denotative meaning** of a word or concept is its *exact definition*. The **connotative meaning** is its *emotional or personal meaning*. The denotative meaning of the word *naked* (having no clothes) is the same for a nudist as it is for a movie censor, but we could expect their connotations to differ. Connotative differences can influence how we think about important issues. For example, the term *enhanced radiation device* has a more positive connotation than *neutron bomb* does (Gruner & Tighe, 1995).

Figure 11–4 ◆   Use of prototypes in concept identification. Even though its shape is unusual, item **(a)** can be related to a model (an ordinary set of pliers) and thus recognized. But what are items **(b)** and **(c)**? If you don't recognize them, look ahead to Fig. 11–6. (After Bransford & McCarrell, 1977.)

Rate this word: **JAZZ**

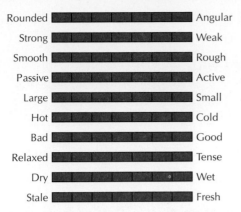

Figure 11–5 ◆   This is an example of Osgood's semantic differential. The connotative meaning of the word *jazz* can be established by rating it on the scales. Mark your own rating by placing dots or X's in the spaces. Connect the marks with a line; then have a friend rate the word and compare your responses. It might be interesting to do the same for *rock and roll, disco,* and *classical.* You also might want to try the word *psychology*. (From C. E. Osgood. Copyright © 1952 American Psychological Association. Reprinted by permission.)

Can you give a clearer statement of what a connotative meaning is?

Researcher Charles Osgood used a method he called the **semantic differential** *as a way to measure connotative meaning* (Fig. 11–5 ◆). When words or concepts are rated on a series of scales, most of their connotative meaning boils down to the dimensions *good-bad, strong-weak,* and *active-passive.* (Sounds like a good movie title, doesn't it: *The Good the Bad the Strong the Weak the Active and the Passive.*) Because concepts vary on these dimensions, words or phrases with roughly the same denotative meaning may have very different connotations. For example, I am *conscientious*; you are *careful*; he is *nit-picking!*

Learning Check	Critical Thinking

Learning Check

1. List three basic units of thought: Image · Concept language

2. Synesthesia is the use of kinesthetic sensations as a vehicle for thought. T or F?

3. Humans appear capable of forming three-dimensional images that can be moved or rotated in mental space. T or F?

4. When a person forms a three-dimensional image of an environment, it is easiest to remember if an object is placed to the right or left of center. T or F?

5. Our reliance on imagery in thinking means that problem solving is impaired by micromovements. T or F?

6. A mup is defined as anything that is small, blue, and hairy. Mup is a conjunctive concept.

7. The connotative meaning of the word *naked* is "having no clothes." T or F?

Critical Thinking

8. It takes longer to answer the question, "Does a frog have lips and a stubby tail?" than the question, "Does a frog have lips?" Can you think of an explanation other than mental rotation to explain this difference?

9. A Democrat and a Republican are asked to rate the word *democratic* on the semantic differential. Under what conditions would their ratings be most alike?

Language—Don't Leave Home without It

As we have seen, thinking sometimes takes place without language. Everyone has searched for a word to express an idea that exists as a vague image or feeling. Nevertheless, most thinking leans heavily on language, because it allows the world to be **encoded** (*translated*) into symbols that are easy to manipulate.

The study of meaning in words and language is known as **semantics.** It is here that the link between language and thought becomes most evident. Suppose, on an intelligence test, you were asked to circle the word that does not belong in this series:

> SKYSCRAPER CATHEDRAL TEMPLE PRAYER

If you circled *prayer*, you answered as most people do. Now try another problem, again circling the odd item:

> CATHEDRAL PRAYER TEMPLE SKYSCRAPER

Had you seen only this question, you probably would have circled *skyscraper*. There is a subtle change in meaning caused by reordering the words (Mayer, 1995).

Semantics may directly influence thinking when the choice of words alters meaning: Has one country's army "invaded" another? Or "effected a protective incursion"? Is the city reservoir "half full" or "half empty"? Would you rather eat "prime beef" or "dead cow"?! (See Fig. 11–7 ◆.)

Cross-culturally, semantic problems may arise when languages are translated. Perhaps the San Jose, California, public library can be excused for displaying a large banner that was supposed to say, "You are welcome" in a native Philippine language. The banner actually meant, "You are circumcised." Likewise, we may forgive Pepsi for translating "Come alive, you Pepsi generation," into Thai as "Pepsi brings your ancestors back from the dead." However, in more important situations, such as in international diplomacy, avoiding semantic confusion may be vital.

The Structure of Language

What does it take to make a language?

First of all, a language must provide *symbols* that can stand for objects and ideas. The symbols we call words are built out of **phonemes** (FOE-neems: *basic speech sounds*) and **morphemes** (MOR-feems: *speech sounds collected into meaningful units,* such as syllables or words). For instance, in English the sounds *m, b, w,* and *a* cannot form a syllable *mbwa*. In Swahili, they can.

The units of speech can be arranged in countless ways. Consider the possibilities with just four morphemes: *reach, to, able,* and *un*. From these, we can make *able to, unable to, reach to, to reach, able to reach, unable to reach, reachable, unreachable, reachable to, unreachable to, unto, unto Able.*

Figure 11–6 ◆ Context can substitute for a lack of appropriate prototypes in concept identification.

| PURPLE | BLUE | GREEN | GREEN |
| RED | PURPLE | RED | GREEN |

Figure 11–7 ◆ The Stroop interference task. Test yourself by naming the colors in the top two rows as quickly as you can. Then name the colors of the *ink* used to print the words in the bottom two rows (do not read the words themselves). The greater difficulty of naming colors in the bottom rows shows how intimately thought is linked to language. The meaning of words has a powerful impact on our response to them. (After Tzeng & Wang, 1983.)

As a second point, a language must have a **grammar,** *or set of rules for making sounds into words and words into sentences.* One part of grammar, known as **syntax,** consists of *rules for word order in sentences.* Syntax is important because rearranging words almost always changes the meaning of a sentence: "Dog bites man" versus "Man bites dog."

Traditional grammar is concerned with "surface" language—the sentences we actually speak. The revolutionary ideas of linguist Noam Chomsky focus instead on the unspoken rules we use to change core ideas into various sentences. Chomsky (1986) argues that we do not learn all the sentences we might ever say. Rather, we actively *create* them by applying **transformation rules** to universal, core patterns. *Such rules allow us to change a simple declarative sentence into other voices or forms.* For example, the core sentence "Dog bites man" can be transformed to the following patterns (and others as well):

Past: The dog bit the man.

Passive: The man was bitten by the dog.

Negative: The dog did not bite the man.

Question: Did the dog bite the man?

Children show evidence of using transformation rules when they form sentences such as "I runned home." The child has applied the past tense rule to the irregular verb *to run.*

There is a tendency to think of languages only as systems of spoken sounds and written symbols. However, as the next highlight explains, language is not limited to speech.

A Voice for the Deaf

At age 24, Ildefonso, who was born deaf, had never communicated with another human, except by mime. Then at last, Ildefonso had a breakthrough: After much hard work with a sign language teacher, he understood the link between a cat and the gesture for it. At that magic moment, he grasped the idea that "cat" could be communicated to another person, just by signing the word. For Ildefonso, it marked the end of his terrible isolation from others.

Ildefonso's long-awaited breakthrough was made possible by **American Sign Language (ASL),** *a gestural language.* Contrary to what many people think, ASL is not pantomime or a code. It is a true language, like German, Spanish, or Japanese. In fact, ASL is not understood by those who use other gestural languages, such as French Sign, Chinese Sign, Yiddish Sign, or Old Kentish Sign.

Psychologists and linguists have realized that our biological tendency to learn a language does not specify if it should be spoken or gestural. Similar universal language patterns are evident in both speech and sign. Of course, ASL has a *spatial* grammar, syntax, and semantics all its own (Fig. 11–8 ◆). Just the same, signing children pass through the same stages of language development at about the same age as speaking children do.

Figure 11–8 ◆ ASL has only 3,000 root signs, compared with roughly 600,000 words in English. However, variations in signs make ASL a highly expressive language. For example, the sign LOOK-AT can be varied in ways to make it mean look at me, look at her, look at each, stare at, gaze, watch, look for a long time, look at again and again, reminisce, sightsee, look forward to, predict, anticipate, browse, and many more variations.

Sign languages naturally arise out of a need to communicate visually. But they also embody a personal identity and define a distinct community. Sign is the true voice of the deaf and hearing impaired. Those who "speak" sign share not just a language, but a rich culture as well. (Sources: Meier, 1991; Petitto & Marentette, 1991; Sacks, 1990; Schaller, 1991.)

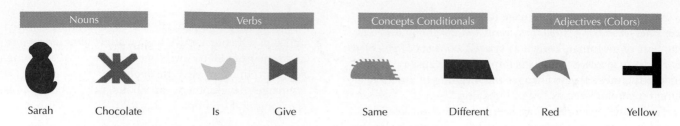

Nouns		Verbs		Concepts Conditionals		Adjectives (Colors)	
Sarah	Chocolate	Is	Give	Same	Different	Red	Yellow

Figure 11–9 ◆ Here is a sample of some of the word-symbols that Sarah the chimpanzee used to communicate with humans. (After Premack & Premack, 1972).

The third, and perhaps most essential, characteristic of language is that it is **productive**—*it can generate new thoughts or ideas.* Because symbols do not resemble the things they represent, words or signs can be rearranged to produce an infinite variety of meaningful sentences. Some are silly: "Please don't feed me to the goldfish." Some are profound: "We hold these truths to be self-evident, that all men are created equal." In either case, it is this productive quality that makes language such a powerful tool for thought.

Do animals use language?

Animals do communicate. The cries, gestures, and mating calls of animals have broad meanings immediately understood by other animals of the same species (Premack, 1983). For the most part, however, natural animal communication is quite limited. Even apes and monkeys make only a few dozen distinct cries, which carry messages such as "attack," "flee," or "food here." More important, animal communication seems to lack the productive quality of human language. For example, when a monkey gives an "eagle distress call," it means something like, "I see an eagle." The monkey has no way of saying, "I don't see an eagle," or "Thank heavens that wasn't an eagle," or "That sucker I saw yesterday was some huge eagle" (Glass et al., 1979).

Could an animal be taught to use language?

Psychologists have made several interesting attempts to teach animals to use language. Let's consider some of their successes and failures.

Talking Chimps

Early attempts to teach chimps to talk were a dismal failure. The world record was held by Viki, a chimp who could say only four words (*mama, papa, cup,* and *up*) after six years of intensive training (Fleming, 1974; Hayes, 1951). (Actually, all four words sounded something like a belch.) Obviously, chimps lack the vocal control needed to speak. The first real success came when Beatrice and Allen Gardner realized that chimps might be able to learn a gestural language. Using operant conditioning and imitation, the Gardners set out to teach a female chimp named Washoe to use American Sign Language.

To the Gardners' delight, Washoe's communication skills blossomed rapidly. Soon she began to put together primitive sentence strings like "Come-gimme sweet," "Out please," "Gimme tickle," and "Open food drink." Washoe's peak vocabulary was about 240 signs and she could construct six-word sentences (Gardner & Gardner, 1969; Rose, 1984).

A chimp named Sarah was another well-known pupil of human language. David Premack (1970) taught Sarah to use 130 "words" consisting of plastic chips arranged on a magnetized board (Fig. 11–9 ◆). From the beginning of her training, Sarah was required to use proper word order. She learned to answer questions, to label things "same" or "different," to classify objects by color, shape, and size, and to construct compound sentences (Premack & Premack, 1983) (Fig. 11–10 ◆). One of Sarah's top achievements was her use of *conditional* sentences. A **conditional statement** *contains a qualification, often in the if-then form:* "If Sarah take apple, then Mary give Sarah chocolate." "If Sarah take banana, then Mary no give Sarah chocolate."

Figure 11–10 ◆ After reading the message "Sarah insert apple pail banana dish" on the magnetic board, Sarah performed the actions as directed. (From "Teaching Language to an Ape" by Ann J. Premack and David Premack. Copyright © 1972 by Scientific American, Inc. All rights reserved.)

Can it be said with certainty that the chimps understand such interchanges?

Most researchers working with chimps believe that they have indeed communicated with them. Especially striking are the chimps' spontaneous responses. Washoe once "wet" on psychologist Roger Fouts' back while riding on his shoulders. When Fouts asked, with some annoyance, why she had done it, Washoe signed, "It's funny!"

Criticisms   Such interchanges are impressive. But communication and actual language use are two different things. Some psychologists doubt that apes can really use language. For one thing, the chimps rarely "speak" without prompting. Many of their seemingly original sentences turn out to be responses to questions or imitations of signs the teacher made. Also, it appears that the apes may be simply performing chains of *operant responses* to get food, play, or other "goodies" (Savage-Rumbaugh et al., 1979; Terrace, 1985). By using such responses, the apes then manipulate their trainers to get what they want.

You might say critics think the apes have made monkeys out of their trainers. However, psychologists Roger and Debbi Fouts believe they can answer such criticisms. An analysis they performed of some 6,000 conversations between chimps showed that only 5 percent had anything to do with food. The Foutses also videotaped conversations between chimps that took place when no humans were present to cue them (Fouts et al., 1984).

A recent study of chimps using a special symbol system (described in the next section) found that the chimps do not merely imitate humans. During "conversations" with humans, the chimps use symbols to express agreement, excitement, to make requests or promises, and to select alternatives. In short, they hold real conversations, in which information is exchanged symbolically (Greenfield & Savage-Rumbaugh, 1993). So, maybe the chimps will make monkeys out of the critics.

Problems with Syntax   At this point, numerous chimps, a gorilla named Koko, and an assortment of dolphins and sea lions have learned to communicate with word symbols of various kinds. Yet, even if some criticisms can be answered, linguists such as Noam Chomsky remain unconvinced that animals can truly use language. The core issue is that problems with syntax (word order) have plagued almost all animal language experiments. For example, when a chimp named Nim Chimpsky (no relation to Chomsky) wanted an orange, he would typically signal a grammarless string of words: "Give orange me give eat orange me eat orange give me eat orange give me you." This might be communication, but it is not language.

Recently, the flames of controversy were fanned again by Kanzi, a pygmy chimpanzee studied by Duane Rumbaugh and Sue Savage-Rumbaugh. Kanzi communicates using gestures and push buttons on a computer keyboard. Each of the 250 buttons is marked with a **lexigram**, *or geometric word-symbol* (Fig. 11–11 ◆). Using the lexigrams, Kanzi can create primitive sentences several words long. He can also understand about 650 spoken sentences. During testing, Kanzi hears spoken words over headphones, so his caretakers cannot prompt him (Savage-Rumbaugh et al., 1990; Savage-Rumbaugh & Lewin, 1996).

Kanzi's sentences consistently follow correct word order. His syntax is good even for new word combinations he has never made before. Like a child learning language, Kanzi picked up some ordering rules from his caregivers (Savage-Rumbaugh & Lewin, 1996). However, he has developed other patterns on his own. For example, Kanzi almost always places two action symbols in the order he wants to carry them out, such as "chase tickle" or "chase hide." That is, he uses symbols to plan and communicate the order of actions. Psycholinguist Patricia Marks Greenfield says that Kanzi's use of grammar is on a par with that of a 2-year-old child (Savage-Rumbaugh et al., 1993).

Kanzi's ability to invent a simple grammar may help us better understand the roots of human language. It is certainly the strongest answer yet to the critics. On the other hand, Chomsky insists that if chimps were biologically capable of language they would have made use of it on their own. Although the issue is far from resolved, such research promises to unravel some of the mysteries of language learning. In fact, it has already been helpful for teaching language to aphasic children (children with serious language impairment) and severely retarded children (Savage-Rumbaugh et al., 1990).

Figure 11–11 ◆ Kanzi's language learning has been impressive. He can comprehend spoken English words. He can identify lexigram symbols when he hears corresponding words. He can use lexigrams when the objects they refer to are absent and he can, if asked, lead someone to the object. All these skills were acquired through observation, not conditioning (Savage-Rumbaugh et al., 1990; Savage-Rumbaugh & Lewin, 1996).

Problem Solving— Getting an Answer in Sight

We have reviewed some of the basic ways that we mentally represent information so that it can be manipulated and used to solve problems. It is now time to take a direct look at problem solving. A good way to start is to solve a problem. Give this one a try.

> A famous ocean liner (the *Queen Ralph*) is steaming toward port at 20 miles per hour. It is 50 miles from shore when a seagull takes off from its deck and flies toward port. At the same instant, a speedboat leaves port at 30 miles per hour. The bird flies back and forth between the speedboat and the *Queen Ralph* at a speed of 40 miles per hour. How far will the bird have flown when the two boats pass?

If you don't immediately see the answer to this problem, read it again. (The answer is revealed shortly in Insightful Solutions.)

We all do a tremendous amount of problem solving every day. Problem solving can be as commonplace as figuring out how to make a non-poisonous meal out of leftovers or as significant as developing a cure for cancer. In either case, we begin with an awareness that an answer probably exists and that by proper thinking, a solution can be found. A number of different approaches to problem solving can be identified.

Mechanical Solutions

A **mechanical solution** *may be achieved by trial and error or by rote*. If I forget the combination to my bike lock, I may be able to discover it by trial and error. In an era of high-speed computers, many trial-and-error solutions are best left to machines. A computer could generate all possible combinations of the five numbers on my lock in a split second. (Of course, it would take me a long time to try them all.)

When a problem is solved by *rote*, thinking is guided by a learned set of rules. If you have a good background in math, you may have solved the problem of the bird and the boats by rote. I hope you didn't. There is an easier solution.

Solutions by Understanding

Many problems cannot be solved mechanically or by habitual modes of thought. In that case, **understanding** (*deeper comprehension of a problem*) is necessary. A classic series of studies on thinking of this type was performed by German psychologist Karl Duncker (1945). Duncker gave college students this problem:

> A person has an inoperable stomach tumor. A device is available that produces rays which at high intensity will destroy tissue

Figure 11–12 ◆ A schematic representation of Duncker's tumor problem. The dark spot represents a tumor surrounded by healthy tissue. How can the tumor be destroyed without injuring surrounding tissue? (After Duncker, 1945.)

(both healthy and diseased). How can the tumor be destroyed without damaging surrounding tissue? (Students were also shown the sketch in Figure 11–12 ◆.)

What did this problem show about problem solving?

Duncker asked the students to think aloud as they worked. He found that there were two phases to successful problem solving. First, students had to discover the *general properties* of a correct solution. A **general solution** *states the requirements for success, but not in enough detail for further action*. This phase was complete when students realized that the intensity of the rays had to be lowered on their way to the tumor. Then, in the second phase, they proposed a number of **functional** (*workable*) **solutions** and selected the best one. (One solution is to focus weak rays on the tumor from several angles. Another is to rotate the person's body. That way, the exposure of healthy tissue will be minimized.)

It might help to summarize with a more familiar example. Almost everyone who tries the Rubik's cube puzzle begins at the mechanical, *trial-and-error* level. If you want to take the easy route, printed instructions are available that give the steps for a *rote* solution. In time, those who persist begin to *understand* the *general properties* of the puzzle. After that, they can solve it consistently.

Heuristics

"You can't get there from here." Or so it often seems when facing a problem. Solving problems often requires a strategy. If the number of alternatives is small, a **random search strategy** may work. This is another example of trial-and-error thinking in which *all possibilities are tried, more or less randomly*. Imagine, for example, that you are traveling and decide to look up an old friend, J. Smith, in a city you are visiting. You open the phone book and find 47 J. Smiths listed. Of course, you could dial each number until you find the right one. "Forget it," you say to yourself. "Is there any way I can narrow the search?" "Oh, yeah! I remember hearing that Janet lives by the beach." Then you take out a map and call only the numbers with addresses near the waterfront (Ellis & Hunt, 1992).

The approach used in this example is a **heuristic** (hew-RIS-tik: *a strategy for identifying and evaluating problem solutions*). Typically, a heuristic is a "rule of thumb" that *reduces the number of alternatives* thinkers must consider. This

Water lilies

Problem: Water lilies growing in a pond double in area every 24 hours. On the first day of spring, only one lily pad is on the surface of the pond. Sixty days later, the pond is entirely covered. On what day is the pond half-covered?

Twenty dollars

Problem: Jessica and Blair both have the same amount of money. How much must Jessica give Blair so that Blair has $20 more than Jessica?

How many pets?

Problem: How many pets do you have if all of them are birds except two, all of them are cats except two, and all of them are dogs except two?

Between 2 and 3

Problem: What one mathematical symbol can you place between 2 and 3 that results in a number greater than 2 and less than 3?

One word

Problem: Rearrange the letters NEWDOOR to make one word.

Solutions to these problems are listed in Table 11–2.

Figure 11–13 ◆

raises the odds of success, although it does not guarantee a solution. Here are some heuristic strategies that often work:

- Try to identify how the current state of affairs differs from the desired goal. Then find steps that will reduce the difference.
- Try working backward from the desired goal to the starting point or current state.
- If you can't reach the goal directly, try to identify an intermediate goal or subproblem that at least gets you closer.
- Represent the problem in other ways, with graphs, diagrams, or analogies, for instance.
- Generate a possible solution and test it. Doing so may eliminate many alternatives, or it may clarify what is needed for a solution.

Ideal Problem Solving Perhaps the most valuable heuristic of all is having a *general* thinking strategy. Psychologist John Bransford and his colleagues list five steps that they believe lead to effective problem solving: **i**dentify, **d**efine, **e**xplore, **a**ct, and **l**ook and learn (Bransford et al., 1986; Bransford & Stein, 1984). Notice that the first letters of the steps spell *ideal*.

To apply the ideal thinking strategy you should *identify* the problem, *define* it clearly, and then *explore* possible solutions and relevant knowledge. Next, you must *act* by trying a possible solution or hypothesis. Finally, you should *look* at the results and *learn* from them. Of course, each

attempted solution may identify further subproblems. These can again be tackled with the "ideal" steps until a final satisfactory solution is found.

Insightful Solutions

During problem solving, we say that **insight** has occurred when *an answer appears suddenly*. An insight is usually so *rapid* and *clear* that we often wonder how the solution could have been missed. Insight usually involves a reorganization of the elements of a problem. Seeing the problem in a new way is what makes its solution seem obvious (Durso, Rea, & Dayton, 1994).

Let's return now to the problem of the boats and the bird. The best way to solve it is by insight. Because the boats will cover the 50-mile distance in exactly one hour, and the bird flies 40 miles per hour, the bird will have flown 40 miles when the boats meet. No math is necessary if you have insight into this problem. Figure 11–13 ◆ lists some additional insight problems you may want to try.

In an interesting experiment, college students rated how "warm" (close to an answer) they felt while solving insight problems. Students who had insights usually jumped directly from "cold" to the correct answer. In contrast, those who gradually felt "warmer" and then "very warm" usually gave wrong answers (Metcalfe, 1986). The surprising message is that you may be headed for a mistake if an insight is *not* rapid. Real insight tends to be an all-or-nothing event (Smith & Kounios, 1996).

The Nature of Insight

What, really, does it mean to have an insight?

Psychologists Robert Sternberg and Janet Davidson (1982) have studied people as they solve problems that require insight or "leaps of logic." According to them, insight involves three abilities. The first is **selective encoding,** which refers to *selecting information that is relevant to a problem*, while ignoring distractions. For example, consider the following problem:

> If you have white socks and black socks in your drawer, mixed in the ratio of 4 to 5, how many socks will you have to take out to make sure of having a pair of the same color?

A person who fails to recognize that "mixed in a ratio of 4 to 5" is irrelevant information will be less likely to come up with the correct answer of three socks.

Insight also relies on **selective combination,** or *bringing together seemingly unrelated bits of useful information*. Try this sample problem:

> With a 7-minute hourglass and an 11-minute hourglass, what is the simplest way to time the boiling of an egg for 15 minutes?

The answer requires using both hourglasses in combination. First, the 7-minute and the 11-minute hourglasses are started running. When the 7-minute hourglass runs out, it's time to begin boiling the egg. At this point, 4 minutes remain on the 11-minute hourglass. Thus, when it runs out it is simply turned over. When it runs out again, 15 minutes will have passed.

A third source of insights is **selective comparison.** This is the ability to *compare new problems with old information or with problems already solved*. A good example is the hat rack problem, in which subjects must build a structure that can support an overcoat in the middle of a room. Each person is given only two long sticks and a C-clamp to work with. The solution, shown in Figure 11–14 ◆, is to clamp the two sticks together so that they are wedged between floor and ceiling. If you were given this problem, you would be more likely to solve it if you first thought of the way pole lamps are wedged between floor and ceiling.

Fixations

One of the most important barriers to problem solving is **fixation,** *the tendency to get "hung up" on wrong solutions or to become blind to alternatives*. Usually this occurs when we place unnecessary restrictions on our thinking (Isaak & Just, 1995). How, for example, could you plant four small trees so that each is an equal distance from all the others? (The answer is shown in Figure 11–15 ◆.)

A prime example of restricted thinking is **functional fixedness,** *an inability to see new uses (functions) for familiar*

Figure 11–14 ◆ Solution to the hat rack problem.

objects or for objects that were used in a particular way. If you have ever used a dime as a screwdriver, you've overcome functional fixedness.

How does functional fixedness affect problem solving?

Karl Duncker, who coined the term *functional fixedness*, performed a clever study to demonstrate it. Duncker challenged students to mount a candle on a vertical board so that the candle could burn normally. Duncker gave each student three candles, some matches, some cardboard boxes, some thumbtacks, and other items. Half of Duncker's subjects received these items *inside* the cardboard boxes. The

Figure 11–15 ◆ Four trees can be placed equidistant from one another by piling dirt into a mound. Three of the trees are planted equal distances apart around the base of the mound. The fourth tree is planted on the top of the mound. If you were fixated on arrangements that involve level ground, you may have been blind to this three-dimensional solution.

(a) (b) (c)

Figure 11–16 ◆ Materials for solving the candle problem were given to subjects in boxes **(a)** or separately **(b).** Functional fixedness caused by condition **(a)** interfered with solving the problem. The solution to the problem is shown in **(c).**

others were given all the items, including the boxes, spread out on a tabletop.

Duncker found that when the items were in the boxes, solving the problem was very difficult. This is because the boxes were seen as *containers*, not as items that might be part of the solution. (If you haven't guessed the solution, check Fig. 11–16 ◆.) Undoubtedly, we could avoid many fixations if we took a more flexible approach to categorizing the world (Langer & Piper, 1987). For instance, creativity could be facilitated in Duncker's container problem by saying, "This *could be* a box," instead of, "This *is* a box."

Common Barriers to Problem Solving

Functional fixedness is just one of the mental blocks that prevent insight. Here's an example of another: A $5 bill is placed on a table and a stack of objects is balanced precariously on top of the bill. How can the bill be removed without touching or moving the objects? A good answer is to split the bill on one of its edges. Gently pulling from opposite ends will tear the bill in half and remove it without toppling the objects. Many people fail to see this solution because they have learned not to destroy money (Adams, 1988). Notice again the impact of placing something in a category, in this case, "things of value" (which should not be destroyed). The list that follows identifies other common mental blocks and fixations that can hinder problem solving.

1. Emotional barriers: Inhibition and fear of making a fool of oneself, fear of making a mistake, inability to tolerate ambiguity, excessive self-criticism.
Example: An architect is afraid to try an unconventional design because she fears that other architects will think it is frivolous.

2. Cultural barriers: Values which hold that fantasy is a waste of time; that playfulness is for children only; that reason, logic, and numbers are good; that feelings, intuitions, pleasure, and humor are bad or have no value in the serious business of problem solving.
Example: A corporate manager wants to solve a business problem, but becomes stern and angry when members of his marketing team joke playfully about possible solutions.

3. Learned barriers: Conventions about uses (functional fixedness), meanings, possibilities, taboos.
Example: A cook doesn't have any clean mixing bowls and fails to see that he could use a frying pan as a bowl.

4. Perceptual barriers: Habits leading to a failure to identify important elements of a problem.
Example: A beginning artist concentrates on drawing a vase of flowers without seeing that the "empty" spaces around the vase are part of the composition, too.

In recent years, studies of thinking have benefitted greatly from computer models of problem solving. Before we explore that topic, it might be a good idea to see if you can answer the following Learning Check questions (without help from a computer).

Table 11–2 ■ Solutions to Insight Problems

Water lilies: Day 59
Twenty dollars: $10
How many pets?: Three (one bird, one cat, and one dog)
Between 2 and 3: A decimal point
One word: ONE WORD (You may object that the answer is two words, but the problem called for the answer to be "one word," and it is.)

1. True languages are *productive* because they can be used to generate new possibilities.

2. The basic speech sounds are called *phonemes* ; the smallest meaningful units of speech are called *morphemes* .

3. One of the chimpanzee Sarah's most outstanding achievements was the construction of sentences involving
   a. negation   **b.** conditional relationships   c. adult grammar   d. unprompted questions

4. Critics consider "sentences" constructed by apes to be simple *operant* responses having little meaning to the animal.

5. Insight refers to rote, or trial-and-error, problem solving. T or **F?**

6. The first phase in problem solving by understanding is to discover the general properties of a correct solution. **T** or F?

7. Problem-solving strategies that guide the search for solutions are called *heuristics* .

8. A common element underlying insight is that information is encoded, combined, and compared
   a. mechanically   b. by rote   c. functionally   **d.** selectively

9. The term *fixation* refers to the point at which a helpful insight becomes fixed in one's thinking. T or **F?**

10. Do you think that it is true that "a problem clearly defined is a problem half solved"?

Answers:

1. productive 2. phonemes, morphemes 3. b 4. operant 5. F 6. T 7. heuristics 8. d 9. F 10. Although that might be an overstatement, it is true that clearly defining a starting point and the desired goal can serve as a heuristic in problem solving.

Artificial Intelligence— I Compute, Therefore I Am

It's been a long time since Johann Sebastian Bach, the 18th-century German composer, last wrote any music. But listeners can be forgiven if they briefly mistake music created by Kemal Ebcioglu for Bach's work. Ebcioglu devised a computer program that writes harmonies remarkably similar to Bach's. Ebcioglu analyzed Bach's music and came up with 350 rules that govern the harmonizing process. The resulting program displays what is known as *artificial intelligence*. Its compositions sound like reasonably good classical music. This shows the power of artificial intelligence. Small but glaring defects in the music and a certain lack of inspiration reveal its shortcomings.

Artificial intelligence (AI) *refers to computer programs capable of doing things that require intelligence when done by people* (Best, 1995). Artificial intelligence is based on the fact that many tasks—from harmonizing music to medical diagnosis—can be reduced to a set of rules applied to a body of information. AI is valuable in situations where speed, vast memory, and persistence are required. In fact, AI programs are better at some tasks than humans are.

AI and Cognition

Artificial intelligence provides a way to probe some of the oldest questions about the mind, such as how we compre-

hend language, make decisions, and solve problems. Increasingly, cognitive psychologists are using AI as a research tool in two basic ways: *computer simulations* and *expert systems*.

Computer simulations *are programs that attempt to duplicate human behavior*, especially thinking, decision making, or problem solving. Here, the computer acts as a "laboratory" for testing models of cognition. If a computer program behaves as humans do (including making the same errors), then the program may be a good model of how we think (Mayer, 1995).

Most computer models of problem solving are based on a **means-ends analysis.** Typically, the program *compares the current state of affairs to the desired end-state or goal and attempts to reduce the difference*. After each step, the program tests to see if the difference is greater or less than before. This cycle is repeated until the problem is solved. Models such as this may seem removed from real life, but much human thinking and problem solving has a means-ends quality to it (Anderson, 1993). The following quotation provides an everyday example:

> I want to take my son to nursery school. What's the difference between what I have and what I want? Distance. What changes distance? My car. My car won't start. What is needed to make it start? A new battery. What has new batteries? An auto repair shop. I need to have the shop come to my house and put in a new battery. But the shop doesn't know I need a battery. What is the problem? Communication. What allows communication? A telephone. (And so on.) (Adapted from Newell & Simon, 1972.)

Expert systems are a second major form of AI. **Expert systems** *are computer programs that respond as a human expert would*. They have demystified some human abilities by

Two composers. The one on the left was a genius who wrote sublime, multi-voiced harmonies. The one on the right has created reasonably good, if uninspired, music. Computer models of thought can approximate intelligent human behavior. However, rule-based computer "thinking" still lacks the flexibility, creativity, and common sense of human intelligence.

converting complex skills into clearly stated rules a computer can follow. Expert systems can predict the weather, analyze geological formations, diagnose disease, play chess, read, tell when to buy or sell stocks, and do many other tasks.

Experts and Novices Working with artificial intelligence has helped especially to clarify differences between novices and experts. Research on chess masters, for example, shows that their skills are based on specific **organized knowledge** (*systematic information*) and **acquired strategies** (*learned tactics*). In other words, becoming a star performer does not come from some general strengthening of the mind. Master

chess players don't necessarily have better memories than beginners (except for realistic chess positions) (Gobet & Simon, 1996). (See Figure 11–17 ◆.) And, typically, they don't explore more moves ahead than lesser players.

What does set master players apart is their ability to recognize *patterns* that suggest what lines of play should be explored next (Best, 1995). This helps eliminate a large number of possible moves. The chess master, therefore, does not waste time exploring unproductive pathways. Experts are better able to see the true nature of problems and to define them in terms of general principles (Anderson, 1993). In general, expert performance at most thinking tasks is based

Figure 11–17 ◆ The left chessboard shows a realistic game. The right chessboard is a random arrangement of pieces. Expert chess players can memorize the left board at a glance, yet they are no better than beginners at memorizing the random board (Saariluoma, 1994). Their superior recall of realistic positions is based on a learned ability to see meaningful patterns among pieces. Such patterns change groups of pieces into large chunks that match knowledge stored in long-term memory (Gorbet & Simon, 1996).

on acquired strategies and knowledge. If you would like to excel at a profession or a mental skill, plan on adding to your knowledge every day—for at least 10 years (Ericsson & Charness, 1994).

Expertise also allows more **automatic processing,** *or fast, fairly effortless thinking based on experience with similar problems.* Automatic processing frees "space" in short-term memory, making it easier to work on the problem. At the highest skill levels, expert performers tend to rise above rules and plans. Their decisions, thinking, and actions become rapid and fluid. Thus, when a chess master recognizes a pattern on the chessboard, the most desirable tactic comes to mind almost immediately (Klein et al., 1995).

Limitations   What the preceding tells us is that experts in one area do not automatically become better problem solvers elsewhere. Nor do they become generally smarter (Ericsson & Charness, 1994). The same conclusion applies to artificial intelligence. Expert systems have been hailed as a possible remedy for human errors in tasks such as air-traffic control, the operation of nuclear power plants, and the control of weapons systems. However, the truth is that expert systems are "idiot geniuses." They are very adept within a narrow range of problem solving, but they are "stone stupid" at everything else.

Eventually, AI may lead to robots that recognize voices and that speak and act "intelligently" (Best, 1995). But cognitive scientists are becoming aware that machine "intelligence" is ultimately "blind" outside its underlying set of rules. In contrast, human cognition is much more flexible. For example, u cann understnd wrds thet ar mizpeld. Computers are very literal and easily stymied by such errors.

Humans are able to take into account exceptions, context, and interpretations as they think. We also make commitments and take responsibility for our actions. A rule-driven expert system processes information without regard for the meaning of actions. Expert systems may never be able to anticipate the infinite number of possible events that could occur. As a result, their actions might be disastrous in unanticipated situations (Denning, 1988).

Clearly, artificial intelligence will play an increasingly visible role in cognitive research and in our lives. However, it is not likely to soon replace the human touch in many areas. Although Bach might have been fascinated by AI, it is doubtful that his musical magic will be eclipsed by a machine.

Creative Thinking— Down Roads Less Traveled

As we have noted, problem solving may be the result of thinking that is mechanical, insightful, or based on understanding. To this we can add that thought may be **inductive** (*going from specific facts or observations to general principles*) or **deductive** (*going from general principles to specific situations*). Thinking may also be **logical** (*proceeding from given information to new conclusions on the basis of explicit rules*) or **illogical** (*intuitive, associative, or personal*).

What distinguishes creative thinking from more routine problem solving?

Creative thinking involves all these styles of thought (in varying combinations) plus *fluency, flexibility,* and *originality.* The meaning of these terms can be illustrated with an example. Let's say that you would like to find a creative use (or uses) for the millions of automobile tires discarded each year. The creativity of your suggestions could be rated in this way: **Fluency** is defined as *the total number of suggestions* you are able to make. **Flexibility** *is the number of times you shift from one class of possible uses to another.* **Originality** refers to *how novel or unusual* your suggestions are. By totaling the number of times you showed fluency, flexibility, and originality, we could rate the creativity of your thinking on this problem. Speaking more generally, we would be rating your capacity for *divergent thinking* (Baer, 1993).

Divergent thinking is the most widely used measure of creative problem solving. In routine problem solving or thinking, there is one correct answer, and the problem is to

Table 11–3 ■ **Convergent and Divergent Problems**

Convergent Problems

- What is the area of a triangle that is 3 feet wide at the base and 2 feet tall?
- Erica is shorter than Zoey but taller than Carlo, and Carlo is taller than Jared. Who is the second tallest?
- If you simultaneously drop a baseball and a bowling ball from a tall building, which will hit the ground first?

Divergent Problems

- What objects can you think of that begin with the letters BR?
- How could discarded aluminum cans be put to use?
- Write a poem about fire and ice.

find it. This leads to **convergent thinking** (*lines of thought converge on the answer*). **Divergent thinking** is the reverse, in which *many possibilities are developed from one starting point* (Baer, 1993). (See Table 11–3 ■ for some examples.)

Divergent thinking is also a characteristic of daydreaming. Before we discuss divergent thinking further, let's take a brief detour into the realm of fantasy (if you're not there already).

A Closer Look

Daydreams, Fantasy, and Creativity

Has your reading of this chapter been interrupted by a **daydream** (*vivid waking fantasy*)? Psychologist Eric Klinger (1990) fitted volunteers with electronic pagers and asked them to record what they were doing or thinking whenever he "beeped" them. Surprisingly, Klinger found that about half of our waking thoughts are occupied by daydreams. What do we know about this unique mental state?

Content In general, daydreams mirror our desires, fears, and anxieties in a fairly direct way. Eric Klinger says that, "When you're happy you have happy daydreams, when you're sad you have sad daydreams, and when you're angry you have angry daydreams." Because daydreams are fairly straightforward in meaning, they can be a good source of personal insights. Sleeping dreams, in contrast, tend to be more complex and difficult to analyze (Klinger, 1990).

Two of the most common daydream plots are the *conquering hero* and the *suffering martyr* themes. In a **conquering hero fantasy**, the daydreamer gets the

starring role as *a famous, rich, or powerful person:* a celebrity, athlete, musician, famous surgeon, brilliant lawyer, or magnificent lover. Themes such as these seem to reflect needs for mastery and escape from the frustrations of everyday life. **Suffering martyr daydreams** center on feelings of being *neglected, hurt, rejected, or unappreciated by others.* In such fantasies, others end up regretting their past actions and realizing what a *wonderful person* the daydreamer was all along.

Benefits Daydreams often fill a need for stimulation during routine or boring tasks. They also improve our ability to delay immediate pleasures so that future goals can be achieved. And in everyday terms, fantasy can be an outlet for frustrated impulses. If you have a momentary urge to kill the fool in front of you on the highway, substituting fantasy for action may avert disaster.

Perhaps the greatest value of fantasy is its contribution to creativity. In the imaginative realm of fantasy, nothing is impossible—a quality allowing for tremendous fluency and flexibility of thought. For most people, fantasy and daydreaming are associated with positive emotional adjustment, lower levels of aggression, and greater mental flexibility or creativity (Klinger, 1990; Singer, 1974). Perhaps that's why Albert Einstein was, in his own words, "disorderly and a dreamer."

Isn't creativity more than divergent thought? What if a person comes up with a large number of useless answers to a problem?

A good question. To be creative, the solution to a problem must be more than novel, unusual, or original. It must also be *practical* if it is an invention and *sensible* if it is an idea (Finke, 1990). This is the dividing line between a "harebrained scheme" and a "stroke of genius" (Fig. 11–18 ◆). In other words, the creative person brings reasoning and critical thinking to bear on new ideas once they are produced (Feldhusen, 1995).

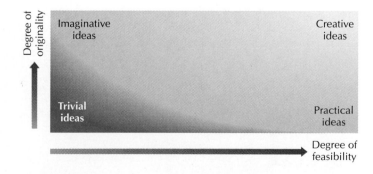

Figure 11–18 ◆ Creative ideas combine originality with feasibility. (Adapted from McMullan & Stocking, 1978.)

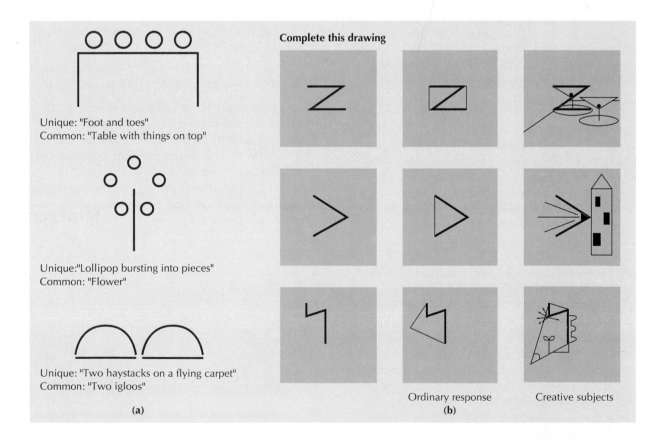

Hat-tipping device. According to the patent, it is for "automatically effecting polite salutations by the elevation and rotation of the hat on the head of the saluting party when said person bows to the person or persons saluted." In addition to being original or novel, a creative solution must fit the demands of the problem. Is this a creative solution to the "problem" of hat tipping?

Problem finding is another major difference between creative thinking and more ordinary problem solving. Many of the problems we solve are "presented" to us—by employers, teachers, circumstances, or life in general. **Problem finding** involves *the active discovery of problems.*

When you are thinking creatively a spirit of discovery prevails: You are more likely to seek out unsolved problems and *choose* to tackle them. Thus, problem finding may be a more creative act than the convergent problem solving that typically follows it (Runco & Chand, 1995).

Tests of Creativity

There are several tests of divergent thinking. In the **Unusual Uses Test,** a person is asked to think of *as many uses as possible for an object* (such as the tires mentioned earlier). In the **Consequences Test,** the goal is to list *the consequences that would follow a basic change in the world.* For example, you might be asked, "What would be the results if everyone suddenly lost the sense of balance and could no longer stay in an upright position?" Subjects try to list as many reactions as possible. In the **Anagrams Test,** people are given a word such as *creativity* and asked to *make as many new words as possible by rearranging the letters.* Each of these tests can be scored for fluency, flexibility, and originality. (For an example of other tests of divergent thought, see Figure 11–19 ◆.)

Creativity tests have been useful, but they are not the whole story. If you want to predict whether a person will be creative in the future, it helps to look at two more kinds of information (Feldhusen & Goh, 1995):

Complete this drawing

Unique: "Foot and toes"
Common: "Table with things on top"

Unique: "Lollipop bursting into pieces"
Common: "Flower"

Unique: "Two haystacks on a flying carpet"
Common: "Two igloos"

(a)

Ordinary response
(b)

Creative subjects

Figure 11–19 ◆ Some tests of divergent thinking. Creative responses are more original and more complex. [**(a)** after Wallach & Kogan, 1965; **(b)** after Barron, 1958.]

- The *products* of creative thinking (such as essays, poems, drawings, or constructed objects) are often more informative than test results. When creative people are asked to actually produce something, others tend to judge their work as creative.

- A simple listing of a person's *past creative activities and achievements* is an excellent guide to the likelihood that she or he will be creative in the future.

Is there any pattern to creative thinking?

Stages of Creative Thought

A good summary of the sequence of events in creative thinking proposes five stages that usually occur:

1. Orientation. As a first step, the problem must be defined and important dimensions identified.

2. Preparation. In the second stage, creative thinkers saturate themselves with as much information pertaining to the problem as possible.

3. Incubation. Most major problems produce a period during which all attempted solutions will have proved futile. At this point, problem solving may proceed on a subconscious level: While the problem seems to have been set aside, it is still "cooking" in the background.

4. Illumination. The stage of incubation is often ended by a rapid insight or series of insights. These produce the "Aha!" experience, often depicted in cartoons as a lightbulb appearing over the thinker's head.

5. Verification. The final step is to test and critically evaluate the solution obtained during the stage of illumination. If the solution proves faulty, the thinker reverts to the stage of incubation.

Of course, creative thought is seldom so neat. Nevertheless, the stages listed are a good summary of the typical sequence of events.

You may find it helpful to attach the stages to the following more or less true story. Legend has it that the king of Syracuse (a city in ancient Greece) once suspected that his goldsmith had substituted cheaper metals for some of the gold in a crown and had pocketed the difference. Archimedes, a famous mathematician and thinker, was given the problem of discovering whether the king had been cheated.

Archimedes began by defining the problem (*orientation*): "How can I determine what metals have been used in the crown without damaging it?" He then checked all known methods of analyzing metals (*preparation*). All involved cutting or melting the crown, so he was forced to temporarily set the problem aside (*incubation*). Then one day as he stepped into his bath, Archimedes suddenly knew he had the solution (*illumination*). He was so excited he is said to have run naked through the streets shouting, "Eureka, eureka!" (I have found it, I have found it!).

The development of modern aircraft has been highly creative and quite rapid. Even so, it has been marked more by incremental progress than by dramatic breakthroughs.

On observing his own body floating in the bath, Archimedes realized that different metals of equal weight would displace different amounts of water. A pound of brass, for example, occupies more space than a pound of gold, which is denser. All that remained was to test the solution (*verification*). Archimedes placed an amount of gold (equal in weight to that given the goldsmith) in a tub of water. He marked the water level and removed the gold. He then placed the crown in the water. Was the crown pure gold? If it was, it would raise the water to exactly the same level. Unfortunately, the purity of the crown and the fate of the goldsmith are to this day unknown!

The preceding account is a good general description of creative thinking. However, creative thinking can be highly complex. Rather than springing from sudden insights, much creative problem solving is **incremental** (Weisenberg, 1986). That is, it is the end result of *many small steps*. This is certainly true of many inventions, which build on earlier ideas.

Some authors believe that truly exceptional creativity requires a rare combination of thinking skills, personality, and a supportive social environment. This mix, they believe, accounts for creative giants such as Edison, Freud, Mozart, Picasso, Tolstoy, and others (Tardif & Sternberg, 1988).

What makes a person creative?

The Creative Personality

According to the popular stereotype, highly creative people are eccentric, introverted, neurotic, socially inept, unbalanced in their interests, and on the edge of madness. Although some well-known artists and musicians cultivate a public image to fit the stereotype, there is little truth in it. Direct studies of creative individuals paint a very different picture (Dacey, 1989).

1. For people of normal intelligence, there is a small positive correlation between creativity and IQ. In other words, smarter people have a slight tendency to also be more creative. But, for the most part, at any given level of IQ, some people are creative and some are not. The average college graduate has an IQ of 120. This is more than high enough to allow a person to write novels, do scientific research, or pursue other creative work (Finke, 1990). IQs above 120 do not seem to add anything more to creative ability (Sternberg & Lubart, 1995).

2. Creative people usually have a greater than average range of knowledge and interests, and they are more fluent in combining ideas from various sources.

3. Creative people have an openness to experience. They accept irrational thoughts and are uninhibited about their feelings and fantasies (McCrae, 1987).

4. Creative people enjoy symbolic thought, ideas, concepts, and possibilities. They tend to be interested in truth, form, and beauty, rather than in recognition or success. Their creative work is an end in itself (Sternberg & Lubart, 1995).

5. Highly creative people value independence and have a preference for complexity (Dacey, 1989). However, they are unconventional and non-conforming primarily in their work; otherwise they do not have particularly unusual, outlandish, or bizarre personalities.

It is widely accepted that people are often creative only in particular areas of skill or knowledge. For example, a person who is a creative writer might be an uncreative artist or businessperson. Perhaps this is because creativity favors a prepared mind. Those who are creative in a particular field often are building on a large store of existing knowledge (Feldhusen, 1995; Sternberg & Lubart, 1995).

As our discussion has already implied, creative persons share a number of general traits, regardless of the field in which they work. Table 11–4 ■ summarizes these characteristics. Of course, a specific creative person may possess many, but not all, of these characteristics.

Can creativity be learned?

It is beginning to look as if some creative thinking skills can be taught. In particular, creativity can be increased by

Table 11–4 ■ Characteristics of Creative Persons

GENERAL TRAITS
  Originality
  Verbal fluency
  Relatively high intelligence
  A good imagination

THINKING ABILITIES
  Uses metaphors in thinking
  Flexible decision maker
  Uses broad categories
  Makes independent judgments
  Uses mental images
  Can cope with novelty
  Thinks logically
  Can break mental sets
  Finds order in chaos

THINKING STYLE
  Challenges assumptions, asks "Why?"
  Looks for novelty and gaps in knowledge
  Draws new ideas out of existing knowledge
  Prefers non-verbal communication
  Enjoys visualizing
  Finds beauty in "good" problems and elegant solutions
  Takes advantage of chance

PERSONALITY CHARACTERISTICS
  Willing to take intellectual risks
  Persistence in problem solving
  Curiosity and inquisitiveness
  Openness to new experiences
  Absorption in tasks of interest
  Discipline and commitment to work
  High spontaneous interest in work
  Uncomfortable with rules and limits imposed by others
  Seeks competence and challenges
  Reflective and preoccupied
  Tolerates ambiguity
  Broad range of interests
  Playful with ideas
  Values creativity and originality
  Intuitive

Adapted from Tardif and Sternberg (1988).

practice in divergent thinking (Baer, 1993). In the Applications section of this chapter you will find a brief discussion of some helpful strategies.

At the same time that irrational, intuitive thought may contribute to creative problem solving, it can also lead to thinking errors. The next section tells how this can happen.

Intuitive Thought— Mental Shortcut? Or Dangerous Detour?

Problem 1: An epidemic breaks out and 600 people are about to die. Doctors have two choices. If they give drug A, 200 lives will be saved. If they give drug B, there is a one-third chance that 600 people will be saved, and a two-thirds chance that none will be saved. Which drug should they choose?

Problem 2: Again, 600 people are about to die, and doctors must make a choice. If they give drug A, 400 people will die. If they give drug B, there is a one-third chance that no one will die, and a two-thirds chance that 600 will die. Which drug should they choose?

Most people choose drug A for the first problem and drug B for the second. This is fascinating because the two problems are identical. The only difference is that the first is stated in terms of lives saved, the second in terms of lives lost. Yet, even people who realize that their answers are contradictory find it difficult to change them (Kahneman & Tversky, 1972, 1973).

Intuition

As the examples show, we often make decisions on the basis of intuition rather than logic. **Intuition** *is quick, impulsive thought that does not rely on clear reasoning.* It may provide rapid answers, but it can also be misleading and sometimes disastrous. Two noted psychologists, Daniel Kahneman (KON-eh-man) and Amos Tversky (tuh-VER-ski), have spent over 20 years studying how people make decisions and predictions in the face of uncertainty. They have found, to put it bluntly, that human judgment is often seriously flawed (Kahneman et al., 1982). Understanding the thinking errors they have identified may help you to avoid them. Let's explore some common errors.

Representativeness One very common pitfall in judgment is illustrated by the following question:

Which is more probable?

1. Steffi Graf will lose the first set of a tennis match but win the match.
2. Steffi Graf will lose the first set.

Tversky and Kahneman (1982) found that most people regard statements like A as more probable than B. However, this intuitive answer overlooks an important fact: The likelihood of two events occurring together is lower than the probability of either alone. (For example, the probability of getting one head when flipping a coin is one half, or .5. The probability of getting two heads when flipping two coins is one fourth, or .25.) Therefore, A is less likely to be true than B.

Tversky and Kahneman believe that such faulty conclusions are based on an intuitive error called the **representativeness heuristic.** That is, a choice is given greater weight *if it seems to be representative of what we already know.* Thus, the information about Steffi Graf is compared to a mental model of what a tennis pro's behavior should be like. The first choice seems to better represent this model and therefore seems more likely, even though it isn't.

Underlying Odds A second common error in judgment involves ignoring the **base rate,** *or underlying probability of an event.* People in one experiment were told that they would be given descriptions of 100 people—70 lawyers and 30 engineers. Subjects were then asked to guess, without knowing anything about a person, whether she or he was an engineer or a lawyer. All correctly stated the probabilities as 70 percent for lawyer and 30 percent for engineer. Participants were then given this description:

> Dick is a 30-year-old man. He is married with no children. A man of high ability and high motivation, he promises to be quite successful in his field. He is well liked by his colleagues.

Notice that the description gives no new information about Dick's occupation. He could still be either an engineer or a lawyer. Therefore, the odds should again be estimated as 70-30. However, most people changed the odds to 50-50. Intuitively it seems that Dick has an equal chance of being either an engineer or a lawyer. But this guess completely ignores the underlying odds.

Perhaps it is fortunate that we do at times ignore underlying odds. Were this not the case, how many people would get married in the face of a 50 percent divorce rate? Or how many would start high-risk businesses? On the other hand, people who smoke, drink and then drive, or skip wearing auto seat belts ignore rather high odds of injury or illness. In many high-risk situations, ignoring base rates is the same as thinking you are an exception to the rule.

Framing Perhaps the most general conclusion from Kahneman and Tversky's work is that *the way a problem is stated,* or **framed,** affects decisions (Tversky & Kahneman, 1981). As the first example in this discussion revealed, people often give different answers to the same problem stated in slightly different ways. Before we continue, here's an exercise that may give you further insight into framing.

Which Parent?

A couple are divorcing. Both parents seek custody of their only child, but custody can be granted to just one parent. If you had to make a decision based on the following information, to which parent would you award custody of the child?

Parent A: average income, average health, average working hours, reasonable rapport with the child, relatively stable social life.

Parent B: above-average income, minor health problems, lots of work-related travel, very close relationship with the child, extremely active social life.

Most people choose to award custody to Parent B, the parent who has some drawbacks but also several advantages (such as above-average income). That's because people tend to look for *positive qualities* that can be *awarded* to the child. However, how would you choose if you were asked this question: Which parent should be denied custody? In this case, most people choose to deny custody to Parent B. Why is Parent B a good choice one moment and a poor choice the next? It's because the second question asked who should be *denied* custody. To answer this question people tend to look for *negative qualities* that would *disqualify* a parent.

As you can see, the way a question is framed can channel people down a narrow path where they attend to only part of the information provided, rather than weighing all the pros and cons (Shafir, 1993).

Usually, the *broadest* way of framing or stating a problem produces the most rational decisions. However, people often state problems in increasingly narrow terms until a single, seemingly "obvious" answer emerges. For example, to select a career, it would be wise to consider pay, working conditions, job satisfaction, needed skills, future employment outlook, and many other factors. Instead, such decisions are often narrowed to thoughts such as, "I like to write, so I'll be a journalist," "I want to make good money and law pays well," or "I can be creative in photography." Framing decisions so narrowly greatly increases the risk of making a poor choice.

A Look Ahead We have discussed only some of the intuitive errors made in the face of uncertainty. The study of intuitive decision making is rapidly finding application to medical diagnosis, business decisions, military strategy, investing and finance, international relations, and more. In each area, people are learning to think twice before they decide. With practice, you, too, can learn to spot errors like those described.

Remember that shortcuts to answers often short-circuit clear thinking—a point we will pursue in the upcoming Applications section. After that, the Explorations section delves briefly into the fascinating topic of animal intelligence.

Learning Check

1. Fluency, flexibility, and originality are characteristics of
   a. convergent thought **b.** deductive thinking **(c.)** creative thought **d.** trial-and-error solutions

2. List the typical stages of creative thinking in the correct order.
   orientation   preparation   incubation   illumination   verification

3. An ability to organize, abstract, and synthesize ideas blocks creativity; these are non-creative qualities. T or (F?)

4. To be creative, an original idea must also be practical or feasible. (T) or F?

5. Intelligence and creativity are highly correlated; the higher a person's IQ, the more likely he or she is to be creative. (T) or F?

6. Kate is single, outspoken, and very bright. As a college student, she was deeply concerned with discrimination and other social issues and participated in several protests. Which statement is more likely to be true?
   (a.) Kate is a bank teller.
   b. Kate is a bank teller and a feminist.

7. The probability of two events occurring together is lower than the probability of either one occurring alone. (T) or F?

8. Usually, the broadest way of ___*framing*___ a problem yields the most rational decisions.

Critical Thinking

9. A coin is flipped four times with one of the following results: (a) H T T H, (b) T T T T, (c) H H H H, (d) H H T H. Which sequence would most likely precede getting a head on the fifth coin flip?

Answers:

1. c   2. orientation, preparation, incubation, illumination, verification   3. F   4. T   5. F   6. a   7. T   8. framing   9. The chance of getting a head on the fifth flip is the same in each case. Each time you flip a coin, the chance of getting a head is 50 percent, no matter what happened before. However, many people intuitively think that b is the answer because a head is "overdue," or that c is correct because the coin is "on a roll" for heads.

*A*t one time or another, we all experience difficulties in thinking and problem solving. The following should alert you to some of the more common problems.

Rigid Mental Set Try the problems pictured in Figure 11–20 ◆. If you have difficulty, try asking yourself what assumptions you are making. The problems are designed to demonstrate the limiting effects of a mental set. (The answers to these problems, along with an explanation of the sets that prevent their solution, are found in Fig. 11–22 ◆.) In addition to the assumptions and mental sets we bring to a problem, problems themselves may produce a disruptive set. A simple example is the following: The name Polk is pronounced "poke," the word folk is pronounced "foke," and the white of an egg is pronounced _____ . Here is another example: See if you can unscramble each set of letters to make a word that uses all the letters:

MEST _____

LFAE _____

DUB _____

STKAL _____

OTOR _____

LTEPA _____

Now try a new list:

FINEK _____

OPONS _____

KROF _____

PUC _____

SDIH _____

LTEPA _____

Did you notice that the last problem was the same in each case? Many people don't and end up solving the problem twice. To complete the first list (*stem, leaf, bud, stalk, root*), the item LTEPA is usually unscrambled as *petal*. In the second list (*knife, spoon, fork, cup, dish*), LTEPA becomes *plate* for many people.

Now that you have been forewarned about the danger of faulty assumptions, see if you can correctly answer the following questions.

1. Argentines do not have a fourth of July. T or F?

2. How many birthdays does the average person have?

3. A farmer had 19 sheep. All but 9 died. How many sheep did the farmer have left?

(a) **(b)**

Figure 11–20 ◆ **(a)** Nine dots are arranged in a square. Can you connect them by drawing four continuous straight lines without lifting your pencil from the paper? **(b)** Six matches must be arranged to make four triangles. The triangles must be the same size, with each side equal to the length of one match. (The solutions to these problems appear in Fig. 11–22.)

4. It is not unlawful for a man living in Winston-Salem, North Carolina, to be buried west of the Mississippi River. T or F?

5. Some months have 30 days, some have 31. How many months have 28 days?

6. I have two coins that together total 30 cents. One of the coins is not a nickel. What are the two coins?

7. It would be far better to have an elephant eat you than a gorilla. T or F?

8. If there are twelve one-cent candies in a dozen, how many two-cent candies are there in a dozen?

These questions are designed to cause thinking errors. Here are the answers:

1. F. Of course they have a fourth of July. What would they do, go from the third to the fifth? **2.** One, celebrated each year. **3.** Nineteen—9 alive and 10 dead. **4.** F. It is against the law to bury a living person anywhere. **5.** All of them. **6.** A quarter and a nickel. One of the coins is not a nickel, but the other one is! **7.** F. It would be better to have the elephant eat the gorilla. (Read it again.) **8.** Twelve.

If you got caught on any of the questions, consider it an additional reminder of the value of actively challenging the assumptions you are making in any instance of problem solving.

Problems with Logic A major thinking difficulty centers on the process of *logical reasoning*. Simple sequences of logical

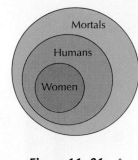

Figure 11–21 ◆

thought can be arranged as a set of *premises* (assumptions) and a *conclusion*. This *format for evaluating logical arguments* is called a **syllogism**. A syllogism can be judged for the *validity* of its reasoning and for the *truth* of its *conclusion*. It is entirely possible to draw true conclusions using faulty logic or to draw false conclusions using valid logic. The following examples show how this is possible.

Syllogism I

All humans are mortal. (**Major premise**)

All women are humans. (**Minor premise**)

Therefore, all women are mortal. (**Conclusion**)

Comment: As you can see from Figure 11–21 ◆, the logic of this syllogism is valid. Since our premises are true, this means the conclusion is true. The diagram shows all women included within the boundaries of mortals.

Syllogism II

All women are humans.

All humans are mortal.

Therefore, all mortals are women.

Comment: In this example, the conclusion drawn is false because the reasoning is invalid. The diagram for Syllogism I shows that all mortals are not women. Notice how little the syllogism has to be changed to produce a false conclusion. Now consider Syllogism III.

Syllogism III

All psychologists are weird.

Mary is a psychologist.

Therefore, Mary is weird.

Comment: In this case the reasoning is valid, but the conclusion is false because the first premise is false. All psychologists are *not* weird. (Honest!) Now let's consider one more syllogism.

Syllogism IV

All ducks have wings.

All birds have wings.

Therefore, all ducks are birds.

Comment: This syllogism shows the importance of paying close attention to logic. The reasoning appears to be valid since the conclusion is true, but substitute *bats* or *airplanes* for *ducks* and see how the conclusion reads. It is a good idea to get in the habit of questioning the logic used by politicians, advertisers, and psychologists, too, for that matter.

Over-simplification   It may be an over-simplification to say so, but over-simplification is another basic source of thinking errors. There are two types of over-simplification that are particularly troublesome. The first is **all-or-nothing thinking** (*one-dimensional thought*). Classifying things as absolutely right or wrong, good or bad, acceptable or unacceptable, or honest or dishonest prevents appreciation of the complexity of most life problems.

The second problem is thinking in terms of **stereotypes** (*over-simplified images*). Stereotypes are particularly troublesome when human relationships are involved (see Chapter 21). An inaccurate or rigid picture of men, African Americans, women, conservatives, liberals, police officers, or any other group of people leads to muddled thinking about individual members of the group. Try to look for this and other errors in your own thinking habits.

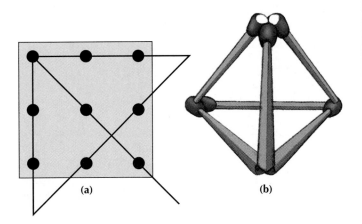

(a)   **(b)**

Figure 11–22 ◆   Problem solutions. **(a)** The dot problem can be solved by extending the lines beyond the square formed by the dots. Most people assume incorrectly that they may not do this. **(b)** The match problem can be solved by building a three-dimensional pyramid. Most people assume that the matches must be arranged on a flat surface. If you remembered the four-tree problem from earlier in the chapter, the match problem may have been easy to solve.

Enhancing Creativity—Brainstorms

Thomas Edison once explained his creativity by saying, "Genius is 1 percent inspiration and 99 percent perspiration." Many studies of creativity show that "genius" and "eminence" owe as much to persistence and dedication as they do to inspiration (Ericsson & Charness, 1994).

Once it is recognized that creativity can be hard work, then something can be done to enhance it. Here are some suggestions on how to begin.

1.   Define the problem broadly. Whenever possible, enlarge the definition of a problem. For instance, assume your problem is: Design a better doorway. This is likely to lead to ordinary solutions. Why not change the problem to: Design a better way to get through a wall? Now your solutions will be more original. Best of all might be to state the problem as: Find a better way to define separate areas for living and working. This could lead to truly creative solutions (Adams, 1988).

Let's say that you are the leader of a group interested in designing a new can opener. Wisely, you ask the group to think about *opening* in general, rather than about can openers. This was just the approach used in developing the pop-top can. As the design group discussed the concept of opening, one member suggested that nature has its own openers, like the soft seam on a pea pod. Instead of a new can-opening tool, the group invented the self-opening can (Stein, 1974).

2.   Create the right atmosphere. Various experiments show that people make more original, spontaneous, and imaginative responses when exposed to others (role models) doing the same. If you want to become more creative, spend more time around creative people (Feldhusen, 1995). This is the premise underlying much education in art, theater, dance, and music (Sternberg & Lubart, 1995).

3.   Allow time for incubation. Trying to hurry or to force a solution may simply encourage fixation on a dead end. Most experts agree that creativity takes time. Creative thinking depends on having a chance to revise or embellish initial solutions, even those based on rapid insight (Tardif & Sternberg, 1988). Incubation can be especially fruitful if you are exposed to external cues that relate to the problem (remember Archimedes' bath?). For example, Johannes Gutenberg, creator of the printing press, realized while at a wine harvest that the mechanical pressure used to crush grapes could also be used to imprint letters on paper (Dorfman, Shames, & Kihlstrom, 1996).

4.   Seek varied input. Remember, creativity requires divergent thinking. Rather than digging deeper with logic, you are attempting to shift your mental "prospecting" to new areas. As an example of this strategy, Edward de Bono (1970, 1992) recommends that you randomly look up words in the dictionary and relate each to the problem. Often the words will trigger a fresh perspective or open a new avenue. For instance, let's say you are asked to come up with new ways to clean oil off a beach, and you draw a blank. Following de Bono's suggestion, you would read the following randomly selected words, relate each to the problem, and see what thoughts are triggered: *weed, rust, poor, magnify, foam, gold, frame, hole, diagonal, vacuum, tribe, puppet, nose, link, drift, portrait, cheese, coal.*

5.   Look for analogies. As the principle of selective comparison (described earlier) suggests, many "new" problems are really old problems in new clothing (Siegler, 1989). Representing a problem in a variety of ways is often the key to solving it. Most problems become easier when they are represented effectively. For example, consider this problem:

> Two backpackers start up a steep trail at 6 A.M. They hike all day, resting occasionally, and arrive at the top at 6 P.M. The next day they start back down the trail at 6 A.M. On the way down they stop several times and vary their pace. They arrive back at 6 P.M. On the way down, one of the hikers, who is a mathematician, tells the other that she has realized that they will pass a point on the trail at exactly the same time as they did the day before. Her non-mathematical friend finds this hard to believe, since on both days they have stopped and started many times and changed their pace. The problem: Is the mathematician right?

Perhaps you will see the answer to this problem immediately. If not, think of it this way: What if there were two pairs of backpackers, one going up the trail, the second coming down, and both hiking on the *same day?* It becomes obvious that the two pairs of hikers will pass each other at some point on the trail. Therefore, they will be at the same place at the same time. The mathematician was right.

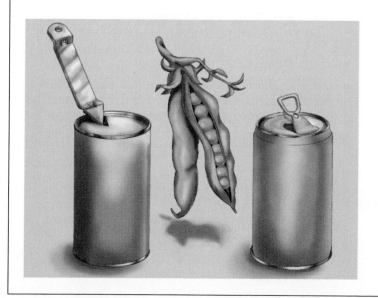

6. Take sensible risks. A willingness to go against the crowd is a key element in doing creative work. Unusual and original ideas may be rejected at first by conventional thinkers. Often, creative individuals must persevere and take some risks before their ideas are widely accepted. Consider, for example, the "Post-it" notes you may have seen stuck all over many offices. They were invented by a scientist who accidentally created a weak adhesive. Rather than throw the mixture out, the scientist put it to a highly creative new use. However, it took him some time to convince others that a "bad" adhesive could be a useful product. Today, stick-on notepapers are one of the 3-M Company's most successful products (Sternberg & Lubart, 1995).

7. Delay evaluation. Various studies suggest that people are most likely to be creative when they are given the freedom to play with ideas and solutions without having to worry about whether they will be evaluated. In the first stages of creative thinking, it is important to avoid criticizing your efforts. Worrying about the correctness of solutions tends to inhibit creativity (Amabile, 1983). This idea is expanded in the discussion that follows.

An alternative approach to enhancing creativity is called *brainstorming.* Although brainstorming is a group technique, it can be applied to individual problem solving as well.

Brainstorming

The essence of **brainstorming** *is that producing and evaluating ideas are kept separate.* In group problem solving, each person is encouraged to produce as many ideas as possible without fear of criticism (Buyer, 1988). This encourages divergent thinking. Some of the most successful brainstorming takes place on computer networks, where each person's fears of being evaluated are minimized (Siau, 1996).

Only at the end of a brainstorming session are ideas reconsidered and evaluated. As ideas are freely generated, an interesting **cross-stimulation effect** takes place in which *one participant's ideas trigger ideas from others.* The four basic rules for successful brainstorming are:

1. Criticism of an idea is absolutely barred. All evaluation is to be deferred until after the session.

2. Modification or combination with other ideas is encour-

aged. Don't worry about giving credit for ideas or keeping them neat. Mix them up!

3. Quantity of ideas is sought. In the early stages of brainstorming, quantity is more important than quality. Try to generate lots of ideas.

4. Unusual, remote, or wild ideas are sought. Let your imagination run amok!

How is brainstorming applied to individual problem solving?

The essential point to remember is to *suspend judgment.* Ideas should first be produced without regard for logic, organization, accuracy, practicality, or any other evaluation. In writing an essay, for instance, you would begin by writing ideas in any order, the more the better, just as they occur to you. Later you would go back and reorganize, rewrite, and criticize your efforts.

As an aid to following rules 2, 3, and 4 of the brainstorming method, you might find this checklist helpful for encouraging original thought. It can be used to see if you have overlooked a possible solution.

Creativity Checklist

1. Redefine. Consider other uses for all elements of the problem. (This is designed to alert you to fixations that may be blocking creativity.)

2. Adapt. How could other objects, ideas, procedures, or solutions be adapted to this particular problem?

3. Modify. Imagine changing anything and everything that could be changed.

4. Magnify. Exaggerate everything you can think of. Think on a grand scale.

5. Minify. What if everything were scaled down? What if all differences were reduced to zero? "Shrink" the problem down to size.

6. Substitute. How could one object, idea, or procedure be substituted for another?

7. Rearrange. Break the problem into pieces and shuffle them.

8. Reverse. Consider reverse orders and opposites, and turn things inside out.

9. Combine. This one speaks for itself.

By making a habit of subjecting a problem to each of these procedures, you should be able to greatly reduce the chances that you will overlook a useful, original, or creative solution.

Learning Check | **Critical Thinking**

1. In evaluating a syllogism, it is possible to draw a true conclusion with faulty logic, or a false conclusion with valid logic. T or F?

2. Stereotyping is an example of over-simplification in thinking. T or F?

---

3. Exposure to creative models has been shown to enhance creativity. T or F?

4. In brainstorming, each idea is critically evaluated as it is generated. T or F?

5. Defining a problem broadly produces a cross-stimulation effect that can inhibit creative thinking. T or F?

6. What mode of thinking does the "Creativity Checklist" (redefine, adapt, modify, magnify, and so forth) encourage?

Answers:

1. T 2. T 3. T 4. F 5. F 6. divergent thinking

Exploration

Animal Intelligence

To what extent are animals capable of thought?

Most pet owners can supply stories of apparent thinking in animals. A friend might say, "Wow, you should have seen Studebaker figure out how to get into the closet where I hid the dog food." Are animals actually thinking in such situations? In a rudimentary sense they are.

Animals demonstrate an ability to mentally represent situations in **delayed response problems.** *These are tasks in which an animal must remember the solution to a problem before responding.* For example, a hungry animal could be allowed to watch as food is hidden under one of three goal boxes. After a delay, the animal is released. Can it select the correct box? If the delay is brief, the answer is yes. Some animals, in fact, can remember the the locations of objects for several days or more (Lea & Kiley-Worthington, 1996).

At times, animal behavior implies far higher levels of thought. In fact, German psychologist Wolfgang Köhler (VOOLF-gong KEAR-ler) believed that animals such as chimpanzees are capable of insight. To test for insight, Köhler challenged Sultan, his brightest chimp, with a **multiple-stick problem.** In this problem *several sticks of increasing length were arranged between the cage and a desired object* (a banana in this case) (Fig. 11–23 ◆). To reach the banana, Sultan

Figure 11–23 ◆ Psychologist Wolfgang Köhler believed that the solution of a multiple-stick problem revealed a capacity for insight in chimpanzees.

had to use the first stick to retrieve the second stick (which was longer than the first). The second stick could then be used to get an even longer stick, which could then be used to reach the banana (Köhler, 1925).

When confronted with this problem, Sultan looked at the banana, then at the sticks . . . then at the banana. Picking up the first stick, Sultan smoothly and without further hesitation solved the problem and raked in the banana.

Psychologists have long debated whether Köhler's chimps actually displayed insight. However, in recent years evidence for animal intelligence and thinking ability has continued to grow. For example, a recent study suggests that three kinds of apes (chimpanzees, bonobos, and orangutans) can use tools intelligently. Each of the apes was shown a food treat in the middle of a long, narrow transparent plastic tube. Each was also given a tool that could be used to poke the food out of the tube. The tool was either a straight wooden stick, a bundle of three sticks held tightly together by a rubber band, or a stick with two shorter sticks stuck through holes drilled in each end (Fig. 11–24 ◆).

The apes could use the straight stick to directly retrieve the food. The bundle of sticks was too wide to fit in the tube unless the rubber band was removed. The H-shaped stick was also too wide

unless the two short sticks were removed from its ends. The apes were able to successfully use tools in all three of these conditions. They also made fewer errors with practice, suggesting that they had a rudimentary understanding of the problem (Visalberghi, Fragaszy, & Savage-Rumbaugh, 1995).

How Intelligent Are Animals?

Evidence for the idea that animals are capable of intelligent thought is varied and, to many researchers, convincing (Lea & Kiley-Worthington, 1996):

- Monkeys can learn to select, from among three objects, the one that differs from the other two.

- When a container of sugar water is moved a set distance farther from a beehive each day, the bees begin to go to the new location *before* the water is moved.

- Pigeons can learn to select photographs of humans from a group of photos that includes various objects.

- A chimp named Lana has learned to remove one, two, or three objects from a computer screen, after first being shown the numbers 1, 2, or 3.

Do such examples really demonstrate thinking by animals? Some psychologists say yes; some say no. What would it take,

then, to verify animal thinking? Psychologist Donald Griffin suggests that we must observe behavior that is *versatile* and *appropriate* to changing circumstances. He also believes that thinking is implied by actions that appear to be planned with an awareness of likely results (Griffin, 1992). As one example, sea otters select suitably sized rocks and use them to hammer shellfish loose for eating. They then use the rock to open the shell (Fig. 11–25 ◆).

As convincing as such examples may seem, they have been challenged. For instance, Epstein, Lanza, and Skinner conditioned pigeons to duplicate seemingly insightful behavior like that claimed for higher animals. Other psychologists, however, reply that the pigeons only achieved the *appearance* of thinking, because their behavior was strongly guided by reinforcement.

As stated before, it seems reasonable to assume that animals do think. However, debate is sure to continue about the limits of their intelligence and about whether specific examples demonstrate thinking, instinct, or conditioning.

Counting on Sheba Psychologist Sarah Boysen recently added to the debate about animal cognition in a fascinating experiment. Boysen and her colleagues taught a chimp named Sheba to count and to recognize numbers from 0 to 8

Figure 11–24 ◆ Researchers recently showed that chimpanzees, bonobos, and orangutans can solve problems that appear to require both thinking and comprehension. A transparent plastic tube was baited with a food treat (such as peanuts) and the apes were given one of three tools to use: a straight stick, a bundle of sticks, or a stick with cross-bars. Successful use of the latter two tools required greater comprehension of the problem (Visalberghi, Fragaszy, & Savage-Rumbaugh, 1995).

Figure 11–25 ◆ Does the seemingly intelligent behavior of sea otters and other animals reflect thinking ability, instinct, or conditioning? The evidence remains inconclusive, so psychologists disagree.

Figure 11–26 ◆ Typical stimuli used in testing chimpanzees for comprehension of the concepts *less and more*. The chimps could not resist choosing the larger amount of candy, even when that choice meant they got the smaller amount of candy and another chimp got the larger amount. The use of numeric symbols freed the chimps to choose the smaller amount of food for the other chimp.

(Boysen et al., 1995). When Boysen decided to test Sheba's understanding of *more* and *less,* a striking thing happened. Boysen placed two plates of gumdrops in front of Sheba, one holding more gumdrops than the other. Sheba was allowed to select one of the plates. Naturally enough, Sheba selected the plate with more candy. When she did, that plate was given to another chimpanzee. Sheba became visibly agitated at this foul turn of events.

The gumdrop test was repeated many more times. Nonetheless, Sheba could not learn to choose the plate with less candy on it. At that point, Boysen decided to place numbers on the plates, rather than gumdrops. The number Sheba chose determined how many gumdrops the second chimp would receive (Fig. 11–26 ◆). Almost immediately, Sheba learned to point to the smaller number. Clearly, she knew the rule: If she chose the larger number the larger amount of candy was given away and she kept the smaller amount; if she pointed to the smaller number, she got to keep the larger amount of candy.

Further testing revealed that knowing the rule and acting on it were two different things. Whenever gumdrops were used, Sheba could not choose the smaller number. When numerals were used, she could. Sheba's behavior suggests that chimpanzees can learn, at a very basic level, to think symbolically. (Symbolic thought uses language or symbols to represent the external world.)

Sheba's inability to choose correctly when faced with plates of candy is intriguing. Very likely, chimps living in the wild are genetically programmed to collect food as efficiently as possible. Only when they have learned to use symbols are chimps freed from the immediate and powerful allure of a plate of gumdrops. In addition to providing insight into the mind of a chimpanzee, Sheba's behavior emphasizes the tremendous advantage that we humans have as symbol-using animals.

(Sources: Boysen & Berntson, 1989; Epstein et al., 1981; Griffin, 1992; Herrnstein, 1979; Premack, 1983; Rose, 1984; Rumbaugh et al., 1989.)

Learning Check

1. There is evidence that chimpanzees are capable of insightful solutions to problems, but some psychologists remain unconvinced that true insight is involved. T or F?

2. Rudimentary thinking abilities are revealed when animals successfully solve _____ _____ problems, which involve mentally representing an external situation.

3. Köhler's ape Sultan was apparently able to solve problems involving numbers and amounts. T or F?

4. Psychologist Donald Griffin suggests that animal cognition is revealed by behavior which is *versatile* and *appropriate* to changing circumstances. T or F?

5. In tests involving the concepts *more* and *less,* Sheba the chimpanzee was only able to perform correctly when the amounts were represented _____ .

Critical Thinking

6. Chimpanzees and other apes are intelligent and entertaining animals. If you were doing research on their cognitive abilities, what major problem would you have to guard against?

Answers:

1. T 2. delayed response 3. F 4. T 5. symbolically 6. The problem of anthropomorphizing (ascribing human characteristics to animals) is especially difficult to avoid when researchers spend many hours interacting with chimps.

Chapter Summary

What is the nature of thought?

◆ Thinking is the manipulation of **internal representations** of external stimuli or situations.

◆ Three basic units of thought are **images, concepts,** and **language** or **symbols.**

In what ways are images related to thinking?

◆ Most people have internal images of one kind or another. Images may be **stored** or **created.** Sometimes they cross normal sense boundaries in a type of imagery called **synesthesia.**

◆ Images used in problem solving may be three-dimensional, they may be rotated in space, and their size may change.

◆ **Kinesthetic images** are created by produced, remembered, or imagined actions. **Kinesthetic sensations** and **micromovements** seem to help structure the flow of thought for many people.

How are concepts learned? Are there different kinds of concepts?

◆ A **concept** is a generalized idea of a class of objects or events.

◆ **Concept formation** may be based on **positive** and **negative instances** or more commonly, on **rule learning.** In practice, concept identification frequently makes use of **prototypes,** or general models of the concept class.

◆ Concepts may be classified as **conjunctive** ("and" concepts), **disjunctive** ("either-or" concepts), or **relational.**

◆ The **denotative** meaning of a word or concept is its dictionary definition. **Connotative** meaning is personal or emotional. Connotative meaning can be measured with the **semantic differential.**

What is the role of language in thinking?

◆ Language allows events to be **encoded** into **symbols** for easy mental manipulation. Thinking in language is influenced by meaning. The study of meaning is called **semantics.**

◆ Language carries meaning by combining a set of symbols or signs according to a set of rules (**grammar**), which includes rules about word order (**syntax**). A true language is **productive,** and can be used to generate new ideas or possibilities.

Can animals be taught to use language?

◆ Animal communication is relatively limited because it lacks symbols that can be rearranged easily.

◆ Attempts to teach chimpanzees systems such as **American Sign Language** suggest to some that primates are capable of language use. Others question this conclusion. Studies that make use of **lexigrams** provide the best evidence yet of animal language use.

What do we know about problem solving?

◆ The solution to a problem may be arrived at **mechanically** (by **trial and error** or by **rote** application of rules), but mechanical solutions are frequently inefficient or ineffective, except where aided by computer.

◆ Solutions by **understanding** usually begin with discovery of the **general properties** of an answer. Next comes proposal of a number of **functional solutions.**

◆ Problem solving is frequently aided by **heuristics.** These are strategies that typically narrow the search for solutions. The **ideal strategy** is a general heuristic.

◆ When understanding leads to a rapid solution, it is said that **insight** has occurred. Three elements of insight are **selective encoding, selective combination,** and **selective comparison.**

◆ Insight and other problem solving can be blocked by **fixation. Functional fixedness** is a common fixation, but **emotional blocks, cultural values, learned conventions,** and **perceptual habits** are also problems.

What is artificial intelligence?

◆ **Artificial intelligence** refers to any artificial system that can perform tasks that require intelligence when done by people.

◆ Two principal areas of artificial intelligence research are **computer simulations** and **expert systems.**

◆ Computer simulations of human problem solving are usually based on a **means-ends analysis.**

◆ Expert human problem solving is based on **organized knowledge** and **acquired strategies,** rather than some general improvement in thinking ability.

◆ Artificial intelligence is helping scientists explore the nature of human thought, knowledge, and expertise.

What is the nature of creative thinking?

◆ To be creative, a solution must be practical and sensible as well as original. Creative thinking requires **divergent thought,** characterized by **fluency, flexibility,** and **originality.** Tests of creativity measure these qualities.

◆ **Daydreaming and fantasy** are a source of much divergent thinking.

◆ Five stages often seen in creative problem solving are **orientation, preparation, incubation, illumination,** and **verification.** Not all creative thinking fits this pattern. Much creative activity is based on **incremental problem solving.**

◆ Studies suggest that **creative persons** share a number of identifiable characteristics, most of which contradict popular stereotypes. There appears to be only a slight correlation between IQ and creativity.

How accurate is intuition?

◆ Intuitive thinking often leads to errors. Wrong conclusions may be drawn when an answer seems highly **representative** of what we already believe is true.

◆ A second problem is ignoring the **base rate** (or **underlying probability**) of an event.

◆ Clear thinking is usually aided by stating or **framing** a problem in broad terms.

What can be done to improve thinking and to promote creativity?

◆ Major sources of thinking errors include **rigid mental set, faulty logic,** and **over-simplification.**

◆ Various strategies, including **brainstorming,** tend to enhance creative problem solving.

Do animals think?

◆ Animals reveal a rudimentary capacity for thought when they solve **delayed response problems** and, in some cases, problems that appear to require understanding or **insight.**

◆ There is also evidence that higher animals, such as chimpanzees, can learn to use rudimentary symbolic thought. For the moment, however, some psychologists remain unconvinced about such abilities.

Intelligence

Preview

What Day Is It?

Ask George in which recent years April 21 fell on a Sunday. With little hesitation he will answer, "1996, 1991, 1985, 1974, 1968, 1963, 1957, 1946." Surprisingly, this gives only the slightest hint of his ability. If encouraged, George will go back as far as 1700—with complete accuracy! His calendar calculations cover a range of at least 6,000 years: With equal ease he can identify February 15, 2002, as a Friday or August 28, 1591, as a Wednesday.

Is he a genius?

George's abilities are all the more amazing in view of the fact that he is mentally retarded. He cannot add, subtract, multiply, or divide even simple numbers (Horwitz et al., 1965). George's strange talent is an example of the *savant syndrome,* in which an island of brilliance is found in a sea of retardation. In the savant syndrome, a person of below normal intelligence shows exceptional mental ability in a very limited area, such as mental arithmetic, calendar calculations, art, or music ("Savant," 1995).

How could George be retarded and have such amazing ability at the same time?

Perpetual calendars have only 14 different yearly "templates." It appears that many calendar calculators memorize the 14 templates and learn how to tell which one applies to a particular year. This allows a person of limited intelligence to perform an impressive mental feat (Young, 1994).

The striking contrast between George's general retardation and his unusual ability is a fitting introduction to the challenge of trying to define and measure intelligence. Quite frankly, we are still searching for answers to questions like these: Is intelligence a general trait or a collection of specific skills? To what extent is intelligence determined by the genetic "wheel of fortune"? How much is it nurtured by environment? Is it possible to construct an intelligence test that is fair to all people? How important is intelligence for "success"? Because our understanding of intelligence is rapidly changing, we cannot hope to give final answers.

For the sake of clarity, we will first assume that intelligence *can* be measured, and we will use IQ scores as a way to answer questions about intelligence. Later, we will consider questions that have been raised about intelligence tests and the meaning of their results.

Chapter Survey

Theme: Measuring intelligence is worthwhile, but tests only provide limited definitions of intelligent behavior.

Key Questions:

Key Questions	Key Topics to Watch for
How do psychologists define intelligence?	A brief history of intelligence testing Intelligence versus aptitudes
What are the qualities of a good psychological test?	Reliability, validity, objectivity, and test standardization
What are typical IQ tests like?	Individual and group tests of intelligence
How do IQ scores relate to gender, age, and occupation?	The concept of IQ Variations in IQ
What does IQ tell us about genius?	The mentally gifted
What causes mental retardation?	Degrees of mental retardation Causes of mental retardation
How do heredity and environment affect intelligence?	Genetic and environmental influences
How have views of intelligence changed in recent years?	Speed of neural processing Cognitive views of intelligence Multiple intelligences
Are IQ tests fair to all racial and cultural groups?	IQ in perspective The Larry P. case

Defining Intelligence— Intelligence Is . . . You Know, It's . . .

Intelligence cannot be observed directly: It has no mass, occupies no space, and is invisible. Nevertheless, we feel certain it exists. Consider the following two children:

> When she was 14 months old, Anne H. wrote her own name. She taught herself to read at age 2. At age 5, she astounded her kindergarten teacher by walking into class with a stack of encyclopedias—which she proceeded to read. At 10 she breezed through an entire high school algebra course in 12 hours.

> At age 10 Billy A. can write his name and can count, but he has trouble with simple addition and subtraction problems and finds multiplication impossible. He has been held back in school twice and is still incapable of doing the work his 8-year-old classmates find easy. His teachers have suggested placing him in a special educational program for slow learners.

Anne is considered a genius; Billy, a slow learner. There seems little doubt that they differ in intelligence.

Wait! Anne's ability is obvious, but how do we know that Billy isn't just lazy?

This is the same dilemma that **Alfred Binet** faced in 1904. The minister of education in Paris had given Binet the task of finding a way to distinguish slower students from the more capable (or the capable but lazy). In a flash of brilliance, Binet and an associate created a test made up of "intellectual"

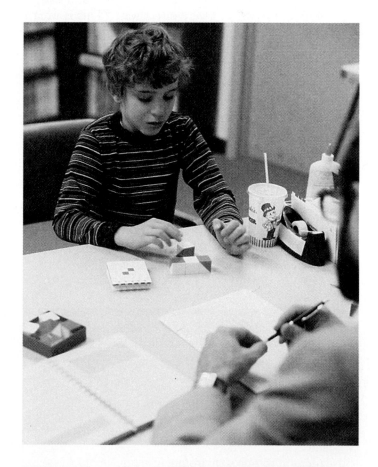

Modern intelligence tests are widely used to measure cognitive abilities. When properly administered, such tests provide an operational definition of intelligence.

questions and problems. Next, they learned which questions an average child could answer at each age. Children low in intellectual ability were identified by below-par scores on the test.

Binet's approach gave rise to modern intelligence tests. At the same time, it launched over 90 years of often heated debate. Part of the debate is related to the basic difficulty of defining intelligence.

Is there an accepted definition of intelligence?

A Definition of Intelligence

Most psychologists would probably agree with David Wechsler's general description of **intelligence** as the *global capacity to act purposefully, to think rationally, and to deal effectively with the environment.* To add to the definition, Table 12–1 ■ shows results from a survey of 1,020 experts on intelligence. At least three quarters agreed that the listed items are important elements of intelligence (Snyderman & Rothman, 1987).

Beyond this, there is so much disagreement that many psychologists simply accept an **operational definition** of intelligence. *(We define a concept operationally by stating the procedures used to measure it.)* By selecting test items, a psychologist is saying in a very direct way, "This is what I mean by intelligence." A test that measures memory, reasoning, and verbal fluency offers a very different definition of intelligence than one that measures strength of grip, shoe size, length of the nose, or a person's best Pac-Man score.

Aptitudes As a child, my friend Hedda displayed an aptitude for art. Today, Hedda is a successful graphic artist. How does an aptitude like Hedda's differ from general intelligence? An **aptitude** *is a capacity for learning certain abilities.* Persons with mechanical, artistic, or musical aptitudes are likely to do well in careers involving mechanics, art, or music, respectively (Fig. 12–1 ◆).

Are there tests for aptitudes? How are they different from intelligence tests?

Table 12–1 ■ Important Elements of Intelligence	
Description	**Percent of Agreement**
Abstract thinking or reasoning	99.3
Problem-solving ability	97.7
Capacity to acquire knowledge	96.0
Memory	80.5
Adaptation to one's environment	77.2
Adapted from Snyderman & Rothman, 1987.	

Figure 12–1 ◆ Special aptitude tests measure a person's potential for achievement in a limited area of ability, such as manual dexterity. Multiple aptitude tests measure potentials in broader areas, such as college work, law, or medicine. Intelligence tests measure a very wide array of aptitudes and mental abilities.

Aptitude tests measure a narrower range of abilities than intelligence tests do. For example, **special aptitude tests** *predict a person's likelihood of succeeding in a single area*, such as clerical work or operating a computer (Fig. 12–2 ◆). (To learn how psychologists use aptitude tests to select people for employment, see Chapter 22.) **Multiple aptitude tests** *measure two or more capacities.* Tests of this type tend to be more like intelligence tests. The well-known *Scholastic Assessment Test* (SAT), which measures aptitudes for language, math, and reasoning, is a multiple aptitude test. The tests required to enter graduate schools of law, medicine, business, and dentistry are also multiple aptitude tests. The broadest aptitude measures are **general intelligence tests,** *which assess a wide variety of mental abilities* (Anastasi, 1996).

Reliability and Validity

Suppose that a deranged psychologist, Professor Ike Q. Tester, decides to write an intelligence test (the *I. Q. Tester IQ Test*). As a concerned citizen, there are two questions you

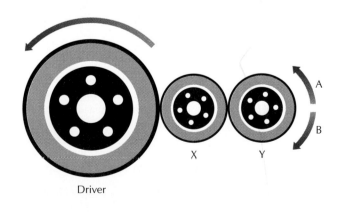

1. If the driver turns in the direction shown, which direction will wheel Y turn?   A   B

2. Which wheel will turn the slowest?   Driver   X   Y

Figure 12–2 ◆ Sample questions like those found on tests of mechanical aptitude.

should ask about Tester's test: "Is it *reliable?*" and "Is it *valid?*"

What does reliability refer to?

If you weigh yourself several times in a row, a reliable bathroom scale gives the same weight each time. Likewise, a **reliable** *test must give approximately the same score each time a person takes it.* In other words, the scores should be *consistent* and highly correlated. It is easy to see that unreliable tests have little value. Imagine a medical test for pregnancy or breast cancer, for instance, that gives positive and negative responses for the same woman on the same day.

To check the reliability of the *I. Q. Tester IQ Test,* we could administer it to a large group of people. Then each person could be tested again a week later to establish *test-retest reliability.* Reliability is also sometimes measured by comparing the score on one half of the test items to the score on the other half (*split-half reliability*). If Tester offered two versions of his test, we could correlate scores on one to scores on the other for each person (*equivalent-forms reliability*).

By comparing such scores we find that the Tester Test is quite reliable. In fact, the scores are identical each time the test is given: Everyone scores zero (except Professor Tester, who scores 100 percent and thereby proclaims himself the only human with any intelligence).

Let's concede to Tester that his test is reliable (but for the wrong reasons). A more important question then becomes, Is the test valid? Obviously we have been playing with a silly example. A test has **validity** *when it measures what it claims to measure.* By no stretch of imagination could a test of intelligence be valid if the person who wrote it is the only one who can pass it.

How is validity established?

Validity is usually demonstrated by comparing test scores to actual performance. This is called *criterion validity.* Scores on a test of legal aptitude, for example, might be compared to grades in law school. If high scores correlate with high grades, or some other standard of success, the test might be considered valid. Unfortunately, many tests you will encounter, such as those found in magazines or offered by commercial self-improvement courses, have little or no validity.

Tester's Last Stand   Let's return to Professor Tester for a final point. Although he admits that his test has problems, Professor Tester claims that at least it is *objective.* Is he right? Actually, he might be. If the *I. Q. Tester IQ Test* gives *the same score when corrected by different people* it is an **objective test.** However, objectivity is not enough to guarantee a fair test. To be useful a psychological test must also be *standardized.*

Test standardization refers to two things. First, it means that *standard procedures are used in giving the test.* The instructions, answer forms, amount of time to work, and so forth, are the same for everyone. Second, it means finding the **norm,** *or average score,* made by a large group of people

like those for whom the test was designed. Without standardization, it would be unfair to compare the scores of people taking a test on different occasions. And without norms, there would be no way to tell if a score is high, low, or average.

Later in this chapter we will address the question of whether intelligence tests are valid. For now, let's take a practical approach and examine some widely used standardized tests.

Testing Intelligence— The IQ and You

American psychologists quickly saw the value of Alfred Binet's test. In 1916, **Lewis Terman** and others at Stanford University revised it for use in the U.S. After more revisions, the **Stanford-Binet Intelligence Scale, Fourth Edition** is still a widely used *individual test of intelligence.* The original Stanford-Binet assumed that intellectual ability improves throughout childhood. Today, the Stanford-Binet (or Binet-4) is still primarily made up of age-ranked questions of increasing difficulty. Table 12–2 ■ lists the subtests of the Binet-4.

Intelligence Quotients

The age-ranked questions of the original Stanford-Binet allowed a person's *mental age* to be measured. **Mental age** *is the average mental ability displayed at a given age.* For example, at ages 8 or 9, very few children can define the word *connection.* At age 10, 10 percent can. At age 13, 60 percent can. In other words, the ability to define *connection* indicates mental ability equal to that of an average 13-year-old and gives a mental age of 13 (on this single item). Table 12–3 ■ is a sample of items that persons of average intelligence can answer at various ages.

Mental age is a good measure of actual ability. But mental age says nothing about whether overall intelligence is *relatively* high or low. To know the meaning of mental age we must also consider a person's **chronological age** (*age in years*). Then we can relate mental age to actual age. This yields an **IQ,** or **intelligence quotient.** When the Stanford-Binet was first used, IQ was defined as *mental age (MA) divided by chronological age (CA) and multiplied by 100:*

$$\frac{MA}{CA} \times 100 = IQ$$

An advantage of the IQ was that intelligence could be compared among children with different chronological and mental ages. For instance, a 10-year-old child with a mental age of 12 has an IQ of 120:

Table 12–2 ■ Stanford-Binet 4: Ability Areas and Subtests

Verbal Reasoning

Vocabulary	Name a pictured object or define a word.
Comprehension	Answer questions requiring logic or common sense.
Absurdities	Tell what is wrong with pictures (for example, a bicycle has square wheels).
Verbal relations	Given four words, tell how three are similar.

Quantitative Reasoning

Quantitative	Use numbered blocks to add and count; solve word problems.
Number series	Given a series of numbers, tell what two numbers would come next. For example, 3, 6, 9, would be followed by 12 and 15.
Equation building	Given a set of numbers and mathematical signs, arrange them to make a true equation. For example, 3, 4, 7, +, = would be arranged as 3 + 4 = 7.

Abstract/Visual Reasoning

Pattern analysis	Put picture puzzles together; reproduce patterns with blocks.
Copying	Copy arrangements of blocks or draw copies of designs.
Matrices	Complete a matrix of shapes that has one part missing.
Paper folding and cutting	Choose pictures that show how a piece of paper would look if folded or cut.

Short-Term Memory

Bead memory	Correctly remember the order of beads placed on a stick.
Memory for sentences	Repeat sentences exactly after hearing them once.
Memory for digits	Repeat a series of digits (forward or backward) after hearing them once.
Memory for objects	After seeing several objects, point to the objects in the same order as they were shown.

$$\frac{(MA)\ 12}{(CA)\ 10} \times 100 = 120\ (IQ)$$

A second child having a mental age of 12, but with a chronological age of 12 would have an IQ of 100:

$$\frac{(MA)\ 12}{(CA)\ 12} \times 100 = 100\ (IQ)$$

The IQ shows that the younger child is brighter than his 12-year-old friend, even though their intellectual skills are actually the same. Notice that IQ equals 100 when MA = CA. An IQ score of 100 is therefore defined as average intelligence.

Then does a person with an IQ score below 100 have below average intelligence?

Not unless the IQ is well below 100. An IQ of 100 is the *mathematical* average (or mean) for such scores. However, *average intelligence* is usually defined as any score from 90 to 109. The important point is that IQ scores will be over 100 when mental age is higher than age in years (Fig. 12–3 ◆). IQ scores below 100 occur when age in years exceeds mental age. An example of the second situation would be a 15-year-old with an MA of 12:

$$\frac{12}{15} \times 100 = 80\ (IQ)$$

Deviation IQs   The preceding examples are offered to give you insight into the history and meaning of IQ scores. However, it is no longer necessary to calculate IQs for modern tests. Instead, *deviation IQs* are used. A **deviation IQ** *is obtained statistically from a person's relative standing in his or her age group.*

Deviation IQs are based on how far above or below average a person's "raw" score is. (A raw score is the actual number of questions answered correctly. See Appendix A for more information.) Tables are used to convert a person's raw score to an IQ score. This approach avoids certain troublesome errors that occur when IQs are calculated directly (Neisser et al., 1996).

How old do children have to be before their IQ scores become stable?

Stability of IQ   IQ scores are not very dependable until about age 6 (Schuerger & Witt, 1989). The correlation between IQ scores from age 2 and those at age 18 is only .31. (Recall that a perfect correlation is 1.00, and a correlation of 0.00 occurs when scores are unrelated.) IQs become more

Table 12–3 ◼ Sample Items from the Stanford-Binet Intelligence Scale

Age	Items
2 years old	On a large paper doll, points out the hair, mouth, feet, ears, nose, hands, and eyes.
	When shown a tower built of four blocks, builds one like it.
3 years old	When shown a bridge built of three blocks, builds one like it.
	When shown a drawing of a circle, copies it with a pencil.
4 years old	Fills in the missing word when asked, "Brother is a boy; sister is a _____."
	"In daytime it is light; at night it is _____."
	Answers correctly when asked, "Why do we have houses?" "Why do we have books?"
5 years old	Defines *ball*, *hat*, and *stove*.
	When shown a drawing of a square, copies it with a pencil.
9 years old	Answers correctly when examiner says, "In an old graveyard in Spain they have discovered a small skull which they believe to be that of Christopher Columbus when he was about 10 years old. What is foolish about that?"
	Answers correctly when asked, "Tell me the name of a color that rhymes with head." "Tell me a number that rhymes with tree."
Adult	Can describe the difference between laziness and idleness, poverty and misery, character and reputation.
	Answers correctly when asked, "Which direction would you have to face so your right hand would be toward the north?"

Terman & Merill, 1960.

Figure 12–3 ◆ With a score of 230, Marilyn Mach vos Savant has the highest IQ ever officially recorded. When she was only 7 years and 9 months old, vos Savant could answer questions that the average 13-year-old can answer. At ages 8, 9, and 10, she got perfect scores on the Stanford-Binet scale. Now in her 40s, she is capitalizing on her celebrity by giving lectures and writing books (Lemley, 1986).

reliable as children grow older. Overall, changes are usually small after middle childhood (Fig. 12–4 ◆). The average change (median change) in IQ on retesting is roughly 5 points in either direction.

How much does aging affect the IQ?

Because IQ reflects education, maturity, and experience, as well as innate intelligence, test scores show a small, gradual increase until about age 40 (Eichorn et al., 1981). This trend,

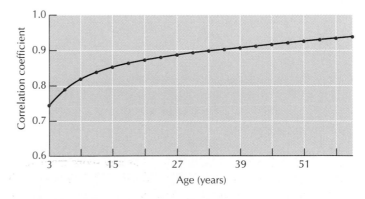

Figure 12–4 ◆ The stability or reliability of IQ scores increases rapidly in early childhood. Scores are very consistent from early adulthood to late middle age. (Source: Schuerger & Witt, 1989.)

of course, is an average. Some people make fairly large gains in IQ, whereas others experience sizable losses. How do the two groups differ? In general, persons with large IQ gains are exposed to stimulating intellectual experiences during early adulthood. Those who decline typically suffer from chronic illnesses, drinking problems, or unstimulating lifestyles (Honzik, 1984).

Some studies of IQ reveal slow declines after middle age, while others indicate little or no change due to aging (Schaie, 1980). As you may recall from Chapter 5, these contradictory results can be explained in this way: When we emphasize general information or comprehension, there is little decline in IQ until advanced age; however, test items requiring speed, rapid insight, or perceptual flexibility show earlier losses and a rapid decline after middle age (Brody, 1992). Overall, age-related losses are small for most healthy, well-educated individuals (Weintraub et al., 1991).

Perhaps the most intriguing link between IQ and aging is the observation that impending death may bring about marked changes in brain function. Certain intellectual skills have been shown to *decline abruptly about five years before death*. This **terminal decline** in IQ can be measured even when a person appears to be in good health (Suedfeld & Piedrahita, 1984).

The Wechsler Tests

Is the Stanford-Binet the only intelligence test?

A widely used alternative to the Stanford-Binet is the **Wechsler Adult Intelligence Scale-Third Edition,** or **WAIS-III.** This test also has a form for use with children, called the **Wechsler Intelligence Scale for Children-Third Edition (WISC-III).**

The Wechsler tests are similar to the Stanford-Binet, but differ in important ways. For one thing, the WAIS-III was designed to test adult intelligence. Of course, the Stanford-Binet may be used with adults, but it tends to be better suited for children and adolescents. The Wechsler tests yield a

Table 12–4 ■ Sample Items Similar to Those Used on the WAIS-III	
Verbal Subtests	**Sample Items**
Information	How many wings does a bird have? Who wrote *Paradise Lost?*
Digit span	Repeat from memory a series of digits, such as 3 1 0 6 7 4 2 5, after hearing it once.
General Comprehension	What is the advantage of keeping money in the bank? Why is copper often used in electrical wires?
Arithmetic	Three men divided 18 golf balls equally among themselves. How many golf balls did each man receive? If 2 apples cost 15¢, what will be the cost of a dozen apples?
Similarities	In what way are a lion and a tiger alike? In what way are a saw and a hammer alike?
Vocabulary	The test consists simply of asking, "What is a ____ ?" or "What does ____ mean?" The words cover a wide range of difficulty or familiarity.
Performance Subtests	**Description of Item**
Picture arrangement	Arrange a series of cartoon panels to make a meaningful story.
Picture completion	What is missing from these pictures?
Block design	Copy designs with blocks (as shown at right).
Object assembly	Put together a jigsaw puzzle.
Digit symbol	Fill in the symbols:

1	2	3	4
X	III	I	0

3	4	1	3	4	2	1	2

Courtesy of The Psychological Corporation.

single overall IQ, just as the Stanford-Binet does. However, the WAIS and WISC also provide separate scores for *performance* and *verbal* intelligence. **Performance intelligence** is measured by solving puzzles, assembling objects, completing pictures, and other *non-verbal tasks*. **Verbal intelligence** is measured by answering questions involving vocabulary, general information, arithmetic, and other *language- or symbol-oriented tasks*. Verbal and non-verbal abilities can be broken down further, to reveal various cognitive strengths and weaknesses. The abilities measured by the Wechsler tests and some sample test items are listed in Table 12–4 ■.

Group Tests

The Binet-4 and the Wechsler tests are **individual intelligence tests,** which must be given to *a single person by a trained specialist*. In contrast, **group intelligence tests** can be administered to *a large group of people with minimal supervision*. Group tests usually require people to read, to follow instructions, and to solve problems of logic, reasoning, mathematics, or spatial skills. The first group intelligence test was the *Army Alpha*, developed for World War I military inductees. As you can see in Table 12–5 ■, intelligence testing has come a long way since then.

Scholastic Aptitude Tests If you're wondering if you have ever taken an intelligence test, the answer is probably yes. As mentioned earlier, the *Scholastic Assessment Test* is a multiple aptitude test. So are the *American College Test* (ACT) and the *College Qualification Test* (CQT). Each of these group tests is designed to predict chances for success in college. Because the tests measure a variety of mental aptitudes, each can also be used to estimate general intelligence.

Table 12–5 ■	Items from the Army Alpha Subtest on "Common Sense"

The *Army Alpha* was given to World War I army recruits in the United States as a way to identify potential officers. In these sample questions, note the curious mixture of folk wisdom, scientific information, and moralism (Kessen & Cahan, 1986). Other parts of the test were more like modern intelligence tests.

1. If plants are dying for lack of rain, you should
   [ ] water them
   [ ] ask a florist's advice
   [ ] put fertilizer around them
2. If the grocer should give you too much money in making change, what is the right thing to do?
   [ ] buy some candy for him with it
   [ ] give it to the first poor man you meet
   [ ] tell him of his mistake
3. If you saw a train approaching a broken track you should
   [ ] telephone for an ambulance
   [ ] signal the engineer to stop the train
   [ ] look for a piece of rail to fit in
4. Some men lose their breath on high mountains because
   [ ] the wind blows their breath away
   [ ] the air is too rare
   [ ] it is always cold there
5. We see no stars at noon because
   [ ] they have moved to the other side of the earth
   [ ] they are much fainter than the sun
   [ ] they are hidden behind the sky

Learning Check	Critical Thinking

Check your comprehension before you continue reading.

1. The first successful intelligence test was developed by Alfred Binet .

2. If we define intelligence by writing a test, we are using
   a. a circular definition   **b.** an abstract definition   **c.** an operational definition
   d. a chronological definition

3. Place an R or a V after each operation to indicate if it would be used to establish the reliability or the validity of a test.
   a. Compare score on one half of test items to score on the other half. (R)
   b. Compare scores on test to grades, performance ratings, or other measures. (V)
   c. Compare scores from the test after administering it on two separate occasions. (R)
   d. Compare scores on alternate forms of the test. (R)

4. IQ was originally defined as $\frac{MA}{CA}$ _____ times 100.

Variations in Intelligence—The Numbers Game

IQ ranges have been classified as shown in Table 12–6 ■. A look at the percentages reveals a definite pattern. The distribution of IQs approximates a **normal** (*bell-shaped*) **curve,** in which most scores fall close to the average, with far fewer at the extremes. Figure 12–5 ◆ shows this characteristic of measured intelligence.

On the average, do males and females differ in intelligence?

Sex IQ does not give a definite answer to this question because test items were selected to be equally difficult for both sexes. It seems safe to assume that men and women do not differ in overall intelligence, and no significant IQ difference has been found. However, tests like the WAIS-R allow us to compare the intellectual strengths and weaknesses of men and women.

For decades, women, as a group, performed best on items that require verbal ability, vocabulary, and rote learning. Men, in contrast, were best at items that require spatial visualization and arithmetic reasoning. However, such male-female differences have almost disappeared in recent years among children and young adults. The small differences that remain appear to be based on a tendency for parents and

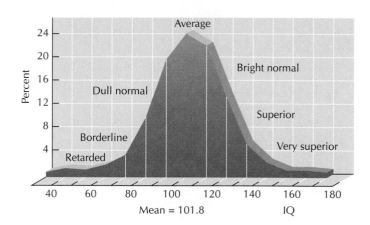

Figure 12–5 ◆ Distribution of Stanford-Binet Intelligence Test scores for 3,184 children. (After Terman & Merrill, 1960.)

educators to encourage males, more than females, to learn math and spatial skills (Hyde & Linn, 1988).

How do IQ scores relate to success in school, jobs, and other endeavors?

IQ and Achievement The correlation between IQ and school grades is .50—a sizable association. If intelligence were the only factor affecting grades, the association might be even higher. However, motivation, special talents, off-campus educational opportunities, and many other factors influence school grades and success. Interestingly, IQ is not a good predictor of out-of-school achievements such as art, music, creative writing, dramatics, science, and leadership. Tests of creativity are much more strongly related to these "real-world" achievements (Neisser et al., 1996; Wallach, 1985).

As you might expect, there is also a relationship between IQ and job classification. Persons holding white-collar, professional positions average higher IQs than those in blue-collar settings. For example, accountants, lawyers, and engineers average about 125 in IQ. In contrast, miners and farm workers average about 90 (Brody, 1992). It is important to note, however, that a range of IQ scores can be found in all occupations. Many people of high intelligence, because of choice or circumstance, have "low-ranking" jobs.

It is tempting to interpret the link between IQ and occupation as evidence that professional jobs require more

Table 12–6 ■	Distribution of Adult IQ Scores on the WAIS-R	
IQ	**Description**	**Percent**
Above 130	Very superior	2.2
120–129	Superior	6.7
110–119	Bright normal	16.1
90–109	Average	50.0
80–89	Dull normal	16.1
70–79	Borderline	6.7
Below 70	Mentally retarded	2.2

John Kirtley has an IQ score of 174, yet he prefers to do custodial work, feeling that his unusual intellect would be "used" by his employers if he pursued a technical occupation.

intelligence. However, since higher status jobs often require an academic degree, the apparent link between IQ and job status may be misleading. Selection for professional jobs appears to be biased in favor of a particular type of intelligence, namely, the kind measured by intelligence tests (McClelland, 1994; Neisser et al., 1996).

When IQs are extreme—below 70 or above 140—the influence on a person's life becomes unmistakable. Only about 3 percent of the population falls into these ranges. Nevertheless, this translates to millions of people who have exceptionally high or low IQs. Discussions of the mentally gifted and mentally retarded follow.

The Mentally Gifted— Is Genius Next to Insanity?

How high is the IQ of a genius?

Only about 2 people out of 100 score above 130 on IQ tests. Such people are usually described as "gifted." Less than one-half percent of the population scores above 140. These people can certainly be considered gifted or perhaps even "geniuses." However, some psychologists reserve the term *genius* for even higher IQs or for other qualities, such as exceptional creativity or insight (Kamphaus, 1993).

Gifted Children

Do high IQ scores in childhood predict later ability? To directly answer this question, Lewis Terman selected 1,500 children with IQs of 140 or more. Terman followed this gifted group (the "Termites" as he called them) into adulthood. By doing so, Terman countered a number of popular misconceptions about high intelligence (Shurkin, 1992).

Misconception: The gifted tend to be peculiar, socially backward people.
Fact: On the contrary, Terman's gifted subjects were socially well adjusted and showed above average leadership capacity.
Misconception: "Early ripe means later rot": The gifted tend to fizzle out as adults.
Fact: This is false. When retested as adults, Terman's subjects again scored in the upper IQ ranges.
Misconception: The very bright are usually physically inferior "eggheads" or weaklings.
Fact: This is also a misconception. As a group, the gifted were above average in height, weight, and physical appearance.
Misconception: The highly intelligent person is more susceptible to mental illness ("Genius is next to insanity").
Fact: Terman demonstrated conclusively that the gifted have better than average mental health records, indicating a greater *resistance* to mental illness. However, the very intelligent (IQ of over 180) may have social and behavioral adjustment problems as children (Janos & Robinson, 1985).
Misconception: Intelligence has nothing to do with success, especially in practical matters.
Fact: The later success of Terman's subjects was the most striking finding of the study. Far more of them than average had completed college, earned advanced degrees, and held professional positions. As a group, the gifted had produced dozens of books, thousands of scientific articles, and hundreds of short stories and other publications (Shurkin, 1992; Terman & Oden, 1959).

As noted earlier, IQ scores are not generally good predictors of real-world success. However, when scores are in the gifted range, the likelihood of outstanding achievement does seem to be higher.

Were all of the gifted children superior as adults?

No. Remember that high IQ reveals intellectual *potential*. A high IQ is no guarantee of success or achievement. Some of the gifted had committed crimes, were unemployable, or were poorly adjusted.

How did the more successful subjects differ from the less successful?

Most had parents who were educated and who valued learning. These parents, it seems, encouraged their children to become avid learners. Successful members of the gifted group also tended to show a high degree of *intellectual*

It is wise to remember that there are many ways in which a child may be gifted. Many schools now offer Gifted and Talented Education programs for students with a variety of special abilities—not just for those who score well on IQ tests.

determination. That is, they had a desire to know, to excel, and to persevere (Tomlinson-Keasey & Little, 1990).

Giftedness and Achievement   As you can see, the most successful gifted persons tend to be *persistent* and *motivated* to learn and succeed. As one educator put it, "No one is paid to sit around being capable of achievement—what you do is always more important than what you should be able to do" (Whimbey, 1980). Plenty of people can be found with high IQs who have learned and accomplished very little. In general, talents are most likely to blossom when combined with support, encouragement, education, and effort (Freeman, 1995).

How might a parent spot an unusually bright child?

Identifying Gifted Children   Early signs of giftedness are not always purely "intellectual." **Giftedness** *can be either the possession of a high IQ or special talents or aptitudes.* The following signs may reveal that a child is gifted:

- A tendency to seek out and identify with older children and adults
- An ability to absorb information rapidly
- An early fascination with explanations and problem solving
- Talking in complete sentences as early as 2 or 3 years of age
- An unusually good memory
- Precocious talent in art, music, or number skills
- An early interest in books, along with early reading (often by age 3)
- Showing of kindness, understanding, and cooperation toward others (Alvino, 1996).

Notice again that children may be gifted in ways other than having a high IQ. If talents in art, mechanics, music, athletics, and so on, were considered, 19 out of 20 children could be labeled as having a special "gift" of some sort. Limiting giftedness to high IQ can shortchange children with special talents or potentials. This is especially true of ethnic minority children, who may be the victims of subtle biases in standardized intelligence tests.

GATE Programs   Being exceptionally bright is not without its problems. The gifted child may become bored in classes designed for average children. Boredom can lead to misbehavior or clashes with teachers who may consider the gifted child a show-off or smart aleck. The extremely bright child may also find classmates less stimulating than older children or adults. In recognition of these problems, many schools now provide special Gifted and Talented Education (GATE) classes for gifted children. Such programs combine classroom enrichment with fast-paced instruction to satisfy the gifted child's appetite for intellectual stimulation (Gottfried & Gottfried, 1994).

Mental Retardation—A Difference That Makes a Difference

A person with mental abilities far below average is termed **mentally retarded** or **developmentally disabled.** *An IQ of approximately 70 or below is regarded as the dividing line for retardation.* However, a person's ability to perform **adaptive behaviors** (*basic skills such as dressing, eating, communicating,* *shopping, and working*) also figures into evaluating retardation (DSM-IV, 1994; Kamphaus, 1993).

Levels of Retardation

Below an IQ of 70, retardation is classified as shown in Table 12–7 ■. The listed IQ ranges are approximate because IQ scores normally vary a few points. The terms in the right-hand column are listed only to give you a general impression of each IQ range. Unless they are used cautiously, such terms can needlessly limit the educational goals of retarded persons (DSM-IV, 1994).

Are the retarded usually placed in institutions?

No. Total care is only necessary for the **profoundly** retarded (*IQ below 25*). Many of these individuals live within the community in group homes or with their families. The **severely** retarded (*IQ of 25–40*) and **moderately** retarded (*IQ of 40–55*) are capable of mastering basic language and self-help skills. Many become self-supporting by working in **sheltered workshops** (*special simplified work environments*). The **mildly** retarded (*IQ of 55–70*) make up about 85 percent of all those affected. This group can benefit from carefully structured education. As adults, these persons, as well as the **borderline retarded** (*IQ 70–85*), are capable of living alone and they may marry. However, they tend to have difficulties with many of the demands of adult life (Zetlin & Murtaugh, 1990).

Causes of Retardation

What causes mental retardation?

In 30 to 40 percent of cases, no known biological problem can be identified. In many such instances the degree of retardation is mild, in the 50–70 IQ range. Often, other family members are also mildly retarded. *Familial retardation*, as this is called, occurs mostly in very poor households, where nutrition, intellectual stimulation, medical care, and emotional support may be inadequate. This suggests that **familial retardation** *is based largely on an*

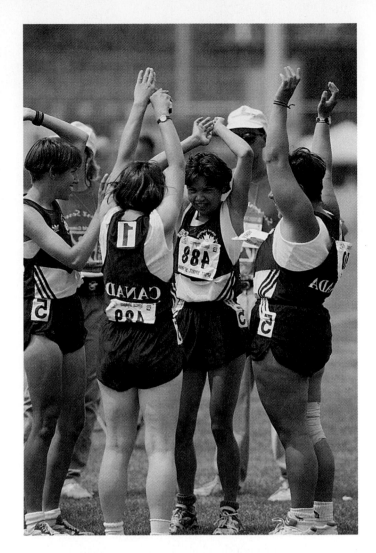

These youngsters are participants in the Special Olympics—an athletic event for the mentally retarded. It is often said of the Special Olympics that "everyone is a winner—participants, coaches, and spectators."

impoverished environment. Thus, many cases of retardation could be prevented by better nutrition, education, and early childhood enrichment programs (Hunt, 1995; Zigler, 1995).

	Table 12–7 ■ Levels of Mental Retardation		
IQ Range	**Degree of Retardation**	**Educational Classification**	**Required Level of Support**
50–55 to 70	Mild	Educable	Intermittent
35–40 to 50–55	Moderate	Trainable	Limited
20–25 to 35–40	Severe	Dependent	Extensive
Below 20–25	Profound	Life support	Pervasive

DSM-IV, 1994; Hodapp, 1994.

Organic Sources of Retardation

About 50 percent of all cases of mental retardation are *organic*, or related to physical disorders, including **birth injuries** (*such as lack of oxygen during delivery*), and **fetal damage** (*prenatal damage from disease, infection, or the mother's abuse of drugs*). **Metabolic disorders** also cause retardation. These are *problems with the rate of energy production and use in the body*. Some forms of retardation are linked to **genetic abnormalities**, *including missing genes, extra genes, or defective genes* (DSM-IV, 1994). Let's briefly look at several distinctive problems.

Phenylketonuria (PKU) The problem called **phenylketonuria** (FEN-ul-KEET-uh-NURE-ee-ah) *is a genetic disease caused by the lack of an important enzyme*. This defect causes *phenylpyruvic* (FEN-ul-pye-ROO-vik) *acid* (a destructive chemical) to collect within the body. PKU is also linked to very low levels of dopamine, an important chemical messenger in the brain. If PKU goes untreated, severe retardation typically occurs by age 3.

PKU can be detected in newborn babies by routine medical testing. Affected children are usually placed on a diet low in phenylalinine, the substance the child's body can't handle. Careful adherence to this diet can usually prevent retardation. (Phenylalinine is present in many foods. You might be interested to know that it is also found in Aspartame, the artificial sweetener in diet colas.)

Microcephaly The term **microcephaly** (MY-kro-SEF-ah-lee) means *small-headedness*. The microcephalic suffers a rare abnormality in which the skull is extremely small or fails to grow. This forces the brain to develop in a limited space, causing severe retardation. Although they are typically institutionalized, microcephalic persons are usually affectionate, well behaved, and easy to work with.

Hydrocephaly **Hydrocephaly** (HI-dro-SEF-ah-lee: "water on the brain") *is caused by a buildup of cerebrospinal fluid within brain cavities*. Pressure from this fluid can damage the brain and greatly enlarge the head. Hydrocephaly is not uncommon—about 10,000 hydrocephalic babies are born each year in the United States and Canada. Thanks to new medical procedures, most of these infants will now lead normal lives. A surgically implanted tube drains fluid from the brain into the abdomen. If this is done within the first 3 months of life, retardation can usually be avoided.

Cretinism **Cretinism** (KREET-un-iz-um) is a form of retardation that appears in infancy. It results from *an insufficient supply of thyroid hormone*. In some parts of the world, cretinism is caused by a lack of iodine in the diet, which the thyroid requires. Iodized salt has made this source of retardation rare in industrialized nations. Cretinism causes stunted physical and intellectual growth that cannot be reversed. Fortunately, cretinism is easily detected in infancy. Once detected, it can be treated with thyroid hormone replacement, before permanent damage is done.

Down Syndrome The disorder known as *Down syndrome* causes *moderate to severe retardation* and a shortened life expectancy (usually around 40 years) in 1 out of 800 babies. Distinctive features of this problem, once referred to as mongolism, are almond-shaped eyes, a slightly protruding tongue, a stocky build, and stubby hands with deep creases on the palms.

It is now known that **Down syndrome** children have an *extra 21st chromosome*. This condition, which is referred to as *trisomy-21*, results from flaws in the parents' egg or sperm cells. Thus, while Down syndrome is *genetic*, it is not usually *hereditary* and doesn't "run in the family."

The age of parents is a major factor in Down syndrome. The reproductive cells of older men and woman are more prone to errors during cell division, which raises the odds that an extra chromosome will be present (see Table 12–8 ■). As you can see, the older a woman is, the greater the risk. Older fathers also add to the risk. In about 25 percent of cases the father is the source of the extra chromosome (de la Cruz & Muller, 1983). Older adults who plan to have children should carefully consider the odds shown in Table 12–8.

There is no "cure" for Down syndrome. However, these children are usually loving and responsive, and they make progress in a caring environment. At a basic level, Down syndrome children can do most of the things that other children can, only slower (Berry et al., 1984). The best hope for Down syndrome children, therefore, lies in specially tailored educational programs that enable them to lead fuller lives.

Fragile-X Syndrome The second most common form of genetic mental retardation (after Down syndrome) is **fragile-X syndrome** (Hodapp, 1994). Unlike Down syndrome, fragile-X syndrome is hereditary—it *does* run in families. The problem is related to *a thin, frail-looking area on the X (male) chromosome*. Because fragile-X is sex linked (like color-blindness), boys are most often affected, at a rate of about 1 out of every 1200 (Rose, 1995).

Table 12–8 ■ Risk of Having a Down Syndrome Baby	
Mother's Age	**Incidence of Down Syndrome**
Early 20s	1/2000
Early 40s	1/105
Late 40s	1/12

Fragile-X males generally have long, thin faces and big ears. Physically, they are usually larger than average during childhood, but smaller than average after adolescence. Up to three-fourths of all fragile-X males suffer from hyperactivity and attention disorders. Many also have a peculiar tendency to avoid eye contact with others.

Fragile-X males are only mildly retarded during early childhood, but they are often severely or profoundly retarded as adults. In learning adaptive behaviors, they tend to do better with daily living skills than with language and social skills (Hodapp, 1994).

Retardation in Perspective

It is valuable to remember that the developmentally disabled have no handicap where feelings are concerned. They are sensitive to rejection and easily hurt by teasing or ridicule. Likewise, they respond warmly to love and acceptance. Everyone has a right to self-respect and a place in the community. This is especially important during childhood, when the support of others adds greatly to the retarded person's chances of becoming a well-adjusted member of society.

Learning Check

1. The distribution of IQs approximates a ___normal___ (bell-shaped) curve.

2. The association between IQ and high-status professional jobs proves that such jobs require more intelligence. T or F?

3. Differences in the intellectual strengths of men and women have grown larger in recent years. T or F?

4. Only about 6 percent of the population scores above 140 on IQ tests. T or F?

5. An IQ score below 90 indicates mental retardation. T or F?

6. Many cases of mental retardation without known organic causes appear to be ___familial___.

Match:

7. _D_ PKU
8. _B_ Microcephaly
9. _E_ Hydrocephaly
10. _A_ Cretinism
11. _C_ Down syndrome
12. _F_ Fragile-X

A. Too little thyroid hormone
B. Very small brain
C. 47 chromosomes
D. Lack of an important enzyme
E. Excess of cerebrospinal fluid
F. Abnormal male chromosome
G. Caused by a lack of oxygen at birth

Critical Thinking

13. Lewis Terman took great interest in the lives of many of the "Termites." He even went so far as to advise them about what kinds of careers they should pursue. What error of observation did Terman make?

Answers:

1. normal 2. F 3. F 4. F 5. F 6. familial 7. D 8. B 9. E 10. A 11. C 12. F 13. Terman may have unintentionally altered the behavior of the people he was studying. Although Terman's observations are generally regarded as valid, he did break a basic rule of scientific observation.

Heredity and Environment—Super Rats and Family Trees

Is intelligence inherited?

This seemingly simple question is loaded with controversy. Some psychologists believe that intelligence is strongly affected by heredity. Others feel that environment is dominant. Let's examine some of the evidence for each view.

In a classic study of genetic factors in learning, Tryon (1929) managed to breed separate strains of "maze-bright" and "maze-dull" rats (animals that were extremely "bright" or "stupid" at learning mazes). After several generations of breeding, the slowest "super rat" outperformed the best "dull" rat. This and other studies of **eugenics** (*selective breeding for desirable characteristics*) suggest that some traits are highly influenced by heredity.

That may be true, but is maze-learning really a measure of intelligence?

No, it isn't. Tryon's study seemed to show that intelligence is inherited, but later researchers found that the "bright" rats were simply more motivated by food and less easily distracted during testing (Whimbey, 1980). When they weren't chasing after rat chow, the "bright" rats were no more intelligent than the supposedly dull rats. Thus, Tryon's study did demonstrate that behavioral characteristics are influenced by heredity, but it was inconclusive concerning intelligence. Because of such problems, animal studies cannot tell us with certainty how heredity and environment affect intelligence. Let's see what human studies reveal.

Hereditary Influences

Most people are aware that there is a moderate similarity in the intelligence of parents and their children, or between

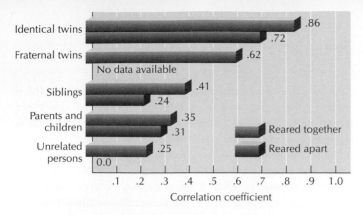

Figure 12–6 ◆ Approximate correlations between IQ scores for persons with varying degrees of genetic and environmental similarity. Notice that the correlations grow smaller as the degree of genetic similarity declines. Also note that a shared environment increases the correlation in all cases. (Estimates from Bouchard, 1983; Henderson, 1982.)

brothers and sisters. As Figure 12–6 ◆ shows, the similarity in IQ scores among relatives grows in proportion to their closeness on the family tree.

Does that indicate that intelligence is hereditary?

Not necessarily. Brothers, sisters, and parents share similar environments as well as similar heredity. To separate heredity and environment, we need to make some selected comparisons.

Twin Studies Notice in Figure 12–6 that the IQ scores of fraternal twins are more alike than those of ordinary siblings. **Fraternal twins** *come from two separate eggs* fertilized at the same time. They are no more genetically alike than ordinary siblings. Why then, should the twins' IQ scores be more similar? The reason is environmental: Parents treat twins more alike than ordinary siblings, resulting in a closer match in IQs.

More striking similarities are observed with **identical twins,** *who develop from a single egg and have identical genes.* At the top of Figure 12–6 you can see that identical twins who grow up in the same family have highly correlated IQs. This is what we would expect with identical heredity and very similar environments. Now, let's consider what happens when identical twins are reared apart. As you can see, the correlation drops, but only from .86 to .72. Psychologists who emphasize genetics believe figures like these show that differences in adult intelligence are roughly 50 percent hereditary (Casto, DeFries, & Fulker, 1995; Neisser et al., 1996; Plomin & Rende, 1991).

How do environmentalists interpret the figures?

Environmentalists point out that some separated twins differ by as much as 20 IQ points. In every case where this occurs there are large educational and environmental differences between the twins (Whimbey, 1980). Also, separated twins are almost always placed in homes socially and educationally similar to those of their birth parents. This would tend to

inflate apparent genetic effects by making the separated twins' IQs more alike (Kamin, 1981).

Environmental Influences

Strong evidence for an environmental view of intelligence comes from families having one adopted child and one biological child. As Figure 12–7 ◆ shows, parents contribute genes *and* environment to their biological child. With an adopted child they contribute only environment. If intelligence is highly genetic, the IQs of biological children should be more like their parents' IQs than are the IQs of adopted children. However, studies show that children reared by the same mother resemble her in IQ to the same degree. It does not matter whether or not they share her genes (Horn et al., 1979; Kamin, 1981; Weinberg, 1989).

Another way to see environmental effects is to compare children adopted by parents of high or low socio-economic status. As you might predict, children who grow up in high-status homes develop higher IQs than those reared by lower status parents. Presumably, the higher socio-economic homes provide an enriched environment, with better nutrition, greater educational opportunities, and other advantages (Capron & Duyme, 1992).

How much can environment alter intelligence?

IQ and Environment In one study, striking increases in IQ occurred in 25 children who were moved from an orphanage to more stimulating environments. The children, all considered mentally retarded and unadoptable, were moved to an institution where they received personal attention from adults. Later, these supposedly retarded children were adopted by parents who gave them love, a family, and a stimulating environment. The IQs of the children showed an average gain of 29 points. For one child, the increase was an amazing 58 points. A second group of initially less "retarded" children who remained in the orphanage *lost* an average of 26 IQ points (Skeels, 1966)!

In another encouraging study, a group of children from low-income families were provided with enriched environments from early infancy through preschool. By age 2 their IQ scores were already higher than those in a control group. More important, they were still 5 points higher 7 years after the program ended (Campbell & Ramey, 1994).

Figure 12–7 ◆ Comparison of an adopted child and a biological child reared in the same family. (After Kamin, 1981.)

A particularly striking environmental effect is the fact that 14 nations have shown average IQ gains of from 5 to 25 points during the last 30 years (Flynn, 1987, 1990; Horgan, 1995). These IQ boosts, averaging 15 points, occurred in far too short a time for genetics to explain them. It is more likely that the gains reflect environmental forces, such as improved education, nutrition, and living in a technologically complex society (Horgan, 1995).

School can also have a large impact on IQ. Stephen Ceci found that people who leave school lose anywhere from .25 point to 6 points in IQ per year. Dropping out of school in the eighth grade can reduce a person's adult IQ by up to 24 points. Conversely, IQ rises as people spend more time in school (Ceci, 1991). This is another clear sign that improved environments can raise intelligence. The following highlight explores this idea further.

Research Frontier

Can Intelligence Be Taught?

The traditional answer to the question, "Can intelligence be taught?" is "No." Coaching, for instance, has little positive effect on aptitude and intelligence test scores (Brody, 1992; Kulik et al., 1984). But is brief coaching a fair test of the elasticity of intelligence? Apparently not. There is growing evidence that extended, in-depth training in thinking skills can increase tested intelligence.

At the forefront of such efforts is Israeli psychologist Reuven Feuerstein (FOY-er-shtine). Feuerstein and his colleagues have developed a program they call Instrumental Enrichment. Through hundreds of hours of guided problem solving, students learn to avoid the thinking flaws that lower IQ scores (Feuerstein et al., 1986). Feuerstein and others have shown that such training can improve thinking abilities and even raise IQs (Skuy et al., 1995; Tzuriel & Alfassi, 1994).

Cognitive skills training is very time consuming. In recognition of this problem, psychologists are now writing computer programs to teach problem solving, effective thinking, and other elements of intelligence. With our growing understanding of how people think, and with the tireless aid of computers, it may indeed become common in schools to "teach intelligence." Most importantly, improved education and training in thinking skills can improve the intellectual abilities of all children, regardless of what their IQ scores may be (Hunt, 1995; Perkins, 1995).

Summary To sum up, few psychologists seriously believe that heredity is not a major factor in intelligence, and all acknowledge that environment affects it. Estimates of the impact of heredity and environment continue to vary. But ultimately, both camps agree that improving social conditions and education can raise intelligence.

There is probably no limit to how far *down* intelligence can go in an extremely poor environment. On the other hand, heredity does seem to impose upper limits on IQ, even under ideal conditions. It is telling, nevertheless, that gifted children tend to come from homes where parents spend time with their children, answer their questions, and encourage intellectual exploration. Genes are fixed at birth. Improving the environments in which children learn and grow is the main avenue by which we can assure that they reach their full potential (Lipsitt, 1990).

As a final summary, it might help to think of inherited intellectual potential as a rubber band that is stretched by outside forces. A long rubber band may be stretched more easily, but a shorter one can be stretched to the same length if enough force is applied. Of course, a superior genetic gift may allow for a higher maximum IQ. In the final analysis, intelligence reflects development as well as potential, nurture as well as nature (Rose, 1995; Weinberg, 1989).

New Approaches to Intelligence—Intelligent Alternatives

Until now, we have treated intelligence as a quality that can be measured, like height or weight. Recently, three new ways of looking at intelligence have emerged:

- Some psychologists are investigating the neural basis for intelligence. How, they ask, does the nervous system contribute to differences in IQ?

- A second new approach views intelligent behavior as an expression of thinking skills. Cognitive psychologists believe that the nervous system is like a fast computer—it's of little value unless you know how to use it.

- A third trend involves newer, broader definitions of intelligence. Many psychologists have begun to question the narrow focus on analytic thinking found in traditional IQ tests (Perkins, 1995).

The Intelligent Nervous System

Do intelligent people have faster nervous systems?

In an attempt to answer this question, researchers are measuring how fast people process various kinds of information. For example, psychologists have looked at how long it takes people to react when making a choice (Fig. 12–8 ◆). The flurry of brain activity that follows exposure to a stimulus has also been recorded. Such studies attempt to

Figure 12–8 ◆ Attempts to measure the speed of mental processing have taken several forms. In this example, the person must make a rapid choice based on the position of a colored stimulus flashed on a computer screen. A faster reaction time is assumed to reflect faster processing of information. In some experiments brain responses are measured directly, through electrodes attached to the scalp.

measure a person's **speed of processing,** which is assumed to reflect *the brain's speed and efficiency* (Deary & Stough, 1996).

Does rapid information processing really have anything to do with intelligence? Let's see.

Research Frontier

Inspecting Intelligence

Look quickly at Figure 12–9a ◆. Which "leg" of the drawing is longer, the right or the left? It's a pretty easy question, isn't it? However, if similar drawings are flashed on a screen for only a split second, the task becomes much harder. And, strange as it may seem, it may reveal something about intelligence.

Stimuli like those in Figure 12–9 are used to measure **inspection time**—*the amount of time a person must inspect (look at) a stimulus to make a correct judgment about it.* In a real inspection time task, a stimulus like the one on the left appears for a few milliseconds. It is then followed immediately by a second stimulus, like 12–9b. (The second stimulus keeps people from using

Figure 12–9 ◆ Stimuli like those used in inspection time tasks.

afterimages or sensory memory to make decisions about the first stimulus.)

In inspection time studies, we want to know how quickly a person's nervous system can take in enough information to make a correct decision. As simple as this measure may seem, it correlates about −.45 with IQ scores. (The correlation is negative because shorter inspection times are associated with higher IQs.) So, to a degree, it appears that having a quick nervous system is, indeed, part of what it means to be quick, smart, swift, or brainy.

(Sources: Bowling & Mackenzie, 1996; Deary & Stough, 1996.)

Intelligent Information Processing

Much intelligent behavior is an expression of good thinking skills. Cognitive psychologist David Perkins believes that how smart you are depends on three factors:

- Relatively fixed **neural intelligence** (*the speed and efficiency of the nervous system*)
- **Experiential intelligence** (*specialized knowledge and skills acquired over time*)
- **Reflective intelligence** (*an ability to become aware of one's own thinking habits*)

Little can be done to change neural intelligence. However, by adding to personal knowledge and learning to think better, people can become more intelligent (Perkins, 1995). The effects of Feurstein's Instrumental Enrichment program (described earlier) are a good example of how reflective intelligence can be improved.

Many psychologists now believe that to make full use of innate intelligence a person must have good **metacognitive skills.** *Meta* means "beyond," so metacognitive skills go above and beyond ordinary thinking. Such skills *involve an ability to manage your own thinking and problem solving.* Typically this means breaking problems into parts, establishing goals and subgoals, monitoring your progress, and making corrections. Learning metacognitive skills is the surest avenue to becoming more intelligent (Hunt, 1995).

Multiple Intelligences

At an elementary school, a student who is two grades behind in reading shows his teacher how to solve a difficult computer programming problem. In a nearby room, one of his classmates, who is poor in math, plays an intricate piece of music on a piano. Both of these children show clear signs of intelligence. And yet, each might score below average on a traditional IQ test.

Such observations have convinced many psychologists that it is time to forge new, broader definitions of intelligence. Their basic goal is to better predict "real-world" success—not just the likelihood of success in school (Sternberg, 1996).

Frames of Mind One such psychologist is Howard Gardner of Harvard University. Gardner (1993) theorizes that there are actually seven different kinds of intelligence. Each is listed below, with examples of pursuits that make use of them.

1. *language*—writer, lawyer, comedian
2. *logic and math*—scientist, accountant, programmer
3. *visual and spatial thinking*—engineer, inventor, artist
4. *music*—composer, musician, music critic
5. *bodily-kinesthetic skills*—dancer, athlete, surgeon
6. *intrapersonal skills* (self-knowledge)—poet, actor, minister
7. *interpersonal skills* (social abilities)—psychologist, teacher, politician

Most of us are probably strong in only a few types of intelligence. In contrast, geniuses like Albert Einstein seem to be able to use all of the intelligences, as needed, to solve problems.

If Gardner's theory of **multiple intelligences** is correct, traditional IQ tests measure only a part of real-world intelligence—namely, linguistic, logical-mathematical, and spatial abilities. A further implication is that our schools may be wasting a lot of human potential. For example, some children might find it easier to learn math or reading if these topics were tied into art, music, dance, drama, and so on.

Not all psychologists agree with Gardner's broader definition of intelligence. His view, in fact, is at odds with

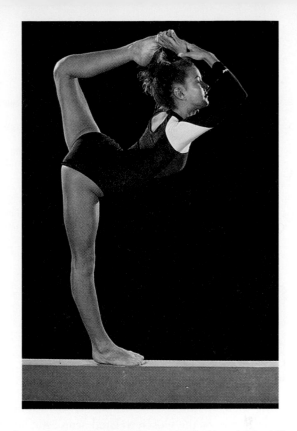

According to Howard Gardner's theory, bodily-kinesthetic skills reflect one of seven distinct types of intelligence.

studies which suggest that scores on IQ tests mainly reflect an underlying "general intelligence" or *general ability factor* (often referred to as *g*) (Neisser et al., 1996). This **g-factor** is said to explain the *high correlations found among scores on various tests of intellectual ability and achievement*. Gardner's reply would probably be that such correlations only show how narrowly traditional tests define intelligence. In any case, it seems likely that in the future intelligence will not be so strongly equated with IQ. Already, many schools are using Gardner's theory to cultivate a wider range of skills and talents (Woo, 1995).

A Look Ahead As promised earlier, the Applications section of this chapter addresses questions concerning the validity of intelligence tests and their fairness to various groups. In the Exploration, we will examine some of the controversial issues raised by intelligence testing in the school system. In addition to being highly interesting, these topics should round out your understanding of intelligence.

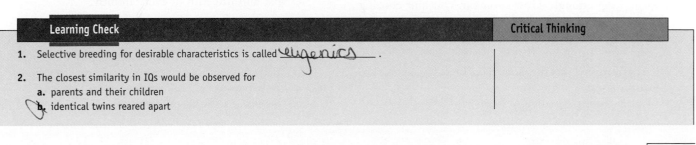

Learning Check	Critical Thinking

1. Selective breeding for desirable characteristics is called ⟨eugenics⟩.
2. The closest similarity in IQs would be observed for
   a. parents and their children
   b. identical twins reared apart

c. fraternal twins reared together

d. siblings reared together

3. Most psychologists believe that intelligence is 90 percent hereditary. T or F?

4. Except for slight variations during testing, IQ cannot be changed. T or F?

5. Environmental effects are probably more capable of lowering IQ than of raising it. T or F?

6. Inspection time has been used as a measure of _____ intelligence.
   a. experiential   **b.** neural   **c.** reflective   **d.** analytical

7. According to Howard Gardner's theory, which of the following is not measured by traditional IQ tests?
   a. intrapersonal skills   **b.** spatial skills   **c.** logical skills   **d.** linguistic skills

8. Dropping out of school can lower tested IQ and attending school can raise it. What do these observations reveal about intelligence tests?

Answers:

1. eugenics 2. b 3. F 4. F 5. T 6. b 7. a 8. Such observations remind us that intelligence tests are affected by learning and that they measure knowledge, as well as innate cognitive abilities.

Applications

How Intelligent Are Intelligence Tests?

During their lifetimes, most people take an intelligence test, or one of the closely related scholastic aptitude tests. If you have ever taken an individually administered IQ test, you may actually know what your IQ is. If not, the following self-administered test will provide a rough estimate of your IQ. Most people are curious about how they would score on an intelligence test. Why not give the Dove test a try?

Dove Counterbalance Intelligence Test

Time limit: 5 minutes.
Circle the correct answer.

1. T-bone Walker got famous for playing what?
   a. trombone *b.* piano *c.* T-flute *d.* guitar
   e. "hambone"

2. A "gas head" is a person who has a
   a. fast-moving car. *b.* stable of "lace."
   c. "process." *d.* habit of stealing cars.
   e. long jail record for arson.

3. If you throw the dice and 7 is showing on the top, what is facing down?
   a. 7 *b.* snake eyes *c.* boxcars *d.* little joes *e.* 11

4. Cheap chitlings (not the kind you purchase at a frozen-food counter) will taste rubbery unless they are cooked long enough. How soon can you quit cooking them to eat and enjoy them?
   a. 45 minutes *b.* two hours *c.* 24 hours
   d. one week (on a low flame) *e.* one hour

5. Bird or Yardbird was the jacket jazz lovers from coast to coast hung on
   a. Lester Young *b.* Peggy Lee

c. Benny Goodman *d.* Charlie Parker
e. Birdman of Alcatraz

6. A "handkerchief head" is
   a. a cool cat. *b.* a porter. *c.* an Uncle Tom.
   d. a hoddi. *e.* a preacher.

7. Jet is
   a. an East Oakland motorcycle club.
   b. one of the gangs in West Side Story.
   c. a news and gossip magazine.
   d. a way of life for the very rich.

8. "Bo Diddly" is a
   a. game for children.
   b. down-home cheap wine.
   c. down-home singer.
   d. new dance.
   e. Moejoe call.

9. Which word is most out of place here?
   a. splib *b.* blood *c.* gray *e.* black *d.* spook

10. If a pimp is uptight with a woman who gets state aid, what does he mean when he talks about "Mother's Day"?
    a. second Sunday in May
    b. third Sunday in June
    c. first of every month
    d. none of these
    e. first and fifteenth of every month

11. How much does a "short dog" cost?
    a. 15¢ *b.* $2 *c.* 35¢ *d.* 5¢ *e.* $1.19 plus tax

12. Many people say that "Juneteenth" (June 10th) should be made a legal holiday because this was the day when
    a. the slaves were freed in the United States.
    b. the slaves were freed in Texas.

c. the slaves were freed in Jamaica.

d. the slaves were freed in California.

e. Martin Luther King was born.

f. Booker T. Washington died.

13. If a man is called a "blood," then he is a

    a. fighter *b.* Mexican-American *c.* Black

    d. hungry hemophile *e.* red man or Indian

14. What are the Dixie Hummingbirds?

    a. a part of the KKK

    b. a swamp disease

    c. a modern gospel group

    d. a Mississippi Negro paramilitary strike force

    e. deacons

15. The opposite of square is

    a. round. *b.* up *c.* down *d.* hip *e.* lame

Answers: 1. *d* **2.** *c* **3.** *a* **4.** *c* **5.** *d* **6.** *c* **7.** *c*

        8. *c* **9.** *c* **10.** *c* **11.** *c* **12.** *b* **13.** *c*

        14. *c* **15.** *d*

If you scored 14 on this exam, your IQ is approximately 100, indicating average intelligence. If you scored 11 or less, you are mentally retarded. With luck and the help of a special educational program, we may be able to teach you a few simple skills!

Isn't the Dove Test a little unfair?

No, it is *very* unfair. It was written by African-American sociologist Adrian Dove as "a half serious attempt to show that we're just not talking the same language." Dove tried to slant his test as much in favor of urban African-American culture as he believes the typical intelligence test is biased toward a white middle-class background. (Because of its age, the test is probably now also unfair for anyone under 30.)

Dove's test is a thought-provoking reply to the fact that African-American children in the United States score an average of about 15 points lower on standardized IQ tests than Anglo-American children. By reversing the bias, Dove has shown that intelligence tests are not equally valid for all groups. As Jerome Kagan says, "If the Wechsler and Binet scales were translated into Spanish, Swahili, and Chinese and given to every 10-year-old in Latin America, East Africa, or China, the majority would obtain IQ scores in the mentally retarded range."

Culture-Fair Testing

Certainly we cannot believe that children of different cultures are all retarded. The fault must lie in the test. Cultural values, traditions, and experiences can greatly affect performance on tests designed for Western cultures (Neisser et al., 1996; Nixon, 1990). To avoid this problem, some psychologists have tried to develop *culture-fair tests* that do not disadvantage certain groups. **A culture-fair test** *is designed to minimize the importance of skills and knowledge that may be more common in some cultures than in others.* (For a sample of culture-fair test items, see Figure 12–10 ◆). Culture-fair tests attempt to measure intelligence without, as much as possible, being influenced by a person's verbal skills, cultural background, and educational level.

The Bell Curve—Race, Culture, and IQ

Biased tests are not the only IQ issue blacks have confronted. In 1994, Richard Hernstein and Charles Murray proclaimed, in a book titled *The Bell Curve*, that African-Americans score below average in IQ because of their "genetic heritage." Hernstein and Murray's most inflammatory claim is that the poor, whatever ethnic group they may belong to, are genetically incapable of climbing out of poverty (Hernstein & Murray, 1994).

Psychologists have responded to such claims with a number of counter-arguments. First, it is no secret that as a

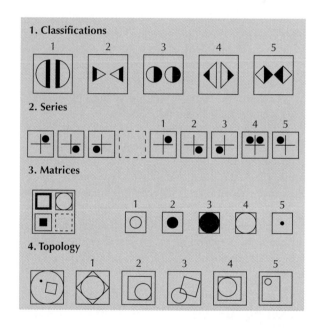

Figure 12–10 ◆ No intelligence test can be entirely free of cultural bias. However, culture-fair intelligence tests try to minimize the effects of growing up in various cultures. The following sample items are from a culture-fair test. 1. Which pattern is different from the remaining four? (Number 3.) 2. Which of the five figures on the right would properly continue the three on the left—that is, fill the blank? (Number 5.) 3. Which of the figures on the right should go in the square on the left to make it look right? (Number 2.) 4. At left, the dot is outside the square and inside the circle. In which of the figures on the right could you put a dot outside the square and inside the circle? (Number 3.) (Courtesy of R. B. Cattell.)

group blacks in the United States are more likely than whites to live in environments that are physically, educationally, and intellectually impoverished. When unequal education is part of the equation, IQs tell us little about how heredity affects intelligence (Neisser et al., 1996).

A second argument against Hernstein and Murray is that they overlook the point made by the Dove Test. The assumptions, biases, and content of standard IQ tests do not always allow meaningful comparisons between ethnic, cultural, or racial groups (Helms, 1992; Miller-Jones, 1989). As Leon Kamin (1981) says, "The important fact is that we cannot say which sex (or race) might be more intelligent, because we have no way of measuring 'intelligence.' We have only IQ tests."

Kamin's point is that the makers of IQ tests decided in advance to use test items that would give men and women equal IQ scores. It would be just as easy to put together an IQ test that would give blacks and whites equal scores. Differences in IQ scores are not a fact of nature, but a decision by the test makers. This is why whites do better on IQ tests written by whites, and blacks do better on IQ tests devised by blacks. Another example of this fact is an intelligence test made up of 100 words selected from the *Dictionary of Afro-American Slang*. Williams (1975) gave the test to 100 black and 100 white high school students in St. Louis and found that the black group averaged 36 points higher than the white group.

Recently, a distinguished group of psychologists evaluated the claims made in *The Bell Curve*. They concluded there is no scientific evidence that group differences in average IQ are based on genetics. In fact, studies that used actual blood-group testing found no significant correlations between ethnic ancestry and IQ scores. The conclusions that Hernstein and Murray drew in *The Bell Curve* reflect their political beliefs and biases, not scientific facts. Group differences in IQ scores are based on cultural and environmental differences, not on heredity (Alva, 1993; Caplan et al., 1992; Neisser et al., 1996; Yee et al., 1993).

Questioning IQ—Beyond the Numbers Game

African Americans are not the only segment of the population with reason to question the validity of intelligence testing and the role of heredity in determining intelligence. The clarifications they have won extend to others as well.

Consider the 9-year-old child confronted with this question on an intelligence test: "Which of the following does not belong with the others? Roller skates, airplane, train, bicycle." If the child fails to answer "airplane," does it reveal a lack of intelligence? It can be argued that an intelligent choice could be based on any of these alternatives:

Roller skates are not typically used for transportation; an airplane is the only non-land item; a train can't be steered; a bicycle is the only item with just two wheels. The parents of a child who misses this question may have reason to be angry since educational systems tend to classify children and then make the label stick.

Recent court decisions have led some states to outlaw the use of intelligence tests in public schools (see the Exploration section). Criticism of intelligence testing has also come from the academic community. Harvard University psychologist David McClelland believes that IQ is of little value in predicting real competence to deal effectively with the world. McClelland concedes that IQ predicts school performance, but when he compared a group of college students with straight A's to another group with poor grades, he found no differences in later career success (McClelland, 1973, 1994).

Standardized Testing

In addition to IQ tests, 400 to 500 million standardized multiple-choice tests are given in schools and workplaces around the nation each year. Many, like the *Scholastic Assessment Test*, may determine whether a person is admitted to college. Other tests—for employment, licensing, and certification—directly affect the lives of thousands by qualifying or disqualifying them for jobs.

Widespread reliance on standardized intelligence tests and aptitude tests raises questions about the relative good and harm they do. On the positive side, tests can open opportunities as well as close them. A high test score may allow a disadvantaged youth to enter college, or it may identify a child who is bright but emotionally disturbed. Test scores may also be fairer and more objective than arbitrary judgments made by admissions officers or employment interviewers. Also, tests *do* accurately predict academic performance. The fact that academic performance *does not* predict later success may call for an overhaul of college course work, not an end to testing.

On the negative side, mass testing can occasionally exclude people of obvious ability. In one case, a student who was seventh in his class at Columbia University, and a member of Phi Beta Kappa, was denied entrance to law school because he had low scores on the *Law School Admissions Test*. Other complaints relate to the frequent appearance of bad or ambiguous questions on standardized tests, overuse of class time to prepare students for the tests (instead of teaching general skills), and in the case of intelligence tests, the charge that tests are often biased. Also, most standardized tests demand passive recognition of facts, assessed with a multiple-choice format. They do not, for the most part, test a person's ability to think critically or creatively or to apply knowledge to solve problems (Jones & Appelbaum, 1989).

What should we make of the positive and negative aspects of standardized testing? Robert Glaser says we should remember that tests are "limited tools for limited purposes." Glaser also says that tests are now used primarily to *select* people. In schools they could instead be used to *adapt* instruction to the strengths, weaknesses, and needs of each student—thereby increasing the chances of success.

Conclusion

An application of the preceding discussion to your personal understanding of intelligence can be summarized in this way: Intelligence tests are a two-edged sword; we have learned much from their use, yet they have the potential to do great harm. In the final analysis, it is important to remember—as Howard Gardner has pointed out—that creativity, motivation, physical health, mechanical aptitude, artistic ability, and numerous other qualities not measured by intelligence tests contribute to achievement of life goals. Also remember that IQ is not intelligence. IQ is an index of intelligence (as narrowly defined by a particular test). Change the test and you change the score. An IQ is not some permanent number stamped on the forehead of a child that forever determines potential. The real issue is what skills people have, not what their test scores are (Hunt, 1995).

Learning Check

1. The WAIS-III, Binet-4, and Dove Test are all culture-fair intelligence scales. T or F?

2. Hernstein and Murray's claim that heredity accounts for racial differences in average IQ ignores environmental differences and the cultural bias inherent in standard IQ tests. T or F?

3. IQ scores predict school performance. T or F?

4. IQ is not intelligence; it is one index of intelligence. T or F?

Critical Thinking

5. Assume that a test of memory for words is translated from English to Spanish. Would the Spanish version of the test be equal in difficulty to the English version?

Answers:

1. F 2. T 3. T 4. T 5. Probably not, because the Spanish words might be longer or shorter than the same words in English. The Spanish words might also sound more or less alike than words on the original test. Translating an intelligence test into another language can subtly change the meaning and difficulty of test items.

The Case: *Larry P. vs. the California State Superintendent of Education.*

The Issue: Larry P. is one of six African-American children who claim that biased IQ test scores were wrongly used to place them in classes for the educable mentally retarded (EMR).

The Outcome: In a landmark decision, a federal judge ruled that IQ test scores alone can no longer be used for EMR placement.

The ruling has virtually eliminated IQ testing in California schools. Similar rulings in other states have had the same effect (Kamphaus, 1993). The bare facts of the Larry P. case only hint at the interesting issues it raised. Testimony during the trial brought out the following:

For Larry P.: All six youngsters suing the state had scored below 75 on standardized IQ tests. But they scored from 17 to 35 points higher when retested by psychologists who used language and examples the children were familiar with.

For the State: Experts admitted that IQ test questions can be easier for some groups than for others. However, they held that IQ tests accurately predict school performance and are therefore valid.

For Larry P.: Witnesses pointed out that EMR assignments are almost always permanent. They also described the devastating effects of placing a child of normal intelligence in an EMR class. One researcher found that other students commonly refer to EMR students with cruel nicknames. EMR students are not expected to progress beyond the third- to fifth-grade level. Thus, by the time of graduation, a child of normal intelligence would be hopelessly behind other students. After graduation, EMR students find it difficult to get jobs, because they have been labeled "retarded."

For the State: Defense experts claimed that IQ tests help prevent mistakes in EMR assignments—for example, by revealing the true potential of a child who might be considered "slow" by a biased teacher. They also defended the EMR program as an effort to help less able students.

For Larry P.: Roughly twice as many African-American and Latino children are found in EMR classes than would be expected based on the percentage of African Americans and Latinos in the general population. This fact suggests a defect in the tests, not in the children.

Ignorance vs. Stupidity In the end, the judge ruled that IQ tests violate federal anti-discrimination laws. He was convinced, he said, that they are based mainly on verbal tasks that are unfair to children whose home environment does not provide practice in formal English or verbal skills. He further held that "if tests suggest that a young child is probably going to be a poor student, the school cannot, on that basis alone, deny that child the opportunity to develop and improve the academic skills necessary for success in our society."

Supporters of the Larry P. decision believe that it affirms the rights of disadvantaged children, whose ignorance—a lack of knowledge—has been mistaken for stupidity—a lack of intelligence. One such supporter is Jane Mercer, a sociologist who gave key testimony in the case.

Six-hour Retardates Mercer testified that the more a child's family is like the average white Anglo middle-class norm, the better the child scores on IQ tests. Mercer believes that schools often label children retarded, when actually the children only lack culturally-tied knowledge. Mercer has found that many African-American or Latino EMR students show abundant signs of normal intelligence. A child who does poorly in the classroom or on an IQ test may function perfectly well at home and in the community. Mercer refers to such children as "six-hour retardates"— youngsters who are "retarded" only during the school day.

If standardized IQ tests cannot be used to assess student abilities, what can?

SOMPA Mercer and her associate June Lewis think they have an answer. They call it SOMPA, which stands for *System of Multicultural Pluralistic Assessment.* SOMPA is not a new test. Rather, it's a different way of looking at children.

How does SOMPA differ from standard IQ tests?

SOMPA combines three ways of assessing a child. First, it looks for any medical problems that may be causing low school performance. Next, the child's behavior outside the classroom is evaluated to avoid the mistake of creating a "six-hour retardate" on the basis of a test score. Third, SOMPA assumes that when everything else is held constant (educational advantages at home, especially), the child who has learned the most probably has the most "learning potential." Off-campus environments, however, are not equal. SOMPA therefore assumes that true potential can be masked by a child's cultural background. To avoid this prob-

lem, SOMPA compares each child's WISC score with that of children from similar backgrounds.

To show how SOMPA works, Mercer offers an example. Maria Gonzales is 7. She lives with her mother, father, and five brothers and sisters in an inner-city barrio. Maria's mother and father both grew up in rural Mexico, where the mother finished fourth grade and the father second grade. Maria's family speaks only Spanish.

The average score for a child like Maria—with a background so different from core Anglo culture—is about 85. Maria's score on the WISC was 114, almost 30 points above this average. Mercer estimates Maria's real learning potential at 133. If her family had been more like the middle-class norm, Maria's score of 114 would have been accepted as accurate. Considering her age and background, Maria's performance on the WISC is truly outstanding. Maria is probably a gifted child whose potential should not be wasted.

More IQ Controversy In 1986, Judge Robert Peckham, who issued the original opinion, reiterated the California IQ test ban. In fact, he added to it, saying "The prohibition on IQ tests goes further and prohibits any use of an IQ test as part of an assessment which could lead to special education placement or services, even if the test is only part of a comprehensive assessment plan" (Landers, 1986). This directive pretty much eliminated any form of IQ tests, even SOMPA, for evaluating African-American children.

Soon after Judge Peckham's ruling, a group of African-American parents filed a suit claiming that the ban on IQ testing discriminated against their children. It was nearly impossible, they pointed out, to use tests to identify learning disabilities or other problems if a child was making poor progress in school. In 1992, Judge Peckham revised his decision again. Children could be tested for learning disabilities, he decided, if their parents requested it. The ban on routine use of IQ tests for placement in EMR classes remains in effect, however (Turkington, 1992).

The State of the Debate   Understandably, the Larry P. decision and those that followed remain controversial. Some psychologists object to the courts making educational decisions. Others point out that they must now resort to nonstandard alternative measures. Many of these alternatives are subjective and open to potential abuse. It may become easier, for instance, to rid classrooms of "problem children"—late bloomers, troublemakers, quirky learners—who may not be intellectually defi-

cient, but just need more attention and understanding. Without IQ tests, how can such children be identified?

A typical reply from critics of IQ testing is that an IQ gives little information about the cause of a low score. It therefore tells little about what corrective action should be taken. To improve mental ability, IQ scores are not needed. The purpose of school is to help children learn and develop skills needed in adjusting to life and work (Baumeister, 1987).

In the years since the Larry P. case, studies of traditional intelligence tests continue to show that IQ tests predict school performance quite well (Neisser et

al., 1996). Thus, it is fair to ask, Should a child who is intelligent, but educationally disadvantaged, be placed in a class that is too advanced for his or her ability level? Certainly, it is damaging to be falsely labeled "retarded." However, it can also be damaging to place children in classes for which they are unprepared.

What Do You Think?   If you were the judge in the Larry P. case, how would you have ruled? If you were a school psychologist, how would you feel about using IQ tests or alternatives such as SOMPA? In your opinion, what role should IQ tests have in a democratic society?

Learning Check

1. The basic issue of the Larry P. case was whether children's IQs are lowered by placement in EMR classes. T or F?

2. Before the Larry P. case, placement in EMR classes was almost always done on the basis of group IQ test scores. T or F?

3. SOMPA is designed to obtain IQ scores from an assessment of a child's physical health and social functioning. T or F?

4. In the SOMPA system, IQ scores are compared to norms for children of similar cultural and social backgrounds. T or F?

5. According to the latest ruling, IQ tests can be used for educational placement in California EMR programs only when they are part of a comprehensive assessment plan. T or F?

Critical Thinking

6. Much of the Larry P. case centered on whether IQ tests are accurate measures of intelligence for all children. In other words, the debate revolved around the _____ of IQ tests.

Answers:
1. F 2. T 3. F 4. T 5. F 6. validity

Chapter Summary

How do psychologists define intelligence?

◆ **Intelligence** refers to one's general capacity to act purposefully, think rationally, and deal effectively with the environment.

◆ In practice, intelligence is **operationally defined** by the creation of intelligence tests.

◆ General intelligence is distinguished from specific **aptitudes. Special aptitude tests** and **multiple aptitude tests** are used to assess a person's capacities for learning various abilities. Aptitude tests measure a narrower range of abilities than **general intelligence tests** do.

What are the qualities of a good psychological test?

◆ To be of any value, a psychological test must be **reliable** (give consistent results). A worthwhile test must also have **validity,** meaning that it measures what it claims to measure.

◆ Widely used intelligence tests are **objective** (they give the same result when scored by different people) and **standardized** (the same procedures are always used in giving the test, and **norms** have been established so that scores can be interpreted).

What are typical IQ tests like?

◆ The first practical intelligence test was assembled by **Alfred Binet.** A modern version of Binet's test is the **Stanford-Binet Intelligence Scale, Fourth Edition.** A second major intelligence test is the **Wechsler Adult Intelligence Scale-Third Edition** (WAIS-III). The WAIS-III measures both **verbal** and **performance** intelligence.

◆ In addition to **individual tests,** intelligence tests have also been produced for use with groups. A **group test** of historical interest is the *Army Alpha.* The SAT, the ACT, and the CQT are group scholastic aptitude tests. Although narrower in scope than IQ tests, they bear some similarities to them.

How do IQ scores relate to gender, age, and occupation?

◆ Intelligence is expressed in terms of an **intelligence quotient** (IQ). IQ is defined as **mental age** (MA) divided by **chronological age** (CA) and then multiplied by 100. An "average" IQ of 100 occurs when mental age equals chronological age.

◆ Modern IQ tests no longer calculate IQs directly. Instead the final score reported by the test is a **deviation IQ.**

◆ IQ scores become fairly stable at about age 6, and they become increasingly reliable thereafter. On the average, IQ scores continue to gradually increase until middle age. Later intellectual declines are moderate for most people until their 70s. Shortly before death, a more significant **terminal decline** in intelligence is often observed.

◆ The distribution of IQ scores approximates a **normal curve.** There are no overall differences between males and females in tested intelligence. However, very small gender differences may result from the intellectual skills our culture encourages males and females to develop.

◆ IQ is related to school grades and job status. The second association may be somewhat artificial because educational credentials are required for entry into many occupations.

What does IQ tell us about genius?

◆ People with IQs in the **gifted** or "genius" range of above 140 tend to be superior in many respects.

◆ By criteria other than IQ, a large proportion of children might be considered gifted or talented in one way or another. Intellectually gifted children often have difficulties in average classrooms and benefit from special accelerated programs.

What causes mental retardation?

◆ The terms **mentally retarded** and **developmentally disabled** are applied to those whose IQ falls below 70 or who lack various **adaptive behaviors.**

◆ Further classifications of retardation are: **mild** (50–55 to 70), **moderate** (35–40 to 50–55), **severe** (20–25 to 35–40), and **profound** (below 20–25). Chances for educational success are related to the degree of retardation.

◆ About 50 percent of the cases of mental retardation are **organic,** being caused by birth injuries, fetal damage, metabolic disorders, or genetic abnormalities. The remaining cases are of undetermined cause.

◆ Many cases of subnormal intelligence are thought to be the result of **familial retardation,** a generally low level of educational and intellectual stimulation in the home, coupled with poverty and poor nutrition.

◆ Six distinct forms of organic retardation are **phenylketonuria** (PKU), **microcephaly, hydrocephaly, cretinism, Down syndrome,** and **fragile-*X* syndrome.**

How do heredity and environment affect intelligence?

◆ Studies of **eugenics** in animals and familial relationships in humans demonstrate that intelligence is partially determined by **heredity.** However, **environment** is also important, as revealed by changes in tested intelligence induced by schooling and stimulating environments.

◆ There is evidence that some elements of intelligence can be taught. Intelligence therefore reflects the combined effects of both heredity and environment in the development of intellectual abilities.

How have views of intelligence changed in recent years?

◆ Some psychologists are investigating the *neural basis* for intelligence, especially the **speed of processing** various kinds of information.

◆ Cognitive psychologists believe that successful intelligence depends on thinking and problem solving skills. **Metacognitive skills**, in particular, contribute greatly to intelligent behavior.

◆ Many psychologists have begun to forge new, broader definitions of intelligence. Howard Gardner's **theory of multiple intelligences** is a good example of this trend.

Are IQ tests fair to all racial and cultural groups?

◆ Traditional IQ tests often suffer from a degree of **cultural bias.** For this and other reasons, it is wise to remember that IQ is merely an **index** of intelligence and that intelligence is narrowly defined by most tests.

◆ The use of standard IQ tests for educational placement of students (especially into special education classes) has been prohibited by law in some states. Whether this is desirable and beneficial to students is currently being debated.

Motivation and Emotion

Preview

Flight of the Gossamer Albatross

What would it feel like to *pedal* an airplane over the English Channel? Cyclist Bryan Allen found out the hard way. Allen was both pilot and "engine" for the first human-powered flight from England to France. Allen pedaled a delicate aircraft, the *Gossamer Albatross,* in a grueling 3-hour flight. The channel crossing took him to the limits of endurance as he fought head winds, thirst, leg cramps, and exhaustion. The following excerpts are from Allen's (1979) account:

> 6:59 A.M. At last, word comes over the radio. . . . "We have France in sight—four miles to go. . . ."
> Four miles or four hundred. I'm fading now and know it. Gradually the head winds have been building up . . . I talk to myself . . . Don't give up now, you *can* do it! As I waver between hope and despair, the radio crackles again:
> "Altitude six inches, six inches; get it up, you've got to get it up!"
> 7:29 A.M. One mile. Less distance than I had flown *Gossamer Condor* two years before for the original Kremer prize. Then, however, there were no head winds or turbulence, no thirst, no cramps. . . . Despite the cramps, I struggle back up to five feet. "Against all hope," I repeat to myself, "against all hope."
> 7:36 A.M. Four hundred yards to shore. . . . One hundred yards now. I am running on reserves I never knew I had. . . .

Motivation and Emotion This chapter is about the motives and emotions underlying Bryan Allen's behavior—and your own. Bryan Allen's final burst of effort ("I am running on reserves I never knew I had") is but one example of the many links between emotion and motivation. Our discussion begins with basic motives, such as hunger and thirst, and ends with a look at how emotions affect us. While emotion can be the spice of life, it is sometimes the spice of death as well.

Chapter Survey

Theme: Behavior is initiated, energized, and directed by motives and emotions.

Key Questions:

Key Topics to Watch for:

Key Questions	Key Topics to Watch for
What is motivation? Are there different types of motives?	A model of motivation Types of motives Homeostasis
What causes hunger? Overeating? Eating disorders?	Mechanisms of hunger Obesity and eating disorders
Is there more than one type of thirst?	Intracellular and extracellular thirst
In what ways are pain avoidance and the sex drive unusual?	Cyclic, episodic, and non-homeostatic drives
How does arousal relate to motivation?	Arousal and body rhythms
What are social motives? Why are they important?	Learned motives Achievement motivation
Are some motives more basic than others?	A hierachy of motives Intrinsic and extrinsic motivation
What happens during emotion?	Elements of emotion
Can "lie detectors" really detect lies?	The polygraph and lie detection
How accurately are emotions expressed by "body language" and the face?	Emotional expressions
How do psychologists explain emotions?	Theories of emotion
Can psychology be applied to weight control?	Behavioral dieting
What is the nature of love?	Types of love

Motivation—Forces that Push and Pull

We move. We seek different goals, some more vigorously than others. The same goal may be pursued for different reasons, or different goals may be pursued for the same reasons. We use the concept of motivation to explain each of these basic aspects of behavior. To be more specific, **motivation** refers to the *dynamics of behavior*—the ways in which our actions are *initiated, sustained*, and *directed* (Petri, 1996).

Can you clarify that?

Yes. Let's relate the concept of motivation to a simple sequence of activity:

> Liz is studying (psychology, of course) in the library. She begins to feel hungry and has difficulty concentrating. Her stomach growls. She grows restless and decides to buy an apple from a vending machine. The machine is empty, so she goes to the cafeteria. Closed. She returns to the library, packs up her books, and drives home, where she prepares a meal and eats. At last her hunger is satisfied, and she again resumes studying.

Liz's food seeking was *initiated* by her bodily need for food; it was *sustained* because her need was not immediately met; and her activities were *directed* by possible sources of food.

Notice too that her food seeking was *terminated* by achieving her goal.

A Model of Motivation

Many motivated activities can be thought of as beginning with a **need** (*an internal deficiency*). The need that initiated Liz's search was a depletion of substances within the cells of her body. Needs cause a **drive** (*an energized motivational state*) to develop. The drive was hunger, in Liz's case. Drives activate a **response** (*an action or series of actions*) designed to attain a **goal** (*the "target" of motivated behavior*). A goal that satisfies the original need ends the motivational sequence. Thus, a simple model of motivation can be shown in this way:

Motivation sequence

Why use the terms need and drive? Aren't they the same thing?

Both terms are necessary because the strength of needs and drives can differ. If you begin fasting today, your bodily need for food will increase each following day. However, you would probably be less "hungry" on the seventh day of

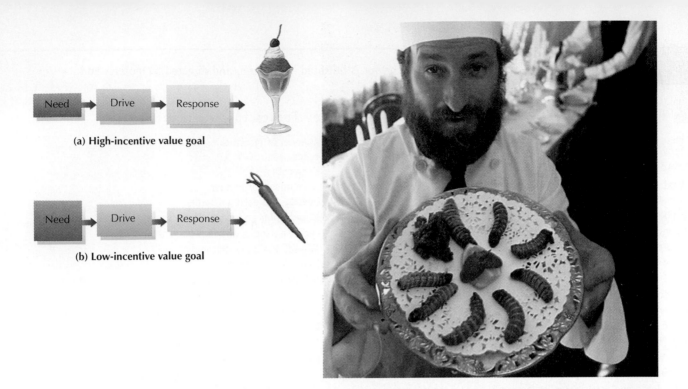

Figure 13–1 ◆ Needs and incentives interact to determine drive strength (*left*). **(a)** Moderate need combined with a high-incentive goal produces a strong drive. **(b)** Even when a strong need exists, drive strength may be moderate if a goal's incentive value is low. It is important to remember, however, that incentive value lies "in the eye of the beholder" (*photo*). No matter how hungry, few people would be able to eat the pictured grubworms.

fasting than you were on the first. While your need for food steadily increases, the hunger drive comes and goes.

Before we assume that we have a complete model of motivation, let us observe Liz's eating behavior on another occasion:

> For dinner, Liz has just eaten soup, salad, a large steak, a large baked potato, one half of a loaf of bread, two pieces of cheesecake, and four cups of coffee. After the meal she remarks about her discomfort from overeating. Soon after, Liz's roommate arrives with a strawberry pie. Liz exclaims that strawberry pie is her favorite dessert and proceeds to eat three good-sized pieces and has a cup of coffee to wash them down.

Is this hunger? Certainly we can believe that Liz's extra-large meal was enough to satisfy her biological needs for food.

How does this change the model of motivation?

Incentives The story illustrates that motivated behavior can be energized by the "pull" of external stimuli, as well as by the "push" of internal needs. The pull exerted by a goal is called its **incentive value** (*a goal's appeal beyond its ability to fill a need*). Some goals are so desirable (strawberry pie, for example) that they motivate behavior in the absence of an internal need. Other goals are so low in incentive value that they will be rejected even though they might meet the internal need. Fresh, live grubworms, for instance, are considered a delicacy in some parts of the world, but it is doubtful that you would eat one no matter how hungry you might be.

In most instances, actions are energized by both internal needs *and* external incentives. In addition, a strong state of need may make a less attractive incentive into a desirable goal. You may never have eaten a grubworm, but chances are you've eaten some pretty horrible leftovers when the refrigerator was bare. Incentives also help account for motives that do not seem to have any identifiable internal need, such as drives for success, status, or approval (Fig. 13–1 ◆).

Types of Motives For the purpose of study, motives can be divided into three major categories:

1. Primary motives *are based on biological needs that must be met for survival.* The most important primary motives are hunger, thirst, pain avoidance, and needs for air, sleep, elimination of wastes, and regulation of body temperature. Primary motives are innate.

2. Stimulus motives *are needs for stimulation and information.* Examples include activity, curiosity, exploration, manipulation, and physical contact. While such motives also appear to be innate, they are not strictly necessary for survival.

3. Secondary motives *are based on learned needs, drives, and goals.* Learned motives account for the great diversity of activities suggested by Bryan Allen's historic flight. Many secondary motives are related to learned needs for power, affiliation (the need to be with others), approval, status, security, and achievement. Fear and aggression also appear to be subject to learning.

Primary Motives and Homeostasis— Keeping the Home Fires Burning

How important is food in your life? Water? Sleep? Air? Temperature regulation? Finding a public rest room? For most of us, satisfying biological needs is so routine that we tend to overlook how much of our behavior they direct. But exaggerate any of these needs through famine, shipwreck, poverty, near-drowning, bitter cold, or drinking 10 cups of coffee, and their powerful grip on behavior becomes evident. We are, after all, still animals in many ways.

Biological drives are essential because they maintain **homeostasis** (HOE-me-oh-STAY-sis), or *bodily equilibrium* (Cannon, 1932).

What is homeostasis?

The term *homeostasis* means "standing steady," or "steady state." Within the body there are "ideal" levels for body temperature, for the concentration of chemicals in the blood,

for blood pressure, and so forth. When the body deviates from these ideal levels, automatic reactions restore equilibrium. You might find it helpful to think of homeostatic mechanisms as being similar to the operation of a *thermostat* set at a particular temperature.

A (Very) Short Course on Thermostats

If room temperature falls below the level set on a thermostat, the heat is automatically turned on to warm the room. When the heat equals or slightly exceeds the ideal temperature, it is automatically turned off. In this way room temperature is kept in a state of equilibrium hovering around the ideal level.

In the human body the first reactions to disequilibrium are also automatic. For example, if you become too hot, blood flow to the surface of your body increases and you begin to perspire, thus lowering body temperature. We become aware of homeostasis only when driven by continued disequilibrium to seek shade, warmth, food, or water.

Since hunger is one of the most interesting and better understood of the primary drives, let's examine it first. Before reading about hunger, you may find it helpful to complete the Learning Check that follows.

Learning Check	Critical Thinking

Learning Check

1. Motives _____ , sustain, and _____ activities.

2. Needs provide the _____ of motivation, whereas incentives provide the _____ .

Classify the following needs or motives by placing the correct letter in the blank.

A. Primary motive   **B.** Stimulus motive   **C.** Secondary motive

3. _B_ curiosity   6. _A_ thirst

4. _C_ status   7. _C_ achievement

5. _A_ sleep   8. _B_ physical contact

9. The maintenance of bodily equilibrium is called thermostasis. T or F?

10. A goal high in incentive value may create a drive in the absence of any internal need. T or F?

Critical Thinking

11. Many people mistakenly believe that they suffer from "hypoglycemia," which is often blamed for fatigue, difficulty concentrating, irritability, and other symptoms. Why is it unlikely that many people actually have hypoglycemia?

Answers:

1. initiate, direct 2. push, pull 3. B 4. C 5. A 6. A 7. C 8. B 9. F 10. T 11. Because of homeostasis: Blood sugar is normally maintained within narrow bounds. While blood sugar levels fluctuate enough to affect hunger, true hypoglycemia is an infrequent medical problem.

Hunger—Pardon Me, That's Just My Hypothalamus Growling

What causes hunger?

When you feel hungry, you probably associate a desire for food with sensations from your stomach. This, sensibly enough, is where the search for hunger began. In an early study, Cannon and Washburn decided to see if the contrac-

tions of an empty stomach cause hunger. To do this, Washburn trained himself to swallow a balloon. The balloon was then inflated inside his stomach, through an attached tube. This allowed Washburn's stomach contractions to be recorded (Fig. 13–2 ◆). Cannon and Washburn observed that when Washburn's stomach contracted, he felt "hunger pangs." They concluded that hunger is nothing more than stomach contractions (Cannon & Washburn, 1912). (Unfortunately, this proved to be an inflated conclusion.)

Perhaps you already guessed that something more than the stomach is involved in hunger. For many people, hunger produces an overall feeling of weakness or shakiness that

Figure 13–2 ◆ In Cannon's early study of hunger, a simple apparatus was used to simultaneously record hunger pangs and stomach contractions. (After Cannon, 1934.)

seems unrelated to the stomach. Of course, eating *is* limited when the stomach is **distended** (*full*). (Remember last Thanksgiving?) However, we now know that the stomach is not essential for feeling hunger (Martin, White, & Hulsey, 1991).

How has that been demonstrated?

For medical reasons, many people have had their stomachs removed surgically. Nevertheless, these people continue to feel hungry and to eat regularly. It would seem that some *central* factor must cause hunger. One important element now appears to be the level of glucose (sugar) in the blood (Campfield et al., 1996). If insulin is injected in humans, it causes **hypoglycemia** (HI-po-gly-SEE-me-ah: *low blood sugar*) and stimulates feelings of hunger and stomach contractions. Strange as it may seem, the liver also affects hunger.

The liver?

Yes, the liver. The liver responds to a lack of bodily "fuel" by sending nerve impulses to the brain, which contribute to a desire to eat (Martin, White, & Hulsey, 1991).

Brain Mechanisms

What part of the brain controls hunger?

When you are hungry, many parts of the brain are affected, so no single "hunger center" exists. However, one area of importance is the **hypothalamus** (HI-po-THAL-ah-mus). This small structure *regulates many aspects of motivation and emotion, especially hunger, thirst, and sexual behavior* (Fig. 13–3 ◆).

 Cells in the hypothalamus are sensitive to levels of sugar (and perhaps other substances) in the blood. The hypothalamus also receives messages from the liver, stomach, intestines, and fat cells in the body (Martin, White, & Hulsey, 1991). These messages combine to produce hunger.

 One area of the hypothalamus seems to be part of a **feeding system** *that initiates eating.* If the *lateral hypothalamus* is "turned on" with an electrified probe, even a well-fed animal will immediately begin eating. (The term *lateral*

simply means the sides of the hypothalamus. See Figure 13–4 ◆.) If the same area is destroyed, the animal will refuse to eat and will die if not force-fed.

 A second area within the hypothalamus seems to be part of a **satiety system,** or *"stop mechanism" for eating.* If the *ventromedial hypothalamus* (VENT-ro-MEE-dee-al) is destroyed, dramatic overeating results. (*Ventromedial* refers to the bottom middle of the hypothalamus.) Rats with such damage will overeat until they balloon up to weights of 1,000 grams or more. Many get so obese that they can barely move (Fig. 13–5 ◆). A normal rat weighs about 180 grams. To put this weight gain in human terms, picture someone you know who weighs 180 pounds growing to a weight of 1,000 pounds.

 A third area of importance in the hypothalamus is the *paraventricular nucleus* (PAIR-uh-ven-TRICK-you-ler) (Fig. 13–4). This area helps keep blood sugar levels steady in the body (Martin, White, & Hulsey, 1991). As a result, it seems to be involved in both starting and stopping eating. The paraventricular nucleus is very sensitive to a substance called **neuropeptide Y (NPY).** *If NPY is present in large amounts in the paraventricular nucleus an animal will eat* until it cannot hold another bite.

Figure 13–3 ◆ Location of the hypothalamus in the human brain.

Corpus callosum · Lateral hypothalamus

Ventromedial hypothalamus · Paraventricular nucleus

Figure 13–4 ◆ This is a cross section through the middle of the brain (viewed from the front of the brain). Indicated areas of the hypothalamus are associated with hunger and the regulation of body weight.

Figure 13–5 ◆ Damage to the hunger satiety system in the hypothalamus can produce a very fat rat, a condition called hypothalamic *hyperphagia* (Hi-per-FAGE-yah: overeating). This rat weighs 1,080 grams. (The pointer has gone completely around the dial and beyond.) (Photo courtesy of Neal Miller.)

Another recently discovered substance acts as a major stop signal for eating. This chemical, called **glucagon-like peptide 1 (GLP-1)** *causes eating to cease.* GLP-1 is released by the intestines after you eat a meal. From there, it travels in the bloodstream to the brain. When enough GLP-1 arrives, your desire to eat ends (Turton et al., 1996).

The discovery of chemical messengers that start and stop eating may make artificial control of hunger possible. If so, better treatments for eating disorders, such as extreme obesity and self-starvation, could follow (Scott, 1996).

Set Point It should come as no surprise that there is more to hunger than immediate "start" and "stop" systems in the brain. In addition to knowing when to start eating, and when a meal is over, your body needs to regulate weight over longer time periods. This task appears to be handled by a system that is sensitive to the amount of fat stored in the body.

Basically, your body has a **set point** *for the proportion of body fat it maintains.* In other words, the set point acts like a "thermostat" for fat levels. Your own set point is the weight you maintain when you are making no effort to gain or lose weight. When your body goes below its set point, you will feel hungry most of the time (Martin, White, & Hulsey, 1991). On the other hand, if your "spare tire" is well inflated, fat cells release a substance called *leptin*. **Leptin** is carried in the bloodstream to the brain, where it *acts as a signal to eat less* (Considine et al., 1996).

Do people have different set points?

Yes. Set points appear to be partly inherited and partly affected by childhood feeding patterns. Studies of adopted children illustrate the impact of heredity: If a child's birth parents are overweight, the child is likely to become obese too (Stunkard et al., 1986). This suggests that genes greatly influence adult weight.

The set point also tends to be higher for people who were overfed as children. Adults whose weight problems began in childhood tend to have *more* fat cells and *larger* fat cells.

The mouse on the left has a genetic defect that prevents its fat cells from producing normal amounts of leptin. Without this chemical signal, the mouse's body acts as if its set point for fat storage is, shall we say, rather high.

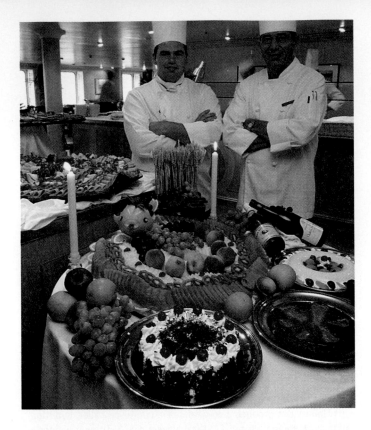

Plentiful, eye-catching foods provide powerful incentives for overeating. In North America, numerous external eating cues and diets high in sweetness, fat, and variety have contributed to excessive weight gains in one adult out of every three.

What if a person doesn't become overweight until adulthood? In that case, the fat cells grow larger, but they usually do not increase in number. Thus, weight problems that begin in childhood are much more difficult to control.

Obesity

Why do people overeat?

Set points are only one piece in a complex puzzle that scientists are still trying to solve. Their search is fueled by the fact that obesity is a major health risk and, for many, a source of social stigma and low self-esteem.

If eating were controlled only by internal needs, fewer people would overeat. However, many people are sensitive to **external eating cues** (*signs and signals linked with food*). If you are sensitive to external cues, you are most likely to eat when food is attractive, highly visible, and easy to obtain. (Have you ever overeaten at a holiday party or buffet?) People of all weights can be found who are unusually sensitive to external eating cues, so this is not strictly a problem of the obese (Rodin, 1981). Just the same, eating cues do appear to be a factor in some overeating.

A *diet* is not just something you go on when you are trying to lose weight. **Diet** *refers to the types and amounts of food you regularly consume.* Diets also contribute to overeating. Placing animals on a "supermarket" diet, for instance, can

lead to gross obesity. In one experiment, rats were given meals of chocolate chip cookies, salami, cheese, bananas, marshmallows, milk chocolate, peanut butter, and fat. Rats on this diet gained almost three times as much weight as animals that ate only laboratory rat chow (Sclafani & Springer, 1976). (Rat chow is a dry mixture of several bland grains. If you were a rat, you'd probably eat more cookies than rat chow, too!)

We humans also appear to be sensitive to dietary content. In general, *sweetness*, high *fat content*, and *variety* tend to encourage overeating (Ball & Grinker, 1981; Lucas & Sclafani, 1990). Sadly, our culture may provide the worst possible kinds of foods for those with a tendency toward obesity.

It is tempting to assume that fatness comes from constant overeating, but this is a myth. Overeating occurs mainly when a person is gaining weight. Once excess weight is gained, it can be maintained with a normal diet. An added problem is that as people gain weight, they reduce their activity levels and burn fewer calories. As a result, some overweight persons continue to gain weight while consuming fewer calories than their slimmer neighbors.

Is it true that people also overeat when they are emotionally upset?

Yes. People with weight problems are just as likely to eat when they are anxious, angry, or sad, as when hungry (Schotte et al., 1990). Of course, unhappiness often accompanies obesity in our fat-conscious culture. The result is a pattern of overeating that leads to emotional distress and still more overeating. This cycle can make weight control extremely difficult.

To summarize, overeating results from a complex interplay of internal and external influences, diet, emotions, genetics, exercise, and many other factors. To answer the question we began with, people become obese in different ways and for different reasons. Clearly, scientists are still a long way from winning the "battle of the bulge."

For your interest, the following highlight offers another perspective on overeating.

The Paradox of Yo-Yo Dieting

If dieting works, why are hundreds of "new" diets published each year? The answer is that while dieters do lose weight, most regain it soon after they quit dieting. Indeed, many people suffer a rebound that pushes weight higher than it was before they began dieting. Why should this be so? The answer is that dieting (starving) slows the body's rate of metabolism (Leibel, Rosenbaum, & Hirsch, 1995).

In effect, a dieter's body becomes highly efficient at *conserving* calories and storing them as fat (Bennett & Gurin, 1982). Any low calorie diet may have this effect, but "yo-yo dieting," or repeated weight loss and gain, is especially troublesome. Frequent **weight cycling** (*losing and gaining weight*) tends to slow the body's **metabolic rate** (*the rate at which energy is used up*). This makes it harder to lose weight each time a person diets and easier to regain weight when the diet ends. Frequent changes in weight also increase susceptibility to heart disease and premature death (Brownell & Rodin, 1994; Lissner et al., 1991).

Apparently, evolution prepared us to save energy when food is scarce and to stock up on fat when food is plentiful. Briefly starving yourself, therefore, may have little lasting effect on weight. To avoid ineffectively bouncing between feast and famine re-

quires a permanent change in eating habits and exercise—a topic we will return to in this chapter's Applications.

Other Factors in Hunger

As research on overeating suggests, "hunger" is affected by more than bodily needs for food. Let's consider some additional factors of interest.

Cultural Factors   Learning to think of some foods as desirable and others as revolting has much to do with eating habits. In North America we would never consider eating the eyes out of the steamed head of a monkey, but in some parts of the world this dish is considered a real delicacy. By the same token, our willingness to eat meat, cows, and fish would be considered barbaric in many cultures. In short, **cultural values** greatly affect the incentive value of foods.

Taste   Even tastes for "normal" foods may vary considerably. One experiment revealed that the hungrier you are, the more pleasant a sweet food tastes (Cabanac & Duclaux, 1970). Another study found that people who are anxious are more likely to choose familiar foods to eat, rather than unusual foods (Pliner, Eng, & Krishnan, 1995). If you have some favorite "comfort foods" that you eat when you are upset, this finding will make sense to you.

Fans cheered as daytime TV host Oprah Winfrey lost 67 pounds on a commercial diet. Over the next year, viewers watched in morbid fascination as Oprah regained all of the weight she had lost. Oprah's rebound came as no surprise to psychologists. Numerous studies show that you can lose weight on almost any diet. However, you will almost certainly gain it back in a few years. Only recently has Oprah been able to stabilize her weight through exercise and revised eating habits (Seligman, 1994).

As you may have noticed, it is easy to acquire a **taste aversion,** *or active dislike,* for a particular food. All that's required is for a food to cause sickness or to be associated with nausea (Jacobsen et al., 1993). Not only will such foods be avoided, they too can become nauseating. A friend of the author's, who once became ill after eating a cheese Danish (well, actually, *several*), has never again been able to come face to face with this delightful pastry.

If getting sick occurs long after eating, how does it become associated with a particular food?

A good question. Taste aversions are a type of classical conditioning. As stated in Chapter 9, a long delay between the CS and US usually prevents conditioning. For this reason, psychologists theorize that we have a biological tendency to associate an upset stomach with foods eaten earlier. Such learning is usually protective (Garcia et al., 1974). Yet, sadly, many human cancer patients suffer taste aversions long after the nausea of their drug treatments has passed (Jacobsen et al., 1993).

If you like animals, you will be interested in an imaginative approach to an age-old problem. In many rural areas, predators are poisoned, trapped, or shot by livestock owners. These practices have nearly wiped out the timber wolf, and in some areas the coyote faces a similar end. How might the coyote be saved without a costly loss of livestock?

In a classic experiment, coyotes were given lamb tainted with lithium chloride. Coyotes who took the bait became nauseated and vomited. After one or two such treatments, they developed **bait shyness**—*a lasting distaste for the tainted food* (Gustavson & Garcia, 1974). If applied consistently, taste aversion conditioning might solve many predator-

livestock problems. (Perhaps this technique could even be used to protect roadrunners from the Wiley Coyote!)

Taste aversions may also help people avoid severe nutritional imbalances. For example, if you go on a fad diet and eat only grapefruit, you will eventually begin to feel ill. In time, associating your discomfort with grapefruit could create an aversion to it and restore some balance to your diet.

One classic study on **self-selection feeding** found that human infants ate a balanced diet when given a free choice of foods. Since the infants sometimes went on food jags, the overall balance of their eating may have been based, in part, on the process just described. It should be noted, however, that the "wisdom of the body" is quite limited. Babies in the study were only allowed to choose from fresh, unseasoned, unsweetened foods. If candy had been a choice, the infants might have gorged themselves on it (Story & Brown, 1987). We humans seem to have an innate preference for sweet and fatty foods—juicy steaks and fried chicken, cookies, cakes and so on. An appetite for candy and junk food can easily override the weaker tendency to eat a balanced diet.

Eating Disorders

Under the sheets of her hospital bed Krystal looks like a starved skeleton. If her self-destructive course cannot be changed, Krystal may die of malnutrition.

Serious cases of undereating like Krystal's are called **anorexia nervosa** (AN-uh-REK-see-yah ner-VOH-sah). Victims of anorexia, who are mostly adolescent females (5 to 10 percent are male), suffer devastating weight loss from *active, self-inflicted starvation* (Wakeling, 1996).

Do anorexics lose their appetite?

No, many anorexics continue to feel hungry, yet struggle to starve themselves. The problem is best described as a *relentless pursuit of excessive thinness.* Often, anorexia starts with "normal" dieting that gradually begins to dominate the person's life. In time, anorexics suffer weakness, an absence of menstrual cycles, and frequent infections. Five to 8 percent (more than 1 in 20) die of malnutrition or related problems. Table 13–1 ■ lists the symptoms of anorexia nervosa.

Bulimia nervosa (bue-LIHM-ee-yah), also known as the *binge-purge syndrome,* is a second major eating disorder. Bulimics gorge on food, then induce vomiting or take laxatives to avoid gaining weight (see Table 13–1). Like anorexia, bulimia is far more prevalent in women than in men. Approximately 5 percent of college women are bulimic and as many as 61 percent have milder eating problems. Bingeing and purging can also seriously damage health. Typical risks include sore throat, hair loss, muscle spasms, kidney damage, dehydration, tooth erosion, swollen salivary glands, menstrual irregularities, loss of sex drive, and even heart attack.

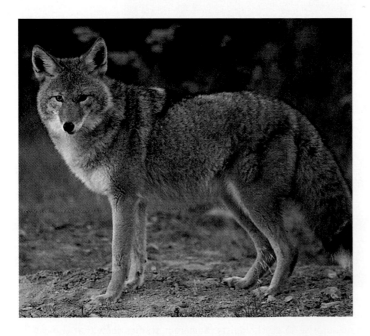

Like humans and other animals, coyotes develop taste aversions when food is associated with nausea.

Table 13–1 ■ Recognizing Eating Disorders

Anorexia nervosa

[ ] Body weight below 85 percent of normal for one's height and age.

[ ] Refusal to maintain body weight in normal range.

[ ] Intense fear of becoming fat or gaining weight, even though underweight.

[ ] Disturbance in one's body image or perceived weight.

[ ] Self-evaluation is unduly influenced by body weight.

[ ] Denial of seriousness of abnormally low body weight.

[ ] Absence of menstrual periods.

[ ] Purging behavior (vomiting or misuse of laxatives or diuretics).

Bulimia nervosa

[ ] Normal or above-normal weight.

[ ] Recurring binge eating.

[ ] Eating within an hour or two an amount of food that is much larger than most people would consume.

[ ] Feeling a lack of control over eating.

[ ] Purging behavior (vomiting or misuse of laxatives or diuretics).

[ ] Excessive exercise to prevent weight gain.

[ ] Fasting to prevent weight gain.

[ ] Self-evaluation is unduly influenced by body weight.

DSM-IV, 1994.

Anorexia nervosa can be far more dangerous than many people realize. This haunting photo shows popular singer Karen Carpenter shortly before her death. Carpenter died of starvation-induced heart failure. More recently, Christy Henrich, a former member of the U.S. National Gymnastics Team, died at age 22. Henrich, too, suffered from anorexia. Many more victims of eating disorders die each year (Witherspoon, 1994).

What causes anorexia and bulimia?

Causes   Both anorexics and bulimics have unrealistic views of their bodies and exaggerated fears of becoming fat (Gardner & Bokenkamp, 1996). Many victims overestimate their body size by 25 percent or more. Almost all continue to see themselves as "fat" when in fact they are wasting away (Fig. 13–6 ◆) (Williamson et al., 1989). In some cases, body image can actually change after a meal. For example, after eating nothing more than a candy bar and a soft drink, bulimic women thought they had grown larger. It's no wonder that bulimic women often panic and attempt to purge themselves of food (McKinzie et al., 1993).

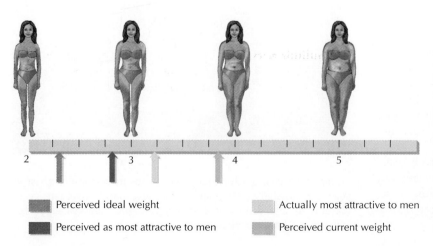

Perceived ideal weight

Perceived as most attractive to men

Actually most attractive to men

Perceived current weight

Figure 13–6 ◆ Women with abnormal eating habits were asked to rate their body shape on a scale similar to the one you see here. As a group, they chose ideal figures much thinner than what they thought their current weights were. (Most women say they want to be thinner than they currently are, but to a lesser degree than women with eating problems.) Notice that the women with eating problems chose an ideal weight that was even thinner than what they thought men prefer. This is not typical of most women. In this study, only women with eating problems wanted to be thinner than what they thought men find attractive (Zellner, Harner, & Adler, 1989).

The relentless parade of atypically thin models in the media contributes to eating disorders. People with eating disorders are much more likely to report being influenced by unrealistic body ideals in the media (Murray, Touyz, & Beumont, 1996).

Control is another issue for people with eating disorders. Anorexics are usually "perfect" daughters—helpful, considerate, conforming, and obedient. Many seem to be trying to have perfect control in one area of their lives, by being perfectly slim (Pliner & Haddock, 1996). Bulimics are also concerned with control. Typically they are obsessed with thoughts of weight, food, eating, and ridding themselves of food. Most feel fat, guilty, shameful, and anxious after a binge. Vomiting reduces these feelings, which makes purging highly reinforcing for many bulimics (Powell & Thelen, 1996).

Treatment In almost all cases, victims of eating disorders need professional help. Treatment for anorexia usually begins with a carefully controlled medical diet to restore weight and health. Next, the client enters counseling to work on the personal conflicts that led to weight loss. For bulimia, psychologists have had some success with behavioral counseling. This approach includes careful self-monitoring of food intake and work on extinguishing the urge to vomit after eating. A related cognitive-behavioral approach focuses on changing the thinking patterns and beliefs about weight and body shape that perpetuate eating disorders (Johnson, Tsoh, & Varnado, 1996).

Most anorexics do not seek help, and many actively resist it. Bulimics will sometimes seek treatment, but usually not until their eating habits become intolerable. In either case, it may take strong urging by family or friends to get victims into treatment.

Primary Motives Revisited—Thirst, Sex, and Pain

The control of most other primary motives is similar to that observed in hunger. For example, thirst is only partially related to dryness of the mouth and throat. When drugs are used to keep the mouth constantly wet or dry, thirst and water intake remain normal. Like hunger, thirst appears to be regulated by the hypothalamus, where separate *thirst* and *thirst satiety* systems are found. Also like hunger, thirst is strongly affected by individual learning and by cultural values.

Thirst

You may not have noticed, but there are actually two kinds of thirst. **Extracellular thirst** occurs when *water is lost from the fluids surrounding the cells of your body.* Bleeding, vomiting, diarrhea, sweating, and drinking alcohol cause this type of thirst (Petri, 1996). When a person loses both water and minerals in any of these ways—especially by perspiration—a slightly salty liquid may be more satisfying than plain water.

Why would a thirsty person want to drink salty water?

The reason is that before the body can retain water, minerals lost through perspiration (mainly salt) must be replaced. In lab tests, animals greatly prefer saltwater after salt levels in their bodies are lowered (Strickler & Verbalis, 1988). Similarly, some nomadic peoples of the Sahara Desert prize

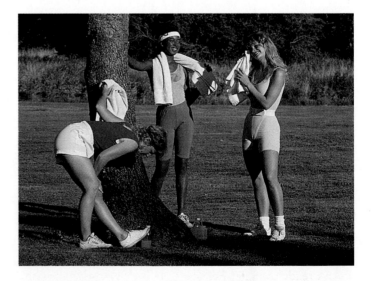

It may seem contradictory, but thirst caused by perspiring is best quenched by slightly salty liquids. The salty snacks offered at taverns are intended to increase beer sales, but they also appeal to people who have perspired heavily at work or play.

blood as a beverage, probably because of its saltiness. (Maybe they should try Gatorade?)

A second type of thirst occurs when you eat a salty meal. In this instance your body does not lose fluid. Instead, excess salt causes *fluid to be drawn out of cells*. As the cells "shrink," **intracellular thirst** is triggered. Thirst of this type is best quenched by plain water.

The drives for food, water, air, sleep, and elimination are all fairly similar in that they are generated by a combination of activities in the body and the brain, are modified by learning and culture, and are influenced by external factors. Two unusual primary drives are the sex drive and the drive to avoid pain.

Pain

How is the drive to avoid pain different?

Drives such as hunger, thirst, and sleepiness come and go in a fairly regular cycle each day. Pain avoidance, by contrast, is an **episodic drive** (ep-ih-SOD-ik). That is, it *occurs in distinct episodes* when damage to the body takes place. Most of the primary drives cause us to actively seek a desired goal (food, drink, warmth, and so forth). The goal in pain avoidance is to eliminate pain.

It may surprise you to discover that pain avoidance is partly learned. Some people, for instance, feel they must be "tough" and not show any discomfort; others complain loudly at the smallest ache or pain. As you might expect, the first attitude raises pain tolerance, and the second lowers it (Kleinke, 1978). Such attitudes explain why members of some societies endure cutting, burning, whipping, tattooing, and piercing of the skin that would agonize the typical member of our society.

The Sex Drive

The sex drive is also unusual. In fact, many psychologists do not think of sex as a primary motive because sex (contrary to anything your personal experience might suggest) is not necessary for *individual* survival. It is necessary, of course, for *group* survival among humans and other creatures.

In lower animals the sex drive is directly related to the effects of hormones. *Female mammals* (other than humans) *are interested in mating only when their fertility cycles are in the stage of* **estrus,** or "heat." Estrus is caused by secretion of **estrogen** (*a female sex hormone*) into the bloodstream. Hormones are important in the male animal as well. In most lower animals, castration will abolish the sex drive. But in contrast to the female, the normal male animal is almost always ready to mate. His sex drive is primarily aroused by the behavior of a receptive female. In many species, mating is therefore closely tied to female fertility cycles.

How much do hormones affect the sex drive in humans?

Tolerance for pain and the strength of a person's motivation to avoid discomfort are greatly affected by cultural practices and beliefs.

The link between hormones and the sex drive grows weaker as we ascend the biological scale. Hormones do affect the human sex drive, but only to a limited degree. For example, there is no connection between female sexual activity and women's monthly menstrual cycles (Udry & Morris, 1977). In humans, mental, cultural, and emotional factors determine sexual expression. However, our liberation from hormones is not total. Human males show a loss of sex drive after castration, and some women lose sexual desire when taking birth control pills.

Human sexual behavior and attitudes are discussed in detail in Chapter 15. For now it is enough to note that the sex drive is largely **non-homeostatic** (*relatively independent of bodily need states*). In humans, the sex drive can be aroused at virtually any time by almost anything. It therefore shows no clear relationship to deprivation (the amount of time since the drive was last satisfied). Certainly, an increase in desire may occur as time passes. But recent sexual activity does not prevent sexual desire from occurring again. Notice, too, that people may seek to arouse the sex drive as well as to reduce it. This unusual quality makes the sex drive capable of motivating a wide range of behaviors. It also explains why sex is used to sell almost everything imaginable.

The non-homeostatic quality of the sex drive can be shown in this way: An animal is allowed to copulate until it seems to have no further interest in sexual behavior. Then a new sexual partner is provided. Immediately the animal resumes sexual activity. This pattern is called the *Coolidge effect* after former U.S. president Calvin Coolidge. What, you might ask, does Calvin Coolidge have to do with the sex drive? The answer is found in the following story.

While touring an experimental farm, Coolidge's wife reportedly asked if a rooster mated just once a day. "No ma'am," she was told, "he mates dozens of times each day." "Tell that to the president," she said, with a faraway look in her eyes. When President Coolidge reached the same part of the tour, his wife's message was given to him. His reaction was to ask if the dozens of matings were with the same hen. No, he was told, different hens were involved. "Tell *that* to Mrs. Coolidge," the president is said to have replied.

Stimulus Drives— Skydiving, Horror Movies, and the Fun Zone

It is sometimes said that curiosity killed the cat, but nothing could be further from the truth. **Stimulus drives,** *which reflect needs for exploration, manipulation, curiosity, and stimulation,* clearly aid survival. As mentioned earlier, such drives might be explained by the life-and-death necessity of keeping track of sources of food, danger, and other important details of the environment. However, stimulus drives seem to go beyond such needs.

Monkey Business

In an experiment, monkeys confined to a dimly lit box learned to perform a simple task in order to open a window that allowed them to view the outside world (Butler & Harlow, 1954). In a similar experiment, monkeys quickly learned to solve a mechanical puzzle made up of interlocking metal pins, hooks, and hasps (Butler, 1954) (Fig. 13–7 ◆). In both situations, no external reward was offered for exploration or manipulation.

The puzzle-solving monkeys seemed to work for the sheer fun of it. An interest in video games, chess, crossword puzzles, Rubik's cube, and the like offers a human parallel. Curiosity—the drive to *know*—also seems to be powerful in humans. Scientific investigation, intellectual curiosity, and other advanced activities may express this basic drive.

Figure 13–7 ◆ Monkeys happily open locks that are placed in their cage. Since no reward is given for this activity, it provides evidence for the existence of stimulus needs. (Photo courtesy of Harry F. Harlow.)

It is well known that humans and animals demand and actively seek stimulation (Reybowski, 1982). As discussed in Chapter 8, many people have undergone prolonged or severe **sensory deprivation** (*a major reduction in the amount or variety of sensory stimulation*). Those who do—such as prisoners, arctic explorers, radar operators, and truck drivers—often report sensory distortions and disturbed thinking.

Are stimulus drives homeostatic?

Arousal Theory

By combining homeostasis with drives for stimulation, we get a useful model of human behavior. **Arousal theory** states that there are *ideal levels of arousal for various activities*. It further assumes *that people try to keep arousal near these ideal levels* (Hebb, 1966).

What do you mean by arousal?

Arousal *refers to activation of the body and the nervous system.* Arousal is zero at death; it is low during sleep; it is moderate during normal daily activities; and it is high at times of excitement, emotion, or panic. Arousal theory assumes that an individual becomes uncomfortable when arousal is too low ("I'm bored") or when it is too high, as in fear, anxiety, or panic ("The dentist will see you now").

Curiosity and stimulation seeking can be interpreted as attempts to raise the level of arousal when it is too

Thrill seeking is an element of the sensation-seeking personality.

low. Most adults vary their activities to maintain a comfortable level of activation. Music, parties, athletics, conversation, sleep, and the like are mixed to keep arousal at moderate levels, thus preventing both boredom and overstimulation.

Do people vary in their needs for stimulation?

Sensation Seekers The city dweller who visits the country complains that it is "too quiet," and seeks some "action." The country dweller finds the city "hectic," "overwhelming," or "too much," and seeks peace and quiet. Arousal theory also assumes that each of us learns to seek a personal "ideal" or preferred level of arousal. Marvin Zuckerman has devised a test to measure such differences. His *Sensation-Seeking Scale* (SSS) includes statements like the samples shown in Table 13–2 ■ (from Zuckerman et al., 1978; Zuckerman, 1996).

Sensation seeking *is a trait of individuals who prefer high levels of stimulation.* High and low sensation seeking probably reflects differences in how each person's body responds to new, unusual, surprising, or intense stimulation (Zuckerman, 1990). People who score high on the full-length version of the SSS tend to be extroverted, independent individuals who value change. They also report more sexual partners than low scorers; they are more likely to smoke, and they prefer spicy, sour, and crunchy foods over bland foods. Tourists who take "adventure" holidays tend to score high on the SSS (Gilchrist et al., 1995)! Low sensation seekers are orderly, nurturant, giving, and they enjoy the company of others. Which are you? (Most people fall somewhere in between.)

Table 13–2 ■ Sample Items from the Sensation-Seeking Scale

Thrill and adventure seeking
- I would like to try parachute jumping.
- I think I would enjoy the sensations of skiing very fast down a high mountain slope.

Experience seeking
- I like to explore a strange city or section of town myself, even if it means getting lost.
- I like to try new foods that I have never tasted before.

Disinhibition
- I like wild, "uninhibited" parties.
- I often like to get high (drinking liquor or smoking marijuana).

Boredom susceptibility
- I can't stand watching a movie that I've seen before.
- I like people who are sharp and witty, even if they do sometimes insult others.

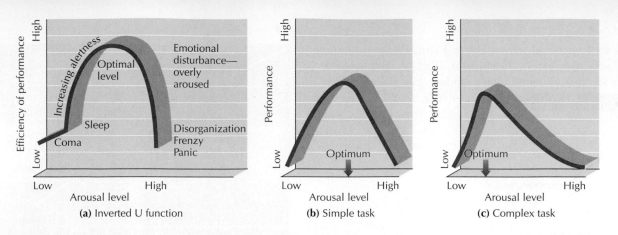

Figure 13–8 ◆ **(a)** The general relationship between arousal and efficiency can be described by an inverted U curve. The optimal level of arousal or motivation is higher for a simple task **(b)** than for a complex task **(c)**.

Levels of Arousal

Is there an ideal level of arousal for peak performance?

If we set aside individual differences, performance is usually best when arousal is *moderate*. Let's say that you have to take an essay exam. If you are sleepy or feeling lazy (arousal level too low), your performance will suffer. If you are in a state of anxiety or panic about the test (arousal level too high), you will also perform below par. This relationship between arousal and efficiency of behavior can be expressed as an **inverted U function** (*a curve, roughly in the shape of an upside-down U*) (Fig. 13–8 ◆) (Anderson, 1990).

At very low levels of arousal the body is not sufficiently energized to perform well. With increased arousal, performance continues to improve up to the middle area of the curve. Then it begins to drop off as a person becomes emotional, frenzied, or disorganized. Such disorganization might occur if you were trying to start a car stalled on a railroad track, with a speeding train bearing down on you. Even when life and death are not at stake, excess arousal is disruptive. For example, the batting averages of professional baseball players drop dramatically during the late innings of close games (Davis & Harvey, 1992).

Is performance always best at moderate levels of arousal?

No, the optimal level of arousal depends on the complexity of the task you are performing. For simple tasks, activation is less harmful. *If a task is relatively simple, the optimal level of arousal will be high. When a task is more complex, the best performance occurs at low levels of arousal.* This relationship is called the **Yerkes-Dodson law** (see Fig. 13–8). It applies to a wide variety of tasks and to measures of motivation other than arousal.

Some examples of how the Yerkes-Dodson law operates might be helpful. At a track meet it is almost impossible for a sprinter to get too aroused for a race. The task is direct and uncomplicated: Run as fast as you can for a short distance. On the other hand, a golfer making the last putt in an important tournament and a basketball player making a game-deciding free throw face more sensitive and complex tasks. Excessive arousal will almost always hurt their performance. In school, most students have experienced "test anxiety," a familiar example of the effects of excessive arousal on performance.

Then is it true that by learning to calm down, a person would do better on tests?

Usually, but not always. Studies of anxious students show that they are typically most anxious when they're unprepared for a test. If this is the case, calming down simply means you will remain calm while failing. Let's see what steps you can take to lower test anxiety.

Using Psychology

Coping with Test Anxiety

Test anxiety is a combination of *heightened physiological arousal* (uneasiness, tension, sweating, pounding heart, nervousness) and *excessive worry*. This combination—worry plus arousal—tends to distract test takers with a rush of upsetting thoughts and feelings (Gierl & Rogers, 1996).

Psychologists have become relatively successful in treating test anxiety. Let's see what we can learn from their efforts.

Preparation The most direct antidote for test anxiety is *hard work*. Many test-anxious students simply study too little and too late for exams (Gross, 1990). If your study skills are poor, improving them is a good way to reduce test anxiety (Jones & Petruzzi, 1995).

Another solution is to *overprepare* by studying well in advance of the "big day." Students who are well prepared score higher, worry less, and are less likely to become overly aroused.

Relaxation Learning to relax is another way to lower test anxiety (Ricketts & Galloway, 1984). You can learn self-relaxation skills by looking at Chapter 19, where a relaxation technique is described. Test-taking is also less threatening if you feel that you have emotional support from others (Sarason, 1981). If you are test anxious, it might help to discuss the problem with your professor. Preparing for tests with a supportive friend or classmate can also help.

Rehearsal Nervousness during tests can be lessened by carefully *rehearsing* how you will cope with upsetting events. Before taking a test, imagine yourself going blank, running out of time, or feeling panicked. Then calmly plan how you will handle each situation—by keeping your attention on the task, by focusing on one question at a time, and so forth (Watson & Tharp, 1996).

Restructuring Thoughts Because worries are a major part of test anxiety, changing self-defeating thinking patterns can be the best solution of all. Test-anxious students benefit from listing the distracting and upsetting thoughts they have during exams. They then work on learning to combat their worries with calming, rational replies (Jones & Petruzzi, 1995). (These are called *coping statements;* see the Applications section in Chapter 14 for more information.)

Let's say, for example, that a student thinks, "I'm going to fail this test and all my friends will think I'm stupid." To counter this upsetting thought, she or he might say, "If I prepare well and control my worries, I will probably pass the test. Even if I don't, it won't be the end of the world. My friends will still like me, and I can try to improve on the next test."

Students who cope well with testing take a practical attitude and try to do the best they can, even under trying circumstances. With practice, most students can learn to be less testy at test time (Zeidner, 1995).

Circadian Rhythms

We have seen that moment-to-moment changes in activation can have a major impact on performance. What about larger cycles of arousal? Do they also affect energy levels, motivation, and performance? Scientists have long known that the body operates like a finely tuned instrument, guided by internal "biological clocks." *Every 24 hours, your body undergoes a cycle of changes* called **circadian** (SUR-kay-dee-AN) **rhythms** (*circa*: about; *diem*: a day) (Orlock, 1993).

Throughout the day, large changes take place in body temperature, blood pressure, urine volume, and amino acid levels (Fig. 13–9 ◆). Also affected are the activities of the liver, kidneys, and endocrine glands. These activities, and

Figure 13–9 ◆ Core body temperature is a good indicator of a person's circadian rhythm. Most people reach a low point 2-3 hours before their normal waking time. It's no wonder that both the Chernobyl and Three-Mile Island nuclear power plant accidents occurred around 4 A.M. Rapid travel to a different time zone, shift work, depression, and illness can throw sleep and waking patterns out of synchronization with the body's core rhythm. Mismatches of this kind are very disruptive (Hauri & Linde, 1990).

many others, peak sometime each day. Output of the hormone adrenaline, which arouses the body, is often 3 to 5 times greater during the day. Most people are more energetic and alert at the high point of their circadian rhythms (Natale & Cicogna, 1996).

Differences in such peaks are so basic that when a "day person" rooms with a "night person," both are more likely to give their relationship a negative rating (Carey et al., 1988). This is easy to understand: What could be worse than having someone bounding around cheerily when you're half asleep, or the reverse?

Shift Work and Jet Lag Circadian rhythms are most noticeable whenever there is a major shift in time schedules. It is well documented, for example, that businesspersons, diplomats, athletes, and other time zone travelers tend to make errors or perform poorly when their body rhythms are disturbed (Rader & Hicks, 1987).

If you travel great distances east or west, the peaks and valleys of your circadian rhythms will be out of phase with the sun and clocks. For example, you might find that your period of peak arousal is at midnight. Your low point, in contrast, occurs during the middle of the day (return to Fig. 13–9). Shift work has the same effect, causing fatigue, inefficiency, irritability, upset stomach, and depression (Akerstedt, 1990).

How fast do people adapt to time shifts?

For major time zone shifts (5 hours or more) it can take from several days to 2 weeks to resynchronize. Adaptation to jet

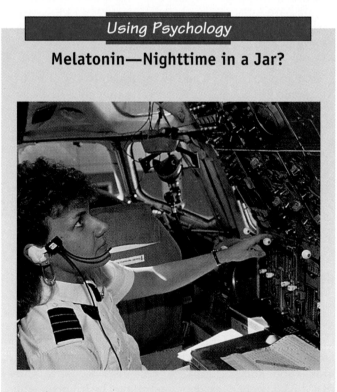

Figure 13–10 ◆ Time required to adjust to air travel across six time zones. The average time to resynchronize was shorter for westbound travel than for eastbound flights. (Data from Beljan et al., 1972; cited by Moore-Ede et al., 1982.)

lag is slowest when you stay indoors, where you can sleep and eat on "home time." Getting outdoors, where you must sleep, eat, and socialize on the new schedule, speeds adaptation. A 5-hour dose of bright sunlight early each day is particularly helpful for resetting your circadian rhythm in a new time zone (Czeisler et al., 1989). The same principle can be applied to shift work by bathing workers in bright light during their first few night shifts (Eastman et al., 1994).

The *direction* of travel also affects adaptation (Harma et al., 1994). If you fly west, adapting is relatively easy, taking an average of 4 to 5 days. If you fly east, adapting takes 50 percent longer, or more (Fig. 13–10 ◆). Why is there a difference? The answer is that when you fly east the sun comes up *earlier* (relative to your "home" time). Let's say that you live in Los Angeles and fly to New York. Getting up at 7 A.M. in New York will be like getting up at 4 A.M. in Los Angeles. If you fly west the sun comes up later. As you may recall from Chapter 8, the sleep-waking cycle naturally runs longer than 24 hours. For this reason, it's easier for most people to "advance" (stay up later and sleep in) than it is to shift backward. Likewise, work shifts that "rotate" backward (night, evening, day) are more disruptive than those that advance (day, evening, night). Best of all are work shifts that do not change: Even continuous night work is less upsetting than rotating shifts (Williamson & Sanderson, 1986).

What does all of this have to do with those of us who are not shift workers or world travelers?

There are few college students who have not at one time or another "burned the midnight oil," especially for final exams. During any strenuous period, it is wise to remember that departing from your regular schedule is likely to cost more than it's worth. Often, you can do as much during 1 hour in the morning as you could have in 3 hours of work after midnight. The 2-hour difference in efficiency might as well be spent sleeping. If you feel you must deviate from your normal schedule, do it gradually over a period of days.

In general, if you can anticipate an upcoming body rhythm change (when traveling, before finals week, or when doing shift work), it is best to *preadapt* to your new schedule. **Preadaptation** *is the gradual matching of sleep-waking cycles to a new time schedule.* Before traveling, for instance, you should go to sleep one hour later (or earlier) each day until your sleep cycle matches the time at your destination. If you are unable to do that, it at least helps to fly early in the day when you fly east. When you fly west, it is better to fly late. (Remember, the E in *east* matches the E in *early*.) The following highlight has one more bit of advice.

Using Psychology

Melatonin—Nighttime in a Jar?

Flight crews often suffer severe disruptions in their sleep cycles. For example, a crew that leaves Los Angeles at 4 P.M., bound for London, will arrive in 8 hours. Crew members' bodies, which are on California time, will act as if it is 12 A.M. Yet in London, it will be 8 A.M. Recent studies confirm that melatonin can help people adjust more rapidly to such time-zone changes.

The latest studies of flight crews show that jet lag can be minimized by taking a synthetic hormone called *melatonin* (mel-ah-TONE-in). **Melatonin** *is normally produced at night by the pineal gland and suppressed during daylight* (Brown, 1994).

Melatonin has a strong impact on the timing of body rhythms and sleep cycles. As far as the brain is concerned, it's bedtime when melatonin levels rise (Attenburrow, Cowen, & Sharpley, 1996).

To reset the body's clock in a new time zone, a small amount of melatonin can be taken about an hour before bedtime. This dose is continued for as many days as necessary to ease jet lag. The same treatment can be used for rotating work shifts, too (Arendt, 1994; Brown, 1994; Comperatore et al., 1996).

Learned Motives—The Pursuit of Excellence

Many motives are acquired directly. It is easy enough to see that praise, money, success, pleasure, and similar reinforcers affect our goals and desires. But how do people learn to enjoy activities that are at first painful or frightening? Why do people climb rocks, jump out of airplanes, run marathons, take sauna baths, or swim in frozen lakes? For an answer, let's examine a related situation.

When a person first tries a drug such as heroin, he or she feels a "rush" of pleasure. However, as the drug wears off, discomfort and craving occurs. The easiest way to end the discomfort is to take another dose—as most drug users quickly learn. But in time, habituation takes place; the drug stops producing pleasure, although it will end discomfort. At the same time, the aftereffects of the drug grow more painful. At this point, the drug user has acquired a powerful new motive. In a vicious cycle, heroin relieves discomfort, but it guarantees that withdrawal will occur again in a few hours.

Opponent-Process Theory

Psychologist Richard Solomon (1980) offers an intriguing explanation for drug addiction and other learned motives. According to his **opponent-process theory,** *if a stimulus causes a strong emotion, such as fear or pleasure, an opposite emotion tends to occur when the stimulus ends.* For example, if you are in pain, and the pain ends, you will feel a pleasant sense of relief. If a person feels pleasure, as in the case of drug use, and the pleasure ends, it will be followed by craving or discomfort. If you are in love and feel good when you are with your lover, you will be uncomfortable when she or he is absent.

What happens if the stimulus is repeated?

Solomon assumes that when a stimulus is repeated, our response to it habituates, or gets weaker. First-time skydivers, for instance, are almost always terrified. But with repeated jumps, fear decreases, until finally the skydiver feels a "thrill" instead of terror (Roth et al., 1996). In contrast, emotional aftereffects get stronger with repetition. After a first jump, beginning parachutists feel a brief but exhilarating sense of relief. After many such experiences, seasoned skydivers can get a "rush" of euphoria that lasts for hours after a jump (Fig. 13–11 ◆). With repetition, the pleasurable aftereffect gets stronger and the initial "cost" (pain or fear) gets weaker. The opponent-process theory thus explains how skydiving, rock climbing, ski jumping, and other hazardous pursuits become reinforcing. If you are a fan of horror movies, carnival rides, or bungee jumping, your motives may be based on the same effect. (Notice, too, the strong link between motivation and emotion in such examples. We will return to this idea later.)

Social Motives

Competition and achievement are highly valued in Western culture. In less industrialized nations, the desire to achieve may be low. Some of your friends are more interested than others in success, money, possessions, status, love, approval, grades, dominance, power, or belonging to groups. In each case we are referring to differences in *social motives* or goals. **Social motives** *are acquired in complex ways through socialization and cultural conditioning.* The behavior of outstanding

Figure 13–11 ◆ A sport parachutist takes the plunge. The typical emotional sequence for a first jump is: anxiety before, terror during, and relief after the jump. After many jumps the emotional sequence becomes: eagerness before, a thrill during, and exhilaration after a jump. The new sequence strongly reinforces skydiving.

artists, scientists, athletes, educators, and leaders is best understood in terms of such learned needs, particularly the need for achievement.

The Need for Achievement

To many people, being "motivated" means being interested in achievement. In later chapters we will investigate aggression, helping, affiliation, seeking approval, and other social motives. For now, let us focus on the need for achievement.

The **need for achievement (nAch)** can be defined as *a desire to meet some internalized standard of excellence* (McClelland, 1961). The person with high needs for achievement strives to do well in any situation in which evaluation takes place.

Is that like the aggressive businessperson who strives for success?

Power   Not necessarily. Needs for achievement may lead to wealth and prestige, but a person who is a high achiever in art, music, science, or amateur athletics may strive for excellence without seeking material reward. The need for achievement differs from a **need for power**, which is *a desire to have impact or control over others* (McClelland, 1975). People with strong needs for power want their importance to be visible: They buy expensive possessions, wear prestigious clothes, and exploit relationships. In some ways the pursuit of power and financial success is the dark side of the American dream. People whose main goal in life is to make lots of money tend to be poorly adjusted and unhappy (Kasser & Ryan, 1993).

Achievement   David McClelland (1958, 1961) and other psychologists have probed the effects of high or low needs for achievement. Using a simple measure of nAch, McClelland found that he could predict the behavior of high and low achievers in many situations. In one study, the occupations of college graduates were compared with scores on a need-for-achievement test given in their sophomore year. Fourteen years after graduation, those who scored high in nAch were found more often in careers involving risk and responsibility (McClelland, 1965).

Characteristics of Achievers

In front of you are five targets. Each is placed at an increasing distance from where you are standing. You are given a beanbag to toss at the target of your choice. Target A, anyone can hit; target B, most people can hit; target C, some people can hit; target D, very few people can hit; target E is rarely if ever hit. If you hit A, you will receive $2; B, $4; C, $8; D, $16; and E, $32. You get only one toss. Which one would you choose? McClelland's research

suggests that if you have a high need for achievement, you will select C or perhaps D.

Those high in nAch are *moderate* risk takers. When faced with a problem or challenge, persons high in nAch avoid goals that are too easy. That's because easy goals offer no sense of satisfaction. They also avoid long shots because there is either no hope of success, or it will be due to luck rather than skill. Persons low in nAch select either sure things or impossible goals. Either way, there is no risk of personal responsibility for failure.

Desires for achievement and calculated risk taking lead to success in many situations. People high in nAch complete difficult tasks, they earn better grades, and they tend to excel in their occupations. College students high in nAch attribute success to their own ability, and failure to insufficient effort. Thus, high nAch students are more likely to renew their efforts when they perform poorly. When the going gets tough, high achievers get going.

In college, a great deal of importance is placed on academic achievement. In light of this, it is understandable that students are sometimes tempted to buy self-help tapes that promise to improve their motivation to study. Such tapes are aggressively advertised and available in many campus bookstores. However, if you're ever tempted to buy one of these tapes, you should ask a crucial question: Do they work?

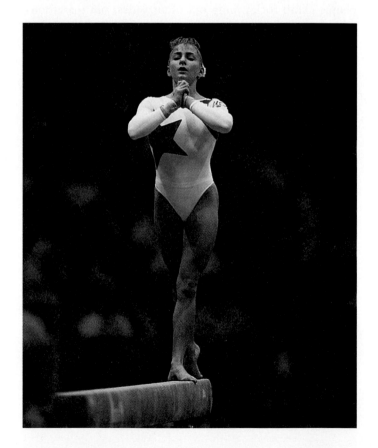

The person with high needs for achievement strives to do well in any situation in which evaluation takes place.

Mail-Order Motivation?

Each year, consumers spend millions of dollars on so-called "subliminal" self-help audiotapes. These tapes supposedly contain messages presented below the level of conscious awareness. Usually, "subliminal messages" are embedded in relaxing music or the soothing sounds of ocean waves. The tapes are purported to "subconsciously" influence motivation to help listeners lose weight, relieve pain, gain intimacy, succeed financially, improve grades, and so forth. Do the tapes work? Tanya Russell, Wayne Rowe, and Albert Smouse (1991) decided to test them under controlled conditions.

Russell, Rowe, and Smouse obtained the tapes "Improve Study Habits" and "Passing Exams" from the largest U.S. manufacturer of subliminal audiotapes. Three groups of university students took part in a 10-week evaluation. An "active treatment group" listened to tapes containing subliminal suggestions. An "inactive treatment group" listened to placebo tapes with ocean wave sounds but no subliminal messages. Students in a control group did not listen to any tapes.

The results of the experiment were certainly not subliminal. The message came through loud and clear: Average final exam grades and semester grade point averages for all three groups revealed no effects or benefits from listening to the tapes (Russell, Rowe, & Smouse, 1991). People who think they have been helped by subliminal tapes apparently have experienced nothing more than a placebo effect (Benoit & Thomas, 1992; Greenwald et al., 1991; Merikle & Skanes, 1992; Moore, 1995; Staum & Brotons, 1992).

Fear of Success

Have you ever hidden your talents in favor of blending into a group? Have you ever backed off from "winning" in sports or school? Have you ever "played dumb" with friends? Everyone has probably done so at times. Each of these actions involves a **fear of success** (*actively avoiding success*). Obviously, fear of success can stifle efforts to achieve. Do you fear success?

Who's Afraid of a Little Success?

With which of the following statements do you agree?

1. I am happy only when I am doing better than others.
2. Achievement commands respect.
3. It is extremely important for me to do well in all things that I undertake.
4. Often the cost of success is greater than the reward.

5. I believe that successful people are often sad and lonely.
6. I think success has been emphasized too much in our culture. (Zuckerman & Allison, 1976)

Agreement with the first three statements shows a positive attitude toward success. People who agree with the last three statements tend to avoid success.

Why would anyone dodge success? Most often because: (1) success can require a stressful shift in self-concept; (2) many people fear rejection when they stand out in a group; and (3) some people fear the extra demands of being a "successful person" (Tresemer, 1977). All three reasons are illustrated by a secretary who quit when she was offered a job as a supervisor. When asked why she quit, she said it was because she didn't want to be a "career woman," because she feared her former friends in the office would reject her, and because she disliked telling others what to do.

Do fears of success occur mainly in women?

Both men and women are subject to general success fears (Canavan, 1989; Kearney, 1984). But there is often an extra conflict for women, who may consider it "unfeminine" to excel. Thus, for many women the issue is not literally a fear of success. Rather, it is a conflict between achievement and social acceptance (Hyland, 1989; Pfost & Fiore, 1990; Sancho & Hewitt, 1990). Understandably, then, successful women are most often those who define achievement as an acceptable feminine quality. Perhaps changing attitudes will help remove this unnecessary stumbling block for future generations of talented and aspiring women.

It might seem that avoiding success is always undesirable. In reality, an overemphasis on achievement can be just as big a handicap. Our society is notorious for its successful but unhappy workaholics. In the final analysis, a truly successful life strikes a balance between achievement and other needs.

The Key to Success?

What does it take to achieve extraordinary success? Psychologist Benjamin Bloom did an interesting study of America's top concert pianists, Olympic swimmers, sculptors, tennis players, mathematicians, and research neurologists. Bloom (1985) found that drive and determination, not great natural talent, led to exceptional success.

The first steps toward high achievement began when parents exposed the child to music, swimming, scientific ideas, and so forth, "just for fun." At first many of the children were quite ordinary in their skills. One Olympic swimmer, for instance, remembers repeatedly losing races as a 10-year-old. At some point, however, the children began to more actively cultivate their abilities. Before long, parents noticed the child's rapid progress and sought out an expert instructor or coach. After more successes, the youngsters began "living" for their talent, practicing many hours daily.

This continued for many years before they reached truly extraordinary heights of achievement.

The upshot of Bloom's work is that talent is nurtured by dedication and hard work. This is most likely to happen when parents give wholehearted support to a child's special interest and emphasize doing one's best at all times. Studies of child prodigies and eminent adults also show that intensive practice and expert instruction are common ingredients of high achievement. Elite performance in music, sports, chess, the arts, and many other pursuits requires at least 10 years of dedicated practice (Ericsson & Charness, 1994). The old belief that "talent will out" of its own accord is largely a myth. This is especially true for talented women who may face a wide variety of social obstacles to exceptional achievement (Noble, Subotnik, & Arnold, 1996).

Achieving elite performance may be reserved for the dedicated few. Nevertheless, there is much that anyone can do to improve everyday motivation.

- Set goals that are specific and challenging, but attainable.
- Advance in small steps.
- When you first acquire a skill, your goal should be to make progress in learning. Later, you can concentrate on improving your performance, compared with other people.
- Get expert instruction that helps you master the skill.
- Find a skilled model (someone good at the skill) to emulate.
- Get support and encouragement from an observer.
- If you fail, regard it as a sign that you need to try harder, not that you lack ability.

(Druckman & Bjork, 1994.)

Self-Confidence—Keeping Your Eye on the Goal

Self-confidence is one of the most important sources of motivation. A person with **self-confidence** believes she or he can successfully carry out an activity or reach a goal. That's why self-confidence affects motivation: It influences the challenges you will undertake, the effort you will make, and how long you will persist when things don't go well.

To enhance self-confidence, it is wise to do the following:

Motives in Perspective—A View from the Pyramid

As you may recall from Chapter 1, humanistic psychologist Abraham Maslow defined self-actualization as the full development of personal potential. As a sidelight to his work on self-actualization, Maslow proposed that there is a **hierarchy of human needs.** By this he meant that *some needs are more basic or powerful than others.* Think for a moment about the needs that influence your behavior. Which seem strongest? Which do you spend the most time and energy satisfying? Now look at Maslow's hierarchy (Fig. 13–12 ◆).

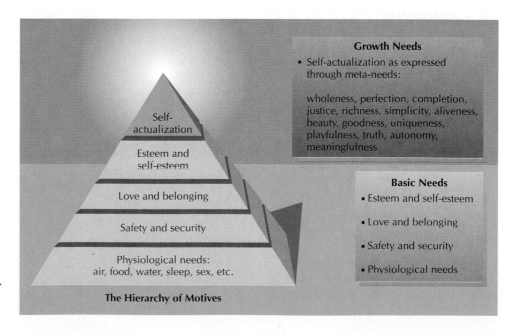

Figure 13–12 ◆ Maslow believed that lower needs in the hierarchy are dominant. Basic needs must be satisfied before growth motives are fully expressed. Desires for self-actualization are reflected in various meta-needs (see text).

Growth Needs
- Self-actualization as expressed through meta-needs:

  wholeness, perfection, completion, justice, richness, simplicity, aliveness, beauty, goodness, uniqueness, playfulness, truth, autonomy, meaningfulness

Basic Needs
- Esteem and self-esteem
- Love and belonging
- Safety and security
- Physiological needs

Self-actualization

Esteem and self-esteem

Love and belonging

Safety and security

Physiological needs: air, food, water, sleep, sex, etc.

The Hierarchy of Motives

Wheelchair athletes engage in vigorous competition. Maslow considered such behavior an expression of the need for self-actualization.

Table 13–3 ■ **Maslow's List of Meta-Needs**

Meta-needs are seen as an expression of tendencies for self-actualization, the full development of personal potential.

1. Wholeness (unity)
2. Perfection (balance and harmony)
3. Completion (ending)
4. Justice (fairness)
5. Richness (complexity)
6. Simplicity (essence)
7. Aliveness (spontaneity)
8. Beauty (rightness of form)
9. Goodness (benevolence)
10. Uniqueness (individuality)
11. Playfulness (ease)
12. Truth (reality)
13. Autonomy (self-sufficiency)
14. Meaningfulness (values)

Note that physiological needs are at the bottom. Since these are necessary for survival, they tend to be prepotent, or dominant over the higher needs. It could be said, for example, that "to a starving person, food is god."

Maslow believed that higher needs are expressed only when the prepotent physiological needs are satisfied. This is also true of needs for safety and security. Until there is a basic amount of order and stability in meeting the lower needs, a person may have little interest in higher pursuits. A person who is extremely thirsty, for instance, might have little interest in writing poetry or making small talk about the weather. For this reason, Maslow described the *first four levels of the hierarchy* as **basic needs.** Other basic needs include love and belonging (family, friendship, caring), and needs for esteem and self-esteem (recognition and self-respect).

All of the basic needs are *deficiency* motives. That is, they are activated by a *lack* of food, water, security, love, esteem, or other basic needs. At the top of the hierarchy we find **growth needs**, represented by *the need for self-actualization*. The need for self-actualization is not based on deficiencies. Rather, it is a positive, life-enhancing force for personal growth.

How are needs for self-actualization expressed?

Maslow called the less powerful but humanly important *actualization motives* **meta-needs** (Maslow, 1970). These are listed in Table 13–3 ■. According to Maslow, there is a tendency to move up the hierarchy to the meta-needs. A person whose survival needs are met, but whose meta-needs are unfulfilled, falls into a "syndrome of decay." Such people experience despair, apathy, and alienation.

Maslow's point is that mere survival or comfort is usually not enough to make a full and satisfying life. It's interesting to note, in this regard, that college students who are primarily concerned with financial success, personal appearance, and social recognition score lower than average in vitality, self-actualization, and general well-being (Kasser & Ryan, 1996).

Maslow's hierarchy is not well documented by research, and many questions can be raised about it. How, for instance, do we explain the use of fasting as a means of social protest? How has the meta-need for justice overcome the more basic need for food? (Perhaps the answer is that fasting is temporary and self-imposed.) Despite such objections, Maslow's views have been influential as a way of understanding and appreciating the rich interplay of human motives. Rather than being a scientific theory, Maslow's hierarchy represents a philosophical viewpoint.

Did Maslow believe that many people are motivated by meta-needs?

Maslow estimated that only about one person in ten is primarily motivated by self-actualization needs. Most are more concerned with esteem, love, or security. Perhaps this is because incentives and rewards in our society are slanted to encourage conformity, uniformity, and security in schools, jobs, and relationships. When was the last time you met a meta-need?

Intrinsic and Extrinsic Motivation

Some people cook for a living and consider it hard work. Others cook for pleasure and dream of opening a restaurant.

For some people, carpentry, gardening, writing, photography, or jewelry making is fun. For others the same activities are drudgery they must be paid to do. How can the same activity be "work" for one person and "play" for another?

When you carry out an activity for enjoyment, to show your ability, or to gain skill, your motivation is usually *intrinsic*. **Intrinsic motivation** occurs when there is *no obvious external reward or ulterior purpose behind your actions.* The activity is enjoyed as an end in itself. Intrinsic motivation is closely related to the higher levels of Maslow's hierarchy. In contrast, **extrinsic motivation** stems from *obvious external factors, such as pay, grades, rewards, obligations, and approval.* Most of the activities we think of as "work" are extrinsically rewarded.

Turning Play into Work   It might seem that increasing extrinsic incentives would strengthen motivation, but this is not always the case (Lepper, Keavney, & Drake, 1996). Research with children shows that excessive rewards can undermine spontaneous interest (Ross et al., 1976). For instance, children lavishly rewarded for drawing with Magic Markers (felt-tip pens) later showed little interest in playing with them (Greene & Lepper, 1974). Apparently, "play" can be turned into "work" by *requiring* a person to do something he or she would otherwise enjoy. In general, the presence of strong extrinsic rewards tends to decrease intrinsic motivation (Tang & Hall, 1995). In addition, people are more likely to be creative when they are intrinsically motivated than when extrinsic rewards are stressed (Sternberg and Lubart, 1995).

Creativity   On the job, the *quantity* of work may be increased by salaries and bonuses. However, the *quality* of work is tied more to intrinsic factors, such as interest, freedom of action, and constructive feedback (Amabile, 1983; Kohn, 1987). Psychologist Teresa Amabile lists the following as "creativity killers" on the job:

- Working under surveillance
- Having your choices restricted by rules
- Working primarily to get a good evaluation (or avoid a bad one)
- Working mainly to get more money

When a person is intrinsically motivated, a certain amount of challenge, surprise, and complexity makes a task rewarding. That's why we tend to be more creative when motivated by enjoyment of the work itself. When extrinsic motivation is stressed, complexity, surprise, and challenge just become barriers to reaching a goal (Pittman & Heller, 1987). A person who is extrinsically motivated wants to take the fastest, most direct route to a goal. Typically, this undermines creativity (Sternberg and Lubart, 1995).

How can the concept of intrinsic motivation be applied?

Motivation can't always be intrinsic. Nor should it be. Not every worthwhile activity is intrinsically satisfying. In

People who are intrinsically motivated feel free to explore creative solutions to problems.

addition, extrinsic motivation is often needed if we are to develop enough skill or knowledge for an activity to become intrinsically rewarding. This effect can be observed in learning to read, to play a musical instrument, or to enjoy a sport.

So, both extrinsic and intrinsic motivation are necessary. But extrinsic motivation should not be overused. Greene and Lepper (1974) summarize: (1) If there is no intrinsic interest in an activity to begin with, there is nothing to lose by using extrinsic rewards; (2) if needed skills are lacking, extrinsic rewards may be necessary to begin; (3) extrinsic rewards may focus attention on an activity so that real interest can develop—this is especially true for motivating learning in children; (4) if extrinsic rewards or incentives are to be used, they should be as small as possible, used only when absolutely necessary, and faded out as soon as possible. A good rule of thumb to remember is that the more complex an activity is, the more it is hurt by extrinsic reward (Kohn, 1987).

By following these rules, you can avoid taking spontaneous interest and satisfaction out of motivation for others, especially children.

Motivation and Emotion

Intrinsic motivation is but one of the many links we find between motivation and emotion. Often, emotions rearrange the priority of goals. Let's say, for example, that you are strolling toward a market. Your goal is to reach the market and buy some groceries. Suddenly, an angry dog begins to chase you. If you find yourself running *away* from the market, fear has changed your immediate goal to self-preservation (Oatley & Jenkins, 1992).

Many of the goals we seek make us feel good. Many of the activities we avoid make us feel bad. Success is usually accompanied by pleasant emotions; failure by unpleasant emotions. For such reasons, the story of human motivation is also an emotional tale. The next section complements our discussion of motivation with a look at emotion.

Dissecting an Emotion— How Do You Feel?

If a mad scientist were to replace your best friend's brain with a computer, how would you know that something was different? One of the first telltale signs might be an absence of emotion. **Emotion** *is a state characterized by physiological arousal, changes in facial expression, gestures, posture, and subjective feelings.*

Emotion adds greatly to the meaning of life and the depth of caring in our relationships. Have you ever waited until someone was in a good mood to ask for a favor? If you have, you are aware that emotions have a powerful influence on motivation. People who are feeling happy are more likely to help others in need (O'Malley & Andrews, 1983). It is equally apparent, however, that emotions can have a negative impact. Hate, anger, contempt, disgust, and fear all disrupt behavior and relationships.

The root of the word *emotion* means "to move," and emotions do indeed move us. First, the body is physically aroused during emotion. Such bodily stirrings are what cause us to say we were "moved" by a play, a funeral, or an act of kindness. Second, we are often motivated, or moved to take action, by emotions such as fear, anger, or joy. Underlying all

this, perhaps, is the fact that emotions are linked to basic *adaptive behaviors*, such as attacking, retreating, seeking comfort, helping others, reproducing, and the like. **Adaptive behaviors** *aid our attempts to survive and adjust to changing conditions* (Plutchik, 1990; 1994). Again, we must realize that emotions can be disruptive, as in having stage fright or choking up in an athletic contest. But more often, emotions aid survival.

Most people closely identify a pounding heart, sweating palms, and "butterflies" in the stomach with emotion. Indeed, **physiological changes** inside the body are a major element of fear, anger, joy, and other emotions. These changes include variations *in heart rate, blood pressure, perspiration, and other bodily stirrings.* (More on this in a moment.) Most of these reactions are caused by **adrenaline**, *a hormone produced by the adrenal glands.* Adrenaline is released into the bloodstream when the sympathetic nervous system is activated. People who have their adrenal glands removed for medical reasons display much less emotional arousal (Hepburn, Deary, & MacLeod, 1996).

Emotional expressions, *or outward signs of what a person is feeling,* are another major element of emotion. For example, when you are intensely afraid, your hands tremble, your face contorts, and your posture becomes tense and defensive. Emotion is also revealed by marked shifts in voice tone or modulation. Other signs of emotion range from shrill rage to the surprisingly subdued last words on flight

Figure 13–13 ◆ How accurately do facial expressions reveal emotion? After you have guessed what emotion these people are feeling, turn to Figure 13–20.

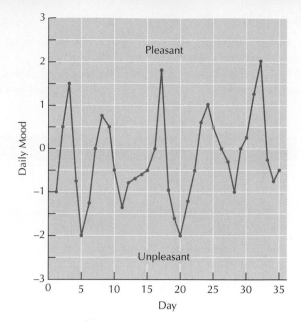

Figure 13–14 ◆ Folklore holds that people who work or attend school on a weekly schedule experience their lowest moods on "Blue Monday." Actually, moods tend to be generally lower for *most* weekdays than they are on weekends. The graph shown here plots the average daily mood ratings made by a group of college students over a 5-week period. As you can see, many people find that their moods rise and fall on a 7-day cycle. For most students, a low point tends to occur around Monday or Tuesday and a peak on Friday or Saturday. (Adapted from Larsen & Kasimatis, 1990.) In other words, moods are often entrained (pulled along) by weekly schedules.

recorders after air disasters (a common last word is "Damn," spoken calmly). Such emotional expressions are particularly important because they communicate emotion from one person to another (Fig. 13–13 ◆). A final major element consists of **emotional feelings,** or a person's *private emotional experience.* This is the part of emotion with which we are typically most familiar.

Primary Emotions

Are some emotions more basic than others?

Based on his research, Robert Plutchik (1990, 1994) believes there are eight **primary emotions: fear, surprise, sadness, disgust, anger, anticipation, joy,** and **acceptance** (receptivity). If the list seems too short, it's because each emotion can vary in *intensity.* Anger, for instance, may vary from rage to simple annoyance.

The mildest forms of various emotions are called *moods* (Fig. 13–14 ◆). A **mood** *is a low intensity, long-lasting emotional state.* Moods act as a subtle emotional undercurrent that affects day-to-day behavior (Clark & Williamson, 1989). Emotions typically last from a few seconds to a few hours. Moods can last for many hours, or even days. Moods often prepare us to act in certain ways. For example, when your neighbor Roseanne is in an irritable mood she may react angrily to almost anything you say. When she is in a happy mood she can easily laugh off an insult (Oatley & Jenkins, 1992). Our moods are closely tied to circadian rhythms. When body temperature is at its daily low point, people tend to feel "down," emotionally. When body temperature is at its peak, your mood is likely to be positive—even if you missed a night of sleep (Boivin, Czeisler, & Waterhouse, 1997).

One of Plutchik's most interesting ideas concerns the mixing of primary emotions. As shown in Figure 13–15 ◆, each pair of adjacent emotions can be mixed to yield a third,

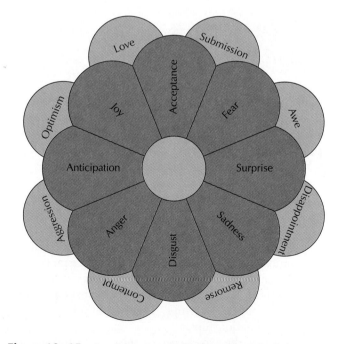

Figure 13–15 ◆ Primary and mixed emotions. In Robert Plutchik's model there are eight primary emotions, as listed in the inner areas. Adjacent emotions may combine to give the emotions listed around the perimeter. Mixtures involving more widely separated emotions are also possible. (Adapted from Plutchik, 1980.)

Frontal lobe
Cerebral cortex
Amygdala
Occipital lobe

Figure 13–16 ◆ An amygdala can be found buried within the temporal lobes on each side of the brain (see Chapter 3). The amygdala appears to provide "quick and dirty" processing of emotional stimuli that allows us to react involuntarily to danger.

more complex emotion. Other mixtures are also possible. For example, five-year-old Shannon feels both joy and fear as she eats a stolen cookie. The result? Guilt—as you may recall from your own childhood. Likewise, jealousy could be a mixture of love, anger, and fear.

The Brain and Emotion

The primary emotions we have discussed can be further reduced to just two categories: positive and negative emotions. Ordinarily, we might think that positive and negative emotions are opposites. But this is not the case. As Shannon's "cookie guilt" implies, people can experience positive and negative emotions at the same time. How is that possible? Recordings of brain activity show that positive emotions are processed mainly in the left hemisphere of the brain. In contrast, negative emotions are processed in the right hemisphere. The fact that positive and negative emotions are based on different brain areas helps explain why we can feel happy and sad at the same time ("Emotion," 1995).

Scientists used to think that all emotions are processed by the cerebral cortex. However, there is new evidence that this is not always the case. Imagine this test of willpower: Go to a zoo and place your face close to the glass in front of a rattlesnake display. Suddenly, the rattlesnake strikes at your face. Do you flinch? Even though you know you are safe, researcher Joseph LeDoux predicts that you will probably recoil from the snake's attack.

LeDoux and other researchers have found that an area of the brain called the **amygdala** (ah-MIG-duh-la) *specializes in producing fear* (Fig. 13–16 ◆). (See Chapter 3 for more information.) The amygdala receives sensory information very directly and quickly, bypassing the cortex. As a result, it allows us to respond to potentially dangerous stimuli before we really know what's happening. This primitive fear response is not under the control of higher brain centers. The role of the amygdala in emotion may explain why people who suffer from phobias and disabling anxiety often feel afraid without knowing why (LeDoux, 1996).

Later we will attempt to put all the elements of emotion together into a single picture. But first, we need to look more closely at physiological arousal and emotional expressions.

Physiology and Emotion— Arousal, Sudden Death, and Lying

To a large degree, the physical aspects of emotion are innate, or built into the body. The physical reactions of an African Bushman frightened by a wild animal and an urbane city dweller frightened by a prowler are quite similar (Mesquita & Frijda, 1992). Reactions to unpleasant emotions are especially consistent. Typically, they include muscle tension, a pounding heart, irritability, dryness of the throat and mouth, sweating, butterflies in the stomach, frequent urination, trembling, restlessness, sensitivity to loud noises, and a large number of internal changes. These reactions are nearly universal because they are caused by the **autonomic nervous system (ANS)** (*the neural system that connects the brain with the internal organs and glands*). As you may recall from Chapter 3, activity of the ANS is *automatic* and not normally under voluntary control. There are two divisions of the ANS, one called the *sympathetic branch* and the other the *parasympathetic branch*.

What do they do during emotion?

Fight or Flight

In general, the **sympathetic branch** *activates the body for emergency action*—for "fighting or fleeing." It does this by arousing a number of bodily systems and inhibiting others. (Sympathetic nervous system effects are listed in Table 13–4 ■.) These changes have a purpose. Sugar is released into the bloodstream for quick energy, the heart beats faster to supply blood to the muscles, digestion is temporarily inhibited, blood flow in the skin is restricted to reduce bleeding, and so forth. Most sympathetic reactions improve the chances of surviving an emergency.

The **parasympathetic branch** *generally reverses emotional arousal and calms and relaxes the body*. After a period of high emotion, the heart is slowed, the pupils return to normal size, blood pressure drops, and so forth. In addition to restoring balance, the parasympathetic system helps build up and conserve bodily energy.

The parasympathetic system responds much more slowly than the sympathetic system. That's why increased heart rate, muscle tension, and other signs of arousal do not fade for 20 or 30 minutes after you feel an intense emotion, such as fear. Moreover, after a strong emotional shock, the parasympathetic system may overreact and lower blood pressure too much. This is why people sometimes become

Table 13–4 ■ Autonomic Nervous System Effects

Organ	Parasympathetic System	Sympathetic System
Pupils of eyes	Constricts to diminish light	Dilates to increase light
Tear glands Mucous membranes of nose and throat Salivary glands	Stimulates secretion	Inhibits secretion, causes dryness
Heart Blood vessels	Slowing of heart, constriction of blood vessels	Acceleration of heart; dilation of blood vessels to increase blood flow
Lungs, windpipe	Constricts bronchi of lungs to relax breathing	Dilates bronchi to increase breathing
Esophagus Stomach Abdominal blood vessels	Stimulates secretion and movement	Inhibits secretion and movement, diverts blood flow
Liver	Liberates bile	Retains bile, releases blood sugar
Pancreas	Stimulates secretion	Inhibits secretion
Intestines Rectum Kidney Bladder	Excitation, expulsion of feces and urine	Inhibition, retention of feces and urine
Skin blood vessels	Dilate, increase blood flow	Constrict; skin becomes cold and clammy
Sweat glands	Inhibited	Stimulated to increase perspiration
Hair follicles	Relaxed	Tensed to make hair stand on end

dizzy or faint at the sight of blood and other such shocks (Kleinknecht, 1986).

To learn about an interesting sidelight of sympathetic arousal, let's take a brief side trip.

A Closer Look

Emotion—Do the Eyes Have It?

Is there any truth to the idea that the eyes can reveal emotion?

The eyes have long been considered "windows on the soul" and indicators of emotion. If you doubt someone's word, you may ask them to "look you in the eye." Many seasoned poker players claim to have detected a bluff by watching the eyes of their opponents. Psychologist Eckhard Hess believes that in such instances we are mainly interested in the size of a person's *pupils*. As shown in Table 13–4, emotion affects the pupils. Specifically, *arousal*, *interest*, or *attention* can activate the sympathetic nervous system and cause the pupils to dilate (enlarge).

Dilation of the pupils can occur during both pleasant and unpleasant emotions. Despite this fact, most people tend to interpret *large* pupils as a sign of pleasant feelings and *small* pupils as a sign of negative feelings. To illustrate, Hess (1975a and b) showed two photos of an attractive young woman to a group of men. In one photograph the woman's pupils were large. In the other they were small. The men consistently described the woman with large pupils as "soft," "feminine," or "pretty." The same woman, with small pupils, was described as "hard," "selfish," and "cold" (Fig. 13–17 ◆).

This effect, of course, does not apply only to women. In another experiment, subjects were introduced to two individuals of the opposite sex and asked to choose one as a partner for the experiment. One person in each pair had been given eye drops to dilate his or her pupils, and the other had not. Subjects of both sexes tended to select the person with the larger pupils as a partner. (Perhaps at long last we know why the bad guys in movies always have beady eyes!)

Figure 13–17 ◆ Select the face you think looks more attractive, warm, or friendly. Research by Eckhard Hess (1975b) suggests you will choose the face on the left because the pupils of the eyes are larger.

Sudden Death As noted, the parasympathetic system *may overreact during intense fear or after any period of intense emotion.* This response is called a **parasympathetic rebound.** When it is severe it can sometimes cause death. In times of war, combat can be so savage that some soldiers literally die of fear (Moritz & Zamchech, 1946). Apparently, such deaths are caused when the parasympathetic nervous system overreacts and slows the heart to a stop. Even in civilian life this is possible. In one case, a terrified young woman was admitted to a hospital because she felt she was going to die. A backwoods midwife had predicted that the woman's two sisters would die before their 16th and 21st birthdays. Both died as predicted. The midwife also predicted that this woman would die before her 23rd birthday. She was found dead in her hospital bed the day after she was admitted. It was two days before her 23rd birthday (Seligman, 1989). The woman was an apparent victim of her own terror.

Is the parasympathetic nervous system always responsible for such deaths?

Probably not. In the case of older persons or those with heart problems, the direct effects of sympathetic activation may be enough to bring about heart attack and collapse. For example, five times more people than usual died of heart attacks on the day of a major 1994 earthquake in Los Angeles (Leor, Poole, & Kloner, 1996). Psychiatrist George Engel (1977) studied hundreds of similar occurrences and concluded that almost half of all sudden deaths are associated with the traumatic disruption of a close relationship, such as the anniversary of the death of a loved one. Recently widowed men, for instance, have a sudden death rate 40 percent higher than married men of the same age. Clearly, relationships are one of the most potent sources of human emotional response.

Lie Detectors

Several ways of measuring bodily changes caused by the ANS have been developed. One common use of these measures is the "lie detector." However, "lie detection" must be questioned for two reasons: its accuracy is doubtful and it is often an invasion of privacy (Lykken, 1981; Saxe, 1991, 1994).

What is a lie detector? Do lie detectors really detect lies?

The lie detector is more accurately called a *polygraph* (Fig. 13–18 ◆). A **polygraph** (the word means "many writings") *is a device that records changes in heart rate, blood pressure, breathing rate, and the galvanic skin response.* (The **galvanic skin response (GSR)** is recorded from the surface of the hand by electrodes *that measure skin conductance* or, more simply, sweating.) The polygraph is popularly known as a lie detector because it is used by the police. In reality, the polygraph is not a lie detector at all. As critic David Lykken points out, there is no unique "lie response" that everyone gives when not telling the truth. The machine only records *general emotional arousal*—it can't tell the difference between lying and fear, anxiety, or excitement (Bashore & Rapp, 1993; Saxe, 1991, 1994).

When trying to detect a lie, the polygraph operator begins by asking **irrelevant** (*neutral, non-emotional*) **questions**, such as, "Is your name (person's name)?" "Did you eat lunch today?" and so forth. This establishes a "baseline" for normal emotional responsiveness. Then *relevant questions* can be asked: "Did you murder Hensley?" **Relevant questions** *are those to which only a guilty person should react.* A person who lies will presumably become anxious or emotional when answering relevant questions.

Wouldn't a person be nervous just from being questioned?

Yes, but to minimize this problem, skilled polygraph examiners ask a *series* of questions with critical items mixed among them. An innocent person may respond emotionally to the whole procedure, but only a guilty person is supposed to respond more to key questions. For example, a suspected bank robber might be shown several pictures and asked, "Was the teller who was robbed this person? Was it this person?"

As an alternative, subjects may be asked *control questions* that can be compared with critical questions (Saxe et al., 1985). **Control questions** *are designed to make almost anyone anxious:* "Have you ever stolen anything from your place of work?" Typically, control questions are very difficult to answer truthfully with an unqualified no. In theory they allow the examiner to see how a person reacts to doubt or misgivings. The person's reaction to critical questions can then be compared with responses to control questions.

Even when questioning is done properly, lie detection may be inaccurate (Dawson, 1990). For example, a man named Floyd Fay was convicted of murdering his friend Fred Ery. To prove his innocence, Fay volunteered to take a lie detector test, which he failed. Fay spent two years in prison

Figure 13–18 ◆ (*Left*) A typical polygraph includes devices for measuring heart rate, blood pressure, respiration, and galvanic skin response. Pens mounted on the top of the machine make a record of bodily responses on a moving strip of paper. (*Right*) Changes in the area marked by the arrow indicate emotional arousal. If such responses appear when a person answers a question, he or she may be lying, but other causes of arousal are also possible.

before the real killer confessed to the crime. Psychologist David Lykken (1981) has documented three such cases in which innocent people spent from one to five years behind bars after being convicted on the basis of polygraph evidence.

If Floyd Fay was innocent, why did he fail the test?

Put yourself in his place, and it's easy to see why. Imagine the examiner asking, "Did you kill Fred?" Since you knew Fred, and you are a suspect, it's no secret that this is a critical question. What would happen to *your* heart rate, blood pressure, breathing, and perspiration under such circumstances?

Proponents of lie detection claim from 90 to 95 percent accuracy. But in one laboratory experiment, accuracy was dramatically lowered when people thought about past emotional situations as they answered irrelevant questions (Ben-Shakhar & Dolev, 1996). Similarly, the polygraph may

be thrown off by self-inflicted pain, by tranquilizing drugs, or by people who can lie without anxiety (Waid & Orne, 1982). Worst of all, the test's most common error is to label an innocent person guilty, rather than a guilty person innocent (Lykken, 1981; Patrick & Iacono, 1989).

In field studies involving real crimes and criminal suspects, an average of approximately 1 innocent person in 5 was rated as guilty by the lie detector (Saxe et al., 1985). In some instances, these false positives caused 75 percent, or 3 out of 4, innocent persons to be labeled guilty. Individuals who believe the polygraph is highly accurate may actually change their statements to be consistent with the test. This, too, can leave an innocent person open to false accusations (Meyer & Youngjohn, 1991).

Despite its unreliability, you could be given a lie detector test for employment or other reasons. Should this occur, the best advice is to remain calm; then actively challenge the outcome if the machine wrongly questions your honesty.

Learning Check

See if you can correctly answer these questions.

1. Many of the physiological changes associated with emotion are caused by secretion of the hormone
   a. atropine   b. adrenaline   c. attributine   d. amoduline

2. Emotional _____ often serve to communicate a person's emotional state to others.

3. Awe, remorse, and disappointment are among the primary emotions listed by Robert Plutchik. T or F?

4. Emotional arousal is closely related to activity of the _____ nervous system.

5. The sympathetic system prepares the body for "fight or flight" by activating the parasympathetic system. T or F?

6. The parasympathetic system inhibits digestion and raises blood pressure and heart rate. T or F?

7. What bodily changes are measured by a polygraph? _____

Critical Thinking

8. Can you explain why people "cursed" by shamans or "witch doctors" sometimes actually die?

Answers:

1. b 2. expressions 3. F 4. autonomic 5. F 6. F 7. heart rate, blood pressure, breathing rate, galvanic skin response 8. In cultures where there is deep belief in magic or voodoo, a person who thinks that she or he has been cursed may become uncontrollably emotional. After several days of intense terror, a parasympathetic rebound is likely. If the rebound is severe enough, it can lead to physical collapse and death.

Expressing Emotions— Making Faces and Talking Bodies

Are human emotional expressions a carryover from more primitive and animal-like stages of human evolution? Charles Darwin thought so. Darwin (1872) observed that tigers, monkeys, dogs, and humans all bare their teeth in the same way during rage. Darwin believed that emotional expressions were retained during the course of human evolution because communicating feelings to others is an aid to survival. Today, emotional expressions give us valuable hints about what others are feeling (Oatley & Jenkins, 1992). It would be difficult to live, work, or play with others without such messages.

Are emotional expressions the same for all people?

The most basic expressions appear to be fairly universal (Fig. 13–19 ◆). Children who are born deaf and blind have little opportunity to learn emotional expressions from others.

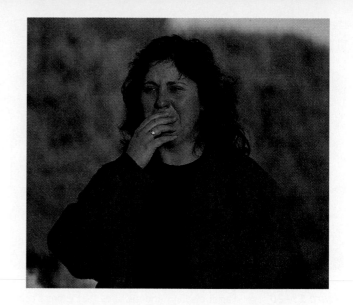

The expression of emotion is strongly influenced by learning. As you have no doubt observed, women cry more often, longer, and more intensely than men do. Men begin learning early in childhood to suppress crying—possibly to the detriment of their emotional health (Williams & Morris, 1996).

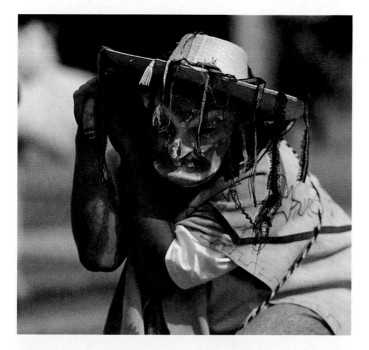

Figure 13–19 ◆ Facial expressions of anger often act as a warning of threat or impending attack. Is anger expressed the same way in different cultures? A study of masks from 18 cultures found that those meant to be frightening or threatening were strikingly similar. Shared features included angular, diagonal, or triangular eyes, eyebrows, nose, cheeks, and chin, together with an open, downward-curved mouth. (Keep this list in mind next Halloween.) Obviously, the pictured mask is not meant to be warm and cuddly. Your ability to "read" its emotional message suggests that basic emotional expressions have universal biological roots (Aronoff, Barclay, & Stevenson, 1988).

Even so, they use the same facial gestures as others to display joy, sadness, disgust, and so on. In fact, the gestures of such children may be one of the few examples of "pure" emotional expression.

By adulthood, most people have learned to control facial expressions so that many gestures become unique to various cultures. Among the Chinese, for example, sticking out the tongue is a gesture of surprise, not of disrespect or teasing. If a person comes from a culture different from your own, it is wise to remember that you can easily misunderstand that person's emotional expressions. Also, different emotions may produce similar expressions. For example, disappointment, sadness, remorse, and guilt all look pretty much alike. At such times, it is important to know the social *context* in which the expression occurred (Ekman, 1993). Situations provide strong cues that affect our interpretations of what others are feeling (Carroll & Russell, 1996).

Despite such variations, facial expressions of *fear, anger, disgust, sadness,* and *happiness* (enjoyment) are recognized by people of all cultures. *Contempt, surprise,* and *interest* may also be universal, although researchers are less certain of these expressions (Ekman, 1993). Notice that this list covers most of the primary emotions described earlier. It's also nice to note that a smile is the most universal and easily recognized facial expression of emotion.

Body Language If a friend approached you and said, "Hey, ugly, what are you doing?" would you be offended? Probably not, because such expressions are usually accompanied by a big grin. The facial and bodily gestures of emotion speak a language all their own and add an additional message to what is said verbally. *The study of communication through body movement, posture, gestures, and facial expressions* is called

Figure 13–20 ◆ Facial displays and gestures that express complex emotions can be difficult to judge accurately. The agonized expression on the face of Frank De Vito is deceptive. When this photograph was taken, Mr. De Vito and his wife had just learned that he won $1 million in a state lottery.

kinesics (kih-NEEZ-iks). Informally, we call it body language. To see a masterful use of body language, turn off the sound on TV sometime and watch a popular entertainer or politician at work.

Body language can have powerful effects. In a recent study, people watched 30-second silent video clips of college professors' body language. Then the observers rated the professors. Amazingly, their ratings were highly similar to end-of-semester student ratings of the same professors (Ambady & Rosenthal, 1993).

What kinds of messages are sent with body language?

Popular books on body language tend to list particular meanings for gestures. For instance, a woman who stands rigidly, crosses her arms over her chest, or sits with her legs tightly crossed is supposedly sending a "hands off" message. But researchers in the field of kinesics emphasize that gestures are rarely this fixed in meaning. The message might simply be, "This room is cold."

It is also important to realize that gestures vary in meaning in different cultures. What, for instance, does it mean if you touch your thumb and first finger together to form a circle? In North America it means "Everything is fine" or "A-okay." In France and Belgium it means "You're worth zero." In southern Italy it means "You're an ass!" (Ekman et al., 1984). Thus, when the layer of culturally defined meanings is removed, it is more realistic to say that an overall **emotional tone** (*underlying emotional state*) is communicated by body language.

The human face is capable of producing some 20,000 different expressions, which makes it the most expressive part of the body. Most of these are **facial blends,** *that mix two or more basic expressions*. Imagine, for example, that you just

received an F on an unfair test. Quite likely, your eyes, eyebrows, and forehead would show anger, while your mouth would express sadness.

Most of us believe we can fairly accurately tell what others are feeling by observing facial expressions. If thousands of facial blends occur, how do we make such judgments? The answer seems to lie in the fact that facial expressions can be boiled down to basic dimensions of **pleasantness-unpleasantness, attention-rejection,** and **activation** (*or arousal*) (Schlosberg, 1954). If you smile when you give a friend a hard time, you add the emotional message of pleasantness and acceptance to the verbal insult, which changes its meaning. As they say in movie Westerns, it makes a big difference to "Smile when you say that, partner."

Other emotional feelings are telegraphed by the body. The most general seem to be **relaxation** or **tension,** and **liking** or **disliking.** Relaxation is expressed by casually positioning the arms and legs, leaning back (if sitting), and spreading the arms and legs. Liking is expressed mainly by leaning toward a person or object. Thus, body positioning can reveal feelings that would normally be concealed. Who do you "lean toward"?

Imagine that you are standing 30 yards from a classroom in which test grades are being announced. As students file out, do you think you could tell—without the aid of facial expressions—who got an A and who got an F? Actually, your task might not be too difficult. Overall *posture* can also indicate one's emotional state. Specifically, when a person is successful, his or her posture is likely to be more erect (Weisfeld & Beresford, 1982) (Fig. 13–21 ◆). Psychologists debate whether this tendency is a product of evolution or is simply learned. In any case, standing tall with pride and slumping with dejection do seem to be consistent patterns.

Emotions are often unconsciously revealed by gestures and body positioning.

Figure 13-21 ◆ Posture and success. These drawings show the end points of a five-point scale used to measure erectness of posture. Success by people in various situations was found to be reflected by a more upright posture. (Adapted from Weisfeld & Beresford, 1982.)

Does body positioning or movement ever reveal lying or deception?

If you know a person well, you may be able to detect deception from expressive changes. But don't count on it. Most people learn to maintain careful control over their facial expressions. A good example is smiling so you won't hurt someone's feelings when you have received a disappointing gift. Because of such control, deception is often best revealed by body language (Ekman & O'Sullivan, 1991). Even a good con artist may be too busy attending to his or her words and face to control certain bodily clues.

Using Psychology

Behavioral Lie Catching

The salesman swears that he is giving you "the buy of a lifetime." If you can't touch his tongue to a hot knife, how else can you tell if he's lying? Most people assume that shifty eyes and squirming are clear signs of lying. But Paul Ekman (1986) found that neither of these clues increases when a person is fibbing. Also contrary to what you might expect, nervous movements that involve touching one's own body (rubbing, grooming, scratching, twisting hair, rubbing hands, biting lips, stroking the chin, and so on) are not consistently related to lying.

On the other hand, the *gestures people use to illustrate what they are saying* may reveal lying. These gestures, called **illustrators**, tend to *decrease* when a person is telling a lie. In other words, persons who usually "talk with their hands" may be much less animated when they are lying.

Other movements, called *emblems*, can also reveal lying. **Emblems** *are gestures that have widely understood meanings within a particular culture.* Some examples are the thumbs-up sign, the A-Okay sign, the middle-finger insult, a head nod for yes, and a head shake for no. Emblems tend to *increase* when a person is lying. More importantly, they often reveal true feelings contrary to what the liar is saying. For example, a person might smile and say, "Yes, I'd love to try some of your homemade candied pig's feet," while slowly shaking her head from side to side.

Among the best clues to lying are the signs of strong emotion produced by the ANS. These include blinking, blushing, blanching, pupil dilation, rapid or irregular breathing, perspiration, frequent swallowing, speech errors, and a louder, higher-pitched voice. All of these clues are hard for the liar to censor. But such clues are like the polygraph: They reveal emotions; they do not always mean a person is lying. Remember, good liars can fool most people most of the time—and that's no lie (Ekman & O'Sullivan, 1991).

Theories of Emotion— Several Ways To Fear a Bear

Is it possible to explain what takes place during emotion? How are arousal, behavior, cognition, expression, and feelings interrelated?

Theories of emotion offer different answers to these questions. Let's investigate some of the most prominent views. Each appears to have a part of the truth, so we will try to put them all together in the end.

The James-Lange Theory (1884–1885)

Common sense tells us that we see a bear, feel fear, become aroused, and run (and sweat and yell). But psychologists have questioned this order of events. In the 1880s, American psychologist William James (the functionalist) and Danish psychologist Carl Lange proposed that common sense had it backward. According to James and Lange, bodily arousal (such as increased heart rate) does not follow a feeling such as fear. Instead, they argued, *emotional feelings follow bodily arousal.* Thus, we see a bear, run, are aroused, and *then* feel fear as we become aware of our bodily reactions.

To support this line of thought, James pointed out that we often do not experience an emotion until after reacting. For example, imagine that you are driving and that a car suddenly pulls out in front of you. You swerve and skid to an abrupt halt at the side of the road. Only after you have come to a stop do you notice your pounding heart, rapid breathing, and tense muscles—and recognize your fear.

The Cannon-Bard Theory (1927)

American physiologist Walter Cannon and his student Phillip Bard found a number of reasons to question the James-Lange theory. While agreeing that the body becomes stirred up during emotion, Cannon (1932) and Bard proposed that emotional feelings and bodily arousal are both organized in the brain. In their theory, seeing a bear activates the thalamus, which in turn alerts both the cortex and the hypothalamus for action. The cortex is responsible for emotional feelings and emotional behavior. The hypothalamus is responsible for arousing the body. Thus, if the bear is seen as dangerous, bodily arousal, running, and feelings of fear will all be generated *at the same time* by brain activity.

Schachter's Cognitive Theory of Emotion (1971)

The previous theories are mostly concerned with physical responses. Stanley Schachter realized that cognitive (mental) factors also enter into emotion. According to Schachter, emotion occurs when a particular *label* is applied to general physical *arousal*. Schachter believes that when we are aroused, we have a need to interpret our feelings. Assume, for instance, that someone sneaks up behind you on a dark street and says, "Boo!" No matter who the person is, your body will be aroused (pounding heart, sweating palms, and so on). If the person is a total stranger, you may interpret this arousal as fear; if the person is a close friend, the arousal may be labeled as surprise or delight. The label (such as anger, fear, or happiness) applied to bodily arousal is influenced by past experience, the situation, and the reactions of others.

Support for the cognitive theory of emotion comes from an experiment in which subjects watched a slapstick movie (Schachter & Wheeler, 1962). Before viewing the movie, one third of the subjects received an injection of adrenaline, one third got a placebo injection, and the remaining subjects were given a tranquilizer. Subjects who received the adrenaline rated the movie funniest and showed the most amusement while watching it. In contrast, those given the tranquilizer were least amused, and the placebo group fell in between.

According to the cognitive theory of emotion, individuals who received adrenaline had a stirred-up body, but no explanation for the way they were feeling. Consequently, they became happy when the movie implied that

Table 13–5	Three Classic Theories of Emotion

James-Lange theory States that emotional feelings follow bodily arousal and come from awareness of such arousal.
Cannon-Bard theory States that activity in the thalamus causes emotional feelings and bodily arousal to occur simultaneously.
Cognitive theory States that emotions occur when physical arousal is labeled or interpreted on the basis of experience and situational cues.

their arousal was due to amusement. This and similar experiments make it clear that emotion is much more than just an agitated body. Perception, experience, attitudes, judgment, and many other mental factors also affect emotion. Schachter would predict, then, that if you met a bear, you would be aroused. If the bear seemed unfriendly, you would interpret your arousal as fear, and if the bear offered to shake your "paw," you would be happy, amazed, and relieved! (Table 13–5 ■ summarizes the three classic theories of emotion.)

Attribution We now move from slapstick movies and fear of bear bodies to appreciation of bare bodies. Researcher Stuart Valins (1967) added an interesting wrinkle to Schachter's theory of emotion. According to Valins, *arousal can be attributed to various sources*—a process that alters perceptions of emotion. To demonstrate such **attribution**, Valins (1966)

Which theory of emotion best describes the reactions of these people? Given the complexity of emotion, each theory appears to possess an element of truth.

showed male college students a series of slides of nude females. While watching the slides, each subject heard an amplified heartbeat that he believed was his own. In reality, subjects were listening to a recorded heartbeat carefully designed to beat *louder* and *stronger* when some (but not all) of the slides were shown.

After viewing the slides, each subject was asked to say which slide he found most attractive. Students exposed to the false heartbeat consistently rated slides paired with a "pounding heart" as the most attractive. In other words, when a student saw a slide and heard his heartbeat become more pronounced, he attributed his "emotion" to the slide. His interpretation seems to have been, "Now that one I like!" His next reaction, perhaps, was "But why?" Later research suggests that subjects persuade themselves that the slide really is more attractive in order to explain their apparent arousal (Truax, 1983).

That seems somewhat artificial. Does it really make any difference what arousal is attributed to?

Yes. To illustrate how attribution works in the "real world," consider what happens when parents interfere with the budding romance of a son or daughter. Often, trying to break up a young couple's relationship *intensifies* their feelings for one another. Parental interference adds frustration, anger, and fear or excitement (as in seeing each other "on the sly") to the couple's feelings. Since they already care for one another, they are likely to attribute all this added emotion to "true love" (Walster, 1971).

Attribution theory predicts that you are most likely to "love" someone who gets you stirred up emotionally, even when fear, anger, frustration, or rejection is part of the formula. Thus, if you want to successfully propose marriage, take your intended to the middle of a narrow, windswept suspension bridge over a deep chasm and look deeply into his or her eyes. As your beloved's heart pounds wildly (from being on the bridge, not from your irresistible charms), say, "I love you." Attribution theory predicts that your companion will conclude, "Oh wow, I must love you too."

The preceding is not as farfetched as it may seem. In an ingenious study, a female experimenter interviewed men in a park, some on a swaying suspension bridge 230 feet above a river, and others on a solid wooden bridge just 10 feet above the ground. After the interview, each subject was given the experimenter's telephone number, so he could "find out about the results" of the study if he wanted to. Men interviewed on the suspension bridge were much more likely to give the "lady from the park" a call (Dutton & Aron, 1974). Apparently, these men experienced heightened arousal, which they interpreted as attraction to the experimenter—a clear case of love at first fright! (Love is discussed further in this chapter's Exploration and Chapter 20.)

The Facial Feedback Hypothesis

Schachter added thinking and interpretation (cognition) to our view of emotion, but the picture still seems incomplete. What about emotional expressions? How do they influence emotion? As Charles Darwin observed, the face seems very central to emotion. Is it really just an "emotional billboard"?

Psychologist Carrol Izard (1977, 1990) was among the first to suggest that the face does, indeed, affect emotion. According to Izard and others, emotional activity causes innately programmed changes in facial expression. *Sensations from the face then provide cues to the brain that help us determine what emotion we are feeling.* This idea is known as the **facial feedback hypothesis** (Adelmann & Zajonc, 1989). Stated another way, it says that having facial expressions and becoming aware of them is what leads to emotional experience. Exercise, for instance, arouses the body, but this arousal is not experienced as emotion because it does not trigger emotional expressions.

Psychologist Paul Ekman takes the idea one step further. Ekman believes that "making faces" can actually cause emotion (Ekman, 1993). In one study, he and his colleagues carefully guided subjects as they arranged their faces, muscle by muscle, into expressions of surprise, disgust, sadness, anger, fear, and happiness (Fig. 13–22 ◆). At the same time, subjects' bodily reactions were monitored.

Contrary to what might be expected, "making faces" brought about changes in the autonomic nervous system, as reflected by heart rate and skin temperature. In addition, each facial expression produced a different pattern of activity. An angry face, for instance, raised heart rate and skin temperature, whereas disgust lowered heart rate and skin temperature (Ekman et al., 1983). In a related experiment, people rated how funny they thought cartoons were while holding a pen crosswise in their mouths. Those who held the pen in their teeth thought the cartoons were funnier than did people who held the pen in their lips. Can you guess why? The answer is that if you hold a pen with your teeth, you are forced to form a smile; holding it with the lips makes a frown. As predicted by the facial feedback hypothesis, subjects' emotional experiences were influenced by their facial expressions (Strack, Martin, & Stepper, 1988). Next time you're feeling sad, bite a pen!

It appears, then, that not only do emotions determine expressions, but expressions may determine emotions (Adelmann & Zajonc, 1989; Ekman, 1992). (See Table 13–6 ■). This could explain an interesting effect you have probably observed. When you are feeling "down," forcing yourself to smile will sometimes be followed by an actual improvement in your mood (Laird, 1974, 1984).

Figure 13–22 ◆ Facial feedback and emotion. Participants in Ekman's study formed facial expressions like those normally observed during emotion. When they did this, emotion-like changes took place in their bodily activity. (After Ekman et al., 1983.)

Table 13-6	Facial Muscles and Felt Emotion
Contracted Facial Muscles	**Felt Emotion**
Forehead	Surprise
Brow	Anger
Mouth (down)	Sadness
Mouth (smile)	Joy

Adelmann & Zajonc, 1989.

A Contemporary Model of Emotion

Current thought holds that each of the theories we have described is partly true. James and Lange were right that feedback from arousal and behavior adds to emotional experience. Cannon and Bard were right about the timing of events (although we now know that the amygdala provides an alternate, faster pathway to fear arousal). Schachter showed that cognition is important. Today, psychologists are increasingly aware that the way a situation is *appraised* greatly affects the course of emotion (Strongman, 1996). **Emotional appraisal** refers to *evaluating the personal meaning of a stimulus:* Is it good/bad, threatening/supportive, relevant/irrelevant, and so on. However, Schachter's theory tends to overlook the role of other parts of emotion, such as facial expressions. Also, the theory doesn't seem to fit all circum-

stances. For example, how can a child who hasn't learned to label emotion have an emotion?

In recent years many new theories of emotion have appeared. Rather than pick one "best" theory, let's put the main points of several theories together in a single **contemporary model of emotion** (Fig. 13–23 ◆).

Imagine that a large snarling dog has just lunged at you with its teeth bared. A modern view of emotion goes something like this: An *emotional stimulus* (the dog) is *appraised* (judged) as a threat or other cause for emotional response (Table 13–7 ■). (You think to yourself, "Uh oh, big trouble!") Your emotional appraisal gives rise to *ANS arousal* (your heart pounds and your body becomes stirred up). The appraisal also releases *innate emotional expressions* (your face twists into a mask of fear and your posture becomes tense). At the same time, the appraisal leads to *adaptive behavior* (running from the dog). It also causes a change in consciousness that you recognize as the subjective experience of fear. (The intensity of this *emotional feeling* is directly related to the amount of ANS arousal.)

Each element of emotion—ANS arousal, adaptive behavior, subjective experience, and emotional expressions—may feed back into your appraisal and alter it. In other words, this feedback changes your thoughts, judgments, or perceptions of emotion. Such changes further alter all of the other reactions, which again alter the appraisal or interpretation of events. Thus, emotion may blossom, change course, or diminish as it proceeds. Note too that the original emotional stimulus can be external, like the attacking dog, or internal, such as a memory of being chased by a dog, rejected by a lover, or praised by a friend. This is why mere thoughts and memories can make us fearful, sad, or happy (Strongman, 1996).

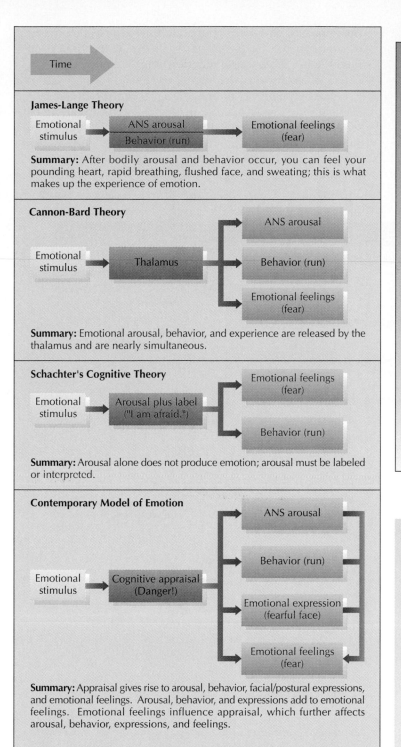

Figure 13–23 ◆ Theories of emotion.

Our discussion suggests that emotion is greatly influenced by how you think about an event. For example, if another driver "cuts you off" on the highway, you could become very angry. But if you do, you will add 5 or 10 minutes of emotional upset to your day. By changing your appraisal, you could just as easily choose to laugh at the other driver's childish behavior—and minimize the emotional wear-and-tear.

Table 13–7 ■ **Appraisals and Corresponding Emotions**

Appraisals	Emotion
You have been slighted or demeaned	Anger
You feel threatened	Anxiety
You have experienced a loss	Sadness
You have broken a moral rule	Guilt
You have not lived up to your ideals	Shame
You desire something another has	Envy
You are near something repulsive	Disgust
You fear the worst but yearn for better	Hope
You are moving toward a desired goal	Happiness
You are linked with a valued object or accomplishment	Pride
You have been treated well by another	Gratitude
You desire affection from another person	Love
You are moved by someone's suffering	Compassion

Paraphrased from Lazarus, 1991a.

Using Psychology

Emotional Intelligence—The Fine Art of Self-Control

The Greek philosopher Aristotle had a recipe for handling relationships smoothly. You must be able, he said, "to be angry with the right person, to the right degree, at the right time, for the right purpose, and in the right way." Psychologist Daniel Goleman calls such self-control "emotional intelligence." It is, he believes, a major element of a satisfying life.

Emotional intelligence refers to a combination of skills. These include *empathy, self-control, self-awareness, sensitivity to the feelings of others, persistence, and self-motivation,* among others.

People who excel in life tend to be emotionally intelligent. On the other hand, the costs of poor emotional skills can be high. They range from problems in marriage and parenting to poor physical health. A lack of emotional intelligence can ruin careers and sabotage achievement. Perhaps the greatest toll falls on children and teenagers. For them, poor emotional skills can contribute to depression, eating disorders, unwanted pregnancy, aggression, and violent crime.

Understandably, Goleman believes that schools should promote emotional competence as well as intellectual skills. The result, he feels, would be greater self-control, altruism, and compassion—all basic capacities needed if our society is to thrive (Goleman, 1995).

A Look Ahead In the next chapter we will look further at the impact of emotional appraisals, especially as they relate to coping with threats and stress. Before we continue, you might want to appraise your learning with the Learning Check questions that follow.

At one point or another, weight control becomes a challenge for many people. In this chapter's Applications section we will return to the topic of hunger to summarize some strategies for winning the battle of the bulge. After that, we will end on a positive note by exploring the powerful emotion of love.

Learning Check

1. Charles Darwin held that emotional expressions aid survival for animals. T or F?

2. A formal term for "body language" is _____ .

3. Which three dimensions of emotion are communicated by facial expressions?
   a. pleasantness-unpleasantness   b. complexity   c. attention-rejection
   d. anger   e. curiosity-disinterest   f. activation

4. According to the James-Lange theory, emotional experience precedes physical arousal and emotional behavior. (We see a bear, are frightened, and run.) T or F?

5. The Cannon-Bard theory of emotion says that bodily arousal and emotional experience occur _____ .

6. According to Schachter's cognitive theory, bodily arousal must be labeled or interpreted for an emotional experience to occur. T or F?

7. Subjects in Valin's false heart rate study attributed increases in their heart rate to the action of a placebo. T or F?

8. As you try to wiggle your ears, you keep pulling the corners of your mouth back into a smile. Each time you do, you find yourself giggling. Which of the following provides the best explanation for this reaction?
   a. attribution   b. the Cannon-Bard theory   c. appraisal   d. facial feedback

Critical Thinking

9. People with high spinal injuries may feel almost no signs of physiological arousal from their bodies. Nevertheless they still feel emotion, which can be intense at times. What theory of emotion does this observation contradict?

Answers:
1. T 2. kinesics 3. a, c, f 4. F 5. simultaneously 6. T 7. F 8. d 9. The James-Lange theory and Schachter's cognitive theory. The facial feedback hypothesis also helps explain the observation.

Applications
Behavioral Dieting—Fat Chance for a Slim Future

The goal of the previous discussion was to help you better understand a number of basic motives and emotions. In this section, we will consider an application of motivational research by looking at psychological techniques for weight control.

What can be done to control weight?

The basic approach for years has been to "diet"; that is, to restrict food intake drastically for a brief period. This, of course, is perfectly sensible in theory: You must eat less to lose weight. As noted earlier, however, most people who lose weight by dieting regain it rapidly. A recent study of an expensive commercial diet program found that most of the weight lost on the diet is regained within about four years (Walsh & Flynn, 1995).

What is really needed if one wishes to lose weight is to overhaul *eating habits and to control cues for eating*. The person who succeeds in changing eating habits can expect a permanent weight reduction. This approach, called **behavioral dieting,** is greatly superior to simple dieting for weight control. The following list summarizes several behavioral techniques that have proved helpful.

1. **Begin any weight-control program with a physical**

checkup. About 5 percent of all weight problems are physical.

2.   Get yourself committed to weight loss. Involve as many people in your program as you can. Formal programs such as Overeaters Anonymous or Take Off Pounds Sensibly can be a good source of social support (Foreyt, 1987b).

3.   Learn your eating habits by observing yourself and keeping a "diet diary." Begin by making a complete record of your eating habits for two weeks. Record when and where you eat, what you eat, and the feelings and events that occur just before and after eating. How do others around you respond to your eating? Is a roommate, relative, or spouse encouraging you to overeat?

4.   Count calories, but don't starve yourself. To lose, you must eat less, and calories allow you to keep an accurate record of your food intake. If you have trouble eating less every day, try dieting 4 days a week. People who diet intensely every other day lose as much as those who diet moderately every day (Viegener et al., 1990).

5.   Develop techniques to control the act of eating. Begin by taking smaller portions. Carry to the table only what you plan to eat. Put all other food away before leaving the kitchen. Eat slowly, finish one mouthful before taking another, sip water between bites of food, count your mouthfuls, and leave food on your plate.

Generally, avoid eating alone, since you're less likely to overeat in front of others. (One exception is eating at social events where food is plentiful and you are urged to eat. Another is eating with someone else who is overeating. In either case, eating may be facilitated.)

6.   Try to base eating on hunger, not on taste, or learned habits that dictate leaving a clean plate. When you see something really appealing, ask yourself, "Am I hungry? Do I need to eat? Or do I just want a good taste?" If your desire to eat is based on taste, turn the food down. Also, during meals, pause for a minute or two and then ask yourself, "Am I full?" If the answer is yes, stop eating (Seligman, 1994).

7.   Learn to weaken your personal eating cues. When you have learned when and where you do most of your eating, avoid these situations. Try to restrict your eating to one room, and do not read, watch TV, study, or talk on the phone while eating. Require yourself to interrupt what you are doing in order to eat. Be especially aware of the "night eating syndrome." Most calories are consumed late in the day or at night. Keep food out of sight and find things to do to keep yourself busy during this dangerous period.

8.   Avoid snacks. Buy low-calorie foods that require preparation, and fix only a single portion at a time. If you have an impulse to snack, set a timer for 20 minutes and see if you are still hungry then. Delay the impulse to snack several times if possible. Dull your appetite by filling up on raw carrots, bouillon, water, coffee, or tea.

9.   Exercise. Physical activity burns calories. Stop saving steps and riding elevators. Add activity to your routine in every way you can think of. Contrary to popular opinion, regular exercise does not increase appetite. For reasons that are not well understood, exercise lowers the body's set point for fat storage. Many psychologists are now convinced that no diet can succeed for long without an increase in exercise. Also, being fit may be more important than being fat. You can be moderately overweight and still be healthy if you get lots of exercise (Seligman, 1994).

Burning as little as 200 extra calories a day can play a major role in preventing regain of weight. A recent study found that the greatest weight loss over a two-year period was produced by regular exercise, not by dieting (Skender et al., 1996).

10.   Make a list of rewards you will receive if you change your eating habits and punishments that will occur if you don't. You may find it helpful to set up specific rewards (see Chapter 19 for more details). Don't reward yourself with food!

11.   Chart your progress daily. Record your weight, the number of calories eaten, and whether you met your daily goal. (Set realistic goals by cutting down calories gradually. Losing about a pound per week is realistic, but remember, you are changing habits, not just dieting. Diets don't work!) Take pride in your successes. Post your chart in a prominent place. This record of your progress is possibly the most important of all the techniques.

12.   Beware of relapses. Try to identify specific high-risk situations in which you are likely to overeat. Then form a plan using the principles already described to help you cope with the risk of relapse (Foreyt, 1987b). It also helps to tell yourself that a single overeating incident does not mean that you have "blown it." Faltering should be interpreted as an isolated slip, not as a sign that you might as well give up (Marlatt & Gordon, 1985).

13.   Set a "threshold" for weight control. A study of Weight Watchers members found that those who successfully maintained their weight loss had a regain limit of 3 pounds or less. In other words, if they gained more than 2 or 3 pounds, they immediately began to make corrections in their eating habits and exercise (Brownell et al., 1986).

Be patient with this program. It takes years to develop eating habits. You can expect it to take at least several months to change them. If you are unsuccessful at losing weight with these techniques, you might find it helpful to seek the aid of a psychologist familiar with behavioral weight-loss techniques.

Learning Check

1. According to behavioral dieting specialists, about 45 percent of all weight problems are physical. T or F?

2. In addition to burning calories, physical exercise can lower the body's set point. T or F?

3. For behavioral dieting you should maintain a diet diary and chart your progress, but you should avoid the trap of counting calories. T or F?

4. Those who successfully control their weight are willing to admit to themselves that they have "blown it" if they deviate from their diet. T or F?

Critical Thinking

5. Charting weight loss makes use of a behavioral principle discussed in Chapter 9, "Conditioning and Learning." Can you name it?

Answers:

1. F 2. T 3. F 4. F 5. Feedback.

Exploration

Love—Stalking an Elusive Emotion

*L*ove is one of the most intense of all human experiences. Moreover, at one time or another, most people must ask themselves, "Is this love or lust?" "Is it real or infatuation?" "What am I really feeling?" All of which raises the question: What is love? Think, for instance, about the different ways we love our parents, friends, and spouses or lovers.

How do various kinds of love differ from one another?

This is the question that led psychologist Robert Sternberg to propose his *triangular theory of love*. Although the theory is preliminary, others have confirmed the value of its core ideas (Aron & Westbay, 1996). Perhaps they will help

you think more clearly about your own loving relationships.

Love Triangles

According to Sternberg's **triangular theory of love** (1988), *love is made up of three elements: intimacy, passion, and commitment.* As you can see in Figure 13–24 ◆ each factor can be visualized as

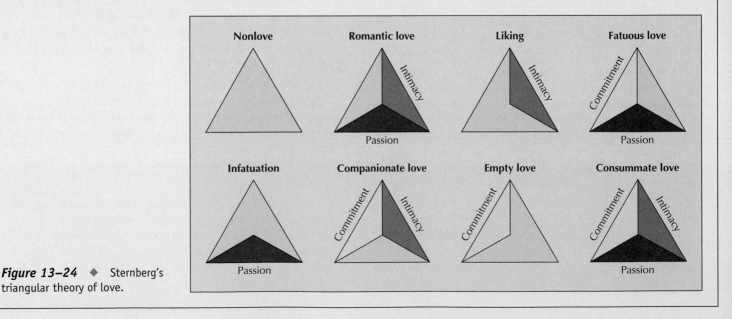

Figure 13–24 ◆ Sternberg's triangular theory of love.

one side of a triangle. Notice also that the three elements can combine to produce seven different types of love. We will return to these types in a moment, but first let's briefly explore love's three "ingredients."

Intimacy A relationship has **intimacy,** or closeness, if *affection, sharing, communication, and support* are present. Intimacy grows steadily at first, but in time it levels off. After it does, people in long-term relationships may gradually lose sight of the fact that they are still very close and mutually dependent.

Passion **Passion** refers mainly to *physiological arousal*. This arousal may be sexual, but it includes other sources too. As discussed earlier in this chapter, arousal, no matter what its cause, may be interpreted as passion in a romantic relationship (Bersheid & Walster, 1974). This is probably why passionate love often occurs against a backdrop of danger, adversity, or frustration—especially in soap operas and romance novels! Passion is the primary source of love's *intensity*. It's not surprising, then, that romance inspires the strongest feelings of love. In contrast, love for siblings is least intense (Sternberg & Grajeck, 1984).

Commitment The third side of the love triangle consists of commitment—*your decision to love another person and your degree of commitment to stay with them.* Commitment starts at zero before you meet a person and it grows steadily as you get acquainted. Like intimacy, commitment tends to level off. However, it may waver up and down with a relationship's good times and bad times. Commitment drops rapidly when a relationship is in serious trouble.

Seven Flavors of Love

The presence or absence of intimacy, passion, and/or commitment produces eight triangles. The first defines **nonlove,** a total absence of all three elements.

In **liking,** you feel close to a person and communicate well with her or him. However, you do not feel any passion or deep commitment to the person. A likable classmate might fall into this category.

Romantic love mixes intimacy (closeness and sharing) with passion (often in the form of physical attraction). Despite its intensity, romantic love does not involve much commitment at first. Think, for example, of a summer romance that ends in a relatively easy parting of ways.

Fatuous love describes commitments made rapidly on the basis of physical attraction (passion), but without much emotional intimacy. Fatuous love is of the boy-meets-girl-and-they-get-married-a-month-later type. Relationships started this way risk failure because lovers make a commitment before they really get to know each other well.

Infatuation is an even more superficial form of love. In this case a person is inflamed with passion, but shares no intimacy or commitment with the beloved. In time, of course, infatuation may lead to more lasting kinds of love.

Companionate love refers to affection and deep attachment that is built on respect, shared interests, and firm friendship. Companionate love is lower key emotionally. However, it is steady and long term and tends to grow in time. Companionate love is the "kind of affection we feel for those with whom our lives are deeply intertwined" (Walster & Walster, 1978).

Couples sometimes reach a point where there is little passion or intimacy left in their relationship. If they stay together merely out of commitment or habit, they experience **empty love.**

Consummate love occurs when two people are passionate, committed to one another, and emotionally close. Complete, balanced love of this kind occurs only in very special relationships. When all three factors are present, a relationship is more likely to be lasting (Whitley, 1993). (Table 13–8 ■ summarizes the seven types of love described here.)

How Do I Love Thee? The categories described here are certainly not the last word on love. Undoubtedly, other kinds of love also exist. In addition, Sternberg's theory may place too much emphasis on passion. In most relationships, intimacy and commitment are a bigger part of love than passion is (Clark & Reis, 1988; Tucker & Aron, 1993).

Our culture also tends to place much emphasis on passion as the main basis for "falling" in love. However, this overlooks the fact that the passionate, breathless stage of love typically lasts only about 6 to 30 months (Walster & Walster, 1978). What happens when this period ends? Quite often, people separate.

Table 13–8 ■ Seven Varieties of Love

Liking Intimacy without passion or commitment.
Romantic love Intimacy plus passion.
Fatuous love Passion with commitment, but lacking intimacy.
Infatuation Passion without commitment or intimacy.
Companionate love Intimacy and commitment without passion.
Empty love Commitment without intimacy or passion.
Consummate love Passion, intimacy, and commitment.

There is a degree of danger in expecting to live forever on a romantic cloud. People who are primarily caught up in passionate love may neglect to build a more lasting relationship. Rather than down-playing companionate love, it is helpful to realize that lovers must also be friends. High-quality relationships are frequently based on secure, companionate love (Hecht et al., 1994). In fact, consummate love is basically a blending of romantic love and companionate love.

You may be tempted to match the love triangles with your own relationships. If you do apply the theory, remember that each love relationship is a unique story, and few are perfect (Sternberg, 1995). In another study, Sternberg and Michael Barnes (1986) found that relationships are generally satisfying if you think the other person feels about you the way you would *like* for her or him to feel about you.

Some politicians have belittled the study of love as "unscientific." But in a world often wracked by violence, hatred, and despair, what could be more important than understanding the elusive state we call love?

Learning Check

1. Essentially, all types of love can be described as a passion for another person. T or F?

2. According to Sternberg's theory, all forms of love involve commitment to another person or to a relationship. T or F?

3. Passion is the primary element of infatuation. T or F?

4. Fatuous love can be defined as commitment based on passion but lacking in intimacy. T or F?

5. The passionate stage of love usually lasts only 6 to 30 weeks. T or F?

Critical Thinking

6. Passionate love tends to decline at each of three major transitions in marriage. Based on your own observations of relationships, what do you think they are?

Answers:

1. F 2. F 3. T 4. T 5. F 6. The transitions are: from engagement to marriage; from childlessness to parenthood; and from children living at home to an empty nest (Tucker & Aron, 1993).

Chapter Summary

What is motivation? Are there different types of motives?

◆ Motives **initiate, sustain,** and **direct** activities. Motivation typically involves the sequence **need, drive, goal,** and **goal attainment** (need reduction).

◆ Behavior can be activated either by **needs** (push) or by **goals** (pull). The attractiveness of a goal and its ability to initiate action are related to its **incentive value.**

◆ Three principal types of motives are **primary motives, stimulus motives,** and **secondary motives.** Most primary motives operate to maintain **homeostasis.**

What causes hunger? Overeating? Eating disorders?

◆ Hunger is influenced by a complex interplay between fullness of the stomach, blood sugar levels, metabolism in the liver, and fat stores in the body.

◆ The most direct control of eating is effected by the **hypothalamus,** which has areas that act like **feeding** and **satiety** systems. The hypothalamus is sensitive to both neural and chemical messages, which affect eating.

◆ Other factors influencing hunger are the body's **set point,** external **eating cues,** the attractiveness and variety of **diet, emotions,** learned **taste preferences** and **taste aversions,** and **cultural values.**

◆ Obesity is the result of a complex interplay of internal and external influences, diet, emotions, genetics, and exercise.

◆ **Anorexia nervosa** (self-inflicted starvation) and **bulimia nervosa** (gorging and purging) are two prominent eating disorders. Both problems tend to involve conflicts about self-image, self-control, and anxiety.

Is there more than one type of thirst?

◆ Like hunger, thirst and other basic motives are affected by a number of bodily factors, but are primarily under the central control of the hypothalamus. Thirst may be either **intracellular** or **extracellular.**

In what ways are pain avoidance and the sex drive unusual?

◆ Pain avoidance is unusual because it is **episodic** as

opposed to **cyclic.** Pain avoidance and pain tolerance are partially learned. The sex drive is also unusual in that it is **non-homeostatic.**

How does arousal relate to motivation?

◆ The stimulus motives include drives for **exploration, manipulation, change,** and **sensory stimulation.**

◆ Drives for stimulation are partially explained by **arousal theory,** which states that an ideal level of bodily arousal will be maintained if possible. The desired level of arousal or stimulation varies from person to person, as measured by the *Sensation-Seeking Scale.*

◆ Optimal performance on a task usually occurs at *moderate* levels of arousal. This relationship is described by an **inverted U function.** The **Yerkes-Dodson law** further states that for simple tasks the ideal arousal level is higher, and for complex tasks it is lower.

◆ **Circadian rhythms** of bodily activity are closely tied to sleep, activity, and energy cycles. Time zone travel and shift work can seriously disrupt sleep and bodily rhythms.

What are social motives? Why are they important?

◆ Social motives are learned through socialization and cultural conditioning. Such motives account for much of the diversity of human motivation. **Opponent-process theory** explains the operation of some acquired motives.

◆ One of the most prominent social motives is the **need for achievement (nAch).** High nAch is correlated with success in many situations, with occupational choice, and with *moderate* risk taking.

◆ There is evidence that at times both men and women experience a **fear of success.** This is especially true if achievement is seen as conflicting with social acceptance.

◆ **Self-confidence** greatly affects motivation in everyday life.

Are some motives more basic than others?

◆ Maslow's **hierarchy of motives** categorizes needs as **basic** and **growth oriented.** Lower needs in the hierarchy are assumed to be **prepotent** (dominant) over higher needs. Self-actualization, the highest and most fragile need, is reflected in **meta-needs.**

◆ Higher needs in Maslow's hierarchy are closely related to the concept of **intrinsic motivation.** In many situations, **extrinsic motivation** (that which is induced by obvious external rewards) can reduce intrinsic motivation, enjoyment, and creativity.

What happens during emotion?

◆ Emotions are linked to many basic **adaptive behaviors.** Other major elements of emotion are **physiological changes** in the body, **emotional expressions,** and **emotional feelings.**

◆ The following are considered to be **primary emotions:** *fear, surprise, sadness, disgust, anger, anticipation, joy,* and *acceptance.* Other emotions seem to represent mixtures of the primaries.

◆ The left hemisphere of the brain primarily processes positive emotions. Negative emotions are processed in the right hemisphere.

◆ The amygdala provides a "quick and dirty" pathway for the arousal of fear that bypasses the cerebral cortex.

◆ Physical changes associated with emotion are caused by the action of **adrenaline,** a hormone released into the bloodstream, and by activity in the **autonomic nervous system** (ANS).

◆ The **sympathetic branch** of the ANS is primarily responsible for arousing the body, the **parasympathetic branch** for quieting it. Sudden death due to prolonged and intense emotion is probably related to a **parasympathetic rebound.** Heart attacks caused by sudden intense emotion are more likely due to sympathetic arousal.

Can "lie detectors" really detect lies?

◆ The **polygraph,** or "lie detector," measures emotional arousal by monitoring *heart rate, blood pressure, breathing rate,* and the *galvanic skin response (GSR).* The accuracy of the lie detector has been challenged by many researchers.

How accurately are emotions expressed by "body language" and the face?

◆ Basic emotional expressions, such as smiling or baring one's teeth when angry, appear to be unlearned. **Facial expressions** appear to be central to emotion.

◆ Body gestures and movements (body language) also express feelings, mainly by communicating **emotional tone.** Three dimensions of facial expressions are **pleasantness-unpleasantness, attention-rejection,** and **activation.** The study of body language is known as **kinesics.**

◆ Lying can sometimes be detected from changes in **illustrators** or **emblems** and from signs of **general arousal.**

How do psychologists explain emotions?

◆ The **James-Lange theory** of emotion says that emotional *experience* follows the bodily reactions of emotion. In contrast, the **Cannon-Bard theory** says that bodily reactions and emotional experience occur at the same time and that emotions are organized in the brain.

◆ Schachter's **cognitive theory** of emotion emphasizes the importance of *labels,* or interpretations, applied to feelings of bodily arousal. Also important is the process of **attribution,** in which bodily arousal is attributed to a particular person, object, or situation.

◆ The **facial feedback hypothesis** holds that sensations and information from emotional expressions help define what emotion a person is feeling.

♦ Contemporary views of emotion place greater emphasis on the effects of **cognitive appraisals** of situations. Also, all of the elements of emotion are seen as interrelated and interacting.

Can psychology be applied to weight control?

♦ Because of the limitations of traditional dieting, changing basic eating patterns and exercise habits is usually more effective. **Behavioral dieting** brings about such changes by use of self-control techniques.

What is the nature of love?

♦ Sternberg's **triangular theory** describes love as a combination of **passion, intimacy,** and **commitment.** Combinations of these three factors produce **non-love, liking, infatuation, romantic love, fatuous love, companionate love, empty love,** and **consummate love.**

Health, Stress, and Coping

Preview

How to Build a Human Time Bomb

When he was arrested, John was sitting atop a 30-ton bulldozer, staring into space. Behind him lay a mile-long path of destruction: John had cut a broad, straight path through yards, roads, and fields. The path led back to his house, where the dozer was usually kept. Why did he do it? John explained that his father had denied him use of the family car that morning. Hours later, his anger exploded.

What would cause someone to react so drastically to a family disagreement?

In John's case, the answer is that he was *frustrated*—very frustrated! Perhaps you have been as frustrated as John must have been when he climbed into the driver's seat. For example, picture yourself looking for a parking space in a crowded lot. Imagine that you are late for a test and have already been delayed by an irritating traffic jam. After 15 minutes of frantic searching, you finally spy an empty space, but as you start toward it, a Volkswagen darts around the corner and into "your" space. A car behind you begins to honk impatiently. Your car's radiator boils over. In such a situation, you might be seized by a colossal desire to run over anything in sight—other cars, pedestrians, lampposts, trees, and flower beds. Few people actually carry out such impulses, but the feeling is common. Aggressive urges frequently accompany frustration (Berkowitz, 1988).

Is frustration the same as anger?

No. *Frustration* can be defined as a negative emotional state that occurs when one is prevented from reaching a goal. John's desire to use the family car was blocked by his father. Similarly, in the imaginary parking lot, the goal of finding a parking space was blocked by the presence of other cars.

Frustration is just one of the many causes of *stress*. Stress occurs whenever a challenge or a threat forces a person to *adjust* or *adapt*. Stress is a normal part of life. But when stress is severe or prolonged it can do tremendous damage to one's health. Stress, in other words, is a *behavioral* factor that directly affects personal well-being.

In the first part of this chapter we will explore a variety of behavioral risks to your health. Then, we will look more closely at what stress is and how it affects us. After that, we will stress effective ways of coping with stress.

Chapter Survey

Theme: Health is affected greatly by lifestyle and behavior patterns, especially those related to stress.

Key Questions:

Key Questions:	Key Topics to Watch for:
What is health psychology? How does behavior affect health?	Health psychology Behavioral risk factors Health-promoting behaviors
What is stress? What factors determine its severity?	Dimensions of stress Emotional appraisals
What causes frustration and what are typical reactions to it?	Variables affecting frustration Typical reactions to frustration
Are there different types of conflict? How do people react to conflict?	Types of conflict Typical reactions to conflict
What are defense mechanisms?	Anxiety and psychological defense Types of defense mechanisms
What do we know about coping with feelings of helplessness and depression?	Learned helplessness Mastery training Depression and the college blues
How is stress related to health and disease?	Life events, hassles, and stress Psychosomatic disorders Biofeedback The general adaptation syndrome
What are the best strategies for managing stress?	Stress management and coping skills
Is meditation useful for coping with stress?	Meditation and the relaxation response

Health Psychology— Here's to Your Good Health

Most people agree that health is important—especially their own. Yet, almost one half of all deaths in North America are primarily due to unhealthy behavior or lifestyles. A specialty called **health psychology** aims to do something about it. The core of this approach is *the use of psychological principles to promote health and to prevent illness* (Taylor, 1990). Psychologists working in the allied field of **behavioral medicine** *apply psychology to manage medical problems.* Their interests include pain control, adjustment to chronic illness, adherence to doctors' instructions, stress-related diseases, and similar topics (Luiselli, 1994).

Behavioral Risk Factors

Around the turn of the century, people primarily died from infectious diseases and accidents. Today, people generally suffer and die from **lifestyle diseases,** *which are related to health-damaging personal habits.* Familiar examples include heart disease, stroke, and lung cancer (McGinnis & Foege, 1993). (See Figure 14–1 ◆.) Clearly, some behaviors and lifestyles promote health, whereas others lead to illness and death. As the cartoon character Pogo put it, "We have met the enemy and he is us."

What kinds of behavior are you referring to as unhealthy?

Of course, some causes of poor health are beyond our control. Nevertheless, a number of *behavioral risk factors* can be controlled. **Behavioral risk factors** *are behaviors that increase the chances of disease, injury, or early death.* Each of the following is a major behavioral risk factor (Dubbert, 1992; Groth-Marnat & Schumaker, 1995):

- high levels of stress
- untreated high blood pressure
- cigarette smoking
- abuse of alcohol or other drugs
- overeating
- inadequate exercise
- unsafe sexual behavior
- exposure to toxic substances
- violence
- driving at excessive speeds
- disregarding personal safety

Table 14–1 ■ shows how many high school students in the U.S. engage in risky behaviors of the kind listed here. As you can see, health-damaging behaviors are usually well established before adulthood (Kolbe, Collins, & Cortese, 1997).

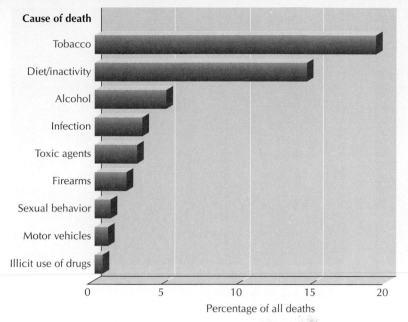

Cause of death

Tobacco
Diet/inactivity
Alcohol
Infection
Toxic agents
Firearms
Sexual behavior
Motor vehicles
Illicit use of drugs

0   5   10   15   20

Percentage of all deaths

Figure 14–1 ◆ The nine leading causes of death in the United States are shown in this graph. As you can see, eight of the top nine causes are directly related to behavioral risk factors (infection is the exception). At least 45 percent of all deaths can be traced to unhealthful behavior. The percentage of day-to-day health problems related to unhealthful behavior is even higher. (Data from McGinnis & Foege, 1993.)

Table 14–1 ■ Percentage of U.S. High School Students Who Engaged in Health-Endangering Behaviors	
Risky Behavior	**Percentage**
Rode with drinking driver (previous month)	35
Were in a physical fight (previous year)	42
Carried a weapon (previous month)	22
Had 5 or more drinks on one occasion (previous month)	30
Have used marijuana	33
Have engaged in sexual intercourse	53
Did not use condom during last sexual intercourse	47
Smoked cigarettes (previous month)	31
Ate high-fat food (previous day)	34
No vigorous exercise (previous week)	34

Source: Kolbe, Collins, & Cortese, 1997.

In addition to specific risk factors, a general **disease-prone personality** type also exists. Such people tend to be *chronically depressed, anxious, hostile, and . . . frequently ill* (Taylor, 1990). In contrast, people who are intellectually resourceful, compassionate, optimistic, and non-hostile tend to enjoy good health (Cartwright, Wink, & Kmetz, 1995).

Lifestyle In your mind's eye, fast-forward an imaginary film of your life all the way to old age. Do it twice—once with a lifestyle including a large number of behavioral risk factors, and the second time without them. It should be obvious that

when countless small risks add up, they dramatically raise the chance of illness. If stress is a frequent part of your life, visualize your body seething with emotion, day after day after day. If you smoke, picture a lifetime's worth of cigarette smoke blown through your lungs in a week or a day. If you drink, take a lifetime of alcohol's assaults on the brain, stomach, and liver and squeeze them into a month: Your body would be poisoned, ravaged, and soon dead. If you eat a high-fat, high-cholesterol diet, fast-forward a lifetime of heart-killing plaque building up in your arteries.

Although it may sound like it, this discussion is not meant to be a sermon. It is merely a reminder that risk factors do make a difference. To make matters worse, unhealthy lifestyles almost always create multiple risks. That is, people who smoke are also likely to drink excessively. Those who overeat usually do not get enough exercise. And so on (Feuerstein et al., 1986a; Matarazzo, 1984).

Health-Promoting Behaviors

To help prevent disease and promote well-being, health psychologists first try to remove behavioral risk factors. All the medicine or surgery in the world may not be enough to restore health without changes in behavior. We all know someone who has had a heart attack or lung disease who cannot or will not change the habits that lead to illness (Matarazzo, 1984).

Beyond this, psychologists are also interested in getting people to increase *behaviors that promote health*. **Health-promoting behaviors** include such obvious practices as getting regular exercise, controlling smoking and alcohol use, maintaining a balanced diet, getting good medical care, and managing stress (Glik, Kronenfeld, & Jackson, 1996). Health-promoting behaviors can also be as simple as using seat belts in a car—a practice that greatly ups life expectancy!

In the long run, behavioral risk factors and lifestyles do make a difference in health and life expectancy.

Basic health practices *should* extend a person's life. But do they? A major study done in California provides an answer (Belloc, 1973; Belloc & Breslow, 1972; Breslow & Enstrom, 1980). Nearly 7,000 people filled out a detailed health questionnaire about seven basic health practices. In ensuing years, researchers kept a close watch on the health and death records of these people. Before we discuss the results, you might find it interesting to check the items listed here that apply to you.

Basic Health-Promoting Behaviors

1. I get 7 to 8 hours of sleep a night.
2. I am currently at or near the ideal weight for my height.
3. I have never smoked cigarettes.
4. I use alcohol moderately or not at all.
5. I get regular physical exercise.
6. I eat breakfast almost every day.
7. I never or rarely eat between meals.

Men who engaged in all seven health practices had a death rate almost 4 times lower than men who engaged in zero to three practices. The death rate was 2 times lower for women who engaged in all seven practices. To state the results another way, a 45-year-old man who regularly engages in only three of the behaviors has a remaining life expectancy of about 22 years. A man of the same age who maintains six or seven of the health practices can expect to live another 33 years. That's a 50 percent increase in life expectancy.

Later work showed that the first five practices are the most important for predicting health. You should note, however, that these are not the only elements of a healthy lifestyle. They are just the ones investigated in this particular study.

In some cases, specific diseases can be treated or prevented through changes in behavior. For example, chronic hypertension (high blood pressure) is often deadly. Yet, for some people simple lifestyle changes can fend off this "silent killer." Effective measures include losing weight, consuming less sodium (salt), moderating alcohol use, and increasing physical activity (Dubbert, 1995).

Early Prevention   Smoking is the largest preventable cause of death and the single most lethal risk factor (McGinnis & Foege, 1993). As such, smoking provides a good example of the behavioral possibilities for preventing illness.

What have health psychologists done to lessen the risks?

Attempts to "immunize" youths against pressures to start smoking provide a glimpse of health psychology in action. The smoker who says, "Quitting is easy, I've done it dozens of times" states a basic truth—only 1 smoker in 10 has long-term success. Thus, the best way to deal with smoking is to prevent it before it becomes a lifelong habit.

Smoking develops slowly, which gives time to expose young people to various prevention efforts (Botvin & Botvin, 1992). Examples include peer quizzes about the effects of smoking, anti-smoking art contests, poster and T-shirt giveaways, anti-smoking pamphlets for parents, and student quizzes of parents (Biglan et al., 1996).

Some of the best anti-smoking programs include **refusal skills training**, *in which youths learn to resist pressures to begin smoking (or using other drugs)*. In one program, junior high students were given "standard" information on the dangers of smoking. Then, for added impact, the students *role-played* ways to resist pressures from peers, adults, and cigarette advertisements. Follow-up checks indicated that the role-playing students were only half as likely to begin smoking as were students in a control group (Hurd et al., 1980). Similar methods can be applied to other health risks, such as sexually transmitted diseases and unwanted pregnancy (Botvin et al., 1995).

The latest school-based health programs also teach students general life skills. The idea is to give kids skills that will help them cope with day-to-day stresses. That way, they will be less tempted to escape problems through drug use or other destructive behaviors. **Life skills training** typically includes *practice in stress reduction, self-protection, decision making, self-control, and social skills* (Jones et al., 1995).

Health Campaigns   In addition to projects like the ones described, health psychologists have had success with **community health campaigns.** These are *community-wide education projects designed to lessen a combination of major risk factors.* Health campaigns help make people aware of risks such as stress, alcohol abuse, high blood pressure, high cholesterol, smoking, sexually transmitted diseases, or excessive sun exposure. This is followed by efforts to motivate people to change their behavior. Many campaigns provide **role models** (*positive examples*) who show people how to improve their own health. They also direct people to community services for health screening, advice, and treatment (Cheadle et al., 1992-93). People may be reached through the mass media, public schools, health fairs, their place of work, or self-help programs (Calvert & Cocking, 1992; Schooler et al., 1993). The following highlight offers an example of one such effort.

A Way to Change Your Habits:
SELF MONITORING

Before you can make any changes, you need to know how much of something you are already doing, such as smoking, eating or exercising.

We have all known people who kept gaining weight on their diets while swearing up and down that they never eat. Their problem was that they were not keeping track of how much they were really eating.

Here are the steps to help you find out what you are doing. Just keeping track may help you decide to make a change.

✪ STEP 1:
Decide which habit you want to watch.

CAUTION: *Keep track of only one habit at a time. You should not try to quit smoking, lose weight and increase your exercise all at the same time.*

The page shown here is reproduced from a booklet prepared as part of a public health campaign conducted in southern Arizona. Such campaigns promote health by calling attention to psychological risk factors and by telling what to do about them. (From Marques et al., 1982.)

Using Psychology

Health Campaigns—Have a Heart

A good example of a community health campaign in action is the Stanford Heart Disease Prevention Program (Meyer et al., 1980). In the Stanford project, a media campaign about risk factors in heart disease—smoking, diet, and exercise—was combined with special group "workshops" for high-risk individuals. The program's success can be seen in the fact that after 2 years, the number of smokers decreased by 17 percent in two test communities. Compare this figure with the 12 percent *increase* observed in similar, untreated communities.

Such progress may seem modest, but it is, in fact, worthwhile, cost effective, and highly promising. Overall, results of the project show a 15 percent reduction in risk of heart disease in the target cities (Farquhar et al., 1984). All you have to do is picture someone you love staying healthy or living longer to appreciate the value of such efforts.

Wellness   Health is not just an absence of disease. People who are truly healthy attain a positive state of **wellness** or *well-being.* Maintaining wellness is a life-long pursuit and, hopefully, a labor of love. People who attain optimal wellness are both physically and psychologically healthy. They engage in positive thinking, show emotional resilience, are optimistic and self-confident (Lightsey, 1996).

People who enjoy a sense of well-being also have supportive relationships with others, they do meaningful work, and they live in a clean environment. Many of these aspects of wellness are addressed in other chapters of this book. In this chapter we will give special attention to the role that stress plays in health and sickness. As stated earlier, stress management is a major activity of health psychologists. Understanding stress, and learning to control it, can improve not only your health, but the quality of your life as well. For these reasons, a discussion of stress and stress management follows.

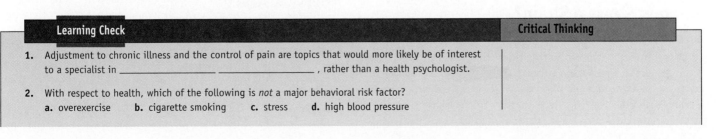

Learning Check	Critical Thinking
1. Adjustment to chronic illness and the control of pain are topics that would more likely be of interest to a specialist in _____ _____ , rather than a health psychologist.	
2. With respect to health, which of the following is *not* a major behavioral risk factor? **a.** overexercise **b.** cigarette smoking **c.** stress **d.** high blood pressure	

3. Eating breakfast almost every day and rarely eating between meals proved to be the two most important health-promoting behaviors in the Alameda County study. T or F?

4. Health psychologists tend to prefer _____ , rather than modifying habits (like smoking) that become difficult to break once they are established.

5. The disease-prone personality is marked by _____ , anxiety, and hostility.

6. The general public is increasingly well informed about health risks and healthful behavior. Can you apply the concept of reinforcement to explain why so many people fail to act on this information?

Answers:
rewards for healthful behavior.
years, greatly lessening the immediate
health payoffs are delayed by months or
4. prevention 5. depression 6. Many
1. behavioral medicine 2. a 3. F

Stress—Thrill or Threat?

Is stress is always bad? Clearly it's not. As stress researcher Hans Selye (SEL-yay) (1976) observed, "To be totally without stress is to be dead." As noted earlier, **stress** *is the mental and physical condition that occurs any time we must adjust or adapt to the environment.* Naturally, unpleasant events such as work pressures, marital problems, or financial troubles produce stress. But so do travel, sports, a new job, mountain climbing, dating, and other pleasant activities. Even if you aren't a thrill seeker, a healthy lifestyle may include a fair amount of stress.

Your body's **stress reaction** begins with the same *autonomic nervous system arousal that occurs during emotion.* If you were standing at the top of a wind-whipped ski jump for the first time, and you found it stressful, we would observe a rapid surge in your heart rate, blood pressure, respiration, muscle tension, and other ANS responses. *Short-term* stresses of this kind can be uncomfortable, but they rarely do any damage. (Your landing might be another matter, however.) Later we will describe *long-term* physical changes that accompany prolonged stress. These changes can do much harm. For now, Table 14–2 ■ gives an overview of typical signs or symptoms of prolonged stress.

Other than when it is long lasting, why is stress sometimes damaging and sometimes not?

Stress reactions are complex. Let's examine some of the chief factors that determine whether or not stress is harmful.

When Is Stress a Strain?

It goes almost without saying that some events are more likely to cause stress than others. A **stressor** *is a condition or event in the environment that challenges or threatens a person.* Police officers, for instance, suffer from a high rate of stress-related diseases. The threat of injury or death, plus occasional confrontations with drunk or belligerent citizens, takes a toll. A major factor here is the *unpredictable* nature of police work. An officer who stops to issue a traffic ticket never knows if a cooperative citizen or an armed gang member is waiting in the car.

An interesting experiment involving three groups of rats shows how unpredictable events add to stress. Rats in one group were given shocks preceded by a warning tone. A second group got shocks without warning. The third group received no shocks, but heard the tone. After a few weeks, the animals that received unpredictable shocks had severe ulcers. Those given predictable shocks showed little or no ulceration. Those receiving no shocks had no stomach ulcers (Weiss, 1972).

Pressure is another element in stress, especially job stress. **Pressure** occurs when activities must be speeded up, when deadlines must be met, when extra work is added unexpectedly, or when a person *must work near maximum capacity for long periods* (Weiten, 1988). Most students who have survived final exams are familiar with the effects of pressure.

Table 14–2 ■ Warning Signs of Stress

Emotional signs
  Anxiety
  Apathy
  Irritability
  Mental fatigue
Behavioral signs
  Avoidance of responsibilities and relationships
  Extreme or self-destructive behavior
  Self-neglect
  Poor judgment
Physical signs
  Excessive worry about illness
  Frequent illness
  Exhaustion
  Overuse of medicines
  Physical ailments and complaints

Doctor & Doctor, 1994.

Although it may not seem so, assembly line work can be quite stressful, due to the lack of control employees have over the pace of work.

What if I set deadlines for myself? Does it make a difference where the pressure comes from?

Yes. People generally feel more stress in situations over which they have little or no control (Taylor, 1990). For example, Douglas DeGood (1975) subjected college students to an unpleasant shock-avoidance task. Some participants were allowed to select their own rest periods, while others rested at times selected for them. Individuals allowed to control their own rest periods showed lower stress levels (as measured by blood pressure) than those given no choice.

To summarize, when emotional "shocks" are *intense* or *repeated*, *unpredictable*, *uncontrollable*, and linked to *pressure*, stress will be magnified and damage is likely to result. (See Table 14–3 ■ for a rating of jobs that contain these elements.) At work, chronic stress sometimes results in *burnout*, a pattern of emotional exhaustion described next.

Table 14–3 ■ The 10 Most Stressful Jobs	
Job	**Rank**
U.S. president	1
firefighter	2
senior corporate executive	3
Indy-class race car driver	4
taxi driver	5
surgeon	6
astronaut	7
police officer	8
NFL football player	9
air-traffic controller	10

Krantz, 1995.

Burnout—The High Cost of Caring

Margo, a young nurse, realizes with dismay that she has changed from a caring person at work to a cynic who has "lost all patience with her patients" and wishes they would "go somewhere else to be sick."

Reactions like Margo's are clear signs of job **burnout,** a condition that exists when an employee is *physically, mentally, and emotionally drained.* What does it mean to be "burned out"? Psychologist Christina Maslach (1982) has identified three aspects of the problem (Lee & Ashforth, 1990; Yadama & Drake, 1995).

First of all, burnout involves *emotional exhaustion.* Affected persons are fatigued, tense, and apathetic. Many suffer from various physical complaints. They feel "used up" and have an "I don't give a damn anymore" attitude toward work.

A second aspect of burnout is *depersonalization*, or detachment from others. "Burned-out" workers coldly treat clients as if they were objects and find it difficult to care about them.

The third aspect of burnout is a feeling of *reduced personal accomplishment.* Burned-out workers do poor work and feel helpless, hopeless, or angry. Their self-esteem suffers and they yearn to change jobs or careers.

Burnout may occur in any job, but it is a marked problem in emotionally demanding helping professions, such as nursing, teaching, social work, child care,

The helping professions require empathy, caring, and emotional involvement. As a result, caregivers risk depleting their emotional resources and ability to cope. Over time, this can lead to burnout.

counseling, caring for AIDs patients, or police work (Bellani et al., 1996; Matthews, 1990; Poulin & Walter, 1993; Yadama & Drake, 1995).

It's ironic that the same work that produces burnout can also be highly challenging and rewarding. If our society wishes to keep caring people in the helping professions, several changes may be needed. A good start would be to redesign jobs to create a better balance between demands and satisfactions. As in other stressful situations, people are more likely to "burnout" if they feel that they have little control over their work (McKnight & Glass, 1995).

Building stronger social support systems at work could also help prevent burnout. A good example is the growing use of **support groups** for nurses and other caregivers. Such groups allow workers to *give and receive emotional support* as they talk about feelings, problems, and stresses (Garside, 1993).

Ultimately, the best solution for burnout may be for each of us to better appreciate the stresses felt by people whose work requires caring about the needs of others (Capner & Caltabiano, 1993).

Appraising Stressors

As important as *external* events may be, they are not the whole story where stress is concerned. As noted in Chapter 13, the emotions we feel are greatly affected by the way in which a situation is appraised. That's why some people are stressed by events that others view as a thrill or a challenge. Ultimately, stress depends on how a situation is perceived. I have a friend who would find it stressful to listen to five of his son's rap CDs in a row. He has a son who would find it stressful to listen to one of his father's opera CDs. To know if a person is stressed, we must know what meaning the person places on events. As we will see in a moment, whenever a stressor is appraised as a **threat** (*potentially harmful*), an especially powerful stress reaction follows (Lazarus, 1991a).

"Am I Okay or in Trouble?"   Situation: You have been selected to give a speech to 300 people. Or, a doctor tells you that you must undergo a dangerous and painful operation. Or, the one true love of your life walks out the door. What would your emotional response to these events be? How do you cope with an emotional threat?

According to Richard Lazarus (1991a), there are two important steps in managing a threatening situation. The first is a **primary appraisal**, in which you decide if a situation is *relevant or irrelevant, positive or threatening*. In essence, this appraisal answers the question, "Am I okay or in trouble?" Then you make a **secondary appraisal**, during which you *assess your resources and choose a way to meet the threat or challenge.* ("What can I do about this situation?") The way a

Figure 14–2 ◆ Stress is the product of an interchange between a person and the environment.

situation is "sized up" therefore becomes very important to coping with it (Fig. 14–2 ◆). Public speaking, for instance, can be appraised as an intense threat or as a challenge and a chance to perform. Emphasizing the threat—by imagining failure, rejection, or embarrassment—obviously invites disaster (Lazarus, 1993).

"The fuel light's on, Frank! We're all going to die! ... Wait, wait. ... Oh, my mistake—that's the intercom light."

The Nature of Threat   What does it mean to feel threatened by a stressor? Certainly in most day-to-day situations it does not mean that you think your life is in danger. Threat has more to do with the idea of control. As psychologist Michael Gazzaniga says, "Animals and people are particularly prone to stress when they can't—or think they can't—control their immediate environment" (Gazzaniga, 1988). In short, a *perceived lack of control* is just as important as actual lack of control in causing us to feel threatened (DasGupta, 1992). If your answer to the question, "What can I do about this situation?" is "nothing," you are likely to feel emotionally stressed.

Your personal sense of control in any situation also comes from believing that you can reach desired goals. Or, to state it another way, it is threatening for a person to feel that she or he lacks *competence* to cope with a particular demand (Bandura, 1986). Thus, the intensity of the body's stress reaction often depends on what we think and tell ourselves about stressors. That's why it can be valuable to train yourself to think in ways that avoid triggering the body's stress response. (Some strategies for controlling upsetting thoughts are described in this chapter's Applications section.)

Coping with Threat

You have appraised a situation as threatening. What will you do next? There are two major choices. **Problem-focused coping** is aimed at *managing or altering the distressing situation itself*. In **emotion-focused coping**, people try instead to *control their emotional reactions* to the situation (Lazarus, 1993).

Couldn't both types of coping occur together?

Yes. Sometimes the two types of coping aid one another. Say, for example, that a woman feels anxious as she steps to the podium to give a speech. If she does some deep breathing to reduce her anxiety (emotion-focused coping), she will be better able to glance over her notes to improve her delivery (problem-focused coping).

It is also possible, unfortunately, for the two types of coping to clash. For instance, if you have to make a difficult decision, you may suffer unbearable emotional distress. In such circumstances there is a temptation to make a quick and ill-advised choice, just to end the emotional suffering. Doing so may allow you to cope with your emotions, but it shortchanges problem-focused coping. In general, problem-focused coping tends to be especially useful when you are facing a controllable stressor—that is, a situation you can actually do something about. Emotion-focused efforts are best suited to managing stressors that you cannot control (Lazarus, 1993; Taylor, 1990). To improve your chances of coping effectively, the stress-fighting strategies described in this chapter include a mixture of both techniques.

We will soon return to another look at stress and its effects. But first, let's examine two major (and all too familiar) causes of stress: frustration and conflict.

Frustration—Blind Alleys and Lead Balloons

What causes frustration?

Obstacles of many kinds cause frustration. A useful distinction can be made between *external* and *personal* sources of frustration. **External frustration** is based on *conditions outside of the individual that impede progress toward a goal*. All of the following are external frustrations: getting stuck with a flat tire; having a marriage proposal rejected; finding the cupboard bare when you go to get your poor dog a bone; finding the refrigerator bare when you go to get your poor tummy a T-bone; finding the refrigerator gone when you return home; being chased out of the house by your starving dog. In other words, external frustrations are based on *delay, failure, rejection, loss,* and other direct blocking of motives.

Notice that external obstacles can be either *social* (slow drivers, tall people in theaters, people who cut into lines) or *non-social* (stuck doors, a dead battery, rain on the day of the game). If you ask 10 of your friends what has frustrated them recently, most will probably mention someone's behavior ("My sister wore one of my dresses when I wanted to wear it," "My supervisor is unfair," "My history teacher grades too hard"). As social animals, we humans are highly sensitive to social sources of frustration (Peeters, Buunk, & Schaufeli, 1995).

Frustration usually increases as the **strength, urgency,** or **importance** of a blocked motive increases. An escape artist submerged in a tank of water and bound with 200 pounds of chain would become *quite* frustrated by the jamming of a trick lock. Remember, too, that motivation becomes stronger as we near a goal. As a result, frustration is more intense when a person runs into an obstacle very close to a goal. If you've ever missed an A grade by two points, you were probably very frustrated. If you've missed an A by one point—well, frustration builds character, right?

A final factor affecting frustration is summarized by the old phrase "the straw that broke the camel's back." The effects of *repeated* frustrations can accumulate until a small irritation sets off an unexpectedly violent response. The boy who bulldozed the countryside (see the chapter Preview) probably had been frustrated many times before by his father.

Personal frustrations are based on *personal characteristics*. If you are 4 feet tall and aspire to be a professional basketball player, you very likely will be frustrated. If you want to go to medical school, but can earn only D grades, you will likewise be frustrated. In both examples, frustration is actually based on personal limitations. Yet, failure may be *perceived* as externally caused. We will return to this point in the Applications section. In the meantime, let's look at some typical reactions to frustration.

Reactions to Frustration

Aggression *is any response made with the intent of harming a person or an object.* It is one of the most persistent and frequent responses to frustration (Berkowitz, 1988). The frustration-aggression link is so common, in fact, that experiments are hardly necessary to show it. A glance at almost any newspaper will provide examples such as the one that follows.

Justifiable Autocide

Burien, Washington (AP)—Barbara Smith committed the assault, but police aren't likely to press charges. Her victim was a 1964 Oldsmobile which failed once too often to start.

When Officer Jim Fuda arrived at the scene, he found one beat-up car, a broken baseball bat and a satisfied 23-year-old Seattle woman.

"I feel good," Ms. Smith reportedly told the officer. "That car's been giving me misery for years and I killed it."

Does frustration always cause aggression? Aren't there other reactions?

Although the connection is strong, frustration does not always provoke aggression. Later, in Chapter 21, we will explore factors that influence when and where aggression is likely to occur. For now, it is enough to note that aggression is not usually the first, or only, reaction to frustration. More often, frustration is met first with **persistence**. This is characterized by more **vigorous efforts** and **varied responses** (Fig. 14–3 ◆). For example, if you put your last quarter in a vending machine and find that pressing the button has no effect, you will probably press harder and faster (vigorous effort). Then you will press all the other buttons (varied response). Persistence may help you get *around* a barrier in order to reach your goal. However, if the machine *still* refuses to deliver, or return your quarter, you may become aggressive and kick the machine (or at least tell it what you think of it).

Persistence can be very adaptive. Overcoming a barrier ends the frustration and allows the need or motive to be satisfied. The same is true of aggression that removes or destroys a barrier. Picture a small band of primitive humans, parched by thirst but separated from a water hole by a menacing animal. It is easy to see that attacking the animal may ensure their survival. In modern society such direct aggression is seldom acceptable. If you find a long line at the drinking fountain, aggression is hardly an appropriate response. Because direct aggression is disruptive and generally discouraged, it is frequently *displaced*.

How is aggression displaced? Does displaced aggression occur often?

Directing aggression toward a source of frustration may be

Figure 14–3 ◆ Frustration and common reactions to it.

impossible, or it may be too dangerous. If you are frustrated by your boss at work or by a teacher at school, the cost of direct aggression may be too high (losing your job or failing a needed class). Instead, the aggression may be **displaced**, or *redirected*, toward whomever or whatever is available.

Targets of displaced aggression tend to be safer, or less likely to retaliate, than the original source of frustration. Bulldozing the countryside when the real source of frustration was one's father is a clear case of displaced aggression. Sometimes long *chains* of displacement occur, in which one person displaces aggression to the next. For instance, a businesswoman who is frustrated by high taxes reprimands an employee, who swallows his anger until he reaches home and then yells at his wife, who in turn yells at the children, who then tease the dog. The dog chases the cat, who later knocks over the canary cage.

Psychologists attribute much hostility and destructiveness in our society to displaced aggression. A disturbing example is the finding that when unemployment increases, so does child abuse (Steinberg et al., 1981). A pattern known as **scapegoating**, *in which a person or group of people are blamed for conditions not of their making,* is particularly damaging. A **scapegoat** is a person who has become *a habitual target of displaced aggression.* A tragic example of scapegoating on a large scale is the fact that in the United States between 1880 and 1930 there was a strong correlation between the price of cotton and the number of lynchings of African Americans in the South. As the price of cotton went down (and frustration increased), the number of lynchings increased (Dollard et al., 1939). Despite recent progress, many minority groups continue to suffer from hostility based on scapegoating.

Some organizations raise money by charging people for the "privilege" of smashing a junk car with a sledge hammer. Are some participants displacing aggressive urges related to frustration in other areas of their lives?

Think, for example, about the hostility expressed toward recent immigrants during times of economic recession or hardship.

I have a friend who dropped out of school to hitchhike around the country. He seemed very frustrated before he quit. What type of response to frustration is that?

Another major reaction to frustration is *escape*, or *withdrawal*. It is stressful and unpleasant to be frustrated. If other reactions do not reduce feelings of frustration, a person may try to escape. **Escape** may mean actually *leaving a source of frustration* (dropping out of school, quitting a job, leaving an unhappy marriage), or it may mean *psychologically escaping*. Two common forms of psychological escape are *apathy* (pretending not to care) and the *use of drugs* such as cocaine, alcohol, marijuana, or narcotics. (See Fig. 14–3 for a summary of common reactions to frustration.)

Conflict—Yes, No, Yes, No, Yes, No, Well, Maybe

Conflict occurs whenever a person must *choose between incompatible or contradictory needs, desires, motives, wishes, or external demands.* Choosing between college and work, marriage and single life, or study and failure are conflicts many students face. There are four basic forms of conflict. As we will see, each has its own effects and characteristics (Figs. 14–4 ◆ and 14–5 ◆).

Approach-Approach Conflicts The simplest conflict comes from having to *choose between two positive, or desirable, alternatives.* Choosing between tutti-fruitti-coconut-mocha-champagne-ice and orange-marmalade-peanut butter-coffee-swirl at the ice cream parlor may throw you into a temporary conflict. However, if you really like both choices, your decision will be quickly made. Even when more important decisions are at stake, **approach-approach conflicts** tend to be the easiest to resolve. The old fable about the mule that died of thirst and starvation while standing between a bucket of water and a bucket of oats is obviously unrealistic. When both options are positive, the scales of decision are easily tipped one direction or the other.

Figure 14–4 ◆ Three basic forms of conflict. For this woman, choosing between pie and ice cream is a minor approach-approach conflict; deciding whether to take a job that will require weekend work is an approach-avoidance conflict; and choosing between paying higher rent and moving is an avoidance-avoidance conflict.

Health, Stress, and Coping | **459**

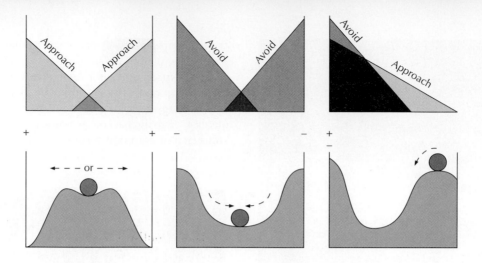

Figure 14–5 ◆ Conflict diagrams. As shown by the colored areas in the graphs, desires to approach and to avoid increase near a goal. The effects of these tendencies are depicted below each graph. The "behavior" of the ball in each example illustrates the nature of the conflict above it. An approach conflict (*left*) is easily decided. Moving toward one goal will increase its attraction (*graph*) and will lead to a rapid resolution. (If the ball moves in either direction, it will go all the way to one of the goals.) In an avoidance conflict (*center*), tendencies to avoid are deadlocked, resulting in inaction. In an approach-avoidance conflict (*right*), approach proceeds to the point where desires to approach and avoid cancel each other. Again, these tendencies are depicted (*below*) by the action of the ball. (Graphs after Miller, 1944.)

Avoidance-Avoidance Conflicts Being forced to *choose between two negative, or undesirable, alternatives* creates an **avoidance-avoidance conflict.** A person in an avoidance conflict is caught between "the devil and the deep blue sea" or between "the frying pan and the fire." In real life, avoidance-avoidance conflicts involve such dilemmas as choosing between studying and failure, unwanted pregnancy and abortion, the dentist and tooth decay, a monotonous job and poverty, or dorm food and starvation.

Suppose I don't object to abortion. Or suppose that I consider any pregnancy sacred and not to be tampered with?

Like many other stressful situations, these examples can be defined as conflicts only on the basis of personal needs and values. If a woman wants to end a pregnancy and does not object to abortion, she experiences no conflict. If she would not consider abortion under any circumstances, there is no conflict.

Double avoidance conflicts often have a "damned if you do, damned if you don't" quality. In other words, both choices are negative, but *not choosing* may be impossible or equally undesirable. To illustrate, imagine the plight of a person trapped in a hotel fire 20 stories from the ground. Should the person jump from the window and almost surely die on the pavement? Or should the person try to dash through the flames and almost surely die of smoke inhalation and burns? When faced with a choice such as this, it is easy to see why people often *freeze*, finding it impossible to decide or take action. A trapped individual may first think about the window, approach it, and then back away after looking down 20 stories. Next, the person may try the door and again back away as heat and smoke billow in. In actual disasters of this sort, people are often found dead in their rooms, victims of an inability to take action.

Indecision, inaction, and freezing are not the only reactions to double avoidance conflicts. Since avoidance conflicts are stressful and rarely solved, people sometimes pull out of them entirely. This reaction, called *leaving the field*, is another form of escape. It may explain the behavior of a student the author knew who could not attend school unless he worked. However, if he worked he could not earn passing grades. His solution after much conflict and indecision? He joined the navy.

Approach-Avoidance Conflicts Approach-avoidance conflicts are also difficult to resolve. Since people seldom escape them, they are in some ways more troublesome than avoidance conflicts. A person in an **approach-avoidance conflict** is "caught" by being *attracted to, and repelled by, the same goal or activity.* Attraction keeps the person in the situation, but its negative aspects cause turmoil and distress. For example, a high school student arrives to pick up his date for the first time. He is met at the door by her father, who is a professional wrestler—7 feet tall, 300 pounds, and entirely covered with hair. The father gives the boy a crushing handshake and growls that he will break him in half if the girl is not home on time. The student considers the girl attractive and has a good time. But does he ask her out again? It depends on the relative strength of his attraction and his fear. Almost certainly he will feel *ambivalent* about asking her out again, knowing that another encounter with her father is involved.

Ambivalence (*mixed positive and negative feelings*) is a central characteristic of approach-avoidance conflicts. Ambivalence is usually translated into *partial approach* (Miller, 1944). Since our student is still attracted to the girl, he may spend time with her at school and elsewhere. But he may not actually date her again. Some more realistic examples of approach-avoidance conflicts are planning marriage to someone your parents strongly disapprove of, wanting to be an actor but suffering stage fright, wanting to buy a car but not wanting to make monthly payments, wanting to eat when overweight, and wanting to go to school but hating to study. Many of life's important decisions have approach-avoidance dimensions.

Aren't real-life conflicts more complex than the ones described here?

Yes. In reality, conflicts are rarely as clear-cut as those described. People in conflict are usually faced with several dilemmas at once, so several types of conflict are intermingled. The fourth type of conflict moves us closer to this realistic state of affairs.

Multiple Conflicts   You are offered two jobs: One has good pay but poor hours and dull work; the second has interesting work and excellent hours, but low pay. Which do you select? This situation is more typical of the choices we must usually make. It offers neither completely positive nor completely negative options. It is, in other words, a **double approach-avoidance conflict,** in which *each alternative has both positive and negative qualities.*

As with single approach-avoidance conflicts, people faced with double approach-avoidance conflicts feel ambivalent about each choice. This causes them to **vacillate,** *or waver between the alternatives.* Just as you are about to choose one such alternative, its undesirable aspects tend to loom large. So, what do you do? You swing back toward the other choice. If you have ever been romantically attracted to two people at once—each having qualities you like and dislike—then you have probably experienced vacillation. Another example that may be familiar is trying to decide between two college majors, each with advantages and disadvantages.

In real life it is common to face **multiple approach-avoidance conflicts** in which *several alternatives each have positive and negative features.* An example would be trying to choose which automobile to buy among several brands. On a day-to-day basis, most multiple approach-avoidance conflicts are little more than an annoyance. When they involve major life decisions, such as choosing a career, a school, a mate, or a job, they can add greatly to the amount of stress experienced.

Learning Check	**Critical Thinking**

Be sure you can answer these questions before continuing.

1. Greater perceived control over a stressor is usually associated with a reduction in the amount of stress experienced. T or F?

2. Emotional exhaustion, depersonalization, and reduced accomplishment are characteristics of job _____ .

3. Stress tends to be greatest when a situation is appraised as a _____ and a person does not feel _____ to cope with the situation.

4. According to Lazarus, coping with threatening situations can be both problem-focused and _____ focused.

5. Which of the following is *not* a common reaction to frustration?
   a. ambivalence   **b.** aggression   **c.** displaced aggression   **d.** persistence

6. Sampson Goliath is 7 feet tall and weighs 300 pounds. He has failed miserably in his aspirations to become a jockey. The source of his frustration is mainly _____ .

7. As a reaction to frustration, apathy may be viewed as a form of _____ .

8. Inaction and freezing are most characteristic of avoidance-avoidance conflicts. T or F?

9. Approach-avoidance conflicts produce mixed feelings called _____ .

10. Which do you think would produce more stress: (a) Appraising a situation as mildly threatening but feeling like you are totally incompetent to cope with it? Or, (b) appraising a situation as very threatening but feeling that you have the resources and skills to cope with it?

Answers:

1. T 2. burnout 3. threat, competent 4. emotion- 5. a 6. personal 7. escape 8. T 9. ambivalence 10. There is no correct answer because individual stress reactions vary greatly. However, the secondary appraisal of a situation often determines just how stressful it is. Feeling incapable of coping is very threatening all by itself.

Psychological Defense— Mental Karate?

Threatening situations are often accompanied by an unpleasant emotion known **as anxiety.** A person who is anxious feels *tense, uneasy, apprehensive, worried, and vulnerable.* This can lead to emotion-focused coping that is *defensive* in nature (Lazarus, 1991b). Since anxiety is unpleasant and uncomfortable, we are usually motivated to avoid it. Anxiety caused by stressful situations or by our own shortcomings and limitations may be lessened by the use of psychological *defense mechanisms.*

What are psychological defense mechanisms and how do they reduce anxiety?

A **defense mechanism** *is any technique used to avoid, deny, or distort sources of threat or anxiety.* Defense mechanisms are also used to maintain an idealized self-image so that we can

Compensation Counteracting a real or imagined weakness by emphasizing desirable traits or seeking to excel in the area of weakness or in other areas.

Denial Protecting oneself from an unpleasant reality by refusing to perceive it.

Fantasy Fulfilling unmet desires in imagined achievements or activities.

Intellectualization Separating emotion from a threatening or anxiety-provoking situation by talking or thinking about it in impersonal "intellectual" terms.

Isolation Separating contradictory thoughts or feelings into "logic-tight" mental compartments so that they do not come into conflict.

Projection Attributing one's own feelings, shortcomings, or unacceptable impulses to others.

Rationalization Justifying your behavior by giving reasonable and "rational," but false, reasons for it.

Reaction formation Preventing dangerous impulses from being expressed in behavior by exaggerating opposite behavior.

Regression Retreating to an earlier level of development or to earlier, less demanding habits or situations.

Repression Unconsciously preventing painful or dangerous thoughts from entering awareness.

Sublimation Working off unmet desires, or unacceptable impulses, in activities that are constructive.

comfortably live with ourselves. Many of the defenses were first identified by Sigmund Freud, who assumed they operated *unconsciously*. Often, defense mechanisms create large "blind spots" in awareness, as when an extremely stingy person fails to recognize that he or she is a tightwad. Everyone has at one time or another used such defenses. Let's consider some of the most common. (A more complete listing is given in Table 14–4 ■.)

Denial One of the most basic defense mechanisms is *denial*. **Denial** *means to protect oneself from an unpleasant reality by refusing to accept it or believe it.* Denial is closely linked with

death, illness, and similar painful and threatening experiences. For instance, if you were told that you had only 3 months to live, how would you react? Your first thoughts might be "Aw, come on, someone must have mixed up the X-rays" or "The doctor must be mistaken" or simply "It can't be true!" Similar denial and disbelief are common reactions to the unexpected death of a friend or relative: "It's just not real. I don't believe it. I just don't believe it!"

Repression Freud noticed that his patients had tremendous difficulty recalling shocking or traumatic events from childhood. It seemed that powerful forces were *holding these painful memories from awareness.* Freud called this **repression.** Apparently, we protect ourselves by repressing thoughts or impulses that are painful or threatening. Feelings of hostility toward a loved one, the names of disliked people, and past failures and embarrassments are common targets of repression.

Reaction Formation **Reaction formation** is a defense in which impulses are not only repressed, but are also *held in check by exaggerated opposite behavior.* For example, a mother who unconsciously resents her children may, through reaction formation, become absurdly overprotective and overindulgent. Her real thoughts of "I hate them" and "I wish they were gone" are replaced by "I love them" and "I don't know what I would do without them." The mother's hostile impulses are traded for "smother" love, so that she won't have to admit her dislike of her children. The basic idea in a reaction formation is that the individual acts out an opposite behavior to block threatening impulses or feelings.

Regression In its broadest meaning, **regression** refers to any *return to earlier, less demanding situations or habits.* Most parents who have a second child have to put up with at least some regression by the older child. Threatened by a new rival for attention, an older child may regress to childish speech, bed-wetting, or infantile play after the new baby arrives. However, regression is usually less severe. The child at summer camp who gets homesick and longs for the security of familiar surroundings is undergoing mild regression. An adult who throws a temper tantrum or a married adult who "goes home to mother" is also regressing.

Projection *Projection* is an unconscious process that protects us from the anxiety that would occur if we were to

JUMP START REPRINTED BY PERMISSION OF UFS, INC.

discern our own faults or unacceptable traits. A person who is projecting tends to see his or her own feelings, shortcomings, or unacceptable impulses in others. **Projection** *lowers anxiety by exaggerating negative traits in others while directing attention away from one's own failings.*

The author once worked for a greedy shop owner who cheated many of his customers. This same man considered himself a pillar of the community and a good Christian. How did he justify to himself his greed and dishonesty? He believed that everyone who entered his store was bent on cheating *him* any way they could. In reality, few, if any, of his customers shared his motives, but he projected his own greed and dishonesty onto them.

Rationalization Every teacher is familiar with this strange phenomenon: On the day of an exam, an incredible wave of disasters sweeps through the city. An amazing number of mothers, fathers, sisters, brothers, aunts, uncles, grandparents, friends, relatives, and pets become ill or die. Motors suddenly fall out of automobiles. Books are lost or stolen. Alarm clocks go belly-up and ring no more.

The making of excuses comes from a natural tendency to explain one's behavior. **Rationalization** *refers to justifying personal actions by giving "rational" but false reasons for them.* When the explanation you give for your behavior is reasonable and convincing—but not the real reason—you are *rationalizing*. Here's an example: A student who fails to turn in an assignment made at the beginning of the semester gives the following explanation.

> My car broke down 2 days ago and I couldn't get to the library until yesterday. Then I couldn't get all the books I needed because some were checked out, but I wrote what I could. Then last night, as the last straw, the cartridge in my printer ran out, and since all the stores were closed, I couldn't finish the paper on time.

If asked why he left the assignment until the last minute (the real reason it's late), the student would probably offer another set of rationalizations. If these are questioned, the student may become emotional as he is forced to see himself without the protection of his rationalizations.

All of the defense mechanisms described seem pretty undesirable. Do they have a positive side?

People who overuse defense mechanisms become less adaptable, because they consume great amounts of emotional energy to control anxiety and maintain an unrealistic self-image. Defense mechanisms do have value, however. Often, they help keep us from being overwhelmed by immediate threats. This can provide time for a person to learn to cope in a more effective, problem-focused manner. If you recognize some of your own behavior in the descriptions here, it is hardly a sign that you are hopelessly defensive. As noted earlier, most people make occasional use of defense mechanisms.

Two defense mechanisms that have a decidedly more positive quality are *compensation* and *sublimation.*

Compensation Compensatory reactions *are defenses against feelings of inferiority.* A person who has a defect or weakness (real or imagined) may go to unusual lengths to *overcome the weakness or to compensate for it by excelling in other areas.* One of the pioneers of "pumping iron" in America is Jack LaLanne. LaLanne made a successful career out of body building in spite of the fact that he was thin and sickly as a young man. Or perhaps it would be more accurate to say *because* he was thin and sickly. There are dozens of examples of compensation at work. A childhood stutterer may excel in debate at college. Franklin D. Roosevelt's outstanding achievements in politics came after he was stricken with polio. As a child, Helen Keller was unable to see or hear, but she became an outstanding thinker and writer. Doc Watson, Ray Charles, Stevie Wonder, and a number of other well-known musicians are blind.

Sublimation The defense called **sublimation** (sub-lih-MAY-shun) is defined as *working off frustrated desires (especially sexual desires) through socially acceptable activities.* Freud believed that art, music, dance, poetry, scientific investigation, and other creative activities can serve to rechannel sexual energies into productive behavior. Freud also felt that almost any strong desire can be sublimated. For example, a very aggressive person may find social acceptance as a professional soldier, boxer, or football player. Greed may be refined into a successful business career. Lying may be sublimated into storytelling, creative writing, or politics.

Sexual motives appear to be the most easily and widely sublimated. Freud would have had a field day with such modern pastimes as surfing, motorcycle riding, drag racing, and dancing to or playing rock music, to name but a few. People enjoy each of these activities for a multitude of reasons, but it is hard to overlook the rich sexual symbolism apparent in each.

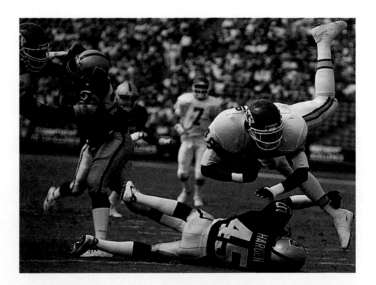

For some players—and fans—football probably allows sublimation of aggressive urges.

Learned Helplessness— Is There Hope?

What would happen if a person's defenses failed or if the person appraised a threatening situation as hopeless?

Bruno Bettelheim (1960), who survived imprisonment in Nazi concentration camps, described a reaction he called "give-up-itis." Many of the prisoners felt so helpless that they developed a "zombie-like" detachment that made them into "walking corpses." Martin Seligman has described a similar reaction in Vietnam prisoner of war camps. Seligman reports the case of a young marine who had adapted unusually well to the stresses of being a POW. His health was apparently related to a promise made by his captors that if he cooperated, he would be released on a certain date. As the date approached, his spirits soared. Then came a devastating blow. He had been deceived. His captors had never really intended to release him. He immediately lapsed into a deep depression, refused to eat or drink, and died shortly thereafter.

Those seem like extreme examples. Does anything similar occur outside of concentration camps?

Apparently so. For example, researchers in Finland recently discovered that even in everyday life, people who feel a sense of hopelessness die at elevated rates (Everson, Goldberg, & Salonen, 1996).

How can we explain the impact of stressful emotions? Recent attempts to understand such events have focused on the concept of *learned helplessness* (Seligman, 1989). **Learned helplessness** *is a learned inability to overcome obstacles and avoid punishing or aversive stimuli.* To observe learned helplessness, let's see what happens when animals are tested in a shuttle box (Fig. 14–6 ◆). If placed in one side of a divided box, dogs will quickly learn to leap to the other side to escape an electric shock. If they are given a warning before the shock occurs (for example, a light that dims), most dogs learn to avoid the shock by leaping the barrier before the shock arrives. This is true of most dogs, but not those who have learned to feel helpless.

How is a dog made to feel helpless?

Before being tested in the shuttle box, some dogs are placed in a harness (from which they cannot escape) and are given several painful shocks. The animal is helpless to prevent these shocks (Overmier & Seligman, 1967). When placed in the shuttle box, these dogs react to the first shock by crouching, howling, and whining. None try to escape. They helplessly resign themselves to their fate. After all, they have already learned that there is nothing they can do about shock. In short, helplessness is a psychological state that frequently occurs when events *appear to be uncontrollable* (Seligman, 1989). Similar effects occur when humans fail or when they receive punishment they cannot predict or prevent. For example, college students who feel helpless about their school work tend to procrastinate and to give up easily. As you might expect, they also earn poor grades and are frequently unhappy (McKean, 1994).

Where humans are concerned, attributions (discussed in Chapter 13) have a large effect on helplessness. Persons who are made to feel helpless in one situation are more likely to act helpless in other situations if they attribute their failure to *lasting, general* factors. An example would be concluding "I must be stupid" after failing to solve a series of puzzles. In contrast, attributing failure to specific factors in the original situation ("I'm not too good at puzzles" or "I wasn't really interested") tends to prevent learned helplessness from spreading (Alloy et al., 1984; Anderson et al., 1984).

(a)

(b)

(c)

(d)

Figure 14–6 ◆ In the normal course of escape and avoidance learning, a light dims shortly before the floor is electrified **(a)**. Since the light does not yet have meaning for the dog, the dog receives a shock (non-injurious, by the way) and leaps the barrier **(b)**. Dogs soon learn to watch for the dimming of the light **(c)** and to jump before receiving a shock **(d)**. Dogs made to feel "helpless" rarely even learn to escape shock, much less to avoid it.

Depression

Seligman and others have drawn attention to the similarities between learned helplessness and **depression**. Symptoms that occur in both depression and learned helplessness include feelings of *despondency, powerlessness, and hopelessness.* Also common are decreased activity, lowered aggression, loss of sexual drive and appetite. In humans there is a tendency to see oneself as failing, even when this is not the case (Seligman, 1989).

Depression is one of the most widespread emotional problems, and it undoubtedly has many causes (see Chapter 18). However, Seligman has made a good case for learned helplessness being a factor in many cases of depression and hopelessness. For example, Seligman (1972a) describes the fate of Archie, a 15-year-old boy. For Archie, school is an unending series of shocks and failures. Other students treat him as if he's stupid; in class he rarely answers questions because he doesn't know some of the words. He feels knocked down every direction he turns. These may not be electric shocks, but they are certainly emotional "shocks," and Archie has learned to feel helpless to prevent them. When he leaves school his chances of success will be poor. He has learned to passively endure whatever shocks life has in store for him.

Does Seligman's research give any clues about how to "unlearn" helplessness?

Hope   With dogs, one effective technique is to forcibly drag them away from the shock into the "safe" compartment. After this is done several times, the animals regain "hope" and feelings of control over the environment. Just how this can be done with humans is a question psychologists are currently exploring. It seems obvious, for instance, that someone like Archie would benefit from an educational program that would allow him to "succeed" repeatedly.

In **mastery training**, *responses are reinforced that lead to mastery of a threat or control over one's environment.* Animals who undergo such training become more resistant to learned helplessness (Volpicelli et al., 1983). For example, animals that first learn to successfully escape shock are more persistent in trying to escape inescapable shock. In effect, they won't give up, even when the situation is "hopeless."

Such findings suggest that we might be able to "immunize" people against helplessness and depression by allowing them to master seemingly impossible challenges. The Outward Bound schools, in which people pit themselves against the rigors of mountaineering, white-water canoeing, and wilderness survival, might serve as a model for such a program. Similarly, psychologists have found that the mental and physical health of elderly persons who live in nursing homes can be improved by giving them more control over their lives (Seligman, 1989). Things as small as choosing what to eat for lunch or being allowed to

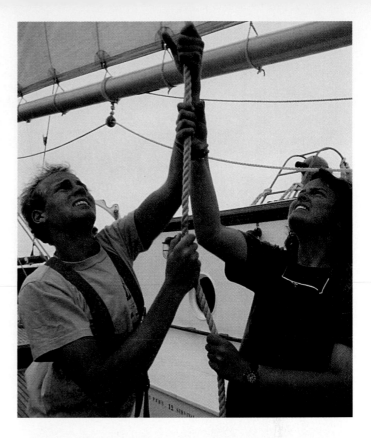

Mastery training can occur informally when people learn to cope with challenges. For example, 18- to 21-year-old trainees on a transatlantic sailing voyage showed marked improvements in their ability to cope with stress (Norris & Weinman, 1996).

decorate one's room can be enough to counteract feelings of helplessness.

The value of hope should not be overlooked. As fragile as this emotion seems to be, it is a powerful antidote to depression and helplessness. As an individual, you may find hope in religion, nature, human companionship, or even technology. Wherever you find it, remember its value: Hope is among the most important of all human emotions. Having positive beliefs, such as optimism, hope, and a sense of meaning and control is closely related to personal well-being (Taylor, 1990).

Depression, a Problem for Everyone

During the school year, up to 78 percent of all college students suffer some symptoms of depression. At any given time, from 16 to 30 percent of the student population is depressed (McLennan, 1992; Wong & Whitaker, 1993).

Why Students Get the Blues   Why should so many students be "blue"? Various problems contribute to depressive feelings. Here are some of the most common:

1.   Stresses from the increased difficulty of college work and pressures to make a career choice often leave students feeling that they are missing out on fun or that all their hard work is meaningless.

In a survey, college students reported that they were depressed from one to two times a month. These episodes lasted from a few hours to several days (Snyder & Smith, 1985).

2. Isolation and loneliness are common when a student leaves his or her support group behind. In the past, family, a circle of high school friends, and often an intimate boyfriend or girlfriend could be counted on for support and encouragement.

3. Problems with studying and grades frequently trigger depression. Many students enter college with high aspirations and little experience with failure. At the same time, many lack basic skills necessary for academic success.

4. Another common cause of college depression is the breakup of an intimate relationship, either with a former boyfriend or girlfriend or with a newly formed college romance.

5. Students who find it difficult to live up to their idealized images of themselves are especially prone to depression (Scott & O'Hara, 1993).

6. Stressful events frequently trigger depression. An added danger is that depressed students are more likely to abuse alcohol, which is a depressant (Camatta & Nagoshi, 1995).

Recognizing Depression Most people know, obviously enough, when they are "down." Aaron Beck, an authority on depression, suggests you should assume that more than a minor fluctuation in mood is involved when five conditions exist:

1. You have a consistently negative opinion of yourself.

2. You engage in frequent self-criticism and self-blame.

3. You place negative interpretations on events that usually wouldn't bother you.

4. The future looks bleak and negative.

5. You feel that your responsibilities are overwhelming.

What can be done to combat depression?

The following highlight gives some suggestions that you may find helpful.

Using Psychology

Coping with Depression

If you don't do well on a test or class assignment, how do you react? If you see it as a small, isolated setback, you probably won't feel too bad. However, if you feel like you have "blown it" in a big way, depression may follow. Psychologists have observed that students who strongly link everyday events to long-term goals (such as a successful career or high income) tend to overreact to day-to-day disappointments (McIntosh, Harlow, & Martin, 1995).

What does the preceding tell us about the college blues? The implication is that it's important to take daily tasks one step at a time and to chip away at them. That way, you are less likely to feel overwhelmed, helpless, or hopeless.

Beck and Greenberg (1974) suggest that when you feel "blue," you should make a *daily schedule* for yourself. Try to schedule activities to fill up every hour during the day. It is best to start with easy activities and progress to more difficult tasks. Check off each activity as it is completed. That way, you will begin to break the self-defeating cycle of feeling helpless and falling further behind. (Depressed students spend much of their time sleeping.) A series of small accomplishments, successes, or pleasures may be all that you need to get going again. However, if you are lacking skills needed for success in college, ask for help in getting them. Don't remain "helpless."

Feelings of worthlessness and hopelessness are usually supported by self-critical or negative thoughts. Beck and Greenberg recommend writing down such thoughts as they occur, especially those that immediately precede feelings of sadness. After you have collected these thoughts, write a rational answer to each. For example, the thought "No one loves me" should be answered with a list of those who do care. (See Chapter 19 for more information.) One more point to keep in mind is this: When events begin to improve, try to accept it as a sign that better times lie ahead. Positive events are most likely to end depression if you view them as stable and continuing, rather than temporary and fragile (Needles & Abramson, 1990).

Attacks of the "college blues" are common and should be distinguished from more serious cases of depression. Severe depression is a serious problem that can lead to suicide or a major impairment of emotional functioning. In such cases it would be wise to seek professional help.

Stress and Health— Unmasking a Hidden Killer

At a university medical school, Dr. Thomas Holmes and his associates confirmed something long suspected: Stressful events can reduce the body's natural defenses against disease. Stress, therefore, can increase the likelihood of illness (Holmes & Masuda, 1972). Holmes found that disaster, depression, and sorrow often precede illness. More surprising is the finding that almost any major *change* in one's life requires adjustment and may increase susceptibility to accidents and illness.

How would I know if I were subjecting myself to too much stress?

Life Events and Stress

Holmes and his associates developed a rating scale to estimate the health hazards faced when stresses add up. Their **Social Readjustment Rating Scale (SRRS)** is reprinted in Table 14–5 ■. Notice that the effect of life events is expressed in **life change units (LCUs)** (*numerical values assigned to each life event*).

As you read the scale, notice too that a positive life event may be as costly as a disaster. Marriage rates 50 life change units, even though it is usually a happy event. Notice also that many items read "Change in. . . ." This means that an improvement in life conditions can be as costly as a decline.

To use the scale, add up the LCUs for all life events you have experienced during the last year and compare the total to the following standards.

0–150: No significant problems
150–199: Mild life crisis (33 percent chance of illness)
200–299: Moderate life crisis (50 percent chance of illness)
300 or more: Major life crisis (80 percent chance of illness)

According to Holmes, there is a high chance of illness or accident in the near future when one's LCU total exceeds 300 points.

A more conservative rating of stress can be obtained by totaling LCU points for only the previous 6 months. Studies of U.S. Navy personnel produced the figures shown here for 6-month totals (Rahe, 1972).

Table 14-5 ■ Social Readjustment Rating Scale (SRRS)

The SRRS lists significant life events and offers a rating of their contribution to susceptibility to illness.

Rank	Life Event	Life Change Units	Rank	Life Event	Life Change Units
1	Death of spouse	100	22	Change in responsibilities at work	29
2	Divorce	73	23	Son or daughter leaving home	29
3	Marital separation	65	24	Trouble with in-laws	29
4	Jail term	63	25	Outstanding personal achievement	28
5	Death of a close family member	63	26	Spouse begins or stops work	26
6	Personal injury or illness	53	27	Begin or end school	26
7	Marriage	50	28	Change in living conditions	25
8	Fired at work	47	29	Revision of personal habits	24
9	Marital reconciliation	45	30	Trouble with boss	23
10	Retirement	45	31	Change in work hours or conditions	20
11	Change in health of family member	44	32	Change in residence	20
12	Pregnancy	40	33	Change in school	20
13	Sex difficulties	39	34	Change in recreation	19
14	Gain of new family member	39	35	Change in church activities	19
15	Business readjustment	39	36	Change in social activities	18
16	Change in financial state	38	37	Take out loan less than $20,000	17
17	Death of close friend	37	38	Change in sleeping habits	16
18	Change to different line of work	36	39	Change in number of family get-togethers	15
19	Change in number of arguments with spouse	35	40	Change in eating habits	15
			41	Vacation	13
20	Take out mortgage or loan for major purchase	31	42	Christmas	12
21	Foreclosure of mortgage or loan	30	43	Minor violation of the law	11

LCUs	Average number of illnesses reported for 6-month period
0–100	1.4
300–400	1.9
500–600	2.1

Many of the listed life changes don't seem relevant to young adults or college students. Does the SRRS apply to these people?

The SRRS tends to be more appropriate for older, more established adults. However, research has shown that the health of college students is also affected by stressful events, such as entering college, changing majors, or the breakup of a steady relationship (Crandall, Preisler, & Aussprung, 1992).

Evaluation The SRRS is not a foolproof way to rate stress, and some studies have failed to confirm the LCU-illness link (Weinberger, 1987). Furthermore, it is debatable whether positive life events are always stressful (Feuerstein et al.,

Marriage is usually a positive life event. Nevertheless, the many changes it brings can be stressful.

1986a). Perhaps the most important criticism of the scale is based on a point made earlier: People differ greatly in their reactions to the same event. For such reasons, the SRRS is, at best, only a rough index of stress. Nevertheless, it's hard to ignore a study in which people were deliberately exposed to the virus that causes common colds. The results were nothing to sneeze at: If a person had a high stress score, she or he was much more likely to actually get a cold (Cohen et al., 1993).

To summarize, a high LCU score should be taken seriously. If your score goes much over 300, an adjustment in your activities or lifestyle may be needed. Remember, "To be forewarned is to be forearmed."

There must be more to stress than major life changes. Isn't there a link between ongoing stresses and health?

The Hazards of Hassles In addition to having a direct impact, major life events spawn countless daily frustrations and irritations (Pillow, Zautra, & Sandler, 1996). Also, many of us face ongoing stresses at work or at home that do not involve major life changes. In view of these facts, psychologist Richard Lazarus and his associates studied the impact of minor but frequent stresses. Lazarus (1981) aptly refers to such *distressing daily annoyances* as **hassles, or microstressors.** Hassles range from traffic jams to losing classroom notes; from an argument with a roommate to an employer's unrealistic demands (see Table 14–6 ■).

In a year-long study, Lazarus had 100 men and women keep track of the frequency and severity of the hassles they endured. Participants also filled out questionnaires about their physical and mental health. As Lazarus had suspected, frequent and severe hassles turned out to be better predictors of day-to-day health than major life events were. However, major life events did predict changes in health 1 or 2 years after the events took place. It appears that daily hassles are closely linked to immediate health and psychological well-being (Roberts, 1995; Ruffin, 1993). Major life changes have more of a long-term impact.

In follow-up work, Lazarus and others found that the personal importance of hassles affects the amount of stress they produce (Lazarus et al., 1985). Microstressors that are viewed as central to one's self-worth are many times more likely to cause trouble. For many people, central hassles are linked to work, family, and relationships. But as psychologist Rand Gruen notes, "Taking care of paperwork or being organized can be central for some people" (Fisher, 1984). This observation again emphasizes that stress occurs in people, not in the environment. Stress is always related to personality, values, perceptions, and personal resources (Moos & Swindle, 1990).

What can be done about a high LCU score or feeling excessively hassled?

A good response is to use stress management skills. For serious problems, stress management should be learned directly from a therapist or a stress clinic. When ordinary stresses are involved, there is much you can do on your own. This chapter's Applications section will give you a start. In the meantime, take it easy!

One way to guarantee that you will experience a large number of life changes and hassles is to live in a foreign culture. The following discussion offers a brief glimpse into some of the consequences of culture shock.

Table 14–6   ■   Examples of Daily Hassles

Too many responsibilities or commitments
Problems with work, boss, or co-workers
Unexpected house guests
Inconsiderate neighbors
Noisy, messy, or quarreling children
Regrets over past decisions
Having trouble making decisions
Money worries or concerns
Not enough time for family, relaxation, entertainment
Loneliness, social isolation, separated from family
Physical illness, symptoms, complaints
Concerns about weight, appearance
Frustrations with daily chores
Delays, transportation problems
Paperwork, filling out forms
Misplacing or losing things
Noise, crime, pollution, bad weather, disturbing news event, deteriorating neighborhoods

---

Cultural Diversity

Acculturative Stress—Stranger in a Strange Land

How stressful is it to be a "stranger in a strange land"? Around the world, an increasing number of emigrants and refugees must adapt to dramatic changes in language, dress, values, and social customs. For many, the result is a period of culture shock or **acculturative stress** (*stress caused by adapting to a foreign culture*). Typical reactions to acculturative stress are anxiety, hostility, depression, alienation, physical illness, or identity confusion (Thomas, 1995).

The severity of acculturative stress is related, in part, to how a person adapts to a new culture. Four main patterns are:

Integration—maintain your old cultural identity but participate in the new culture

Separation—maintain your old cultural identity and avoid contact with the new culture

---

Health, Stress, and Coping | **469**

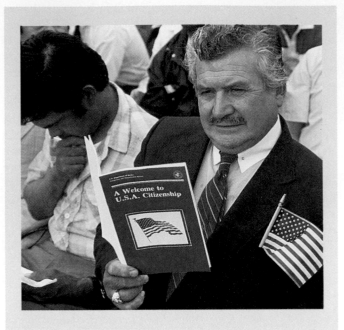

One of the best antidotes for acculturative stress is a society that tolerates or even celebrates ethnic diversity. While some people find it hard to accept new immigrants, the fact is, nearly everyone's family tree includes people who were once strangers in a strange land.

> Assimilation—adopt the new culture as your own and have contact with its members
>
> Marginalization—reject your old culture but suffer rejection by members of the new culture

To illustrate each pattern, let's consider a family that has migrated to the United States from the imaginary country of Farlandia.

The father favors integration. He is learning English and wants to get involved in American life. At the same time, he is a leader in the Farlandian-American community and spends much of his leisure time with other Farlandian-Americans. His level of acculturative stress is low.

The mother only speaks Farlandish and only interacts with other Farlandian-Americans. She remains almost completely separate from American society. Her stress level is high.

The teenage daughter is annoyed by hearing Farlandish spoken at home, by her mother's serving only Farlandian food, and by having to spend her leisure time with her extended Farlandian family. She would prefer to speak English and to be with her American friends. Her desire to assimilate creates moderate stress.

The son doesn't particularly value his Farlandian heritage, yet he is rejected by his schoolmates because he speaks with a Farlandian accent. He feels trapped between two cultures. His position is marginal and his stress level is high.

To summarize, those who feel marginalized tend to be highly stressed; those who seek to remain separate are also highly stressed; those who pursue integration into their new culture are minimally stressed; and those who assimilate are moderately stressed. (Sources: Berry, 1990; Rogler, Cortes, & Malgady, 1991; Williams & Berry, 1991.)

Psychosomatic Disorders

As we have seen, chronic or repeated stress can damage physical health, as well as upset emotional well-being. Prolonged stress reactions are closely related to a large number of psychosomatic (SIKE-oh-so-MAT-ik) illnesses. In **psychosomatic disorders** (*psyche:* mind; *soma:* body), *psychological factors contribute to actual bodily damage or to damaging changes in bodily functioning.* Psychosomatic problems, therefore, are *not* the same as *hypochondria.* **Hypochondriacs** (HI-po-KON-dree-aks) *imagine that they suffer from diseases.* There is nothing imaginary about asthma, a migraine headache, or high blood pressure. Severe psychosomatic disorders can be fatal. The person who says, "Oh it's *just* psychosomatic" misunderstands the seriousness of stress-related diseases.

Are stomach ulcers psychosomatic?

For many years, stomach ulcers were thought to be primarily caused by stress. However, recent medical research has

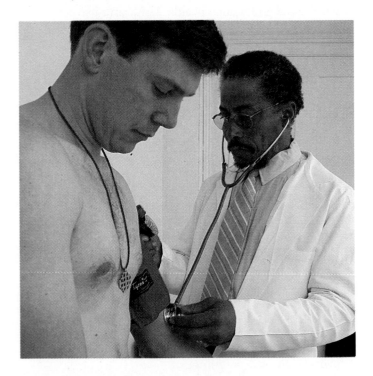

It is estimated that at least half of all patients who see a doctor have a psychosomatic disorder or an illness that is complicated by psychosomatic symptoms.

traced some ulcers to bacterial infections of the stomach. This does not rule out the possibility that ulcers may occasionally be psychosomatic. Stress and lifestyle factors may contribute to the development of stomach infections (Doctor & Doctor, 1994). However, it is more likely that a person suffering from stomach pain has functional dyspepsia. This psychosomatic disorder causes ulcer-like pain, but does not make holes in the stomach lining (Whitehead, 1992).

The most common psychosomatic problems are gastrointestinal and respiratory (dyspepsia and asthma, for example), but many others exist. Typical problems include eczema (skin rash), hives, migraine headaches, rheumatoid arthritis, hypertension (high blood pressure), colitis (ulceration of the colon), and heart disease. Actually, these are only the major problems. Lesser health complaints are also frequently stress related. Typical examples include sore muscles, headaches, neckaches, backaches, indigestion, constipation, chronic diarrhea, fatigue, insomnia, premenstrual problems, and sexual dysfunctions (Brown, 1980; De Benedittis et al., 1990). For some of these problems biofeedback may be helpful. The next section explains how.

Biofeedback

Psychologists have discovered that people can learn to control bodily activities once thought to be involuntary. This is done by applying *informational feedback to bodily control*, a process called **biofeedback.** If I were to say to you, "Raise the temperature of your right hand," you probably couldn't, because you wouldn't know if you were succeeding. To make your task easier, we could attach a sensitive thermometer to your hand. The thermometer could be wired so that an increase in temperature would activate a signal light. Then, all you would have to do is try to keep the light on as much as possible. With practice and the help of biofeedback, you could learn to raise your hand temperature at will.

Biofeedback holds promise as a way to treat psychosomatic problems (Fig. 14–7 ◆). People have been successfully trained to treat migraine headaches with biofeedback. Sensors are taped to patients' hands and foreheads. Patients then learn to redirect blood flow away from the head to their extremities. Since migraine headaches involve excessive blood flow to the head, biofeedback helps patients reduce the frequency of their headaches (Gauthier et al., 1994; Grimsley & Karriker, 1996).

Early successes led many to predict that biofeedback would offer a cure for psychosomatic illnesses, anxiety, phobias, drug abuse, chronic pain, and a long list of other problems. In reality, biofeedback has proved helpful, but not an instant cure (Amar, 1993). Biofeedback can help relieve muscle-tension headaches, migraine headaches, and chronic pain (Arena et al., 1995; Flor & Birbaumer, 1993; Gauthier et al., 1994). It shows promise for lowering blood pressure and controlling heart rhythms (Blanchard et al., 1996; McGrady, 1994). The technique has been used with some success to control epileptic seizures and hyperactivity in

Figure 14–7 ◆ In biofeedback training bodily processes are monitored and processed electronically. A signal is then routed back to the patient through headphones, signal lights, or other means. This information helps the patient alter bodily activities not normally under voluntary control.

children (Potashkin & Beckles, 1990; Sterman, 1996). Insomnia also responds to biofeedback therapy (Barowsky et al., 1990).

How does biofeedback help? Some researchers believe that many of its benefits arise from *general relaxation*. Others stress that there is no magic in biofeedback itself. The method simply acts as a "mirror" to help a person perform tasks involving *self-regulation* (Green & Shellenberger, 1986; Norris, 1986). Just as a mirror does not comb your hair, biofeedback does not do anything by itself. It can, however, help people make desired changes in their behavior (Amar, 1993).

Does biofeedback apply to brain activity?

For the moment, it seems that we have not yet reached the age of "electronic yoga" or "instant bliss." This is especially true of low-cost home "alpha-feedback" machines. These devices are so inaccurate that many "blissed out" users are actually listening to electrical noise from their house wiring, rather than their own brain waves (Beyerstein, 1985). Likewise, commercial programs that claim to teach people to produce alpha waves are essentially worthless (Beyerstein, 1990). Although biofeedback is a useful therapy, it must be applied skillfully to be of value (Amar, 1993).

It would be a mistake to assume that stress is the sole cause of psychosomatic diseases. Usually, several factors combine to produce damage. These include hereditary differences, specific organ weaknesses, and learned reactions to stress. Personality also enters the picture. As mentioned earlier, there may be a general disease-prone personality. To a degree, there are also "headache personalities," "asthma personalities," and so on. The best documented of such patterns is the "cardiac personality"—a person at high risk for heart disease.

The Cardiac Personality

Two noted cardiologists, Meyer Friedman and Ray Rosenman, offer a glimpse at how some people create unnecessary stress. In a landmark study of heart problems, Friedman and Rosenman (1974) classified people into two categories: **Type A personalities** (*those who run a high risk of heart attack*) and **Type B personalities** (*those who are unlikely to have a heart attack*). Friedman and Rosenman then did an 8-year follow-up, finding more than twice the rate of heart disease in Type A's than in Type B's (Rosenman et al., 1975).

What is the Type A personality like?

Type A   Type A people are hard driving, ambitious, highly competitive, achievement oriented, and striving. Type A people believe that with enough effort they can overcome any obstacle, and they "push" themselves accordingly.

Perhaps the most telltale signs of a Type A personality are *time urgency* and chronic *anger* or *hostility*. Type A's seem to chafe at the normal pace of events. They hurry from one activity to another, racing the clock in self-imposed urgency. As they do, they feel a constant sense of frustration and anger. Feelings of anger and hostility, in particular, are strongly related to increased risk of heart attack (Miller et al., 1996). One study found that 15 percent of a group of 25-year-old doctors and lawyers who scored high on a hostility test were dead by age 50.

Some news reports have stated that Type A behavior is not a factor in heart attacks. Why is that?

It's true that some studies have failed to show a link between

Individuals with Type A personalities feel a continuous sense of anger, irritation, and hostility.

Type A behavior and heart attacks. However, many of these failures appear to be a result of using less accurate ways to classify people as A's and B's. (Friedman and Rosenman did probing interviews to classify people. Many later studies have used paper-and-pencil tests.) There is also growing evidence that anger or hostility may be the core *lethal factor* of Type A behavior (Chesney & Rosenman, 1985; Denollet, 1993; Friedman & Booth-Kewley, 1987). Placing such disputes aside, hundreds of studies *have* supported the validity of the Type A concept. At this point, it still seems that Type A's would be wise to take their increased health risks seriously (Miller et al., 1991; Sprafka et al., 1990).

How are Type A people identified?

Characteristics of Type A people are summarized in the short self-identification test presented in Table 14–7 ■. If most of the list applies to you, you may be a Type A. However, confirmation of your type would require more powerful testing methods. Also, remember that the original definition of Type A behavior was probably too broad. The key psychological factors that increase heart disease risk appear to be anger, hostility, and mistrust (Suls & Swain, 1994).

A large-scale study of heart attack victims found that modifying Type A behavior significantly reduces the rate of repeat heart attacks (Friedman et al., 1984). Since our society places a premium on achievement, competition, and mastery, it is not surprising that many people develop Type A personalities. The best way to avoid the self-made stress this causes is to adopt behavior that is the opposite of that listed in Table 14–7 (Nakano, 1996).

It is entirely possible to succeed in life without sacrificing your health or happiness in the process. People who

Table 14–7 ■ **Characteristics of the Type A Person**

Check the items that apply to you. Do you:

_____ Have a habit of explosively accentuating various key words in ordinary speech even when there is no need for such accentuation?

_____ Finish other persons' sentences for them?

_____ *Always* move, walk, and eat rapidly?

_____ Quickly skim reading material and prefer summaries or condensations of books?

_____ Become easily angered by slow-moving lines or traffic?

_____ Feel an impatience with the rate at which most events take place?

_____ Tend to be unaware of the details or beauty of your surroundings?

_____ Frequently strive to think of or do two or more things simultaneously?

_____ Almost always feel vaguely guilty when you relax, vacation, or do absolutely nothing for several days?

_____ Tend to evaluate your worth in quantitative terms (number of A's earned, amount of income, number of games won, and so forth)?

_____ Have nervous gestures or muscle twitches, such as grinding your teeth, clenching your fists, or drumming your fingers?

_____ Attempt to schedule more and more activities into less time and in so doing make fewer allowances for unforeseen problems?

_____ Frequently think about other things while talking to someone?

_____ Repeatedly take on more responsibilities than you can comfortably handle?

Shortened and adapted from Meyer Friedman and Ray H. Rosenman, *Type A Behavior and Your Heart* (New York: Knopf, 1983).

frequently feel angry and hostile toward others may benefit from the advice of Redford Williams, a physician interested in Type A behavior. The following highlight summarizes his advice.

Using Psychology

Strategies for Reducing Hostility

According to Redford Williams, reducing hostility involves three goals. First, you must stop mistrusting the motives of others. Second, you must find ways to reduce how often you feel anger, indignation, irritation, and rage. Third, you must learn to be kinder and more considerate of others. Based on his clinical experience, Williams (1989) recommends 12 strategies for reducing hostility and increasing trust.

1. Become aware of your angry, hostile, and cynical thoughts by logging them in a notebook. Record what happened, what you thought and felt, and what actions you took. Review your hostility log at the end of each week.

2. Admit to yourself and to someone you trust that you have a problem with excessive anger and hostility.

3. Interrupt hostile, cynical thoughts whenever they

occur. (The Applications for Chapter 19 explains a thought-stopping method you can use for this step.)

4. When you have an angry, hostile, or cynical thought about someone, silently look for the ways in which it is irrational or unreasonable.

5. When you are angry, try to mentally put yourself in the other person's shoes.

6. Learn to laugh at yourself and use humor to defuse your anger.

7. Learn reliable ways to relax. Two methods are described in this chapter's Applications section. Another can be found in the Applications for Chapter 19.

8. Practice trusting others more. Begin with situations where no great harm will be done if the person lets you down.

9. Make an effort to listen more to others and to really understand what they are saying.

10. Learn to be assertive, rather than aggressive in upsetting situations. (See Chapter 21 for information about self-assertion skills.)

11. Rise above small irritations by pretending that today is the last day of your life.

12. Rather than blaming people for mistreating you, and becoming angry over it, try to forgive them. We all have shortcomings.

How do Type A people who do not develop heart disease differ from those who do?

Hardy Personality

Psychologists Salvatore Maddi and Suzanne Kobasa (1984) studied people who have what they call a **hardy personality.** Such people seem to be *unusually resistant to stress.* Maddi and Kobasa's studies began with a comparison of two groups of managers at a large utility company. All of the managers held high-stress positions. Yet, some tended to get sick after stressful events, while others were rarely ill. How did the people who were thriving differ from their "stressed-out" colleagues? Both groups seemed to have traits typical of the Type A personality, so that wasn't the explanation. They were also quite similar in most other respects. The main difference was that the hardy group seemed to hold a world view that consisted of the following:

1. They had a sense of personal *commitment* to self, work, family, and other stabilizing values.
2. They felt that they had *control* over their lives and their work.
3. They had a tendency to see life as a series of *challenges,* rather than as a series of threats or problems.

These traits seem to allow the hardy personality to transcend stresses. Basically, hardy persons react to stressors with less arousal and negative emotion than their non-hardy neighbors do. Non-hardy persons tend to exaggerate the negative impact of life experiences (Wiebe, 1991). Hardy persons, in contrast, are less likely to feel threatened in stressful situations. Clearly, a willingness to commit yourself to active coping can do much to change stress into a healthy challenge (Florian, Mikulincer, & Taubman, 1995). Hardiness lowers the negative impact of stress and increases personal satisfaction with one's work (Rush, Schoel, & Barnard, 1995).

A very basic question remains unanswered in our discussion of stress. How does stress, and our response to it, translate into bodily damage? The answer seems to lie in the body's defenses against stress, a pattern known as the *general adaptation syndrome.*

The General Adaptation Syndrome

The **general adaptation syndrome (G.A.S.)** is a series of bodily reactions to prolonged stress. Study of the general adaptation syndrome began when Canadian physiologist Hans Selye (1976) noticed that the first symptoms of almost any disease or trauma (poisoning, infection, injury, or stress) are almost identical. After more research, Selye concluded that the body responds in the same way to any stress, be it infection, failure, embarrassment, adjustment to a new job, trouble at school, or a stormy romance.

What pattern does the body's response to stress take?

Figure 14–8 ◆ The General Adaptation Syndrome. During the initial alarm reaction to stress, resistance falls below normal. It rises again as bodily resources are mobilized, and it remains high during the stage of resistance. Eventually, resistance falls again as the stage of exhaustion is reached. (From *The Stress of Life* by Hans Selye. Copyright © 1976 by Hans Selye. Used by permission of McGraw-Hill Book Company.)

The G.A.S. consists of three stages: an *alarm reaction,* a *stage of resistance,* and a *stage of exhaustion* (Selye, 1976).

In the **alarm reaction,** the *body mobilizes its resources* to cope with added stress. The pituitary gland secretes a hormone that causes the adrenal glands to step up their output of adrenaline and noradrenaline. As these hormones are dumped into the bloodstream, some bodily processes are speeded up and others are slowed so that bodily resources are applied where they are needed.

We should all be thankful that our bodies instantly and automatically respond to emergencies. But brilliant as this automatic emergency system is, it can also cause problems (Wilson, 1986). In the first phase of the alarm reaction, people have such symptoms as headache, fever, fatigue, sore muscles, shortness of breath, diarrhea, upset stomach, loss of appetite, and lack of energy. Notice that these are also the symptoms of being sick, of stressful travel, of high-altitude sickness, of final exams week, and (possibly) of falling in love!

Soon the body's defenses are stabilized, and symptoms of the alarm reaction disappear. Physically, the body has made adjustments to resist stress. However, the outward appearance of normality comes at a high cost. During the **stage of resistance,** *bodily adjustments to stress stabilize,* but at a high physical cost. The body is better able to cope with the original source of stress, but its resistance to other stresses is lowered (Fig. 14–8 ◆). For example, animals placed in an extremely cold environment become more resistant to the cold, but more susceptible to infection. It is during the stage of resistance that the first signs of psychosomatic disorders begin to appear.

If stress continues, the **stage of exhaustion** may be reached. In this stage *the body's resources are exhausted* and the stress hormones are depleted. Unless a way of relieving stress is found, the result will be a psychosomatic disease, a serious loss of health, or complete collapse.

The stages of the G.A.S. may sound melodramatic if you are young and healthy or if you have never endured prolonged stress. However, stress should not be taken lightly. When Selye examined animals in the later stages of the G.A.S., he found enlargement and discoloration of their adrenal glands, intense shrinkage of the thymus, spleen, and lymph nodes, and deep bleeding stomach ulcers. In addition to such direct effects, stress can disrupt the body's *immune system*, making people more vulnerable to illness. The **immune system** *mobilizes bodily defenses (such as white blood cells) against invading microbes and other disease agents* (Ader & Cohen, 1993).

Research Frontier

Stress, Illness, and the Immune System

Health experts have uncovered fascinating evidence that the body and the brain work together as a kind of "health care system." The body's immune system is regulated, in part, by the brain. Because of this link, stress and upsetting emotions may affect the immune system in ways that increase susceptibility to disease (Ader & Cohen, 1993). (By the way, *study of the links among behavior, disease, and the immune system* is called **psychoneuroimmunology.** Try dropping that into a conversation sometime if you want to observe a stress reaction!)

Psychologists have found that the immune system is weakened in students during major exam times, and by divorce, bereavement, a troubled marriage, job loss, depression, and similar stresses (Gilbert et al., 1996; Herbert & Cohen, 1993; Stein et al., 1990). Findings such as these suggest that stress leads to illness by affecting the immune system. This is probably why the "double whammy" of getting sick when you are trying to cope with prolonged or severe stress is so common (Ader & Cohen, 1993).

Could reducing stress help prevent illness?

Yes. Various psychological approaches, such as support groups, relaxation exercises, guided imagery, and stress management training can actually boost immune system functioning (Kiecolt-Glaser & Glaser, 1992). By doing so, they help promote and restore health. There is even evidence that such measures improve the chances of survival following life-threatening diseases, such as cancer (Anderson et al., 1994). No one is immune to stress. Nevertheless, it's reassuring to know that managing stress can help protect your immune system and health.

A Look Ahead The work we have reviewed here has drawn new attention to the fact that each of us has a personal responsibility for maintaining and promoting health. In the Applications section that follows, we will look at what you can do to better cope with stress and the health risks that it entails. The concluding Exploration looks at meditation as a potential stress-reducing technique. But first, the following Learning Check may help you maintain a healthy grade on your next psychology test.

Learning Check

1. Holmes' SRRS appears to predict long-range changes in health, whereas the frequency and severity of daily microstressors is closely related to immediate ratings of health. T or F?

2. Ulcers, migraine headaches, and hypochondria are all frequently psychosomatic disorders. T or F?

3. Which of the following is *not* classified as a psychosomatic disorder?
   a. hypertension **b.** colitis **c.** eczema **d.** thymus

4. Biofeedback is a type of meditation in which the body is made very quiet so that bodily functioning can be detected. T or F?

5. Two major elements of biofeedback training appear to be relaxation and self-regulation. T or F?

6. Evidence is beginning to suggest that the most important feature of the Type A personality is a sense of time urgency, rather than feelings of anger and hostility. T or F?

7. A sense of commitment, challenge, and control characterizes the hardy personality. T or F?

8. The first stage of the G.A.S. is called the _____ reaction.

9. Whereas stressful incidents suppress the immune system, stress management techniques have almost no effect on immune system functioning. T or F?

10. Acculturative stress tends to be minimal when a person who has moved to a different country maintains a high degree of separation from the new "host" culture. T or F?

Critical Thinking

11. In addition to being stress resistant, persons with hardy personalities appear to be good at avoiding a problem discussed earlier in this chapter. Can you name it?

Answers:
11. Learned helplessness.
7. T 8. alarm 9. F 10. F
1. T 2. F 3. d 4. F 5. T 6. F

Stress management *is the application of behavioral strategies to reduce stress and improve coping skills.* As promised, this section describes techniques for managing stress. Before you continue, you may want to assess your level of stress again, this time using a scale developed for undergraduate students. (See Table 14–8 ■.) Like the SRRS, high scores on the *Undergraduate Stress Questionnaire* (USQ) are associated with greater susceptibility to illness (Crandall, Preisler, & Aussprung, 1992).

The USQ is scored by simply counting the number of items you checked. (Notice that the questionnaire is a mixture of major life events and daily hassles.) The scale below is an approximate guide to the meaning of your score. But remember, stress is an internal state. If you are good at coping with stressors, a high score may not be a problem for you.

0–7	Low
8–15	Below average
16–23	Average
24–31	Above average
32–39	High
40+	Very high

Now that you have a picture of your current level of stress, what can you do about it? The simplest way of coping with stress is to modify or remove its source—by leaving a stressful job, for example. Obviously this is often impossible, which is why learning to manage stress is so important.

As shown in Figure 14–9 ◆, stress triggers *bodily effects*, *upsetting thoughts*, and *ineffective behavior*. Also shown is the fact that each element worsens the others in a vicious cycle. Indeed, the basic idea of the "Stress Game" is that once it begins, *you lose*—unless you take action to break the cycle. The information that follows tells how.

Managing Bodily Reactions

Much of the immediate discomfort of stress is caused by the body's fight-or-flight emotional response. The body is ready to act, with tight muscles and a pounding heart. When action is prevented, we merely remain "uptight." A sensible remedy is to learn a reliable, drug-free way of relaxing.

Exercise Because stress prepares the body for action, its effects can be dissipated by using the body. Any full-body exercise can be effective. Swimming, dancing, jumping rope, yoga, most sports, and especially walking are valuable outlets (Anshel, 1995b).

Be sure to choose activities that are vigorous enough to relieve tension, yet enjoyable enough to be done repeatedly. Exercising for stress management is most effective when it is done daily (Wheeler & Frank, 1988). Remember, though, that this refers to light exercise, such as walking. If you do more vigorous exercise to maintain aerobic fitness, 3 to 4 times a week is about right.

Meditation Many stress counselors recommend **meditation** *for quieting the body and promoting relaxation.* We will consider meditation techniques and their effects in the upcoming Exploration section. For now, it is enough to note that meditation is easy to learn—taking an expensive commercial course is unnecessary.

Meditation is one of the most effective ways to relax (Eppley, Abrams, & Shear, 1989). But be aware that listening to or playing music, taking nature walks, enjoying hobbies, and the like can be meditations of sorts. Anything that reliably interrupts upsetting thoughts and promotes relaxation can be helpful.

Progressive Relaxation **Progressive relaxation** refers to a method for *relaxing systematically, completely, and by choice.* To learn the full technique, consult Chapter 19 of this book. The basic idea is to tighten all the muscles in a given area of your body (the arms, for instance) and then voluntarily relax them. By first tensing and relaxing each area of the body, you can learn to be highly aware of how muscle tension feels. Then when each area is relaxed, the change is more noticeable and more controllable. In this way it is possible, with practice, to greatly reduce tension. People who have difficulty learning progressive relaxation may find biofeedback helpful.

Guided Imagery In a technique called **guided imagery,** people *visualize images that are calming, relaxing, or beneficial* in other ways. Relaxation, for instance, can be promoted by visualizing peaceful scenes. Pick several places where you feel safe, calm, and at ease. Typical locations might be a beach or lake, the woods, floating on an air mattress in a warm pool, or lying in the sun at a quiet park. To relax, vividly imagine yourself in one of these locations. In the visualized scene, you should be alone and in a comfortable position. It is important to visualize the scene as realistically as possible. Try to feel, taste, smell, hear, and see what you would actually experience in the calming scene. Practice forming such images several times a day for about 5 minutes each time. When your scenes become familiar and detailed they can be used to reduce anxiety and encourage relaxation (Rosenthal, 1993).

Table 14–8 ■ Undergraduate Stress Questionnaire

Have any of the following stressful events happened to you at any time during the last 2 weeks?

If any has, please check the space next to it. If an item has not occurred, then please leave it blank.

_____ Death (family member or friend)
_____ Death of a pet
_____ Working while in school
_____ Parents getting a divorce
_____ Registration for classes
_____ Trying to decide on major

_____ Talked with a professor
_____ Trying to get into your college
_____ Had a class presentation
_____ Had projects, research papers due
_____ Had a lot of tests
_____ It's finals week

_____ Applying to graduate school
_____ You have a hard upcoming week
_____ Lots of deadlines to meet
_____ Missed your menstrual period and waiting
_____ Had an interview
_____ Applying for a job

_____ Sat through a boring class
_____ Can't understand your professor
_____ Did badly on a test
_____ Went into a test unprepared
_____ Crammed for a test
_____ Used a fake I.D.

_____ Breaking up with boy/girlfriend
_____ Holiday
_____ Bad haircut today
_____ Victim of a crime
_____ Can't concentrate
_____ Coping with addictions

_____ Found out boy/girlfriend cheated on you
_____ Did worse than expected on test
_____ Stayed up late writing a paper
_____ Problems with your computer
_____ Favorite sports team lost
_____ Ran out of typewriter ribbon while typing

_____ Change of environment (new doctor, dentist, etc.)
_____ Bothered by not having family's social support
_____ Arguments, conflict of values with friends
_____ Had a visit from a relative and entertained him/her
_____ Noise disturbed you while trying to study
_____ Maintaining a long distance boy/girlfriend

_____ Assignments in all classes due the same day
_____ Dealt with incompetence at the registrar's office
_____ Someone borrowed something without your permission
_____ Exposed to upsetting TV show, book, or movie
_____ Problem getting home when drunk
_____ Had confrontation with an authority figure

_____ Got to class late
_____ Parents controlling with money
_____ Feel isolated
_____ Decision to have sex on your mind
_____ No sex in a while
_____ Living with boy/girlfriend

_____ Felt some peer pressure
_____ Felt need for transportation
_____ Couldn't find a parking space
_____ Property stolen
_____ Car/bike broke down, flat tire, etc.
_____ Got a traffic ticket

_____ No time to eat
_____ Having roommate conflicts
_____ Had to ask for money
_____ Lack money
_____ Checkbook didn't balance
_____ You have a hangover

_____ Someone you expected to call did not
_____ Lost something (especially, wallet)
_____ Erratic schedule
_____ Thoughts about future
_____ Dependent on other people
_____ No sleep

_____ Sick, injury
_____ Fought with boy/girlfriend
_____ Performed poorly at a task
_____ Heard bad news
_____ Thought about unfinished work
_____ Feel unorganized

_____ Someone cut ahead of you in line
_____ Job requirements changed
_____ Someone broke a promise
_____ Someone did a "pet peeve" of yours
_____ Can't finish everything you need to do

Source: Crandall, Preisler, & Aussprung, 1992.

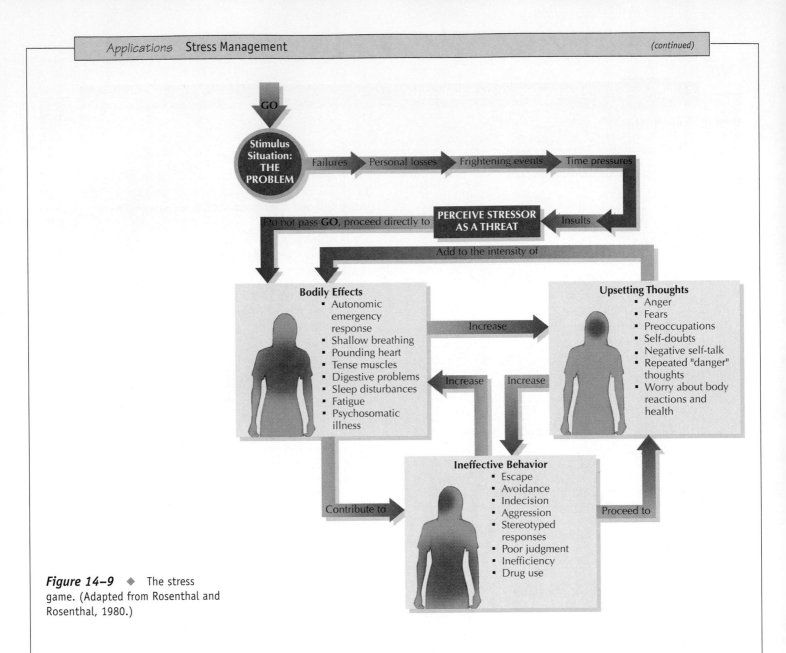

Figure 14–9 ◆ The stress game. (Adapted from Rosenthal and Rosenthal, 1980.)

Modifying Ineffective Behavior

Stress is often made worse by our response to it. The following suggestions may help you deal with stress more effectively.

Slow Down Remember that stress can be self-generated. Try to deliberately do things at a slower pace—especially if your pace has speeded up over the years. Tell yourself, "What counts most is not if I get there first, but if I get there at all" or, "My goal is distance, not speed."

Organize Disorganization creates stress. Try to take a fresh look at your situation and get organized. Setting priorities can be a real stress fighter. Ask yourself what's really important and concentrate on the things that count. Learn to let go of trivial but upsetting irritations. And above all, when you are feeling stressed, remember to K.I.S.: **K**eep **I**t **S**imple. (Some people prefer K.I.S.S.: Keep It Simple, Stupid.)

Strike a Balance Work, school, family, friends, interests, hobbies, recreation, community, church—there are many important elements in a satisfying life. Damaging stress often comes from letting one element—especially work or school—get blown out of proportion. Your goal should be quality in life, not quantity. Try to strike a balance between challenging "good stress" and relaxation (Wheeler & Frank, 1988). Remember, when you are "doing nothing" you are actually doing something very important: Set aside time for "me acts" such as loafing, browsing, puttering, playing, and napping.

Recognize and Accept Your Limits Many of us set unrealistic and perfectionistic goals. Given that no one can ever be perfect, this attitude leaves many people feeling inadequate, no matter how well they have performed. Set gradual, achievable goals for yourself. Also, set realistic limits on what you try to do on any given day. Learn to say no to added demands or responsibilities.

Seek Social Support Social support (*close, positive relationships with others*) facilitates good health and morale (Flannery & Wieman, 1989). One reason for this is that support from family and friends serves as a buffer to cushion the impact of stressful events (Taylor, 1990). Talking out problems and expressing tensions can be incredibly helpful. If things really get bad, seek help from a therapist, counselor, or clergyman (please note that bartender is not on the list).

Write about Your Feelings If you don't have someone you can talk to about stressful events, you might try expressing your thoughts and feelings in writing. Several studies have found that students who write about their upsetting experiences, thoughts, and feelings are better able to cope with stress. They also experience fewer illnesses and they get better grades (Pennebaker & Francis, 1996).

Avoiding Upsetting Thoughts

Assume you are taking a test. Suddenly you realize that you are running short of time. If you say to yourself, "Oh no, this is terrible, I've blown it now," your body's response will probably be sweating, tenseness, and a knot in your stomach. On the other hand, if you say, "I should have watched the time, but getting upset won't help now, I'll just take one question at a time," your stress level will be much lower.

As stated earlier, stress is greatly affected by the views we take of events. Physical symptoms and a tendency to make poor decisions are increased by negative thoughts or "self-talk." In many cases what you say to yourself can be the difference between coping and collapsing (Matheny et al., 1996).

Coping Statements Psychologist Donald Meichenbaum has popularized a technique called **stress inoculation.** In it, clients learn to *fight fear and anxiety with an internal monologue of positive coping statements.* First, clients learn to identify and monitor **negative self-statements** (*self-critical thoughts that increase anxiety*). Negative thoughts are a problem because they tend to directly elevate physical arousal. To counter this effect, clients learn to replace negative statements with coping statements from a supplied list. Eventually they are encouraged to make their own lists (Saunders et al., 1996).

How are coping statements applied?

Coping statements *are reassuring and self-enhancing.* They are used to block out, or counteract, negative self-talk in stressful situations. Before giving a short speech, for instance, you would replace "I'm scared," "I can't do this," "My mind will go blank and I'll panic," or "I'll sound stupid and boring" with "I'll give my speech on something I like," or "I'll breathe deeply before I start my speech," or "My pounding heart just means I'm psyched up to do my best." Additional examples of coping statements follow.

Preparing for Stressful Situation

I'll just take things one step at a time.
If I get nervous I'll just pause a moment.
Tomorrow I'll be through it.
I've managed to do this before.
What exactly do I have to do?

Confronting the Stressful Situation

Relax now, this can't really hurt me.
Stay organized, focus on the task.
There's no hurry, take it step by step.
Nobody's perfect, I'll just do my best.
It will be over soon, just be calm.

Meichenbaum cautions that saying the "right" things to yourself may not be enough to improve stress tolerance. You must practice this approach in actual stress situations. Also, it is important to develop your own personal list of coping statements by finding what works for you. Ultimately, the value of learning this, and other stress management skills, ties back into the idea that much stress is self-generated. Knowing that you can manage a demanding situation is in itself a major antidote for stress.

Coping with Frustration and Conflict

A psychologist studying frustration placed rats on a small platform at the top of a tall pole. Then he forced them to jump off the platform toward two elevated doors, one locked and the other unlocked. If the rat chose the correct door, it swung open and he landed safely on another platform. If he chose the locked door, he bounced off it and fell into a net far below.

The problem of choosing the open door was made unsolvable and very frustrating by randomly alternating which door was locked. After a time, most rats adopted a stereotyped response. That is, they chose the same door every time. This door was then permanently locked. All the rat had to do was to jump to the other door to avoid a fall, but time after time the rat bounced off the locked door (Maier, 1949).

Isn't this an example of persistence?

No. Persistence that is not *flexible* can become "stupid," stereotyped behavior like that of a rat on a jumping stand. It is important when dealing with frustration to know when to quit and establish a new direction. Here are some suggestions to help you avoid needless frustration.

1. Try to identify the source of your frustration. Is it external, or personal?

2. Is the source of frustration something that can be changed? How hard would you have to work to change it? Is it under your control at all?

3. If the source of your frustration can be changed or removed, are the necessary efforts worth it?

The answers to these questions help determine if persistence will be futile. There is value in learning to accept gracefully those things that cannot be changed.

It is also important to distinguish between *real* barriers and *imagined* barriers. All too often we create our own imaginary barriers. For example:

> Anita wants a part-time job to earn extra money. At the first place she applied, she was told that she didn't have enough "experience." Now she complains of being frustrated because she wants to work but cannot. She needs "experience" to work, but can't get experience without working. She has quit looking for a job.

Is Anita's need for experience a real barrier? Unless she applies for *many* jobs it is impossible to tell if she has overestimated its importance. For her the barrier is real enough to prevent further efforts, but with persistent looking she might locate an "unlocked door." If a reasonable amount of persistence does show that experience is essential, it might be obtained in other ways—through temporary volunteer work, for instance.

How can I handle conflicts more effectively?

Most of the suggestions just made also apply to conflict. However, here are some additional things to remember when you are in conflict or must make a difficult decision.

1. Don't be hasty when making important decisions. Take time to collect information and to weigh pros and cons. Hasty decisions are often regretted. Even if you do make a faulty decision, it will trouble you less if you know that you did everything possible to avoid a mistake.

2. Try out important decisions *partially* when possible. If you are thinking about moving to a new town, try to spend a few days there first. If you are choosing between colleges, do the same. If classes are in progress, sit in on some. If you want to learn to scuba dive, rent equipment for a reasonable length of time before buying.

3. Look for workable compromises. Again, it is important to get all available information. If you think that you have only one or two alternatives and they are undesirable or unbearable, seek the aid of a teacher, counselor, minister, or social service agency. You may be overlooking possible alternatives these people will know about.

4. When all else fails, make a decision and live with it. Indecision and conflict exact a high cost. Sometimes it is best to select a course of action and stick with it unless it is very obviously wrong after you have taken it.

In class you may want to describe some of the frustrations and conflicts you have experienced and how you handled them. Prepare to discuss frustrations and conflicts you have resolved unusually effectively or that you might have handled better. Do you have some additional hints to share with other students?

Learning Check	**Critical Thinking**
1. Exercise, meditation, and progressive relaxation are considered effective ways of countering negative self-statements. T or F?	5. Steve always feels extremely pressured when the due date arrives for his major term papers. How could he reduce stress in such instances?
2. Research shows that social support from family and friends has little effect on the health consequences of stress. T or F?	**Answers:**
3. One element of stress inoculation is training in the use of positive coping statements. T of F?	1. F 2. F 3. T 4. T 5. The stress associated with doing term papers can be almost completely eliminated by making a long-term assignment into many small daily or weekly assignments. Students who habitually procrastinate are often amazed at how pleasant college work can be once they renounce "brinkmanship."
4. Stereotyped responding can be particularly troublesome in coping with frustration. T or F?	

*M*editation refers to a family of mental exercises designed to focus attention in a way that interrupts the typical flow of thoughts, worries, and analysis (Wilson, 1986). Meditation takes many forms and has many meanings in various cultures. Here we are interested in meditation as a self-control strategy for lowering physical and mental arousal. People who regularly use meditation as a stress reduction technique often report less daily physical arousal and anxiety. Even if meditation is not practiced daily, it may be a useful technique for interrupting worries and fearful thinking (Wilson, 1986).

Receptive Meditation Meditation takes two major forms. In **concentrative meditation,** *attention is given to a single focal point,* such as an object, a thought, or one's own breathing. In contrast, **receptive meditation** *is "open," or expansive.* That is, the person widens attention to embrace a total, non-judgmental awareness of his or her experience of the world (Walsh, 1984). An example of this type of meditation is losing all self-consciousness while walking in the wilderness with a quiet and receptive mind. To gain insight into receptive meditation, try the following exercise sometime.

> While walking outdoors, silently complete this statement four or five times: Right now I see . . . . Then complete each of the following statements four or five times and proceed to the next one: Right now I hear . . . . Right now I smell . . . . Right now I feel . . . . Each time, become aware of what you see, hear, smell, and feel. Then repeat the process as many times as you like.

At first you will tend to name what you are experiencing. If you can stop doing that and just be intensely aware of your surroundings—without thinking—you will have some idea of what receptive meditation is like. If you can learn to be openly aware without using any words, you will be even closer.

Although it may not seem so, receptive meditation is regarded as more difficult to attain than concentrative meditation (Smith, 1986). For this reason, we will discuss concentrative meditation as a practical self-control method.

How is concentrative meditation done?

Concentrative Meditation The basic idea in concentrative meditation is to sit still and quietly focus on some external object or on a repetitive internal stimulus such as a word or your own breathing (Wilson, 1986). In one experiment, college students were instructed to concentrate on breathing:

> While you are sitting, let your breath become relaxed and natural. Let it set its own pace and depth if you can. Then focus your attention on your own breathing: the movements of your belly, not your nose and throat. Do not allow extraneous thoughts or stimuli to pull your attention away from your breathing. This may be hard to do at first, but keep directing your attention back to it. Turn everything else aside if it comes up. (Maupin, 1965)

Not all subjects responded to this exercise, but at the end of a 2-week period, those who did reported experiences of deep concentration, pleasant bodily sensations, and extreme detachment from outside worries and distractions.

An alternative approach you may want to try involves the use of a *mantra*. **Mantras** *are words used as the focus of attention in concentrative meditation.* Typically they are smooth, flowing sounds that are easily repeated. Instead of focusing on breathing, you can silently repeat a mantra. One widely used mantra is the word "om." If you belong to an organized religion, your mantra could be a phrase from a familiar prayer. Like breathing, a mantra is basically used as a focus for attention. If other thoughts arise during meditation, one should return attention to the mantra as often as necessary to maintain meditation.

The Relaxation Response A principal claim of many commercial meditation courses is that they offer a mantra tailored to the needs of each individual. But medical researcher Herbert Benson found that the physical benefits of meditation are the same no matter what word is used. These include lowered heart rate, blood pressure, muscle tension, and other signs of stress.

Benson believes that the core of meditation is the **relaxation response—***an innate physiological pattern that opposes activation of the body's fight-or-flight mechanisms.* Benson feels, quite simply, that most of us have forgotten how to relax deeply. Subjects in his experiments have had considerable success in producing the relaxation response by following these instructions:

> Sit quietly in a comfortable position. Close your eyes. Deeply relax all your muscles, beginning at your feet and progressing up to your face. Keep them deeply relaxed.
> Breathe through your nose. Become aware of your breathing. As you breathe out, say the word "one" silently to yourself.
> Do not worry about whether you are successful in achieving a deep level of relaxation. Maintain a passive attitude and permit relaxation to occur at its own pace. Expect distracting thoughts. When these distracting thoughts occur, ignore them and continue repeating "one." (Adapted from Benson, 1977.)

What effects does meditation have, other than producing relaxation?

Effects of Meditation Many extravagant claims have been made about meditation. For example, members of the Transcendental Meditation (TM) movement have stated that 20 minutes of meditation is as restful as a full night's sleep. This, however, is simply not true. One study, for instance, found that merely "resting" for 20 minutes produces the same bodily effects as meditation (Holmes, 1984; Holmes et al., 1983). Long-term meditators have also claimed improvement in memory, alertness, creativity, and intuition. Again, such claims must be regarded as unproven. Most are based on personal testimonials or poorly controlled studies. A major problem with most studies of TM is that they use devoted meditators. It is quite likely that the beliefs and lifestyles of these people influence the results of the studies as much as meditation does (Druckman & Bjork, 1994).

In defense of meditation, it is important to remember that relaxation can be mental as well as physical. As a stress-control technique, meditation may be a good choice for people who find it difficult to "turn off" upsetting thoughts when they need to relax. For example, college students who tried meditation in a recent study felt happier, less anxious, and less depressed after just two weeks of twice-a-day meditation (Smith, Compton, & West, 1995).

While many of the claimed benefits of meditation appear to be overstated, meditation does reliably elicit the relaxation response (Janowiak & Hackman, 1994; Kelly, 1996). Benson (1975) believes that the following elements are the keys for inducing relaxation.

1. A quiet environment
2. Decreased muscle tension
3. A mental device (such as a repeated word) that helps shift thoughts away from ordinary, rational concerns
4. A passive attitude toward whether you are "succeeding" at becoming relaxed

Summary   To summarize, research suggests that concentrative meditation is only one of several ways to elicit the relaxation response. For many people, sitting quietly and "resting" can be as effective. However, if you are the type of person who finds it difficult to ignore upsetting thoughts, then concentrative meditation might be a better way to promote relaxation. More important than the method you choose, however, is a willingness to set aside time each day to intentionally relax. Meditation and similar techniques provide a valuable, stress-lowering "time-out" from the normal clamor of thoughts and worries—something almost everyone could use in our fast-paced society.

Learning Check

1. The focus of attention in concentrative meditation is "open," or expansive. T or F?

2. Mantras are words said silently to oneself to end a session of meditation. T or F?

3. Research conducted by Herbert Benson indicates that careful selection of a mantra is necessary to obtain the physical benefits of meditation. T or F?

4. The most immediate benefit of meditation appears to be its capacity for producing the relaxation response. T or F?

Critical Thinking

5. Meditation tends to interrupt negative self-statements and other upsetting internal "talk." In this sense, the effects of meditation are similar to what technique?

Answers:

1. F 2. F 3. F 4. T 5. Stress inoculation (the use of coping statements).

Chapter Summary

What is health psychology? How does behavior affect health?

◆ **Health psychologists** are interested in behavior that helps maintain and promote health.

◆ Studies of health and illness have identified a number of **behavioral risk factors** and **health-promoting behaviors.**

◆ Health psychologists have pioneered efforts to *prevent* the development of unhealthy habits and to improve well-being through **community health campaigns.**

What is stress? What factors determine its severity?

◆ **Stress** occurs when demands are placed on an organism to adjust or adapt.

◆ Stress is more damaging in situations involving *pressure*, a *lack of control*, *unpredictability* of the stressor, and *intense* or *repeated* emotional shocks.

◆ Stress is intensified when a situation is perceived as a *threat* and when a person does not feel *competent* to cope with it.

◆ In work settings, prolonged stress can lead to **burnout.**

◆ The **primary appraisal** of a situation greatly affects our emotional response to it. Stress reactions, in particular, are related to an appraisal of threat.

◆ During a **secondary appraisal,** some means of coping with a situation is selected. Coping may be either **problem-focused** or **emotion-focused,** or both.

What causes frustration and what are typical reactions to it?

◆ **Frustration** is the negative emotional state that occurs when progress toward a goal is blocked. Sources of frustration may be usefully classified as *external* or *personal.*

◆ External frustrations are based on *delay, failure, rejection, loss,* and other direct blocking of motives. Personal frustration is related to *personal characteristics* over which one has little control.

◆ Frustrations of all types become more intense as the *strength, urgency,* or *importance* of the blocked motive increases.

◆ Major behavioral reactions to frustration include *persistence, more vigorous responding, circumvention, direct aggression, displaced aggression* (including *scapegoating*), and *escape* or *withdrawal.*

Are there different types of conflict? How do people react to conflict?

◆ **Conflict** occurs when one must choose between contradictory alternatives.

◆ Five major types of conflict are **approach-approach** (choice between two positive alternatives), **avoidance-avoidance** (both alternatives are negative), **approach-avoidance** (a goal or activity has both positive and negative aspects), **double approach-avoidance** (both alternatives have positive and negative qualities) and **multiple approach-avoidance** (several alternatives each have good and bad qualities).

◆ Approach-approach conflicts are usually the easiest to resolve.

◆ Avoidance conflicts are difficult to resolve and are characterized by *inaction, indecision, freezing,* and a *desire to escape* (called *leaving the field*).

◆ People usually remain in approach-avoidance conflicts, but fail to fully resolve them. Approach-avoidance conflicts are associated with *ambivalence* and *partial approach. Vacillation* is probably the most common reaction to double approach-avoidance conflicts.

What are defense mechanisms?

◆ Anxiety, threat, or feelings of inadequacy frequently lead to the use of **defense mechanisms.** These are habitual psychological strategies used to avoid or reduce anxiety.

◆ A large number of defense mechanisms have been identified, including *compensation, denial, fantasy, intellectualization, isolation, projection, rationalization, reaction formation, regression, repression,* and *sublimation.*

What do we know about coping with feelings of helplessness and depression?

◆ The concept of **learned helplessness** has been used to explain the failure to cope with threatening situations and as a model for understanding **depression. Mastery training** acts as one major antidote to helplessness.

◆ **Depression** is a major, and surprisingly common, emotional problem. Actions and thoughts that counter feelings of helplessness tend to reduce depression.

How is stress related to health and disease?

◆ Work with the *Social Readjustment Rating Scale* indicates that an accumulation of **life changes** can increase susceptibility to accident or illness. However, immediate psychological and mental health is more closely related to the intensity and severity of daily annoyances, known as **hassles** or **microstressors.**

◆ Intense or prolonged stress (especially when it is associated with negative emotional response), may cause damage in the form of *psychosomatic* problems. **Psychosomatic** (mind-body) **disorders** have no connection to **hypochondria,** the tendency to imagine that one has some terrible disease.

◆ During **biofeedback training,** bodily processes are monitored and converted to a signal that indicates what the body is doing. With practice, biofeedback allows alteration of many bodily activities. It shows promise for the alleviation of some psychosomatic illnesses.

- People with **Type A personalities** are competitive, striving, and frequently angry or hostile, and they have a chronic sense of time urgency. These characteristics—especially anger and hostility—combine to double the chances of heart attack.
- People who have traits of the **hardy personality** seem to be resistant to stress, even if they also have Type A traits.
- The body reacts to stress in a series of stages called the **general adaptation syndrome** (G.A.S.).
- The stages of the G.A.S. are **alarm, resistance,** and **exhaustion.** The pattern of bodily reactions and changes in resistance observed in the G.A.S. follows closely the pattern observed in the development of psychosomatic disorders.
- Studies of **psychoneuroimmunology** show that stress also lowers the body's immunity to disease.

What are the best strategies for managing stress?

- A sizable number of coping skills can be applied to manage stress. Most of these focus on one of three areas: **bodily effects, ineffective behavior,** and **upsetting thoughts.**

Is meditation useful for coping with stress?

- **Receptive meditation** and **concentrative meditation** are self-control techniques that can be used to reduce stress. Two major benefits of meditation are its ability to interrupt anxious thoughts and its ability to elicit the **relaxation response.**

Gender and Sexuality

Preview

That Magic Word

> **Sex** \seks\ n 1. One of the two divisions of organisms formed on the distinction of male and female.

"Sex" has many meanings: reproduction, gender, sexual identity, intimacy, and much more. Of the various meanings, the simplest would seem to be *gender*. What, really, could be simpler? Females are females and males are males, right? Wrong. Even something as basic as gender is complicated and many sided.

Gender   The complexity of gender is illustrated by the attempt of Dr. René Richards to enter a women's tennis tournament. Dr. Richards is a transsexual. Formerly she was Dr. Richard Raskin, an ophthalmologist. As a man, Richard Raskin was a modestly successful tennis player. After a sex-change operation, Dr. Richards tried to launch a new tennis career as a woman. Understandably, other women players protested. Officials finally decided to use a genetic sex test to decide if Dr. Richards could compete. She, in turn, protested this test. Genetically she is still male, but psychologically she is female—she has female genitals, and she functions socially as a female (Hyde, 1996). Is Dr. Richards, then, female or male?

You might view the case of René Richards as an unfair example because transsexuals seek to alter natural gender. For most people, the various indicators of gender are in agreement. Nevertheless, it is not unusual to find occasional ambiguities among the dimensions of a person's "sex." Contrary to common belief, gender is not a simple either-or classification. In the first part of this chapter, we will consider some basic dimensions of "maleness" and "femaleness." An essential question we will address is, How does one become female or male?

Sexual Behavior   Each of us is by nature a sexual creature. This inescapable reality springs from the basic biology of reproduction. With this in mind, later sections of this chapter discuss sexual behavior, sexual arousal and response, sexual problems, and attitudes toward sexuality.

Sex is probably a topic you already know a lot about. It should be interesting, then, for you to compare your knowledge with the information that follows. Sexuality has a tremendous impact on relationships, personal identity, and health.

Gender Development— Circle One: *XX* or *XY*?

It is said that the one thing you will never forget about a person is that person's sex. Considering the number of activities, relationships, conflicts, and choices influenced by gender, it is no wonder that we pay close attention to it. Let's begin with a few basic questions: What does it mean to be female or male? What are the dimensions of gender? How do gender and sex role differences develop?

Female or Male?

Basic physical differences between males and females can be divided into *primary* and *secondary* sexual characteristics. **Primary sexual characteristics** *refer to the sexual and reproductive organs themselves:* the vagina, ovaries, and uterus in females and the penis, testes, and scrotum in males. (See Figures 15–1 ◆ and 15–2 ◆. Also see Table 15–1 ■.) As described in Chapter 5, **secondary sexual characteristics** *are more superficial sexual features that appear at puberty in response to hormonal signals from the pituitary gland.* In females,

secondary sexual characteristics involve development of the breasts, broadening of the hips, and other changes in body shape. Males develop facial and body hair, and the voice deepens. These changes signal readiness for reproduction. Reproductive maturity is especially evident in the female **menarche** (MEN-ar-kee: *the onset of menstruation*). Soon after menarche, monthly *ovulation* begins. **Ovulation** refers to *the release of ova (eggs) from the ovaries.* From the first ovulation until **menopause** (*the end of regular monthly fertility cycles*), women can bear children.

What causes the development of sex differences?

Sex Hormones In general, sexual characteristics are related to the action of sex hormones. (Hormones are chemical substances secreted by endocrine glands.) The **gonads** (*or sex glands*) affect sexual development and behavior by secreting **estrogens** (*female hormones*) and **androgens** (*male hormones*). The gonads in the male are the testes; female gonads are the ovaries. The adrenal glands (located above the kidneys) also supply sex hormones in both females and males. At puberty, adrenal hormones add to the development of secondary sexual characteristics.

Interestingly, all individuals normally produce both estrogens and androgens. It is their proportion that influences sex differences. In fact, the development of male

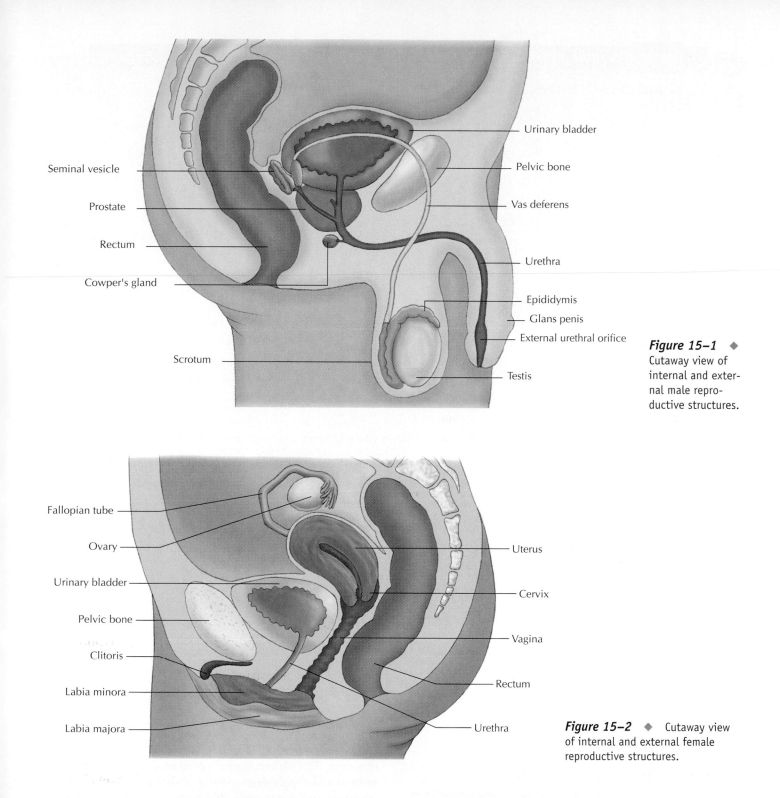

Figure 15–1 ◆ Cutaway view of internal and external male reproductive structures.

Seminal vesicle
Prostate
Rectum
Cowper's gland
Scrotum
Urinary bladder
Pelvic bone
Vas deferens
Urethra
Epididymis
Glans penis
External urethral orifice
Testis

Figure 15–2 ◆ Cutaway view of internal and external female reproductive structures.

Fallopian tube
Ovary
Urinary bladder
Pelvic bone
Clitoris
Labia minora
Labia majora
Uterus
Cervix
Vagina
Rectum
Urethra

or female anatomy is largely due to the presence or absence—before birth—of **testosterone** (tes-TOSS-teh-rone: *one of the androgens, secreted mainly by the testes*) (Breedlove, 1994).

Then is biological sex determined by the sex hormones?

Not entirely. As suggested by our discussion in the chapter Preview, gender cannot be reduced to a single dimension.

Dimensions of Gender   At the very least, any evaluation of gender must include (1) **genetic sex** (*XX or XY chromosomes*), (2) **gonadal sex** (*ovaries or testes*), (3) **hormonal sex** (*predominance of androgens or estrogens*), (4) **genital sex** (*clitoris and vagina in females, penis and scrotum in males*), and (5) **gender identity** (*one's personal sense of maleness or femaleness*). To see why gender must be defined along several dimensions, let's follow the sequence of events involved in becoming female or male.

Table 15-1 ■ **Male and Female Sexual Anatomy**

Female Reproductive Structures

Cervix (SER-vix)   The lower end of the uterus that projects into the vagina.

Clitoris (KLIT-er-iss)   Small, sensitive organ made of erectile tissue; located above the vaginal opening.

Fallopian tube (feh-LOPE-ee-en)   One of two tubes that carry eggs from the ovaries to the uterus.

Labia majora (LAY-bee-ah mah-JOR-ah)   The larger outer lips of the vulva.

Labia minora (LAY-bee-ah mih-NOR-ah)   Inner lips of the vulva, surrounding the vaginal opening.

Ovary (OH-vah-ree)   One of the two female reproductive glands; ovaries are the source of hormones and eggs.

Uterus (YOO-ter-us)   The pear-shaped muscular organ in which the fetus develops during pregnancy; also known as the womb.

Vagina (vah-JINE-ah)   Tube-like structure connecting the external female genitalia with the uterus.

Male Reproductive Structures

Cowper's glands   Two small glands that secrete a clear fluid into the urethra during sexual excitement.

Epididymis (ep-ih-DID-ih-mus)   A coiled structure at the top of the testes in which sperm are stored.

External urethral orifice (yoo-REE-thral OR-ih-fis)   The opening at the tip of the penis through which urine and semen pass.

Glans penis (glanz PEA-nis)   The tip of the penis.

Prostate (PROSS-tate)   A gland located at the base of the urinary bladder that supplies most of the fluid that makes up semen.

Scrotum (SKROE-tehm)   The sac-like pouch that holds the testes.

Seminal vesicles (SEM-in-uhl VES-ih-kuhlz)   These two small organs (one on each side of the prostate) supply fluid that becomes part of semen.

Testis (TES-tis, singular; testes, plural)   One of the two male reproductive glands; the testes are a source of hormones and sperm.

Vas deferens (vaz DEH-fur-enz)   The duct that carries sperm from the testes to the urethra.

Related Structures

Pelvic bone   One of the bones at the front of the pelvis (the pelvis connects the spine with the legs).

Rectum   The lowest section of the large intestine.

Urethra (yoo-REE-thra)   The tube through which urine drains as it leaves the body. In males, semen also passes through the urethra.

Urinary bladder   The sac that collects urine before it is eliminated from the body.

Prenatal Gender Development

Becoming male or female starts simply enough. Genetic sex is determined at the instant of conception: Two **X chromosomes** initiate development of a *female*; an X chromosome plus a **Y chromosome** produces a *male*. Genetic sex remains the same throughout life. But it alone does not determine gender. We must also consider hormonal effects before birth.

For the first 6 weeks of prenatal growth, there is no difference between genetically female or male embryos.

However, if a Y chromosome is present, testes develop in the embryo and supply testosterone. This stimulates growth of the penis and other male structures (Fig. 15-3 ●). In the absence of testosterone, the embryo will develop female reproductive organs and genitals, regardless of genetic sex (Breedlove, 1994). It might be said, then, that nature's primary impulse is to make a female.

Development of the embryo usually matches genetic sex, but not always. A genetic male will fail to develop male genitals if too little testosterone is formed during prenatal growth. Even if testosterone is present, an inherited **androgen insensitivity** (*unresponsiveness to testosterone*)

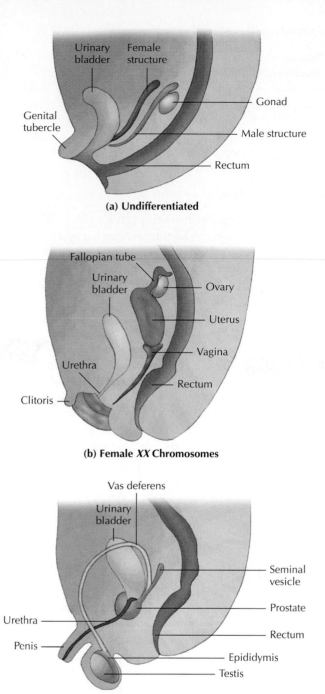

(a) Undifferentiated

(b) Female *XX* Chromosomes

(c) Male *XY* Chromosomes

Figure 15–3 ◆ Prenatal development of the reproductive organs. Early development of ovaries or testes affects hormonal balance and alters sexual anatomy. **(a)** At first the sex organs are the same in the human female and male. **(b)** When androgens are absent, female structures develop. **(c)** Male sex organs are produced when androgens are present.

may exist, again resulting in female development (Breedlove, 1994).

Similarly, androgens must be either at low levels or absent for an *XX* embryo to develop as a female. Thus, for both genetic females and males, hormonal problems before birth may result in **hermaphroditism** (her-MAF-ro-dite-

ism). This term refers to defects in sexual development that result in *dual or ambiguous sexual anatomy*. For instance, a developing female may be masculinized by progestin (a drug given to prevent miscarriage) or by a problem known as the *androgenital syndrome* (an-dro-JEN-ih-tal). In the **androgenital syndrome,** the child's body produces estrogen, but *a genetic abnormality causes the adrenal glands to release too much androgen*. In such cases a female child may be born with male genitals.

Would such a child be reared as a male?

Some are. Usually, however, the condition is detected and corrected by surgery. If necessary, extra estrogen may be given after birth.

Origins of Male-Female Differences Some researchers believe that in addition to guiding physical development, the interplay of sex hormones before birth may also "sex-type" the brain (Breedlove, 1994; Money, 1987). Changes in the brain are then thought to alter later chances of developing feminine or masculine characteristics (Witelson, 1991).

Does that mean there is a physical basis for female and male traits?

In animals, clear links exist between prenatal hormones and male or female behaviors. For humans, however, the evidence suggests that most sex-linked behavior is learned (Caplan et al., 1985, 1987; Hare-Mustin & Marecek, 1988). Be that as it may, some researchers believe that a **biological biasing effect** occurs, in which *prenatal androgens or estrogens subtly influence development of the body, nervous system, and later behavior patterns.*

Is there any evidence for that?

Consider females exposed to androgens before birth. After birth, their hormone balance shifts to female and they are raised as girls. Does prenatal exposure to male hormones have any masculinizing effect? Psychologist John Money has observed that during childhood, such girls are typically "tomboys" who prefer the company of boys to girls. However, this masculinization does not persist into adulthood. After adolescence, the girls' tomboyism usually gives way to traditional interests in marriage and motherhood (Money, 1987; Money & Mathews, 1982). Cases like these seem to show that both prenatal hormones and later social factors contribute to adult sexual identity.

At the risk of getting mired in the "battle of the sexes," let's consider one more idea. Some researchers believe that biology underlies female-male differences in thinking abilities. Women, they contend, are more often "left brained," and men, "right brained." The left brain, you may recall, is largely responsible for language and rote learning. The right brain is superior at spatial reasoning. Thus, some psychologists believe that biological differences explain why men (as a group) do slightly better on spatial tasks and math and why women are slightly better at language skills. Others, however, strongly reject this theory. To them, such claims are based on shaky evidence and sexist thinking (Caplan et al.,

1985; Hellige, 1990). The most telling evidence on this point may be the fact that differences between female and male scores on the *Scholastic Assessment Test* are rapidly declining. The same applies to tests of math ability (Buss, 1995). These observations are probably explained by the growing similarity of male and female interests, experiences, and educational goals.

The one thing that is certain in the gender debate is that males and females are more alike than they are different (Maccoby & Jacklin, 1974; Tavris, 1992). Of various gender differences measured by psychologists, 25 percent are close to zero. An additional 62 percent are in the small to moderate range. Thus, 87 percent of the differences between the sexes that have been studied fall between zero and moderate in size (Hyde & Plant, 1995).

It is important to realize that the differences that do exist between women and men are based on *averages* (Fig. 15–4 ◆). Many women are better than men at math and many men are better than women at verbal skills. Scores for women and men overlap so much that it is impossible to predict if any one individual will be good or bad at math or language simply from knowing his or her gender. There is no biological basis for the unequal treatment women have often faced at work, school, and elsewhere. The important differences between women and men are not in our genes or hormones. Instead, most male-female differences can be traced to *social* differences in power, opportunities, and the ways that women and men are treated in society (Tavris, 1992).

Gender Identity   Your personal, *private sense of femaleness or maleness*, which is referred to as **gender identity,** can be distinguished from *sex roles*. Sex roles are observable traits, mannerisms, interests, and behaviors defined by one's culture as "male" or "female."

Gender identity is a *learned* self-perception. This point is emphasized by cases of hermaphroditism. What happens if we compare two individuals having the same degree of gender ambiguity, one raised as a girl and the other as a boy? Usually, we will find that the person raised as a girl will regard herself as a girl and act like a girl. Likewise, the individual raised as a boy will act like a boy and identify himself as a boy (Money, 1987).

At what age is gender identity acquired?

Gender identity is essentially formed by 3 or 4 years of age. Accordingly, children born with ambiguous gender have few problems as long as a final decision concerning their sex is made by the age of 18 months. If the parents consistently treat the child *only* as a girl or as a boy, the child should develop a clear sense of gender. If the decision is delayed, the child may develop a gender identity at odds with his or her biological sex, or a confused sexual identity.

How is gender identity acquired?

Obviously, it begins with *labeling* ("It's a girl," "It's a boy"). The powerful impact of labeling is revealed by an interesting study. In an experiment, people were shown videotapes of four male and four female babies. Each baby was randomly labeled with a male or female name. Regardless of a baby's real sex, infants labeled male were perceived as more masculine and stronger than those labeled as female (Burnham & Harris, 1992).

Labeling is important because it influences **sex role socialization** (*the process of learning behaviors considered appropriate for one's gender in a given culture*). Sex role socialization refers to the countless subtle pressures exerted by parents, peers, and cultural forces that urge boys to "act like boys" and girls to "act like girls." In the next section we will investigate sex roles and sex role socialization in more detail.

Sex Roles

Sex roles are probably as important as chromosomal, genital, or hormonal sex in their influence on adult sexual behavior. A **sex role** *is the favored pattern of behavior expected of individuals on the basis of their gender.* In our culture, boys are usually encouraged to be strong, fast, aggressive, dominant, achieving, and otherwise "male." Traditionally, females have been expected to be sensitive, intuitive, passive, emotional, and "naturally" interested in child rearing. All cultures define sex roles. As the following highlight points out, this often leads to stereotyped thinking about females and males.

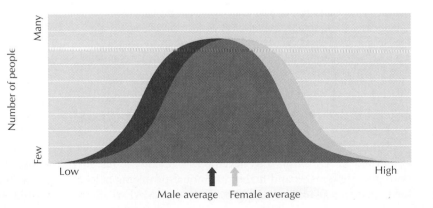

Figure 15–4 ◆   Recorded differences in various abilities that exist between women and men are based on *averages.* For example, if we were to record the number of men and women who have low, medium, or high scores on tests of language ability, we might obtain graphs like those shown. For other abilities, men would have a higher average. However, such average differences are typically small. As a result, the overlap in female abilities and male abilities is very large (Breedlove, 1994).

Sex Role Stereotypes

Question: How many men does it take to change a light bulb?

Answer: None. Real men aren't afraid of the dark.

This joke pokes fun at the North American stereotype of manhood. Despite much progress in the last 20 years, *sex role stereotypes* continue to have a major impact on women and men. **Sex role stereotypes** *are over-simplified and widely held beliefs about what men and women are actually like.* Sex roles tend to dictate how we act. Sex role stereotypes, in contrast, treat learned sex roles as if they were real gender differences.

Are women suited to be fighter pilots, corporate presidents, military commanders, or race car drivers? A person with strong sex role stereotypes might say, "No, because women are not sufficiently aggressive, dominant, or mechanically inclined for such roles." Yet, today we know that women have performed successfully in virtually all realms of human endeavor. Nevertheless, sex role stereotypes persist. The United States has never had a woman president, and it wasn't until 1984 that a woman was even nominated as a vice-presidential candidate.

"The committee on women's rights will now come to order."
HUCK/PUNCH/LONDON

In many occupations women continue to score "firsts" of the kind just mentioned. Nonetheless, sex role stereotypes are a major obstacle where employment is concerned. Unequal pay for comparable work and experience is a major problem for women (Frieze, Olson, & Good, 1990). For many jobs your chances of being hired could be reduced by your gender, be it male or female. Like all stereotypes, those based on sex roles ignore the wonderful diversity of humanity and human potential.

The "naturalness" of sex roles becomes questionable when different cultures are compared. For example, Ethel

Albert (1963) identified numerous cultures in which women do the heavy work because men are considered too weak for it. In Russia, roughly 75 percent of all medical doctors are women, and women make up a large portion of the work force. Many more examples could be cited, but perhaps one of the most interesting is anthropologist Margaret Mead's (1935) observations of the Tchambuli people of New Guinea.

Sex roles for the Tchambuli are a nearly perfect reversal of American stereotypes. Tchambuli women do the fishing and manufacturing and are expected to control the power and economic life of the community. Women also take the initiative in courting and sexual relations. Tchambuli men, on the other hand, are expected to be dependent, flirtatious, and concerned with their appearance. Art, games, and theatrics occupy most of the Tchambuli males' time, and males are particularly fond of adorning themselves with flowers and jewelry.

As the Tchambuli demonstrate, activities regarded as "appropriate" for females and males vary in different cultures. The arbitrary nature of sex roles is also apparent. A man is no less a man if he cooks, sews, or cares for children. A woman is no less a woman if she excels in sports, succeeds in business, or works as an auto mechanic. Still, adult personality and gender identity are closely tied to cultural definitions of "masculinity" and "femininity."

An interesting side effect of sex role socialization is the imprint it leaves on activities having nothing to do with gender. For example, boys are more aggressive than girls and girls have more emotional empathy than boys (Block, 1979; Maccoby & Jacklin, 1974).

How are such differences created?

Sex Role Socialization Learning sex roles begins immediately after birth. Infant girls are held more gently and treated more tenderly than boys. Both parents play more roughly with sons than with daughters (who are presumed to be more "delicate"). Later, boys are allowed to roam over a wider area without special permission. They are also expected to run errands earlier than girls. Daughters are told that they are pretty and that "nice girls don't fight." Boys are told to be strong and that "tough guys don't cry." Sons are more often urged to control their emotions, except for anger and aggression, which parents tolerate more in boys than in girls.

Toys are strongly sex typed: Parents buy dolls for girls; trucks and guns for boys. Fathers, especially, tend to encourage their children to play with "appropriate" sex-typed toys (Bradley & Gobbart, 1989) (Fig. 15–5 ◆). By the time children reach kindergarten they have learned to think that doctors, firefighters, and pilots are men and that nurses, secretaries, and hairdressers are women (Blaske, 1984; Stroeher, 1994). And why not? The work force is still highly segregated by sex, and children learn from what they observe. Stereotyped sex roles are even the norm in children's picture books (McDonald, 1989)!

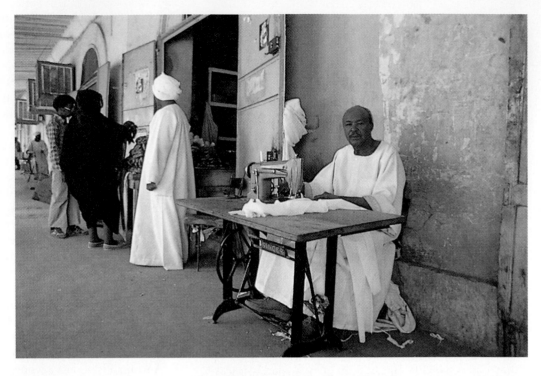

Behaviors that are considered typical and appropriate for each sex (sex roles) vary a great deal from culture to culture. Undoubtedly some cultures magnify sex differences more than others (Breedlove, 1994).

Overall, parents tend to encourage their sons to engage in **instrumental** (*goal-directed*) **behaviors,** to control their emotions, and to prepare for the world of work. Daughters, on the other hand, are encouraged in **expressive** (*emotion-*

oriented) **behaviors** and, to a lesser degree, are socialized for motherhood.

As they are growing up, children tend to segregate themselves into same-sex groups. During much of childhood, this limits conflicts between male and female patterns of behavior. However, as children move into adolescence they begin to spend more time with members of the opposite sex. This brings the dominant, competitive style of boys into conflict with the nurturant, expressive style of girls, often placing girls at a disadvantage (Maccoby, 1990).

When told that they respond differently to girls and boys, many parents explain that it is because there are "natural" differences between the sexes. But what comes first, "natural differences" or the expectations that create them? In our culture, "male" seems—for many—to be defined as "not female." That is, parents often have a vague fear of expressive and emotional behavior in male children, because to them it seems to imply effeminacy. Many parents who would not be troubled if their daughters engaged in "masculine" play might be upset if their sons played with dolls or imitated "female" mannerisms.

To summarize, sex role socialization in our society prepares children for an adult world in which men are expected to be instrumental, conquering, controlling, and unemotional and in which women are expected to be expressive, emotional, passive, and dependent. Thus, sex role socialization prepares us to be highly competent in some respects and handicapped in others (Levant, 1996).

Of course, many people find traditional sex roles perfectly comfortable. It seems evident, however, that just about everyone will benefit when the more stereotyped and burdensome aspects of sex roles are set aside. The next section explains why.

Figure 15–5 ◆ One study found that even the parents of 2-year-olds strongly encourage their toddlers to play with "sex-appropriate" toys. Parents' non-verbal responses to toys were consistently more positive when a toy matched stereotypes for the child's gender (Caldera, Huston, & O'Brien, 1989).

Androgyny—Are You Masculine, Feminine, or Androgynous?

Are you aggressive, ambitious, analytical, assertive, athletic, competitive, decisive, dominant, forceful, independent, individualistic, self-reliant, and willing to take risks? If so, you are quite "masculine." Are you affectionate, cheerful, childlike, compassionate, flatterable, gentle, gullible, loyal, sensitive, shy, soft spoken, sympathetic, tender, understanding, warm, and yielding? If so, then you are quite "feminine."

What if I have traits from both lists?

Then you may be *androgynous* (an-DROJ-ih-nus). The two lists you just read are from the work of psychologist Sandra Bem. By combining a list of 20 "masculine" traits (self-reliant, assertive, and so forth), 20 "feminine" traits (affectionate, gentle), and 20 neutral traits (truthful, friendly) Bem created the *Bem Sex Role Inventory* (BSRI). Next, she and her associates gave the BSRI to thousands of people, asking them to say whether each trait applied to them. Of those surveyed, 50 percent fell into traditional feminine or masculine categories; 15 percent scored higher on traits of the opposite gender; and 35 percent were androgynous, getting high scores on both feminine and masculine items.

Psychological Androgyny

You haven't said yet what it means to be androgynous. Is it having both female and male traits?

The word **androgyny** (an-DROJ-ih-nee) literally means "man-woman." Androgyny sounds as if it might have something to do with androids, asexuality, or sex-change operations, but it actually refers to *having both feminine and masculine traits.*

Bem's interest in androgyny stems from her belief that our complex society requires flexibility with respect to sex roles. She believes that it is more than ever necessary for men to be gentle, compassionate, sensitive, and yielding and for women to be forceful, self-reliant, independent, and ambitious—*as the situation requires.* In short, Bem feels that more people should be androgynous.

Adaptability In an interesting series of experiments, Bem showed that androgynous individuals are more adaptable and less hindered by images of "feminine" or "masculine" behavior. For example, in one experiment Bem gave people

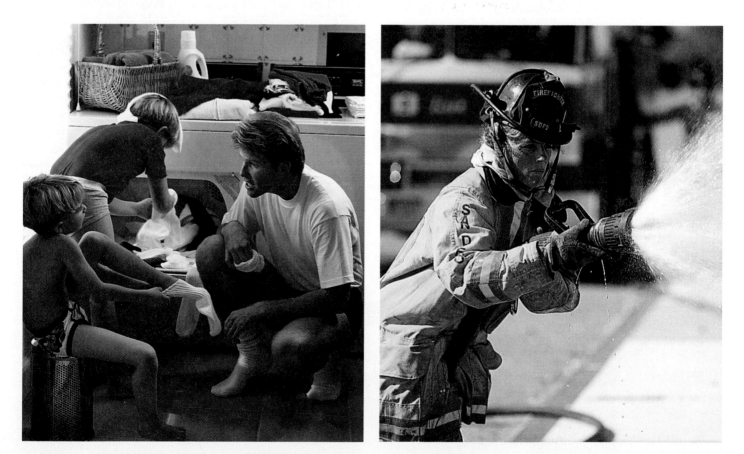

Androgynous individuals adapt easily to both traditionally "feminine" and "masculine" situations.

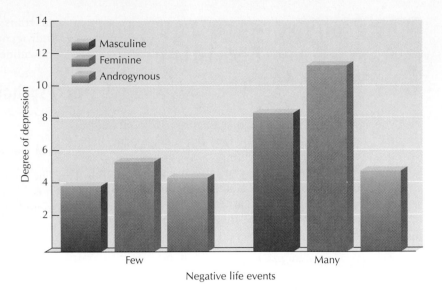

Figure 15–6 ◆ Another indication of the possible benefits of androgyny is found in a study of reactions to stress. When confronted with an onslaught of negative events, strongly masculine or feminine persons become more depressed than androgynous individuals do (adapted from Roos & Cohen, 1987).

the choice of performing either a "masculine" activity (oil a hinge, nail boards together, and so forth) or a "feminine" activity (prepare a baby bottle, wind yarn into a ball, and so on). Masculine men and feminine women consistently chose gender-appropriate activities, even when the opposite choice paid more!

Bem concluded that rigid sex roles can seriously restrict behavior, especially for men (Bem, 1975, 1981). She believes that masculine males have great difficulty expressing warmth, playfulness, and concern—even when appropriate. Masculine men, it seems, tend to view such traits as unacceptably "feminine." Masculine men also find it hard to accept emotional support from others, especially from women (Ashton & Fuehrer, 1993). Problems faced by highly feminine women are the reverse of those faced by masculine men. Such women have trouble being independent and assertive, even when these qualities are desirable.

Over the years androgyny has been variously supported, attacked, and debated. Now, as the dust begins to settle, the picture looks like this:

■ Having "masculine" traits primarily means that a person is independent and assertive. Scoring high in "masculinity,"

therefore, is related to high self-esteem and to success in many situations (Long, 1989).

■ Having "feminine" traits primarily means that a person is nurturant and interpersonally oriented. People who score high in "femininity," therefore, tend to experience greater social closeness with others and more happiness in marriage.

In sum, there are advantages to possessing both "feminine" and "masculine" traits, whatever one's gender may be (Ickes, 1993; Spence, 1984). In general, androgynous persons are more flexible when it comes to coping with difficult situations (Jurma & Powell, 1994; Spangenberg & Lategan, 1993). (See Figure 15–6 ◆.) Androgynous persons also tend to be more satisfied with their lives. Apparently, this is because they can use both instrumental and emotionally expressive capacities to enhance their lives and relationships (Dean-Church & Gilroy, 1993; Ramanaiah, Detwiler, & Byravan, 1995).

It is worth saying again that many people remain comfortable with traditional views of masculinity and femininity. Nevertheless, researchers have done much to show that "feminine" traits and "masculine" traits can exist in the same person and that androgyny can be a highly adaptive balance.

Learning Check	Critical Thinking

To check your progress, answer the following questions:

1. _____ sexual characteristics refer to the sexual and reproductive organs; _____ sexual characteristics refer to other bodily changes that take place at puberty.

2. All individuals normally produce both androgens and estrogens, although the proportions differ in females and males. T or F?

3. The five basic dimensions of gender are: _____

4. In females, hermaphroditism may result from
   a. an androgen insensitivity **b.** the androgenital syndrome **c.** excessive estrogen **d.** all of these

5. For humans, the biological biasing effect of prenatal hormones tends to override all other influences. T or F?

6. One's private sense of maleness or femaleness is referred to as _____ _____ .

7. Traditional sex role socialization encourages ____ behavior in males.
   a. instrumental **b.** emotional **c.** expressive **d.** dependent

8. A person who is androgynous is one who scores high on ratings of traits usually possessed by the opposite sex. T or F?

9. For both women and men, having masculine traits is associated with greater happiness in marriage. T or F?

10. A problem known as transsexualism exists when a person feels that she or he is trapped in a body of the wrong sex. This problem is therefore defined almost entirely on the basis of which dimension of gender?

Sexual Behavior— Mapping the Erogenous Zone

When does sexual behavior first appear in humans?

A capacity for sexual arousal is apparent at birth or soon after. Sexual researcher Alfred Kinsey verified instances of **orgasm** (*sexual climax*) in boys as young as 5 months old and girls as young as 4 months (Kinsey et al., 1948, 1953). Kinsey also found that children aged 2 to 5 years spontaneously touch and exhibit their genitals.

Sexual behavior continues in various forms throughout childhood. But as a child matures, cultural norms place greater restrictions on sexual activities. Still, 25 percent of females and 50 percent of males report having engaged in preadolescent sex play. In adulthood, norms continue to shape sexual activity along socially approved lines. In our culture, sex between children, incest (sex between close relatives), prostitution, and extramarital sex all tend to be discouraged.

As was the case with sex role behavior, it can be seen that such restrictions are somewhat arbitrary. Comparing various cultures shows that less restriction is usually accompanied by more sexual activity of all kinds. Apart from cultural norms, it can be said that any sexual act engaged in by consenting adults is "normal" if it does not hurt anyone.

Sexual Arousal

Sexual arousal in humans is complex. It may, of course, be produced by direct stimulation of the body's **erogenous zones** (eh-ROJ-eh-nus: *productive of pleasure or erotic desire*). Human erogenous zones include the genitals, mouth, breasts, ears, anus, and to a lesser degree, the surface of the entire body. It is clear, however, that more than physical contact is involved: A urological or gynecological examination rarely results in any sexual arousal. Human sexual arousal obviously includes a large cognitive element. Indeed, arousal may be triggered by mere thoughts or images.

Sexual Scripts In a restaurant we commonly expect certain things to occur. It could even be said that each of us has a restaurant "script" that defines a plot, dialogue, and actions that should take place. Researcher John Gagnon (1977) believes that, similarly, we learn a variety of **sexual scripts**, *or unspoken mental plans that guide our sexual behavior.* Such scripts determine when and where we are likely to express sexual feelings, and with whom. They provide a "plot" for the order of events in lovemaking, and they outline "approved" actions, motives, and outcomes.

When two people follow markedly different scripts, misunderstandings are almost sure to occur. Consider, for instance, what happens when a woman acting out a "friendly-first-date" script is paired with a man following a "seduction" script: The result is often anger, hurt feelings, or worse. Even newlyweds may find that their sexual "agendas" differ. In such cases, considerable "rewriting" of scripts is often needed for sexual compatibility.

1996 ZIGGY AND FRIENDS, INC. DISTRIBUTED BY UNIVERSAL PRESS SYNDICATE. REPRINTED WITH PERMISSION. ALL RIGHTS RESERVED.

However you may feel about the reality of sexual scripts, one implication of this line of thought is inescapable: For humans the mind (or brain) is the ultimate erogenous zone.

Are men more easily sexually aroused than women?

Women are no less *physically* responsive than men are (Laan et al., 1995). However, compared with men, women more often have a negative *emotional* response to erotic stimuli, such as explicit pictures of sex. That is, women more often report feeling upset or disgusted by these stimuli (Mosher & MacIan, 1994).

One reason for women's emotional responses may lie in the erotic stimuli themselves. Most erotic materials (such as films and videos) are made by men, for men. The next highlight reports on this interesting aspect of female sexuality.

A Closer Look

"What Do Women Want?"

Sigmund Freud was perplexed by what he regarded as a great mystery. "What," he wondered, "do women want?" Psychologist Ellen Laan thinks she may have an answer. Laan is studying differences between subjective sexual arousal—whether a woman says she feels sexually aroused, and physical arousal—how her body is actually responding (Laan et al., 1995).

In one of Laan's studies, women watched excerpts from two erotic films. One was made by a man for male viewers. The other was directed by a woman and presented from a female point of view. Using a medical recording device, Laan found that women's physical arousal was nearly identical to both types of films. However, their subjective experiences differed greatly. Many women reported being repulsed, disgusted, and decidedly not aroused by the male-oriented film. When viewing the film made for women, Laan's subjects reported more subjective feelings of sexual arousal, more positive emotions, and more interest in the film (Laan et al., 1994).

Why did the women respond so differently? Basically, the male-centered film was a macho fantasy in which the woman character was little more than a sexual prop—her pleasure and fulfillment were portrayed as largely unimportant. In the woman-made film, the female character took the initiative in lovemaking and obviously enjoyed it.

Clearly, women and men have equal potential for sexual arousal. However, a woman's subjective feelings of arousal tend to be more closely tied to her emotional response to erotic cues. It would appear that many women want to be active partners in lovemaking and they want their needs and preferences to be acknowledged. There's no mystery in that, Dr. Freud.

If the capacity for sexual arousal is measured by frequency of orgasm (brought about by masturbation or intercourse), the peak of male sexual activity is at age 18. The peak rate of female sexual activity appears to occur a little later (Janus & Janus, 1993). However, male and female sexual behavior is rapidly becoming more alike (Oliver & Hyde, 1993). Figure 15–7 ◆ shows the results of a recent major survey of sexual behavior among American adults. As you can see, the frequency of sexual intercourse is very similar for men and women (Laumann et al., 1994).

Sex Drive The term **sex drive** *refers to the strength of one's motivation to engage in sexual behavior.*

What causes differences in sex drive?

Attitudes toward sex, sexual experience, and recency of sexual activity are all obviously important, but physical factors also play a role. In males the strength of the sex drive is related to the amount of androgens secreted by the testes. When the supply of androgens dramatically increases at puberty, sex drive increases too.

Surprisingly, "male" hormones also affect the female sex drive. In addition to estrogen, a woman's body produces small amounts of androgens, which can increase the sex drive

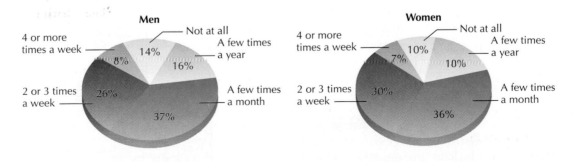

Figure 15–7 ◆ These graphs show the frequency of sexual intercourse for American adults. To generalize, about one third of the people surveyed have sex twice a week or more, one third a few times a month, and one third a few times a year or not at all. The overall average is about once a week (Laumann et al., 1994).

Figure 15–8 ◆ Average frequency of sexual intercourse per week for adults in the United States. Average intervals for intercourse decline from once every 4–5 days in young adulthood, to once every 16 days in the 60s. Remember that averages such as these are lowered by the inclusion of people who are abstinent or who do not have sexual partners (such as many widowed persons). However, the age declines noted here also show up for people who are married, ranging from an average rate of intercourse of twice a week for couples under 30 to once every 3 weeks for those over 70. This suggests that the average frequency of intercourse does decline with advancing age (Smith, 1990).

in women, just as they do in men. When women are given androgens for medical reasons, they report increased sexual desire (Van Goozen et al., 1995). Some women also report changes in sex drive at various times during their monthly cycles. However, such effects are probably small, because women may have sex at any time, including during menstruation.

Do nocturnal emissions ("wet dreams") reveal an unusually strong sex drive? Do they ever indicate sexual disorders? Do both men and women experience nocturnal orgasms?

About 85 percent of males and 35 percent of females have had *erotic dreams that resulted in sexual climax* (**nocturnal orgasms**). These incidents typically begin during adolescence and may continue throughout adulthood. Nocturnal orgasm, therefore, may be considered a completely normal (if relatively infrequent) form of sexual release.

Does alcohol stimulate the sex drive?

In general, no. Alcohol is a *depressant*. As such, it may, in small doses, stimulate erotic desire by lowering inhibitions. This effect no doubt accounts for alcohol's reputation as an aid to seduction. (Humorist Ogden Nash once summarized this bit of folklore by saying, "Candy is dandy, but liquor is quicker.") However, in larger doses alcohol suppresses orgasm in women and erection in men. Increasing levels of drunkenness cause a progressive *decrease* in sexual desire, arousal, pleasure, and performance (Crowe & George, 1989).

Does removal of the testes or ovaries abolish the sex drive? Also, what happens to the sex drive in old age?

In lower animals, **castration** (*surgical removal of the testicles*) or removal of the ovaries usually completely abolishes sexual activity in *inexperienced* animals. In humans, the effects of male and female castration vary. Initially, the sex drive declines in some individuals, while others experience no

change. This is why castration of sex offenders is unlikely to be effective in curbing their behavior. However, after several years have passed, almost all subjects do report a decrease in sex drive.

The preceding observations have nothing to do with the effects of **sterilization** (*surgery to make a man or woman infertile*). The vast majority of men and women who choose surgically based birth control (such as a tubal ligation or a vasectomy) experience no loss of sex drive. If anything, they may become more sexually active when pregnancy is no longer a concern.

A natural decline in sex drive typically accompanies aging and reduced sex hormone output (Segraves & Segraves, 1995). (See Figure 15–8 ◆.) However, sexual activity does not come to an unavoidable end. In some cases, women and men in their 80s and 90s have continued active sex lives (Skoog, 1996). The crucial factor for an extended sex life appears to be regularity and opportunity. ("Use it or lose it.") Individuals who fairly regularly engage in intercourse have little difficulty in later years. Many people in their 70s, 80s, and 90s report that sex is at least as gratifying as ever (Janus & Janus, 1993).

Masturbation One of the most basic human sexual behaviors is masturbation. **Masturbation** may be defined as *deliberate self-stimulation that causes sexual pleasure or orgasm*. Rhythmic self-stimulation has been observed in infants under 1 year of age. In adulthood, female masturbation most often centers on stimulation of the clitoris or the areas immediately surrounding it. Masturbation in the male usually takes the form of stroking or other manipulation of the penis. Some questions commonly asked about masturbation follow.

In adulthood, do more men masturbate than women?

Yes. Of the women who took part in a recent national survey, 89 percent reported that they had masturbated at some time. Of the males, 95 percent reported that they had masturbated. (Some cynics add, "And the other 5 percent lied!") As Figure 15–9 ◆ shows, masturbation is a regular feature of the sex lives of many people (Janus & Janus, 1993).

What purpose does masturbation serve?

Through masturbation, people discover what is pleasing sexually and what their natural rhythms and preferences are. Masturbation is therefore an important part of the psychosexual development of most adolescents. Among other things, it provides a healthy substitute for sexual intercourse at a time when sexual activity is discouraged and young people are maturing emotionally (Strong & DeVault, 1994).

Is it immature for masturbation to continue after marriage?

If it is, there are many "immature" people around! Approximately 70 percent of married women and men masturbate at least occasionally. Generally speaking, masturbation is a valid sexual activity at any age, and it may continue after marriage without posing any threat to a relationship. Contrary to popular myths, people are not compelled to masturbate because they lack a sexual partner. Actually, people who are most sexually active are also the ones who masturbate the most. Masturbation is just "one more item on the menu" for people with active sex lives (Laumann et al., 1994).

Is there any way in which masturbation can cause harm?

Fifty years ago, a child might have been told that masturbation would cause insanity, acne, sterility, or other such nonsense. "Self-abuse," as it was often called, has enjoyed a long and unfortunate history of religious and medical condemnation. The contemporary view is that masturbation is a normal and acceptable sexual behavior. Enlightened parents are well aware of this fact. Still, many children are punished or made to feel guilty for touching their genitals. This is unfortunate since masturbation itself is harmless. Typically, its only negative effects are fear, guilt, or anxiety, which arise when people learn negative attitudes toward it. In an age when people are being urged to practice "safer sex," masturbation remains the safest sex of all.

Sexual Orientation— Who Do You Love?

Sexual behavior and romantic relationships are strongly influenced by a person's sexual orientation. **Sexual orientation** refers to *one's degree of emotional and erotic attraction to members of the same gender, opposite gender, or both genders.* A person who is **heterosexual** *is romantically and erotically attracted to members of the opposite sex.* Those who are **homosexual** *are attracted to persons whose gender matches their own.* An individual who is **bisexual** *is attracted to both men and women.* In short, sexual orientation answers these questions: Who are you attracted to? Who do you have erotic fantasies about? Do you love men, or women, or both? (Garnets & Kimmel, 1991; Seligman, 1994).

Sexual orientation is a very deep part of personal identity. Starting with their earliest erotic feelings, most people remember being attracted to either the opposite sex or the same sex. The chances are practically nil of an exclusively heterosexual or homosexual person being "converted" from one orientation to the other. If you are heterosexual, you are probably certain that nothing could ever make you have homoerotic feelings. If so, then you know how homosexual persons feel about the prospects for changing *their* sexual orientation (Seligman, 1994).

But what about people who have had both heterosexual and homosexual relationships?

Many such instances involve homosexual persons who temporarily date or marry members of the opposite sex because of pressures to fit into a predominantly heterosexual society. When these people realize they are being untrue to themselves, their personal identity and relationships may shift accordingly. Other apparent shifts in orientation probably involve people who are fundamentally bisexual. Overall, sexual orientation is a very stable personal characteristic (Garnets & Kimmel, 1991).

What determines a person's sexual orientation?

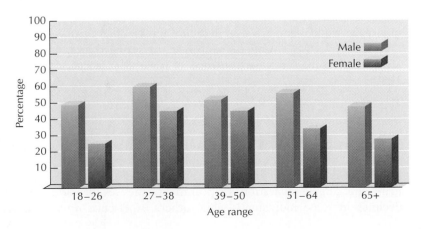

Figure 15–9 ◆ Percentage of women and men who masturbate. (Data from Janus & Janus, 1993.)

Research suggests that a combination of hereditary, biological, social, cultural, and psychological influences combine to produce one's sexual orientation (Money, 1987; Van Wyk & Geist, 1995). As one author summarizes, "Like much of human behavior, a combination of biological and social factors are most likely involved in the development of sexuality" (Gladue, 1987).

The following highlight summarizes some interesting recent findings about the origins of sexual orientation.

Genes, the Brain, and Sexual Orientation

Why are some people attracted to the opposite sex while others prefer members of the same sex? New evidence suggests that sexual orientation is at least partly hereditary. One recent study found that if one identical twin is homosexual or bisexual, there is a 50 percent chance that the other twin is too. This and related findings leads some researchers to estimate that sexual orientation is from 30 to 70 percent genetic (Bailey et al., 1993; Bailey & Pillard, 1991).

How could genes affect sexual orientation? Possibly, heredity shapes areas of the brain that orchestrate sexual behavior. Support for this idea comes from the work of neurobiologist Simon LeVay. He and other scientists have shown that various brain structures do indeed differ in heterosexuals and homosexuals (LeVay, 1993). Other research suggests that sexual orientation is influenced by a gene or genes found on the X chromosome. Thus, genetic tendencies for homosexuality may be passed from mothers to their children (Hamer et al., 1993; Hu et al., 1995).

Many people mistakenly believe that homosexuality is caused by a hormone imbalance. However, it is *highly unlikely* that hormone levels during adulthood affect sexual orientation. Hormone levels of most gay men and lesbians are within the normal range (Banks & Gartrell, 1995). If hormones do have a role in determining sexual orientation, their impact occurs before birth (Berenbaum & Snyder, 1995; Meyer-Bahlburg et al., 1995).

It is also a mistake to think that parenting makes children homosexual. There is little difference between the development of children with gay or lesbian parents and those who have heterosexual parents (Bailey et al., 1995; Flaks et al., 1995; Golombok & Tasker, 1996; Patterson, 1995).

All of these findings tend to discredit myths about parental behavior making children homosexual or claims that homosexuality is merely a preference. While learning contributes to one's sexual orientation, it appears that nature strongly prepares people to be either homosexual or heterosexual (LeVay, 1993). In view of this, discriminating against homosexuals is much like rejecting a person for being blue-eyed or left-handed (Hamill, 1995).

Homosexuality

As the preceding discussion implies, homosexuality is part of the normal range of variations in sexual orientation (Garnets & Kimmel, 1991). Gay men, lesbians, and bisexuals encounter hostility because they are members of a minority group, not because there is anything inherently wrong with them (Meyer, 1995).

Based on a recent national survey, it is estimated that about 7 percent of all adults regard themselves as homosexual or bisexual (see Table 15–2 ■). Among men, 1 in 25 is homosexual. Among women, 1 in 50 is a lesbian. About 1 person in 25 is bisexual. These percentages are small, but they indicate that roughly 7 persons out of every 100 are bisexual or homosexual (Janus & Janus, 1993). That means about 50 million people in the U.S. alone are gay, lesbian, or have a family member who is homosexual (Patterson, 1995).

When evaluating homosexuality, it is important to remember that cultural standards vary greatly. A survey of 76 cultures found that almost two thirds accept some form of homosexuality. About 20 percent of all females and 25 percent of all males have had at least one homosexual experience. Historically, homosexuality has been a part of human sexuality since the dawn of time.

In contrast to heterosexuals, homosexual persons tend to discover their sexual orientation at a fairly late date—often not until early adolescence. Very likely, this is because they are surrounded by powerful cultural images that contradict their natural feelings. It is probably difficult for most heterosexual persons to imagine how stressful it is to deny something as basic as one's sexual orientation. Yet, understandably, homosexual persons may be reluctant to accept or acknowledge their sexual orientation. Doing so risks rejection by family, friends, and others (Krivascka, Savin-Williams, & Slater, 1992).

Testing consistently shows no differences in personality or adjustment between heterosexuals and homosexuals (Bell

Table 15–2 ■ Sexual Orientation among Adults		
	Men	**Women**
Heterosexual	91%	95%
Homosexual	4%	2%
Bisexual	5%	3%
Janus & Janus, 1993.		

et al., 1981; Marmor, 1980). Emotional adjustment, then, appears to be independent of sexual preference (Siegelman, 1987). For these and other reasons, homosexuality is not considered a sexual disorder (DSM-IV, 1994). Sexual orientation is not related to a person's ability to function in society, work constructively, maintain mental health, care for children, or form caring relationships (Seligman, 1994).

The problems faced by lesbians and gay men tend to be related to rejection by family, discrimination in employment and housing, and the undercurrents of *homophobia* and *heterosexism* in our society (Meyer, 1995). (**Homophobia** *refers to prejudice, fear, and dislike aimed at homosexuals.* **Heterosexism** *is the belief that heterosexuality is better or more natural than homosexuality.*)

Most gay males and lesbian women have at one time or another suffered verbal abuse—or worse—because of their sexual orientation (Pilkington & D'Augelli, 1995). Much of this rejection is based on false stereotypes about gay and lesbian people. The following points are a partial reply to such stereotypes (Melton, 1989). Gay and lesbian people:

- Do not try to convert others to homosexuality.
- Do not molest children.
- Are not mentally ill.
- Do not hate persons of the opposite sex.
- Do not, as parents, make their own children gay.
- Do frequently have long-term, caring, monogamous relationships.
- Are no less able to contribute to society than heterosexuals.

Homosexual persons are found in all walks of life, at all social and economic levels, and in all cultural groups. They are as diverse in terms of race, ethnicity, age, parenthood, relationships, careers, health, education, politics, and sexual behavior as the heterosexual community (Garnets & Kimmel, 1991). Perhaps as more people come to see gay and lesbian people in terms of their humanity, rather than their sexuality, the prejudices they have faced will wane.

Learning Check | Critical Thinking

1. A capacity for sexual arousal is apparent at birth or soon after. T or F?

2. Areas of the body that produce erotic pleasure are called _____ zones.

3. When exposed to erotic stimuli, men and women vary in their most common emotional reactions, but there appears to be no difference in their levels of physical arousal. T or F?

4. There is some evidence to suggest that sexual activity and sex drives peak later for males than they do for females. T or F?

5. It is possible (and normal) for sexual activity to continue to ages of 80 or 90. T or F?

6. More males than females report that they masturbate. T or F?

7. Masturbation can cause physical harm, according to the latest research reports. T or F?

8. Whether a person has erotic fantasies about women or men is a strong indicator of his or her sexual orientation. T or F?

9. Research suggests that homosexuality is closely related to hormonal imbalances found in roughly 7 percent of all adults. T or F?

10. Why do you think that fidelity in marriage is strongly encouraged by law and custom?

Answers:
10. Through marriage laws and customs, human societies tend to foster enduring bonds between sexual partners to help ensure that children are cared for and not just produced (Ainsworth, 1989).
1. T 2. erogenous 3. T 4. F
5. T 6. T 7. F 8. T 9. F

Human Sexual Response—Sexual Interactions

Before the pioneering work of gynecologist William Masters and psychologist Virginia Johnson (1966, 1970), surprisingly little was known about human sexual response. In a series of experiments, interviews, and controlled observations, Masters and Johnson directly studied sexual intercourse and masturbation in nearly 700 males and females.

The information they obtained has greatly improved our understanding of human sexuality.

According to Masters and Johnson, sexual response can be divided into four phases: (1) *excitement,* (2) *plateau,* (3) *orgasm,* and (4) *resolution* (Fig. 15–10 ◆ and Fig. 15–11 ◆). These four phases can be described as follows:

Excitement phase *The first level of sexual response, indicated by initial signs of sexual arousal.*

Plateau phase *The second level of sexual response, during which physical arousal intensifies.*

Orgasm *A climax and release of sexual excitement.*

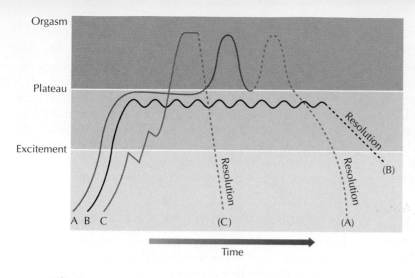

Figure 15-10 ◆ Female sexual response cycle. The green line shows that sexual arousal rises through the excitement phase and levels off for a time during the plateau phase. Arousal peaks during orgasm and then returns to pre-excitement levels. In pattern A, arousal rises from excitement, through the plateau phase, and peaks in orgasm. Resolution may be immediate, or it may first include a return to the plateau phase and a second orgasm (dotted line). In pattern B, arousal is sustained at the plateau phase and slowly resolved without sexual climax. Pattern C shows a fairly rapid rise in arousal to orgasm. Little time is spent in the plateau phase and resolution is fairly rapid. (Reproduced by permission from Frank A. Beach [ed.], *Sex and Behavior*, NY: John Wiley & Sons, Inc., 1965.)

Resolution *The final phase of sexual response, involving a return to lower levels of sexual tension and arousal.*

These four phases are the same for people of all sexual orientations (Garnets & Kimmel, 1991).

Female Response In women, the excitement phase is marked by a complex pattern of changes that prepare the vagina for intercourse. At the same time, the nipples become erect, pulse rate rises, and the skin may become flushed. If sexual stimulation ends, the excitement phase will gradually subside. If the person moves into the plateau phase, physical changes and subjective feelings of arousal become more intense. An end to sexual arousal during this phase will be resolved more slowly and may produce considerable frustration. On some occasions women skip the plateau phase (see Fig. 15-10). For some women, this is almost always the case.

During orgasm, from 3 to 10 muscular contractions of the vagina, uterus, and related structures discharge sexual tension. A small amount of fluid is sometimes released from the urethra during orgasm. However, vaginal lubrication produced during the excitement phase probably accounts for the perceptions of women who believe they have ejaculated. Orgasm is usually followed by resolution, a

return to lower levels of sexual tension and arousal. After orgasm, about 15 percent of all women return to the plateau phase and may have one or more additional orgasms before resolution.

Before the work of Masters and Johnson, there was considerable debate about whether female orgasms associated with the vagina are different from those derived from stimulation of the clitoris. Sigmund Freud claimed that a clitoral orgasm is an "immature" form of female response. Since the clitoris is the female structure comparable to the penis, Freud believed that women whose orgasms centered on the clitoris had not fully accepted their femininity.

Masters and Johnson exploded the Freudian myth by showing that there is no difference in physical response no matter how an orgasm is produced. As a matter of fact, the inner two thirds of the vagina is relatively insensitive to touch. Most sensations during intercourse, therefore, come from stimulation of the clitoris and other external areas.

It now seems apparent that sensations from many sources are fused together into the total experience of orgasm. For the majority of women, one of the more important sources of pleasurable sensations is the clitoris. When women in one study were asked to express a

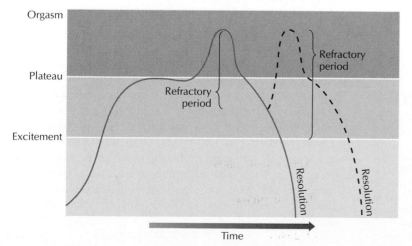

Figure 15-11 ◆ Male sexual response cycle. The green line shows that sexual arousal rises through the excitement phase and levels off for a time during the plateau phase. Arousal peaks during orgasm and then returns to pre-excitement levels. During the refractory period, immediately after orgasm, a second sexual climax is typically impossible. However, after the refractory period has passed, there may be a return to the plateau phase, followed by a second orgasm (dotted line). (Reproduced by permission from Frank A. Beach [ed.], *Sex and Behavior*, NY: John Wiley & Sons, Inc., 1965.)

preference for vaginal or clitoral stimulation, most said they would rather not choose. But if they were forced to choose, two thirds said they would prefer clitoral sensations (Fisher, 1973). Similarly, researcher Shere Hite reported the results of an unscientific yet thought-provoking survey of 3,000 women. Among these women, only 26 percent reported regularly reaching orgasm during intercourse without separate massaging of the clitoris (Hite, 1976). Thus, to downgrade the "clitoral orgasm" ignores the basic physiology of female sexual response.

Male Response Sexual arousal in the male is signaled by erection of the penis during the excitement phase. There is also a rise in heart rate, increased blood flow to the genitals, enlargement of the testicles, erection of the nipples, and numerous other bodily changes. As was true of female sexual response, continued stimulation moves the male into the plateau phase. Again, physical changes and subjective feelings of arousal become more intense. Further stimulation during the plateau phase brings about a reflex release of tension resulting in sexual climax, or orgasm.

In the mature male, orgasm is usually accompanied by **ejaculation** (*release of sperm and seminal fluid*). Afterward, it is followed by a short **refractory period** *during which a second orgasm is impossible.* (Many men cannot even have an erection until the refractory phase has passed.) Only rarely is the male refractory period immediately followed by a second orgasm. Both orgasm and resolution in the male usually do not last as long as they do for females.

Comparing Male and Female Responses

Similarities between male and female sexual responses far outweigh the differences. However, differences that do exist may have an effect on sexual adjustment. For example, women typically go through the sexual phases more slowly than men do. During lovemaking, from 10 to 20 minutes is often required for a woman to go from excitement to orgasm.* Males may experience all four stages in as little as 4 minutes. These differences should be kept in mind by couples seeking sexual compatibility.

Does that mean that a couple should try to time lovemaking to promote simultaneous orgasm?

At one time simultaneous orgasm (both partners reaching

---

* There is much variation, however. In a study of 1,000 married women, it was found that 50 percent of them reached orgasm if intercourse lasted 1 to 11 minutes; if intercourse lasted 15 minutes or more, the rate increased to 66 percent. Twenty-five percent of the wives said that orgasm occurred within 1 minute of the start of intercourse (Brewer, 1981). (Note that these times refer only to intercourse, not to an entire arousal sequence.)

sexual climax at the same time) was considered the ideal "goal" of lovemaking. More recently, it has been rejected as an artificial concern that may reduce sexual enjoyment. It is more advisable for couples to seek mutual satisfaction through a combination of intercourse and manual stimulation than it is to inhibit spontaneity, communication, and pleasure. A recent national survey found that the vast majority of American adults no longer feel that simultaneous orgasm is necessary for satisfying lovemaking (Janus & Janus, 1993).

Does slower response mean that women are less sexual than men?

Definitely not. During masturbation, 70 percent of females reach orgasm in 4 minutes or less. This finding casts serious doubts on the idea that women actually respond more slowly. Slower female response during intercourse probably occurs because stimulation to the clitoris is less direct. It might be said that the male simply provides too little stimulation for more rapid female response, not that the female is in any way inferior.

Does penis size affect female response?

Masters and Johnson found that the vagina adjusts to the size of the penis and that subjective feelings of pleasure and intensity of orgasm are not related to penis size. They also found that while individual differences exist in flaccid penis size, there tends to be much less variation in size during erection. This is why erection has been referred to as the "great equalizer." Contrary to popular belief, there is no relationship between penis size and male sexual potency.

Men almost always reach orgasm during intercourse, but many women do not. Does this indicate that women are less sexually responsive?

Again, the evidence argues against any lack of female sexual responsiveness. It is true that about 1 woman in 3 does not experience orgasm during the first year of marriage, and only about 30 percent regularly reach orgasm through intercourse alone. However, this does not imply lack of physical responsiveness since approximately 90 percent of all women reach orgasm when masturbating.

In another regard, the female is clearly more responsive. Only about 5 percent of males are capable of multiple orgasm (and then only after an unavoidable refractory period). Most males are limited to a second orgasm at best. In contrast, Masters and Johnson's findings suggest that most women who regularly experience orgasm are capable of multiple orgasm. According to one recent survey, 48 percent of all women have experienced multiple orgasms (Darling et al., 1992). Remember, though, that only about 15 percent regularly experience multiple orgasms. A woman should not assume that something is wrong if she isn't orgasmic or multi-orgasmic. Many women have satisfying sexual experiences even when orgasm is not involved.

Sexual Attitudes and Behavior—Choice, Risk, and Responsibility

Has there been a "sexual revolution"?

If a woman and a man living before the turn of the century could be transported to the present, what would they think about today's sexual values and practices? Undoubtedly, they would be stunned by the major changes that have taken place. Unmarried couples falling into bed on television; advertisements for bras, skimpy men's underwear, tampons, and cures for "jock itch"; near nudity at the beaches; sexually explicit movies—these and many other elements of contemporary culture would be shocking to a person from the Victorian era (Strong & DeVault, 1994).

The word *revolution*, however, suggests rapid change. Has there been a sexual revolution? A look at social changes that took place in the 1960s and '70s now makes it clear that some fundamental changes have occurred. Liberalized attitudes toward sexual expression, coupled with the availability of reliable contraceptives, have significantly changed sexual behavior. Compared with earlier decades, the gap between sexual values and actual behavior has narrowed. For example, traditional morality called for female virginity before marriage. Yet, in the 1940s and '50s, as many as 75 percent of women who married had engaged in premarital sexual relations (Strong & DeVault, 1994).

Attitudes Changing attitudes are illustrated by the issue of premarital intercourse. In a 1959 Roper poll, 88 percent of those interviewed agreed that premarital sex is wrong. By 1973, only 48 percent felt likewise. In a more recent survey, only 22 percent of young adults believed that premarital sex is unacceptable (Lord, 1985). Similar changes have been observed in attitudes toward extramarital sex, homosexuality, sex education, and a variety of related issues.

Have changing attitudes been translated into behavior?

Behavior Changes in attitudes are still larger than changes in actual sexual behavior. Mostly, there is greater *tolerance* for sexual activity, especially that *engaged in by others*. For example, a magazine poll found that 80 percent of all readers considered extramarital sex acceptable under some circumstances (Athenasiou et al., 1970). But two other polls found that, in practice, only about 30 percent of married persons actually had extramarital sexual experience (Rubenstein, 1983; Rubenstein & Tavris, 1987). This percentage has not changed greatly in the last 40 years. More importantly, faithfulness in marriage is a widely shared norm. Over a year, only 1.5 percent of married people have sex partners other than their spouse. Americans actually seem to live up to the norm of marital fidelity fairly well, despite much talk in pop psychology about "open" marriages (Laumann et al., 1994; Smith, 1990).

Premarital intercourse rates have traditionally been considered a good indication of overall sexual activity. The social upheaval that began in the 1960s led to an especially sharp rise in sexual activity among teenagers. This increase continued into the 1980s, although it has slowed recently. In the 1950s, Kinsey found that 70 percent of males and 33 percent of females had engaged in premarital intercourse by age 25. In the 1970s, Morton Hunt obtained premarital intercourse rates of 97 percent for males and about 70 percent for females. Now, according to the most recent

Twenty years ago, television soap operas were tame, gossipy melodramas. Today they are sexy, gossipy melodramas that frequently feature steamy on-screen lovemaking.

figures, 83 percent of all women and 91 percent of all men have had premarital sexual experience (Janus & Janus, 1993). To some extent these changes are related to a tendency to postpone marriage. In the United States alone, over 2 million unmarried couples are living together.

Another major element of the sexual revolution is earlier participation in sexual behavior by both sexes. A poll conducted in 1986 found that 57 percent of the nation's 17-year-olds were sexually experienced. For 16-year-olds, the figure was 46 percent; for 15-year-olds it was 29 percent; and for 14-year-olds, 19 percent. This particular aspect of increased sexual behavior remains troubling. Today, the United States has one of the highest teenage pregnancy rates among all industrialized nations. A partial solution may be to give youths a better understanding of their sexuality. A recent study confirmed that sex education delays the age at which young people first engage in sexual intercourse (Sawyer & Smith, 1996).

Is the Revolution Over?

Talk of a sexual revolution has quieted somewhat in recent years, and a conservative counter-movement has been visible. Some of the reaction may reflect concern about sexually transmitted diseases. However, a gradual liberalization continues, albeit at a much slower pace (Janus & Janus, 1993).

In all, there is ample evidence that sexual behavior has increased in the last 30 years. While this trend has brought problems, it does not seem to represent a wholesale move toward sexual promiscuity. While it is true that sexual intercourse by unmarried couples is more common today, most couples emphasize mutual commitment and a loving relationship as a requirement for sexual involvement (Strong & DeVault, 1994). In this regard, premarital sex can be said to parallel the behavior of engaged couples in past years. Or, as one author has noted (Hyde, 1996), many young people today have just changed the sequence of events. For their parents, the sequence was: fall in love, marry, and begin a sexual relationship. For many, the sequence now is fall in love, begin a sexual relationship, and marry. Most women have only one premarital sexual partner, whom they eventually marry. And men typically have about six premarital partners (Hyde, 1996). Overall, an image of rampant sexual behavior is not supported.

Even premarital intercourse does not appear to represent a major rejection of traditional values and responsible behavior. The association between sexuality and love or affection remains strong for the majority of the population. Both premarital sex and cohabitation are still widely viewed as preludes to marriage or as temporary substitutes for it (Strong & DeVault, 1994). Likewise, other changes in attitudes and behavior appear to reflect a greater acceptance of sexuality rather than a total rejection of earlier values.

Slow Death of the Double Standard

A good summary of one of the major changes that has occurred in sexual behavior is found in the phrase, "the slow death of the double standard."

The **double standard** *refers to applying different standards for judging the appropriateness of male and female sexual behavior.* In past decades, for example, males were largely forgiven for engaging in premarital sex. Young males who "sowed wild oats" were not only tolerated, but in some cases tacitly encouraged to do so as a step toward manhood. On the other hand, women who were sexually active before marriage ran the risk of being labeled "easy," "bad," or "promiscuous." Clearly, women are more aware of the double standard than men are: 79 percent of men believe it exists, whereas 91 percent of women do (Janus & Janus, 1993).

Similar differences pervade sexual mores and place women in a "separate but not equal" position with regard to sexual behavior (Sprecher & Hatfield, 1996). However, as the gap between female and male sexual patterns has continued to close, it is increasingly likely that an end to the double standard is in sight.

Choices   A more comfortable acceptance of human sexuality is the positive side of changing sexual attitudes and values. The negative side is represented by the plight of people who are not ready for, or interested in, greater sexual freedom. Apparently, some individuals feel pressured into sexual behavior because it is "expected." Six percent of first sexual intercourse experiences are against the person's will (Bajracharya, Sarvela, & Isberner, (1995).

Pressures to engage in sex probably come as much from the individual as from others. For a greater acceptance of human sexuality to be constructive, people must feel that they have the right to say no, as well as the right to choose when, where, how, and with whom their sexuality will be expressed. As is true elsewhere, freedom must be combined with responsibility, commitment, and caring if it is to have meaning.

The importance of respecting the right to say no is underscored by the recent dramatic increase in cases of **acquaintance** (or **date**) **rape** (*forced intercourse that occurs in the context of a date or other voluntary encounter*). From *5 to 15 percent* of all female college students report having been raped. Roughly one half of these rapes were by first dates, casual dates, or romantic acquaintances (Finkelson & Oswalt, 1995; Koss et al., 1987).

Men who commit date rape often believe they have done nothing wrong. A typical explanation is, "Her words were saying no, but her body was saying yes." But forced sex is rape, even if the rapist doesn't use a knife or become violent.

The effects of acquaintance rape are no less devastating than rape committed by a stranger. The next highlight lists some persistent myths about rape.

Rape Myths and Facts

The following points are a sampling of some damaging and all too common misinformation about rape.

Myth: Only women who "ask for it" by wearing sexy or provocative clothes get raped.

Fact: Anyone can be sexually assaulted. Victims of sexual assault include both men and women and people of all ages, races, and sexual orientations. Appearance and style of dress have little to do with rape.

Myth: Rape is a spontaneous, impulsive act.

Fact: Over half of all rapes are planned in advance. In the case of gang rape, about 90 percent are planned.

Myth: Rapists are sexually frustrated and can't control their sexual desires.

Fact: Nearly all rapists have available sexual partners. Rape is based on violent impulses and needs for power, not a simple desire for sex.

Myth: If a woman stays at home and avoids suspicious strangers, her chances of ever being raped are very small.

Fact: Sixty-five to 80 percent of all rapes are committed by a friend or acquaintance of the victim. About 60 percent of all sexual assaults occur in the victim's home.

Myth: Rape is impossible unless a woman consents.

Fact: Even if no weapon is used, a woman may be physically intimidated or paralyzed by fear. Some women cooperate with an assailant in an attempt to live through the assault.

Myth: Most women secretly want to be raped.

Fact: Rape is painful, degrading, terrifying, and emotionally devastating. No one wants to be a victim of sexual assault.

As a final point, it is worth noting that men who embrace traditional masculine sex roles are more likely to believe such myths (Truman, Tokar, & Fischer, 1996).

AIDS, STDs, and Sexual Responsibility

A **sexually transmitted disease (STD)** *is passed from one person to another by intimate physical contact.* The incidence of STDs has been rising for the last 20 years. Today, sexually active individuals run an elevated risk of getting chlamydia (klah-MID-ee-ah), gonorrhea, hepatitis B, herpes, syphilis, and other STDs (see Table 15–3 ■). As you read through Table 15–3, remember that many people who carry STDs remain **asymptomatic** (a-SIMP-teh-mat-ik: *lacking obvious symptoms*). It is quite possible to be infected without knowing it. Likewise, it is often impossible to tell if a sexual partner is infectious.

For many sexually active people, **acquired immune deficiency syndrome (AIDS)** has added a new threat. Whereas most other STDs are treatable, AIDS is almost always fatal. Check your knowledge about AIDS against the following summary.

AIDS

AIDS is caused by the **human immunodeficiency virus (HIV).** In time, this virus *disables the immune system, allowing other "opportunistic" diseases to invade the body* without resistance. Most AIDS victims eventually die of multiple infections (although a new drug therapy has improved the odds of survival). The first symptoms of AIDS may show up as little as 2 months after infection, or they may not appear for up to 7 years. Because of this long incubation period, infected persons often pass the AIDS virus on to others without knowing it. Medical testing can detect the presence of an HIV infection. However, for at least the first 6 months after becoming infected, a person can test negative while carrying the virus. A negative test result, therefore, is no guarantee that a person is a "safe" sex partner.

HIV infections are spread by direct contact with body fluids—especially blood, semen, and vaginal secretions. The AIDS virus cannot be transmitted by casual contact. People do not get AIDS from shaking hands, touching or using objects used by an AIDS patient, eating food prepared by an infected person, social kissing, from sweat or tears, from sharing drinking glasses, sharing towels, and so forth.

Populations at Risk   AIDS has been called the gay plague because male homosexuals were its first highly visible victims. However, this label is in error. AIDS can be spread by all forms of sexual intercourse, and it has affected persons of all sexual orientations. Recently, the AIDS epidemic has spread more quickly among heterosexuals, women, African Americans, Hispanics, and children. HIV infection is now the leading cause of death among women and men between the ages of 25 and 44 (Knowles, 1995).

Those who are at greatest risk for HIV infection remain men who have had sex with other men (homosexual and bisexual men), people who have shared needles (for tattoos or for intravenous drug use), blood transfusion recipients (between 1977 and spring 1985), hemophiliacs (who require frequent blood transfusions), sexual partners of people in the preceding groups, and heterosexuals with a

Table 15-3 ■ Common Sexually Transmitted Diseases

STD	Male Symptoms	Female Symptoms	Prevention	Treatment
gonorrhea	milky discharge from urethra; painful, frequent urination	vaginal discharge and inflammation, painful urination	condom/safer sex practices	antibiotics
chlamydia	painful urination, discharge from urethra	painful urination, discharge from vagina, abdominal pain	condom/safer sex practices	antibiotics
syphilis	painless sores on genitals, rectum, tongue, or lips, skin rash, fever, headache, aching bones and joints	same	condom/safer sex practices	antibiotics
genital herpes	pain or itching on the penis; water blister or open sores	pain or itching in the genital area; water blisters or open sores	condom/safer sex practices	symptoms can be treated but not cured
genital warts	warty growths on genitals	same	condom/safer sex practices	removal by surgery or laser
HIV/AIDS	prolonged fatigue, swollen lymph nodes, fever lasting more than 10 days, night sweats, unexplained weight loss, purplish lesions on skin, persistent cough or sore throat, persistent colds, persistent diarrhea, easy bruising or unexplained bleeding	same	condom/safer sex practices	can be treated with various drugs, but not cured
hepatitis B	mild cases may have no symptoms, but infection can cause chronic liver disease, cirrhosis of the liver, or liver cancer	same	vaccination	none available
pelvic inflammatory disease	does not apply	intense pain in lower back and/or abdomen, fever	condom/safer sex practices	antibiotics

history of multiple partners. Thus, the vast majority of people are not at high risk of HIV infection. Still, 1 in 75 men and 1 in 700 women in North America are now infected with HIV. As a result, people who engage in unsafe sex are gambling with their lives—at very poor odds (Fig. 15–12 ◆). Six percent of all new AIDS cases are now heterosexual—and the incidence is rising. In addition, new strains of the HIV virus are appearing. One in particular, which has spread explosively among heterosexuals in Africa, was recently detected in North America (Knowles, 1995).

Behavioral Risk Factors The behaviors listed here are risky when performed with an infected person.

Risky Behaviors

- Sharing drug needles and syringes
- Anal sex, with or without a condom
- Vaginal or oral sex with someone who injects drugs or engages in anal sex
- Sex with someone you don't know well, or with someone you know has several partners
- Unprotected sex (without a condom) with an infected partner

The AIDS Memorial Quilt was begun in 1985 to commemorate those who have died from AIDS. Today, the quilt has grown to immense size, symbolizing the extent of the AIDS epidemic. Originally the quilt memorialized only homosexual victims. It now includes heterosexual men, women, and children, signifying that AIDS respects no boundaries (Zucker, 1995).

Figure 15–12 ◆ Popular professional basketball star Earvin "Magic" Johnson stunned fans in 1991 when he announced that he had tested positive for the HIV virus. Johnson, who is heterosexual, emphasized that his infection is a warning that anyone who is sexually active can contract the AIDS virus if he or she doesn't follow safe sex practices. Johnson further stressed that abstinence is the surest way to prevent AIDS. Johnson's infection increased public awareness about AIDS. Unfortunately, though, it has resulted in little real change in risky behavior (Brown et al., 1996).

■ Having two or more sex partners (additional partners further increase the risk)

With respect to the preceding, it's important to remember that you can't tell from appearance if a person is infected. Many people would be surprised to learn that their partners have engaged in behavior that places them both at risk (Seal & Palmer-Seal, 1996). Generally speaking, people who ignore future consequences of their actions are more likely to engage in risky sex (Rothspan & Read, 1996).

The preceding high-risk behaviors can be contrasted with the following list of safer sexual practices. Note, however, that unless a person completely abstains, sex can be made safer, but not entirely risk-free (Hawkins, Gray, & Hawkins, 1995).

Safer Sex Practices

■ Not having sex
■ Sex with one mutually faithful, uninfected partner
■ Not injecting drugs
■ Discussing contraception with partner

■ Being selective regarding sexual partners
■ Reducing the number of sexual partners
■ Discussing partner's sexual health prior to engaging in sex
■ Not engaging in sex while intoxicated
■ Using a condom

Sexually active persons should practice safer sex until their partner's sexual history and/or health has been clearly established. And remember, a condom offers little or no protection if it is misused.

Perhaps because it is fatal, AIDS is having a strong impact on sexual behavior in some groups. Among gay men there has been a sharp increase in monogamous relationships and in abstention from sex. Gay men have also significantly reduced their participation in high-risk sexual behaviors.

Other groups are not getting the message. The AIDS epidemic has thus far had little impact on the willingness of college students to engage in risky behavior (casual sex) or to use condoms (Clark, 1990; DeBuono et al., 1990). A recent study of heterosexually active adults found that 62 percent did not practice safer sex with their last partner. Most of these "gamblers" knew too little about their partners to be assured that they were not taking a big risk. Table 15–4 ■

| | Percentage |
Reasons For Not Having Safer Sex	**Giving Excuse**
Condom not available	20
Didn't want to use a condom	19
"Couldn't stop ourselves"	15
Partner didn't want to use a condom	14
Alcohol or drug use	11

Table 15–4 ■ Common Excuses for Not Practicing Safer Sex

Kusseling et al., 1996.

lists the excuses they gave for engaging in risky sex (Kusseling et al., 1996).

Apparently, heterosexual people still don't feel that they are truly at risk. However, worldwide *75 percent* of people with the AIDS virus were infected through heterosexual sex. In Europe and North America, only 3 percent of men, but 34 percent of women contracted the AIDS virus from a person of the opposite sex. Over the next 20 to 30 years, heterosexual transmission is expected to become the primary means of spreading HIV infection in most industrialized countries. A special concern is the fact that approximately 20 percent of all AIDS victims are teenagers. Adolescents tend to see themselves as invulnerable and are prone to risk taking that ranges from speeding to unprotected sex. Many sexually active teens are under the mistaken impression that precautions are unnecessary. However, among North American adolescents, straight sex has surpassed gay sex as the primary source of HIV infections (Radetsky, 1992).

Risk and Responsibility The threat of AIDS has forced many people to face new issues of risk and responsibility. Anyone who does not ensure their own safety is playing Russian roulette with their health. One chilling study of HIV patients—who knew they were infectious—found that 41 percent of those who were sexually active did not always use condoms (Sobel et al., 1996)! Thus, responsibility for "safer sex" rests with each sexually active individual. It is unwise to count on a sexual partner for protection against HIV infection.

Unprotected sex might seem safe if both partners know that they are HIV-negative. However, HIV can be extremely contagious during the first two months of infection. During that time, routine HIV testing cannot detect the infection. A special risk that befalls people in committed relationships is that they often interpret practicing safer sex as a sign of mistrust. Taking precautions could, instead, be defined as a way of showing that you really care about the welfare of your partner (Hammer et al., 1996).

The sexual revolution was fueled, in part, by the "pill" and other birth control methods. Will the threat of AIDS reverse the tide of changes that occurred in previous decades? Will STD come to mean Sudden Total Disinterest in sex? Will the "germs of endearment" change the terms of endearment? The answers may depend on how quickly people learn to respect the AIDS virus and whether its prevention or cure can be achieved.

A Look Ahead Even without STDs to worry about, sexual problems are quite common. In the Applications section we will consider the most frequent complaints and how they are remedied. After that, the Exploration section addresses an interesting question: What do patterns of touching reveal about personal relationships?

Learning Check **Critical Thinking**

1. List the four phases of sexual response identified by Masters and Johnson:

2. Males typically experience _____ after ejaculation.
   a. an increased potential for orgasm **b.** a short refractory period **c.** the excitement phase
   d. muscular contractions of the uterus

3. The research of Masters and Johnson suggests that the similarities between female and male sexual responses outweigh the differences. T or F?

4. During lovemaking, from 10 to 20 minutes is often required for a woman to go from excitement to orgasm, while a male may experience all four stages of sexual response in as little as 4 minutes. T or F?

5. Simultaneous orgasm of the female and male should be the ultimate goal in lovemaking. T or F?

6. Recent research shows that more liberal views regarding sexual behavior have erased the traditional values that link sexual involvement with committed relationships. T or F?

7. Contrary to long-standing belief, it now appears that much female sexual pleasure is focused on
   a. the uterus   **b.** the clitoris   **c.** the urethra   **d.** the cervix

8. The term _____ _____ describes the long-standing tendency for the sexual behavior of women and men to be judged differently.

9. Because AIDS is spread by direct contact with body fluids, it can be transmitted by social kissing or contact with food or dishes handled by an AIDS patient. T or F?

10. Of the following reasons that teenage boys and girls give for engaging in sex—love, curiosity, sexual gratification, peer pressure, and "everyone's doing it"—which do you think they rank first, and which last?

Answers:

1. excitement, plateau, orgasm, resolution 2. b 3. T 4. T 5. F 6. F
7. b 8. double standard 9. F
10. Peer pressure ranks first (cited by
30 percent of those surveyed) and love
ranked last (cited by 8 percent) ("Teen
sex," 1989).

Applications
Sexual Problems—When Pleasure Fades

What are the most common sexual problems? How are they treated?

Because they are so often endured in private, sexual dysfunctions are far more common than many people realize. Most people who seek sexual counseling have one or more of the following types of problems (DSM-IV, 1994):

1. **Desire Disorders:** *The person has little or no sexual motivation or desire.*

2. **Arousal Disorders:** *The person desires sexual activity, but does not become sexually aroused.*

3. **Orgasm Disorders:** *The person does not have orgasms or experiences orgasm too soon or too late.*

4. **Sexual Pain Disorders:** *The person experiences pain that makes lovemaking uncomfortable or impossible.*

There was a time when people suffered such problems in silence. However, in recent years effective treatments have been found for many of the major complaints. Let's briefly investigate the nature, causes, and treatments of sexual dysfunctions.

Desire Disorders

Desire disorders, like most sexual problems, must be defined in relation to a person's age, gender, partner, expectations, and sexual history. It is not at all unusual for a person to briefly lose sexual desire. Typically, erotic feelings return when anger toward a partner fades, or fatigue, illness, and similar temporary problems end. Under what circumstances, then, is loss of desire a dysfunction? First, the loss of desire must be *persistent*. Second, the person must be *troubled by it*. When these two conditions are met, **hypoactive sexual desire** is said to exist. Diminished desire can apply to both sexes. However, it is somewhat more common in women (Beck, 1995; Read, 1995).

Some people don't merely lack sexual desire; they are *repelled* by sex and seek to avoid it. A person who suffers from **sexual aversion** *feels fear, anxiety, or disgust about engaging in sex.* Often, the afflicted person still has some erotic feelings. For example, he or she may still masturbate or have sexual fantasies. Nevertheless, the prospect of having sex with another person causes panic or revulsion (DSM-IV, 1994).

Sexual desire disorders are common. Possible physical causes include illness, fatigue, hormonal difficulties, and the side effects of medicines. Desire disorders are also associated with psychological factors such as depression, fearing loss of control over sexual urges, strict religious beliefs, fear of pregnancy, marital conflict, fear of closeness, and simple loss of attraction to one's partner (Allgeier & Allgeier, 1995; Read, 1995). It is also not uncommon to find that people with desire disorders were sexually mistreated as children (Bakich, 1995).

Treatment Desire disorders are complex problems. Unless they have a straightforward physical cause, they are difficult to treat. Desire disorders are often deeply rooted in a person's childhood, sexual history, personality, and relationships. In such instances, counseling or psychotherapy is recommended (Allgeier & Allgeier, 1995).

Arousal Disorders

A person suffering from an arousal disorder wants to make love, but experiences little or no physical arousal. For women, this means vaginal dryness. For men, it means an inability to maintain an erection. Basically, in arousal disorders the body does not cooperate with the person's desire to make love.

Male Erectile Disorder *An inability to maintain an erection for lovemaking* is called **male erectile disorder.** This problem, which is also known as erectile dysfunction, was once referred to as *impotence.* However, psychologists now discourage use of the term impotence because of its many negative connotations.

Erectile disorders can be primary or secondary. Men suffering from primary erectile dysfunction have never had an erection. Those who previously performed successfully, but then developed a problem, suffer from secondary erectile dysfunction. Either way, persistent erectile difficulties tend to be very disturbing to the man and his sexual partner.

How often must a man experience failure for a problem to exist?

Ultimately, only the man and his partner can make this judgment. Nevertheless, sex therapists Masters and Johnson (1970) believe that a problem exists when failure occurs on 25 percent or more of a man's lovemaking attempts. Repeated erectile dysfunction should therefore be distinguished from *occasional* erectile problems. Fatigue, anger, anxiety, and drinking too much alcohol can cause temporary erectile difficulties in healthy males. True erectile disorders typically persist for months or years.

It is important to recognize that occasional erectile problems are normal. In fact, "performance demands" or overreaction to the temporary loss of an erection may generate fears and doubts that contribute to a further inhibition of arousal (Abrahmson et al., 1989). At such times, it is particularly important for the man's partner to avoid expressing anger, disappointment, or embarrassment. Patient reassurance helps prevent the establishment of a vicious cycle.

What causes erectile disorders?

For years, experts held that erectile disorders are rarely caused by physical illness, disease, or damage. Now it is recognized that roughly 40 percent of all cases are organic, or physically caused. The origin of the remaining cases is **psychogenic** (*a result of emotional factors*). Even when erectile dysfunction is organic, however, it is almost always made worse by anxiety, anger, and dejection. If a man can have an erection at times other than lovemaking (during sleep, for instance) the problem probably is not physical (Ackerman & Carey, 1995).

Organic erectile problems have many causes. Typical sources of trouble include alcohol or drug abuse, diabetes, vascular disease, prostate and urological disorders, neurological problems, and reactions to medication for high blood pressure, heart disease, or stomach ulcers. Erectile problems are also a normal part of aging. As men grow older they typically experience a decline in sexual desire and arousal and an increase in sexual dysfunction (Segraves & Segraves, 1995).

According to Masters and Johnson (1970), primary erectile disorders are often related to harsh religious training, early sexual experiences with a seductive mother, sexual molestation in childhood, or other experiences leading to guilt, fear, and sexual inhibition.

Secondary erectile disorders may be related to anxiety about sex in general, guilt because of an extramarital affair, resentment or hostility toward a sexual partner, fear of inability to perform, and similar emotions and conflicts. Often the problem starts with repeated sexual failures caused by drinking too much alcohol or by premature ejaculation. In any event, initial doubts soon become severe fears of failure—which further inhibit sexual response.

Treatment Drugs or surgery may be used in medical treatment of organic erectile disorders. Treatment for both organic and psychogenic disorders also usually includes counseling to remove fears and psychological blocks (Althof & Seftel, 1995). The man learns that he cannot consciously will an erection and that his manhood is not in doubt. To further free him of fears (particularly fear of failure), the man and his partner are usually assigned a series of exercises to perform. This technique, called **sensate focus,** *directs attention to natural sensations of pleasure* and builds communication skills (McCabe, 1992).

In sensate focus, the couple is told to take turns caressing various parts of each other's bodies. They are further instructed to carefully avoid any genital contact. Instead, they are to concentrate on giving pleasure and on signaling what feels good to them. This takes the pressure to perform off the man and allows him to learn to give pleasure as a means of receiving it.

Over a period of days or weeks, the couple proceeds to more intense physical contact involving the breasts and genitals. As inhibitions are reduced and natural arousal begins to replace fear, the successful couple moves on to mutually satisfying lovemaking.

Female Sexual Arousal Disorder Women who suffer from **female sexual arousal disorder** *respond with little or no physical arousal to sexual stimulation.* The problem thus appears to correspond directly to male erectile difficulties. As in the male, female sexual arousal disorder may be primary or secondary. Also, it is again important to remember that all women occasionally experience inhibited arousal. In some instances the problem may reflect nothing more than a lack of sufficient sexual stimulation before attempting lovemaking (Allgeier & Allgeier, 1995; Read, 1995).

The causes of inhibited arousal in women are similar to those seen in men. Sometimes the problem is medical, being related to illness or the side effects of medicines or contraceptives. Psychological factors include anxiety, anger or hostility toward one's partner, depression, stress, or distracting worries. Some women can trace their arousal difficulties to frightening childhood experiences, such as molestations (often by older relatives), incestuous relations that produced lasting guilt, a harshly religious background in which sex was considered evil, or to cold, unloving childhood relationships. Also common is a need to maintain control over emotions, deep-seated conflicts over being female, and extreme distrust of others, especially males (Read, 1995).

How does treatment proceed?

Treatment   Treatment typically includes sensate focus, genital stimulation by the woman's partner, and "non-demanding" intercourse controlled by the woman. With success in these initial stages, full intercourse is gradually introduced. As sexual training proceeds, psychological conflicts and dynamics typically appear, and as they do, they are treated in separate counseling sessions.

Orgasm Disorders

A person suffering from an orgasm disorder either fails to reach orgasm during sexual activity or reaches orgasm too soon or too late. Notice that such disorders are very much based on expectations. For instance, if a man experiences delayed orgasm, one couple might define it as a problem, whereas another might welcome it. It is also worth noting again that some women rarely or never have orgasm and still find sex pleasurable (Allgeier & Allgeier, 1995; Read, 1995).

Female Orgasmic Disorder   The most prevalent sexual complaint among women is a *persistent inability to reach orgasm during lovemaking*. It is often clear in **female orgasmic disorder** that the woman is not completely unresponsive. Rather, she is unresponsive in the context of a relationship—she may easily reach orgasm by masturbation, but not in lovemaking with her partner.

Then couldn't the woman's partner be at fault?

Sex therapists try to avoid finding fault or placing blame. However, it is true that the woman's partner must be committed to ensuring her gratification. Roughly two thirds of all women need direct stimulation of the clitoris to reach orgasm. Therefore, some apparent instances of female orgasmic disorder can be traced to inadequate stimulation or faulty technique on the part of the woman's partner. Even when this is true, sexual adjustment difficulties are best viewed as a problem the couple shares, not just as the "woman's problem," the "man's problem," or her "partner's problem."

Treatment   If we focus only on the woman, the most common source of orgasmic difficulties is overcontrol of sexual response. Orgasm requires a degree of abandonment to erotic feelings. It is inhibited by ambivalence or hostility toward the relationship, by guilt, by fears of expressing sexual needs, and by tendencies to control and intellectualize erotic feelings. The woman is unable to let go and enjoy the flow of pleasurable sensations.

In Helen Kaplan's treatment program at Cornell University, anorgasmic women (those who do not have orgasms) are first trained to focus on their sexual responsiveness through masturbation or vigorous stimulation by a partner. As the woman becomes consistently orgasmic in these circumstances, her responsiveness is gradually transferred to lovemaking with her partner. Couples also typically learn alternative positions and techniques of lovemaking designed to increase clitoral stimulation (Hurlbert & Apt, 1995). At the same time, communication between partners is stressed, especially with reference to the woman's sexual value system (expectations, motivations, and preferences).

Male Orgasmic Disorder   Among males, *an inability to reach orgasm* was once considered a rare problem. But milder forms of **male orgasmic disorder** account for increasing numbers of clients seeking therapy. Typical background factors are strict religious training, fear of impregnating, lack of interest in the sexual partner, symbolic inability to give of oneself, unacknowledged homosexuality, or the recent occurrence of traumatic life events. Power and commitment struggles within relationships may be important added factors.

Treatment   Treatment for male orgasmic disorder (also known as retarded ejaculation) consists of sensate focus, manual stimulation by the man's partner (which is designed to orient the male to his partner as a source of pleasure), and stimulation to the point of orgasm followed by immediate intercourse and ejaculation. Work also focuses on resolving personal conflicts and marital difficulties underlying the problem.

Premature Ejaculation   Defining premature ejaculation is tricky because of large variations in the time different women take to reach orgasm. Helen Kaplan says that **premature ejaculation** exists when it occurs reflexively or the man cannot tolerate high levels of excitement at the plateau stage of arousal. Basically, ejaculation is premature *if it consistently occurs before the man and his partner want it to occur.*

Do many men have difficulties with premature ejaculation?

Approximately 50 percent of young adult men have problems with premature ejaculation. Theories advanced to explain it have ranged from the idea that it may represent hostility toward the man's sexual partner (since it deprives the partner of satisfaction) to the suggestion that most early male sexual experiences tend to encourage rapid climax (such as those taking place in the back seat of a car and masturbation). Kaplan (1974) adds that excessive arousal and anxiety over performance are usually present, and that some men simply engage in techniques that maximize sensation and make rapid orgasm inevitable.

Ejaculation is a reflex. To control it, a man must learn to recognize the physical signals that it is about to occur. Some men have simply never learned to be aware of these signals. Whatever the causes, premature ejaculation can be a serious difficulty, especially in the context of long-term relationships.

Treatment   Treatment for premature ejaculation is highly successful and relatively simple. The most common treatment is a "stop-start" procedure called the **squeeze technique** (Grenier & Byers, 1995). The man's sexual partner stimulates him manually until he signals that ejaculation is about to occur. The man's partner then firmly *squeezes the tip of his penis to inhibit orgasm.* When the man feels he has control, stimulation is repeated. Later the squeeze technique is used during lovemaking. Gradually, the man acquires the ability to delay orgasm sufficiently for mutually satisfactory lovemaking. During treatment, skills that improve communication between partners are developed, along with a better understanding of the male's sexual response cues (Larson, 1990).

Sexual Pain Disorders

Pain in the genitals before, during, or after sexual intercourse is called **dyspareunia** (DIS-pah-ROO-nee-ah). Both females and males can experience dyspareunia. However, this problem is actually rare in males. In women, dyspareunia is often related to **vaginismus** (VAJ-ih-NIS-mus), a condition in which *muscle spasms of the vagina prevent intercourse* (DSM-IV, 1994).

Vaginismus is often accompanied by obvious fears of intercourse, and where fear is absent, high levels of anxiety are present. Vaginismus therefore appears to be a phobic response to intercourse. Predictably, its causes include experiences of painful intercourse, rape and/or brutal and frightening sexual encounters, fear of men and of penetration, misinformation about sex (belief that it is injurious), fear of pregnancy, and fear of the specific male partner (Read, 1995; Ward & Ogden, 1994).

Treatment   Treatment of vaginismus is similar to what might be done for a non-sexual phobia. It includes extinction of conditioned muscle spasms by progressive relaxation of the vagina, desensitization of fears of intercourse, and masturbation or manual stimulation to associate pleasure with sexual approach by the woman's partner. Hypnosis has also been used successfully in some cases.

Summary   Solving sexual problems can be difficult. The problems described here are rarely solved without professional help (a possible exception is premature ejaculation). If a serious sexual difficulty is not resolved in a reasonable amount of time, the aid of an appropriately trained psychologist, physician, or counselor should be sought. The longer the problem is ignored, the more difficult it is to solve. But professional help is available.

Relationships and Sexual Adjustment

What can be done to improve sexual adjustment?

Often, it is best to view sexual adjustment within the broader context of a relationship. Conflict and unresolved anger in other areas frequently take their toll in sexual adjustment, and mutually satisfying relationships tend to carry over into sexual relations. Sex is not a performance or a skill to be mastered like playing tennis. It is a form of communication within a relationship. Couples with strong and caring relationships can probably survive most sexual problems. A couple with a satisfactory sex life but a poor relationship rarely lasts. Marriage expert John Gottman believes that a couple must have at least five times as many positive as negative moments in their marriage if it is to survive (Gottman, 1994).

Disagreements about Sex   When disagreements arise over issues such as frequency of lovemaking, who initiates lovemaking, or what behavior is appropriate, Masters and Johnson believe that the rule should be, "Each partner must accept the other as the final authority on his or her own feelings." Partners are urged to give feedback about their feelings by following what therapists call the "touch and ask" rule: Touching and caressing should often be followed by questions such as, "Does that feel good?" "Do you like that?" and so forth (Knox, 1984). Satisfying erotic relationships focus on enhancing sexual pleasure for both partners, not on selfish interest in one's own gratification (Kleinplatz, 1996).

When problems do arise, partners are urged to be *responsive* to each other's needs at an *emotional* level and to recognize that all sexual problems are *mutual*. "Failures" should always be shared without placing blame. Masters and

Johnson believe that it is particularly important to avoid the "numbers game." That is, couples should avoid being influenced by statistics on the average frequency of lovemaking, by stereotypes about sexual potency, and by the superhuman sexual exploits portrayed in movies and magazines.

Bridges to Sexual Satisfaction   According to sex therapist Barry McCarthy, four elements are necessary for a continuing healthy sexual relationship:

1. *Sexual anticipation.* Looking forward to lovemaking is inhibited by routine and poor communication between partners. It is wise for busy couples to set aside time to spend together. Unexpected, spontaneous lovemaking should also be encouraged.

2. *Valuing one's sexuality.* This is most likely to occur when you develop a respectful, trusting, and intimate relationship with your partner. Such relationships allow both partners to deal with negative sexual experiences when they occur.

3. *Feeling that you deserve sexual pleasure.* As previously noted, the essence of satisfying lovemaking is the giving and receiving of pleasure.

4. *Valuing intimacy.* A sense of closeness and intimacy with one's partner helps maintain sexual desire, especially in long-term relationships (McCarthy, 1995).

Are there any other guidelines for maintaining a healthy relationship?

Intimacy and Communication

A study that compared happily married couples with unhappily married couples found that, in almost every regard, the happily married couples showed superior *communication* skills. Three patterns that are almost always related to serious long-term problems in relationships are defensiveness (including whining), stubbornness, and refusal to talk with your partner (the "big freeze") (Gottman & Krokoff, 1989). Many couples find that communication is facilitated by observing the following guidelines.

Avoid "Gunnysacking"   Persistent feelings, whether positive or negative, need to be expressed. Gunnysacking refers to saving up feelings and complaints. These are then "dumped" during an argument or are used as ammunition in a fight. Gunnysacking is very destructive to a relationship.

Be Open about Feelings   Happy couples not only talk more, they convey more personal feelings and show greater sensitivity to their partners' feelings. As one expert put it, "In a healthy relationship, each partner feels free to express his likes, dislikes, wants, wishes, feelings, impulses, and the other

person feels free to react with like honesty to these. In such a relationship, there will be tears, laughter, sensuality, irritation, anger, fear, baby-like behavior, and so on" (Jourard, 1963).

Don't Attack the Other Person's Character   Whenever possible, expressions of negative feelings should be given as statements of one's own feelings, not as statements of blame. It is far more constructive to say, "It makes me angry when you leave things around the house" than it is to say, "You're a slob!" Remember too, that if you use the words "always" or "never," you are probably mounting a character attack.

Don't Try to "Win" a Fight   Constructive fights are aimed at resolving shared differences, not at establishing who is right or wrong, superior or inferior.

Recognize that Anger Is Appropriate   Constructive and destructive fights are not distinguished by whether or not anger is expressed. A fight is a fight, and anger is appropriate. As is the case with any other emotion in a relationship, anger should be expressed. However, constructive expression of anger requires that couples fight fair by sticking to the real issues and not "hitting below the belt." Resorting to threats, such as announcing, "This relationship is over," is especially damaging.

Try to See Things through Your Partner's Eyes   Marital harmony is closely related to the ability to put yourself in another person's place (Long & Andrews, 1990). When a conflict arises, always pause and try to take your partner's perspective. Seeing things through your partner's eyes can be a good reminder that no one is ever totally right or wrong in a personal dispute.

Don't Be a "Mind-Reader"   The preceding suggestion should not be taken as an invitation to engage in "mind-reading." Assuming that you know what your partner is thinking or feeling can muddle or block communication. Hostile or accusatory mind-reading, like the following examples, can be very disruptive: "You're just looking for an excuse to criticize me, aren't you?" "You don't really want my mother to visit, or you wouldn't say that." Rather than *telling* your partner what she or he thinks, *ask* her or him.

To add to these guidelines, Bryan Strong and Christine DeVault (1994) suggest that if you really want to mess up a relationship, you can almost totally avoid intimacy and communication by doing the following.

Ten Ways to Avoid Intimacy

1. Don't talk about anything meaningful, especially about feelings.

2. Never show your feelings; remain as expressionless as possible.

3. Always be pleasant and pretend everything is okay even if you are upset or dissatisfied.

4. Always win, never compromise.

5. Always keep busy; that way you can avoid intimacy and make your partner feel unimportant in your life.

6. Always be right; don't let on that you are human.

7. Never argue or you may have to reveal differences and make changes.

8. Make your partner guess what you want. That way, you can tell your partner that she or he doesn't really understand or love you.

9. Always take care of your own needs first.

10. Keep the television set on. Wouldn't you rather be watching TV than talking with your partner?

Remember, to encourage intimacy, wise couples *avoid* the practices in the preceding list.

As a last point, it is worth restating that sexual adjustment and loving relationships are interdependent. As one observer put it, when sex goes well, it's 15 percent of a relationship, and when it goes badly it's 85 percent (Knox, 1984). As a shared pleasure, a form of intimacy, a means of communication, and a haven from everyday tensions, a positive sexual relationship can do much to enhance a couple's mutual understanding and caring. Likewise, an honest, equitable, and affectionate out-of-bed relationship contributes greatly to sexual satisfaction (Hatfield et al., 1982).

Learning Check

1. Males suffering from primary erectile dysfunction have never been able to have or maintain an erection. T or F?

2. According to the latest figures, most erectile disorders are caused by physical problems. T or F?

3. Sensate focus is the most common treatment for premature ejaculation. T or F?

4. Premature ejaculation is considered the rarest of the male sexual adjustment problems. T or F?

5. As it is for female sexual arousal disorder, the sensate focus technique is a primary treatment mode for male sexual arousal disorder. T or F?

6. Vaginismus, which appears to be a phobic response to sexual intercourse, can also cause dyspareunia. T or F?

7. Masters and Johnson urge sexual partners to recognize that all sexual problems are mutual and not just one partner's problem. T or F?

8. The term *gunnysacking* refers to the constructive practice of hiding anger until it is appropriate to express it. T or F?

Critical Thinking

9. Who would you expect to have the most frequent sex and the most satisfying sex, married couples or single persons?

Answers:

1. T 2. F 3. F 4. F 5. T 6. T 7. T 8. F 9. Contrary to mass media portrayals of sexy singles, married couples have the most sex and are most likely to have orgasms when they do (Laumann et al., 1994). Greater opportunity, plus familiarity with a partner's needs and preferences probably account for these findings.

*T*he whole thing began because Sidney Jourard is a people watcher. One day, sitting in a coffeehouse in San Juan, Puerto Rico, where he was a Peace Corps consultant, he wondered how many times the couple at the next table would touch each other in 1 hour. During the next 2 years, he did the same thing in London and Paris while studying at London's Tavistock Clinic. When he went to Gainesville, Florida, to teach psychology at the University of Florida, he checked out an American couple for the 1 hour. The two people at the Gainesville table touched each other 2 times in 1 hour. In Paris the touch total for 1 hour was 110. In San Juan, 180. And in London? In

London, the two people touched each other not at all.

From this information you must draw your own conclusions. Jourard—back in Gainesville, Florida, teaching, being a therapist, and practicing hatha yoga—refused to. But his interest led him to make further surveys.

He gave booklets to his Gainesville students, 54 males and 84 females. Each booklet contained four diagrams of the body divided into 24 zones, the idea lifted (he says with a straight face) from a butcher's meat chart. He then asked his students to report, anonymously of course, which area of their bodies had been touched by their mother, father,

best-friend-same-sex, and best-friend-opposite-sex. Furthermore, each student was asked to show which zones he or she had touched on these four persons. Time range: within the last year. The charts in Figure 15–13 ◆ show the result. Here Jourard will draw conclusions about "body accessibility."

"If you're out of love," says the professor, "you're out of touch."

"There isn't a great deal of body contact going on outside the strictly sexual context. It's almost as if all possible meanings of a touch are eliminated except the caress with the sexually arousing intent. . . . Most regions of a young adult's body remain untouched

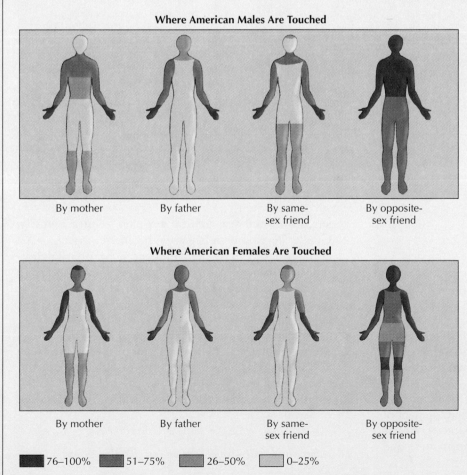

Where American Males Are Touched

By mother   By father   By same-sex friend   By opposite-sex friend

Where American Females Are Touched

By mother   By father   By same-sex friend   By opposite-sex friend

■ 76–100%   ■ 51–75%   ■ 26–50%   □ 0–25%

Figure 15–13 ◆ Results of Jourard's study of interpersonal touch. Figures shown are the percentages of young adults touched in each body area, during a 1-year period, by the persons listed. Touching patterns are highly influenced by culture. People in other countries touch much more, or less, than is customary in North America. (After Jourard, 1966.) A more recent study found that women and androgynous persons are more likely to touch same-sex friends and acquaintances than shown here (Crawford, 1994a, 1994b). Also, touching patterns change over time. More recent studies of touching show significant increases in women's reports of being touched in the area from the thighs to the shoulders by an opposite-sex friend. Men show similar increases in being touched in the pelvic area and upper torso by an opposite-sex friend. These trends seem to reflect a liberalization of intimate touching in love and dating relationships (Thayer, 1988).

unless one has a close friend of the opposite sex, and that depends on the relationship going on between them."

One of our touch taboos, then, is that we equate touch with sexuality. Therefore, unless the relationship is sexual, *mustn't touch*.

Jourard goes on to say that in family physical contact, the daughters are "the favored ones." A girl's parents touch her more than they would if she were a boy. Right up into her 20s. Parents stop touching boys about the time they reach what used to be called the Age of Reason—when one can commit sin. Furthermore, a girl's mother is allowed, or allows herself (having herself once been a favored one), to give frequent touches to a girl's hair. One half of the parents

get to touch her on the lips, and half manage a literal pat on the back. But—taboo, taboo—only 13 percent of the girls received a paternal pat on the bottom, and none of the girls touched or were touched by their fathers in the genital area. (Not quite the case with regard to male students and Mamma.)

Outside the best-friend-opposite-sex category, very little touching goes on, but when it does happen between lovers, the professor says, "There is a virtual deluge of physical contact all over the body. . . . I suspect that the transformation from virginity or even preorgasmic existence to the experience of having a sexual climax is so radical as to be equivalent to a kind of rebirth."

For Jourard, in our maddeningly

crowded world, touch may be our salvation. "I think that body contact has the function of confirming one's bodily being," he says. Yet, how can one learn to touch lovingly if one is not permitted to touch and be touched when young? To touch and be touched at times other than when making love?

"It's a blunted way of life," Jourard says. "People need physical contact to increase awareness and sensitivity to the body. But, instead, we use our relationship with others as a means to increase our status and social position. We are afraid to let others get close because then we are trapped. . . . The price we pay for this estrangement is loneliness." (The preceding article was written by H. E. F. Donohue, 1968.)

Learning Check

1. In his first casual observations, Jourard noted the highest rates of touching in
   a. Florida   **b.** France   **c.** Puerto Rico   **d.** England

2. Within the family, boys are typically touched more by parents than girls are. T or F?

3. Jourard recorded the highest rates of touching by
   a. mothers   **b.** fathers   **c.** same-sex friends   **d.** opposite-sex friends

4. In North American culture, the hands are the most accepted areas of the body for touching by others. T or F?

Critical Thinking

5. If a man touches a woman on the arm or shoulder while talking to her at work, has he sexually harassed her?

Answers:

1. c 2. F 3. d 4. T 5. It depends on her wishes: Even touching that involves "public" areas of the body can be harassing if it is an unwanted intrusion on personal privacy.

Chapter Summary

What are the basic dimensions of gender?

◆ Physical differences between males and females can be divided into **primary sexual characteristics** (genital and reproductive organs) and **secondary sexual characteristics** (other bodily features).

◆ Reproductive maturity in females is signaled by **menarche** (the onset of menstruation). The development of both primary and secondary sexual characteristics is influenced by **estrogens** (female sex hormones) and **androgens** (male sex hormones).

◆ Gender can be broken down into **genetic sex, gonadal sex, hormonal sex, genital sex,** and **gender identity.**

◆ Gender development begins with genetic sex (*XX* or *XY* chromosomes). It is then influenced by prenatal hormonal influences. **Androgen insensitivity,** exposure to *progestin,* the **androgenital syndrome,** and similar problems can affect formation of the genitals. Resulting gender ambiguities are called **hermaphroditism.**

◆ Many researchers believe that prenatal hormones can exert a **biological biasing effect** that combines with **social factors** present after birth to influence psychosexual development. On most psychological dimensions, women and men are more alike than they are different.

How does one's sense of maleness or femaleness develop?

◆ Social factors are especially apparent in learned **gender**

identity and the effect of **sex roles** and **sex role socialization** on behavior.

◆ Sex roles contribute to the development of **sex role stereotypes** that often distort perceptions about the kinds of occupations for which men and women are suited.

◆ Gender identity, which is based to a large extent on labeling, usually becomes stable by age 3 or 4 years. Sex role socialization in particular seems to account for most observed female/male differences. Parents tend especially to encourage boys in **instrumental behaviors** and girls in **expressive behaviors.**

What is psychological androgyny (and is it contagious)?

◆ Research conducted by Sandra Bem and others indicates that roughly one third of all persons are **androgynous.** Approximately 50 percent are traditionally feminine or masculine.

◆ Psychological androgyny (possessing both masculine and feminine traits) appears related to greater adaptability or flexibility in behavior.

What are the most typical patterns of human sexual behavior?

◆ Sexual behavior is quite "natural," being apparent soon after birth and expressed in various ways throughout life. "Normal" sexual behavior is defined differently by various cultures. There appears to be little difference in sexual responsiveness between females and males.

◆ Sexual arousal is partly related to the body's **erogenous zones,** but mental and emotional reactions are the ultimate source of sexual response.

◆ There is some evidence that the sex drive peaks at a later age for females than it does for males, although this difference is diminishing. Sex drive in both females and males may be related to bodily levels of androgens.

◆ **Nocturnal orgasms** are a normal, but relatively minor, form of sexual release. **Castration** may or may not influence sex drive in humans. **Sterilization** does not alter sex drive.

◆ There is a gradual decline in the frequency of sexual intercourse with increasing age. However, many elderly persons remain sexually active and great variations exist at all ages.

◆ **Masturbation** is a normal and completely acceptable behavior practiced by a large percentage of the population. For many, masturbation is an important part of sexual self-discovery. It is valid in marriage and normally has no harmful effects.

◆ **Sexual orientation** refers to one's degree of emotional and erotic attraction to members of the same gender, opposite gender, or both genders. A person may be **heterosexual, homosexual,** or **bisexual.**

◆ A combination of hereditary, biological, social, and psychological influences combine to produce one's sexual orientation.

◆ As a group, homosexual men and women do not differ psychologically from heterosexuals.

To what extent do females and males differ in sexual response?

◆ Human sexual response can be divided into four phases: (1) **excitement;** (2) **plateau;** (3) **orgasm;** and (4) **resolution.** Both females and males may go through all four stages in 4 or 5 minutes. But during lovemaking, most females typically take longer than this, averaging from 10 to 20 minutes.

◆ There do not appear to be any differences between "vaginal orgasms" and "clitoral orgasms" in the female. Fifteen percent of women are consistently multi-orgasmic, and at least 50 percent are capable of multiple orgasm.

◆ Males experience a **refractory period** after orgasm and only 5 percent of men are multi-orgasmic. Mutual orgasm has been abandoned by most sex counselors as the ideal in lovemaking.

Have recent changes in attitudes affected sexual behavior?

◆ Attitudes toward sexual behavior, especially the behavior of others, have been significantly liberalized, but actual changes in sexual behavior have been more gradual.

◆ Another change has been earlier and more frequent sexual activity among adolescents and young adults. Also evident are a greater acceptance of female sexuality and a narrowing of differences in female and male patterns of sexual behavior.

◆ **Acquaintance rape** and rape-supportive myths and attitudes remain major problems.

What impact have sexually transmitted diseases had on sexual behavior?

◆ During the last 20 years there has been a steady increase in the incidence of **sexually transmitted diseases.** This increase, coupled with the emergence of **acquired immune deficiency syndrome,** has had a sizable impact on patterns of sexual behavior, including increased awareness of high-risk behaviors and some curtailment of risk taking.

What are the most common sexual adjustment problems? How are they treated?

◆ The principal problems in sexual adjustment are **desire disorders, arousal disorders, orgasm disorders,** and **sexual pain disorders.**

◆ Behavioral methods and counseling techniques have been developed to alleviate each problem. However, most sexual adjustment problems are closely linked to the general health of a couple's *relationship*. For this reason, *communication skills* that foster and maintain intimacy are the key to successful relationships.

What is the role of touching in personal relationships?

◆ Patterns of touching vary from culture to culture, and they depend on the nature of the relationship between two people. Touch can therefore have a variety of meanings, most of which are non-sexual.

16

Personality

Preview

The Hidden Essence

Rural Colorado. The car lurched over the last few yards of brain-jarring ruts. Before us stood an ancient farmhouse, a hulking monument to neglect. Annette was out of the house—hooting and whooping—before we had stopped.

If anyone was suited for a move to the "wilds" of Colorado, it was Annette, the "terror of Tenth Street." Still, it was hard to imagine a more radical change. After separating from her husband, she had traded housewifery in the city for survival in the high country. Survival, by the way, is no exaggeration. Annette was working as a ranch hand and as a lumberjack (lumberjill?), trying to make it alone through some hard winters.

So radical were the changes in Annette's life, I must confess I expected just as radical a change in her. She was, on the contrary, more her "old self" than ever.

Perhaps you have had a similar experience. After several years of separation it is always intriguing to see an old friend. Often you will be struck at first by ways in which the person has changed. Soon, however, you will probably be pleased to discover how superficial such changes really are. Under it all there is a core that ties the semi-stranger before you to the person you once knew. It is exactly this core of consistency that psychologists have in mind when they use the term *personality*.

The Extra Dimension
Despite our advanced technology, the human dimension still determines success or failure in many situations. Errors in human judgment contributed significantly to the *Challenger* spacecraft disaster. Similarly, it is often said that the most dangerous part of an automobile is "the nut at the wheel." Without doubt, personality touches many aspects of our daily lives. Selecting a mate, choosing friends, getting along with co-workers, voting for a president, and numerous other activities raise questions about personality.

What is personality? How does it differ from temperament, character, or attitudes? Is it possible to measure personality? These and related questions are the concerns of this chapter.

Theme: Personality refers to the consistency we see in personal behavior patterns. Measures of personality reveal individual differences and help predict future behavior.

Key Questions:	Key Topics to Watch for:
How do psychologists use the term *personality*?	Definitions of personality, character, and temperament
What core concepts make up the psychology of personality?	Traits, types, self-concept, and self-esteem Theories of personality
Are some personality traits more basic or important than others?	Classifying traits Source traits and the 16 PF The five-factor model
How do psychodynamic theories explain personality?	Psychoanalytic theory Neo-Freudian theories
What do behaviorists emphasize in their approach to personality?	Behavioral theories Social learning theory
How do humanistic theories differ from other perspectives?	Maslow and self-actualization Carl Rogers' self theory
How do psychologists measure personality?	Interviews, direct observation, questionnaires, and projective tests
What causes shyness? What can be done about it?	Understanding shyness
How does self-monitoring affect behavior?	Characteristics of high and low self-monitors

Do You Have Personality?

"**J**im's not handsome, but he has a great personality." "My father's business friends think he's a nice guy, but they should see him at home where his real personality comes out." "It's hard to believe Tanya and Nikki are sisters. They have such opposite personalities."

It's obvious from such statements that we all frequently use the term *personality*. But when asked, many people seem hard pressed to define personality. Most simply end up saying something about "charm," "charisma," or "style." If you use *personality* in such ways, you are giving it a different meaning than psychologists do. To a psychologist it makes little sense to ask, "Do I have personality?" or to proclaim, "She has lots of personality." In psychological terms, everyone has personality.

Then how do psychologists use the term?

Most psychologists regard **personality** *as a person's unique and relatively stable behavior patterns*. In other words, personality refers to the consistency in who you are, have been, and will become. It also refers to the special blend of talents, attitudes, values, hopes, loves, hates, and habits that makes each of us a unique person.

How is that different from the way most people use the term?

Many people confuse personality with *character*. The term **character** *implies that a person has been judged or evaluated*, not

just described. If, by saying someone has "personality," you mean the person is friendly, outgoing, and attractive, you are really referring to what we regard as good character in our culture. But in some cultures it is deemed good for a person to be fierce, warlike, and cruel. So, while everyone in a particular culture has personality, not everyone has character—or at least not good character. (Do you know any good characters?)

Personality is also distinct from *temperament*. As mentioned in Chapter 4, temperament is the "raw material" from which personality is formed. **Temperament** *refers to the hereditary aspects of personality*, including sensitivity, activity levels, prevailing mood, irritability, and adaptability (Kagan, 1989). As you may recall, even newborn babies differ in temperament.

Psychology Looks at Personality

Psychologists use a large number of concepts to explain personality. It might be wise, therefore, to start with a few key terms. These ideas should help you keep your bearings as you read this chapter.

Traits

We use the idea of traits every day in talking about the personalities of friends and acquaintances. For instance, my friend Dan is *sociable, orderly*, and *intelligent*. His sister Andrea is *shy, sensitive*, and *creative*. In general, psychologists think of

Do these men have personality? Do you?

Psychologists and employers are especially interested in the personality traits of individuals who hold high-risk, high-stress positions involving public safety, such as police, air-traffic controllers, and nuclear power plant employees.

personality traits *as specific lasting qualities within a person.* Typically, traits are inferred from observed behavior. If you see Dan talking to strangers—first at a supermarket and later at a party—you might deduce that he is "sociable." You might then predict from this trait that he will also be sociable at school or at work. As you can see, we often use traits to predict future behavior from past behavior (Hogan, Hogan, & Roberts, 1996). Traits also imply some consistency in behavior. As an example, think about how little the personality traits of your best friends have changed in the last 5 years. It would be strange indeed to feel like you were talking with a different person each time you met a friend or acquaintance.

Personality—When Is the Plaster Set?

At what age are the major outlines of personality firmly established? When is the "plaster set"? Certainly, it is possible for personality to change dramatically at any age. This is rare, however. Studies show that in your 20s the mold of your personality begins to harden. By age 30, personality has typically become quite stable. After that, major shifts in who you are tend to be unusual. When major changes do occur, they are associated with dramatic life events, such as personal catastrophes or tragedies.

After age 30, simply moving to a new city, changing your looks, or finding new friends won't reshape your basic personality. The person you are at age 30 is, for the most part, the person you will be at age 60. (Sources: Costa & McCrae, 1992; Roan, 1992.)

Types

Have you ever asked the question, "What type of person is she (or he)?" before meeting someone new? An interest in personality *types* is quite natural. People who have *several traits in common* are said to have the same **personality type** (Potkay & Allen, 1986). Informally, it is quite common to speak of personality types. Your own thinking might include the executive type, the athletic type, the motherly type, the Yuppie type, the strong silent type, and so forth. If I asked you to define these informal types, you would probably list a different collection of traits for each one.

How valid is it to speak of personality "types"?

Over the years, psychologists have proposed many ways to categorize personalities into types. Consider the idea, first advanced by Swiss psychiatrist Carl Jung (yoong), that a person is either an *introvert* or *extrovert*. An **introvert** *is a shy, self-centered person whose attention is focused inward.* An

The four basic personality types

extrovert *is a bold, outgoing person whose attention is directed outward.* These terms are so widely used that you may think of yourself and your friends as being one type or the other. However, the wildest, wittiest, most party-loving "extrovert" you know is introverted at times, and extremely introverted persons are assertive and sociable in some situations. In short, two categories (or even several) are often inadequate to fully describe differences in personality. That's why rating people on a list of traits is often more informative than classifying them into two or three types.

Even though types tend to oversimplify personality, they do have value. Most often, types are used as a shorthand way of labeling people who have several key traits in common.

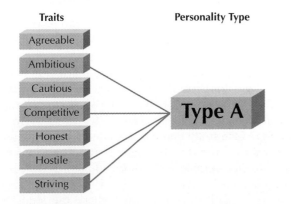

Figure 16–1 ◆ Personality types are defined by the presence of several specific traits. For example, several possible personality traits are shown in the left column. A person who has a Type A personality typically possesses all or most of the highlighted traits. Type A persons are especially prone to heart disease.

You might recall from Chapter 14, for instance, that classifying people as Type A or Type B personalities helps predict their chances of suffering a heart attack (see Fig. 16–1 ◆). Similarly, you will read in the next chapter about unhealthy personality types such as the paranoid personality, the dependent personality, and the antisocial personality. Each is defined by a specific collection of maladaptive traits.

Self-Concept

Another way of understanding personality is to focus on a person's self-concept. The rough outlines of your own self-concept would be revealed by this request: "Please tell us about yourself." In other words, **self-concept** *is a person's perception of his or her own personality traits.* It consists of all your ideas and feelings about who you are (Potkay & Allen, 1986).

Many psychologists believe that self-concepts have a major impact on behavior. We creatively build our self-concepts out of daily experience. Then we slowly revise them as we have new experiences. Once a stable self-concept exists, it tends to shape our subjective world by guiding what we attend to, remember, and think about (Markus & Nurius, 1986).

An individual's self-concept can greatly affect personal adjustment—especially when the self-concept is *inaccurate* or *inadequate* (Potkay & Allen, 1986). As an example, consider Maryanne, a student who thinks she is stupid, worthless, and a failure, despite getting good grades in college. With such a negative self-concept, Maryanne will probably be depressed or anxious no matter how well she does.

Self-Esteem In addition to having an inaccurate self-concept, note that Maryanne suffers from low self-esteem. **Self-esteem** *refers to how you evaluate yourself.* A person who has high self-esteem is confident, proud, and self-respecting. Low self-esteem reveals that a person is insecure, lacking in confidence, and self-critical. Like Maryanne, people who have low self-esteem usually show signs of stress and unhappiness.

Self-esteem tends to rise when we experience success. It is also enhanced by praise from others. Thus, a person who is competent and effective and who is loved, admired, and respected by others will almost always have high self-esteem (Baumeister, 1994).

What really sets people of low self-esteem apart is that they typically have poor self-knowledge. Like Maryanne, their self-concepts are inconsistent, inaccurate, and confused. Problems of this type are explored later in this chapter.

Personality Theories

Personality is so complex that we might easily become lost without a guiding framework for understanding it. How do the observations we make about personality fit together?

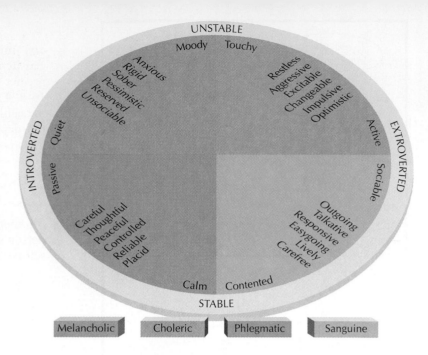

Figure 16–2 ◆ English psychologist Hans Eysenck believes that many personality traits are related to whether you are mainly introverted or extroverted and whether you tend to be emotionally stable or unstable (highly emotional). These characteristics, in turn, are related to four basic types of temperament first recognized by the early Greeks. The types are: *melancholic* (sad, gloomy), *choleric* (hot-tempered, irritable), *phlegmatic* (sluggish, calm), and *sanguine* (cheerful, hopeful). (Adapted from Eysenck, 1981.)

How does personality develop? Why do people become emotionally unhealthy? How can they be helped? To answer such questions, psychologists have created a dazzling array of theories. A **personality theory** *is a system of concepts, assumptions, ideas, and principles proposed to explain personality* (Fig. 16–2 ◆).

There are dozens of personality theories, so it is possible to introduce only a few of the most influential ones here. The four broad perspectives we will consider are:

1. **Trait theories** *attempt to learn what traits make up personality and how they relate to actual behavior.*

2. **Psychodynamic theories** *focus on the inner workings of personality, especially internal conflicts and struggles.*

3. **Behavioristic theories** *place importance on the external environment and on the effects of conditioning and learning.*

4. **Humanistic theories** *stress private, subjective experience and personal growth.*

Now that you are oriented, let's take a deeper look at personality.

The Trait Approach— Describe Yourself in 18,000 Words or Less

How many words can you think of to describe the personality of a close friend? You should have little trouble making a long list: Over 18,000 English words refer to personal characteristics. As we have said, **traits** *are relatively permanent and enduring qualities that a person shows in most situations.* For example, if you are usually optimistic,

reserved, and friendly, these qualities might be considered stable traits of your personality.

What if I am sometimes pessimistic, uninhibited, or shy?

The first three qualities are still traits as long as they are most *typical* of your behavior. Let's say Ima Student approaches most situations with optimism, but has a habit of expecting the worst each time she takes a test. If her pessimism is limited to this situation or to a few others, it is still accurate and useful to describe her as an optimistic person. In the following example, notice again that traits help us predict behavior.

Introversion and Extroversion— Extroverted Study Habits

As we have noted, separating people into broad types, such as "introvert" or "extrovert," may oversimplify personality. However, introversion/extroversion can also be thought of as a trait. Knowing how you rate on this single dimension of personality would allow us to predict how you will behave in a variety of settings. Where, for example, do you prefer to study in the library? One study found that students scoring high in the trait of extroversion choose study locations that have higher noise levels and provide more chances for socializing (Campbell & Hawley, 1982). In the campus library at Colgate University (where the study was done), you can find extroverted students in the second floor lounge. Or, if you prefer, more introverted students can be found studying in the carrels on the first and third floors!

Table 16-1 ■ Adjective Checklist

Check the traits you feel are characteristic of your personality. Are some more basic than others?

aggressive	organized	ambitious	clever
confident	loyal	generous	calm
warm	bold	cautious	reliable
sensitive	mature	talented	jealous
sociable	honest	funny	religious
dominant	dull	accurate	nervous
humble	uninhibited	visionary	cheerful
thoughtful	serious	helpful	emotional
orderly	anxious	conforming	good-natured
liberal	curious	optimistic	kind
meek	neighborly	passionate	compulsive

In general, the trait approach attempts to identify traits that best describe a person. Take a moment to check the traits in Table 16–1 ■ that you feel describe your personality. Are the traits you checked of equal importance? Are some stronger or more basic than others? Do any overlap? For example, if you checked "dominant," did you also check "confident" and "bold"? Answers to these questions would interest a *trait theorist*. To better understand personality, **trait theorists** *attempt to analyze, classify, and interrelate traits.*

Are there different kinds of traits?

Classifying Traits

Psychologist Gordon Allport (1961) identified several kinds of traits. **Common traits** *are those shared by most members of a culture.* Common traits show how people from a particular nation or culture are similar, or which traits the culture emphasizes. In American culture, for example, competitiveness is a fairly common trait. Among the Hopi of Northern Arizona, it is a relatively rare trait.

Of course, common traits tell us little about individuals. While many people are competitive in American culture, each person may rate high or low in this trait. Usually we are also interested in these **individual traits,** *which define a person's unique personal qualities.*

If the difference between common traits and individual traits is unclear, consider this analogy: If you were going to buy a pet dog, you would want to know the general characteristics of a particular breed (its common traits). In addition, you would want to know about the "personality" of a specific dog before selecting it (its individual traits).

Allport also made distinctions between *cardinal traits, central traits,* and *secondary traits.* A **cardinal trait** *is so basic that all of a person's activities can be traced to the trait's existence.* It is said, for instance, that an overriding factor in the life of Albert Schweitzer was "reverence for every living thing."

Likewise, Abraham Lincoln's personality was dominated by the cardinal trait of honesty. According to Allport, few people have cardinal traits.

How do central and secondary traits differ from cardinal traits?

Central Traits   **Central traits** *are the core qualities or basic building blocks of personality.* Allport found that a surprisingly small number of central traits are enough to capture the essence of a person. College students asked to describe someone they knew well mentioned an average of only seven central traits (Allport, 1961).

In contrast, **secondary traits** *are less consistent, relatively superficial aspects of a person.* For this reason, any number of secondary traits could be listed in a personality description. Your own secondary traits include such things as food preferences, attitudes, political opinions, musical tastes, and so forth. In Allport's terms, a personality description might therefore include the following items.

Name: Jane Doe

Age: 22

Cardinal traits: None

Central traits: Possessive, autonomous, artistic, dramatic, self-centered, trusting

Secondary traits: Prefers colorful clothes, likes to work alone, politically liberal, always late (and so forth).

Source Traits   A second major approach to the study of traits is illustrated by the work of Raymond B. Cattell (1965). Cattell was dissatisfied with merely classifying traits. Instead, he wanted to reach deeper into personality to learn how traits are organized and interlinked.

Cattell began by studying features that make up the *visible areas of personality.* He called these **surface traits.** Through the use of questionnaires, direct observation, and life records, Cattell assembled data on the surface traits of a

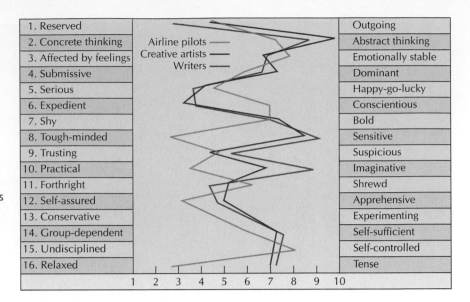

1. Reserved		Outgoing
2. Concrete thinking	Airline pilots ──	Abstract thinking
3. Affected by feelings	Creative artists ──	Emotionally stable
4. Submissive	Writers ──	Dominant
5. Serious		Happy-go-lucky
6. Expedient		Conscientious
7. Shy		Bold
8. Tough-minded		Sensitive
9. Trusting		Suspicious
10. Practical		Imaginative
11. Forthright		Shrewd
12. Self-assured		Apprehensive
13. Conservative		Experimenting
14. Group-dependent		Self-sufficient
15. Undisciplined		Self-controlled
16. Relaxed		Tense

1 2 3 4 5 6 7 8 9 10

Figure 16–3 ◆ The 16 source traits measured by Cattell's 16 PF are listed beside the graph. Scores can be plotted as a profile for an individual or a group. The profiles shown here are group averages for airline pilots, creative artists, and writers. Notice the similarity between artists and writers and the difference between these two groups and pilots. (After Cattell, 1973.)

large number of people. He then noted that surface traits often appear in *clusters*, or groups. In fact, some traits appeared together so often that they seemed to represent a single more basic trait. Cattell called such *underlying personality characteristics* **source traits.**

How do source traits differ from Allport's central traits?

The main difference is that Allport classified traits subjectively, whereas Cattell used a statistical technique called *factor analysis* to reduce surface traits to source traits.

In a **factor analysis,** *psychologists look at the correlations among several measurements.* If patterns emerge in these correlations they are assumed to reflect general, underlying factors. Using this approach, Cattell developed a list of 16 source traits. He considers this the basic number necessary to describe an individual personality.

Cattell's source traits are measured by a test called the *Sixteen Personality Factor Questionnaire* (often referred to as the 16 PF). Like many tests of its type, the 16 PF can be used to produce a **trait profile,** *or graph of a person's scores for each trait.* Trait profiles can be very helpful for obtaining a "picture" of an individual personality or for making comparisons between the personalities of two or more persons (Fig. 16–3 ◆).

The Big Five Noel is outgoing and friendly, conscientious, emotionally stable, and smart. His brother Joel is introverted, hostile, irresponsible, emotionally unpredictable, and disinterested in ideas (stupid). You will be spending a week in a space capsule with either Noel or Joel. Who would you choose? If the answer seems obvious, it may be because we have described Noel and Joel in terms of the **five-factor model,** *a system that identifies the five most basic dimensions of personality.*

The "Big Five" factors listed in Figure 16–4 ◆ are the result of attempts to further reduce Cattell's 16 factors to just five universal dimensions (Digman, 1990; Goldberg, 1993).

The Big Five may be the best answer of all to the question, What are the most basic dimensions of personality?

If you would like to compare the personalities of two people, try rating them informally on the five dimensions shown in Figure 16–4. For factor 1, *extroversion*, rate how introverted or extroverted each person is. Factor 2, *agreeableness*, refers to how friendly, nurturant, and caring a

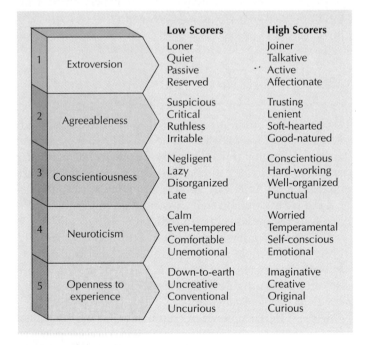

		Low Scorers	High Scorers
1	Extroversion	Loner Quiet Passive Reserved	Joiner Talkative Active Affectionate
2	Agreeableness	Suspicious Critical Ruthless Irritable	Trusting Lenient Soft-hearted Good-natured
3	Conscientiousness	Negligent Lazy Disorganized Late	Conscientious Hard-working Well-organized Punctual
4	Neuroticism	Calm Even-tempered Comfortable Unemotional	Worried Temperamental Self-conscious Emotional
5	Openness to experience	Down-to-earth Uncreative Conventional Uncurious	Imaginative Creative Original Curious

Figure 16–4 ◆ The Big Five. According to the five-factor model, basic differences in personality can be "boiled down" to the dimensions shown here. The five-factor model answers these essential questions about a person: Is she/he extroverted or introverted? Agreeable or difficult? Conscientious or irresponsible? Emotionally stable or unstable? Smart or unintelligent? These questions cover a large measure of what we might want to know about someone's personality. (Trait descriptions adapted from McCrae & Costa, 1990.)

Knowing where a person stands on the "Big Five" personality factors helps predict his or her behavior. For example, people who score high on conscientiousness tend to be safe drivers who are unlikely to have automobile accidents (Arthur & Graziano, 1996).

person is, as opposed to cold, indifferent, self-centered, or spiteful. A person who is *conscientious* (factor 3) is self-disciplined, responsible, and achieving. People low on this factor are irresponsible, careless, and undependable. Factor 4, *neuroticism*, refers to the presence of negative, upsetting emotions. People who are high in neuroticism tend to be anxious, emotionally "sour," and irritable. Finally, people who rate high on factor 5, *openness to experience*, are intelligent, open to new ideas, and interested in cultural pursuits (Digman, 1990). The beauty of this model is that almost any trait you might name will be related to one of the five factors.

Before you read the next section, take a moment to answer the questions in the following highlight. Doing so will add to your understanding of a long-running controversy in the psychology of personality.

Rate Yourself

How Do You View Personality?

The questions that follow may help you gain insight into the assumptions you make about personality. Answer true or false for each statement.

1. My friends' actions are fairly consistent from day to day and in different situations. T or F?

2. Whether a person is honest or dishonest, kind or cruel, a hero or a coward, depends mainly on circumstances. T or F?

3. Most people that I have known for several years have pretty much the same personalities now as they did when I first met them. T or F?

4. The reason that people in some professions (such as teachers, lawyers, or doctors) seem so much alike is because their work requires that they act in particular ways. T or F?

5. One of the first things I would want to know about a potential roommate is what the person's personality is like. T or F?

6. I believe that immediate circumstances usually determine how people act at any given time. T or F?

7. To be comfortable in a particular job, a person's personality must match the nature of the work. T or F?

8. Almost anyone would be polite at a wedding reception; it doesn't matter what kind of personality the person has. T or F?

Now count the number of times you marked true for the odd-numbered items. Do the same for the even-numbered items.

If you agreed with most of the odd-numbered items, you tend to view behavior as strongly influenced by personality traits or lasting personal dispositions.

If you agreed with most of the even-numbered items, you view behavior as strongly influenced by external situations and circumstances.

If the number of times you answered true is nearly equal for odd and even items, you place equal weight on traits and situations as sources of behavior. This is the view now held by many personality psychologists.

Traits, Consistency, and Situations

For many years, psychologists debated this question: Which most affects our behavior, personality traits or external circumstances? There is now little doubt that personality traits remain consistent over long periods of time (Costa & McCrae, 1992; Roan, 1992). And yet, *situations* also exert a powerful influence on behavior. For instance, it would be unusual to find someone reading a book at a football game or dancing at a movie. Likewise, few people sleep in roller coasters or tell jokes at funerals. On the other hand, your personality traits may help predict whether you choose to read a book, go to a movie, or attend a football game in the first place. Most psychologists now agree that traits *interact* with situations to determine behavior. (This point is expanded later in this chapter.) **Trait-situation interactions,** then, refer to the fact that *external settings and circumstances influence the expression of personality traits.*

To illustrate some trait-situation interactions, imagine what would happen if you moved from a church to a classroom to a party to a football game. As the setting changed, your behavior would probably become more loud and boisterous. This change would demonstrate situational effects on behavior. At the same time, your personality traits would also be apparent: If you were quieter than average in class, you would probably be quieter than average in the other settings too (Rorer & Widiger, 1983).

Do We Inherit Personality?

How much does heredity affect personality traits?

Some breeds of dogs have reputations for being friendly, aggressive, intelligent, calm, or emotional. Such differences fall in the realm of **behavioral genetics**—*the study of inherited behavioral traits.* We know that facial features, eye color, body type, and other physical characteristics are inherited. So too are many behavioral tendencies. For instance, selective breeding of animals can lead to striking differences in social behavior, emotionality, learning ability, aggression, activity, and other behaviors (Steen, 1996).

To what extent do such findings apply to humans?

Genetic studies of humans rely on comparisons of identical twins and other close relatives (Rose, 1995). Such studies are not as conclusive as work done with animals. Nonetheless, they show that intelligence, some mental disorders, temperament, and other complex qualities are influenced by heredity. (For examples of behavioral genetic research, see Chapters 4, 12, and 18.) In view of findings like these, we also might wonder, Do genes affect personality?

Wouldn't comparing the personalities of identical twins help answer the question?

It would indeed—especially if the twins were separated at birth or soon after.

Twins and Traits Over the past decade and a half, psychologists at the University of Minnesota have been studying identical twins who grew up in different homes. At the university, reunited twins take a wide range of medical and psychological tests (Fig. 16–5 ◆). The results of such tests indicate that identical twins are much alike, even when they are reared apart (Bouchard et al., 1990; Lykken et al., 1992).

Like all identical twins, reunited twins are astonishingly similar in appearance and voice quality. Observers are struck by how often the twins display identical facial gestures, hand movements, and nervous tics, such as nail biting or finger tapping. Separated twins also tend to share similar talents. If one twin excels at art, music, dance, drama, or athletics, the other is likely to also—despite wide differences in childhood environment. However, the next highlight explains why it's wise to be cautious about some reports of extraordinary similarities in reunited twins.

Critical Thinking

The Minnesota Twins

Many reunited twins in the Minnesota study displayed similarities far beyond what would be expected on the basis of heredity. A good example is provided by the "Jim twins," James Lewis and James Springer. Both Jims had married and divorced women named Linda. Both had undergone police training. Both had named their firstborn sons James Allan. Both drove Chevrolets and vacationed at the same beach each summer. Both listed carpentry and mechanical drawing among their hobbies. Both had built benches around trees in their yards. And so forth (Holden, 1980).

Figure 16–5 ◆ Reunited identical twins Terry and Margaret undergo lung function tests at the University of Minnesota. Researchers collected a wide range of medical and psychological data for each set of twins.

Such coincidences may seem amazing at first. But the astute reader will realize that they have little to do with genetics. Equally "amazing" similarities may also occur for unrelated persons. In fact, one study compared twins with unrelated pairs of students of the same age and sex. The unrelated pairs were almost as alike as the twins with respect to political beliefs, musical interests, religious preferences, jobs held, hobbies, favorite foods, and so on (Wyatt et al., 1984). This is true because people of the same age and sex live in the same historical times and select from a similar range of societal options.

Imagine that you were separated at birth from a twin brother or sister. If you were reunited with your twin today, what would you do? Quite likely, you would spend the next several days comparing every imaginable detail of your lives. Under such circumstances it is virtually certain that you and your twin would compile a long list of similarities. ("Wow! I use the same brand of toothpaste you do!") Yet, two unrelated persons of the same age, sex, and race could probably rival your list—*if* they were as motivated to find similarities.

To summarize, many of the seemingly "astounding" coincidences shared by reunited twins may be a special case of the fallacy of positive instances, described in Chapter 1. Similarities blaze brightly in the memories of reunited twins, while differences are ignored.

Studies of separated twins make it clear that heredity has a sizable effect on each of us. All told, it seems reasonable to conclude that there is a genetic factor in personality (Gatz, 1990). Heredity appears to be responsible for 20 to 45 percent of the variation in some personality traits (Loehlin et al., 1988; Pedersen et al., 1988; Plomin, 1989). Notice, however, that the same figures imply personality is shaped as much, or more, by environment as it is by heredity (Gatz, 1990). That's why the personalities of separated twins slowly become more and more different the longer they live apart (Baker & Daniels, 1990; McCartney, Bernieri, & Harris, 1990).

In summary, each personality is a unique blend of heredity and environment, biology and culture. We are not—thank goodness—genetically programmed robots whose behavior and personality traits are "wired in" for life. Where you go in life is the result of the choices you make. These choices may be influenced by inherited tendencies, but they are not the simple result of our genetic fortunes (Rose, 1995).

Learning Check

1. _____ refers to the hereditary aspects of a person's emotional nature.

2. The term _____ refers to the presence or absence of desirable personal qualities.
   a. personality   **b.** source trait   **c.** character   **d.** temperament

3. A system that classifies all people as either introverts or extroverts is an example of a _____ approach to personality.

4. An individual's perception of his or her own personality constitutes that person's _____ .

5. According to Allport, few people have _____ traits.

6. Central traits are those shared by most members of a culture. T or F?

7. Cattell believes that clusters of _____ traits reveal the presence of underlying _____ traits.

8. Cattell's personality questionnaire provides ratings on 16 surface traits. T or F?

9. Which of the following is *not* one of the Big Five personality factors?
   a. submissiveness   **b.** agreeableness   **c.** extroversion   **d.** neuroticism

10. To understand personality it is wise to remember that traits and situations _____ to determine our behavior.

11. _____ _____ is the study of how heredity influences personality, intelligence, and other behavioral traits and patterns.

Critical Thinking

12. How does memory contribute to the formation of an accurate or inaccurate self-image?

Answers:

1. Temperament 2. c 3. type 4. self-concept 5. cardinal 6. F 7. surface, source 8. F 9. a 10. interact 11. Behavioral genetics 12. As discussed in Chapter 10, memory is highly selective, and long-term memories are often revised or distorted to fit new information. Such properties add to the moldability of self-concepts.

Psychoanalytic Theory—Id Came to Me in a Dream

Psychodynamic theorists are not content with studying personality traits. Instead, they want to probe under the surface of personality—to learn what drives, conflicts, and energies animate us. **Psychoanalytic theory,** *the best-known* psychodynamic approach, grew out of the work of Sigmund Freud, a Viennese physician. Freud became interested in personality when he realized that many of his patients' problems seemed to lack physical causes. Starting about 1890 and continuing until he died in 1939, Freud evolved a theory of personality that deeply influenced modern thought. Freud's theory is far more complex than a short sketch can show. We will consider only its main features.

How did Freud view personality?

Table 16-2 ■ Key Freudian Concepts	
Anal stage *The psychosexual stage corresponding roughly to the period of toilet training (ages 1 to 3).*	**Neurotic anxiety** *Apprehension felt when the ego struggles to control id impulses.*
Anal-expulsive personality *A disorderly, destructive, cruel, or messy person.*	**Oedipus conflict** *A boy's sexual attraction to his mother, and feelings of rivalry with his father.*
Anal-retentive personality *A person who is obstinate, stingy, or compulsive, and who generally has difficulty "letting go."*	**Oral stage** *The period when infants are preoccupied with the mouth as a source of pleasure and means of expression.*
Conscience *The part of the superego that causes guilt when its standards are not met.*	**Oral-aggressive personality** *A person who uses the mouth to express hostility by shouting, cursing, biting, and so forth. Also, one who actively exploits others.*
Conscious *Region of the mind that includes all mental contents a person is aware of at any given moment.*	**Oral-dependent personality** *A person who wants to passively receive attention, gifts, love, and so forth.*
Ego *The executive part of personality that directs rational behavior.*	**Phallic personality** *A person who is vain, exhibitionistic, sensitive, and narcissistic.*
Ego ideal *The part of the superego representing ideal behavior; a source of pride when its standards are met.*	**Phallic stage** *The psychosexual stage (roughly ages 3 to 6) when a child is preoccupied with the genitals.*
Electra conflict *A girl's sexual attraction to her father and feelings of rivalry with her mother.*	**Pleasure principle** *A desire for immediate satisfaction of wishes, desires, or needs.*
Erogenous zone *Any body area that produces pleasurable sensations.*	**Preconscious** *An area of the mind containing information that can be voluntarily brought to awareness.*
Eros *Freud's name for the "life instincts."*	**Psyche** *The mind, mental life, and personality as a whole.*
Fixation *A lasting conflict developed as a result of frustration or over-indulgence.*	**Psychosexual stages** *The oral, anal, phallic, and genital stages, during which various personality traits are formed.*
Genital stage *Period of full psychosexual development, marked by the attainment of mature adult sexuality.*	**Reality principle** *Delaying action (or pleasure) until it is appropriate.*
Id *The primitive part of personality that remains unconscious, supplies energy, and demands pleasure.*	**Superego** *A judge or censor for thoughts and actions.*
Latency *According to Freud, a period in childhood when psychosexual development is more or less interrupted.*	**Thanatos** *The death instinct postulated by Freud.*
Libido *In Freudian theory, the force, primarily pleasure oriented, that energizes the personality.*	**Unconscious** *Region of the mind that is beyond awareness, especially impulses and desires not directly known to a person.*
Moral anxiety *Apprehension felt when thoughts, impulses, or actions conflict with the superego's standards.*	

The Structure of Personality

Freud viewed personality as a dynamic system directed by three mental structures, the **id,** the **ego,** and the **superego.** According to Freud, most behavior involves activity of all three systems. (Freud's theory includes a large number of concepts. For your convenience, they are defined in Table 16–2 ■.)

The Id   The id is made up of innate biological instincts and urges. It is self-serving, irrational, impulsive, and totally **unconscious.** The id operates on the **pleasure principle.** This means that pleasure-seeking urges of all kinds are freely expressed. If everyone's personality were solely under control of the id, the world would be chaotic beyond belief.

Freud thought of the id as a well of energy for the entire **psyche** (sie-KEY), or personality. This energy, called **libido** (lih-BEE-doe), flows from the **life instincts** (called **Eros**). According to Freud, libido promotes survival, underlies sexual desires, and is expressed whenever we seek pleasure. Freud also described a **death instinct. Thanatos,** as he called it, is responsible for aggressive and destructive urges. Freud offered humanity's long history of wars and violence as evidence of such urges. Most id energies, then, are aimed at discharging tensions related to sex and aggression.

The Ego   The ego is sometimes described as the "executive," because it directs energies supplied by the id. The id is like a blind king or queen whose power is awesome but who must rely on others to carry out orders. The id can only form mental images of things it desires. The ego wins power to direct behavior by relating the desires of the id to external reality.

Are there other differences between the ego and the id?

Yes. Recall that the id operates on the pleasure principle. The ego, in contrast, is guided by the **reality principle.** That is, the ego delays action until it is practical or appropriate. The ego is the system of thinking, planning, problem solving, and deciding. It is in conscious control of the personality.

What is the role of the superego?

The Superego   The superego acts as a judge or censor for the thoughts and actions of the ego. One part of the superego, called the **conscience,** reflects actions for which a person has been punished. When standards of the conscience are not met, you are punished internally by *guilt* feelings.

A second part of the superego is the **ego ideal.** The ego ideal reflects all behavior one's parents approved of or rewarded. The ego ideal is a source of goals and aspirations. When its standards are met, we feel *pride.*

By these processes, the superego acts as an "internalized

Freud considered personality an expression of two conflicting forces, life instincts and the death instinct. Both are symbolized in this drawing by Allan Gilbert. (If you don't immediately see the death symbolism, stand farther from the drawing.)

parent" to bring behavior under control. In Freudian terms, a person with a weak superego will be a delinquent, criminal, or antisocial personality. In contrast, an overly strict or harsh superego may cause inhibition, rigidity, or unbearable guilt.

The Dynamics of Personality

How do the id, ego, and superego interact?

It is important to recognize that Freud did not picture the id, ego, and superego as parts of the brain or as "little people" running the human psyche. In reality, they are separate and conflicting mental processes. Freud theorized a delicate balance of power among the three. For example, the demands of the id for immediate pleasure often clash with the superego's moral restrictions. Perhaps an example will help clarify the role of each part of the personality.

Freud in a Nutshell

Let's say you are sexually attracted to an acquaintance. The id clamors for immediate satisfaction of its sexual desires, but is opposed by the superego (which finds the very thought of sex shocking). The id says, "Go for it!" The superego icily replies, "Never even think that again!" And what does the ego say? The ego says, "I have a plan!"

Of course, this is a drastic simplification, but it does capture the core of Freudian thinking. To reduce tension, the ego could begin actions leading to friendship, romance, courtship, and marriage. If the id is unusually powerful, the ego may give in and attempt a seduction. If the superego prevails, the ego may be forced to *displace* or *sublimate* sexual energies to other activities (sports, music, dancing, push-ups, cold showers). According to Freud, internal struggles and rechanneled energies typify most personality functioning.

Is the ego always caught in the middle?

Basically yes, and the pressures on it can be intense. In addition to meeting the conflicting demands of the id and superego, the overworked ego must deal with external reality.

According to Freud, you feel anxiety when your ego is threatened or overwhelmed. Impulses from the id cause **neurotic anxiety** when the ego can barely keep them under control. Threats of punishment from the superego cause **moral anxiety.** Each person develops habitual ways of calming these anxieties, and many resort to using *ego-defense mechanisms* to lessen internal conflicts. (Defense mechanisms are discussed in Chapter 14.)

Levels of Awareness A major principle of psychoanalytic theory, and other psychodynamic theories, is that behavior often expresses unconscious (or hidden) internal forces. The **unconscious** contains repressed memories and emotions, plus the instinctual drives of the id. Interestingly, modern scientists have found brain areas that seem to have the kinds of unconscious effects that Freud described. Especially important are areas linked with emotion and memory—such as the hippocampus and the amygdala in the limbic system (LeDoux, 1996).

Even though they are beyond awareness, unconscious thoughts, feelings, or urges may slip into behavior in disguised or symbolic form. For example, if you meet someone you would like to know better, you may unconsciously leave a book or a jacket at the person's house to ensure another meeting.

Earlier you said that the id is completely unconscious. Are the actions of the ego and superego unconscious?

At times, yes, but they also operate on two other levels of awareness (Fig. 16–6 ◆). The **conscious** level includes everything you are aware of at a given moment, including thoughts, perceptions, feelings, and memories. The **preconscious** contains material that can be easily brought to awareness. If you stop to think about a time when you felt angry or rejected, you will be moving this memory from the preconscious to the conscious level of awareness.

The operation of the superego gives another sign of the levels of awareness. At times we consciously try to live up to moral codes or standards. Yet, at other times a person may feel guilty without knowing why. Psychoanalytic theory credits this kind of guilt to unconscious workings of the

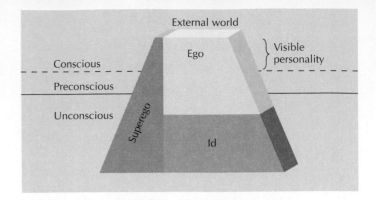

Figure 16–6 ◆ The approximate relationship between the id, ego, and superego, and the levels of awareness.

superego. Freudian psychology holds that truly unconscious events cannot be easily brought to awareness or directly known.

Personality Development

Let's continue with a look at how psychoanalytic theory explains personality development. Freud theorized that the core of personality is formed before age 6 in a series of **psychosexual stages.** His account holds that childhood urges for erotic pleasure have lasting effects on development. Freud's emphasis on infantile sexuality remains controversial. However, Freud used the term *sex* very broadly to refer to several different physical sources of pleasure.

A Freudian Fable? Freud identified four psychosexual stages, the **oral, anal, phallic,** and **genital.** (He also described a period of "latency" between the phallic and genital stages. Latency is explained in a moment.) At each stage, a different part of the body becomes a child's primary **erogenous zone** (an area capable of producing pleasure). Each area then serves as the main source of pleasure, frustration, and self-expression. Freud believed that many adult personality traits can be traced to **fixations** in one or more of the stages.

What is a fixation?

A fixation is an unresolved conflict or emotional hang-up caused by overindulgence or by frustration. As we describe the psychosexual stages you'll see why Freud considered fixations important.

The Oral Stage During the first year of life, most of an infant's pleasure comes from stimulation of the mouth. If a child is overfed or frustrated, oral traits may be created. Some examples of adult expressions of oral needs are gum chewing, nail biting, smoking, kissing, overeating, and alcoholism.

What if there is an oral fixation?

Fixation early in the oral stage produces an **oral-dependent**

Was Freud's ever-present cigar a sign of an oral fixation? Was it a phallic symbol? Was it both? Or was it neither? An inability to say for sure is one of the shortcomings of psychoanalytic theory.

personality. Oral-dependent persons are gullible (they swallow things easily!), passive, and need lots of attention (they want to be mothered). Frustrations later in the oral stage may cause aggression, often in the form of biting. Fixation here creates an **oral-aggressive** adult who likes to argue ("biting sarcasm" is their forte!), is cynical, and exploits others.

The Anal Stage   Between the ages of 1 and 3, the child's attention shifts to the process of elimination. When parents attempt toilet training, the child can gain approval or express rebellion or aggression by "holding on" or by "letting go." Therefore, harsh or lenient toilet training can cause an anal fixation that may lock such responses into personality. Freud described the **anal-retentive** (holding-on) personality as obstinate, stingy, orderly, and compulsively clean. The **anal-expulsive** (letting-go) personality is disorderly, destructive, cruel, or messy.

The Phallic Stage   Adult traits of the **phallic personality** are vanity, exhibitionism, sensitive pride, and narcissism (excessive vanity and self-love). Freud theorized that phallic fixations develop between the ages of 3 and 6. At this time, increased sexual interest causes the child to be physically attracted to the parent of the opposite sex. In males this attraction leads to an **Oedipus conflict.** In it, the boy feels rivalry with his father for the affection of the mother. Freud believed that the male child feels threatened by the father (specifically, the boy fears castration). To ease his anxieties, the boy must **identify** with the father. Their rivalry ends when the boy seeks to become more like his father. As he does, he begins to accept the father's values and form a conscience.

What about the female child?

In a parallel to the Oedipus conflict, called the **Electra conflict,** the girl loves her father and competes with her mother. However, according to Freud, the girl identifies with the mother more gradually. This, he said, is less effective in creating a conscience. Freud believed that females already feel castrated. Because of this, they are less driven to identify with their mothers than boys are with their fathers. This particular part of Freudian thought has been thoroughly (and rightfully) rejected by modern feminists. It is probably best understood as a reflection of the male-dominated times in which Freud lived.

Latency   According to Freud there is a period of *latency* from age 6 to puberty. Latency is not actually a stage. Rather, it is a quiet time during which psychosexual development is dormant or interrupted. Freud's belief that psychosexual development is "on hold" at this time is hard to accept. Nevertheless, Freud saw latency as a relatively quiet time compared to the stormy first 6 years of life.

The Genital Stage   At puberty an upswing in sexual energies activates all the unresolved conflicts of earlier years. This upsurge, according to Freud, is the reason why adolescence can be such a trying time, filled with emotion and turmoil. The genital stage begins at puberty. It is marked, during adolescence, by a growing potential for responsible social-sexual relationships. The genital stage ends with a mature capacity for love and the realization of full adult sexuality.

Critical Comments   As bizarre as Freud's developmental theory might seem, it has been influential for several reasons. First, it pioneered the idea that the early years of life help shape adult personality. Second, it identified feeding, toilet training, and infantile sexual experiences as critical events in personality formation. Third, Freud was among the first to propose that development proceeds through a series of stages. (Erik Erikson's psycho*social* stages, described in Chapter 5, are a modern offshoot of Freudian thinking.)

Is the Freudian view of development widely accepted?

Despite his contributions, few psychologists wholeheartedly embrace Freud's theory today. In some cases Freud was clearly wrong. His portrayal of the elementary school years (latency) as free from sexuality and unimportant for personality development is hard to believe. His idea of the role of a stern or threatening father in the development of a strong conscience in males has also been challenged. Studies show that a son is more likely to develop a strong conscience if his father is affectionate and accepting, rather than stern and punishing. Freud also overemphasized sexuality in personality development; other motives and cognitive factors are of equal importance.

Recently, Freud has been criticized for his views of patients who believed they were sexually molested as children. Freud assumed that such events were merely childhood fantasies. This view has led to a long-standing tendency to disbelieve children who have been molested and women who have been raped (Brannon, 1996).

Many more criticisms of Freud could be listed, but the fact remains that there is an element of truth to much of what he said. The major remaining problem with Freud's theory is that it is almost impossible to verify scientifically.

Psychodynamic Theories—Freud's Descendants

Freud's ideas quickly attracted a brilliant following. Just as rapidly, the importance Freud placed on instinctual drives and sexuality caused many to disagree with him. Those who stayed close to the core of Freud's thinking are called *neo-Freudians* (*neo* means "new"). **Neo-Freudians** *accepted the broad features of Freud's theory but revised parts of it.* Some of the better-known neo-Freudians are Karen Horney, Anna Freud (Freud's daughter), Otto Rank, and Erich Fromm. Other early followers broke away more completely from Freud and created their own opposing theories. This group includes people such as Alfred Adler, Harry Sullivan, and Carl Jung.

How did the thinking of these people differ from Freud's ideas?

The full story of other psychodynamic theories must await your first course in personality. For now, let's sample two views. The first embraces most but not all of Freud's theory (Horney). The second involves a carry-over of Freudian ideas into a related but unique theory (Jung).

Karen Horney (1885–1952)

Karen Horney (HORN-eye) remained faithful to most of Freud's theory, but she resisted his more mechanistic, biological, and instinctive ideas. For example, as a woman, Horney rejected Freud's claim that "anatomy is destiny." This view, woven into Freudian psychology, held that males are dominant or superior to females. Horney was among the first to challenge the obvious male bias in Freud's thinking.

Horney also disagreed with Freud about the causes of neurosis. Freud held that neurotic (anxiety-ridden) individuals are struggling with forbidden id drives that they fear they cannot control. Horney's view was that a core of **basic anxiety** *occurs when people feel isolated and helpless in a hostile world.* These feelings, she believed, are rooted in childhood. Trouble occurs when an individual tries to control basic anxiety by exaggerating a single mode of interacting with others.

What do you mean by "mode of interacting"?

According to Horney, each of us can move **toward** others (*by depending on them for love, support, or friendship*), we can move **away** from others (*by withdrawing, acting like a "loner," or being "strong" and independent*), or we can move **against** others (*by attacking, competing with, or seeking power over them*). Horney believed that emotional health reflects a balance in moving toward, away from, and against others. In her view, emotional problems tend to lock people into overuse of one of the three modes—an insight that remains valuable today.

Carl Jung (1875–1961)

Carl Jung was a student of Freud's, but the two parted ways as Jung began to develop his own ideas. Like Freud, Jung called the conscious part of the personality the ego. However, he further noted that a *persona*, or "mask" exists between the ego and the outside world. The **persona** *is the "public self" presented to others.* It is most apparent when we adopt particular roles or hide our deeper feelings. As mentioned earlier, Jung believed that actions of the ego may reflect attitudes of **introversion** (*in which energy is mainly directed inward*), or of **extroversion** (*in which energy is mainly directed outward*).

Was Jung's view of the unconscious the same as Freud's?

Jung used the term *personal unconscious* to refer to what Freud simply called the unconscious. The **personal unconscious** *is a mental storehouse for a single individual's experiences, feelings, and memories.* But Jung also described a deeper **collective unconscious,** *or mental storehouse for unconscious ideas and images shared by all humans.* Jung believed that, from the beginning of time, all humans have had experiences with birth, death, power, god figures, mother and father figures, animals, the earth, energy, evil, rebirth, and so on. According to Jung, such universals create **archetypes** (AR-KEH-types: *original ideas, images, or patterns*).

Archetypes, found in the collective unconscious, are unconscious images that cause us to respond emotionally to *symbols* of birth, death, energy, animals, evil, and the like. Jung believed that he detected symbols of such archetypes in the art, religion, myths, and dreams of every culture and age. Let us say, for instance, that a man dreams of dancing with his sister. To Freud this would probably be a sign of hidden incestuous feelings. To Jung the image of the sister might represent an unexpressed feminine side of the man's personality and the dream might represent the cosmic dance that intertwines "maleness" and "femaleness" in all lives.

Are some archetypes more important than others?

Two particularly important archetypes are the **anima** (*female principle*) and the **animus** (*male principle*). In men, the anima is an unconscious, idealized image of women. This image is based, in part, on real experiences with women (the man's mother, sister, friends). However, the experiences men have had with women throughout history form the true core of the anima. The reverse is true of women, who possess an animus or idealized image of men. The anima in males and the animus in females enable us to relate to members of the opposite sex. The anima and animus also make it possible for people to learn to express both "masculine" and "feminine" sides of their personalities.

Jung regarded the *self archetype* as the most important of all. The **self archetype** *represents unity*. Its existence causes a gradual movement toward balance, wholeness, and harmony within the personality. Jung felt that we become richer and more completely human when a balance is achieved between the conscious and unconscious, the anima and animus, thinking and feeling, sensing and intuiting, the persona and the ego, introversion and extroversion.

Was Jung talking about self-actualization?

Essentially he was. Jung was the first to use the term *self-actualization* to describe a striving for completion and unity. He believed that the self archetype is symbolized in every culture by **mandalas** (*magic circles*) of one kind or another.

Jung's theory may not be scientific, but clearly he was a man of genius and vision. If you would like to know more about Jung and his ideas, a good starting place is his autobiography, *Memories, Dreams, Reflections*.

Learning Check

1. List the three divisions of personality postulated by Freud.

   _____

2. Which division is totally unconscious? _____

3. Which division is responsible for moral anxiety? _____

4. Freud proposed the existence of a life instinct known as Thanatos. T or F?

5. Freud's view of personality development is based on the concept of _____ stages.

6. Arrange these stages in the proper order: phallic, anal, genital, oral.

   _____

7. Freud considered the anal-retentive personality to be obstinate and stingy. T or F?

8. Karen Horney theorized that people control basic anxiety by moving toward, away from, and _____ others.

9. Carl Jung's theory states that archetypes, which are found in the personal unconscious, exert an influence on behavior. T or F?

Critical Thinking

10. Many adults would find it embarrassing or humiliating to drink from a baby bottle. Can you explain why?

Answers:

1. id, ego, superego 2. id 3. superego 4. F 5. psychosexual 6. oral, anal, phallic, genital 7. T 8. against 9. F 10. A psychoanalytic theorist would say that it is because the bottle rekindles oral conflicts and feelings of vulnerability and dependence.

Jung regarded circular designs as symbols of the self-archetype and representations of unity, balance, and completion within the personality.

Learning Theories of Personality— Habit I Seen You Before?

How do behaviorists approach personality?

According to some critics, as if people are robots like R2D2 of *Star Wars* fame. Actually, the behaviorist position is not nearly that mechanistic, and its value is well established. The behaviorists have shown repeatedly that children can *learn* things like kindness, hostility, generosity, or destructiveness. But what does that have to do with personality? Everything, according to the behavioral viewpoint.

The behaviorist position is that personality is no more (or less) than a collection of learned behavior patterns. Personality, like other learned behavior, is acquired through classical and operant conditioning, observational learning,

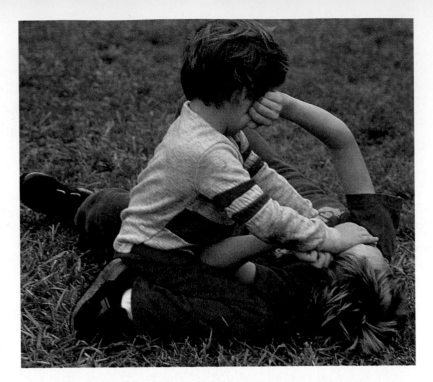

Freud believed that aggressive urges are "instinctual." In contrast, behavioral theories assume that personal characteristics such as aggressiveness are learned. Is this boy's aggression the result of observational learning, harsh punishment, or prior reinforcement?

reinforcement, extinction, generalization, and discrimination. When Mother says, "It's not nice to make mud pies with Mommy's blender. If we want to grow up to be a big girl, we won't do it again, will we?" she serves as a model and in other ways shapes her daughter's personality.

A **learning theorist** *is a psychologist interested in the ways that learning shapes and explains personality.* Strict learning theorists reject the idea that personality is made up of consistent traits. They would assert, for instance, that there is no such thing as a trait of "honesty" (Bandura, 1973; Mischel, 1968).

Certainly some people are honest while others are not. How can honesty not be a trait?

A learning theorist would agree that some of the people you know are honest *more often* than others. But knowing this does not allow us to predict for certain whether a person will be honest in a specific situation. It would not be unusual, for example, to find that a person honored for returning a lost wallet had cheated on a test or broken the speed limit. If you were to ask a learning theorist, "Are you an honest person?" the reply might be, "In what situation?"

A good example of how situations influence behavior is shown in Figure 16–7 ◆. The graphs give the results of a role-playing experiment in which college students had to ask a professor for an extension on an assigned paper. For some students the paper was worth 15 percent of their final grade; for others it was worth 75 percent. Each student was assigned one of three reasons why the paper was late: they had a hangover, had too much work to do, or had the flu. The students were then sent in to plead their cases. As Figure 16–7 shows, most students lied about why their paper was late when they had an illegitimate excuse (a hangover) and the paper was critical to their grade. When their excuse was legitimate (the flu) none lied (Greene & Saxe, 1990).

As you can see, learning theorists are interested in the external causes of our actions. However, this emphasis on **situational determinants** (*external conditions that strongly influence behavior*) does not entirely remove the person from

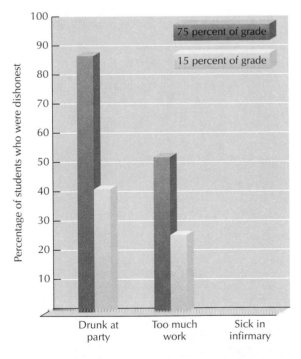

Figure 16–7 ◆ Honesty is greatly influenced by circumstances. Many students were dishonest when the true reason for wanting an extension on an overdue paper was a poor excuse ("drunk at party"). Fewer were dishonest when the excuse was semi-legitimate ("too much work") and none lied when their excuse was legitimate ("sick in infirmary"). The importance of the paper for a course grade also influenced honesty. (Data from Greene & Saxe, 1990.)

the picture. Situations always interact with a person's prior learning history to activate behavior.

Situations vary greatly in their impact. Some are especially powerful, whereas others are trivial and have little effect on behavior. The more powerful the situation, the easier it is to see what is meant by situational determinants. For example, each of the following situations would undoubtedly have a strong influence on behavior: an escaped lion walks into the supermarket; you accidentally sit on a lighted cigarette; you find your lover in bed with your best friend. Yet even these situations could provoke very different reactions from different personalities. That's why behavior is always a product of both prior learning and the situations in which people find themselves.

As discussed earlier, trait theorists also believe that situations affect behavior. But in their view, situations interact with *traits*, rather than a person's learning history. So, in essence, learning theorists favor replacing "traits" with "prior learning" to explain behavior.

How do learning theorists view the structure of personality?

Personality = Behavior

The behavioral view of personality can be illustrated with an early theory proposed by John Dollard and Neal Miller (1950). In their view, **habits** (*learned behavior patterns*) make up the structure of personality. As for the dynamics of personality, Dollard and Miller believe that habits are governed by four elements of learning: *drive, cue, response,* and *reward*. A **drive** *is any stimulus strong enough to goad a person to action* (such as hunger, pain, lust, frustration, or fear). **Cues** *are signals from the environment.* These signals guide **responses** (*actions*) so that they are most likely to bring about **reward** (*positive reinforcement*).

How does that relate to personality?

An example may clarify this viewpoint. Let's say a child is frustrated by an older brother who takes a toy from her. The child could make any of several responses. She could throw a temper tantrum, hit her brother, tell Mother, and so forth. The response she chooses is guided by available cues and the previous effects of each response. If telling Mother has paid off in the past, and the mother is present, telling again may be her immediate response. If a different set of cues exists (if Mother is absent or if the older brother looks particularly menacing), the girl may select some other response. To an outside observer, the child's actions seem to reflect her personality. To the learning theorist, they are a direct reaction to the combined effects of drive, cue, response, and reward.

Doesn't this analysis leave out a lot?

Yes. Learning theorists first set out to provide a simple, clear model of personality. But in recent years they have had to face a fact that they originally tended to overlook. The fact is: People think. The new breed of behavioral psychologists—who include perception, thinking, expectations, and other mental events in their views—are called social learning theorists. *Learning principles, modeling, cognition, and the effects of social relationships* are combined in **social learning theory** to explain personality.

Social Learning Theory The "cognitive behaviorism" of social learning theory can be illustrated by three concepts proposed by Julian Rotter. They are: the psychological situation, expectancy, and reinforcement value. Let's examine each (Rotter & Hochreich, 1975).

Someone trips you. How do you respond? Your response probably depends on whether you think it was planned or an accident. It is not enough to know the setting in which a person responds. We also need to know the person's **psychological situation;** *that is, how the person interprets or defines the situation.* Here's another example. Let's say you score low on an exam. Do you consider it a challenge to work harder, a sign that you should drop the class, or an excuse to get drunk? Again, your interpretation is important.

An **expectancy** *refers to your anticipation that making a response will lead to reinforcement.* To continue the example, if working harder has paid off in the past, it is a likely reaction to a low test score. But to predict your response, we would also have to know if you *expect* your efforts to pay off in the present situation. In fact, expected reinforcement may be more important than actual past reinforcement. And what about the *value* you attach to grades, school success, or personal ability? Rotter's third concept, **reinforcement value,** *states that humans attach different subjective values to various activities or rewards.* This, too, must be taken into account to understand personality.

One more idea deserves mention here. At times, we all evaluate our actions and may reward ourselves with special privileges or treats when the evaluation is positive. With this in mind, social learning theory adds the concept of *self-reinforcement* to the behavioristic view. **Self-reinforcement** *refers to praising or rewarding oneself for having made a particular response* (such as completing a school assignment). Thus, habits of self-praise and self-blame become an important part of personality. In fact, self-reinforcement can be thought of as the behaviorist's counterpart to the superego.

Through self-reinforcement we reward ourselves for personal achievements and other "good" behavior.

- I often think positive thoughts about myself.
- I frequently meet standards that I set for myself.
- I try not to blame myself when things go wrong.
- I usually don't get upset when I make mistakes because I learn from them.
- I can get satisfaction out of what I do even if it's not perfect.
- When I make mistakes I take time to reassure myself.
- I don't think talking about what you've done right is too boastful.
- Praising yourself is healthy and normal.
- I don't think I have to be upset every time I make a mistake.
- My feelings of self-confidence and self-esteem stay pretty steady.

People who agree with all or most of the preceding statements tend to have high rates of self-reinforcement. And, as the last item suggests, high rates of self-reinforcement are related to high self-esteem. The reverse is also true: Numerous studies have shown that mildly depressed college students tend to have low rates of self-reinforcement (Heiby, 1983).

It is not known if low self-reinforcement leads to depression, or the reverse. But in any case, learning to be more self-reinforcing appears to lessen depression (Fuchs & Rehm, 1977). From a behavioral viewpoint, there is value in learning to be "good to yourself."

Behavioristic View of Development

How do learning theorists account for personality development?

Many of Freud's major points can be restated in terms of learning theory. Miller and Dollard (1950) agree with Freud that the first 6 years are crucial for personality development, but for different reasons. Rather than thinking in terms of psychosexual urges and fixations, they ask, "What makes early learning experiences so lasting in their effects?" Their answer is that childhood is a time of urgent and tearing drives, powerful rewards and punishments, and crushing frustrations. Also important is **social reinforcement,** *which is based on the effects of praise, attention, or approval from others.* These forces combine to shape the core of personality.

Critical Situations Miller and Dollard believe that during childhood four **critical situations** *are capable of leaving a lasting imprint on personality.* These are (1) **feeding,** (2) **toilet** or **cleanliness training,** (3) **sex training,** and (4) learning to express **anger** or **aggression.**

Why are these of special importance?

Feeding serves as an illustration. If children are fed when they cry, they are encouraged to actively manipulate their parents. The child allowed to cry without being fed learns to be passive. Thus, a basic active or passive orientation toward the world may be created by early feeding experiences. Feeding can also affect later social relationships because the child learns to associate people with satisfaction and pleasure or with frustration and discomfort.

Toilet and cleanliness training can be a particularly strong source of emotion for both parents and children. Parents are usually aghast the first time they find a child smearing feces about with gay abandon. Their reaction is often sharp punishment. For the child, the result is frustration and confusion. Many attitudes toward cleanliness, conformity, and bodily functions are formed at such times. Studies also show that severe, punishing, or frustrating toilet training can have undesirable effects on personality development (Sears et al., 1957). Toilet and cleanliness training therefore demand patience and a sense of humor.

What about sex and anger?

When, where, and how a child learns to express anger and aggression is of obvious importance. So too is expression of sexual behavior. Both types of experiences can leave an imprint on personality. Specifically, permissiveness for sexual and aggressive behavior in childhood is linked to adult needs for power (McClelland & Pilon, 1983). This link probably occurs because permitting such behaviors allows children to get pleasure from asserting themselves.

Sex training also involves learning "male" and "female" behaviors—which creates an even broader basis for shaping personality.

Becoming Male or Female From birth onward, children are identified as boys or girls and encouraged to learn sex-appropriate behavior. According to social learning theory, identification and imitation contribute greatly to personality development in general and to sex training in particular. **Identification** *refers to the child's emotional attachment to admired adults*, especially to those the child depends on for love and care. Identification typically encourages **imitation,** *a desire to act like the admired person.* Many "male" or "female" traits come from children's conscious or unconscious attempts to imitate the behavior of a same-sex parent with whom they identify.

If children are around parents of both sexes, why don't they imitate behavior typical of the opposite sex as well as of the same sex?

You may recall from Chapter 9 that Albert Bandura and others have shown that learning takes place vicariously as well as directly. This means that we can learn without direct reward by observing and remembering the actions of others. But the actions we choose to imitate depend on their outcomes. For example, boys and girls have equal chances to observe adults and other children acting aggressively. However, girls are less likely than boys to imitate aggressive behavior because they rarely see female aggression rewarded or approved. Thus, many arbitrary "male" and "female" qualities are passed on at the same time sexual identity is learned.

A study of preschool children by Lisa Serbin and Daniel O'Leary (1975) found that teachers are 3 times more likely to pay attention to boys who are aggressive or disruptive than to girls acting the same way. Boys who hit other students or who broke things typically got loud scoldings and became the center of attention for the whole class. When teachers responded to disruptive girls, they gave brief, soft rebukes

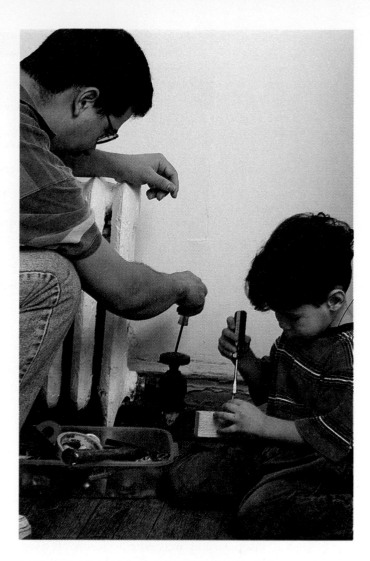

Adult personality is influenced by identification with parents.

that others couldn't hear. Since we know that attention of almost any kind reinforces children's behavior, it is clear that the boys were being encouraged to be active and aggressive. Serbin and O'Leary found that girls got the most attention when they were within arm's reach, more or less clinging to the teacher.

The pattern just described grows stronger throughout elementary school. In all grades, boys are louder, faster, and more boisterous than girls. Day after day, boys receive a disproportionate amount of the teacher's attention (Sadker & Sadker, 1994).

It's easy to see that teachers unwittingly encourage girls to be submissive, dependent, and passive. Similar differences in reinforcement probably explain why males are responsible for much more aggression in society than females are. By age 10, boys expect to get less disapproval from parents for aggression than girls do. This is especially true if the aggression is provoked by another boy (Perry, Perry, & Weiss, 1989). Among adults, rates of murder and assault are consistently higher for men (Deaux, 1985). The roots of this difference appear to lie in childhood.

1. Learning theorists believe that personality "traits" really are _____ acquired through prior learning. They also emphasize _____ determinants of behavior.

2. Dollard and Miller consider cues the basic structure of personality. T or F?

3. To explain behavior, social learning theorists include mental elements, such as _____ (the anticipation that a response will lead to reinforcement).

4. Self-reinforcement is to behavioristic theory as superego is to psychoanalytic theory. T or F?

5. Which of the following is *not* a "critical situation" in the behaviorist theory of personality development?
   a. feeding   b. sex training   c. language training   d. anger training

6. In addition to basic rewards and punishments, a child's personality is also shaped by _____ reinforcement.

7. Social learning theories of development emphasize the impact of identification and _____ .

Humanistic Theory— Peak Experiences and Personal Growth

Humanism *focuses on human experience, problems, potentials, and ideals.* It is a reaction to the static quality of trait theories, the pessimism of psychoanalytic theory, and the mechanical nature of learning theory. At its core is a positive image of what it means to be human. Humanists reject the Freudian view of personality as a battleground for biological instincts and unconscious forces. Instead, they view *human nature* as inherently *good* and seek ways to allow our potentials to emerge. (**Human nature** *consists of the traits, qualities, potentials, and behavior patterns most characteristic of the human species.*) Humanists also oppose the mechanical, "thing-like" overtones of the behaviorist viewpoint. We are not, they say, merely a bundle of moldable responses; rather, we are creative beings capable of *free choice.* To a humanist the person you are today is largely the product of all of your previous choices. The humanistic viewpoint also places greater emphasis on immediate **subjective experience** (*private perceptions of reality*), rather than on prior learning. Humanists believe that there are as many "real worlds" as there are people. To understand behavior we must learn how a person subjectively views the world—what is "real" for her or him.

Who are the major humanistic theorists?

There are many psychologists whose theories fall within the humanistic tradition. Of these, the best known are Carl Rogers (1902–1987) and Abraham Maslow (1908–1970). Since Maslow's idea of self-actualization was introduced in Chapter 1, let's begin with a more detailed look at this facet of his thinking.

Maslow and Self-Actualization

Abraham Maslow became interested in people who were living unusually effective lives. How were they different from the average person? To find an answer, Maslow began by studying the lives of great men and women, such as Albert Einstein, William James, Jane Adams, Eleanor Roosevelt, Abraham Lincoln, John Muir, and Walt Whitman. From there he moved on to directly study artists, writers, poets, and other creative individuals.

Along the way, Maslow's thinking changed radically. At first he studied only people of obvious creativity or high achievement. However, it eventually became clear that a housewife, carpenter, clerk, or student could be living a rich, creative, and satisfying life. Maslow referred to *the process of fully developing personal potentials as* **self-actualization** (Maslow, 1954).

A Closer Look

Self-Actualizers—Lives of the Emotionally Rich

A **self-actualizer** *is a person who is living creatively and making full use of his or her potentials.* In his studies, Maslow found that self-actualizers shared many similarities. Whether famous or unknown, academically distinguished or uneducated, rich or poor, self-actualizers tend to fit the following profile.

1. Efficient perceptions of reality. Maslow's subjects were able to judge situations correctly and honestly and were very sensitive to the fake and dishonest.

2. Comfortable acceptance of self, others, nature. Subjects accepted their own human nature with all its shortcomings. The shortcomings of others and the contradictions of the human condition were also accepted with humor and tolerance.

3. Spontaneity. Maslow's subjects extended their creativity into everyday activities. They tended to be unusually alive, engaged, and spontaneous.

4. Task centering. Most subjects tended to focus on the task at hand, rather than their own feelings or needs. Typically they had a mission to fulfill in life or some task or problem outside of themselves to pursue. Humanitarians such as Albert Schweitzer or Mother Teresa represent this quality.

5. Autonomy. Subjects were free from dependence on external authority or other people. They tended to be resourceful and independent.

6. Curiosity and continued freshness of appreciation. The self-actualizer seems to constantly renew appreciation of life's basic goods. A sunset or a flower will be experienced as intensely time after time as it was at first. There is an "innocence of vision," like that of an artist or child.

7. Fellowship with humanity. Maslow's subjects felt a deep identification with others and the human situation in general.

8. Profound interpersonal relationships. The interpersonal relationships of self-actualizers are marked by deep, loving bonds.

9. Comfort with solitude. Despite their satisfying relationships with others, self-actualizing persons are comfortable being alone and they value solitude (Sumerlin & Bundrick, 1996).

10. Non-hostile sense of humor. This refers to the wonderful capacity to laugh at oneself. It also refers to the kind of humor a man like Abraham Lincoln had. Lincoln probably never made a joke that hurt anybody. His wry comments were a gentle prodding at human shortcomings.

11. Peak experiences. All of Maslow's subjects reported the frequent occurrence of **peak experiences** (*temporary moments of self-actualization*). These were marked by feelings of ecstasy, harmony, and deep meaning. Subjects reported feeling at one with the universe, stronger and calmer than ever before, filled with light, beautiful and good, and so forth. In short, self-actualizers feel safe, non-anxious, accepted, loved, loving, and alive.

Maslow's choice of self-actualizing people for study seems pretty subjective. Is it really a fair representation of self-actualization?

Although Maslow tried to investigate self-actualization empirically, his choice of people to study was subjective.

Undoubtedly there are many ways to reach full development of personal potential. Maslow's primary contribution was to draw attention to the *possibility* of continued personal growth. Maslow considered self-actualization an ongoing process, not a simple end point to be attained only once.

What steps can be taken to promote self-actualization?

Maslow made few specific recommendations about how to proceed. Nevertheless, a number of helpful suggestions can be gleaned from his writings (Maslow, 1954, 1967, 1971).

Steps toward Self-Actualization There is no magic formula for leading a more creative life. Self-actualization is primarily a *process*, not a goal or an end point. As such, it requires hard work, patience, and commitment. Here are some ways to begin.

1. Be willing to change. Begin by asking yourself, "Am I living in a way that is deeply satisfying to me and which truly expresses me?" If not, be prepared to make changes in your life. Indeed, ask yourself this question often and accept the need for continual change.

2. Take responsibility. You can become an architect of self by acting as if you are personally responsible for every aspect of your life. Shouldering responsibility in this way helps end the habit of blaming others for your own shortcomings.

3. Examine your motives. Self-discovery involves an element of risk. If most of your behavior seems to be directed by a desire for safety or security, it may be time to test the limits of these needs. Try to make each life decision a choice for growth, not a response to fear or anxiety.

4. Experience honestly and directly. Wishful thinking is another barrier to personal growth. Self-actualizers trust themselves enough to accept all kinds of information without distorting it to fit their fears and desires. Try to see yourself as others do. Be willing to admit, "I was wrong" or, "I failed because I was irresponsible."

5. Make use of positive experiences. Maslow considered peak experiences temporary moments of self-actualization. Therefore, you might actively repeat activities that have caused feelings of awe, amazement, exaltation, renewal, reverence, humility, fulfillment, or joy.

6. Be prepared to be different. Maslow felt that everyone has a potential for "greatness," but most fear becoming what they might. As part of personal growth, be prepared to trust your own impulses and feelings; don't automatically judge yourself by the standards of others. Accept your uniqueness.

7. Get involved. Maslow found with few exceptions that self-actualizers tend to have a mission or "calling" in life. For these people, "work" is not done just to fill deficiency needs, but to satisfy higher yearnings for truth, beauty, brotherhood, and meaning. Get personally involved and committed. Turn your attention to problems outside yourself.

8. Assess your progress. Since there is no final point at which one becomes self-actualized, it is important to gauge your progress frequently and to renew your efforts. If you feel bored at school, at a job, or in a relationship, consider it a challenge or an indication that you have not taken responsibility for personal growth. Almost any activity can be used as a chance for self-enhancement if it is approached creatively.

Carl Rogers' Self Theory

Like Freud, Carl Rogers based his theory on clinical experience. Unlike Freud, who portrayed the normal personality as "adjusted" to internal conflict, Rogers saw a greater possibility for inner harmony. The **fully functioning person,** he said, *lives in harmony with her or his deepest feelings and impulses.* Such people have achieved an openness to their experiences and they trust their inner urges and intuitions (Rogers, 1961). Rogers believed that this attitude is most likely to occur when a person receives ample amounts of love and acceptance from others.

Personality Structure and Dynamics Rogers' theory of personality centers on the concept of the **self,** *a flexible and changing perception of personal identity.* The self is made up of those experiences identified as "I" or "me" that are separated from "not-me" experiences. Much human behavior can be understood as an attempt to maintain consistency between one's *self-image* and one's actions. (**Self-image** *is your total subjective perception of your body and personality.*) For example, individuals who think of themselves as kind and considerate will act that way in most situations.

Let's say I know a person who thinks she is kind and considerate, but she really isn't. How does that fit Rogers' theory?

According to Rogers, experiences that match the self-image are **symbolized** (*admitted to awareness*) and contribute to gradual changes in the self. Information or feelings inconsistent with the self-image are said to be *incongruent.* Thus, a state of **incongruence** *exists when there is a discrepancy between one's experiences and self-image.* It is incongruent, for example, to think of yourself as a considerate person if others frequently mention your rudeness. It is also incongruent to

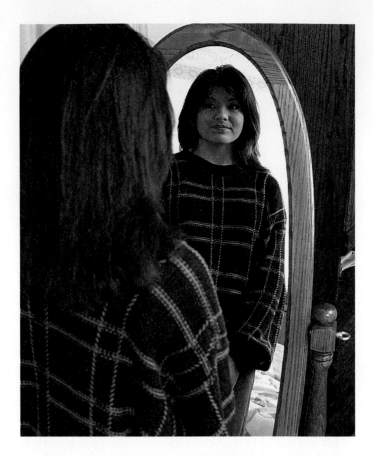

Humanists consider self-image a central determinant of behavior and personal adjustment.

pretend you are kind when you are feeling callous or to say you are not angry when you are seething inside.

Experiences seriously incongruent with the self-image can be threatening, and they are often distorted or denied conscious recognition. Blocking, denying, or distorting experiences prevents the self from changing. This creates a gulf between the self-image and reality. As the *self-image grows more unrealistic,* the **incongruent person** becomes confused, vulnerable, dissatisfied, or seriously maladjusted (Fig. 16–8 ◆). (For more information, also see Chapter 17.) Studies have confirmed that people who know themselves well tend to like and feel good about themselves

Figure 16–8 ◆ Incongruence occurs when there is a mismatch between any of these three entities: the ideal self (the person you would like to be), your self-image (the person you think you are), and the true self (the person you actually are). Self-esteem suffers when there is a large difference between one's ideal self and self-image. Anxiety and defensiveness are common when the self-image does not match the true self.

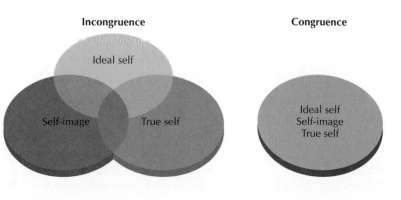

(Baumgardner, 1990). Poor self-knowledge is associated with low self-esteem (Campbell, 1990).

When your self-image is consistent with what you really think, feel, do, and experience, you are best able to actualize your potentials. Rogers also considered it essential to have congruence between the self-image and the **ideal self.** The ideal self is similar to Freud's ego ideal. *It is an image of the person you would most like to be.*

Is it really incongruent not to live up to one's ideal self?

Rogers was aware that we never fully attain our ideals, but the greater the gap between the way you see yourself and the way you would like to be, the greater the tension and anxiety experienced. The Rogerian view of personality can therefore be summarized as a process of maximizing potentials by accepting information about oneself as honestly as possible. In accord with Rogers' thinking, researchers have found that people with a close match between their self-image and ideal self tend to be socially poised, confident, and resourceful. Those with a poor match tend to be depressed, anxious, insecure, and lacking in social skills (Gough et al., 1983; Scott & O'Hara, 1993). The next highlight provides another perspective on the ways in which self-image can influence our behavior.

Research Frontier

Possible Selves—Trying on a Self for Size

Your ideal self is only one of many personal identities you may have pondered. Psychologists Hazel Markus and Paula Nurius (1986) believe that each of us harbors images of many **possible selves** (*persons one could become*). These selves include the person we would most like to be (the ideal self), as well as other selves we could become or are afraid of becoming.

Possible selves translate our hopes, fears, fantasies, and goals into specific images of who we *could* be. Thus, a beginning law student might picture herself as a successful attorney; the husband in a troubled marriage might picture himself as a divorcé; and a person on a diet might imagine both slim and grossly obese possible selves. Such self-images tend to direct future behavior. They also give meaning to current behavior and help us evaluate it. For example, the unhappy spouse might be moved by upsetting images of his "divorcé self" to try saving the marriage.

Even day-to-day decisions may be guided by possible selves. Purchasing clothes, a car, cologne, membership in a health club, and the like may be influenced by images of a valued future self. Of course, identities are not all equally possible. As Markus and

Nurius point out, almost everyone over age 30 has probably felt the anguish of realizing that some cherished possible selves will never be realized.

Humanistic View of Development

Why do mirrors, photographs, tape recorders, and the reactions of others hold such fascination and threat for most people? Carl Rogers' theory suggests it is because they provide information about one's self. The development of a self-image depends greatly on information from the environment. It begins with a sorting of perceptions and feelings: my body, my toes, my nose, I want, I like, I am, and so on. Soon, it expands to include self-evaluation: I am a good person, I did something bad just now, and so forth.

How does development of the self contribute to later personality functioning?

Rogers believed that positive and negative evaluations by others cause children to develop *internal standards of evaluation* he called **conditions of worth.** In other words, we learn that some actions win our parents' love and approval whereas others are rejected. More important, parents often label many of a child's *feelings* as bad or wrong. For example, a child might be told that it is wrong to feel angry toward a brother or sister—even when anger is justified. Likewise, a little boy might be told that he must not cry or be afraid, two very normal emotions.

Learning to evaluate some experiences or feelings as "good" and others as "bad" is directly related to a later capacity for self-esteem, *positive self-evaluation*, or **positive self-regard,** to use Rogers' term. To think of yourself as a good, lovable, worthwhile person, your behavior and experiences must match your internal conditions of worth. The problem is that this can cause incongruence by leading to the denial of many true feelings and experiences.

To put it simply, Rogers regarded many adult adjustment problems as an attempt to live by the standards of others. He believed that congruence and self-actualization are encouraged by replacing conditions of worth with **organismic valuing** (*a natural, undistorted, full-body reaction to an experience*). Organismic valuing is a direct, gut-level response to life that avoids the filtering and distortion of incongruence. It involves trusting one's own feelings and perceptions and being one's own "locus of evaluation." Organismic valuing is most likely to develop, Rogers felt, when children (or adults) receive **unconditional positive regard** (*unshakable love and approval*) from others. That is, when they are "prized" as worthwhile human beings, just for being themselves, without any conditions or strings attached.

Personality Theories—Overview and Comparison

Which personality theory is right?

Each theory has added to our understanding of personality by organizing observations of human behavior. Nevertheless, theories can never be fully proved or disproved. We can only determine if evidence tends to support a theory or to disconfirm it. At the same time that theories are neither true nor false, their implications or predictions may be. The best way to judge a theory, then, is in terms of its *usefulness* for explaining behavior, for stimulating research, and for suggesting ways of treating psychological disorders. Each theory has fared differently in these areas.

Trait Theories   Traits are very useful for describing and comparing personalities. Many of the personality tests used by clinical psychologists are based on trait theories. However, trait theories can be criticized for having a circular quality. For example, how do we know that a young man named Delon has the trait of shyness? Because we frequently observe Delon avoiding conversations with others. And why doesn't Delon socialize with others? Because shyness is a trait of his personality. And how do we know he has the trait of shyness? Because we observe that he avoids socializing with others. And so on.

Psychoanalytic Theory   By present standards, psychoanalytic theory seems to over-emphasize sexuality and biological instincts. These distortions were corrected somewhat by the neo-Freudians, but problems remain. One of

the most telling criticisms of Freudian theory is that it can explain any psychological event *after* it has occurred. But beforehand, it offers little help in predicting future behavior. For this reason, many psychoanalytic concepts are difficult or impossible to test scientifically (Schick & Vaughn, 1995).

Behavioristic Theory   Learning theories have provided a good framework for personality research. Of the three major perspectives, the behaviorists have made the best effort to rigorously test and verify their ideas. They have, however, been criticized for understating the impact that temperament, emotion, thinking, and subjective experience have on personality. Social learning theory can be regarded as an attempt to answer some of these criticisms.

Humanistic Theory   A great strength of the humanists is the light they have shed on positive dimensions of personality. As Maslow (1968) put it, "Human nature is not nearly as bad as it has been thought to be. It is as if Freud supplied us with the sick half of psychology and we must now fill it out with the healthy half." Despite their contributions, the humanists can be criticized for using imprecise concepts that are difficult to measure or study objectively. Even so, humanistic thought has encouraged many people to seek greater self-awareness and personal growth. Also, humanistic concepts are widely used in counseling and psychotherapy.

In the final analysis, we need all four major perspectives to explain personality. Each perspective provides a sort of lens through which personality can be viewed. In many instances, a balanced picture emerges only when each theory is considered. Table 16–3 ■ provides a final overview of the four principal approaches.

Table 16-3 ■ Comparison of Four Views of Personality

	Trait Theories	Psychoanalytic Theory	Behaviorist Theory	Humanistic Theory
View of human nature	neutral	negative	neutral	positive
Is behavior free or determined?	determined	determined	determined	free choice
Principal motives	depends on one's traits	sex and aggresion	drives of all kinds	self-actualization
Personality structure	traits	id, ego, superego	habits	self
Role of unconscious	minimized	maximized	practically non-existent	minimized
Conception of conscience	traits of honesty, etc.	superego	self-reinforcement punishment history	ideal self, valuing process
Developmental emphasis	combined effects of heredity and environment	psychosexual stages	critical learning situations identification and imitation	development of self-image
Barriers to personal growth	unhealthy traits	unconscious conflicts, fixations	maladaptive habits; unhealthy environment	conditions of worth, incongruence

Personality Assessment—Psychological Yardsticks

One of the great values of studying personality is the refinement it brings to personality measurement and testing. The results are highly useful in research, industry, education, and clinical work.

How is personality "assessed"?

Psychologists use *interviews*, *observation*, *questionnaires*, and *projective tests* to measure personality. Each method is a refinement of more informal ways of judging a person. All forms of personality assessment have limitations (described later). For this reason, they are often used in combination.

At one time or another, you have probably "sized up" a potential date, friend, or employer by engaging in conversation (interview). Perhaps you have asked a friend, "When I am delayed I get angry. Do you?" (questionnaire). Maybe you watch your professors when they are angry or embarrassed to learn what they are "really" like (observation). Or possibly you have noticed that when you say, "I think people feel . . . ," you may be expressing your own feelings (projection). Let's see how psychologists apply each of these approaches to probe personality.

The Interview

In an **interview,** *questioning is used to gain information about an individual's personal history, personality traits, or current psychological state.* Interviews can identify personality disturbances and provide information to guide counseling or therapy. They are also used to select persons for employment, college, or special programs.

An interview is **unstructured** *if the conversation is informal* and topics are taken up freely as they arise. In a **structured** interview, the interviewer obtains information *by asking a series of planned questions.* Many such questions are straightforward requests for information. Could a computer ask the questions and record the answers? Let's see.

Tell It to the Computer

If you were emotionally distressed and sought help from a psychologist or psychiatrist, the first thing she or he might do is a **diagnostic interview.** *The purpose of such interviews is to find out how a person is feeling and* *what complaints or symptoms he or she may have.* In many cases, diagnostic interviews are based on a specific series of questions. Because the questions are always the same, some researchers have begun to wonder, Why not let a computer ask them?

So far, the results of computer-administered interviews have been promising. In one study, people were interviewed by both a computer and a psychiatrist. Eighty-five percent of these people thought the computer did an acceptable interview (Dignon, 1996). Another study examined the ability of a computerized interview to identify psychiatric disorders and symptoms. The computer-based interview proved to be highly accurate and in close agreement with interviews done by psychiatrists (Marion, Shayka, & Marcus, 1996). Thus, it may soon become common for people to "Tell it to the computer," at least in the initial stages of seeking psychiatric or psychological help.

One of the major limitations of computerized interviews is that they would miss an important source of information. In live, face-to-face interviews it is possible to observe a person's tone of voice, hand gestures, posture, and facial expressions. Such "body language" cues are important because they may radically alter the message sent, as when a person claims to be "completely calm," but trembles uncontrollably. In addition, skillful interviewing goes well beyond simply collecting information. For instance, a counselor might ask a depressed person, "Have you ever contemplated suicide? What were the circumstances?" The counselor might then follow up by asking, "How did you feel about it?" or, "How is what you are now feeling different from what you felt then?"

Limitations Interviews give rapid insight into personality, but they have certain limitations. For one thing, interviewers can be swayed by preconceptions. A person identified as a "housewife," "college student," "high school athlete," "punk," or "ski bum" may be misjudged because of an interviewer's bias toward a particular lifestyle. Second, an interviewer's own personality may influence the interviewee's behavior. When this occurs, it can accentuate or distort the interviewee's apparent traits. A third problem is that people sometimes try to deceive interviewers. For example, a person accused of a crime might pretend to be mentally disabled to avoid punishment.

A fourth problem is the *halo effect*. The **halo effect** *is a tendency to generalize a favorable or unfavorable impression to unrelated details of personality.* A person who is likable or physically attractive may be rated more mature, intelligent, or adjusted than she or he actually is. The halo effect is something to keep in mind when interviewing for employment. First impressions do make a difference (Lance, LaPointe, & Stewart, 1994).

Even with their limitations, interviews are a respected method of personality assessment. In many cases, interviews are an essential step to additional personality testing and to counseling or therapy.

Direct Observation and Rating Scales

Are you fascinated by bus depots, airports, subway stations, or other public places? Many people relish a chance to observe the actions of others. When used as an assessment procedure, **direct observation** (*looking at behavior*) is a simple extension of this natural interest in "people watching." For instance, a psychologist might arrange to observe a disturbed child playing with other children. Does the child remain withdrawn from others? Does she become hostile or

What is your initial impression of the person wearing the gray jacket? If you think that she looks friendly, attractive, or neat, your subsequent perceptions might be altered by a positive first impression. Interviewers are often influenced by the halo effect (see text).

aggressive without warning? By careful observation, the psychologist will identify personality characteristics and clarify the nature of the child's problems.

Wouldn't observation be subject to the same problems of misperception as an interview?

Yes. Misperceptions can be a difficulty. For this reason, *rating scales* are sometimes used (Fig. 16–9 ◆). A **rating scale** *is a list of personality traits or aspects of behavior on which a person is evaluated.* Rating scales limit the chance that some traits will be overlooked while others are exaggerated (Merenda, 1996). Perhaps they should be standard procedures for choosing a roommate, spouse, or lover!

An alternative to rating scales is to do a **behavioral assessment** *by recording the frequency of various behaviors.* In this case, observers record *actions*, not what traits they think a person has. For example, psychologists working with hospitalized mental patients may find it helpful to record the frequency of patients' aggression, self-care, speech, and unusual behaviors (Alevizos & Callahan, 1977). Behavioral assessments are not strictly limited to visible behavior. They can also be helpful in probing thought processes. In one study, for example, students high in math anxiety were asked to think aloud while doing math problems. Then their thoughts were analyzed to pinpoint the causes of their anxiety (Blackwell et al., 1985).

Situational Testing A specialized form of direct observation is called *situational testing*. A **situational test** *simulates real-life conditions so that a person's reactions can be directly observed.* Situational testing is based on the premise that the best way to learn how a person reacts to certain types of

situations is to simulate those situations. Situational tests expose a person to frustration, temptation, pressure, boredom, or other conditions capable of revealing personality characteristics.

How are situational tests done?

An interesting example of situational testing is the judgmental firearms training provided by many police departments. At times, police officers must make split-second decisions about using their weapons. A mistake may be fatal. In a shoot–don't shoot test, actors play the part of armed criminals. As various high-risk scenes are acted out live or on videotape, officers must decide to shoot or hold fire. A newspaper reporter who once took the test (and failed it) gives this account (Gersh, 1982):

> I judged wrong. I was killed by a man in a closet, a man with a hostage, a woman interrupted when kissing her lover, and a man I thought was cleaning a shotgun. . . . I shot a drunk who reached for a comb, and a teenager who pulled out a black water pistol. Looked real to me.

In addition to the training it provides, situational testing uncovers police cadets who lack the good judgment needed to carry a gun out on the street.

Personality Questionnaires

Most **personality questionnaires** *are paper-and-pencil tests that reveal personality characteristics.* As measures of personality, questionnaires are more *objective* than interviews or observation. (An **objective test** *gives the same score when*

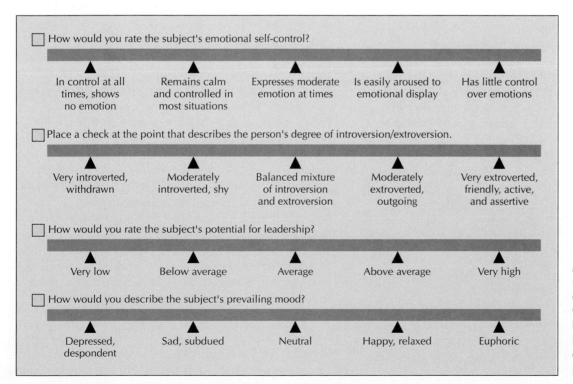

Figure 16–9 ◆ Sample rating scale items. To understand how the scale works, imagine someone you know well. Where would you place check marks on each of the scales to rate that person's characteristics?

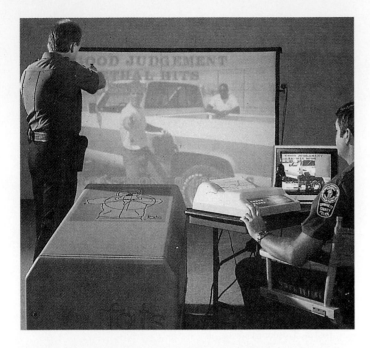

A police officer undergoes judgmental firearms training. Variations on this situational test are used by a growing number of police departments. All officers must score a passing grade.

different people correct it.) Questions, administration, and scoring are all standardized so that scores are unaffected by the opinions or prejudices of the examiner. However, this is not enough to ensure a test's accuracy. It must also be both *reliable* and *valid*. A test is **reliable** *if it yields close to the same score each time it is given to the same person*. A test has **validity** when it *measures what it claims to measure*. Unfortunately, many personality tests you will encounter, such as those found in magazines or offered by commercial self-improvement courses, have little or no validity. (Reliability and validity are discussed further in Chapter 12.)

Many personality tests have been developed, including the *Guilford-Zimmerman Temperament Survey*, the *California Psychological Inventory*, the *Allport-Vernon Study of Values*, the 16 PF, and many more. One of the *best-known and most widely used objective tests of personality* is the **Minnesota Multiphasic Personality Inventory-2** (**MMPI-2**). The MMPI-2 is composed of 567 items to which a test taker must respond "true," "false," or "cannot say." Items include statements such as the following.

> Everything tastes the same.
> There is something wrong with my mind.
> I enjoy animals.
> Whenever possible I avoid being in a crowd.
> I have never indulged in any unusual sex practices.
> Someone has been trying to poison me.
> I daydream often.*

---

* Reproduced by permission. Copyright 1989, by the University of Minnesota Press.

How can these items show anything about personality? For instance, what if a person has a cold so that "everything tastes the same"?

The following highlight offers an answer to this question (and a little bit of fun).

A Closer Look

Personality Tests—A Roast and a Rationale

Humorist Art Buchwald (1965) once lampooned personality questionnaires by writing his own test. The following is a sample of his items. Answer "Yes," "No," or "Don't bother me, I can't cope!"

> I would enjoy the work of a chicken flicker.
> My eyes are always cold.
> Frantic screams make me nervous.
> I believe I smell as good as most people.
> Most of the time I go to sleep without saying good-bye.
> I use shoe polish to excess.
> The sight of blood no longer excites me.

More recently, psychologist Carol Sommer added the following gems to Buchwald's list.

> I salivate at the sight of mittens.
> As an infant I had very few hobbies.
> Spinach makes me feel alone.
> Dirty stories make me think about sex.
> I stay in the bathtub until I look like a raisin.
> I like to put chameleons on plaid cloth.
> I never finish what I

Such questions may seem ridiculous, but they are not very different from the real thing. How, then, do the items on tests such as the MMPI-2 reveal anything about personality? The answer is that a single item tells little about personality. For example, a person who agrees that "Everything tastes the same" might simply have a cold. It is only through *patterns* of response that personality dimensions are revealed.

Items on the MMPI-2 were selected for their ability to correctly identify persons with particular psychiatric problems. For instance, if a series of items is consistently answered in a particular way by depressed persons, it is assumed that others who answer the same way are also prone to depression. As silly as the gag items in the preceding lists may seem, it is possible that some could actually work in a legitimate test. But before an item could become part of a test, it would have to be shown to correlate highly with some trait or dimension of personality.

The MMPI-2 measures 10 major aspects of personality (listed in Table 16–4 ■). After the MMPI-2 is scored, results

Table 16–4	■	MMPI-2 Basic Clinical Subscales

1. **Hypochondriasis** (HI-po-kon-DRY-uh-sis). Exaggerated concern about one's physical health.
2. **Depression.** Feelings of worthlessness, hopelessness, and pessimism.
3. **Hysteria.** The presence of physical complaints for which no physical basis can be established.
4. **Psychopathic deviate.** Emotional shallowness in relationships and a disregard for social and moral standards.
5. **Masculinity/feminity.** One's degree of traditional "masculine" aggressiveness or "feminine" sensitivity.
6. **Paranoia.** Extreme suspiciousness and feelings of persecution.
7. **Psychasthenia** (sike-as-THEE-nee-ah). The presence of obsessive worries, irrational fears (phobias), and compulsive (ritualistic) actions.
8. **Schizophrenia.** Emotional withdrawal and unusual or bizarre thinking and actions.
9. **Mania.** Emotional excitability, manic moods or behavior, and excessive activity.
10. **Social introversion.** One's tendency to be socially withdrawn.

are *charted graphically* as an **MMPI-2 profile** (Fig. 16–10 ◆). By comparing a person's profile to scores produced by normal adults, a psychologist can identify various personality disorders. Additional scales are capable of identifying substance abuse, eating disorders, Type A behavior, repression, anger, cynicism, low self-esteem, family problems, inability to function in a job, and other problems of interest to clinicians and employers (Hathaway & McKinley, 1989).

How accurate is the MMPI-2?

The accuracy of the MMPI-2 or any other personality questionnaire rests on the assumption that people are willing to tell the truth about themselves. Because of the importance of this assumption, the MMPI-2 has additional **validity scales** *that tell whether test scores should be invalidated.* The validity scales detect attempts by test takers to "fake good" (make themselves look good) or "fake bad" (make it look like they have problems). Other scales help adjust final scores that are affected by personal defensiveness or by tendencies to exaggerate shortcomings and troubles.

Unfortunately, the validity scales are not enough to ensure accuracy. If MMPI-2 scores alone are used to classify a person as emotionally disturbed, large numbers of normal people will be incorrectly labeled (Cronbach, 1990). (The next highlight discusses a related controversy.) Fortunately, such judgments usually take into account information from interviews or other sources.

Focus on a Controversy

Honesty Tests—Do They Tell the Truth?

Each year, millions of anxious job seekers take paper-and-pencil *honesty tests* given by companies that hope to avoid hiring dishonest workers. **Honesty tests** (also known as integrity tests) *assume that poor attitudes toward various dishonest acts predispose a person to dishonest behavior.* Examples include attitudes toward taking office supplies home from work or leaving work early. Most of the tests also ask people how honest they think the average person is, and how honest they are in comparison. Surprisingly, many job applicants willingly rate their own honesty as below average. (You have to admire them for being honest about it!) Honesty tests also ask about prior brushes with the law, past acts of theft or deceit, and attitudes toward use of illicit drugs and alcohol.

Is honesty testing valid?

This question is still very much in dispute. Some psychologists believe that the best honesty tests are

Figure 16–10 ◆ An MMPI-2 profile showing hypothetical scores indicating normality, depression, and psychosis. High scores begin at 66 and very high scores at 76. An unusually low score (40 and below) may also reveal personality characteristics or problems.

sufficiently valid to be used for making employment decisions (Ones et al., 1993). Others, however, remain unconvinced. Most studies have failed to demonstrate that honesty tests can accurately *predict* if a person will be a poor risk on the job (Saxe, 1991). Psychologists are also concerned because honesty tests are often administered by untrained businesspersons. Yet another cause for concern is the fact that 96 percent of test takers who fail are incorrectly labeled as dishonest (Camara & Schneider, 1994). In North America alone, that means well over a million workers a year are falsely accused of being dishonest (Rieke & Guastello, 1995).

Some states have banned the use of honesty tests as the sole basis for deciding whether to hire a person. Yet, it's easy to understand why employers want to do whatever they can to reduce theft and dishonesty in the workplace. The pressures to use honesty tests are intense. No doubt, the debate about honesty testing will continue. Honest.

Projective Tests of Personality—Inkblots and Hidden Plots

Projective tests take a very different approach to personality than the techniques already discussed. Interviews, observation, rating scales, and inventories try to directly identify overt, observable traits (Vane & Guarnaccia, 1989). By contrast, projective tests attempt to indirectly uncover deeply hidden or *unconscious* wishes, thoughts, and needs.

As a child you may have delighted in finding faces and objects in cloud formations. Or perhaps you have learned something about your friends' personalities from their reactions to movies or paintings. If so, you will have some insight into the rationale for projective tests. In a **projective test,** *a person is asked to describe ambiguous stimuli or make up stories about them.* Describing an unambiguous stimulus (a picture of an automobile, for example) tells little about your personality. But when you are faced with an unstructured stimulus or situation, you must organize what you see in terms of your own life experiences. Everyone sees something different in a projective stimulus, and what is perceived can reveal the inner workings of one's personality.

Because projective tests have no right or wrong answers, the ability of subjects to fake or "see through" such tests is greatly reduced (Vane & Guarnaccia, 1989). Moreover, projective tests can be a rich source of information, since responses are not restricted to simple true/false or yes/no answers.

Is the inkblot test a projective technique?

The Rorschach Inkblot Test

The inkblot test, or **Rorschach Technique** (ROR-shock), is one of the oldest and most widely used projective tests. Developed by Swiss psychologist Hermann Rorschach in the 1920s, *it consists of 10 standardized inkblots.* These vary in color, shading, form, and complexity.

How does the test work?

First, a person is shown each blot and asked to describe what she or he sees in it (Fig. 16–11 ◆). Later the psychologist may return to a blot, asking the person to identify specific sections of it, to elaborate on previous descriptions, or to give new impressions about what it contains. Obvious differences in content—such as "blood dripping from a dagger" versus "flowers blooming in a field"—are important for identifying personal conflicts and fantasies. But surprisingly, content is considered less important than what parts of the inkblot are

Figure 16–11 ◆ Inkblots similar to those used on the Rorschach. What do you see?

used to form an image and how the image is organized. These factors allow psychologists to view the ways in which a person perceives the world and to detect emotional disturbances. The Rorschach is especially good at detecting psychosis, one of the most serious of all mental disorders (Ganellen, 1996).

The Thematic Apperception Test

Another popular projective test is the **Thematic Apperception Test (TAT)** developed by Harvard psychologist and personality theorist Henry Murray (1893-1988).

How does the TAT differ from the Rorschach?

The TAT *consists of 20 sketches depicting various scenes and life situations* (Fig. 16–12 ◆). The person being tested is shown each sketch and is asked to make up a story about the people in it. Later the person is shown each sketch a second or, perhaps, a third time and asked to elaborate on previous stories or to construct new stories for each.

To score the TAT, a psychologist analyzes the content of the stories. Interpretations focus on how people feel, how they interact, what events led up to the incidents depicted in the sketch, and how the story will end. The psychologist might also count the number of times the central figure in

Figure 16–12 ◆ This is a picture like those used for the Thematic Apperception Test. If you wish to simulate the test, tell a story that explains what led up to the pictured situation, what is happening now, and how the action will end.

each story is angry, overlooked, apathetic, jealous, or threatened. For example, here is a story written by a student to describe Figure 16–12.

> The girl has been seeing this guy her mother doesn't like. The mother is telling her that she better not see him again. The mother says, "He's just like your father." The mother and father are divorced. The mother is smiling because she thinks she is right. But she doesn't really know what the girl wants. The girl is going to see the guy again, anyway.

As this example implies, the TAT is especially good at revealing feelings about a person's social relationships (Alvarado, 1994).

How accurate are projective tests?

Limitations of Projective Testing   Although projective tests have been popular with clinical psychologists, their validity is considered lowest among tests of personality. Objectivity and reliability (consistency) of judgments are also low among different users of the TAT and Rorschach. Note that after the subject interprets an ambiguous stimulus, the scorer must interpret the subject's (sometimes) ambiguous responses. In a sense, the interpretation of a projective test may be a projective test for the scorer!

Despite the drawbacks of projective tests, many psychologists believe they still have value, especially as part of a **test battery** (*collection of assessment devices and interviews*). In the hands of a skillful clinician, projective tests can detect major conflicts and aid in setting goals for therapy (Weiner, 1996). Moreover, since projective tests are unstructured, they may be a better way to get clients to talk about anxiety-provoking topics than direct questions are.

Sudden Murderers—A Research Example

Personality assessments provide us with clues to some of the most perplexing human events. Consider Fred Cowan, a model student in school and described by those who knew him as quiet, gentle, and a man who loved children. Despite his size (6 feet tall, 250 pounds), Fred was described by a co-worker as "someone you could easily push around."

Fred Cowan is representative of a puzzling phenomenon: the sudden murderer—a gentle, quiet, shy, good-natured person who explodes without warning into violence (Lee et al., 1977). Two weeks after he was suspended from his job, Fred returned to work determined to get even with his supervisor. Unable to find the man, he killed four co-workers and a policeman before taking his own life.

Isn't such behavior contrary to the idea of personality traits?

It might seem that sudden murderers are newsworthy simply because they seem to be such unlikely candidates for violence. On the contrary, research conducted by Melvin Lee, Philip Zimbardo, and Minerva Bertholf suggests that sudden murderers explode into violence *because* they are shy, restrained, and inexpressive, not in spite of it. These researchers studied prisoners at a California prison. Ten were inmates whose homicide was an unexpected first offense. Nine were criminals with a record of habitual violence prior to murder. Sixteen were inmates convicted of non-violent crimes.

Did the inmates differ in personality makeup?

Lee and his associates administered a battery of tests to the inmates. Included were the MMPI, a test measuring shyness, an adjective checklist, and personal interviews with each inmate. As expected, the sudden murderers were passive, shy, and overcontrolled (restrained) individuals. The habitually violent inmates were "masculine" (aggressive), undercontrolled (impulsive), and less likely to view themselves as shy than the average person (Lee et al., 1977).

Interviews and other observations have revealed that quiet, overcontrolled individuals are likely to be especially violent if they ever lose control. Their attacks are usually triggered by a minor irritation or frustration, but the attack reflects years of unexpressed feelings of anger and belittlement. When sudden murderers finally release the strict controls they have maintained on their behavior, a furious and frenzied attack ensues. Usually it is totally out of proportion to the offense against them, and often they have amnesia for some or all of their violent actions.

In comparison, the previously violent murderers showed very different reactions. Although they killed, their violence was moderate—usually only enough to do the necessary damage. Typically, they felt they had been cheated or betrayed and that they were doing what was necessary to remedy the situation or to maintain their manhood (Lee et al., 1977).

A Look Ahead The preceding example illustrates how some of the concepts and techniques discussed in this chapter can be applied to further our understanding. The Applications section that follows should add balance to your view of personality. Following that, the concluding Exploration discusses some interesting ideas about how we define and present ourselves to others. Don't be shy. Read on!

Learning Check	Critical Thinking

Learning Check

1. Planned questions are used in a _____ interview.

2. The halo effect is the tendency of an interviewer to influence what is said by the interviewee. T or F?

3. Which of the following is considered the most objective measure of personality?
   a. rating scales   **b.** personality questionnaires   **c.** projective tests   **d.** TAT

4. Situational testing allows direct _____ of personality characteristics.

5. A psychotic person would probably score highest on which MMPI-2 scale?
   a. depression   **b.** hysteria   **c.** schizophrenia   **d.** mania

6. The use of ambiguous stimuli is most characteristic of
   a. interviews   **b.** projective tests   **c.** personality inventories   **d.** direct observation

7. The content of one's responses to the MMPI-2 is considered an indication of unconscious wishes, thoughts, and needs. T or F?

8. Doing a behavioral assessment requires direct observation of the person's actions or a direct report of the person's thoughts. T or F?

9. A surprising finding is that sudden murderers are usually undercontrolled, very masculine, and more impulsive than average. T or F?

10. A test is considered valid if it consistently yields the same score when the same person takes it on different occasions. T or F?

Critical Thinking

11. Projective testing would be of greatest interest to which type of personality theorist?

Answers:

1. structured 2. F 3. b 4. observation 5. c 6. b 7. F 8. T 9. F 10. F 11. Psychodynamic, because projective testing is designed to uncover unconscious thoughts, feelings, and conflicts.

*A*s a personality trait, **shyness** *refers to a tendency to avoid others, as well as feelings of social inhibition (uneasiness and strain when socializing)* (Buss, 1980). Shy persons fail to make eye contact, retreat when spoken to, speak too quietly, and display little interest or animation in conversations. Do you:

- Find it hard to talk to strangers?
- Lack confidence with people?
- Feel uncomfortable in social situations?
- Feel nervous with people who are not close friends?

If so, you may be part of the *50 percent* of college students who consider themselves shy (Carducci & Stein, 1988). Mild shyness may be no more than a nuisance. However, extreme shyness is often associated with depression, loneliness, fearfulness, social anxiety, inhibition, and low self-esteem (Schmidt & Fox, 1995).

What causes shyness?

Elements of Shyness

To begin with, shy persons often lack **social skills** (*proficiency at interacting with others*). Many simply have not learned how to meet people or how to start a conversation and keep it going. **Social anxiety** (*a feeling of apprehension in the presence of others*) is also a factor in shyness. Almost everyone feels nervous in some social situations (such as meeting an attractive stranger). Typically, this is a reaction to **evaluation fears** (*fears of being inadequate, embarrassed, ridiculed, or rejected*). In general, however, evaluation fears are more frequent or intense for shy persons. A third problem for shy persons is a **self-defeating bias** (*distortion*) in their thinking. Specifically, shy persons almost always blame themselves when a social encounter doesn't go well.

Situational Causes of Shyness   Shyness is most often triggered by *novel* or *unfamiliar* social situations. A person who does fine with family or close friends may become shy and awkward when meeting a stranger. Shyness is also magnified by formality, by meeting someone of higher status, by being noticeably different from others, or by being the focus of attention (as in giving a speech) (Buss, 1980).

Don't most people become cautious and inhibited in such circumstances?

Yes. That's why we need to see how the personalities of shy and non-shy persons differ.

Dynamics of the Shy Personality

There is a tendency to think that shy persons are wrapped up in their own feelings and thoughts. But surprisingly, researchers Jonathan Cheek and Arnold Buss (1979) found no connection between shyness and **private self-consciousness** (*attention to inner feelings, thoughts, and fantasies*). Instead, they discovered that shyness is linked to **public self-consciousness** (*acute awareness of oneself as a social object*).

Persons who rate high in public self-consciousness are intensely concerned about what others think of them (Buss, 1980). They worry about saying the wrong thing or appearing foolish. In public, they may feel "naked" or as if others can "see through them." Such feelings trigger anxiety or outright fear during social encounters, leading to awkwardness and inhibition (Buss, 1986). The shy person's anxiety, in turn, often causes her or him to misperceive others in social situations (Schroeder, 1995).

As mentioned, almost everyone feels anxious in at least some social situations. But there is a key difference in the way shy and non-shy persons *label* this anxiety. Shy persons tend to consider their social anxiety a *lasting personality trait*. Shyness, in other words, becomes part of their self-concept. In contrast, non-shy persons believe that *external situations* cause their occasional feelings of shyness. When non-shy persons feel anxiety or "stage fright," they assume that almost anyone would feel as they do under the same circumstances (Zimbardo et al., 1978).

Labeling is important because it affects *self-esteem*. In general, non-shy persons tend to have higher self-esteem than shy persons. This is because non-shy persons give themselves credit for their social successes and they recognize that failures are often due to circumstances. In contrast, shy people blame themselves for social failures and never give themselves credit for successes (Buss, 1980; Girodo, 1978).

What can be done to reduce shyness?

Shy Beliefs

While directing a shyness clinic, psychologist Michel Girodo (1978) observed that shyness is often maintained by unrealistic or self-defeating beliefs. Here's a sample of such beliefs.

1. *If you wait around long enough at a social gathering, something will happen.*
Comment: This is really a cover-up for fear of starting a conversation. For two people to meet, at least one has to make an effort and it might as well be you.

2. *Other people who are popular are just lucky when it comes to being invited to social events or asked out.*

Comment: Except for times when a person is formally introduced to someone new, this is false. People who are more active socially typically make an effort to meet and spend time with others. They join clubs, invite others to do things, strike up conversations, and generally leave little to luck.

3. *The odds of meeting someone interested in socializing are always the same, no matter where I am.*

Comment: This is another excuse for inaction. It pays to seek out situations that have a higher probability of leading to social contact, such as clubs, teams, and school events.

4. *If someone doesn't seem to like you right away, they really don't like you and never will.*

Comment: This belief leads to much needless shyness. Even when a person doesn't show immediate interest, it doesn't mean the person dislikes you. Liking takes time and opportunity to develop.

Unproductive beliefs like the preceding can be replaced with statements such as the following.

1. I've got to be active in social situations.

2. I can't wait until I'm completely relaxed or comfortable before taking a social risk.

3. I don't need to pretend to be someone I'm not; it just makes me more anxious.

4. I may think other people are harshly evaluating me, but actually I'm being too hard on myself.

5. I can set reasonable goals for expanding my social experience and skills.

6. Even people who are very socially skillful are never successful 100 percent of the time. I shouldn't get so upset when an encounter goes badly. (Adapted from Girodo, 1978.)

Social Skills

Learning social skills takes practice. There is nothing "innate" about knowing how to meet people or start a conversation. Social skills can be directly practiced in a variety of ways. It can be helpful, for instance, to get a tape recorder and listen to several of your conversations. You may be surprised by the way you pause, interrupt, miss cues, or seem disinterested. Similarly, it can be useful to look at yourself in a mirror and exaggerate facial expressions of surprise, interest, dislike, pleasure, and so forth. By such methods, most people can learn to put more animation and skill into their self-presentation. (For a discussion of related skills, see the section on self-assertion in Chapter 20.)

Opening Lines If you would like to start a conversation to meet someone new, what's the best way to begin? In a study reported by psychologist Chris Kleinke (1986), 1,000 men and women rated typical "opening lines." An analysis of these statements revealed that they fell into three categories: *direct*, *innocuous* (mild or harmless), and *cute-flippant*. The examples that follow illustrate each category (adapted from Kleinke, 1986).

Direct

I feel a little embarrassed about this, but I'd like to meet you.
Since we're both sitting alone, would you care to join me?
That's a very pretty (sweater, jacket, skirt) you have on.

Innocuous

Hi.
Would you watch my books for a minute?
It's beautiful today, isn't it?
Can you give me directions to _____?

Cute-Flippant

Do you think I deserve a break today?
I play the field, and I think I just hit a home run.
Your place or mine?
I'm easy. Are you?

By a large margin, both men and women preferred opening lines that were direct or innocuous. Cute or flippant statements were least liked, especially by women. The kinds of opening lines so often used by male and female characters in the movies appear to be duds in real life.

Conversation One of the simplest ways to make better conversation is by learning to ask questions. A good series of questions shifts attention to the other person and shows you are interested. Nothing fancy is needed. You can do fine with questions such as, "Where do you (work, study, live)? Do you like (dancing, travel, music)? How long have you (been at this school, worked here, lived here)?" After you've broken the ice, the best questions are often those that are *open ended*:

"What parts of the country have you seen?" (as opposed to: "Have you ever been to Florida?")
"What's it like living on the west side?" (as opposed to: "Do you like living on the west side?")
"What kinds of food do you like?" (as opposed to: "Do you like Chinese cooking?")

It's easy to see why open-ended questions are helpful. In replying to open-ended questions, people often give "free information" about themselves. This extra information can be used to ask other questions or to lead into other topics of conversation.

This brief sampling of ideas is no substitute for actual

practice. Overcoming shyness requires a real effort to learn new skills and test old beliefs and attitudes. It may even require the help of a counselor or therapist. At the very least, a shy person must be willing to take social risks. Breaking down the barriers of shyness will always include some awkward or unsuccessful encounters. Nevertheless, the rewards are powerful: human companionship and personal freedom.

Learning Check	Critical Thinking
1. Surveys show that 14 percent of American college students consider themselves shy. T or F?	**6.** Shyness is a trait of Leshaun's personality. Like most shy people, Leshaun is most likely to feel shy in unfamiliar social settings. Leshaun's shy behavior demonstrates that the expression of traits is governed by what concept?
2. Social anxiety and evaluation fears are seen almost exclusively in shy individuals; the non-shy rarely have such experiences. T or F?	
3. Unfamiliar people and situations most often trigger shyness. T or F?	
4. Public self-consciousness plus a tendency to label oneself as shy are major characteristics of the shy personality. T or F?	**Answers:**
5. Changing personal beliefs and practicing social skills can be helpful in overcoming shyness. T or F?	1. F 2. F 3. T 4. T 5. T 6. trait-situation interactions

Exploration

Self-Monitoring—Which Me Do You See?

As you walk into the room, you face a dilemma that challenges party-goers everywhere: On the left, a conversation is taking place between three similar people—a film lover, an art lover, and a music lover. On the right side of the room, a mixed group has formed, including a member of the peace movement, a military "hawk," and a feminist. Which group do you join? Your answer may depend on whether you are high or low in *self-monitoring* (Snyder & Harkness, 1984).

Self-monitoring refers to how much people *monitor (observe, regulate, and control) the image of themselves they display to others in public*. Some of us are **high self-monitors,** *who actively change the impression we make to fit situations and expectations.* It is as if high self-monitors ask, "Who does this situation want me to be, and how can I be that person?" In contrast, **low self-monitors** are less interested in controlling the impression they make. Such people seek to *faithfully express what they really think and feel.* It is as if they want to know, "Who am I, and how can I be me in this situation?" (Snyder, 1987).

The Public Self

Self-monitoring has been extensively studied by psychologist Mark Snyder. In general, persons high in self-monitoring take a flexible approach to defining themselves. They are very interested in their public "image." Low self-monitors, on the other hand, try to accurately present their beliefs and principles no matter what the situation is. Snyder believes that the way people define what they regard as "me" has an impact on their lives and behavior.

To return to the party, Snyder and Harkness (1984) found that in similar situations high self-monitors preferred to join clearly defined groups. At the party, for example, they could strike a "cultured" pose if they joined the first group. However, the second group would put them in a difficult position: Any image they projected could offend at least one member of the group. Such group differences had far less impact on low self-monitors. Basically, they chose whichever group had someone with whom they could identify.

How can you tell if you are high or low in self-monitoring?

High or Low? To measure this characteristic, Snyder developed the *Self-*

Monitoring Scale. Although the entire scale cannot be reprinted here, the items that follow are examples of statements that separate highs from lows.

High Self-Monitors

I would probably make a good actor.
I'm not always the person I appear to be.
I guess I put on a show to impress and entertain others.

Low Self-Monitors

I have never been good at games like charades or improvisational acting.
In a group, I am rarely the center of attention.
At a party, I let others keep the jokes and stories going.

If you are still not sure what your self-monitoring style is, the following comparisons may be helpful. Each difference has been verified in studies of self-monitoring (Snyder, 1987).

■ **Highs** are keenly interested in the actions of others and in trying to "read" their motives, attitudes, and traits. Presumably, high self-monitors do this so that they will know how to present themselves to a particular person, such as a date.

■ **Lows** seek to match their public behavior to their private attitudes, feelings, and beliefs. Lows tend to speak their minds no matter who is listening.

■ **Highs** are flexible and adaptable, and they display different behavior from situation to situation.

■ **Lows** change little from situation to situation. They value a match between who they believe they are and what they do. Lows do not want to change opinions to please others or win their favor.

■ **Highs** tend to declare who they are by listing their roles and memberships (student, post office employee, member of the school orchestra, third-ranking player of the tennis team, and so on).

■ **Lows** identify themselves in terms of their beliefs, emotions, values, and personality.

■ **Highs** choose friends who are skilled or knowledgeable in various areas. They also tend to have specific friends for specific activities.

■ **Lows** have friends who tend to all be alike in basic ways. No matter what the activity, they prefer to get together with the same friends.

■ **Highs** are concerned with outer appearances. They choose their clothes, hair style, jewelry, and so forth, to project an image (Graeff, 1996).

■ **Lows** have a wardrobe that is less varied; they do not have to look different as often as high self-monitors do.

■ **Highs** initiate dating based mainly on the date's appearance. (In the personals column their ads are the ones that emphasize appearance.)

■ **Lows** are more interested in a potential date's personality.

■ **Highs** believe it is possible to love two people at the same time.

■ **Lows** believe that there is only one real love for a person.

■ **Highs** prefer jobs where their role is very clearly defined.

■ **Lows** prefer jobs where they can "just be themselves."

Implications   As you can see, there are advantages and disadvantages to being either high or low in self-monitoring. In general, high self-monitors are adaptable and present themselves well in social situations. However, they tend to reveal little about their private feelings, beliefs, and intentions. This, plus gaps between their attitudes and actions, may have a negative effect on relationships. The primary drawback to being low in self-monitoring is a tendency to be unresponsive to the demands of different situations. Low self-monitors want to "just be themselves," even when adjustments in self-presentation would make them more effective.

One True Self?   Is there a single "true self" that underlies the many roles we play in daily life? Studies of self-monitoring raise questions about the idea that each person has a "true self." High self-monitors, in particular, act as if they have many selves. For these people, controlling the image they impart is a way of life, at parties, in meetings, in classes, and elsewhere. The "public self" of high self-monitors may or may not be backed by a perceived "real me" on the inside. In many cases, it may be better to try to understand the self *in action* by looking at the ways people define themselves. Just as the answer to the question "Who am I?" varies for each person, the answer to the question "Do I have a single true self?" may vary too.

Do you have a single true self? Give the question some thought the next time you go to a party!

Learning Check   **Critical Thinking**

1. Self-monitoring refers to how much people compare their self-image to the images others hold of them. T or F?

2. Low self-monitors tend to ask, "Who does this situation want me to be?" T or F?

3. In social situations, high self-monitors prefer clearly defined groups that do not create self-presentation conflicts. T or F?

4. A low self-monitor would probably agree with the statement, "I usually prefer to wear my most comfortable clothes, no matter what the occasion is." T or F?

5. "Handsome Tom Cruise look-alike seeking slim fashion-model-type fox for flights of fancy." This ad would most likely be placed by a person high in self-monitoring. T or F?

6. Which of Carl Jung's concepts is most relevant to the behavior of high self-monitors?

Answers:

6. persona

1. F 2. F 3. T 4. T 5. T

Chapter Summary

How do psychologists use the term personality?

◆ **Personality** is made up of one's unique and enduring behavior patterns.

◆ **Character** is personality evaluated, or the possession of desirable qualities.

◆ **Temperament** refers to the hereditary and physiological aspects of one's emotional nature.

What core concepts make up the psychology of personality?

◆ Personality **traits** are lasting personal qualities that are inferred from behavior.

◆ Personality **types** group people into categories on the basis of shared traits or similar characteristics.

◆ Behavior is influenced by **self-concept,** which is a perception of one's own personality traits.

◆ A positive self-evaluation leads to high **self-esteem.** Low self-esteem is associated with stress, unhappiness, and depression.

◆ **Personality theories** combine interrelated assumptions, ideas, and principles to explain personality.

Are some personality traits more basic or important than others?

◆ **Trait theories** attempt to specify qualities of personality that are most lasting or characteristic of a person.

◆ Allport made useful distinctions between **common traits** and **individual traits** and between **cardinal, central,** and **secondary traits.**

◆ A second trait approach, developed by Cattell, attributes visible **surface traits** to the existence of 16 underlying **source traits.**

◆ Source traits are measured by the *Sixteen Personality Factor Questionnaire* (16 PF). The outcome of the 16 PF may be graphically presented as a **trait profile.**

◆ The **five-factor model** of personality reduces traits to five universal dimensions of personality.

◆ Traits appear to **interact** with **situations** to determine behavior.

◆ **Behavioral genetics** and studies of separated **identical twins** suggest that **heredity** contributes significantly to adult personality traits.

How do psychodynamic theories explain personality?

◆ Like other **psychodynamic** approaches, Sigmund Freud's **psychoanalytic theory** emphasizes unconscious forces and conflicts within the personality.

◆ In Freud's theory, personality is made up of the **id, ego,** and **superego.**

◆ **Libido,** derived from the life instincts, is the primary energy running the personality. Conflicts within the personality may cause **neurotic anxiety** or **moral anxiety** and motivate use of **ego-defense mechanisms.**

◆ The personality operates on three levels, the **conscious, preconscious,** and **unconscious.**

◆ The Freudian view of personality development is based on a series of **psychosexual stages:** the **oral, anal, phallic,** and **genital** stages. **Fixation** at any stage can leave a lasting imprint on personality.

What do behaviorists emphasize in their approach to personality?

◆ **Behavioral theories** of personality emphasize learning, conditioning, and immediate effects of the environment.

◆ **Learning theorists** generally stress the effects of **prior learning** and **situational determinants** of behavior.

◆ Learning theorists John Dollard and Neal Miller consider **habits** the basic core of personality. Habits express the combined effects of **drive, cue, response,** and **reward.**

◆ **Social learning theory** adds cognitive elements, such as perception, thinking, and understanding to the behavioral view of personality. Examples of such concepts include the **psychological situation, expectancies,** and

reinforcement value. Some social learning theorists treat "conscience" as a case of **self-reinforcement.**

◆ The behavioristic view of personality development holds that **social reinforcement** in four situations is critical. The **critical situations** are **feeding, toilet** or **cleanliness training, sex training,** and **anger** or **aggression training. Identification** and **imitation** are of particular importance in sex training.

How do humanistic theories differ from other perspectives?

◆ **Humanistic theory** emphasizes **subjective experience** and needs for **self-actualization.**

◆ Abraham Maslow's study of **self-actualizers** identified characteristics they share, ranging from efficient perceptions of reality to frequent peak experiences.

◆ Carl Rogers' theory views the **self** as an entity that emerges from personal experience. Experiences that match the **self-image** are **symbolized** (admitted to consciousness), while those that are **incongruent** are excluded.

◆ The **incongruent person** has a highly unrealistic self-image and/or a mismatch between the self-image and the ideal self. The **congruent** or **fully functioning** person is flexible and open to experiences and feelings.

◆ In the development of personality, humanists are primarily interested in the emergence of a **self-image** and in **self-evaluations.**

◆ As parents apply **conditions of worth** to children's behavior, thoughts, and feelings, children begin to do the same. Internalized conditions of worth then contribute to incongruence and disrupt the **organismic valuing process.**

How do psychologists measure personality?

◆ Techniques typically used for **personality assessment** are **interviews, observation, questionnaires,** and **projective tests.**

◆ **Structured** and **unstructured interviews** provide much information, but they are subject to interviewer bias and misperceptions. The **halo effect** may also lower the accuracy of an interview.

◆ **Direct observation,** sometimes involving **situational tests, behavioral assessment,** or the use of **rating scales,** allows evaluation of a person's actual behavior.

◆ **Personality questionnaires,** such as the *Minnesota Multiphasic Personality Inventory-2* (MMPI-2), are **objective** and **reliable,** but their **validity** is open to question.

◆ **Honesty tests,** which are essentially personality questionnaires, are widely used by businesses to make hiring decisions. Their validity is hotly debated.

◆ **Projective tests** ask a subject to project thoughts or feelings to an ambiguous stimulus or unstructured situation.

◆ The *Rorschach Technique,* or inkblot test, is a well-known projective technique. A second is the *Thematic Apperception Test* (TAT).

◆ The validity and objectivity of projective tests are quite low. Nevertheless, projective techniques are considered useful by many clinicians, particularly as part of a **test battery.**

What causes shyness? What can be done about it?

◆ Shyness is a mixture of social inhibition and social anxiety. It is marked by heightened **public self-consciousness** and a tendency to regard one's shyness as a lasting trait. Shyness can be lessened by changing *self-defeating beliefs* and by improving *social skills.*

How does self-monitoring affect behavior?

◆ People vary in their degree of **self-monitoring** or desire to control the impression they make on others.

◆ **High self-monitoring** persons try to fit their public image to various situations. **Low self-monitors** are interested in accurately expressing their feelings, beliefs, and values, regardless of the situation.

Abnormal Behavior: Deviance and Disorder

Preview

Catch-22: A Practical Definition of "Crazy"

"Is Orr crazy?"

"He sure is," Doc Daneeka said.

"Can you ground him?"

"I sure can. But first he has to ask me to. That's part of the rule."

"Then why doesn't he ask you to?"

"Because he's crazy," Doc Daneeka said. "He has to be crazy to keep flying combat missions after all the close calls he's had. Sure, I can ground Orr. But first he has to ask me to."

"That's all he has to do to be grounded?"

"That's all. Let him ask me."

"And then you can ground him?" Yossarian asked.

"No. Then I can't ground him."

"You mean there's a catch?"

"Sure there's a catch," Doc Daneeka replied. "Catch-22. Anyone who wants to get out of combat duty isn't really crazy."

There was only one catch and that was Catch-22, which specified that a concern for one's own safety in the face of dangers that were real and immediate was the process of a rational mind. Orr was crazy and could be grounded. All he had to do was ask; and as soon as he did, he would no longer be crazy and would have to fly more missions. Orr would be crazy to fly more missions and sane if he didn't, but if he was sane he had to fly them. If he flew them he was crazy and didn't have to; but if he didn't want to he was sane and had to. Yossarian was moved very deeply by the absolute simplicity of this clause of Catch-22 and let out a respectful whistle.

"That's some catch, that Catch-22," he observed.

"It's the best there is," Doc Daneeka agreed.*

This excerpt from Joseph Heller's novel, *Catch-22*, captures the ambiguities of the classic question, What is normal? In the 1800s, doctors and non-professionals alike used terms such as "crazy," "insane," "cracked," and "lunatic" quite freely. The "insane" were thought of as bizarre and definitely different from you or me.

Today our understanding of mental disorders is growing ever more sophisticated. Drawing the line between normal and abnormal can be done only by weighing some complex issues. In this chapter we will summarize major psychological problems and their characteristics.

---

* *Catch-22*, Copyright 1955, 1961 by Joseph Heller. Reprinted by permission of Simon and Schuster, Inc., a division of Gulf & Western Corporation.

Chapter Survey

Theme: Judgments of normality are relative, but mental and emotional disorders clearly exist and need to be classified and explained.

Key Questions:

How is normality defined, and what are the major psychological disorders?	Psychopathology Normal and abnormal behavior Mental disorders
What is a personality disorder?	Personality disorders and the antisocial personality
What are the most common sexual disorders?	Sexual deviance and paraphilias
What problems result when a person suffers high levels of anxiety?	Adjustment, anxiety, dissociative, and somatoform disorders
How do psychologists explain anxiety-based disorders?	Psychodynamic, humanistic, existential, behavioral, and cognitive views of maladaptive behavior
Is psychiatric labeling damaging?	Dangers of psychiatric labeling
What role does the concept of insanity play in criminal trials?	The insanity defense

Key Topics to Watch for:

Abnormal Behavior— What Is Normal?

"The helicopters. Oh no, not the helicopters. Have come to tear the feathers out of my frontal lobes. Help me, nurse, help me, can't you hear them? Gotta get back into my body to save it . . . The doctor is thinking I would make good glue." These are the words of Carol North, a psychiatrist who survived a long bout of schizophrenia (North, 1987).

Unlike the fictional excerpt from *Catch-22*, Carol North's tortured journey into madness was real. Mental illness left Dr. North incapacitated for nearly two decades. Her case is but one hint of the magnitude of mental health problems. Here are the facts on *psychopathology:*

- During their lifetimes, 1 out of every 100 persons will become so severely disturbed as to require hospitalization.

- Some 3 to 6 percent of the aged suffer from organic psychoses.

- In any given week, 7 percent of the population is experiencing an anxiety-related disorder.

- 1 out of every 8 school-aged children is seriously maladjusted.

- 10 to 20 percent or more of all adults will suffer a major depression in their lifetime.

- Each year over 2 million persons in North America are

The self-portraits shown here were painted by Andy Wilf between 1978 and 1981. During that time, Wilf is said to have increasingly abused drugs and alcohol. This dramatic series of images is a record of his self-destructive descent into a private hell. The third painting shows a shrouded skull—and foretells the artist's fate. Wilf died of a drug overdose early in 1982. Drug abuse is but one of the many psychopathologies, or "problems in living," psychologists seek to alleviate. (Courtesy of Ulrike Kantor, Ulrike Kantor Gallery.)

admitted or readmitted for psychiatric treatment in hospitals.

Psychopathology

Psychopathology *is the scientific study of mental, emotional, and behavioral disorders. The term also refers to abnormal or maladaptive behavior itself.* Thus, psychopathology may be further defined as an *inability to behave in ways that foster the well-being of the individual and ultimately of society.* This definition covers not only obviously maladaptive behavior, such as drug addiction, compulsive gambling, or loss of contact with reality, but also any behavior that interferes with personal growth and self-fulfillment (Carson, Butcher, & Mineka, 1996).

Defining Abnormality

"That guy is really wacko, I think his porch lights are dimming." "Yeah, the butter's sliding off his waffle. I'd say he's at least a half-bubble short of level. I think he's ready to go postal." Informally, it's tempting to make snap judgments about mental health. However, to seriously classify certain behaviors or certain people as psychologically unhealthy raises complex and age-old issues.

Defining normality can be tricky. We might begin by saying that psychopathology is characterized by **subjective discomfort.** *That is, the unhealthy personality is marked by unhappiness, anxiety, depression, or other signs of emotional distress.*

But couldn't a person be psychotic without feeling subjective discomfort?

Yes. A problem with this definition is that a person's behavior might be quite maladaptive without causing personal discomfort. A psychotic person displaying obviously bizarre and maladjusted behavior might feel "on top of the world." It could be said, also, that a *lack* of discomfort may reveal a problem. If you were to show no signs of grief or depression after the death of a friend or loved one, we might suspect psychopathology. In practice, subjective discomfort accounts

for most instances in which people voluntarily seek professional help.

Some psychologists have tried to pin down normality more objectively by using *statistical* definitions. **Statistical abnormality** *refers to extreme scores on some dimension, such as IQ or anxiety.* For example, since we know that anxiety is a property of several disorders, we could devise a test to learn how many people show low, medium, or high levels of anxiety. Usually, the results of such a test will form a **normal** (*bell-shaped*) **curve** (Fig. 17–1 ◆). (Normal in this case is a statistical concept referring only to the shape of the curve.) Notice that most people score in the center region of such a curve. Those people who deviate from the average by being anxious all the time (high anxiety) might be considered abnormal. Incidentally, a person who never feels anxiety might also be considered abnormal.

Then a statistical definition of abnormality tells us nothing about the meaning of a deviation from the norm?

Right. It is as statistically "abnormal" (unusual) for a person to score above 145 on an IQ test as it is to score below 55, but only in the second case would we consider the score "abnormal" or undesirable (Wakefield, 1992).

Another major problem with statistical definitions is the question of *where to draw the line* between normality and abnormality. Most behavioral problems range from mild to severe. To take a new example, we could obtain the average frequency of sexual intercourse for persons of a particular age, sex, and marital status. Obviously, a person who feels driven to seek sexual release dozens of times a day has a problem. But as we move back toward the norm we face the statistical problem of drawing lines. How often must an otherwise normal behavior occur before it becomes abnormal? As you can see, statistical boundary lines are often somewhat arbitrary (Widiger & Trull, 1991).

Non-conformity may also reveal abnormality. **Social non-conformity** *refers to disobeying societal standards for acceptable conduct.* In this case, abnormality is based on poor socialization, in which a person learns destructive or self-destructive behavior. However, we must be careful to distinguish unhealthy non-conformity from the behavior of

Figure 17–1 ◆ The number of people displaying a personal characteristic may help define what is statistically abnormal.

Social non-conformity does not automatically indicate psycho-pathology.

creative individuals and those with unique lifestyles. Personal eccentricities can be charming and perfectly healthy. Note, too, that strict adherence to social norms is no guarantee of mental health. In some cases, psychopathology takes the form of rigid conformity.

Before any behavior can be defined as normal or abnormal, we must consider the **situational context** (*social situation, behavioral setting, or general circumstances*) in which it occurs. Is it normal to stand outside and water a lawn? It depends on whether or not it is raining. Is it abnormal for a grown man to remove his pants and expose himself to another man or woman in a place of business? It depends on whether the other person is a bank clerk or a doctor! Almost any imaginable behavior can be considered normal in some context, as the following example indicates.

> In mid-October, 1972, an airplane carrying a rugby team called the Old Christians crashed in the snow-capped Andes of South America. Incredibly, 16 of the 45 people who had been aboard at the time of the crash survived 73 days in deep snow and subfreezing temperatures. They were forced to use extremely grim measures to do so—they ate the bodies of those who had died in the crash.

Culture is one of the most influential contexts in which any behavior is judged. In some cultures it is considered normal to defecate or urinate in public or to appear naked in public. In our culture such behaviors would be considered unusual or abnormal. Thus, **cultural relativity** (*the idea that judgments are made relative to the values of one's culture*) can affect the diagnosis of mental disorders (Alarcon, 1995). Still, all known cultures classify people as abnormal if they fail to communicate with others or are consistently unpredictable in their actions.

The Politics of "Madness"

The year is 1840. You are a slave who has tried repeatedly to escape from a cruel and abusive master. An expert is consulted about your "abnormal" behavior. His conclusion? You are suffering from "drapetomania," a mental "disorder" that causes slaves to run away (Wakefield, 1992).

As this example suggests, psychiatric terms are easily abused. Historically, some have been applied to culturally disapproved behaviors that are not really disorders. For example, all of the following were once considered disorders: "drapetomania," "childhood masturbation disorder," "lack of vaginal orgasm," "self-defeating personality disorder" (applied mainly to women), and "nymphomania" (a woman with a healthy sexual appetite) (Wakefield, 1992).

In judging normality, gender is probably the most common source of bias, because standards tend to be based on males (Tavris, 1992). According to psychologist Marcie Kaplan (1983) and others, women are penalized both for conforming to female stereotypes and for ignoring them. If a woman is independent, aggressive, and unemotional, she may be considered "unhealthy." Yet at the same time, a woman who is vain, emotional, irrational, and dependent on others (all "feminine" traits in our culture) may be classified as a histrionic, or dependent personality (Bornstein, 1996).

Perhaps the most easily abused diagnosis women face is "premenstrual dysphoric disorder." This "disorder" is essentially a list of some of the normal changes that precede many women's menstrual periods. If a man experiences similar changes in mood, they are regarded as just "normal ups and downs" (Tavris, 1992). Such differences help illustrate the subtle influence that culture may have on perceptions of disorder and normality.

If abnormality is so hard to define, how are judgments of psychopathology made?

It should be clear that all definitions of abnormality are *relative*. Consider Joan, for example, who has an intense fear of heights. Joan can't look out the window of a tall building or fly in an airplane. Are her fears a mental disorder? Most likely Joan will *not* be diagnosed as suffering from a phobic disorder (described later) because she lives in a small town without tall buildings and has no need to fly. To be a problem, Joan's fears must interfere with her normal activities and cause her marked distress (Widiger & Trull, 1991).

In spite of the difficulty of defining abnormality, we know that psychological disturbances occur and that they must be identified. Each of the standards we have discussed helps define abnormality. As Joan's example suggests, an additional core feature of all abnormal behavior is that it is **maladaptive:** *Rather than helping a person to cope successfully, abnormal behavior makes it more difficult for the person to meet the demands of day-to-day life.* In her particular life circumstances, Joan's fears are not seriously maladaptive. For another person they could be a major problem.

Various levels of functioning—from superior to severely disturbed—are described in Table 17–1 ■. Note that the bottom of the scale reads "persistent danger of hurting self or others." Clearly, behavior at this level is maladaptive.

In practice, the judgment that a person needs help usually occurs when the person *does something* (hits a person, hallucinates, stares into space, collects rolls of toilet paper, and so forth) that *annoys* or *gains the attention* of a person in a *position of power* in the person's life (an employer, teacher, parent, spouse, or the person himself or herself). That person then *does something* about it. (A police officer may be called, the person may be urged to see a psychologist, a relative may start commitment proceedings, or the person may voluntarily seek help.)

Table 17–1 ■ **Levels of Functioning**

Scale	Level of Functioning	Examples
100	Superior functioning in a wide range of activities. No symptoms.	Life's problems never seem to get out of hand. Person is sought out by others because of his or her many positive qualities.
90	Absent or minimal symptoms, functioning well in all areas, no more than everyday problems.	Has mild anxiety before exams, occasional arguments with family members.
80	If symptoms are present, they are brief and common reactions to stressors. No more than slight impairment in relationships, work, or school.	Has difficulty concentrating after family arguments, is falling behind in schoolwork.
70	Some mild symptoms, or some difficulty with relationships, work, or school.	Mood is depressed and has mild insomnia. Has been truant at school and has stolen things at home.
60	Moderate symptoms or moderate problems with relationships, work, or school.	Emotions are blunted, speech evasive, occasional panic attacks, no friends, unable to keep a job.
50	Serious symptoms or any serious impairments in relationships, work, or school.	Person has suicidal thoughts, engages in obsessional rituals, shoplifts, has no friends, unable to keep a job.
40	Some impairment in grasp of reality or in communication, plus major impairments in work or school, relationships, judgment, thinking, or mood.	Speech is illogical, obscure, or irrelevant. Person is depressed and avoids friends, neglects family, and is unable to work.
30	Behavior is considerably affected by delusions or hallucinations; or, person is seriously impaired in communication or judgment; or, is unable to function in almost all areas.	Person is sometimes incoherent, acts grossly inappropriately, is preoccupied with suicide, stays in bed all day, has no job, home, or friends.
20	Some danger of hurting self or others; or, occasionally fails to maintain minimal personal hygiene; or, communication is grossly impaired.	Person makes tentative suicide attempts, is frequently violent and manically excited, smears own feces, is either incoherent or mute.
10	Persistent danger of severely hurting self or others; or, persistent inability to maintain minimal personal hygiene; or, serious suicidal acts.	Repeatedly violent, maintains almost no personal hygiene, has made potentially lethal suicide attempts.

Adapted from *Global Assessment of Functioning Scale,* DSM-IV, 1994.

Classifying Mental Disorders— Problems by the Book

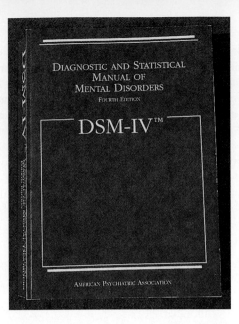

Psychological problems can be grouped into broad categories. The most widely used classification system is found in the *Diagnostic and Statistical Manual of Mental Disorders* (DSM-IV, 1994). The manual provides a common language for therapists, researchers, social agencies, and health workers. It also helps professionals diagnose mental disorders and select appropriate therapies.

A **mental disorder** *is a significant impairment in psychological functioning* (Widiger & Trull, 1991). If you were to glance through DSM-IV, you would find a wide range of disorders described, including those listed in Table 17–2 ■. It is not possible here to discuss all of the problems in the table. (However, many are covered in other chapters.) The descriptions that follow will give you an overview of some of the major disorders. Most of these, and some not mentioned, are discussed in more detail in this chapter and the next. Some major risk factors for developing mental disorders are listed in Table 17–3 ■.

DSM-IV is not the only system for classifying mental disorders. Nevertheless, most activities in mental health settings—from diagnosis to therapy to billing of insurance companies—are influenced by the DSM. DSM-IV is both a scientific document and a social one. Major disorders are well-documented problems. Some problems, however, have little to do with "mental illness." Instead, they are primarily socially disapproved behaviors.

An Overview of Mental Disorders

Psychotic disorders *are characterized by hallucinations and delusions, social withdrawal, and a retreat from reality.* Psychotic disorders tend to be severe and may lead to hospitalization. At times, psychotic persons cannot tell what is fantasy or hallucination and what is real. In addition, their ability to control thoughts and actions is severely impaired. Here's what a young college student who became psychotic told his father:

> It's the strangest thing. I hear voices, hundreds of them, telling me that everyone wants me dead. It's like all the radios of the world blaring all the stations at once, and it doesn't stop. It jams my brain. (Weisburd, 1990)

Schizophrenia, delusional disorders, and some mood disorders are forms of psychosis. Psychotic symptoms may also accompany medical problems (such as brain diseases), drug abuse, and other conditions (DSM-IV, 1994). (Table 17–4 ■ provides a simplified list of major disorders.)

Organic mental disorders *are problems caused by brain pathology;* that is, by senility, drug damage, diseases of the brain, injuries, poisons, and so on (Fig. 17–2 ◆). Organic disorders may be accompanied by severe emotional disturbances, impaired thinking, memory loss, personality changes, delirium, or psychotic symptoms (Costello & Costello, 1992).

It could be argued that almost all mental disorders are at least partly biological. For this reason, DSM-IV does not list "organic mental disorders" as a separate category. Never-

theless, all of the following problems are closely associated with organic damage: delirium, dementia, amnestic, and other cognitive disorders; mental disorders due to a general medical condition; and substance related disorders.

Substance related disorders *are defined by abuse of or dependence on mood- or behavior-altering drugs.* Typical culprits include alcohol, barbiturates, opiates, cocaine, amphetamines, hallucinogens, marijuana, and nicotine. Problems of this type center on damaged functioning at home or on the job, and an inability to stop using the drug. Active drug intoxication or drug withdrawal, delirium, dementia, amnesia, psychosis, emotional problems, sexual problems, and sleep disturbances may also be substance related (Boutros & Bowers, 1996).

Mood disorders *primarily involve disturbances in affect, or emotion.* Individuals suffering from mood disorders may be *manic,* meaning agitated, euphoric, and hyperactive, or they may be *depressed,* or both. In any case, extremes of mood are intense or long lasting. In addition, depressed individuals run a high risk of suicide (DSM-IV, 1994). (Mood disorders are discussed in the next chapter.)

Anxiety disorders *are marked by feelings of fear, apprehension, or anxiety, as well as anxiety-based distortions in behavior.* Anxiety disorders may take the form of *panic* (in which the person suffers sudden unexplainable feelings of panic), *phobias* (excessive, irrational fears), or *generalized anxiety* (chronic and persistent anxiety). Other anxiety disorders are *post-traumatic stress disorder* (high anxiety that persists long after an extremely distressing event, such as military combat) and *acute stress disorder* (high anxiety that occurs immediately

Table 17-2 ■ **Major DSM-IV Categories**

DISORDERS USUALLY FIRST DIAGNOSED IN INFANCY, CHILDHOOD, OR ADOLESCENCE

- **Mental Retardation**
  Example: Mild Mental Retardation
- **Learning Disorders**
  Example: Reading Disorder
- **Motor Skills Disorder**
  Example: Developmental Coordination Disorder
- **Pervasive Developmental Disorders**
  Example: Autistic Disorder
- **Disruptive Behavior and Attention-Deficit Disorders**
  Example: Attention-Deficit/Hyperactivity Disorder

- **Feeding and Eating Disorders of Infancy or Early Childhood**
  Example: Pica
- **Tic Disorders**
  Example: Transient Tic Disorder
- **Communication Disorders**
  Example: Stuttering
- **Elimination Disorders**
  Example: Enuresis
- **Other Disorders of Infancy, Childhood, or Adolescence**
  Example: Separation Anxiety Disorder

DELIRIUM, DEMENTIA, AMNESTIC, AND OTHER COGNITIVE DISORDERS

- **Delirium**
  Example: Delirium Due to a General Medical Condition
- **Dementia**
  Example: Dementia of the Alzheimer's Type

- **Amnestic Disorders** (memory loss)
  Example: Amnestic Disorder Due to a General Medical Condition
- **Cognitive Disorder Not Otherwise Specified**

MENTAL DISORDERS DUE TO A GENERAL MEDICAL CONDITION NOT ELSEWHERE CLASSIFIED

- **Catatonic Disorder Due to a General Medical Condition**
- **Personality Change Due to a General Medical Condition**

- **Mental Disorder Not Otherwise Specified Due to a General Medical Condition**

SUBSTANCE RELATED DISORDERS

Example: Cocaine Use Disorder

SCHIZOPHRENIA AND OTHER PSYCHOTIC DISORDERS

- **Schizophrenia**
  Example: Schizophrenia, Paranoid Type
- **Schizophreniform Disorder**
- **Schizoaffective Disorder**
- **Delusional Disorder**
  Example: Delusional Disorder, Grandiose Type

- **Brief Psychotic Disorder**
- **Shared Psychotic Disorder (Folie à Deux)**
- **Psychotic Disorder Due to a General Medical Condition**
- **Substance-Induced Psychotic Disorder**
- **Psychotic Disorder Not Otherwise Specified**

MOOD DISORDERS

- **Depressive Disorders**
  Example: Major Depressive Disorder
- **Bipolar Disorders**
  Example: Bipolar I Disorder

- **Mood Disorder Due to a General Medical Condition**
- **Substance-Induced Mood Disorder**
- **Mood Disorder Not Otherwise Specified**

ANXIETY DISORDERS

Example: Panic Disorder

SOMATOFORM DISORDERS

Example: Conversion Disorder

FACTITIOUS DISORDERS (faked disability or illness)

Example: Factitious Disorder

Table 17-2 ■ **Major DSM-IV Categories—Continued**

DISSOCIATIVE DISORDERS

Example: Dissociative Identity Disorder

SEXUAL AND GENDER IDENTITY DISORDERS

- **Sexual Dysfunctions**
  Example: Sexual Arousal Disorder
- **Paraphilias**
  Example: Voyeurism

- **Sexual Disorder Not Otherwise Specified**
- **Gender Identity Disorders**
  Example: Gender Identity Disorder

EATING DISORDERS

Example: Anorexia Nervosa

SLEEP DISORDERS

- **Primary Sleep Disorders**
  - **Dyssomnias**
    Example: Primary Insomnia
  - **Parasomnias**
    Example: Sleep Terror Disorder

- **Sleep Disorders Related to Another Mental Disorder**
  Example: Insomnia Related to Post-Traumatic Stress Disorder
- **Other Sleep Disorders**
  Example: Substance-Induced Sleep Disorder

IMPULSE CONTROL DISORDERS NOT ELSEWHERE CLASSIFIED

Example: Kleptomania

ADJUSTMENT DISORDERS

Example: Adjustment Disorder

PERSONALITY DISORDERS

Example: Antisocial Personality Disorder

---

after a highly distressing event, such as an airliner crash). A pattern known as *obsessive-compulsive* behavior is also associated with anxiety (more on this later).

Somatoform disorders (so-MAT-oh-form) are indi-

Table 17-3 ■ **Risk Factors for Mental Disorder**

Social conditions: poverty, stressful living conditions, homelessness, social disorganization, overcrowding
Family factors: parents who are immature, mentally disturbed, criminal, or abusive; severe marital strife; extremely poor child discipline; disordered family communication patterns
Psychological factors: stress, low intelligence, learning disorders, lack of control or mastery
Biological factors: genetic defects or inherited vulnerabilities, poor prenatal care, very low birth weight, chronic physical illness or disability, exposure to toxic chemicals or drugs, head injuries

Table 17-4 ■ **Some Selected Categories of Psychopathology**

Problem	Primary Symptom
Psychotic disorders	Loss of contact with reality
Mood disorders	Mania or depression
Anxiety disorders	High anxiety or anxiety-based distortions in behavior
Somatoform disorders	Bodily complaints
Dissociative disorders	Fragmented awareness
Personality disorders	Unhealthy personality patterns
Sexual and gender identity disorders	Disturbed gender identity, deviant sexual behavior, problems in sexual adjustment
Substance related disorders	Drug abuse

Figure 17–2 ◆ This MRI scan of a human brain (viewed from the top) reveals a tumor (dark spot). Mental disorders sometimes have organic causes of this sort. However, in many instances no organic damage can be found.

cated when a person has *physical symptoms that mimic disease or injury* (paralysis, blindness, illness, or chronic pain, for example) *for which there is no identifiable cause.* In such cases it is assumed that psychological factors underlie the symptoms.

Dissociative disorders *include cases of sudden temporary amnesia and instances of multiple identity (multiple personality). Also included are frightening episodes of depersonalization.* Depersonalization refers to feelings of being outside one's body, of behaving like a robot, or of being in a dream world.

Personality disorders *are deeply ingrained, unhealthy personality patterns.* Such patterns are usually apparent by adolescence and continue throughout much of adult life. They include paranoid (overly suspicious), narcissistic (self-loving), dependent, borderline, and antisocial personality types, as well as others.

Sexual and gender identity disorders *include any of a wide range of difficulties with sexual identity, deviant sexual behavior, or sexual adjustment.* In *gender identity disorders,* sexual identity does not match a person's physical gender. Deviations in sexual behavior known as *paraphilias* include exhibitionism, fetishism, voyeurism, and so on. Also found in this category are a variety of *sexual dysfunctions* (problems in sexual desire, arousal, or response; see Chapter 15).

Shouldn't neurosis be included in the list of problems?

The term *neurosis* is fading from use because it tends to lump together too many separate problems. Behavior once considered "neurotic" is now classified as an anxiety, somatoform, or dissociative disorder (or in some cases as a mild mood disorder). Even so, you may sometimes hear the term *neurosis* used to loosely refer to problems associated with excessive anxiety.

Is insanity the same as psychosis?

No. Psychosis is a mental disorder. **Insanity** *is a legal term that refers to an inability to manage one's affairs or foresee the consequences of one's actions.* Persons who are declared insane are not legally responsible for their actions and they can be involuntarily committed to a mental hospital. Legally, insanity is established by testimony from *expert witnesses* (psychologists and psychiatrists). An **expert witness** *is a person recognized by a court of law as being qualified to give opinions on a specific topic.*

In practice, those who are committed are usually judged to be a danger to themselves or to others, or they are severely mentally disabled (Turkheimer & Parry, 1992). (See this chapter's Exploration for further discussion of insanity.)

To what extent are mentally disordered persons a danger to others?

By amazing coincidence, the following highlight addresses that very question.

Are the Mentally Ill Prone to Violence?

Jeffrey Dahmer was everyone's worst nightmare brought to life. Dahmer drugged his victims, drilled holes in their skulls, sexually molested their lifeless bodies, dismembered them, and ate their body parts, which he stored in a refrigerator.

Although Jeffrey Dahmer's case is extreme, he is typical of the mentally disordered persons who make the evening news. Most have committed murder or some other heinous crime. This gives the impression that the mentally ill are violent and dangerous. In reality, only a tiny percentage of all mentally disordered persons are more violent than average. (Dahmer was killed in prison by another inmate in 1994.)

How accurately does a case like Dahmer's reflect the risk of violence by the mentally ill? Are the mentally ill or formerly mentally ill likely to be violent? Extensive research on this question leads to the following conclusions.

- Only persons who are *actively psychotic* are more violence prone than non-patients. That is, if a person is experiencing delusions and hallucinations, the risk of violence is elevated. Other mental problems are unrelated to violence.

- Only persons *currently* experiencing psychotic symptoms are at increased risk for violence. Violent behavior is not related to being a former mental patient or having had psychotic symptoms *in the past*.

Thus, Dahmer's case, like many others in the news, gives a false impression. Even when we consider people who are actively psychotic, we find that the vast majority are not violent. The risk of violence from mental patients is actually many times lower than that posed by persons who have the following attributes: young, male, poor, and intoxicated.

Beliefs about mental disorders are important because they affect laws and personal attitudes toward the mentally ill. People who strongly believe that the mentally ill are prone to violence are typically afraid to have former mental patients as neighbors, co-workers, or friends. But as you can see, only a small minority of the actively mentally ill pose an increased risk. Former mental patients, in particular, are no more likely to be violent than people in general. The overwhelming majority of violent crimes are committed by people who are not mentally ill. (Sources: Monahan, 1992; Rice, 1997; Teplin, Abram, & McClelland, 1994.)

The sections that follow provide more details about some of the problems already mentioned. A full discussion of schizophrenia and other more severe problems is reserved for the next chapter. Before you read further, see if you can answer these questions.

Learning Check

1. Amnesia, multiple identities, and depersonalization are possible problems in
   a. mood disorders   **b.** somatoform disorders   **c.** psychosis   **d.** dissociative disorders

2. Which among the following is *not* a major psychological problem listed in DSM-IV?
   a. mood disorders   **b.** personality disorders   **c.** insanity   **d.** anxiety disorders

3. A major difference between psychotic disorders and anxiety disorders (or other milder problems) is that in psychosis the individual has lost contact with reality as shown by the presence of
   _____ or _____ .

4. In a court of law, sanity is determined by tests administered by court-appointed lawyers. T or F?

5. Statistical definitions of abnormality successfully avoid the limitations of other approaches. T or F?

6. One of the most powerful contexts in which judgments of normality and abnormality are made is
   a. the family   **b.** occupational settings   **c.** religious systems   **d.** culture

Critical Thinking

7. Bryan, a fan of grunge rock, occasionally wears a skirt in public. Does Bryan's cross-dressing indicate that he has a mental disorder?

Answers:

1. d   2. c   3. delusions, hallucinations   4. F   5. F   6. d   7. Probably not. Undoubtedly Bryan's cross-dressing is socially disapproved by many people. Nevertheless, to be classified as a mental disorder it must cause him to feel disabling shame, guilt, depression, or anxiety. The cultural relativity of behavior like Bryan's is revealed by the fact that it is fashionable and acceptable for women to wear men's clothing.

Personality Disorders— Blueprints for Maladjustment

As stated earlier, personality disorders are maladaptive personality patterns. For example, the paranoid personality is overly suspicious, mistrusting, hypersensitive, guarded, and distrustful of others. Narcissistic persons are preoccupied with their own self-importance: They need constant admiration and they are absorbed in fantasies of power, wealth, brilliance, beauty, and love. The dependent personality is marked by an extreme lack of self-confidence. Dependent persons allow others to run their lives and they place their own needs after others'. In a histrionic personality disorder, the person seeks attention through exaggerated emotion and dramatic actions. Typically, personality disorders such as these can be traced back to adolescence or even childhood. The case described next captures the flavor of a severe personality disorder.

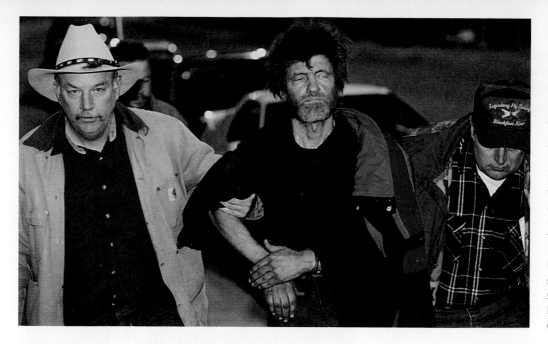

Over a period of years, Theodore Kaczynski allegedly mailed bombs to unsuspecting victims, many of whom were maimed or killed. As a young adult, Kaczynski was a brilliant mathematician. At the time of his arrest, he had become the Unabomber—a reclusive "loner" who deeply mistrusted other people and modern technology. Kaczynski's hostility, rigidity, driven need for self-sufficiency, and hatred of society are all typical features of a paranoid personality. His blunted emotions and nearly total lack of close social relationships are features of a schizoid personality. Thus, Kaczynski appears to suffer from a combination of paranoid and schizoid personality disorders.

Borderline Personality—The Sad Case of Judy

"Get out of here and leave me alone so I can die in peace," Judy screamed at her nurses. Although only 42 years old and normally very attractive, Judy looked old, disheveled, and haggard in the seclusion room of the psychiatric hospital. On one of her arms, long dark red marks mingled with the scars of previous suicide attempts. Judy once bragged that her record was 67 stitches. Today, the nurses had to strap her into restraints to keep her from gouging her eyes out. She was given a sedative and slept for 12 hours. She woke calmly and asked for her therapist—even though this latest incident was ostensibly triggered by his canceling her morning appointment and re-scheduling it for later that afternoon.

Judy has a borderline personality disorder. Although she is capable of working, Judy has repeatedly lost jobs because of her turbulent relationships with others. At times she can be friendly and a real charmer. At other times she is extremely unpredictable, moody, and even suicidal. Being a friend to Judy means accepting a burden that is nearly unbearable at times. The cancellation of an appointment, special dates that are forgotten, a wrong turn of phrase—these and similar small incidents may trigger Judy's anger or, worse yet, a suicide attempt. Judy's only hope lies in intensive, long-term therapy.

The list of personality disorders is long (Table 17–5 ■), so let us focus on a single frequently misunderstood problem, the antisocial personality.

Antisocial Personality

What are the characteristics of an antisocial personality?

The individual with an **antisocial personality** *lacks a conscience, is impulsive, selfish, emotionally shallow, and tends to manipulate others* (Lykken, 1995). Such people, who are sometimes referred to as *sociopaths* or *psychopaths*, typically have a long history of conflict with society. Antisocial persons are irresponsible, lacking in judgment and morals, and unable to learn from experience. They are also incapable of deep feelings, including guilt, shame, fear, loyalty, and love. In short, the sociopath is poorly socialized and has a general disregard for the truth (DSM-IV, 1994).

Are sociopaths dangerous?

Many sociopaths are delinquents or criminals who may pose a threat to the general public (Rice, 1997). However, sociopaths are rarely the crazed murderers you have seen portrayed on TV and in movies. In fact, many sociopaths are "charming" and create a good first impression. Their lying, self-serving manipulation and lack of dependability only gradually become evident. Many successful businesspersons, entertainers, politicians, and other seemingly normal people reveal psychopathic leanings by coldly using others. Basically, psychopaths cheat their way through life (Rice, 1997).

What causes sociopathy?

People with antisocial personalities usually have a childhood history of emotional deprivation, neglect, and physical abuse (Pollock et al., 1990). As mentioned in Chapter 4, some psychologists believe that infants who fail to form a healthy emotional attachment to a caregiver may become prone to antisocial behavior (Magid, 1988). Adult psychopaths also display subtle physical problems. For example, they produce

Table 17–5	■	Personality Disorders and Typical Degree of Impairment

Moderate Impairment

Dependent Unhealthy submissiveness and dependence on others (clinging)

Histrionic Excessive emotion and attention-seeking behavior

Narcissistic Exaggerated self-importance and desire for constant admiration

Antisocial Irresponsible and antisocial behavior, such as aggression, deceit, recklessness, and lack of remorse

High Impairment

Obsessive-compulsive Orderliness, perfectionism, and rigid routine

Schizoid Limited emotion and a lack of interest in close personal relationships with others

Avoidant Discomfort in social situations, fear of evaluation, timidity

Severe Impairment

Borderline Extremely unstable self-image, relationships, moods, and impulses

Paranoid A deep distrust and suspiciousness of the motives of others, which are seen as demeaning or threatening

Schizotypal Social isolation, extremely odd behavior, and disturbed thought patterns, but not actively psychotic

From DSM-IV, 1994 and Millon, 1981.

Studies show that more than 65 percent of all persons with anti-social personalities have been arrested, usually for crimes such as robbery, vandalism, or rape.

unusual brain-wave patterns suggesting under-arousal of the brain (Fig. 17–3 ◆). This condition may explain why many psychopaths are thrill seekers. Quite likely, they are searching for stimulation strong enough to overcome their chronic under-arousal and "boredom" (Carson, Butcher, & Mineka, 1996; Hare, 1996).

In a revealing study, psychopaths were shown extremely grisly and unpleasant photographs. The photos were so upsetting that normal people are visibly startled by them. The psychopaths, however, showed no startle response to the photos (Patrick et al., 1993). (They didn't "bat an eyelash.") Those with antisocial personalities might therefore be described as *emotionally cold*. They simply do not feel normal pangs of conscience, guilt, or anxiety (Hare, 1996). This coldness seems to account for an unusual ability to calmly lie, cheat, steal, or manipulate others (Lykken, 1995).

Can sociopathy be treated?

Antisocial personality disorders are rarely treated with success. All too often, sociopaths manipulate therapy like any other situation. If it is to their advantage to act "cured," they will do so, but they return to former patterns of behavior at the first opportunity. There is some evidence, however, that antisocial behavior declines somewhat after age 40.

Sexual Deviance—Trench Coats, Whips, Leathers, and Lace

Sexual deviance implies a departure from socially accepted standards of behavior. By strict standards (including the law in some states), any sexual activity other than face-to-face heterosexual intercourse between married adults is "deviant." But public standards are often at odds with behavior found privately acceptable. By private standards, large numbers of people regard oral sex, masturbation, and premarital sex as perfectly normal. None of these behaviors is listed in DSM-IV. Neither is homosexuality, which is a variation in sexual preference, not a sexual disorder. (See the discussion of sexual orientation in Chapter 15 for more information.)

Paraphilias

From a psychological point of view, the mark of true sexual deviations, or **paraphilias** (PAIR-eh-FIL-ih-ahs), *is that they are compulsive and destructive.* Typically, they cause guilt, anxiety, or discomfort for one or both participants. The paraphilias cover a wide variety of behaviors, including:

Figure 17–3 ◆ Using PET scans, Canadian psychologist Robert Hare found that the normally functioning brain (top) lights up with activity when a person sees emotion-laden words such as "maggot" or "cancer." But the brain of a psychopath (bottom) remains inactive, especially in areas associated with feelings and self-control. When Dr. Hare showed the bottom image to several neurologists, one asked, "Is this person from Mars?" (Images courtesy of Robert Hare.)

Pedophilia—*sex with children, or child molesting*

Fetishism—*sexual arousal associated with inanimate objects*

Exhibitionism—*"flashing," or displaying the genitals to unwilling viewers*

Voyeurism—*"peeping," or viewing the genitals of others without their permission*

Transvestic fetishism—*achieving sexual arousal by wearing clothing of the opposite sex*

Sexual sadism—*deriving sexual pleasure from inflicting pain*

Sexual masochism—*desiring pain as part of the sex act*

Frotteurism—*sexually touching or rubbing against a nonconsenting person, usually in a public place such as a subway*

Sexual deviance is a highly emotional subject, and many misconceptions exist about it. Two of the most misunderstood problems are exhibitionism and pedophilia. Check your understanding against the information that follows.

Exhibitionism Exhibitionism is a common problem. Roughly 35 percent of all sexual arrests are for "flashing." Exhibitionists are typically male and married, and most come from strict and repressive backgrounds. Exhibitionists have the highest repeat rate among sexual offenders. Most of them feel a deep sense of inadequacy, which produces a compulsive need to prove their "manhood" by frightening women. While exhibitionists are usually harmless, those who approach closer than arm's reach may be dangerous (Sue et al., 1994). In general, a woman confronted by an exhibitionist can assume that his goal is to shock and alarm her. By becoming visibly upset she actually encourages him (Hyde, 1996).

Child Molestation Child molesters, who also are usually males, are often pictured as despicable perverts lurking in dark alleys. In fact, most are married and two thirds are fathers. Many are rigid, passive, puritanical, or religious. In one half to two thirds of all cases of pedophilia, the offender is a friend, acquaintance, or relative of the child. Molesters are also often thought of as child rapists, but most molestations rarely exceed fondling (Sue et al., 1994).

How serious are the effects of a molestation?

The impact varies widely. It is affected by how long the abuse lasts and whether genital sexual acts are involved (Freize, 1987). Many authorities believe that a single incident of fondling is unlikely to cause severe emotional harm to a child. For most children the event is frightening, but not a lasting trauma. This is why parents are urged not to overreact to such incidents or to become hysterical. Doing so only further frightens the child. This does not mean, however, that parents should ignore hints from a child that a molestation may have occurred. Here are some hints of trouble that parents should watch for.

Recognizing Signs of Child Molestation

1. The child fears being seen nude (for instance, during bathing), when such fears were absent before.
2. The child develops physical complaints, such as headaches, stomachaches, and other stress symptoms.
3. The child displays anxiety, fidgeting, shame, or discomfort when any reference to sexual behavior occurs.
4. The child becomes markedly emotional and irritable.
5. The child engages in hazardous risk taking, such as jumping from high places or riding a bicycle dangerously in traffic.
6. The child reveals self-destructive or suicidal thoughts, self-blame.
7. The child shows a loss of self-esteem or self-worth.

(Adapted from Frederick, 1987.)

How can children protect themselves?

Children should be taught to shout "No" if an adult tries to engage them in sexual activity. If children are asked to keep a secret, they should reply that they don't keep secrets. It also helps if children know the tactics typically used by molesters. Recent interviews with convicted sex offenders revealed the following patterns (Elliott, Browne, & Kilcoyne, 1995):

Tactics of Child Molesters

1. Most molesters act alone.
2. Most assaults take place in the abuser's home.
3. Many abusers gain access to the child through caretaking.
4. Children are targeted at first through bribes, gifts, and games.
5. The abuser tries to lull the child into participation through touch, talking about sex, and persuasion.
6. The abuser then uses force, anger, threats, and bribes to gain continued compliance.

Repeated molestations, those that involve force or threats, and incidents that exceed fondling can leave lasting emotional scars. As adults, many victims of incest or molestation develop sexual phobias. For them, lovemaking may evoke vivid and terrifying memories of the childhood victimization. Serious harm is especially likely to occur if the molester is someone the child deeply trusts. Molestations by parents, close relatives, teachers, priests, youth leaders, and similar persons can be quite damaging. In such cases professional counseling is often needed.

Rape

As the preceding discussion suggests, the picture of sexual deviance that most often emerges is one of sexual inhibition and immaturity. Typically, some relatively infantile sexual expression (like exhibitionism or pedophilia) is selected because it is less threatening than healthy sexuality. Rapists are a notable exception to this pattern, however.

Forcible rape *refers to sexual intercourse carried out against the victim's will, under the threat of force.* Rapists often inflict more violence on their victims than is necessary to achieve their goal. Many women feel confident that their chances of being raped are low. But the facts tell a different story (Koss, 1993).

The Facts on Rape

- At least 1 woman in 7 will be raped in her lifetime. Because many rapes go unreported, the true figure is probably 1 in 4.
- Approximately 1 college woman in 6 is a victim of rape.
- In 65 to 80 percent of all cases the rapist is a friend or acquaintance of the victim.
- Rape by an acquaintance is as devastating as rape by a stranger.
- Five percent of rapes result in pregnancy.
- Four to 30 percent of rape victims contract sexually transmitted diseases.

Rape is not a sexual disorder. It is a crime. Indeed, most authorities no longer think of rape as a primarily sexual act. Rather, it is an act of brutality or aggression based on the need to debase others. Many rapists are antisocial personalities who impulsively take what they want without concern for the feelings of the victim or guilt about their deed. Others harbor deep-seated resentment or outright hatred of women. However, the problem may reach far deeper, as indicated in the following highlight.

A Closer Look

Is Ours a Rape-Supportive Culture?

Rape is related to sex role socialization. Many people learn to believe that women should not show direct interest in sex. Men, on the other hand, are taught to take the initiative and to persist in attempts at sexual intimacy—even when the woman says no.

Psychologists James Check and Neil Malamuth believe that such attitudes create a "rape-supportive culture." In their view, rape is only an extreme expression of a system that condones coercive (forced) sexual intimacy. They point out, for instance, that the single most used cry of rapists to their victims is, "You know you want it." And afterward, "There now, you really enjoyed it, didn't you."

To test the hypothesis that stereotyped images contribute to rape, male college students were classified as either high or low in sex role stereotyping. Each student then read one of three stories: The first described voluntary intercourse; the second depicted stranger rape; and the third described acquaintance rape (forced intercourse on a date).

As predicted, college males high in sex role stereotyping were more aroused by the rape stories. Their arousal patterns, in fact, were similar to those found among actual rapists. Moreover, a chilling 44 percent of those tested said they would consider rape—especially if they could be sure of not being caught (Check & Malamuth, 1983). In general, sexually aggressive men tend to be emotionally insensitive to others (Lisak & Ivan, 1995).

In view of such attitudes—and the continuing widespread belief that when a woman says no she means yes—it is little wonder that rape occurs every 6 minutes in the United States. Perhaps the time has come for our culture to make it clear that no means no.

Quite often, the rapist's goal is not strictly sexual intercourse; it is to attack, subordinate, humiliate, and degrade the victim. Typical after-effects for the victim include rage, guilt, depression, loss of self-esteem, shame, sexual adjustment problems, and in many cases, a lasting mistrust of male-female relationships (Freize, 1987). The impact is so great that most women continue to report fear, anxiety, and sexual dysfunction a year and a half or more after being raped. Even years later, rape survivors are more likely to suffer from depression, alcohol or drug abuse, and other emotional problems (Koss, 1993).

Any man who doubts the seriousness of rape should imagine himself mistakenly placed in jail, where he is violently raped (sodomized) by other inmates. There is no pleasure in rape for victims of either sex. It is truly a despicable crime.

Anxiety-Based Disorders—When Anxiety Rules

Imagine for a moment the feeling of waiting to take an important test for which you are unprepared; or waiting to give a speech to a large audience of strangers; or being followed by a police car while you are driving. You have almost certainly felt *anxiety* in one of these situations.

Anxiety *refers to feelings of apprehension, dread, or uneasiness.* As you may have noticed, the physical reactions that accompany anxiety are similar to fear. However, anxiety is a response to an *unclear or ambiguous threat.* For instance, what we commonly call "stage fright" is actually anxiety, because an audience poses no real threat to safety (except, perhaps, at extremely bad talent shows). Compared to anxiety, fear is more focused and intense. Typically it is the result of a specific, identifiable threat. When we are fearful we say to ourselves, "A terrible event is happening and I must take action right now to stop it." When we are anxious we say, "A terrible event may happen. I may not be able to deal with it, but I've got to be ready to try" (Zinbarg et al., 1992).

Disruptive Anxiety

We all occasionally feel anxiety, and at times of great stress, anxiety may be intense. But anxiety that is out of proportion to a situation may reveal a problem. An example is a college student named Jian who appeared at the counseling center because he was deathly afraid of tests. He had already skipped three exams because he stayed home in bed, petrified by fears of failure.

Jian shows clear signs of having a disruptive emotional problem, but one that did not involve a loss of contact with reality. As mentioned earlier, such problems were once called neuroses. Now they are classified separately as anxiety disorders, dissociative disorders, and somatoform disorders. In general, these problems involve the following features:

- High levels of anxiety and/or restrictive, self-defeating behavior patterns

- A tendency to use elaborate defense mechanisms or avoidance responses to maintain minimal functioning

- Pervasive feelings of stress, insecurity, inferiority, unhappiness, and dissatisfaction with life

- The person feels threatened, but doesn't do anything about it

In short, affected persons struggle to preserve control, but they remain ineffective and unhappy (Zinbarg et al., 1992).

If fear and anxiety are normal emotions, when do they signal a problem?

A problem exists when anxiety becomes intense or persistent enough to prevent a person from doing what she or he wants or needs to do. Also, persons with anxiety disorders feel that their anxieties are out of control—that they cannot stop worrying. Anxiety, fears, and phobias are probably the most common psychological disturbances today. On any given day, roughly 7 percent of the adult population could be diagnosed as having an anxiety disorder (Landers, 1989).

Do such problems cause a "nervous breakdown"?

Adjustment Disorders Anxiety-based problems seriously disrupt people's lives and almost always cause misery. However, they rarely bring about a total "breakdown." Actually, the term *nervous breakdown* has no formal meaning. What many people have in mind when they use the term is properly called an *adjustment disorder.*

Adjustment disorders *occur when ordinary life stresses push people beyond their ability to cope effectively.* Examples of such stresses are prolonged unemployment, severe marital strife, and chronic physical illness. Some signs that a person may be suffering from an adjustment disorder are extreme irritability, sleep disturbances, loss of appetite, physical complaints, and apathy, anxiety, or depression (DSM-IV, 1994). Often, these problems are successfully treated with rest, sedation, supportive counseling, and a chance to "talk through" fears and anxieties.

How is an adjustment disorder different from an anxiety disorder?

The outward symptoms can be similar. However, adjustment disorders typically disappear when life circumstances improve. This shows their link to stressful events.

Anxiety Disorders

In most anxiety disorders, the person's distress seems greatly out of proportion to the situation. Consider, for example, the following description of Ethel B:

> She was never completely relaxed, and complained of vague feelings of restlessness, and a fear that something was "just around the corner." Although she felt that she had to go to work to help pay the family bills, she could not bring herself to start anything new for fear that something terrible would happen on the job. She had experienced a few extreme anxiety attacks during which she felt "like I couldn't breathe, like I was sealed up in a transparent envelope. I thought I was going to have a heart attack. I couldn't stop shaking." (Suinn, 1975*)

Distress like Ethel B's is a key element in anxiety disorders. Many psychologists believe that it also underlies dissociative and somatoform disorders, where maladaptive behavior serves to reduce anxiety and discomfort. To deepen your understanding, let's examine several anxiety-based disorders. (Table 17–6 ■ lists the anxiety disorders.)

Generalized Anxiety Disorder The essential feature of a **generalized anxiety disorder** *is at least 6 months of unrealistic or excessive anxiety and worry* (DSM-IV, 1994). The person's discomfort is sometimes described as **free-floating anxiety** *because it is triggered by so many different situations.* Affected individuals typically complain of sweating, racing heart,

---

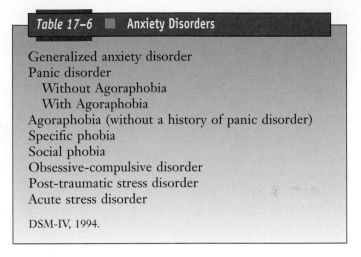

Table 17-6 ■ **Anxiety Disorders**

Generalized anxiety disorder
Panic disorder
  Without Agoraphobia
  With Agoraphobia
Agoraphobia (without a history of panic disorder)
Specific phobia
Social phobia
Obsessive-compulsive disorder
Post-traumatic stress disorder
Acute stress disorder

DSM-IV, 1994.

---

clammy hands, dizziness, upset stomach, and rapid breathing. They are continually preoccupied by worries, which makes them irritable and unable to concentrate. Generalized anxiety disorder affects more women than men (Brawman-Mintzer & Lydiard, 1996).

Was Ethel B's problem a generalized anxiety disorder?

No. The added presence of *anxiety attacks* indicates she suffered from *panic disorder.*

Panic Disorder (without Agoraphobia) In a **panic disorder** (without agoraphobia) *the person is in a chronic state of anxiety, and also has moments of sudden, intense, unexpected panic.* During a panic attack victims experience heart palpitations or chest pain, choking or smothering sensations, vertigo, feelings of unreality, trembling, and fears of losing control. Many believe that they are having a heart attack, are going insane, or are about to die. Needless to say, this pattern leaves victims unhappy and uncomfortable much of the time (Katerndahl, 1996).

Panic attacks may also occur in other anxiety disorders. What sets panic disorder apart is that the panic attacks seem to appear without warning ("out of the blue"), rather than just in certain situations (DSM-IV, 1994).

Panic Disorder (with Agoraphobia) In a **panic disorder** (with agoraphobia) *the person suffers from chronic anxiety and brief moments of sudden panic. In addition, the person suffers from agoraphobia* (ah-go-rah-FOBE-ee-ah). **Agoraphobia** *is an intense, irrational fear that a panic attack will occur in a public place or unfamiliar situation.* More simply, agoraphobia is an intense fear of leaving the house and familiar surroundings. Typically, the agoraphobic person finds ways of avoiding areas of insecurity—such as crowds, open roads, supermarkets, automobiles, and so on. As a result, some agoraphobics are literally housebound (DSM-IV, 1994).

Agoraphobia **Agoraphobia** can also occur without panic. In this case, *the person fears that something extremely embarrassing will happen if she or he leaves home or enters an unfamiliar*

---

* From *Fundamentals of Behavior Pathology* by R. M. Suinn. Copyright © 1975. Reprinted by permission of John Wiley & Sons, Inc. Additional Suinn quotes in this chapter and the next are from the same source.

situation. For example, an agoraphobic person may refuse to go outside because she fears having a sudden attack of dizziness, or diarrhea, or shortness of breath. Being outside the home alone, being in a crowd, standing in line, being on a bridge, or in a car, bus, or train can be impossible for an agoraphobic (DSM-IV, 1994). About 7 percent of all adults suffer from agoraphobia (with or without panic) during their lifetime (Magee et al., 1996).

Specific Phobia   As stated earlier, phobias are intense, irrational fears that persist even when there is no real danger. In a **specific phobia,** *persistent fears, anxiety, and avoidance are focused on objects, activities, or situations.* Persons affected by phobias recognize that their fears are unreasonable and excessive, but they cannot control them.

Specific phobias can be classified according to the object or situation that is feared. The most common types are listed here.

Animal type—*fear of a specific type of animal, such as a dog, spider, or snake*

Natural environment type—*fear of heights, storms, the ocean, caves, and the like*

Blood, injection, injury type—*fear of blood, injections, injuries, medical procedures*

Situational type—*fear of specific situations, such as airplanes, elevators, enclosed spaces*

Other type—*fear of a wide range of other situations, such as those that may lead to choking, vomiting, or catching an illness*

These types, of course, only outline the possibilities. Specific phobias may be attached to nearly any object or situation. Many of the more common specific phobias have been given names, such as those listed in Table 17–7 ■.

Obviously, by combining the appropriate root word with the word *phobia,* any number of unlikely fears can be named. Some are *acarophobia,* a fear of itching; *zemmiphobia,* fear of the great mole rat; *phobosophobia,* fear of fear; *arachibutyrophobia,* fear of peanut butter sticking to the roof of the mouth, and *hippopotomonstrosesquipedaliophobia,* fear of long words!

Almost everyone has a few mild phobias: Fears of heights, closed spaces, or bugs and crawly things are common. A phobic disorder differs from such garden-variety fears in that it produces overwhelming anxiety. The result can be vomiting, wild climbing and running, or fainting. For a phobic disorder to exist, the person's fear must disrupt his or her daily life. Phobic persons are so threatened that they will go to almost any length to avoid the feared object or situation. About 11 percent of all adults have phobic disorders during their lifetime (Magee et al., 1996).

Social Phobia   In a **social phobia,** *the person fears social situations in which he or she can be observed, evaluated, embarrassed, or humiliated by others.* This leads affected persons to avoid certain social situations, such as eating, writing, using the rest room, or speaking in public. When the situation cannot be avoided, the person endures it with intense anxiety or distress. Social phobias greatly impair functioning at work, at school, in social activities, or in personal relationships (DSM-IV, 1994). About 13 percent of

Table 17–7 ■ Common Phobias
Acrophobia—*fear of heights*
Astraphobia—*fear of storms, thunder, lightning*
Arachnophobia—*fear of spiders*
Aviophobia—*fear of airplanes*
Claustrophobia—*fear of closed spaces*
Hematophobia—*fear of blood*
Microphobia—*fear of germs*
Nyctophobia—*fear of darkness*
Pathophobia—*fear of disease*
Pyrophobia—*fear of fire*
Xenophobia—*fear of strangers*
Zoophobia—*fear of animals*

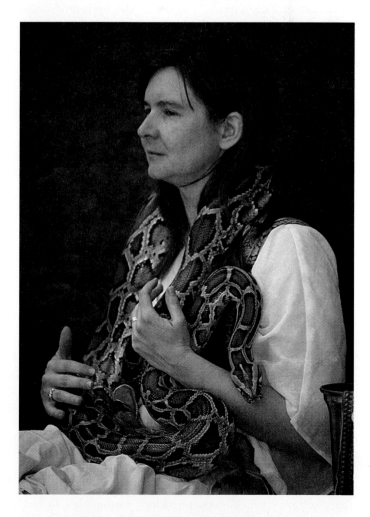

For a person with a strong fear of snakes (ophidiophobia), merely looking at this picture may be unsettling.

all adults are affected by social phobias at one time or another (Magee et al., 1996).

Obsessive-Compulsive Disorder

In an **obsessive-compulsive disorder** *the person is preoccupied with certain distressing thoughts and feels compelled to perform certain behaviors.* You have probably experienced a mild obsessional thought in the form of some song or stupid commercial jingle that is repeated over and over in your mind. This may be irritating, but it is usually not terribly disturbing. True **obsessions** *are images or thoughts that intrude into consciousness against a person's will.* They are so disturbing that they cause anxiety or extreme discomfort. The most common obsessions are about violence (such as poisoning one's spouse or stabbing a child), about being "dirty" or "unclean," about whether one has performed some action (such as turning off the stove), and about committing immoral acts (Wilson, 1986).

Obsessions usually give rise to **compulsions.** *These are irrational acts a person feels driven to repeat.* Often, the compulsive act helps control or block out anxiety caused by an obsession. For example, a minister who finds profanities popping into his mind might take up compulsively counting his heartbeat to prevent himself from thinking "dirty" words.

Many people with compulsions can be classified as *checkers* or *cleaners.* Thus, a person who feels unclean because of a conflict about masturbation might be driven to wash his or her hands hundreds of times a day, even after they become raw (Tallis, 1996). And a young mother who repeatedly has an image of a knife plunging into her infant might count all the knives in the house several times a day and check repeatedly to see that they are locked away. Doing this is motivated by an urgent need to reduce her anxieties, at least temporarily.

Of course, not all obsessive-compulsive disorders are so dramatic. Many simply involve extreme orderliness and rigid routine. Compulsive attention to detail and rigid adherence to procedures and rules make the highly anxious person feel more secure. That way, activities remain totally structured and under control. Notice, too, that when such patterns are long-standing, but less intense, they may be classified as a personality disorder.

Stress Disorders

Most anxiety disorders have little connection to the actual degree of threat. A notable exception is found in **stress disorders.** *These problems occur when stresses outside the range of normal human experience cause a significant emotional disturbance* (DSM-IV, 1994). Such reactions frequently follow sudden disasters, such as floods, tornadoes, earthquakes, or serious accidents. Research shows that stress disorders also affect many political hostages, combat veterans, prisoners of war,

The severe obsessions and compulsions of billionaire Howard Hughes led him to live as a recluse for over 20 years. Hughes had an intense fear of contamination. To avoid infection, he constructed sterile, isolated environments in which his contact with people and objects was strictly limited by complicated rituals. Before handling a spoon, for instance, Hughes had his attendants wrap the handle in tissue paper and seal it with tape. A second piece of tissue was then wrapped around the first before he would touch it (Hodgson & Miller, 1982). A spoon prepared as Hughes required is shown here.

and victims of terrorism, violent crime, child molestation, rape, or witnessing the death or injury of another person (Berman et al., 1996; Coyne & Downey, 1991).

Symptoms of stress disorders include repeatedly reliving the traumatic event, avoiding stimuli associated with the event, and a numbing of emotions. Also common are insomnia, nightmares, guardedness, an inability to concentrate, irritability, and explosions of anger or aggression. *If such reactions last less than a month after a traumatic event*, the problem is called an **acute stress disorder.** *If they last more than a month*, the person is suffering from **post-traumatic stress disorder (PTSD)** (DSM-IV, 1994). PTSD may persist for years after the stress has passed—as has happened to many veterans of the Vietnam War (Fontana et al., 1992). PTSD is far more common than once believed. Nearly 1 adult out of 12 in the United States has suffered from post-traumatic stress disorder at some time during his or her life (Kessler, Sonnega, & Nelson, 1995).

Dissociative Disorders

In a dissociative reaction we see striking episodes of *amnesia, fugue,* or *multiple identity.* **Dissociative amnesia** *is the inability to recall one's name, address, or past.* **Dissociative fugue** (sounds like "fewg") *involves fleeing to escape extreme conflict or threat.* Dissociations are often triggered by highly traumatic events, as the following case illustrates (Lipschitz et al., 1996).

An American soldier in the Vietnam war wandered into the countryside and ambushed Vietcong soldiers without any

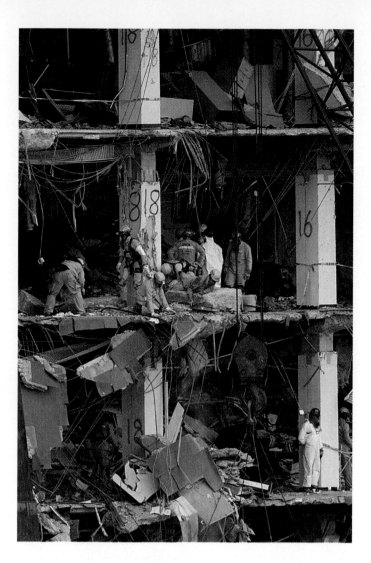

A terrorist bomb destroyed the Alfred P. Murrah Building in Oklahoma City on April 19th, 1995. The bomb killed 169 people and left over 600 injured. In the aftermath of such disasters, many survivors suffer from acute stress reactions. For some, the flare-up of anxiety and distress may occur months or years after the stressful event is over, an example of a post-traumatic stress reaction. Many witnesses, survivors, and rescue workers have suffered PTSD in the years following the Oklahoma City bombing.

memory of his actions. His fugue and amnesia were triggered when he discovered the dead body of a Vietnamese child he had adopted. Later, in therapy, he was able to remember the incident: "After 15 years in the Army, he was all I had. It's all my fault! It's all my fault! If I had just taken you over to the hooch, you wouldn't be there, man! It's not fair. They ain't gotta kill kids." (Spiegel, 1986)

It can easily be seen that forgetting one's identity and fleeing unpleasant situations can serve as defenses against intolerable anxiety.

A person suffering from a **dissociative identity disorder** *has two or more separate identities or personality states* (DSM-IV, 1994). Note that identity disorders are *not* the same as schizophrenia. Schizophrenia is a form of psychosis, dis-

cussed in the next chapter. One of the most dramatic examples of multiple identity disorder is described in the book *Sybil* (Schreiber, 1973). Sybil had 16 different personality states. Each identity had a distinct voice, vocabulary, and posture. One personality could play the piano (not Sybil), but the others could not.

When an identity other than Sybil was in control, Sybil experienced a "time lapse," or memory blackout. Sybil's amnesia and alternate identities developed during childhood when she was regularly beaten, locked in closets, perversely tortured, sexually abused, and almost killed. Sybil's first dissociations allowed her to escape by creating another person who would suffer torture in her place. Dissociative identity disorders often begin with similar unbearable childhood experiences. A history of childhood trauma, especially sexual abuse, is found in over 95 percent of persons whose personalities split into multiple identities (Ross et al., 1990; Tutkun, Yargic, & Sar, 1995).

Therapy for dissociative identity disorders may make use of hypnosis, which allows contact with the various personality states. The goal of therapy is *integration* and *fusion* of the various identities into a single, balanced personality. Fortunately, multiple identity disorders are far rarer in real life than they are in TV dramas!

Somatoform Disorders

Perhaps you have known someone, particularly someone prone to anxiety, who seems to be practically obsessed by fears of having a serious disease. Usually these individuals are preoccupied with bodily functions, such as their heartbeat or digestion. Minor physical problems, a small sore, or an occasional cough, can convince them that they have cancer or some other disease. Typically, their unwarranted fear of having a disease persists despite the fact that there is no medical basis for their complaints (DSM-IV, 1994).

Are you describing hypochondria?

Yes. In **hypochondriasis** (HI-po-kon-DRY-uh-sis), *the person interprets normal sensations and small bodily signs as proof that she or he has a terrible disease.* Persons who have a related problem called **somatization disorder** (som-ah-tuh-ZAY-shun) *express their anxieties in the form of various bodily complaints* such as vomiting or nausea, shortness of breath, difficulty swallowing, or painful menstruation. Typically, they feel ill much of the time and visit doctors repeatedly. Most take medicines or other treatments, but no organic cause can be found for their distress (Ford, 1995). Similarly, a person suffering from **pain disorder** *is disabled by pain that has no identifiable physical basis* (DSM-IV, 1994).

A rarer somatoform disorder ("body-form" disorder) is called a *conversion reaction*. In a **conversion disorder** *severe emotional conflicts are "converted" into symptoms that actually disturb physical functioning or closely resemble a physical disability.* For instance, a soldier might become deaf or lame or develop "glove anesthesia" just before a battle.

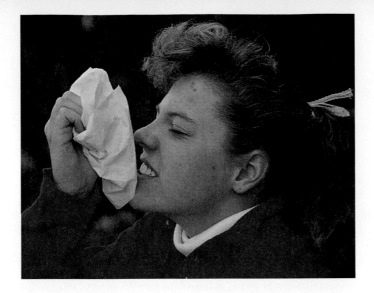

Uncontrollable sneezing, which may continue for days or weeks, is often a conversion disorder. In such cases sneezing is atypical in rate and rhythm. In addition, the person's eyes do not close during a sneeze and sneezing does not occur during sleep. All of these signs suggest that the cause of the sneezing is psychological, not physical (Fochtmann, 1995).

What is "glove anesthesia"?

"Glove anesthesia" is a loss of sensitivity in the areas of the skin that would normally be covered by a glove. Glove anesthesia shows that conversion symptoms often contradict known medical facts. The system of nerves in the hands does not form a glove-like pattern and could not cause the observed symptoms (Fig. 17–4 ◆).

If symptoms disappear when a victim is asleep, hypnotized, or anesthetized a conversion reaction must be suspected. Another sign to watch for is a victim's seeming lack of concern about suddenly becoming disabled. (Be careful not to confuse somatoform disorders with psychosomatic disorders. As discussed in Chapter 14, psychosomatic disorders are illnesses in which actual physical damage or dysfunction results from emotional reactions to stress.)

The physical symptoms of a conversion disorder usually excuse the person from a threatening situation. In one case, a college student had a minor traffic accident. The following morning he woke with numbness in his legs and could not move them. A conversion reaction was suspected because he did not seem at all disturbed by his sudden inability to walk. (This sign is referred to as *la belle indifférence*). Investigation revealed that his parents were pressuring him to stay in school (although he wanted to quit) and that he was not prepared for his final exams. If he failed his exams, he expected to be drafted (Suinn, 1975).

A final note of interest: Conversion disorders probably account for many of the so-called miracle cures attributed to faith healers or medical quacks. Persons with conversion symptoms who firmly believe they are being helped may undergo a "miraculous" cure, but they usually develop new symptoms later.

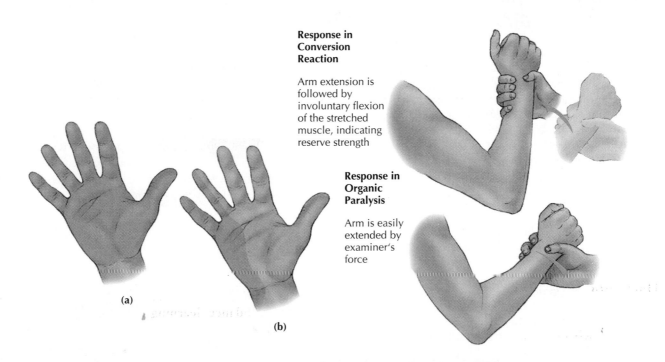

Response in Conversion Reaction

Arm extension is followed by involuntary flexion of the stretched muscle, indicating reserve strength

Response in Organic Paralysis

Arm is easily extended by examiner's force

(a)

(b)

Figure 17–4 ◆ (*Left*) "Glove" anesthesia is a conversion reaction involving loss of feeling in areas of the hand that would be covered by a glove (a). If the anesthesia were physically caused, it would follow the pattern shown in (b). (*Right*) To test for organic paralysis of the arm, an examiner can suddenly extend the arm, stretching the muscles. A conversion reaction is indicated if the arm pulls back involuntarily. (Adapted from Weintraub, 1983.)

Four Pathways to Anxiety and Disorder

What causes the problems described in the preceding discussion?

Because we are both biological and social creatures, it is not surprising that susceptibility to anxiety-based disorders appears to be partly inherited. Studies of parents suffering from panic disorder, for instance, show that an unusually large number (60 percent) of their children are born with a fearful, inhibited temperament (Rosenbaum et al., 1989). Such children are irritable and wary as infants, shy and fearful as toddlers, and by school age they are quiet and cautious introverts. Authorities believe that such children are at high risk for anxiety problems, such as panic attacks, in adulthood (Rosenbaum et al., 1991).

At least four major psychological perspectives on the causes of dissociative, anxiety, and somatoform disorders can be identified. These are (1) the *psychodynamic* approach, (2) the *humanistic-existential* approach, (3) the *behavioral* approach, and (4) the *cognitive* approach.

Psychodynamic Approach

Recall that the term **psychodynamic** *refers to internal motives, conflicts, unconscious forces, and other dynamics of mental life.* Freud was the first to propose a psychodynamic explanation for what was then known as neurosis. According to Freud, disturbances like those we have described represent a raging conflict among subparts of the personality—the id, ego, and superego.

Freud particularly emphasized that intense anxiety can be caused by forbidden id impulses for sex or aggression that threaten to break through into behavior. It is as if the person is in a constant state of fear that the ego will be overwhelmed and that the person may do something "crazy" or unacceptable. Also important in the Freudian view is guilt generated by the superego in response to these impulses. Caught in the middle, the ego eventually is overwhelmed. This forces the person to adopt rigid defense mechanisms and misguided, inflexible behavior to prevent a disastrous loss of control.

Humanistic-Existential Approaches

Humanistic *thought emphasizes subjective experience and human problems and potentials.* Humanistic psychologist Carl Rogers interpreted emotional disorders as the end product of a faulty **self-image** (*the total perception of oneself; another term for self-concept*) (Rogers, 1959). Rogers believed that anxious individuals have built up unrealistic mental images of themselves. This leaves them vulnerable to contradictory information. Let's say, for example, that an essential part of a student's self-image is the idea that she is highly intelligent.

If the student does poorly in school, she may deny or distort her perceptions of herself and her perceptions of the situation. Rigid use of defense mechanisms, a conversion reaction, anxiety attacks, or similar symptoms may result from threats to one's self-image. These symptoms in turn become new threats that provoke further distortions. We have, in other words, a classic example of a vicious cycle of maladjustment and anxiety that feeds on itself once started.

Existential *thought focuses on the elemental problems of existence, such as death, meaning, choice, and responsibility.* Some psychologists take a more existential view and stress that unhealthy anxiety reflects a loss of *meaning* in one's life. According to them, we must show *courage* and *responsibility* in our choices if life is to have meaning. Too often, they say, we give in to "existential anxiety" and back away from life-enhancing choices. Existential anxiety is the unavoidable anguish that comes from knowing that we are personally responsible for our lives. Hence, we have a crushing need to choose wisely and courageously as we face life's empty and impersonal void.

From the existential view, people who are unhappy and anxious are living in "bad faith." That is, they have collapsed in the face of the awesome responsibility to choose a meaningful existence. In short, they have lost their way in life.

Behavioral Approach

Behavioristic *approaches emphasize overt, observable behavior and the effects of learning and conditioning.* Consequently, behaviorists assume that the "symptoms" we have discussed are learned, just as other behaviors are. You might recall from Chapter 9, for instance, that phobias can be acquired through classical conditioning. Similarly, anxiety attacks may reflect conditioned emotional responses that are generalized to new situations. As another example, the hypochondriac's "sickness behavior" may be reinforced by the sympathy and attention he or she gets.

One point that theorists agree on is that disordered behavior is ultimately self-defeating and paradoxical. A paradox is a contradiction. The contradiction in self-defeating behavior is that it makes the person more miserable in the long run, but its immediate effect is to temporarily lower anxiety.

But if the person becomes more miserable in the long run, how does the pattern get started?

The behavioral explanation is that self-defeating behavior begins with *avoidance learning* (described earlier, in Chapter 9). **Avoidance learning** *occurs when making a particular response delays or prevents the onset of a painful or unpleasant stimulus.* Here's a quick review to refresh your memory:

> An animal is placed in a special cage. After a few minutes a light comes on, followed a moment later by a painful shock. Quickly, the animal escapes into a second chamber. After a few minutes, a light comes on in this chamber, and the shock is repeated.

Soon the animal learns to avoid pain by moving before the shock occurs. Once an animal learns to avoid the shock, it can be turned off altogether. A well-trained animal may avoid the non-existent shock indefinitely.

The same analysis can be applied to disordered human behavior. A behaviorist would say that *the powerful reward of immediate relief from anxiety keeps self-defeating avoidance behavior alive*. This view, known as the **anxiety reduction hypothesis,** seems to explain why the behavior patterns we have discussed often look very "stupid" to outside observers.

Cognitive Approach

The **cognitive view** *is that distorted thinking causes people to magnify ordinary threats and failures, leading to distress* (Foa et al., 1996). For example, Terrie, who is socially phobic, constantly has upsetting thoughts about being evaluated. One reason for this is that social phobics tend to be perfectionists. Like other social phobics, Terrie is excessively concerned about mistakes and she perceives criticism where there is none (Juster et al., 1996). In addition, she focuses too much attention on herself, which intensifies her anxiety in social situations (Woody, 1996). Even when they are successful, distorted thinking leads socially phobic persons to think they have failed (Alden & Wallace, 1995). In short, changing the thinking patterns

of anxious individuals can greatly lessen their fears (Poulton & Andrews, 1996).

There is probably a core of truth to each of the four psychological explanations. For this reason, understanding anxiety-based disorders may be aided by combining parts of all four perspectives. Each viewpoint also suggests a different approach to treatment. Because there are many possibilities, a full discussion of therapy is found later, in Chapter 19.

A Final Note—You're Okay, Really! It is your author's hope that you will not fall prey to the psychological equivalent of "medical student's disease" after reading this chapter. Medical students, it seems, have a tendency to notice in themselves the symptoms of each dreaded disease they study. As a psychology student you may have noticed what seem to be abnormal tendencies in your own behavior. If so, don't panic. In the majority of instances, this only shows that pathological behavior is an *exaggeration* of normal defenses and reactions, not that your behavior is abnormal.

A Look Ahead Two interesting topics conclude our discussion in this chapter. The upcoming Applications describes a classic experiment that asked the question, If a normal person were placed in a mental hospital, how would she or he be perceived by other patients and by the hospital staff? The answer is fascinating and instructive. After that, an Exploration discusses the validity of pleading "not guilty by reason of insanity" in the courtroom.

Learning Check	Critical Thinking

See if you can correctly answer the following questions about the anxiety disorders we have discussed.

1. Excessive anxiety over ordinary life stresses is characteristic of which of the following disorders?
   a. free-floating anxiety disorder **b.** agoraphobia **c.** hypochondriasis **d.** adjustment disorder

2. Panic disorder can occur with or without agoraphobia, but agoraphobia cannot occur alone, without the presence of a panic disorder. T or F?

3. Alice has a phobic fear of blood. The formal term for her fear is
   a. nyctophobia **b.** hematophobia **c.** pathophobia **d.** pyrophobia

4. A person who intensely fears eating, writing, or speaking in public suffers from

   _____ _____ .

5. "Checkers" and "cleaners" suffer from which disorder?
   a. acarophobia **b.** panic disorder with agoraphobia **c.** generalized anxiety disorder
   d. obsessive-compulsive disorder

6. The symptoms of acute stress disorders last less than one month; post-traumatic stress disorders last more than one month. T or F?

7. Which of the following is *not* a dissociative disorder?
   a. fugue **b.** amnesia **c.** conversion reaction **d.** multiple identity

8. Freud's original psychodynamic explanation of "neurosis" was based on the avoidance learning hypothesis. T or F?

9. The existential explanation of unhealthy anxiety is based on a conflict between subparts of the personality. T or F?

10. The anxiety reduction hypothesis is a _____ explanation of anxiety disorders.

    a. psychodynamic   **b.** humanistic   **c.** behavioristic   **d.** cognitive

11. Many of the physical complaints associated with anxiety disorders are closely related to activity of what part of the nervous system?

Answers:

Applications

Psychiatric Labeling—On Being Sane in Insane Places

Suppose someone were committed to a psychiatric hospital by accident. Would the staff notice? Would the person be able to get out?

David Rosenhan of Stanford University set out to answer these questions and another: How accurately do psychiatric hospitals distinguish between people who are psychotic and those who are healthy?

To find out, Rosenhan and several colleagues had themselves committed (Rosenhan, 1973). Entrance to mental hospitals was gained by faking only one symptom. Rosenhan and the others complained of hearing voices that said "empty," "hollow," and "thud." In 11 out of 12 tries, they were admitted with a diagnosis of "schizophrenia."

Pseudo-patients

After being admitted, these "pseudo-patients" dropped all pretense of mental illness. Yet, even though they acted completely normal, none of the researchers was ever recognized by hospital *staff* as a phony patient. Other patients were not so easily fooled. It was not unusual for a real patient to say to one of the researchers, "You're not crazy, you're checking up on the hospital!" or, "You're a journalist."

Rosenhan and the others spent from 1 to 7 weeks in hospitals before being discharged. The hospitals ranged from very modern and plush to ancient and shoddy. No matter how good the facilities or how good the hospital's reputation, Rosenhan found some disturbing conditions. Contact between staff and patients was very limited and sometimes marked by fear or hostility. It was found that attendants and staff only spent an average of 11 percent of their time out of the "cage," the glassed-in central compartment in the ward.

It was not unusual for the morning attendants to wake patients with a hostile call of: "Come on, you m____ f____s, out of bed!" When patients tried to talk with staff, they were often ignored or received strange replies. One pseudo-patient approached a psychiatrist and politely asked when he might get grounds privileges. The doctor's reply was, "Good morning, Dave. How are you today?"

Rosenhan found that therapy other than drugs was very limited. Daily contact of patients with psychiatrists, psychologists, or physicians averaged about 7 minutes. On the other hand, the researchers were given a total of 2,100 pills to swallow, an average of 7 pills a day per patient. (Only 2 of the 2,100 pills were actually taken, the rest being pocketed or flushed down the toilet.)

Non-persons Patients tended to be treated as non-persons. A nurse unbuttoned her uniform to adjust her bra in front of a room full of male patients. She was not being sexy; she just didn't consider the patients men. Patients would often be discussed by the staff while the patient was standing nearby. It was as if patients were invisible or pieces of furniture.

A situation that sums up Rosenhan's findings better than any other is his note-taking. Rosenhan began taking notes by carefully jotting things on a small piece of paper hidden in his hand. He learned quickly that hiding was totally unnecessary. He was soon walking around with a clipboard and note pads, recording observations and collecting data.

No one questioned this behavior. Note-taking was simply seen as a symptom of his "illness." As a matter of fact, Rosenhan found that anything he did was ignored. When a staff member manhandled a patient (as happened occasionally), Rosenhan would be right there—taking notes on the whole incident!

Psychiatric Labels

These observations clarify the failure of staff members to detect the fake patients. Because they were seen in the context of a mental ward, and because they had been *labeled* schizophrenic, anything the pseudo-patients did was seen as a symptom of their psychotic "illness."

To return to the original hypothetical question about talking your way out of an accidental commitment, it should be clear that it could be quite futile to say, "Look, this is all a mistake. I'm not crazy. You've got to let me out." The response might very well be, "Have you had these paranoid delusions for long?"

Many mental health professionals found Rosenhan's findings hard to believe. This led to a follow-up study, in which the staff of another hospital was warned that one or more pseudo-patients were going to try to gain admission over the next 3 months. Thus alerted, the staff at this hospital tried to identify fake incoming patients. Among 193 candidates, 41 were labeled fakes by at least one staff member, and 19 more were labeled "suspicious." This only served to confirm Rosenhan's original findings since he never sent any patients—fake or otherwise—to this hospital!

Stigma   It is important to note that all of the normal people who served as pseudo-patients in the original studies were discharged as schizophrenics (psychotics) "in remission" (temporarily free of symptoms). In other words, the label that prevented hospital staff from seeing the normality of the researchers stayed with them when they left. Such labels frequently stigmatize their bearers. Psychiatrist Karl Menninger (1964) once commented that:

> A label can blight the life of a person even after his recovery from mental illness. A young doctor I knew suffered for a time from some anxiety and indecision. He consulted a psychiatrist and soon recovered. Unfortunately, a "tentative" diagnosis of schizophrenia got abroad—I don't know how—and the young doctor's professional career was seriously impaired. He was injured, not by mental illness but by a word.

If you doubt that psychiatric labels can be stigmatizing, try to make a list of politicians you know of who have publicly revealed that they have suffered from mental illness. Your list is likely to be *very* short.

Implications   Rosenhan's findings carry a cautionary message for professionals and non-professionals alike: Labels can be dangerous. As Stoller (1967) said, "When a person is labeled—neurotic, psychotic, executive, teacher, salesman, psychologist—either by himself or by others, he restricts his behavior to the role and even may rely upon the role for security."

The terms presented in this chapter and the next can, and do, aid communication about human problems. But if used carelessly, they may do great damage. Everyone has felt or acted "crazy" during brief periods of stress or high emotion. A person whose emotional problems extend over a longer period of time is different from you or me only in the severity of his or her difficulty.

It is therefore more productive to label problems than to label people. Think of the difference in impact between saying, "He is experiencing a serious emotional disorder" and saying, "He is a psychotic." Which statement would you choose to have said about yourself?

Even such careful usage of labels can cause difficulties. Some people are relieved to learn that their problem has a name and that it is shared by others. Others, however, may be upset to learn that they are considered "mentally ill." The stigma that still clings to this term discourages some people from seeking needed professional help (McReynolds, 1989).

As a final point, it is important to realize that even severely disturbed persons appreciate being treated normally. Rosenhan's research makes it clear that people are not helped by being thrust into the patient role. One former patient's comments clarify this last point:

> After I got back from the hospital, my friends tried to *act* like nothing had changed. But I could tell they weren't being honest. For instance, a friend invited me to dinner and everything went fine until I dropped my fork. Both my friend and his wife jumped up and stared at me like they thought I might explode. I was quite embarrassed.

Remember, no matter how disturbed a person may be, she or he continues to merit respect and compassion.

Learning Check	Critical Thinking

1. In the majority of their attempts, Rosenhan's pseudo-patients were admitted to mental hospitals after complaining only that they were hearing voices. T or F?

2. Although they were often detected by professional staff members, the normality of the pseudo-patients was never recognized by other patients. T or F?

3. During a short hospital stay, one pseudo-patient was denied psychiatric drugs even though he requested them. T or F?

4. Rosenhan found that almost anything pseudo-patients said or did was interpreted as a symptom of their "illness." T or F?

5. When they were alerted that a number of pseudo-patients might try to gain entry, hospital staff members were able to more accurately detect the fakes. T or F?

6. The powerful impact of psychiatric labels is related to what perceptual principle (discussed in Chapter 7)?

Answers:

1. T   2. F   3. F   4. T   5. F   6. perceptual expectancy (set)

Exploration

Psychology and the Law—The "Twinkie Defense"

Mark David Chapman claimed that devils forced him to kill former Beatle John Lennon. In court, his lawyer asserted that Chapman was "not guilty by reason of insanity." However, at mid-trial Chapman decided to plead guilty to second-degree murder. His reason? He said that God had visited him in his cell and told him to confess.

Chapman's case was one of thousands each year that mingle law, psychiatry, psychology, and public opinion. For over 150 years, the *insanity defense* has bedeviled the courts and raised difficult legal, moral, and psychological questions.

What exactly is the insanity defense?

The **insanity defense** *is a plea that a person was incapable of knowing right from wrong at the time of a crime.*

Insanity

The insanity defense entered Western law as the **M'Naghten rule,** *a standard in English common law for judging sanity and legal responsibility.* In 1843 the English House of Lords ruled on the case of Daniel M'Naghten, a "madman" who attempted to kill a member of Parliament, but murdered another man instead. The court held that a defendant—in this case M'Naghten—must understand the wrongfulness of his or her actions to be held responsible for them. Persons suffering from "mental disease or other defects" that prevent them from knowing right from wrong are "insane." In the U.S. legal system, the taking of life by an insane person is not murder.

Defendants may also claim they knew their act was wrong, but they had an **irresistible impulse** (*uncontrollable urge*) to act. An example is the person who finds his or her spouse in a stranger's arms and kills in a jealous rage. A related defense claims **diminished capacity** (*impaired mental competence*) to control actions or to know right from wrong. A person who commits a crime while under the influence of drugs might make this plea.

The Twinkie Defense The problems posed by the insanity defense are vividly shown by three legal cases. In Oakland, California, a jury declared Darlin June Cromer sane in the racial killing of a 5-year-old boy. This was the verdict, despite the fact that one psychiatrist testified that Cromer was "the most psychotic person" he'd ever seen. Cromer was sentenced to life in prison.

On the opposite side of the Bay, Dan White admitted killing San Francisco Mayor George Moscone and Supervisor Harvey Milk. However, White's lawyer convinced the jury that White acted with diminished capacity. The defense claimed, among other things, that White was deranged from eating too much "junk food"—an argument that became known as the "Twinkie Defense." (For those unschooled in junk food, a Twinkie is a small sponge cake with a sugary cream filling.)

Testimony in the trial established that White planned the murders beforehand and carefully avoided security guards to reach his victims. White received a 7-year jail sentence. (He was paroled 3 years later.) The verdict so outraged many citizens that a new law in California now bans claims of "diminished capacity." In yet another case, "Vampire Killer" Richard Chase was convicted of killing six people and drinking the blood of some of his victims. Chase was declared sane.

These cases point to the inconsistencies of a system that allows people who appear sane to be judged insane, and apparently insane people to be judged sane.

How is sanity determined?

Expert Testimony The most sensational criminal trials involving insanity have a typical pattern: Defense psychiatrists interview the defendant and then testify that he or she was insane at the time of the crime; prosecution psychiatrists examine the defendant and testify to his or her sanity. After these expert witnesses contradict one another's testimony, it's up to the jury to decide who is right.

But more often, this "battle of the experts" never takes place. In almost all cases, prosecutors, defense attorneys, medical experts, and judges agree *before* trial that the defendant is mentally ill. Thus, if a person really is psychotic, in most cases experts agree fairly readily (Janofsky et al., 1996).

Opinion, Please The preceding brief discussion raises several interesting questions.

1. The states of Montana, Idaho, and Utah have banned the insanity plea, but in most states it remains intact. Several other states now allow only a "guilty, but insane" plea. (Jeffrey Dahmer pleaded "guilty, but insane.") In your opinion, should questions of sanity be considered in criminal trials? Should the insanity defense be allowed?

Before you answer, you should know that pleas of insanity are actually relatively rare, being used in only about 1 out of every 100 court cases. In only about 1 out of 500 of these cases does the insanity defense succeed. Nationally, this amounts to about 150 cases a year in the United States (Silver et al., 1994).

More important, a verdict of innocence by reason of insanity does not set a person free. In most states it requires automatic commitment to a mental hospital. Thereafter, the law places the burden of proof on patients. To be released, they must show that they are no longer a danger to themselves or others. Moreover, in most cases, persons declared "insane" are hospitalized longer than they would have been imprisoned for a criminal conviction. The average hospital stay is about 3 years (Silver et al., 1994). Nevertheless, in some instances, the public may still rightly ask if justice has been served.

2. Should the courts accept pleas of diminished capacity? Before you answer this question, think about the

"guilt" of a severely retarded person or someone with a brain tumor who commits a crime.

3. In your opinion, who should decide if a person should be committed? Should it be a judge? A jury? A psychiatrist? A psychologist? Who should decide when an "insane" person can be released? Should a person have the right to refuse treatment? What if the person committed a crime?

Before answering, it may be useful to know that psychiatric predictions of violent behavior are largely inaccurate. Follow-ups of arrests and mental hospital records show that from two thirds to nine tenths of the time, experts are *wrong* in forecasting violence. At present, there is no way to accurately predict which individuals are likely to be dangerous to themselves or to others (Teplin, Abram, & McClelland, 1994).

As you can see, there are no easy answers to the preceding questions. Nevertheless, when the issues are "madness," personal freedom, criminal responsibility, and justice, everyone has an opinion. What's yours?

Learning Check

1. Daniel M'Naghten was a lawyer who defended a member of the British House of Lords who was accused of murder, but who pleaded insanity. T or F?

2. In a court of law, the insanity defense is based on the premise that persons who are mentally defective cannot be held fully responsible for their actions. T or F?

3. A person who committed a crime while suffering from a mind-altering reaction to a prescription medicine might have some success in claiming innocence due to diminished capacity. T or F?

4. In every state of the United States, insanity can be used as a legal defense as long as expert witnesses are willing to testify that the defendant was insane at the time of the crime. T or F?

5. Psychiatric predictions of future violence are correct only in about one tenth to one third of all forecasts. T or F?

Critical Thinking

6. Many states began to restrict use of the insanity defense after John Hinkley, Jr., who tried to murder President Ronald Reagan, was acquitted by reason of insanity. What does this trend reveal about insanity?

Answers:

1. F 2. T 3. T 4. F 5. T 6. It emphasizes again that insanity is a legal concept, not a psychiatric diagnosis. Laws reflect community standards. When those standards change, lawmakers may seek to alter definitions of legal responsibility.

Chapter Summary

How is normality defined, and what are the major psychological disorders?

◆ Formal definitions of abnormality usually take into account all or most of the following: *subjective discomfort*, *statistical definitions* (or *norms*), *social non-conformity*, and the *cultural* or *situational context* of behavior.

◆ Problems exist with each definition in that all are *relative* standards.

◆ A key element in judgments of disorder is that a person's behavior must be *maladaptive*. In practice, judging normality is a social act influenced by many factors.

◆ Major categories of **psychopathology** are described in the *Diagnostic and Statistical Manual of Mental Disorders* (*DSM-IV*).

◆ Major problems include *psychotic disorders, organic mental disorders, substance related disorders, mood disorders, anxiety disorders, somatoform disorders, dissociative disorders, personality disorders,* and *sexual disorders.*

◆ Traditionally, the term *neurosis* has been used to describe milder, anxiety related disorders. However, the term is fading from use.

◆ **Insanity** is a legal term defining whether a person may be held responsible for his or her actions. Sanity is determined in court by **expert witnesses.**

What is a personality disorder?

◆ **Personality disorders** are deeply ingrained maladaptive personality patterns.

◆ A frequently misunderstood personality disorder is **antisocial personality.** Antisocial persons seem to lack a *conscience.* They are emotionally unresponsive, manipulative, and have shallow personal relationships.

What are the most common sexual disorders?

◆ Definitions of **sexual deviance** are highly subjective. Many "sexually deviant" behaviors are acceptable in private or in some cultures.

◆ Deviations that often cause difficulty are called **paraphilias.** The paraphilias include: **pedophilia, fetishism, voyeurism, exhibitionism, transvestic fetishism, sexual sadism, sexual masochism,** and **frotteurism.**

◆ Exhibitionists are rarely dangerous and can best be characterized as sexually inhibited and immature.

◆ The effects of **child molestation** vary greatly, depending on the severity of the molestation and the child's relationship to the molester.

◆ **Rape** is primarily a violent crime of aggression.

What problems result when a person suffers high levels of anxiety?

◆ Anxiety, dissociative, and somatoform disorders are characterized by *high levels of anxiety*, *rigid defense mechanisms*, and *self-defeating behavior patterns.*

◆ The term *nervous breakdown* has no formal meaning. However, "emotional breakdowns" do correspond somewhat to **adjustment disorders.**

◆ **Anxiety disorders,** characterized by excessive anxiety or anxiety-based behaviors, include **generalized anxiety disorder** (chronic anxiety and worry), **panic disorder** with or without agoraphobia (anxiety attacks, panic, free-floating anxiety), **agoraphobia** (fear of public places or leaving the home), **specific phobias** (irrational fear of specific objects or situations), **social phobia** (fear of various social situations), **obsessive-compulsive disorders** (obsessions and compulsions), and **post-traumatic stress disorder** or **acute stress disorder** (emotional disturbances triggered by severe stress).

◆ **Dissociative disorders** may take the form of **dissociative amnesia** (loss of memory and personal identity), **dissociative fugue** (flight from familiar surroundings), or **dissociative identity disorder**.

◆ **Somatoform disorders** center on physical complaints that mimic disease or disability. In **hypochondriasis,** persons think that they have specific diseases. In a **somatization disorder,** the person has numerous physical complaints and repeatedly seeks medical treatment, but no organic problems can be found. **Somatoform pain** refers to discomfort for which there is no identifiable physical cause. In **conversion disorders,** actual symptoms of disease or disability develop but their origins are psychological.

How do psychologists explain anxiety-based disorders?

◆ The **psychodynamic** approach emphasizes unconscious conflicts as the cause of disabling anxiety.

◆ The **humanistic** approach emphasizes the effects of a *faulty self-image.* The related **existential** approach stresses a loss of meaning in one's life.

◆ The **behavioral** approach emphasizes the effects of previous learning, particularly *avoidance learning.*

◆ **Cognitive** theories of anxiety focus on the effects of distortions in thinking, judgment, and attention.

Is psychiatric labeling damaging?

◆ David Rosenhan's use of *pseudo-patients* to study mental hospitals suggests that problems in diagnosis exist and that *psychiatric labeling* can affect our perceptions of others' behavior.

What role does the concept of insanity play in criminal trials?

◆ In Western law, the **insanity defense** evolved from the **M'Naghten rule.** Insanity is closely related to claims of **diminished capacity** or claims that a person had an **irresistible impulse.** Inconsistencies in the application of the insanity defense have fueled debate about its validity.

18

Major Mental Disorders

Preview

Psychosis—"Losing It"

The excerpts that follow are from a letter written by a man suffering a psychosis. They illustrate some of the severe disturbances in thinking, behavior, speech, and emotions that occur in psychosis.

> They changed the flag of the United States of America once by adding Alaska as a State to the Union and thus paving the way for Hawaii to become a state in 1959. That of course, gives me the *"capacity of the flag itself"* and therefore like any Congressional Medal of Honor winner, gives me the *"capacity of the President of the United States of America . . . ."*
>
> Some "small time" politicians got together on me and sand-bagged me brainwashed me and bugged me with a *"short-wave* Radio grid center, with an ultra-violet cross grid" called a "bug." Its sole purpose is to use a person's senses against himself so as to perjure and distort him to no end of humiliation . . . they vibrate your nerves physically with it and never ceases. Once on the grounds they started frequencing my time all the more, vibrating the back of my neck, first flicking it to the front of my face, like a "whip" or a cat of 9 tails. (Suinn, 1975)

Psychosis reflects a loss of contact with reality. The following comments, made by several psychotic patients, illustrate what is meant by a "split" from reality (Torrey, 1988).

> Everything is in bits. You put the picture up bit by bit into your head. It's like a photograph that's torn in bits and put together again. If you move it's frightening.
>
> I felt I had the power to determine the weather, which responded to my inner moods, and even to control the movement of the sun.
>
> I like talking to a person but not in audible words. I try to force my thoughts into someone. I concentrate on how they move.
>
> Last week I was with a girl and suddenly she seemed to get bigger and bigger, like a monster coming nearer and nearer.

What is psychosis really like? What causes it? What can be done about it? For answers to these and related questions, read on.

Psychosis—Life in the Shadow of Madness

A person who is psychotic undergoes striking changes in thinking, behavior, and emotion. The following descriptions identify some of the major features of psychoses (psycho*sis*, singular; psycho*ses*, plural).

Delusional Thinking   Delusions *are false beliefs held against all contrary evidence.* Disturbed persons insist their delusions are true, even when the facts contradict them. For example, a recent case report tells of a 43-year-old schizophrenic man who was convinced he was pregnant (Mansouri & Adityanjee, 1995).

Are there different types of delusions?

Some common types of delusions are: (1) *depressive* delusions, in which people feel that they have committed horrible crimes or sinful deeds; (2) *somatic* delusions, such as belief that one's body is "rotting away" or that it is emitting foul odors; (3) delusions of *grandeur,* in which individuals think they are extremely important persons; (4) delusions of *influence,* in which people feel they are being controlled or influenced by others or by unseen forces; (5) delusions of *persecution,* in which people feel that others are "out to get them"; and (6) delusions of *reference,* in which unrelated events are given personal significance (as when it is assumed that a newspaper article or a television program is giving a special personal message to the person) (DSM-IV, 1994).

   If you reread the first quote of the Chapter Preview, you will find evidence of delusions of grandeur, influence, and persecution.

Hallucinations and Sensations   Hallucinations *are imaginary sensations, such as seeing, hearing, or smelling things that don't exist in the real world.* The most common psychotic hallucination is hearing voices. The person may answer these voices, which are frequently insulting (DSM-IV, 1994). Sometimes hallucinated voices command patients to hurt themselves. Unfortunately, many obey (Kasper, Rogers, & Adams, 1996).

   More rarely, psychotic individuals may feel "insects crawling under their skin," taste "poisons" in their food, or smell "gas" their "enemies" are using to "get" them. It is easy to understand why hallucinations are highly disruptive. Images and feelings conjured up by the psychotic person's own mind can seem as "real" and vivid as external stimuli (Benwall, 1990).

   Along with hallucinations, sensory changes in psychosis may bring about extreme sensitivity to heat, cold, pain, or touch. Anesthesia, a loss of normal sensitivity, is also possible.

Disturbed Emotions   Emotions may swing violently between the extremes of elation and depression, or the psychotic person may be hyper-emotional, depressed, emotionally "flat," or apathetic. In instances of **flat affect**, *there are almost no signs of emotion.* Typically, the person's face is frozen in a blank expression. Behind their "frozen masks," however, psychotic persons continue to feel emotions as strongly as ever (Sison et al., 1996).

Disturbed Communication   An almost universal symptom of psychosis is difficulty in communicating with others. Psychotic speech tends to be garbled and chaotic. Sometimes it sounds like a "word salad," as the following example illustrates.

The lion will have to change from dogs into cats until I can meet my father and mother and we dispart from rats . . . . It's all over for a squab true tray and there ain't no squabs, there ain't no men, there ain't no music, there ain't nothing besides my mother and my father who stand alone upon the Island of Capri where is no ice. Well it's my suitcase sir. (Rodgers, 1982)

Personality Disintegration Major disturbances such as those just described—as well as added problems in thought, memory, and attention—bring about *personality disintegration* and a break with reality. **Personality disintegration** *refers to a loss of coordination among thoughts, actions, and emotions.* The result is almost always serious impairment in a person's work, social relations, and self-care.

When psychotic disturbances and a fragmented personality are evident for weeks or months (often including a period of deterioration, an active phase, and a residual phase), the person has suffered a psychosis (DSM-IV, 1994).

How could a person function with such problems?

Actually, the preceding description is somewhat exaggerated. It is rare to find all these symptoms occurring at once. As a matter of fact, you would probably find a trip to a psychiatric ward disappointing if you expected to see flamboyant, dramatic, or bizarre behavior. Extremely psychotic behavior typically occurs in brief *episodes*. The symptoms of psychosis come and go. Much of the time they are quite subtle.

Does psychosis occur without warning?

No. Usually there are signs of impending trouble. Symp-

toms such as insomnia, emotional changes, or feeling "high" signal a coming crisis for most psychotic patients (Brier & Strauss, 1983). (See Table 18–1 ■.) In fact, most patients are aware of their symptoms and try to fight off the coming psychotic break. An exception to this observation is a pattern called a **brief reactive psychosis.** In this case, *psychotic symptoms typically appear after an extremely stressful event,* such as horrifying military combat or the murder of a loved one. The onset of a brief reactive psychosis tends to be sudden, with symptoms rarely lasting more than a month (Larson, 1990).

Even after a psychotic break, people are not totally unresponsive to their surroundings. In one interesting experiment, psychotic patients were interviewed in two ways. Some were told that the purpose of the interview was to determine if they were "ready for discharge." In this group, patients who were known to like the hospital acted very bizarre during the interviews. A second group was told that the interview was to decide which patients should be given "open ward" privileges. In this case, disturbed patients suddenly became amazingly free of symptoms (Braginsky & Braginsky, 1967). This experiment shows that some psychotic symptoms can be thought of as a primitive form of communication. By their actions, many patients are saying, "I need help," or, "I can't handle it any more."

Are there different types of psychosis?

An **organic psychosis** *is based on known brain pathology, such as disease, a gunshot wound, an accidental injury, or other physical causes.* In contrast, a **functional psychosis** *is based on unknown causes or psychological factors.*

As we will see later, functional psychoses may also involve physical changes in the brain. In a sense, then, all psychoses are partly organic. However, the term organic psychosis is usually reserved for disorders involving clear-cut brain injuries or diseases. Some examples follow.

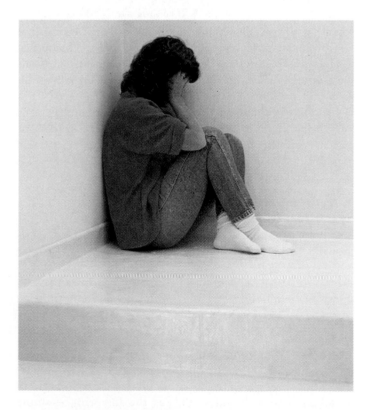

A scene in a state mental hospital.

Table 18–1 ■	Common Warning Signs of Psychosis and Major Mood Disorders

- Expresses bizarre thoughts or beliefs that defy reality
- Has withdrawn from family members and other relationships
- Hears unreal voices, sees things others don't
- Is extremely sad, persistently despondent, or suicidal
- Is excessively energetic, has little need for sleep
- Loses appetite, sleeps excessively, has no energy
- Exhibits extreme mood swings
- Believes someone is trying to harm her or him
- Has engaged in anti-social, destructive, or self-destructive behavior

Sources: Harvey et al., 1996; Sheehy & Cournos, 1992.

Organic Psychosis

Psychotic disorders are sometimes directly related to diseases of the brain. One example is **general paresis** (pah-REE-sis), *which occurs when syphilis attacks brain cells.* In advanced cases of untreated syphilis a patient's behavior may become disorganized and uninhibited. This can lead to shocking profanity and obscene behavior—the "dirty old man" syndrome.

A source of organic psychosis that gives special cause for alarm is poisoning by lead and mercury (Fig. 18–1 ◆). Although relatively rare, such poisoning can damage the brain and cause hallucinations, delusions, and a loss of emotional control. A particularly dangerous situation is found in many old buildings, which contain leaded paints. Children who eat this paint may become psychotic or retarded (Dyer, 1993). Leaded paints also release powdered lead into the air. Children may breathe the powder or eat it after handling contaminated toys. Other sources of lead are soldered water pipes, old lead-lined drinking fountains, lead-glazed pottery, and lead from automobile exhaust. On a much larger scale, "poisoning" of another type, in the form of drug abuse, can also produce psychosis (DSM-IV, 1994).

The most common organic problem is **senile dementia** (duh-MEN-sha), *a serious mental impairment in old age caused by deterioration of the brain.* In senile dementia, we see major disturbances in memory, reasoning, judgment, impulse control, and personality. This combination usually leaves the person confused, suspicious, apathetic, or withdrawn (Larson, 1990). The most common cause of senile dementia is *Alzheimer's disease* (described in our first highlight). Other common causes are circulatory problems, repeated strokes, or general shrinkage and atrophy of the brain.

Figure 18–1 ◆ The Mad Hatter, from Lewis Carroll's *Alice in Wonderland.* History provides numerous examples of psychosis caused by toxic chemicals. Carroll's Mad Hatter character is modeled after an occupational disease of the 18th and 19th centuries. In that era, hatmakers were heavily exposed to mercury used in the preparation of felt. Consequently, many suffered brain damage and became psychotic, or "mad" (Kety, 1979).

A Closer Look

Alzheimer's Disease

Alzheimer's disease (ALLS-hi-merz) is one of the most fearsome problems of aging, affecting about 5 to 10 percent of all people over age 65. **Alzheimer's disease** *is an age-related disorder characterized by impaired memory, confusion, and a progressive loss of mental abilities.*

Alzheimer's victims at first have difficulty remembering recent events. Then they slowly become more disoriented, suspicious, and confused. In time they lose the ability to work, cook, drive, or use tools. As their condition worsens, victims can no longer read, write, and calculate. Eventually they are mute, bedridden, and unable to walk, sit up, or smile (Larson, 1990).

Former U.S. President Ronald Reagan was diagnosed with Alzheimer's disease in 1995. Like many Alzheimer's victims, Reagan slipped into a slow mental decline that severely restricted his activities.

Researchers suspect that Alzheimer's disease is caused by unusual webs and tangles in brain cells leading to and from the hippocampus (Nagy et al., 1996). (This area, you may recall, is important for learning and memory.) Changes also take place in an area called the nucleus basalis and in chemicals that carry messages within the brain. In roughly 20 percent of all cases of Alzheimer's disease the cause is genetic. Hereditary Alzheimer's disease runs in families and strikes its victims early, between the ages of 45 and 55 (Murrell et al., 1991).

By the year 2000, 1 out of every 10 adults over age 65 will be a victim of Alzheimer's disease. Although the disease tends to progress slowly, it is ultimately fatal.

Yet, there is no established treatment. Understandably, efforts to find a cure for Alzheimer's disease are expanding. For some of us, such efforts may be a race against time.

Three major types of functional psychosis are *delusional disorders*, *schizophrenia*, and *psychotic mood disorders*. Information on each is provided in the following sections. (Remember, too, that a general category called *psychotic disorders not otherwise specified* also exists.)

Delusional Disorders— An Enemy behind Every Tree

People with delusional disorders usually do not suffer from hallucinations, emotional excesses, or personality disintegration. Even so, their break with reality is unmistakable. The main feature of **delusional disorders** *is the presence of deeply held false beliefs*. The content of such delusions may involve grandiosity, jealousy, persecution, bodily complaints, or romantic attraction (Table 18–2 ■). Although they are false, these delusions concern experiences that could conceivably occur in real life (Manschreck, 1996).

The most common delusional disorder, often called **paranoid psychosis,** *centers on delusions of persecution*. Many self-styled reformers, crank letter writers, "communist hunters," "UFO abductees," and the like, suffer paranoid delusions. Paranoid individuals often believe that they are being cheated, spied on, followed, poisoned, harassed, or plotted against. Usually they are intensely suspicious, believing they must be on guard at all times.

The evidence such people find to support their beliefs is usually unconvincing to others. Every detail of the paranoid person's existence is woven into a private version of "what's really going on." Buzzing during a telephone conversation

Table 18–2 ■ Delusional Disorders
Erotomanic type   *Marked by erotic delusions that one is loved by another, especially by someone famous or of higher status.*
Grandiose type   *Delusion that one has some great, unrecognized talent, knowledge, or insight or a special relationship with an important person or with God, or that one is a famous person (who, if alive, is regarded as an imposter).*
Jealous type   *An all-consuming, unfounded belief that one's spouse or lover is unfaithful.*
Persecutory type   *Delusion that one is being conspired against, cheated, spied on, followed, poisoned, maligned, or harassed.*
Somatic type   *Belief that one's body is diseased or rotting, or infested with insects or parasites, or that parts of the body are misshapen or defective.*
DSM-IV, 1994.

may be interpreted as "someone listening"; a stranger who comes to the door asking for directions may be seen as "really trying to get information"; and so forth.

Persons suffering paranoid delusions are rarely treated. It is almost impossible for them to accept that they need help. Anyone who suggests that they have a problem simply becomes part of the "conspiracy" to "persecute" them.

Paranoid persons frequently lead lonely, isolated, and humorless lives dominated by constant suspicion and hostility. While they are not necessarily dangerous to others, they can be. A person who believes that "the Mafia" is slowly closing in on him may be moved to violence by his irrational fears. If a stranger came to the door with his hand in his coat pocket, he could become the target of a paranoid attempt at "self-defense."

Because the topics we will consider next involve several new terms and ideas, let's stop for a quick Learning Check before proceeding.

Learning Check	Critical Thinking
1. A person who wrongly believes that his or her body is "rotting away" is suffering from **a.** depressive delusions **b.** somatic delusions **c.** delusions of grandeur **d.** delusions of persecution	**7.** The following quotation is an example of which symptom of psychosis? "I felt I had the power to determine the weather, which responded to my inner moods, and even to control the movement of the sun."
2. Persons suffering from psychoses are almost totally unresponsive to their surroundings. T or F?	
3. A psychosis caused by lead poisoning would be termed a functional disorder. T or F?	
4. Hallucinations and personality disintegration are the principal features of paranoid psychosis. T or F?	
5. In *flat affect*, a sensory experience—such as hearing voices—occurs in the absence of a stimulus. T or F?	**Answers:**
6. Alzheimer's disease is thought to be caused by lead poisoning of the hippocampus. T or F?	7. Delusions of grandeur. 1. b 2. F 3. F 4. F 5. F 6. F

Schizophrenia—Shattered Reality

Schizophrenia (SKIT-soh-FREE-nee-uh) *is a type of psychosis characterized by delusions, hallucinations, apathy, and a "split" between thought and emotion.* One person in 100 will become schizophrenic and roughly half of all the people admitted to mental hospitals are schizophrenic. Most are young adults, but schizophrenia can occur at any age.

In schizophrenia, emotions may become blunted or very inappropriate. For example, a schizophrenic person might smile or giggle when told his mother just died, or might describe her death with no visible emotion. In addition, schizophrenia is marked by all of the following: withdrawal from contact with others; a loss of interest in external activities; a breakdown of personal habits; an inability to deal with daily events; and the delusions, hallucinations, and thought abnormalities found in other types of psychosis.

Remember the schizophrenic person who said, "Everything is in bits. . . . It's like a photograph that's torn in bits and put together again"? Many schizophrenic symptoms appear to arise from impaired *selective attention* (Hirt & Pithers, 1991; Lenzenweger et al., 1991; Ward et al., 1991). In other words, it is hard for schizophrenics to focus on one item of information at a time. This may be why they are overwhelmed by a jumble of thoughts, sensations, images, and feelings.

Schizophrenic delusions can be bizarre. They often include the idea that the person's thoughts and actions are being controlled, that his or her thoughts are being broadcast so others can hear them, that thoughts have been "inserted" into the person's mind, or that thoughts have been removed.

Does a schizophrenic person have two personalities?

Schizophrenia does not refer to having more than one personality. Recall from the previous chapter that multiple identity is a non-psychotic, dissociative disorder. The next highlight clarifies the differences between schizophrenia and other problems that are easily confused with it.

Critical Thinking

"Schizophrenic" Confusion

"David was so warm and friendly yesterday, but today he's as cold as ice. He's so schizophrenic sometimes that I don't know how to react." Such statements illustrate how often the term *schizophrenic* is misused. As you know, even a person who displays two or more personalities (a dissociative disorder) is not "schizo-

phrenic." Neither, of course, is a person like David, whose behavior is merely inconsistent.

On a more technical level, schizophrenia is often confused with a personality disorder that resembles it somewhat. Recall from Chapter 17 that personality disorders are maladaptive personality patterns. One such pattern is the **schizotypal personality,** *a non-psychotic disorder involving withdrawal, social isolation, and odd behavior—but no break with reality.* Starting in adolescence, affected persons slowly become isolated, emotionally withdrawn, listless, and apathetic. Many are considered "odd," "shiftless," or eccentric. Their behavior at times may be markedly peculiar (collecting garbage, eating cigarette butts, talking to themselves, and so forth).

Problems of this type do resemble some aspects of schizophrenia. But the schizotypal personality, like other personality disorders, does not involve a psychotic "break with reality." Many individuals with a schizotypal personality simply live colorless and isolated lives on the fringes of society as vagrants, eccentrics, derelicts, or prostitutes.

Is there more than one type of schizophrenia?

Schizophrenia may be a group of related disturbances. For now, we can identify four major subtypes of schizophrenia (Table 18–3 ■).

Disorganized Schizophrenia The disorder known as *disorganized schizophrenia* (sometimes called hebephrenic schizophrenia) comes close to matching the stereotyped images of "madness" seen in movies and on television. In disorganized schizophrenia, personality disintegration is almost complete: Emotions, speech, and behavior are all highly disorganized. The result is silliness, laughter, and

Table 18–3   Types of Schizophrenia

Catatonic type   *Schizophrenia marked by stupor, rigidity, unresponsiveness, posturing, mutism, and, sometimes, agitated, purposeless behavior.*
Disorganized type   *Schizophrenia marked by incoherence, grossly disorganized behavior, bizarre thinking, and flat or grossly inappropriate emotions.*
Paranoid type   *Schizophrenia marked by a preoccupation with delusions or by frequent auditory hallucinations related to a single theme, especially grandeur or persecution.*
Undifferentiated type   *Schizophrenia in which there are prominent psychotic symptoms, but none of the specific features of catatonic, disorganized, or paranoid types.*

DSM-IV, 1994.

In disorganized schizophrenia, behavior is marked by silliness, laughter, and bizarre or obscene behavior.

bizarre or obscene behavior, as shown by this intake interview of a patient:

Dr.: I am Dr. _____ . I would like to know something more about you.
Patient: You have a nasty mind. Lord! Lord! Cat's in a cradle.
Dr.: Tell me, how do you feel?
Patient: London's bell is a long, long dock. Hee! Hee! (Giggles uncontrollably.)
Dr.: Do you know where you are now?
Patient: D____n! S____t on you all who rip into my internals! The grudgerometer will take care of you all! (Shouting) I am the Queen, see my magic, I shall turn you all into smidgelings forever!
Dr.: Your husband is concerned about you. Do you know his name?
Patient: (Stands, walks to and faces the wall) Who am I, who are we, who are you, who are they, (turns) I . . . I . . . I . . . I! (Makes grotesque faces.)
    Edna was placed in the women's ward where she proceeded to masturbate. Occasionally, she would scream or shout obscenities. At other times she giggled to herself. She was known to attack other patients. She began to complain that her uterus was attached to a "pipeline to the Kremlin" and that she was being "infernally invaded" by Communism. (Suinn, 1975)

Disorganized schizophrenia typically develops in early adolescence or young adulthood. It is often preceded by serious personality disorganization in earlier years. Chances of improvement are limited, and social impairment is usually extreme (DSM-IV, 1994).

Catatonic Schizophrenia   The catatonic person seems to be in a state of total panic. This brings about a stuporous condition in which odd positions may be held for hours or even days. Sometimes, a condition called *waxy flexibility* occurs. While in this state, the catatonic person can be arranged into any position, like a mannequin. These periods of immobility may be similar to the tendency to "freeze" at times of great emergency or panic. Catatonic individuals appear to be struggling desperately to control their inner turmoil. One sign of this is the fact that stupor may occasionally give way to agitated outbursts or violent behavior. The following excerpt describes a **catatonic episode** (*a period of extreme stupor, immobility, and unresponsiveness*).

> Manuel appeared to be physically healthy upon examination. Yet he did not regain his awareness of his surroundings. He remained motionless, speechless, and seemingly unconscious. One evening an aide turned him on his side to straighten out the sheet, was called away to tend another patient, and forgot to return. Manuel was found the next morning, still on his side, his arm tucked under his body, as he had been left the night before. His arm was turning blue from lack of circulation but he seemed to be experiencing no discomfort. Further examination confirmed that he was in a state of waxy flexibility. (Suinn, 1975)

Notice that Manuel did not speak. *Mutism*, along with a marked decrease in responsiveness to the environment, makes the catatonic patient difficult to "reach." Fortunately, this bizarre form of schizophrenia has become rare in Europe and North America (DSM-IV, 1994).

Paranoid Schizophrenia   Paranoid schizophrenia is the most common schizophrenic disorder. *Paranoid schizophrenia*, like a paranoid delusional disorder, centers around delusions of grandeur and persecution. However, paranoid schizophrenics also hallucinate and their delusions are more bizarre and unconvincing than those seen in a delusional disorder.

Thinking that their minds are being controlled by God, the government, or "cosmic rays from space," or that someone is trying to poison them, paranoid schizophrenics may feel forced into violence to "protect" themselves. An example is James Huberty, who brutally murdered 21 people at a McDonald's restaurant in San Ysidro, California. Some observers believe that Huberty was a paranoid schizophrenic who felt persecuted and cheated by life. Shortly before he announced to his wife that he was "going hunting humans," Huberty had been hearing hallucinated voices.

Undifferentiated Schizophrenia   The three types of schizophrenia just described occur most often in textbooks. In reality, patients may shift from one pattern to another at different times (Heinrichs, 1993). Many patients, therefore, are simply classified as suffering from *undifferentiated schizophrenia*.

The diagnosis of schizophrenia is fairly subjective and

open to error. For example, when 72 "schizophrenic" patients in a state hospital were re-evaluated, only 45 were confirmed to be schizophrenic (Wilson, 1989). All things considered, however, there is no doubt that schizophrenia is real or that its treatment is a major challenge.

The Causes of Schizophrenia

Former British Prime Minister Winston Churchill once described a question that perplexed him as "a riddle wrapped in a mystery inside an enigma." The same words might be used to describe the causes of schizophrenia, the most common and devastating of the psychoses.

What do we know about the causes of schizophrenia?

Environment   An increased risk of developing schizophrenia may begin at birth or even before. Women who are exposed to the influenza (flu) virus during the middle of pregnancy have children who run a higher risk for becoming schizophrenic. Malnutrition during pregnancy and complications at the time of birth can have a similar impact. Possibly, such events disturb early brain development, leaving people more vulnerable to psychosis (Cannon et al., 1993; Murray et al., 1992; Pilowski et al., 1993; Takei et al., 1994; "Twins with," 1995).

Early **psychological trauma** (*a psychological injury or shock*) may also contribute to the risk of becoming schizophrenic. Often, the victims of schizophrenia were exposed to violence, sexual abuse, death, divorce, separation, or other stresses in childhood (Mirsky & Duncan, 1986). An unanswered question is why early trauma leaves some individuals emotionally crippled and others not. The same question arises in adulthood, where severely disturbed and mildly disturbed individuals appear to have experienced similar levels of stress prior to the onset of their illness (Harder et al., 1989).

Living in a troubled family is another risk factor in schizophrenia. In a **disturbed family environment**, *stressful relationships, communication patterns, and negative emotions prevail.* For example, a 15-year study found that the chance of developing schizophrenia is related to *deviant communication* within families (Goldstein, 1985). **Deviant communication patterns** *cause anxiety, confusion, anger, conflict, and turmoil.* Typically, disturbed families interact in ways that are laden with guilt, prying, criticism, negativity, and emotional attacks (Fowles, 1992; Wichstrom et al., 1996).

How could communication patterns make a difference? British psychiatrist Ronald Laing (1928-1989) claimed that the families of schizophrenics frequently engage in **double-bind communication.** *A double-bind message is one that places the listener in an unsolvable emotional conflict, or "no-win" situation.* For example, the mother of a schizophrenic patient might issue this typical double-bind message: "You don't really love me; you're only pretending you do." This statement asks for a showing of love but makes showing love

Can the catatonic's rigid postures and stupor be understood in terms of abnormal body chemistry? Environment? Heredity?

impossible. It wouldn't be surprising if such conflicts left the person feeling "crazy" or agitated (Laing, 1970).

Although they are attractive, environmental explanations alone are not enough to account for schizophrenia (Fowles, 1992). For instance, when the children of schizophrenic parents are raised away from their chaotic home environment, they are still likely to become psychotic.

Does that mean that heredity is a factor in schizophrenia?

Heredity   Evidence for heredity as a factor in schizophrenia has grown quite strong in recent years. It now appears that some individuals inherit a *potential* for developing schizophrenia. They are, in other words, more *vulnerable* to the disorder than others are (Fowles, 1992).

How can that be shown?

Here is a prime example: If one identical twin becomes schizophrenic (remember, identical twins have identical genes), then the other twin has a *48 percent* chance of also becoming schizophrenic (Lenzenweger & Gottesman, 1994). There is even a case on record of *four* identical quadruplets *all* developing schizophrenia. (This fascinating case is described in a moment.)

What about other family relationships?

If *both* parents are schizophrenic, their children have a 46 percent chance of developing the disorder. Persons with a brother or sister and one parent who are schizophrenic run a 17 percent risk themselves. Persons with a schizophrenic brother or sister have a 9 percent chance of also becoming schizophrenic. For *fraternal* twins the chance of mutual schizophrenia is about 17 percent (Lenzenweger & Gottesman, 1994). These figures can be compared to the risk of developing schizophrenia for the population in general, which is 1 percent (Fig. 18–2 ◆). Comparisons such as these have shown that schizophrenia is more common among close relatives than among distant relatives and that it tends to run in families (Plomin & Rende, 1991). The following highlight provides a striking example of heredity influencing schizophrenia.

The Genain Sisters—Trouble Times Four

By the time the Genain quadruplets reached high school, they began to act strangely. Hester broke light bulbs and tore buttons off her clothes. By age 20, Nora moaned at meals and complained that the bones in her neck were slipping. At night she stood on her knees and elbows in bed until they bled. At age 22, Iris quit her job, complaining that "I am pinned down. Someone wants to fight and I don't want to." Soon after, she "went to pieces." She screamed, drooled at meals, and talked of hearing voices. Myra, who was the fourth identical quad, panicked easily and couldn't be reassured, but did not actually break down until age 24 (Rosenthal & Quinn, 1977).

In addition to sharing identical heredity, the Genain sisters—Nora, Iris, Myra, and Hester—have something else in common: All four became schizophrenic before age 25. The women, who are now in their early 60s, have been in and out of mental hospitals all their lives.

You may be immediately tempted to assume that the Genain quads' psychoses were caused by heredity. However, it would be a mistake to overlook the nightmarish family life in which the girls grew up. Mr. Genain was an alcoholic who hounded, spied on, terrorized, and sexually molested the girls.

For the most part, Mrs. Genain was curiously blind to her husband's actions and offered the girls little support. Instead, she added her own bizarre thinking and sexual preoccupations to the family's already warped relationships. To put it mildly, the girls' mother and father failed spectacularly as parents.

In the final analysis, it seems that both heredity and an unhealthy environment led to the Genain sisters' problems (Carson, Butcher, & Mineka, 1996). Further support for this conclusion comes from the fact that Myra, the least ill of the four, was her mother's favorite. Myra also was the only sister able to keep some distance from her father.

In sum, it appears that heredity may set higher or lower thresholds for psychosis. Whether a person becomes actively disturbed, however, may depend on the kind of stresses to which she or he is exposed (Ventura et al., 1989).

How could someone inherit a susceptibility to schizophrenia?

Brain Chemistry

Amphetamine, LSD, PCP ("angel dust"), and similar drugs produce effects that partially mimic the symptoms of psychosis. Also, the same drugs (phenothiazines) used to treat LSD overdoses tend to alleviate the symptoms of

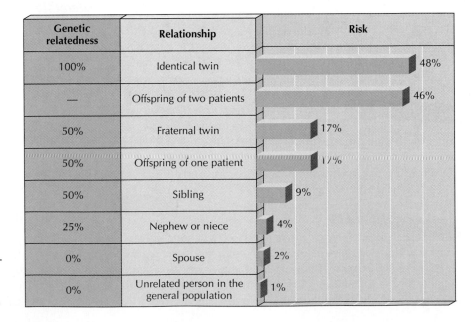

Genetic relatedness	Relationship	Risk
100%	Identical twin	48%
—	Offspring of two patients	46%
50%	Fraternal twin	17%
50%	Offspring of one patient	17%
50%	Sibling	9%
25%	Nephew or niece	4%
0%	Spouse	2%
0%	Unrelated person in the general population	1%

Figure 18–2 ◆ Lifetime risk of developing schizophrenia is associated with how closely a person is genetically related to a schizophrenic person. A shared environment also increases the risk. (Estimates from Lenzenweger & Gottesman, 1994.)

This series of paintings by Louis Wain reflects a troubled personality. Wain was a British illustrator who became schizophrenic in middle age. As Wain's psychosis progressed, his cat paintings became highly abstract and fragmented. In many ways, Wain's paintings resemble the perceptual changes caused by psychedelic drugs such as mescaline and LSD. Recent research suggests that psychosis may, in fact, be the result of mind-altering changes in brain chemistry. (Derik Bayes/Courtesy Guttman-Maclay *Life* Picture Service.)

schizophrenia. Facts such as these suggest that **biochemical abnormalities** (*disturbances in brain chemicals or neurotransmitters*) in schizophrenics may produce some substance similar to a *psychedelic* (mind-altering) drug. At present, one of the most likely candidates is **dopamine** (DOPE-ah-meen), *an important chemical messenger found in the brain* (Fowles, 1992).

How does dopamine fit into the picture?

Many researchers now believe that schizophrenia is directly

related to overactivity in brain dopamine systems (Heinrichs, 1993). Early hints of a dopamine-psychosis link came when researchers noted that large doses of amphetamines (speed) produce symptoms that are almost identical to paranoid schizophrenia. Amphetamines, it turns out, raise brain dopamine levels. Another piece of the puzzle fell into place when it was discovered that all major *antipsychotic* drugs *block* the action of dopamine at receptor areas in the brain (Fowles, 1992). (See Fig. 18–3 ◆.)

Then is schizophrenia a "dopamine high"?

For a time it seemed so. But no extra or abnormal amounts of dopamine could be found in the brains of schizophrenics. So much for the dopamine theory!

But wait. Our story is not over. In a dramatic breakthrough, a team of researchers at the University of Toronto, Canada, found nearly *double* the normal number of dopamine receptors in the brains of schizophrenics. These extra receptors exist in especially large numbers in the limbic system (a major emotional system of the brain). Another possibility is that dopamine receptors become extra responsive to normal amounts of dopamine (Port & Seybold, 1995).

Many scientists now believe that dopamine activation triggers a flood of unrelated thoughts, feelings, and perceptions. This directly accounts for the voices, hallucinations, delusions, and other disturbances of schizophrenia (Gottesman, 1991). The implication is that schizophrenics

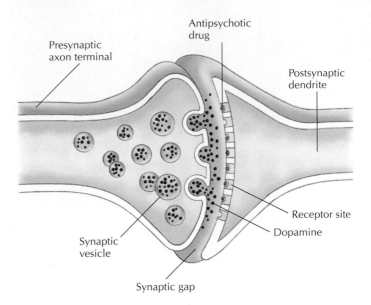

Figure 18–3 ◆ Dopamine normally crosses the synapse between two neurons, activating the second cell. Antipsychotic drugs bind to the same receptor sites as dopamine does, blocking its action. In people suffering from schizophrenia, a reduction in dopamine activity can quiet a person's agitation and psychotic symptoms.

Figure 18–4 ◆ *(Left)* CT scan of would-be presidential assassin John Hinkley, Jr., taken when he was 25. The X-ray image shows widened fissures in the wrinkled surface of Hinkley's brain. *(Right)* CT scan of a normal 25-year-old's brain. In most young adults the surface folds of the brain are pressed together too tightly to be seen. As a person ages, surface folds of the brain normally become more visible. Pronounced brain fissuring in young adults may be a sign of schizophrenia, chronic alcoholism, or other problems.

NORMAL   SCHIZOPHRENIC   MANIC-DEPRESSIVE

Figure 18–5 ◆ Positron emission tomography produces PET scans of the human brain. In the scans shown here, red, pink, and orange indicate lower levels of brain activity; white and blue indicate higher activity levels. Notice that activity in the schizophrenic brain is quite low in the frontal lobes (top area of each scan) (Velakoulis & Pantelis, 1996). Activity in the manic-depressive brain is low in the left brain hemisphere and high in the right brain hemisphere. The reverse is more often true of the schizophrenic brain. Researchers are trying to identify consistent patterns like these to aid diagnosis of mental disorders.

may be on a sort of drug trip caused by their own bodies. One of the most effective treatments for schizophrenia is a drug called clozapine. This drug blocks the action of dopamine within the brain. In short, most evidence suggests that schizophrenia is a brain disease (Heinrichs, 1993).

The Schizophrenic Brain   Medical researchers have long hoped for a way to directly observe the schizophrenic brain. Three medical techniques are now making it possible. One, called a *CT scan*, provides an X-ray picture of the brain. CT stands for computed tomography. **CT scans** *are computer-enhanced X-ray images.* (See the Exploration in Chapter 3 for more information.) Figure 18–4 ◆ shows a CT scan of the brain of John Hinkley, Jr. As you may recall, Hinkley shot President Ronald Reagan and three other men in 1981. In the ensuing trial, Hinkley was judged insane.

The CT scan promises to aid in diagnosing schizophrenia, and to provide new information on its causes. As you can see, Hinkley's brain differed from the norm. Specifically, it had wider surface fissuring.

MRI scans (*magnetic resonance imaging*) are allowing researchers to peer inside the schizophrenic brain. What they are finding is that schizophrenics tend to have enlarged ventricles (fluid-filled spaces within the brain). The areas that appear to be abnormal are crucial for regulating motivation, emotion, perception, and attention (Degreef et al., 1992; Frazier et al., 1996).

A third technique, called a **PET scan** (*positron emission tomography*), provides an image of brain *activity*. To make a PET scan, a radioactive sugar solution is injected into a vein. When the sugar reaches the brain, a device measures how much is used in each area. This information is then translated into a colored map, or scan, of brain activity (Fig. 18–5 ◆). (Again, the Exploration in Chapter 3 gives more information.) Researchers are finding patterns in such scans that are consistently linked with schizophrenia, affective disorders, and other problems. For instance, activity tends to be abnormally low in the frontal lobes of the schizophrenic brain (Velakoulis & Pantelis, 1996). In the future, PET scans may be routinely used to accurately diagnose schizophrenia. For now, PET scans show that there is a clear difference in schizophrenic brain activity.

Summary   In summary, the emerging picture of psychosis takes this general form: *Anyone* subjected to enough stress may be pushed to a psychotic break. (Battlefield psychosis is an example.) However, some people inherit a difference in brain chemistry or brain structure that makes them more susceptible, even to normal life stresses.

Thus, the right combination of inherited potential and environmental stress brings about mind-altering changes in brain chemicals. This explanation, which is called a **stress-vulnerability model,** *attributes psychosis to a combination of environmental stress and inherited susceptibility.* It seems to apply to other forms of psychopathology as well, such as depression (Fowles, 1992; Gottesman, 1991; Yank et al., 1993). (See Figure 18–6 ◆.)

Ultimately, distinctions between organic and functional psychoses may be dropped, and treatment of major disturbances may become more chemical than psychological. But for now, psychosis remains "a riddle wrapped in a mystery inside an enigma." Let us hope the recent advances that we have so briefly explored are as promising as they appear to be.

Figure 18–6 ◆ Various combinations of vulnerability and stress may produce psychological problems. The top bar shows low vulnerability and low stress. The result? No problem. The same is true of the next bar down, where low vulnerability is combined with moderate stress. Even high vulnerability (third bar) may not lead to problems if stress levels remain low. However, when high vulnerability combines with moderate or high stress (bottom two bars) the person "crosses the line" and suffers from psychopathology.

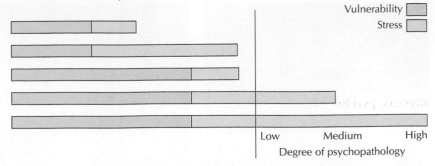

Mood Disorders— Peaks and Valleys

Nobody loves you when you're down and out—or so it seems. Psychologists have gradually come to realize that **mood disorders** (*major disturbances in emotion*) are among the most serious of all. Two general types of mood disorder are *depressive disorders* and *bipolar disorders*. (See Table 18–4.) In **depressive disorders,** *sadness and despondency are exaggerated, prolonged, or unreasonable*. Indications of a depressive disorder are dejection, hopelessness, and an inability to feel pleasure or to take interest in anything. Also common are fatigue, disturbed sleep and eating patterns, feelings of worthlessness, a very negative self-image, and thoughts of suicide. In **bipolar disorders,** *persons go both "up" and "down" emotionally* (DSM-IV, 1994).

In terms of sheer numbers, studies show that in Europe and North America, between 10 and 20 percent of the adult population has had a major depressive episode at some time (DSM-IV, 1994). At any given time, roughly 5 percent of the population is suffering from a mood disorder (Landers, 1989).

Moderate Mood Disorders

If a person is moderately depressed for at least 2 years, the problem is called a **dysthymic disorder** *(dis-THY-mik). If depression alternates with periods when the person's mood is elevated, expansive, or irritable, the problem is a* **cyclothymic disorder** *(SIKE-lo-THY-mik)* (DSM-IV, 1994).

In serious cases of depression it becomes impossible for a person to function at work or at school. Sometimes, depressed individuals cannot even feed or dress themselves. When depression and/or mania is even more severe, the person may become psychotic and lose touch with reality.

How are mood disorders different from milder, more normal feelings of depression?

A **reactive depression** *is an episode of despondency that follows some identifiable event*. If a loved one dies or a person suffers a major failure, loss, or setback, a period of mourning or depression is to be expected. Depression at such times represents an emotional adjustment that is completed within a reasonable time.

When someone is continuously or intensely depressed, we must look for causes that go beyond the apparent triggering incident. In many reactive depressions, we find that the person was unprepared to cope with a major loss because of a previous series of disappointments. For example, after his car is stolen and he fails a class, a college student learns that his girlfriend back home has become engaged to someone else. The student stops eating regularly, withdraws from friends, and neglects studying. In other instances, the person is simply emotionally dependent or immature. In any case, the triggering incident for depression is often merely the "last straw" that reveals an underlying emotional disturbance.

Major Mood Disorders

Major mood disorders *are marked by lasting extremes of emotion*. About 14 percent of patients admitted to mental hospitals suffer from major mood disorders. Usually, one of the following patterns predominates. In a **bipolar I disorder,** *the individual is mostly loud, elated, hyperactive, and energetic, but has also had one or more periods of depression*. In a **bipolar II disorder** *the person is mostly sad and guilt ridden, but has had one or more manic episodes. The person who only goes "down" emotionally suffers from a* **major depressive disorder**

Table 18-4	DSM-IV Classification of Mood Disorders
Bipolar Disorders	**Depressive Disorders**
Cyclothymic disorder	Dysthymic disorder
Bipolar I disorder (mostly manic)	Major depressive disorder
Bipolar II disorder (mostly depressed)	Single episode
	Recurrent
DSM-IV, 1994.	

(DSM-IV, 1994). Incidentally, people suffering from bipolar disorders are at very high risk of attempting suicide (Chen & Dilsaver, 1996).

Major mood disorders can be limited primarily to emotional extremes. Quite often, however, persons with major mood disorders also have psychotic symptoms. *This combination of mood disorder and a break with reality is called an* **affective psychosis.**

How do such problems differ from other types of psychosis?

Affective Psychoses Manic individuals throw themselves into fits of activity characterized by extreme distractibility, rapid shifts in thoughts ("flights of ideas"), constant talking, and restless movement. In advanced stages, manic behavior becomes more and more incoherent, agitated, and out of control. Eating or sleeping may be ignored until manic individuals push themselves into states of total delirium. (This behavior accounts for public images of the "raving maniac.") The following excerpt illustrates manic-psychotic behavior.

Her husband had returned home to find her twirling around the living room bizarrely draped in her wedding gown tied with a bath towel and wearing a lamp shade. She gaily greeted him, laughed with an ear-piercing shrillness, and invited him to stay for the exciting "coming-out" party she was giving. Strewn on the table were a thousand handwritten invitations signed with a flourish and addressed to such dignitaries as the president of the United States, the justices of the Supreme Court, the emperor of Japan. She made incessant noises: singing her own ballads, shouting mottoes, which she devised, reciting limericks, making rhyming sounds, and yelling obscenities. (Suinn, 1970)

Depressive reactions show a reverse pattern in which feelings of failure, sinfulness, worthlessness, and total despair are dominant. The person becomes extremely subdued or withdrawn and may be intensely suicidal. Depressive reactions pose a serious threat to survival. Suicide attempted during a psychotic depression is rarely a simple "plea for help." Usually, the person intends to succeed and may give no prior warning.

Manic and depressive states appear to be related in bipolar disorders. That is, when manic behavior occurs, it may still be a reaction to depression. The manic person may seek to escape feelings of worthlessness and depression in an unending rush of activity.

How do major mood disorders differ from dysthymic and cyclothymic disorders?

The major mood disorders usually involve more severe emotional changes. Also, of course, the person's emotional excesses can be accompanied by psychotic delusions and hallucinations. As a further distinction, major mood disorders and affective psychoses more often appear to be **endogenous** (en-DODGE-eh-nus: *produced from within*), rather than a reaction to external events.

In a depressive psychosis, suicidal impulses can be intense and despair total.

The Causes of Mood Disorders

How is depression explained?

Depression and other mood disorders have resisted adequate explanation and treatment. Some scientists are focusing on the biology of mood changes. These researchers are interested in brain chemicals and transmitter substances, especially serotonin, noradrenaline, and dopamine levels (Ricci & Wellman, 1990). Their findings are complex and inconclusive, but progress has been made. For example, the chemical *lithium carbonate* can be effective for treating some cases of depression, particularly those also showing manic behavior.

Other researchers seek psychological explanations. Psychoanalytic theory, for instance, holds that depression is caused by repressed anger that is displaced and turned inward as self-blame and self-hate (Isenberg & Schatzberg, 1976). As discussed in Chapter 14, behavioral theories of depression emphasize learned helplessness (Seligman, 1989). Cognitive psychologists believe that self-criticism and negative, distorted, or self-defeating thoughts underlie many cases of depression. (This view is discussed in Chapter 19.) Clearly, life stresses trigger many mood disorders. This is especially true for people who have personality traits and thinking patterns that make them vulnerable to depression (Franche & Dobson, 1992; Gatz, 1990; Miranda, 1992).

Overall, women are twice as likely as men to experience depression (Culertson, 1997). Authorities believe that social and environmental conditions are the main reason for this difference. Factors that contribute to women's greater risk of depression include conflicts between work and parenting, reproductive stresses, the strain of providing emotional support for others, marital strife, sexual and physical abuse, and poverty. Nationwide, poverty is concentrated among women and children. As a result, poor women frequently suffer the stresses associated with single parenthood, loss of control over their lives, poor housing, and dangerous neighborhoods (Russo, 1990).

As you might guess, the fact that major mood disorders appear to be endogenous implies that genetics may be involved, especially in bipolar disorders (Gatz, 1990; Plomin & Rende, 1991). As a case in point, the rate of depression among children of depressed parents is higher even if the children are adopted (Dunner, 1985). If one identical twin is depressed, the other has an 80 percent chance of suffering depression, too. For non-twin siblings the probability is 35 percent. As we have noted, psychological causes are important in many cases of depression. But for major mood disorders, biological factors seem to play a larger role.

Research Frontier

Feeling Sad? It Could Be SAD.

Unless you have experienced a winter of "cabin fever" in the far north, you may be surprised to learn that the rhythms of the seasons underlie some depressions. Researcher Norman Rosenthal has found that some people suffer from **seasonal affective disorder (SAD),** *or depression that only occurs during the fall and winter months.* Almost anyone can get a little depressed when days are short, dark, and cold. But when a person's symptoms are lasting and disabling, the problem may be SAD. Here are some of the major symptoms of SAD (Rosenthal, 1993):

- **Oversleeping and difficulty staying awake:** Your sleep patterns may be disturbed and waking very early in the morning is common.

- **Fatigue:** You feel too tired to maintain a normal routine.

- **Craving:** You hunger for carbohydrates and sweets, leading to overeating and weight gain.

- **Inability to cope:** You feel irritable and stressed.

- **Social withdrawal:** You become unsocial in the winter but are socially active during other seasons.

Starting in the fall, people with SAD sleep longer but more poorly. During the day they feel tired and drowsy and they tend to overeat. With each passing day they become more sad, anxious, irritable, and socially withdrawn.

Although their depressions are usually only moderately severe, many victims of SAD face each winter

with a sense of foreboding. SAD is especially prevalent in northern latitudes, where days are very short during the winter (Booker & Hellekson, 1992) (Fig. 18–7 ◆). Without treatment, SAD can return winter after winter (Schwartz et al., 1996).

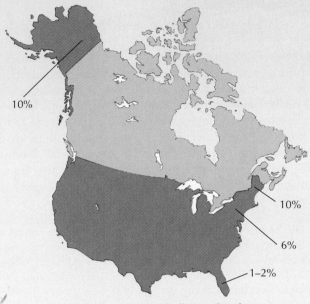

Rates of seasonal affective disorder, by latitude

Figure 18–7 ◆ Seasonal affective disorder is related to reduced exposure to daylight during the winter. SAD affects 1 to 2 percent of Florida's population, about 6 percent of the people living in Maryland and New York City, and nearly 10 percent of the residents of New Hampshire, Alaska, and the Canadian provinces (Booker & Hellekson, 1992).

Seasonal depressions are related to the release of more melatonin during the winter. This hormone, which is secreted by the pineal gland, regulates the body's response to changing light conditions. That's why 80 percent of SAD patients can be helped by extra doses of bright light, an approach called *phototherapy* (Fig. 18–8 ◆). **Phototherapy** *involves exposing SAD patients to one or more hours of very bright fluorescent light each day.* As an alternative, some patients benefit from a one hour walk outside in the morning light (Wirz-Justice et al., 1996). For many SAD sufferers these hearty doses of light appear to be the next best thing to vacationing in the tropics.

While we await the outcome of attempts to understand and treat depression, a problem remains: Thousands of depressed people commit suicide each year. What can be done about it? Later in this chapter the Applications section will provide some answers.

Figure 18–8 ◆ An hour or more of bright light a day can dramatically reduce the symptoms of seasonal affective disorder. Treatment is usually necessary from fall through spring. Some people respond best to artificial light in the early morning that creates a false "dawn" 2 hours earlier than normal (Avery et al., 1993).

Learning Check

Match the following:

1. _____ Schizotypal
2. _____ Disorganized schizophrenia
3. _____ Catatonic schizophrenia
4. _____ Paranoid schizophrenia
5. _____ Major mood disorders

A. Manic or depressive behavior
B. Mutism, odd postures, immobility
C. Non-psychotic disorder
D. Silliness, bizarre behavior, personality disintegration
E. Delusions of grandeur or persecution
F. Anxiety attacks, irrational fears

6. Major mood disorders, especially bipolar disorders, often appear to be endogenous. T or F?

7. Learned helplessness is emphasized by _____ theories of depression.
   a. humanistic   b. biological   c. behavioristic   d. psychoanalytic

8. The drug lithium carbonate has been shown to be an effective treatment for schizophrenia. T or F?

9. Environmental explanations of schizophrenia emphasize prenatal trauma, early emotional trauma, and
   a. manic parents   b. schizoaffective interactions   c. psychedelic interactions
   d. disturbed family relationships

10. The _____ _____ of a schizophrenic person runs a 48 percent chance of also becoming psychotic.

11. Enlarged surface fissures and ventricles, as revealed by CT scans, are frequently found in the brains of chronic schizophrenics. T or F?

12. Abnormally high numbers of noradrenaline receptors have been found in the brains of schizophrenics. T or F?

13. The acronym SAD stands for schizotypal affective disorder. T or F?

Critical Thinking

14. Enlarged surface fissures and ventricles are frequently found in the brains of chronic schizophrenics. Why is it a mistake to conclude that such features cause schizophrenia?

Answers:
1. C 2. D 3. B 4. E 5. A 6. T
7. c 8. F 9. d 10. Identical twin
11. T 12. F (dopamine receptors)
13. F 14. Because correlation does not confirm causation. Structural brain abnormalities are merely *correlated* with schizophrenia. They could be additional symptoms, rather than causes, of the disorder.

Treatment—Medical Approaches

Is psychosis incurable? If a person's symptoms temporarily disappear, can an unexpected relapse occur?

An organic psychosis cannot be "cured" in the usual sense,

but it may be controlled with drugs and other techniques. With functional psychoses the outlook is still rather negative, but many people do recover (Fig. 18–9 ◆). It is wrong to fear "former mental patients" or to exclude them from work, friendships, and other social situations. A psychotic episode does not inevitably lead to lifelong dysfunction. Too often, however, it leads to unnecessary rejection based on groundless fears. As we noted in Chapter 17, only persons who are *actively psychotic* have an elevated chance of being

Figure 18–9 ◆ At least 1 schizophrenic patient in 4 had completely recovered 10 years after being diagnosed. Three out of 4 had improved. New treatments for schizophrenia and other major mental disorders may improve these odds. (Source: FDA Consumer, 1993.)

Schizophrenic patients 10 years after diagnosis

violent. Even this group is responsible for only a tiny percentage of all the violent incidents in any given community (Monahan, 1992).

What can be done about psychosis?

Two basic forms of treatment exist. The first, called **psychotherapy,** *is any psychological treatment for behavioral or emotional problems.* Psychotherapy is a special relationship between a psychologist and a person in trouble. Often, it involves two people talking about one person's problems. Psychotherapy may be applied to anything from a brief crisis to a full-scale psychosis. However, psychologists tend *not* to treat patients with major depressive disorders, schizophrenia, or similarly severe conditions. Major mental disorders are more often treated medically (Knesper et al., 1989). Because approaches vary greatly, a complete discussion of psychotherapy is found in the next chapter.

A second major approach to treatment is **somatic** (*bodily*) **therapy.** The main somatic treatments are *pharmacotherapy, electroconvulsive therapy,* and *psychosurgery.* Somatic therapy is often done in the context of psychiatric *hospitalization.* All the somatic approaches have a medical slant and they are mostly used to treat psychoses and major mood disorders.

Drugs

The atmosphere in mental hospitals changed radically in the mid-1950s with the widespread adoption of pharmaco-

therapy (FAR-meh-ko-THER-eh-pea). **Pharmacotherapy** *is the use of drugs to alleviate the symptoms of emotional disturbance.* Drugs may relieve the anxiety attacks and other discomforts of non-psychotic disorders. More often, however, they are used to combat psychosis and major mood disorders.

What types of drugs are used in pharmacotherapy?

The three major classes of drugs are *minor tranquilizers, major tranquilizers (antipsychotics),* and *antidepressants.* **Minor tranquilizers** *are drugs (such as Valium) that produce relaxation or reduce anxiety.* **Antidepressants** *are mood elevating drugs used to combat depression.* **Antipsychotics** *are drugs that, in addition to having tranquilizing effects, also tend to reduce hallucinations and delusional thinking.* (See Table 18–5 ■ for examples of each class of drugs.)

Are drugs a valid approach to treatment?

Drugs have shortened hospital stays and greatly improved the chances for recovery from psychiatric disorders. Because of drug therapy, it has become possible for many individuals to return to the community, where they can be treated on an "out-patient" basis.

Few experts would argue for a return to the conditions that existed before pharmacotherapy became available. But there are some drawbacks. First of all, drugs generally do not *cure* mental illness—they only relieve symptoms. If a patient stops taking his or her medication, the symptoms may return. Nevertheless, relief from symptoms may allow

Table 18-5 ■ **Commonly Prescribed Psychiatric Drugs**		
Class	**Examples (trade names)**	**Effects**
Minor tranquilizers (anti-anxiety drugs)	Ativan, Halcion, Librium, Restoril, Valium, Zanax	Reduce anxiety, tension, fear
Antidepressants	Anafranil, Elavil, Nardil, Norpramin, Parnate, Paxil, Prozac, Tofranil, Zoloft	Counteract depression
Antipsychotics (major tranquilizers)	Clozaril, Haldol, Mellaril, Navane, Risperdal, Thorazine	Reduce agitation, delusions, hallucinations, thought disorders

patients to benefit more fully from psychotherapy and other attempts to help them.

Limitations of Drug Therapy Many psychiatric drugs have adverse side effects. For example, 15 percent of patients taking major tranquilizers develop **tardive dyskinesia** (TAR-div dis-cah-NEE-zyah). *This neurological disorder is marked by rhythmic facial and mouth movements*, such as chewing, sucking, or smacking the lips. Unusual movements of the arms (such as "fly-catching" motions) and other restless movements are also common (Chakos et al., 1996).

Perhaps the most valid criticism of pharmacotherapy is the simple observation that it is easily overused. Only about 50 percent of the victims of disabling mental illness are helped by drugs, but nearly all receive them. Apparently, there is a great temptation to reach for the prescription pad. Many observers agree that too many drugs are being given to too many people. Researcher David Rosenhan (whose work was described in the Applications section of Chapter 17) believes that drugs often are not merely given at therapeutic levels. Rather, they are sometimes used to keep patients docile and easy to manage. Many critics believe that the locks that came off the doors of old-style institutions have been replaced at times by "chemical locks" or "chemical straitjackets." Another problem is that the ease with which drugs can be given may discourage the use of psychotherapy. This and related controversies are explored further in the next highlight.

Focus On A Controversy

Psychiatric "Wonder Drugs"

New psychiatric drugs are often hailed as medical "miracles." However, all drugs involve a trade-off between benefits and risks. For example, the drug Clozaril (clozapine) can relieve the symptoms of schizophrenia in some previously "hopeless" cases. But Clozaril is nearly as dangerous as it is helpful: 2 out of 100 patients taking the drug suffer from a potentially fatal blood disease. Because of this risk, all patients must have a blood test once a week. Those whose white blood cell count drops below normal must immediately stop taking the drug or they will die. Is the risk worth it? Many experts think it is, because chronic schizophrenia robs people of almost everything that makes life worth living.

It's possible, of course, that newer drugs will improve the risk-benefit ratio in the treatment of schizophrenia. For example, the recently approved drug Risperdal (risperidone) appears to be as effective as Clozaril, without the lethal risk. It also shows no signs of causing tardive dyskinesia (Kane, 1996).

Prozac (fluoxetine) is another drug that has raised

hopes for improved treatment. Prozac, an antidepressant, is used primarily to treat mood disorders. Prozac is popular because it causes fewer side effects than other antidepressants. Soon after it was introduced, however, claims began to surface that people using Prozac tended to become suicidal. The verdict today? The risk of suicide is actually *lower* for patients taking Prozac than those taking a placebo (Tollefson et al., 1993).

While the suicide controversy has cooled, another is still blazing. Psychiatrist Peter Kramer (1993) has charged that Prozac alters the personalities of people who take it. In some cases, he believes, Prozac may be used to transform people into improved, but unnatural, versions of themselves. (Kramer calls this effect "cosmetic psychopharmacology.") Defenders of Prozac and similar drugs respond that what Kramer has observed is just the natural response to correcting a biochemical imbalance. Instead of becoming someone they're not, they say, patients feel more like themselves than they have in years (Metzner, 1994).

Criticisms like Kramer's remain open to debate. What isn't disputed is that even the best new drugs are not cure-alls. They help some people for some problems, but not for all. It is noteworthy that, for serious mental disorders, a combination of medication and psychotherapy almost always works better than drugs alone. Drugs can be therapeutic, but they are seldom "miraculous." (Additional sources: Kemper, 1991; Maugh, 1992.)

In the long run, concern over side effects and the overuse of drugs may bring about a better balance between pharmacotherapy and psychotherapy. But where psychosis and mood disorders are concerned, drugs will undoubtedly remain a major mode of treatment (Thase & Kupfer, 1996).

Shock

In **electroconvulsive therapy (ECT)** *a 150-volt electrical current is passed through the brain for slightly less than a second.* This rather drastic medical treatment for depression triggers a convulsion and causes the patient to lose consciousness for a short time. Muscle relaxants and sedative drugs are given before ECT to soften its impact. Treatments are given in a series of 6 to 8 sessions spread over 3 to 4 weeks.

How does shock help?

Actually, it is the seizure that is believed to be helpful. Proponents of ECT claim that shock-induced seizures alter the biochemical balance in the brain, bringing an end to severe depression and suicidal behavior (Swartz, 1993). Others have charged that ECT works only by confusing

In electroconvulsive therapy, electrodes are attached to the head, and a brief electrical current is passed through the brain. ECT is used in the treatment of severe depression.

patients so they can't remember why they were depressed (Kohn, 1988).

The ECT Debate Many people consider ECT a distasteful procedure, and not all professionals support its use. In fact, experts continue to debate the value of ECT and the seriousness of its side effects. Critics claim that ECT causes permanent memory losses and occasional brain damage. Proponents of ECT argue that detailed brain scans show no evidence of damage (Kohn, 1988). Also, it has been reported that if electrodes are applied to only one side of the head, memory loss is greatly reduced. However, ECT done in this way may not end depression (Sackheim et al., 1987).

Those who support ECT view it as being like any other medical treatment: It involves calculated risks. As is true of pharmacotherapy, the major problem with ECT seems to lie in overuse and misuse. Some patients have had hundreds of shock treatments and have suffered damage in the process.

What, then, can be said about ECT? Most experts seem to agree on the following: (1) At best, ECT produces only temporary improvement—it gets the patient out of a bad spot, but it must be combined with other treatments; (2) ECT does cause permanent memory losses in many patients; and (3) ECT should be used only as a last resort after drug therapy has failed (Kohn, 1988). All told, ECT is considered by many to be a valid treatment for selected cases of depression—especially when it rapidly ends wildly self-destructive or suicidal behavior (Abrams, 1997; Isaac & Armat, 1990).

Psychosurgery

The most extreme biological treatment is **psychosurgery,** a general term applied to *any surgical alteration of the brain.* The best-known psychosurgery is the *lobotomy.* In the **prefrontal lobotomy** and related techniques, *the frontal lobes are surgically disconnected from other areas of the brain.* The original goal of this procedure was to calm persons who had not responded to any other type of treatment.

When the lobotomy was first introduced in the 1940s, there were enthusiastic claims for its success. But later studies suggested that some patients were calmed, some showed no noticeable change, and some became "veg-etables." Lobotomies also produced a high rate of undesirable side effects, such as seizures, extreme lack of emotional response, and even stupor. At about the same time that such problems became apparent, the first antipsychotic drugs became available. Soon after, the lobotomy was abandoned (Swayze, 1995).

To what extent is psychosurgery used now?

Psychosurgery is still considered a valid treatment by many neurosurgeons. However, most now use sophisticated **deep lesioning** techniques. In this approach, *small target areas are destroyed in the brain's interior.* The appeal of deep lesioning is that it can have fairly specific effects. For instance, patients suffering from a severe type of obsessive-compulsive disorder may be helped by psychosurgery (Cumming et al., 1995).

It is worth remembering that all forms of psychosurgery are *irreversible.* A drug can be given or taken away. You can't take back psychosurgery. Many critics argue that psychosurgery should be banned altogether. Others continue to report success with psychosurgical procedures. All things considered, it is perhaps most accurate, even after decades of use, to describe psychosurgery as an experimental technique.

Hospitalization

Somatic therapy, psychotherapy, and other techniques may require a special setting or special control for a period of time. Traditionally, this has meant a trip to a psychiatric hospital or state institution. **Mental hospitalization** *consists of confinement to a protected environment that provides therapy for emotional and behavioral problems.* Hospitalization by itself is a form of treatment. Staying in a psychiatric ward removes patients from situations that may be provoking or maintaining their problems. At its best, the hospital is a sanctuary that provides diagnosis, support, refuge, and psychotherapy. At worst, an institution can be a brutalizing experience that leaves a person less prepared to face the world than before.

Hospitals are ideally used as a last resort after other forms of treatment within the community have been exhausted. It has become clear that most psychiatric patients do as well with short-term hospitalization as they do with longer periods. For this reason, the average stay in psychiatric hospitals is now just 20 days, rather than 3 to 4 months, as it was 20 years ago.

A new trend in psychiatric treatment is **partial hospitalization,** *in which patients spend only part of their time at the hospital.* Even for the acutely disturbed, over-night hospital

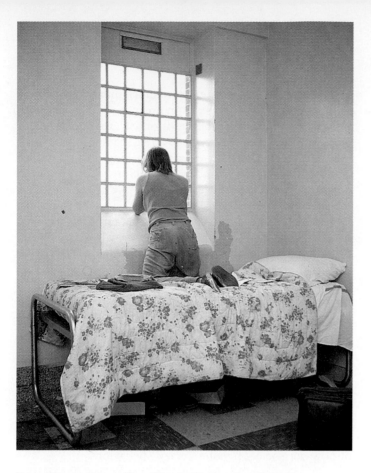

Depending on the quality of the institution, hospitalization may be a refuge or a brutalizing experience. Many state "asylums" or mental hospitals are antiquated and in need of drastic improvement.

is comparable to that seen with traditional hospitalization (Sledge et al., 1996).

Deinstitutionalization In the last 30 years the population in large mental hospitals has dropped by two thirds. This is largely the result of a trend toward **deinstitutionalization,** *or reduced use of full-time commitment to mental institutions.* This change is based, in part, on a desire to improve the odds that hospitalization will be helpful. Long-term hospitalization can lead to dependency, isolation, and continued emotional disturbance. As a result, many patients become so "institutionalized" that it's hard for them to return to the community (Chamberlin & Rogers, 1990).

How successful have such policies been?

In truth, their success has been limited. Many states welcomed smaller mental hospital populations as a way to save money. But the upsetting result has been that many chronic patients are discharged into hostile communities without adequate care. Many former patients have joined the ranks of the homeless (Susnick & Belcher, 1996). Others are repeatedly jailed for minor crimes such as trespassing, vagrancy, and disturbing the peace. Ultimately, former patients who suffer from unemployment, homelessness, and social isolation all too often are jailed or rehospitalized (Rossi, 1990; Turkheimer & Parry, 1992).

Large mental hospitals may no longer be warehouses for society's unwanted, but many former patients are no better off in bleak nursing homes, single-room hotels, board-and-care homes, jails, or shelters. Ironically, high-quality care is available in almost every community. As much as anything, a simple lack of sufficient funding prevents large numbers of people from getting the help they need (Torrey, 1996).

It would help greatly if better rehabilitation programs were offered after hospital treatment (Anthony, Cohen, & Kennard, 1990). One such approach is the use of *half-way houses,* which can ease a patient's return to the community. **Half-way houses** *are short-term group living facilities for individuals making the transition from an institution (mental hospital, prison, and so forth) to independent living.* Typically,

stays are becoming less common. For example, some patients spend their days in the hospital, but go home at night. Others attend therapy sessions during the evening, after work. A major advantage of partial hospitalization is that patients can go home and practice what they've been learning. Gradually, the number of hours patients spend at the hospital is reduced. Eventually, most people return to normal life. The effectiveness of partial hospitalization

A well-run half-way house can be a humane and cost-effective way to ease former mental patients back into the community (Coursey, Ward-Alexander, & Katz, 1990).

Major Mental Disorders 603

they offer supervision and support, without being as restrictive and medically slanted as hospitals. They also keep people near their families. Most important, half-way houses can reduce a person's chances of being readmitted to a hospital (Coursey, Ward-Alexander, & Katz, 1990).

Community Mental Health Programs

Community mental health centers are a bright spot in the area of mental health care. **Community mental health centers** *offer a wide range of mental health services, such as prevention, counseling, consultation, and crisis intervention.* Such centers try to minimize hospitalization and seek new answers to mental health problems. Typically, they provide short-term treatment, out-patient care, and special crisis or emergency services.

If it is like most, the primary aim of the mental health center in your community is to directly aid troubled citizens. The second goal of mental health centers is *prevention.* Consultation, education, and **crisis intervention** (*skilled management of a psychological emergency*) are used to end or prevent problems before they become serious. Also, some centers attempt to raise the general level of mental health in target areas by combating problems such as unemployment, delinquency, and drug abuse (Levine et al., 1993).

How have community mental health centers fared in meeting their goals?

In practice, they have concentrated much more on providing clinical services than they have on prevention. This situation appears to be primarily the result of wavering government support (translation: money). Overall, community mental health centers have succeeded in making mental health services more accessible than ever before. Many of their programs are made possible by **paraprofessionals** (*individuals who work in a near-professional capacity under the supervision of more highly trained staff*). Some paraprofessionals are ex-addicts, ex-alcoholics, or ex-patients who have "been there." Many more are persons (paid or volunteer) who have skills in tutoring, crafts, or counseling or who are simply warm, understanding, and skilled at communication. A career as a paraprofessional should not be overlooked by students planning to work in the field of mental health.

A Look Ahead By the time you finish reading this page, someone in North America will have attempted suicide. Suicide is a disturbing and widely misunderstood problem. In the Applications section we will examine what is known about suicide and how it can sometimes be prevented. The Exploration section concludes with a provocative discussion of how our society handles "crazy" behavior.

Learning Check	Critical Thinking
1. The use of pharmacotherapy has required longer hospital stays, since drugs can only be given under hospital supervision. T or F?	9. The residents of Berkeley, California, once voted on a referendum to ban the use of ECT within city limits. Do you think that the use of certain psychiatric treatments should be controlled by law?
2. ECT is a modern form of pharmacotherapy. T or F?	
3. Electroconvulsive therapy is used mainly as a treatment for depression. T or F?	
4. Tardive dyskinesia is a possible complication in long-term use of **a.** major tranquilizers **b.** antidepressants **c.** minor tranquilizers **d.** ECT	
5. Currently, the frontal lobotomy is the most widely used form of psychosurgery. T or F?	
6. Psychosurgery can be reversed if it is unsuccessful. T or F?	**Answers:**
7. Whenever possible, the community mental health movement emphasizes prevention of mental health problems. T or F?	*making medical decisions.*
8. Research indicates that relatively short periods of psychiatric hospitalization are as beneficial as long-term hospital stays. T or F?	1. F 2. F 3. T 4. a 5. F 6. F 7. T 8. T 9. The question of who can prescribe drugs, do surgery, and administer ECT is controlled by law. However, psychiatrists strongly object to residents, city councils, or government agencies

"Suicide: A permanent solution to a temporary problem."

Suicide ranks as the seventh cause of death in North America. Roughly 1 person out of 100 attempts suicide during his or her lifetime. Sooner or later you are likely to be affected by the suicide attempt of a friend, relative, neighbor, or co-worker. Check your knowledge of suicide against the following information.

What factors affect suicide rates?

Season Suicide rates vary greatly, but some general patterns emerge. Contrary to popular belief, suicide rates are lower than average between Thanksgiving and Christmas (Phillips & Wills, 1987). On the other hand, more suicides take place at New Year's than during any other 24 hour period. A "Monday effect" also exists, with higher suicide rates occurring on the first day of the week. This pattern applies mainly to men, especially those between the ages of 41 and 65. It probably reflects the fact that traditional "breadwinners" can be especially depressed as they begin another work week—or another week of looking for a job (McCleary et al., 1991).

Sex Men have the questionable honor of being better at suicide than women. Three times as many men as women *complete* suicide, but women make more attempts. More men than women die by suicide because they typically use a gun or an equally fatal method (Garland & Zigler, 1993). Women most often attempt a drug overdose—a method that leaves greater chance of help arriving before death occurs. Sadly, women are beginning to use more lethal methods than in the past (Rogers, 1990). This, combined with a higher rate of attempts, may soon place women and men at equal risk of death by suicide.

Age Age is also a factor in suicide. Suicide rates gradually rise during adolescence. They then sharply increase during young adulthood (ages 20-24). From then until age 84 the rate continues to gradually rise with advancing age (Shneidman, 1987a). As a result, more than half of all suicides are committed by individuals over 45 years old. However, there has been a steady increase in the suicide rates for adolescents and young adults (Diekstra & Garnefski, 1995).

Part of the increase in youth suicide comes from the ranks of college students, where suicide is the leading cause of death. Contrary to popular belief, the most dangerous time for student suicide is the first 6 weeks of a semester, not during final exams.

School is a factor in some suicides, but only in the sense that suicidal students were not living up to their own extremely high standards. Many were good students. Other important factors in student suicide are chronic health problems (real or imagined) and interpersonal difficulties (some suicides are rejected lovers, but others are simply withdrawn and friendless people).

Of special concern to psychologists is the recent dramatic increase in adolescent suicides. At present, about 1 million teenagers attempt suicide each year in the United States and 7,000 of those die (Cimons, 1991). This total—about 19 deaths per day—is triple the suicide rate reported 20 years ago (Garland & Zigler, 1993). Also distressing is the fact that an increasing number of youths employ such highly lethal methods as shooting themselves to commit suicide (Fig. 18–10 ◆).

Income Some professions, such as medicine and psychiatry, have higher than average suicide rates. Overall, however, suicide is quite democratic. It is equally a problem of the rich and the poor.

Marital Status An additional factor in suicide is marital status. Marriage (when successful) may be the best natural guard against suicidal impulses. The highest suicide rates are

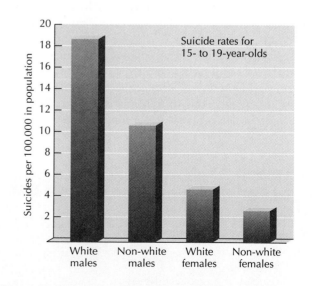

Figure 18–10 ◆ Adolescent suicide rates vary for different racial and ethnic groups. Higher rates occur among whites than among non-whites. White male adolescents run the highest risk of suicide. Considering gender alone, it is apparent that more male than female adolescents commit suicide. This is the same as the pattern observed for adults.

found among the divorced, the next-highest rates occur among the widowed, lower rates are recorded for single persons, and married individuals have the lowest rates of all.

Why do people try to kill themselves?

Immediate Causes of Suicide

Suicides typically combine three emotions: despair, guilt, and anger. In other words, the person wants to die (escape), wants to be killed (punished), and wants to hurt (or punish) others. Where do such feelings come from? Usually they are preceded by a history of interpersonal troubles with family, in-laws, or a lover or spouse. Often there are drinking problems, sexual adjustment problems, or job difficulties. (The highest risk for suicide involves this combination: Older divorced white male, physically ill, substance abuser, living alone.) Table 18–6 ■ lists major risk factors for suicide.

A combination of factors such as these leads to severe depression and a preoccupation with death as the "answer" to the person's suffering. There is usually a break in communication with others that causes the person to feel isolated and misunderstood. Self-image becomes very negative. The person feels worthless and helpless and wants to die. Severe feelings of *hopelessness* are a warning that the risk of suicide is very high (Beck et al., 1990).

A long history of such conditions is not always necessary to produce a wish to die. People who attempt suicide are not necessarily "mentally ill." Anyone may temporarily reach a state of depression severe enough to attempt suicide. Most dangerous for the average person are times of divorce, separation, failure, and bereavement. Each can create what seems like an intolerable situation and can motivate an intense desire for escape.

The causes of increased adolescent suicide remain unclear. As with adults, there is often a backdrop of problems with drugs, depression, school, peers, family, divorced parents, or the breakup of a romance. To make matters worse, most adolescents who attempt suicide are socially isolated and poor at solving problems in their personal relationships (Cole et al., 1992; Sadowski & Kelley, 1993).

Some experts suggest that many cases of adolescent suicide result from unrealistic expectations. For example, parents may create feelings of despair by pressuring their children to meet impossibly high standards. Even without parental pressure, teenagers may expect the impossible of themselves in school, sports, romance, or progress toward a future career. Extremely high expectations and an unusual degree of sensitivity to hurt and disappointment can bring self-esteem to rock bottom over even the smallest "failure" (Cole et al., 1992; Mack, 1986). Again, the outcome is feelings of helplessness, hopelessness, and a desire to escape. Similar patterns have been observed for adult suicides, who are sometimes victims of an intense need for perfection (Blatt, 1995).

Preventing Suicide

Is it true that people who talk about or threaten suicide are rarely the ones who try it?

No. This is one of the major fallacies about suicide. Of every 10 potential suicides, 8 give warning beforehand. A person who threatens suicide should be taken seriously—even one who seems to be "crying wolf." (See Figure 18–11 ◆). A potential suicide may say nothing more than, "I feel sometimes like I'd be better off dead." Warnings may also come indirectly. If a friend gives you a favorite ring and says, "Here, I won't be needing this anymore," or comments, "I guess I won't get my watch fixed—it doesn't matter anyway," it may be a plea for help. The warning signs listed in Table 18–7 ■, especially if observed in combination, can signal an impending suicide attempt (Leenaars, 1995; Slaby, Garfinkel, & Garfinkel, 1994).

Is it true that suicide can't be prevented, that the person will find a way to do it anyway?

No. The decision to attempt suicide usually comes when a person is alone, depressed, and unable to view matters objectively. You *should* intervene if someone seems to be threatening suicide.

It is estimated that about two thirds of all suicide attempts fall in the "to be" category. That is, they are made by people who do not really want to die. Almost a third more

---

Table 18–6 ■ Major Risk Factors for Suicide

- Drug or alcohol abuse
- A prior suicide attempt
- Depression or other mood disorder
- Hopelessness
- Antisocial or aggressive behavior
- Family history of suicidal behavior
- Shame, humiliation, failure, or rejection
- Availability of a firearm

Garland & Zigler, 1993.

Figure 18–11 ◆ Suicidal behavior usually progresses from suicidal thoughts, to threats, to attempts. A person is unlikely to make an attempt without first making threats. Thus, suicide threats should be taken seriously (Garland & Zigler, 1993).

Table 18–7 ■ Warning Signs of Potential Suicide

- Withdrawal from contact with others
- Sudden swings in mood
- Recent occurrence of life crisis or emotional shock
- Personality change
- Gift giving of prized possessions
- Depression/hopelessness
- Aggression and/or risk taking
- Single-car accident
- Preoccupation with death
- Drug use
- Death imagery in art
- Direct threats to commit suicide

are characterized by a "to be or not to be" attitude. These people are *ambivalent* or undecided about dying.

Only about 3 to 5 percent of cases represent individuals who definitely want to die. Most people, therefore, are relieved when someone comes to their aid. Remember that suicide is almost always a cry for help and that you *can* help. As suicide expert Edwin Shneidman (1987a) puts it, "Suicidal behavior is often a form of communication, a cry for help born out of pain, with clues and messages of suffering and anguish and pleas for response."

What is the best thing to do if someone hints they are thinking about suicide?

How to Help

It helps to know some of the common characteristics of suicidal thoughts and feelings. Edwin Shneidman (1987) has identified several.

1. Escape. Everyone at times feels like running away from an upsetting situation. Running away from home, quitting school, abandoning a marriage—these are all departures. Suicide, of course, is the ultimate escape. It helps when suicidal persons see that the natural wish for escape doesn't have to be expressed by ending it all.

2. Unbearable psychological pain. Emotional pain is what the suicidal person is seeking to escape. A goal of anyone hoping to prevent suicide should be to reduce the pain in any way possible. Ask the person, "Where does it hurt?"

3. Frustrated psychological needs. Often, suicide can be prevented if a distraught person's frustrated needs can be identified and eased. Is the person deeply frustrated in his or her search for love, achievement, trust, security, or friendship?

4. Constriction of options. The suicidal person feels helpless and decides that death is the *only* solution. The person has narrowed all his or her options solely to death. The rescuer's goal, then, is to help broaden the suicidal person's perspective. Even when all the choices are unpleasant, suicidal persons can usually be made to see that their *least unpleasant option* is better than death.

Knowing these patterns will give some guidance in talking to a suicidal person. In addition, your most important task may be to establish *rapport* with the person. You should offer support, acceptance, and legitimate caring.

Remember that a suicidal person feels misunderstood. You should therefore try to accept and understand the feelings the person is expressing. Shneidman (1987b) gives the example of a college senior who made straight A's for three and one half years and then received a B. The student became deeply depressed and was determined to kill himself. His friends pointed out that he still had a 3.98 grade average. But by talking about grades they missed the point. The student's problem was the loss of his perfect record. It would be better to say, "I understand your desire to keep your perfect average. That grade must seem devastating." Acceptance should also extend to the idea of suicide itself. It is completely acceptable to ask, "Are you thinking of suicide?"

Establishing communication with suicidal persons may be enough to carry them through a difficult time. You may also find it helpful to get day-by-day commitments from them to meet for lunch, share a ride, and the like. Let the person know you *expect* her or him to be there. Such commitments, even though small, can be enough to tip the scales when a person is alone and thinking about suicide.

Don't end your efforts too soon. One of the most dangerous times for suicide is when a person suddenly seems to get better after a severe depression. Many experts agree that this often means that the person has finally made the decision to end it all. The improvement in mood is deceptive because it comes from an anticipation that suffering is at an end.

Crisis Intervention   Most cities have mental health crisis intervention teams or centers for suicide prevention. Both services have staff trained to talk with suicidal persons over the phone. Give a person who seems to be suicidal the number of one of these services. Urge the person to call you or the other number if she or he becomes frightened or impulsive. Or better yet, help the person make an appointment to get psychological treatment (Garland & Zigler, 1993).

The preceding applies mainly to persons who are having mild suicidal thoughts. If a person actually threatens suicide, you must act more quickly. Ask how the person plans to carry out the suicide. A person who has a *concrete, workable plan,* and the means to carry it out, should be asked to accompany you to the emergency ward of a hospital.

If a person seems on the verge of attempting suicide, don't worry about overreacting. Call the police, crisis intervention, or a rescue unit. Needless to say, you should call immediately if a person is in the act of attempting suicide or if a drug has already been taken. The majority of suicide attempts come at temporary low points in a person's life and may never be repeated. Get involved—you may save a life!

Suicide: A Summary of Facts

The following is a list of useful facts to know about suicide (Leenaars, 1995).

1. More men than women commit suicide; but women make more attempts.

2. College students are most likely to attempt suicide during the first part of the school quarter or semester.

3. Many people temporarily become depressed enough to contemplate suicide. Those who would attempt suicide are not all psychotic or suffering from lasting mental illness.

4. Suicide strikes both the rich and the poor.

5. A person who is suicidal once may never again become suicidal. Preventing suicide is well worth the effort.

6. Most potentially suicidal persons give warning.

7. People who talk about suicide *do* often attempt it.

8. The majority of people (two thirds) who attempt suicide do not really want to die, and most of the remainder are ambivalent about dying.

9. A *sudden* improvement in mood after a suicidal depression can mean that the person has decided to carry out a suicide attempt.

10. Four major characteristics of the suicidal state are (1) psychological pain, (2) frustrated needs, (3) a desire to escape, and (4) constricted options.

11. Suicide can often be prevented by the efforts of family, friends, and mental health professionals.

Learning Check

1. More women use guns in their suicide attempts than do men. T or F?

2. While the overall suicide rate has remained about the same, there has been a decrease in adolescent suicides. T or F?

3. Suicide is equally a problem of the rich and the poor. T or F?

4. The highest suicide rates are found among divorced males. T or F?

5. The majority (two thirds) of suicide attempts fall in the "to be" category. T or F?

Critical Thinking

6. What two major risk factors contributed to the 1994 suicide of Kurt Cobain, lead singer for the rock group Nirvana?

Answers:

1. F   2. F   3. T   4. T   5. T   6. Drug or alcohol abuse and availability of a firearm.

Exploration

Who Is "Crazy" and What Should Be Done about It?

The best-known critic of traditional psychiatric treatment for "mental illness" is psychiatrist Thomas Szasz (pronounced saz). Szasz (1966, 1983, 1987) believes that mental illness is a myth. Szasz charges that traditional medical concepts of diseases have been wrongly applied to emotional problems. The *medical model*, as it is called, treats such problems as "diseases" with "symptoms" that can be "cured."

Szasz believes that brain diseases eventually may be found, but that they are not empirically demonstrated as yet. He thus regards "mental illness" as just an idea used when trying to deal with disturbing behavior. If "mental patients" starve themselves, attack members of their families, commit arson or theft, kill themselves, or kill prominent persons, what does psychiatry do? It pardons them (says they are not responsible for their actions) and imprisons them (commits them to a mental hospital for "treatment"). Or, it says they are sane, responsible, and guilty of a crime. In this case they are imprisoned in jail. Szasz believes that labels such as *psychosis* are used mainly to transform people from being responsible for their actions to being non-responsible "patients" who need pity and therapy.

Another of Szasz's points is that "mental illness" and all its categories are merely descriptions of the unlimited variety of human behavior. The labels used to classify mental illness do not explain anything. They are merely applied to behaviors that violate social or psychiatric norms. Thus, the concept of mental illness is used to deal with persons whose behavior creates a *social disturbance* or violates social rules. If a person acts in a way that "offends" society and a law exists against such acts, the person may be jailed. If no law exists, the person may be "treated." In this sense, the distinction between madness and badness, or mental illness and criminality, is a *moral judgment,* not a medical reality.

In light of such thinking, Szasz and a number of other experts prefer to view emotional disturbances as "problems in living." This view makes the goal of therapy "change" rather than "cure" and changes "patients" to "clients." It has also led Szasz to question the handling of the civil rights of psychiatric "patients." Szasz estimates that 90 percent of all patients in mental hospitals are there involuntarily. He sees this as a serious mistake. To commit people because they *might* be dangerous to themselves is indefensible by Szasz's standards.

According to Szasz, the only legitimate reason for depriving a person of freedom is for being "dangerous to others," but then only if the person has broken the law by committing violence or by threatening to do so. Szasz considers the vast majority of "disturbed" persons as no more dangerous than a randomly selected group of citizens. He therefore rejects involuntary commitment as "punishment without trial, imprisonment without limit, and stigmatization without hope of redress."

Point and Counterpoint Szasz does not assert that bizarre behavior is normal. His position is merely that it cannot be explained or sensibly treated using a strict medical model. Szasz's critics reply that advances in neuroscience increasingly call his ideas into question. Certainly, a brain damaged by disease, accident, or drugs can lead to illness, including mental or emotional illness. Szasz's reply is that clearly demonstrated brain abnormalities still apply to only a small percentage of all cases of psychopathology.

It is undoubtedly a mistake to assume that the arguments raised by Szasz justify abandoning the tremendous advances in mental health care found in current approaches. All societies have classified some of their members into categories analogous to our term "mentally ill." The social problems created by "crazy" behavior will not vanish by changing the words used to describe it. Szasz does, however, raise serious questions about civil rights and involuntary commitment. As other critics point out, the medical model of mental illness can strip people of their humanity, autonomy, and self-respect (Hall, 1996).

Recently, several states have made it easier to force the mentally ill into hospitals (Shogren, 1994). Forced treatment might appear to be humane in some instances. But as a final bit of food for thought, consider the following incident, recorded by a reporter visiting a large state mental hospital.

A thin man, old and dry, stopped the guide and said, "When the hell you gonna get me a suit and let me outa here? How about it? . . ." The guide said something indefinite and the man walked away, nodding. This was the section for killers, I had been told, so I asked what the thin man had done. "He painted a horse." "He what?" "He painted a horse." "What's wrong with that?" "It was in a field. A live horse. He was drunk and somebody bet him he couldn't make a horse look like a zebra, I think, so he painted it and they put him here. For being drunk probably." "How long has he been in?" "Thirty-seven years. By the time they got around to letting him out he really was crazy . . . . For his own good we just can't let him go out of here."*

On what basis should we as a society involuntarily commit people? How often would ending involuntary commitment mean freedom to wander lost and neglected on the streets, without family, friends, or hope? Is it better to force mentally ill persons off the streets and into hospitals? What do you think is the right way to deal with "crazy" behavior?

---

* Bruce Jackson, "Our prisons are criminal," *New York Times Magazine,* September 22, 1973, pp. 54-57.

Learning Check   **Critical Thinking**

1. Szasz has argued that it is inappropriate to apply a medical or disease model to what he terms "problems in living." T or F?

2. Szasz points out that most people in mental hospitals are there voluntarily. T or F?

3. Psychosis is the only disorder that Szasz recognizes as a legitimate mental disease. T or F?

4. The new trend that favors forcing the chronically mentally ill off the streets and into hospitals is a reversal of an earlier trend. Can you name the former pattern?

Answers:

4. Deinstitutionalization.

1. T 2. F 3. F

Chapter Summary

What are the general characteristics of psychosis?

◆ **Psychosis** is a break in contact with reality that is marked by **delusions, hallucinations, sensory changes, disturbed emotions and communication,** and in some cases, **personality disintegration.**

◆ Psychotic symptoms tend to be most prominent during short *episodes* of increased disturbance.

◆ A **brief reactive psychosis** may follow extremely stressful life events.

◆ An **organic psychosis** is based on known injuries or diseases of the brain. Other problems of unknown origin are termed **functional psychoses.**

◆ Three common causes of organic psychosis are *untreated syphilis* (**general paresis**), *poisoning*, and **senile dementia** (especially **Alzheimer's disease**).

How do delusional disorders differ from other forms of psychosis?

◆ A diagnosis of **delusional disorder** is almost totally based on the presence of delusions of grandeur, persecution, infidelity, romantic attraction, or physical disease.

◆ The most common delusional disorder is **paranoid psychosis.** Because they often have intense and irrational delusions of persecution, paranoids may be violent if they believe they are threatened.

What forms does schizophrenia take?

◆ **Schizophrenia** is the most frequently occurring psychosis. It is distinguished by a split between thought and emotion, and by delusions, hallucinations, and communication difficulties.

◆ Schizophrenia should not be confused with multiple identity disorder or with **schizotypal personality disorder,** which involves gradual withdrawal into isolation from others and odd, apathetic behavior.

◆ **Disorganized schizophrenia** is marked by extreme personality disintegration and silly, bizarre, or obscene behavior. Social impairment is usually extreme.

◆ **Catatonic schizophrenia** is associated with *stupor, mutism,* and odd postures. Sometimes violent and agitated behavior also occurs.

◆ In **paranoid schizophrenia** (the most common subtype), outlandish delusions of grandeur and persecution are coupled with psychotic symptoms and personality breakdown.

◆ **Undifferentiated schizophrenia** is the term used to indicate a lack of clear-cut patterns of disturbance.

What causes schizophrenia?

◆ Current explanations of schizophrenia emphasize a combination of *early trauma, environmental stress, inherited susceptibility,* and *biochemical abnormalities* in the body or brain.

◆ A number of environmental factors appear to increase the risk of developing schizophrenia. These include viral infection or malnutrition during the mother's pregnancy, birth complications, early **psychological trauma,** and a **disturbed family environment,** especially one marked by **deviant communication.**

◆ Studies of twins and other close relatives strongly support *heredity* as a major factor in schizophrenia. Recent biochemical studies have focused on abnormalities in brain transmitter substances, especially **dopamine** and its receptor sites.

◆ Additional abnormalities in brain structure or activity have been detected in schizophrenic brains by the use of **CT scans, MRI scans,** and **PET scans.**

◆ The dominant explanation of schizophrenia, and other problems as well, is the **stress-vulnerability model.**

What are mood disorders? What causes depression?

◆ **Mood disorders** primarily involve disturbances of mood or emotion, producing *manic* (agitated, elated, hyperactive) or *depressive* (sad, apathetic, suicidal) states.

◆ Long-lasting, though relatively moderate, depression is called a **dysthymic disorder.** Chronic, though moderate, swings in mood between depression and elation are called a **cyclothymic disorder. Reactive depressions** are often triggered by external events; however, they are more intense or prolonged than normal.

◆ **Major mood disorders** involve extremes of mood or emotion. **Bipolar disorders** combine mania and depression.

◆ In a **bipolar I disorder** the person is mostly manic, but has had at least one major depression. In a **bipolar II disorder** the person is mostly depressed, but has had at least one manic episode.

◆ The problem known as **major depressive disorder** involves extreme sadness and despondency, but no evidence of mania.

◆ When a major mood disorder is accompanied by psychotic symptoms, it is called an **affective psychosis.**

◆ **Seasonal affective disorder** (**SAD**), which occurs during the winter months, is another common form of depression. SAD is typically treated with **phototherapy.**

◆ *Biological, psychoanalytic, cognitive,* and *behavioral* theories of depression have been proposed. Heredity is clearly a factor in susceptibility to mood disorders. Research on the causes and treatment of depression continues.

How are major mental disorders treated?

◆ Three **somatic** approaches to treatment of psychosis are **pharmacotherapy** (use of drugs), **electroconvulsive therapy** (**ECT**) (brain shock for the treatment of depression), and **psychosurgery** (surgical alteration of the brain). All three techniques are capable of producing serious side effects, and all are controversial to a degree because of questions about effectiveness and side effects.

◆ **Hospitalization** is often associated with the administration of somatic therapy, and it is also considered a form of treatment.

◆ Prolonged hospitalization has been discouraged by **deinstitutionalization,** by **partial hospitalization,** and by the use of **half-way houses.**

◆ A development in mental health care that seeks to avoid or minimize hospitalization is the creation of **community mental health centers.** Community mental health centers also have as their goal the prevention of mental health problems through education, consultation, and **crisis intervention.**

Why do people commit suicide? Can suicide be prevented?

◆ Suicide is statistically related to such factors as age, sex, and marital status. However, in individual cases the potential for suicide is best identified by a *desire to escape, unbearable psychological pain, frustrated psychological needs,* and a *constriction of options.*

◆ Suicide can often be prevented by the efforts of family, friends, and mental health professionals.

What does it mean to be "crazy"? What should be done about it?

◆ Thomas Szasz has raised challenging questions about the nature of abnormal behavior and its relationship to personal responsibility and civil rights.

◆ Public policies concerning treatment of the chronically mentally ill continue to evolve as authorities try to strike a balance between providing help and taking away personal freedoms.

19

Therapies

Preview

Cold Terror on a Warm Afternoon

The warm Arizona sun was shining brightly. Outside my office window an assortment of small birds sang sweetly. I could hear them between Susan's frightened sobs.

As a psychologist, I see many students with personal problems. Still, I was somewhat surprised to see Susan at my office door. Her excellent work in class and her healthy, casual appearance left me unprepared for her first words. "I feel like I'm losing my mind," she said. "Can I talk to you?"

In the next hour, Susan sketched the features of her own private hell. Her calm exterior hid a world of overwhelming fear, anxiety, and depression. She had lost several jobs because she was overwhelmed by fear when she spoke to co-workers and customers. Her social phobia led to embarrassing misunderstandings and frequent absenteeism. At each job she held, it was only a matter of time until she got fired.

At school Susan felt "different" and was sure that other students could tell she was "weird." Several disastrous romances had left her terrified of men. Lately she had become so depressed that she had begun to think of suicide. Often, she became terrified for no apparent reason. Each time, her heart pounded wildly and she felt she was about to completely lose control.

Susan's visit to my office was an important turning point. Emotional conflicts had made her existence a nightmare. At a time when she was becoming her own worst enemy, Susan realized she needed the help and support of another person. In Susan's case, that person was a talented psychologist to whom I referred her. By combining various forms of psychotherapy, the psychologist was able to help Susan come to grips with her emotions and restore her balance.

This chapter discusses psychological methods used to alleviate problems like Susan's. First, we will describe therapies that emphasize the value of gaining *insight* into personal problems. Later, we will focus on *behavior therapies* and *cognitive therapies,* which are used to directly change troublesome actions and thoughts.

Chapter Survey

Theme: Although there are many forms of psychotherapy, all are based on a common core of therapeutic principles.

Key Questions:

Key Questions	Key Topics to Watch for
How do psychotherapies differ?	Dimensions of therapy
How did modern therapies originate?	Origins of psychotherapy
Is Freudian psychoanalysis still used?	Psychoanalysis and short-term dynamic therapy
What are the major humanistic therapies?	Client-centered, existential, and Gestalt therapies
What is aversion therapy?	Behavior therapy and aversion therapy
How is behavior therapy used to treat phobias, fears, and anxieties?	Desensitization, EMDR, and virtual reality exposure therapy
What role does reinforcement play in behavior therapy?	Extinction, token economies
Can therapy change thoughts and emotions?	Cognitive therapy, rational-emotive behavior therapy
Can psychotherapy be done with groups of people?	Group therapies
What do various therapies have in common?	Core features of psychotherapy Basic counseling skills
How are behavioral principles applied to everyday problems?	Modifying troublesome behaviors
How would a person go about finding professional help?	Seeking professional help
Do cultural differences affect counseling and psychotherapy?	The culturally skilled counselor

Psychotherapy—Getting Better by the Hour

Humpty-Dumpty sat on a wall.

Humpty-Dumpty had a great fall.

All the King's horses and all the King's men,

Couldn't put Humpty together again.

In our age of stress, conflict, and anxiety, who will put you together again, and how will they do it? Actually, the odds are that you will *not* experience an emotional problem like Susan's. But if you did, what help is available? In most cases, the answer is some form of *psychotherapy.*

What is psychotherapy?

Psychotherapy is any psychological technique used to facilitate positive changes in personality, behavior, or adjustment. The psychotherapist has many approaches to choose from: psychoanalysis, desensitization, Gestalt therapy, logotherapy, client-centered therapy, reality therapy, and behavior therapy—to name but a few.

Due to an explosive growth in the number of therapies, some confusion may exist about how they differ. To begin, it is helpful to recognize that psychotherapies vary widely in emphasis (as described in the first highlight). For this reason, the best approach may differ for a particular person or problem.

A Closer Look

Dimensions of Therapy

The term *psychotherapy* most often refers to verbal interaction between trained mental health professionals and their clients. Many therapists also use learning principles to directly alter troublesome behaviors.

The terms listed here describe basic aspects of various therapies. Notice that more than one term may apply to a particular therapy. For example, it would be possible to have a directive, action-oriented group therapy or a non-directive, individual, insight-oriented therapy.

- **Individual therapy** *A therapy involving only one client and one therapist.*

- **Group therapy** *A therapy session in which several clients participate at the same time.*

- **Insight therapy** *Any psychotherapy whose goal is to lead clients to a deeper understanding of their thoughts, emotions, and behavior.*

- **Action therapy** *Any therapy designed to bring about direct changes in troublesome thoughts, habits, feelings, or behavior, without seeking insight into their origins or meanings.*

- **Directive therapy** *Any approach in which the therapist provides strong guidance.*

- **Non-directive therapy** *A style of therapy in which clients assume responsibility for solving their own* problems; the therapist assists, but does not guide or give advice.

- **Time-limited therapy** *Any therapy begun with the expectation that it will last only a limited number of sessions.*

- **Supportive therapy** *An approach in which the therapist's goal is to offer support, rather than to promote personal change. A person trying to get through an emotional crisis or one who wants to solve day-to-day problems may benefit from supportive therapy.*

Myths Popular accounts tend to depict psychotherapy as a complete personal transformation—a sort of "major overhaul" of the psyche. But this ignores the realities of solving human problems. Therapy is *not* equally effective for all problems. Chances of improvement are fairly good for phobias, low self-esteem, some sexual problems, and marital conflicts. More complex problems, however, can be difficult to solve. Also, contrary to what many people think, therapy usually does not bring about dramatic changes in behavior or an end to personal difficulties. For many people, the major benefit of therapy is that it provides comfort, support, and a way to make constructive changes (Zilbergeld, 1983).

In short, it is often unrealistic to expect psychotherapy to undo a person's entire past history. Yet even when problems are severe, therapy may help a person gain a new perspective or learn behaviors to better cope with life (Carson, Butcher, & Mineka, 1996). Psychotherapy can be hard work for both client and therapist. But when it succeeds, there are few activities more worthwhile.

As a final point, you should note that psychotherapy is not always undertaken to solve problems or end a crisis. Therapy can also promote personal growth and enrichment for people who are already doing well (Buck, 1990). Table 19–1 ■ lists some of the elements of positive mental health that therapists seek to restore or promote (Bergin, 1991).

Origins of Therapy— Bored Skulls and Hysteria on the Couch

Early treatments for mental problems give ample reason for appreciating modern therapies. Archaeological findings dating to the Stone Age suggest that most primitive approaches were marked by fear and superstitious belief in demons, witchcraft, and magic. One of the more dramatic "cures" practiced by primitive "therapists" was a process called *trepanning* (treh-PAN-ing; also sometimes spelled *trephining*). In modern usage, **trepanning** *is any surgical procedure in which a hole is bored in the skull.* In the hands of primitive therapists it meant boring, chipping, or bashing holes into a patient's head. Presumably this was done to

Table 19–1 ■ Elements of Positive Mental Health

- Personal autonomy and independence
- A sense of identity
- Feelings of personal worth
- Skilled in interpersonal communication
- Sensitivity, nurturance, and trust
- Genuine and honest with self and others
- Self-control and personal responsibility
- Committed and loving in personal relationships
- Capacity to forgive others and oneself
- Personal values and a purpose in life
- Self-awareness and motivation for personal growth
- Adaptive coping strategies for managing stresses and crises
- Fulfillment and satisfaction in work
- Good habits of physical health

Adapted from Bergin, 1991.

relieve pressure or release evil spirits (Fig. 19–1 ◆). Actually, trepanning may have simply been an excuse to kill people who were unusual, since many "patients" didn't survive the "treatment."

During the Middle Ages, treatment for the mentally ill in Europe focused on **demonology,** *the study of demons and persons plagued by spirits.* Medieval "therapists" commonly blamed abnormal behavior on supernatural forces, such as possession by the devil or curses from witches and wizards. As a treatment, they used **exorcism,** *or "casting out" of "evil*

Figure 19–1 ◆ Primitive "treatment" for mental disorders sometimes took the form of boring a hole in the skull. This example shows signs of healing, which means the patient survived the treatment. Many didn't.

spirits." For the fortunate, exorcism was a religious ritual. More often, it took the form of physical torture to make the body an inhospitable place for the devil to reside.

One explanation for the rise of demonology may lie in **ergotism** (AIR-got-ism), *a psychotic-like condition caused by ergot poisoning.* In the Middle Ages, rye fields were often infested with ergot fungus. Ergot, we now know, is a natural source of LSD and other mind-altering chemicals. Eating bread made from tainted grain can cause symptoms that easily could be interpreted as possession, bewitchment, or madness. Pinching sensations, convulsions, muscle twitches, facial spasms, delirium, and visual hallucinations are all common reactions to ergot poisoning (Kety, 1979; Matossian, 1982). Thus, many of the "patients" of demonology may have been doubly victimized.

The idea that the emotionally disturbed are "mentally ill" and that they should be treated compassionately emerged after 1793. That was the year **Philippe Pinel** *changed the Bicêtre Asylum in Paris from a squalid "madhouse" into a mental hospital by personally unchaining the inmates.* Although over 200 years have passed since Pinel began humane treatment

(Top) Supernatural explanations attributed abnormal behavior to the work of the devil or "possession" by demons. A modern analysis of "demonic possession" suggests that some victims were suffering from dissociative disorders (van der Hart, Lierens, & Goodwin, 1996). *(Bottom)* Many other cases of "possession" in medieval Europe and "bewitchment" in colonial New England may be explained by the psychedelic effects of ergot fungus. Two ears of rye infested with the fungus (dark areas) are shown here.

for the emotionally disturbed, the process of improving psychiatric care continues today.

When was psychotherapy developed?

The first true psychotherapy was developed around the turn of the century by Sigmund Freud. As a physician in Vienna, Freud was intrigued by cases of **hysteria**, *in which physical symptoms (such as paralysis or numbness) occur without known physical causes.* As you may recall, such problems are now called *somatoform disorders* (see Chapter 18). Slowly, Freud became convinced that the symptoms of hysteria were only the tip of the iceberg. Freud believed that deeply hidden unconscious conflicts (frequently sexual in nature) were to blame. Based on this insight, Freud went on to develop his own form of therapy, which he called *psychoanalysis.* Since it is the "granddaddy" of more modern therapies, let us examine psychoanalysis in some detail.

Psychoanalysis— Expedition into the Unconscious

Isn't psychoanalysis the therapy where the patient lies on a couch?

Freud's patients usually reclined on a couch while he sat out of sight taking notes and offering interpretations. Freud used this arrangement to encourage relaxation and a free flow of thoughts and images from the unconscious. It is the least important characteristic of psychoanalysis and many modern analysts have abandoned it.

How did Freud treat emotional problems?

Freud's theory stressed that neurosis is caused by repressed memories, motives, and conflicts—particularly those stemming from instinctual drives for sex and aggression. Although they are hidden, these factors remain active in the personality. This forces the person to develop rigid ego-defense mechanisms. She or he then devotes excessive amounts of time and energy to compulsive and self-defeating behavior. *Thus, the main goal of* **psychoanalysis** *is to resolve internal conflicts that lead to emotional suffering* (Wolitzky, 1995).

Freud relied on four basic techniques to uncover the unconscious roots of neurosis (Freud, 1949). These are *free association, dream analysis, analysis of resistance,* and *analysis of transference.*

Free Association During psychoanalysis, the patient engages in **free association**, *by saying whatever comes to mind.* Patients must speak without concern for whether ideas are painful, embarrassing, or illogical. The person's thoughts are allowed to move freely from one association to the next. The

(*Left*) Many early asylums were no more than prisons with inmates held in chains. (*Right*) One late 19th-century "treatment" was based on swinging the patient in a harness—presumably to calm the patient's nerves.

purpose of free association is to lower defenses so that unconscious material may emerge (Wolitzky, 1995).

Dream Analysis   Freud also considered dreams an unusually good way to tap the unconscious. Freud called dreams "the royal road to the unconscious" because he felt that forbidden desires and unconscious feelings are more freely expressed in dreams. Usually, they are found in the **latent content** (*hidden, symbolic meaning*) of dreams, rather than in a dream's **manifest content** (*obvious, visible meaning*).

Freud was very interested in the unconscious messages revealed by **dream symbols** (*images that have personal or emotional meanings*). Let's say a young husband reports a dream in which he pulls a pistol from his waistband and aims at a target while his wife watches. The pistol repeatedly fails to discharge, and the man's wife laughs at him. Freud might see this as an indication of repressed feelings of sexual impotence, with the gun serving as a disguised image of the penis.

Analysis of Resistance   When free associating or describing dreams, the patient may *resist* talking about or thinking about certain topics. Such **resistances** (*blockages in the flow of ideas*) are said to reveal particularly important unconscious

conflicts. As the analyst becomes aware of resistances, she or he brings them to the patient's awareness so they can be dealt with realistically (Wolitzky, 1995). Rather than being roadblocks in therapy, resistances can be challenges and guides (May, 1996).

Analysis of Transference   **Transference** *is the tendency to "transfer" feelings to a therapist that match those the patient had for important persons in his or her past.* At times the patient may act as if the analyst is a rejecting father, an unloving or overprotective mother, or a former lover. As the patient re-experiences repressed emotions, the therapist can help the patient recognize and understand them. Troubled individuals often provoke anger, rejection, boredom, criticism, and other negative reactions from others. Effective therapists learn to avoid reacting as others do, and playing the patient's habitual "games." This, too, contributes to therapeutic change (Strupp, 1989).

Is psychoanalysis still used?

Psychoanalysis Today   Traditional psychoanalysis called for three to five therapy sessions a week, often for many years. Because of the huge amounts of time and money this

Pioneering psychotherapist Sigmund Freud in his office.

requires, psychoanalysts have become relatively rare. Today, most psychodynamic therapists have switched to doing **short-term dynamic therapy,** *which is designed to produce insights in less time than traditional psychoanalysis.* In this approach, therapists rely on direct interviewing to rapidly uncover unconscious conflicts. They also seek to actively provoke emotional reactions that will lower defenses and provide insights (Davanloo, 1995). Interestingly, brief therapy seems to accelerate recovery. It is as if patients recognize that they need to get to the heart of their problems quickly (Reynolds et al., 1996).

The development of newer, more streamlined dynamic therapies is in part due to questions about the effectiveness of traditional psychoanalysis. One critic, Hans J. Eysenck (1967; 1994), has suggested that psychoanalysis simply takes so long that there is a **spontaneous remission** of symptoms (*improvement due to the mere passage of time*). How could we tell if a particular therapy, or the passage of time is responsible for a person's improvement? Typically, some

patients are randomly assigned for treatment, while others are placed on a waiting list. If members of this **waiting-list control group,** *who receive no treatment,* improve at the same rate as those in therapy, the therapy may be of little value.

How seriously should the possibility of spontaneous remission be taken? It is true that problems ranging from hyperactivity to anxiety improve with the passage of time. However, researchers have confirmed that 60 to 90 percent of patients in psychoanalysis show marked improvement (Bachrach et al., 1991).

The value of Eysenck's critique is that it encouraged psychologists to try new ideas and techniques. Researchers began to ask: "When psychoanalysis works, why does it work? What procedures are essential, and which are unnecessary?" Based on intuition, personal philosophy, clinical experience, and the personality theory they prefer, modern therapists have given surprisingly varied answers to these questions. Upcoming sections will acquaint you with some of the therapies currently in use.

Learning Check

See if you can answer the following questions. If you miss any, review the previous sections.

Match:

_____ **1.** Directive therapies   **A.** Change behavior

_____ **2.** Action therapies   **B.** Place responsibility on client

_____ **3.** Insight therapies   **C.** The client is guided strongly

_____ **4.** Non-directive therapies   **D.** Seek understanding

5. Pinel is famous for his use of exorcism. T or F?

6. Freud developed trepanning. T or F?

7. In psychoanalysis, an emotional attachment to the therapist by the patient is called
   a. free association   **b.** manifest association   **c.** resistance   **d.** transference

Critical Thinking

8. Waiting-list control groups help separate the effects of therapy from improvement related to the mere passage of time. What other type of control group might be needed to learn if therapy is truly beneficial?

Answers:

7. d 8. Placebo therapy is sometimes used to assess the benefits of real therapy. Placebo therapy superficially resembles the real thing, but lacks key elements that are thought to be therapeutic.

1. C 2. A 3. D 4. B 5. F 6. F

Humanistic Therapies—Restoring Human Potential

The goal of traditional psychoanalysis is adjustment. Freud was actually quite conservative in his claims: Any of his patients, he said, could expect only to change their "hysterical misery into common unhappiness"! Humanistic therapies are generally more optimistic. Most assume that it is possible for people to live rich and rewarding lives and to make full use of their potentials. Psychotherapy is seen as a means of giving natural tendencies toward mental health a chance to emerge.

What is client-centered therapy? How is it different from psychoanalysis?

Client-Centered Therapy

Psychoanalysts delve into the unconscious. Psychologist Carl Rogers (1902–1987) found it more beneficial to explore *conscious* thoughts and feelings. The psychoanalyst tends to take a position of authority, stating what dreams, thoughts, or memories "mean." In contrast, Rogers believed that what is right or valuable for the therapist may not be right and valuable for the client. Consequently, the client determines what will be discussed during each session. (Rogers preferred the term *client* to *patient* because "patient" implies a person is "sick" and needs to be "cured.") In summary, **client-centered therapy** *(also called person-centered therapy) is non-directive and based on insights from conscious thoughts and feelings* (Bohart, 1995).

If the client runs things, what does the therapist do?

The therapist's job is to create an "atmosphere of growth." The therapist provides opportunities for change, but the client must actively seek to solve his or her problems. The therapist cannot "fix" the client (Bohart & Tallman, 1996).

Health-Promoting Conditions Rogers believed that effective therapists maintain four basic conditions. First, the therapist offers the client **unconditional positive regard** *(unshakable personal acceptance)*. The therapist refuses to react with shock, dismay, or disapproval to anything the client says or feels. Total acceptance by the therapist is the first step to self-acceptance by the client.

Second, the therapist attempts to achieve genuine **empathy** *by trying to see the world through the client's eyes and feeling some part of what the client is feeling.*

As a third essential condition, the therapist strives to be **authentic** *(genuine and honest)*. The therapist must not hide behind a professional role. Rogers believed that phony fronts destroy the growth atmosphere sought in client-centered therapy.

Fourth, the therapist does not make interpretations, propose solutions, or offer advice. Instead, the therapist **reflects** *(rephrases, summarizes, or repeats)* the client's thoughts and feelings. This allows the therapist to act as a psychological "mirror" so that clients can see themselves more clearly. Rogers believed that a person armed with a realistic self-image and greater self-acceptance will gradually discover solutions to life's problems. His faith in the capacity for emotional health is movingly expressed in the following highlight.

A Closer Look

Carl Rogers and Personal Growth

Like other humanistic psychologists, Carl Rogers (1980) believed deeply that humans have a natural urge to seek health and self-growth. Rogers' belief is vividly expressed by the following words:

I remember that in my boyhood the bin in which we stored our winter's supply of potatoes was in the basement, several feet below a small window. The conditions were unfavorable, but pale white sprouts . . . would grow two or three feet in length as they reached toward the light of the distant window. The sprouts were, in their bizarre, futile growth, a sort of desperate expression of the directional tendency I have been describing. . . . In dealing with clients whose lives have been terribly warped, in working with men and women on the back wards of state hospitals, I often think of those potato sprouts. . . . The clue to understanding their behavior is that they are striving, in the only ways that they perceive as available to them, to move toward growth, toward becoming. To healthy persons, the results may seem bizarre and futile but they are life's desperate attempt to become itself. This potent constructive tendency is an underlying basis of the person-centered approach.

Existential Therapy

According to the existentialists, "being in the world" (existence) creates deep conflicts. Each of us, they say, must deal with the realities of death. We must face the fact that we create our private world by making choices. We must overcome isolation on a vast and indifferent planet. Most of all, we must confront feelings of meaninglessness.

What do these concerns have to do with psychotherapy?

Existential therapy *focuses on the problems of existence, such as meaning, choice, and responsibility.* Like client-centered therapy, it promotes self-knowledge and self-actualization. However, there are important differences. Client-centered therapy seeks to uncover a "true self" hidden behind an

Psychotherapist Carl Rogers, who originated client-centered therapy.

artificial screen of defenses. In contrast, existential therapy emphasizes **free will,** *the human ability to make choices.* Accordingly, existential therapists believe you can *choose to become* the person you want to be.

Existential therapists try to give clients the *courage* to make rewarding and socially constructive choices. Typically, therapy focuses on **death, freedom, isolation,** and **meaninglessness,** *the "ultimate concerns" of existence* (Yalom, 1980). These universal human challenges include: an awareness of one's mortality; the responsibility that comes with freedom to choose; being alone in one's private world; and the reality that meaning must be created in life.

What does the existential therapist do?

The therapist helps clients discover self-imposed limitations in personal identity. To be successful, the client must fully accept the task of changing his or her life (Bugental & Sterling, 1995).

One example of existential therapy is Victor Frankl's **logotherapy,** *which emphasizes the need to find and maintain meaning in life.* Frankl (1955) based his approach on experiences he had as a prisoner in a Nazi concentration camp. In the camp Frankl saw countless prisoners break down as they were stripped of all hope and human dignity. Those who survived with their sanity did so because they managed to hang on to a sense of *meaning* (logos). Even in less dire circumstances, a sense of meaning in life contributes greatly to psychological well-being (Reker, 1994).

A key aspect of existential therapy is **confrontation,** *in which clients are challenged to examine their values and choices.* Ideally, this prompts the person to take responsibility for the quality of his or her existence. An important part of confrontation is the unique, intense, here-and-now *encounter* between two human beings.

When existential therapy is successful, it brings about a renewed sense of purpose and a reappraisal of what's important in life (Dyck, 1987). Some clients even experience an emotional rebirth like that seen when people survive a close brush with death. As Marcel Proust wrote, "The real voyage of discovery consists not in seeing new landscapes but in having new eyes."

Gestalt Therapy

Gestalt therapy, which is most often associated with Frederick (Fritz) Perls (1969), is built around the idea that perception, or *awareness*, is disjointed and incomplete in the maladjusted individual. The Gestalt approach is more directive than client-centered or existential therapy and it emphasizes immediate experience.

What does Gestalt mean?

The German word *Gestalt* means "whole," or "complete." **Gestalt therapy** *helps individuals rebuild thinking, feeling, and acting into connected wholes.* This is achieved by expanding personal awareness, by accepting responsibility for one's thoughts, feelings, and actions, and by filling in gaps in experience (Yontef, 1995).

What do you mean by gaps in experience?

Gestalt therapists believe that we often shy away from expressing or "owning" upsetting feelings. This creates a gap in self-awareness that may become a barrier to personal growth. For example, a person who feels anger after the death of a parent might go for years without expressing it. This and similar threatening gaps may affect emotional health.

Working either one-to-one or in a group setting, the Gestalt therapist encourages clients to become more aware of their immediate experiences. Rather than discussing *why* clients feel guilt, anger, fear, or boredom, they are encouraged to have these feelings in the "here and now" and to become fully aware of them. The therapist helps promote awareness by drawing attention to a client's posture, voice, and eye or hand movements. The client may also be asked to exaggerate a vague feeling until it becomes clear. Gestalt therapists believe that expressing such feelings allows people to "take care of unfinished business" and break through emotional impasses.

In all his writings, Perls' basic message comes through clearly: Emotional health comes from knowing what you

Therapies | **619**

want to do, not dwelling on what you *should* do, *ought* to do, or *should want* to do. Another way of stating this idea is that emotional health comes from taking full responsibility for one's feelings and actions. For example, it means changing "I can't" to "I won't," or "I must" to "I choose to."

How does Gestalt therapy help people discover their real wants?

Above all else, Gestalt therapy emphasizes *present* experi-

ence. Clients are urged to stop intellectualizing and talking *about* feelings. Instead they learn to: live now; live here; stop imagining; experience the real; stop unnecessary thinking; taste and see; express rather than explain, justify, or judge; give in to unpleasantness and pain just as to pleasure; surrender to being as you are (Naranjo, 1970). Gestalt therapists believe that, paradoxically, the best way to change is to become who you really are (Yontef, 1995).

Learning Check

See if you can answer the following questions.

Match:

_____ 1. Client-centered therapy   A. Meaning

_____ 2. Gestalt therapy   B. Unconditional positive regard

_____ 3. Existential therapy   C. Gaps in awareness

_____ 4. Logotherapy   D. Choice and becoming

5. The Gestalt therapist tries to *reflect* a client's thoughts and feelings. T or F?

6. Client-centered therapy is directive. T or F?

7. Confrontation and encounter are concepts of existential therapy. T or F?

Critical Thinking

8. How might using the term *patient* affect the relationship between a person seeking help and a therapist?

Answers:

1. B 2. C 3. D 4. A 5. F 6. F 7. T 8. The terms *doctor* and *patient* imply a large gap in status and authority between a person and his or her therapist. Client-centered therapy attempts to narrow this gap by making the person the final authority concerning solutions to his or her problems.

Behavior Therapy— Healing by Learning

Five times a day, for several days, Brooks Workman stopped what she was doing and vividly imagined opening a soft-drink can. She then pictured herself bringing the can to her mouth and placing her lips on it. Just as she was about to drink, hordes of roaches poured out of the can and scurried into her mouth—writhing, twitching, and wiggling their feelers (Williams & Long, 1991).

Why would anyone imagine such a thing?

Brooks Workman's behavior is not as strange as it sounds. Her goal was self-control: Brooks felt that she was drinking too many colas and she wanted to cut down. The method she chose (called *covert sensitization*) is a form of *behavior therapy* (Cautela & Kearney, 1986). **Behavior therapy** *is the use of learning principles to make constructive changes in behavior.* Behavioral approaches include behavior modification, aversion therapy, desensitization, token economies, and other techniques.

Behavior therapists believe that insight, or deep understanding of one's problems, is often unnecessary for improvement. Instead, behavior therapists try to directly alter troublesome thoughts and actions. Brooks Workman didn't need to probe into her past or her emotions and conflicts; she simply wanted to break her habit of drinking too many colas.

Even when serious problems are at stake, techniques like the one she used have proved valuable.

In general, how does behavior therapy work?

Behavior therapists assume that people have *learned* to be the way they are. If they have learned responses that cause problems, then they can change them by *relearning* more appropriate responses. Broadly speaking, **behavior modification** *is any use of classical or operant conditioning to directly alter human behavior.*

How does classical conditioning work? I'm not sure I remember.

Classical conditioning was described in Chapter 9. Here is a brief review of conditioning principles:

> A neutral stimulus is followed by an *unconditioned stimulus* (*US*) that consistently produces an unlearned reaction, called the *unconditioned response* (*UR*). Eventually the previously neutral stimulus begins to produce this response directly. The response is then called a *conditioned response* (*CR*), and the stimulus becomes a *conditioned stimulus* (*CS*). Thus, for a child the sight of a hypodermic needle (CS) is followed by an injection (US), which causes anxiety or fear (UR). Eventually the sight of a hypodermic (the conditioned stimulus) may produce anxiety or fear (a conditioned response) *before* the child gets an injection.

What does classical conditioning have to do with behavior modification?

Classical conditioning can be used to associate discomfort with a bad habit, as in the case of the woman who wanted to drink fewer colas. More powerful versions of this approach are called *aversion therapy*.

Aversion Therapy—A Little Pain Goes a Long Way

Imagine that you are eating an apple. Suddenly you discover that you just bit a large green worm in half. You vomit. Months pass before you can eat an apple again without feeling ill. You now have a *conditioned aversion* to apples. (A **conditioned aversion** *is a learned dislike or negative emotional response to some stimulus*.)

How are conditioned aversions used in therapy?

In **aversion therapy,** *an individual learns to associate a strong aversion to an undesirable habit* such as smoking, drinking, or gambling. Aversion therapy has been used to cure hiccups, sneezing, stuttering, vomiting, nail-biting, bed-wetting, compulsive hair-pulling, alcoholism, and the smoking of tobacco, marijuana, or crack cocaine. It is also used to treat fetishism, transvestism, pedophilia, and other "maladaptive" sexual behaviors. (To learn how aversion therapy can help people quit smoking, see the next highlight.) There is little doubt that aversive conditioning is an everyday occurrence. For example, not many physicians who treat lung cancer are smokers nor do many emergency room doctors drive without using their seat belts (Rosenthal & Steffek, 1991).

Using Psychology

Puffing Up an Aversion

The fact that nicotine is toxic makes it easy to create an aversion to smoking. Behavior therapists have found that electric shock, nauseating drugs, and similar aversive stimuli are not required to make smokers uncomfortable. All that is needed is for the smoker to smoke—rapidly and for a long time.

Rapid smoking (*prolonged smoking at a forced pace*) is the most widely used aversion therapy for smoking (Lichtenstein, 1982). In this method, clients are told to smoke continuously, taking a puff every 6 to 8 seconds. Rapid smoking continues until the smoker is miserable and can stand it no more. By then, most people are thinking, "I never want to see another cigarette for the rest of my life."

Studies suggest that rapid smoking is one of the most effective behavior therapies for smoking (Tiffany et al., 1986). Nevertheless, anyone tempted to try rapid smoking should realize that it is very unpleasant. Without the help of a therapist, most people quit too

soon for the procedure to succeed. (An alternative method that is more practical is described in the Applications section of this chapter.)

The most basic problem with rapid smoking—as with other stop-smoking methods—is that about one half of those who quit smoking begin again. During at least the first year after quitting, there is no "safe point" after which relapse becomes less likely (Swan & Denk, 1987).

Because the "evil weed" calls so strongly to former smokers, support from a stop-smoking group or a close, caring person can make a big difference. Former smokers who get encouragement from others are much more likely to stay smoke free (Gruder et al., 1993). Those whose social groups include many smokers are more likely to begin smoking again (Mermelstein, 1986).

An excellent example of aversion therapy is provided by the work of Roger Vogler and his associates (1977). Vogler works with alcoholics who were unable to stop drinking. For many clients, aversion therapy is a last chance. Here is a typical aversion procedure:

> While drinking an alcoholic beverage, painful (although non-injurious) electric shocks are delivered to the client's hand. From the client's point of view, the shocks are unpredictable; he or she never knows for sure when one is due. Most of the

Aversion therapy for drinking. The sights, smells, and tastes of drinking are associated with unpleasant electric shocks applied to the hand.

time, however, the shocks come as the client is beginning to take a drink of alcohol.

This **response-contingent** (*response-connected*) shock obviously takes the pleasure out of drinking. Shocks also cause the alcohol abuser to develop a conditioned aversion to drinking. Normally, misery caused by alcohol abuse comes long after the act of drinking—too late to have much effect. But if we can link the sight and smell of alcohol with *immediate* discomfort, then drinking will begin to make the individual very uncomfortable.

But can't the person tell when it is "safe" to drink and when it is not?

Yes, *generalization* of aversion conditioning to the "real world" is a problem. With this in mind, Vogler constructed in his office a vivid re-creation of a "friendly neighborhood tavern," complete with a bar, tables, soft lights, music, and a bartender. Also provided are a "living room," a "bedroom," and a "kitchen." Clients undergo aversion therapy in a setting as much like the normal site of their drinking as possible, and carryover of the aversion training is improved.

Vogler also added an interesting twist to his program: Alcohol abusers are videotaped as they go from sober to drunk. Later, they watch the videotaped drinking bout and see themselves with slurred speech, dropping cigarette ashes in their drinks and saying stupid and belligerent things. Most are ashamed and embarrassed when they see the tapes. Apparently, few people have any idea how unattractive they are when drunk.

To add to the effect, the bartender is trained to provoke clients into becoming argumentative and obnoxious. Presumably, this is not too hard to do by the time the client is saying, "I am 'masshhhed'." In the videotape self-confrontation held later, grossly drunken behaviors are replayed until the client says, "Okay, okay, I've seen enough." Seeing themselves as obnoxious drunks adds to the aversion people feel for drinking, and it increases their determination to quit.

I'm not sure I'm comfortable with the idea of treating humans this way.

People are often disturbed (shocked?) by such methods. It must be emphasized that clients usually volunteer for aversion therapy because it helps them overcome a destructive habit. Indeed, commercial aversion programs for overeating, smoking, and alcohol abuse have attracted many willing customers. And more importantly, aversion therapy can be justified by its long-term benefits. As behaviorist Donald Baer put it, "A small number of brief, painful experiences is a reasonable exchange for the interminable pain of a lifelong maladjustment."

Desensitization—Who's Afraid of a Big, Bad Hierarchy?

Assume that you are a swimming instructor who wants to help a child overcome fear of the high diving board. How might you proceed? Directly forcing a terrified child off the high board could be a psychological disaster. Obviously, a better approach would be to begin by teaching the child to dive off the edge of the pool. Then the child could be taught to dive off the low board, followed by a platform 6 feet above

Programs for treating fears of flying combine relaxation, systematic desensitization, group support, and lots of direct exposure to airliners. Many such programs conclude with a brief flight, so that participants can "test their wings" (Roberts, 1989).

Figure 19–2 ◆ Treatment of a snake phobia by vicarious desensitization. The photographs show models interacting with snakes. To overcome their own fears, phobic subjects observed the models. (Bandura et al., 1969. Photos courtesy of Albert Bandura.)

the water and then an 8-foot platform. As a last step, the child could try the high board.

This *rank-ordered series of steps* is called a **hierarchy.** The hierarchy allows the child to undergo *adaptation.* Gradually the child adapts to the high dive and overcomes fear, much as one adapts to a cool swimming pool on a hot day. When the child has overcome the fear, a psychologist would say that *desensitization* (dee-SEN-sih-tih-ZAY-shun) has occurred.

Desensitization is also based on the principle of *reciprocal inhibition,* a term coined by Joseph Wolpe (1974). In **reciprocal inhibition,** *one emotional state is used to block another.* For instance, it is impossible to be anxious and relaxed at the same time. If we can get our subject onto the high board in a relaxed state, anxiety and fear responses will be inhibited. Repeated visits to the high board should cause fear in the situation to disappear. Again we would say that the person has been *desensitized.* In general, **systematic desensitization** (*a guided reduction in fear, anxiety, or aversion*) is usually accomplished by gradually approaching a feared stimulus while maintaining relaxation.

What is desensitization used for?

Desensitization is primarily used to help people unlearn or countercondition **phobias** (*intense, unrealistic fears*) or strong anxieties. Almost everyone has a phobia or two. Many people fear heights, snakes, public speaking, spiders, and so forth. Usually these cause little difficulty because the person carefully avoids feared situations. However, consider the following: a teacher with stage fright, a student with test anxiety, a salesperson who fears people, an aspiring pole-vaulter who fears heights, or a newlywed with a fear of sexual intimacy. Each may be hampered enough by fears or anxieties to seek aid.

How is desensitization done?

Systematic desensitization usually involves three steps. First, the client and the therapist *construct a hierarchy.* This is a list of fear-provoking situations involving the phobia and ranging from the least disturbing situation to the most disturbing one. Second, the client is taught *exercises that produce deep relaxation* (described in this chapter's Applications section). Once the client is relaxed, she or he proceeds to the third step by trying to *perform the least disturbing item* on the list. For a fear of heights (acrophobia), this might be: "(1) Stand on a chair." The first item is repeated until no anxiety is felt. Any change from complete relaxation is a signal that clients must repeat the relaxation process before continuing. Slowly clients move up the hierarchy: "(2) Climb to the top of a small stepladder"; "(3) Look down a flight of stairs"; and so on, until the last item is performed without fear: "(20) Fly in an airplane." For many fears, desensitization is most effective when people are directly exposed to the stimuli and situations they fear (Menzies & Clarke, 1993). For something like a simple spider phobia, this can even be done in groups (Ost, 1996).

I understand how some fears could be desensitized by gradual approach—as in the case of the child on the high dive. But how would a therapist use desensitization to combat fear of sexual intimacy?

For a person with a fear of heights, the steps of the hierarchy might be acted out. Often, however, this is totally impractical. In some cases the problem can be handled by having clients observe *models* who are performing the feared behavior (Fig. 19–2 ◆) (Rosenthal & Steffek, 1991). A **model** *is a person who serves as an example for observational learning.* If such **vicarious desensitization** (*secondhand learning*) is not practical, there is yet another alternative. Fortunately, desensitization works almost as well when a person *vividly imagines* each step in the hierarchy (Deffenbacher & Suinn, 1988). If the steps can be visualized without anxiety, fear in the actual situation is reduced.

Here is a sample of the hierarchy imagined by a 24-year-old married woman to overcome the fear and disgust she felt for sexual intercourse. (Some steps are left out to shorten the list.)

1. Dancing with and embracing husband while fully clothed.
2. Being kissed on cheeks and forehead.
3. Being kissed on lips.
4. Sitting on husband's lap, both fully dressed.
5. Husband kisses neck and ears.
6. Husband caresses hair and face.

   .
   .
   .

17. Having intercourse in bed in the dark.
18. Having intercourse in the nude in a dining room or living room.
19. Changing positions during intercourse.
20. Having intercourse in the nude while sitting on husband's lap. (Adapted from Lazarus, 1964.)

Mrs. A was able to imagine the last steps in this hierarchy without anxiety after a 3-month period of desensitization. Accordingly, she and her husband reported that their sexual relationship was greatly improved.

In an important new development, psychologists are beginning to use *virtual reality* to treat phobias. Virtual reality is a computer-generated, three-dimensional "world" that viewers enter by wearing a head-mounted video display. **Virtual reality exposure** *allows computerized fear stimuli to be presented to patients in a controlled fashion.* It has already been used successfully to treat acrophobia (fear of heights) and fear of flying (Fig. 19–3 ◆) (Rothbaum, et al., 1995; Rothbaum, et al., 1996).

Desensitization has been one of the most successful behavior therapies. A second new technique may provide yet another way to lower fears, anxieties, and psychological pain. The following highlight has the details.

Research Frontier

Eye Movement Desensitization— Watching Trauma Fade?

Traumatic events produce painful memories. Victims of accidents, disasters, molestations, muggings, rapes, or emotional abuse are often haunted by disturbing images and flashbacks. Recently, Dr. Francine Shapiro developed a technique called **eye movement desensitization and reprocessing (EMDR)** *to help ease traumatic memories and post-traumatic stress.*

In a typical EMDR session, the client is asked to visualize the images that most upset her or him. At the same time, a pencil (or other object) is moved rapidly from side to side in front of the person's eyes. Watching the moving object causes the person's eyes to dart swiftly back and forth. After about 30 seconds, patients describe any memories, feelings, and thoughts that emerged and discuss them with the therapist. These steps are repeated until troubling thoughts and emotions no longer surface (Shapiro, 1995).

Results of initial studies indicate that EMDR lowers anxieties and takes the pain out of traumatic memories (Carlson et al., 1996; Wilson, Becker, & Tinker, 1995). However, EMDR is highly controversial. Some studies, for example, have found that eye

Figure 19–3 ◆ (*Right*) Dr. Barbara Rothbaum and Dr. Larry Hodges show how a virtual reality system is used to expose people to feared stimuli. Many patients say that they would rather face exposure to feared stimuli in a virtual environment than in a real physical environment. (*Left*) A computer image from a virtual elevator. Over an 8-week period, patients who suffered from acrophobia "rode" in the elevator. Each session took them to greater heights. (Image courtesy of Larry Hodges, Thomas Meyer, and Rob Kooper.)

movements add nothing to the treatment. The apparent success of EMDR may simply be based on gradual exposure to upsetting stimuli, like in other forms of desensitization (Lilienfeld, 1996).

Is EMDR a breakthrough? Or will it prove to be a case of wishful thinking? Given the frequency of traumas in modern society, it shouldn't be long before we find out.

Operant Principles— All the World Is a Skinner Box?

Aversion therapy and desensitization are based on classical conditioning. Where does operant conditioning fit in?

The principles of operant conditioning were developed by B. F. Skinner and other psychologists, mostly through laboratory research with animals. As you may recall, **operant conditioning** *refers to learning based on the consequences of making a response.* The operant principles most frequently used by behavior therapists to deal with human behavior are:

1. Positive reinforcement. An action that is followed by reward will occur more frequently. If children whine and get attention, they will whine more frequently. If you get A's in your psychology class, you may become a psychology major.

2. Non-reinforcement. An action that is not followed by reward will occur less frequently.

3. Extinction. If a response is not followed by reward after it has been repeated many times, it will go away. After winning three times, you pull the handle on a slot machine 30 times more without a payoff. What do you do? You go away. So does the response of handle pulling (for that particular machine, at any rate).

4. Punishment. If a response is followed by discomfort or an undesirable effect, the response will be suppressed (but not necessarily extinguished).

5. Shaping. Shaping means rewarding actions that are closer and closer approximations to a desired response. If a response is complicated, it may never occur and thus may never be rewarded. If I want to reward a retarded child for saying "ball," I may begin by rewarding the child for saying anything that starts with a *b* sound.

6. Stimulus control. Responses tend to come under the control of the situation in which they occur. If I set my clock 10 minutes fast, I can get to work on time in the morning. My departure is under the stimulus control of the clock, even though I know it is fast.

7. Time out. A time-out procedure usually involves removing the individual from a situation in which reinforcement occurs. Time out, which prevents reward from following an undesirable response, is a variation of non-reinforcement. For example, children who fight with each other can be sent to separate rooms and allowed out only when they are able to behave more calmly (Olson & Roberts, 1987). (For a more thorough review of operant learning, return to Chapter 9.)

As simple as these principles may seem, they have been used very effectively to overcome difficulties in work, home, school, and industrial settings. Let's see how.

Non-Reinforcement and Extinction—Time Out in the Attention Game

An extremely overweight mental patient had a persistent and disturbing habit: She stole food from other patients. No one could persuade her to stop stealing or to diet. For the sake of her health, a behavior therapist assigned her to a special table in the ward dining room. If she approached any other table, she was immediately removed from the dining room. Since her attempts to steal food went unrewarded, they rapidly disappeared. Additionally, any attempt to steal from others usually resulted in the patient's missing her own meal (Ayllon, 1963).

What operant principles did the therapist in this example use?

The therapist used *non-reward* to produce *extinction*. The most frequently occurring human behaviors lead to some form of reward. An undesirable response can be eliminated by *identifying* and *removing* the rewards that maintain it. But people don't always do things for food, money, or other obvious rewards. Most of the rewards maintaining human behavior are more subtle. *Attention, approval,* and *concern* are common yet powerful reinforcers for humans (Fig. 19–4 ◆).

In school we often find that misbehaving children are surrounded by others who giggle and pay attention to them. If seating is rearranged so that the disruptive children are surrounded by less responsive students, misbehavior decreases. Attention from a teacher (even a scolding) can also be a reinforcer. An experiment showed that when teachers paid extra attention to classroom misbehavior, it increased. It increased even when the attention took the form of saying things such as "Sit down!" When misbehaving children were *ignored* and attention was given to children who were *not* misbehaving, misbehavior decreased (Madsen et al., 1968).

How are non-reward and extinction applied in therapy?

Non-reward and extinction can eliminate many problem behaviors, especially in schools, hospitals, and institutions. Often, difficulties center around a limited number of particularly disturbing responses. A typical strategy used in institutions is called *time out*. Time out means refusing to reward maladaptive responses, usually by refusing to play the *attention* game. Another form of time out is to remove an individual immediately from the setting in which an undesirable response occurs, so that the response will not be rewarded. For example:

Fourteen-year-old Josh periodically appeared in the nude in the activity room of a training center for disturbed juveniles. This behavior always generated a great deal of attention from staff and other patients. Usually Josh was returned to his room and confined there. During this "confinement," he often missed doing his usual chores. As an experiment he was placed on time out. The next time he appeared nude, counselors and other staff

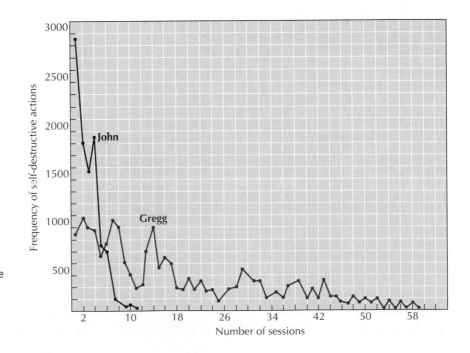

Figure 19–4 ◆ This graph shows extinction of self-destructive behavior in two autistic boys. Before extinction began, the boys received attention and concern from adults for injuring themselves. During extinction, self-damaging behavior was ignored. (Adapted from Lovaas & Simons, 1969.)

members greeted him normally and then ignored him. Attention from other patients rapidly subsided. Sheepishly he returned to his room and dressed.

Reinforcement and Token Economies—The Target Is Health

This section might be called "Throwing a Lifeline to the Unreachable." A distressing problem faced when dealing with the severely disturbed is how to "break through" to a patient who cannot, or will not, communicate. Mental patients sometimes spend years in hospitals without noticeable improvement.

What can be done in such circumstances?

One widely used approach is based on **tokens** (*symbolic rewards, such as plastic chips, that can be exchanged for real rewards*). (As you may recall from Chapter 9, tokens are secondary reinforcers.)

Tokens may be printed slips of paper, check marks, points, or gold stars. Whatever form they take, tokens serve as rewards because they may be exchanged for candy, food, cigarettes, recreation, or other privileges, such as private time with a therapist, outings, or using the stereo. Tokens are used in mental hospitals, half-way houses, schools for the retarded, programs for delinquents, and ordinary classrooms. They usually produce dramatic improvements in behavior (Sullivan & O'Leary, 1990).

By using tokens, a therapist can *immediately reward* a positive response. This allows a therapist to influence behavior directly, through operant shaping, instead of vaguely urging patients to "get themselves together." For maximum impact, the therapist selects specific **target behaviors** (*actions or other behaviors the therapist seeks to modify*). Target behaviors are then reinforced with tokens. For example, a mute mental patient might first be given a token each time he or she says a word. Next, tokens may be given for speaking a complete sentence. Later, the patient could gradually be required to speak more often, then to answer questions, and eventually to carry on a short conversation in order to receive tokens. In this way, patients who have not spoken more than a few words for months or years have been returned to the world of normal communication.

Full-scale use of tokens in an institutional setting produces a *token economy*. In a **token economy,** *patients are rewarded with tokens for a wide range of socially desirable or productive activities.* They must *pay* tokens for privileges and for engaging in problem behavior (Fig. 19–5 ◆). For example, tokens are given to patients who get out of bed, dress themselves, take required medication, arrive for meals on time, and the like. Constructive activities, such as gardening, cooking, or custodial duties, may also earn tokens. Patients must *exchange* tokens for meals and private rooms, movies, passes, off-ward activities, and other privi-

Credit Card

OXNARD DAY TREATMENT CENTER CREDIT INCENTIVE SYSTEM

EARN CREDITS BY		SPEND CREDITS FOR	
MONITOR DAILY	15	COFFEE	5
MENU PLANNING CHAIRMAN	50	LUNCH	10
PARTICIPATE	5	EXCEPT THURSDAY	15
BUY FOOD AT STORE	10	BUS TRIP	5
COOK FOR/PREPARE LUNCH	5	BOWLING	8
WIPE OFF KITCHEN TABLE	3	GROUP THERAPY	5
WASH DISHES	5-10	PRIVATE STAFF TIME	5
DRY AND PUT AWAY DISHES	5	DAY OFF	5-20
MAKE COFFEE AND CLEAN URN	15	WINDOW SHOPPING	5
CLEAN REFRIGERATOR	20	REVIEW WITH DR.	10
ATTEND PLANNING CONFERENCE	1	DOING OWN THING	1
OT PREPARATION	1-5	LATE 1 PER EVERY 10 MIN	
COMPLETE OT PROJECT	5	PRESCRIPTION FROM DR.	10
RETURN OT PROJECT	2		
DUST AND POLISH TABLES	5		
PUT AWAY GROCERIES	3		
CLEAN TABLE	5		
CLEAN 6 ASH TRAYS	2		
CLEAN SINK	5		
CARRY OUT CUPS & BOTTLES	5		
CLEAN CHAIRS	5		
CLEAN KITCHEN CUPBOARDS	5		
ASSIST STAFF	5		
ARRANGE MAGAZINES NEATLY	3		
BEING ON TIME	5		
MONITOR-ANN			

Figure 19–5 ◆ Shown here is a token used in one token economy system; also pictured is a list of credit values for various activities. Tokens may be exchanged for items or for privileges listed on the board. (After photographs by Robert P. Liberman.)

leges. Patients are *charged* tokens for staying in bed, disrobing in public, talking to themselves, fighting, crying, and similar target behaviors (Morisse et al., 1996).

Token economies can radically change a patient's overall adjustment and morale. Patients are given an incentive to change and they are held responsible for maladaptive habits and actions. Many "hopelessly" retarded, mentally ill, and delinquent people have been returned to productive lives by means of token economies.

Wouldn't there be a problem with generalization of improvements brought about by a token economy?

Yes. Lack of generalization can again be a problem. To minimize this, patients are praised and given *social* recognition when they receive tokens. Each time a token is given, the therapist says something like, "That was very good," or "You're doing so well."

By the time they are ready to leave the program, patients may be earning tokens on a weekly basis for maintaining sane, responsible, and productive behavior. Typically, the most effective token economies are those that gradually switch from tokens to *social rewards* such as recognition and approval. Such rewards are what patients will receive when they return to family, friends, and community.

Cognitive Therapy— Think Positive!

How would a behavior therapist treat a problem like depression? None of the techniques described seem to apply.

As we have discussed, behavior therapists usually try to change troublesome actions. However, in recent years a new breed of therapist has appeared. *Cognitive therapists*, as they are called, are interested in thoughts, as well as visible behavior. Rather than looking only at actions, cognitive therapists try to learn what people think, believe, and feel. In general, **cognitive therapy** *helps clients change thinking patterns that lead to troublesome emotions or behaviors* (Freeman & Reinecke, 1995).

Cognitive Therapy for Depression

Cognitive therapy has been especially effective for treating depression. As you may recall from Chapter 14, Aaron Beck (1991) believes that negative, self-defeating thoughts underlie depression. According to Beck, depressed persons see themselves, the world, and the future in negative terms. Beck believes this occurs because of several major distortions in thinking. The first is **selective perception,** *which refers to perceiving only certain stimuli in a larger array.* If five good things happen during the day and three bad things, the depressed person will focus only on the bad. A second

thinking error underlying depression is **overgeneralization,** *the tendency to apply an upsetting event to unrelated situations.* An example would be considering yourself a total failure, or completely worthless, if you were to lose a job or fail one class. To complete the picture, Beck says that depressed persons tend to *magnify* the importance of undesirable events, and they engage in **all-or-nothing thinking,** *by seeing each event as completely good or bad, right or wrong, successful or a failure* (Beck, 1985).

What do cognitive therapists do to alter such patterns?

Cognitive therapists make a step-by-step effort to correct negative thoughts that lead to depression or similar problems. At first, clients are taught to recognize and keep track of their own thoughts. The client and therapist then look for ideas and beliefs that cause depression, anger, and avoidance. For example, here's how a therapist might challenge all-or-nothing thinking (Burns & Persons, 1982):

> *Patient:* I'm feeling even more depressed. No one wants to hire me, and I can't even clean up my apartment. I feel completely incompetent!
> *Therapist:* I see. The fact that you are unemployed and have a messy apartment proves that you are completely incompetent?
> *Patient:* Well . . . I can see that doesn't add up.

Next, clients are asked to gather information to test their beliefs. For instance, a depressed person might list his or her activities for a week. The list is then used to challenge all-or-nothing thoughts, such as "I had a terrible week" or "I'm a complete failure." With more coaching, clients learn to alter thoughts in ways that improve their moods, actions, and relationships.

Cognitive therapy is as effective as pharmacotherapy for treating many cases of depression. More important, people who have adopted new thinking patterns are less likely to become depressed again—a benefit that drugs can't impart (Fava et al., 1996; Hollon et al., 1992).

In an alternate approach, cognitive therapists look for an *absence* of effective coping skills and thought patterns, not for the *presence* of self-defeating thinking (Freeman & Reinecke, 1995). The aim is to teach clients how to cope with anger, depression, shyness, stress, and similar problems. Stress inoculation, which is described in Chapter 14, is a good example of this approach.

Cognitive therapy is a promising and rapidly expanding specialty. Before we leave the topic, let's explore one more widely used form of cognitive therapy.

Rational-Emotive Behavior Therapy

Rational-emotive behavior therapy (REBT) *attempts to change or remove irrational beliefs that cause emotional problems.* According to Albert Ellis (1973, 1995), the basic idea of rational-emotive therapy is as easy as ABC. Ellis assumes that people become unhappy and develop self-defeating habits because they have unrealistic or faulty *beliefs.*

How are beliefs important?

Ellis analyzes problems in this way: The letter A stands for an *activating experience,* which the person assumes to be the cause of C, an *emotional consequence.* For instance, a person who is rejected (the activating experience) feels depressed, threatened, or hurt (the consequence). Rational-emotive therapy shows the client that the real problem is what comes between A and C: In between is B, the client's irrational and unrealistic *beliefs.* In this example, the unrealistic belief leading to unnecessary suffering is: "I must be loved and approved by almost everyone at all times." REBT holds that events do not *cause* us to have feelings. We feel as we do because of our beliefs (Kottler & Brown, 1996).

Using Psychology

Ten Irrational Beliefs— Which Do You Hold?

1. I must be loved and approved by almost every significant person in my life or it's awful and I'm worthless.
   Example: "One of my roommates doesn't seem to like me. I must be a total zero."

2. I should be completely competent and achieving in all ways to be a worthwhile person.
   Example: "I don't understand my chemistry class. I guess I really am a stupid person."

3. Certain people I must deal with are thoroughly bad and should be severely blamed and punished for it.
   Example: "The old man next door is such a pain. I'm going to play my stereo even louder the next time he complains."

4. It is awful and upsetting when things are not the way I would very much like them to be.
   Example: "I should have gotten a B in that class. The teacher is unfair."

5. My unhappiness is always caused by external events; I cannot control my emotional reactions.
   Example: "You make me feel awful. I would be happy if it weren't for you."

6. If something unpleasant might happen, I should keep dwelling on it.
   Example: "I'll never forget the time my boss insulted me. I think about it every day at work."

7. It is easier to avoid difficulties and responsibilities than to face them.
   Example: "I don't know why my wife seems angry. Maybe it will just pass by if I ignore it."

8. I should depend on others who are stronger than I am.
   Example: "I couldn't survive if he left me."

9. Because something once strongly affected my life, it will do so indefinitely.
   Example: "My girlfriend dumped me during my junior year in college. I don't know if I can ever trust a woman again."

10. There is always a perfect solution to human problems and it is awful if this solution is not found.
    Example: "I'm so depressed about politics in this country. It all seems hopeless."

(Adapted from Rohsenow & Smith, 1982.)

Ellis (1979, 1987) says that most irrational beliefs come from three core ideas, each of which is unrealistic:

1. I *must* perform well and be approved of by significant others. If I don't, then it is awful, I cannot stand it, and I am a rotten person.

2. You *must* treat me fairly. When you don't, it is horrible, and I cannot bear it.

3. Conditions *must* be the way I want them to be. It is terrible when they are not, and I cannot stand living in such an awful world.

It's easy to see that such beliefs can lead to much grief and needless suffering in a less than perfect world. Rational-emotive behavior therapists are very directive in their attempts to change a client's irrational beliefs and "self-talk." The therapist may attack clients' logic, challenge their thinking, confront them with evidence contrary to their beliefs, and even assign "homework." Here, for instance, are some examples of statements that dispute irrational beliefs (after Kottler & Brown, 1996):

- "Where is the evidence that you are a loser just because you didn't do well this one time?"
- "Who said the world should be fair? That's your rule."
- "What are you telling yourself to make yourself feel so upset?"
- "Is it really terrible that things aren't working out as you would like? Or is it just inconvenient?"

Many of us would probably do well to give up our irrational beliefs. Improved self-acceptance and a better tolerance of daily annoyances are the benefits of doing so.

The value of cognitive approaches is further illustrated by three techniques (*covert sensitization, thought stopping,* and *covert reinforcement*) described in the Applications section that concludes this chapter. A little later you can see what you think of them.

Learning Check

1. Behavior modification programs aimed at extinction of an undesirable behavior typically make use of what operant principles?
   a. punishment and stimulus control   **b.** punishment and shaping
   c. non-reinforcement and time out   **d.** stimulus control and time out

2. Attention can be a powerful _____ for humans.

3. Token economies depend on the time-out procedure. T or F?

4. Tokens basically allow the operant shaping of desired responses or "target behaviors." T or F?

5. According to Beck, selective perception, overgeneralization, and _____ thinking are cognitive habits that underlie depression.

6. REBT teaches people to change the antecedents of irrational behavior. T or F?

Critical Thinking

7. In Aron Beck's terms, a belief such as "I must perform well or I am a rotten person" involves two thinking errors. These are:

Answers:
1. c 2. reinforcer 3. F 4. T 5. all-or-nothing 6. F 7. Overgeneralization and all-or-nothing thinking.

Group Therapy—People Who Need People

Group therapy *is psychotherapy done with more than one person.* Most of the psychotherapies we have discussed can be adapted for use in groups. Psychologists first tried working with groups as a practical response to the need for more therapists. To their surprise, group therapy not only worked, it also offered some special advantages (Dies, 1995).

What are the advantages of group therapy?

In group therapy, a person can *act out* or directly experience problems. Doing so often produces insights that might not occur from merely talking about one person's difficulties. In addition, other group members with similar problems can offer support and useful input. Groups can help form a bridge between therapy and real-life problems. For reasons such as these, a number of specialized groups and techniques have emerged. Because they range from Alcoholics Anonymous to Marriage Encounter, we will sample only a few representative approaches.

Psychodrama

One of the first group approaches was developed by Jacob L. Moreno (1953), who called his technique *psychodrama*. In **psychodrama,** *clients act out personal conflicts and feelings with others who play supporting roles.* The client's **role-playing** *usually involves re-enacting dramatic incidents that cause problems in real life.* For example, Don, a disturbed teenager, might act out a typical family fight, with the therapist playing his father and with other patients playing his mother, brothers, and sisters. Moreno believed that insights from these enactments transfer to real-life situations.

Therapists using psychodrama often find *role reversals* especially helpful. A **role reversal** *refers to taking the part of* another person in order to learn how that person feels. For instance, Don would be asked to role-play his father or mother, to better understand their feelings. A related method is the **mirror technique,** *in which clients observe another person re-enact their own behavior.* Thus, Don might briefly join the audience and watch as another group member plays his role. This allows the teenager to see himself as others do (Shaffer & Galinsky, 1989).

Family Therapy

Family relationships are the source of great pleasure, and all too often, of great pain for many people. In **family therapy,** *husband, wife, and children work as a group to resolve the problems of each family member.* Family therapy tends to be brief and focused on specific problems, such as frequent fights or a depressed teenager. For some types of problems, family therapy may be superior to other approaches (Pinsof, Wynne, & Hambright, 1996).

Family therapists believe that problems are rarely limited to a single family member: A problem for one is considered a problem for all. That is, families often contribute to and maintain maladaptive behavior. If changes are not made in the *family system,* changes in any single family member may not last. A **family system** *is an entire family unit,* including all its members, their relationships, and their typical patterns of behavior. Thus, family members work together to improve communication, to change destructive patterns, and to see themselves and each other in new ways. This helps them reshape distorted perceptions and interactions directly, with the very persons with whom they have troubled relationships (Goldfried, Greenberg, & Marmar, 1990).

Does the therapist work with the whole family at once?

The family therapist treats the family as a unit, but may not meet with the entire family at each session. If a family crisis is at hand, the therapist may first try to identify the most resourceful family members, who can help solve the

A group therapy session. Group members offer mutual support while sharing problems and insights.

immediate problem. The therapist and family members may then work on resolving more basic conflicts and on improving family relationships. In some instances, family therapists look beyond the present family to previous generations. Understanding a troubled marriage, for example, may be aided by identifying conflicts that have carried over from each spouse's parents or even grandparents (Dies, 1995).

Group Awareness Training

During the 1960s and 1970s, the human potential movement led many people to become interested in personal growth experiences. Often, their interest was expressed by participation in sensitivity training or encounter groups.

What is the difference between sensitivity and encounter groups?

Sensitivity groups tend to be less confrontive than encounter groups. Participants in **sensitivity groups** *take part in exercises that gently enlarge self-awareness and sensitivity to others.* For example, in a "trust walk," participants expand their confidence in others by allowing themselves to be led about while blindfolded.

Encounter groups *are based on an honest expression of feelings and reactions to other participants.* Intense emotion and communication may take place in an encounter group. Typically, the emphasis is on tearing down defenses and false fronts. Because there is a danger of hostile confrontation and psychological damage, encounter group participation is safest when members are carefully screened and when a trained leader guides the group. Encounter group "casualties" are rare, but they do occur (Shaffer & Galinsky, 1989).

In business settings, psychologists still use the basic principles of sensitivity and encounter groups—truth, self-awareness, and self-determination—to improve employee

relationships. Specially designed encounter groups for married couples are also widely held. However, in the last decade there has been a shift away from public participation in sensitivity and encounter groups. Instead, hundreds of thousands of people have taken part in various forms of *large-group awareness training* (Finkelstein et al., 1982). **Large-group awareness training** *refers to programs that claim to increase self-awareness and facilitate constructive personal change.* Lifespring, Actualizations, est, the Forum, and similar commercial programs are well-known examples. Like the smaller groups that preceded them, large-group trainings combine psychological exercises, confrontation, new viewpoints, and group dynamics to promote personal change.

Are sensitivity, encounter, and awareness groups really psychotherapies?

These experiences tend to be positive, but they produce only moderate benefits (Faith, Wong, & Carpenter, 1995). Moreover, many of the claimed benefits may simply result from a kind of **therapy placebo effect,** *in which improvement is based on a client's belief that therapy will help.* Positive expectations, a break in daily routine, and an excuse to act differently can have quite an impact. The importance of such factors is easily illustrated: Participants in a weekend "retreat" that featured nothing more than volleyball, charades, and ballroom dancing reported enhanced mental health (McCardel & Murray, 1974)! Kurt Back may have summarized it best when he said, "Encounter groups may comfort, but they do not cure anything."

A danger you should be aware of in some large-group training programs is that participants may be verbally attacked by a "trainer" as part of the "educational" process. For some people, such attacks *create* an emotional crisis that did not exist before. Unwary participants then resolve this crisis by converting to the organization that promotes the training (Cushman, 1989). Don't expect your life to be transformed by a large-group experience. (The same can be said of various forms of "media" therapy, as discussed in the next section.)

Psychotherapy at a Distance—Psych Jockeys and Cybertherapy

How valid are psychological services offered over the phone and on the Internet?

For better or worse, psychotherapy and counseling are rapidly entering the electronic age. Today, psychological services are available through radio, telephone, and e-mail. What are the advantages and disadvantages of getting help "online"? What are the risks and possible benefits?

By now, you have probably heard a phone-in radio psychologist. On a typical program, callers describe problems arising from child abuse, loneliness, love affairs, phobias, sexual adjustment, or depression. The radio psychologist then offers reassurance, advice, or suggestions for getting help. How valid are their efforts?

Critical Thinking

Media Psychologists

Talk-radio psychology may seem harmless, but it raises some important questions. For instance, is it reasonable to give advice without knowing anything about a

Media psychologists have been urged to educate without actually doing therapy on the air. Some overstep this boundary, however.

person's background? Might the advice do harm? What good can a psychologist do in 3 minutes?

In defense of themselves, radio psychologists point out that listeners may learn solutions to their own problems by hearing others talk. Many also stress that their work is educational, not therapeutic. Nevertheless, the question arises, When does advice become therapy? The American Psychological Association urges media psychologists to discuss problems only of a general nature, instead of actually counseling anyone. For example, if a caller complains about insomnia, the radio psychologist should talk about insomnia in general, not probe the caller's personal life (Schommer, 1984).

By giving information, advice, and social support, radio psychologists probably do help some listeners (Levy, 1989). Even so, a good guide for anyone tempted to call a radio psychologist might be "let the consumer beware."

Telephone Therapists

The same cautions we have noted for "psych jockeys" apply to telephone therapists. These "counselors" can be reached through 900-number services for $3 to $4 per minute. To date, there is no evidence that telephone counseling is effective. Successful face-to-face therapy is based on a continuing *relationship* between two people. Telephone therapy is seriously undermined by a lack of visual cues (such as facial expressions and body language) and by limited personal contact (Haas, Benedict, & Kobos, 1996).

It's important to note that legitimate therapists occasionally use the phone to calm, console, or advise clients between therapy sessions. Also, use of the telephone for suicide hotlines and crisis counseling is well established. However, where commercial telephone therapists are concerned, consumers might well ask themselves, How much confidence would I place in a physician who would make a diagnosis over the phone? Many telephone "therapists" may be nothing more than untrained operators (Newman, 1994).

Cybertherapy

It has been said that you can find almost anything on the Internet. Recently, "cybertherapy," psychological advice, support groups, and self-help magazines have been added to the list. Some services, such as support groups, are free. Online counseling or advice, in contrast, is typically offered for a fee. Some online therapists will "discuss" problems with you through e-mail messages. Others merely answer questions or give advice concerning specific problems.

Psychologists who have gone online emphasize that they're not engaged in therapy. Rather, they offer guidance and advice to help people solve everyday problems in living. However, many online services imply in advertising that they are a substitute for therapy. Consequently, some people may be contacting online counselors when they actually need face-to-face therapy.

Online counseling and advice services do have some advantages. For one thing, clients can remain anonymous. Thus, a person who might hesitate to see a psychologist can seek help privately, online. Likewise, the Internet can link people who live in rural areas with professional psychologists living in large cities. And, compared with traditional office visits, cybertherapy is relatively inexpensive.

As with radio talk shows and telephone counselors, many objections can be raised about online psychological services. Clearly, brief e-mail messages are no way to make a diagnosis. And forget about facial expressions or body language—not even tone of voice reaches the cybertherapist. Typing little smiley faces or frowns is a poor substitute for real human interaction. Another problem is that e-mail counseling may not be completely confidential. In some cases, highly personal messages could be intercepted and misused. Of special concern is the fact that "cybershrinks" may or may not be trained professionals. And even if they are, questions have been raised about whether a psychologist licensed in one state can legally conduct therapy in another state, via the Internet.

Summary As you can see, psychological services that rely on electronic communication may serve some useful purposes some of the time. However, the effectiveness of therapy conducted by telephone or over the Internet has not been established. As a result, the very best advice given by media psychologists, telephone counselors, or cybertherapists may be, "You should consider discussing this problem with a psychologist or counselor in your own community." (Additional sources: Hannon, 1996; Sleek, 1995; Zgodzinski, 1996.)

Psychotherapy— An Overview

How effective is psychotherapy?

Judging the outcome of therapy is tricky. Nevertheless, there is ample evidence that therapy is beneficial. Hundreds of experimental studies show a strong pattern of positive effects for psychotherapy and counseling (Lambert, & Cattani-Thompson, 1996; Lipsey & Wilson, 1993). Even more convincing, perhaps, are the findings of a recent national survey. Nearly 9 out of 10 people who have sought mental health care say their lives improved as a result of the treatment (Consumer, 1995; Kotkin, Daviet, & Gurin, 1996).

In general, then, psychotherapy works. Of course, results vary in individual cases. For some people therapy is tremendously helpful; for others it is unsuccessful; overall it is effective for more people than not. Speaking more subjectively, one real success—in which a person's life is lastingly changed for the better—can be worth the frustration of several cases in which little progress is made.

It is common to think of therapy as a long, slow process. But this is not always the case. Research reveals that most people can expect improvement in a reasonably brief time. About 50 percent of all patients feel better after only eight therapy sessions. After 26 sessions, roughly 75 percent have improved (Howard et al., 1986b) (Fig. 19–6 ◆). The typical "dose" of therapy is one hourly session per week. This means that the majority of patients improve after 6 months of therapy, and half feel better in just 2 months. Keep in mind that people often suffer for several years before seeking help. In view of this, such rapid improvement is impressive.

What do psychotherapies have in common?

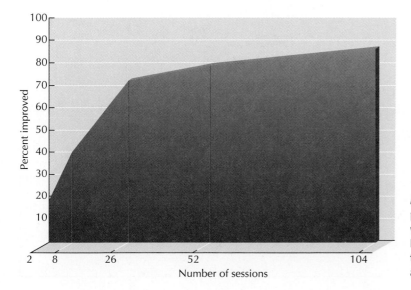

Figure 19–6 ◆ The dose-improvement relationship in psychotherapy. This graph shows the percentage of patients who improved after varying numbers of therapy sessions. Notice that the most rapid improvement took place during the first 6 months of once-a-week sessions. (From Howard et al., 1986b.)

Core Features of Psychotherapy

The therapies we have sampled are but a few of the many approaches in use today. They represent some of the basic variations in approach and they may offer ideas you can use. For a summary of major differences among psychotherapies, see Table 19–2 ■. To add to your understanding, let us briefly summarize what all techniques have in common.

All the psychotherapies we have discussed embrace some of the following goals: insight, resolution of conflicts, an improved sense of self, a change in unacceptable patterns of behavior, better interpersonal relations, and an improved picture of oneself and the world.

How do psychotherapists achieve these goals?

1. Therapy provides a *caring relationship between the client and therapist*, called a **therapeutic alliance.** Emotional rapport, warmth, friendship, understanding, acceptance, and empathy are the basis for this relationship. The therapeutic alliance unites the client and therapist as they work together to solve the client's problems. The strength of this alliance has a major impact on whether therapy succeeds (Krupnick et al., 1996).

2. Therapy offers a *protected setting* in which emotional *catharsis* (release) can take place. Therapy is a sanctuary in which the client is free to express fears, anxieties, and personal secrets without fearing rejection or loss of confidentiality (Weiss, 1990).

3. All therapies to some extent offer an *explanation* or *rationale* for the client's suffering. Additionally, they propose a line of action that will end this suffering.

4. Therapy provides clients with a *new perspective* about themselves and their situations and a chance to practice *new behaviors* (Crencavage & Norcross, 1990; Stiles et al., 1986).

Because therapies have much in common, a majority of psychologists have become *eclectic* in their work (Jensen, Bergin, & Greaves, 1990). Eclectic therapists use whatever methods best fit a particular problem. In addition, some seek to combine the best elements of various therapies into more general systems.

If you recall that our discussion began with trepanning and demonology, it is clear that psychotherapy has come a long way. Still, the search for ways to improve psychotherapy remains an urgent challenge for those who devote their lives to helping others.

Basic Counseling Skills

A number of general helping skills can be distilled from the various approaches to therapy. These suggest several points to keep in mind when you would like to comfort a person in distress, such as a troubled friend or relative. (Also, see Table 19–3 ■.)

Active Listening People frequently talk "at" each other without really listening. A person with problems needs to be heard. Make a sincere effort to listen to and understand the person. Try to accept the person's message without judging

Table 19–2 ■ Comparison of Psychotherapies				
	Insight or Action?	**Directive or Non-Directive?**	**Individual or Group?**	**Therapy's Strength***
Psychoanalysis	Insight	Directive	Individual	Searching honesty
Short-term dynamic therapy	Insight	Directive	Individual	Productive use of conflict
Client-centered therapy	Insight	Non-directive	Individual	Acceptance, empathy
Existential therapy	Insight	Both	Individual	Personal empowerment
Gestalt therapy	Insight	Directive	Both	Focus on immediate awareness
Behavior therapy	Action	Directive	Both	Observable changes in behavior
Cognitive therapy	Action	Directive	Individual	Constructive guidance
Rational-emotive behavior therapy	Action	Directive	Individual	Clarity of thinking and goals
Psychodrama	Insight	Directive	Group	Constructive reenactments
Family therapy	Both	Directive	Group	Shared responsibility for problems

*This column based in part on Andrews (1989).

Table 19–3 ■ **Helping Behaviors**

To help another person gain insight into a personal problem it is valuable to keep the following comparison in mind.

Behaviors that Help	Behaviors that Hinder
Active listening	Probing painful topics
Acceptance	Judging/moralizing
Reflecting feelings	Criticism
Open-ended questioning	Threats
Supportive statements	Rejection
Respect	Ridicule/sarcasm
Patience	Impatience
Genuineness	Placing blame
Paraphrasing	Opinionated statements

Adapted from Kottler & Brown, 1996.

it or immediately leaping to conclusions (Kottler & Brown, 1996). Let the person know you are listening, with eye contact, posture, your tone of voice, and your replies (Ivey & Galvin, 1984).

Clarify the Problem   People who have a clear idea of what is wrong in their lives are in a better position to discover solutions. Try to understand the problem from the person's point of view. As you do, check your understanding often. For example, you might ask, "Are you saying that you feel depressed just at school? Or in general?" Remember, a problem well defined is often half solved.

Focus on Feelings   Feelings are neither right nor wrong. By focusing on feelings you can avoid making the person defensive. Passing judgment on what is said prevents the free outpouring of emotion that is the basis for catharsis. For example, a friend confides that he has failed a test. Perhaps you know that he studies very little. If you say, "Maybe if you studied a little more you would do better," he will probably become defensive or hostile. Much more can be accomplished by saying, "You must feel very frustrated" or simply, "How do you feel about it?" (Ivey & Galvin, 1984).

Avoid Giving Advice   Many people mistakenly think that they must solve others' problems for them. Remember that your goal is to provide understanding and support, not solutions (Egan, 1984). Of course, it is reasonable to give advice when you are asked for it, but beware of the trap of the "Why don't you . . . ? Yes, but . . ." game. According to psychotherapist Eric Berne (1964), this "game" follows a pattern: Someone says, "I have this problem." You say, "Why don't you do thus and so?" The person replies, "Yes, but . . ." and then gives several reasons why your suggestion won't work. If you make a new suggestion, the reply will once again be, "Yes, but . . ." because the person either knows more about his or her personal situation than you do or because she or he has reasons for avoiding your advice. The student described earlier knows he needs to study. His problem is to understand why he doesn't *want* to study.

Accept the Person's Frame of Reference   W. I. Thomas said, "Things perceived as real are real in their effect." Try to resist the temptation to contradict the person with your point of view. Since we all live in different psychological worlds, there is no single "correct" view of a life situation. A person who feels that his or her point of view is understood feels freer to examine it objectively and to question it. (Accepting and understanding the perspective of another person can be especially difficult when cultural differences exist. See this chapter's Exploration for more information.)

Teams of psychologists and counselors are often assembled to provide support to victims of major accidents and natural disasters. Because their work is stressful and often heart wrenching, relief workers also benefit from on-site counseling. Expressing emotions and talking about feelings are major elements of disaster counseling.

Reflect Thoughts and Feelings One of the best things you can do when offering support to another person is to give feedback by simply restating what is said. This is also a good way to encourage a person to talk. If your friend seems to be at a loss for words, *restate* or *paraphrase* his or her last sentence. Here's an example.

> *Friend:* I'm really down about school. I can't get interested in any of my classes. I flunked my Spanish test, and somebody stole my notebook for psychology.
> *You:* You're really upset about school, aren't you?
> *Friend:* Yeah, and my parents are hassling me about my grades again.
> *You:* You're feeling pressured by your parents?
> *Friend:* Yeah, damn.
> *You:* It must make you angry to be pressured by them.

As simple as this sounds, it is very helpful to someone trying to sort out feelings. Try it. If nothing else, you'll develop a reputation as a fantastic conversationalist!

Silence Studies show that counselors tend to wait longer before responding than do people in everyday conversations. Pauses of 5 seconds or more are not unusual, and interrupting is rare. Listening patiently lets the person feel unhurried and encourages her or him to speak freely (Goodman, 1984).

Questions Because your goal is to encourage free expression, *open questions* tend to be the most helpful (Goodman, 1984). A *closed question* is one that can be answered yes or no.

Open questions call for an open-ended reply (see Chapter 16). Say, for example, that a friend tells you, "I feel like my boss has it in for me at work." A closed question would be, "Oh yeah? So, are you going to quit?" Open questions, such as, "Do you want to tell me about it?" or "How do you feel about it?" are more likely to be helpful.

Maintain Confidentiality Your efforts to help will be wasted if you fail to respect the privacy of someone who has confided in you. Put yourself in the person's place. Don't gossip.

These guidelines are not an invitation to play "junior therapist." Professional therapists are trained to approach serious problems with skills far exceeding those described here. However, the points made help define the qualities of a therapeutic relationship. They also emphasize that each of us can supply two of the greatest mental health resources available at any cost: friendship and honest communication.

A Look Ahead In the Applications section that follows we will return briefly to behavioral approaches. There you will find a number of useful techniques that you may be able to apply to your own behavior. You'll also find a discussion of when to seek professional help, and how to go about doing it. Here's your author's professional advice: This is an Applications you won't want to skip reading.

Learning Check

1. In psychodrama, people attempt to form meaningful wholes out of disjointed thoughts, feelings, and actions. T or F?

2. Most large-group awareness trainings make use of Gestalt therapy. T or F?

3. There are no dangers in participating in an encounter group. T or F?

4. Which therapy places great emphasis on role-playing?
   a. psychodrama   **b.** awareness training   **c.** family therapy   **d.** encounter

5. According to the APA, media psychologists should educate, they should not do therapy on the air. T or F?

6. Emotional _____ (release) in a protected setting is an element of most psychotherapies.

7. To aid a troubled friend, you should focus on facts rather than feelings, and you should critically evaluate what the person is saying to help him or her grasp reality. T or F?

8. One danger of giving advice is the tendency for the interchange to slip into the "Yes, but" game. T or F?

Critical Thinking

9. In your opinion, do psychologists have a duty to protect others who may be harmed by their clients? For example, if a patient has homicidal fantasies about his ex-wife, should she be informed?

Answers:
1. F 2. F 3. F 4. a 5. T 6. catharsis 7. F 8. T 9. According to the law, there is a duty to protect others where a therapist could, with little effort, prevent serious harm. However, this duty can conflict with a client's rights to confidentiality and with client-therapist trust. Therapists often must make difficult choices in such situations.

"*T*hrow out the snake oil, ladies and gentlemen, and throw away your troubles. Doctor B. Havior Modification is here to put an end to all human suffering."

True? Well, not quite. Behavior therapy is not a cure-all. Its use is often quite complicated and requires a great deal of experience and expertise. Also, there are times when therapists regard insight therapy as more appropriate than behavior therapy. Still, behavior therapy offers a straightforward solution to many problems.

It would be a serious mistake to presume that you could effectively apply the principles of behavior therapy to major personal problems. As mentioned elsewhere in this book, professional help is available and should be sought when a significant problem exists. For lesser difficulties there is a good chance that you might succeed in modest attempts to apply the principles of behavior therapy to yourself. Let us see how this might be done.

Covert Reward and Punishment—Boosting Your "Willpower"

"Have you ever decided to quit smoking cigarettes, watching television too much, eating too much, drinking too much, or driving too fast?"

"Well, one of those applies. I have decided several times to quit smoking."

"When have you decided?"

"Usually after I am reminded of how dangerous smoking is—like when I heard that my uncle had died of lung cancer. He smoked constantly."

"If you have decided to quit 'several times,' I assume you haven't succeeded."

"No, the usual pattern is for me to become upset about smoking and then to cut down for a day or two."

"You forget the disturbing image of your uncle's death, or whatever, and start smoking again."

"Yes, I suppose if I had an uncle die every day or so, I might actually quit!"

The use of electric shock to condition an aversion seems remote from everyday problems. Even naturally aversive actions are hard to apply to personal behavior. As mentioned earlier, for instance, rapid smoking is difficult for most smokers to carry out on their own. And what about a problem like overeating? It would indeed be a challenge to eat enough to create a lasting aversion to overeating. (Although it is sometimes tempting to try.)

In view of such limitations, psychologists have developed an alternative procedure that can be used to curb smoking, overeating, and other habits (Cautela & Bennett, 1981; Cautela & Kearney, 1986).

Covert Sensitization In a technique called **covert sensitization,** *aversive imagery is used to reduce the occurrence of an undesired response.* Here's how it's done: Obtain six 3 X 5 cards and on each write a brief description of a scene related to the habit you wish to control. The scene should be so *disturbing* or *disgusting* that thinking about it would temporarily make you very uncomfortable about indulging in the habit. For smoking, the cards might read:

- I am in a doctor's office. The doctor looks at some reports and tells me I have lung cancer. He says a lung will have to be removed and sets a date for the operation.

- I am in bed under an oxygen tent. My chest feels caved in. There is a tube in my throat. I can barely breathe.

- I wake up in the morning and smoke a cigarette. I begin coughing up blood.

- Other cards would continue along the same line.

For overeating the cards might read:

- I am at the beach. I get up to go for a swim and I overhear people whispering to each other, "Isn't that fat disgusting?"

- I am at a store buying clothes. I try on several things that are too small. The only things that fit look like rumpled sacks. Salespeople are staring at me.

And so forth.

The trick, of course, is to get yourself to imagine or picture vividly each of these disturbing scenes *several times* a day. Imagining the scenes can be accomplished by placing them under *stimulus control.* Simply choose something you do *frequently* each day (such as getting a cup of coffee or getting up from your chair). Next make a rule: Before you can get a cup of coffee or get up from your chair, or whatever you have selected as a cue, you must take out your cards and *vividly picture* yourself engaging in the action you wish to curb (eating or smoking, for example). Then *vividly picture* the scene described on the top card. Imagine the scene for 30 seconds.

After visualizing the top card, move it to the bottom so the cards are rotated. Make up new cards each week. The scenes can be made much more upsetting than the samples given here. The samples are toned down to keep you from being "grossed out."

Covert sensitization can also be used directly in situations that test your self-control. If you are trying to lose weight, for instance, you might be able to turn down a tempting dessert in this way: As you look at the dessert, visualize maggots crawling all over it. If you make this image as vivid and nauseating as possible, losing your appetite is almost a certainty. If you want to apply this technique to other situations, be aware that vomiting scenes are especially effective. Covert sensitization may sound as if you are "playing games with yourself," but it can be a great help if you want to cut down on a bad habit (Cautela & Kearney, 1986). Try it!

Thought Stopping As discussed earlier, behavior therapists have begun to realize that thoughts, like visible responses, can also cause trouble. Think of times when you have repeatedly "put yourself down" mentally or when you have been preoccupied by needless worries, fears, or other negative and upsetting thoughts. If you would like to gain control over such thoughts, *thought stopping* may help you do it.

In **thought stopping,** *aversive stimuli are used to interrupt or prevent upsetting thoughts.* The simplest thought-stopping technique makes use of mild punishment to suppress upsetting mental images and internal "talk." Simply place a large, flat rubber band around your wrist. As you go through the day apply this rule: Each time you catch yourself thinking the upsetting image or thought, pull the rubber band away from your wrist and snap it. You need not make this terribly painful. Its value lies in drawing your attention to how often you form negative thoughts and in interrupting the flow of thoughts. Strong punishment is not required.

It seems like this procedure might be abandoned rapidly. Is there an alternative?

A second thought-stopping procedure requires only that you interrupt upsetting thoughts each time they occur. Begin by setting aside time each day during which you will deliberately think the unwanted thought. As you begin to form the thought, shout "stop!" aloud, with conviction. (Obviously, you should choose a private spot for this part of the procedure!)

Repeat the thought-stopping procedure 10 to 20 times for the first 2 or 3 days. Then switch to shouting "stop!" covertly (to yourself) rather than aloud. Thereafter, thought stopping can be carried out throughout the day, whenever upsetting thoughts occur (Williams & Long, 1991). After several days of practice, you should be able to stop unwanted thoughts whenever they occur.

Covert Reinforcement Earlier we discussed how punishing images can be linked to undesirable responses, such as smoking or overeating, to decrease their occurrence. Many people also find it helpful to covertly *reinforce* desired actions. **Covert reinforcement** *is the use of positive imagery to reinforce desired behavior.* For example, suppose your target behavior is, once again, not eating dessert. If this were the case, you could

do the following (Cautela & Bennett, 1981; Cautela & Kearney, 1986):

> Imagine that you are standing at the dessert table with your friends. As dessert is passed, you politely refuse and feel good about staying on your diet.

These images would then be followed by imagining a pleasant, reinforcing scene:

> Imagine that you are your ideal weight. You look really slim in your favorite color and style. Someone you like says to you, "Gee, you've lost weight. I've never seen you look so good."

For many people, of course, actual direct reinforcement (as described in the Chapter 9 Applications) is the most powerful way to alter behavior. Nevertheless, covert or "visualized" reinforcement can have similar effects. To make use of covert reinforcement, choose one or more target behaviors and rehearse them mentally. Then follow each rehearsal with a vivid, rewarding image.

Self-Directed Desensitization—Overcoming Common Fears

You have prepared for 2 weeks to give a speech in a large class. As your turn approaches, your hands begin to tremble and perspire. Your heart pounds and you find it difficult to breathe. You say to your body, "Relax!" What happens? Nothing!

Relaxation The key to desensitization is relaxation. To inhibit fear, one must *learn* to relax. Here is a method for achieving deep-muscle relaxation.

> Tense the muscles in your right arm until they tremble. Hold them tight for about 5 seconds and then let go. Allow your hand and arm to go limp and to relax completely. Repeat the procedure. Releasing tension two or three times will allow you to feel whether or not your arm muscles have relaxed. Repeat the tension-release procedure with your left arm. Compare it with your right arm. Repeat until the left arm is equally relaxed. Apply the tension-release technique to your right leg; to your left leg; to your abdomen; to your chest and shoulders. Clench and release your chin, neck, and throat. Wrinkle and release your forehead and scalp. Tighten and release your mouth and face muscles. As a last step, curl your toes and tense your feet. Then release.

Practice the tension-release method until you can achieve complete relaxation quickly (5 to 10 minutes).

After you have practiced relaxation once a day for a week or two, you will begin to be able to tell when your body (or a group of muscles) is tense. Also, you will begin to be able to relax on command. As an alternative, you might want to try imagining a very safe, pleasant, and relaxing scene. Some people find such images as relaxing as the tension-release method (Rosenthal, 1993b). Once you have learned to relax, the next step is to identify the fear you would like to control and construct a hierarchy.

Procedure for Constructing a Hierarchy   Make a list of situations (related to the fear) that make you anxious. Try to list at least 10 situations. Some should be very frightening and others only mildly frightening. Write a short description of each situation on a separate 3 X 5 card. Place the cards in order from the least disturbing situation to the most disturbing. Here is a sample hierarchy for a student afraid of public speaking:

1. Being given an assignment to speak in class
2. Thinking about the topic and the date the speech must be given
3. Writing the speech; thinking about delivering the speech
4. Watching other students speak in class the week before the speech date
5. Rehearsing the speech alone; pretending to give it to the class
6. Delivering the speech to my roommate; pretending my roommate is the teacher
7. Reviewing the speech on the day it is to be presented
8. Entering the classroom; waiting and thinking about the speech
9. Being called; standing up; facing the audience
10. Delivering the speech

Using the Hierarchy   When you have mastered the relaxation exercises and have the hierarchy constructed, set aside time each day to work on reducing your fear. Begin by performing the relaxation exercises. When you are completely relaxed, visualize the scene on the first card (the least frightening scene). If you can *vividly* picture and imagine yourself in the first situation twice *without a noticeable increase in muscle tension*, proceed to the next card. Also, as you progress, relax yourself between cards.

Each day, stop when you reach a card that you cannot visualize without becoming tense in three attempts. Each day, begin one or two cards before the one on which you stopped the previous day. Continue to work with the cards until you can visualize the last situation without experiencing tension (techniques are based on Wolpe, 1974).

Don't be discouraged if you are unable to relax completely while imagining the upsetting scenes. Research shows that in many instances your fear will still lessen after repeated exposure to the feared situations (Kleinknecht, 1986).

By using this approach you should be able to reduce the fear or anxiety associated with things such as public speaking,

entering darkened rooms, asking questions in large classes, heights, talking to members of the opposite sex, and taking tests. Even if you are not always able to reduce a fear, you will have learned to place relaxation under voluntary control. This alone is valuable because controlling unnecessary tension can increase energy and efficiency.

Seeking Professional Help—When, Where, and How?

How would I know if I should seek professional help at some point in my life?

Although there is no simple answer to this question, the following guidelines may be helpful.

1. If your level of psychological discomfort (unhappiness, anxiety, or depression, for example) becomes comparable to a level of physical discomfort that would cause you to see a doctor or dentist, you should consider seeing a psychologist or a psychiatrist.
2. Another sign that should influence your decision is the occurrence of significant changes in observable behavior such as the quality of your work (including schoolwork), your rate of absenteeism, your use of drugs (including alcohol), or your relationships with others who are important to you.
3. Perhaps you have at some time urged a friend or relative to seek professional help and were then dismayed because he or she refused to recognize the problem. If *you* find friends or relatives making a similar suggestion, recognize that they may be seeing things more objectively than you.
4. If you have persistent or disturbing suicidal thoughts or impulses, you should seek help immediately.

Table 19–4 ■ lists the reasons most often given by people who voluntarily sought help from a mental health professional.

Locating a Therapist

If I wanted to talk to a therapist, how would I find one?

1.   *The yellow pages.* Psychologists are listed in the telephone book under "Psychologist" or in some cases under "Counseling Services." Psychiatrists are generally listed as a subheading under "Physicians." Counselors are usually found under the heading "Marriage and Family Counselors." These listings will usually put you in touch with individuals in private practice.

2.   *Community or county mental health centers.* Most counties and many cities offer public mental health services. (These

Table 19–4 ■ Reasons for Consulting a Mental Health Professional	
Reason	**Percent**
Depression	21.2
Marital problems	16.8
Child-rearing problems	9.7
Difficulty in social relationships	5.3
Difficulty in work relationships	5.3
Suicidal thoughts	5.3
Alcohol/drug dependence	3.5
Desire to quit smoking	2.6
Obsession about something	2.6
Sexual dysfunction	2.6
Weight loss/eating disorders	1.8
Spousal/partner abuse	1.8
Hallucinations/hearing voices	1.8
Other	19.5

Note: Respondents could list more than one reason.
Adapted from Murstein & Fontaine, 1993.

Table 19–5 ■ Mental Health Resources

- Family doctors
- Mental health specialists, such as psychiatrists, psychologists, social workers, or mental health counselors
- Health maintenance organizations
- Community mental health centers
- Hospital psychiatry departments and outpatient clinics
- University- or medical school-affiliated programs
- State hospital outpatient clinics
- Family service/social agencies
- Private clinics and facilities
- Employee assistance programs
- Local medical, psychiatric, or psychological societies

Source: National Institute of Mental Health.

are listed in the phone book.) Public mental health centers usually provide counseling and therapy services directly and can make referrals to private therapists.

3. *Mental health associations.* Many cities have mental health associations organized by concerned citizens. Groups such as these usually keep listings of qualified therapists and of other services and programs in the community.

4. *Colleges and universities.* If you are a student, don't overlook counseling services offered by a student health center or special student counseling facilities.

5. *Newspaper advertisements.* Some psychologists advertise their services in newspapers. Also, low-cost "outreach" clinics occasionally try to make their presence known to the public by advertising. In either case, you should carefully inquire into a therapist's training and qualifications. Without the benefit of a referral from a trusted person, it is wise to be cautious.

6. *Crisis hotlines.* The typical crisis hotline is a telephone service staffed by community volunteers. These people are trained to provide information concerning a wide range of mental health problems. They also have lists of organizations, services, and other resources in the community to which they can refer you for help.

Table 19–5 ■ summarizes all of the sources for psychotherapy, counseling, and referrals we have discussed, as well as some additional possibilities.

How would I know what kind of a therapist to see? How would I pick one?

Options The choice between a psychiatrist and a psychologist is somewhat arbitrary. Both are trained to do psychotherapy. While a psychiatrist can administer somatic therapy and prescribe drugs, a psychologist can work in conjunction with a physician if such services are needed. Psychologists and psychiatrists are equally effective as therapists (Consumer, 1995; Seligman, 1995).

Fees for psychiatrists are usually higher, averaging about $100 an hour. Psychologists average about $85 an hour. Counselors and social workers typically charge about $70 per hour. Group therapy averages only $40 because the therapist's fee is divided among several people (Engler & Goleman, 1992).

With fees in mind, your decision may be influenced by whether you have health insurance that will cover the expense. If fees are a problem, keep in mind that many individual therapists charge on a sliding scale, or ability-to-pay basis, and that community mental health centers almost always charge on a sliding scale.

Some communities and college campuses have counseling services staffed by sympathetic *paraprofessionals* or *peer counselors*. A **paraprofessional** *is a person who works in a near-professional capacity under the supervision of a more highly trained person.* **Peer counselors** *are non-professional persons who have learned basic counseling skills.* These services are free or very low cost. There is a natural tendency, perhaps, to doubt the abilities of paraprofessionals. However, many studies have shown that paraprofessional counselors are often as effective as professionals (Christensen & Jacobson, 1994).

Also, don't overlook *self-help groups*, which can add valuable support to professional treatment. Members of a self-help group typically share a particular type of problem, such as eating disorders or coping with an alcoholic parent. **Self-help groups** *offer members mutual support and a chance to discuss problems*. In many instances helping others also serves as therapy for those who give help (Levine, Toro, & Perkins, 1993). For some problems, self-help groups may be the best choice of all (Christensen & Jacobson, 1994).

What about self-help books?

Large numbers of people turn to self-help books each year. At their best, self-help books can provide valuable information and advice. At their worst, self-help books are like a fast-food version of psychotherapy: They are quick and inexpensive, but low in nutritional value (Marx et al., 1992).

Some self-help books simply promise too much or make personal change sound too easy. Such books can lead readers to unfairly blame themselves for conditions over which they have little control. A person who is already feeling overwhelmed might end up feeling utterly hopeless if she or he can't follow the advice given in a self-help book (Gambrill, 1992).

About one third of all therapists at least occasionally recommend self-help books to their clients. This practice, which is called **bibliotherapy** (*book-therapy*), suggests that certain books do have value. Bibliotherapy is typically used to support traditional therapy. People who read self-help books on their own run a risk of getting bad advice or actually being harmed by what they read (Gambrill, 1992; Marx et al., 1992). Nevertheless, for some problems, such as passivity, anxiety, and milder forms of sexual dysfunction, bibliotherapy can be effective (Marrs, 1995).

In summary, if the problem is not too serious, and you read with a healthy dose of skepticism, some self-help books can actually be helpful. Table 19–6 ■ lists several books given favorable ratings by therapists and other experts (Marx et al., 1992; Santrock, Minnett, & Campbell, 1994.).

Qualifications You can usually get information about the training and qualifications of a therapist simply by asking. A reputable therapist will be glad to reveal his or her background. If you have any doubts, credentials may be checked and other helpful information can be obtained from local branches of any of the following organizations. You can also write to the addresses listed here.

American Family Therapy Association
2020 Pennsylvania Ave. N.W., Suite 273
Washington, DC 20006

Table 19–6 ■ Favorably Rated Self-Help Books
Adult Children of Alcoholics (Woititz, 1983)
Anger: The Misunderstood Emotion (Tavris, 1989)
Anxiety Disorders and Phobias (Beck & Emery, 1985)
Cognitive Therapy and Emotional Disorders (Beck, 1976)
Feeling Good (Burns, 1980)
Learned Optimism (Seligman, 1991)
On Death and Dying (Kübler-Ross, 1969)
Parent Effectiveness Training (Gordon, 1970)
Passages (Sheehy, 1977)
Shyness (Zimbardo, 1977)
The Hurried Child (Elkind, 1981)
The Relaxation Response (Benson, 1975)
The Road Less Traveled (Peck, 1980)
What Color Is Your Parachute (Bolles, 1987)
When Bad Things Happen To Good People (Kushner, 1981)
When I Say No I Feel Guilty (Smith, 1975)
Women Who Love Too Much (Norwood, 1985)
You Just Don't Understand (Tannen, 1990)

Marx et al., 1992; Santrock, Minnett, & Campbell, 1994.

American Psychiatric Association
1400 K Street N.W.
Washington, DC 20005

American Psychological Association
750 1st Street N.E.
Washington, DC 20002

American Association of Humanistic Psychology
7 Hartwood Dr.
Amherst, NY 14226

Canadian Psychiatric Association
200-237 Argyle
Ottawa, ONT K2P1B8

National Mental Health Association
1021 Prince St.
Alexandria, VA 22314

The question of how to pick a particular therapist remains. The best way is to start with one short consultation with a respected psychiatrist or psychologist or with a counselor at a mental health center. This will allow the person you consult to evaluate the nature of your difficulty and recommend an appropriate type of therapy or a therapist who is likely to be helpful. As an alternative you might ask the person teaching this course for a referral.

How would I know whether or not to quit or ignore a therapist?

Evaluating a Therapist A balanced look at psychotherapies suggests that all *techniques* are about equally successful (Omer & London, 1988; Stiles et al., 1986). However, all *therapists* are not equally successful. Far more important than the approach used are the therapist's personal qualities (Luborsky et al., 1986). The most consistently successful therapists are those who are willing to use whatever method seems most helpful for a client. They are also marked by personal characteristics of warmth, integrity, sincerity, and empathy (Patterson, 1989; Strupp, 1989).

It is perhaps most accurate to say that at this stage of development, psychotherapy is an art, not a science. The *relationship* between a client and therapist is the therapist's most basic tool (Strupp, 1989). This is why you must trust and easily relate to a therapist for therapy to be effective. (See Table 19–7 ■.) Clients who like their therapist are generally more successful in therapy (Talley et al., 1990). An especially important part of the therapeutic alliance is agreement about the goals of therapy. It is therefore a good idea to think about what you would like to accomplish by entering therapy. Write down your goals and discuss them with your therapist during the first session (Goldfried et al., 1990). Your first meeting with a therapist should also answer all of the following questions (Somberg et al., 1993):

- Will the information I reveal in therapy remain completely confidential?

- What risks do I face if I begin therapy?

Table 19–7 ■ **Psychotherapy Danger Signals**
■ Sexual advances by therapist
■ Therapist makes repeated verbal threats or is physically aggressive
■ Therapist is excessively blaming, belittling, hostile, or controlling
■ Therapist makes excessive small talk; talks repeatedly about his/her own problems
■ Therapist encourages prolonged dependence on him/her
■ Therapist demands absolute trust or tells client not to discuss therapy with anyone else

- How long do you expect treatment to last?

- What form of treatment do you expect to use?

- Are there alternatives to therapy that might help me as much or more?

It's always tempting to avoid facing up to personal problems. With this in mind, you should give a therapist a fair chance and not give up too easily. But don't hesitate to change therapists or to terminate therapy if you lose confidence in the therapist or if you don't relate well to the therapist as a person.

Learning Check	Critical Thinking
1. Covert sensitization and thought stopping combine aversion therapy and cognitive therapy. T or F?	9. Would it be acceptable for a therapist to urge a client to break all ties with a troublesome family member?
2. Like covert aversion conditioning, covert reinforcement of desired responses is also possible. T or F?	
3. Exercises that bring about deep-muscle relaxation are an essential element in covert sensitization. T or F?	
4. Items in a desensitization hierarchy should be placed in order from the least disturbing to the most disturbing. T or F?	
5. The first step in desensitization is to place the visualization of disturbing images under stimulus control. T or F?	
6. Persistent emotional discomfort is a clear sign that professional psychological counseling should be sought. T or F?	**Answers:**
7. Community mental health centers rarely offer counseling or therapy themselves, they only do referrals. T or F?	borders on unethical behavior. ing a client to sever a relationship sions and feelings about significant persons in their lives. However, actively urg-
8. In many instances, a therapist's personal qualities have more of an effect on the outcome of therapy than does the type of therapy used. T or F?	can help clients evaluate important deci- made by clients themselves. Therapists 7. F 8. T 9. Such decisions must be 1. T 2. T 3. F 4. T 5. F 6. T

Western nations are rapidly moving toward cultural pluralism. A pluralistic society combines the traditions of many racial and ethnic groups in a rich and varied tapestry. Our own multicultural society increasingly calls for therapists who can work with clients from varied cultural backgrounds (Montague, 1996). Consider the following case history:

David Chan

David Chan, a 21-year-old college student majoring in engineering, was failing his classes and suffering from headaches, indigestion, and insomnia. A medical doctor could find no physical cause for David's illness, so David sought counseling. During his first session David seemed depressed and anxious. He responded to questions with short, polite, but impersonal statements that revealed little about his feelings. After several more sessions, the counselor was able to see that David did not like engineering and felt pressured by his parents to go into this field. The counselor felt that David was too dependent on his parents and unable to express his anger towards them. To help him vent his feelings, the counselor used a Gestalt technique called the "empty chair." The counselor asked David to imagine that his parents were seated in two chairs placed opposite him. After much prompting, David was able to express his true feelings toward his parents. However, in the following counseling sessions, David seemed more withdrawn and guilt-ridden than ever (Sue & Sue, 1991).

David's counselor had a history of success with other clients. What went wrong in his work with David? The fault lies in subtle cultural differences between the counselor, an Anglo-American, and David, a Chinese American.

David's cultural heritage emphasizes moderation, self-discipline, patience, humility, and respect for one's parents.

David's counselor was trained to value independence, openness, and free expression of personal thoughts and feelings. Using his own experience as a guide, the counselor misunderstood David's restrained answers to questions, which merely reflect David's deference to authority. The counselor's use of the empty chair technique was also a mistake. "Honor thy parents" is a very basic Chinese-American value. Asking David to "talk back" to his parents actually made his conflicts worse. For David, a less direct, more culturally aware approach might have been more helpful (Sue & Sue, 1991).

Traditional theories of counseling and psychotherapy tend to emphasize values like those listed in Table 19-1. However, these values are not shared by all cultures or ethnic groups. For example, North American culture strongly emphasizes competition and individualism, whereas others stress cooperation and group effort. What is considered healthy or ideal in one culture can be undesirable in another. In David's case, the behavior that his counselor saw as overly passive is actually a preferred way of interacting in Chinese-American culture. In short, therapists and counselors are learning that they need to use strategies and techniques that are consistent with the life experiences and cultural values of their clients (Lee, 1991b).

Cultural Barriers

Counseling and psychotherapy rely on honest and direct communication. Yet, when a client and therapist come from different cultural backgrounds, misunderstandings are common. Cultural groups vary greatly in their beliefs, values, religious convictions, lifestyles, sexual attitudes, family structures, and preferred languages. The culturally aware therapist must be very careful to not make false assumptions about a

client's personal history, values, goals for therapy, or expectations (Montague, 1996).

Psychologists Derald Sue and David Sue (1990) believe there are four main **cultural barriers** to effective counseling. *These include differences in language, social class, cultural values, and non-verbal communication.* Non-verbal communication provides a good example of how even small cultural differences can lead to misunderstandings. In most Native American cultures, one of the ways you show respect is by not making eye contact. This is why American Indians who enter therapy may spend much of their time looking at their feet or at the ground. To look a therapist in the eye is to challenge his or her authority and be disrespectful. But if the therapist doesn't understand Native American culture, the client's behavior looks like a textbook case of poor self-esteem. In light of such misunderstandings, it's not surprising that over half of all Native Americans do not return after a first therapy session with non-native therapists (Heinrich, Corbine, & Thomas, 1990).

Culturally Skilled Counselors

A **culturally skilled counselor** *is a therapist who has the awareness, knowledge, and skills necessary to intervene successfully in the lives of clients from diverse cultural backgrounds.* Counselors, of course, need to be aware of issues faced by almost everyone, such as problems with personal relationships, education and achievement, work and career, parenting, and personal growth. In addition, the culturally skilled counselor must know about the special conflicts and problems typical of members of various racial or ethnic groups (Montague, 1996; Zayas et al., 1996).

A major step toward competence as a culturally skilled counselor is to become more aware of one's own cultural values and biases. Whatever a counselor's own ethnocultural background, she or he must try to avoid thinking of clients in terms of stereotypes. The therapist must also affirm that minority cultural beliefs and values are different, but not inferior to his or her own (Heinrich, Corbine, & Thomas, 1990). He or she needs to gain knowledge about the history and culture of diverse groups of people, often by direct experience in the community (Lee, 1991b). This allows the culturally skilled counselor to use appropriate methods and choose appropriate goals.

Contrary to what our discussion may imply, cross-cultural counseling can be quite successful. Cultural barriers are transcended on a regular basis by counselors who can achieve empathy with their clients. This is aided by being able to mentally take the role of the client (Scott & Borodovsky, 1990).

What do you mean by "mentally take the role of the client"?

Multicultural counselors attempt to put themselves in their clients' shoes by making sure they understand the client's sense of ethnic identity, degree of ac-

culturation, family influences, sex role socialization, religious or spiritual beliefs, and immigration experiences (Lee, 1991a). The more the counselor's and client's backgrounds differ, the more important it is for such factors to guide therapy.

If a therapist is knowledgeable enough, it can also be valuable to incorporate cultural beliefs and healing practices into therapy. Many ethnic groups make little distinction between religious and secular life. As a consequence, spiritual beliefs may greatly influence everyday life and personal adjustment. For this reason, therapists sometimes work with clergy or tribal healers to bridge the gap between cultures (Heinrich, Corbine, & Thomas, 1990; Richardson, 1991).

In summary, the culturally skilled counselor must be able to do all of the following (Lee, 1991b):

- Establish rapport with a person from a different cultural background

- Adapt traditional theories and techniques to meet the needs of clients from non-European ethnic or racial groups

- Be sensitive to cultural differences without resorting to stereotypes

- Treat members of racial or ethnic communities as individuals

- Be aware of a client's ethnic identity and degree of acculturation to the majority society

- Use existing helping resources within a cultural group to support efforts to resolve problems

Conclusion Multicultural awareness has helped broaden our ideas about mental health and optimal development. Furthermore, the lessons learned in cross-cultural counseling draw attention to other differences that may have an impact on therapy. Effective therapists need to be sensitive not only to racial and ethnic differences, but also to differences related to age, sexual orientation, religious beliefs, handicaps, and other such dimensions. It is also worth remembering that cultural barriers apply to communication in all areas of life, not just therapy. While such differences can be challenging, they are also frequently enriching.

Learning Check

1. As the case history of David Chan shows, it is almost impossible for counseling or psychotherapy to succeed when the cultural backgrounds of a client and therapist are very different. T or F?

2. A major difference in social class between a client and a therapist, such as urban poor versus upper middle-class, is considered less of a barrier than differences in non-verbal communication. T or F?

3. The culturally skilled counselor must be highly aware of his or her own cultural background, as well as that of clients. T or F?

4. Although Marsha cannot really know what it is like to leave a war-torn nation and emigrate to a strange country, she has talked extensively with members of the Vietnamese-American community and feels great empathy for them. Marsha has met a key requirement for effective cross-cultural counseling of Vietnamese immigrants. T or F?

Critical Thinking

5. The essence of culturally skilled counseling could be summarized as an awareness of the social and cultural _____ in which people live.

Answers:

1. F 2. F 3. T 4. T 5. contexts

Chapter Summary

How do psychotherapies differ?

◆ Psychotherapies may be classified as **insight, action, directive, non-directive,** or **supportive** therapies, and combinations of these. Therapies may be conducted either *individually* or in *groups*, and they may be *time limited*.

How did modern therapies originate?

◆ Primitive approaches to mental illness were often based on superstition. **Trepanning** involved boring a hole in the skull. **Demonology** attributed mental disturbance to supernatural forces and prescribed **exorcism** as the cure. In some instances, the actual cause of bizarre behavior may have been **ergot poisoning.** More humane treatment began in 1793 with the work of *Philippe Pinel* in Paris.

Is Freudian psychoanalysis still used?

◆ Freud's **psychoanalysis** was the first formal psychotherapy. Psychoanalysis seeks to release repressed thoughts and emotions from the unconscious. The psychoanalyst uses **free association, dream analysis,** and analysis of **resistance** and **transference** to reveal health-producing insights.

◆ Some critics argue that traditional psychoanalysis receives credit for *spontaneous remission* of symptoms. However, psychoanalysis has been shown to be successful for many patients. Also, **short-term dynamic therapy** (which relies on psychoanalytic theory but is brief and focused) is as effective as other major therapies.

What are the major humanistic therapies?

◆ **Client-centered** (or **person-centered**) **therapy** is non-directive and is dedicated to creating an atmosphere of growth. *Unconditional positive regard, empathy, authenticity,* and *reflection* are combined to give the client a chance to solve his or her own problems.

◆ **Existential therapies,** such as Frankl's **logotherapy,** focus on the end result of the choices one makes in life. Clients are encouraged through *confrontation* and *encounter* to exercise *free will* and to take responsibility for their choices.

◆ **Gestalt therapy** emphasizes immediate awareness of thoughts and feelings. Its goal is to rebuild thinking, feeling, and acting into *connected wholes* and to help clients break through emotional blocks.

What is aversion therapy?

◆ Behavior therapists use various **behavior modification** techniques that apply learning principles to change human behavior.

◆ In **aversion therapy,** classical conditioning is used to associate maladaptive behavior (such as smoking or drinking) with pain or other aversive events in order to inhibit undesirable responses.

How is behavior therapy used to treat phobias, fears, and anxieties?

◆ Classical conditioning also underlies **systematic desensitization,** a technique used to overcome fears and anxieties. In desensitization, gradual **adaptation** and **reciprocal inhibition** break the link between fear and particular situations.

◆ Typical steps in desensitization are: Construct a **fear hierarchy;** learn to produce total relaxation; and perform items on the hierarchy (from least to most disturbing).

◆ Desensitization may be carried out with real settings or it may be done by *vividly imagining* the fear hierarchy.

◆ Desensitization is also effective when it is administered **vicariously;** that is, when clients watch **models** perform the feared responses.

◆ In some cases, **virtual reality exposure** can be used to present fear stimuli in a controlled manner.

◆ A new technique called **eye movement desensitization and reprocessing (EMDR)** shows promise as a treatment for traumatic memories and stress disorders. At present, however, EMDR is highly controversial.

What role does reinforcement play in behavior therapy?

◆ Behavior modification also makes use of operant principles, such as **positive reinforcement, non-reinforcement, extinction, punishment, shaping, stimulus control,** and **time out.** These principles are used to extinguish undesirable responses and to promote constructive behavior.

◆ Non-reward can extinguish troublesome behaviors. Often this is done by simply *identifying* and *eliminating* reinforcers, particularly *attention* and *approval*.

◆ To apply positive reinforcement and operant shaping, symbolic rewards known as **tokens** are often used. Tokens allow *immediate reinforcement* of selected **target behaviors.**

◆ Full-scale use of tokens in an institutional setting produces a **token economy.** Toward the end of a token economy program, patients are shifted to **social rewards** such as recognition and approval.

Can therapy change thoughts and emotions?

◆ **Cognitive therapy** emphasizes changing thought patterns that underlie emotional or behavioral problems. Its goals are to correct distorted thinking and/or teach improved coping skills.

- In a variation of cognitive therapy called **rational-emotive behavior therapy (REBT)**, clients learn to recognize and challenge their own **irrational beliefs**.

Can psychotherapy be done with groups of people?

- **Group therapy** may be a simple extension of individual methods or it may be based on techniques developed specifically for groups.
- In **psychodrama**, individuals enact roles and incidents resembling their real-life problems. In **family therapy**, the family group is treated as a unit.
- Although they are not literally psychotherapies, **sensitivity** and **encounter groups** attempt to encourage positive personality change. In recent years, commercially offered **large-group awareness trainings** have become popular. However, the therapeutic benefits of such programs are questionable.
- Media psychologists, telephone counselors, and cybertherapists may, on occasion, do some good. However, each has serious drawbacks and the effectiveness of telephone counseling and cybertherapy has not been established.

What do various therapies have in common?

- To alleviate personal problems, all psychotherapies offer a *caring relationship, emotional rapport*, a *protected setting, catharsis, explanations* for the client's problems, a *new perspective*, and a chance to practice *new behaviors*.
- Many **basic counseling skills** underlie a variety of therapies. These include *listening actively*, helping to *clarify the problem, focusing on feelings*, avoiding the giving of *unwanted advice*, accepting the person's *perspective*, *reflecting* thoughts and feelings, being *patient* during

silences, using *open questions* when possible, and maintaining *confidentiality*.

How are behavioral principles applied to everyday problems?

- Cognitive techniques can be an aid to managing personal behavior. In **covert sensitization**, aversive images are used to discourage unwanted behavior. **Thought stopping** uses mild punishment to prevent upsetting thoughts. **Covert reinforcement** is a way to encourage desired responses by mental rehearsal. *Desensitization* pairs relaxation with a hierarchy of upsetting images in order to lessen fears.

How would a person go about finding professional help?

- Sources of psychological help exist in most communities. A competent and reputable therapist can usually be located through public sources of information or a *referral*.
- Practical considerations such as cost and qualifications enter into choosing a therapist. However, the therapist's personal characteristics are of equal importance.

Do cultural differences affect counseling and psychotherapy?

- Many **cultural barriers** to effective counseling and therapy have been identified. Aware therapists are beginning to seek out the knowledge and skills needed to intervene successfully in the lives of clients from diverse cultural backgrounds.
- The **culturally skilled counselor** must be able to establish rapport with a person from a different cultural background and adapt traditional theories and techniques to meet the needs of clients from non-European ethnic or racial groups.

Social Behavior

Preview

"To live alone, one must be either an animal or a god."
Aristotle

"No man is an Iland, intire of itselfe."
John Donne

The Social Animal

Your assignment is this: You have been given a written message and the name, address, and occupation of the person who should receive it. This "target person" lives over 1,500 miles away in a city you have never visited. You are allowed to move the message through the mail, but you may send it only to a first-name acquaintance. That person, in turn, must mail the message only to one of his or her first-name acquaintances. The message is to be moved in this manner until it reaches the target person, whom the previous person must know by name.

Sound impossible? Social psychologist Stanley Milgram and his associates asked a number of people to try moving a message in this way. Amazingly, about 1 message in 5 made it. Even more amazing was the number of people needed to complete a chain between two strangers separated by half a continent. The average number of "links" required was about seven people (Korte & Milgram, 1970; Milgram, 1967)!

How is that possible?

Actually, the seven-link average is not as astounding as it might seem. Each of us is en-meshed in a complex network of social relationships, and each person's network overlaps with many others. If you know hundreds of people, and each of them knows hundreds more, a chain of seven people can create millions of possible interconnections. Undeniably, humans are social animals.

Social psychology *is the scientific study of how individuals behave, think, and feel in social situations* (that is, in the presence, actual or implied, of others) (Baron & Byrne, 1994). Every day, there is a fascinating interplay between our own behavior and that of people around us. Social behavior has been the target of an immense amount of study—too much, in fact, for us to cover in detail. Therefore, this chapter and the next are social psychology "samplers." It is hoped that you will find the topics interesting and thought provoking.

Theme: Humans are social animals. Our behavior is frequently influenced by the presence of others.

Key Questions:

Key Questions	Key Topics to Watch for:
How does group membership affect individual behavior?	Culture, roles, status, group structure, and norms
What unspoken rules govern the use of personal space?	Proxemics and personal space Spatial norms
How do we perceive the motives of others, and the causes of our own behavior?	Attribution theory Errors in attribution Self-handicapping
Why do people affiliate?	The need to affiliate Social comparison theory
What factors influence interpersonal attraction?	Patterns of interpersonal attraction Self-disclosure Social exchange theory Romantic love and attachment
What have social psychologists learned about conformity, social power, obedience, and compliance?	Conformity, groupthink, social power, obedience to authority, and compliance strategies
How does self-assertion differ from aggression?	Assertiveness training
What is a social trap?	Social traps and the tragedy of the commons

Humans in a Social Context—People, People, Everywhere

We are born into an organized society. Established values, expectations, and behavior patterns are present when we arrive. So too is **culture,** *an ongoing pattern of life that is passed from one generation to the next.* Some readily visible aspects of culture are language, marriage customs, concepts of ownership, and sex roles.

Roles The groups to which you belong form your most immediate day-to-day social environment. Each person is a member of many groups: the family, teams, church groups, work groups, and so on. Some groups are formal and organized. Others are informal and loosely defined. All groups influence the behavior of their members.

In each group we occupy a *position* in the *structure* of the group. **Social roles** *are patterns of behavior expected of persons in various social positions.* For instance, expectations exist for playing the roles of mother, teacher, employer, and student. Some roles are **ascribed** (*they are assigned to a person or not under the person's control*): male or female, son, adolescent, inmate. **Achieved roles** *are attained voluntarily or by special effort:* spouse, teacher, scientist, band leader.

What effect does role-playing have on behavior?

In general, roles streamline our daily interactions by allowing us to anticipate the behavior of others. When a person is acting as a physician, mother, clerk, or police

Roles have a powerful impact on social behavior. What kinds of behavior do you expect from your teachers? What behaviors do they expect from you? What happens if either of you fails to match the other's expectations?

officer, we expect certain behaviors. However, roles have a negative side too. It is not unusual for a person to experience **role conflict,** *in which two or more roles make conflicting demands on behavior.* Getting caught in a role conflict can be very uncomfortable. Consider, for example, a judge whose neighbor's son is brought in with a traffic violation, or the teacher who must flunk a close friend's daughter. Likewise, the clashing demands of work and family create role conflicts for many parents.

A study done by Philip Zimbardo and his students at Stanford University dramatically shows the impact of social roles. In this experiment, normal, healthy, male college students were paid to serve as "inmates" and "guards" in a simulated prison (Zimbardo et al., 1973).

On the second day of "imprisonment," the prisoners staged a disturbance. The guards, however, quickly suppressed this rebellion. Over the next few days the guards' actions grew increasingly brutal. In a surprisingly short time, the prisoners became traumatized, passive, and dehumanized. Four of them had to be released because of hysterical crying, confusion, or severe depression. Each day, the guards tormented the prisoners with more frequent commands, insults, and demeaning tasks. After 6 days the experiment was halted.

What had happened? Zimbardo believes the assigned roles—prisoner and guard—were so powerful that in just a few days the experiment became "reality" for those involved. Afterward, many of the guards found it hard to believe their own behavior. As one recalls, "I was surprised at myself. I made them call each other names and clean toilets out with their bare hands. I practically considered the prisoners cattle" (Zimbardo et al., 1973). It would seem that the origins of many destructive human relationships can be found in destructive roles.

Status   Social position also determines one's **status**, *or level of power and importance within a group.* In most groups, higher status bestows special privileges and respect. For example, in one classic experiment, researchers left dimes in phone booths. When subjects entered the booths they were approached by a researcher who said, "Excuse me, I think I left a dime in this phone booth a few minutes ago. Did you find it?" Seventy-seven percent of the people returned the money when the researcher was well dressed, but only 38 percent returned it to poorly dressed researchers (Bickman, 1974). Perhaps the better treatment given "higher status" individuals in this example explains some of our society's preoccupation with status symbols.

The following highlight discusses another subtle dimension of status.

Touch and Status

Pause for a moment and think about who you touch during a typical day. Do you think that social status affects your patterns of touching and being touched by others?

It would be surprising if touching weren't affected by status. Touch is one of the most basic forms of communication. Its message can be one of warmth, friendship, caring, nurturance, or sexual interest (see Chapter 15). In addition, touching is a "privilege" of power and high status. Older persons, for instance, are more likely to touch younger persons than the reverse. Likewise, people of high socioeconomic status are more likely to touch those of lower status.

Even in situations where persons touch each other equal amounts, there is an important difference. When a person of higher status touches one of lower status, the contact is more likely to be "personal" or familiar. When lower status persons touch those of higher status, it is more likely to be formal or impersonal, such as a handshake (Hall, 1996b).

There is one more difference worth noting. Men, by virtue of their higher status and greater power in society, are more likely to touch women than women are to touch men (Major, Schmidlin, & Williams, 1990). This difference is highly visible in most work settings: Picture a male boss touching his female secretary on the shoulder or arm to get her attention; she, in turn, never touches him. While women have moved toward equal status with men, patterns of social touching suggest that subtle inequalities in power and dominance persist.

Are there other dimensions of group membership?

Structure and Cohesion   Groups are made up of people who are in some way interrelated. Two very important dimensions of any group are its *structure* and *cohesiveness.* **Group structure** *consists of the network of roles, communication pathways, and power in a group.* Organized groups such as an army or an athletic team have a high degree of structure. Informal friendship groups may or may not be highly structured. **Group cohesiveness** *is basically the degree of attraction among group members or their commitment to remaining in the group.* Members of cohesive groups literally stick together: They are more likely to stand or sit close together and focus attention on one another. They also show more signs of mutual affection and their behavior tends to be closely coordinated (Levine & Moreland, 1990). Cohesiveness is the basis for much of the power that groups exert over their members. Therapy groups, businesses, sports teams, and the like often actively seek to strengthen group cohesion.

Norms   The functioning of any group is greatly affected by its norms. A **norm** *is an accepted (but often unspoken) standard of conduct for appropriate behavior.* If you have the slightest doubt about the existence of powerful group norms, try this test: Board a crowded bus, find a seat, and begin singing loudly in your fullest voice. Probably not more than one person in 100 could actually carry out these instructions.

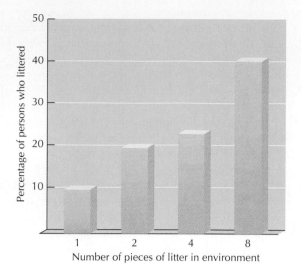

Figure 20–1 ◆ Results of an experiment on norms concerning littering. The prior existence of litter in a public setting implies that littering is acceptable. This encourages others to "trash" the area. (From Cialdini, Reno, & Kallgren, 1990.)

The impact of norms is illustrated by an interesting experiment on littering. The question in this study was, Does the amount of trash already discarded in an area affect the likelihood that people will add to the litter? As subjects walked into a public parking garage, they were given a handbill. As you can see in Figure 20–1 ◆, the more litter there was in the garage, the more likely people were to drop their handbill on the floor. Apparently, seeing that others had littered implied a lax norm about whether littering is acceptable. The moral? The cleaner a public area is kept, the less it will need to be cleaned (Cialdini, Reno, & Kallgren, 1990).

How are norms formed?

One early study of how group norms are formed made use of a striking illusion called the **autokinetic effect.** *In a completely darkened room, a stationary pinpoint of light will appear to drift or move about.* (The light is therefore "autokinetic," or "self-moving.") Muzafer Sherif (1906–1988) found that estimates of how far the light moves vary widely from person to person. However, when two or more people give estimates at the same time, their judgments rapidly converge. A similar convergence of attitudes, beliefs, and behaviors takes place among members of most groups.

Norms are often based on our *perceptions* of what others think and do. For example, a majority of college students believe that they are more troubled about excessive drinking on campus than other students are. Apparently, many students are fooled by a false norm that they help create by not speaking up. If disapproving students actually outnumber "party animals," then campus norms for acceptable drinking should be more conservative than they typically are (Prentice & Miller, 1993).

A vivid example of the influence that norms have on

behavior is found in the unspoken rules governing the use of *personal space.* Since personal space is an intriguing topic in its own right, let's take a moment to examine it.

Personal Space— Invisible Boundaries

An interesting aspect of social behavior is the effort people make to regulate the space around their bodies. Each person has an invisible "spatial envelope" that defines his or her **personal space.** *This is an area surrounding the body that is regarded as private, and subject to personal control.* Basically, personal space extends "I" or "me" boundaries past the skin.

What effect does personal space have on behavior?

Maintaining and regulating personal space affects many social interactions. Powerful norms define the interpersonal distance considered appropriate for formal business, casual conversation, waiting in line with strangers, and other situations.

The systematic study of rules for the use of personal space is called **proxemics** (Hall, 1974b). The existence of personal space and the nature of proxemics can be demonstrated by "invading" the space of another person. The next time you are talking with an acquaintance, move closer and watch the reaction. Most people show immediate signs of discomfort and step back to re-establish their original distance. Those who hold their ground will turn to the side, look away, or position an arm in front of themselves as a kind of barrier to intrusion. If you persistently edge toward your subjects, it should be easy to move them several feet from their original positions. The existence of spatial norms may explain why people who feel offended by another person sometimes say, "Get out of my face."

Would this technique work with a good friend?

Possibly not. Conventions governing comfortable or acceptable distances vary according to relationships as well as activities. Hall (1966b) identified four basic zones: *intimate, personal, social,* and *public* distance (Fig. 20–2 ◆).

Spatial Norms

The distances listed below apply to face-to-face interactions in North America. Norms for personal distance vary greatly from culture to culture. In many Middle Eastern countries, for instance, people hold their faces only inches apart when conversing. In Western Europe, the English sit closer together when talking than the French do. The Dutch, on the other hand, sit farther apart than the French (Remland,

The use of space in public places is governed by unspoken norms, or "rules," about what is appropriate.

Jones, & Brinkman, 1991). In many parts of the world, merely crossing a border results in a noticeable change in spatial norms.

1. **Intimate distance.** For the majority of North American adults, *the most private and exclusive space extends about 18 inches out from the skin.* Entry within this space (face to face) is reserved for special people or special circumstances. Lovemaking, comforting others, and cuddling children all take place within this space.

2. **Personal distance.** *This is the distance maintained in comfortable interaction with friends.* It extends from about 1½ to 4 feet from the body. Personal distance basically keeps people within "arm's reach" of each other.

3. **Social distance.** *Impersonal business and casual social gatherings take place in a range of about 4 to 12 feet.* This distance eliminates most touching, and it formalizes conversation by requiring greater voice projection. "Important people" in many business offices use the imposing width of their desks to maintain social distance. A big smelly cigar helps, too.

4. **Public distance.** *This is the distance at which formal interactions occur (about 12 feet or more from the body).* When people are separated by more than 12 feet, people look "flat" and the voice must be raised. Formal speeches, lectures, business meetings, and the like, are conducted at public distance.

Because spatial behavior is very consistent, you can learn much about your relationship to others by observing the distance you comfortably hold between yourselves. Watch for this dimension in your daily social activities. But be aware of cultural differences, too. Otherwise, you might misread another person's spatial behavior. People of different nationalities often have different norms for personal space. When they do, both are likely to be uncomfortable when talking, as one tries to move closer and the other keeps moving back. This can lead to misunderstandings in which one person feels that the other is being too familiar, while that person feels rejected.

We have now explored some basic facts of social life and a striking example of group norms. In the next section we will consider a kind of impromptu detective work that we engage in as we try to guess the motives of others and the causes of their actions. Let's see how this is done.

Intimate (0–1.5) Personal (1.5–4) Social (4–12) Public (12+)

Figure 20–2 ◆ Typical spatial zones (in feet) for face-to-face interactions in North America. Often, we must stand within intimate distance of others in crowds, buses, subways, elevators, and other public places. At such times, privacy is maintained by avoiding eye contact, by standing shoulder to shoulder or back to back, and by positioning a purse, bag, package, or coat as a barrier to spatial intrusions.

Social Perception— Behind the Mask

It is probably impossible to completely know another person. In fact, in many instances we must form impressions of people from only the smallest shreds of evidence. How do we form such impressions? How do they affect our behavior? Many of the answers lie in **attribution,** *the process of making inferences about the causes of behavior.* (Attribution was also discussed briefly in Chapter 13.) To learn how we fill in the "person behind the mask," let's explore the making of attributions.

Attribution Theory

Two people enter a restaurant and order different meals. Nell tastes her food, then salts it. Bert salts his food before he tastes it. How would you explain their behavior? In Nell's case, you might assume that the *food* needed salt. If so, you have attributed her actions to an **external cause** (*one assumed to lie outside a person*). With Bert, you might be more inclined to conclude that he must really *like* salt. If so, you would be saying that the cause of his behavior is *internal* (McGee & Snyder, 1975). **Internal causes** *of behavior are assumed to lie*

During the 1996 Olympics, U.S. gymnast Kerri Strug performed an important vault after severely spraining her ankle. Later she was carried to the award stand by her coach, Bela Karoli. As you watched these events, did you attribute Karoli's actions to selfless concern for his young protégée? Or was Karoli motivated by a selfish desire to hog the limelight? Such attributions greatly affect how we perceive and respond to the social behavior of others.

within a person. Examples include needs, preferences, and personality traits.

What effects do such interpretations have?

It is difficult to fully understand social behavior without considering internal and external attributions. For instance, let's say that Jim, who is in one of your classes, seems to avoid you. You see Jim at a market. Do you say hello to him? It could depend on how you have explained Jim's actions to yourself. Have you assumed his avoidance is caused by shyness? Coincidence? Dislike?

How do people make such judgments?

Making Attributions Two factors that greatly influence attribution are the *consistency* and *distinctiveness* of a person's behavior (Kelley, 1967). **Consistency** *refers to the fact that a behavior changes very little on different occasions.* If Jim has consistently avoided you, it is clear that he was not just in a bad mood on each occasion, so coincidence is ruled out. Still, Jim's avoidance could mean he is shy, not that he dislikes you. That's why distinctiveness is also important. **Distinctiveness** *refers to the fact that a behavior occurs only under specific circumstances.* If Jim seems to avoid others, too, you may conclude that he is shy. If his avoidance is consistently and distinctively linked with you, you will probably assume that he dislikes you. You could be wrong, of course, but your behavior toward Jim will change just the same.

To infer causes, we typically take into account the behavior of the **actor** (*the person of interest*), the **object** (*target or aim*) of the action, and the **setting** (*social or physical environment*) in which the action occurs (Kelley, 1967). Imagine, for example, that someone compliments your taste in clothes. If you are at a picnic, you may attribute this compliment to what you are wearing (the "object") unless, of course, you're wearing your worst "grubbies." If you are, you may simply assume that the person (or "actor") is friendly, or tactful. However, if you are at a clothing store and a salesperson compliments you, you will probably attribute it to the setting—not to what you are wearing or the salesperson's true feelings. In making attributions we are very sensitive to **situational demands.** *These are pressures to behave in certain ways that are associated with various settings and social situations.* When a person is quiet and polite in church or at a funeral, it tells us little about the individual's motives. The situation demands such behavior.

When situational demands are strong, we tend to *discount* claims that a person's actions are internally caused. **Discounting** *refers to downgrading internal explanations of a person's actions when they appear to have strong external causes.* For example, you have probably discounted the sincerity of professional athletes who endorse shaving creams, hair tonics, deodorants, and the like. Obviously, the athletes' endorsements are well explained by the large sums of money they receive. It's not necessary to assume they actually *like* the potions they sell.

Consensus (*or agreement*) is another factor affecting

attribution. A consensus in the behavior of a number of people implies that the behavior has an external cause. If millions of people go to see a particular movie, we tend to say *the movie* is good. If someone you know goes to see a movie six times, when others are staying away in droves, the tendency is to assume that *the person* likes "that type of movie."

A Closer Look

Self-Handicapping—Smoke Screen for Failure

Have you ever known someone who got drunk before taking an exam? Why would a person risk failure in this way? Often, the reason lies in **self-handicapping** *(arranging to perform under conditions that impair performance)*. If a person fails, self-handicapping makes her or him feel better because it provides an excuse for poor performance (Drexler, Ahrens, & Haaga, 1995).

What if a person succeeds while "handicapped"?

Well, then, so much the better. The person's self-image then gets a boost because she or he succeeded under conditions that normally lower performance (Murray & Warden, 1992).

Do you believe that "you either have it or you don't" where ability is concerned? If so, you may be particularly prone to self-handicapping. By working with a handicap, people can avoid any chance of discovering that they "don't have it" (Rhodewalt, 1994)!

Drinking alcohol is one of the most popular—and dangerous—self-handicapping strategies. A person who is drunk can attribute failure to being "loaded," while accepting success if it occurs. Examples of using alcohol for self-handicapping include being drunk for school exams, job interviews, or an important first date. A person who gets drunk at such times should be aware that coping with anxiety in this way can lead to serious alcohol abuse.

Any time you set up excuses for a poor performance, you are self-handicapping. Other examples of self-handicapping include making a halfhearted effort, claiming to be ill, and procrastinating. Most of us have used self-handicapping at times. Indeed, life would be harsh if we didn't sometimes give ourselves a break from accepting full responsibility for success or failure. Self-handicapping, therefore, becomes a problem mainly when it is habitual. So, watch out for self-handicapping, but don't be too hard on yourself.

Actor and Observer   Let's say that at the last five parties you have attended, you've seen a woman named Pam. Based on this, you assume that Pam is very outgoing and likes to socialize. You see Pam at yet another gathering and mention that she seems to like parties. She says, "Actually, I hate these parties, but I get invited to play my tuba at them. My music teacher says I need to practice in front of an audience, so I keep attending these dumb events. Want to hear a Sousa march?"

We seldom know the real reasons for others' actions. That is why we tend to infer causes from *circumstances*. However, in doing so, we often make mistakes of the type just described. *The most common error is to attribute the actions of others to internal causes, while attributing our own behavior to situations (external causes)* (Jones & Nisbett, 1971). This mistake is made so often that it is called the **fundamental attributional error.**

Because of errors in judgment, we consistently attribute the behavior of others to their wants, motives, and personality traits. In contrast, we tend to find external explanations for our own behavior (Krueger, Ham, & Linford, 1996). No

Distressed couples tend to attribute their partners' actions to the worst possible motives, such as bad intentions or selfishness. Thus, attributional styles may lead to serious conflicts in marriage and other relationships (Holtzworth-Munroe & Hutchinson, 1993; Noller & Ruzzene, 1991).

doubt you chose *your* major in school because of what it has to offer. Other students choose *their* majors because of the kind of people they are. Other people who don't leave tips in restaurants are cheapskates. If you don't leave a tip it's because the service was bad. And, of course, other people are always late because they are irresponsible. I am late because I have a good reason.

Implications   As you can see, attribution theory summarizes how we think about ourselves and others, including the errors we tend to make. In addition, attribution theory has highlighted some practical problems. Let's conclude with a brief example.

Ye Old Double Standard   Research on attribution has revealed an interesting double standard regarding the abilities of men and women. In a study by Kay Deaux and Tim Emswiller (1974), men and women overheard a male or female perform extremely well on a perception task. Each person was then asked to rate whether the test taker's success was due to ability, luck, or some combination of the two. Both men and women attributed male success mainly to skill and women's performances mainly to luck! This was true even though male and female performances were identical. As early as *kindergarten*, boys tend to take credit for successes. Girls, in contrast, tend to discount their own performances ("put themselves down") (Burgner & Hewstone, 1993). In general, there is a strong tendency to assume, "He's skilled, she's lucky," when assessing the performances of men and women (Swim & Sanna, 1996).

Throughout life, such attributions no doubt dog the heels of many talented and successful women.

Learning Check

1. Male, female, and adolescent are examples of _____ roles.

2. Status refers to a set of expected behaviors associated with a social position. T or F?

3. Research has shown that the number of first-name acquaintances needed to interconnect two widely separated strangers averages about 7 people. T or F?

4. The Stanford prison experiment demonstrated the powerful influence of the autokinetic effect on behavior. T or F?

5. Social psychology is the study of how people behave in _____ .

6. If two people position themselves 5 feet apart while conversing, they are separated by a gap referred to as _____ distance.

7. When situational demands are strong, we tend to attribute a person's actions to internal causes. T or F?

8. The fundamental attributional error is to attribute the actions of others to internal causes, while attributing our own behavior to external causes. T or F?

Critical Thinking

9. The Stanford prison experiment also illustrates a major concept of personality theory (Chapter 16), especially social learning theory. Can you name it?

Answers:

1. ascribed 2. F 3. T 4. F 5. social situations or the presence of others 6. social 7. F 8. T 9. It is the idea that behavior is often strongly influenced by situations rather than by personal traits.

The Need for Affiliation—Come Together

Why do people choose to congregate with others?

We have already observed that the **need to affiliate** (*a desire to associate with other people*) appears to be a basic human characteristic. But why? Probably because affiliation helps meet needs for approval, support, friendship, and information. We also seek company to alleviate fear or anxiety. An experiment in which college women were threatened with painful electric shock serves as an illustration.

Zilstein's Shock Shop

A man introduced as Dr. Gregor Zilstein ominously explained to arriving subjects, "We would like to give each of you a series of electric shocks . . . these shocks will hurt, they will be painful." In the room was a frightening electrical device that seemed to verify Zilstein's plans. While waiting to be shocked, each subject was given a choice of waiting alone or with other subjects. Women frightened in this way more often chose to wait with others than did subjects told that the shock would be a mild tickle or tingle (Schachter, 1959).

Apparently, the frightened women found it comforting or reassuring to be with others. The tempting conclusion is that "misery loves company." But this is not completely accurate.

In a later experiment, women expecting to be shocked

were given the option of waiting with other shock subjects, with women waiting to see their advisors, or alone. Most subjects chose to wait with other future "victims." In short, misery seems to love miserable company! In general, we tend to seek the company of people in circumstances similar to our own (Gump & Kulik, 1997).

Is there a reason for that?

Yes. Other people provide information for evaluating one's own reactions. When a situation is threatening or unfamiliar, or when a person is in doubt, *social comparisons* serve as a guide for behavior (Banaji & Prentice, 1994).

Social Comparison Theory

In some cases objective standards for self-evaluation exist. If I want to know how tall I am, I simply get out a tape measure. But how do I know if I am a good athlete, guitarist, worker, parent, or friend? How do I know if my views on politics, religion, or grunge rock are unusual or widely shared? When there are no objective standards, comparing yourself to others is the only yardstick available.

Eminent social psychologist Leon Festinger (1919–1989) was among the first to point out that group membership fills needs for **social comparison** (*comparing your own actions, feelings, opinions, or abilities to those of other persons*). When students gather to compare notes after a classroom exam, they satisfy needs for social comparison.

Festinger (1954) emphasized that social comparisons are not made randomly. To illustrate, let's say we ask a student named Wendy if she is a good tennis player. If Wendy compares herself to a professional, the answer will be no. But this tells little about her relative ability. In Wendy's group of tennis partners, she might be considered an excellent player. Useful personal evaluation requires comparison with people of similar backgrounds, abilities, and circumstances (Miller, Turnbull, & McFarland, 1988). On a fair scale of comparison, Wendy knows she is good and takes pride in her tennis skills. In the same way, thinking of yourself as successful, talented, responsible, or fairly paid depends entirely on whom you compare yourself with.

In addition to providing information, social comparisons may, at times, be made in ways that reflect a desire for self-protection or self-enhancement. If you feel threatened, you may make a **downward comparison** by *contrasting yourself with a person who ranks lower on some dimension* (Banaji & Prentice, 1994). For example, if you have a part-time job and your employer cuts your hours, you may comfort yourself by thinking about a friend who just lost a job.

What about upward comparisons? Do they occur, too?

As Wendy's tennis playing suggests, comparing yourself with people of much higher ability will probably just make you feel bad (Wheeler and Miyake, 1992). However, **upward comparisons,** *in which we compare ourselves to a person who ranks higher on some dimension*, are sometimes used for

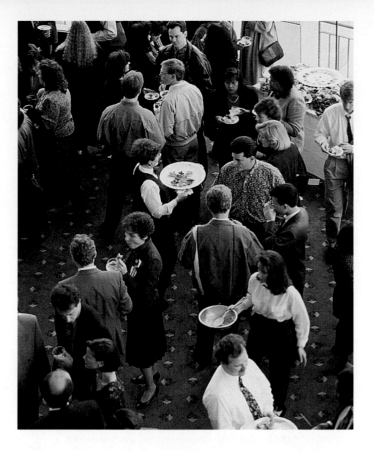

High school class reunions are notorious for the rampant social comparison they often encourage. Apparently it's hard to resist comparing yourself to former classmates to see how you are doing in life.

self-improvement. One way that Wendy can learn to improve her tennis skills is to compare herself with players who are only a little better than she is (Collins, 1996).

In general, social comparison theory holds that desires for self-evaluation, self-protection, and self-enhancement provide motives for associating with others. In doing so, they influence which groups we join.

Don't people also affiliate out of attraction for one another?

They do, of course. The next section tells why.

Interpersonal Attraction—Social Magnetism?

"**B**irds of a feather flock together." "Familiarity breeds contempt." "Opposites attract." "Absence makes the heart grow fonder." Interest in what attracts people to one another has spawned an extensive folklore about what factors are important. This is understandable, since **interpersonal attraction** (*affinity to another person*) is the basis for most voluntary social relationships.

What attracts people to each other? Proximity and frequency of contact have a surprisingly large impact.

What attracts people to each other?

Several factors determine with whom you are likely to become friends. A brief discussion of each follows.

Physical Proximity

It may be difficult to admit, but our selection of friends (and even lovers) is based more on opportunity than we might like to believe. **Physical proximity** (*nearness*) plays a powerful role in making friends. A classic study in a married-student housing complex found that the closer people lived to each other, the more likely they were to become friends (Festinger et al., 1950). People in love like to think they have found the "one and only" person in the universe for them. In reality, they have probably found the one and only person in a 5-mile radius—or at least within driving distance (Buss, 1985)!

A main reason for proximity's effect is that it increases the *frequency of contact* between people. A variety of experiments show that we are generally attracted to people with whom we have frequent contact (Saegert et al., 1973). In other words, there does seem to be a "boy-next-door" or "girl-next-door" effect in romantic attraction, and a "folks-next-door" effect in friendship.

Physical Attractiveness

Physical attractiveness *refers to a person's degree of physical beauty, as defined by his or her culture.* As might be expected, beautiful people are consistently rated more appealing than those of average appearance. This is due, in part, to the **halo effect,** *a tendency to generalize a favorable impression to unrelated personal characteristics.* Because of it, we assume that attractive people are also likable, intelligent, warm, witty, mentally healthy, and socially skilled (Feingold, 1992). Basically, we act as if "what is beautiful is good." However, there are limits to the traits we associate with beauty. For instance, we do not expect beautiful people to be more honest or concerned about others (Johnson, 1991)! And in reality, physical attractiveness has almost *no* connection to intelligence, talents, or abilities (Feingold, 1992).

Being physically attractive can be an advantage for both males and females. Good-looking people are less lonely, less socially anxious, more popular, more socially skilled, and

Physical beauty can be socially advantageous because of the widespread belief that "what is beautiful is good." However, physical beauty is generally unrelated to actual personal traits and talents.

more sexually experienced than unattractive people (Feingold, 1992). Where romance is concerned, physical attractiveness has more influence on a woman's fate than on a man's (Feingold, 1990). For instance, there is a strong relationship between a woman's physical beauty and her frequency of dating. For men, looks are unrelated to dating frequency.

If you view this state of affairs as rather shallow and sexist, it may be reassuring to know that beauty is a factor mainly in initial acquaintance (Keller & Young, 1996). Later, more substantial personal qualities become important (Berscheid, 1994). It takes more than appearance to make a lasting relationship. Even first impressions are less affected by beauty if we are given information that helps us see a person as an individual (Johnson, 1991).

Competence

Competence *is the degree of ability or proficiency a person displays.* Not surprisingly, we are also attracted to people who are talented or competent. However, there is an interesting twist to this, as revealed in the following example.

Clever but Clumsy

In an experiment on attraction, college students listened to one of four tapes of a supposed candidate for the "College Quiz Bowl." On two of the tapes the person was represented as highly intelligent; on the other two he was depicted as average in ability. One of the "intelligent" and one of the "average" tapes included an incident in which the candidate clumsily spilled coffee on himself. Those listening to the tapes rated as *most* attractive the superior candidate who blundered, and as *least* attractive the student who was average and clumsy. The superior but clumsy student was more attractive than the student who was only superior. (Aronson, 1969)

The upshot of this experiment seems to be that we like people who are competent but imperfect—which makes them more "human."

Similarity

Take a moment to mentally list as many of your friends as you can. What do they have in common (other than the joy of knowing you)? It is highly likely that most are close to you in age and of the same sex and race as you. There will be exceptions, of course. However, similarity on these three dimensions is the general rule for friendships.

Similarity *refers to the extent to which two people are alike in background, age, interests, attitudes, beliefs, and so forth.* One of the most consistent findings about interpersonal attraction is that similar people are attracted to each other (Carli, Ganley, & Pierce-Otay, 1991). This is probably at least partially due to the reinforcing value of seeing our beliefs and attitudes affirmed by others. It shows we are "right" and

In college dormitories, roommates who are similar in personality and physical attractiveness tend to be more satisfied with their relationship (Carli, Ganley, & Pierce-Otay, 1991).

reveals that they are clever people as well (Alicke, Yurak, & Vredenburg, 1996)!

Does similarity also influence mate selection? The next highlight provides an answer.

A Closer Look

Selecting a Mate—Reflections in a Social Mirror

Ninety percent of all people in Western societies marry at some point. What, beyond attraction, determines how people pair up? The answer is that *we tend to marry someone who is like us in almost every way,* a pattern called **homogamy** (huh-MOG-ah-me) (Caspi & Herbener, 1990).

Studies show that married couples are highly similar in age, education, race, religion, and ethnic background. In addition, the correlation between their attitudes and opinions is .5. For mental abilities it is .4, and for socioeconomic status, height, weight, and eye color it is .3. In general, you are far more likely to choose someone similar to yourself as a mate than someone very different. This is probably a good thing. Personality traits tend to be closely matched in the most stable marriages (Kim, Martin, & Martin, 1989). Conversely, the risk of divorce is highest among couples with sizable differences in age and education (Tzeng, 1992).

A second question of interest concerns what traits people look for in a mate. In the United States, both men and women agree that the following are the first six most important qualities: kindness and understanding, intelligence, exciting personality, good health, adaptability, and physical attractiveness. Despite such agreement, men and women do differ on some rankings. Men, for instance, rank physical attractiveness as the third most important feature, whereas women rank it sixth. A second major difference concerns good earning capacity: Men rank it eleventh; women rank it eighth (Buss, 1985).

Apparently, for most people, romance is leavened with a dash of practicality. Another study found that women in the U.S., Russia, and Japan regard intelligence, ambition, success, and status as more important in a potential mate than men do. Notice, though, that kindness and understanding are ranked first by almost everyone (Hatfield & Sprecher, 1995).

Self-Disclosure

How do people who are not yet friends learn if they are similar?

Getting to know others requires a willingness to talk about more than just the weather, sports, or nuclear physics. At some point you must begin to *share private thoughts and feelings and reveal yourself to others.* This process, which is called **self-disclosure,** is a basic skill for developing close relationships. Lack of self-disclosure is associated with anxiety, unhappiness, and loneliness (Meleshko & Alden, 1993; Mikulincer & Nachshon, 1991).

We more often reveal ourselves to persons we like than to those we find less attractive. Disclosing oneself to others also requires a degree of trust. Many people play it safe, or "close to the vest," with people they do not know well. Indeed, there are definite norms about when self-disclosure is acceptable and when it is not. Moderate self-disclosure leads to **reciprocity** (*a return in kind*). *Overdisclosure,* however, gives rise to suspicion and reduced attraction. **Overdisclosure** *is self-disclosure that exceeds what is appropriate for a particular relationship or social situation.* For example, imagine standing in line at a market and having the person in front of you say, "Lately I've been thinking about how I really feel about myself. I think that I'm pretty well adjusted, but I occasionally have some questions about my sexual adequacy."

When self-disclosure proceeds at a moderate pace, it is accompanied by growing levels of liking, trust, and intimacy (Miller, 1990; Vera & Betz, 1992). When it is too rapid or inappropriate, we are likely to "back off" and wonder about the person's motives. The following highlight provides another interesting angle on patterns of self-disclosure.

Excessive self-disclosure is a staple of many television talk shows. Guests frequently reveal intimate details about their personal lives, including private family matters, sex and dating, physical or sexual abuse, major embarrassments, and criminal activities. Viewers probably find such intimate disclosures entertaining, rather than threatening, because they don't have to reciprocate.

Cultural Diversity

Gendered Friendships

Two male friends share lunch at a restaurant. In the next hour they talk about sports, cars, sports cars, the *Sports Illustrated* swimsuit edition, sports, cars, and golf. (Did I mention sports and cars?) Janis, who was at a nearby table, overheard the entire conversation. Here's her summary of what the men said to each other: "Absolutely nothing!"

In North American culture most male friendships are *activity-based.* That is, men tend to do things together—a pattern that provides companionship without closeness.

The friendships of women are more often based on *shared feelings and confidences.* If two female friends spent an afternoon together and did not reveal problems, private thoughts, and feelings to one another, they would assume that something was wrong. For women, friendship is a matter of talking about shared concerns and intimate matters.

Actually, the differences between male and female

friendships are smaller than implied here. Men do know *something* about the private thoughts and feelings of their friends. Nevertheless, most contemporary men do not form close friendships with other men. Many could probably learn something from female friendships: Men live their friendships side by side; women live them face to face. (Sources: Archer, 1996; Nardi, 1992; Reid & Fine, 1992).

Social Exchange Theory

Many relationships can be understood as an ongoing series of **social exchanges** (*transfers of attention, information, affection, favors, or the like, between two people*). In such exchanges, we tend to maximize rewards while minimizing our "costs." When a relationship ceases to be attractive, people often say, "I'm not getting anything out of it any more." Actually, they probably are. But their costs—in terms of effort, irritation, or lowered self-esteem—have begun to exceed their rewards.

According to **social exchange theory,** *a relationship must be profitable (its rewards must exceed its costs) for both participants.* Otherwise, it will not last. For instance, John and Ruthie have been dating for 2 years. While they still have fun at times, they also frequently argue and bicker. If the friction in their relationship gets much stronger, it will exceed the rewards of staying together. When that happens they will probably split up (Gottman, 1994).

Actually, just being profitable is not the whole story. It is more accurate to say that a relationship needs to be profitable *enough.* Generally, the balance between rewards and costs is judged in comparison with what we have come to expect from past experience. *The personal standard a person uses to evaluate rewards and costs is called the* **comparison level.** The comparison level is high for a person with a history of satisfying and rewarding relationships. It is lower for someone whose relationships have been unsatisfying. Thus, the decision to continue a relationship is affected by your personal comparison level. A lonely person, or one whose friendships have been marginal, might stay in a relationship that you would consider unacceptable.

Loving and Liking— Dating, Rating, Mating

Does romantic attraction differ from interpersonal attraction?

In Chapter 13 we noted that **romantic love** *is marked by high levels of interpersonal attraction and emotional arousal.* We also discussed various types of love that result from combinations of intimacy, passion, and commitment. To get another angle

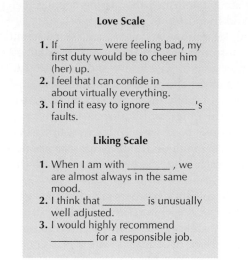

Love Scale

1. If _____ were feeling bad, my first duty would be to cheer him (her) up.
2. I feel that I can confide in _____ about virtually everything.
3. I find it easy to ignore _____'s faults.

Liking Scale

1. When I am with _____ , we are almost always in the same mood.
2. I think that _____ is unusually well adjusted.
3. I would highly recommend _____ for a responsible job.

Figure 20–3 ◆ Sample love-scale and liking-scale items. Each scale consists of 13 items similar to those shown. Scores on these scales correspond to other indications of love and liking. (Reprinted by permission of Zick Rubin.)

on love, psychologist Zick Rubin (1973) chose to think of it as an attitude held by one person toward another. This allowed him to develop "liking" and "love" scales to measure each "attitude" (see Fig. 20–3 ◆). Next, he asked dating couples to complete each scale twice; once with their date in mind and once for a close friend of the same sex.

What were the results?

Scores for love of partner and love of friend differed more than those for **liking** (*affection without passion or deep commitment*) (Table 20–1 ■). In other words, dating couples liked *and* loved their partners, but mostly liked their friends. Women, however, were a little more "loving" of their friends than were men. Does this reflect real differences in the strength of male friendships and female friendships? Maybe not, since it is more acceptable in our culture for women to express love for one another than it is for men. Nevertheless,

Table 20–1 ■ Average Love and Liking Scores for Date and Same-Sex Close Friend		
Attitude toward dating partner		
	Love score	Liking score
Women	89.5	88.5
Men	89.4	84.7
Attitude toward close friend		
	Love score	Liking score
Women	65.3	80.5
Men	55.0	79.1

Source: Rubin, 1970.

another study confirmed that dating couples feel a mixture of love and friendship for their partners. In fact, 44 percent of a group of dating persons named their romantic partner as their closest friend (Hendrick & Hendrick, 1993).

Another way in which love and friendship differ is the degree of mutual absorption. Romantic love, in contrast to simple liking, usually involves deep **mutual absorption** of the lovers. In other words, lovers (unlike friends) *attend almost exclusively to one another.* It's not surprising then, that couples scoring high on Rubin's love scale spend more time gazing into each other's eyes than do couples who score low on the scale.

What do romantic partners see when they gaze into each other's eyes? A final interesting characteristic of romantic love is lovers' ability to see their partners in idealized ways. Nobody's perfect, of course. That's why it's no surprise that relationships are most likely to persist when lovers idealize one another. Doing so doesn't just blind them to their partner's faults, it actually helps them create the relationship they wish for (Murray, Holmes, & Griffin, 1996).

Love and Attachment

Sheela has been dating Paul for over a year. Although they have had some rough spots, Sheela is comfortable, secure, and trusting in her love for Paul. Charlene, in contrast, has had a long series of unhappy romances with men. She is basically a loner who has difficulty trusting others. Like Sheela, Eduardo has been dating the same person for a year. However, his relationship with Helen has been stormy and troubled. Eduardo is strongly attracted to Helen. Yet, he is also in a constant state of anxiety over whether she really loves him.

Sheela, Charlene, and Eduardo might be surprised to learn that the roots of their romantic relationships may lie in childhood. There is growing evidence that early attachments to caregivers (see Chapter 4) can have a lasting impact on how we relate to others (Shaver & Hazen, 1993). For example, recent studies of dating couples have identified secure, avoidant, and ambivalent attachment patterns similar to those seen in early child development (Mikulincer & Nachshon, 1991).

Secure attachment *is a stable and positive emotional bond.* A secure attachment style like Sheela's is marked by caring, intimacy, supportiveness, and understanding in love relationships. Secure persons regard themselves as friendly, good natured, and likable. They think of others as generally well intentioned, reliable, and trustworthy. People with a secure attachment style find it relatively easy to get close to others. They are comfortable depending on others and having others depend on them. In general, they don't worry too much about being abandoned or about having someone become too emotionally close to them. Most people prefer to have a secure partner, whatever their own style might be (Latty-Mann & Davis, 1996).

Charlene's **avoidant attachment style** *reflects a fear of*

intimacy and a tendency to resist commitment to others. Avoidant persons tend to pull back when things don't go well in a relationship. The avoidant person is suspicious, aloof, and skeptical about love. She or he tends to see others as either unreliable or overly eager to commit to a relationship. As a result, avoidant persons find it hard to completely trust and depend on others. Avoidant persons get nervous when anyone gets too close emotionally. Basically, they avoid intimacy (Tidwell, Reis, & Shaver, 1996).

Persons like Eduardo have an **ambivalent attachment style,** *marked by mixed emotions about relationships.* Conflicting feelings of affection, anger, emotional turmoil, physical attraction, and doubt leave them in an unsettled, ambivalent state. Often, ambivalent persons regard themselves as misunderstood and unappreciated. They tend to see their friends and lovers as unreliable and unable or unwilling to commit themselves to lasting relationships. Ambivalent persons worry that their romantic partners don't really love them or may leave them. While they want to be extremely close to their partners, they are also preoccupied with doubts about the partner's dependability and trustworthiness.

How could emotional attachments early in life affect adult relationships?

It appears that we use early attachment experiences to build mental models about affectionate relationships. Later, we use these models as a sort of blueprint for forming, maintaining, and breaking bonds of love and affection (Simpson, 1990). Thus, the quality of childhood bonds to parents or other caregivers may hold a key to understanding how we approach romantic relationships (Shaver & Hazen, 1993). Maybe it's no accident that persons who are romantically available are often described as "unattached."

It is fascinating to think that our relationships may be influenced by events early in childhood. Could the source of adult mating patterns reach even farther back? The next section explores that possibility.

Evolution and Mate Selection

Evolutionary psychology *is the study of the evolutionary origins of human behavior patterns.* Many psychologists have come to believe that evolution left an imprint on men and women that influences everything from sexual attraction and infidelity to jealousy and divorce. According to David Buss, the key to understanding human mating patterns is not found just in learning, socialization, attachment, or culture. Rather, we must also understand how evolved behavior patterns guide our choices (Buss, 1994).

In a study of 37 cultures on six continents, Buss found the following patterns: Compared with women, men are more interested in casual sex; they prefer younger, more physically attractive partners; and they get more jealous over real or imagined sexual infidelities than they do over a loss of emotional commitment. Compared with men, women prefer slightly older partners who appear to be industrious, higher

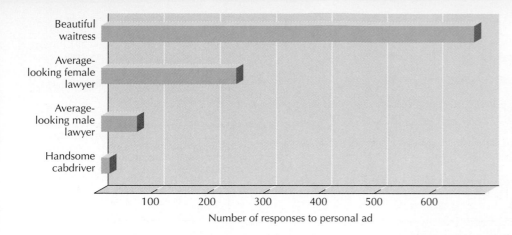

Beautiful
waitress

Average-
looking female
lawyer

Average-
looking male
lawyer

Handsome
cabdriver

100   200   300   400   500   600

Number of responses to personal ad

Figure 20–4 ◆ What do people look for when considering potential dating partners? Here are the results of a study in which personal ads were placed in newspapers. As you can see, men were more influenced by looks, and women by success (Goode, 1996).

in status, or economically successful; women are more upset by a partner who becomes emotionally involved with someone else, rather than one who is sexually unfaithful (Buss, 1994; Buss et al., 1992) (Fig. 20–4 ◆).

Why do such differences exist? Buss and other researchers believe that evolutionary psychology explains many human mating patterns. Mating preferences, they say, evolved in response to the differing reproductive challenges faced by men and women.

As a rule, women must invest more time and energy in reproduction and nurturing the young than men do. Consequently, women evolved an interest in whether their partners will stay with them and whether their mates have the resources to provide for their children (Archer, 1996).

In contrast, the reproductive success of men depends on their mates' fertility. Men, therefore, tend to look for health and youth in a prospective mate, as signs of suitability for reproduction. This preference, perhaps, is why some older men abandon their first wives in favor of young, beautiful "trophy wives." Evolutionary theory further explains that the male emphasis on mates' sexual fidelity is based on concerns about the paternity of offspring. From a biological perspective, men do not benefit from investing resources in children they did not sire (Schmitt & Buss, 1996).

A sizable body of evidence supports the evolutionary view of mating preferences. However, it is important to remember that evolved mating tendencies are subtle at best and easily overruled by other factors. Indeed, some mating

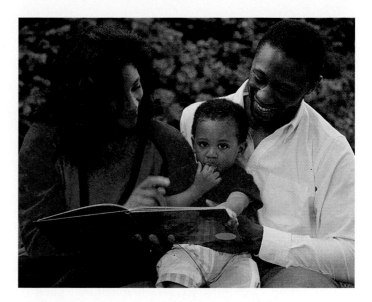

According to evolutionary psychologists, women tend to be concerned with whether mates will devote time and resources to a relationship. Men place more emphasis on physical attractiveness and sexual fidelity.

patterns may simply reflect the fact that men still tend to control the power and resources in most societies (Feingold, 1992). Most important of all, remember that when either men or women choose mates, kindness and intelligence still rate highest. They are love's greatest allies.

Learning Check	Critical Thinking

Before you read more, check your comprehension with the following questions.

1. Women threatened with electric shock in an experiment generally chose to wait alone or with other women not taking part in the experiment. T or F?

2. The need to affiliate is related to interest in social comparison. T or F?

3. Social comparisons are made pretty much at random. T or F?

4. Interpersonal attraction is increased by all but one of the following. (Which does not fit?)
   a. physical proximity   **b.** competence   **c.** similarity   **d.** social costs

5. High levels of self-disclosure are reciprocated in most social encounters. T or F?

6. Women rate their friends higher on the love scale than do men. T or F?

7. The most striking finding about marriage patterns is that most people choose mates whose personalities are quite unlike their own. T or F?

8. Both ambivalent and avoidant attachment patterns are associated with difficulties in trusting a romantic partner. T or F?

9. Compared with men, women tend to be more upset by sexual infidelity than by a loss of emotional commitment on the part of their mates. T or F?

10. How have contemporary communications networks altered the effects of proximity on interpersonal attraction?

Answers:

1. F 2. T 3. F 4. d 5. F 6. T 7. F 8. T 9. F 10. It is now possible to interact with another person by telephone, fax, short-wave radio, modem, or similar means. This makes actual physical proximity less crucial in interpersonal attraction, because frequent contact is possible even at great distances.

Social Influence— Follow the Leader

No topic lies nearer the heart of social psychology than **social influence,** *or changes in a person's behavior induced by the actions of others.* When people interact, they almost always affect one another's behavior. Let's probe the ways in which this takes place.

Imagine a traffic signal brightly flashing the word WAIT. As you other pedestrians wait for it to change, a well-dressed man in a suit crosses against the light. How many people follow him? Do you think the answer would be different if the man were dressed in a denim shirt, patched pants, and scuffed shoes? This street-corner setting was used in an early experiment on social influence. As you might have guessed, more people followed the well-dressed man than the one dressed in shabby clothes (Lefkowitz et al., 1955).

In another sidewalk experiment, various numbers of people were assembled on a busy New York City street. On cue they all looked at a sixth-floor window across the street. A camera recorded the number of passersby who also stopped to stare. The larger the influencing group, the more people were swayed to join in staring at the window (Milgram et al., 1969).

Are there different kinds of social influence?

Social influence ranges from simple suggestion to intensive indoctrination (brainwashing). Everyday behavior is probably most influenced by group pressures for conformity. Conformity situations develop when individuals become aware of differences between themselves and group actions, norms, or values (Baron & Byrne, 1994). Let us consider this important dimension of social life in more detail.

Conformity

When John first started working at the Fleegle Flange Factory, he found it easy to process 300 flanges an hour,

Conformity is a subtle dimension of daily life. Notice the similarities in clothing and hairstyles among these couples.

while those around him averaged only 200. Other workers told him to slow down and take it easy. "I get bored," he said and continued to do 300 flanges an hour. At first John had been welcomed, but now conversations broke up when he approached and other workers laughed at him or ignored him when he spoke. Although he never made a conscious decision to conform, in another week John's output had slowed to 200 flanges an hour.

As mentioned earlier, all groups have unspoken rules of conduct called *norms.* The broadest norms, defined by society as a whole, establish "normal" or acceptable behavior in most situations. Comparing hairstyles, habits of speech, dress, eating habits, and social customs in two or more cultures makes it clear that we all conform to social norms. In fact, a degree of uniformity is necessary if we are to interact comfortably. Imagine being totally unable to anticipate the actions of others. In stores, schools, and homes this would be frustrating and disturbing. On the highways it would be lethal.

Perhaps the most basic of all group norms is, as John discovered, "Thou shalt conform." This is equally true for the Hell's Angels, the Daughters of the American Revolution, a street-corner gang, or the board of directors of a large corporation. Groups of all kinds exert considerable pressures toward uniformity on their members. Like it or not, everyday life is filled with instances of **conformity** (*bringing one's own behavior into agreement with norms or the behavior of others.*)

How strong are group pressures for conformity?

The Asch Experiment One of the better known experiments on conformity was staged by Solomon Asch in the early 1950s. Asch's experiment is best appreciated by placing yourself in the position of a subject. Assume that you are seated at a table with six other students. Your task is actually quite simple. On each trial you are asked to select from among three lines the one that matches a standard line (Fig. 20–5 ◆).

As the testing begins, each person announces an answer for the first card. When your turn comes, you find yourself in complete agreement with the others. "This isn't hard at all," you say to yourself. For several more trials your answers correspond to those of the group. Then comes a shock. All six people announce that line 1 matches the standard, and you were about to say line 2 matches. Suddenly you feel alone and upset. You nervously look at the lines again as the room falls silent. Everyone seems to be staring at you as the experimenter awaits your answer. Do you yield to the group?

In this experiment the other "students" were all accomplices coached to give the wrong answer on about a third of the trials. Few real subjects suspected trickery; hence, the group pressure created was very realistic (Asch, 1956).

How many people yielded to group pressure?

Subjects conformed to the group on about one third of the critical trials. Of those tested, 75 percent yielded at least once. The significance of these results is underscored by the fact that people tested alone erred in less than 1 percent of their judgments. Those who yielded to group pressures were clearly denying what their eyes told them.

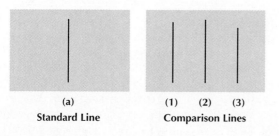

(a)		(1)	(2)	(3)
Standard Line		**Comparison Lines**		

Figure 20–5 ◆ Stimuli used in Solomon Asch's conformity experiments.

Are some people more susceptible to group pressures than others?

A variety of experiments have shown that people with high needs for structure or certainty are more likely to be influenced. So are people who are anxious, low in self-confidence, or concerned with the approval of others. If you live in a culture that emphasizes group cooperation (such as many Asian cultures) you may be more likely to conform (Bond & Smith, 1996).

In addition to personal characteristics, certain situations tend to encourage conformity—sometimes with disastrous results. The following highlight offers a prime example.

Groupthink—Agreement at Any Cost

What happens when people in positions of power fall prey to pressures for conformity? To find out, Yale psychologist Irving Janis (1918–1990) analyzed a series of disastrous decisions made by government officials. His conclusion? Many such fiascoes are the result of **groupthink**—*a compulsion by decision makers to maintain each other's approval, even at the cost of critical thinking* (Janis, 1989).

Groupthink has been blamed for many embarrassments, such as John F. Kennedy's backing of the Bay of Pigs invasion in Cuba or Ronald Reagan's Iran-Contra scandal. It also seems to have contributed to the *Challenger* space shuttle disaster. A recent analysis of 19 international crises found that groupthink contributed to most (Schafer & Crichlow, 1996).

The core of groupthink is misguided loyalty that prevents group members from "rocking the boat" or questioning weak arguments and sloppy thinking. In other words, groupthink is more likely to occur when group members emphasize their emotional bonds, rather than the task at hand. The resulting conformity pressures and self-censorship cause people to believe that they agree more than they actually do (Bernthal & Insko, 1993; Turner et al., 1992).

To prevent groupthink, group leaders should take the following steps:

- Define each group member's role as a "critical evaluator."
- Avoid revealing any personal preferences in the beginning.
- State the problem factually, without bias.
- Invite a group member or outside person to play devil's advocate.
- Make it clear that group members will be held accountable for decisions.

- Encourage open inquiry and a search for alternate solutions (Chen et al., 1996; Kroon et al., 1992).

In addition, Janis suggested that there should be a "second-chance" meeting to re-evaluate important decisions. That is, each decision should be reached twice. In an age clouded by the threat of war, meltdowns, and similar disasters, even stronger solutions to the problem of groupthink would be welcome. Perhaps we should form a group to think about it?!

How do groups enforce norms?

Group Factors in Conformity In most of our experiences with groups, we have been rewarded with acceptance and approval for conformity and threatened with rejection or ridicule for non-conformity. These reactions are called **group sanctions** (*rewards and punishments administered by groups to enforce conformity*). Negative sanctions range from laughter, staring, or social disapproval to complete rejection or formal ostracism. This is illustrated by experiments in which Asch made up groups of six real subjects and one trained dissenter. When "Mr. Odd" announced his wrong answers, he was greeted with derisive laughter and sidelong glances. Treatment such as this helps explain why we are especially likely to conform when we are concerned about whether our views are right or wrong (Alicke & Doherty, 1992).

Wouldn't the effectiveness of group sanctions depend on the importance of the group?

Yes. The more important group membership is to a person, the more he or she will be influenced by other group members. That's why the Asch experiments are impressive. Since these were only temporary groups, sanctions were informal and rejection had no lasting importance. Just the same, the power of the group was evident.

What other factors, besides importance of the group, affect the degree of conformity?

Earlier we described an experiment in which passersby were influenced by people staring at a building. We noted that the larger the group, the greater the number of people influenced. In Asch's face-to-face groups the size of the majority also made a difference, but a surprisingly small one. In other experiments, the number of conforming subjects increased dramatically as the majority grew from 2 to 3 people. However, a majority of 3 produced about as much yielding as a majority of 8. The next time you want to talk someone into (or out of) something, take 2 friends along and see what a difference it makes! (Sometimes it helps if the two are large and mean looking.)

Even more important than the size of the majority is its **unanimity** (*unanimous agreement*). Having at least one person in your corner can greatly reduce pressures to conform. When Asch gave subjects an ally (who also opposed the majority by giving the correct answer), conformity was lessened. In terms of numbers, a unanimous majority of 3 is more powerful than a majority of 8 with one dissenting. Perhaps this accounts for the rich diversity of human attitudes, beliefs, opinions, and lifestyles. If you can find at least one other person who sees things as you do (no matter how weird), you can be relatively secure in your opposition to other viewpoints.

In 1991, television viewers all over the world saw a graphic videotape of Los Angeles police officers beating Rodney King as they arrested him. Jurors at the officers' assault trial saw the same incriminating videotape. Nevertheless, the officers were acquitted. In response to social pressure from other jurors, one key juror had changed her vote from "guilty" to "not guilty." You may be confident that you would not change your vote under similar circumstances. However, social pressures can be intense in the jury room.

1. The effect one person's behavior has on another is called _____ _____ .

2. Conformity is a normal aspect of social life. T or F?

3. Subjects in Solomon Asch's conformity study yielded on about 75 percent of the critical trials. T or F?

4. Non-conformity is punished by negative group _____ .

5. Janis used the term _____ to describe a compulsion among decision-making groups to maintain an illusion of unanimity.

6. Would it be possible to be completely non-conforming (that is, to not conform to *some* group norm)?

Answers:

1. social influence 2. T 3. F 4. sanctions 5. groupthink 6. A person who did not follow at least *some* norms concerning normal social behavior would very likely be perceived as extremely bizarre, disturbed, or psychotic.

Social Power—Who Can Do What to Whom?

Here's something to think about: Whereas *strength* is a quality possessed by individuals, *power* is always social—it arises when people come together and disappears when they disperse. In trying to understand the ways in which people are able to influence each other, it is helpful to distinguish among five types of **social power** (*the capacity to control, alter, or influence the behavior of another person*) (Raven, 1974).

Reward power *lies in the ability to reward a person for complying with desired behavior.* Teachers try to exert reward power over students with grades. Employers command reward power by their control of wages and bonuses.

Coercive power *is based on an ability to punish a person for failure to comply.* Coercive power is the basis for most laws, in that fines or imprisonment are used to control behavior.

Legitimate power *comes from accepting a person as an agent of an established social order.* For example, elected leaders and supervisors have legitimate power. So does a teacher in the classroom. Outside the classroom that power would have to come from another source.

Referent power *is based on respect for or identification with a person or a group.* The person "refers to" the source of referent power for direction. Referent power is responsible for much of the conformity we see in groups.

Expert power *is based on recognition that another person has knowledge necessary for achieving a goal.* We allow teachers, lawyers, and other experts to guide behavior because of their ability to produce desired results. Physicians, psychologists, programmers, and plumbers have expert power.

A person who has power in one situation may have very little in another. In those situations where a person has power, she or he is described as an *authority.* In the next section we will investigate **obedience,** *a special type of conformity to the demands of an authority.*

Obedience—Would You Electrocute a Stranger?

The question is this: If ordered to do so, would you shock a man with a known heart condition who is screaming and asking to be released? Certainly we can assume that few people would do so. Or can we? In Nazi Germany, obedient soldiers (once average citizens) helped slaughter over 9 million people in concentration camps. Another example of the same phenomenon was an infamous incident during the Vietnam War. To the horror of many under his command, Lt. William Calley led a bloody massacre of helpless civilians at a village called My Lai. Do such inhumane acts reflect deep character flaws? Are they the acts of heartless psychopaths or crazed killers? Or are they simply the result of obedience to authority? What are the limits of obedience? These are the questions that puzzled social psychologist Stanley Milgram (1965) when he began a provocative series of studies on obedience.

How did Milgram study obedience?

As was true of the Asch experiments, Milgram's research is best appreciated by imagining yourself as a subject. Place yourself in the following situation.

Milgram's Obedience Studies

Imagine answering a newspaper ad to take part in a "learning" experiment at Yale University. When you arrive, a coin is flipped and a second subject, a pleasant-looking man in his 50s, is designated the "learner." By chance you have become the "teacher."

Your task is to read a list of word pairs. The learner's task is to memorize them. You are to punish him with an electric shock each time he makes a mistake. The learner is taken to an adjacent room and you watch as he is seated in an "electric chair" apparatus. Electrodes are attached to his wrists. You

Figure 20–6 ◆ Scenes from Stanley Milgram's study of obedience: the "shock generator," strapping a "learner" into his chair, and a "teacher" being told to administer a severe shock to the learner.

are then escorted to your position in front of a "shock generator." On this device is a row of 30 switches labeled from 15 to 450 volts. Accompanying descriptions range from "Slight Shock" to "Extreme Intensity Shock" and finally "Danger Severe Shock." Your instructions are to administer a shock each time the learner makes a mistake. You are to begin with 15 volts and then move one switch (15 volts) higher for each additional mistake (Fig. 20–6 ◆).

The experiment begins, and the learner soon makes his first error. You flip a switch. More mistakes. Rapidly you reach the 75-volt level. The learner moans after each shock. At 100 volts he complains that he has a heart condition. At 150 volts he says he no longer wants to continue and demands release. At 300 volts he screams and says he can no longer give answers.

At some point during the experiment, you begin to protest to the experimenter. "That man has a heart condition," you say; "I'm not going to kill that man." The experimenter says, "Please continue." Another shock and another scream from the learner and you say, "You mean I've got to keep going up the scale? No, sir. I'm not going to give him 450 volts!" The experimenter says, "The experiment requires that you continue." For a time the learner refuses to answer any more questions and screams with each shock

(Milgram, 1965). Then he falls chillingly silent for the remainder of the experiment.

I can't believe many people would do this. What happened?

Milgram also doubted that many people would obey his orders. When he polled a group of psychiatrists before the experiment, they predicted that less than 1 percent of those tested would obey. The astounding fact is that 65 percent obeyed completely by going all the way to the 450-volt level. Virtually no one stopped short of 300 volts ("Severe Shock") (Fig. 20–7 ◆).

Was the learner injured?

The time has come to reveal that the "learner" was actually an actor who turned a tape recorder on and off in the shock room. No shocks were ever administered, but the dilemma for the "teacher" was quite real. Subjects protested, sweated, trembled, stuttered, bit their lips, and laughed nervously. Clearly they were disturbed by what they were doing. Nevertheless, most obeyed the experimenter's orders. (The ethical questions raised by this experiment are discussed in the Exploration for Chapter 2.)

Why did so many people obey?

Figure 20–7 ◆ Results of Milgram's obedience experiment. Only a minority of subjects refused to provide shocks, even at the most extreme intensities. The first substantial drop in obedience occurred at the 300-volt level (Milgram, 1963).

Shock level

Slight	15 Volts	
Moderate	
Strong	
Very strong	
Intense	Victim screams
Extreme intensity	Victim pounds on wall
Danger: severe shock	Victim silent
XXX	450 Volts	Victim silent

10 20 30 40 50 60 70 80 90 100
Percentage of subjects obeying
command at each shock level

Milgram's Follow-Up   Some have suggested that the prestige of Yale University contributed to subjects' willingness to obey. Might it be that they assumed the professor running the experiment would not really allow anyone to be hurt? To investigate this possibility, the experiment was rerun in a shabby office building in nearby Bridgeport, Connecticut. There was nothing in either the location or the experimenter's appearance to inspire confidence. Under these conditions fewer people obeyed (48 percent), but the reduction was minor.

Milgram was quite disturbed by the willingness of people to knuckle under to authority and senselessly shock someone. In later experiments, he tried in various ways to reduce obedience. He found that the distance between the teacher and the learner was important. When subjects were in the *same room* as the learner, only 40 percent obeyed fully. When they were *face to face* with the learner and required to force his hand down on a simulated "shock plate," only 30 percent obeyed (Fig. 20–8 ◆). Distance from the authority also had an effect. When the experimenter gave his orders over the phone, only 22 percent obeyed. You may doubt that Milgram's study of obedience applies to you. If so, take a moment to read the following highlight.

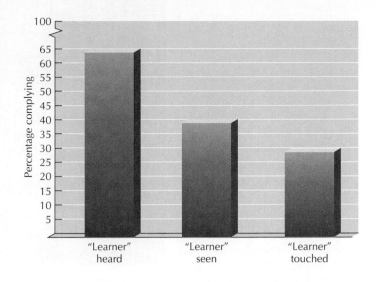

Figure 20–8 ◆ Physical distance from the "learner" had a significant effect on the percentage of subjects obeying orders.

Quack Like a Duck

The demonstration described here has become a favorite of many psychology teachers (Halonen, 1986). Imagine your response to the following events. On the first day of class, your professor begins to establish the basic rules of behavior for the course. Seats are assigned and you must move to a new location. You are told not to talk during class. Your professor tells you that you must have permission to leave early. You are told to bring your textbook to class at all times.

Up to this point you might not have any difficulty obeying your professor's orders. Then the demands become less reasonable. The professor says, "Use only a pencil for taking notes. Borrow one if you must." "Take off your watch." "Keep both hands on your desktop at all times." "All students who are freshmen stand at the back of the class." The demonstration is capped by orders that you cannot follow without looking silly: "Stick two fingers up your nose and quack like a duck."

Where do you think you would draw the line in obeying such orders? In reality, you might find yourself obeying a legitimate authority long after that person's demands had become unreasonable. What would happen, though, if a few students resisted orders early in the sequence? Would that help free others to disobey? For an answer, let's return to some final remarks on Milgram's experiment.

Implications   Milgram's research raises nagging questions about our willingness to commit antisocial or inhumane acts commanded by a "legitimate authority." The excuse so often given by war criminals—"I was only following orders"—takes on new meaning in this light. Milgram suggested that when directions come from an authority, people rationalize that they are not personally responsible for their actions. Others have pointed out that "crimes of obedience" may be committed by ordinary people responding to normal social psychological processes. In locales as diverse as Vietnam, Rwanda, Bosnia, South Africa, Nicaragua, Sri Lanka, and Laos the tragic result has been "sanctioned massacres" of chilling proportions (Kelman & Hamilton, 1989). Even in ordinary life, crimes of obedience happen every day. In order to keep their jobs, many people obey orders to do things that they regard as dishonest, unethical, or harmful (Hamilton & Sanders, 1995).

Aren't you taking an overly dim view of obedience?

Obedience to authority is obviously necessary and desirable in many circumstances. Just the same, it is probably true, as C. P. Snow (1961) observed, "When you think of the long and gloomy history of man, you will find more hideous crimes have been committed in the name of obedience than in the name of rebellion." With this in mind, let us end on a more positive note. In one of his experiments, Milgram found that group support can greatly reduce destructive obedience. When real subjects saw two other "teachers" (both actors) resist orders and walk out of the experiment, only 10 percent continued to obey. Thus, a personal act of courage or moral fortitude by one or two members of a group may free others to disobey misguided or unjust authority.

Obedience to authority is often necessary and reasonable; however, it can also be destructive.

Compliance—A Foot in the Door

In *conformity* situations the pressure to "get in line" is usually indirect. When an authority commands *obedience* the pressure is direct and difficult to resist. There is a third possibility. The term **compliance** *refers to situations in which one person bends to the requests of another person who has little or no authority or social power* (Deaux, Dane, & Wrightsman, 1993).

Pressures to comply are quite common. For example, a stranger might ask you to yield a phone booth so he can make a call; a saleswoman might suggest that you buy a more expensive watch than you had planned on; or a co-worker might ask you for 50 cents to buy a cup of coffee.

What determines whether a person will comply with a request?

Many factors could be listed, but three stand out as especially interesting. Let's briefly consider each.

The Foot-in-the-Door Effect People who sell door-to-door have long recognized that once they get a foot in the door, a sale is almost a sure thing. To state the **foot-in-the-door principle** more formally, *a person who first agrees to a small request is later more likely to comply with a larger demand* (Dillard, 1991). For instance, if someone asked you to put a large, ugly sign in your front yard to promote safe driving, you would probably refuse. If, however, you had first agreed to put a small sign in your window, you would later be much more likely to allow the big sign in your yard (Freedman & Fraser, 1966).

Apparently, the foot-in-the-door effect is based on observing one's own behavior. Seeing yourself agree to a small request helps convince you that you didn't mind doing what was asked. After that, you are more likely to comply with a larger request (Dillard, 1991).

The Door-in-the-Face Effect Let's say that a neighbor comes to your door and asks you to feed his dogs, water his plants, and mow his yard while he is out of town for a month. This is quite a major request—one that most people would probably turn down. Feeling only slightly guilty, you tell your neighbor that you're sorry but you can't help him. Now, what if the same neighbor returns the next day and asks if you would at least pick up his mail while he is gone. Chances are very good that you would honor this request, even if you might have resisted it otherwise. Psychologist Robert Cialdini coined the term **door-in-the-face effect** *to describe the tendency for a person who has refused a major request to comply with a smaller request* (Cialdini et al., 1975). In other words, after a person has turned down a major request ("slammed the door in your face"), he or she may be more willing to agree to a lesser demand. This strategy works because a person who abandons a large request appears to have given up something. In response, many people feel that they must repay her or him by giving in to the smaller request (Dillard, 1991).

The Low-Ball Technique Anyone who has purchased an automobile will recognize a third way of inducing compliance. Automobile dealers are notorious for convincing customers to buy cars by offering "low-ball" prices that undercut the competition. The dealer first gets the customer to agree to buy at an attractively low price. Then, once the customer is committed, various techniques are used to bump the price up before the sale is concluded. (This ploy is described further in a moment.)

The **low-ball technique** *consists of getting a person committed to act and then making the terms of acting less desirable.* Here's another example: A fellow student asks to borrow $25 for a day. This seems reasonable and you agree. However, once you have given your classmate the money, he explains that it would be easier to repay you after payday, in 2 weeks. If you agree, you've succumbed to the low-ball technique. Here's another example: Let's say you ask someone to give you a ride to school in the morning. Only after the person has agreed do you tell her that you have to be there at 6 A.M.

How To Drive a Hard Bargain

Your local car lot is a good place to see compliance take place. Automobile salespersons play the compliance game daily and get very good at it. If you understand what they are up to, you will have a far better chance of resisting their tactics.

A Foot in the Door   The salesperson offers you a test drive. If you accept, you will have made a small commitment of time to a particular car and to the salesperson. The salesperson will then ask you to go to an office and fill out some papers, "just to see what kind of a price" she or he can offer. If you go along, you will be further committed.

The Low-Ball Technique   To get things underway the salesperson will offer you a very good price for your trade-in or will ask you to make an offer on the new car, "any offer, no matter how low." The salesperson will then ask if you will buy the car if she or he can sell it for the price you state. If you say yes, you have virtually bought the car. Most people find it very difficult to walk away once bargaining has reached this stage.

The Hook Is Set   Once buyers are "hooked" by a low-ball offer, the salesperson goes to the manager to have the sale "approved." On returning, the salesperson will tell you with great disappointment that the dealership would lose money on the deal. "Couldn't you just take a little less for the trade-in or pay a little more for the car?" the salesperson will ask. At this point many people hesitate and grumble, but most give in and accept some "compromise" price or trade-in amount.

Milking the Sale   By the time you strike a deal, you can be sure that the price you accept will give the dealership the minimum profit it requires on all sales—and probably much more. To add insult to injury, the salesperson will then try to increase the profit by convincing you to add various options to your car—extra mirrors, a stereo system, cruise control, and so forth. All of these items cost less from independent suppliers, so many people pay hundreds of dollars too much for them alone.

Evening the Odds   To combat all of the preceding, get a final "best offer" in writing. Then walk out. Go to another dealer and see if the salesperson will better the price, in writing. When he or she does, return to the first dealership and negotiate for an even better price. Then decide where to buy.

Passive Compliance

Complying with requests is a normal part of daily social life. At times, however, a willingness to comply can exceed what is reasonable. Researcher Thomas Moriarty (1975) has demonstrated excessive, *passive compliance* under realistic conditions. **Passive compliance** *refers to quietly bending to unreasonable demands or unacceptable conditions.* Moriarty became interested in the "little murders" of daily life—the personal insults, rebuffs, and sacrifices of dignity that have become so common. Moriarty observed that many people will put up with almost anything to avoid a confrontation. He decided to put this passive, "no-hassle" attitude to experimental test.

In one experiment, two people (one actually an accomplice) were given a difficult test in a very small room. The subjects were seated back to back and left alone to work. As soon as the experimenter left, the phony subject turned on a portable cassette player at full volume. Real subjects who failed to complain were treated to a 17-minute blast of nerve-wracking rock music. The accomplice was instructed to turn the music off only after a third request. In this particular experiment, 80 percent of the subjects said nothing, although they glared, covered their ears, stopped work, and so forth. An interview later showed that most were angry or annoyed, but were afraid to tell the other person to be quiet.

Could it be that people failed to complain because they didn't want to disrupt the testing?

Yes, it is possible that the passivity observed in this study is unique to the experimental setting. However, when Moriarty and his students staged loud conversations behind theater patrons or people studying in a library, very few protested. In other naturalistic experiments, people were accosted in phone booths. The experimenter explained that he had left a ring in the booth and asked if the person had found it. When subjects said no, the experimenter demanded that they empty their pockets. Most did.

In these and similar situations, people passively accepted having their personal rights trampled, even when objecting presented no threat to their safety (Fig. 20–9 ◆). Overly passive women, in particular, tend to be ripe targets for exploitation, especially by men (Richards, Rollerson, & Phillips, 1991). Have we become "a nation of willing victims"? Certainly, we hope not. Nevertheless, researchers such as Milgram and Moriarty have identified a significant social problem. We will address the problem again in the Applications section of this chapter.

A Look Ahead In the upcoming Applications, we will return to the problem of passive behavior to learn how you can better handle difficult social situations. Then, in the

Figure 20–9 ◆ In a recent experiment done at an airport, a smoker intentionally sat or stood near non-smokers. Only 9 percent of the non-smokers asked the smoker to stop smoking, even when no-smoking signs were clearly visible nearby (Gibson & Werner, 1994).

Exploration, we will examine the nature of social traps. A social trap is a situation in which individuals blindly act in ways that do collective harm.

Learning Check	**Critical Thinking**

Learning Check

1. An ability to punish others for failure to obey is the basis for
   a. referent power **b.** legitimate power **c.** expert power **d.** coercive power

2. The term *compliance* refers to situations in which a person complies with commands made by a person who has authority. T or F?

3. Obedience in Milgram's experiments was related to
   a. distance between learner and teacher
   b. distance between experimenter and teacher
   c. obedience of other teachers
   d. all of these

4. Obedience is conformity to the commands of an _____ .

5. By repeating his obedience experiment in a downtown office building, Milgram demonstrated that the prestige of Yale University was the main reason for subjects' willingness to obey in the original experiment. T or F?

6. The research of Thomas Moriarty and others has highlighted the problem of _____ _____ , rather than obedience to authority.

Critical Thinking

7. Modern warfare allows killing to take place impersonally and at a distance. How does this relate to Milgram's experiments?

Answers:

1. d 2. F 3. d 4. authority 5. F 6. passive compliance 7. There is a big difference between killing someone in hand-to-hand combat and killing someone by lining up images on a video screen. Milgram's research suggests that it is easier for a person to follow orders to kill another human when the victim is at a distance and removed from personal contact.

Most of us have been rewarded, first as children and later as adults, for compliant, obedient, or "good" behavior. Perhaps this is why so many people find it difficult to assert themselves. Or perhaps non-assertion is related to anxiety about "making a scene" or feeling disliked by others. Whatever the causes, some people suffer tremendous anguish in any situation requiring poise, self-confidence, or self-assertion. Have you ever done any of the following?

- Hesitated to question an error on a restaurant bill because you were afraid of making a scene?
- Backed out of asking for a raise or a change in working conditions?
- Said yes when you wanted to say no?
- Been afraid to question a grade that seemed unfair?

If you have ever had difficulty asserting yourself in similar situations, behavior therapist Joseph Wolpe has a solution for you: a technique called **assertiveness training** (*instruction in how to be self-assertive*).

What is done in assertiveness training?

Assertiveness training is a very direct procedure. By using group exercises, videotapes, mirrors, and staged conflicts, the instructor teaches assertive behavior. People learn to practice honesty, disagreeing, questioning authority, and assertive postures and gestures. As their self-confidence improves, non-assertive clients are taken on "field trips" to shops and restaurants where they practice what they have learned.

Non-assertion requiring therapy is unusual. Neverthe-less, many people become tense or upset in at least some situations in which they must stand up for their rights. For this reason, many people have found the techniques and exercises of assertiveness training helpful. If you have ever eaten a carbonized steak when you ordered it rare, or stood in silent rage as a clerk ignored you, the following discussion will be of interest.

Self-Assertion

The first step in assertiveness training is to convince yourself of three basic rights: You have the right to refuse, to request, and to right a wrong. **Self-assertion** *involves standing up for these rights by speaking out in your own behalf.*

Is self-assertion just getting things your own way?

Not at all. A basic distinction can be made between *self-assertion* and *aggressive* behavior. Self-assertion is a direct, honest expression of feelings and desires. It is not exclusively self-serving. People who are non-assertive are usually patient to a fault. Sometimes their pent-up anger explodes with unexpected fury, which can be very destructive to relationships. In contrast to assertive behavior, **aggression** *involves hurting another person or achieving one's goals at the expense of another.* Aggression does not take into account the feelings or rights of others. It is an attempt to get one's own way no matter what. Assertion techniques emphasize firmness, not attack (Table 20–2 ■).

Assertiveness Training The basic idea in assertiveness training is that each assertive action is practiced until it can be repeated even under stress. For example, let's say it really

Table 20–2 ■ Comparison of Assertive, Aggressive, and Non-assertive Behavior		
	Actor	**Receiver of Behavior**
Non-assertive behavior	Self-denying, inhibited, hurt, and anxious; lets others make choices; goals not achieved	Feels sympathy, guilt, or contempt for actor; achieves goals at actor's expense
Aggressive behavior	Achieves goals at others' expense; expresses feelings, but hurts others; chooses for others or puts them down	Feels hurt, defensive, humiliated, or taken advantage of; does not meet own needs
Assertive behavior	Self-enhancing; acts in own best interests; expresses feelings; respects rights of others; goals usually achieved, self-respect maintained	Needs respected and feelings expressed; may achieve goal; self-worth maintained

angers you when a store clerk waits on several people who arrived after you did. To improve your assertiveness in this situation, you would begin by *rehearsing* the dialogue, posture, and gestures you would use to confront the clerk or the other customer. Working in front of a mirror can be very helpful. If possible, you should *role-play* the scene with a friend. Be sure to have your friend take the part of a really aggressive or irresponsible clerk, as well as a cooperative one. Rehearsal and role-playing should also be used when you expect a possible confrontation with someone—for example, if you are going to ask for a raise, challenge a grade, or confront a landlord.

Is that all there is to it?

No. Another important principle is **overlearning** (*practice that continues after initial mastery of a skill*). When you rehearse or role-play assertive behavior, it is essential to continue to practice until your responses become almost automatic. This helps prevent you from getting flustered in the actual situation.

One more technique you may find useful is the **broken record**. *This is a self-assertion technique involving repeating a request until it is acknowledged.* A good way to prevent assertion from becoming aggression is to simply restate your request as many times and in as many ways as necessary. As an illustration, let's say you are returning a pair of shoes to a store. After two wearings the shoes fell apart, but you bought them 2 months ago and no longer have a receipt. The broken record could sound something like this:

Customer: I would like to have these shoes replaced.
Clerk: Do you have a receipt?
Customer: No, but I bought them here, and since they are defective, I would like to have you replace them.
Clerk: I can't do that without a receipt.
Customer: I understand that, but I want them replaced.
Clerk: Well, if you'll come back this afternoon and talk to the manager.
Customer: I've brought these shoes in because they are defective.

Clerk: Well, I'm not authorized to replace them.
Customer: Yes, well, if you'll replace these, I'll be on my way.

Notice that the customer did not attack the clerk or create an angry confrontation. Simple persistence is often all that is necessary for successful self-assertion.

How would I respond assertively to a put-down?

Responding assertively to verbal aggression (a "put-down") is a real challenge. The tendency is to respond aggressively, which usually makes things worse. A good way to respond to a put-down uses the following steps: (1) If you are wrong, admit it; (2) acknowledge the person's feelings; (3) assert yourself about the other person's aggression; (4) briskly end the interchange.

Psychologists Robert Alberti and Michael Emmons (1995) offer an example of how to use the four steps. Let's say you accidentally bump into someone. The person responds angrily, "Damn it! Why don't you watch where you're going! You fool, you could have hurt me!" A good response would be to say, "I'm sorry I bumped you. I didn't do it intentionally. It's obvious you're upset, but I don't like your calling me names, or yelling. I can get your point without that."

Now, what if someone insults you indirectly ("I love your taste in clothes, it's so 'folksy'")? Alberti and Emmons suggest you ask for a clarification ("What are you trying to say?"). This will force the person to take responsibility for the aggression. It can also provide an opportunity to change the way the person interacts with you: "If you really don't like what I'm wearing, I'd like to know it. I'm not always sure I like the things I buy, and I value your opinion."

To summarize, self-assertion does not supply instant poise, confidence, or self-assurance. However, it is a way of combating anxieties associated with life in an impersonal and sometimes intimidating society. If you are interested in more information, you can consult a book entitled *Your Perfect Right* by Alberti and Emmons (1995).

Learning Check

1. In assertiveness training, people learn techniques for getting their way in social situations and angry interchanges. T or F?

2. Non assertive behavior causes hurt, anxiety, and self-denial in the actor, and sympathy, guilt, or contempt in the receiver. T or F?

3. Overlearning should be avoided when rehearsing assertive behaviors. T or F?

4. The "broken record" must be avoided, because it is a basic non-assertive behavior. T or F?

Critical Thinking

5. When practicing self-assertion, do you think it would be better to improvise your own responses or imitate those of a person skilled in self-assertion?

Answers:
1. F 2. T 3. F 4. F 5. A recent study found that imitating an assertive model is more effective than improvising your own responses (Kipper, 1992). If you know an assertive and self-assured person, you can learn a lot by watching how they handle difficult situations.

You are in a packed theater in an older building. Halfway through the feature movie (*Bambi Meets Godzilla*) you begin to smell smoke. The screen goes dark. You try to stay calm as you shuffle toward a distant exit sign. Suddenly someone screams. You lunge for the door. Instantly, you are caught in a crush of people. The crowd jams together so tightly that only a few people can squeeze through the door. If the fire moves swiftly, many lives will be lost.

This situation—panic during a fire—is a classic example of a *social trap*. Each person in a theater who runs toward the exits has acted in his or her immediate self-interest. Yet if *everyone* bolts at once the chances that anyone will survive may be very low.

Social Traps

What exactly is a social trap?

A **social trap** *is any social situation that rewards individual actions that have undesired collective effects in the long run* (Cross & Guyer, 1980). On an individual level, it is quite common for people to be "trapped" by immediate rewards that are followed by delayed costs or suffering. For instance, many people are enticed into drinking too much at parties because their pleasure is immediate and their discomfort (a hangover) comes later. Many people go into debt because they get the immediate reward of owning desirable goods; only later do they suffer when a staggering credit card bill arrives. For the immediate pleasures of intimacy, many teenagers later pay the price of pregnancy, forced marriage, early divorce, curtailed education, and so on.

Behavioral traps that involve groups of people, or social traps, as we have called them, are especially interesting. In a social trap no one individual intentionally acts against the group interest, but if many people act alike, collective harm is done. For example, each person

who leaves work at 5 P.M. in a congested city expects to gain by getting home earlier. Yet if everyone leaves at 5:00, the resulting traffic jam ensures that everyone will, in fact, arrive home late and emotionally frazzled. The problem could be solved if some people would wait a half hour or more before leaving. However, no one does this because immediate self-interest encourages a "fast getaway."

A related example is the fact that many large cities now have rapid transit systems that are underused by their citizens. Each person decides that it is more convenient to own and drive a separate car (in order to run errands and so on). However, we see again that individual behavior affects the welfare of others. Because everyone wants to drive for "convenience," driving becomes inconvenient: The mass of cars in most cities causes irritating traffic snarls and a lack of parking spaces. Each car owner has been drawn into a trap.

The Tragedy of the Commons

Social traps are especially damaging when we are enticed into overuse of scarce resources. This is exactly what happened a few years ago to crab fishermen in Alaska.

Initially, crabs were plentiful and fishermen were few. Each fisherman was therefore able to make large, lucrative catches. To raise their profits, fishermen began to add second, third, and fourth boats to their operations. For a while this did, in fact, increase individual profits. But as the size of the fishing fleet continued to grow, the number of crabs available to be caught by any boat decreased.

Eventually, so many crabs were caught that their rate of reproduction slowed. As a result, crab fishermen began to go bankrupt in large numbers. Individually their actions made sense. But collectively the group suffered greatly.

Ecologist Garrett Hardin (1968, 1985) calls situations like the one just described the **tragedy of the commons.** *Tragedies of this sort occur when people share a scarce resource. Each person acts in his or her self-interest, which causes the resource to be used up so that everyone suffers.* More familiar examples of this dilemma are the lack of individual incentives to conserve gasoline, water, or electricity. Whenever one's personal comfort or convenience is involved, it is highly tempting to "let others worry about it." Yet in the long run everyone stands to lose. The tragedy of the commons is especially likely to occur when people are uncertain about how much of a resource exists or how fast it is being replaced (Hine & Gifford, 1996).

Social Problems

Many major social problems can be thought of as social traps. In most cases of environmental pollution, for instance, there are immediate benefits for polluting and major long-term costs. If one person pollutes a river or trashes the roadside, it has little noticeable effect. But as many people do the same, problems that affect everyone quickly mount. As another example, consider the farmer who applies pesticides to a crop to save it from insect damage. The farmer benefits immediately. However, if other farmers follow suit, the local water system may be permanently damaged.

Traps also exist at the international level. Countries that add to their nuclear stockpiles hope to be more "secure." Yet, doing so may eventually increase the chances of a final nuclear holocaust (Nevin & Fuld, 1993). It's no wonder that people who study international conflicts often come away shaking their heads and wondering, "How did we get into this mess?"

What can be done to avoid social traps?

Escaping Traps In some situations it might be possible to dismantle social traps by rearranging rewards and costs. For example, many companies are tempted to pollute because it saves them money and increases profits. To reverse the situation, a pollution tax could be levied so that it would cost more, not less, for a business to pollute. As another example, we could reward lower individual consumption of resources. Some power companies have already experimented with a meter that charges lower rates for using power at "off-peak" periods (also see Chapter 22).

There is evidence that in real social traps, people are more likely to restrain themselves when they believe others will too (Messick et al., 1983). Otherwise they are likely to think, "Why should I be a sucker? I don't think anyone else is going to conserve" (fuel, electricity, water, paper, crabs, or whatever). In some cases, people can be forced to limit their use of a scarce resource. However, some will see this as an infringement of their rights. Others, who are already non-abusers, may feel like they are being punished for a problem they did not cause (Baron & Jurney, 1993). Fortunately, just being aware that a social trap exists is sometimes enough to help people avoid it (Neidert & Linder, 1990).

Some problems may be harder to solve. What, for instance, can be done about truck drivers who cause dangerous traffic jams because they will not pull over on narrow roads? How can littering be discouraged or prevented? How would you make car-pooling or using public transportation the first choice for most people? Or how could people simply be encouraged to stagger their departure times to and from work? All of these and more are social traps that need springing. It is important that we not fall into the trap of ignoring them.

Learning Check

1. A social trap is any situation in which undesired actions are rewarded in the long run. T or F?

2. Individuals in a social trap act in ways that appear to be rational, but that create problems for the group as a whole. T or F?

3. The tragedy of the commons occurs when individuals use a shared resource too quickly because they get immediate rewards for doing so. T or F?

4. Rearranging individual rewards and costs is one way to dismantle social traps. T or F?

Critical Thinking

5. What social trap accompanies most major holidays?

Answers:

1. F 2. T 3. T 4. T 5. Travel nightmares are the rule as people jam trains, planes, and highways on major holidays.

Chapter Summary

How does group membership affect individual behavior?

◆ Humans are social animals enmeshed in a complex network of social relationships. **Social psychology** studies how individuals behave, think, and feel in social situations.

◆ **Culture** provides a broad social context for our behavior. One's *position* in groups defines a variety of **roles** to be played.

◆ **Social roles,** which may be *achieved* or *ascribed*, are particular behavior patterns associated with social positions. When two or more contradictory roles are held, **role conflict** may occur. The Stanford prison experiment showed that destructive roles may override individual motives for behavior.

◆ Positions within groups typically carry higher or lower levels of **status**. High status is associated with special privileges and respect.

◆ **Group structure** refers to the organization of roles, communication pathways, and power within a group. **Group cohesiveness** is basically the degree of attraction among group members.

◆ **Norms** are standards of conduct enforced (formally or informally) by groups. The **autokinetic effect** has been used to demonstrate that norms rapidly form even in temporary groups.

What unspoken rules govern the use of personal space?

◆ The study of personal space is called **proxemics.** Four basic spatial zones around each person's body are

intimate distance (0–18 inches), **personal distance** (1½–4 feet), **social distance** (4–12 feet), and **public distance** (12 feet or more).

How do we perceive the motives of others, and the causes of our own behavior?

◆ **Attribution theory** is concerned with how we make inferences about behavior. A variety of factors affect attribution, including **consistency, distinctiveness, situational demands,** and **consensus.**

◆ The **fundamental attributional error** is to ascribe the actions of others to internal causes, while attributing one's own behavior to external causes.

◆ **Self-handicapping** involves arranging excuses for poor performance as a way to protect one's self-image or self-esteem.

Why do people affiliate?

◆ The **need to affiliate** is tied to additional needs for approval, support, friendship, and information. Additionally, research indicates that affiliation is related to reducing anxiety and uncertainty.

◆ **Social comparison theory** holds that we affiliate to evaluate our actions, feelings, and abilities. Social comparisons are also made for purposes of self-protection and self-enhancement.

What factors influence interpersonal attraction?

◆ **Interpersonal attraction** is increased by **physical proximity** (nearness), **frequent contact, physical attractiveness, competence,** and **similarity.** A large degree of similarity on many dimensions is characteristic of *mate selection.*

◆ **Self-disclosure** occurs more when two people like one another. Self-disclosure follows a **reciprocity norm:** Low levels of self-disclosure are met with low levels in return, whereas moderate self-disclosure elicits more personal replies. However, **overdisclosure** tends to inhibit self-disclosure by others.

◆ According to **social exchange theory,** we tend to maintain relationships that are *profitable;* that is, those for which perceived rewards exceed perceived costs.

◆ **Romantic love** has been studied as a special kind of attitude. Love can be distinguished from liking by the use of attitude scales. Dating couples like *and* love their partners but only like their friends. Love is also associated with greater *mutual absorption* between people.

◆ Adult love relationships tend to mirror patterns of **emotional attachment** observed in infancy and early childhood. **Secure, avoidant,** and **ambivalent** patterns can be defined on the basis of how a person approaches romantic and affectionate relationships with others.

◆ **Evolutionary psychology** attributes human mating patterns to the differing reproductive challenges faced by men and women since the dawn of time.

What have social psychologists learned about conformity, social power, obedience, and compliance?

◆ In general, **social influence** refers to alterations in behavior brought about by the behavior of others. **Conformity** to group pressure is a familiar example of social influence.

◆ Virtually everyone conforms to a variety of broad social and cultural norms. **Conformity pressures** also exist within smaller groups. The famous Asch experiments demonstrated that various **group sanctions** encourage conformity.

◆ **Groupthink** refers to compulsive conformity in group decision making. Victims of groupthink seek to maintain each other's approval, even at the cost of critical thinking.

◆ Social influence is also related to five types of **social power: reward power, coercive power, legitimate power, referent power,** and **expert power.**

◆ **Obedience** to authority has been investigated in a variety of experiments, particularly those by Milgram. Obedience in Milgram's studies decreased when the victim was in the same room, when the victim and subject were face to face, when the authority figure was absent, and when others refused to obey.

◆ **Compliance** with direct requests is another means by which behavior is influenced. Three strategies for inducing compliance are the **foot-in-the-door technique,** the **door-in-the-face approach,** and the **low-ball technique.**

◆ Recent research suggests that in addition to excessive obedience to authority, many people show a surprising **passive compliance** to unreasonable requests.

How does self-assertion differ from aggression?

◆ **Self-assertion,** as opposed to **aggression,** involves clearly stating one's wants and needs to others. Learning to be assertive is accomplished by *role-playing, rehearsing* assertive actions, *overlearning,* and use of specific techniques, such as the *"broken record."*

What is a social trap?

◆ A **social trap** is a social situation in which immediately rewarded actions have undesired effects in the long run. One prominent social trap occurs when limited public resources are overused, a problem called the **tragedy of the commons.**

Attitudes, Culture, and Human Relations

Preview

Doomsday for the Seekers

Hardly a year passes, it seems, without a doomsday group of one kind or another making the news. In one classic example of such groups, a woman named Mrs. Keech claimed she was receiving messages from beings on a planet called Clarion. The aliens told Mrs. Keech they had detected a fault in the earth's crust that would plunge North America into the sea on December 21st. However, Mrs. Keech and her followers, who called themselves the Seekers, had no fear: On December 20th they expected to be met at midnight by a flying saucer and taken to safety in outer space.

December 20th arrived, and the Seekers gathered at Mrs. Keech's house. Many had given up jobs and possessions to prepare for departure. Expectations were high and commitment was total. But as the night wore on, midnight passed and the world continued to exist. It was a bitter and embarrassing disappointment for the Seekers.

Did the group break up then?

Our story now takes an amazing twist—one that intrigued social psychologists. Instead of breaking up, the Seekers became *more* convinced than ever before that they were right. At about 5 A.M. Mrs. Keech said she had received a new message explaining that the Seekers had saved the world.

Before December 20th, the Seekers were uninterested in persuading other people that the world was coming to an end. Now they called newspapers and radio stations to convince others of their accomplishment.

How do we explain this strange turn in the behavior of Mrs. Keech's doomsday group? An answer may lie in the concept of *cognitive dissonance*. Cognitive dissonance also helps explain many aspects of attitude change. Watch for Mrs. Keech and a discussion of cognitive dissonance later in this chapter.

Chapter Survey

Theme: Social life is complex, but consistent patterns can be found in our attitudes, as well as our positive and negative interactions with others.

Key Questions:

What are attitudes? How are they acquired?	
How are attitudes measured and changed?	
Under what conditions is persuasion most effective?	
What is cognitive dissonance? What does it have to do with attitudes and behavior?	
Is brainwashing actually possible? How are people converted to cult membership?	
What causes prejudice and intergroup conflict? What can be done about these problems?	
How do psychologists explain human aggression?	
Why are bystanders so often unwilling to help in an emergency?	
What can be done to lower prejudice and promote social harmony?	
How does the theory of sociobiology try to explain social behavior?	

Key Topics to Watch for:

Attitudes and attitude formation

Measuring attitudes
Sources of attitude change

Persuasion
Characteristics of the communicator, message, and audience

Cognitive dissonance theory

Brainwashing and forced attitude change
Cult recruitment and membership

Types and sources of prejudice
Stereotypes and group conflict
Reducing prejudice

Theories of aggression

Bystander apathy and helping others

Living with diversity

Sociobiology and biological determinism

Attitudes—Belief + Emotion + Action

What is your attitude toward affirmative action, environmental groups, the death penalty, imported automobiles, k. d. lang, psychology? The answers can have far-reaching effects on your behavior. Attitudes are intimately woven into our actions and views of the world. Our tastes, friendships, votes, preferences, and goals are all touched by attitudes.

What specifically is an attitude?

An **attitude** *is a mixture of belief and emotion that predisposes a person to respond to other people, objects, or institutions in a positive or negative way.* Attitudes summarize past experience and predict or direct future actions. For example, an approach known as the *misdirected letter technique* demonstrates that actions are closely connected to attitudes.

The Luck of the Irish

During a period of violence in Northern Ireland, attitudes toward the Irish were measured in a sample of English households. Later, wrongly addressed letters were sent to the same households. Each letter had either an English name or an Irish name on it. The question was: Would the "Irish" letters be returned to the Post Office or thrown away? As predicted, letters were more often thrown away by people living in households where anti-Irish attitudes had been measured earlier (Howitt et al., 1977).

"Your attitude is showing," is sometimes said. Actually, attitudes are expressed in three ways: through beliefs, emotions, and actions. The **belief component** *of an attitude is what a person believes about the attitudinal object.* The **emotional component** *consists of feelings toward the attitudinal object.* The **action component** *refers to one's actions toward various people, objects, or institutions.* Consider, for example, your attitude toward gun control. You will have beliefs about whether or not gun control would affect rates of crime or violence. You will have emotional responses to guns, finding them either attractive and desirable or threatening and destructive. And, you will have a tendency to seek out or avoid gun ownership. The action component of your attitude will probably also include support of organizations that urge or oppose gun control. As you can see, attitudes orient us to the social world. In doing so, they prepare us to act in certain ways (Olson & Zanna, 1993). (For another example, please see Fig. 21–1 ◆.)

How do people acquire attitudes?

Attitude Formation

Attitudes are acquired in several basic ways. Sometimes, attitudes come from **direct contact** (*personal experience*) with the object of the attitude—such as opposing pollution when a nearby factory ruins your favorite river. Attitudes are also learned through **interaction with others;** *that is, through discussion with people holding a particular attitude.* For instance,

Belief component
Restores justice
Provides equal opportunity

Emotional component
Optimism

Action component
Vote for affirmative action
Donate to groups that support affirmative action

Belief component
Unfair to majority
Reverse discrimination

Emotional component
Anger

Action component
Vote against affirmative action
Donate to groups that oppose affirmative action

Figure 21–1 ◆ Elements of positive and negative attitudes towards affirmative action.

if three of your friends are volunteers at a local recycling center, and you talk with them about their beliefs, you will probably come to favor recycling too. **Child rearing** (*the effects of parental values, beliefs, and practices*) also affects attitudes. For example, if both parents belong to the same political party, chances are 2 out of 3 that their children will belong to that party as adults.

In the previous chapter we discussed group forces that operate to bring about conformity. There is little doubt that many of our attitudes are influenced by **group membership.** In one classic study, for example, groups were formed to discuss the case of a juvenile delinquent. Most participants believed the boy needed love, kindness, and friendship. To test group pressures on attitudes, a person who advocated severe punishment was added to each group.

How did group members react to the "deviate"?

At first they directed almost all of their comments to him.

But when he stuck to his position, an interesting thing happened. Soon, he was almost completely excluded from conversation. And later, the deviate was strongly rejected in ratings made by other group members (Schachter, 1951). Group pressures for conformity and the difficulty of holding deviant attitudes can be clearly seen in this outcome.

Attitudes are also influenced by the **mass media** (*all media, such as magazines and television, that reach large audiences*). As Marshall McLuhan put it, we are "massaged" by the media, meaning we are coaxed, persuaded, and skillfully manipulated. Ninety-nine percent of North American homes have a television set, which is on an average of over 7 hours a day. The information thus channeled into homes has a powerful impact. For instance, frequent viewers mistrust others and overestimate their chances of being harmed (Gerbner & Gross, 1976; Roberts & Bachen, 1981). This suggests that a steady diet of TV violence leads some people to develop a **"mean" world view,** *in which they regard*

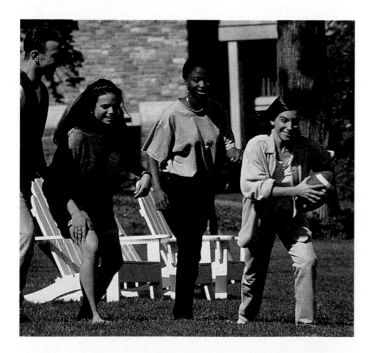

Attitudes are an important dimension of social behavior. They are often greatly influenced by the groups to which we belong.

FOR BETTER OR FOR WORSE COPYRIGHT 1991 LYNN JOHNSTON PROD. INC. REPRINTED WITH PERMISSION OF UNIVERSAL PRESS SYNDICATE. ALL RIGHTS RESERVED.

the world as a dangerous and threatening place (Heath & Gilbert, 1996).

Some attitudes are simply formed through **chance conditioning** (*learning that takes place by chance or coincidence*) (Olson & Zanna, 1993). Let's say, for instance, that you have had three encounters in your lifetime with psychologists. If all three were negative, you might take an unduly dim view of psychology and psychologists. In the same way, people often develop strong attitudes toward cities, restaurants, or parts of the country on the basis of one or two unusually good or bad experiences. The following highlight provides an interesting example of how conditioning contributes to attitude formation.

Research Frontier

Rock Music Videos and Antisocial Attitudes

Many rock music videos are filled with rebellion, violence, intoxication, sexual promiscuity, and degrading images of women. Rock videos almost always show such behavior in a positive light, making it seem commonplace. Does this affect viewers' attitudes toward antisocial behavior? To find out, Christine and Ranald Hansen (1990) staged an experiment in which college students watched three antisocial rock videos or three neutral music videos. Afterward, subjects "accidentally" saw one of two "job applicants" (who were actually accomplices in the experiment) make an obscene gesture with his hand. Later, each student was asked how likable the job applicants were and if they should be hired.

As you might expect, students who only watched neutral videos liked the antisocial job applicant less and gave him low ratings.

What about the students who had watched antisocial videos? Were their attitudes influenced?

Clearly they were. Subjects who had just seen a barrage of antisocial images rated the "job applicant" who made the obscene gesture just as highly as the one who didn't.

As the Hansens point out, music elicits positive emotions. What if these good feelings are associated with antisocial themes? Quite likely, classical conditioning will contribute to the creation of positive attitudes toward antisocial behavior (Hansen & Hansen, 1990).

Why are some attitudes acted on, while others are not?

To answer this question, let's consider an example. Assume that a woman named Lorraine knows that automobiles add to air pollution, and strongly objects to smog. Why would Lorraine continue to drive to work every day? Probably it is because the *immediate consequences* of our actions weigh heavily on the choices we make. No matter what Lorraine's attitude may be, it is difficult for her to resist the immediate convenience of driving. Our expectations of how *others will evaluate* our actions are also important. By taking this factor into account, researchers have been able to predict family planning choices, alcohol use by adolescents, re-enlistment in the National Guard, voting on a nuclear power plant initiative, and so forth (Cialdini et al., 1981). Finally, we must not overlook the effects of long-standing *habits* (Triandis, 1977). Let's say that a "male chauvinist" boss vows to change his sexist attitudes toward female employees. Two months later it would not be unusual for his behavior to show the effects of habit rather than his intention to change.

In short, there are often large differences between attitudes and behavior—particularly between privately held attitudes and public behavior. However, barriers to action typically fall when a person holds an attitude with *conviction.* If you have **conviction** *about an issue it evokes strong feelings, you think about it and discuss it often, and you are knowledgeable about it* (Abelson, 1988). Attitudes held with passionate conviction often lead to major changes in personal behavior (Olson & Zanna, 1993).

Can attitudes be measured?

Attitude Measurement

Attitudes can be measured several ways. In an **open-ended interview,** *individuals are simply asked to freely express attitudes toward a particular issue.* For example, a person might be asked, "What are your thoughts about freedom of speech on college campuses?" Attitudes toward social groups can be measured with a **social distance scale.** *On such scales people state their willingness to admit members of a particular group to various levels of social closeness.* These levels range from "would exclude from my country" to "would admit to marriage in my family." If a person is prejudiced toward a group, she or he will prefer to remain socially distant from members of the group (Cover, 1995).

The use of *attitude scales* is one of the most common methods of measurement. **Attitude scales** *consist of statements expressing various possible views on an issue* (for example, "Socialized medicine would destroy the quality of health care in this country" or "This country needs a national health care program"). *People typically respond to each item on a 5-point scale by ranking it from "strongly agree" to "strongly disagree."* By combining scores on all items, a person can be rated for overall acceptance or rejection of a particular issue. When used in public polls, attitude scales provide useful information about the feelings of large segments of the population.

Attitude Change—Why the "Seekers" Went Public

Although attitudes are relatively stable, they do change. Some attitude change can be understood in terms of **reference groups** (*any group a person identifies with and uses as a standard for social comparison*). It is not necessary to have face-to-face contact with other people for them to serve as a reference group. It depends instead on whom you identify with or whose attitudes and values you care about.

In the 1930s Theodore Newcomb studied real-life attitude change among students at Bennington College. Most students came from conservative homes, but Bennington was a very liberal school. Newcomb found that most students shifted significantly toward more liberal attitudes during their 4 years at Bennington. Those who didn't change kept their parents and hometown friends as primary reference groups. This is typified by one student's statement, "I decided I'd rather stick to my father's ideas." Those who did change identified primarily with the campus community. Notice that all students could count the college and their families as *membership* groups. However, one group or the other tended to become their point of reference.

What about advertising and other direct attempts to change attitudes? Are they effective?

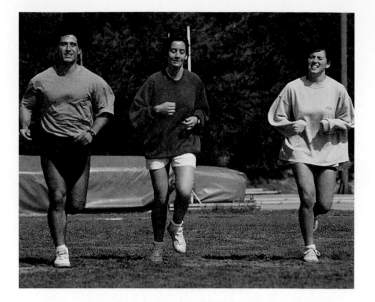

Do you exercise regularly? Like students in the Bennington study, your intentions to exercise are probably influenced by the exercise habits of your reference groups (Terry & Hogg, 1996).

Persuasion

Persuasion *is any deliberate attempt to change attitudes or beliefs through information and arguments.* Businesses, politicians, and others who seek to persuade us obviously believe that attitudes can be changed. Over $12 billion is spent yearly on television advertising in the United States and Canada alone. Persuasion can range from the daily blitz of media commercials to personal discussion among friends. In most cases, the success or failure of persuasion can be understood if we consider the **communicator,** the **message,** and the **audience.**

Let's say you have a chance to promote an issue important to you (for or against nuclear power, for instance) at a community gathering. Whom should you choose to make the presentation, and how should that person present it? Research suggests that attitude change is encouraged when the following conditions are met.

1. The communicator is likable, expressive, trustworthy, an expert on the topic, and similar to the audience in some respect.

2. The message appeals to emotions, particularly to fear or anxiety.

3. The message also provides a clear course of action that

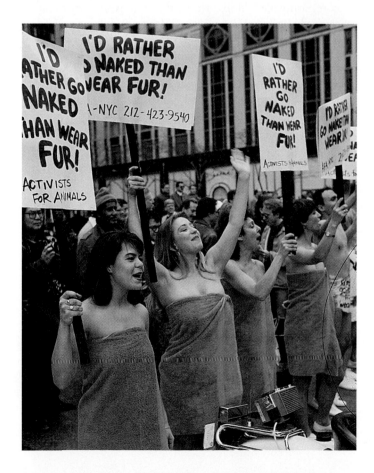

Persuasion. Would you be likely to be swayed by this group's message? Successful persuasion is related to characteristics of the communicator, the message, and the audience.

will, if followed, reduce fear or produce personally desirable results.

4. The message states clear-cut conclusions.

5. The message is backed up by facts and statistics.

6. Both sides of the argument are presented in the case of a well-informed audience.

7. Only one side of the argument is presented in the case of a poorly informed audience.

8. The persuader appears to have nothing to gain if the audience accepts the message.

9. The message is repeated as frequently as possible (Aronson, 1992; Eagly & Chaiken, 1992; Johnson, 1991).

You should have little trouble seeing how these principles are applied to sell everything from underarm deodorants to presidents. With selling in mind, let's make a brief side visit to the topic of consumer psychology.

Using Psychology

Consumer Psychology

Whether it's buying a car, toothpaste, a record, or lunch, we are all consumers. **Consumer psychology** *is an applied field that focuses on how consumers behave* (Robertson & Kassarjian, 1991).

Many people give little thought to why they buy what they do. But in fact, **consumer behavior** *consists of deciding to spend, selecting a brand, shopping, making a purchase, and evaluating the product in use* (Robertson & Kassarjian, 1991). At each step, advertising, packaging, and a host of other factors affect our behavior. To pinpoint such factors, **marketing research** is often done. *This is a type of public opinion polling in which people are asked to give their personal impressions of products, services, or advertising.* In this way, researchers have learned that powerful, widely held *brand images* often develop. A **brand image** *is the mental "picture" that consumers have of a product, especially with regard to its emotional meaning.* A case in point is the images many people have of automobiles, such as: Mercedes-Benz (high status), Corvette (power and sportiness), Buick (conservatism), and so forth (Robertson & Kassarjian, 1991). Brand images tend to direct buying behavior and they help explain why many people purchase products for their labels as much as for their performance. (The importance of product names is illustrated by the difficulty Chevrolet had in initial attempts to market its *Nova* model in South America. Until the name was changed, consumers shunned the car. The problem? In Spanish, *no va* means "doesn't go"!)

It sounds like consumer psychology is concerned with persuading people to buy things they don't need. Is that the case?

Not all consumer psychology is profit oriented. For instance, principles of consumer behavior may be used to encourage people to conserve gasoline, water, and electricity, or to use "green" (environmentally friendly) products (Shrum et al., 1995). The same principles that are used to get us to buy products can persuade us to act in our own best interest. Advertising campaigns concerning auto seat belt use, drug abuse prevention, healthful behavior, and the like, all draw on an understanding of consumer behavior (Olander, 1990).

Role-Playing We all know from personal observation that emotional experiences can dramatically alter attitudes. A good example is the person who gives up drinking after nearly dying in an automobile accident caused by drunkenness. To actively bring about such attitude change, psychologists sometimes create similar experiences through role-playing. For instance, Janis and Mann (1965) asked women who were known smokers to play the role of cancer patients. A doctor told each of the women that he had some bad news: She had lung cancer and would have to undergo immediate surgery. The women played out the part by asking questions about the surgery, if it might fail, and so on. Women in the role-playing group drastically reduced their smoking. Those who listened to a tape recording of similar information showed little change.

Why does role-playing have more effect than hearing the same information?

Cognitive Dissonance Theory Certainly emotional impact and realism have some effect, but part of the explanation also lies in *cognitive dissonance*. Cognitions are thoughts. Dissonance means clashing. The influential theory of **cognitive dissonance** *states that contradicting or clashing thoughts cause discomfort.* That is, we have a need for *consistency* in our thoughts, perceptions, and images of ourselves (Festinger, 1957; Thibodeau & Aronson, 1992).

What happens if people act in ways that are inconsistent with their attitudes or self-images? Typically, the contradiction makes them uncomfortable. Such discomfort can motivate people to make their thoughts or attitudes agree with their actions. For example, smokers are told on every pack that cigarettes endanger their lives. They light up and smoke anyway. How do they resolve the tension between this information and their actions? They could quit smoking, but it may be easier to convince themselves that smoking is not really so dangerous. To do this, many smokers seek examples of heavy smokers who have lived long lives; they spend their time with other smokers; and they avoid information about the link between smoking and cancer. According to cognitive dissonance theory we also tend to reject new information

Table 21-1 ■ Strategies for Reducing Cognitive Dissonance

Celia, who is a college student, has always thought of herself as an environmental activist. Recently, Celia "inherited" a car from her parents, who were replacing the family "barge." In the past, Celia biked or used public transportation to get around. Her parent's old car is an antiquated gas-guzzler, but she has begun to drive it on a daily basis. How might Celia reduce the cognitive dissonance created by the clash between her environmentalism and her use of an inefficient automobile?

Strategy	Example
■ Change your attitude	■ "Cars are not really a major environmental problem."
■ Add consonant thoughts	■ "This is an old car, so keeping it on the road makes good use of the resources consumed when it was manufactured."
■ Change the importance of the dissonant thoughts	■ "It's more important for me to support the environmental movement politically than it is to worry about how I get to school and work."
■ Reduce the amount of perceived choice	■ "My schedule has become too hectic, I really can't afford to bike or take the bus anymore."
■ Change your behavior	■ "I'm only going to use the car when it's impossible to bike or take the bus."

After Franzoi, 1996.

that contradicts ideas we already hold. We're all guilty of this "don't bother me with the facts, my mind is made up" strategy at times.

Now recall Mrs. Keech and her doomsday group. Why did their belief in Mrs. Keech's messages *increase* after the world failed to end? Why did the group suddenly become interested in convincing others that their beliefs were correct? Cognitive dissonance theory explains that after publicly committing themselves to their beliefs, they had a strong need to maintain their consistency. In effect, convincing others was a way of adding proof that they were right (see Table 21–1 ■).

Cognitive dissonance also underlies attempts to convince *ourselves* that we've done the right thing. Here's an example you may recognize: As romantic partners become better acquainted, they sooner or later begin to notice things they don't like about each other. How do they reduce the cognitive dissonance and doubts caused by their partners' shortcomings? A recent study found that we tend to create stories that change our partners' faults into virtues: he seems cheap, but he's really frugal; she seems egotistical, but she's really self-confident; he's not stubborn, he just has integrity; she's not undependable, she's a free spirit; and so on (Murray & Holmes, 1993).

Acting contrary to one's attitudes doesn't always bring about change. How does cognitive dissonance account for that?

The amount of *justification* for acting contrary to your attitudes and beliefs affects how much dissonance you feel. (**Justification** *is the degree to which a person's actions are*

explained by rewards or other circumstances.) In a classic study, college students did an extremely boring task (turning wooden pegs on a board), for a *long* time. Afterward, they were asked to help lure others into the experiment by pretending that the task was interesting and enjoyable. Students paid $20 for lying to others did not change their own negative opinion of the task. Those who were paid only $1 later rated the experience as actually being pleasant and interesting. How can we explain these results? Apparently, students paid $20 experienced no dissonance. These students

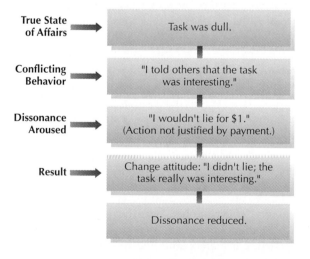

Figure 21–2 ◆ Summary of the Festinger and Carlsmith (1959) study from the viewpoint of a person experiencing cognitive dissonance.

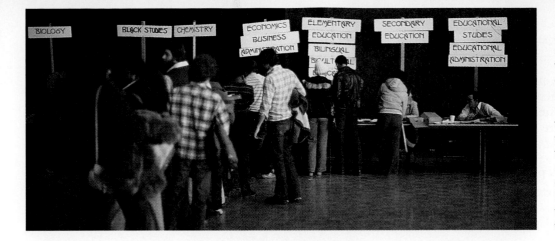

Making choices often causes dissonance. This is especially true if the rejected alternative is perceived as better than the one selected. To minimize such dissonance, we tend to emphasize positive aspects of what we choose, while downgrading other alternatives. Thus, college students are more likely to think their courses will be good after they have registered than they did before making a commitment (Rosenfeld et al., 1983).

could reassure themselves that anybody would tell a little white lie for $20. Those paid $1 were faced with the conflicting thoughts, "I lied. But I had no good reason to do it." Rather than admit to themselves that they had lied, these students changed their attitude toward what they had done (Festinger & Carlsmith, 1959) (Fig. 21–2 ◆).

Other studies indicate that we are especially likely to experience dissonance after we cause an event to occur that

we wish hadn't taken place (Cooper & Fazio, 1984). Let's say, for example, that you agree to help a friend move to a new apartment. The big day arrives and you feel like staying in bed. Actually, you wish you hadn't promised to help. To reduce dissonance, you may convince yourself that the work will actually be "good exercise," "sort of fun," or that your friend really deserves the help. We often make such adjustments in attitudes to minimize cognitive dissonance.

Learning Check

1. Attitudes have three parts, a _____ component, an _____ component, and an _____ component.

2. Which of the following is associated with attitude formation?
   a. group membership   **b.** mass media   **c.** chance conditioning   **d.** child rearing
   e. all of the preceding   **f.** a and d only

3. Because of the immediate consequences of actions, behavior contrary to one's stated attitudes is often enacted. T or F?

4. Items such as "would exclude from my country" or "would admit to marriage in my family" are found in which attitude measure?
   a. a reference group scale   **b.** a social distance scale   **c.** an attitude scale
   d. an open-ended interview

5. In presenting a persuasive message, it is best to give both sides of the argument if the audience is already well informed on the topic. T or F?

6. Consumer psychology is exclusively concerned with profits and increasing the sales of commercial products. T or F?

7. Much attitude change is related to a desire to avoid clashing or contradictory thoughts, an idea summarized by _____ _____ theory.

Critical Thinking

8. Students entering a college gym are asked to sign a banner promoting water conservation. Later, the students shower at the gym. What effect would you expect signing the banner to have on how long students stay in the showers?

Answers:

1. belief, emotional, action 2. e
3. T 4. b 5. T 6. F 7. cognitive dissonance 8. Cognitive dissonance theory predicts that students who sign the banner will take shorter showers, to be consistent with their publicly expressed support of water conservation. This is exactly the result observed in a study done by social psychologist Elliot Aronson.

Forced Attitude Change—Brainwashing and Cults

Many people associate *brainwashing* with techniques used by the Communist Chinese on prisoners during the

Korean War. Through various types of "thought reform," the Chinese were able to coerce approximately 16 percent of these prisoners to sign false confessions (Schein et al., 1957). More recently, the mass murder/suicide at Jonestown, the Branch Davidian tragedy at Waco, and the Heaven's Gate group suicide in San Diego have rekindled public interest in forced attitude change.

What is brainwashing? How does it differ from other persuasive techniques?

As we have noted, advertisers, politicians, educators, religious organizations, and others actively seek to alter attitudes and opinions. To an extent, their persuasive efforts resemble brainwashing, but there is an important difference: **Brainwashing,** *or forced attitude change, requires a captive audience.* If you are offended by a television commercial, you can tune it out. Prisoners in the POW camps in Korea (and later in Vietnam) were completely at the mercy of their captors. Complete control over the environment allows a degree of psychological manipulation that would be impossible in a normal setting.

How does captivity facilitate persuasion?

Brainwashing

Psychologist James McConnell identified three techniques used in brainwashing: (1) The target person is isolated from other people who would support his or her original attitudes; (2) the target is made completely dependent on his or her captors for satisfaction of needs; and (3) the indoctrinating agent is in a position to reward the target for changes in attitudes or behavior.

Brainwashing typically begins with an attempt to make the target person feel completely helpless. Physical and psychological abuse, lack of sleep, humiliation, and isolation serve to **unfreeze,** *or loosen,* former values and beliefs. When exhaustion, pressure, and fear become unbearable, **change** *occurs as the person abandons former beliefs.* Typically, prisoners who reach the breaking point sign a false confession or

cooperate to gain relief. When they do, they are suddenly rewarded with praise, privileges, food, or rest. Continued coupling of hope and fear with additional pressures to conform then serves to **refreeze** (*solidify*) new attitudes (Schein et al., 1961).

How permanent are changes caused by brainwashing?

In most cases, the dramatic shift in attitudes brought about by brainwashing is temporary. Most "converted" prisoners who returned to the United States after the Korean War eventually reverted to their original beliefs and repudiated their indoctrinators.

Cults

Exhorted by their leader, some 900 members of the Reverend Jim Jones' People's Temple picked up paper cups and drank purple Kool-Aid laced with the deadly poison cyanide. Psychologically, the mass suicide at Jonestown in 1978 is not so incredible as it might seem. The inhabitants of Jonestown were isolated in the jungles of Guyana, intimidated by guards and lulled with sedatives. They were also cut off from friends and relatives and totally accustomed to obeying rigid rules of conduct, which primed them for Jones' final "loyalty test." Of greater psychological interest is the question of how people reach such a state of commitment and dependency.

Why do people join groups such as the People's Temple?

The People's Temple was a classic example of a *cult.* A **cult** *is a group in which the leader's personality is more important than the beliefs she or he preaches.* Cult members give their

In April 1993, David Koresh and members of his Branch Davidian group perished in an inferno at their Waco, Texas, compound. Authorities believe the fire was set by a cult member, under the direction of Koresh. Like Jim Jones had done years before in Jonestown, Koresh took nearly total control of his followers' lives. He told them what to eat, dictated sexual mores, and directed the paddling of errant followers. Followers were persuaded to surrender money, property, and even their children and wives. Like Jones, Koresh also took mistresses and had children out of wedlock. Like other cult leaders, Jones and Koresh demanded absolute loyalty and obedience, with tragic results (Reiterman, 1993).

allegiance to this person, who is regarded as infallible, and they follow his or her dictates without question. Almost always, cult members are victimized by their leaders in one way or another.

Psychologist Margaret Singer has studied and aided hundreds of former cult members. Her interviews reveal that in recruiting new members, cults use a powerful blend of guilt, manipulation, isolation, deception, fear, and escalating commitment. In this respect, cults employ high-pressure indoctrination techniques not unlike those used in brain-washing (Isser, 1991; Singer & Addis, 1992).

Recruitment Some of those interviewed by Singer were suffering from marked psychological distress when they joined a cult. Most, however, were simply undergoing a period of mild depression, indecision, or alienation from family and friends. Cult members try to catch potential converts at a time of need—especially when a sense of belonging will be attractive to the convert. For instance, many converts were approached just after a romance had broken up, or when they were struggling with exams, were trying to choose a major, or were simply at loose ends and "on the street." Another dangerous time is when young adults are having difficulty becoming independent from their families (Sirkin, 1990). At such times, people are easily persuaded that joining the group is all they must do to be happy again (Schwartz, 1991).

How is conversion achieved?

Conversion Often it begins with intense displays of affection and understanding ("love bombing"). Next comes isolation from non-cult members and drills, discipline, and rituals (all-night meditation or continuous chanting, for instance). These rituals wear down physical and emotional resistance and generate feelings of commitment. In short, cults tend to appeal to recruits' emotions, while discouraging critical thinking (Galanti, 1993).

At first, recruits make small commitments (to stay after a meeting, for example). Then, larger commitments are encouraged (to stay an extra day, to call in sick at work, and so forth). Making a major commitment is usually the final step. The new devotee signs over a bank account or property to the group, moves in with the group, and so forth. Such major public commitments create a powerful cognitive dissonance effect. Before long it becomes virtually impossible for converts to admit they have made a mistake.

Once in the group, members are cut off from family and friends (former reference groups), and the cult can control the flow and interpretation of information to them. Members are isolated from their former value systems and social structures. Conversion is complete when they come to think of themselves more as group members than as individuals. At this point obedience is nearly total (Schwartz, 1991; Wexler, 1995).

Why do people stay in cults?

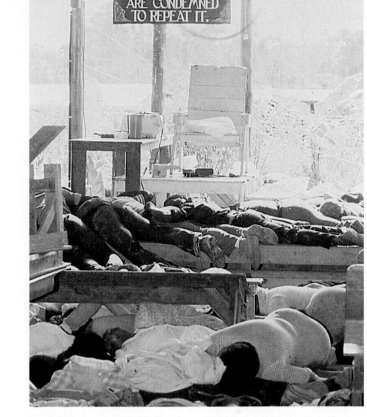

Aftermath of the mass suicide at Jonestown. How do cult-like groups recruit new devotees? (See text.)

Most former members mention guilt and fear as the main reasons for not leaving when they wished they could. Most had been reduced to child-like dependency on the group for meeting all their daily needs (Singer, 1979). After they leave, many former cult members suffer from anxiety, panic attacks, and emotional disturbances much like post-traumatic stress syndrome (West, 1993).

Behind the "throne" from which Jim Jones ruled Jonestown was a sign bearing these words: "Those who do not remember the past are condemned to repeat it." If we are to take the Reverend Jones at his word, then we should remember that cults are but one example of the danger of trading independence for security. Cults are merely the most visible sign of how we all can be influenced by sophisticated psychological coercion and by our need for approval from others.

Prejudice—Attitudes That Injure

Prejudice *is a negative emotional attitude held against members of a particular social group.* Prejudice is usually marked by unreasonable suspicion, fear, or hatred. Often prejudices are institutionalized, or reflected in government policy, schools, and so forth, and enforced by social power structures. In such cases prejudice is referred to as *racism, sexism, ageism,* or *heterosexism* depending on the group affected. Since sexism, ageism, and heterosexism were discussed in earlier chapters, let's focus on racism. Both racial prejudice and racism lead to **discrimination**, *or unequal treatment of people whose rights should be identical to those of others.* Discrimination frequently prevents people from doing things they should be able to do, such as buying a house, riding a bus, or attending a high-quality school.

Discrimination is deeply woven into society. One remarkable study, for instance, involved 15 college students who had received no traffic citations in the previous year. Each student attached a bumper sticker for a well-known, militant black organization to his or her car (Heussenstamm, 1971). During the next 17 days the group received a total of 33 traffic citations! The power relationship between the white establishment and black militants in this instance (at least as interpreted by individual police officers) is clear.

How do prejudices develop?

Becoming Prejudiced

One major theory suggests that prejudice is a form of **scapegoating** (*blaming a person or a group for the actions of others or for conditions not of their making*). Scapegoating, you may recall, is a type of *displaced aggression* in which hostilities triggered by frustration are redirected at "safe" targets. One interesting test of this hypothesis was conducted at a summer camp for young men. The men were given a difficult test they were sure to fail. Additionally, completing the test caused them to miss a trip to the theater, which was normally the high point of their weekly entertainment. Attitudes toward Mexicans and Japanese were measured before the test and after the men had failed the test and missed the entertainment. Subjects in this study consistently rated members of these two groups lower after being frustrated (Miller & Bugelski, 1970).

At times, the development of prejudice (like other attitudes) can be traced to direct experiences with members of the rejected group. A child who is repeatedly bullied by members of a particular racial or ethnic group might develop a lifelong dislike for all members of the group. The tragedy in such cases is that once prejudices are established, they prevent us from accepting additional, more positive experiences that could reverse the damage (Wilder, Simon, & Faith, 1996).

Distinguished psychologist Gordon Allport (1958) concluded that there are two important sources of prejudice. **Personal prejudice** *occurs when members of another racial or ethnic group are perceived as a threat to one's own interests.* For example, members of another group may be viewed as competitors for jobs. **Group prejudice** *occurs when a person conforms to group norms.* For instance, you might have no personal reason for disliking out-group members, but your friends, acquaintances, or co-workers may expect it of you.

The Prejudiced Personality   Other research suggests that prejudice at times is a general personality characteristic.

Do you mean some people are more prone to prejudice than others?

Apparently, some are. Theodore Adorno and his associates (1950) carefully probed what they called the *authoritarian personality* (ah-thor-ih-TARE-ee-un). These researchers started out by studying anti-Semitism as a means of understanding the social climate that existed in Germany during World War II. In the process, they found that people who are prejudiced against one group tend to be prejudiced against *all* out-groups.

What are the characteristics of the prejudice-prone personality?

The **authoritarian personality** *is marked by rigidity, inhibition, prejudice, and over-simplification.* Authoritarians also tend to be very *ethnocentric.* **Ethnocentrism** *refers to placing one's own group "at the center," usually by rejecting all other groups.* Put more simply, authoritarians consider their own ethnic or racial group superior to others. In addition to rejecting out-groups, authoritarians are overwhelmingly concerned with power, authority, and obedience. To measure these qualities, the *F scale* was created (the *F* stands for "fascism"). This attitude scale is made up of statements such as the ones that follow—to which authoritarians readily agree (Adorno et al., 1950).

Authoritarian Beliefs

Obedience and respect for authority are the most important virtues children should learn.

People can be divided into two distinct classes: the weak and the strong.

If people would talk less and work more, everybody would be better off.

What this country needs most, more than laws and political programs, is a few courageous, tireless, devoted leaders, in whom the people can put their faith.

Nobody ever learns anything really important except through suffering.

Every person should have complete faith in some supernatural power whose decisions are obeyed without question.

Certain religious sects that refuse to salute the flag should be forced to conform to such patriotic action or else be abolished.

As children, authoritarians were usually severely punished. Most learned to fear authority (and to covet it) at an early age. In general, people are more likely to express authoritarian beliefs when they feel threatened (Doty, Peterson, & Winter, 1991). An example would be calling for more severe punishment in schools when the economy is bad and job insecurities are high. Authoritarians are not happy people.

It should be readily apparent from the list of authoritarian beliefs that the F scale is slanted toward politically conservative authoritarians. To be fair, psychologist Milton Rokeach (1918–1988) noted that rigid and authoritarian personalities can be found at both ends of the political spectrum. Rokeach, therefore, preferred to describe rigid and intolerant thinking as *dogmatism*. (**Dogmatism** *is an unwarranted positiveness or certainty in matters of belief or opinion.*) Dogmatic persons find it difficult to change their beliefs, even when the evidence contradicts them (Davies, 1993).

Even if we discount the obvious bigotry of the dogmatic or authoritarian personality, racial prejudice runs deep in many nations. To illustrate, one experiment showed that liberal, white, male college students were more willing to give shocks (under laboratory conditions) to a black victim than to a white victim (Shulman, 1974). We will probe deeper into the roots of such prejudiced behavior in an upcoming discussion, but first let's stop for a Learning Check.

Intergroup Conflict— The Roots of Prejudice

An unfortunate by-product of group membership is that it often limits contact with people in other groups. Additionally, groups themselves may come into conflict. Both events tend to foster unpleasant feelings and prejudices toward the out-group. The bloody clash of opposing forces in Bosnia, Israel, Ireland, South Africa, and Hometown, U.S.A., are reminders that intergroup conflict is widespread. Daily we read of jarring strife between nations, communities, and political, religious, or ethnic groups. In many cases, intergroup conflict is accompanied by *stereotyped* images of out-group members and by bitter prejudice.

What exactly do you mean by a stereotype?

Social stereotypes *are oversimplified images of people who belong to a particular social group.* There is a good chance that you have stereotyped images of some of the following categories: redneck, politician, show-off, do-gooder, juvenile delinquent, business executive, housewife, snob, playboy, teenager, slob, spoiled brat, billionaire. Stereotypes have a powerful effect on how we treat others (Andersen, Klatzky, & Murray, 1990). In general, the top three categories on which most stereotypes are based are gender, age, and race (Fiske, 1993a).

Stereotypes tend to simplify people into "us" and "them" categories. Actually, aside from the fact that they always oversimplify, stereotypes may be either *positive* or *negative*. Table 21–2 ■ shows stereotyped images of various national and ethnic groups and their changes over a 34-year period. Notice that many of the qualities listed are desirable. Note too, that while the overall trend was a decrease in negative stereotypes, belief in the existence of some negative traits increased.

Even though stereotypes sometimes include positive traits, they are mainly used to maintain control over other people. When a person is stereotyped, the easiest thing for her or him to do is to abide by others' expectations—even if the expectations are demeaning. That's why no one likes to be stereotyped. Being forced into a small, distorted social "box" by stereotyping is limiting and insulting. Stereotypes rob people of their individuality. Without stereotypes there would be far less hate, prejudice, exclusion, and conflict (Fiske, 1993b).

Trait	Percent Checking Trait 1933	Percent Checking Trait 1967	Trait	Percent Checking Trait 1933	Percent Checking Trait 1967	Trait	Percent Checking Trait 1933	Percent Checking Trait 1967
Americans			**Italians**			**Jews**		
Industrious	48	23	Artistic	53	30	Shrewd	79	30
Intelligent	47	20	Impulsive	44	28	Mercenary	49	15
Materialistic	33	67	Musical	32	9	Grasping	34	17
Progressive	27	17	Imaginative	30	7	Intelligent	29	37
Germans			**Irish**			**Blacks**		
Scientific	78	47	Pugnacious	45	13	Superstitious	84	13
Stolid	44	9	Witty	38	7	Lazy	75	26
Methodical	31	21	Honest	32	17	Ignorant	38	11
Efficient	16	46	Nationalistic	21	41	Religious	24	8

Source: M. Karlins, T. L. Coffman, and G. Walters, "On the fading of social stereotypes: Studies in three generations of college students," *Journal of Personality and Social Psychology* 13 (1969): 1–16.

Research Frontier

Choking on Stereotypes

Bill, a retired aircraft mechanic, has agreed to talk to a group of high school students about the early days of commercial aviation. During his talk, Bill is concerned that any slip in his memory will confirm stereotypes about older people being forgetful. Because he is anxious and preoccupied about possible memory lapses, Bill actually does have problems with his memory.

As Bill's example suggests, negative stereotypes can have a self-fulfilling quality. This is especially true in situations in which a person's abilities are evaluated. For example, African Americans must often cope with negative stereotypes about their academic abilities. Could such stereotypes actually impair school performance?

Psychologist Claude Steele has amassed evidence that people tend to feel threatened when they think they are being judged in terms of a stereotype. The anxiety that this causes can then lower performance, seemingly confirming the stereotype. An experiment Steele did demonstrates this effect. In the study, black and white college students took a very difficult verbal test. Some students were told the test measured *academic ability*. Others were told that the test was a laboratory *problem-solving task* unrelated to ability. In the ability condition, black students performed worse than whites. In the problem-solving condition they performed the same as whites.

In light of such findings, Steele and his colleagues are currently working on ways to remove stereotype threat, so that all students can use their potentials more fully (Steele, 1997).

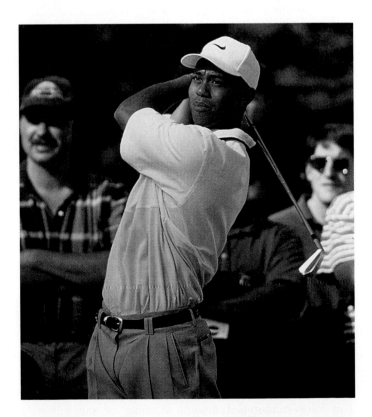

Racial and ethnic pride are gradually replacing stereotypes and discrimination, but the problem of prejudice is far from solved.

In the years since 1967, there have been further declines in negative stereotypes, but also some recent reversals. Some observers believe that racial and ethnic prejudice is on the upswing. But often, today's racism takes the form of **symbolic prejudice,** *which is expressed in a disguised fashion* (Brewer & Kramer, 1985). That is, many people realize that crude and obvious racism is socially unacceptable. However, this may not stop them from expressing prejudice in thinly veiled forms when they state their opinions on issues such as affirmative action programs, busing, immigration, crime, and so on. In effect, modern racists find ways to rationalize their prejudice so that it seems to be based on issues other than raw racism.

Stereotypes held by the prejudiced tend to be unusually irrational. When given a list of negative statements about other groups, prejudiced individuals agree with most of them. It's particularly revealing that they often agree with conflicting statements. Thus, a prejudiced person may say that Jews are both "pushy" and "standoffish" or that African Americans are both "ignorant" and "sly." In one study, prejudiced persons even expressed negative attitudes toward two non-existent groups, the "Piraneans" and the "Danirians." Note, too, that when a prejudiced person meets a pleasant or likable member of a rejected group, the out-group member tends to be perceived as "an exception to the rule," not as evidence against the stereotype. Even when such "exceptional" experiences begin to accumulate, a prejudiced person may not change his or her stereotyped belief (Fiske, 1993a; Wilder, Simon, & Faith, 1996).

Cultural Diversity

Enemy Images

"Huns, Krauts, Japs." If you've watched many vintage war movies you've probably heard these ugly and hateful terms. During World War II, as in all wars, public images of "the enemy" were monstrous and dehumanizing. Even today, in the absence of active hostilities, enemy images tend to depict our national rivals as evil or less than human. For example, media images of Russians have long depicted them as inhumane, vicious torturers who enjoy murder and inflicting pain. In the movie *Rambo*, for instance, two Russian soldiers are shown enjoying themselves as they torture Sylvester Stallone with electric shock and hot knives (Silverstein, 1989). (Given a chance, some movie critics might join in.)

In times of war, dehumanizing images are used to make it seem that a nation's enemies *deserve* hatred and even death. Undoubtedly, such images provide a degree of emotional insulation that makes it easier for soldiers to harm other humans. Yet during times of peace, enemy images can lead to dangerous misper-

ceptions of the motives and actions of other nations (Silverstein, 1989).

During the recent civil war in parts of the former Yugoslavia, Bosnian Serbs described mass killing of Muslim civilians as "ethnic cleansing." In reality, the Serb attacks were genocide, in which mothers, fathers, daughters, and sons were slaughtered.

In many ways, ethnic jokes, racial stereotypes, degrading names, out-group slurs, and the like are small-scale examples of the damage that "enemy" images can do. Clashes ranging from those between street gangs, to those between nations, are fueled, in part, by dehumanizing images of "the enemy."

How do stereotypes and intergroup tensions develop?

Two experiments, both in unlikely settings and both using children as subjects, offer some insight into these problems.

Experiments in Prejudice

What is it like to be discriminated against? Those who have never experienced discrimination probably can't imagine it. In a unique experiment, elementary school teacher Jane Elliot sought to give her pupils direct experience with prejudice.

On the first day of the experiment, Elliot announced that brown-eyed children were to sit in the back of the room and that they could not use the drinking fountain. Blue-eyed children were given extra recess time and got to leave first for lunch. At lunch, brown-eyed children were prevented from taking second helpings because they would "just waste it." Brown-eyed and blue-eyed children were kept from mingling, and the blue-eyed children were told they were "cleaner" and "smarter" (Peters, 1971).

At first, Elliot had to maintain these imposed conditions of prejudice. She also made an effort to constantly criticize and belittle the brown-eyed children. To her surprise, the blue-eyed children rapidly joined in and were soon outdoing her in the viciousness of their attacks. The blue-eyed children began to feel superior, and the brown-eyed children felt just plain awful. Fights broke out. Test scores of the brown-eyed children fell.

How lasting were the effects of this experiment?

The effects were short lived, because two days later the roles of the children were reversed. Before long, the same destructive effects occurred again, but this time in reverse. The implications of this experiment are unmistakable. In less than one day it was possible to get children to hate each other because of eye color and **status inequalities** (*differences in power, prestige, or privileges*). Certainly the effects of a lifetime of real racial or ethnic prejudice are infinitely more powerful and destructive.

What can be done to combat prejudice?

Equal-Status Contact   Progress has been made through attempts to educate the general public about the lack of justification for prejudice. Changing the belief component of an attitude is one of the most direct means of changing the entire attitude. Thus, when people are made aware that members of various racial and ethnic groups share the same goals, ambitions, feelings, and frustrations as they do, intergroup relations may be improved.

However, this is not the whole answer. As we noted earlier, there is often a wide difference between attitudes and actual behavior. Until non-prejudiced behavior is engineered, changes can be quite superficial. Several lines of thought (including cognitive dissonance theory) suggest that more frequent *equal-status contact* between groups in conflict should reduce prejudice and stereotyping (Olson & Zanna, 1993).

Equal-status contact *refers to social interaction that occurs on an equal footing, without obvious differences in power or status.* Much evidence suggests that equal status contact does, in fact, lessen prejudice. For example, in one early study white women who lived in integrated and segregated housing projects were compared for changes in attitude toward their African-American neighbors. Women in the integrated project showed a favorable shift in attitudes toward members of the other racial group. Those in the segregated project showed no change or actually became more prejudiced than before (Deutsch & Collins, 1951). In other studies, mixed-race groups have been formed at work, in the laboratory, and at schools. The conclusion from such research is that personal contact with a disliked group will induce friendly behavior, respect, and liking. However, these benefits occur only when personal contact is cooperative and on an equal footing (Grack & Richman, 1996).

To test the importance of equal-status contact directly, Gerald Clore and his associates set up a unique summer camp for children. The camp was directed by one white male, one white female, one black male, and one black female. Each campsite had three black and three white campers and one black and one white counselor. Thus, blacks and whites were equally divided in number, power, privileges, and duties. Did the experience make a difference? Apparently it did: Testing showed that the children had significantly more positive attitudes toward opposite-race children after the camp than they did before (Clore, 1976).

Superordinate Goals   Let us now consider a revealing study of intergroup conflict and its reduction. Muzafer Sherif and his associates did an ingenious experiment, also at a summer camp, with 11-year-old boys. When the boys arrived at camp, they were split into two groups and housed in separate cabins. At first the groups were kept apart to build up in-group friendships. During this time, cooperative games and activities were used to develop group pride and identification. Soon each group had a flag and a name (the "Rattlers" and the "Eagles"), and had staked out its territory. At this point the two groups were placed in competition with each other. After a number of clashes, disliking between the groups bordered on hatred. Outright hostility erupted as the boys baited each other, started fights, and raided each other's cabins (Sherif et al., 1961).

Were they allowed to go home hating each other?

As an experiment in reducing intergroup conflict, and to prevent the boys from remaining enemies, various strategies to reduce tensions were tried. Holding meetings between leaders from each group did nothing. Just getting the groups together also did little. When the groups were invited to eat together, the event became a free-for-all.

Finally, emergencies that required cooperation among members of both groups were staged at the camp. For example, the water supply was damaged in a way so that all the boys had to work together to repair it. Creation of this and other *superordinate goals* helped restore peace between the two groups. (A **superordinate goal** *exceeds or overrides other lesser goals.*)

As members of the groups were forced to cooperate, hostilities subsided. Cooperation and shared goals seem to help reduce conflict by encouraging people in opposing groups to see themselves as members of a single, larger group (Gaertner et al., 1990). Superordinate goals, in other words, have a "we're all in the same boat" effect on perceptions of group membership (Olson & Zanna, 1993).

A Closer Look

Superordinate Goals—Finding Common Ground

Superordinate goals unite groups in the pursuit of a common goal. Can such goals exist on a global scale?

One example might be a desire to avoid nuclear holocaust. Politically, this goal may be far from universal. But its superordinate quality is clearly evident. Scientists now project that if *any* country suffers a nuclear attack, all other countries would suffer a terrifying "nuclear winter." In effect, almost everyone, friend and foe alike, would share the same fate (Sagan & Turco, 1990).

Nuclear winter refers to a devastating drop in global temperature that would follow the fire storms, dust, and smoke of a nuclear strike. The probable result would be global crop failure, famine, and death on a large scale. Even if there were no counter-attack, a hostile country could pay dearly for its aggression (Turco et al., 1983).

It is probably fair to say that nations need to find more commonalities and shared goals. It's true that the former Soviet Union has become less of a threat to world peace. But at the same time, other "unstable" nations are gaining nuclear weapons capability. In view of the implications of nuclear winter, perhaps finding a way to reduce the threat of nuclear warfare will prove to be a superordinate goal. Another that comes quickly to mind is the need to preserve the natural environment on a global scale.

In a "jigsaw" classroom, children help each other prepare for tests. As they teach each other what they know, the children learn to cooperate and to respect the unique strengths of each individual.

"Jigsaw" Classrooms   Contrary to the hopes of many, integrating public schools often has little positive effect on racial prejudice. In fact, prejudice may be made worse, and the self-esteem of minority students frequently decreases (Aronson, 1992).

If integrated schools provide equal-status contact, shouldn't prejudice be reduced?

Theoretically, yes. But in practice, minority group children often enter newly integrated schools unprepared to compete on an equal footing. Elliot Aronson and his colleagues argue that the competitive nature of schools almost guarantees that children will *not* learn to like and understand each other. In the typical classroom, children compete fiercely for the teacher's approval. Successful students learn to feel superior and often show contempt for unsuccessful students. This is a high-stakes game in which only a few can win. It is clearly not a good way to reduce prejudice.

With the preceding in mind, Aronson pioneered a way to apply the concept of superordinate goals to ordinary classrooms. According to Aronson, such goals are effective because they create a condition of **mutual interdependence,** *in which people must depend on one another to meet each person's goals.* When each person's needs are linked to those of others in the group, cooperation is encouraged (Deutsch, 1993).

How has this idea been applied?

Aronson has successfully created *"jigsaw"* classrooms that emphasize cooperation rather than competition. The term *jigsaw* refers to the pieces of a jigsaw puzzle. In a **jigsaw classroom,** *each child is given a "piece" of the information needed to complete a project or prepare for a test.*

In a typical session, children are divided into groups of 5 or 6 and given a topic to study for a later exam. Each child is given his or her "piece" of information and asked to learn it. For example, one child might have information on Thomas Edison's invention of the light bulb; another, facts about his invention of the long-playing phonograph record; and a third, information on Edison's childhood. After the children have learned their individual parts, they teach them to others in the group. Even the most competitive children quickly realize that they cannot do well without the aid of everyone in the group. Each child makes a unique and essential contribution, so the children learn to listen to, and respect, each other.

Does the jigsaw method work? Compared to children in traditional classrooms, children in jigsaw groups are less prejudiced, they like their classmates more, they have more positive attitudes toward school, their grades improve, and their self-esteem increases (Aronson et al., 1979; Webb & Farivar, 1994). Such results are quite encouraging. As Kenneth Clark (1965) has said, "Racial prejudice . . . debases all human beings—those who are its victims, those who victimize, and in quite subtle ways, those who are merely accessories."

Aggression—The World's Most Dangerous Animal

Ritualized human aggression. Violent and aggressive behavior is so commonplace it may be viewed as entertainment. How "natural" is aggressive behavior?

For a time, the City Zoo of Los Angeles, California, had on display two examples of the world's most dangerous animal—the only animal capable of destroying the earth and all other animal species. Perhaps you have already guessed which animal it was. In the cage were two college students, representing the species *Homo sapiens!*

The human capacity for *aggression* seems staggering. It has been estimated that during the 125-year period ending with World War II, 58 million humans were killed by other humans (an average of nearly 1 person per minute). Murder now ranks as a major cause of death in the United States. One American kills another every 23 minutes—making the United States one of the world's most violent nations. It is estimated that more than 1.4 million American children are subjected to physical abuse by parents each year. Over 25 percent of all married American men and women have physically attacked their spouses (O'Leary et al., 1989). War, homicide, riots, family violence, assassination, rape, assault, forcible robbery, and other violent acts offer sad testimony to the realities of human aggression.

What causes aggression?

Aggression *refers to any action carried out with the intention of harming another person.* The complexity of aggression has given rise to a number of potential explanations for its occurrence. Brief descriptions of some of the major possibilities follow.

Instincts

Some theorists argue that as humans, we are naturally aggressive, having inherited a "killer instinct" from our animal ancestors. *Ethologists* theorize that aggression is a biologically rooted behavior observed in all animals, including humans. (An **ethologist** *is a person who studies the natural behavior patterns of animals.*) Noted ethologist Konrad Lorenz (1966, 1974) also believed that humans lack certain innate patterns that inhibit aggression in animals. For example, in a dispute over territory or dominance, two wolves may growl, lunge, bare their teeth, and fiercely threaten each other. In most instances, though, neither is killed or even wounded. One wolf, recognizing the dominance of the other, will typically bare its throat in a gesture of submission. The dominant wolf could kill in an instant, but it is inhibited by the submissive gesture. In contrast, human confrontations of equal intensity almost always end in injury or homicide.

The idea that humans are "naturally" aggressive has an intuitive appeal, but many psychologists question it. Many of Lorenz's "explanations" of aggression are little more than loose comparisons between human and animal behavior. Just labeling a behavior as "instinctive" does little to explain it. More important, we are left with the question of why some individuals or human groups (the Arapesh, the Senoi, the Navajo, the Eskimo, and others) show little hostility or aggression. And, thankfully, the vast majority of humans *do not* kill or harm others.

Biology

Despite problems with the instinctive view, there is evidence that aggression may have a biological basis. Physiological studies have shown that there are brain areas capable of triggering or ending aggressive behavior (see Chapter 3). Also, researchers have found a relationship between aggression and such physical factors as hypoglycemia (low blood sugar), allergy, and specific brain injuries and disorders. For both men and women higher levels of the hormone testosterone are associated with more aggressive behavior (Banks & Dabbs, 1996; Dabbs, Hargrove, & Heusel, 1996; Harris et al., 1996). None of these conditions, however, can be considered a direct *cause* of aggression. Instead, they probably lower the threshold for aggression, making hostile behavior more likely to occur (Baron & Richardson, 1994).

The effects of alcohol and other drugs provide another indication of the role of the brain and biology in violence and aggression. A variety of studies show that alcohol is involved in large percentages of murders and violent crimes. Like the conditions already noted, intoxicating drugs seem to lower inhibitions to act aggressively—often with tragic results (Bushman & Cooper, 1990; Ito, Miller, & Pollock, 1996).

To summarize, the fact that we are biologically *capable* of aggression does not mean that aggression is inevitable or "part of human nature." Twenty eminent scientists who studied the question concluded that, "Biology does not condemn humanity to war. . . . Violence is neither in our evolutionary legacy nor in our genes. The same species that invented war is capable of inventing peace" (Scott & Ginsburg, 1994; UNESCO, 1990). Humans are fully capable of learning to inhibit their use of violence (Lore & Schultz, 1993).

Frustration

Step on a dog's tail and you may get nipped. Frustrate a human and you may get insulted. The **frustration-aggression hypothesis** *states that frustration tends to lead to aggression* (Dollard et al., 1939). At several points in earlier chapters we have considered examples of the link between frustration and aggression.

Does frustration always produce aggression?

Although the connection is strong, a moment's thought will show that frustration does not *always* lead to aggression. Frustration, for instance, may lead to stereotyped responding or perhaps to a state of "learned helplessness" (see Chapter 14). Also, aggression can occur in the absence of frustration. This possibility is illustrated by sports spectators who start fights, throw bottles, tear down goal posts, and so forth, after their team has *won*.

Aversive Stimuli Frustration probably encourages aggression because it is uncomfortable. Various **aversive stimuli,** *which produce discomfort or displeasure,* can heighten hostility and aggression (Anderson, Anderson, & Deuser, 1996; Berkowitz, 1990) (Fig. 21–3 ◆). Examples include insults, high temperatures, pain, and even disgusting scenes or odors. Such stimuli probably raise overall arousal levels so that we become more sensitive to **aggression cues** (*signals that are associated with aggression*) (Carlson, Marcus-Newhall, & Miller, 1990). Aversive stimuli also tend to activate ideas, memories, and expressions associated with anger and aggression (Berkowitz, 1990).

Some cues for aggression are internal (angry thoughts, for instance). Many are external: Certain words, actions, and gestures made by others are strongly associated with aggressive responses. A raised middle finger, for instance, is an almost universal invitation to aggression in North America.

Even inanimate objects may serve as aggression cues. In one classic experiment, subjects gave shocks to another person in a laboratory. Before doing so, they were ridiculed and shocked by the other person. Just before subjects got a chance to "return the favor," they saw either two badminton rackets or a shotgun and a revolver on a table in the testing room. In either case, the experimenter explained that someone had left the objects there, and he casually moved them aside. Subjects who glimpsed the guns gave stronger shocks to the person who had angered them than did subjects who saw the sports equipment (Berkowitz, 1968). Thus, we

Some freeway shootings may be a reaction to the frustration of traffic congestion. The fact that automobiles provide anonymity, or a loss of personal identity, may also encourage aggressive actions that would not otherwise occur.

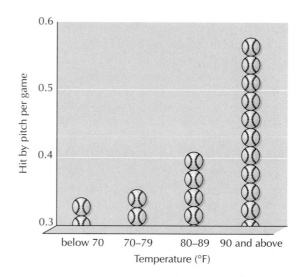

Figure 21–3 ◆ Personal discomfort caused by aversive (unpleasant) stimuli can make aggressive behavior more likely. For example, studies of crime rates show that the incidence of highly aggressive behavior, such as murder, rape, and assault, rises as the air temperature goes from warm to hot to sweltering (Anderson, 1989). The results you see here further confirm the heat-aggression link. The graph shows that there is a strong association between the temperatures at major league baseball games and the number of batters hit by a pitch during those games. When the temperature goes over 90°, watch out for that fastball! (Reifman, Larrick, & Fein, 1991.)

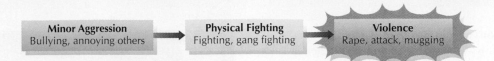

Minor Aggression	Physical Fighting	Violence
Bullying, annoying others	Fighting, gang fighting	Rape, attack, mugging

Figure 21–4 ◆ Violent behavior among delinquent boys doesn't appear overnight. Usually, their capacity for violence develops slowly, as they move from minor aggression to increasingly brutal acts. Overall aggression increases dramatically in early adolescence as boys gain physical strength and more access to weapons (Loeber & Hay, 1997).

see that *weapons serve as strong cues for aggressive behavior.* The implication of this **weapons effect** seems to be that the symbols and trappings of aggression encourage aggression. A prime example is the fact that murders are almost 3 times more likely to occur in homes where guns are kept. Nearly 80 percent of the victims in such homes are killed by a family member or acquaintance. Only 4 percent are murdered by strangers (Kellermann et al., 1993).

Social Learning

One of the most widely accepted explanations of aggression is also the simplest. *Social learning theory* holds that we learn to be aggressive by observing aggression in others (Bandura, 1973). **Social learning theory** *combines learning principles with cognitive processes, socialization, and modeling, to explain behavior.* According to this view, there is no instinctive human programming for fist-fighting, pipe-bombing, knife wielding, gun loading, 95-mile-an-hour "bean balls," or other violent or aggressive behaviors. Hence, aggression must be learned (Fig. 21–4 ◆).

Social learning theorists predict that individuals growing up in non-aggressive cultures will themselves be non-aggressive. Those raised in a culture with aggressive models and heroes will learn aggressive responses. Considered in such terms, it is no wonder that America has become one of the most violent of all countries. It is estimated that a violent crime occurs every 54 seconds in the United States. Approximately 40 percent of the population owns firearms. Nationally, 70 percent agree that "When a boy is growing up, it is very important for him to have a few fist-fights." Eighteen percent of the population admit to having slapped or kicked another person. Children and adults are treated to an almost nonstop parade of aggressive models, in the media as well as in actual behavior. We are, without a doubt, an aggressive culture.

The debate on the effects of pornography is heating up again. Until recently, most evidence suggested that viewing pornography has no major adverse effects.

This conclusion appears to remain valid for stimuli that can be described as merely erotic or sexual in content (Pollard, 1995). However, in the last 10 years there has been a dramatic increase in aggressive-pornographic stimuli appearing in the mass media. **Aggressive pornography** *refers to depictions in which violence, threats, or obvious power differences are used to force someone (usually a woman) to engage in sex.*

The principal finding of studies on aggressive-pornographic stimuli is that they do increase male aggression against females (Pollard, 1995). In a summary of various experiments, researchers Neil Malamuth and Ed Donnerstein (1982) concluded that "exposure to mass media stimuli that have violent *and* sexual content increases the audience's aggressive-sexual fantasies, beliefs in rape myths, and aggressive behavior." Donnerstein and Daniel Linz (1986) further conclude that it is media *violence* that is most damaging. As they put it, "Violent images, rather than sexual ones, are most responsible for people's attitudes about women and rape." The problem, then, extends far beyond X-rated films and books. Mainstream movies, magazines, music videos (like those mentioned earlier), and television programs are equally to blame for reinforcing the myth that women find force or aggression pleasurable. It is very telling that rapists respond with sexual arousal to both sexual and non-sexual violence. Clearly, violence is a major dimension of rape (Seto & Kuban, 1996).

The World According to TV Did you know that the world is populated primarily by males, professionals, whites, and members of the middle class? Did you know that women make up only 28 percent of the population; that one half of all women are teenagers or in their early 20s; that more than one third are unemployed or have no purpose beyond offering emotional support to men or serving as objects of sexual desire? That minorities are generally service workers, criminals, victims, or students? That over one half of all villains have accents? That most victims are single women, young boys, or non-whites? If you watch much TV, these are the impressions you get daily on the tube (Carlson, 1986; Charren & Sandler, 1983).

It is clear that TV reality does not match the real world. Every day, TV provides an endless stream of bad models, especially concerning violence. In the United States there

Figure 21–5 ◆ Although TV violence does not cause aggression, it can encourage it. The likelihood of committing criminal acts by age 30 is related to the amount of TV watching a person did when she or he was a child (Eron, 1987). (Graph copyright 1987 by the American Psychological Association, Inc. Reprinted by permission of the author.)

are about 188 hours of violent programs per week. Eighty-one percent of all programs contain violence. Murder, robbery, kidnapping, and assault make up 85 percent of TV crimes. In real life, they total about 5 percent. Television is particularly unrealistic about the effects of violence. An astounding 73 percent of violent characters go unpunished and 58 percent of violent acts don't lead to painful results. Only 16 percent of all programs show any realistic long-term consequences for violence. For children's programs the rate falls to just 5 percent (*National Television Violence Study,* 1995–96).

How much does TV violence affect children?

As Albert Bandura showed in his studies of imitation (Chapter 9), children may learn new aggressive actions by watching violent or aggressive behavior, or they may learn that violence is "okay." Either way, they are more likely to act aggressively. It is important to remember that younger children do not grasp the nuances of TV plots. A child may simply remember that when good guys were bothered in some way by others, they aggressed. Heroes on TV are as violent as the villains, and they usually receive praise for their violence.

In addition to teaching new antisocial actions, television may *disinhibit* dangerous impulses that viewers already have. **Disinhibition** (*the removal of inhibition*) results in acting out behavior that normally would be restrained. For example, many TV programs give the message that violence is acceptable behavior that leads to success and popularity. For some people, this message can lower inhibitions against acting out hostile feelings (Berkowitz, 1984).

Another effect of TV violence is that it tends to lower sensitivity to violent acts. As anyone who has seen a street fight or a mugging can tell you, TV violence is sanitized and unrealistic. The real thing is gross, ugly, and gut wrenching. Even when it is graphic, TV violence is viewed

in the relaxed and familiar setting of the home. For at least some viewers, this combination diminishes emotional reactions to violent scenes. When Victor Cline and his associates showed a bloody fight film to a group of boys, they found that heavy TV viewers (averaging 42 hours a week) showed much less emotion than those who watched little or no TV (Cline et al., 1972). Television, it seems, can cause a **desensitization** (*reduced emotional sensitivity*) to violence.

Preventing Aggression

What can be done about aggression?

Social learning theory implies that "aggression begets aggression." In other words, watching a prize fight, sporting event, or violent television program may increase aggression, rather than drain off aggressive urges. A case in point is provided by psychologist Leonard Eron, who spent 22 years following over 600 children into adulthood. Eron (1987) observes, "Among the most influential models for children were those observed on television. One of the best predictors of how aggressive a young man would be at age 19 was the violence of the television programs he preferred when he was 8 years old" (Fig. 21–5 ◆). According to Eron, children learn aggressive strategies and actions from TV violence (also see Chapter 9). Because of this, they are more prone to aggress when they face frustrating situations or cues. Others have found that viewers who watch violent videotapes have more aggressive thoughts. As we have noted, violent thoughts often precede violent actions (Bushman & Geen, 1990). Thus, the spiral of aggression might be broken if we did not so often portray it, reward it, and glorify it (Hughes & Hasbrouck, 1996).

Buffering Television's Impact

Other than pulling the plug, what can parents do about television's negative effects on children? Actually, quite a lot. Children typically model parents' TV viewing habits, and they are guided by parents' reactions to programs. Parents can make a big difference if they do the following (Eron, 1986; Huesmann, 1986; Schneider, 1987).

Parents as TV Guides

1. Limit total viewing time so that television does not dominate your child's view of the world. If necessary, set schedules for when watching TV is allowed.

2. Closely monitor what your child does watch. Change channels or turn off the TV if you object to a program. Be prepared to offer games and activities that stimulate your child's imagination and creativity.

3. Actively seek programs your child will enjoy, especially those that model positive behavior and social attitudes.

4. Watch television with your child so that you can counter what is shown. Help your child distinguish between reality and TV fantasies. Reply to distortions and stereotypes as they appear on screen.

5. Discuss the social conflicts and violent solutions shown on television. Ask your child in what ways the situations are unrealistic and why the violence shown would not work in the real world. Encourage the child to propose more mature, realistic, and positive responses to situations.

6. Show by your own disapproval that violent TV heroes are not the ones to emulate. Remember, children who identify with TV characters are more likely to be influenced by televised aggression.

By following these guidelines you can help children learn to enjoy television without being overly influenced by programs and advertisers.

Couldn't TV's impact also be used constructively?

TV as a Positive Model There is no denying TV's tremendous power to inform and to entertain. When these features are combined, as they were in specials such as *Roots* or *Holocaust*, the effect can be quite constructive. Perhaps the best examples of TV as a positive social force are educational programs such as *Barney and Friends*, *Sesame Street*, and *Mr. Rogers' Neighborhood*. Numerous research reports have found that the impact of these programs is positive. Clearly, television can teach children while holding their interest and attention.

Prosocial behavior *consists of actions toward others that are helpful, constructive, or altruistic.* As a model for positive

A recent study by Jerome and Dorothy Singer found that preschoolers who watch *Barney and Friends* show improved cognitive skills and knowledge—such as knowing colors and shapes, numbers, vocabulary, good manners, and facts about nature and health (deGroot, 1994).

attitudes and responses, TV could be used to promote helping, cooperation, charity, and brotherhood in the same way that it has tended to stereotype and encourage aggression. Over 200 studies have now shown that prosocial behavior on TV increases prosocial behavior by viewers (Hearold, 1987). To illustrate, a program called "Youth Against Violence: Choose to De-Fuse" was developed in New York City to help inner-city youths resist violence. The program focused on creating positive peer pressure for choosing non-violent solutions to conflict. The use of real-life situations, speech, and body language added to the effectiveness of the program (Zimmerman, 1996b).

Anger Control On a personal level, psychologists have succeeded in teaching some people to control their anger and aggressive impulses. **Anger control** *refers to personal strategies for reducing or curbing anger.* The key to remaining calm is to define upsetting situations as *problems to be solved.* Therefore, to limit anger, people are taught to:

1. Define the problem as precisely as possible.

2. Make a list of possible solutions.

3. Rank the likely success of each solution.

4. Choose a solution and try it.

5. Assess how successful the solution was, and make adjustments if necessary.

Taking these steps has helped many people to lessen tendencies toward child abuse, family violence, and other destructive outbursts (Meichenbaum et al., 1982).

Beyond this, the question remains, How shall we tame the world's most dangerous animal? There is no easy answer. Only a challenge of pressing importance. The solution will undoubtedly involve the best efforts of thinkers and researchers from many disciplines.

For the more immediate future, it is clear that we need more people who are willing to engage in helpful, altruistic, prosocial behavior. In the next section we will examine some of the forces that operate to prevent people from helping others. Also discussed are a few glimmerings about how to encourage prosocial behavior.

Prosocial Behavior— Helping Others

Late one night, tenants of a Queens, New York, apartment building watched and listened in horror as a young woman named Kitty Genovese was murdered on the sidewalk outside. From the safety of their rooms, no fewer than 38 people heard the agonized screams as her assailant stabbed her, was frightened off, and returned to stab her again.

Kitty Genovese's murder took over 30 minutes, but none of her neighbors tried to help. None even called the police until after the attack had ended. Perhaps it is understandable that no one wanted to get involved. After all, it could have been a violent lovers' quarrel. Or helping might have meant risking personal injury. But what prevented these people from at least calling the police?

Isn't this an example of the alienation of city life?

News reports treated this incident as evidence of a breakdown in social ties caused by the impersonality of the city. While it is true that urban living can be dehumanizing, this does not fully explain such **bystander apathy** (*unwillingness of bystanders to offer help during emergencies*). According to psychologists Bibb Latané and John Darley (1968), failure to help is related to the number of people present. Over the years many studies have shown that the *more* potential helpers present, the *lower* the chances that help will be given (Latané et al., 1981).

Why would people be less willing to help when others are present?

In Kitty Genovese's case, the answer is that everyone thought *someone else* would help. The dynamics of this effect are easily illustrated: Suppose that two motorists have stalled at roadside, one on a sparsely traveled country road and the other on a busy freeway. Who gets help first?

On the freeway, where hundreds of cars pass every minute, each driver can assume that someone else will help.

Does the person lying on the ground need help? What factors determine whether a person in trouble will receive help in an emergency? Surprisingly, more potential helpers tend to lower the chances that help will be given.

Personal responsibility for helping is spread so thin that no one takes action. On the country road, one of the first few people to arrive will probably stop, since the responsibility is clearly theirs. In general, Latané and Darley assume that bystanders are not apathetic or uncaring; they are inhibited by the presence of others.

Bystander Intervention

There are four decision points individuals must pass through before giving help. First they must notice that something is happening. Next they must define the event as an emergency. Then they must take responsibility. Finally, they must select a course of action (Fig. 21–6 ◆). Laboratory experiments have shown that each step can be influenced by the presence of other people.

Noticing What would happen if you fainted and collapsed on the sidewalk? Would someone stop to help? Would people think you were drunk? Would they even notice you? Latané and Darley suggest that if the sidewalk is crowded, few people will even see you. This has nothing to do with people blocking each other's vision. Instead, it is related to widely accepted norms against staring at others in public. People in crowds typically "keep their eyes to themselves."

Is there any way to show that this is a factor in bystander apathy?

To test this idea, students were asked to fill out a questionnaire either alone or in a room full of people. While the students worked, a thick cloud of smoke was blown into the room through a vent.

Most students left alone in the room noticed the smoke immediately. Few of the people in groups noticed the smoke

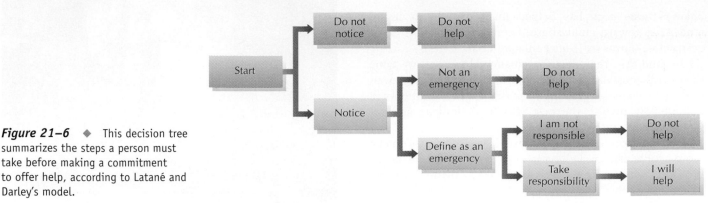

Figure 21–6 ◆ This decision tree summarizes the steps a person must take before making a commitment to offer help, according to Latané and Darley's model.

until it actually became difficult to see through it. Subjects working in groups politely kept their eyes on their papers and avoided looking at others (or the smoke). In contrast, those who were alone scanned the room from time to time.

Defining an Emergency   The smoke-filled room also shows the influence others have on defining a situation as an emergency. When subjects in groups finally noticed the smoke, they cast sidelong glances at others in the room. Apparently, they were searching for clues to help interpret what was happening. No one wanted to overreact or act like a fool if there was no emergency. However, as subjects coolly surveyed the reactions of others, they were themselves being watched. In real emergencies, people sometimes underestimate the need for action because each person attempts to appear calm. In short, until someone acts, no one acts.

Taking Responsibility   Perhaps the most crucial step in the helping sequence is assuming responsibility. In this case, groups limit helping by causing a **diffusion of responsibility** (*spreading responsibility among several people*).

Is that like the unwillingness of drivers to offer help on a crowded freeway?

Exactly. It is the feeling that no one is personally responsible for helping. This problem was demonstrated in an experiment in which students took part in a group discussion over an intercom system. Actually, there was only one real subject in each group; the others were tape-recorded actors. Each subject was placed in a separate room (supposedly to maintain confidentiality), and discussions of college life were begun. During the discussion, one of the "students" simulated an epileptic-like seizure and called out for help. In some cases, subjects thought they were alone with the seizure victim. Others believed they were members of 3- or 6-person groups.

Subjects who thought they were alone with the "victim" of this staged emergency reported it immediately or tried to help. Some subjects in the 3-person groups failed to respond, and those who did were slower. In the 6-person groups, over a third of the subjects took no action at all. People in this experiment were obviously faced with a conflict like that in many real emergencies: Should they be helpful and respon-

sible, or should they mind their own business? Many were influenced toward inaction by the presence of others.

People do help in some emergencies. How are these different?

It is not always clear what makes the difference. Helping behavior is complex and influenced by many variables. One naturalistic experiment staged in a New York City subway gives a hint of the kinds of things that may be important. When a "victim" (actor) "passed out" in a subway car, he received more help when carrying a cane than when carrying a liquor bottle. More important, however, was the fact that most people were willing to help in either case (Piliavin et al., 1969).

To better answer the question we need to consider some factors not included in Latané and Darley's account of helping.

Who Will Help Whom?

Many studies suggest that when we see a person in trouble, it tends to cause *heightened arousal* (Dovido, 1984). This aroused, keyed-up feeling can motivate us to give aid, but only if the rewards of helping outweigh the costs. Higher costs (such as great effort, personal risk, or possible embarrassment) almost always decrease helping (Foss, 1986). In addition to general arousal, potential helpers may also feel **empathic arousal.** *This means they empathize with the person in need or feel some of the person's pain, fear, or anguish.* Helping is much more likely when we are able to take the perspective of others and feel sympathy for their plight (Eisenberg, 1991).

If people feel sad or distressed when another person is in trouble, couldn't it be that they help just to make themselves feel better?

It is certainly possible that some helping is actually "selfish." But research has shown that empathy (empathic arousal) really does unleash altruistic motivation based on sympathy and compassion. Most helping, including such altruistic acts as making donations or being kind, is motivated by a true desire to relieve the distress of others (Dovido, Allen, & Schroeder, 1990).

Empathic arousal is especially likely to motivate helping

when the person in need seems to be similar to ourselves (Eisenberg & Miller, 1987). In fact, a feeling of connection to the victim may be one of the most important factors in helping. This, perhaps, is why being in a good mood also increases helping. When we are feeling successful, happy, or fortunate, we may also feel more connected to others (Dovido, 1984). In summary, there is a strong **empathy-helping relationship:** *We are most likely to help someone in need when we "feel for" that person and experience emotions such as empathy, sympathy, and compassion* (Batson, 1990).

Is there anything that can be done to encourage prosocial behavior?

People who see others helping are more likely to offer help themselves. As you may recall from Chapter 2, for example, motorists were much more likely to stop to help a woman fix a tire when they had just passed another woman being helped by someone (Bryan & Test, 1967). Also, persons who give help in one situation tend to perceive themselves as helpful people. This change in self-image encourages them to help in other situations. One more point is that norms of fairness encourage us to help others who have helped us (Dovido, 1984). For all these reasons, helping others not only assists them directly, it encourages others to help too.

"De-victimize" Yourself If you should find yourself in need of help during an emergency, what can you do to avoid being a victim of bystander apathy? The work we have reviewed here suggests that you should make sure that you are noticed, that people realize there's an emergency, and that they need to take action. Being noticed can be promoted in some situations by shouting "Fire!" Bystanders who might run away from a robbery or an assault may rush to see where the fire is. At the very least, remember not to just scream. Instead, you should call out "Help," or "I need help right now." Whenever possible, define your situation for bystanders. Say, for instance, "I'm being attacked, call the police." Or, "Stop that man, he has my purse." You can also directly assign responsibility to a bystander by pointing to someone and saying, "You, call the police" or "I'm injured, I need you to call an ambulance" (Cummins, 1995).

A Look Ahead The Applications for this chapter returns to the topic of prejudice for some further thoughts about how to promote tolerance. Sociobiology, which is discussed in the Exploration section, is a controversial theory that relates social behavior to heredity and evolution. Don't miss this interesting conclusion to our discussion of social psychology.

Learning Check

1. Social stereotypes may be both positive and negative. T or F?

2. The stereotypes underlying racial and ethnic prejudice tend to evolve from the superordinate goals that often separate groups. T or F?

3. The term *symbolic prejudice* refers to racism or prejudice that is expressed in disguised or hidden form. T or F?

4. Jane Elliot's classroom experiment in prejudice showed that children could be made to dislike one another
   a. by setting up group competition **b.** by imposing status inequalities **c.** by role-playing
   d. by frustrating all the students

5. Research suggests that prejudice and intergroup conflict may be reduced by _____ interaction and _____ goals.

6. Social learning theorists view aggression as related to biological instincts for aggression. T or F?

7. Frustration is more likely to produce aggression when cues for aggressive behavior are present. T or F?

8. Social learning theory holds that exposure to aggressive models helps drain off aggressive energies. T or F?

9. Defining an event as an emergency is the first step toward bystander intervention. T or F?

10. Seeing that a person in need is similar to ourselves tends to increase empathic arousal and the likelihood that help will be given. T or F?

Critical Thinking

11. Cognitive dissonance theory predicts that equal-status contact should help reduce prejudice. Can you explain how?

Answers:

1. T 2. F 3. T 4. b 5. equal-status, superordinate 6. F 7. T 8. F 9. F 10. T 11. A prejudiced person who has positive contacts with out-group members will experience dissonance as that person's prejudiced beliefs clash with his or her actual behavior and experiences. One way to reduce this dissonance is to change the prejudiced attitudes.

*J*erry, who is Japanese American, is married to an Irish Catholic American. Here is what Jerry, his wife, and children did on New Year's Day:

> We woke up in the morning and went to Mass at St. Brigid's, which has a black gospel choir. . . . Then we went to the Japanese-American Community Center for the Oshogatsu New Year's program and saw Buddhist archers shoot arrows to ward off evil spirits for the year. Next, we ate traditional rice cakes as part of the New Year's service and listened to a young Japanese-American storyteller. On the way home, we stopped in Chinatown and after that we ate Mexican food at a taco stand. (Adapted from Njeri, 1991)

Jerry and his family reflect a new social reality: Cultural diversity is becoming the norm. By the year 2000 about one third of the population in the United States will be African American, Latino, Asian American, and Native American. In some large cities "minority" groups are already the majority. By 2056 the "average" U.S. resident will no longer trace his or her roots to Europe (U.S. Bureau of the Census, 1995).

Multiculturalism   Today's society is more like a "tossed salad" than a cultural "melting pot." Rather than expecting everyone to be alike, psychologists believe that we must learn to respect and appreciate our differences. **Multiculturalism,** as this is called, *gives equal status to different ethnic, racial, and cultural groups. It is a recognition and acceptance of human diversity* (Fowers & Richardson, 1996).

Breaking the Prejudice Habit

Most people publicly support policies of equality and fairness. Yet, many still have lingering biases and negative images of blacks, Latinos, Asians, and other racial and ethnic minorities. How can we make sense of such conflicting attitudes? Patricia Devine, a social psychologist, has shown that a decision to forsake prejudice does not immediately eliminate prejudiced thoughts and feelings. Non-prejudiced people may continue to respond emotionally to members of other racial or ethnic groups. Quite likely this reflects lingering stereotypes and prejudices learned in childhood (Devine et al., 1991).

Devine's work gives insight into how prejudice reduction takes place. For many people the process begins with sincerely accepting values of tolerance and equality. Persons who count tolerance as an important personal value feel pangs of guilt, conscience, or self-criticism when they have intolerant thoughts or feelings (Zuwerink, et al., 1996). This motivates them to try to alter their own biased reactions. But doing so is not easy. Typically, it requires repeated efforts to learn to think, feel, and act differently. Fully overcoming the "prejudice habit" can be challenging. Nevertheless, many people are succeeding (Devine et al., 1991). If you would like to be more tolerant, the following points may be helpful to you.

Beware of Stereotyping

Stereotypes make the social world more manageable. But placing people in categories almost always causes them to appear more similar than they really are. As a result, we tend to see out-group members as very much alike, even when they are as varied as our friends and family.

Patricia Devine found that both prejudiced and non-prejudiced persons are equally aware of stereotypes. Non-prejudiced persons, however, work hard to actively inhibit stereotyped thoughts and to emphasize fairness and equality (Devine, 1990). A good way to tear down stereotypes is to get to know individuals from various racial, ethnic, and cultural groups.

Seek Individuating Information   When are we most tempted to apply stereotypes? Typically it is when we only have minimal information about a person. Stereotypes help us guess what a person is like and how she or he will act. Unfortunately, these inferences are usually wrong.

One of the best antidotes for stereotypes is **individuating information** (*information that helps us see a person as an individual, rather than as a member of a group*) (Click, Zion, & Nelson, 1988). Anything that keeps us from placing a person in a particular social category tends to negate stereotyped thinking. When you meet individuals from various backgrounds, focus on the *person*, not the *label* attached to her or him.

A good example of the effects of individuating information comes from a study in Canada of English-speaking students in a French language program. Students who were "immersed" (spent most of their waking hours with French Canadians) became more positive toward them. Immersed students were more likely to say they had come to appreciate and like French Canadians; they were more willing to meet and interact with them; and they saw themselves as less different from French Canadians (Lambert, 1987).

Don't Fall Prey to Just-World Beliefs   Do you believe that the world is basically fair? Even if you don't, you may believe that the world is sufficiently just so that people generally get what they deserve. It may not be obvious, but beliefs of this sort can directly increase prejudiced thinking.

As a result of discrimination, social conditions, and circumstances (such as recent immigration), minorities may occupy lower socio-economic positions. **Just-world beliefs** (*belief that people generally get what they deserve*) can lead us to assume that minority group members wouldn't be in such positions if they weren't inferior in some way. This bit of faulty thinking amounts to blaming people who are *victims* of prejudice and discrimination for their plight.

Be Aware of Self-Fulfilling Prophecies   You may recall from Chapter 2 that people tend to act in accordance with the behavior expected by others. If you hold strong stereotypes about members of various groups, a vicious cycle can be set up. When you meet someone who is different from yourself, you may treat her or him in a way that is consistent with your stereotypes. If the other person is influenced by your behavior, she or he may act in ways that seem to match your stereotype. This creates a *self-fulfilling prophecy* and reinforces your belief in the stereotype. (A **self-fulfilling prophecy** *is an expectation that prompts people to act in ways that make the expectation come true.*)

Remember, Different Does Not Mean Inferior   Some conflicts between groups cannot be avoided. What *can* be avoided is unnecessary **social competition** (*rivalry among groups, each of which regards itself as superior to others*). The concept of social competition refers to the fact that some individuals seek to enhance their self-esteem by identifying with a group. However, this works only if the group can be seen as superior to others. Because of social competition, groups tend to view themselves as better than their rivals (Baron & Byrne, 1994). In a recent survey, every major ethnic group in the United States rated itself as better than any other group (Njeri, 1991). This is a little like the fabled town of Lake Woebegone, where all the children are above average.

A person who has high self-esteem does not need to treat others as inferior in order to feel good about himself or herself. Similarly, it is not necessary to degrade other groups in order to feel positive about one's own group identity (Messick & Mackie, 1989).

Look for Commonalities   We live in a society that puts a premium on competition and individual effort. One problem with this is that competing with others fosters desires to demean, defeat, and vanquish them. When we cooperate with others we tend to share their joys and suffer when they are in distress (Lanzetta & Englis, 1989). If you feel that you have nothing in common with people whose backgrounds are very different from your own, remember this: If we don't find ways to cooperate and live in greater harmony, everyone will suffer. That, if nothing else, is one thing that we all have in common.

Everyone knows what it feels like to be different. Greater tolerance comes from remembering those times.

Cultural Awareness

Living comfortably in a multicultural society means getting to know a little about other groups. Getting acquainted with a person whose cultural background is different from your own can be a wonderful learning experience. No one culture has all the answers or the best ways of doing things. Multicultural populations enrich a community's food, music, arts, and philosophy. Likewise, learning about different racial, cultural, and ethnic groups can be personally rewarding.

The importance of cultural awareness often lies in subtleties and details. For example, in large American cities, many small stores are owned by Korean immigrants. Some of these Korean-American merchants have been criticized for being cold and hostile to their customers. Refusing to place change directly in customers' hands, for instance, helped trigger an African-American boycott of Korean grocers in New York City. The core of the problem was a lack of cultural awareness on both sides.

In America, if you walk into a store, you expect the clerk to be courteous to you. One way of showing politeness is by smiling. But in the Confucian-steeped Korean culture, a smile is reserved for family members and close friends. If a Korean or Korean American has no reason to smile, he or she just doesn't smile. There's a Korean saying: "If you smile a lot, you're silly." Expressions such as "thank you" and "excuse me" are also used sparingly and strangers rarely touch each other—not even to return change.

Here's another example of how ignorance of cultural practices can lead to needless friction and misunderstanding: An African-American woman who wanted to ease racial tensions took a freshly baked pie to her neighbors across the way, who were Orthodox Jews. At the front door the woman extended her hand, not knowing that Orthodox Jews don't shake women's hands, unless the woman is a close family member. Once she was inside, she picked up a kitchen knife to cut the pie, not knowing the couple kept a kosher household and used different knives for different foods. The woman's well-intentioned attempt at neighborliness ended in an argument! Knowing a little more about each other's cultures could have prevented both of the conflicts just described.

Learning Check

1. Multiculturalism refers to the belief that various subcultures and ethnic groups should be blended into a single emergent culture. T or F?

2. Patricia Devine found that many people who hold non-prejudiced beliefs still have prejudiced thoughts and feelings in the presence of minority group individuals. T or F?

3. Individuating information tends to be a good antidote for stereotypes. T or F?

4. Just-world beliefs are the primary cause of social competition. T or F?

Critical Thinking

5. Why is it valuable to learn the terms by which members of various groups prefer to be addressed (for example, Mexican-American, Latino [or Latina], Hispanic, or Chicano [Chicana])?.

Answers:

1. F 2. T 3. T 4. F 5. Because labels might have negative meanings that are not apparent to persons outside the group. People who are culturally aware allow others to define their own identities, rather than imposing labels on them.

Exploration

Sociobiology—Do Genes Guide Social Behavior?

A small band of men moves cautiously through a rubble-strewn battlefield. Without warning, a grenade sails overhead and lands at their feet. There is no time for escape. Instinctively, one of the men dives at the grenade, covers it with his own body, and shields his comrades from certain death. Scenes such as this have occurred in almost every modern war. How are such altruistic actions explained?

Sociobiology   According to a viewpoint called **sociobiology,** *many human social behaviors have roots in heredity.* Sociobiology is a more extreme form of evolutionary psychology, discussed briefly in Chapter 20. Sociobiologists, such as Harvard zoologist Edward Wilson, believe that competition, war, territoriality, aggression, sibling rivalry, conformity, male-female differences, fear of strangers, altruism, and many other behaviors are "in our genes."

The core idea in sociobiology is that social behavior evolves in ways that maximize fitness for survival. For instance, animals who compete successfully for food, territory, mates, and so forth, are more likely to survive and reproduce. Thus, competitiveness gradually becomes an inborn trait. Sociobiologists believe that many human traits evolved through similar patterns of natural selection.

Applying the concept of natural selection to explain human nature may make sense for some behaviors. But how do sociobiologists explain altruistic actions like the selfless heroism of the soldier described earlier? The answer is intriguing. Sociobiologists point out that altruistic suicides can be observed in many animal species. For example, if a honeybee stings an intruder to protect its hive, the bee will die. How could such behavior evolve if altruistic bees never get a chance to reproduce and pass on their genes? Sociobiologists reply that altruistic actions help im-

prove chances that an animal's *kin* will survive.

Each individual shares some genes in common with close family members. So, while the altruistic individual's genes may not be passed on directly, they are perpetuated by close kin. In human terms, sociobiologists argue that a person might sacrifice his or her own chance of survival to ensure the survival of several close relatives. Of course, heroic soldiers are typically unrelated to their comrades. Nevertheless, a soldier may act for the good of the group because altruism was "bred into" humans during eons of evolution.

Biological Determinism Sociobiology deserves credit for offering a fresh perspective on human behavior. In fact, sociobiology produces some fascinating images when it is taken to its logical extremes: It is almost as if genes are at the helms of great hulking machines (our bodies) that they use for protection and self-preservation. Sociobiology seems to say that genes manipulate our behavior to ensure *their* survival (or at least the survival of duplicate genes in the bodies of our relatives).

Sociobiology's major strength is that it helps relate human behavior to biology. Its major weakness is that it probably overstates its case. The degree of biological determinism assumed by sociobiologists is so extreme that even most biologists question it.

Critique Thinking about the biological foundations of human behavior is always interesting. However, the conclusions drawn by sociobiologists are highly questionable (Lerner & von Eye, 1992). Evolution and natural selection, for instance, may have favored development of the human brain, rather than of specific behavioral traits. Humans equipped with large brains are resourceful, adaptable, and flexible. Intelligence,

in fact, would seem to have much more to do with our survival than strict genetic programming does. Likewise, development during each person's own lifetime provides a powerful explanation for most behavior patterns (Lerner & von Eye, 1992).

Critics of sociobiology point out that evolution progresses too slowly to account for many behavioral adaptations. The spread of ideas, traditions, and cultural patterns is much more rapid. To return to our earlier example, altruism may indeed be a necessity for a society to endure. However, selfless acts need not be coded into our nature by genes; they may be explained equally well by learning.

The danger inherent in sociobiology is that it can be used to support the social status quo. By defining human nature as relatively fixed and (in the short run) unchanging, sociobiology discourages attempts to change current

cultural practices. Edward Wilson has said, for instance, that since males are typically more aggressive than females, "Even with identical education and equal access to all professions, men are more likely to continue to play a disproportionate role in political life, business, and science." If you are a female, that should make you angry. If you are a male, it should make you angry on behalf of your mother, sisters, daughters, wife, lover, or female friends.

Conclusion In the realm of ideas it's also a matter of survival of the fittest. To many observers it appears that sociobiology will have to evolve greatly if it is going to survive. In the meantime, the sociobiology debate should prove interesting. (Sources: Blaustein, 1983; Gould, 1976; Kamin, 1985; Kitcher, 1985; Lerner & von Eye, 1992; Lumsden & Wilson, 1983; Snowdon, 1983; Wilson, 1975)

Learning Check

1. The core idea of sociobiology is that social behavior evolved in ways that maximize individual fitness for survival. T or F?

2. Sociobiologists believe that altruistic behavior evolved because individual sacrifice can improve chances that immediate family members and close kin will survive. T or F?

3. The majority of biologists endorse sociobiological explanations of behavior. T or F?

4. Critics of sociobiology point out that natural selection among humans might have favored enlargement of the brain and behavioral flexibility—not selection of specific behavioral traits. T or F?

Critical Thinking

5. Sociobiology is highly controversial because it takes an extreme position in an age-old debate that also applies to human development, intelligence, and personality. What is the debate and what is sociobiology's position?

Answers:

1. F 2. T 3. F 4. T 5. The nature-nurture debate. Sociobiology places an extreme emphasis on nature (inborn behavioral tendencies).

Chapter Summary

What are attitudes? How are they acquired?

◆ **Attitudes** are learned dispositions made up of a **belief component,** an **emotional component,** and an **action component.**

◆ Attitudes may be formed by *direct contact, interaction* with others, *child-rearing practices,* and *group pressures. Peer group influences,* the *mass media,* and *chance conditioning* also appear to be important in attitude formation.

How are attitudes measured and changed?

◆ Attitudes are typically measured by use of techniques such as **open-ended interviews, social distance scales,** and **attitude scales.** Attitudes expressed in these ways do not always correspond to actual behavior.

◆ Attitude change is related to **reference group** membership, to *deliberate* **persuasion,** and to significant personal experiences (which may be engineered through *role-playing*).

Under what conditions is persuasion most effective?

◆ Effective persuasion occurs when characteristics of the **communicator,** the **message,** and the **audience** are well matched. In general, a likable and believable communicator who repeats a credible message that arouses emotion in the audience and states clear-cut conclusions will be persuasive.

What is cognitive dissonance? What does it have to do with attitudes and behavior?

◆ The maintenance and change of attitudes is closely related to needs for consistency in thoughts and actions. **Cognitive dissonance theory** explains the dynamics of such needs.

◆ Cognitive dissonance occurs when there is a clash between thoughts or between thoughts and actions. The amount of reward or justification for one's actions influences whether dissonance occurs. We are motivated to reduce dissonance when it occurs, often by changing beliefs or attitudes.

Is brainwashing actually possible? How are people converted to cult membership?

◆ **Brainwashing** is a form of forced attitude change. It depends on control of the target person's total environment. Three steps in brainwashing are **unfreezing, changing,** and **refreezing** attitudes and beliefs.

◆ Many cults recruit new members with high-pressure indoctrination techniques resembling brainwashing. Such groups attempt to catch people when they are vulnerable. Then they combine *isolation,* displays of *affection, discipline and rituals, intimidation,* and *escalating commitment* to bring about conversion.

What causes prejudice and intergroup conflict? What can be done about these problems?

◆ **Prejudice** is a negative attitude held toward members of various out-groups. One theory attributes prejudice to **scapegoating.** A second account says that prejudices may be held for personal reasons (**personal prejudice**) or simply through adherence to group norms (**group prejudice**).

◆ Prejudiced individuals tend to have an **authoritarian** or **dogmatic personality,** characterized by rigidity, inhibition, intolerance, over-simplification, and **ethnocentrism.**

◆ Intergroup conflict gives rise to hostility and the formation of **social stereotypes. Status inequalities** tend to build prejudice. **Equal-status contact** tends to reduce it.

◆ Psychologists have emphasized the concept of **superordinate goals** as a key to reducing intergroup conflict, be it racial, religious, ethnic, or national. On a smaller scale, **jigsaw classrooms** (which encourage cooperation through **mutual interdependence**) have been shown to be an effective way of combating prejudice.

How do psychologists explain human aggression?

◆ **Aggression** and violence are serious social problems and the subject of much current research. **Ethological explanations** of aggression attribute it to inherited instincts. **Biological explanations** emphasize brain mechanisms and physical factors related to thresholds for aggression.

◆ According to the **frustration-aggression hypothesis,** frustration and aggression are closely linked. Frustration is only one of many **aversive stimuli** that can arouse a person and make aggression more likely. Aggression is especially likely to occur when **aggression cues** are present.

◆ **Social learning theory** has focused attention on the role of **aggressive models** in the development of aggressive behavior.

Why are bystanders so often unwilling to help in an emergency?

◆ Four decision points that must be passed before a person gives help are: **noticing, defining** an emergency, **taking responsibility,** and **selecting** a course of action. Helping is less likely at each point when other potential helpers are present.

◆ Helping is encouraged by general arousal, **empathic arousal,** being in a good mood, low effort or risk, and perceived similarity between the victim and the helper.

For several reasons, giving help tends to encourage others to help too.

What can be done to lower prejudice and promote social harmony?

◆ **Multiculturalism** is an attempt to give equal status to different ethnic, racial, and cultural groups.
◆ Greater tolerance can be encouraged by neutralizing stereotypes with **individuating information;** by looking for **commonalities** with others; and by avoiding the effects of **just-world beliefs, self-fulfilling prophecies,** and **social competition.**

◆ **Cultural awareness** is a key element in promoting greater social harmony.

How does the theory of sociobiology try to explain social behavior?

◆ **Sociobiology** attempts to explain human social behavior by relating it to natural selection and human evolution. Although some elements of the theory are difficult to defend, sociobiology has prompted a healthy debate about the biological origins of human behavior.

22

Applied Psychology

Preview

The Towering Inferno

Alarmed, you sniff the air. "Is that smoke?," you say to yourself. "Yes, something's definitely burning!" You throw open your hotel room door. Outside, a thick black cloud fills the hallway. Somewhere in the choking haze you hear a voice shout "Fire!" "Oh my," you think, "I'm on the 22nd floor. I'd better find the elevator—fast." At that instant you hear the following:

> *Female voice:* "May I have your attention, please. May I have your attention, please."
> *Male voice:* "There has been a fire reported on the 20th floor. While this report is being verified, the building manager would like you to proceed to the stairways and walk down to the 18th floor. Please do not use the elevators, as they may be needed. Please do not use the elevators, but proceed to the stairways." (Loftus, 1979)

All too often, fires in high-rise buildings lead to needless deaths. Using the elevators, for instance, can be fatal. During a fire, they act as chimneys for smoke and poisonous fumes.

In the confusion following a fire alarm, many people ignore posted instructions for safe escape. To remedy the situation, psychologists Jack Keating and Elizabeth Loftus created an unusual, life-saving "fire alarm." The best alarm, they found, is a *voice* that tells people exactly what to do, like the message reproduced above.

As simple as the message seems, it contains certain key elements: (1) Research has shown that switching from a female to a male voice (or the reverse) is very *attention getting;* (2) during emergencies, people like to feel that some *authority* is in control (the "building manager" in this case); (3) the crucial reminder to avoid the elevators is *repeated,* so it will be remembered.

Applied psychology *refers to the use of psychological principles and research methods to solve practical problems.* Escaping from fires may be a dramatic example of applying psychology, but it is far from unusual. The largest applied areas are clinical and counseling psychology. But there are many others. In fields as diverse as business, education, sports, law, and the environment, psychology is being applied to our lives. Let's see how.

Chapter Survey

Theme: Psychology can be used to solve practical problems in a variety of settings.

Key Questions:	Key Topics to Watch for:
How is psychology applied in business and industry?	Industrial/organizational psychology Personnel psychology Theories of management
What have psychologists learned about the effects of our physical and social environments?	Environmental psychology Stressful environments Environmental problem solving
How has psychology improved education?	Educational psychology
What does psychology reveal about juries and court verdicts?	Law and psychology Jury behavior, jury selection
Can psychology enhance athletic performance?	Sports psychology Motor skills and peak performance
What can be done to improve communication at work?	Effective communication Being a good listener
How is psychology being applied in space missions?	Space psychology Designing space habitats

Industrial/Organizational Psychology—Psychology at Work

Do you consider work a blessing? Or a curse? Or do you simply agree that it is "better to wear out than to rust out"? Whatever your attitude, the simple fact is that most adults work for a living.

Industrial/organizational psychologists *study the behavior of people at work and in organizations.* Very likely, their efforts will affect how you are selected for a job and tested, trained, or evaluated for promotion. Most I/O psychologists are employed by government, industry, and businesses. Typically, they work in two major areas. These are (1) testing and placement (personnel psychology) and (2) human relations at work. To get a fuller flavor of what I/O psychologists do, look at Table 22–1 ■. As you can see, their interests are quite varied. As a further illustration, our first highlight gives an interesting sample of I/O research.

Table 22-1 ■ Topics of Special Interest to Industrial/Organizational Psychologists

Absenteeism	Pay schedules
Decision making	Personnel selection
Design of organizations	Personnel training
Employee stress	Productivity
Employee turnover	Promotion
Interviewing	Task analysis
Job enrichment	Task design
Job satisfaction	Work behavior
Labor relations	Work environment
Machine design	Worker evaluations
Management styles	Work motivation
Minority workers	

Using Psychology

Flexitime

If you've ever worked "9 to 5," you know that traditional time schedules can be confining. They also doom many workers to a daily battle with rush-hour traffic. To improve worker morale, industrial psychologists sometimes recommend the use of **flexitime,** *or flexible working hours.* The basic idea of flexitime is that starting and quitting times are flexible, as long as employees are present during a core work period (Owen, 1976). For example, employees might be allowed to arrive between 7:30 A.M. and 10:30 A.M. and depart between 3:30 P.M. and 6:30 P.M.

Is flexitime really an improvement? Studies of two groups of clerical workers suggest that in many cases it is. After a switch to flexitime, workers experienced more job satisfaction, better work-group relations, better relations with supervisors, and less absenteeism (Narayan & Nath, 1982; Orpen, 1981). Perhaps it is better, when possible, to bend hours instead of people.

Figure 22–1 ◆ Analyzing complex skills has also been valuable to the U.S. Air Force. When million-dollar aircraft and the lives of pilots are at stake, it makes good sense to do as much training and research as possible on the ground. Air Force psychologists use flight simulators like the one pictured here to analyze the complex skills needed to fly jet fighters. Skills can then be taught without risk on the ground. The General Electric simulator shown here uses a computer to generate full-color images that respond realistically to a pilot's use of the controls. (Photograph supplied courtesy of General Electric Company.)

Personnel Psychology

The mark of maturity, Sigmund Freud said, is a capacity for love and work. While most people gladly embrace love, many would just as soon forget work. Yet the fact is, employed adults spend an average of over 2,000 hours a year at their jobs. With so much time at stake, understanding the world of work is clearly a "survival skill."

At present, the odds are 9 out of 10 that you are, or will be, employed in business or industry. Thus, nearly everyone who holds a job is sooner or later placed under the "psychological microscope" of personnel selection. **Personnel psychology** *is concerned with testing, selection, placement, and promotion of employees.* Clearly, there is value in knowing how selection for hiring and promotion is done.

How do personnel psychologists make employee selections?

Job Analysis Personnel selection begins with **job analysis,** *a detailed description of the skills, knowledge, and activities required by a particular job* (Borman et al., 1997). A job analysis may be done by interviewing expert workers or supervisors, by giving them questionnaires, by directly observing work, or by identifying *critical incidents.* **Critical incidents** *are situations with which competent employees must be able to cope.* The ability to deal calmly with a mechanical emergency, for example, is a critical incident for airline pilots. Once job requirements are known, psychologists can state what skills, aptitudes, and interests are needed (Fig. 22–1 ◆).

Selection Procedures After desirable skills and traits are identified, the next step is to learn which job applicants have them. Today, the methods most often used for evaluating job candidates include collecting *biodata,* conducting *interviews,* giving *standardized psychological tests,* and the *assessment center* approach. Let's see what each entails.

As simple as it may seem, one good way to predict job success is to collect **biodata** (*detailed biographical information*) from applicants. The idea behind biodata is that looking at past behavior is a good way to predict future behavior. By learning in detail about a person's life, it is often possible to say whether the person is suited for a particular type of work. Some of the most useful items of biodata include past athletic interests, academic achievements, scientific interests, extracurricular activities, religious activities, social popularity, friction with brothers and sisters, attitudes toward school, and parents' socioeconomic status (Eberhardt & Muchinsky, 1982). Such facts tell quite a lot about personality, interests, and abilities. In addition to earlier experiences, a person's recent life activities also help predict job success (Schmidt, Ones, & Hunter, 1992).

The traditional personal interview is still one of the most popular ways to select people for jobs or promotions. A **personal interview** *involves questioning job applicants to learn their qualifications and to gain an impression of their personalities* (Borman et al., 1997).

As we discussed in Chapter 16, interviews are subject to the *halo effect* and similar problems. (Recall that the **halo effect** *is the tendency of interviewers to extend favorable or unfavorable impressions to unrelated aspects of an individual's personality.*) That's why psychologists continue to study interviews, with an eye on improving their accuracy (see the next highlight). Nevertheless, even with their limitations, interviews are a valid and effective way of predicting how people will perform on the job (Landy et al., 1994).

A Closer Look

The Sweet Smell of Success? Not Always.

Each year, clothing and cosmetics manufacturers spend huge sums to convince us that their products make us more attractive. Actually, such claims are somewhat justified. You might recall from Chapter 16, for instance, that physically attractive people are often given more positive evaluations in interviews—even on traits that have no connection with appearance. Presumably, this might also apply to the effects of wearing a pleasant perfume or cologne. But does it? In an interesting study, *female* interviewers did, in fact, give higher ratings to job applicants who wore pleasant scents. But *males*, in contrast, gave *lower* ratings to persons who wore perfume or cologne (Baron, 1983).

Psychologist Robert Baron, who did this experiment, speculates that the male interviewers were more aware of the scents and resented the implied attempt to influence their ratings. Whatever the case, one thing is clear: If possible, you should learn an interviewer's sex beforehand—if you want to avoid making a flagrant, fragrant error, that is.

In general, a direct effort to make a good impression—such as emphasizing your positive traits and past successes—is most effective in interviews (Gilmore & Ferris, 1989). However, beware of blatant self-promotion. Excessively "blowing your own horn" tends to lower interviewers' perceptions of competence and suitability for a job (Howard & Ferris, 1996).

What kinds of tests do personnel psychologists use?

In addition to general intelligence and personality tests (described in Chapters 12 and 16), personnel psychologists often use **vocational interest tests.** *These paper-and-pencil tests assess a person's interests and match them to interests found among successful workers in various occupations.* Tests such as the *Kuder Occupational Interest Survey* and the *Strong-Campbell Interest Inventory* probe interests with items like the following:

I would prefer to
a. visit a museum
b. read a good book
c. take a walk outdoors

Table 22–2	Vocational Interest Themes	
Theme	Sample College Major	Sample Occupation
Realistic	Agriculture	Mechanic
Investigative	Physics	Chemist
Artistic	Music	Writer
Social	Education	Counselor
Enterprising	Business	Sales
Conventional	Economics	Clerk

Holland, 1985; Snow, 1986.

Interest inventories typically reflect the six major themes shown in Table 22–2 ■. If you take an interest test and your choices match those of people in a given occupation, it is assumed that you, too, would be comfortable doing the work they do.

Aptitude tests are another mainstay of personnel psychology. *Such tests rate a person's potential to learn tasks or skills used in various occupations.* Tests exist for clerical, verbal, mechanical, artistic, legal, and medical aptitudes, plus many others. For example, tests of clerical aptitude emphasize the capacity to do rapid, precise, and accurate office work. One section of a clerical aptitude test might therefore ask a person to mark all identical numbers and names in a long list of pairs like those shown here.

49837266	49832766
Global Widgets, Inc.	Global Wigets, Inc.
874583725	874583725
Sevanden Corp.	Sevanden Corp.
B/C Publishing	B/C Puhlishing

Paper-and-pencil tests sometimes seem far removed from the day-to-day challenges of work. In recent years, psychologists have tried to make employment testing more interesting and relevant. For example, personnel psychologists are developing **multi-media computerized tests.** *These tests use computers to present realistic work situations*—in living color and stereo sound. As potential employees watch typical work scenes unfold, the action freezes on various problems. The applicant is then asked what she or he would do in that situation. In addition to screening job applicants, multi-media presentations can be used to improve the job skills of current employees. It won't be long before multi-media tests are widely used (Landy et al., 1994).

After college, chances are good that you will encounter an *assessment center.* **Assessment centers** *are set up by many large organizations to do in-depth evaluations of job candidates.*

Aptitude tests are used to select job candidates and to advise people about what types of work they are likely to be good at.

This approach has become so popular that the list of businesses using it—Ford, IBM, Kodak, Exxon, Sears, AT&T, and thousands of others—reads like a corporate *Who's Who*.

How do assessment centers differ from the selection methods already described?

Assessment centers are primarily used to fill management and executive positions. First, applicants are tested and interviewed. Then they are observed and evaluated in simulated work situations. For example, in one exercise applicants are given an **in-basket test** *that simulates the decision-making challenges executives face.* The test consists of a basket full of memos, requests, and typical business problems. Each applicant is asked to quickly read all of the materials and to take appropriate action. In another, more stressful test, applicants take part in a **leaderless group discussion.** *This is a test of leadership that simulates group decision making and problem solving.* While the group grapples with a realistic business problem, "clerks" bring in price changes, notices about delayed supplies, and so forth. By observing applicants, it is possible to evaluate leadership skills and to see how job candidates cope with stress.

How well does this approach work?

Assessment centers have had considerable success in predicting performance in a variety of jobs, careers, and advanced positions (Landy et al., 1994). One study of women, for instance, found that assessment center predictions of management potential were closely related to career progress 7 years later (Ritchie & Moses, 1983). On the basis of long-range studies, it appears that future success is most clearly predicted by oral communication skills, leadership, energy, resistance to stress, tolerance for uncertainty, need for advancement, and planning skills (Ritchie & Moses, 1983).

As you will soon learn, psychologists working in business do far more than match people with jobs. Let's see how they contribute to management and the quality of work.

Theories of Management

At 7 A.M. each morning at a major manufacturing plant, more than 400 assembly line workers, supervisors, and top executives begin their day talking, joking, and exercising together, all to the beat of amplified music. To say the least, these are unusual working conditions. To understand the rationale behind them, let's consider two basic theories of employee management.

Theory X and Theory Y One of the earliest attempts to improve worker efficiency was made in 1923 by Frederick Taylor, an engineer. To speed up production, Taylor standardized work routines and stressed careful planning, control, and orderliness. Today, modern versions of Taylor's approach are called *scientific management* (also known as

Theory X, for reasons explained shortly). **Scientific management** *uses time-and-motion studies, task analysis, job specialization, assembly lines, pay schedules, and the like to increase productivity.*

It sounds like scientific management treats people as if they were machines. Is that true?

To some extent it is. Managers who follow Theory X tend to assume that workers must be goaded or guided into being productive. Many psychologists working in business, of course, are concerned with improving **work efficiency** (*defined as maximum output at lowest cost*). As a result, they alter conditions they believe will affect workers (such as time schedules, work quotas, bonuses, and so on). Some might even occasionally wish that people would act like well-oiled machines. However, most recognize that *psychological efficiency* is just as important as work efficiency. **Psychological efficiency** *refers to maintaining good morale, labor relations, employee satisfaction, and similar aspects of work behavior.* Management styles that ignore or mishandle the human element can be devastatingly costly.

The term *Theory X* was coined by psychologist Douglas McGregor (1960) as a way to distinguish scientific management from a newer management style. McGregor dubbed this newer approach, which emphasizes human relations at work, *Theory Y.*

How is this approach different?

Theory Y *managers assume that workers enjoy autonomy and are willing to accept responsibility.* They also assume that worker needs and goals can be meshed with the company's goals, and that people are not naturally passive or lazy. In short, Theory Y assumes that people are industrious, creative, and rewarded by challenging work. It appears that given the proper conditions of freedom and responsibility, many people *will* work hard to gain competence and use their talents.

Many features of Theory Y are illustrated by the Honda plant at Marysville, Ohio. As you may already know, the automobile industry has a long history of labor-management clashes and worker discontent. In fact, outright sabotage by assembly line workers is not uncommon. To avoid such problems, Honda initiated a series of simple, seemingly successful measures. They include the following practices.

- Regardless of their position, all employees wear identical white uniforms. This allows workers and supervisors to interact on a more equal footing and builds feelings of teamwork.

- To further minimize status differences, all employees hold the title *associate.*

- Private offices, separate dining halls, and reserved parking spaces for executives were abolished.

- Employees work alongside company executives, to whom they have easy access.

- Every employee has a say in, and responsibility for, quality control and safety.

- Departmental meetings are held daily. At this time, announcements are discussed, decisions are made, and thoughts are freely shared (Abrams, 1983).

Management Strategies   Two elements that make Theory Y methods effective are *participative management* and *management by objectives*. In **participative management,** *employees at all levels are directly involved in decision making.* By taking part in decisions that affect them, employees like those at the Honda factory come to see work as a cooperative effort—not as something imposed on them by an egotistical boss. The benefits include greater productivity, more involvement in work, greater job satisfaction, and less job-related stress (Coye & Belohlav, 1995; Jackson, 1983).

What does "management by objectives" refer to?

In **management by objectives,** *workers are given specific goals to meet,* so they can tell if they are doing a good job. Typical objectives include reaching a certain sales total, making a certain number of items, or reducing waste by a specific percentage. In any case, workers are free to choose (within limits) how they will achieve their goals. As a result, they feel more independent and take personal responsibility for their work.

Recently, many companies have begun to give *groups* of workers greater freedom and responsibility as well. This is typically done by creating self-managed teams. A **self-managed team** *is a group of employees who work together toward shared goals.* Self-managed teams can typically choose their own methods of achieving results, as long as they are effective. Self-managed teams tend to make good use of the strengths and talents of individual employees. They also promote new ideas and improve motivation. Most of all, they encourage cooperation and teamwork within organizations (Lewis, Goodman, & Fandt, 1995).

How can workers below the management level be involved more in their work? One popular answer is the use of **quality circles.** *These are voluntary discussion groups that seek ways to solve business problems and improve efficiency* (Jewell, 1990). In contrast to self-managed teams, quality circles usually do not have the power to put their suggestions into practice directly. But good ideas speak for themselves and many are adopted by management. Quality circles have many limitations. Nevertheless, studies verify that greater personal involvement can lead to better performance and job satisfaction (Buch & Spangler, 1990; Geehr et al., 1995).

Job Satisfaction

It often makes perfect sense to apply Theory X methods to work. However, doing so without taking worker needs into account can be a case of winning the battle while losing the war. That is, immediate productivity may be enhanced while job satisfaction is lowered. And when job satisfaction is low, absenteeism skyrockets, morale falls, and there is a high rate of employee turnover (leading to higher training costs and inefficiency). Understandably, many of the methods used by enlightened Theory Y managers ultimately improve **job satisfaction,** *or the degree to which a person is pleased with his or her work.*

Under what conditions is job satisfaction highest?

Basically, job satisfaction comes from a good fit between work and a person's interests, abilities, needs, and expectations. What, then, do workers consider important? In the early 1970s, American workers were asked to rate the importance of 25 aspects of work. Their first eight choices were as follows (*Work in America*, 1973):

1. Interesting work
2. Enough help and equipment to get the job done

Participative management techniques encourage employees at all levels to become involved in decision making. Quite often this arrangement leads to greater job satisfaction.

3. Enough information to get the job done

4. Enough authority to get the job done

5. Good pay

6. Opportunity to develop special abilities

7. Job security

8. Seeing the results of one's work

A second survey in the early 1980s again found that satisfying, rewarding work ranked first in worker preference. However, high income rose to second place (Weaver & Matthews, 1987). Some observers worry that a swing toward greater materialism has occurred in the last 10 to 15 years. Even if this is true, intrinsically interesting work still tops the list. To summarize much research, we can say that job satisfaction is highest when workers are (1) allowed ordinary social contacts with others; (2) given opportunities to use their own judgment and intelligence; (3) recognized for doing well; (4) given a chance to apply their skills; (5) given relative freedom from close supervision; and (6) given opportunities for promotion and advancement. Understandably, the most productive employees are those who are happy at work (Staw et al., 1994).

Job Enrichment For years, the trend in business and industry was to make work more streamlined and efficient and to tie better pay to better work. There is now ample evidence that incentives such as bonuses, earned time off, and profit sharing can increase productivity (Horn, 1987). However, in recent years far too many jobs have become routine, repetitive, boring, and unfulfilling. To combat the discontent this can breed, many psychologists recommend a strategy called *job enrichment.*

Job enrichment *involves making a job more personally rewarding, interesting, or intrinsically motivating.* Job enrichment has been used with great success by large corporations such as IBM, Maytag, Western Electric, Chrysler, and Polaroid. It usually leads to lower production costs, increased job satisfaction, reduced boredom, and less absenteeism (Lewis, Goodman, & Fandt, 1995).

How is job enrichment done?

Job enrichment applies many of the principles we have discussed. Usually it involves removing some of the controls and restrictions on employees, giving them greater freedom, choice, and authority. In some cases, employees also switch to doing a complete cycle of work. That is, they complete an entire item or project, instead of doing an isolated part of a larger process. Whenever possible, workers are given feedback about their work or progress. This feedback comes to them directly, instead of to a supervisor.

Merely assigning a person more tasks is usually not enriching. Overloaded workers just feel stressed and they tend to make more errors. True job enrichment increases workers' *knowledge.* That is, workers are encouraged to learn a broad range of skills and information related to their occupations (Campion & McClelland, 1993). In short, most people seem to enjoy being good at what they do.

Although we have only scratched the surface of industrial/organizational psychology, it is time to move on for a look at another applied area of great personal relevance. Before we begin, here's a Learning Check on the preceding discussion.

Learning Check	**Critical Thinking**

1. To gain attention for an emergency announcement, it is better to switch from a male voice to a female voice than it is to do the reverse. T or F?

2. Identifying critical work incidents is sometimes included in a thorough _____ _____ .

3. Detailed biographical information about a job applicant is referred to as _____ .

4. The Strong-Campbell Inventory is a typical aptitude test. T or F?

5. A leaderless group discussion is most closely associated with which approach to employee selection?
   a. aptitude testing   b. personal interviews   c. job analysis   d. assessment center

6. Theory X, or scientific management, is concerned primarily with improving _____ _____ .

7. Participative management is often a feature of businesses that adhere to Theory Y. T or F?

8. For the majority of workers, job satisfaction is almost exclusively related to the amount of pay received. T or F?

9. Job enrichment is a direct expression of scientific management principles. T or F?

10. Job enrichment basically increases what type of motivation?

Answers:
1. F 2. job analysis 3. biodata 4. F 5. d 6. work efficiency 7. T 8. F 9. F 10. Intrinsic motivation.

Environmental Psychology—Life in the Big City

If cities were drivers, some would get lots of speeding tickets. Others would spend most of their time in the slow lane, watching the scenery go by. Informally, you may have noticed that the pace of life varies from city to city. Psychologist Robert Levine and his students decided to measure the overall tempo of 36 American cities to see how they compare.

To rate a city's pace, Levine looked at four indicators: walking speed, working speed, talking speed, and the percentage of men and women wearing watches. The results? The three fastest American cities were Boston, Buffalo, and New York—all in the Northeast. The three slowest cities were in the South and West: Shreveport, Sacramento, and Los Angeles. No surprises here. But Levine's other findings are surprising. Levine and his team also found that there is a correlation between the pace of life and heart disease. Just as there are Type A personalities (heart attack-prone personalities; see Chapter 14), there also seem to be Type A cities. Very likely, Type A people are attracted to fast-paced Type A cities—where they then do their best to keep the pace (Levine, 1990).

The work of Robert Levine, and psychologists like him, falls into an area known as **environmental psychology,** *a specialty concerned with the relationship between environments and human behavior* (Stokols, 1995). Environmental psychologists are interested in both **physical environments** (*natural or constructed*) and **social environments** (*defined by groups of people, such as a dance, business meeting, or party*)

Various behavioral settings place strong demands on people to act in expected ways.

Table 22–3 ■ Topics of Special Interest to Environmental Psychologists	
Architectural design	Personal space
Behavioral settings	Personality and
Cognitive maps	environment
Constructed environments	Pollution
Crowding	Privacy
Energy conservation	Proxemics
Environmental stressors	Resource
Heat	management
Human ecology	Territoriality
Littering	Urban planning
Natural environment	Vandalism
Noise	

(Gifford, 1987). They also give special attention to **behavioral settings** (*smaller areas within an environment whose use is well defined, such as an office, locker room, church, casino, or classroom*) (Schoggen, 1989). As you have no doubt noticed, various environments and behavioral settings tend to "demand" certain actions. Consider, for example, the difference between a library and a campus center lounge. In which would a conversation be more likely to occur?

Other major interests of environmental psychologists are personal space, territorial behavior (discussed in the next highlight), stressful environments, architectural design, environmental protection, and many related topics (Table 22–3 ■).

A Closer Look

Territoriality

In Chapter 20 we noted that powerful norms govern the use of the space immediately surrounding each person's body. As we move farther from the body, it becomes apparent that personal space also extends to adjacent areas that we claim as our "territory." **Territorial behavior** *refers to actions that define a space as one's own or that protect it from intruders.* For example, in the library, you might protect your space with a coat, handbag, book, or other personal belonging. "Saving a place" at a theater or a beach also demonstrates the tendency to identify a space as "ours."

Respect for the temporary ownership of space is widespread. It is not unusual for a person to "take over" an entire table or study room by looking annoyed when others intrude. Your own personal territory may include your room, specific seats in many of your classes, or a particular table in the cafeteria or library that "belongs" to you and your friends.

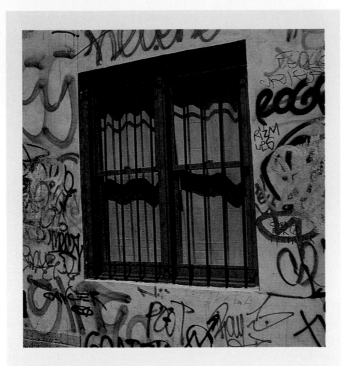

Graffiti, one of the blights of urban life, is an obvious form of territorial marking.

Researchers have found that the more attached you are to an area, the more likely you are to adorn it with obvious **territorial markers** *that signal your "ownership."* Typical markers include decorations, plants, photographs, or posters. College dorms and business offices are prime places to observe this type of territorial marking. Interestingly, burglars are less likely to break into houses that have lots of obvious territorial cues, such as fences (even if small), parked cars, lawn furniture, exterior lights, and security signs (Brown & Bentley, 1993). (A highly territorial bulldog may help, too.)

Environmental Influences A major finding of environmental research is that much of our behavior is controlled, in part, by specific types of environments (Gifford, 1987). For example, many shopping malls and department stores are designed like mazes. Their twisting pathways encourage shoppers to linger and wander while looking at merchandise. Likewise, many college classrooms clearly define a speaker-audience relationship. Discussion among students tends to be discouraged by seats that are bolted to the floor, facing an authority at the front of the room (Wong, Somer, & Cook, 1992). Even public bathrooms influence behavior. Since the seating is limited, few people hold meetings there!

Psychologists have also found that a variety of environmental factors influence the amount of vandalism that occurs in public places. On the basis of psychological research, many architects now "harden" and "de-opportunize" public settings to discourage vandalism and graffiti (Wise, 1982).

Some such efforts limit opportunities for vandalism (doorless toilet stalls, tiled walls). Others weaken the lure of likely targets. (Strangely enough, a raised flower bed around signs helps protect them because people resist trampling the flowers to get to the sign.)

Given the personal impact that environments have, it is important to know how we are affected by stressful or unhealthy environments—a topic we will consider next.

Stressful Environments

Everyone has his or her own list of complaints about large cities. Traffic congestion, pollution, crime, and impersonality are urban problems that immediately come to mind. To this list psychologists have added crowding, noise, and over-stimulation as major sources of urban stress. Psychological research has begun to clarify the impact of each of these conditions on human functioning.

Crowding Over-population ranks as one of the most serious problems facing the world today. The world's population is now over 5.5 billion. World population doubled in the period from 1950 to 1987. It will double again in the next 39 years (Erlich & Erlich, 1990) (Fig. 22–2 ◆). Each day, the world population grows by 250,000 (a quarter of a million) people (United Nations Population Fund, 1993).

Experts estimate that the maximum sustainable population of the Earth is between 5 billion and 20 billion persons. What this means is that the Earth has already entered the lower range of its carrying capacity (Cohen, 1996). Further population increases at the present rate could be disastrous. How many more people can the forests, oceans, croplands, and atmosphere support? The most pessimistic experts believe we have *already* exceeded the number of people the Earth can sustain indefinitely (Oskamp, 1995a).

Nowhere are the effects of over-population more evident than in the teeming cities of many under-developed nations. Closer to home, the jammed buses, subways, and living quarters of our own large cities are ample testimony to the stresses of crowding.

Is there any way to assess the effect crowding has on people?

One approach is to study the effects of overcrowding among animals. Although the results of animal experiments cannot be considered conclusive for humans, they point to some disturbing effects.

For example?

In an interesting experiment, John Calhoun (1962) let a group of laboratory rats breed without limit in a confined space. Calhoun provided plenty of food, water, and nesting material for the rats. All that the rats lacked was space. At its peak, the colony numbered 80 rats. Yet, it was housed in a cage designed to comfortably hold about 50. Overcrowding in the cage was heightened by the actions of the two most

Figure 22–2 ◆ Population growth has slowed slightly in recent years, but world population still threatens to double again in less than 40 years (graph source: Population Institute). Over-population and rapid population growth are closely connected with environmental damage, international tensions, and rapid depletion of non-renewable resources. Some demographers predict that if population growth is not limited voluntarily before it reaches 10 billion, it will be limited by widespread food shortages, disease, infant mortality, and early death (Erlich & Erlich, 1990).

dominant males. These rascals staked out private territory at opposite ends of the cage, gathered harems of 8 to 10 females, and prospered. Their actions forced the remaining rats into a small, severely crowded middle area.

What effect did crowding have on the animals?

A high rate of pathological behavior developed in both males and females. Females gave up nest building and caring for their young. Pregnancies decreased, and infant mortality ran extremely high. Many of the animals became indiscriminately aggressive and went on rampaging attacks against others. Abnormal sexual behavior was rampant, with some animals displaying hypersexuality and others total sexual passivity. Many of the animals died, apparently from stress-caused diseases. The link between these problems and overcrowding is unmistakable.

But does that apply to humans?

Many of the same pathological behaviors can be observed in crowded inner-city ghettos. It is therefore tempting to assume that violence, social disorganization, and declining birthrates as seen in these areas are directly related to crowding. However, the connection has not been so clearly demonstrated with humans. People living in the inner city suffer disadvantages in nutrition, education, income, and health care. These, more than crowding, may deserve the blame. In fact, most laboratory studies using human subjects have failed to produce any serious ill effects by crowding people into small places. Most likely, this is because *crowding* is a psychological condition that is separate from **density** (*the number of people in a given space*).

How does crowding differ from density?

Crowding *refers to subjective feelings of being over-stimulated by social inputs or a loss of privacy*. Whether high density is experienced as crowding may depend on relationships among those involved. In an elevator, subway, or prison, high

densities may be uncomfortable. In contrast, a musical concert, party, or reunion may be most pleasant at high density levels. Thus, physical crowding may interact with situations to intensify existing stresses or pleasures. When crowding causes a *loss of control* over one's immediate social environment, however, stress is likely to result (Fuller et al., 1996; Lepore, Evans, & Schneider, 1992).

Stress probably explains why death rates increase among prison inmates and mental hospital patients who live in crowded conditions. Even milder instances of crowding can

Woodstock '94. High densities do not automatically produce feelings of crowding. The nature of the situation and the relationship between crowd members are also important.

As the late Carl Sagan once said, "When you look closely, you find so many things going wrong with the environment, you are forced to reassess the hypothesis of intelligent life on Earth."

have a negative impact. People who live in crowded conditions often become guarded and withdrawn from others (Evans & Lepore, 1993).

Overload One unmistakable result of high densities and crowding is a state that psychologist Stanley Milgram called **attentional overload.** *This is a stressful condition that occurs when sensory stimulation, information, and social contacts make excessive demands on attention.* Large cities, in particular, tend to bombard residents with continuous input. The resulting sensory and cognitive overload can be quite stressful. The following highlight describes an added dimension of this sensory assault.

A Closer Look

The High Cost of Noise

How serious are the effects of daily exposure to noise? A study of children attending schools near Los Angeles International Airport suggests that constant noise can be quite damaging. Children from the noisy schools were compared with similar students attending schools farther from the airport (Cohen et al., 1981). These comparison students were from families of comparable social and economic makeup. Testing showed that children attending the noisy schools had higher blood pressure than those from the quieter schools. They were more likely to give up attempts to solve a difficult puzzle. And they were poorer at proofreading a printed paragraph—a task that requires close attention and concentration.

The greater tendency of the noisy-school children

to give up or become distracted is a serious handicap. It may even reveal a state of "learned helplessness" (described in Chapter 14) caused by daily, uncontrollable blasts of sound. Even if such damage proves to be temporary, it is clear that **noise pollution** (*annoying and intrusive noise*) is a major source of environmental stress. Other researchers have linked noise with impaired learning ability, less tolerance for frustration, and a reduced willingness to help others (Staples, 1996).

Milgram (1970) believed that city dwellers learn to prevent attentional overload by engaging only in brief, superficial social contacts, by ignoring non-essential events, and by fending off others with cold and unfriendly expressions. In short, many city dwellers find that a degree of callousness is essential for survival.

Is there any evidence that such strategies are actually adopted?

A fascinating study suggests they are. In several large American cities and smaller nearby towns, a young child stood on a busy street corner and asked passing strangers for help, saying, "I'm lost. Can you call my house?" About 72 percent of those approached in small towns offered to help. Only about 46 percent of those who were asked for help in the cities gave aid. In some cities (Boston and Philadelphia) only about one third were willing to help (Takooshian et al., 1977). An analysis of 65 studies confirmed that country people are more likely to help than city people (Steblay, 1987). Thus, a blunting of sensitivity to the needs of others may be one of the more serious costs of urban stresses and crowding.

Toxic Environments Human activities drastically change the natural environment. We burn fossil fuels, destroy forests, use chemical products, strip, clear, and farm the land. In doing so, we alter natural cycles, animal populations, and the very face of the Earth. The long-range impact of such activities is already becoming evident through global warming, the extinction of plants and animals, a hole in the ozone layer, and polluted land, air, water, and oceans (McKenzie-Mohr & Oskamp, 1995).

On a smaller scale there is plenty of evidence that unchecked environmental damage will be costly to our children and descendants. For example, studies show that exposure to toxic hazards, such as radiation, pesticides, and industrial chemicals leads to an elevated risk of physical and mental disease (Baum & Fleming, 1993).

How can people be encouraged to help preserve the environment? Research has shown that it is best to combine several strategies. Persuasion and education can be used to get individuals and businesses to voluntarily reduce activities that damage the environment. Effective appeals may be based on self-interest (cost savings), the collective good (protecting one's own children and future generations), or

People tend to have prolonged emotional responses to technological disasters. Long after an accidental release of radioactivity by the Three Mile Island Nuclear Power Plant, nearby residents continued to feel stressed and apprehensive (Baum & Fleming, 1993).

simply a personal desire to take better care of the planet. Changing the consequences of wasteful energy use, polluting, and the like can also alter behavior. For example, energy taxes can be used to increase the cost of using fossil fuels; rebates can be offered for installing insulation or buying energy-efficient appliances; and tax breaks can be given to companies that take steps to preserve the environment (Dwyer et al., 1993; Kempton, Darley, & Stern, 1992).

Environmental Problem Solving

While overcrowding and pollution rank high on the list of environmental stresses, they are only two of the many challenges that press for attention. To conclude, let's sample some of the solutions that psychologists have provided for environmental problems.

Problem The way people think about the environment greatly affects their behavior. Mental "maps" of various areas, for instance, often guide actions and alter decisions. A case in point is a study done in Philadelphia. There, researchers found that an existing school bus route contributed to truancy. The problem was that many of its stops were at corners where children were afraid of being attacked and beaten (Conyne & Clack, 1981).

Solution By doing an **environmental assessment,** *psychologists develop a picture of environments as they are perceived*

by the people using them. An assessment often includes such things as charting areas of highest use in buildings, using attitude scales to measure reactions to various settings (such as schools, businesses, and parks) and even having people draw a version of their cognitive map of a building, campus, or city (Coulton et al., 1996).

In the case of the school children, residents of the neighborhood were asked to rate how much stress they felt when walking in various areas. The result was a contour map (somewhat like a high- and low-pressure weather map) that showed the areas of highest perceived stress. This "stress map" was then used to reroute school buses to "low-pressure" areas.

Problem Anyone who has ever lived in a college dorm knows that at times a dorm hall can be quite a "zoo." Most architects aim to create buildings in which people will be comfortable, happy, and healthy. But sometimes they miss the mark with human behavior. In one well-known experiment, Baum and Valins (1977) found that students housed in long, narrow, corridor-design dormitories often feel crowded and stressed. The crowded students tended to withdraw from others and even made more trips to the campus health center than students living in less crowded buildings.

Solution **Architectural psychology** *is the study of the effects buildings have on behavior.* By analyzing buildings, psychologists are often able to suggest design changes that solve or avoid problems. For example, Baum and Valins (1979) studied two basic dorm arrangements. One dorm had a long corridor with one central bathroom. As a result, residents were constantly forced into contact with one another. The other dorm had rooms clustered in threes. Each of these suites shared a small bathroom. Even though the amount of space available to each student was the same in both dorms, students in the long-corridor dorm reported feeling more crowded. They also made fewer friends in their dorm and showed greater signs of withdrawing from social contact.

What sort of solution does this suggest?

A later study showed that small architectural changes can greatly reduce stress in high-density living conditions. Baum and Davis (1980) compared students living in a long-corridor dorm housing 40 students to those living in an altered long-corridor dorm. In the altered dorm, Baum and Davis divided the hallway in half with unlocked doors and made three center bedrooms into a lounge area (Fig. 22–3 ◆). At the end of the term, students living in the divided dorm reported less stress from crowding. They also formed more friendships and were more open to social contacts. In comparison, students in the long-corridor dorm felt more crowded, stressed, and unfriendly, and they kept their doors shut much more frequently—presumably because they "vahnted to be alone." Similar improvements have been made by altering the interior design of businesses, schools,

(a)   (b)

☐ Bedroom   ☐ Bathroom   ☐ Lounge

Figure 22–3 ◆ An architectural solution for crowding. Psychologists divided a dorm hall like that shown in the left diagram **(a)** into two shorter halls separated by unlocked doors and a lounge area **(b)**. This simple change minimized unwanted social contacts and greatly reduced feelings of crowding among dorm residents. (Adapted from Baum & Davis, 1980.)

apartment buildings, mental hospitals, and prisons. In general, the more spaces one must pass through to get from one part of a building to another, the less stressed and crowded people feel (Evans et al., 1996).

Problem The rapid worldwide consumption of natural resources is one of the most devastating of all social problems. Industrialized nations, in particular, are consuming world resources at an alarming rate. The United

Shown here are the Skeen family of Pearland, Texas, and the Yadev family of Ahraura, India. Each was photographed by the Material World Project, which documented typical families and their possessions around the world. Developed countries presently consume the largest share of world resources. However, population growth is fastest in developing countries and their hunger for material possessions is rapidly expanding. Achieving sustainable levels of population and consumption are two of the greatest challenges of the coming century. (From *Material World,* Sierra Club Books, 1994.)

States and Canada, for instance, have a little over 5 percent of the world's population. Yet we consume 25 to 30 percent of all the fossil fuels and raw materials used annually. The typical resident of Vancouver, Chicago, or Miami consumes 10 to 1000 times more resources each day than the average resident of Chile, Ghana, or Zaire (Cohen, 1996). In the face of projected shortages and squandered resources, what can be done to encourage conservation on a personal level?

Solution Try as you might to reduce your use of energy (electricity, for instance), you would probably find it difficult to do. A major problem is that *feedback* about energy use (the monthly bill) arrives long after the temptation to turn up the heat or to leave lights on (see Chapter 9). Psychologists aware of this problem have shown that lower energy bills result from simply giving families daily feedback about their use of gas or electricity.

Programs that give monetary rewards for energy conservation are even more effective. This is especially true for "master-metered" apartment complexes. In such apartments, families do not receive individual bills for their utilities. Consequently, they have no reason to save gas and electricity. Often, they consume about 25 percent more energy than they would in an individually metered apartment (McClelland & Cook, 1980). At this rate of waste, apartment owners can split any savings (from reduced consumption) with their tenants—and still be ahead. Similar factors can greatly increase recycling, as described in the next feature.

People are much more likely to recycle if proper attention is given to psychological factors that promote recycling behavior.

Using Psychology

Reduce, Reuse, Recycle

What can be done to lighten the environmental impact of our "throw-away" society? As we have discussed, reducing consumption is a start. Personally reusing products and materials that would normally be thrown away is also important. In addition, we can recycle materials such as paper, steel, glass, aluminum, and plastic that can be used to make new products. What can be done to encourage people to recycle? Psychological research has shown that all of the following strategies promote recycling (Oskamp, 1995b).

Provide monetary rewards. As mentioned before, monetary rewards encourage conservation. Requiring refundable deposits on glass bottles is a good example of using incentives to increase recycling.

Remove barriers. Anything that makes recycling more convenient helps. A good example is cities that offer curbside pickup of household recyclables. Some cities even accept unsorted recycling

materials, which greatly increases participation in recycling programs.

Use persuasion. Many recycling programs benefit from media campaigns to persuade people to participate.

Obtain public commitment. People who feel they have committed themselves to recycling are more likely to follow through and actually recycle. Sometimes, people are asked to sign "pledge cards" on which they promise to recycle. Another technique involves having people sign a list committing themselves to recycling. Such lists may or may not be published in a local newspaper. They are just as effective either way.

Encourage goal setting. People who set their own goals for recycling tend to meet them. Goal setting has been used successfully with families, dorms, neighborhoods, offices, factories, and so forth.

Give feedback. Again, feedback proves to be very valuable. Recycling typically increases when families, work groups, dorms, and the like are simply told, on a weekly basis, how much they recycled. Even impersonal feedback can be effective. In one study, signs were placed on recycling containers on a college campus. The signs showed how many aluminum cans had been deposited in the previous week. This simple procedure increased recycling by 65 percent (Larson et al., 1995).

Conclusion We have had room here only to hint at the creative and highly useful work being done in environmental psychology. While many environmental problems remain, it is encouraging to see that behavioral solutions exist for at least some of them. Surely, creating and maintaining healthy environments is one of the major challenges facing coming generations (Oskamp, 1995a).

We have discussed work and the environment at some length because both have major effects on our lives. To provide a fuller account of the diversity of applied psychology, let's conclude by briefly sampling three additional topics of interest: educational psychology, psychology and law, and sports psychology. But first, here's a Learning Check.

Learning Check	Critical Thinking

Learning Check

1. Although male rats in Calhoun's crowded animal colony became quite pathological, female rats continued to behave in a relatively normal fashion. T or F?

2. To clearly understand behavior, it is necessary to make a distinction between crowding and _____ (the number of people in a given space).

3. Milgram believed that many city dwellers prevent attentional overload by limiting themselves to superficial social contacts. T or F?

4. Performing an environmental _____ might be a good prelude to redesigning college classrooms to make them more comfortable and conducive to learning.

5. So far, the most successful approach for bringing about energy conservation is to add monetary penalties to monthly bills for excessive consumption. T or F?

Critical Thinking

6. Many of the most damaging changes to the environment being caused by humans will not be felt until sometime in the future. How does this complicate the problem of preserving environmental quality?

Answers:

1. F 2. density 3. T 4. assessment 5. F 6. A delay of consequences (rewards, benefits, costs, and punishers) tends to reduce their impact on immediate behavior.

Educational Psychology—An Instructive Topic

You have just been asked to teach a class of fourth-graders for a day. What will you do? (Assume that bribery, showing them films, and a field trip to a video arcade are out.) If you ever do try teaching, you might be surprised at how challenging it is. Effective teachers must understand learning, instruction, classroom dynamics, and testing.

What are the best ways to teach? Is there an optimal teaching style for different age groups, topics, or individuals? These and related questions lie at the heart of educational psychology (Table 22–4 ◆). Specifically, **educational psychology** *seeks to understand how people learn and how teachers instruct.*

Table 22–4 ■ Topics of Special Interest to Educational Psychologists	
Aptitude testing	Language learning
Classroom management	Learning theory
Classroom motivation	Moral development
Classroom organization	Student adjustment
Concept learning	Student attitudes
Curriculum development	Student needs
Disabled students	Teacher attitudes
Exceptional students	Teaching strategies
Gifted students	Teaching styles
Individualized instruction	Test writing
Intellectual development	Transfer of learning
Intelligence testing	

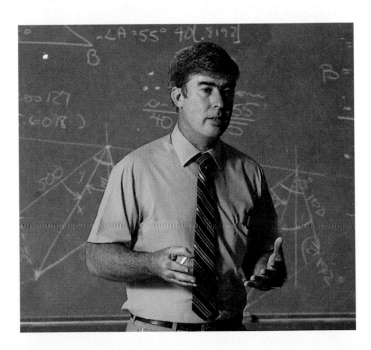

Educational psychologists are interested in enhancing learning and improving teaching.

Elements of a Teaching Strategy Whether it's "breaking in" a new co-worker, instructing a friend in a hobby, or helping a child learn to read, the fact is, we all teach at times. The next time you are asked to share your knowledge, how will you do it? One good way to become more effective is to use a specific **teaching strategy,** *or planned method of instruction.* The example that follows was designed for classroom use, but it applies to many other situations as well (Thornburg, 1984).

Step 1: Learner preparation. Begin by gaining the learner's attention, and focus interest on the topic at hand.

Step 2: Stimulus presentation. Present instructional stimuli (information, examples, and illustrations) deliberately and clearly.

Step 3: Learner response. Allow time for the learner to respond to the information presented (by repeating correct responses or asking questions, for example).

Step 4: Reinforcement. Give positive reinforcement (praise, encouragement) and feedback ("Yes, that's right," "No, this way," and so on) to strengthen correct responses.

Step 5: Evaluation. Test or assess the learner's progress so that both you and the learner can make adjustments when needed.

Step 6: Spaced review. Periodic review is an important step in teaching because it helps strengthen responses to key stimuli.

As a student, I've encountered many different teaching styles. Do different styles affect classroom learning?

Effects of Teaching Styles There is little doubt that teachers can greatly affect student interest, motivation, and creativity. But what styles have what effects? To answer this question, psychologists have compared a number of teaching styles. Two of the most basic are *direct instruction* and *open teaching.*

In **direct instruction,** *factual information is presented by lecture, demonstration, and rote practice.* In **open teaching,** *active teacher-student discussion is emphasized* (Peterson, 1979). And now, the winner: As it turns out, both approaches have certain advantages. Students of direct instruction do slightly better on achievement tests than students in open classrooms (Thornburg, 1984). However, students of open teaching do somewhat better on tests of abstract thinking, creativity, and problem solving. They also tend to be more independent, curious, and positive in their attitudes toward school (Peterson, 1979). At present, it looks as if a balance of teaching styles goes hand in hand with a balanced education.

Although we have viewed only a small sample of educational research, its value for improving teaching and learning should be apparent. Before we leave the topic of education, let's take a brief peek into the future.

Research Frontier

The School of the Future

What will schools of the future look like? Psychologist Wayne Holtzman offers an intriguing answer. Holtzman believes schools should enhance children's mental and physical health just as actively as they encourage learning the "three R's."

To explore the possibilities, Holtzman and his colleagues have created several "full-service" Schools of the Future. How are these schools different? First, they integrate a large array of health services and human services into the schools themselves. In conventional schools, children and families needing special help must travel all over town to get it. Many parents simply never make the effort or find the appropriate agencies. In the School of the Future, everything is available on campus. In this way, efforts to prevent mental health problems, drug abuse, school dropouts, teen pregnancy, and gang activity are made an integral part of each school.

A second major feature of the School of the Future is a very high level of teacher, parent, and community involvement. Parents, in particular, are encouraged to help set goals for the schools and to identify their children's needs. Many parents participate on campus as volunteers and they meet frequently with teachers to monitor their children's progress. In addition, the schools form links with neighborhood groups, churches, recreation programs, and volunteer organizations. As a result, the School of the Future becomes an active part of the surrounding community (Holtzman, 1997).

Ideally, schools of the future will enrich and enhance the lives of children in ways that traditional schools cannot. The School of the Future program has been highly successful in Texas. Perhaps it could be in other communities, too.

Psychology and Law— Judging Juries

One of the best places to see psychology in action is the local courthouse. Jury trials are often fascinating studies in human behavior. Does the defendant's appearance affect the jury's decision? Do the personality characteristics or attitudes of jurors influence how they vote? These and many more questions have been investigated by psychologists interested in law (Davis, 1989). Specifically, the **psychology of law** *is the study of the behavioral dimensions of the legal system* (see Table 22–5 ■).

Table 22-5 ■	Topics of Special Interest in the Psychology of Law
Arbitration	Juror attitudes
Attitudes toward law	Jury decisions
Bail setting	Jury selection
Capital punishment	Mediation
Conflict resolution	Memory
Criminal personality	Parole board decisions
Diversion programs	Police selection
Effects of parole	Police stress
Expert testimony	Police training
Eyewitness testimony	Polygraphy accuracy
Forensic hypnosis	Sentencing decisions
Insanity plea	White-collar crime

Jury Behavior

When a case goes to trial, jurors must listen to days or weeks of testimony and then decide guilt or innocence. How do they reach their decision? Psychologists use **mock juries** (*simulated juries*) to probe such questions. In some mock juries volunteers are simply given written evidence and arguments to read before making a decision. Others watch videotaped trials staged by actors. Either way, studying the behavior of mock juries helps us understand what determines how real jurors vote.

Some of the findings of jury research are unsettling. Studies show that jurors are rarely able to put aside their biases, attitudes, and values while making a decision (Watson et al., 1984). For example, jurors are less likely to find attractive defendants guilty (on the basis of the same evidence) than unattractive defendants (Perlman & Cozby, 1983). There is an interesting twist, however. If good looks helped a person commit a crime, it can work against her or him in court (Tedeschi et al., 1985). An example would be a handsome man accused of swindling money from an unmarried middle-aged woman.

A second major problem is that jurors are not very good at separating evidence from other information, such as their perceptions of the defendant, attorneys, witnesses, and what they think the judge wants. For example, if complex scientific evidence is presented, jurors tend to be swayed more by the expertise of the witness than by the evidence itself (Cooper et al., 1996).

Often, jurors' final verdict is influenced by inadmissible evidence, such as mention of a defendant's prior conviction. When jurors are told to ignore information that slips out in court, they find it very hard to do so. A related problem occurs when jurors take into account the severity of the punishment a defendant faces (Sales & Hafemeister, 1985). Jurors are not supposed to let this affect their verdict, but many do.

A fourth area of difficulty arises because jurors usually cannot suspend judgment until all the evidence is in. Typically, they form an opinion early in the trial. It then becomes hard for them to fairly judge evidence that contradicts their opinion.

Problems like these are troubling in a legal system that prides itself on fairness. However, all is not lost. The more severe the crime and the more clear-cut the evidence, the less a jury's quirks affect the verdict (Tedeschi et al., 1985). Although it is far from perfect, the jury system works reasonably well in most cases.

Jury Selection

Before a trial begins, opposing attorneys are allowed to disqualify potential jurors who may be biased. For example, a person who knows anyone connected with the trial can be excluded. Beyond this, attorneys try to use jury selection to remove people who may cause trouble for them. For instance, jurors who believe rape myths (that some women "ask for it" by their actions or style of dress, for example) are less likely to convict an accused rapist (Watson et al., 1984).

Only a limited number of potential jurors can be excused. As a result, many attorneys ask psychologists for help in identifying people who will favor or harm their efforts. In **scientific jury selection,** *social science principles are applied to the process of choosing a jury.* Several techniques are typically used. As a first step, *demographic information* may be collected

The behavior of juries and jurors has been extensively studied. The findings of such studies are applied by psychologists who act as advisors to attorneys during the jury selection process. Jury selection in the O. J. Simpson murder trial took two months, as defense and prosecution lawyers struggled for the advantage in jury makeup.

for each juror. Much can be guessed by knowing a juror's age, sex, race, occupation, education, political affiliation, religion, and socioeconomic status. Most of this information is available from public records.

To supplement demographic information, a *community survey* may be done to find out how local citizens feel about the case. The assumption is that jurors probably have attitudes similar to people with backgrounds like their own. Although talking with potential jurors outside the courtroom is not permitted, other information networks are available. For instance, a psychologist may interview relatives, acquaintances, neighbors, and co-workers of potential jurors.

Back in court, psychologists also often watch for *authoritarian personality* traits in potential jurors (see Chapter 21). Authoritarians tend to believe that punishment is effective, and they are more likely to vote for conviction (Narby et al., 1993). At the same time, the psychologist typically observes potential jurors' *non-verbal behavior*. The idea is to try to learn from body language which side the person favors (Sales & Hafemeister, 1985).

In the United States, murder trials require a special jury—one made up of people who are not opposed to the death penalty. The following highlight examines the implications of this practice.

Critical Thinking

Death-Qualified Juries

People in a **death-qualified jury** *must favor the death penalty or at least be indifferent to it.* That way, jurors are capable of voting for the death penalty if they think it is justified.

In order for the death penalty to have meaning, death-qualified juries may be a necessity. However, psychologists have discovered that the makeup of such juries tends to be biased. Specifically, death-qualified juries are likely to contain a disproportionate number of people who are male, white, high income, conservative, and authoritarian. Such juries are much more likely than average to convict a defendant (Haney et al., 1994; Narby et al., 1993).

Could death-qualified juries be too willing to convict? It is nearly impossible to say how often the bias inherent in death-qualified juries results in bad verdicts. However, the possibility that some innocent persons have been executed may be one of the inevitable costs of using death as the ultimate punishment.

Many of the techniques of scientific jury selection were used some years ago in the defense of automaker John DeLorean. As you may recall, DeLorean was charged with setting up a $25 million cocaine deal. Before the trial, DeLorean's attorneys had a national survey done to see if he would have a better chance if the trial were held away from Los Angeles. As it turned out, the public attitude was the same all over the country: Everyone thought DeLorean was guilty. (He was eventually acquitted.)

Cases like DeLorean's, the Menendez brothers', William Kennedy Smith's, and O. J. Simpson's raise troubling ethical questions. In each case, wealthy clients had the advantage of psychological jury selection—something most people cannot afford. Attorneys, of course, can't be blamed for trying to improve their odds of winning a case. And since both sides help select jurors, the net effect in most instances is probably a more balanced jury (Sales & Hafemeister, 1985). At its worst, jury analysis leads to unjust verdicts. At its best, it helps to identify and remove only people who would be highly biased.

Jury research is perhaps the most direct link between psychology and law, but there are others. Psychologists evaluate people for sanity hearings, do counseling in prisons, advise lawmakers on public policy, help select and train police cadets, and more (Sales & Hafemeister, 1985). In the future, it is quite likely that psychology will have a growing impact on law and the courts.

Sports Psychology— The Athletic Mind

What does psychology have to do with sports?

Sports psychology *is the study of the behavioral dimensions of sports performance.* As almost all serious athletes soon learn, peak performance requires more than physical training. Mental and emotional "conditioning" are also important. Recognizing this fact, many teams, both professional and amateur, now include psychologists on their staffs. On any given day, a sports psychologist might teach an athlete how to relax, how to ignore distractions, or how to cope with emotions. The sports psychologist might also provide personal counseling for performance-lowering stresses and conflicts (Neff, 1990). Other psychologists are interested in studying factors that affect athletic achievement, such as skill learning, the personality profiles of champion athletes, the effects of spectators, and related topics (Table 22–6 ■). In short, **sports psychologists** *seek to understand and improve sports performance and to enhance the benefits of participating in sports* (Williams, 1995).

Sports often provide valuable information on human behavior in general. For example, a study of Little League baseball found that children's self-esteem improved significantly after a season of play (Hawkins & Gruber, 1982). In other work, psychologists have learned that such benefits are most likely to occur when competition, rejection, criticism, and the "one-winner mentality" are minimized. When working with children in sports, it is also important to

Table 22–6 ■ Topics of Special Interest to Sports Psychologists	
Achievement motivation	Hypnosis
Athletic personality	Mental practice
Athletic task analysis	Motor learning
Coaching styles	Peak performance
Competition	Positive visualization
Control of attention	Self-regulation
Coping strategies	Skill acquisition
Emotions and performance	Social facilitation
Exercise and mental health	Stress reduction
Goal setting	Team cooperation
Group (team) dynamics	Training procedures

Before the advent of sports psychology, it was debatable whether athletes improved because of "homespun" coaching methods, or in spite of them. For example, in early studies of volleyball and gymnastics, it became clear that people teaching these sports had very little knowledge of crucial, underlying skills (Salmela, 1974, 1975).

How has psychology helped?

An ability to do detailed studies of complex skills has been one of the major contributions. In a **task analysis,** *sports skills are broken into subparts,* so that key elements can be identified and taught. Such methods are an extension of techniques first used for job analyses, as described earlier, and illustrated in the following highlight.

emphasize fair play, intrinsic rewards, self-control of emotions, independence, and self-reliance (Orlick, 1975).

Adults, of course, may also benefit from sports. For many, the payoffs are stress reduction, a better self-image, and improved general health. Researchers have reported, for instance, that running is associated with lower levels of tension, anxiety, fatigue, and depression than is found in the non-running population (Gondola & Tuckman, 1982).

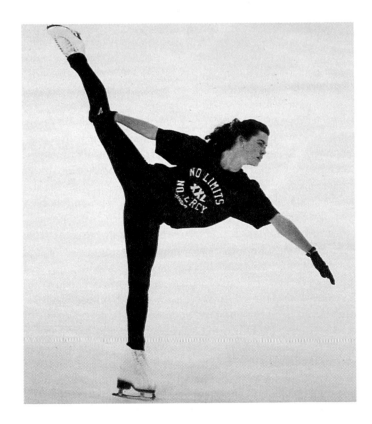

Sports psychologists have played a significant role in helping prepare athletes for peak performance in the Olympic Games. Stress management, attention regulation, mental imagery, motivation, self-confidence, and many other psychological factors greatly affect athletic performance.

Using Psychology

Taking the Pulse of a Bull's-Eye

It doesn't take much to be off-target in the Olympic sport of marksmanship. The object is to hit a bull's-eye the size of a dime at the end of a 165-foot-long shooting range. Nevertheless, an average of 50 bull's-eyes out of 60 shots is not unusual in international competition (prone position).

What does it take—beyond keen eyes and steady hands—to achieve such accuracy? The answer is surprising. Sports psychologists have found that top marksmen consistently squeeze the trigger *between* heartbeats (Fig. 22–4 ◆). Apparently the tiny tremor induced by a heartbeat is enough to send the shot astray (Pelton, 1983). Without careful psychological study, it is doubtful that this element of marksmanship would have been identified. Now that its importance is known, competitors have begun to use various techniques—from relaxation training to biofeedback—to steady and control their heartbeat. In the future, the best marksmen may be those who set their sights on mastering their hearts.

Motor Skills Sports psychologists are very interested in how we learn motor skills. A **motor skill** *is a series of actions molded into a smooth and efficient performance.* Typing, walking, pole-vaulting, shooting baskets, playing golf, driving a car, writing, and skiing are all motor skills.

A basketball player may never make exactly the same shot twice in a game. This makes it almost impossible to practice every shot that might occur. How, then, do athletes become skillful? Typically, athletic performances involve learning *motor programs.* A **motor program** *is a mental plan or model of what a skilled movement should be like.* Motor programs allow an athlete—or a person simply walking across a room—to perform complex movements that fit changing conditions. If, for example, you have learned a

Figure 22–4 ◆ The target on the top shows what happens when a marksman fires during the heart's contraction. Higher scores, as shown by the three shots on the bottom, are more likely when shots are made between heartbeats. (Adapted from Pelton, 1983.)

"bike-riding" motor program, you can easily ride bicycles of different sizes and types on a large variety of surfaces.

Throughout life you will face the challenge of learning new motor skills. How can psychology make your learning more effective? Studies of sports skills suggest that you should keep the following points in mind for optimal skill learning:

1. Begin by observing and imitating a *skilled model*. Modeling provides a good mental picture of the skill. At this point, try simply to grasp a visual image of the skilled movement.

2. Learn *verbal rules* to back up motor learning. Such rules

are usually most helpful in the early phases of skill learning. When first learning cross-country skiing, for example, it is helpful to say, "left arm, right foot, right arm, left foot." Later, as a skill becomes more automated, internal speech may actually get in the way.

3. Practice should be as *lifelike* as possible so that artificial cues and responses do not become a part of the skill. A competitive diver should practice on the board, not on a trampoline. If you want to learn to ski, try to practice on snow, not straw.

4. Get *feedback* from a mirror, videotape, coach, or observer. Whenever possible, get someone experienced in the skill to direct attention to *correct responses* when they occur.

5. When possible, it is better to practice *natural units* rather than breaking the task into artificial parts. When learning to type, it is better to start with real words rather than nonsense syllables.

6. Learn to *evaluate* and *analyze* your own performance. Remember, you are trying to learn a motor program, not just train your muscles. Motor skills are actually very mental.

The last point leads to one more suggestion. Research has shown that **mental practice,** *or merely imagining a skilled performance,* can aid learning (Hinshaw, 1991). This technique seems to help by refining motor programs. Of course, mental practice is not superior to actual practice. Mental practice tends to be most valuable after you have mastered a task at a basic level (Tenenbaum et al., 1996). When you begin to get really good at a skill, give mental practice a try. You may be surprised at how effective it can be.

Peak Performance One of the most interesting topics in sports psychology is the phenomenon of *peak performance*. During **peak performance,** *physical, mental, and emotional states are harmonious and optimal.* Many athletes report episodes during which they felt almost as if they were in a trance. The experience has also been called "flow" because the athlete becomes one with his or her performance and flows with it. At such times, athletes experience intense concentration, detachment, a lack of fatigue and pain, a subjective slowing of time, and feelings of unusual power and control (Browne & Mahoney, 1984). It is at just such times that "personal bests" tend to occur.

A curious aspect of flow is that it cannot be forced to happen. In fact, if a person stops to think about it, the flow state goes away. Psychologists are now seeking to identify conditions that facilitate peak performance and the unusual mental state that usually accompanies it.

Even though flow may be an elusive state, there is much that athletes can do mentally to improve performance. A starting point is to make sure that their *arousal level is appropriate for the task* at hand. For a sprinter at a track meet, that may mean elevating arousal to a very high level. The sprinter could, for example, try to become angry by picturing a rival cheating. For a golfer or a gymnast, lowering arousal may be crucial, in order to avoid "choking" during a big event. One way of controlling arousal is to go through a *fixed routine* before each game or event. Athletes also learn to use *imagery and relaxation techniques* to adjust their degree of arousal (Gould & Udry, 1994).

Imaging techniques can be used to *focus attention* on the athlete's task and to *mentally rehearse* it beforehand. For example, golf great Jack Nicklaus "watches a movie" in his head before each shot. During events, athletes learn to *use cognitive-behavioral strategies to guide their efforts* in a supportive, positive way (Beauchamp et al., 1996). For instance, instead of berating herself for being behind in a match, a tennis player could use the time between points to savor a good shot or put an error out of mind. In general, athletes benefit from avoiding negative, self-critical thoughts that distract them and undermine their confidence. Finally, top athletes tend to use more *self-regulation strategies*, in which they evaluate their performance and make adjustments to keep it at optimum levels (Anshel, 1995a; Kim et al., 1996).

At present, sports psychology is a very young field, and still much more an art than a science. Nevertheless, interest in the field is rapidly expanding (Petrie & Diehl, 1995).

A Look Ahead   Although we have sampled several major areas of applied psychology, they are by no means the only applied specialties. Others that immediately come to mind are community psychology, school psychology, military psychology, health psychology (discussed in Chapter 14) and space psychology (a skyrocketing field that is really looking up—see this chapter's Exploration). Before we explore the "final frontier," the upcoming Applications section returns to the work environment with some advice on how to be an effective communicator.

Learning Check

1. Evaluation of learning is typically the first step in a systematic teaching strategy. T or F?

2. Compared to direct instruction, open teaching produces better scores on achievement tests. T or F?

3. The School of the Future program created _____ schools with close links to the surrounding community. T or F?

4. Despite their many limitations, one thing that jurors are good at is setting aside inadmissible evidence. T or F?

5. Which of the following is *not* commonly used by psychologists to aid jury selection?
   a. mock testimony   **b.** information networks   **c.** community surveys
   d. demographic data

6. Mental models, called _____ _____ , appear to underlie well-learned motor skills.

7. Learning verbal rules to back up motor learning is usually most helpful in the early stages of acquiring a skill. T or F?

8. The flow experience is closely linked with instances of _____ performance.

Critical Thinking

9. When an athlete follows a set routine before an event, what source of stress has she or he eliminated?

Answers:

1. F 2. F 3. full-service 4. F 5. a 6. motor programs 7. T 8. peak 9. As discussed in Chapter 14, stress is reduced when a person feels in control of a situation. Following a routine helps athletes maintain a sense of order and control so that they are not overly aroused when the time comes to perform.

*J*ust a minute, I want to expand on the confusion. This is where I'm assuming we're just going to throw it up for air. I mean, let's tie all this up in loose ends.

The bottom line is we've got to round-file this puppy ASAP before it goes belly-up. Stan says we're talking mouth-breather here. Copy Monica, Steve, and the bean-counters with your input and let's circle the wagons in the A.M.

I was just, like, totally embarrassed, I mean, like abso-double-lutely, totally incinerated, you know? I mean, to the max. I'm all, "I'm just totally sorry, Mr. Thompson." And he's all, "If this is the way you do business, I'm not interested."

Each of the people just quoted probably intended to express his or her ideas clearly. As you can see, however, their efforts are less than a model of clarity.

Getting the Message Across Effective communication is crucial in many work settings. When communication is muddled, important messages may get lost. Feelings can be crushed. Trust may be damaged. Poor decisions are made. Almost always, group effectiveness is impaired.

Clearly, people who work together depend on good communication. Service-oriented work with customers, and ethno-cultural diversity in the work force also put a premium on communication skills. For such reasons, getting a job, keeping it, and excelling in your work all depend on knowing how to communicate clearly with others (Goldstein & Gilliam, 1990).

Effective Communication

To improve your communication skills, or to keep them sharp, remember the following points.

1. State your ideas clearly and decisively. News reporters learn to be precise about the "who, what, when, where, how, and why" of events. At work, the same list is a good guide when you are making a request, giving instructions, or answering a question. Rather than saying, "I need someone to give me a hand sometime with some stuff," it would be better to say, "Blake, would you please meet me in the storeroom in 5 minutes? I need help lifting a box." Notice that the second request answers all of these questions: Who? Blake. What? Could you help me? How? By lifting a box. When? In 5 minutes. Where? In the storeroom. Why? It takes two people.

As you speak, avoid overuse of ambiguous words and phrases ("wiggle words") such as *I guess, I think, kinda, sort of, around, some, about, you know,* and *like.* Here's an example: "Basically, I sort of feel like we should kinda pause. I mean, and, let's see, maybe reconsider, you know, rethink some of

this stuff." It would be better to say: "I believe we should revise our plans immediately." Ambiguous messages leave others in doubt as to your true thoughts and wishes.

Also try not to overuse intensifiers (*very, really, absolutely, extra, super, awesome, ultimate, completely,* and so on). Super extra frequent use of such awesome words really causes them to completely lose their ultimate effectiveness.

2. Eschew the meretricious utilization of polysyllabic locutions. (Don't overuse big words.) Overuse of obscure vocabulary is often a sign of insecurity. Big words may make you sound important, but they can also blur your message. Which of the following two statements is clearer? "Pulchritude possesses solely cutaneous profundity." Or, "Beauty is only skin deep"?

Trendy, overused "buzz words" or phrases should also be avoided. Often they are just a way of *sounding like* you are saying something: "Personally, I feel we've got to be more synergistically proactive and start networking in a programmatic fashion if we want to avoid being negatively impacted by future megatrends in the client-purveyor interface." Translation: "I don't have any worthwhile thoughts on the topic."

3. Avoid excessive use of jargon or slang. Most professions have their own specialized terminology. Here's an example of some printers' jargon: "TR the last two lines but STET the leading." (Reverse the order of the last two lines but don't change the spacing between them.) Jargon can provide a quick, shorthand way of expressing ideas. However, jargon and technical lingo should be avoided unless you are sure that others are familiar with it. Otherwise, people may misunderstand you or feel left out. Using slang can have the same effect as jargon. Slang that excludes people from a conversation makes them feel belittled. (The second quotation at the beginning of this Application is full of slang.)

4. Avoid loaded words. Words that have strong emotional meanings (loaded words) can have unintended effects on listeners. For example, the observation "What a stupid-looking tie" implies that anyone who likes the tie is stupid. In the same way, saying "I think the supervisor's new schedule is a *dumb* idea" brands anyone who agrees with the schedule as foolish. Good decision making and problem solving require an atmosphere in which people feel that their ideas are respected, even when they disagree.

5. Use people's names. Work relationships go more smoothly when you learn names and use them. An impersonal request such as, "Hey you, could you make five copies of this for me?" is not likely to promote future cooperation. Of course, whether you use a first or last name will depend on how formal your relationship to a person is. In any case, learning names is well worth the effort. (The Applications in Chapter 10 tells how to improve your memory for names.)

6. Be polite and respectful. Being polite is important, but don't be artificially servile or stilted. Overuse of expressions such as *sir, madame, with your permission, if you would be ever so kind,* and so on, can actually be insulting. True politeness puts others at ease. Phony politeness makes people feel that they are being made fun of, or manipulated, or that you are faking it to win approval. Being polite can be difficult when tempers flare. If you have a dispute with someone at work, remember to use the techniques of self-assertion described in Chapter 20.

In addition to *what* you say, *how* you say it can be important. Psychologist Chris Kleinke (1986) has noted several speech cues that communicate self-confidence and add credibility to your message.

7. Use an expressive tone of voice. People who know a subject well or who believe in their point of view usually speak with an expressive, animated tone of voice. Speaking energetically, with good voice inflection, typically adds to one's credibility. Don't, however, use a higher pitched voice, as this suggests nervousness.

8. Speak fluently. Before you speak, try to collect your thoughts so that you can get right to the point. Stammering, repeating yourself, frequent pauses, and overuse of "ahs," "uhms," and "you knows," implies incompetence or nervousness.

9. Speak quickly. A brisk rate of speech tends to be persuasive because it implies knowledge, competence, enthusiasm, and confidence. It also helps hold your listener's attention.

10. Make use of non-verbal cues. Remember that non-verbal cues, such as facial expressions and hand gestures, can help accentuate your message and structure it for listeners. In Western cultures, making eye contact while speaking is a particularly important non-verbal cue. In a group, don't talk to the ceiling, or to just one person. Try to make eye contact with each person in the group. That way, each feels included and knows that your message is meant for her or him. Another advantage of eye contact is that it lets you watch for feedback from listeners, whose reactions can guide your communication efforts.

Be aware that your behavior sends messages, too. Actions can parallel, amplify, contradict, or undermine what you are saying. For example, being late for a meeting tells others that they are not very important to you. Likewise, your manner of dress, personal grooming—even the way you decorate your personal work space—all send messages. Think about the message you want to send and be sensitive to non-verbal channels of information.

Being a Good Listener

Effective communication is a two-way street. In addition to expressing yourself clearly, you must also be a good listener. We have already discussed good classroom listening habits (Introduction) and listening in counseling situations (Chapter 19). Here are some additional pointers that apply to work settings.

1. Make an honest effort to pay attention. Stop what you are doing, actively give the speaker your attention, and resist distractions. Communicate your interest by posture and body position. Make eye contact with the speaker to show your interest.

2. Try to identify the speaker's purpose. Is he or she informing, requesting, discussing, persuading, correcting, digressing, or entertaining? Listen for main themes rather than isolated facts. A good listener will be able to answer the question: What is this person's central message? Thus, as you listen, pretend that you will have to summarize the speaker's message for someone else.

3. Suspend evaluation. As you listen, try to keep an open mind. Avoid hasty judging, disagreeing, rejecting, or criticizing. There will be time later to think about what was said. After you have heard an entire message, evaluate the information it contains and decide how to use it. Then reply or take action.

4. Check your understanding. Let the other person talk, but occasionally acknowledge and confirm what she or he is saying. Restate important parts of the message in your own words to make sure you understand it. Ask questions and clarify points you don't understand. Don't let doubts or ambiguities go unresolved.

5. Pay attention to non-verbal messages. Listeners must also be aware of the information provided by gestures, facial expressions, eye contact, touching, body positioning, and voice qualities such as volume, rate, pitch, emphasis, hesitations, and silences. Good listeners are also good observers.

6. Accept responsibility for effective communication. As a listener, it is up to you to actively search for meaning and value in what is said. You can facilitate communication as much by being a good listener as you can by being an effective speaker.

The art of effective communication is well worth cultivating. The points made here are basic, but they can go a long way toward ensuring your success at work—like, totally, abso-double-lutely, you know what I mean?

(Sources: Hartgrove-Freile, 1990; Hellriegel, Slocum, & Woodman, 1995; Jewell, 1989; Kleinke, 1986; Timm & Peterson, 1993.)

Learning Check

1. The sentence, "Copy Monica, Steve, and the bean-counters with your input and let's circle the wagons in the A.M.," shows the danger of using loaded words. T or F?

2. "You've got to REM out some of the TSRs in your AUTOEXEC.BAT file and reboot if you want that software to run." For a beginning computer user, the problem with this message is its overuse of _____ .

3. An expressive, higher pitched tone of voice tends to be more persuasive and credible. T or F?

4. Paying attention to non-verbal messages is an element of effective communication for both speakers and listeners. T or F?

Critical Thinking

5. From the perspective of social psychology, effective communication is likely to increase what dimension of group membership?

Answers:

1. F 2. Jargon 3. F 4. T 5. Group cohesion.

Exploration

Space Psychology—Life on the High Frontier

*T*he first long-term outpost in space is drawing nearer. By the year 2002 the United States, Canada, France, Japan, Russia, and other countries hope to orbit a continuously inhabited space station. Many engineering problems must be solved before the International Space Station becomes a reality (Guterl, 1997). Yet, the real challenge may lie in the psychological adjustments needed for life in space (Preiser, 1997).

The Challenge of Living Aloft

Life in the "mini-world" of a space station won't be easy, physically or mentally. For months at a time, space station residents will be restricted to tiny living quarters with little privacy. Living aloft would be similar to spending several months among strangers in a small room from which you cannot escape. In addition to confinement, long-term space inhabitants will face other trying conditions. These include restricted movement, separation from loved ones, sensory monotony, noise, limited recreation, and other stresses.

Space Habitats

Space psychologists *study the many behavioral challenges that accompany space flight and life in restricted environments.* Clearly, space habitats must be designed with human behavior in mind. What will it take to sustain emotional well-being and efficient performance? To begin, the *social* environment on a space station must operate as smoothly as possible. For this reason, many problems can be avoided by carefully selecting and training future space residents *before* they go aloft.

It also would be wise to identify—and ease—stressors in space station living quarters. To this end, psychologists have studied people confined to submarines, missile silos, Antarctic stations, simulated space stations on Earth, and the like. Let's sample some expected problems and possible solutions.

General Environment   Space station design must take many human factors into account. For instance, researchers have learned that astronauts prefer rooms

with clearly defined "up" and "down"—even in the weightlessness of space. Provisions must be made for regular exercise and full-body showers. As trivial as it might seem, a lack of showers has been a major complaint among people in confinement experiments.

Ideally there should be some flexibility in the use of living and work areas inside a space station. Behavior patterns change over time, and being able to control one's environment helps lower stress. At the same time, people need stability. Psychologists have found, for instance, that eating becomes an important high point in monotonous environments. Eating at least one meal together each day can help keep crew members working as a social unit.

Sleep cycles must be carefully controlled in space to avoid disrupting bodily rhythms. In past space missions, some astronauts found they couldn't sleep while other crew members continued to work and talk. Problems with sleep will be worsened by the constant noise on a space station. At first, such noise is annoying. After weeks or months, it can become a serious stressor. Researchers are experimenting with various earmuffs, eyeshades, and sleeping arrangements to alleviate such difficulties.

Privacy Psychologists are helping engineers design space habitats so they meet human needs for privacy. However, privacy must be based mainly on temporarily blocking out visual and auditory contact with others. In the first permanent space station, there will be too little room for separate quarters.

Forced togetherness is stressful mainly because temporary retreat from others is difficult or impossible. Thus, control over the amount of group contact is more important than actually having a private room. Designers do recognize, however, the need to define private territories. It will be important to identify small areas that can be personalized and "owned" by each individual. Desks, lockers, sleep stations, and the like, could fill this need if they are not shared with others.

Sensory Restriction Sensory monotony will be a problem in space, even with the magnificent vistas of Earth below. (How many times would you have to see the North American continent before you lost interest?)

Researchers are developing stimulus environments that will use music, videotapes, and other diversions to combat monotony and boredom. Again, they are trying to provide choice and control for space crews. Studies of confined living make it clear that one person's symphony is another's grating noise. Where music is concerned, individual earphones may be all that is required to avoid problems.

Most people in restricted environments find that they prefer noninteractive pastimes such as reading, listening to music, looking out windows, writing, and watching films or television. As much as anything, this preference may show again the need for privacy. Reading or listening to music is a good way to psychologically withdraw from

the group. A variety of passive entertainments looks like a must for any space station. Russian astronauts, who make much use of music, have also reacted with delight to grab bags containing unexpected toys or novelties.

Cultural Differences The International Space Station will pose a special psychological challenge only hinted at in previous space missions. Astronauts from different cultures will live and work together for many months at a time. In previous space flights, crew members from different countries have reported occasional incidents of misunderstanding and interpersonal friction (Santy et al., 1993).

How important will such differences become when time aloft stretches beyond 6 months? Most likely they will be magnified. For instance, Japanese astronauts felt that Americans paid too much attention to hair care and personal grooming. Americans, in turn, were surprised by the Japanese indifference to

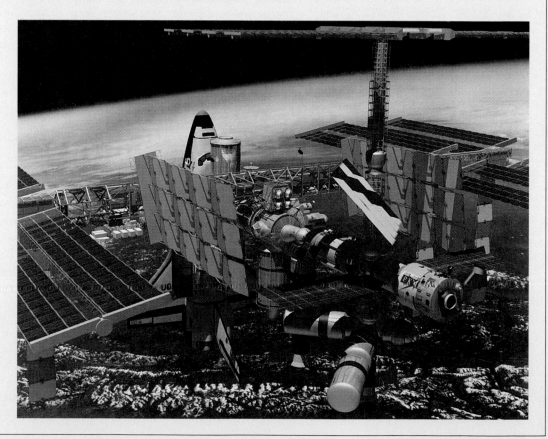

The permanently inhabited International Space Station will be assembled in orbit by space shuttle crews beginning in 1998. The station will provide the United States and its partners—Canada, Japan, and nine European nations—with a habitat in which men and women will live and work in space for extended periods of time. Solving the behavioral problems of living in space will be an important step toward human exploration of the solar system. (Art courtesy of NASA.)

tooth brushing. Likewise, European astronauts felt that Americans did not appreciate the ritual of eating. For their part, Americans were troubled by the fuss European astronauts made over food (Preiser, 1997).

Food itself may be a problem. Norm Thagard, who spent time aboard the Russian space station *Mir,* gagged on canned, jellied fish, a major part of the Russian diet in space. Russians, in contrast, are repulsed by steamed green beans, buttered carrots, and other plain vegetables, all typical foods on American space missions (Preiser, 1997).

Clearly, long-term space inhabitants could benefit from training in cultural awareness. Beyond that, one saving grace is that crew members will have common backgrounds in aviation and spaceflight. Such similarities may, in fact, create a shared "space culture" capable of bridging national differences.

Social Isolation   Separation from family, friends, and one's home community will be a major source of stress. However, the ability to talk regularly with family via two-way televised meetings should help ease feelings of social isolation. Emotional problems could also be prevented by allowing crew members to talk with a psychological support group on Earth. In short, the best antidote for social isolation will probably be abundant opportunities to communicate with associates and loved ones back home (Kelly & Kanas, 1993).

Conflict Resolution and Mental Health
Many studies of long-term isolation show steady declines in motivation. Most inhabitants intend to use their free time for creative pursuits. In reality, they end up marking time and may become apathetic. Judging from submarine missions and Antarctic bases, as many as 5 percent of space inhabitants might experience some psychological disturbance. Most often the problem will be depression. However, in rare instances people have become paranoid, psychotic, suicidal, or

uncontrollably aggressive. As stated earlier, the risk of such problems can be minimized by carefully selecting personnel. Even so, it will be important to teach crew members basic counseling skills for solving conflicts. Effective leaders, in particular, will need to be sensitive to crew members' feelings and able to maintain group harmony and cohesion (Nicholas & Penwell, 1995).

Life on Spaceship Earth
Why is the idea of living in space so fascinating? Perhaps it is because human strengths and weaknesses are magnified in the miniature world of a space station. As psychologist Yvonne Clearwater (1985) says:

> The space station represents the first glimmerings of recognition that some of the toughest challenges in space—as on Earth—concern human behavior, not technology. . . . Ironically, the farther we go from Earth and the longer we stay away, the more we will need to know about ourselves. Scientists working on the space effort believe that psychological factors will become increasingly important for the success or failure of future space missions.

It is curiously fitting that the dazzling technology of space travel has highlighted the inevitable importance of human behavior. Here on Earth, as in space, we cannot count on technology alone to solve problems. The threat of nuclear war, social conflict, crime, prejudice, infectious disease, over-population, environmental damage, famine, homicide, economic disaster—these and most other major problems facing us are behavioral (Kirk & Picard, in press).

Will spaceship Earth endure? It's a psychological question.

Conclusion   Work, leisure, family, community, and environment all contribute to the quality of our lives. And as we have seen throughout this text, psychology has much to offer in each of these areas. It is my sincere hope that you have found enough relevance and value in this book to kindle a lifelong interest in psychology. Psychology's future looks exciting. What role will it play in your life?

(Additional sources: Clearwater, 1985; Connors, Harrison, & Akins, 1985; Engle & Lott, 1980)

Learning Check	Critical Thinking

Learning Check

1. Depression is the most common major psychological disturbance that occurs during prolonged isolation in confined living conditions. T or F?

2. Researchers have learned that astronauts don't really care if living quarters have clearly defined "up" and "down" orientations. T or F?

3. Research shows that needs for privacy can be met by providing ways to temporarily withdraw from social contact with a group, even when physical withdrawal is impossible. T or F?

4. Most people in restricted environments prefer group pastimes, such as playing card games, skits, or group singing. T or F?

Critical Thinking

5. On a spacecraft, how would blocking visual and auditory contact with others affect crowding?

Answers:

1. T 2. F 3. T 4. F 5. While density would remain high, the sense of crowding would be reduced because crew members would feel that they have some control over their immediate social environment.

Chapter Summary

How is psychology applied in business and industry?

◆ **Applied psychology** refers to the use of psychological principles and research methods to solve practical problems.

◆ **Industrial/organizational psychologists** are interested in the problems people face at work and in organizations. Typically they specialize in **personnel psychology** and **human relations** at work.

◆ Personnel psychologists try to match people with jobs by combining **job analysis** with a variety of selection procedures. These include gathering **biodata, interviewing,** giving **standardized psychological tests (interest inventories, aptitude tests,** and **computerized tests),** and using **assessment centers.**

◆ Two basic approaches to business and industrial management are **scientific management (Theory X)** and **human relations** approaches **(Theory Y).** Theory X is most concerned with **work efficiency,** whereas Theory Y emphasizes **psychological efficiency.**

◆ Theory Y methods include **participative management, management by objectives, self-managed teams** and **quality circles.**

◆ **Job satisfaction** is not directly related to productivity, but it is linked to absenteeism, morale, employee turnover, and other factors that affect overall business efficiency. Job satisfaction is usually enhanced by Theory Y-oriented **job enrichment.**

What have psychologists learned about the effects of our physical and social environments?

◆ **Environmental psychologists** are interested in the effects of **behavioral settings, physical** or **social environments,** and human **territoriality,** among many other topics.

◆ Over-population is a major world problem, often reflected at an individual level in crowding.

◆ Animal experiments indicate that excessive crowding can be unhealthy. However, human research shows that psychological feelings of **crowding** do not always correspond to **density** (the number of people in a given space).

◆ One major consequence of crowding is **attentional overload.**

◆ A large number of practical problems—from *noise pollution* to architectural design—have come under the scrutiny of environmental psychologists. In many cases, effective behavioral solutions to such problems have been found, often as a result of first doing a careful **environmental assessment.**

How has psychology improved education?

◆ **Educational psychologists** seek to understand how people learn and teachers instruct. They are particularly interested in **teaching strategies** and **teaching styles,** such as **direct instruction** and **open teaching.**

What does psychology reveal about juries and court verdicts?

◆ The **psychology of law** includes studies of courtroom behavior and other topics that pertain to the legal system.

Psychologists also serve various consulting and counseling roles in legal, law enforcement, and criminal justice settings.

- Studies of **mock juries** show that jury decisions are often far from objective.
- **Scientific jury selection** is used in attempts to choose jurors who have particular characteristics. In some instances, this may result in juries that have a particular bias or that do not represent the community as a whole. A bias toward convicting defendants is characteristic of many **death-qualified juries.**

Can psychology enhance athletic performance?

- **Sports psychologists** seek to enhance sports performance and the benefits of sports participation. A careful **task analysis** of sports skills is one of the major tools for improving coaching and performance.
- A **motor skill** is a non-verbal response chain assembled into a smooth performance. Motor skills are guided by internal mental models called **motor programs.**
- Motor skills are refined through direct practice, but **mental practice** can also contribute to improvement.

- During moments of **peak performance,** physical, mental, and emotional states are optimal.

What can be done to improve communication at work?

- State your message clearly and precisely. Try to avoid overuse of obscure vocabulary, jargon, slang, and loaded words. Learn and use people's names. Be polite, but not servile. Be expressive when you speak. Pay attention to non-verbal cues and the messages they send.
- To be a good listener, actively pay attention, identify the speaker's purpose and core message, suspend evaluation while listening, check your understanding, and make note of non-verbal information.

How is psychology being applied in space missions?

- **Space psychologists** study the many behavioral challenges that accompany space flight and life in restricted environments.
- Space habitats must be designed with special attention to environmental stressors, privacy, social isolation, conflict resolution, and the maintenance of mental health.

Appendix A

Statistics

Statistics from "Heads" to "Tails"

Let's say a friend of yours invites you to try your hand at a "game of chance." He offers to flip a coin and pay you a dollar if the coin comes up heads. If the coin shows tails, you must pay him a dollar. He flips the coin: tails—you pay him a dollar. He flips it again: tails. Again: tails. And again: tails. And again: tails.

At this point you are faced with a choice. Should you continue the game in an attempt to recoup your losses? Or should you assume that the coin is biased and quit before you really get "skinned"? Taking out a pocket calculator (and the statistics book you carry with you at all times), you compute the odds of obtaining 5 tails in a row from an unbiased coin. The probability is 0.031 (roughly 3 times out of 100).

If the coin really is honest, 5 consecutive tails is a rare event. Wisely, you decide that the coin is probably biased and refuse to play again. (Unless, of course, your "friend" is willing to take "tails" for the next 5 tosses!)

Perhaps a decision could have been made in this hypothetical example without using statistics. But notice how much clearer the situation becomes when it is expressed statistically.

Statistics in Psychology   Psychologists try to extract and summarize useful information from the observations they make. To do so, they use two major types of statistics. **Descriptive statistics** *summarize or "boil down" numbers so they become more meaningful and easier to communicate to others.* In comparison, **inferential statistics** *are used for decision making, for generalizing from small samples, and for drawing conclusions.* As was the case in the coin-flipping example, psychologists must often base decisions on limited data. Such decisions are much easier to make with the help of inferential statistics.

Portions of this appendix were contributed by Danniel Downey, Ph.D.

Descriptive Statistics

Statistics bring greater clarity and precision to psychological thought and research. To see how, let's begin by considering three basic types of descriptive statistics: *graphical statistics*, measures of *central tendency*, and measures of *variability*. Let's start with **graphical statistics,** *which present numbers pictorially, so they are easier to visualize.*

Graphical Statistics   Table A–1 ■ shows simulated scores on a test of hypnotic susceptibility given to 100 college students. With such disorganized data, it is hard to form an overall "picture" of the differences in hypnotic susceptibility. But by using a *frequency distribution*, large amounts of information can be neatly organized and summarized. A **frequency distribution** *is made by breaking down the entire range of possible scores into classes of equal size. Next, the number of scores falling into each class is recorded.* In Table A–2 ■, the raw data from Table A–1 have been condensed into a frequency distribution. Notice how much clearer the pattern of scores for the entire group becomes.

Frequency distributions are often shown *graphically* to make them more "visual." A **histogram,** *or graph of a frequency distribution,* is made by labeling class intervals on the *abscissa* (horizontal line) and frequencies (the number of scores in each class) on the *ordinate* (vertical line). Next, bars are drawn for each class interval; the height of each bar is determined by the number of scores in each class (Fig. A–1 ◆). An alternate way of graphing scores is the more familiar **frequency polygon** (Fig. A–2 ◆). *Here, points are placed at the center of each class interval to indicate the number of scores. Then the dots are connected by straight lines.*

Measures of Central Tendency   Notice in Table A–2 that more scores fall in the range 40–59 than elsewhere. How can we show this fact? A measure of **central tendency** *is simply a number describing a "typical score" around which other scores fall.* A familiar measure of central tendency is the mean, or "average." But as we shall see in a moment, there are other types of "averages" that can be used. To illustrate each we need an example: Table A–3 ■ shows the raw data

Table A-1 — Raw Scores of Hypnotic Susceptibility

55	86	52	17	61	57	84	51	16	64
22	56	25	38	35	24	54	26	37	38
52	42	59	26	21	55	40	59	25	57
91	27	38	53	19	93	25	39	52	56
66	14	18	63	59	68	12	19	62	45
47	98	88	72	50	49	96	89	71	66
50	44	71	57	90	53	41	72	56	93
57	38	55	49	87	59	36	56	48	70
33	69	50	50	60	35	67	51	50	52
11	73	46	16	67	13	71	47	25	77

Table A-2 — Frequency Distribution of Hypnotic Susceptibility Scores

Class Interval	Number of Persons in Class
0–19	10
20–39	20
40–59	40
60–79	20
80–99	10

for an imaginary experiment in which two groups of subjects were given a test of memory. Assume that one group was given a drug that might improve memory (let's call the drug Rememberine). The second group received a placebo. Is there a difference in memory scores between the two groups? It's difficult to tell without computing an average.

As one type of "average," the **mean** *is calculated by adding all the scores for each group and then dividing by the total number of scores in that group.* Notice in Table A–3 that the means reveal a difference between the two groups.

The mean is sensitive to extremely high or low scores in a distribution. For this reason it is not always the best measure of central tendency. (Imagine how distorted it would be to calculate average yearly incomes from a small sample of people that happened to include a multimillionaire.) In such cases the middle score in a group of scores—called the *median*—is used instead.

The **median** *is found by arranging scores from the highest to the lowest and selecting the score that falls in the middle.* Consider, for example, the following weights obtained from a small class of college students: 105, 111, 123, 126, 148, 151, 154, 162, 182. The median for the group is 148, the middle score. Of course, if there is an even number of scores, there will be no "middle score." This problem is handled by averaging the

Figure A–1 ◆ Frequency histogram of hypnotic susceptibility scores contained in Table A–2.

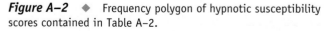

Figure A–2 ◆ Frequency polygon of hypnotic susceptibility scores contained in Table A–2.

Subject	Group 1 Rememberine	Group 2 Placebo
1	65	54
2	67	60
3	73	63
4	65	33
5	58	56
6	55	60
7	70	60
8	69	31
9	60	62
10	68	61
Sum	650	540
Mean	65	54
Median	66	60

$$\text{Mean} = \frac{\Sigma X}{N} \text{ or } \frac{\text{Sum of all scores, X}}{\text{number of scores}}$$

$$\text{Mean Group 1} = \frac{65 + 67 + 73 + 65 + 58 + 55 + 70 + 69 + 60 + 68}{10}$$

$$= \frac{650}{10} = 65$$

$$\text{Mean Group 2} = \frac{54 + 60 + 63 + 33 + 56 + 60 + 60 + 31 + 62 + 61}{10}$$

$$= \frac{540}{10} = 54$$

Median = the middle score or the mean of the two middle scores*

Median Group 1 = 55 58 60 65 $\boxed{65 \quad 67}$ 68 69 70 73

$$= \frac{65 + 67}{2} = 66$$

Median Group 2 = 31 33 54 56 $\boxed{60 \quad 60}$ 60 61 62 63

$$= \frac{60 + 60}{2} = 60$$

*□ indicates middle score(s).

two scores that "share" the middle spot. This procedure yields a single number to serve as the median (see bottom panel of Table A–3).

A final measure of central tendency is the *mode*. The **mode** *is simply the most frequently occurring score in a group of scores*. If you were to take the time to count the scores in Table A–3, you would find that the mode of Group 1 is 65, and the mode of Group 2 is 60. The mode is usually easy to obtain. However, the mode can be an unreliable measure, especially in a small group of scores. The mode's advantage is that it gives the score actually obtained by the greatest number of people.

Measures of Variability Let's say a researcher discovers two drugs that lower anxiety in agitated patients. However, let's also assume that one drug consistently lowers anxiety by moderate amounts, whereas the second sometimes lowers it by large amounts, sometimes has no effect, or may even increase anxiety in some patients. Overall, there is no difference in the *average* (mean) amount of anxiety reduction. Even so, an important difference exists between the two drugs. As this example shows, it is not enough to simply know the average score in a distribution. Usually, we would also like to know if scores are grouped closely together or scattered widely.

Measures of **variability** *provide a single number that tells how "spread out" scores are.* When the scores are widely spread, this number gets larger. When they are close together it gets smaller. If you look again at the example in Table A–3, you will notice that the scores within each group vary widely. How can we show this fact?

The simplest way would be to use the **range,** *which is the difference between the highest and lowest scores.* In Group

1 of our experiment, the highest score is 73, and the lowest is 55; thus, the range is 18 (73 − 55 = 18). In Group 2, the highest score is 63, and the lowest is 31; this makes the range 32. Scores in Group 2 are more spread out than those in Group 1.

A better measure of variability is the **standard deviation** (*an index of how much a typical score differs from the mean of a group of scores*). To obtain the standard deviation, we find the deviation (or difference) of each score from the mean and then square it (multiply it by itself). These squared deviations are then added and averaged (the total is divided by the number of deviations). Taking the square root of this average yields the standard deviation (Table

---

Table A–4 ■ Computations of the Standard Deviation

Group 1 Mean = 65

Score	Mean	Deviation (d)	Deviation Squared (d^2)
65 − 65 =		0	0
67 − 65 =		2	4
73 − 65 =		8	64
65 − 65 =		0	0
58 − 65 =		−7	49
55 − 65 =		−10	100
70 − 65 =		5	25
69 − 65 =		4	16
60 − 65 =		−5	25
68 − 65 =		3	9
			292

$$SD = \sqrt{\frac{\text{sum of } d^2}{n}} = \sqrt{\frac{292}{10}} = \sqrt{29.2} = 5.4$$

Group 2 Mean = 54

Score	Mean	Deviation (d)	Deviation Squared (d^2)
54 − 54 =		0	0
60 − 54 =		6	36
63 − 54 =		9	81
33 − 54 =		−21	441
56 − 54 =		2	4
60 − 54 =		6	36
60 − 54 =		6	36
31 − 54 =		−23	529
62 − 54 =		8	64
61 − 54 =		7	49
			1276

$$SD = \sqrt{\frac{\text{sum of } d^2}{n}} = \sqrt{\frac{1276}{10}} = \sqrt{127.6} = 11.3$$

A–4 ■). Notice again that the variability for Group 1 (5.4) is smaller than that for Group 2 (where the standard deviation is 11.3).

Standard Scores   A particular advantage of the standard deviation is that it can be used to "standardize" scores in a way that gives them greater meaning. For example, John and Susan both took psychology midterms, but in different classes. John earned a score of 118, and Susan scored 110. Who did better? It is impossible to tell without knowing what the average score was on each test, and whether John and Susan scored at the top, middle, or bottom of their classes. We would like to have one number that gives all this information. A number that does this is the *z-score.*

To convert an original score to a **z-score,** *we subtract the mean from the score. The resulting number is then divided by the standard deviation for that group of scores.* To illustrate, Susan had a score of 110 in a class with a mean of 100 and a standard deviation of 10. Therefore, her z-score is +1.0 (Table A–5 ■). John's score of 118 came from a class having a mean of 100 and a standard deviation of 18; thus his z-score is also +1.0 (see Table A–5). Originally it looked as if John did better on his midterm than Susan did. But we now see that relatively speaking, their scores were equivalent. Compared to other students, each was an equal distance above average.

The Normal Curve

When chance events are recorded, we find that some outcomes have a high probability and occur very often; others have a low probability and occur infrequently; still others have little probability and occur rarely. As a result, the distribution (or tally) of chance events typically resembles a *normal curve* (Fig. A–3 ◆). A **normal curve** *is bell-shaped, with a large number of scores in the middle,* tapering to very few extremely high and low scores. Most psychological traits or events are determined by the action of a large number of factors. Therefore, like chance

Table A–5 ■ Computation of a z-Score
$z = \dfrac{X - \overline{X}}{SD}$ or $\dfrac{score - mean}{standard\ deviation}$
Susan: $z = \dfrac{110 - 100}{10} = \dfrac{+10}{10} = +1.0$
John: $z = \dfrac{118 - 100}{18} = \dfrac{+18}{18} = +1.0$

Figure A–3 ◆   The normal curve. The normal curve is an idealized mathematical model. However, many measurements in psychology closely approximate a normal curve. The scales you see here show the relationship of standard deviations, z-scores, and other measures to the curve.

2.14% 13.59% 34.13% 34.13% 13.59% 2.14%

−3 SD   −2 SD   −1 SD   Mean   +1 SD   +2 SD   +3 SD

Figure A–4 ◆ Relationship between the standard deviation and the normal curve.

Table A–6	Area Under the Normal Curve as a Percentage of Total Area for a Variety of z-Scores	
z-Score	Percentage of Area to the Left of This Value	Percentage of Area to the Right of This Value
−3.0 SD	00.1	99.9
−2.5 SD	00.6	99.4
−2.0 SD	02.3	97.7
−1.5 SD	06.7	93.3
−1.0 SD	15.9	84.1
−0.5 SD	30.9	69.1
0.0 SD	50.0	50.0
+0.5 SD	69.1	30.9
+1.0 SD	84.1	15.9
+1.5 SD	93.3	06.7
+2.0 SD	97.7	02.3
+2.5 SD	99.4	00.6
+3.0 SD	99.9	00.1

events, measures of psychological variables tend to roughly match a normal curve. For example, direct measurement has shown such characteristics as height, memory span, and intelligence to be distributed approximately along a normal curve. In other words, many people have average height, memory ability, and intelligence. However, as we move above or below average, fewer and fewer people are found.

It is very fortunate that so many psychological variables tend to form a normal curve, because much is known about the curve. One valuable property concerns the relationship between the standard deviation and the normal curve. Specifically, the standard deviation measures off set proportions of the curve above and below the mean. For example, in Figure A–4 ◆, notice that roughly 68 percent of all cases (IQ scores, memory scores, heights, or whatever) fall between one standard deviation above and below the mean (± 1 SD); 95 percent of all cases fall between ± 2 SD; and 99 percent of the cases can be found between ± 3 SD from the mean.

Table A–6 ■ gives a more complete account of the relationship between z-scores and the percentage of cases

found in a particular area of the normal curve. Notice, for example, that 93.3 percent of all cases fall below a z-score of +1.5. A z-score of 1.5 on a test (no matter what the original, or "raw," score was) would be a good performance, since roughly 93 percent of all scores fall below this mark. Relationships between the standard deviation (or z-scores) and the normal curve do not change. This makes it possible to compare various tests or groups of scores if they come from distributions that are approximately normal.

Learning Check

1. _____ statistics summarize numbers so they become more meaningful or easier to communicate; _____ statistics are used for decision making, generalizing, or drawing conclusions.

2. Histograms and frequency polygons are graphs of frequency distributions. T or F?

3. Three measures of central tendency are the mean, the median, and the _____ .

4. If scores are placed in order, from the smallest to the largest, the median is defined as the middle score. T or F?

5. As a measure of variability, the standard deviation is defined as the difference between the highest and lowest scores. T or F?

6. A z-score of −1 tells us that a score fell one standard deviation below the mean in a group of scores. T or F?

7. In a normal curve, 99 percent of all scores can be found between +1 and −1 standard deviations from the mean. T or F?

Answers:

1. Descriptive, inferential 2. T 3. mode 4. T 5. F 6. T 7. F

Inferential Statistics

Let's say that a researcher studies the effects of a new therapy on a small group of depressed individuals. Is she or he interested only in these particular individuals? Usually not, since except in rare instances, psychologists seek to discover general laws of behavior that apply widely to humans and animals. Undoubtedly the researcher would like to know if the therapy holds any promise for all depressed people. As stated earlier, **inferential statistics** *are techniques that allow us to make inferences.* That is, they allow us to generalize from the behavior of small groups of subjects to that of the larger groups they represent.

Samples and Populations

Samples and Populations In any scientific study, we would like to observe the *entire set, or* **population,** *of subjects, objects, or events of interest.* However, this is usually impossible or impractical. Observing all Catholics, all cancer patients, or all mothers-in-law could be both impractical (since all are large populations) and impossible (since people change denominations, may be unaware of having cancer, and change their status as relatives). In such cases, **samples** (*smaller cross sections of a population*) are selected, and observations of the sample are used to draw conclusions about the entire population.

For any sample to be meaningful, it must be **representative.** That is, *the sample group must truly reflect the membership and characteristics of the larger population.* In our earlier hypothetical study of a memory drug, it would be essential for the sample of 20 people to be representative of the general population. A very important aspect of representative samples is that their members are chosen at **random.** In other words, *each member of the population must have an equal chance of being included in the sample.*

Significant Differences

Significant Differences In our imaginary drug experiment, we found that the average memory score was higher for the group given the drug than it was for persons who didn't take the drug (the placebo group). Certainly this result is interesting, but could it have occurred by chance? If two groups were repeatedly tested (with neither receiving any drug), their average memory scores would sometimes differ. How much must two means differ before we can consider the difference "real" (not due to chance)?

Notice that the question is similar to one discussed earlier: How many tails in a row must we obtain when flipping a coin before we can conclude that the coin is biased? In the case of the coin, we noted that obtaining 5 tails in a row is a rare event. Thus, it became reasonable to assume that the coin was biased. Of course, it is possible to get 5 tails in a row when flipping an honest coin. But since this outcome is unlikely, we have good reason to suspect that something other than chance (a loaded coin, for instance)

caused the results. Similar reasoning is used in tests of statistical significance.

Tests of **statistical significance** *provide an estimate of how often experimental results could have occurred by chance alone.* The results of a significance test are stated as a probability. This probability gives the odds that the observed difference was due to chance. In psychology, any experimental result that could have occurred by chance 5 times (or less) out of 100 (in other words, a probability of .05 or less) is considered *significant.* In our memory experiment, the probability is .025 ($p = .025$) that the group means would differ as they do by chance alone. This allows us to conclude with reasonable certainty that the drug actually did improve memory scores.

Correlation

Many of the statements that psychologists make about behavior do not result from the use of experimental methods. Rather, they come from keen observations and measures of existing phenomena. A psychologist might note, for example, that the higher a couple's socioeconomic and educational status, the smaller the number of children they are likely to have. Or that grades in high school are related to how well a person is likely to do in college. Or even that as rainfall levels increase within a given metropolitan area, crime rates decline. In these instances, we are dealing with the fact that two variables are **co-relating** (*varying together in some orderly fashion*).

The simplest *way of visualizing a correlation* is to construct a **scatter diagram.** In a scatter diagram, two measures (grades in high school and grades in college, for instance) are obtained. One measure is indicated by the X axis and the second by the Y axis. The scatter diagram plots the intersection (crossing) of each pair of measurements as a single point. Many such measurement pairs give pictures like those shown in Figure A–5 ◆.

Figure A–5 also shows scatter diagrams of three basic kinds of relationships between variables (or measures). Graphs A, B, and C show *positive relationships* of varying strength. As you can see, in a **positive relationship,** *increases in the X measure (or score) are matched by increases in the Y measure (or score).* An example would be finding that higher IQ scores (X) are associated with higher college grades (Y). A **zero correlation** *suggests that no relationship exists between two measures* (see graph D). This might be the result of comparing subjects' hat sizes (X) to their college grades (Y). Graphs E and F both show a **negative relationship** (or correlation). *Notice that as values of one measure increase, those of the second become smaller.* An example might be the relationship between amount of alcohol consumed and scores on a test of coordination: Higher alcohol levels are correlated with lower coordination scores.

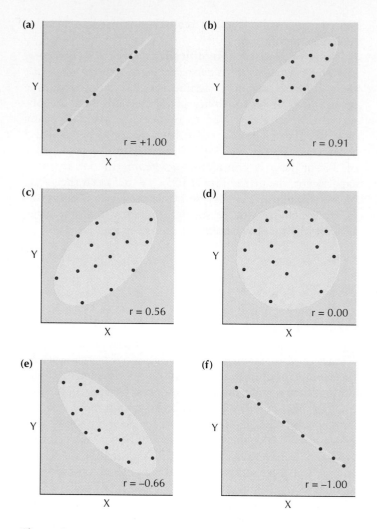

Figure A–5 ◆ Scatter diagrams showing various degrees of relationship for a positive, zero, and negative correlation. (Adapted from Pagano, 1981.)

The strength of a correlation can also be expressed as a **coefficient of correlation**. This coefficient is simply a number falling somewhere between +1.00 and −1.00. If the number is zero or close to zero, it indicates a weak or nonexistent relationship. If the *correlation is +1.00*, a **perfect positive relationship** exists; if the *correlation is −1.00*, a **perfect negative relationship** has been discovered. The most commonly used correlation coefficient is called the Pearson *r*. Calculation of the Pearson *r* is relatively simple, as shown in Table A–7 ■. (The numbers shown are hypothetical.)

As stated in Chapter 2, correlations in psychology are rarely perfect. Most fall somewhere between zero and plus or minus 1. The closer the correlation coefficient is to +1.00 or −1.00, the stronger the relationship. An interesting example of some typical correlations is provided by a study that compared the IQs of adopted children with the IQs of their biological mothers. At age 4, the children's IQs correlated .28 with their mothers' IQs. By

age 7 the correlation was .35. And by age 13 it had grown to .38.

Correlations often provide highly useful information. For instance, it is valuable to know that there is a correlation between cigarette smoking and lung cancer rates. Another example is the fact that higher consumption of alcohol during pregnancy is correlated with lower birth weight and a higher rate of birth defects. There is a correlation between the number of recent life stresses experienced and the likelihood of emotional disturbance. Many more examples could be cited, but the point is, correlations help us to identify relationships that are worth knowing.

Correlations are particularly valuable for making *predictions*. If we know that two measures are correlated, and we know a person's score on one measure, we can predict his or her score on the other. For example, most colleges have formulas that use multiple correlations to decide which applicants have the best chances for success. Usually the formula includes such predictors as high school GPA, teacher ratings, extracurricular activities, and scores on the *Scholastic Assessment Test* (SAT) or some similar test. Although no single predictor is perfectly correlated with success in college, together the various predictors correlate highly and provide a useful technique for screening applicants.

There is an interesting "trick" you can do with correlations that you may find useful. It works like this: If you *square* the correlation coefficient (multiply *r* by itself), you will get a number telling the **percent of variance** (*amount of variation in scores*) accounted for by the correlation. For example, the correlation between IQ scores and college grade point average is .5. Multiplying .5 times .5 gives .25, or 25 percent. This means that 25 percent of the variation in college grades is accounted for by knowing IQ scores. In other words, with a correlation of .5, college grades are "squeezed" into an oval like the one shown in graph C, Figure A–5. IQ scores take away some of the possible variation in corresponding grade point averages. If there were no correlation between IQ and grades, grades would be completely free to vary, as shown in Figure A–5, graph D.

Along the same line, a correlation of +1.00 or −1.00 means that 100 percent of the variation in the Y measure is accounted for by knowing the X measure: If you know a person's X score, you can tell exactly what the Y score is. An example that comes close to this state of affairs is the high correlation (.86) between the IQs of identical twins. In any group of identical twins, 74 percent of the variation in the "Y" twins' IQs is accounted for by knowing the IQs of their siblings (the "X's").

Correlation and Causation It is very important to recognize that finding a correlation between two measures does not automatically mean that one causes the other: *Correlation does not demonstrate causation.* When a correlation exists, the

Student No.	IQ X	Grade Point Average Y	X Score Squared X^2	Y Score Squared Y^2	X Times Y XY
1	110	1.0	12,100	1.00	110.0
2	112	1.6	12,544	2.56	179.2
3	118	1.2	13,924	1.44	141.6
4	119	2.1	14,161	4.41	249.9
5	122	2.6	14,884	6.76	317.2
6	125	1.8	15,625	3.24	225.0
7	127	2.6	16,124	6.76	330.2
8	130	2.0	16,900	4.00	260.0
9	132	3.2	17,424	10.24	422.4
10	134	2.6	17,956	6.76	348.4
11	136	3.0	18,496	9.00	408.0
12	138	3.6	19,044	12.96	496.8
Total	1503	27.3	189,187	69.13	3488.7

$$r = \frac{\Sigma XY - \dfrac{(\Sigma X)(\Sigma Y)}{N}}{\sqrt{\left[\Sigma X^2 - \dfrac{(\Sigma X)^2}{N}\right]\left[\Sigma Y^2 - \dfrac{(\Sigma Y)^2}{N}\right]}}$$

$$= \frac{3488.7 - \dfrac{1503(27.3)}{12}}{\sqrt{\left[189{,}187 - \dfrac{(1503)^2}{12}\right]\left[69.13 - \dfrac{(27.3)^2}{12}\right]}}$$

$$= \frac{69.375}{81.088} = 0.856 = 0.86$$

Adapted from Pagano, 1981.

best we can say is that two variables are related. Of course, this does not mean that it is impossible for two correlated variables to have a cause-and-effect relationship. Rather, it means that we cannot *conclude*, solely on the basis of correlation, that a causal link exists. To gain greater confidence that a cause-and-effect relationship exists, an experiment must be performed (see Chapter 2).

Often, two correlated measures are related as a result of the influence of a third variable. For example, we might observe that the more hours students devote to studying, the better their grades. Although it is tempting to conclude that more studying produces (causes) better grades, it is possible (indeed, it is probable) that grades and the amount of study time are both related to the amount of motivation or interest a student has.

The difference between cause-and-effect data and data that reveal a relationship of unknown origin is one that should not be forgotten. Since we rarely run experiments in daily life, the information on which we act is largely correlational. This should make us more humble and more tentative in the confidence with which we make pronouncements about human behavior.

Learning Check

1. In inferential statistics, observations of a _____ are used to make inferences and draw conclusions about an entire _____ .

2. A representative sample can be obtained by selecting members of the sample at _____ .

3. If the results of an experiment could have occurred by chance alone less than 25 times out of 100, the result is considered statistically significant. T or F

4. A scatter diagram can be used to plot and visualize a _____ between two groups of scores.

5. In a negative relationship, increases in X scores correspond to decreases in Y scores. T or F?

6. A perfect positive correlation exists when the correlation coefficient is 0.00. T or F?

7. It is important to remember that correlation does not demonstrate _____ .

Answers:

1. sample, population   2. random
3. F   4. correlation   5. T   6. F
7. causation

Appendix B

Using Electronic Media in Psychology

In the past, when students or researchers wanted to gather information on a topic, they typically headed for the library. There, they often spent hours or days reading catalogs or journals and making notes. All of this was very time consuming and inefficient. Eventually, professional organizations, such as the American Psychological Association, compiled abstracts and indexes of journals and books. This greatly reduced the time required to find needed information. Still, the process involved searching manually through books and papers. Today, all of this has changed. Personal computers, electronic databases, and computer networks have greatly enlarged the information available and increased the speed with which it can be found.

Electronic Gateways

Taking advantage of the revolution in knowledge retrieval requires that you have access to a computer plus a modem or CD-ROM. However, you can usually use the necessary "hardware" on campus, even if you don't own a personal computer. For this reason, electronic media are rapidly becoming the primary gateway to psychological information.

This appendix is designed to help you locate and retrieve information about psychology. First, let's consider some of the resources that are available to you.

The "Net"

The **Internet** *is an electronic network that enables computers to communicate directly with each other through the phone system.* The Internet was originally developed in the early 1970s for the U.S. Defense Department. In the 1980s it was turned over to the private sector and to other government agencies.

This appendix was contributed by Karen Casto.

Since then, its growth has been phenomenal. By the year 2000 it is estimated that more than 100 million computers will be interconnected via the Internet.

In 1989 a system known as the *World Wide Web* was developed to allow researchers in different locations to rapidly exchange information. The **World Wide Web** *is a system of information "sites" or "pages" that can be accessed through the Internet.* You can view a Web site by using any of a number of software "browsers." Each Web site is just a collection of information stored on a computer that is linked to the World Wide Web. If you know the electronic "address" of the site, you can connect to it and retrieve the information it contains. A browser allows you to see text, images, sounds, movies, and other information contained on a Web page. Many Web pages also have *links* to other Web sites. These **links** *allow you to jump around the Internet to find additional information.* In seconds you can connect with university computers, services that search the Internet for specific topics, electronic journals, and even virtual libraries, where all the books are electronic.

Gophers Because the Internet holds vast amounts of information, various systems have been devised to organize it. For example, *gopher* computers have been set up with information on almost any subject you can imagine. A **gopher** *is a system for organizing information on the Internet, usually in the form of simple lists, called menus.* Gophers are designed to "tunnel" through the Internet to provide information in a structured way. If you select an item from a gopher menu, you may see another, lower level menu that offers more choices. Selecting an item on that menu can lead to another list of topics or options, and so on.

Figure B–1 ◆ is an example of what is retrieved when the University of Minnesota's gopher is accessed. Selecting the menu item "Other Gopher and Information Servers" presents you with another menu, as shown in Figure B–2 ◆. *The software used by gophers to search the Internet is called* **Veronica.** Veronica uses keywords to locate specific gophers or gopher menu items. Most colleges and universities have their own gophers and most allow you to visit other gopher sites as well. Next time you are in the campus library, ask for instructions about using your school's gopher. At the same

Select one of:

- Information About Gopher
- Computer Information
- Discussion Groups
- Fun & Games
- Internet File Server (ftp) Sites
- Libraries
- News
- Other Gopher and Information Servers
- Phone Books
- Search Gopher Titles at the University of Minnesota
- Search Lots of Places at the University of Minnesota
- University of Minnesota Campus Information

= Contains submenu(s)
= Use for searching
= File or form (no submenu)

Figure B–1 ◆ Main gopher menu of the University of Minnesota.

time, get acquainted with Veronica. You may be surprised by the amount of interesting information you can find by working with a gopher system.

Finding and Retrieving Files Another useful tool for exploring the Internet is called a **File Transfer Protocol (FTP) site.** *These sites contain information "files" that can be copied from one computer to another.* After connecting to an FTP site through the Internet, you can select a file that interests you and transfer it to your computer. After you have

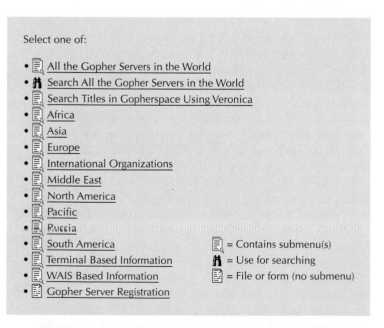

Select one of:

- All the Gopher Servers in the World
- Search All the Gopher Servers in the World
- Search Titles in Gopherspace Using Veronica
- Africa
- Asia
- Europe
- International Organizations
- Middle East
- North America
- Pacific
- Russia
- South America
- Terminal Based Information
- WAIS Based Information
- Gopher Server Registration

= Contains submenu(s)
= Use for searching
= File or form (no submenu)

Figure B–2 ◆ Submenu obtained when "Other Gopher and Information Servers" is selected on the University of Minnesota's main gopher menu.

retrieved a file, you can read it at your leisure. Many college and university psychology departments have FTP sites with articles and reports that are free for the taking. Some sites, however, charge usage fees. If you work on a computer in a campus library, even these sites may be free.

If you know the Internet address of an FTP site you can just connect to it and see what's available for downloading. If you would like to search more broadly for information on a particular topic, Archie will help you do it. **Archie** *is the name of software designed to explore FTP sites.* Archie uses keywords to locate specific information. If you examine Figure B–1 again, you will see a menu item for FTP sites on the University of Minnesota's gopher. Selecting this menu item will connect you to these sites and allow you to use Archie to search FTP sites. Your own campus may have a system that provides the same service.

Wide Area Information Server The **Wide Area Information Server (WAIS)** *was designed to process huge amounts of information and extract only items of interest to a researcher.* Unlike Archie and Veronica, which only search for topics by looking at file names or gopher menus, WAIS *actually searches through the text of entire documents.* When WAIS finds words related to a topic you are researching, it will alert you that it has found something that may be of interest. Look once again at Figure B–1. If the item described as "Other Gopher and Information Servers" is selected, you will see the menu shown in Figure B–2. The second-to-last item, "WAIS Based Information," provides access to WAIS searching.

As you have probably noticed from this discussion, it is easy to jump back and forth from Web pages, to gopher sites, to FTP sites, and so forth. Each source of information has a different purpose, but they are all available on the Internet.

Bulletin Boards **Usenet groups** *are electronic "bulletin boards" that allow discussion of a variety of topics* through **e-mail** (*electronic mail*). The most convenient way to gain access to usenet groups is through commercial information services such as America Online or CompuServe. Usenet groups work very much like real bulletin boards. That is, you post your own e-mail messages and read others' messages. The best way to get the hang of these groups is to locate one you are interested in and just spend some time reading the messages that have been posted. Then, jump into the fray with a posting of your own!

There are many usenet groups on psychology or psychological topics. It is important, however, to keep in mind the freewheeling nature of some of the discussions you may encounter. The Internet is not regulated for content. Keep this fact in mind, especially when participating in usenet groups.

Accessing Electronic Information

Most college and university libraries provide computer terminals that can be used to search electronic databases and sometimes even the Internet. Check with your library to find out what's available and how to use it. If the library doesn't provide Internet access, you can connect on your own with a personal computer and a modem linked to a telephone line. Commercial online services, such as CompuServe or America Online, provide Internet access at relatively low cost. In most cities, direct Internet access is also available (for a fee) from various Internet providers.

URLs   Once you have access to the Internet, you can't go anywhere without knowing your destination. On the Internet the location of each site is known as a **URL.** *URL stands for Uniform Resource Locator. A URL really is nothing more than an electronic address.* It tells your computer where on the Internet to look for information. Usually a URL begins with a prefix that tells in what form information will be transferred. For a World Wide Web page the prefix is *http.* For an FTP site it is *ftp.* For a gopher computer, it is *gopher.* The next part of the address is usually a colon and two forward slashes, as in http://, or gopher://. The subsequent part of the address usually identifies the computer where the site is stored. The final part of each URL states the directory where the file of interest can be found, and the name of the file. Each of these elements is separated by a slash. For example, examine the following URL:

http://ourworld.compuserve.com/homepages/Dev_ Research_Associates/

The http followed by a colon and two forward slashes indicates that this is a World Wide Web address. The computer where the information is stored is called ourworld. compuserve.com. The directory where the file can be found is homepages, and the actual file name is Dev_Research_ Associates/. Make careful note of this address. It will connect you to a Web page that was designed to accompany this appendix.

Your Link to the Internet   The easiest way to explore psychology on the Internet is to visit the Web page described above. Once you have reached the page, you can use it to effortlessly jump to other sites. Links built into the page will take you to a great variety of psychological research sources all over the Internet.

The psychology page is updated at least monthly. As a result, you don't need to make a long list of Internet addresses to start exploring psychology electronically. Also, as the Internet and the World Wide Web change, the site will change accordingly. For instance, if the address of a psychological site changes, the appropriate link on the Web page will change, too. Likewise, new sites of interest will be added as they emerge. If you have access to the Internet, check out the psychology page!

Boolean Searching   *Search engines* are *software programs that allow you to find specific topics in a larger body of information.* Veronica and Archie, which were mentioned earlier, are examples of search engines. Most search engines look for a specific keyword (or sometimes two or three keywords) as they conduct a search. Some search programs are specialized for finding psychological information. Although each search program may have its own procedures, most use *Boolean logic* to define the scope of a search. **Boolean logic** *is a system developed in the 19th century by English mathematician George Boole. Boolean logic merely combines the operators AND, OR, and NOT to make searches narrower or broader.* Typically, searches must be limited in some way because so much information is available on the Internet and in databases. Searching for the keyword *psychology,* for instance, would retrieve an overwhelming amount of information.

Let's say that you are interested in finding information concerning both depression and stress. In this case, you would use the AND operator in a keyword search. That is, you would tell the search program to FIND depression AND stress. Using the AND instruction will retrieve references that contain *both* the keywords "depression" and "stress." Thus, using the AND operator helps to limit the scope of a search.

If you are interested in finding information on either depression or stress, you would use the OR operator. This time you would tell the program to FIND depression OR stress. Doing so would retrieve references to depression and also references to stress. As you can see, using the OR instruction widens a search.

What if you were interested in finding references to stress in animals? In this instance, you could use the AND operator, as in FIND stress AND animal. Alternatively, you could use the NOT operator to *exclude* human subjects from the search. This time, your search would read: FIND stress NOT human. Use of the Boolean logic operator NOT limits the scope of a search.

Online Databases

Psychology and psychological topics can be found all over the Internet. But the largest collections of psychological information are stored in a small number of specialized databases. These databases hold immense amounts of information on psychology and closely related fields. In some cases, they are so comprehensive that you can practically do "one-stop shopping" for information. One such database is PsycINFO. Let's begin with PsycINFO and then consider some other collections that you may find helpful.

PsycINFO   The premier electronic database available in psychology is PsycINFO, offered by the American Psychological Association. PsycINFO provides brief summaries and references to the scientific and scholarly literature in psychology. It also covers work from related fields, such as psychiatry, education, medicine, and social work. PsycINFO indexes roughly 1,300 professional journals, as well as dissertations and technical reports. Each record contains information about the authors, the title of the publication, the source of the record, and an abstract of the article. All records are indexed using key terms that describe the main topics covered in the article or report.

You can gain access to PsycINFO in several ways. Many colleges and universities subscribe to PsycINFO or to a related CD-ROM version called PsycLIT. (PsycLIT is described in a moment.) If this is the case, you can usually search PsycINFO from a terminal in the college library or computer center. PsycINFO can also be accessed through the Internet, but not directly. To reach PsycINFO you must go through a "gateway" such as CompuServe or other Internet providers.

If you would like to search PsycINFO using your own computer, you can reach it through CompuServe's Knowledge Index. Knowledge Index is a collection of databases on a variety of topics. Table B–1 ■ lists the subject areas included in Knowledge Index. As you can see, Knowledge Index provides access to additional databases that are very useful for psychological research. For example, even though a sizable amount of research in psychiatry is covered in PsycINFO, far more is covered in the medical databases. A major drawback to using Knowledge Index is that you must have an account with CompuServe and pay extra for each minute you spend searching PsycINFO. The Knowledge Index databases are also only available at night and on weekends. For more information about how to access PsychINFO you can consult the Web page associated with this appendix.

The American Psychological Association has published a free booklet containing search tips for this system, titled *Searching PsycINFO on CompuServe Knowledge Index*. The booklet is available for free from the APA or you can read an electronic version on the Internet. Check the Web site associated with this appendix for a direct link to the booklet.

Once you have accessed the PsycINFO database, how do you begin a search? The APA suggests that the first thing to do is to write a statement of the research question to be answered. An example would be:

Does tobacco smoking during pregnancy affect a mother's unborn child?

Next, you could begin a search by choosing keywords from the statement. That is, you could search for "smoking," "pregnancy," or perhaps "smoking AND pregnancy." Searches done this way can turn up useful information and are worth trying. However, there is a way to search with greater precision. The APA suggests that you look up each keyword in the *Thesaurus of Psychological Index Terms*. The *Thesaurus* will help you find out what words were used to index PsycINFO reports. In the above example, tobacco smoking and pregnancy are terms you could look up in the *Thesaurus*. Each entry in PsycINFO is indexed using the narrowest possible descriptive words. Consequently, the *Thesaurus* is really useful for narrowing your search. By selecting the same terms used to index PsycINFO, you can retrieve the most relevant entries. Your college library probably has a copy of the *Thesaurus* if it subscribes to PsycINFO.

After you have decided what terms you are interested in, it may be useful to use AND, OR, and NOT operators to further limit or expand your search. Again, be aware that PsycINFO contains an immense amount of information. A scattergun approach to searching will produce too much information—most of it irrelevant. It is almost always worthwhile to target your searches as precisely as possible. To help you do this, PsycINFO allows you to search only specific years, journals, or authors. You can also limit your search to reports about animals or humans or specific age groups. If you choose to, you can select only records that appear in English, or you can exclude dissertations, and so

---

Table B–1 ■ Knowledge Index Database Sections

Each database section is composed of several databases.

1	Agriculture	14	Food
2	Arts	15	Government
3	Biology, Biosciences & Biotechnology	16	History
4	Books	17	Legal Information
5	Business Information	18	Literature & Language
6	Chemistry	19	Magazines
7	Computers & Electronics	20	Mathematics
8	Corporate News	21	Medicine
9	Drug Information	22	News
10	Economics	23	Psychology
11	Education	24	Reference
12	Engineering	25	Religion
13	Environment	26	Social Sciences

forth. The booklet *Searching PsycINFO on CompuServe Knowledge Index* contains examples and detailed instructions on how to do such searches.

Grateful Med The United States National Library of Medicine maintains a series of databases containing medical and biogenetic information. Medline is its primary database. Many of the medical databases are also available on Knowledge Index through CompuServe, as previously noted. In addition, you can gain direct access to the medical databases through the Internet at a site called Grateful Med. Check the Web site associated with this appendix for a link to Medline.

Searches of Medline on Knowledge Index are very similar to PsycINFO searches. You can search Medline using key terms, by author, by year of publication, and by journal name. If you search Medline through the Internet, you'll want to consult a thesaurus known as the *Metathesaurus*. This is very useful for finding the exact medical term that matches common lay phrases. For example, if you enter the term "mad cow," a lay term, into the *Metathesaurus*, and click "Find Related," it returns with the medical term "Encephalopathy, Bovine Spongiform," which you can then use to search the medical database for articles on mad cow disease. For further details about searching these databases, an electronic booklet titled "Internet Grateful Med: New User's Survival Guide" has been published by the U.S. National Library of Medicine. Check the Web page associated with this appendix for a link to the booklet.

ERIC ERIC (Educational Resources Information Center) is a national clearinghouse that provides information and services on education-related issues. The ERIC database is available through Knowledge Index, and also directly on the Internet. Accessing ERIC through Knowledge Index requires an account with CompuServe and also involves paying a fee, whereas searches performed on the Internet are free.

ERIC "digests" are short reports on current education topics. The ERIC database contains research reports, teaching guides, conference papers, books, and journal articles related to education. The ERIC database can be accessed through the AskERIC Virtual Library and the ERIC Clearinghouse on Assessment and Evaluation. As with the other databases, you can search by keyword and by using Boolean logic.

AskERIC is the Internet education information service of ERIC. It has three parts: (1) a question-and-answer service that educators can use to ask experts for information; (2) the AskERIC Virtual Library, which is an Internet site for selected resources in education; and (3) AskERIC R & D, which was formed to provide cutting-edge services and technology to educators. The Virtual Library is one jumping-off point to search the ERIC databases. Check the Web site associated with this appendix for URL links to the ERIC system.

CD-ROM Databases

A very effective way to locate interesting research reports in psychology is to use a CD-ROM database. In the previous section we discussed how to find information stored on computers at remote locations, via the Internet. With CD-ROM databases, all of the information is stored on a compact disc. To use a CD database you would typically go to your college library or computer center. There, you would check out a CD and place it in a computer for viewing and searching. As an alternative, computers are sometimes set up as permanent CD workstations with a CD left in the computer at all times.

Using a "database on a disc" is fast and free. Other than the fact that you must work on campus to use a CD database, CD-ROM searching is convenient and enjoyable. In fact, it may be the easiest way of all to explore the psychological literature.

APEL The American Psychiatric Electronic Library (APEL) CD contains the complete text, including graphics, of ten psychiatric journals, fifteen psychiatric textbooks, and the American Psychiatric Association's Practice Guidelines. Searching APEL is similar to working with other databases in that you can use key words and Boolean logic operators. The major drawback of APEL is that it only covers 1992 to the present and it is limited in scope.

PsycLIT and ClinPSYC PsycLIT and ClinPSYC are computerized CD-ROM databases that are produced by the American Psychological Association. PsycLIT is stored on two discs. The first contains references to journal articles from 1974 through 1989. The second lists articles from 1990 to the present. Disc two also contains a database of book chapters and books published from 1987 to the present. ClinPSYC is a collection of information related to abnormal and clinical psychology.

As with the PsycINFO database, PsycLIT provides references to the scientific literature in psychology and fields related to psychology. It is updated quarterly. PsycLIT is most likely to be found at a college or university library. The database is far too expensive for individual purchase. Table B–2 ■ outlines similarities and differences between PsycINFO, PsycLIT, and the *Psychological Abstracts* (a collection of printed abstracts from psychological journals).

An electronic booklet describing how to search PsycLIT and ClinPSYC is available on the Internet. Check the Web page associated with this appendix for a link to this booklet. The booklet is also available on the American Psychological Association's gopher.

Searching the PsycLIT databases is very similar to searching PsycINFO. It is best to start with a research question, identify the narrowest key terms by using the *Thesaurus*, and use Boolean logic to further focus the search.

Table B–2 ■ Comparison of Searchable Databases Produced by the American Psychological Association

	Psychological Abstracts	PsycINFO	PsycLIT
Format	Printed book	Online or institutional lease	CD-ROM (compact disc)
Sources covered	Journals, technical reports, book chapters, books	Journals, technical reports, dissertations, book chapters, books	Journals, book chapters, books
Dates of coverage	1927–present	1967–present	Journals: 1974–present Books: 1984–present
Updates	Monthly	Monthly	Quarterly
Languages covered	All languages (1927–1987) English Only (1988–present)	All languages	Journals: All languages Books: English
Sources	Subscription from APA (usually found in college and university libraries)	Commercial online services (through the Internet), or institutional lease (usually colleges and universities)	Subscription through CD-ROM vendors (usually found in college and university libraries)

Source: After American Psychological Association, 1996.

Multimedia CD-ROMs

The creation of multimedia CD-ROMs is an exciting recent development in education. A single compact disc can store reams of text and thousands of pieces of art. Thus, all of the information contained in traditional print textbooks can fit on a CD for display on a computer screen. In addition, CDs are capable of presenting animations, audio clips, film clips, and interactive exercises. Although such CDs are just now becoming available, they have the potential to dramatically enhance the process of learning psychology. Two new CDs you may be interested in trying are described here.

PsychNow! *PsychNow!* is an interactive CD-ROM that lets you explore the world of psychology. *PsychNow!* has an easy-to-use graphical interface. Simply follow the on-screen

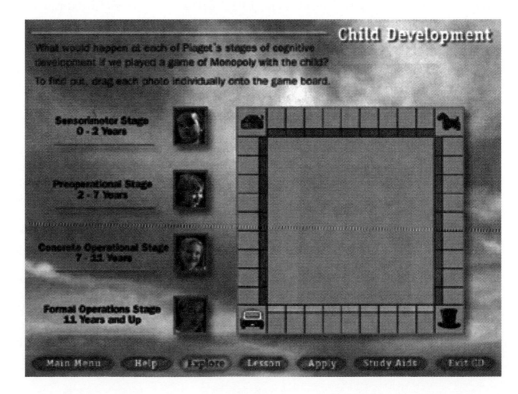

Figure B–3 ◆ A sample screen from *PsychNow!*.

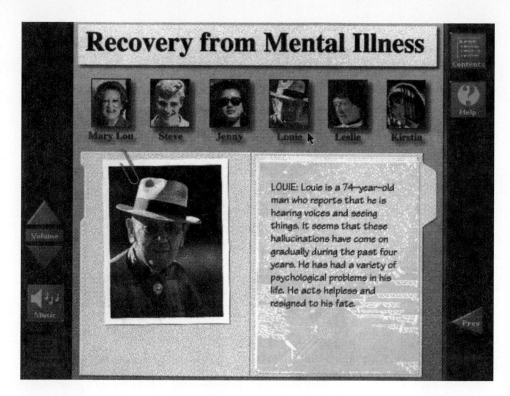

Recovery from Mental Illness

Mary Lou Steve Jenny Louie Leslie Kirstin

LOUIE: Louie is a 74-year-old man who reports that he is hearing voices and seeing things. It seems that these hallucinations have come on gradually during the past four years. He has had a variety of psychological problems in his life. He acts helpless and resigned to his fate.

Figure B–4 ◆ A sample screen from *The Integrator.*

menus and instructions, and *PsychNow!* will introduce you to the fascinating world of psychology. *PsychNow!* will help you delve into psychological topics, learn more about them, and evaluate your understanding (Fig. B–3 ◆).

The most exciting part of *PsychNow!* is the interactive learning experience it offers. The core of *PsychNow!* is a collection of 40 learning modules in eight subject areas of psychology. Each module begins with an interactive exploration of a topic. Demonstrations, experiments, games, and full audio and video presentations make these explorations stimulating and instructive. For example, Piaget's stages of cognitive development are demonstrated in the Child Development module. In this "Explore" feature you can watch how children of different ages play a game of Monopoly. By doing so, you will gain insight into Piaget's theory. Then, you can use the lesson feature of the module to learn more about topics introduced in the "Explore" feature. As you encounter new concepts, you will get immediate feedback to reinforce learning and improve your understanding. To enrich your learning experience, an "Apply" feature in each module challenges you to relate concepts to new examples and situations.

PsychNow! also contains a glossary of over 500 terms, a handy electronic note pad, plus numerous graphics, animations, and video clips that bring psychology to life.

The Integrator *The Integrator* CD contains more than 1,600 audio clips, video clips, transparencies, animated sequences, and much more. All of these materials are designed to help you master introductory psychology. With the click of a mouse you can call up interactive experiments, animations, homework assignments, demonstrations, study pages, interactive surveys, and other helpful materials (Fig. B–4 ◆). This rich collection of information and activities is easy to use and makes exploring psychology more dynamic than ever.

Using Multimedia CD-ROMs Both *PsychNow!* and *The Integrator* can be obtained either directly from Brooks/Cole Publishing Company (ITP) or from your campus bookstore. (You can reach Brooks/Cole at 800-354-0092.) It is also possible that your instructor may provide one of these CDs for classroom use. Both CDs can be used alone or in conjunction with a textbook. *PsychNow!*, in particular, was designed to supplement this book. Using it in conjunction with your reading assignments will allow you to "see" psychology come to life in ways that are not possible in a printed text. If you would like to be part of the electronic revolution in psychology, give either *PsychNow!* or *The Integrator* a try.

Glossary

Ablation Surgical removal of tissue.

Absolute threshold The minimum amount of physical energy necessary to produce a sensation.

Accommodation (perceptual) Changes in the shape of the lens of the eye that serve to focus objects at varying distances.

Accommodation (Piaget) The modification of existing mental patterns to fit new demands.

Acculturative stress Stress caused by the many changes and adaptations required when a person moves to a foreign culture.

Acetylcholine The neurotransmitter released by neurons to activate muscles.

Achieved role A role that is assumed voluntarily.

Achievement motivation A need for success or the attainment of excellence.

Acquisition The period in conditioning during which a response is reinforced.

Action component That part of an attitude consisting of how one tends to act toward the object of the attitude.

Action potential The nerve impulse, which is a rapid change in electrical charge across the cell membrane.

Activation As reflected in facial expressions, the degree of arousal experienced by the person making the expression.

Activation-synthesis hypothesis Theory that relates dream content to motor commands in the brain, which are made, but not carried out during sleep.

Active euthanasia Deliberately inducing death.

Activity theory Theory of aging stating that the best adjustment to aging occurs for individuals who remain active mentally, socially, and physically.

Actor In making attributions, the person whose behavior is being interpreted.

Acuity That aspect of visual perception having to do with the sharpness or resolution of images.

Acupuncture The Chinese medical art of relieving pain and treating illness by inserting thin needles at various points on the body.

Acute stress disorder Psychological disturbance lasting up to one month following stresses, such as natural disasters or military combat, that would produce anxiety in anyone who experienced them.

Adaptation level An internal or mental "average" or "medium" point that is used to judge amounts.

Adaptive behaviors (emotion) Actions that aid humans and animals in their attempts to survive and adapt to changing conditions.

Adaptive behaviors (retardation) Basic skills and actions considered necessary for self-care and for dealing successfully with the environment.

Addiction Development of physical dependence on a drug such that craving and physical discomfort (withdrawal symptoms) occur in its absence.

Adjustment disorder Emotional disturbance caused by stressors within the range of common experience; stress is ongoing and produces anxiety and physical symptoms.

Adolescence The socially defined period between childhood and adulthood.

Adrenal glands Endocrine glands whose hormones arouse the body, regulate salt balance, adjust the body to stress, and affect sexual functioning.

Adrenaline A hormone produced by the adrenal glands that tends, in general, to arouse the body.

Affect Pertaining to emotion or feelings.

Affectional needs One's emotional needs in general but, especially, needs for love, attention, and affection.

Affective psychosis A general term for any major mood disorder that includes psychotic symptoms.

Afterimage A visual sensation that persists after a stimulus is removed.

Ageism Discrimination or prejudice based on a person's age.

Aggression Any action carried out with the intent of harming another person.

Aggression cues Stimuli or signals that are associated with aggression and tend to elicit it.

Agnosia A disturbance in the ability to perceive the meaning of stimuli, such as words, objects, or pictures.

Agoraphobia (without panic) Persons fear that something extremely embarrassing will happen to them if they leave the house or enter unfamiliar situations.

Alarm reaction First stage of the G.A.S., during which bodily resources are mobilized to cope with a stressor.

Alcohol Common name for ethyl alcohol, the intoxicating element in fermented and distilled liquors.

All-or-nothing thinking Classifying objects or events as absolutely right or wrong, good or bad, acceptable or unacceptable, and so forth.

Altered state of consciousness A condition of awareness distinctly different in quality or pattern from waking consciousness.

Alzheimer's disease An age-related disease characterized by memory loss, mental confusion, and in its later stages, by a nearly total loss of mental abilities.

Ambiguous stimuli Patterns that allow more than one perceptual organization.

Ambivalence Mixed positive and negative feelings or simultaneous attraction and repulsion.

Ambivalent attachment An emotional bond marked by conflicting feelings of affection, anger, and emotional turmoil.

American Sign Language A language system of hand gestures used by deaf and hearing-impaired persons.

Ames room An intentionally distorted room that interrupts perceptual constancies.

Amnesia Loss of memory (partial or complete) for past events and, especially, loss of memory for one's identity.

Amniocentesis Testing of the amniotic fluid from a pregnant woman's womb to identify fetal sex and to detect genetic defects in the fetus.

Amphetamine psychosis A severe disruption of psychological functioning caused by abuse of amphetamines.

Amphetamines A class of synthetic drugs having stimulant effects on the nervous system.

Anagrams Test A test of creativity in which subjects try to make as many new words as possible from the letters in a given word.

Anal stage In Freud's theory, the psychosexual stage corresponding roughly to the period of toilet training (age 1 to 3) and characterized by a preoccupation with the process of elimination.

Androgen Any of a number of male sex hormones, especially testosterone.

Androgen insensitivity An inherited disorder in which male embryos fail to develop male genitals because of an unresponsiveness to testosterone.

Androgenital syndrome An inherited disorder that causes the adrenal glands to produce excess androgens, sometimes masculinizing developing females before birth.

Androgyny The presence of both "masculine" and "feminine" traits in a single person (as masculinity and femininity are traditionally defined within one's culture).

Animal model In research, an animal whose behavior is used to discover principles that may apply to human behavior.

Anorexia nervosa Active self-starvation or a sustained loss of appetite that has psychological origins.

Anosmia Loss or impairment of the sense of smell.

Antecedents Events that precede a response.

Anterograde amnesia Loss of the ability to form or retrieve memories for events that occur after an injury or trauma.

Anthropomorphic fallacy The error of attributing human thoughts, feelings, or motives to animals.

Antidepressant A mood-elevating drug.

Antipsychotic A drug that, in addition to having tranquilizing effects, also tends to reduce hallucinations and delusional thinking.

Antisocial personality A person who seems to lack a conscience, is emotionally shallow, impulsive, selfish, and tends to manipulate others; also referred to as a sociopath or psychopath.

Anxiety Apprehension, dread, or uneasiness similar to fear but based on an unclear threat.

Anxiety disorder A disorder characterized by disruptive feelings of fear, apprehension, or anxiety or by distortions in behavior that are anxiety related.

Anxiety reduction hypothesis An explanation of the self-defeating nature of many avoidance responses that emphasizes the immediate reinforcing effects of relief from anxiety.

Aphasia A speech disturbance resulting from damage to language areas on the temporal lobes of the brain.

Apparent distance hypothesis An explanation of the moon illusion stating that the horizon seems more distant than the night sky because there are more depth cues near the horizon.

Applied psychology The use of psychological principles and research methods to solve practical problems.

Applied research Scientific study undertaken to solve immediate practical problems.

Approach-approach conflict A condition in which a person or animal must choose between two positive, or desirable, alternatives.

Approach-avoidance conflict An unpleasant condition in which a person or animal is simultaneously attracted to and repelled by the same goal.

Aptitude A capacity for learning certain abilities.

Aptitude test A test that rates a person's potential to learn skills required by various occupations.

Archetype A universal idea, image, or pattern, found in the collective unconscious.

Architectural psychology Study of the effects buildings have on behavior and the design of buildings using behavioral principles.

Arousal The overall level of excitation or activation in a person or animal.

Arousal theory A theory of motivation that assumes people prefer to maintain "ideal," or comfortable, levels of arousal.

Artificial insemination Medically engineered impregnation.

Artificial intelligence Any artificial system (often a computer program) that is capable of human-like problem solving or skilled responding.

Ascribed role A role that is assigned to a person; a role one has no choice about playing.

Assertiveness training Instruction in how to be self-assertive.

Assessment Evaluation or measurement.

Assessment center A program set up within an organization to conduct in-depth evaluations of job candidates.

Assimilation In Piaget's theory, the application of existing mental patterns to new situations (that is, the new situation is assimilated to existing mental schemes).

Association cortex All areas of the cerebral cortex that are not specifically sensory or motor in function.

Astigmatism Defects in the cornea, lens, or eye that cause some areas of vision to be out of focus.

Astrology False system based on the belief that human behavior is influenced by the position of stars and planets.

Attention Orienting toward or focusing on some stimulus.

Attention-deficit hyperactivity disorder A behavioral problem characterized by short attention span and restless movement.

Attentional overload A stressful condition caused when sensory stimulation, information, and social contacts make excessive demands on attention.

Attitude A learned tendency to respond to people, objects, or institutions in a positive or negative way.

Attitude scale A collection of attitude statements with which respondents indicate agreement or disagreement.

Attribution The process of making inferences about the causes of one's own behavior, and that of others. In emotion, the process of attributing perceived arousal to a particular source.

Auditory area Sites on the temporal lobes where auditory information registers.

Auditory ossicles The three small bones that link the eardrum to the inner ear.

Authenticity In Carl Rogers' terms, the ability of a therapist to be genuine and honest regarding his or her feelings.

Authoritarian parents Parents who enforce rigid rules and demand strict obedience to authority.

Authoritarian personality A personality pattern characterized by rigidity, inhibition, prejudice, and an excessive concern with power, authority, and obedience.

Authoritative parents Parents who supply firm and consistent guidance combined with love and affection.

Autism A severe disorder of childhood involving mutism, sensory spin-outs, sensory blocking, tantrums, unresponsiveness to others, and other difficulties.

Autokinetic effect The apparent movement of a stationary pinpoint of light displayed in a darkened room.

Autonomic nervous system The neural system that connects the brain with the internal organs and glands.

Autonomy A freedom from dependence on external authority or the opinions of others.

Aversion therapy Suppression of an undesirable response by associating it with aversive (painful or uncomfortable) stimuli.

Aversive stimulus Any stimulus that produces discomfort or displeasure.

Avoidance learning Learning that occurs when making a particular response delays or prevents the onset of a painful or unpleasant stimulus.

Avoidance-avoidance conflict An unpleasant condition requiring a choice between two negative, or mutually undesirable, alternatives.

Avoidant attachment An emotional bond marked by a tendency to resist commitment to others.

Axon A thin fiber that conducts information away from the cell body of a neuron.

Babbling The repetition by infants of meaningless language sounds (including both vowel and consonant sounds).

Bait shyness An unwillingness or hesitation on the part of animals to eat a particular food; often caused by the presence of a taste aversion.

Barbiturate One of a large group of sedative drugs.

Barnum effect The tendency to consider a personal description accurate if it is stated in very general terms.

Base rate The basic rate at which an event occurs over time; the basic probability of an event.

Baseline A record of the initial frequency of a target behavior.

Basic (or "pure") research Scientific study undertaken without concern for immediate practical application.

Basic needs The first four levels of needs in Maslow's hierarchy; lower needs tend to be more potent than higher needs.

Basic research Scientific inquiry done to advance basic knowledge, not to solve a practical problem.

Basic suggestion effect The tendency of hypnotized persons to carry out suggested actions as if they were involuntary.

Behavior modification The application of learning principles to change human behavior, espe-

cially maladaptive behavior.

Behavior therapy The use of learning principles to make constructive changes in behavior.

Behavioral assessment Recording the frequency of various behaviors.

Behavioral genetics The study of inherited behavioral traits and tendencies.

Behavioral medicine The study of behavioral factors associated with physical illness and its treatment.

Behavioral personality theory Any model of personality that emphasizes observable behavior, stimuli and responses, and the impact of learning.

Behavioral risk factors Behaviors that increase the chances of disease or injury or that shorten life expectancy.

Behavioral setting A smaller area within an environment whose use is well defined, such as a bus depot, waiting room, or lounge.

Behaviorism The study of overt, observable behavior.

Bem Sex Role Inventory (BSRI) A list of 60 personal traits including "masculine," "feminine," and "neutral" traits; used to rate one's degree of androgyny.

Bereavement Period of emotional adjustment that follows the death of a loved one.

Beta-endorphin A natural chemical produced by the pituitary gland that is similar in structure and pain-killing effect to opiate drugs such as morphine.

Biased sample A sample that does not accurately reflect the population from which it was drawn.

Bibliotherapy Use of books to impart helpful information, either alone or as an adjunct to other forms of therapy.

Binocular depth cues Depth cues that function only when both eyes are used.

Biochemical abnormality A disturbance of the body's chemical systems, especially in brain chemicals or neurotransmitters.

Biodata Detailed biographical information about a job applicant.

Biofeedback Information about bodily activities that aids voluntary regulation of bodily states.

Biological aging Physiological changes that accompany increasing age and alter a variety of physical and psychological functions.

Biological biasing effect Hypothesized effect that prenatal exposure to male or female hormones has on development of the body, nervous system, and later behavior patterns.

Biological constraints Biological limits on what an animal or person can easily learn.

Biological determinism Belief that behavior is controlled by biological processes, such as heredity or evolution.

Biological predisposition The presumed biological readiness of humans to learn certain skills, such as how to use language.

Biological rhythm Any cycle of biological activity, such as sleep and waking cycles or changes in body temperature.

Biopsychologist A psychologist who studies the relationship between behavior and biological processes, especially activity in the nervous system.

Biopsychology The study of biological processes as they relate to behavior.

Bipolar disorders Emotional disorders involving both depression and extremely elevated or manic moods and behavior.

Bipolar I disorder A mood disorder in which a person is mostly manic (excited, hyperactive, energetic), but has also had one or more periods of depression.

Bipolar II disorder A mood disorder in which a person is mostly depressed (sad, despondent, guilt ridden), but has also had one or more manic episodes.

Birth injury Any injury or damage that occurs to an infant during delivery.

Birthing room A room designed to minimize the medical aspects of giving birth.

Bisexual A person romantically and erotically attracted to both men and women.

Blind spot A portion of the retina lacking visual receptors (the point where the optic nerve leaves the eye).

Bottom-up processing Organizing perceptions by beginning with low-level features.

Brain dominance The language-producing cerebral hemisphere.

Brainstem The lowest portions of the brain, including the cerebellum, medulla, and reticular formation.

Brainstorming Method of creative thinking that separates the production and evaluation of ideas.

Brainwashing Engineered or forced attitude change involving a captive audience.

Branching program A computer program that gives learners corrective information and exercises based on the nature of their errors.

Brand image The image that consumers have of various products, especially with regard to their personal or emotional meanings.

Brief reactive psychosis A sudden, brief psychotic break that follows the occurrence of an extremely stressful event.

Brightness The intensity of light reflected from or emanating from a surface.

Brightness constancy The apparent (or relative) brightness of various objects remains the same as long as each object is illuminated by the same amount of light.

Broca's area A language area in the brain related to grammar and pronunciation.

Bulimia nervosa Excessive eating (gorging) usually followed by self-induced vomiting and/or taking laxatives.

Burnout A job-related condition of mental, physical, and emotional exhaustion.

Caffeine A natural drug with stimulant properties; found in coffee and tea and added to artificial beverages and medicines.

Caffeinism Excessive consumption of caffeine, leading to dependence and a variety of physical and psychological complaints.

Camouflage Designs that break up figure-ground organization, making objects more difficult to see.

Cannabis sativa The hemp plant, from whose leaves and flowers marijuana and hashish are derived.

Cannon-Bard theory According to this theory, emotional feelings and bodily arousal occur simultaneously and both begin with activity in the thalamus.

Cardinal trait A personality trait so basic or powerful that all or most of a person's activities spring from existence of the trait.

Career center A counseling facility that offers testing, career guidance, and information on various careers.

Career development One's entire career path, from choosing an initial vocation through retirement.

Caregiving styles Identifiable patterns of parental caretaking and interaction with children.

Caretaker speech An exaggerated pattern of speech used by adults when talking to infants.

Case study An intensive investigation of the behavior of a single person.

Castration Surgical removal of the testicles. Cas-

tration differs from sterilization, a procedure (such as vasectomy or tubal ligation) that merely makes a man or woman infertile.

Cataplexy A sudden temporary paralysis of the muscles.

Catatonic episode Period of extreme stupor, immobility, and unresponsiveness.

Catatonic schizophrenia Schizophrenia marked by stupor, rigidity, unresponsiveness, posturing, mutism, and, sometimes, agitated, purposeless behavior.

Causation The act of causing some effect.

Central nervous system The brain and spinal cord.

Central traits The core traits that characterize an individual personality.

Cerebellum A cauliflower-shaped projection at the base of the brain that controls posture and coordination.

Cerebral cortex The layer of tissue that forms the outer layer and surface of the cerebrum; the cerebral cortex is responsible for basic sensory and motor functions as well as higher mental processes in humans.

Cerebral hemispheres The right and left halves of the cerebrum.

Cerebrum The two large hemispheres that cover the upper part of the brain.

Character Personal characteristics that have been judged or evaluated; a person's desirable or undesirable qualities.

Chemical senses Senses, such as smell and taste, that respond to chemical molecules.

Chemotherapy Use of psychoactive drugs to treat mental or emotional disturbances.

Chorionic villus sampling Testing of a small piece of the placenta early in pregnancy to detect genetic defects in the fetus.

Chromosomes Thread-like structures ("colored bodies") in the nucleus of each cell that are made up of DNA, which carries the genes. Normal human cells have 23 pairs of chromosomes (46 total).

Chronological age A person's age in years.

Circadian rhythms Cyclical changes in bodily function and arousal that vary on a schedule approximating one 24-hour day.

Clairvoyance The purported ability to perceive events at a distance or through physical barriers.

Classical conditioning A basic form of learning in which existing reflex responses come to be elicited by new stimuli (also known as respondent conditioning).

Client-centered therapy A non-directive therapy based on drawing insights from conscious thoughts and feelings; emphasizes accepting one's true self.

Climacteric A time in late middle age when males experience a significant change in health, vigor, or appearance.

Clinging A problem in which a child literally clings to a parent or refuses to leave the parent's side.

Clinical psychologist A specialist who treats or does research on psychological problems.

Clinical study An intensive investigation of the behavior of a single person, especially one suffering from some injury, disease, or disorder.

Cloning The production of an entire organism using the DNA from a single cell.

Closure Gestalt term for the perceptual tendency to complete figures by "closing" or ignoring small gaps.

Cocaine A crystalline drug derived from coca leaves; used as a central nervous system stimulant and local anesthetic.

Cochlea The snail-shaped organ that makes up the inner ear.

Coefficient of correlation A statistical index ranging from -1.00 to +1.00 that indicates the direction and degree of correlation.

Coercive power Social power based on the ability to punish others.

Cognition The process of thinking, knowing, or mentally processing information.

Cognitive behavior therapy The use of learning principles to change maladaptive thoughts, beliefs, and feelings that underlie emotional and behavioral problems.

Cognitive behaviorism An approach that combines behavioral principles with cognition (perception, thinking, anticipation) to explain behavior.

Cognitive dissonance An uncomfortable clash between self-image, thoughts, beliefs, attitudes, or perceptions and one's behavior.

Cognitive learning Higher level learning involving thinking, knowing, understanding, and anticipation.

Cognitive map A mental image of an area (building, city, country) that guides movement from one location to another.

Cognitive psychology The study of human thinking, knowing, understanding, and information processing.

Cognitive therapy The use of learning principles and other methods to change maladaptive thoughts, beliefs, and feelings.

Collective unconscious A mental storehouse for unconscious ideas and images shared by all humans.

Color blindness A total inability to perceive colors.

Color weakness An inability to fully distinguish some colors from others.

Colostrum The first milk produced by a woman for a few days after giving birth. Colostrum is rich in antibodies to disease.

Commitment In a relationship, the degree to which you feel bound to another person.

Common traits Personality traits that are shared by most members of a particular culture.

Communicator In persuasion, the person presenting arguments or information.

Community health campaign A community-wide education program that provides information about factors that affect health and what to do about them.

Community mental health center A facility offering a wide range of mental health services, such as prevention, counseling, consultation, and crisis intervention.

Community psychology Use of community resources to promote mental health and treat or prevent mental health problems.

Companionate love Intimacy and commitment without passion.

Comparative psychology The study and comparison of the behavior of different species, especially animals.

Compensation Counteracting a real or imagined weakness by emphasizing desirable traits or by seeking to excel in other areas.

Competence As a factor in interpersonal attraction, the degree of general ability or proficiency a person displays.

Compliance Bending to the requests of a person who has little or no authority or other form of social power.

Compulsion An act an individual feels driven to repeat, often against his or her will.

Computer simulations Computer programs that mimic some aspect of human thinking, decision making, or problem solving.

Computer-assisted instruction (CAI) Learning aided by computer-presented information and

Concentrative meditation Mental exercise based on focusing attention on a single target of contemplation.

Concept A generalized idea representing a class of related objects or events.

Concept formation The process of classifying information into meaningful categories by direct experience, rule learning, or exposure to prototypes (idealized models).

Conceptual rule A formal rule by which one may decide if an object or event is an example of a particular concept.

Concrete operational stage Period of cognitive development during which children become able to use the concepts of time, space, volume, and number, but in ways that remain simplified and concrete.

Condensation Combining several people, objects, or events into a single dream image.

Conditional statement A statement that contains a qualification, often of the *if-then* form.

Conditioned aversion A learned dislike or conditioned negative emotional response to some stimulus.

Conditioned emotional response An emotional response that has been linked to a previously non-emotional stimulus by classical conditioning.

Conditioned response A reflex response linked to a new stimulus through learning.

Conditioned stimulus A previously neutral stimulus that acquires the capacity to evoke a response by being paired with an unconditioned stimulus.

Conditioning chamber An apparatus designed for the study of operant conditioning in animals; a Skinner box.

Conditions of worth Internal standards used to judge the value of one's thoughts, actions, feelings, or experiences.

Conduction deafness Poor transfer of sounds from the eardrum to the inner ear.

Cones Visual receptors for colors and daylight visual acuity.

Conflict A stressful condition that occurs when a person must choose between incompatible or contradictory alternatives.

Conformity Bringing one's behavior into agreement or harmony with norms or with the behavior of others in a group.

Confrontation In existential therapy, the process of confronting clients with their own values and with the need to take responsibility for the quality of their existence.

Congenital problems Problems or defects that originate during prenatal development.

Conjunctive concept A concept defined by the presence of two or more specific features. (For example, to qualify as an example of the concept an object must be both red *and* triangular.)

Connector neuron A nerve cell that serves as a link between two others.

Connotative meaning The subjective, personal, or emotional meaning of a word or concept.

Conscience In Freudian theory, the part of the superego that causes guilt when its standards are not met.

Conscious Region of the mind that includes all mental contents (thoughts, images, feelings, memories, and so on) a person is aware of at any given moment.

Consciousness A person's experience of mental awareness, including current sensations, perceptions, memories, and feelings.

Consensus The degree to which people respond alike. In making attributions, consensus implies that

responses are externally caused.

Consequences Effects that follow a response.

Consequences Test A test of creativity based on listing the consequences that would follow a basic change in the world.

Conservation In Piaget's theory, mastery of the concept that the volume of matter remains unchanged (is conserved) even when the shape or appearance of objects changes.

Consistency When making attributions, noticing that a behavior changes very little on different occasions.

Consolidation Process by which relatively permanent memories are formed in the brain.

Constructive processing Reorganizing memories on the basis of logic, inference, or the addition of new information.

Consumer behavior All of the actions involved in deciding what to spend, selecting a brand, shopping, making the purchase, and evaluating a product in use.

Consumer psychology Specialty area that focuses on understanding consumer behavior and applying psychology to advertising, marketing, product testing, and the like.

Consumerism Formal attempts to enhance consumer knowledge, rights, and welfare.

Consummate love A loving relationship that combines passion, commitment, and intimacy.

Contact comfort A pleasant and reassuring feeling human and animal infants get from touching or clinging to something soft and warm, usually the mother.

Context Information surrounding a stimulus that gives meaning to the stimulus; with regard to behavior, the social situation, behavioral setting, or other surrounding circumstances in which an action takes place.

Continuous reinforcement A schedule of reinforcement in which every correct response is followed by a reinforcer.

Control (experimental) Eliminating, identifying, or equalizing all factors in an experiment that could affect the outcome.

Control (human factors) Any knob, handle, button, lever, or other device used to alter the activity of a machine.

Control (stress) With regard to stress, the ability to exert some influence over one's circumstances.

Control group In an experiment, subjects exposed to all conditions *except* the independent variable.

Control questions In a polygraph exam, questions that almost always provoke anxiety, thus providing a baseline of emotional responsiveness.

Conventional moral reasoning Moral thinking based on a desire to please others or to follow accepted rules and values.

Convergence The simultaneous turning inward of the two eyes as they focus on nearby objects.

Convergent thought Thinking directed toward discovery of a single established correct answer; conventional thinking.

Conversion disorder A symptom or disability that appears to be physical but that actually results from anxiety, stress, or emotional conflict.

Cooing Spontaneous repetition of vowel sounds by infants.

Coping statements Reassuring, self-enhancing statements that are used to stop self-critical thinking.

Corpus callosum The large bundle of fibers connecting the right and left cerebral hemispheres.

Correlation An orderly relationship between two events, measures, or variables.

Correlational study A non-experimental study

designed to measure the degree of relationship (if any) between two or more events, measures, or variables.

Corticalization An increase in the relative size of the cerebral cortex.

Counseling psychologist A specialist who treats milder emotional and behavioral disturbances.

Counselor An adviser who helps people solve problems with marriage, career, schoolwork, or the like.

Counterirritation Using mild pain to block more intense or long-lasting pain.

Courtesy bias The tendency to give "polite" answers so as not to hurt an interviewer's feelings.

Covert behavior A response that is internal or hidden from view.

Covert reinforcement Using positive imagery to reinforce desired behavior.

Covert sensitization Use of aversive imagery to reduce the occurrence of an undesired response.

Cranial nerve One of 12 major nerves that leave the brain without passing through the spinal cord.

Created image A mental image that has been assembled or invented rather than simply remembered.

Cretinism Stunted growth and mental retardation caused by an insufficient supply of thyroid hormone.

Critical incidents Situations that arise in a job, with which a competent worker must be able to cope.

Critical period During development, a period of increased sensitivity to environmental influences. Also, a time during which certain events must take place for normal development to occur.

Critical situations Situations during childhood that are capable of leaving a lasting imprint on personality.

Critical thinking An ability to evaluate, compare, analyze, critique, and synthesize information.

Cross-cultural psychologist A psychologist who studies the ways in which culture affects human behavior.

Crowding A subjective feeling of being overstimulated by a loss of privacy or by the nearness of others (especially when social contact with them is unavoidable).

Cryonic suspension Freezing the body or head at death in hopes that future revival will become possible.

Crystalized abilities Abilities that a person has intentionally mastered; accumulated knowledge and skills.

CT scan Computed tomography scan; a computer-enhanced X-ray image of the brain.

Cue External stimuli or signs that guide responses, especially those that signal the likely presence or absence of reinforcement.

Cult A group that professes great devotion to some person, idea, or thing.

Cultural psychologist A psychologist who studies the ways in which culture affects human behavior.

Cultural relativity Perceptions and judgments made relative to the values of one's culture.

Cultural values The values attached to various objects and activities by people in a given culture.

Culture An ongoing pattern of life, characterizing a society at a particular stage in its development or at a given point in history.

Culture-fair test A test (such as an intelligence test) designed to minimize the importance of skills and knowledge that may be more common in some cultures than in others.

Curare A drug that competes with acetylcholine, causing paralysis.

Curiosity drive A hypothesized drive assumed to

underlie a wide range of investigative and stimulus-seeking behaviors.

Curve of forgetting A graph that shows the amount of memorized information remembered after varying lengths of time.

Curvilinear relationship A relationship that forms a curved line when graphed.

Cyclothymic disorder Moderate manic and depressive behavior that persists for two years or more.

Dark adaptation The process by which the eye adapts to low illumination and becomes more light sensitive, principally by a shift to rod vision.

Data Observed facts or evidence (*data*: plural; *datum*: singular).

Data reduction system Any system that selects, analyzes, or condenses information.

Daydream A vivid waking fantasy.

Declarative memory That part of long-term memory containing factual information.

Deductive thought Thought that applies a general set of rules to specific situations; for example, using the laws of gravity to predict the behavior of a single falling object.

Deep lesioning Use of an electrode (electrified wire) to destroy small areas deep within the brain.

Deep sleep Stage 4 sleep; the deepest form of normal sleep.

Defense mechanisms Habitual and often unconscious psychological strategies used to avoid or reduce anxiety.

Deinstitutionalization Reduced use of full-time commitment to mental institutions to treat mental disorders.

Delayed speech Speech that is developmentally delayed; that is, speech that begins well after the normal age for language development has passed.

Delta waves Large, slow brain waves that occur in deeper sleep (stage 3 and stage 4).

Delusion A false belief held against all contrary evidence.

Delusional disorder A psychosis marked by severe delusions of grandeur, jealousy, persecution, or similar preoccupations.

Demonology In medieval Europe, the study of demons and the treatment of persons "possessed" by demons.

Dendrites Fibers projecting from nerve cells that receive information from other neurons and carry it to the cell body.

Denial Protecting oneself from an unpleasant reality by refusing to perceive it or believe it.

Denotative meaning The exact, dictionary definition of a word or concept; its objective meaning.

Density The number of people in a given space or, inversely, the amount of space available to each person.

Dependent variable In an experiment, the condition (usually a behavior) that reflects the effects of the independent variable.

Depressant A substance that decreases activity in the body and nervous system.

Depression A state of deep despondency marked by apathy, emotional negativity, and behavioral inhibition.

Depressive disorders Emotional disorders primarily involving sadness, despondency, and depression.

Deprivation In development, the loss or withholding of normal stimulation, nutrition, comfort, love, and so forth; a condition of lacking.

Deprivation dwarfism Stunted growth caused by isolation, rejection, or general deprivation.

Depth cues Perceptual features that impart information about distance and three-dimensional space.

Depth perception The ability to see three-dimensional space and to accurately estimate distances.

Desensitization Reducing fear or anxiety by repeatedly exposing a person to emotional stimuli while the person is deeply relaxed.

Determinism The doctrine that all behavior has prior causes.

Detoxification To remove poison or the effects of poison; in the treatment of alcoholism, the withdrawal of the patient from alcohol.

Developmental level An individual's current state of physical, emotional, and intellectual development.

Developmental milestone A significant turning point or marker in personal development.

Developmental psychologist A psychologist who studies the course of human growth and development.

Developmental psychology The study of progressive changes in behavior and abilities from conception to death.

Developmental task Any skill that must be mastered, or personal change that must take place, for optimal development at a particular life stage.

Deviant communication Patterns of communication that cause guilt, anxiety, confusion, anger, conflict, and emotional turmoil.

Deviation IQ An IQ obtained statistically from a person's relative standing in his or her age group.

Diet The types and amounts of food and drink regularly consumed over a period of time.

Difference threshold The smallest change in stimulus intensity that can be detected by an observer.

Digit-span test A test of attention and short-term memory in which a string of digits is recalled.

Diminished capacity Impaired mental competence to control actions or know right from wrong.

Direct instruction Presentation of factual information by lecture, demonstration, and rote practice.

Direct observation (personality) Any observation of a person's behavior in a natural or prearranged situation undertaken to form an impression of his or her personality.

Discounting Downgrading internal explanations of behavior when a person's actions appear to have strong external causes.

Discovery learning Learning based on insight or understanding rather than on mechanical application of rules.

Discrimination Treating members of various social groups differently in circumstances where their rights or treatment should be identical.

Discriminative stimuli Stimuli that precede rewarded and non-rewarded responses in operant conditioning and that come to exert some control over whether the response is made.

Disease-prone personality A personality style associated with poor health; marked by persistent negative emotions, including anxiety, depression, and hostility.

Disengagement theory of aging States that it is normal and desirable for the aged to withdraw from roles they held earlier.

Dishabituation A reversal of habituation.

Disinhibition The removal of inhibition, resulting in the acting out of behavior that normally would be restrained.

Disjunctive concept A concept defined by the presence of at least one of several possible features. (For example, to qualify an object must be either blue *or* circular.)

Disorganized schizophrenia Schizophrenia marked by incoherence, disorganized behavior, bizarre thinking, and flat or grossly inappropriate emotions.

Displaced aggression Redirecting aggression to a target other than the actual source of one's frustration.

Display Any dial, screen, light, or other device used to provide information about a machine's activity to a human operator.

Dissection Separation of tissues into their parts.

Dissociative amnesia Loss of memory (partial or complete) for past events and, especially, loss of memory for one's personal identity.

Dissociative disorder Temporary amnesia, multiple personality, or depersonalization.

Dissociative fugue Fleeing to escape extreme emotional conflict, anxiety, or threat.

Dissociative identity disorder The presence of two or more distinct personalities or personal identities (multiple personality).

Distinctiveness As a basis for making causal attributions, noticing that a behavior occurs only under a specific (distinct) set of circumstances.

Distractors False items included with a correct item to form a test of recognition memory (for example, the wrong answers on a multiple-choice test).

Disuse Theory that memory traces weaken when memories are not periodically used or retrieved.

Divergent thought Thinking that produces many ideas or alternatives; a major element in original or creative thought.

Divided attention Allotting mental space or effort to various tasks or parts of a task.

DNA Deoxyribonucleic acid; a twisted, ladder-like molecular structure containing the chemical code for genetic information.

Dogmatism An unwarranted positiveness or certainty in matters of belief or opinion.

Dominant gene A gene whose influence will be expressed each time the gene is present.

Door-in-the-face effect The tendency for a person who has refused a major request to subsequently be more likely to comply with a minor request.

Dopamine An important transmitter substance found in the brain, especially in the limbic system, an area associated with emotional response.

Double approach-avoidance conflict An unpleasant state in which one is simultaneously attracted to and repelled by each of two alternatives.

Double standard Applying different standards for judging the appropriateness of male and female sexual behavior.

Double-blind experiment A test in which neither subjects nor experimenters know which subjects are in the experimental group.

Down syndrome A genetic disorder caused by the presence of an extra chromosome; results in mental retardation.

Dream symbols Images in dreams that serve as visible signs of hidden ideas, desires, impulses, emotions, relationships, and so forth.

Drill and practice A basic computer-assisted learning format, typically consisting of questions and answers.

Drive The psychological expression of a motive; for example, hunger, thirst, or a drive for success.

Drug interaction A combined effect of two drugs that exceeds the addition of one drug's effects to the other.

Drug tolerance A reduction in the body's response to a drug.

Dyslexia An inability to read with understanding, often caused by a tendency to misread letters (by seeing their mirror images, for instance).

Dyspareunia Genital pain before, during, or after sexual intercourse.

Dysthymic disorder A moderate level of depression that has persisted for two years or more but has not included periods of severe depression.

Early childhood education program Programs that provide stimulating intellectual experiences, typically for disadvantaged preschoolers.

Easy child A child who is temperamentally relaxed and agreeable.

Echo A brief continuation of sensory activity in the auditory system after a sound is heard.

Echolalia A compulsion, sometimes observed in autistic children, to repeat everything that is said.

Eclectic Selected from many sources.

Educational psychology The study of learning, teaching, and related topics.

Educational simulations Computer programs that simulate real-world settings or situations to promote learning.

Effective parents Parents who supply firm and consistent guidance combined with love and affection.

Effector cells Cells in muscles and glands specialized for the production of responses.

Ego In Freudian theory, the executive part of personality that directs rational, realistic behavior.

Ego ideal In Freudian theory, the part of the superego representing ideal behavior; a source of pride when its standards are met.

Egocentric thought Thought that is self-centered and fails to consider the viewpoints of others.

Eidetic imagery The ability to retain a "projected" mental image long enough to use it as a source of information.

Ejaculation The release of sperm and seminal fluid by the male at the time of orgasm.

Elaborative rehearsal Rehearsal that links new information with existing memories and knowledge.

Electra conflict Freudian concept referring to a girl's sexual attraction to her father and resultant feelings of rivalry with her mother.

Electrical stimulation of the brain (ESB) Direct electrical stimulation and action of brain tissue.

Electroconvulsive therapy (ECT) A medical treatment for severe depression, consisting of an electric shock passed directly through the brain, which produces a convulsion.

Electrode Any wire, needle, or metal plate used to electrically stimulate nerve tissue or to record its activity.

Electroencephalograph (EEG) A device designed to detect, amplify, and record electrical activity in the brain.

Electromagnetic spectrum The full range of electrical and magnetic wavelengths, including X-rays, radio waves, light waves, and so forth.

Emblems Gestures that have widely understood meanings within a particular culture.

Emotion A state characterized by physiological arousal, subjective feelings, changes in facial expression, and adaptive behaviors.

Emotion-focused coping Managing or controlling one's emotional reaction to a stressful or threatening situation.

Emotional appraisal Evaluating the personal meaning of a situation; specific emotions are assumed to result from various appraisals, such as an appraisal of threat leading to anxiety.

Emotional attachment A close emotional bond that infants form with their parents, caregivers, or others.

Emotional bonding An especially close emotional bond between infants and their parents, caregivers, or others (another term for attachment).

Emotional component One's feelings toward the object of an attitude.

Emotional expression Any behavior that gives an outward sign of emotion, especially those signs that communicate emotional states to others.

Emotional feelings The private, subjective experience of having an emotion.

Emotional tone The underlying emotional state an individual is experiencing at any given moment.

Empathy A capacity for taking another's point of view; the ability to feel what another is feeling.

Empirical evidence Facts or information gained by direct observation or experience.

Empty love A relationship based almost entirely on commitment.

Encoding Changing information into a form that allows it to be stored in memory and manipulated in thought.

Encoding failure Failure to store sufficient information to form a useful memory.

Encopresis A lack of bowel control; "soiling."

Encounter group A group experience based on intensely honest expressions of feelings and reactions of participants to one another.

Endocrine system Glands whose secretions pass directly into the bloodstream or lymph system.

Endogenous depression Depression that appears to be produced from within (perhaps by chemical imbalances in the brain), rather than as a reaction to life events.

Endorphins A class of chemicals produced by the pituitary gland that are similar in structure and pain-killing effect to opiate drugs such as morphine.

Energizers Mood-elevating drugs.

Engineering psychology A specialty concerned with the design of machines and work environments so that they are compatible with human perceptual and physical capacities.

Engram Hypothesized physical changes that take place in the brain as it stores information; a memory trace.

Enkephalins Opiate-like brain chemicals that regulate reactions to pain and stress.

Enriched environment An environment deliberately made more novel, complex, and perceptually stimulating.

Enrichment In development, any attempt to make a child's environment more novel, complex, and perceptually or intellectually stimulating.

Enuresis An inability to control urination, particularly with regard to bed-wetting.

Environment ("nurture") The sum total of all external conditions affecting development.

Environmental assessment Measurement and analysis of the effects an environment has on the behavior of people within that environment.

Environmental psychology The formal study of how environments affect behavior.

Episodic drive A drive that occurs in distinct episodes associated with particular conditions (for example, pain avoidance, sexual motivation).

Episodic memory A subpart of declarative memory that records personal experiences that are linked with specific times and places.

Equal-status contact Social interaction that occurs on an equal footing, without obvious differences in power or status.

Ergotism A pattern of psychotic-like symptoms that accompanies poisoning by ergot fungus.

Erogenous zone Any body area that produces pleasurable sensations.

Eros Freud's name for the "life instincts" postulated by his theory.

Escape Reducing discomfort by leaving frustrating situations or by psychologically withdrawing from them.

Escape learning Learning to make a response in order to end an aversive (painful or uncomfortable) stimulus.

Establishment phase The period during which a person enters a career and builds competence in it.

Estrogen Any of a number of female sex hormones.

Estrus Changes in the reproductive organs and sexual drives of animals that create a desire for mating; particularly used to refer to females in heat.

Ethnocentrism Placing one's own group or race at the center—that is, tending to reject all other groups but one's own.

Ethologist A person who studies the natural behavior patterns of animals.

Eugenics Selective breeding for desirable characteristics.

Evolutionary psychology Study of the evolutionary origins of human behavior patterns.

Excitement General emotional arousal associated with activation of the autonomic nervous system.

Excitement phase The first phase of sexual response, indicated by initial signs of sexual arousal.

Exhibitionism Deriving sexual pleasure from displaying the genitals (usually), to an unwilling viewer ("flashing").

Existential therapy An insight therapy that focuses on the problems of existence, such as death, meaning, choice, and responsibility; emphasizes making courageous life choices.

Exorcism In medieval Europe, the practice of expelling or driving off an "evil spirit," especially one residing in the body of a person who is "possessed."

Expectancy An anticipation concerning future events or relationships.

Experiment A formal trial undertaken to confirm or disconfirm a fact or principle.

Experimental group In a controlled experiment, the group of subjects exposed to the independent variable or experimental manipulation.

Experimental psychologist One who scientifically studies human and animal behavior.

Experimental self-observation Wilhelm Wundt's technique of combining trained introspection with objective measurement.

Experimental subjects Humans or animals whose behavior is investigated in an experiment.

Experimenter effect Changes in subjects' behavior caused by the unintended influence of an experimenter's actions.

Expert power Social power derived from possession of knowledge or expertise.

Expert systems Computer programs designed to respond as a human expert would; programs based on the knowledge and rules that underlie human expertise in specific topics.

Expert witness A person recognized by a court of law as being qualified to give expert testimony on a specific topic.

Explicit memory A memory that a person is aware of having; a memory that is consciously retrieved.

Exploration drive Drive to investigate unfamiliar areas of the environment.

Exploration phase The period during which career alternatives are explored.

Expressive behavior Behavior that expresses or communicates emotion.

External cause A cause of behavior that is assumed to lie outside a person.

External eating cue Any external stimulus that tends to encourage hunger or to elicit eating.

External frustration A negative emotional state caused by events or conditions that hinder satisfaction of a motive or that block progress toward a goal.

Extinction A gradual decrease in the frequency of a non-reinforced response.

Extracellular thirst Thirst caused by a reduction in the volume of fluids found between body cells.

Extraneous variable In an experiment, any condition prevented from influencing the outcome.

Extrasensory perception The purported ability to perceive events in ways that cannot be explained by known capacities of the sensory organs.

Extrinsic motivation Motivation based on obvious external rewards, obligations, or similar factors.

Extrovert A person whose attention is directed outward; a bold, sociable, outgoing person.

Eye movement desensitization A reduction in fear or anxiety that occurs when a person holds upsetting thoughts in mind while rapidly moving the eyes from side to side.

Facial agnosia An inability to recognize familiar faces.

Facial blend A facial gesture that mixes parts of two or more basic facial expressions.

Facial feedback hypothesis Explanation that says facial expressions generate feelings that help define what emotion a person is feeling.

Fact memory That part of long-term memory containing factual information (declarative memory).

Factor analysis A statistical technique used to correlate multiple measurements. Measurements that form "clusters" of correlations are assumed to reflect some general underlying factor.

Fallacy of positive instances The tendency to remember or notice information that fits one's expectations, while forgetting discrepancies.

False positive An erroneous sense of recognition.

Familial retardation Mild mental retardation associated with homes that are intellectually, nutritionally, and emotionally impoverished.

Family system The family as an entire unit, including all its members, their relationships, and their typical patterns of behavior.

Family therapy Technique in which all family members participate, both individually and as a group, to change destructive relationships and communication patterns.

Fantasy A product of the imagination determined mainly by one's motives or feelings. Fantasy may be used as an escape mechanism.

Fantasy stage Stage of career exploration in which persons imagine themselves filling unlikely roles.

Fatuous love A relationship based on commitment and passion that lacks intimacy.

Feature detector A sensory system highly attuned to a specific stimulus pattern.

Feedback Information on the effects a response has had that is returned to the person performing the response (also known as knowledge of results).

Feeding system Areas on each side of the hypothalamus that initiate eating when stimulated.

Feeling of knowing The ability to predict beforehand whether one will be able to remember something.

Female orgasmic disorder An inability to reach orgasm during intercourse.

Female sexual arousal disorder A lack of physical arousal to sexual stimulation.

Fetal alcohol syndrome A pattern of birth complications and bodily defects in infants caused by consumption of alcohol by the mother during pregnancy.

Fetal damage A congenital problem; that is, damage or injury that occurs to the fetus during prenatal development.

Fetishism Gaining sexual gratification from inanimate objects; especially, an inability to achieve sexual arousal without the object.

Field experiment An experiment conducted in a natural setting.

Figure-ground organization A basic perceptual organization in which part of a stimulus appears to stand out as an object (figure) against a less prominent background (ground).

Five-factor model A model proposing that the five most universal dimensions of personality are extroversion, agreeableness, conscientiousness, neuroticism, and openness to experience.

Fixation (cognition) The tendency to repeat wrong solutions or faulty responses, especially as a result of becoming blind to alternatives.

Fixation (Freudian) In Freudian theory, lasting conflicts developed during a particular psychosexual stage as a result of frustration or over-indulgence.

Fixed action pattern (FAP) An instinctual chain of movements found in almost all members of a species.

Fixed interval schedule A pattern in which a reinforcer is given only when a correct response is made after a set amount of time has passed since the last reinforced response. Responses made before the time interval has ended are not reinforced.

Fixed ratio schedule A pattern in which a set number of correct responses must be made to get a reinforcer. For example, a reinforcer is given for every 4 correct responses.

Flashbulb memories Memories created at times of high emotion that seem especially vivid.

Flat affect An extreme lack of emotion.

Flexitime A work schedule that allows flexible starting and quitting times, centered around a core work period.

Fluency In tests of creativity, fluency refers to the total number of solutions produced.

Fluid abilities Innate abilities based on perceptual, motor, or intellectual speed and flexibility; abilities that are not based on prior intentional learning.

Foot-in-the-door effect The tendency for a person who has first complied with a small request to be more likely later to fulfill a larger request.

Forcible rape Sexual intercourse carried out against the victim's will, under the threat of force.

Forebrain The highest brain areas, including the hypothalamus, thalamus, corpus callosum, and cerebrum.

Formal operations stage Period of cognitive development marked by a capacity for abstract, theoretical, and hypothetical thinking.

Fovea A small depression at the center of the retina containing only cones and providing the greatest sharpness of vision.

Frame of reference A mental or emotional perspective used for evaluating events.

Framing In thought, the terms in which a problem is stated or the way that it is structured.

Fraternal twins Twins conceived from two separate eggs. Fraternal twins are no more alike genetically than other siblings.

Free association In psychoanalysis, the technique of having a client say anything that comes to mind, regardless of how embarrassing or unimportant it may seem.

Free choice The ability to freely make choices that are not controlled by genetics, learning, or unconscious forces.

Free will The doctrine that human beings are capable of freely making choices.

Free-floating anxiety Anxiety that is very general and pervasive.

Frequency theory Holds that, in hearing, the cochlea converts tones up to about 4000 hertz into nerve impulses that match the frequency of each tone.

Frontal lobes Areas at the top front of the cerebral cortex that include sites associated with the control of movement, the processing of smell, and higher mental functions.

Frontal lobotomy The destruction of brain tissue in frontal areas of the brain.

Frotteurism Sexually touching or rubbing against a non-consenting person.

Frustration An internal emotional state resulting from interference with satisfaction of a motive or blocking of goal-directed behavior.

Frustration-aggression hypothesis Hypothesis stating that frustration tends to lead to aggression.

Fugue Taking flight to escape extreme emotional conflict, anxiety, or threat.

Fully functioning person Carl Rogers' term for persons living in harmony with their deepest feelings, impulses, and intuitions.

Functional fixedness A rigidity in problem solving caused by an inability to see new uses for familiar objects.

Functional MRI An MRI scan that records brain activity.

Functional psychosis A psychosis of unknown origin or one presumed to be caused by psychological factors.

Functional solution A detailed, practical, and workable solution.

Functionalism School of psychology concerned with how behavior and mental abilities help people adapt to their environments.

Fundamental attributional error The tendency to attribute the behavior of others to internal causes (personality, likes, and so forth) while attributing one's own behavior to external causes (situations and circumstances).

Galvanic skin response (GSR) A change in the electrical resistance (or inversely, the conductance) of the skin, due to activity in the sweat glands associated with arousal or anxiety.

Gate control theory Proposes that pain messages pass through neural "gates" in the spinal cord.

Gender bias A tendency for researchers to base conclusions solely on subjects of one gender (usually males).

Gender identity One's personal, private sense of maleness or femaleness.

General adaptation syndrome (G.A.S.) A series of bodily reactions to prolonged stress, occurring in three stages: alarm, resistance, and exhaustion.

General intelligence test A test that measures a wide variety of mental abilities.

General negativism A tendency to respond negatively to almost all situations or social interactions.

General paresis A disease that occurs when syphilis attacks the brain; can cause an organic psychosis.

General solution A solution that states the requirements for success, but not in enough detail for further action.

Generalization Transfer of a learned response from one stimulus situation to other similar situations.

Generalized anxiety disorder The person is in a chronic state of tension and worries about work, relationships, ability, or impending disaster.

Generalized reinforcer A secondary reinforcer that has become independent of direct association with primary reinforcers.

Genes Specific areas on a strand of DNA that carry hereditary information affecting various personal characteristics.

Genetic abnormality Any abnormality in the

genes, including missing genes, extra genes, or defective genes.

Genetic sex   Gender as indicated by the presence of *XX* (female) or *XY* (male) chromosomes.

Genital sex   Gender as indicated by the presence of male or female genitals.

Genital stage   In Freud's theory, the culmination of personality development, marked, among other things, by the attainment of mature adult sexuality.

Gerontologist   One who scientifically studies aging and its effects.

Gestalt   A German word meaning form, pattern, or whole.

Gestalt psychology   The school of psychology emphasizing the study of thinking, learning, and perception in whole units, not by analysis into parts.

Gestalt therapy   An approach that focuses on immediate experience and awareness to help clients rebuild thinking, feeling, and acting into connected wholes; emphasizes the integration of fragmented experiences.

Giantism   Excessive bodily growth caused by too much growth hormone.

Giftedness   Either the possession of a high IQ or special talents or aptitudes.

Goal   The target or objective of a motivated and directed chain of behaviors.

Gonadal sex   Gender as indicated by the presence of ovaries (female) or testes (male).

Gonads   The primary sex glands—the testes in males and ovaries in females.

Grammar   A set of rules for combining language units into meaningful speech or writing.

Graphology   False system based on the belief that handwriting can reveal personality traits.

Grasping reflex   A neonatal reflex consisting of grasping objects placed in the palms.

Gray matter   Areas in the nervous system that have a grayish color due to a high concentration of nerve cell bodies.

Grief   An intense emotional state that follows the death of a lover, friend, or relative.

Group cohesiveness   The degree of attraction among group members or their degree of commitment to remaining in the group.

Group intelligence test   Any intelligence test that can be administered to a group of people with minimal supervision.

Group prejudice   Prejudice held out of conformity to group views.

Group sanctions   Rewards and punishments (such as approval or disapproval) administered by groups to enforce a degree of conformity among members.

Group structure   The network of roles, communication pathways, and power in a group.

Group therapy   Psychotherapy conducted with a group of people.

Groupthink   A compulsion by members of decision-making groups to maintain agreement, even at the cost of critical thinking.

Growth needs   In Maslow's hierarchy, the higher level needs associated with self-actualization (needs that contribute to personal growth and full development of personal potential).

Growth spurt   An often dramatic acceleration in physical growth that coincides with puberty.

Guided imagery   Intentional visualization of images that are calming, relaxing, or beneficial in other ways.

Gustation   The sense of taste.

Habit   A deeply ingrained, learned pattern of behavior.

Habituation   A decrease in perceptual response to a repeated stimulus.

Hair cells   Receptor cells within the cochlea that transduce vibrations into nerve impulses.

Half-way house   A community-based facility for individuals making the transition from an institution (mental hospital, prison, and so forth) to independent living.

Hallucination   An imaginary sensation—such as seeing, hearing, or smelling something that does not exist in the external world.

Hallucinogen   Any substance that alters or distorts sensory impressions.

Halo effect   The tendency of an interviewer to extend a favorable or unfavorable impression to unrelated aspects of an individual's personality.

Handedness   A preference for the right or left hand in most activities.

Hardy personality   A personality style associated with superior stress resistance.

Hassle   Any distressing, day-to-day annoyance; also called a microstressor.

Health psychology   Study of the ways in which psychological principles can be used to maintain and promote health.

Heredity ("nature")   The transmission of physical and psychological characteristics from parents to offspring through genes.

Hermaphroditism   The condition of having genitals suggestive of both sexes; ambiguous genital sexuality.

Hertz   One cycle (or vibration) per second.

Heterosexism   The belief that heterosexuality is better or more natural than homosexuality.

Heterosexual   A person romantically and erotically attracted to members of the opposite sex.

Heuristic   Any strategy or technique that aids problem solving, especially by limiting the number of possible solutions to be tried.

Hidden observer   A detached part of the hypnotized person's awareness that silently observes events.

Hierarchy   A rank-ordered series of higher and lower amounts, levels, degrees, or steps.

Hierarchy of needs   A rank ordering of needs based on their presumed strength or potency.

High self-monitors   Persons who try to adapt their public image to the demands of various situations by managing the impression they make on others.

Higher order conditioning   Classical conditioning in which a conditioned stimulus is used to reinforce further learning; that is, a CS is used as if it were a US.

Hippocampus   A structure in the brain associated with the regulation of emotions and the transfer of information from short-term memory to long-term memory.

Homeostasis   A steady state of bodily equilibrium normally maintained automatically by various physiological mechanisms.

Homogamy   Marriage of two people who are similar to one another.

Homophobia   A powerful fear of homosexuality.

Homosexual   A person romantically and erotically attracted to same-sex persons.

Honesty test   A paper-and-pencil test designed to detect attitudes, beliefs, and behavior patterns that predispose a person to engage in dishonest behavior.

Hormonal sex   Gender as indicated by a preponderance of estrogens (female) or androgens (male) in the body.

Hormone   A glandular secretion that affects bodily functions or behavior.

Hospice   A medical facility or program dedicated to providing optimal care for persons who are dying.

Hospitalism   A pattern of deep depression observed in institutionalized infants marked by weeping and sadness and a lack of normal responsiveness to other humans.

Hue   Classification of colors into basic categories of red, orange, yellow, green, blue, indigo, and violet.

Human genome   The entire set of human genes.

Human growth sequence   The general pattern of physical development from conception to death.

Human immunodeficiency virus (HIV)   The sexually transmitted virus that disables the immune system and causes AIDS.

Human nature   Those traits, qualities, potentials, and behavior patterns most characteristic of the human species.

Humanism   An approach to psychology that focuses on human experience, problems, potentials, and ideals.

Hydrocephaly   A buildup of cerebrospinal fluid within brain cavities.

Hyperactivity   A behavioral state characterized by short attention span, restless movement, and impaired learning capacity.

Hyperopia   Difficulty focusing nearby objects (farsightedness).

Hypersomnia   Extreme daytime sleepiness.

Hyperthyroidism   Faster metabolism and excitability caused by an overactive thyroid gland.

Hypnic jerk   A reflex muscle twitch throughout the body that often occurs as one is falling asleep.

Hypnogogic images   Vivid mental images that may occur just as one enters stage 1 sleep; although somewhat dream-like, the images are usually not associated with REMs.

Hypnosis   An altered state of consciousness characterized by narrowed attention and increased suggestibility.

Hypnotic susceptibility scale   Any test designed to assess an individual's capacity for becoming hypnotized.

Hypoactive sexual desire   A persistent loss of sexual motivation.

Hypochondriac   A person who is excessively preoccupied with minor bodily problems or who complains about illnesses that appear to be imaginary.

Hypochondriasis   A preoccupation with minor bodily problems and the presence of illnesses that appear to be imaginary.

Hypoglycemia   Below-normal blood sugar level.

Hypopituitary dwarfism   Shortness and smallness caused by too little growth hormone.

Hypothalamus   A small area at the base of the brain that regulates many aspects of motivation and emotion, especially hunger, thirst, and sexual behavior.

Hypothesis   The predicted outcome of an experiment or an educated guess about the relationship between variables.

Hypothetical possibilities   Suppositions, guesses, or projections.

Hypothyroidism   Slower metabolism and sluggishness caused by an underactive thyroid gland.

Hysteria   Wild emotional excitability sometimes associated with the development of apparent physical disabilities (numbness, blindness, and the like) without known physical cause.

Icon   A mental image or representation.

Id   According to Freud, the most primitive part of personality, which remains unconscious, supplies energy to other parts of the psyche, and demands immediate gratification.

Ideal self   An idealized image of oneself (the person one would like to be).

Identical twins Twins who develop from the same egg and who, therefore, have identical genes.

Identification Incorporating the goals and values of another person into one's own behavior; feeling emotionally connected to a person and wanting to be like him or her.

Illogical thought Thought that is intuitive, invalid, or haphazard.

Illusion A misleading or distorted perception.

Illusory figure An implied shape that is not actually bounded by an edge or an outline.

Illustrators Gestures used while speaking to illustrate what one is saying.

Image Most often, a mental representation that has picture-like qualities; an icon.

Imaginary audience The group of people a person imagines is watching (or will watch) his or her actions.

Imitation An attempt to match one's own behavior to another person's behavior.

Immune system System that mobilizes bodily defenses (such as white blood cells) against invading microbes and other disease agents.

Implicit memory A memory that a person does not know exists; a memory that is retrieved unconsciously.

Impossible figure A stimulus pattern that cannot be organized into a stable perception.

Impotence An outdated term for male erectile disorder.

Imprinting A rapid and relatively permanent type of learning that occurs during a limited time period early in life.

In vitro fertilization Fertilization of an ovum outside a woman's body.

In-basket test A testing procedure that simulates the individual decision-making challenges that executives face.

Incentive value The value a goal holds for a person or animal above and beyond the goal's ability to fill a need.

Incest Sexual contact with a close relative or family member.

Incongruence State that exists when there is a discrepancy between one's experiences and self-image or between one's self-image and ideal self.

Incongruent person A person who has an inaccurate self-image or a person whose self-image differs greatly from the ideal self.

Independent variable In an experiment, the condition being investigated as a possible cause of some change in behavior. The values that this variable takes do not depend on any other condition; they are chosen by the experimenter.

Individual intelligence test A test of intelligence designed for administration to a single individual by a trained specialist.

Individual traits Personality traits that comprise a person's unique individual qualities.

Individuating information Information that helps define a person as an individual, rather than as a member of a group or social category.

Inductive thought A type of thinking in which a general rule or principle is inferred from a series of specific examples; for instance, inferring the laws of gravity by observing many falling objects.

Industrial-organizational psychology The psychology of work and organizations, especially with respect to personnel selection, human relations, and management.

Infatuation Passionate attraction to another person in the absence of intimacy and commitment.

Information bits Meaningful units of information, such as numbers, letters, words, or phrases.

Information chunks Information bits grouped into larger units.

Innate behavior Inborn, unlearned behavior.

Insanity Legally, a mental disability shown by an inability to manage one's affairs or to be aware of the consequences of one's actions.

Insecure-ambivalent attachment An anxious emotional bond marked by a desire to be with a parent or caregiver and resistance to being reunited.

Insecure-avoidant attachment An anxious emotional bond marked by a tendency to avoid reunion with a parent or caregiver.

Insight A sudden mental reorganization of a problem that causes the solution to seem self-evident.

Insomnia Difficulty in getting to sleep or staying asleep.

Instinctive drift The tendency of learned responses to shift toward innate response patterns.

Instructional games Educational computer programs designed to resemble games in order to motivate learning.

Instrumental behavior Behavior directed toward the achievement of some goal; behavior that is instrumental in producing some effect.

Intelligence An overall capacity to think rationally, act purposefully, and deal effectively with the environment.

Intelligence quotient (IQ) An index of intelligence defined as a person's mental age divided by his or her chronological age and multiplied by 100.

Interference The tendency for new memories to impair retrieval of older memories, and the reverse.

Internal cause A cause of behavior that is assumed to lie within a person—for instance, a need, preference, or personality trait.

Internal representation Any image, concept, precept, symbol, or process used to mentally represent information during thought.

Internet A connection of networks that enables computers to communicate with one another, usually through the telephone system.

Interpersonal attraction Social attraction to another person.

Interview (personality) A face-to-face meeting held for the purpose of gaining information about an individual's personal history, personality traits, current psychological state, and so forth.

Intimacy The presence of affection, sharing, communication, and mutual support in a relationship.

Intimate distance The most private space immediately surrounding the body (about 18 inches from the skin).

Intra-cranial stimulation Direct electrical stimulation and activation of brain tissue.

Intracellular thirst Thirst triggered when fluid is drawn out of cells due to an increased concentration of salts and minerals outside the cell.

Intrauterine environment The physical and chemical environment within the uterus during prenatal development.

Intrinsic motivation Motivation that comes from personal enjoyment of an activity, rather than from external rewards.

Introspection To look within; to examine one's own thoughts, feelings, or sensations.

Introvert A person whose attention is focused inward; a shy, reserved, self-centered person.

Intuitive thought Quick, impulsive thinking that makes little or no use of formal reasoning and logic.

Inverted U function A curve, roughly in the shape of an upside-down U, that relates the quality of performance to levels of arousal.

Ion An electrically charged molecule.

Ion channels Channels through the axon membrane.

Iris Colored circular muscle of the eye that opens and closes to admit more or less light into the eye.

Irrelevant questions In a polygraph exam, neutral, non-threatening, or non-emotional questions.

Ishihara test A test for color blindness and color weakness.

James-Lange theory According to this theory, emotional feelings follow bodily arousal and come from awareness of such arousal.

Jigsaw classroom A method of reducing prejudice in which each student receives a different part of a body of information needed to complete a project or prepare for a test.

Job analysis A detailed description of the skills, knowledge, and activities required by a particular job.

Job enrichment A deliberate attempt to make a job more personally rewarding, interesting, or intrinsically motivating.

Job satisfaction The degree to which a person is comfortable with or satisfied with his or her work.

Just noticeable difference The amount of increase or decrease in a stimulus that can be reliably detected as a change in amount, value, or intensity.

Just-world beliefs Belief that people generally get what they deserve.

Justification In cognitive dissonance theory, the degree to which one's actions are justified by rewards or other circumstances.

Keyword method As an aid to memory, using a familiar word or image to link two items.

Kinesics Study of the meaning of body movements, posture, hand gestures, and facial expressions, commonly called body language.

Kinesthetic imagery Images created by produced, remembered, or imagined muscular sensations.

Kinesthetic senses The senses of body movement and positioning.

Knowledge of results During learning, feedback or information provided about the correctness of responses or other aspects of performance.

Language A collection of words or symbols and rules for combining them, which allows them to be used for thinking and communication.

Large-group awareness training Any of a number of programs (many of them commercialized) that claim to increase self-awareness and facilitate constructive personal change.

Latency (Freudian) According to Freud, a period in childhood when psychosexual development is more or less interrupted.

Latency (response) The amount of time that passes between the presentation of a stimulus and the occurrence of a response.

Latent dream content The hidden or symbolic meaning of a dream, as revealed by dream interpretation and analysis.

Latent learning Learning that occurs without obvious reinforcement and that remains unexpressed until reinforcement is provided.

Later career phase The concluding career phase prior to retirement; marked by high status and respect arising from long experience.

Lateralization Specialization in the abilities of the brain hemispheres.

Law of effect Responses that lead to desirable effects are repeated; those that produce undesirable results are not.

Leaderless group discussion A test of leadership that simulates group decision making and problem solving.

Learned helplessness A learned inability to overcome obstacles or to avoid punishment. A learned state of passivity and inaction in the face of aversive stimuli.

Learning Any relatively permanent change in behavior that can be attributed to experience but not to fatigue, malnutrition, injury, and so forth.

Learning disability Any substantial problem with reading, math, or writing.

Learning psychologist A psychologist who studies how learning occurs.

Learning theorist A psychologist interested in the ways that learning shapes and explains personality.

Legitimate power Social power based on a person's position as an agent of an accepted social order.

Lesbianism Female homosexuality.

Lexigram A geometric shape used as a symbol for a word.

Libido In Freudian theory, the force, primarily pleasure oriented, that energizes the subparts of personality.

Life change units (LCUs) Numerical values assigned to each life event on the Social Readjustment Rating Scale and used to predict the likelihood of illness.

Life expectancy The average number of years a person of a given sex, race, and nationality can expect to live.

Life stages Widely recognized periods of life corresponding to various ages and broad phases of development.

Light sleep Stage 1 sleep, marked by small, irregular brain waves and some alpha waves.

Liking A relationship based on intimacy, but lacking passion and commitment.

Limbic system A system of interconnected structures in the forebrain that are closely associated with emotional response.

Limen A threshold or a limit.

Linear relationship A relationship that forms a straight line when graphed.

Lithium carbonate A drug used to lessen mood swings in persons suffering from some types of affective disorders.

Living will A written declaration stating that a person prefers not to have his or her life artificially prolonged in the event of a terminal illness.

Lobes (cerebral cortex) Areas on the cortex bordered by major fissures or associated with particular functions.

Localization of function The principle stating that sensations are determined by the area of the brain that is activated.

Lock and key theory The theory of olfaction that holds that odors are related to the shapes of chemical molecules.

Logical thought Drawing conclusions on the basis of formal principles of reasoning.

Logotherapy A form of existential therapy that emphasizes the need to find and maintain meaning in one's life.

Long-term memory (LTM) The memory system used for relatively permanent storage of meaningful information.

Looking chamber An experimental apparatus used to test infant perception by presenting visual stimuli and observing infant responses.

Loudness The intensity of a sound; determined by the amplitude of sound waves.

Low self-monitor A person who seeks to faithfully express who she or he is, regardless of the situation.

Low-ball technique A strategy in which commitment is gained first to reasonable or desirable terms, which are then made less reasonable or desirable.

Lucid dream A dream in which the dreamer feels awake and capable of normal thought and action.

M'Naghten rule A rule in English common law for judging sanity and legal responsibility.

Maintenance rehearsal Silently repeating or mentally reviewing information to hold it in short-term memory.

Major depressive disorder A mood disorder in which the person has suffered one or more intense episodes of depression.

Major mood disorders Disorders marked by lasting extremes of mood or emotion and often accompanied by psychotic symptoms.

Major tranquilizers (antipsychotics) Drugs that, in addition to having tranquilizing effects, also tend to reduce hallucinations and delusional thinking.

Maladaptive behavior Behavior that makes it more difficult for a person to adapt to his or her environment and meet the demands of day-to-day life.

Male erectile disorder An inability to maintain an erection for sexual intercourse.

Male orgasmic disorder An inability to reach orgasm during intercourse.

Management by objectives A management technique in which employees are given specific goals to meet in their work.

Mandala A circular design representing balance, unity, and completion.

Manic Extremely excited, hyperactive, or irritable.

Manifest dream content The surface, "visible" content of a dream; dream images as they are remembered by the dreamer.

Manipulation drive Drive to investigate objects by touching and handling them.

Mantra A word or sound used as the focus of attention in concentrative meditation.

Marijuana The leaves and flowers of the hemp plant, *Cannabis sativa*.

Marketing research A type of public opinion polling used to assess consumer views of products, services, and advertising.

Masochism Deriving sexual arousal or pleasure from having pain inflicted during the sex act.

Mass media Collectively, all media that reach very large audiences (magazines, for instance, are a medium of mass communication).

Massed practice A practice schedule in which studying continues for long periods, without interruption.

Mastery training Reinforcement of responses that lead to mastery of a threat or control over one's environment.

Masturbation Production of sexual pleasure or orgasm by manipulation of the genitals other than by intercourse.

Maternal influences The aggregate of all psychological effects mothers have on their children.

Maternity blues A brief and relatively mild state of depression often experienced by mothers 2 or 3 days after giving birth.

Maturation The physical growth and development of the body and nervous system.

Maximum life span The biologically determined maximum number of years humans could live under optimal conditions.

Mean world view Viewing the world and other people as dangerous and threatening.

Means-ends analysis An analysis of how to reduce the difference between the present state of affairs and a desired goal.

Mechanical solution A problem solution achieved by trial and error or by a fixed procedure based on learned rules.

Medicated birth The common practice in Western medicine of giving painkilling drugs during labor and birth.

Meditation A mental technique for quieting the mind and body.

Medulla The enlarged stalk at the base of the brain that connects to the spinal cord and controls vital life functions.

Melatonin A hormone produced by the pineal gland in response to cycles of light and dark.

Memory The mental system for receiving, storing, organizing, altering, and recovering information.

Memory cue Any stimulus associated with a particular memory. The presence of such cues usually enhances memory retrieval.

Memory decay The fading or weakening of memories assumed to occur when memory traces become weaker.

Memory structure The pattern of associations among bits of information stored in memory.

Memory traces Hypothesized physical changes that take place in the brain as it stores information; engrams.

Menarche The onset of menstruation; a woman's first menstrual period.

Menopause An end to regular monthly menstrual periods.

Mental age The average mental ability displayed by people of a given age.

Mental disorder A significant impairment in psychological functioning.

Mental hospitalization Confinement to a protected environment that provides various forms of therapy for mental, emotional, and behavioral problems.

Mental retardation The presence of a developmental disability, a formal IQ score below 70, or a significant impairment of adaptive behavior.

Mental rotation The ability to change the position of an image in mental space in order to examine it from a new perspective.

Mesmerize To hypnotize.

Meta-needs In Maslow's hierarchy, those needs above and beyond the ordinary; needs associated with impulses for self-actualization.

Metabolic disorder Any disorder in metabolism (the rate of energy production and use in the body).

Metabolic rate The rate at which energy is consumed by bodily activity.

Micro-electrode An electrode small enough to record the activity of a single neuron.

Microcephaly A disorder in which the head and brain are abnormally small.

Micromovements Tiny, nearly imperceptible movements associated with changes in muscular tension and activity.

Microsleep A momentary shift in brain-wave patterns to those of sleep.

Midbrain The area of the brain consisting of structures linking the forebrain and the brainstem.

Midcareer phase A stable central career phase marked by high competence and full status.

Mild punishment Punishment that has a relatively weak effect, especially punishment that only temporarily slows responding.

Minimal brain dysfunction (MBD) A hypothesized explanation for hyperactivity, involving a lag in brain development or low-level damage to the brain.

Minnesota Multiphasic Personality Inventory-2 (MMPI-2) The latest version of one of the best-known and most widely used objective personality questionnaires.

Minor tranquilizers Drugs (such as Valium) that

Mirror technique Observing another person re-enact one's own behavior, like a character in a play; designed to help persons to see themselves more clearly.

Misdirected letter technique A way of measuring attitudes toward a group; letters addressed to the group are sent to households and the number forwarded is counted.

MMPI-2 profile A graphic representation of an individual's scores on each of the primary scales of the MMPI-2.

Mnemonic A memory system or aid.

Mock jury A group that realistically simulates a courtroom jury.

Model (learning) A person (either live or filmed) who serves as an example for observational learning or vicarious conditioning.

Model (scientific) In research, an animal whose behavior is used to derive principles that may apply to human behavior.

Modeling Any process in which information is imparted by example, before direct practice is allowed.

Monocular depth cues Depth cues that can be sensed with one eye.

Mood A low-intensity, long-lasting emotional state.

Mood disorder A major disturbance in mood or emotion, such as depression or mania.

Moon illusion The apparent change in size that occurs as the moon moves from the horizon (large moon) to overhead (small moon).

Moral anxiety Apprehension felt when one's thoughts, impulses, or actions conflict with standards enforced by the superego.

Moral development The development of values, beliefs, and thinking abilities that act as a guide regarding what is acceptable behavior.

Moro reflex Neonatal reflex evoked by sudden loss of support or the sounding of a loud noise; in response, the arms are extended and then brought toward each other.

Morphemes The smallest meaningful units in a language, such as syllables or words.

Motivation Mechanisms within an organism that initiate, sustain, and direct activities.

Motor cortex An area on the top of the brain directly associated with control of voluntary movements.

Motor neuron A nerve cell that carries motor commands from the central nervous system to muscles and glands.

Motor program A mental plan or model that guides skilled movement.

Motor skill A series of actions molded into a smooth and efficient performance.

MRI scan Magnetic resonance imaging; a computer-enhanced three-dimensional representation of the brain or body, based on the body's response to a magnetic field.

Müller-Lyer illusion A stimulus consisting of two parallel lines tipped with inward- or outward-pointing Vs. Although they are of equal length, one of the lines appears longer than the other.

Multiculturalism Giving equal status, recognition, and acceptance to different ethnic, racial, and cultural groups.

Multiple approach-avoidance conflict Being simultaneously attracted to and repelled by each of several alternatives.

Multiple aptitude test Test that measures two or more aptitudes.

Multiple personality A form of dissociative disorder in which a person develops two or more distinct personalities.

Muscular imagery Any mental representation based on produced, remembered, or imagined muscular sensations; for instance, the images produced when one imagines hammering a nail.

Muscular responses Visible movement of the muscles or unseen changes in their tension, which creates kinesthetic sensations.

Mutual absorption With regard to romantic love, the almost exclusive attention lovers give to one another.

Mutual interdependence A condition in which two or more persons must depend on one another to meet each person's needs or goals.

Myelin A fatty layer coating some axons that increases the rate at which nerve impulses travel along the axon.

Myoclonus Restless spasms of the leg muscles that disturb sleep.

Myopia A visual defect that makes it difficult to focus distant objects (nearsightedness).

Narcolepsy A serious sleep disturbance in which the individual suffers uncontrollable sleep attacks.

Natural clinical test An accident or other natural event that provides psychological data.

Natural design Human factors engineering that makes use of perceptual signals that are understood by people without any need to learn them.

Natural selection Darwin's theory that evolution favors those plants and animals best suited to their living conditions.

Natural setting The environment in which an organism typically lives.

Naturalistic observation Observation and recording of naturally occurring behavior that is not manipulated experimentally.

Near-death experience A pattern of experiences that may occur when a person is clinically dead and then resuscitated.

Need An internal deficiency that may energize behavior.

Need for achievement (nAch) The desire to excel or meet some internalized standard of excellence.

Need for power The desire to have social impact and control over others.

Need to affiliate The desire to associate with other people.

Negative after-potential A drop in electrical charge below the resting potential.

Negative attention seeking A pattern, seen especially in children, in which misbehavior is used to gain attention.

Negative instance In concept learning, an object or event that does not belong to the concept class.

Negative reinforcement Occurs when a response is followed with an end to discomfort or with the removal of a negative state of affairs.

Negative relationship A relationship in which increases in one measure correspond to decreases in the other.

Negative self-statements Self-critical thoughts that increase anxiety and lower performance.

Negative transfer Mastery of one task conflicts with learning or performing another.

Neglect Ignoring one side of vision or of the body after damage to a brain hemisphere.

Neo-Freudian A personality theorist who accepts the broad features of Freud's theory but has revised the theory to fit his or her own concepts.

Neonate A newborn infant during the first weeks following birth.

Nerve A bundle of neuron fibers supported by connective tissue; nerves can be seen with the unaided eye; neuron fibers are microscopic projections from single cells.

Nerve deafness Deafness caused by damage to the hair cells or auditory nerve.

Network model A model of memory that views it as an organized system of linked information.

Neurilemma A layer of living cells that encases the axons of many neurons.

Neurons Individual nerve cells.

Neuropeptides Brain chemicals that regulate the activity of neurons, thereby influencing memory, emotion, pain, hunger, and other behavior.

Neurosis An outdated term once used to refer, as a group, to anxiety disorders, somatoform disorders, dissociative disorders, and some forms of depression.

Neurotic anxiety Apprehension felt when the ego must struggle to maintain control over id impulses.

Neurotransmitter Any of a number of chemical substances secreted by neurons that alter activity in other neurons.

Neutral stimulus A stimulus that fails to elicit a response.

Nicotine A potent stimulant drug found primarily in tobacco; nicotine is a known carcinogen.

Night blindness A visual defect in which daylight vision is normal, but blindness occurs under conditions of low illumination.

Night terror A very frightening NREM sleep episode.

Nightmare An upsetting dream.

Nocturnal orgasm An orgasm that occurs spontaneously during sleep or dreaming.

Noise pollution Stressful and intrusive noise; usually artificially generated by machinery, but also including noises made by animals and humans.

Non-homeostatic drive A drive that is relatively independent of physical deprivation cycles or bodily need states.

Non-love An absence of intimacy, passion, and commitment in a relationship.

Non-reinforcement Withholding reinforcement after selected responses (in other words, extinction training).

Nonsense syllables Invented three-letter words used to test learning and memory.

Noradrenaline A hormone produced by the adrenal glands that tends to arouse the body; noradrenaline is associated with anger.

Norm (social) An accepted (but often unspoken) standard of conduct for appropriate behavior.

Norm (testing) An average score for a designated group of people.

Normal curve A bell-shaped curve with a large number of scores in the middle, tapering to very few extremely high and low scores.

NREM sleep Non-rapid eye movement sleep characteristic of stages 2, 3, and 4, and largely dream free.

Nystagmus Any involuntary vibration, oscillation, or movement of the eye.

Obedience Conformity to the demands of an authority.

Object In making attributions, the aim, motive, or target of an action.

Object permanence Concept, gained in infancy, that objects continue to exist even when they are hidden from view.

Objective test A test that gives the same score when different people correct it.

Observation Directly gathering data by recording facts or events.

Observational learning Learning achieved by watching and imitating the actions of another or noting the consequences of those actions.

Observer bias The tendency of an observer to distort observations or perceptions to match his or her expectations.

Observer effect Changes in a person's behavior brought about by an awareness of being observed.

Obsession Recurring irrational or disturbing thoughts or mental images a person cannot prevent.

Obsessive-compulsive disorder An extreme, unavoidable preoccupation with certain thoughts and compulsive performance of certain behaviors.

Occipital lobes Portion at the back of the cerebral cortex that includes areas where vision registers in the brain.

Oedipus conflict Freudian concept referring to a boy's sexual attraction to his mother, and feelings of rivalry with his father.

Olfaction The sense of smell.

Olfactory area Sites on the frontal lobes where information on smell registers.

Open teaching Instruction based on active teacher-student discussion.

Open-ended interview An interview in which persons are allowed to freely state their views.

Operant conditioning Learning based on the consequences of responding.

Operant extinction The weakening or disappearance of a non-reinforced operant response.

Operant reinforcer Any event that reliably increases the probability or frequency of responses it follows.

Operant shaping Gradually molding responses by rewarding ever-closer approximations to a final desired pattern.

Operant stimulus discrimination The tendency to make a response when stimuli previously associated with reward are present and to withhold the response when stimuli associated with non-reward are present.

Operant stimulus generalization The tendency to respond to stimuli similar to those present when an operant response was acquired.

Operational definition Defining a scientific concept by stating the specific actions or procedures used to measure it. For example, "hunger" might be defined as "the number of hours of food deprivation."

Opponent-process theory (motivation) States that strong emotions tend to be followed by an opposite emotional state; also, the strength of both emotional states changes over time.

Opponent-process theory (sensation) The theory of color vision stating that three coding systems (red or green, yellow or blue, black or white) are used by the visual system to analyze color information.

Oral stage In Freud's theory, the period early in life when infants are preoccupied with the mouth as a source of pleasure and means of expression.

Organ of Corti Center part of the cochlea, containing hair cells, canals, and membranes.

Organic mental disorder A mental or emotional problem caused by malfunction of the brain.

Organic psychosis A psychosis caused by a known brain injury or disease.

Organismic valuing Placing value on an experience on the basis of how one responds to it as an entire organism; judgment made directly on the basis of one's perceptions and feelings.

Organizational psychology A field that focuses on the psychology of work and on behavior within organizations.

Orgasm A climax and release of sexual excitement.

Orientation response The pattern of changes occurring throughout the body that prepares an organism to receive information from a particular stimulus.

Originality In tests of creativity, originality refers

to the degree of novelty or unusualness of the solutions produced.

Otolith organs Vestibular structures sensitive to movement, acceleration, and gravity.

Oval window A membrane on the cochlea connected to the third auditory ossicle.

Overdisclosure Self-disclosure that exceeds what is appropriate for a particular relationship or social situation.

Overeating Eating in excess of one's daily caloric needs.

Overgeneralization Blowing a single event out of proportion by extending it to a large number of unrelated situations.

Overlearning Study or learning that continues after initial mastery of skills or information.

Overly permissive parents Parents who give their children little guidance, allow them too much freedom, or who do not require the child to take responsibility for his or her actions.

Overprotection Excessively guarding and shielding a child from possible stresses.

Overt behavior An action or response that is directly observable.

Ovulation The release of an ovum (egg cell) by the ovaries; ova combine with sperm cells to begin the growth of an embryo.

Pain disorder Pain that has no identifiable physical cause and appears to be of psychological origin.

Palmistry False system that claims to reveal personality traits and to predict the future by "reading" lines on the palms of the hands.

Panic disorder (with agoraphobia) The person is in a chronic state of anxiety and also has brief moments of sudden, intense, unexpected panic. In addition, the person fears that these panic attacks will occur in public places or unfamiliar situations.

Panic disorder (without agoraphobia) The person is in a chronic state of anxiety, and also has brief moments of sudden, intense, unexpected panic.

Paranoid psychosis A delusional disorder centered especially on delusions of persecution.

Paranoid schizophrenia Schizophrenia marked by a preoccupation with delusions or by frequent auditory hallucinations related to a single theme, especially grandeur or persecution.

Paraphilias Compulsive or destructive deviations in sexual preferences or behavior.

Paraprofessional An individual who works in a near-professional capacity under the supervision of a more highly trained person.

Parapsychology The study of extranormal psychological events, such as extrasensory perception.

Parascience A system that resembles science but is not truly scientific.

Parasympathetic rebound Excess activity in the parasympathetic nervous system following a period of intense emotion.

Parasympathetic system A branch of the autonomic system responsible for quieting the body and conserving energy.

Parental responsiveness Caregiving that is based on sensitivity to a child's feelings, needs, rhythms, and signals.

Parietal lobes Area at the top of the brain that includes sites where bodily sensations register in the brain.

Part learning Separately studying subparts of a larger body of information (such as sections of a textbook chapter).

Partial hospitalization Treatment in which patients spend only part of their time at the hospital.

Partial reinforcement A pattern in which only a portion of responses are reinforced (also called in-

termittent reinforcement).

Partial reinforcement effect Greater resistance to extinction is found in responses acquired on a schedule of partial reinforcement.

Participative management An approach to management that allows employees at all levels to participate in decision making.

Passion The presence of heightened arousal in one's emotional response to another person.

Passive compliance Passively bending to unreasonable demands or circumstances.

Passive euthanasia Allowing death to occur without trying to prevent it or encourage it.

Paternal influences The aggregate of all psychological effects fathers have on their children.

Peak experiences Temporary moments of self-actualization, marked by feelings of ecstasy, harmony, and deep meaning.

Peak performance A performance during which physical, mental, and emotional states are harmonious and optimal.

Pedophilia Sex with children, or child molesting.

Peer counselor A non-professional person who has learned basic counseling skills.

Peer group A group of people who share similar social status.

Perception The mental process of organizing sensations into meaningful patterns.

Perceptual category A pre-existing class, type, or grouping.

Perceptual defense Resistance to perceiving threatening or disturbing stimuli.

Perceptual expectancy (or set) A readiness to perceive in a particular manner, induced by strong expectations.

Perceptual features Important elements of a stimulus pattern, such as lines, shapes, edges, spots, and colors.

Perceptual habits Established patterns of perceptual organization and attention.

Perceptual hypothesis An initial guess regarding the correct way to organize (perceive) a stimulus pattern.

Perceptual stimulation Varied, patterned, and meaningful sensory input.

Performance intelligence Intelligence measured by solving puzzles, assembling objects, completing pictures, and other non-verbal tasks.

Peripheral nervous system All parts of the nervous system lying outside the brain and spinal cord.

Peripheral vision Vision at the periphery (edges) of the visual field.

Persistence As a response to frustration, persistence refers to repeated, more vigorous efforts and more variable responding.

Persona The "mask" or public self presented to others.

Personal distance The distance maintained when interacting with close friends (about 18 inches to 4 feet from the body).

Personal frustration A negative emotional state caused by personal characteristics that hinder satisfaction of a motive or that block progress toward a goal.

Personal interview Formal or informal questioning of job applicants to learn their qualifications and to gain an impression of their personalities.

Personal prejudice Prejudicial attitudes held toward persons who are perceived as a direct threat to one's own interests.

Personal space An area immediately surrounding the body that is regarded as private and subject to personal control.

Personal unconscious A mental storehouse for a single individual's unconscious thoughts.

Personality An individual's unique and relatively

unchanging psychological characteristics and behavior patterns.

Personality disintegration A shattering of the coordination among thoughts, actions, and emotions normally found in personality.

Personality disorder A deeply ingrained, unhealthy, maladaptive personality pattern.

Personality psychologist A psychologist who studies personality traits and dynamics.

Personality questionnaire A paper-and-pencil test consisting of questions designed to reveal various aspects of the respondent's personality.

Personality theory An interrelated system of concepts and principles used to understand and explain personality.

Personality trait A behavioral characteristic displayed in most situations.

Personality type A style of personality defined by a group of related traits.

Personnel psychology Branch of industrial/organizational psychology concerned with testing, selection, placement, and promotion of employees.

Persuasion A deliberate attempt to change attitudes or beliefs with information and arguments.

PET scan Positron emission tomography; a computer-generated image of brain activity, based on glucose consumption in the brain.

Phallic stage In Freud's theory, the psychosexual stage (roughly age 3 to 6) when a person is preoccupied with the genitals as a source of pleasure.

Phenylketonuria A genetic disease that allows phenylpyruvic acid to accumulate in the body.

Pheromone An airborne chemical signal.

Philosophy The study of knowledge, reality, and human nature.

Phobia An intense and unrealistic fear of some object or situation.

Phobic disorder A type of anxiety disorder in which irrational fears (phobias) are focused on specific objects, activities, or situations.

Phonemes The basic sounds of a language that can be joined into syllables and words.

Phosphene A visual sensation caused by mechanical excitation of the retina.

Photon One quantum of light energy.

Photoreceptor Sensory receptors sensitive to light and specialized for the transduction of light stimuli into neural impulses.

Phototherapy A treatment for seasonal affective disorder that involves exposure to bright, full-spectrum light.

Phrenology False and antiquated system based on the belief that personality traits are revealed by the shape of the skull.

Physical attractiveness A person's degree of physical beauty, as defined by his or her culture.

Physical dependence Physical addiction, as indicated by the presence of drug tolerance and withdrawal symptoms.

Physical environments Natural settings, such as forests and beaches, as well as environments built by humans, such as buildings, ships, cities.

Physical proximity As a factor in interpersonal attraction, one's actual physical nearness to others in terms of housing, work, school, and so forth.

Physiological changes in emotion Changes in bodily activities (especially involuntary responses) that accompany emotional states.

Physiological nystagmus An involuntary tremor of the eye.

Physiological psychologist A psychologist who studies the relationship between the nervous system and behavior.

Pica A craving for unnatural foods or substances such as chalk, ashes, and the like.

Pictorial depth cues Features found in paintings, drawings, and photographs that impart information about space, depth, and distance.

Pineal gland Gland in the brain that helps regulate body rhythms and sleep cycles.

Pitch Higher or lower tones; related to the frequency of sound waves.

Pituitary gland The "master gland" at the base of the brain whose hormones influence the output of other endocrine glands.

Place theory Theory of hearing that says that higher and lower frequency tones are detected at specific locations in the cochlea.

Placebo A substance that resembles a drug but has no chemical effect.

Placebo effect Changes in behavior due to expectations that a drug (or other treatment) will have some effect.

Plasticity The brain's capacity for revising its organization.

Plateau phase The second phase of sexual response during which physical arousal is further heightened.

Pleasure principle The principle under which the id operates, consisting of a desire for immediate satisfaction of wishes, desires, or needs.

Polygenic characteristics Personal characteristics that are influenced by a combination of genes.

Polygraph A device for recording several physiological activities, typically including heart rate, blood pressure, respiration, and galvanic skin response; commonly called a "lie detector."

Population An entire group of animals or people belonging to a particular category (for example, all college students or all married women).

Positive instance In concept learning, an object or event that belongs to the concept class.

Positive reinforcement Occurs when a response is followed with a reward or other positive event.

Positive relationship A relationship in which increases in one measure correspond to increases in the other.

Positive self-regard Thinking of oneself as a good, lovable, worthwhile person.

Positive transfer Mastery of one task aids learning or performing another.

Positron emission tomography An image of brain activity based on glucose consumption.

Possible self A collection of thoughts, beliefs, feelings, and images concerning a self one could become.

Post-traumatic stress disorder Psychological disturbance lasting more than one month following stresses, such as natural disasters or military combat, that would produce anxiety in anyone who experienced them.

Postconventional moral reasoning Moral thinking based on carefully examined and self-chosen moral principles.

Postpartum depression A mild to moderately severe depression that begins within 3 months following childbirth.

Power assertion The use of physical punishment or coercion to enforce child discipline.

Preadaptation Gradual matching of sleep-waking cycles to a new time schedule before an anticipated major change in circadian rhythms.

Precognition The purported ability to accurately predict future events.

Preconscious An area of the mind that contains information not currently in consciousness, but that can be voluntarily brought to awareness.

Preconventional moral reasoning Moral thinking based on the consequences of one's choices or actions (punishment, reward, or an exchange of favors).

Prefrontal lobotomy An antiquated surgery in which portions of the frontal lobes were destroyed or disconnected from other brain areas.

Prejudice A negative attitude or prejudgment held against members of a particular group of people.

Premack principle Any high-frequency response can be used to reinforce a low-frequency response.

Premature ejaculation Ejaculation that consistently occurs before the man and his partner want it to occur.

Premature puberty The development of sexual maturity in childhood.

Preoperational stage Period of intellectual development during which children begin to use language and think symbolically, yet remain intuitive and egocentric in their thought.

Prepared childbirth Techniques to manage discomfort and facilitate birth with a minimum of painkilling drugs.

Prepared childbirth training System for preparing women and their partners for childbirth.

Prepared fear theory Holds that people and animals are prepared by evolution to readily learn fears of certain stimuli.

Presbyopia Farsightedness caused by a loss of elasticity in the lens due to aging.

Pressure A stressful condition that occurs when a person must respond at, or near, maximum capacity for long time periods.

Primary appraisal The first step in coping with a threatening situation, consisting of deciding if the situation is indeed a threat.

Primary auditory area Main area on the temporal lobes where hearing registers.

Primary emotions According to Plutchik, the most basic emotions are fear, surprise, sadness, disgust, anger, anticipation, joy, and acceptance.

Primary motives Innate motives based on biological needs.

Primary reinforcers Unlearned reinforcers; usually those that satisfy physiological needs.

Primary sexual characteristics Gender as defined by the genitals and internal reproductive organs.

Primary visual area Main area of the cerebral cortex that processes visual information.

Primate A member of the family of mammals including humans, apes, and monkeys.

Priming Activating implicit (hidden) memories by providing partial information that is linked with them.

Principle of motor primacy Principle that motor, muscular, and physical development must precede the learning of certain skills.

Proactive interference The tendency for old memories to interfere with the retrieval of newer memories.

Proactive maternal involvement Sensitive caregiving in which a mother actively provides her child with educational experiences.

Problem-focused coping Directly managing or remedying a stressful or threatening situation.

Procedural memory That part of long-term memory made up of conditioned responses and learned skills.

Productivity The capacity of language for generating new ideas and possibilities.

Programmed instruction Any learning format that presents information in small amounts, gives immediate practice, and provides continuous feedback to learners.

Progressive relaxation A method for producing deep relaxation of all parts of the body.

Projection Attributing one's own feelings, shortcomings, or unacceptable impulses to others.

Projective tests Psychological tests making use of

ambiguous or unstructured stimuli. Subjects are presumed to project their own thoughts and impulses onto these stimuli.

Prosocial behavior   Behavior toward others that is helpful, constructive, or altruistic.

Prototype   An ideal, or model, used as a prime example of a particular concept.

Proxemics   Systematic study of the human use of space, particularly interpersonal space in various social settings.

Pseudo-memories   False memories that a person believes are real or accurate.

Pseudo-psychology   Any false and unscientific system of beliefs and practices that is offered as an explanation of behavior.

Psi phenomena   Events that seem to lie outside the realm of accepted scientific laws.

Psyche   The mind, mental life, and personality as a whole.

Psychiatric social worker   A professional who applies social science principles to help patients in clinics and hospitals.

Psychiatrist   A medical doctor who specializes in treating mental disorders.

Psychoactive drug   A substance capable of altering attention, memory, judgment, time sense, self-control, mood, or perception.

Psychoanalysis   A Freudian approach to psychotherapy emphasizing the exploration of unconscious conflicts.

Psychoanalyst   A mental health professional (usually a medical doctor) trained to practice psychoanalysis.

Psychoanalytic theory   Freudian theory of personality that emphasizes unconscious forces and internal conflicts in its explanations of behavior.

Psychobiology   A viewpoint that seeks to explain behavior through biological processes, such as activity in the brain and nervous system, genetics, the endocrine system, and evolution.

Psychodrama   A therapy in which clients act out personal conflicts and feelings in the presence of others who play supporting roles.

Psychodynamic theory   Any theory of behavior that emphasizes internal conflicts, motives, and unconscious forces.

Psychokinesis   The purported ability to mentally alter or influence objects or events.

Psycholinguist   A specialist in the psychology of language and language development.

Psychological androgyny   The presence of both "masculine" and "feminine" traits in a single person (as masculinity and femininity are defined within one's culture).

Psychological dependence   Drug dependence that is based primarily on emotional or psychological needs.

Psychological efficiency   Maintenance of good morale, labor relations, employee satisfaction, and similar aspects of work behavior.

Psychological situation   A situation as it is perceived and interpreted by an individual, not as it exists objectively

Psychological trauma   A psychological injury or shock, such as that caused by violence, abuse, neglect, separation, and so forth.

Psychologist   An individual highly trained in the methods, factual knowledge, and theories of psychology.

Psychology   The scientific study of human and animal behavior.

Psychometrics   Mental measurement or testing.

Psychoneuroimmunology   Study of the links among behavior, disease, and the immune system.

Psychopath   An individual who appears to make no distinctions between right and wrong and who

feels no guilt about destructive or antisocial behavior.

Psychopathology   The scientific study of mental, emotional, and behavioral disorders; also, abnormal or maladaptive behavior.

Psychophysics   The study of the relationship between physical stimuli and the sensations they evoke in a human observer.

Psychosexual stages   In Freud's theory of personality development, the oral, anal, phallic, and genital stages, during which various personality traits are formed.

Psychosis   A severe psychological disorder characterized by a retreat from reality, hallucinations and delusions, disturbed emotions, and social withdrawal.

Psychosocial dilemma   A conflict, between personal impulses and the social world, that affects development.

Psychosomatic disorder   Illness in which psychological factors contribute to bodily damage or to damaging changes in bodily functioning.

Psychosurgery   Any surgical alteration of the brain designed to bring about desirable behavioral or emotional changes.

Psychotherapist   Anyone who does psychological therapy. Persons who call themselves psychotherapists are not always psychologists.

Psychotherapy   Any form of psychological treatment for behavioral or emotional problems.

Psychotic disorder   A severe psychological disorder characterized by a retreat from reality, by hallucinations and delusions, and by social withdrawal.

Puberty   The biologically defined period during which a person matures sexually and becomes capable of reproduction.

Public distance   Distance at which formal interactions, such as giving a speech, occur (about 12 feet or more from the body).

Punisher   Any event that decreases the probability or frequency of responses it follows.

Punishment   Occurs when a response is followed with pain or an otherwise negative event or when a response is followed with the removal of a positive reinforcer (response cost).

Pupil   The dark spot at the front of the eye through which light passes.

Quality circle   A discussion group in which employees voluntarily seek to solve business problems.

Racism   Racial prejudice that has become institutionalized (that is, it is reflected in government policy, schools, and so forth) and that is enforced by the existing social power structure.

Random assignment   The use of chance (for example, flipping a coin) to assign subjects to experimental and control groups.

Random search strategy   Trying possible solutions to a problem in a more or less random order.

Rapid eye movements (REMs)   Swift eye movements during sleep.

Rapid smoking   Forced cigarette smoking designed to make smoking aversive and unappealing.

Rating scale   A list of various personality traits or aspects of behavior on which a person is rated, during or after observation of the person's behavior.

Rational-emotive therapy (RET)   An approach that attempts to change or remove irrational beliefs that cause emotional problems.

Rationalization   Justifying one's own behavior by giving reasonable and "rational" but false reasons for it.

Reaction formation   Preventing dangerous or threatening impulses from being expressed by exaggerating opposite behavior.

Reactive depression   A serious depression that appears to be a reaction to some identifiable event.

Readiness   Sufficient maturation for rapid acquisition of a skill.

Realistic stage   Stage of career exploration in which career options are narrowed and more specific plans are made.

Reality principle   The principle by which the ego functions, involving delaying action (or pleasure) until it is appropriate.

Reality testing   Obtaining additional information to check on the accuracy of perceptions.

Recall   To supply or reproduce memorized information with a minimum of external cues.

Receptive meditation   Meditation in which attention is widened to include an awareness of one's total subjective experience.

Receptor sites   Areas on the surface of neurons and other cells that are sensitive to neurotransmitters or hormones.

Recessive gene   A gene whose influence will only be expressed when it is paired with a second recessive gene (it cannot be expressed when paired with a dominant gene).

Reciprocal inhibition   Principle that one emotional state can block another, such as joy preventing fear, or anxiety inhibiting pleasure.

Reciprocity   A reciprocal interchange or return in kind.

Recitation   As a memory aid, repeating aloud information one wishes to retain.

Recoding   Reorganizing or otherwise transforming information to facilitate storage in memory.

Recognition   Memory in which previously learned material is correctly identified as that which was seen before.

Redintegration   The process of reconstructing an entire complex memory after observing or remembering only a part of it.

Reference group   Any group that an individual identifies with and uses as a standard for social comparison.

Referent power   Social power gained when one is used as a point of reference by others.

Referred pain   Pain that is felt in one part of the body, but comes from another.

Reflection   In client-centered therapy, the process of rephrasing or repeating thoughts and feelings so that clients become aware of what they are saying about themselves.

Reflex   An innate, automatic response to a stimulus; for example, an eye blink, knee jerk, or dilation of the pupil.

Reflex arc   The simplest behavior pattern, involving only three neurons; leads from a stimulus to an automatic response, such as an eye blink or knee jerk.

Refractory period   A short time period after orgasm during which males are unable to again reach orgasm.

Refreezing   In brainwashing, the process of rewarding and strengthening new attitudes and beliefs.

Refusal skills training   Training that teaches youngsters how to resist influences to begin smoking (can also be applied to other drugs, such as alcohol or cocaine).

Regression   Any return to an earlier, more infantile behavior pattern.

Rehearsal   Silently repeating or mentally reviewing information to hold it in short-term memory or aid its long-term storage.

Reinforcement   Any event that brings about learning or increases the probability that a particular response will occur.

Reinforcement value   The subjective value a person attaches to a particular activity or reinforcer.

Relational concept A concept defined by the relationship between features of an object or between an object and its surroundings (for example, "greater than," "lopsided").

Relaxation response The pattern of physiological changes that occurs in the body at times of relaxation.

Relearning Learning again something that was previously learned. Used to measure one's memory of prior learning.

Relevant questions In a polygraph exam, questions to which only a guilty person should react.

Reliability The ability of a test to yield the same score, or nearly the same score, each time it is given to the same person.

REM behavior disorder A failure of normal muscle paralysis, leading to violent actions during REM sleep.

REM rebound The occurrence of extra amounts of rapid eye movement sleep in a person who has been deprived of REM sleep.

REM sleep Sleep marked by rapid eye movements, a return to stage 1 EEG patterns; usually associated with dreaming.

Replicate To reproduce or repeat.

Representative sample A small, randomly selected part of a larger population that accurately reflects characteristics of the whole population.

Representativeness hueristic A tendency to select wrong answers because they seem to match pre-existing mental categories.

Repression Unconsciously pushing out or barring from awareness unwanted memories.

Research method A systematic approach to answering scientific questions.

Resistance Blocking that occurs in psychoanalysis during free association; topics the client resists thinking or talking about.

Resolution (grief) With respect to grief, an acceptance of loss and the need for building a new life.

Resolution (sexual) The fourth phase of sexual response, involving a return to lower levels of sexual tension and arousal.

Respondent conditioning Another term for classical conditioning.

Respondent reinforcement In classical conditioning, reinforcement that occurs when the unconditioned stimulus closely follows the conditioned stimulus.

Response Any muscular action, glandular activity, or other identifiable behavior.

Response chaining The assembly of a series of responses into a chain of actions leading to reinforcement.

Response cost Punishment that occurs when a response leads to the removal of a positive reinforcer.

Response cost Removal of a positive reinforcer after a response is made.

Response-contingent Applying reinforcement, punishment, or other consequences only when a certain response is made.

REST Restricted Environmental Stimulation Therapy.

Resting potential The electrical charge that exists between the inside and outside of a neuron at rest.

Retardation Mental capacity significantly below average; traditionally defined as an IQ score below 70.

Reticular activating system (RAS) A part of the reticular formation that activates the cerebral cortex.

Reticular formation A network of fibers within

the medulla associated with attention, alertness, and activation of higher brain areas.

Retina The light-sensitive layer of cells at the back of the eye.

Retinal Part of the chemical compound that makes up rhodopsin (also known as retinene).

Retinal disparity Small discrepancies in the images falling on each retina caused by separation of the eyes.

Retrieval Recovering information from memory.

Retroactive interference The tendency for new memories to interfere with the retrieval of old memories.

Retrograde amnesia Loss of memory for events that preceded a head injury or other amnesia-causing event.

Reversibility of thought Recognition that relationships involving equality or identity can be reversed (for example, if A = B, then B = A).

Reversible figure A stimulus pattern that allows perceivers to reverse figure-ground organization.

Reward Anything that produces pleasure or satisfaction; a positive reinforcer.

Reward power Social power based on the capacity to reward a person for acting as desired.

Rhodopsin The photosensitive pigment in the rods.

Rods Visual receptors that are responsive to dim light but produce only black and white sensations.

Role conflict An upsetting condition that exists when a person tries to occupy two or more roles that make conflicting demands on behavior.

Role model A person who serves as a positive example of desirable behavior.

Role-playing The dramatic enactment or re-enactment of significant life events.

Role reversal Taking the role of another person to learn how one's own behavior appears from the other person's perspective.

Romantic love A combination of intimacy and passion that does not include much commitment.

Rooting reflex Neonatal reflex elicited by a light touch to the cheek, causing the infant to turn toward the object and attempt to nurse.

Rorschach Inkblot Test A projective test comprised of 10 standardized inkblots that are described by the person taking the test.

Run of luck A statistically unusual outcome (as in getting 5 heads in a row when flipping a coin) that could still occur by chance alone.

Sadism Deriving erotic satisfaction by the infliction of pain on another; more broadly, love of cruelty.

Sample A subset or portion of a population.

Satiety system Areas on the bottom middle of the hypothalamus that terminate eating.

Saturation That quality of colors related to their being very pure, from a narrow area of the spectrum, or free from mixture with other colors.

Savings score The amount of time saved (expressed as a percentage) when relearning information.

Scapegoating Selecting a person or group of people to take the blame for conditions not of their making; habitual redirection of aggression toward some person or group.

Schedule of reinforcement A rule or plan for determining which responses will be reinforced.

Schizophrenia A psychosis characterized by delusions, hallucinations, apathy, and a "split" between thought and emotion.

Schizotypal personality A non-psychotic personality disorder involving withdrawal, social isolation, and odd behavior, but no break with reality.

Science A body of knowledge gained through systematic observation and experimentation.

Scientific Conducted strictly according to the principles of evidence used in the natural sciences.

Scientific management (Theory X) An approach to managing employees that emphasizes work efficiency.

Scientific method Testing the truth of a proposition by careful measurement and controlled observation.

Scientific observation Orderly observation designed to answer questions about the world.

Scientist-practitioner model Training of clinical psychologists to do both research and therapy.

Seasonal affective disorder Depression that occurs during fall and winter; presumably related to decreased exposure to sunlight.

Secondary appraisal Deciding how to cope with a threat or challenge.

Secondary elaboration Making a dream more logical and complete while remembering it.

Secondary motives Motives based on learned psychological needs.

Secondary reinforcer A learned reinforcer; often one that gains reinforcing properties by association with a primary reinforcer.

Secondary sexual characteristics Sexual features other than the genitals and reproductive organs—such as the breasts, body shape, and facial hair.

Secondary traits Personality traits that are inconsistent or relatively superficial.

Secure attachment A stable and positive emotional bond.

Sedative A substance that calms, tranquilizes, or induces sleep by depressing activity in the nervous system.

Selective attention Voluntarily focusing on a selected portion of sensory input, most likely by re-routing messages within the brain.

Selective combination In problem solving, the ability to connect seemingly unrelated items of information.

Selective comparison The ability to relate a present problem to similar problems solved in the past or to prior experience.

Selective encoding The mental ability to select relevant information while ignoring useless or distracting information.

Selective perception Perceiving only certain stimuli among a larger array of possibilities.

Self A continuously evolving conception of one's personal identity.

Self archetype An unconscious image representing, unity, wholeness, completion, and balance.

Self-actualization The on-going process of fully developing one's personal potential.

Self-assertion A direct, honest expression of feelings and desires.

Self-awareness Consciousness of oneself as a person.

Self-concept Personal perception of one's own personality traits; a collection of beliefs, ideas, and feelings about one's own identity.

Self-disclosure The process of revealing private thoughts, feelings, and personal history to others.

Self-esteem Regarding oneself as a worthwhile person; a positive evaluation of oneself.

Self-evaluation Positive and negative feelings held toward oneself.

Self-fulfilling prophecy A prediction that prompts people to act in ways that make the prediction come true.

Self-handicapping Arranging to perform under conditions that usually lower performance, so as to have an excuse available for a poor showing.

Self-help group A group of people who share a particular type of problem and provide mutual support to one another.

Self-hypnosis A state of hypnosis attained without the aid of a hypnotist; autosuggestion.

Self-image Total subjective perception of one's body and personality (another term for self-concept).

Self-instruction Use of silent questions and instructions to structure learning.

Self-monitoring Regulation and control of the image one displays to others in public.

Self-recording Self-management based on keeping records of response frequencies.

Self-regulated learning Active, self-guided learning.

Self-reinforcement Praising or rewarding oneself for having made a particular response (such as completing a school assignment).

Self-selection feeding Free choice concerning the foods eaten.

Self-testing Answering self-administered questions.

Semantic differential A measure of connotative meaning obtained by rating words or concepts on several dimensions.

Semantic memory A subpart of declarative memory that records impersonal knowledge about the world.

Semantics The study of meanings in language.

Semicircular canals Fluid-filled vestibular canals; the sensory organs for balance.

Senile dementia Serious mental impairment in old age caused by physical deterioration of the brain.

Sensate focus Form of therapy that directs a couple's attention to natural sensations of sexual pleasure.

Sensation The immediate response in the brain caused by excitation of a sensory organ.

Sensation and perception psychologist A psychologist with expert knowledge on the sense organs and the processes involved in perception.

Sensation seeking A personality characteristic of persons who prefer high levels of stimulation.

Sensitivity group A group experience designed to increase self-awareness and sensitivity to others.

Sensorimotor stage Stage of intellectual development during which sensory input and motor responses become coordinated.

Sensory adaptation A decrease in sensory response to an unchanging stimulus.

Sensory analysis The capacity of sensory systems to separate incoming information into important elements.

Sensory coding Various codes used by the sense organs to transmit information to the brain.

Sensory conflict theory Attributes motion sickness to mismatched information from vision, the vestibular system, and kinesthesis.

Sensory deprivation Any major reduction in the amount or variety of sensory stimulation.

Sensory gating Alteration of incoming sensory messages in the spinal cord, before they reach the brain.

Sensory memory The first stage of memory, which holds an explicit and literal record of incoming information for two seconds or less.

Sensory neuron A nerve cell that carries information from the senses toward the central nervous system.

Separation anxiety Distress displayed by infants when they are separated from their parents or principal caregivers.

Serial position effect The tendency for the greatest number of memory errors to occur in the middle portion of an ordered list.

Set A predisposition to respond in a certain way.

Set point A theoretical proportion of body fat that tends to be maintained by changes in hunger and eating.

Setting In making attributions, the social and/or physical environment in which an action occurs.

Severe punishment Intense punishment; by definition, punishment capable of suppressing a response for long periods.

Sex drive The strength of one's motivation to engage in sexual behavior.

Sex role socialization The process of learning behaviors considered appropriate for one's gender in a given culture.

Sex role stereotypes Over-simplified and widely held beliefs about the basic characteristics of men and women.

Sex roles Separate patterns of traits, mannerisms, interests, and behaviors that are regarded as "male" and "female" by one's culture.

Sex-linked trait Traits other than gender that are influenced by genes carried on an X or a Y chromosome.

Sexism Institutionalized prejudice against members of either sex, based solely on their gender.

Sexual and gender identity disorders Any of a wide range of difficulties with sexual identity, deviant sexual behavior, or sexual adjustment.

Sexual aversion Fear, anxiety, or disgust about engaging in sex.

Sexual disorder Any of a wide range of difficulties with sexual identity, sexual behavior, or sexual adjustment.

Sexual masochism Deriving sexual pleasure from having pain inflicted during the sex act.

Sexual orientation One's degree of emotional and erotic attraction to members of the same gender, opposite gender, or both genders.

Sexual sadism Gaining sexual pleasure by inflicting pain during the sex act.

Sexual script An unspoken mental plan that defines a "plot," dialogue, and actions expected to take place in a sexual encounter.

Sexually transmitted disease A disease that is typically passed from one person to the next by intimate physical contact; a venereal disease.

Shape constancy The perceived shape of objects is unaltered by changes in the shape of their images on the retina.

Shaping Gradually molding responses to a final desired pattern.

Short-term dynamic therapy Modern psychodynamic therapy designed to produce insights within a shorter time than traditional psychoanalysis.

Short-term memory (STM) The memory system used to hold small amounts of information for relatively brief time periods.

Shyness A tendency to avoid others plus uneasiness and strain when socializing.

Sibling rivalry Competition among brothers and sisters for attention, dominance, status within the family, and so forth.

Signal In early language development, any behavior, such as touching, vocalizing, gazing, or smiling, that allows non-verbal interaction and turn-taking between parent and child.

Similarity In interpersonal attraction, the extent to which two people are alike in background, age, interests, attitudes, beliefs, and so forth.

Single-blind experiment An arrangement in which subjects remain unaware of whether they are in the experimental group or the control group.

Single-word stage In language development, the period during which a child first begins to use single words.

Situational context The social situation, behavioral setting, or general circumstances in which an action takes place.

Situational demands Unstated expectations that define desirable or appropriate behavior in various settings and social situations.

Situational determinants External conditions that strongly influence behavior.

Situational test Simulating real-life conditions so that a person's reactions may be directly observed.

Size constancy The perceived size of objects remains unchanged despite changes in the size of the images they cast on the retina.

Size-distance invariance The strict relationship that exists between the distance an object lies from the eyes and the size of its image.

Skin receptors Sensory organs for touch, pressure, pain, cold, and warmth.

Skin senses The senses of touch, pressure, pain, heat, and cold.

Sleep apnea Repeated interruption of breathing during sleep.

Sleep deprivation Being deprived of desired or needed amounts of sleep.

Sleep patterns The order and duration of daily sleep and waking periods.

Sleep spindles Distinctive bursts of brain-wave activity that indicate a person is asleep.

Sleep stages Various levels of sleep depth identified by brain-wave patterns and behavioral changes.

Sleep-deprivation psychosis A major disruption of mental and emotional functioning brought about by lack of sleep.

Sleeptalking Speaking while asleep.

Slow-to-warm-up child A child who is temperamentally restrained, unexpressive, or shy.

Social comparison Making judgments about ourselves through comparison with others.

Social development The development of self-awareness, attachment to caregivers, and relationships with other children and adults.

Social distance Distance at which impersonal interaction takes place (about 4 to 12 feet from the body).

Social distance scale An attitude measure that asks people to rate the degree to which they would be willing to have contact with a member of another group.

Social environment An environment defined by a group of people and their activities or interrelationships (such as a parade, revival meeting, or sports event).

Social exchange Any exchange between two people of attention, information, affection, favors, or the like.

Social exchange theory Theory stating that rewards must exceed costs for relationships to endure.

Social influence Changes in a person's behavior induced by the presence or actions of others.

Social learning theory An approach that combines learning principles with cognitive processes (perception, thinking, anticipation), plus the effects of observational learning, to explain behavior.

Social markers Visible or tangible signs that indicate a person's social status or role.

Social motives Learned motives acquired as part of growing up in a particular society or culture.

Social non-conformity Failure to conform to societal norms or the usual minimum standards for social conduct.

Social phobia An intense, irrational fear of being observed, evaluated, embarrassed, or humiliated by others in social situations, such as eating, writing, blushing, or speaking in public.

Social power The capacity to control, alter, or influence the behavior of another person.

Social psychology The study of human social behavior (behavior that is influenced by one's relationship with others).

Social Readjustment Rating Scale (SRRS) A scale that rates the impact of various life events on the likelihood of illness.

Social referencing Observing others in social situations to obtain information or guidance.

Social reinforcement Praise, attention, approval, and/or affection from others.

Social role Expected behavior patterns associated with particular social positions (such as daughter, worker, student).

Social stereotypes Oversimplified images of the traits of individuals who belong to a particular social group.

Social support Close, positive relationships with other people.

Social trap A social situation that tends to provide immediate rewards for actions that will have undesired effects in the long run.

Socialization The process of learning to live in a particular culture by adopting socially acceptable values and behavior.

Sociobiology Theory that social behavior evolved in ways that maximize fitness for survival of the species.

Sociopath Another name for the psychopath or antisocial personality.

Soma The main body of a neuron or other cell.

Somatic pain Pain from the skin, muscles, joints, and tendons.

Somatic system The system of nerves linking the spinal cord with the body and sense organs.

Somatic therapy Any bodily therapy, such as drug therapy, electroconvulsive therapy, or psychosurgery.

Somatization disorder Afflicted persons have numerous physical complaints. Typically, they have consulted many doctors, but no organic cause for their distress can be identified.

Somatoform disorder The presence of physical symptoms that mimic disease or injury for which there is no identifiable physical cause.

Somatoform pain Pain that has no identifiable physical cause and appears to be of psychological origin.

Somatosensory area The part of the parietal lobes that serves as a receiving area for bodily sensations.

Somesthetic sense Pertaining to sensations produced by the skin, muscles, joints, viscera, and organs of balance.

Somnambulist One who sleepwalks.

Sound wave A cyclic compression of air molecules.

Source traits Basic underlying traits of personality; each source trait is reflected in a larger number of surface traits.

Space adaptation syndrome Motion sickness caused by weightlessness.

Spaced practice A practice schedule that alternates study periods with brief rests. (Massed practice, in comparison, continues for long periods, without interruption.)

Spatial neglect A tendency to ignore the left or right side of one's body and the left or right side of visual space after damage to one of the brain hemispheres.

Special aptitude test Test to predict a person's likelihood of succeeding in a particular area of work or skill.

Species-specific behavior Behavior patterns that occur with little variation in almost all members of a species.

Species-typical behavior Behavior patterns that are typical of a species, but not automatic.

Specific phobia An intense, irrational fear of specific objects, activities, or situations.

Spinal nerve One of 62 major nerves that channel sensory and motor information in and out of the spinal cord.

Split-brain operation A surgical technique in which the corpus callosum is cut, functionally disconnecting the two cerebral hemispheres.

Spontaneous recovery The reappearance of a learned response after its apparent extinction.

Spontaneous remission The disappearance of a psychological disturbance without the aid of therapy.

Sports psychology Study of the psychological and behavioral dimensions of sports performance.

SQ3R method A reading method based on these steps: survey, question, read, recite, and review.

Squeeze technique Method for inhibiting ejaculation by compressing the tip of the penis.

Stage ESP The simulation of ESP for the purpose of entertainment.

Stage hypnosis Use of hypnosis to entertain; often, merely a simulation of hypnosis.

Stage of exhaustion Third stage of the G.A.S., at which time the body's resources are exhausted and serious health consequences occur.

Stage of resistance Second stage of the G.A.S., during which bodily adjustments to stress stabilize but at a high physical cost.

Staining Chemically treating tissues to make their details more visible.

Stanford-Binet Intelligence Scale A widely used individual test of intelligence; a direct descendant of Alfred Binet's first intelligence test.

State-dependent learning Memory influenced by one's bodily state at the time of learning and at the time of retrieval. Improved memory occurs when the bodily states match.

Statistical abnormality Abnormality defined on the basis of an extreme score on some measure or dimension, such as IQ or anxiety.

Statistical significance Experimental results that would rarely occur by chance alone.

Status An individual's position in a group or social structure, especially with respect to power, privilege, importance, and so forth.

Status inequalities Differences in the power, prestige, or privileges of two or more persons or groups.

Stereocilia Bristle-like structures on hair cells.

Stereoscopic vision Perception of space and depth caused chiefly by the fact that the eyes receive different images.

Stereotype An inaccurate, rigid, and oversimplified image of members of a social group, especially an outgroup.

Stereotyped response A rigid, repetitive, and non-productive response made mechanically and without regard for its appropriateness.

Stimulant A substance that produces a temporary increase of activity in the body and nervous system.

Stimulation deafness Deafness resulting from damage caused by exposure to excessively loud sounds.

Stimulus Any physical energy sensed by an organism.

Stimulus control The tendency of stimuli present when an operant response is acquired to subsequently control when and where the response is made.

Stimulus discrimination The learned ability to detect differences in stimuli, often produced by reinforcing responses to one stimulus but not another.

Stimulus generalization The tendency to respond to stimuli similar to, but not identical to, a conditioned stimulus.

Stimulus motives Innate needs for stimulation

and information.

Stress The condition that occurs when a challenge or a threat forces a person to adjust or adapt to the environment.

Stress inoculation Use of positive coping statements to control fear and anxiety.

Stress management The application of behavioral strategies to reduce stress and improve coping skills.

Stress reaction The physical response to stress, consisting mainly of bodily changes related to autonomic nervous system arousal.

Stressor A specific condition or event in the environment that challenges or threatens a person.

Stroboscopic movement Illusion of movement in which an object is shown in a rapidly changing series of positions.

Structuralism The school of thought in psychology concerned with analyzing sensations and personal experience into basic elements.

Structured interview An interview that follows a prearranged plan, usually defined by asking a series of planned questions.

Stuttering Chronic hesitation or stumbling in speech.

Subcortex All brain structures below the cerebral cortex.

Subjective discomfort Personal, private feelings of discomfort or unhappiness.

Subjective experience Reality as it is perceived and interpreted, not as it exists objectively; personal, private, non-objective experience.

Sublimation Working off frustrated desires or unacceptable impulses in substitute activities that are constructive or accepted by society.

Subliminal perception Perception of a stimulus presented below the threshold for conscious recognition.

Substance related disorder Abuse of or dependence on a mood- or behavior-altering drug.

Successive approximations A series of steps that change behavior to a desired response pattern.

Sucking reflex Rhythmic sucking movements elicited by touching the neonate's mouth.

Sudden infant death syndrome The sudden, unexplained death of an apparently healthy infant.

Superego In Freudian theory, an internalization of parental values and societal standards.

Superordinate goal A goal that exceeds or overrides all others; a goal that renders other goals relatively less important.

Superstitious behavior In conditioning, a behavior repeated because it seems to produce reinforcement, even though it is actually unnecessary.

Support group A group formed to provide emotional support for its members through discussion of shared stresses and concerns.

Suppression A conscious effort to not think of something or to keep it from awareness.

Surface traits The visible or observable traits of one's personality.

Surrogate mother A substitute mother (often an inanimate dummy in animal research).

Survey method The use of public polling techniques to answer psychological questions.

Syllogism A format for analyzing logical arguments.

Symbolic prejudice Prejudice that is expressed in disguised fashion.

Symbolization In Carl Rogers' theory, the process of admitting an experience to awareness.

Sympathetic system A branch of the autonomic system responsible for arousing and activating the body at times of stress.

Synapse The microscopic space, between an axon terminal and another neuron, over which neurotransmitters pass.

Synesthesia Experiencing one sense in terms normally associated with another sense; for example, "seeing" sounds as colors.

Syntax Rules for ordering words when forming sentences.

Systematic desensitization A guided reduction in fear, anxiety, or aversion.

Tardive dyskinesia A neurological disorder associated with excessive use of major tranquilizers.

Target behaviors Actions or other behaviors (such as speech) that a behavior therapist seeks to modify.

Task centering Focusing on the task at hand, rather than on one's own feelings or needs.

Taste aversion An active dislike for a particular food; frequently created when the food is associated with illness or discomfort.

Taste bud The receptor organ for taste.

Telegraphic speech In language development, the formation of simple two-word sentences that "telegraph" (communicate) a simple idea.

Telepathy The purported ability to directly know another person's thoughts.

Temperament The physical foundation of personality, including emotional and perceptual sensitivity, energy levels, typical mood, and so forth.

Temporal lobes Areas on each side of the cerebral cortex that include the sites where hearing registers in the brain.

Temporary threshold shift A temporary decrease in sensitivity to sound.

Tentative stage Stage of career exploration in which planning becomes more realistic, although still broad.

Terminal decline An abrupt decline in measured intelligence about five years before death.

Territorial behavior Any behavior that tends to define a space as one's own or that protects it from intruders.

Territorial markers Objects and other signals whose placement indicates to others the "ownership" of a particular area.

Test anxiety High levels of arousal and worry that seriously impair test performance.

Test battery A group of tests and interviews given to the same individual.

Test standardization Establishing standards for administering a test and interpreting scores.

Testosterone Male sex hormone, secreted mainly by the testes and responsible for the development of male sexual characteristics.

Thalamus A structure at the center of the brain that relays sensory information to the cerebral cortex.

Thanatologist A specialist who studies emotional and behavioral reactions to death and dying.

Thanatos The death instinct postulated by Freud.

THC Tetrahydrocannabinol, the main active chemical in marijuana.

Thematic Apperception Test (TAT) A projective test consisting of 20 different scenes and life situations about which respondents make up stories.

Theory A system designed to interrelate concepts and facts in a way that summarizes existing data and predicts future observations.

Theory Y A management style that emphasizes human relations at work and that views people as industrious, responsible, and interested in challenging work.

Therapy placebo effect Improvement caused not by the actual process of therapy but by a client's expectation that therapy will help.

Thought stopping Use of aversive stimuli to interrupt or prevent upsetting thoughts.

Threat An event or situation perceived as potentially harmful to one's well-being.

Thyroid gland Endocrine gland whose hormones help regulate metabolism (the production and expenditure of energy within the body).

Time out Removing a person from a situation in which rewards for maladaptive behavior are available, in order to produce extinction; also, the withholding of social reinforcers (attention, approval) when undesirable responses are made.

Tinnitus A ringing or buzzing sensation in the ears not caused by an external stimulus.

Tip-of-the-tongue state The experience of feeling that a memory is available, while being unable to retrieve it.

Token economy A therapeutic program in which desirable behaviors are reinforced with tokens that can be exchanged for goods, services, activities, and privileges.

Token reinforcer A tangible secondary reinforcer such as money, gold stars, poker chips, and the like.

Tokens Symbolic rewards, or secondary reinforcers (such as plastic chips, gold stars, or points) that can be exchanged for real reinforcers.

Top-down processing Applying higher-level knowledge to rapidly organize sensory information into a meaningful perception.

Tragedy of the commons A social trap in which individuals, each acting in his or her immediate self-interest, overuse a scarce group resource.

Trait profile A graphic representation of the ratings obtained by an individual (or sometimes a group) on each of several personality traits.

Trait theorist A psychologist who is interested in classifying, analyzing, and interrelating traits, and in discovering their origins, to understand and explain personality.

Trait-situation interaction Variations in behavior that occur when the expression of a trait is influenced by settings or circumstances.

Traits (personality) Relatively permanent and enduring qualities of behavior that a person displays in most situations.

Transducer A device that converts energy from one system into energy in another.

Transference In psychoanalysis, the tendency of a client to transfer to the therapist feelings that correspond to those the client had for important persons in his or her past.

Transformation In Piaget's theory, the mental ability to change the shape or form of a substance (such as clay or water) and to perceive that its volume remains the same.

Transformation rules Rules by which a simple declarative sentence may be changed to other voices or forms (past tense, passive voice, and so forth).

Transition period Time span during which a person leaves an existing life pattern behind and moves into a new pattern.

Transvestic fetishism Achieving sexual arousal by wearing clothing of the opposite sex.

Trepanning In modern usage, any surgical procedure in which a hole is bored in the skull; historically, the chipping or boring of holes in the skull to "treat" mental disturbance.

Triangular theory of love Theory that love is composed of three elements: intimacy, passion, and commitment; different types of love are defined by the presence or absence of each element.

Trichromatic theory The theory of color vision based on the assumption that there are three types of cones, with peak sensitivity to red, green, or blue.

Tryptophan A sleep-promoting amino acid.

Tunnel vision Vision restricted to the center of the visual field.

Turn-taking In early language development, the tendency of parent and child to alternate in the sending and receiving of signals or messages.

Two-factor learning Learning that involves both classical conditioning and operant conditioning.

Tympanic membrane The eardrum.

Type A personality A personality type with an elevated risk of heart disease; characterized by time urgency, anger, and hostility.

Type B personality All personality types other than Type A; a low-cardiac-risk personality.

Unconditional positive regard Unshakable love and approval given without qualification.

Unconditioned response An innate reflex response elicited by an unconditioned stimulus.

Unconditioned stimulus A stimulus innately capable of eliciting a response.

Unconscious Region of the mind that is beyond awareness, especially impulses and desires not directly known to a person.

Undifferentiated schizophrenia Schizophrenia lacking the specific features of catatonic, disorganized, or paranoid types.

Unfreezing In brainwashing, a loosening of convictions about former values, attitudes, and beliefs.

Unipolar disorder A mood disorder in which a person experiences extended periods of deep depression but has no history of ever having been manic.

Unstructured interview An interview in which conversation is informal and topics are taken up freely as they arise.

Unusual Uses Test A test of creativity in which subjects try to think of new uses for a common object.

Vacillation Wavering in intention or feelings.

Vaginismus Muscle spasms of the vagina that prevent intercourse or cause pain.

Validity The ability of a test to measure what it purports to measure.

Validity scales Scales that tell whether test scores should be invalidated for lying, inconsistency, or "faking good."

Variable Any condition that changes or can be made to change; a measure, event, or state that may vary.

Variable interval schedule A schedule in which a reinforcer is given for the first correct response made after a varied amount of time has passed (measured from the previous reinforced response). Responses made before the time interval has ended are not reinforced.

Variable ratio schedule A pattern in which a varied number of correct responses must be made to get a reinforcer. For example, a reinforcer is given after 3 to 7 correct responses; the actual number changes randomly.

Verbal intelligence Intelligence measured by answering questions involving vocabulary, general information, arithmetic, and other language- or symbol-oriented tasks.

Vestibular senses The senses of balance, body position, and acceleration.

Vicarious classical conditioning Classical conditioning brought about by observing another person react to a particular stimulus.

Vicarious desensitization A reduction in fear or anxiety that takes place vicariously ("secondhand") when a client watches models perform the feared behavior.

Virilism The development of male sexual characteristics in a female.

Visceral pain Pain originating in the internal organs.

Visible spectrum   That portion of the electro-magnetic spectrum to which the eyes are sensitive.

Visual acuity   The clarity or sharpness of visual perception.

Visual cliff   An apparatus that looks like the edge of an elevated platform or cliff; used to test for depth perception in infants and baby animals.

Visual pigment   A chemical found in the rods and cones that is sensitive to light.

Visually directed reaching   Coordinated, visually guided reaching for a particular object.

Vocational counselor   A counseling psychologist who helps people match their interests, talents, and goals with available careers.

Vocational interest test   A paper-and-pencil test that assesses a person's interests and matches them to interests found among successful workers in various occupations.

Volume transmission   The spread of neuropeptides into groups of neurons, affecting their behavior.

Vomeronasal organ   A sensory organ sensitive to pheromones.

Voyeurism   Deriving sexual pleasure from viewing the genitals of others, usually without their knowledge or permission (peeping).

Waiting-list control group   A group of people who receive no treatment in experiments designed to test the effectiveness of psychotherapy.

Waking consciousness   A state of normal, alert awareness.

Warning system   Pain based on large nerve fibers; warns that bodily damage may be occurring.

Weapons effect   The observation that weapons serve as strong cues for aggressive behavior; also, the tendency for eyewitnesses to focus almost entirely on an assailant's weapon.

Weber's law   States that the just noticeable difference is a constant proportion of the original stimulus intensity; actually applies most accurately to stimuli in the mid-range of intensities.

Wechsler Adult Intelligence Scale-Third Edition (WAIS-III)   A widely used adult intelligence test that rates both verbal and performance intelligence.

Wechsler Intelligence Scale for Children-Third Edition (WISC-III)   A widely used intelligence test for children that rates both verbal and performance intelligence.

Weight cycling   Repeated swings between losing and gaining weight.

Wellness   A positive state of good health; more than the absence of disease.

Wernicke's area   An area related to language comprehension.

White matter   Portions of the nervous system that appear white due to the presence of myelin.

Whole learning   Studying an entire package of information (such as a complete poem) at once.

Wish fulfillment   Freudian belief that the content of many dreams reflects unfulfilled desires that cannot be consciously expressed.

Withdrawal of love   Withholding affection to enforce child discipline.

Withdrawal symptoms   Physical illness and discomfort that accompany the withdrawal of an addictive drug.

Work efficiency   Maximum output (productivity) at lowest cost.

Working memory   Another name for short-term memory, especially as it is used for thinking and problem solving.

X chromosome   The female chromosome contributed by the mother; produces a female when paired with another X chromosome, and a male when paired with a Y chromosome.

Y chromosome   The male chromosome contributed by the father; produces a male when paired with an X chromosome. Fathers may give either an X or a Y chromosome to their offspring.

Yerkes-Dodson law   A qualification of the inverted U function that states the relationships among arousal, task complexity, and performance.

Zener cards   A deck of 25 cards bearing various symbols and used in early parapsychological research.

References

A nation's shame: Fatal child abuse and neglect in the United States. (1995). United States Advisory Board on Child Abuse and Neglect, United States Department of Health and Human Services.

Abbott, A. & Concar, D. (1992). A trip into the unknown. *New Scientist,* Aug., 30–34.

Abe, K., Amatomi, M., & Oda, N. (1984). Sleepwalking and recurrent sleeptalking in children of childhood sleepwalkers. *American Journal of Psychiatry, 141,* 800–801.

Abelson, R. P. (1988). Conviction. *American Psychologist. 43*(4), 267–275.

Abrahamson, D. J., Barlow, D. H., & Abrahamson, L. S. (1989). Differential effects of performance demand and distraction on sexually functional and dysfunctional males. *Journal of Abnormal Psychology, 98*(3), 241–247.

Abrams, A. (1983). Honda Ohio plant transplants Japan methods, harmony. *Los Angeles Times,* Jan. 7, IV, 1–2.

Abrams, R. (1997). *Electroconvulsive therapy.* New York: Oxford University Press.

Abramson, R. (1993). EPA officially links passive smoke, cancer. *Los Angeles Times,* Jan. 8, A27.

Ackerman, M. D. & Carey, M. P. (1995). Psychology's role in the assessment of erectile dysfunction. *Journal of Consulting & Clinical Psychology, 63*(6), 862–876.

Adams, H.E., Wright, L. W., & Lohr, B. A. (1996). Is homophobia associated with homosexual arousal? *Journal of Abnormal Psychology, 105*(3), 440–445.

Adams, J. (1988). *Conceptual blockbusting.* New York: Norton.

Adelmann, P. K. & Zajonc, R. B. (1989). Facial efference and the experience of emotion. *Annual Review of Psychology, 40,* 249–280.

Ader, R. & Cohen, N., (1993). Psychoneuroimmunology: Conditioning and stress. In L. W. Porter and M. R. Rosenzweig (Eds.), *Annual Review of Psychology, 44,* 53–85.

Adler, T. (1992). Are hormone's benefits real—or a tall tale? *APA Monitor,* Dec., 42, 43.

Adorno, T. W., Frenkel-Brunswik, E., Levinson, D. J., & Sanford, R. N. (1950). *The authoritarian personality.* New York: Harper.

Agnati, L. F., Bjelke, B., & Fuxe, K. (1992). Volume transmission in the brain. *American Scientist, 80*(Jul-Aug), 362–373.

Ahles, T. A., Blanchard, E. B., & Leventhal, H. (1983). Cognitive control of pain: Attention to the sensory aspects of the cold pressor stimulus. *Cognitive Therapy and Research, 7,* 159–178.

Ainsworth, M. D. (1989). Attachments beyond infancy. *American Psychologist, 44*(4), 709–716.

Akerstedt, T. (1990). Psychological and psychophysiological effects of shift work. *Scandinavian Journal of Work, Environment & Health, 16*(Suppl. 1), 67–73.

Akerstedt, T., Hume, K., Minors, D., & Waterhouse,
J. (1993). Regulation of sleep and naps on an irregular schedule. *Sleep, 16*(8), 736–743.

Alarcon, R. D. (1995). Culture and psychiatric diagnosis: Impact on DSM-IV and ICD-10. *Psychiatric Clinics of North America, 18*(3), 449–465.

Albert, E. M. (1963). The roles of women: Question of values. In Farber & Wilson (Eds.), *The potential of women.* New York: McGraw-Hill.

Alberti, R., & Emmons, M. (1995). *Your perfect right.* San Luis Obispo, CA: Impact.

Alberto, P. A. & Troutman, A. C. (1995). *Applied behavior analysis for teachers.* Englewood Cliffs, NJ: Merrill.

Alcock, J. E. (1990). *Science and supernature: A critical appraisal of parapsychology.* Buffalo, NY: Prometheus.

Alden, L. E. & Wallace, S. T. (1995). Social phobia and social appraisal in successful and unsuccessful social interactions. *Behaviour Research & Therapy, 33*(5), 497–505.

Alevizos, P. N., & Callahan, E. J. (1977). Assessment of psychotic behavior. In A. R. Ciminero, K. S. Calhoun, & H. E. Adams (Eds.), *Handbook of behavioral assessment.* New York: Wiley.

Alicke, M. D. & Doherty, K. (1992). Social disagreement and conformity. *Journal of Social Behavior & Personality, 7*(1), 125–137.

Alicke, M. D., Yurak, T. J., & Vredenburg, D. S. (1996). Using personal attitudes to judge others. *Journal of Research in Personality, 30*(1), 103–119.

Allen, B. (1979). Winged victory of "Gossamer Albatross." *National Geographic, 156,* 642–651.

Allgeier, A. R. & Allgeier, E. R. (1995). *Sexual interactions.* Lexington, MA: Heath.

Alloy, L. B., Peterson, C., Abramson, L. Y., & Seligman, M. E. (1984). Attributional style and the generality of learned helplessness. *Journal of Personality & Social Psychology, 46,* 681–687.

Allport, G. W. (1958). *The nature of prejudice.* Garden City, NY: Anchor Books, Doubleday.

Allport, G. W. (1961). *Pattern and growth in personality.* New York: Holt, Rinehart, and Winston.

Alsaker, F. D. (1992). Pubertal timing, overweight, and psychological adjustment. *Journal of Early Adolescence, 12*(4), 396–419.

Alsaker, F. D. (1995). Is puberty a critical period for socialization? *Journal of Adolescence, 18*(4), 427–444.

Althof, S. E. & Seftel, A. D. (1995). The evaluation and management of erectile dysfunction. *Psychiatric Clinics of North America, 18*(1), 171–192.

Alva, S. A. (1993). Differential patterns of achievement among Asian-American adolescents. *Journal of Youth and Adolescence, 22*(4), 407–423.

Alvarado, N. (1994). Empirical validity of the Thematic Apperception Test. *Journal of Personality Assessment, 63*(1), 59–79.

Alvino, J. (1996). *Parents' guide to raising a gifted child.* New York: Ballantine.

Amabile, T. M. (1983). *The social psychology of creativity.*
New York: Springer-Verlag.

Amar, P. B. (1993). Biofeedback and applied psychophysiology at the crossroads. *Biofeedback & Self-Regulation, 18*(4), 201–209.

Ambady, N. & Rosenthal, R. (1993). Half a minute: Predicting teacher evaluations from thin slices of non-verbal behavior and physical attractiveness. *Journal of Personality & Social Psychology, 64*(3), 431–441.

American Psychological Association. (1995). *Behavioral research with animals.* Washington, DC: Author.

Anastasi, A. (1996). *Psychological tests.* Englewood Cliffs, NJ: Prentice Hall.

Andersen, S. M., Klatzky, R. L., & Murray, J. (1990). Traits and social stereotypes: Efficiency differences in social processing. *Journal of Personality & Social Psychology, 59*(2), 192–201.

Anderson, B. L., Kiecolt-Glaser, J. K., & Glaser, R. (1994). A biobehavioral model of cancer stress and disease course. *American Psychologist, 49*(5), 389–404.

Anderson, C. A. (1989). Temperature and aggression. *Psychological Bulletin, 106,* 74–96.

Anderson, C. A., Anderson, K. B., & Deuser, W. E. (1996). Examining an affective aggression framework. *Personality & Social Psychology Bulletin, 22*(4), 366–376.

Anderson, J. R. (1993). Problem solving and learning. *American Psychologist, 48*(1), 35–44.

Anderson, J. R. (1995). *Cognitive psychology.* New York: Freeman.

Anderson, J. R., Reder, L. M., & Lebiere, C. (1996). Working memory: Activation limitations on retrieval. *Cognitive Psychology, 30*(3), 221–256.

Anderson, R. H., Anderson, K., Flemming, D. E., & Kinghorn, E. (1984). A multidimensional test of the attributional reformulation of learned helplessness. *Bulletin of the Psychonomic Society, 22,* 211–213.

Andreasen, N. C., Glaum, M., Swayze, V. W., O'Leary, D. S. et al. (1993). Intelligence and brain structure in normal individuals. *American Journal of Psychiatry, 150*(1), 130–143.

Animal rights: CSICOP takes a new direction, (1990). *Skeptical Inquirer, 15,* 4–5.

Annett, M. & Manning, M. (1990). Arithmetic and laterality. *Neuropsychologia, 28*(1), 61–69.

Anshel, M. H. (1995a). An examination of self-regulatory cognitive-behavioural strategies of Australian elite and non-elite competitive male swimmers. *Australian Psychologist, 30*(2), 78–83.

Anshel, M. H. (1995b). Effect of chronic aerobic exercise and progressive relaxation on motor performance and affect following acute stress. *Behavioral Medicine, 21*(4), 186–196.

Anthony, W. A., Cohen, M., & Kennard, W. (1990). Understanding the current facts and principles of mental health systems planning. *American Psycholo-*

gist, 45(11), 1249–1252.

Archer, J. (1996). Sex differences in social behavior. *American Psychologist, 51*(9), 909–917.

Arena, J. G., Bruno, G. M., Hannah, S. L., & Meador, K. J. (1995). A comparison of frontal electromyographic biofeedback training, trapezius electromyographic biofeedback training, and progressive muscle relaxation therapy in the treatment of tension headache. *Headache, 35*(7), 411–419.

Arendt, J. (1994). Clinical perspectives for melatonin and its agonists. *Biological Psychiatry, 35*(1), 1–2.

Aron, A. & Westbay, L. (1996). Dimensions of the prototype of love. *Journal of Personality & Social Psychology, 70*(3), 535–551.

Aronoff, J., Barclay, A. M., & Stevenson, L. A. (1988). The recognition of threatening facial stimuli. *Journal of Personality & Social Psychology, 54*(4), 647–655.

Aronson, E. (1969). Some antecedents of interpersonal attraction. In W. J. Arnold & D. Levine (Eds.), *Nebraska Symposium on Motivation.* Lincoln: University of Nebraska Press.

Aronson, E. (1992). *The Social Animal.* San Francisco: W. H. Freeman.

Aronson, E., with Blaney, N., Sikes, J., Stephan, C., & Snapp, M. (1979). Busing and racial tension: The jigsaw route to learning and liking. In V. J. Derlega & L. H. Janda (Eds.), *Personal adjustment, selected readings.* Glenview, IL: Scott, Foresman.

Arthur, A. G. & White, H. (1996). Children's assignment of gender to animal characters in pictures. *Journal of Genetic Psychology, 157*(3), 297–301.

Arthur, W. Jr. & Graziano, W. G. (1996). The five-factor model, conscientiousness, and driving accident involvement. *Journal of Personality, 64*(3), 593–618.

Asch, S. E. (1956). Studies of independence and conformity: A minority of one against a unanimous majority. *Psychological Monographs, 70*(416).

Aschoff, J. (1994). Naps as integral parts of the wake time within the human sleep-wake cycle. *Journal of Biological Rhythms, 9*(2), 145–155.

Asendorpf, J. B. (1996). Self-awareness and other-awareness. II: Mirror self-recognition, social contingency awareness, and synchronic imitation. *Developmental Psychology, 32*(2), 313–321.

Ash, D. W. & Holding, D. H. (1990). Backward versus forward chaining in the acquisition of a keyboard skill. *Human Factors, 32*(2), 139–146.

Ashton, W. A. & Fuehrer, A. (1993). Effects of gender and gender role identification of participant and type of social support resource on support seeking. *Sex Roles, 28*(7–8), 461–476.

Aslin, R. N. & Smith, L. B. (1988). Perceptual development. *Annual Review of Psychology, 39*, 435–473.

Astronomical Society of the Pacific. (1983). *Astrology and astronomy.* San Francisco.

Athenasiou, R., Shaver, P., & Tavris, C. (1970). Sex. *Psychology Today, 4*(2), 37–52.

Attenburrow, M. E. J., Cowen, P. J., & Sharpley, A. L. (1996). Low dose melatonin improves sleep in healthy middle-aged subjects. *Psychopharmacology, 126*(2), 179–181.

Avery, D. H., Bolte, M. A., Dager, S. R. et al. (1993). Dawn simulation of winter depression. *American Journal of Psychiatry, 150*(1), 113–117.

Axel, R. (1995). The molecular logic of smell. *Scientific American, 273*(4), 154.

Ayllon, T. (1963). Intensive treatment of psychotic behavior by stimulus satiation and food reinforcement. *Behavior Research and Therapy, 1,* 53–61.

Ayllon, T., & Azrin, N. H. (1965). The measurement and reinforcement of behavior of psychotics. *Journal of the Experimental Analysis of Behavior, 8,* 357–383.

Azrin, N. H., Hutchinson, R. R., & McLaughlin, R. (1965). The opportunity for aggression as an operant reinforcer during aversive stimulation. *Journal of Experimental Analysis of Behavior, 8,* 171–180.

Bachman, J. G., & Johnson, L. D. (1979). The freshmen. *Psychology Today, 13,* 78–87.

Bachrach, H., Galatzer-Levy, R., Skolnikoff, A., & Waldron, S. (1991). On the efficacy of psychoanalysis. *Journal of the American Psychoanalytic Association, 39,* 871–916.

Baddeley, A. (1990). *Human memory.* Needham Heights, MA: Allyn and Bacon.

Baddeley, A. (1996). *Your memory: A user's guide.* North Pomfret: Trafalgar Square.

Baer, J. M. (1993). *Creativity and divergent thinking.* Hillsdale, NJ: Erlbaum.

Bahrick, H. P. (1984). Semantic memory content in permastore: Fifty years of memory for Spanish learned in school. *Journal of Experimental Psychology: General, 113*(1), 1–37.

Bahrick, Harry P., Hall, Lynda K., & Berger, Stephanie A. (1996). Accuracy and distortion in memory for high school grades. *Psychological Science, 7*(5), 265–271.

Bailey, J. M. & Pillard, R. C. (1991). A genetic study of male sexual orientation. *Archives of General Psychiatry, 48*(12), 1089–1096.

Bailey, J. M., Bobrow, D., Wolfe, M., & Mikach, S. (1995). Sexual orientation of adult sons of gay fathers. *Developmental Psychology, 31*(1), 124–129.

Bailey, J. M., Pillard, R. C., Neale, M. C., & Agyei, Y. (1993). Heritable factors influence sexual orientation in women. *Archives of General Psychiatry, 50*(3), 217–223.

Bailey, M. B. & Bailey, R. E. (1993). "Misbehavior": A case history. *American Psychologist,* Nov., 1157–1158.

Baillargeon, R. (1991). Reasoning about the height and location of a hidden object in 4.5- and 6.5-month-old infants. *Cognition, 38*(1), 13–42.

Baillargeon, R. & DeVos, J. (1992). Object permanence in young infants: Further evidence. *Child Development, 62*(6), 1227–1246.

Baillargeon, R., De Vos, J., & Graber, M. (1989). Location memory in 8-month-old infants in a non-search AB task. *Cognitive Development, 4,* 345–367.

Baisden, R. H. (1995). Therapeutic uses for neural grafts: Progress slowed but not abandoned. *Behavioral & Brain Sciences, 18*(1), 47–48, 90–107.

Bajracharya, S. M., Sarvela, P. D., & Isberner, F. R. (1995). A retrospective study of first sexual intercourse experiences among undergraduates. *Journal of American College Health, 43*(4), 169–177.

Bak, M., Girvin, J. P., Hambrecht, F.T., Kufta, C. V., Loeb, G. E., & Schmidt, E. M. (1990). Visual sensations produced by intracortical microstimulation of the human occipital cortex. *Medical and Biological Engineering and Computing, 28*(3), 257–259.

Baker, L. A. & Clark, R. (1990). Genetic origins of behavior: Implications for counselors. *Journal of Counseling & Development, 68*(6), 597–600.

Baker, L. A. & Daniels, D. (1990). Nonshared environmental influences and personality differences in adult twins. *Journal of Personality & Social Psychology, 58*(1), 103–110.

Bakich, I. (1995). Hypnosis in the treatment of sexual desire disorders. *Australian Journal of Clinical & Experimental Hypnosis, 23*(1), 70–77.

Bakker, F. C., Boschker, M. S. J., & Chung, T. (1996). Changes in muscular activity while imagining weight lifting using stimulus or response propositions. *Journal of Sport & Exercise Psychology, 18*(3),

313–324.

Balaban, M. T. (1995). Affective influences on startle in five-month-old infants: Reactions to facial expressions of emotion. *Child Development, 66*(1), 28–36.

Ball, G. G., & Grinker, J. A. (1981). Overeating and obesity. In S. J. Mule (Ed.), *Behavior in Excess,* 194–220. New York: Free Press.

Baltes, P. B. (1987). Theoretical propositions of life-span developmental psychology: On the dynamics between growth and decline. *Developmental Psychology, 23*(5), 611–626.

Banaji, M. R. & Prentice, D. A. (1994). The self in social contexts. *Annual Review of Psychology, 45,* 297–332.

Bandura, A. (1971). *Social learning theory.* New York: General Learning Press.

Bandura, A. (1973). *Aggression: A social learning analysis.* Englewood Cliffs, NJ: Prentice-Hall.

Bandura, A. (1986). *Social foundations of thought and action: A social cognitive theory.* Englewood Cliffs, NJ: Prentice-Hall.

Bandura, A., & Rosenthal, T. L. (1966). Vicarious classical conditioning as a function of arousal level. *Journal of Personality & Social Psychology, 3,* 54–62.

Bandura, A., & Walters, R. (1959). *Adolescent aggression.* New York: Ronald.

Bandura, A., & Walters, R. (1963a). Aggression. In H. W. Stevenson (Ed.), *Child psychology.* Chicago: University of Chicago Press.

Bandura, A., & Walters, R. (1963b). *Social learning and personality development.* New York: Holt.

Bandura, A., Blanchard, E. B., & Ritter, B. (1969). Relative efficacy of desensitization and modeling approaches for inducing behavioral, affective, and attitudinal changes. *Journal of Personality & Social Psychology, 13*(3), 173–199.

Bandura, A., Ross, D., & Ross, S. A. (1963). Vicarious reinforcement and imitative learning. *Journal of Abnormal and Social Psychology, 67,* 601–607.

Bank, S. P., & Kahn, M. D. (1982). *The sibling bond.* New York: Basic Books.

Banks, A. & Gartrell, N. K. (1995). Hormones and sexual orientation: A questionable link. *Journal of Homosexuality, 28*(3–4), 247–268.

Banks, T. & Dabbs, J. M. Jr. (1996). Salivary testosterone and cortisol in delinquent and violent urban subculture. *Journal of Social Psychology, 136*(1), 49–56.

Barber, T. X. (1970). *Suggested ("hypnotic") behavior: The trance paradigm versus an alternative paradigm.* Harding, Mass. Medfield Foundation, Report No. 103.

Bard, C., Fleury, M., & Goulet, C. (1994). Relationship between perceptual strategies and response adequacy in sport situations. *International Journal of Sport Psychology, 25*(3), 266–281.

Barker, E. A. (1993). Evaluating graphology. *Skeptical Inquirer, 17*(Spring), 312–315.

Baron, J. & Jurney, J. (1993). Norms against voting for coerced reform. *Journal of Personality & Social Psychology, 64*(3), 347–355.

Baron, R. A. (1983). "Sweet smell of success"? The impact of pleasant artificial scents on evaluations of job applicants. *Journal of Applied Psychology, 68,* 709–713.

Baron, R. A. & Byrne, D. (1994). *Social psychology.* Boston: Allyn & Bacon.

Baron, R. A. & Richardson, D. R. (1994). *Human aggression.* New York: Plenum.

Barowsky, E. I., Moskowitz, J., & Zweig, J. B. (1990). Biofeedback for disorders of initiating and maintaining sleep. *Annals of the New York Academy of Sciences, 602,* 97–103.

Barrett, D. (1993). The "committee of sleep": A study of dream incubation for problem solving. *Dreaming,*

3(2), 115–122.

Barrett, R. J. (1985). Behavioral approaches to individual differences in substance abuse. In Galizio, M. & Maisto, S. A. (Eds.), *Determinants of substance abuse treatment: Biological, psychological, and environmental factors.* New York: Plenum.

Barron, F. (1958). The psychology of imagination. *Scientific American, 199*(3), 150–170.

Barsalou, L. W. (1992). *Cognitive psychology.* Hillsdale, NJ: Lawrence Erlbaum.

Bartlett, J. C. & Searcy, J. (1993). Inversion and configuration of faces. *Cognitive Psychology, 25*(3), 281–316.

Bartoshuk, L. M., Duffy, V. B., & Miller, I. J. (1994). PTC/PROP taste: Anatomy, psychophysics, and sex effects. *Physiology & Behavior, 56*(6), 1165–1171.

Bartz, W. (1990). The basics of critical thought. Personal communication.

Bashore, T. R. & Rapp, P. E. (1993). Are there alternatives to traditional polygraph procedures? *Psychological Bulletin, 113*(1), 3–22.

Basic Behavioral Science Task Force. (1996). Basic behavioral science research for mental health: Vulnerability and resilience. *American Psychologist, 51*(1), 22–28.

Bath, H. (1996). Everyday discipline or control with care. *Journal of Child & Youth Care,* 10(2), 23–32.

Batson, C. D. (1990). How social an animal? The human capacity for caring. *American Psychologist, 45*(3), 336–346.

Bauer, P. J. (1996). What do infants recall of their lives? *American Psychologist, 51*(4), 29–41.

Bauer, W. D., & Twentyman, C. T. (1985). Abusing, neglectful, and comparison mothers' response to child-related and non-child-related stressors. *Journal of Consulting and Clinical Psychology, 53,* 335–343.

Baum, A. & Fleming, I. (1993). Implications of psychological research on stress and technological accidents. *American Psychologist, 48*(6), 665–672.

Baum, A., & Davis, G. E. (1980). Reducing the stress of high-density living: An architectural intervention. *Journal of Personality & Social Psychology, 38,* 471–481.

Baum, A., & Valins, S. (1979). Architectural mediation of residential density and control: Crowding and the regulation of social contact. *Advances in Experimental and Social Psychology, 12,* 131–175.

Baum, A., & Valins, S. (Eds.). (1977). *Human response to crowding: Studies of the effects of residential group size.* Hillsdale, NJ: Erlbaum.

Baumeister, A. A. (1987). Mental retardation: Some conceptions and dilemmas. *American Psychologist, 42*(2), 796–800.

Baumeister, R. F. (1994). Self-esteem. *Encyclopedia of human behavior, Vol. 4.* San Diego, CA: Academic.

Baumgardner, A. H. (1990). To know oneself is to like oneself: Self-certainty and self-affect. *Journal of Personality & Social Psychology, 58*(6), 1062–1072.

Baumrind, D. (1980, July). New directions in socialization research. *American Psychologist, 35,* 639–652.

Baumrind, D. (1991). The influence of parenting style on adolescent competence and substance use. *Journal of Early Adolescence, 11*(1), 56–95.

Baumrind, D. (1993). The average expectable environment is not good enough. *Child Development, 64*(5), 1299–1317.

Beauchamp, P. H., Halliwell, W. R., Fournier, J. F., & Koestner, R. (1996). Effects of cognitive-behavioral psychological skills training on the motivation, preparation, and putting performance of novice golfers. *Sport Psychologist, 10*(2), 157–170.

Beck, A. T. (1985). Cognitive therapy of depression: New perspectives. In P. Clayton (Ed.), *Depression.* New York: Raven.

Beck, A. T. (1991). Cognitive therapy. *American Psychologist, 46*(4), 368–375.

Beck, A. T., & Greenberg, R. L. (1974). *Coping with depression.* Institute For Rational Living.

Beck, A. T., Brown, C., Berchick, R. J., Stewart, B. L. et al. (1990). Relationship between hopelessness and ultimate suicide. *American Journal of Psychiatry, 147*(2), 190–195.

Beck, J. G. (1995). Hypoactive sexual desire disorder: An overview. *Journal of Consulting & Clinical Psychology, 63*(6), 919–927.

Beckwith, L., Rodning, C., & Cohen, S. (1992). Preterm children at early adolescence and continuity and discontinuity in maternal responsiveness from infancy. *Child Development, 63*(5), 1198–1208.

Beebe, B., Gerstman, L., Carson, B., Dolins, M., Zigman, A., Rosenweig, H., Faughey K., & Korman, M. (1982). Rhythmic communication in the mother-infant dyad. In M. Davis (Ed), *Interaction rhythms, periodicity in communicative behavior.* New York: Human Sciences Press.

Begg, I. M., Needham, D. R., & Bookbinder, M. (1993). Do backward messages unconsciously affect listeners? No. *Canadian Journal of Experimental Psychology, 47*(1), 1–14.

Beilin, H. (1992). Piaget's enduring contribution to developmental psychology. *Developmental Psychology, 28*(2), 191–204.

Beljan, J. R., Rosenblatt, L. S., Hetherington, N. W., Layman, J., Flaim, S. E. T., Dale, G. T., & Holley, D. C. (1972). *Human performance in the aviation environment.* NASA Contract No 2-6657, Pt. Ia, 253–259.

Bell, A. P., Weinberg, M. S., & Hammersmith, S. K. (1981). *Sexual preference.* Indiana University Press.

Bellani, M. L., Furlani, F., Gnecchi, M., & Pezzotta, P. (1996). Burnout and related factors among HIV/AIDS health care workers. *AIDS Care, 8*(2), 207–221.

Bellezza, F. S., Six, L. S., & Phillips, D. S. (1992). A mnemonic for remembering long strings of digits. *Bulletin of the Psychonomic Society, 30*(4), 271–274.

Belloc, N. B. (1973). Relationship of physical health practices and mortality. *Preventive Medicine, 2,* 67–81.

Belloc, N. B. & Breslow, L. (1972). Relationship of physical health status and healthy practices. *Preventive Medicine, 1,* 409–421.

Belsky, J. (1996). Parent, infant, and social-contextual antecedents of father-son attachment security. *Developmental Psychology, 32*(5), 905–913.

Belsky, J., Gilstrap, B., & Rovine, M. (1984). The Pennsylvania infant and family development project, I: Stability and change in mother-infant and father-infant interactions in a family setting at one, three, and nine months. *Child Development, 55,* 692–705.

Bem, S. L. (1975). Sex-role adaptability: One consequence of psychological androgyny. *Journal of Personality & Social Psychology, 31,* 634–643.

Bem, S. L. (1981). Gender schema theory. A cognitive account of sex typing. *Psychological Review, 88,* 354–364.

Ben-Shakhar, G. & Dolev, K. (1996). Psychophysiological detection through the guilty knowledge technique: Effect of mental countermeasures. *Journal of Applied Psychology, 81*(3), 273–281.

Ben-Shakhar, G., Bar-Hillel, M., Bilu, Y., Ben-Abba, E., & Flug, A. (1986). Can graphology predict occupational success? Two empirical studies and some methodological ruminations. *Journal of Applied Psychology, 71,*4, 645–653.

Benbow, C. P. (1986). Physiological correlates of extreme intellectual precocity. *Neuropsychologia, 24*(5), 719–725.

Beneke, W. M., & Harris, M. B. (1972). Teaching self-control of study behavior. *Behavior Research and Therapy, 10,* 35–41.

Benloucif, S., Bennett, E. L., & Rosenzweig, M. R. (1995). Norephinephrine and neural plasticity: The effects of xylamine on experience-induced changes in brain weight, memory, and behavior. *Neurobiology of Learning & Memory, 63*(1), 33–42.

Bennett, W., & Gurin, J. (1982). *The dieter's dilemma.* New York: Basic.

Benoit, S. C. & Thomas, R. L. (1992). The influence of expectancy in subliminal perception experiments. *Journal of General Psychology, 119*(4), 335–341.

Benson, H. (1975). *The relaxation response.* New York: Morrow.

Benson, H. (1977). Systematic hypertension and the relaxation response. *The New England Journal of Medicine, 296,* 1152–1156.

Benton, A. L. (1980, Feb.). The neuropsychology of facial recognition. *American Psychologist, 35,* 176–186.

Benwall, R. P. (1990). The illusion of reality. *Psychological Bulletin, 107*(1), 82–95.

Berenbaum, S. A. & Snyder, E. (1995). Early hormonal influences on childhood sex-typed activity and playmate preferences. *Developmental Psychology, 31*(1), 31–42.

Bergin, A. E. (1991). Values and religious issues in psychotherapy and mental health. *American Psychologist, 46*(4), 394–403.

Berkowitz, L. (1968). The frustration-aggression hypothesis revisited. In L. Berkowitz (Ed.), *Roots of aggression: A re-examination of the frustration-aggression hypothesis.* New York: Atherton.

Berkowitz, L. (1984). Some effects of thoughts on anti- and prosocial influences of media events: A cognitive-neoassociation analysis. *Psychological Bulletin, 95,* 410–427.

Berkowitz, L. (1988). Frustrations, appraisals, and aversively stimulated aggression. *Aggressive Behavior, 14*(1), 3–11.

Berkowitz, L. (1990). On the formation and regulation of anger and aggression. *American Psychologist, 45*(4), 494–503.

Berlyne, D. (1966). Curiosity and exploration. *Science, 153,* 25–33.

Berman, S. L., Kurtines, W. M., Silverman, W. K., & Serafini, L. T. (1996). The impact of exposure to crime and violence on urban youth. *American Journal of Orthopsychiatry, 66*(3), 329–336.

Berne, E. (1964). *Games people play.* New York: Grove.

Bernt, T. J. (1992). *Child development.* Fort Worth: Harcourt Brace Jovanovich.

Bernthal, P. R. & Insko, C. A. (1993). Cohesiveness without groupthink: The interactive effects of social and task cohesion. *Group & Organization Management, 18*(1), 66–87.

Berry, J. W. (1990). The psychology of acculturation. In R. A. Dienstbier and J. J. Berman (Eds.), *Nebraska Symposium on Motivation 1989: Cross-cultural perspectives, 37.* Lincoln: Univsersity of Nebraska Press.

Berry, P., Groeneweg, G., Gibson, D., & Brown, R. I. (1984). Mental development of adults with Down syndrome. *American Journal of Mental Deficiency, 89,* 252–256.

Bersheid, E. (1994). Interpersonal relations. *Annual Review of Psychology, 45,* 79–129.

Bersheid, E. & Walster, E. (1974b). A little bit about love. In T. L. Huston (Ed.), *Foundations of interpersonal attraction.* New York: Academic.

Bertsch, G. J. (1976). Punishment of consummatory and instrumental behavior: A review. *Psychological Record, 26,* 13–31.

Best, J. B. (1995). *Cognitive psychology.* St. Paul, MN: West.

Betancur, C., Velez, A., Cabanieu, G., le Moal, M. et al. (1990). Association between left-handedness and allergy: A reappraisal. *Neuropsychologia, 28*(2), 223–227.

Bettelheim, B. (1960). *The informed heart.* New York: Free Press.

Beyerstein, B. (1985). The myth of alpha consciousness. *The Skeptical Inquirer, 10,* 42–59.

Beyerstein, B. L. & Beyerstein, D. F. (1992). *The write stuff: Evaluations of graphology.* Buffalo, NY: Prometheus.

Beyerstein, B. L. (1990). Brainscams: Neuromythologies of the New Age. Special Issue: Unvalidated, fringe, and fraudulent treatment of mental disorders. *International Journal of Mental Health, 19*(3), 27–36.

Bickman, L. (1974). Clothes make the person. *Psychology Today,* April.

Bierley, C., McSweeney, F. K., & Vannieuwerk, R. (1985). Classical conditioning of preferences for stimuli. *Journal of Consumer Research, 12,* 316–323.

Biglan, A., Ary, D., Yudelson, H., & Duncan, T. E. (1996). Experimental evaluation of a modular approach to mobilizing antitobacco influences of peers and parents. *American Journal of Community Psychology, 24*(3), 311–339.

Bigler, E. D., Johnson, S. C., Anderson, C. V., & Blatter, D. D. (1996). Traumatic brain injury and memory: The role of hippocampal atrophy. *Neuropsychology, 10*(3), 333–342.

Birch, J. & McKeever, L. M. (1993). Survey of the accuracy of new pseudoisochromatic plates. *Ophthalmic & Physiological Optics, 13*(1), 35–40.

Birnbaum, I. M., Parker, E. S., Hartley J. T., & Nobel, E. P. (1978). Alcohol and memory: Retrieval processes. *Journal of Verbal Learning and Verbal Behavior, 17,* 325–335.

Birren, J. E. & Fisher, L. M. (1995a). Rules and reason in the forced retirement of commercial airline pilots at age 60. *Ergonomics, 38*(3), 518–525.

Birren, J. E. & Fisher, L. M. (1995b). Aging and speed of behavior *Annual Review of Psychology, 46,* 329–353.

Blackmore, S. (1989). What do we really think? A survey of parapsychologists and sceptics. *Journal of the Society for Psychical Research, 55*(814), 251–262.

Blackmore, S. (1991a). Lucid dreaming. *Skeptical Inquirer, 15,* 362–370.

Blackmore, S. (1991b). Near-death experiences: In or out of the body? *Skeptical Inquirer, 16*(Fall), 34–45.

Blackmore, S. (1993). *Dying to live.* Buffalo, NY: Prometheus.

Blackmore, S. (1995). What's in the box? An ESP test with Chris Robinson. *Journal of the Society for Psychical Research, 60*(840), 322–324.

Blackwell, R. T., Galassi, J. P., Galassi, M. D., & Watson, T. E. (1985). Are cognitive assessments equal? A comparison of think aloud and thought listing. *Cognitive Therapy and Research, 9,* 399–413.

Blanchard, E. B., Eisele, G., Vollmer, A., & Payne, A. (1996). Controlled evaluation of thermal biofeedback in treatment of elevated blood pressure in unmedicated mild hypertension. *Biofeedback & Self Regulation, 21*(2), 167–190.

Blanck, P. D., Bellack, A. S., Rosnow, R. L., et al. (1992). Scientific rewards and conflicts of ethical choices in human subjects research. *American Psychologist, 47*(7), 959–965.

Blane, H. T. (1988). Prevention issues with children of alcoholics. *British Journal of Addiction, 83*(7), 793–798.

Blaske, D. M. (1984). Occupational sex-typing by kindergarten and fourth-grade children. *Psychological Reports, 54,* 795–801.

Blatt, S. J. (1995). The destructiveness of perfectionism. *American Psychologist, 50*(12), 1003–1020.

Blaustein, A. R. (1983). The situation of sociobiology. *Science, 220,* 188–189.

Blechman, E. U. (1992). Mentors for high-risk minority youths. *Journal of Clinical Child Psychology, 2*(2), 160–169.

Block, J. (1979). Socialization influence of personality development in males and females. American Psychological Association Master Lecture, Convention of the American Psychological Association, New York City, Sept., 1979.

Bloom, B. (1985). *Developing talent in young people.* New York: Ballantine.

Bloom, K., Russell, A., & Wassenberg, K. (1987). Turn taking affects the quality of infant vocalizations. *Journal of Child Language, 14*(2), 211–227.

Blumberg, M. S. & Wasserman, E. A. (1995). Animal mind and the argument from design. *American Psychologist, 50*(3), 133–144.

Bohan, J. S. (1990). Social constructionism and contextual history: An expanded approach to the history of psychology. *Teaching of Psychology, 17*(2), 82–89.

Bohannon, J. N. & Stanowicz, L. B. (1988). The issue of negative evidence: Adult responses to children's language errors. *Developmental Psychology, 24*(5), 684–689.

Bohart, A. C. & Tallman, K. (1996). The active client: Therapy as self-help. *Journal of Humanistic Psychology, 36*(3), 7–30.

Bohart, W. (1995). The person-centered therapies. In A. S. Gurman & S. B. Messer, *Essential Psychotherapies.* New York: Guilford.

Boivin, D. B., Czeisler, C. A., & Waterhouse, J. W. (1997). Complex interaction of the sleep-wake cycle and circadian phase modulates mood in healthy subjects. *Archives of General Psychiatry, 54*(2), 145.

Bolles, R. C. (1979). *Learning theory.* New York: Holt, Rinehart & Winston.

Bonanno, G. A., Keltner, D., Holen, A., & Horowitz, M. J. (1995). When avoiding unpleasant emotions might not be such a bad thing. *Journal of Personality & Social Psychology, 69*(5), 975–989.

Bond, R. & Smith, P. B. (1996). Culture and conformity: A meta-analysis of studies using Asch's (1952b, 1956) line judgment task. *Psychological Bulletin, 119*(1), 111–137.

Bond, T. & Wooten, V. (1996). The etiology and management of insomnia. *Virginia Medical Quarterly, 123*(4), 254–255.

Bonnet, M. H., & Moore, S. E. (1982). The threshold of sleep: Perception of sleep as a function of time asleep and auditory threshold. *Sleep, 5*(3), 267–276.

Booker, J. M. & Hellekson, C. J. (1992). Prevalance of seasonal affective disorder in Alaska. *American Journal of Psychiatry, 149*(9), 1176–1182.

Borman, W. C., Hanson, M. A., & Hedge, J. W. (1997). Personnel psychology. *Annual Review of Psychology, 48,* 299–337.

Bornstein, M. H. (1989). Sensitive periods in development: Structural characteristics and causal interpretations. *Psychological Bulletin, 105*(2), 179–197.

Bornstein, R. F. (1996). Sex differences in dependent personality disorder prevalence rates. *Clinical Psychology: Science & Practice, 3*(1), 1–12.

Borrie, R. A., & Suedfeld, P. (1980). Restricted environmental stimulation therapy in a weight reduction program. *Journal of Behavioral Medicine, 3,* 147–161.

Bosse, R., Aldwin, C. M., Levenson, M. R., & Workman-Daniels, K. (1991). How stressful is retirement? *Journal of Gerontology, 46*(1), 9–14.

Botvin, G. J. & Botvin, E. M. (1992). Adolescent tobacco, alcohol, and drug abuse. *Journal of Developmental & Behavioral Pediatrics, 13*(4), 290–301.

Botvin, G. J., Schinke, S., & Orlandi, M. A. (1995). School-based health promotion: Substance abuse and sexual behavior. *Applied & Preventive Psychology, 4*(3), 167–184.

Bouchard, T. J., Lykken, D. T., McGue, M., Segal, N. L., & Tellegen, A. (1990). Sources of human psychological differences: The Minnesota study of twins reared apart. *Science, 250,* 223–228.

Bouchard, T. J., Jr. (1983). Twins—Nature's twice-told tale. *Yearbook of science and the future,* 66–81. Chicago: Encyclopedia Britannica.

Boutros, N. N. & Bowers, M. B. Jr. (1996). Chronic substance-induced psychotic disorders. *Journal of Neuropsychiatry & Clinical Neurosciences, 8*(3), 262–269.

Bower, B. (1990). Gone but not forgotten. *Science News,* 138(Nov. 17), 312–314.

Bower, G. H. (1973). How to . . . uh . . . remember. *Psychology Today,* Oct., 63–70.

Bower, G. H. (1981). Mood and memory. *American Psychologist, 36,* 129–148.

Bower, G. H., & Springston, F. (1970). Pauses as recoding points in letter series. *Journal of Experimental Psychology, 83,* 421–430.

Bower, G. H., Wagner, A. D., Newman, S. E., & Randle, J. D. (1996). Does recoding interfering material improve recall? *Journal of Experimental Psychology: Learning, Memory, & Cognition, 22*(1), 240–245.

Bowers, K. S. & Farvolden, P.. (1996). Revisiting a century-old Freudian slip—From suggestion disavowed to the truth repressed. *Psychological Bulletin, 119*(3), 355–380.

Bowers, K. S. & Woody, E. Z. (1996). Hypnotic amnesia and the paradox of intentional forgetting. *Journal of Abnormal Psychology, 105*(3), 381–390.

Bowling, A. C. & Mackenzie, B. D. (1996). The relationship between speed of information processing and cognitive ability. *Personality & Individual Differences, 20*(6), 775–800.

Boyatzis, C. J., Matillo, G. M., & Nesbitt, K. M. (1995). Effects of "The Mighty Morphin Power Rangers" on children's aggression with peers. *Child Study Journal, 25*(1), 45–55.

Boysen, S. T. & Berntson, G. G. (1989). Numerical competence in a chimpanzee (Pan troglodytes). *Journal of Comparative Psychology, 103*(1), 23–31.

Boysen, S. T., Berntson, G. G., Shreyer, T. A., & Hannan, M. B. (1995). Indicating acts during counting by a chimpanzee (*Pan troglodytes*). *Journal of Comparative Psychology, 109*(1), 47–51.

Bradley, B. S. & Gobbart, S. K. (1989). Determinants of gender-typed play in toddlers. *Journal of Genetic Psychology, 150*(4), 453–455.

Bradley, L. P. (1995). Changing American birth through childbirth education. *Patient Education & Counseling, 25*(1), 75–82.

Bradley, R. H., Caldwell, B. M., Rock, S. L., Ramey, C. T. et al. (1989). Home environment and cognitive development in the first 3 years of life: A collaborative study involving six sites and three ethnic groups in North America. *Developmental Psychology, 25*(2), 217–235.

Braginsky, B. M., & Braginsky, D. D. (1967). Schizophrenic patients in the psychiatric interview: An experimental study of their effectiveness at manipulation. *Journal of Consulting Psychology, 31,* 543–547.

Brakke, K. E. & Savage-Rumbaugh, E. S. (1995). The development of language skills in bonobo and chimpanzee: I. Comprehension. *Language & Communication, 15*(2), 121–148.

Brandstadter, J., Wentura, D., & Greve, W. (1993). Adaptive resources of the aging self. *International Journal of Behavioral Development, 16*(2), 323–349.

Brannon, L. (1996). *Gender.* Boston: Allyn & Bacon.

Bransford, J. & Stein, B. S. (1984). *The IDEAL problem solver.* New York: Freeman.

Bransford, J. D., & McCarrell, N. S. (1977). A sketch of cognitive approach to comprehension: Some thoughts about understanding what it means to comprehend. In P. N. Johnson-Laird & P. C. Wason (Eds.), *Thinking: Readings in cognitive science*. Cambridge: Cambridge University Press.

Bransford, J., Sherwood, R., Vye, N., & Rieser, J. (1986). Teaching thinking and problem solving. *American Psychologist*, *41*(10), 1078–1089.

Braungart, J. M., Plomin, R., DeFries, J. C., & Fulker, D. W. (1992). Genetic influence on tester-rated infant temperament as assessed by Bayley's Infant Behavior Record. *Developmental Psychology*, *28*(1), 40–47.

Brawman-Mintzer, O., & Lydiard, R. B. (1996). Generalized anxiety disorder: issues in epidemiology. *Journal of Clinical Psychiatry*, *57*(Suppl 7), 3–8.

Brazelton, T. B., Koslowski, B., & Main, M. (1974). The origins of reciprocity: The early mother-infant interaction. In M. Lewis & L. A. Rosenblum, (Eds.), *The effect of the infant on its caregiver*. New York: Wiley-Interscience.

Brecher, E. M., & the Editors of *Consumer Reports*. (1972). *Licit and illicit drugs*. Boston: Little, Brown.

Breedlove, S. M. (1994). Sexual differentiation of the human nervous system. *Annual Review of Psychology*, *45*, 389–418.

Breland, K., & Breland, M. (1961). The misbehavior of organisms. *American Psychologist*, *16*, 681–684.

Bremner, J. D., Southwick, S. M., Darnell, A., & Charney, D. S. (1996). Chronic PTSD in Vietnam combat veterans. *American Journal of Psychiatry*, *153*(3), 369–375.

Bresler, D. E., & Trubo, R. (1979). *Free yourself from pain*. New York: Simon & Schuster.

Breslow, L. & Enstrom, J. E. (1980). Persistence of health habits and their relationship to mortality. *Preventive Medicine*, *9*, 469–483.

Brewer, J. S. (1981). Duration of intromission and female orgasm rates. *Medical Aspects of Human Sexuality*, *15*(4), 70–71.

Brewer, M. B. & Kramer, R. K. (1985). The psychology of intergroup attitudes and behavior. *Annual Review of Psychology*, *36*, 219–243.

Bridges, K. M. B. (1932). Emotional development in early infancy. *Child Development*, *3*, 324–334.

Britton, B. K. & Tesser, A. (1991). Effects of time-management practices on college grades. *Journal of Educational Psychology*, *83*(3), 405–410.

Brody, N. (1992). *Intelligence*. San Diego, CA: Academic Press.

Brooks-Gunn, J. & Warren, M. P. (1988). The psychological significance of secondary sexual characteristics in nine- to eleven-year-old girls. *Child Development*, *59*(4), 1061–1069.

Broughton, W. A. & Broughton, R. J. (1994). Psychosocial impact of narcolepsy. *Sleep*, *17*(8, Suppl), S45–S49.

Brown, A. M. (1990). Development of visual sensitivity to light and color vision in human infants: A critical review. *Vision Research*, *30*(8), 1159–1188.

Brown, B. (1980). Perspectives on social stress. In H. Selye (Ed.), *Selye's guide to stress research*, *Vol. 1*. New York: Van Nostrand Reinhold.

Brown, B. B. & Bentley, D. L. (1993). Residential burglers judge risk. *Journal of Environmental Psychology*, *13*(1), 51–61.

Brown, B. R. Jr., Baranowski, M. D., Kulig, J. W., & Stephenson, J. N. (1996). Searching for the Magic Johnson effect: AIDS, adolescents, and celebrity disclosure. *Adolescence*, *31*(122), 253–264.

Brown, G. M. (1994). Light, melatonin and the sleep-wake cycle. *Journal of Psychiatry & Neuroscience*, *19*(5), 345–353.

Brown, R. T. (1991). Helping students confront and deal with stress and procrastination. *Journal of College Student Psychotherapy*, *6*(2), 87–102.

Brown, R., & McNeill, D. (1966). The "tip of the tongue" phenomenon. *Journal of Verbal Learning*

and *Verbal Behavior*, *5*, 325–337.

Brown, S. A., Goldman, M. S., & Christiansen, B. A. (1985). Do alcohol expectancies mediate drinking patterns of adults? *Journal of Consulting and Clinical Psychology*, *53*(4), 512–519.

Browne, M. A., & Mahoney, M. J. (1984). Sport psychology. *Annual Review of Psychology*, *35*, 605–625.

Brownell, K. D. & Rodin, J. (1994). The dieting maelstrom. *American Psychologist*, *49*, 781–791.

Brownell, K. D., Greenwood, M. R. C., Stellar, E., & Shrager, E. E. (1986). The effects of repeated cycles of weight loss and regain in rats. *Physiology and Behavior*, *38*, 459–464.

Brownlee, S. (1997). The senses. *U.S. News & World Report*, Jan. 13, 51–59.

Brugger, P., Landis, T., & Regard, M. (1990). A "sheep-goat" effect in repetition avoidance: Extrasensory perception as an effect of subjective probability? *British Journal of Psychology*, *81*(4), 455–468.

Bruner, J. (1983). *Child's Talk*. New York: Norton.

Bruner, J. S., & Postman, L. (1949). On the perception of incongruity: A paradigm. *Journal of Personality*, *18*, 206–223.

Bryan, J. H., & Test, M. A. (1967). Models and helping. Naturalistic studies in aiding behavior. *Journal of Personality & Social Psychology*, *6*, 400–407.

Bryan, J. H., & Walbek, N. H. (1970). Preaching and practicing generosity: Children's actions and reactions. *Child Development*, *41*, 329–353.

Buch, K. & Spangler, R. (1990). The effects of quality circles on performance and promotions. *Human Relations*, *43*(6), 573–582.

Buchwald, A. (1965). Psyching out. *The Washington Post*, June 20.

Buck, L. A. (1990). Abnormality, normality and health. *Psychotherapy*, *27*(2), 187–194.

Buckhout, R. (1974). Eyewitness testimony. *Scientific American*, *231*, 23–31.

Bugental, J. F. T. & Sterling, M. M. (1995). Existential-humanistic psychotherapy: New perspectives. In A. S. Gurman & S. B. Messer, *Essential Psychotherapies*. New York: Guilford.

Bunge, M. (1984). What is pseudoscience? *The Skeptical Inquirer*, *9*, 36–46.

Burgner, D. & Hewstone, M. (1993). Young children's causal attributions for success and failure. *British Journal of Developmental Psychology*, *11*(2), 125–129.

Burka, J. B., & Yuen, L. M. (1983). *Procrastination*. Menlo Park, CA: Addison-Wesley.

Burnham, D. K. & Harris, M. (1992). Effects of real gender and labeled gender on adults' perceptions of infants. *Journal of Genetic Psychology*, *153*(2), 165–183.

Burns, D. D., & Persons, J. (1982). Hope and hopelessness: A cognitive approach. In L. E. Abt, & I. R. Stuart (Eds.), *The newer therapies: A sourcebook*. New York: Van Nostrand Reinhold.

Burtt, H. E. (1941). An experimental study of early childhood memory: Final report. *Journal of General Psychology*, *58*, 435–439.

Bushman, B. J. & Cooper, H. M. (1990). Effects of alcohol on human aggression. *Psychological Bulletin*, *107*(3), 341–354.

Bushman, B. J. & Geen, R. G. (1990). Role of cognitive-emotional mediators and individual differences in the effects of media violence on aggression. *Journal of Personality & Social Psychology*, *58*(1), 156–163.

Bushnell, L. W., Sai, F. & Mullin, L. T. (1989). Neonatal recognition of the mother's face. *British Journal of Developmental Psychology*, *7*(1), 3–15.

Buss, A. H. (1980). *Self-consciousness and social anxiety*. San Francisco: Freeman.

Buss, A. H. (1986). A theory of shyness. In Jones, W. H., Cheek, J. M., & Briggs, S. R., *Shyness: Perspec-*

tives on research and treatment. New York: Plenum.

Buss, D. M. (1985). Human mate selection. *American Scientist*, *73*, 47–51.

Buss, D. M. (1994). *The evolution of desire*. New York: Basic.

Buss, D. M. (1995). Psychological sex differences. *American Psychologist*, *50*(3), 164–168.

Buss, D. M., Larsen, R. J., Western, D., & Semmelroth, J. (1992). Sex differences in jealousy. *Psychological Science*, *3*, 251–255.

Butler, R. (1954). Curiosity in monkeys. *Scientific American*, *190*(18), 70–75.

Butler, R., & Harlow, H. F. (1954). Persistence of visual exploration in monkeys. *Journal of Comparative Physiological Psychology*, *47*, 258–263.

Buyer, L. S. (1988). Creative problem solving: A comparison of performance under different instructions. *Journal of Creative Behavior*, *22*(1), 55–61.

Byrd, K. R. (1994). The narrative reconstructions of incest survivors. *American Psychologist*, *49*(5), 439–440.

Cabanac, M. & Duclaux, P. (1970). Obesity: Absence of satiety aversion to sucrose. *Science*, *168*, 496–497.

Caldera, Y. M., Huston, A. C. & O'Brien, M. (1989). Social interactions and play patterns of parents and toddlers with feminine, masculine, and neutral toys. *Child Development*, *60*(1), 70–76.

Calhoun, J. B. (1962). A "behavioral sink." In E. L. Bliss (Ed.), *Roots of behavior*. New York: Harper & Row.

Calvert, S. L. & Cocking, R. R. (1992). Health promotion through mass media. *Journal of Applied Developmental Psychology*, *13*(2), 143–149.

Camara, W. J. & Schneider, D. L. (1994). Integrity tests. *American Psychologist*, *49*(2), 112–119.

Camatta, C. D. & Nagoshi, C. T. (1995). Stress, depression, irrational beliefs, and alcohol use and problems in a college student sample. *Alcoholism: Clinical & Experimental Research*, *19*(1), 142–146.

Campbell, F. A. & Ramey, C. T. (1994). Effect of early intervention on intellectual and academic achievement. *Child Development*, *65*, 684–698.

Campbell, J. B., & Hawley, C. W. (1982). Study habits and Eysenck's theory of extraversion-introversion. *Journal of Research in Personality*, *16*, 139–146.

Campbell, J. D. (1990). Self-esteem and clarity of the self-concept. *Journal of Personality & Social Psychology*, *59*(3), 538–549.

Campfield, L. A., Smith, F. J., Rosenbaum, M., & Hirsch, J. (1996). Human eating: Evidence for a physiological basis using a modified paradigm. *Neuroscience & Biobehavioral Reviews*, *20*(1), 133–137.

Campion, M. A. & McClelland, C. L. (1993). Follow-up and extension of interdisciplinary costs and benefits of enlarged jobs. *Journal of Applied Psychology*, *78*(3), 339–351.

Campos, A. & Gonzalez, M. A. (1995). Effects of mental imagery on creative perception. *Journal of Mental Imagery*, *19*(1–2), 67–75.

Campos, J. J., Hiatt, S., Ramsay, D., Henderson, C., & Svejda, M. (1978). The emergence of fear on the visual cliff. In M. Lewis & L. A. Rosenblum (Eds.), *The development of affect*, 149–182. New York: Plenum Press.

Camras, L. A., Sullivan, J., & Michel, G. (1993). Do infants express discrete emotions? *Journal of Nonverbal Behavior*, *17*(3), 171–186.

Canavan, D. (1989). Fear of success. In R. C. Curtis (Ed.). *Self-defeating behaviors*. New York: Plenum.

Cannon, T. D., Mednick, S. A., Parnas, J. et al. (1993). Developmental brain abnormalities in the offspring of schizophrenic mothers. *Archives of General Psychiatry*, *50*(7), 551–564.

Cannon, W. B. (1932). *The wisdom of the body*. New

York: Norton.

Cannon, W. B. (1934). Hunger and thirst. In C. Murchinson (Ed.), *Handbook of general experimental psychology.* Worcester, MA: Clark University Press.

Cannon, W. B., & Washburn, A. L. (1912). An exploration of hunger. *American Journal of Physiology, 29,* 441–454.

Caplan, N., Choy, M. H., & Whitmore, J. K. (1992). Indochinese refugee families and academic achievement. *Scientific American,* Feb., 36–42.

Caplan, P. J., MacPherson, G. M., & Tobin, P. (1985). Do sex-related differences in spatial abilities exist? A multilevel critique with new data. *American Psychologist, 40,* 786–799.

Capner, M. & Caltabiano, M. L. (1993). Factors affecting the progression towards burnout. *Psychological Reports, 73*(2), 555–561.

Capron, C. & Duyme, M. (1992). Assessment of effects of socio-economic status on IQ in a full cross-fostering study. *Nature, 340,* 552–554.

Carducci, B. J. & Stein, N. D. (1988). *The personal and situational pervasiveness of shyness in college students: A nine-year comparison.* Paper presented at the meeting of the Southeastern Psychological Association, New Orleans, April, 1988.

Carew, J. V., Chan, I., & Halfor, C. (1976). *Observing intelligence in young children: Eight case studies.* Englewood Cliffs, NJ: Prentice-Hall.

Carey, A. R. & McLean, E. A. (1997). What's on your mind? *USA Today,* Jan. 6, 1.

Carey, J. C., Stanley, D. A., & Biggers, J. (1988). Peak alert time and rapport between residence hall roommates. *Journal of College Student Development, 29*(3), 239–243.

Carey, S. (1986). Cognitive science and science education. *American Psychologist, 41*(10), 1123–1130.

Carli, L. L., Ganley, R., & Pierce-Otay, A. (1991). Similarity and satisfaction in roommate relationships. *Personality & Social Psychology Bulletin, 17*(4), 419–426.

Carlson, J. G., Chemtob, C. M., Rusnak, K., & Hedlund, N. L. (1996). *Psychotherapy, 33*(1), 104–113.

Carlson, J. M. (1986). *Prime time law enforcement.* New York: Praeger.

Carlson, M., Marcus-Hewhall, A., & Miller, N. (1990). Effects of situational aggression cues: A quantitative review. *Journal of Personality & Social Psychology, 58*(4), 622–633.

Carlson, N. R. (1994). *Physiology of behavior (5th ed.).* Boston: Allyn & Bacon.

Carman, R., & Adams, W. R. (1985). *Study skills: A student's guide for survival.* New York: Wiley.

Carnegie Corporation of New York. (1994). *Starting points: Meeting the needs of our youngest children.* New York: The Carnegie Corporation.

Carpendale, J. I. M. & Krebs, D. L. (1995). Variations in level of moral judgment as a function of type of dilemma and moral choice. *Journal of Personality, 63*(2), 289–313.

Carroll, J. M., Russell, J. A. (1996). Do facial expressions signal specific emotions? Judging emotion from the face in context. *Journal of Personality & Social Psychology, 70*(2), 205–218.

Carson, R. C., Butcher, J. N., & Mineka, S. (1996). *Abnormal psychology and modern life.* NY: HarperCollins.

Carter, W. E. (Ed.) (1980). *Cannabis in Costa Rica: A study of chronic marihuana use.* Philadelphia: Institute for the Study of Human Issues.

Cartwright, L. K., Wink, P., Kmetz, C. (1995). What leads to good health in midlife women physicians? Some clues from a longitudinal study. *Psychosomatic Medicine, 57*(3), 284–292.

Cartwright, R. & Lamberg, L. (1992). *Crisis dreaming.*

New York: HarperCollins.

Caspi, A. & Herbener, E. S. (1990). Continuity and change: Associative marriage and the consistency of personality in adulthood. *Journal of Personality & Social Psychology, 58*(2), 250–258.

Casto, S. D., DeFries, J. C., & Fulker, D. W. (1995). Multivariate genetic analysis of Wechsler Intelligence Scale for Children—Revised (WISC—R) factors. *Behavior Genetics, 25*(1), 25–32.

Cattell, R. B. (1965). *The scientific analysis of personality.* Baltimore: Penguin.

Cattell, R. B. (1973). Personality pinned down. *Psychology Today,* July, 40–46.

Cautela, J. R. & Kearney, A. J. (1986). *The covert conditioning handbook.* New York: Springer.

Cautela, J. R., & Bennett, A. K. (1981). Covert conditioning. In R. J. Corsini (Ed.), *Handbook of innovative psychotherapies,* 189–204. New York: Wiley.

Ceci, S. J. (1991). How much does schooling influence general intelligence and its cognitive components? *Developmental Psychology, 27*(5), 703–722.

Cecil, H., Evans, R. J., & Stanley, M. A. (1996). Perceived believability among adolescents of health warning labels on cigarette packs. *Journal of Applied Social Psychology, 26*(6), 502–519.

Chakos, M. H., Alvir, J. M. J., Woerner, M., & Koreen, A. (1996). Incidence and correlates of tardive dyskinesia in first episode of schizophrenia. *Archives of General Psychiatry, 53*(4), 313–319.

Chamberlin, J. & Rogers, J. A. (1990). Planning a community-based mental health system. *American Psychologist, 45*(11), 1241–1244.

Chance, P. (1982). Your child's self-esteem. *Parents,* Jan.

Chapanis, A., & Lindenbaum, L. E. (1959). A reaction time study of four control-display linkages. *Human Factors, 1,* 1–7.

Chapman, A. J. & Perry, D. (1995). Applying the Cognitive Interview Procedure to child and adult eyewitnesses of road accidents. *Applied Psychology: An International Review, 44*(4), 283–294.

Charren, P. & Sandler, M. W. (1983). *Changing channels.* Reading, MA: Addison-Wesley.

Chastain, G. & Thurber, S. (1989). The SQ3R study technique enhances comprehension of an introductory psychology textbook. *Reading Improvement, 26*(1), 94.

Cheadle, A., Psaty, B. M., Diehr, P., Koepsell, T. et al. (1992–93). An empirical exploration of a conceptual model for community-based health-promotion. *International Quarterly of Community Health Education, 13*(4), 329–363.

Check, J. V. P., & Malamuth, N. M. (1983). Sex role stereotyping and reactions to depictions of stranger versus acquaintance rape. *Journal of Personality & Social Psychology, 45,* 344–356.

Cheek, J. & Buss, A. H. (1979). Scales of shyness, sociability and self-esteem and correlations among them. Unpublished research, University of Texas. (Cited by Buss, 1980.)

Chen, K. & Kandel, D. B. (1995). The natural history of drug use from adolescence to the mid-thirties in a general population sample. *American Journal of Public Health, 85*(1), 41–47.

Chen, Y. & Dilsaver, S. C. (1996). Lifetime rates of suicide attempts among subjects with bipolar and unipolar disorders. *Biological Psychiatry, 39*(10), 896–899.

Chen, Z., Lawson, R. B., Gordon, L. R., & McIntosh, B. (1996). Groupthink: Deciding with the leader and the devil. *Psychological Record, 46*(4), 581–590.

Cheng, H., Cao, Y., & Olson, L. (1996). Spinal cord repair in adult paraplegic rats: Partial restoration of hind limb function. *Science, 273*(5274), 510.

Chesney, M. A., & Rosenman, R. H. (Eds.). (1985).

Anger and hostility in cardiovascular and behavioral disorders. Washington, DC: Hemisphere.

Chess, S. & Thomas, A. (1986). *Know your child.* New York: Basic.

Chess, S., Thomas, A. & Birch, H. G. (1976). *Your child is a person: A psychological approach to parenthood without guilt.* New York: Penguin.

Chiras, D. D. (1991). *Human biology.* St. Paul: West.

Chisholm, K., Carter, M. C., Ames, E. W., & Morison, S. J. (1995). Attachment security and indiscriminately friendly behavior in children adopted from Romanian orphanages. *Development & Psychopathology, 7*(2), 283–294.

Chollar, S. (1989). Dreamchasers. *Psychology Today,* April, 60–61.

Chomsky, N. (1975). *Reflections on language.* New York: Pantheon.

Chomsky, N. (1986). *Knowledge of language.* New York: Praeger.

Christensen, A. & Jacobson, N. S. (1994). Who (or what) can do psychotherapy. *Psychological Science, 5*(1), 8–14.

Christian, A. G. & McDonald, J. L. (1987). Smokeless tobacco country: From nicotine dependency to oral problems and cancer. *Aviation, Space, & Environmental Medicine, 58*(2), 97–104.

Christiansen, B.A., Smith, G. T., Roehling, P. V., & Goldman, M. S. (1989). Using alcohol expectancies to predict adolescent drinking behavior after one year. *Journal of Consulting & Clinical Psychology, 57*(1), 93–99.

Christianson, S., Saisa, J., & Silfvenius, H. (1995). The right hemisphere recognises the bad guys. *Cognition & Emotion, 9*(4), 309–324.

Cialdini, R. B., Petty, R. E., & Cacippo, T. J. (1981). Attitude and attitude change. *Annual Review of Psychology, 32,* 357–404.

Cialdini, R. B., Reno, R. R., & Kallgren, C. A. (1990). A focus theory of normative conduct: Recycling the concept of norms to reduce littering in public places. *Journal of Personality & Social Psychology, 58*(6), 1015–1026.

Cimons, M. (1991). Study shows a million teen suicide attempts. *The Los Angeles Times,* Sept. 20, A26.

Cincirpini, P. M., Labitsky, L., Seay, S. Wallfisch, A. et al. (1995). The effects of smoking schedules on cessation outcome. *Journal of Consulting and Clinical Psychology, 63*(3), 388–399.

Clair, J. M., Karp, D. A., & Yoels, W. C. (1994). *Experiencing the life cycle.* Springfield, IL: Charles C Thomas.

Clark, J. L. & Hill, O. W. (1994). Academic procrastination among African-American college students. *Psychological Reports, 75*(2), 931–936.

Clark, K. B. (1965). *Dark ghetto.* New York: Harper & Row.

Clark, M. S. & Reis, H. T. (1988). Interpersonal processes in close relationships. *Annual Review of Psychology, 39,* 609–672.

Clark, M. S. & Williamson, G. M. (1989). Moods and social judgments. In H. Wagner & A. Manstead (Eds.). *Handbook of Social Psychophysiology.* New York: Wiley.

Clark, R. D. (1990). The impact of AIDS on gender differences in willingness to engage in casual sex. *Journal of Applied Social Psychology, 20*(9, Pt 2), 771–782.

Clarke-Stewart, A., Gruber, C. P., & Fitzgerald, L. M. (1994). *Children at home and in day care.* Hillsdale, NJ: Lawrence Erlbaum.

Clearwater, Y. (1985). A human place in outer space. *Psychology Today,* July, 34–43.

Click, P., Zion, C. & Nelson, C. (1988). What mediates sex discrimination in hiring decisions? *Journal of Personality & Social Psychology, 55*(2), 178–186.

Cline, V. B., Croft, R. G., & Courrier, S. (1972). Desensitization of children to television violence. *Journal of Personality & Social Psychology, 27,* 360–365.

Clore, G. L. (1976). Interpersonal attraction: An overview. In *Contemporary topics in social psychology.* Morristown, NJ: General Learning Press.

Coates, W., Lehle, D. & Cottington, E. (1989). Trauma and the full moon: A waning theory. *Annals of Emergency Medicine, 18,* 763–765.

Cohen, J. E. (1996). *How many people can the earth support?* New York: Nortion.

Cohen, N. L., Waltzman, S. B., & Fisher, S. G. (1993). A prospective, randomized study of cochlear implants. *New England Journal of Medicine, 328(4),* 233–237.

Cohen, S. & Lichtenstein, E. (1990). Partner behaviors that support quitting smoking. *Journal of Consulting & Clinical Psychology, 58(3),* 304–309.

Cohen, S., Evans, G. W., Krantz, D. S., & Stokols, D. (1981). Cardiovascular and behavioral effects of community noise. *American Scientist, 69,* 528–535.

Cohen, S., Tyrrell, D. A., & Smith, A. P. (1993). Negative life events, perceived stress, negative affect, and susceptibility to the common cold. *Journal of Personality and Social Psychology, 64(1),* 131–140.

Cole, D. E., Protinsky, H. O., & Cross, L. H. (1992). An empirical investigation of adolescent suicidal ideation. *Adolescence, 27(108),* 813–818.

Colin, A. K. & Moore, K., & West, A. N. (1996). Creativity, oversensitivity, and rate of habituation. *EDRA: Environmental Design Research Association, 20(4),* 423–427.

Collins, A. M., & Quillian, M. R. (1969). Retrieval time from semantic memory. *Journal of Verbal Learning and Verbal Behavior, 8,* 240–247.

Collins, R. L. (1996). For better or worse: The impact of upward social comparison on self-evaluations. *Psychological Bulletin, 119(1),* 51–69.

Collins, W. A. & Gunnar, M. R. (1990). Social and personality development. *Annual Review of Psychology, 41,* 387–416.

Comperatore, C. A., Lieberman, H. R., Kirby, A. W., & Adams, B. (1996). *Melatonin* efficacy in aviation missions requiring rapid deployment and night operations. *Aviation, Space, & Environmental Medicine, 67(6),* 520–524.

Coni, N., Davison, W., & Webster, S. (1984). *Ageing.* Oxford: Oxford University Press.

Connolly, J. A., Doyle, A. B., & Reznick, E. (1988). Social pretend play and social interaction in preschoolers. *Journal of Applied Developmental Psychology, 9(3),* 301–313.

Connors, M. M., Harrison, A. A., & Akins, F. R. (1985). *Living Aloft.* Washington, DC: National Aeronautics and Space Administration.

Considine, R. V., Sinha, M. K., Heiman, M. L., Kriauciunas, A., et al. (1996). Serum immunoreactive-leptin concentrations in normal-weight and obese humans. *New England Journal of Medicine, 334(5),* 292–295.

Consumer Reports. (1995). Mental health: Does therapy help? Nov., 734–739.

Conway, M. A., Cohen, G., & Stanhope, N. (1992). Very long-term memory for knowledge acquired at school and university. *Applied Cognitive Psychology, 6(6),* 467–482.

Conway, Martin A., Anderson, Stephen J. Larsen, Steen F. Donnelly, C. M. (1994). The formation of flashbulb memories. *Memory & Cognition, 22(3),* 326–343.

Conyne, R. K., & Clack, R. J. (1981). *Environmental assessment and design.* New York: Praeger.

Cooper, J., & Fazio, R. H. (1984). A new look at dissonance theory. *Advances in Experimental Social Psychology, 17,* 226–229.

Cooper, J., Bennett, E. A., & Sukel, H. L. (1996). Complex scientific testimony: How do jurors make decisions? *Law & Human Behavior, 20(4),* 379–394.

Coopersmith, S. (1968). Studies in self-esteem. *Scientific American, 218,* 96–106.

Corballis, M. C. (1980, March). Laterality and myth. *American Psychologist, 35,* 284–295.

Coren, S. (1992). *The left-hander syndrome.* New York: Free Press.

Coren, S. & Aks, D. J. (1990). Moon illusion in pictures: A multimechanism approach. *Journal of Experimental Psychology: Human Perception & Performance, 16(2),* 365–380.

Coren, S. & Halpern, D. F. (1991). Left-handedness: A marker for decreased survival fitness. *Psychological Bulletin, 109(1),* 90–106.

Coren, S., Ward, L. M., & Enns, J. T. (1994). *Sensation and perception.* Ft. Worth: Harcourt Brace.

Cornsweet, T. N. (1970). *Visual perception.* New York: Academic.

Corteen, R. S. & Williams, T. M. (1986). Television and reading skills. In T. M. Williams (Ed.), *The impact of television: A natural experiment in three communities.* Orlando, FL: Academic.

Costa, P. T. & McCrae, R. R. (1992). Multiple uses for longitudinal personality data. *European Journal of Personality, 6(2),* 85–102.

Costello, T. W. & Costello, J. T. (1992). *Abnormal psychology.* New York: HarperCollins.

Coulton, C. J., Korbin, J. E., & Su, M. (1996). Measuring neighborhood context for young children in an urban area. *American Journal of Community Psychology, 24(1),* 5–32.

Coursey, R. D., Ward-Alexander, L., & Katz, B. (1990). Cost-effectiveness of providing insurance benefits for posthospital psychiatric halfway house stays. *American Psychologist, 45(10),* 1118–1126.

Covell, K., Grusec, J. E., & King, G. (1995). The intergenerational transmission of maternal discipline and standards for behavior. *Social Development, 4(1),* 32–43.

Cover, J. D. (1995). The effects of social contact on prejudice. *Journal of Social Psychology, 135(3),* 403–405.

Cowles, J. T. (1937). Food tokens as incentives for learning by chimpanzees. *Comparative Psychology, Monograph, 14(5,* Whole No. 71).

Cox, W. E. (1994). Exceptional evidence of ESP by a reputed sensitive. *Journal of the Society for Psychical Research, 60(836),* 16–28.

Coye, R. W. & Belohlav, J. A. (1995). An exploratory analysis of employee participation. *Group & Organization Management, 20(1),* 4–17.

Coyne, J. C. & Downey, G. (1991). Social factors and psychopathology. In M. R. Rosenzweig and L. W. Porter (Eds.), *Annual Review of Psychology, 42,* 401–425.

Craik, F. I. M. (1970). The fate of primary items in free recall. *Journal of Verbal Learning and Verbal Behavior, 9,* 143–148.

Crandall, C. S., Preisler, J. J., & Aussprung, J. (1992). Measuring life event stress in the lives of college students: The Undergraduate Stress Questionnaire (USQ). *Journal of Behavioral Medicine, 15(6),* 627–662.

Cravatt, B. F., Prospero-Garcia O., Siuzdak G., Gilula, N. B., et al. (1995). Chemical characterization of a family of brain lipids that induce sleep. *Science, 268(5216),* 1506–1509.

Crawford, C. B. (1994a). Effects of sex and sex roles on avoidance of same- and opposite-sex touch. *Perceptual & Motor Skills, 79(1, Pt 1),* 107–112.

Crawford, C. B. (1994b). Effects of sex and sex roles on same-sex touch. *Perceptual & Motor Skills, 78(2),* 391–394.

Crawford, H. J., Brown, A., & Moon, C. E. (1993). Sustained attentional and distractional abilities: Differences between low and highly hypnotizable persons. *Journal of Abnormal Psychology, 102(4),* 534–543.

Crawley, S. B., & Sherrod, K. B. (1984). Parent-infant play during the first year of life. *Infant Behavior & Development, 7,* 65–75.

Cregler, L.L., & Mark, H. (1985). Medical complications of cocaine abuse. *New England Journal of Medicine, 315(23),* 1495–1500.

Crencavage, L. M. & Norcross, J. C. (1990). Where are the commonalities among the therapeutic common factors? *Professional Psychology: Research & Practice, 21(5),* 372–378.

Crick, F. & Mitchison, G. (1995). REM sleep and neural nets. *Behavioural Brain Research, 69(1–2),* 147–155.

Croll, C. (1986). Personal communication.

Cronbach, L. (1990). *Essentials of psychological testing.* Reading, PA: Addison-Wesley.

Cross, J. G., & Guyer, M. J. (1980). *Social traps.* Ann Arbor: The University of Michigan Press.

Crowe, L. C. & George, W. H. (1989). Alcohol and human sexuality: Review and integration. *Psychological Bulletin, 105(3),* 374–386.

Culertson, F. M. (1997). Depression and gender. *American Psychologist, 52(1),* 25–31.

Culver, B., & Ianna, P. (1979). *The gemini syndrome.* Tucson, AZ: Pachart Publishing.

Cumming, E., & Henry, W. E. (1961). *Growing old: The process of disengagement.* New York: Basic.

Cumming, S., Hay, P., Lee, T., & Sachdev, P. (1995). Neuropsychological outcome from psychosurgery for obsessive-compulsive disorder. *Australian & New Zealand Journal of Psychiatry, 29(2),* 293–298.

Cummins, D. D. (1995). *The other side of psychology.* New York: St. Martins.

Cushman, P. (1989). Iron fists/velvet gloves: A study of a mass marathon psychology training. *Psychotherapy, 26(1),* 23.

Cutright, P. (1996). How to achieve racial accommodation by the year 2068. *Social Science Research, 25(1),* 32–49.

Cutting, J. E. (1987). Rigidity in cinema seen from the front row, side aisle. *Journal of Experimental Psychology: Human Perception and Performance, 13(3),* 323–334.

Cytowic, R. E. (1993). *The man who tasted shapes.* Putnam's Sons.

Czeisler, C. A., Kronauer, R. E., Allan, J. S. et al., (1989). Bright light induction of strong (Type O) resetting of the human circadian pacemaker. *Science, 244* (June), 1328–1333.

Czeisler, C. A., Richardson, G. S., Zimmerman, J. C., Moore-Ede, M. C., & Weitzman, E. D. (1981). Entrainment of human circadian rhythms by light-dark cycles: A reassessment. *Photochemistry, Photobiology, 34,* 239–247.

Dabbs, J. M. Jr., Hargrove, M. F., & Heusel, C. (1996). Testosterone differences among college fraternities. *Personality & Individual Differences, 20(2),* 157–161.

Dacey, J. S. (1989). *Fundamentals of creative thinking.* Lexington, MA: Lexington.

Dalgleish, T., Rosen, K., & Marks, M. (1996). Rhythm and blues: The theory and treatment of seasonal affective disorder. *British Journal of Clinical Psychology, 35(2),* 163–182.

Darley, J. M. & Latané, B. (1968). Bystander intervention in emergencies: Diffusion of responsibility. *Journal of Personality & Social Psychology, 8,* 377–383.

Darling, C. A., Davidson, J. K., & Passarello, L. C. (1992). The mystique of first intercourse among college youth: The role of partners, contraceptive practices, and psychological reactions. *Journal of*

Youth & Adolescence, 21(1), 97–117.

Darwin, C. (1872). *The expression of emotion in man and animals.* Chicago: The University of Chicago Press.

Darwin, M. & Wowk, B. (1992). Cryonics: Reaching for tomorrow. *Skeptic, 1*(2), 32–43.

DasGupta, B. (1992). Perceived control and examination stress. *Psychology: A Journal of Human Behavior, 29*(1), 31–34.

Davanloo, H. (1995). Intensive short-term dynamic psychotherapy. *International Journal of Short-Term Psychotherapy, 10*(3–4), 121–155.

David, H., Borgeat, F., & Saucier, J. (1990). The relation between tachystoscopic pictures and neurotic postpartum depression. *Pre- & Peri-Natal Psychology Journal, 4*(3), 219–227.

Davies, M. F. (1993). Dogmatism and the persistence of discredited beliefs. *Personality & Social Psychology Bulletin, 19*(6), 692–699.

Davis, J. H. (1989). Psychology and law: The last 15 years. *Journal of Applied Social Psychology, 19*(3, Pt. 1), 199–230.

Davis, J. R., Vanderploeg, J. M., Santy, P. A., Jennings, R. T. et al. (1988). Space motion sickness during 24 flights of the Space Shuttle. *Aviation, Space, & Environmental Medicine, 59*(12), 1185–1189.

Davis, M. H. & Harvey, J. C. (1992). Declines in major league batting performance as a function of game pressure. *Journal of Applied Social Psychology, 22*(9), 714–735.

Dawson, M. E. (1990). Where does the truth lie? A review of the polygraph test: Lies, truth, and science. *Psychophysiology, 27*(1), 120–121.

De Benedittis, G., Lorenzetti, A., & Pieri, A. (1990). The role of stressful life events in the onset of chronic primary headache. *Pain, 40*(1), 65–75.

De Bono, E. (1992). *Serious creativity.* New York: HarperCollins.

De Haan, E. H. F., Heywood, C. A., Young, A. W., Edelstyn, N. et al. (1995). Ettlinger revisited: The relation between agnosia and sensory impairment. *Journal of Neurology, Neurosurgery & Psychiatry, 58*(3), 350–356.

De La Cruz, F. F., & Muller, J. Z. (1983). Facts about Down syndrome. *Children Today, 12*(6), 2–7.

de Luccie, M. F. & Davis, A. J. (1991). Father-child relationships from the preschool years through mid-adolescence. *Journal of Genetic Psychology, 152*(2), 225–238.

de Roiste, A. & Bushnell, I. W. R. (1996). Tactile stimulation: Short- and long-term benefits for pre-term infants. British Journal of Developmental Psychology, 14(Mar), 41–53.

De Toffol, B., Autret, A., Gaymard, B., & Degiovanni, E. (1992). Influence of lateral gaze on electroencephalographic spectral power. *Electroencephalography and Clinical Neurophysiology, 82*, 432–437.

Dean-Church, L. & Gilroy, F. D. (1993). Relation of sex-role orientation to life satisfaction in a healthy elderly sample. *Journal of Social Behavior & Personality, 8*(1), 133–140.

Deary, I. J. & Stough, C. (1996). Intelligence and inspection time. *American Psychologist, 51*(6), 599–608.

Deaux, K. (1985). Sex and gender. *Annual Review of Psychology, 36*, 49–81.

Deaux, K., & Emswiller, T. (1974). Explanation of successful performance on sex-linked tasks: What is skill for the male is luck for the female. *Journal of Personality & Social Psychology, 29*, 80–85.

Deaux, K., Dane, F., & Wrightsman, L. S. (1993). *Social psychology in the '90s.* Monterey: Brooks/Cole.

DeBell, C. S. & Harless, D. K. (1992). B. F. Skinner: Myth and misperception. *Teaching of Psychology, 19*(2), 68–73.

DeBono, E. (1970). *Lateral Thinking: Creativity step by step.* New York: Harper & Row.

DeBuono, B. A., Zinner, S. H., Daamen, M., & McCormack, W. M. (1990). Sexual behavior of college women in 1975, 1986, and 1989. *New England Journal of Medicine, 322*(12), 821–825.

Deese, J., & Hulse, S. J. (1967). *The psychology of learning* (3rd. ed.). New York: McGraw-Hill.

Deffenbacher, J. L. & Suinn, R. M. (1988). Systematic desensitization and the reduction of anxiety. *Counseling Psychologist, 16*(1), 9–30.

DeGood, D. E. (1975). Cognitive factors in vascular stress responses. *Psychophysiology, 12*, 399–401.

Degreef, G., Ashtari, M., Bogerts, B. et al. (1992). Volumes of ventricular system subdivisions measured from magnetic resonance images in first-episode schizophrenic patients. *Archives of General Psychiatry, 49*(7), 531–537.

deGroot, G. (1994). Psychologists explain Barney's power. *APA Monitor,* June, 4.

DeLeon, P. H., Sammons, M. T., & Sexton, J. L. (1995). Focusing on society's real needs. *American Psychologist, 50*(12), 1022–1032.

Dement, W. (1972). *Some must watch while some must sleep.* Stanford, CA: Stanford Alumni Association.

Demyttenaere, K. Lenaerts, H., Nijs, P., & Van Assche, F. A. (1995). Individual coping style and psychological attitudes during pregnancy predict depression levels during pregnancy and during postpartum. *Acta Psychiatrica Scandinavica, 91*(2), 95–102.

Denmark, F. L. (1994). Engendering psychology. *American Psychologist, 49*(4), 329–334.

Denning, P. J. (1988). Blindness in designing intelligent systems. *American Scientist, 76*, 118–120.

Denollet, J. (1993). Biobehavioral research on coronary heart disease. *Journal of Behavioral Medicine, 16*(2), 115–141.

Deregowski, J. B. (1972, Nov.). Pictorial perception and culture. *Scientific American,* 82–88.

Desimone, R. & Duncan, J. (1995). Neural mechanisms of selective visual attention. *Annual Review of Neuroscience, 18*, 193–222.

DeSpelder, L. A., & Strickland, A. L. (1995). *The last dance.* Mountain View, CA: Mayfield.

Deutsch, M. (1993). Educating for a peaceful world. *American Psychologist, 48*(5), 510–517.

Deutsch, M., & Collins, M. E. (1951). *Interracial housing.* Minneapolis: University of Minnesota Press.

Devine, D. P. & Spanos, N. P. (1990). Effectiveness of maximally different cognitive strategies and expectancy in attenuation of reported pain. *Journal of Personality & Social Psychology, 58*(4), 672–678.

Devine, P. G. (1990). Stereotypes and prejudice: Their automatic and controlled components. *Journal of Personality & Social Psychology, 56*(1), 5–18.

Devine, P. G., Monteith, M. J., Zuerink, J. R., & Elliot, A. J. (1991). Prejudice with and without compunction. *Journal of Personality & Social Psychology, 60*(6), 817–830.

Dewhurst, S. A. & Conway, M. A. (1994). Pictures, images, and recollective experience. *Journal of Experimental Psychology: Learning, Memory, and Cognition, 20*, 1088–1098.

Dickinson, D. J. & O'Connell, D. Q. (1990). Effect of quality and quantity of study on student grades. *Journal of Educational Research, 83*(4), 227–231.

Diekstein, S. & Parke, R. D. (1988). Social referencing in infancy: A glance at fathers and marriage. *Child Development, 59*(2), 506–511.

Diekstra, R. F. & Garnefski, N. (1995). On the nature, magnitude, and causality of suicidal behaviors: An international perspective. *Suicide & Life-Threatening Behavior, 25*(1), 36–57.

Dies, R. R. (1995). Group psychotherapies. In A. S. Gurman & S. B. Messer, *Essential Psychotherapies.* New York: Guilford.

Digman, J. M. (1990). Personality structure: Emergence of the five-factor model. *Annual Review of Psychology, 41*, 417–440.

Dignon, A. M. (1996). Acceptability of a computer-administered psychiatric interview. *Computers in Human Behavior, 12*(2), 177–191.

Dillard, J. P. (1991). The current status of research on sequential-request compliance techniques. *Personality & Social Psychology Bulletin, 17*(3), 283–288.

Dinkmeyer, D. & McKay, G. D. (1989). *The parent's handbook.* Circle Pines, MN: American Guidance Service.

Dixon, J. (1975). Jeanne Dixon strikes back at scientists who knock astrology. *National Star,* Sept. 30, 5.

Dobratz, M. C. (1995). Analysis of variables that impact psychological adaptation in home hospice patients. *Hospice Journal, 10*(1), 75–88.

Doctor, R. M. & Doctor, J. N. (1994). Stress. *Encyclopedia of human behavior, Volume 4,* 311–323. San Diego, CA: Academic.

Dodge, K. A., Pettit, G. S., & Bates, J. E. (1994). Socialization mediators of the relation between socioeconomic status and child conduct problems. *Child Development, 65*(April), 649–665.

Dollard, J. et al. (1939). *Frustration and aggression.* New Haven: Yale University Press.

Dollard, J., & Miller, N. E. (1950). *Personality and psychotherapy: An analysis in terms of learning, thinking and culture.* New York: McGraw-Hill.

Donnerstein, E. I., & Linz, D. G. (1986). The question of pornography. *Psychology Today,* Dec., 56–59.

Donohue, H. E. F. (1968). *Where should you touch?* New York: Hearst.

Dooling, D. J., & Lachman, R. (1971). Effects of comprehension on retention of prose. *Journal of Experimental Psychology, 88*, 216–222.

Dorfman, J., Shames, J., & Kihlstrom, J. F. (1996). Intuition, incubation, & insight. In G. Underwood (Ed.), *Implicit cognition.* New York: Oxford University Press.

Doty, R. M., Peterson, B. E., & Winter, D. G. (1991). *Journal of Personality & Social Psychology, 61*(4), 629–640.

Dovido, J. F. (1984). Helping behavior and altruism: An empirical and conceptual overview. In L. Berkowitz (Ed.), *Advances in experimental social psychology, Vol. 17.* New York: Academic.

Dovido, J. F., Allen, J. L., & Schroeder, D. A. (1990). Specificity of empathy-induced helping: Evidence for altruistic motivation. *Journal of Personality & Social Psychology, 59*(2), 249–260.

Drake, R. A. & Ulrich, G. (1992). *Acta Psychologica, 79*(3), 219–226.

Drake, R. A. (1994). Personal communication.

Drake, R. A., & Seligman, M. E. P. (1989). Self-serving biases in causal attributions as a function of altered activation asymmetry. *International Journal of Neuroscience, 45*, 199–204.

Dretzke, Beverly J. & Levin, Joel R. (1996). Assessing students' application and transfer of a mnemonic strategy. *Contemporary Educational Psychology, 21*(1), 83–93.

Drexler, L. P., Ahrens, A. H., & Haaga, D. A. (1995). The affective consequences of self-handicapping. *Journal of Social Behavior & Personality, 10*(4), 861–870.

Drowatzky, J. N. (1975). *Motor learning: Principles and practices.* Minneapolis, MN: Burgess.

Druckman, D. & Bjork, R. A. (1994). *Learning, remembering, believing: Enhancing human performance.* Washington, D.C.: National Academy Press.

DSM-IV: Diagnostic and statistical manual of mental disorders (4th ed.). American Psychiatric Association. Washington, D.C., 1994.

Duan, D. W. & Cuvo, A. J. (1996). Comparison of prototype and rote instruction of English names for Chinese visual characters. *Journal of Applied Behavior Analysis, 29*(1), 125–127.

Dubbert, P. M. (1995). Behavioral (life-style) modification in the prevention and treatment of hypertension. *Clinical Psychology Review, 15*(3), 187–216.

Dubbert, P. M. (1992). Exercise in behavioral medicine. *Journal of Consulting and Clinical Psychology, 60*(4), 613–618.

Dubow, E. F., Huesmann, L. R., & Eron, L. D. (1987). Childhood correlates of adult ego development. *Child Development, 58*(3), 859–869.

Dubreuil, D. L., Endler, N. S., & Spanos, N. P. (1988). Distraction and redefinition in the reduction of low and high intensity experimentally-induced pain. *Imagination, Cognition and Personality, 7*(2), 155–164.

Duncan, G. S., Brooks-Gunn, J., & Klebanov, P. K. (1994). Economic deprivation and early childhood development. *Child Development, 65*(April), 296–318.

Duncker, K. (1945). On problem solving. *Psychological Monographs, 58*(270).

Dunner, D. L. (1985). Recent genetic studies of bipolar and unipolar depression. In J. C. Coyne (Ed.), *Essential papers on depression*. New York: New York University Press.

Durso, F. T., Rea, C. B., & Dayton, T. (1994). Graph-theoretic confirmation of restructuring during insight. *Psychological Science, 5*(2), 94–98.

Dutton, D. G., & Aron, A. P. (1974). Some evidence for heightened sexual attraction under conditions of high anxiety. *Journal of Personality & Social Psychology, 30*, 510–517.

Dwyer, W. O., Leeming, F. C., Cobern, M. K., Porter, B. E. et al. (1993). Critical review of behavioral interventions to preserve the environment. *Environment and Behavior, 25*(3), 275–321.

Dyck, M. J. (1987). Assessing logotherapeutic constructs: Conceptual and psychometric status of Purpose in Life and Seeking of Noetic Goals tests. *Clinical Psychology, 7*(4), 439–447.

Dyer, F. J. (1993). Clinical presentation of the lead-poisoned child on mental ability tests. *Journal of Clinical Psychology, 49*(1), 94–101.

Dywan, J., & Bowers, K. S. (1983). The use of hypnosis to enhance recall. *Science, 222*, 184–185.

Eagly, A. H. & Chaiken, S. (1992). *The psychology of attitudes*. San Diego, CA: Harcourt Brace Jovanovich.

Eastman, C. I., Stewart, K. T., Mahoney, M. P., Liu, L. et al. (1994). Dark goggles and bright light improve circadian rhythm adaptation to night-shift work. *Sleep, 17*(6), 535–543.

Ebbinghaus, H. (1885). *Memory: A contribution to experimental psychology*. Translated by H. A. Ruger & C. E. Bussenius, 1913. New York: New York Teacher's College, Columbia University.

Eberhardt, B. J., & Muchinsky, P. M. (1982). An empirical investigation of the factor stability of Owens' biographical questionnaire. *Journal of Applied Psychology, 67*, 138–145.

Eccles, J. S., Midgley, C., Wigfield, A., Buchanan, C. M., Reuman, K. D., Flanagan, C., & Mac Iver, D. (1993). Development during adolescence. *American Psychologist, 48*, 90–101.

Edinger, J. D., Marsh, G. R., McCall, W. V., Erwin, C. W. et al. (1990). Daytime functioning and nighttime sleep before, during, and after a 146-hour tennis match. *Sleep, 13*(6), 526–532.

Egan, G. (1984). Skilled helping: A problem-management framework for helper training. In D. Larson (Ed.), *Teaching psychological skills*, 133–150. Monterey, CA: Brooks/Cole.

Egeland, B., Jacobvitz, D., & Sroufe, L. A. (1988). Breaking the cycle of abuse. *Child Development, 59*(4), 1080–1088.

Eich, E., Rachman, S., & Lopatka, C. (1990). Affect, pain, and autobiographical memory. *Journal of Abnormal Psychology, 99*(2) 174–178.

Eichorn, D. H., Hunt, J. V., & Honzik, M. P. (1981). Experience, personality, and IQ: Adolescence to middle age. In D. H. Eichorn, J. A. Clausen, N. Haan, M. P. Honzik, & P. H. Mussen (Eds.), *Present and past in middle life*. New York: Academic.

Eimas, P. D., Quinn, P. C., & Cowan, P. (1994). Development of exclusivity in perceptually based categories of young infants. *Journal of Experimental Child Psychology, 58*(3), 418–431.

Einspieler, C., Widder, J., Holzer, A., & Kenner, T. (1988). The predictive value of behavioural risk factors for sudden infant death. *Early Human Development, 18*(2–3), 101–109.

Eisenberg, N. (1991). Meta-analytic contributions to the literature on prosocial behavior. *Personality & Social Psychology Bulletin, 17*(3), 273–282.

Eisenberg, N. & Miller, P. A. (1987). The relation of empathy to prosocial and related behaviors. *Psychological Bulletin, 101*(1), 91–119.

Ekman, P. (1986). *Telling Lies*. New York: Berkley.

Ekman, P. (1992). Facial expression of emotion. *Psychological Science, 3*, 34–38.

Ekman, P. (1993). Facial expression and emotion. *American Psychologist, 48*(4), 384–392.

Ekman, P. & O'Sullivan, M. (1991). Who can catch a liar? *American Psychologist, 46*(9), 913–920.

Ekman, P., Friesen, W. V., & Bear, J. (1984). The international language of gestures. *Psychology Today*, May, 64–69.

Ekman, P., Levenson, R. W., & Friesen, W. V. (1983). Autonomic nervous system activity distinguishes among emotions. *Science, 221*, 1208–1210.

Elkind, D. (1981). *The hurried child*. Reading, MA: Addison-Wesley.

Elkind, D. (1984). *All grown up & no place to go*. Reading, MA: Addison-Wesley.

Elkind, D. (1995). *Ties that stress*. Cambridge, MA: Harvard University Press.

Elliott, M., Browne, K., & Kilcoyne, J. (1995). Child sexual abuse prevention: What offenders tell us. *Child Abuse & Neglect, 19*(5), 579–594.

Ellis, A. (1973). The no cop-out therapy. *Psychology Today*, 7 (Feb.), 56–60, 62.

Ellis, A. (1979). The practice of rational-emotive therapy. In A. Ellis & J. Whiteley (Eds.) *Theoretical and empirical foundations of rational-emotive therapy*. Monterey, CA: Brooks/Cole.

Ellis, A. (1987). A sadly neglected cognitive component in depression. *Cognitive Therapy & Research, 11*(1), 121–145.

Ellis, A. (1995). Changing rational-emotive therapy (RET) to rational emotive behavior therapy (REBT). *Journal of Rational-Emotive & Cognitive Behavior Therapy, 13*(2), 85–89.

Ellis, H. C. & Hunt, R. R. (1992). *Fundamentals of cognitive psychology*. Madison, WI: Brown & Benchmark.

Emotion and Motivation. (1995). *American Psychologist, 50*(10), 838–845.

Engel, G. (1977, Nov.). Emotional stress and sudden death. *Psychology Today*, 144.

Engle, E., & Lott, A. S. (1980). *Man in flight*. Annapolis, MD: Leeward.

Engler, J. & Goleman, D. (1992). *The consumer's guide to psychotherapy*. New York: Simon & Schuster.

Enns, J. T. & Coren, S. (1995). The box alignment illusion. *Perception & Psychophysics, 57*(8), 1163–1174.

Enright, J. T. (1996). Sequential stereopsis: A simple demonstration. *Vision Research, 36*(2), 307–312.

Eppley, K. R., Abrams, A. I., & Shear, J. (1989). Differential effects of relaxation techniques on trait anxiety: A meta-analysis. *Journal of Clinical Psychology, 45*(6), 957–974.

Epstein, R., Langa, R. P., & Skinner, B. F. (1981). "Self-awareness" in the pigeon. *Science, 212*, 695–696.

Erdelyi, M. H., & Appelbaum, A. G., (1973). Cognitive masking: The disruptive effect of an emotional stimulus upon the perception of contiguous neutral items. *Bulletin of the Psychonomic Society, 1*, 59–61.

Ericsson, K. A. & Charness, N. (1994). Expert performance. *American Psychologist, 49*(8), 725–747.

Ericsson, K. A., & Chase, W. G. (1982). Exceptional memory. *American Scientist, 70*, 607–615.

Erikson, E. H. (1963). *Childhood and society*. New York: Norton.

Erk, R. R. (1995). The conundrum of attention deficit disorder. *Journal of Mental Health Counseling, 17*(2), 131–145.

Erlich, P. R. & Erlich, A. H. (1990). The population explosion. *The Amicus Journal*, Winter, 18–29.

Ernst, E. (1994). Is acupuncture effective for pain control? *Journal of Pain & Symptom Management, 9*(2), 72–74.

Eron, L. D. (1986). Interventions to mitigate the psychological effects of media violence on aggressive behavior. *Journal of Social Issues, 42*(3), 155–169.

Eron, L. D. (1987). The development of aggressive behavior from the perspective of a developing behaviorism. *American Psychologist, 42*, 435–442.

Ethical principles of psychologists and code of conduct (1992). The American Psychological Association. *American Psychologist, 47*(12), 1597–1611.

Evans, G. W. & Lepore, S. J. (1993). Household crowding and social support. *Journal of Personality & Social Psychology, 65*(2), 308–316.

Evans, G.W., Lepore, S. J., & Schroeder, A. (1996). The role of interior design elements in human responses to crowding. *Journal of Personality & Social Psychology, 70*(1), 41–46.

Evans, S. (1993). Keeping cool when the baby won't stop crying. *The Los Angeles Times*, Jan. 25, E–2.

Everson, S. A., Goldberg, D. E., & Salonen, J. T. (1996). Hopelessness and risk of mortality and incidence of myocardial infarction and cancer. *Psychosomatic Medicine, 58*(2), 113.

Eyer, D. (1993). *Mother-infant bonding: A scientific fiction*. New Haven, CT: Yale University Press.

Eyer, Diane E. (1994). Mother-infant bonding: A scientific fiction. *Human Nature, 5*(1), 69–94.

Eysenck, H. J. (1967). New ways in psychotherapy. *Psychology Today*, June, 40.

Eysenck, H. J. (1994). The outcome problem in psychotherapy: What have we learned? *Behaviour Research & Therapy, 32*(5), 477–495.

Eysenck, H. J. (Ed.). (1981). *A model for personality*. New York: Springer-Verlag.

Eysenck, M. W. & Keane, M. T. (1995). *Cognitive psychology*. Hove, East Sussex, U.K.: Erlbaum.

Fackelmann, K. A. (1993). Marijuana and the brain. *Science News, 143*(2), 88–89, 94.

Faigel, H.C., Sznajderman, S., Tishby, O. et al. (1995). Attention deficit disorder during adolescence: A review. *Journal of Adolescent Health, 16*(3), 174–184.

Faith, M. S., Wong, F. Y., & Carpenter, K. M. (1995). Group sensitivity training: Update, meta-analysis, and recommendations. *Journal of Counseling Psychology, 42*(3), 390–399.

Famularo, R., Kinscherff, R., & Fenton, T. (1992). Psychiatric diagnoses of abusive mothers. *Journal of Nervous & Mental Disease, 180*(10), 658–661.

Fantz, R. L. (1961). The origin of form perception. *Scientific American*, May, 71.

Fantz, R. L. (1963). Pattern vision in newborn infants. *Science, 140,* 296–297.

Farah, M. J. (1988). Is visual imagery really visual? Overlooked evidence from neuropsychology. *Psychological Review, 95*(3), 307–317.

Farah, M. J., Weisberg, L. L., Monheit, M. A., & Peronnet, F. (1989). Brain activity underlying mental imagery. *Journal of Cognitive Neuroscience, 1*(4), 302–316.

Farquhar, J. W., Fortmann, S. P., Maccoby, N., Wood, P. D. et al. (1984). The Stanford Five City Project: An overview. In J. D. Matarazzo, S. M. Weiss, J. A. Herd, N. E. Miller, & S. M. Weiss (Eds.), *Behavioral health: A handbook of health enhancement and disease prevention.* New York: Wiley.

Farrimond, T. (1990). Effect of alcohol on visual constancy values and possible relation to driving performance. *Perceptual & Motor Skills, 70*(1), 291–295.

Farthing, G. W. (1992). The psychology of consciousness. Englewood Cliffs, NJ: Prentice Hall.

Fath, J. L., Mitchell, C. M., & Govindaraj, T. (1990). An ICAI architecture for troubleshooting in complex, dynamic systems. *IEEE Transactions on Systems, Man, & Cybernetics, 20*(3), 537–558.

Fava, G. A., Grandi, S., Zielezny, M., Rafanelli, C. (1996). Four-year outcome for cognitive behavioral treatment of residual symptoms in major depression. *American Journal of Psychiatry, 153*(7), 945–947.

Fehr, L. (1976). J. Piaget and S. Claus: Psychology makes strange bedfellows. *Psychological Reports, 39,* 740–742.

Feingold, A. (1990). Gender differences in effects of physical attractiveness on romantic attraction. *Journal of Personality & Social Psychology, 59*(5), 981–993.

Feingold, A. (1992a). Gender differences in mate selection preferences. *Psychological Bulletin, 111,* 304–341.

Feldhusen, J. F. (1995). Creativity: A knowledge base, metacognitive skills, and personality factors. *Journal of Creative Behavior, 29*(4), 255–268.

Feldhusen, J. F. & Goh, B. E. (1995). Assessing and accessing creativity: An integrative review of theory, research, and development. *Creativity Research Journal, 8*(3), 231–247.

Feldman, R. S. & Meyer, J. (1996). *Fundamentals of neuropsychopharmacology.* Sunderland, MA: Sinauer Associates.

Felsenfeld, S. (1996). Progress and needs in the genetics of stuttering. *Journal of Fluency Disorders, 21*(2), 77–103.

Fernald, A. & Mazzie, C. (1991). Prosody and focus in speech to infants and adults. *Developmental Psychology, 27*(2), 209–221.

Fernald, A. (1989). Intonation and communicative intent in mothers' speech to infants: Is the melody the message? *Child Development, 60*(6), 1497–1510.

Fernandez, E. & Turk, D. C. (1989). The utility of cognitive coping strategies for altering pain perception. *Pain, 38*(2), 123–135.

Ferrari, J. R. (1991). Self-handicapping by procrastinators: Protecting self-esteem, social-esteem, or both? *Journal of Research in Personality, 25*(3), 245–261.

Ferrari, J. R. (1992). Procrastinators and perfect behavior. *Journal of Research in Personality, 26*(1), 75–84.

Ferster, C. B., Nurnberger, J. I., & Levitt, E. B. (1962). The control of eating. *Journal of Mathematics, 1,* 87–109.

Festinger, L. (1954). A theory of social comparison processes. *Human Relations, 7,* 117–140.

Festinger, L. (1957). *A theory of cognitive dissonance.* Stanford, CA: Stanford University Press.

Festinger, L., & Carlsmith, J. M. (1959). Cognitive consequences of forced compliance. *Journal of Abnormal and Social Psychology, 58,* 203–210.

Festinger, L., Schachter, S., & Back, K. (1950). *Social pressures in informal groups: A study of a housing project.* New York: Harper.

Feuerstein, M., Labbé, E. E., & Kuczmierczyk, A. R. (1986a). *Health psychology: A psychobiological perspective.* New York: Plenum.

Feuerstein, R., Hoffman, M. B., Rand, Y., & Jensen, M. R. (1986b). Learning to learn: Mediated learning experiences and instrumental enrichment. *Special Services in the Schools, 3*(1–2), 49–82.

Finke, R. (1990). *Creative imagery.* Hillsdale, NJ: Erlbaum.

Finkelhor, D. & Dziuba-Leatherman, J. (1994). Victimization of children. *American Psychologist, 49*(3), 173–183.

Finkelson, L. & Oswalt, R. (1995). College date rape: Incidence and reporting. *Psychological Reports, 77*(2), 526.

Finkelstein, P., Wenegrat, B., & Yalom, I. (1982). Large group awareness training. *Annual Review of Psychology, 33,* 515–539.

Firth, U. (1993). Autism. *Scientific American,* June, 108–114.

Fisher, C. B. & Fyrberg, D. (1994). Participant partners. *American Psychologist, 49*(5), 417–427.

Fisher, K. (1984, Dec.). Berkeley study finds stress is value-laden. *APA Monitor, 26,* 30.

Fisher, K. (1986). Animal research: Few alternatives seen for behavioral studies. *APA Monitor,* March, 16–17.

Fisher, R. P. & Geiselman, R. E. (1987). Enhancing eyewitness memory with the cognitive interview. In M. M. Gruneger, P. E. Morris, & R. N. Sykes (Eds.), *Practical aspects of memory: Current research and issues.* Chinchester, U.K.: Wiley.

Fisher, S. (1973). *The female orgasm.* New York: Basic.

Fiske, S. T. (1993a). Social cognition and social perception. In L. W. Porter & M. R. Rosenzweig (Eds.), *Annual Review of Psychology, 44,* 155–194.

Fiske, S. T., (1993b). Controlling other people. *American Psychologist, 48*(6), 621–628.

Flaks, D. K., Ficher, I., & Joseph, G. (1995). Lesbians choosing motherhood: A comparative study of lesbian and heterosexual parents and their children. *Developmental Psychology, 31*(1), 105–114.

Flannery, R. B. & Wieman, D. (1989). Social support, life stress, and psychological distress: An empirical assessment. *Journal of Clinical Psychology, 45*(6), 867–872.

Flavell, J. H. (1992). Cognitive development: Past, present, and future. *Developmental Psychology, 28*(6), 998–1005.

Fleming, J. (1974). Field report: The state of the apes. *Psychology Today,* Jan., 46.

Flor, H. & Birbaumer, N. (1993). Comparison of the efficacy of electromyographic biofeedback, cognitive-behavioral therapy, and conservative medical interventions in the treatment of chronic musculoskeletal pain. *Journal of Consulting & Clinical Psychology, 61*(4), 653–658.

Florian, V., Mikulincer, M., & Taubman, O. (1995). Does hardiness contribute to mental health during a stressful real-life situation? *Journal of Personality & Social Psychology, 68*(4), 687–695.

Flynn, J. R. (1987). Massive IQ gains in 14 nations: What IQ tests really measure. *Psychological Bulletin, 101*(2), 171–191.

Flynn, J. R. (1990). Massive IQ gains on the Scottish WISC: Evidence against Brand et al.'s hypothesis. *Irish Journal of Psychology, 11*(1), 41–51.

Foa, E. B., Franklin, M. E., Perry, K. J., & Herbert, J. D. (1996). Cognitive biases in generalized social phobia. *Journal of Abnormal Psychology, 105*(3), 433–439.

Fochtmann, L. J. (1995). Intractable sneezing as a conversion symptom. *Psychosomatics, 36*(2), 103–112.

Fontana, A., Rosenheck, R., & Brett, E. (1992). War zone traumas and posttraumatic stress disorder symptomatology. *Journal of Nervous & Mental Disease, 180*(12), 748–755.

Fontenelle, D. H. (1989). *How to live with your children.* Tucson, AZ: Fisher Books.

Foos, P., & Clark, M. C. (1984). *Human learning, 2*(3).

Ford, C. V. (1995). Dimensions of somatization and hypochondriasis. *Neurologic Clinics, 13*(2), 241–253.

Foreyt, J. P. (1987a). Behavioral medicine. In Wilson, G. T., Franks, C.M., Kendall, P. C., & Foreyt, J. P. *Review of behavior therapy: Theory and practice, Vol. I.* New York: Guilford.

Foreyt, J. P. (1987b). The addictive disorders. In Wilson, G. T., Franks, C. M., Kendall, P. C., & Foreyt, J. P. *Review of behavior therapy: Theory and practice, Vol. II.* New York: Guilford.

Forgays, D. G. & Belinson, M. J. (1986). Is flotation isolation a relaxing environment? *Journal of Environmental Psychology, 6*(1), 19–34.

Foss, R. D. (1986). Using social psychology to increase altruistic behavior: Will it help? In Saks, M. J. & Saxe, L. (Eds.), *Advances in applied social psychology, Vol. 3.* Hillsdale, NJ: Erlbaum.

Foster, G., & Ysseldyke, J. (1976). Expectancy and halo effects as a result of artificially induced teacher bias. *Contemporary Educational Psychology, 1,* 37–45.

Foulds, J., Stapleton, J., Swettenham, J., & Bell, N. (1996). Cognitive performance effects of subcutaneous nicotine in smokers and never-smokers. *Psychopharmacology, 127*(1), 31–38.

Foulkes, D., & Schmidt, M. (1983). Temporal sequence and unit composition in dream reports from different stages of sleep. *Sleep, 6*(3), 265–280.

Fouts, R., Fouts, D., & Schoenfield, D. (1984). Sign language conversational interaction between chimpanzees. *Sign Language Studies, 42,* 1–12.

Fowers, B. J. & Richardson, F. C. (1996). Why is multiculturalism good? *American Psychologist, 51*(6), 609–621.

Fowles, D. C. (1992). Schizophrenia: Diathesis-stress revisited. *Annual Review of Psychology, 43,* 303–336.

Franche, R. & Dobson, K. S. (1992). Self-criticism and interpersonal dependency as vulnerability factors to depression. *Cognitive Therapy & Research, 16*(4), 419–435.

Frankenburg, W. K., & Dodds, J. B. (1967). The Denver Developmental Screening Test. *The Journal of Pediatrics, 1,* 181–191.

Frankl, V. (1955). *The doctor and the soul.* New York: Knopf.

Franklin, D. (1984). Growing up short. *Science News, 125*(6), 92–94.

Franklin, D. (1984, Oct. 20). Crafting sound from silence. *Science News, 126,* 252–254.

Franklin, N. & Tversky, B. (1990). Searching imagined environments. *Journal of Experimental Psychology: General, 119*(1), 63–76.

Franks, C. M. (1987). Behavior therapy with children and adolescents. In Wilson, G. T., Franks, C. M., Kendall, P. C. & Foreyt, J. P. *Review of behavior therapy: Theory and practice, Vol. II.* New York: Guilford.

Franzoi, S. L. (1996). *Social psychology.* Dubuque, IA: Brown & Benchmark.

Frazier, J. A., Giedd, J. N., Hamburger, S. D., & Albus, K. E. (1996). Brain anatomic magnetic resonance imaging in childhood-onset schizophrenia. *Archives of General Psychiatry, 53*(7), 617–624.

Frederick, C. J. (1987) Psychic trauma in victims of crime and terrorism. In VandenBos, G. R. & Bryant, B. K. (Eds.), *Cataclysms, crises, and catastrophes: Psychology in action.* Washington, DC:

American Psychological Association.

Freedman, J. L. (1984). Effect of television violence on aggressiveness. *Psychological Bulletin, 96,* 227–246.

Freedman, J. L., & Fraser, S. C. (1966). Compliance without pressure: The foot-in-the-door technique. *Journal of Personality & Social Psychology, 4,* 195–202.

Freeman, A. & Reinecke, M. A. (1995). Cognitive therapy. In A. S. Gurman & S. B. Messer, *Essential Psychotherapies.* New York: Guilford.

Freeman, J. (1995). Recent studies of giftedness in children. *Journal of Child Psychology & Psychiatry & Allied Disciplines, 36*(4), 531–547.

Freeman, W. J. (1991). The physiology of perception. *Scientific American,* Feb., 78–85.

Freize, I. H. (1987). The female victim. In Vanden-Bos, G. R. & Bryant, B. K. (Eds.), *Cataclysms, crises, and catastrophes: Psychology in action.* Washington, DC: American Psychological Association.

French, C. C., Fowler, M., McCarthy, K. & Peers, D. (1991). A test of the Barnum effect. *Skeptical Inquirer, 15*(4), 66–72.

Freud, S. (1900). *The interpretation of dreams.* London: Hogarth.

Freud, S. (1949). *An outline of psychoanalysis.* New York: Norton.

Fried, P. A., O'Connell, C. M., & Walkinson, B. (1992). 60- and 72-month follow-up of children prenatally exposed to marijuana, cigarettes, and alcohol. *Journal of Developmental & Behavioral Pediatrics, 13*(6), 383–391.

Friedman, H. S. & Booth-Kewley, S. (1987). The "disease-prone personality." *American Psychologist, 42*(6), 539–555.

Friedman, M., & Rosenman, R. (1983). *Type A behavior and your heart.* New York: Knopf.

Friedman, M., Thoresen, C. E., Gill, J. J., Powell et al. (1984). Alteration of Type A behavior and reduction in cardiac recurrences in postmyocardial infarction patients. *American Heart Journal, 108*(2), 237–248.

Frieze, I. H., Olson, J. E., & Good, D. C. (1990). Perceived and actual discrimination in the salaries of male and female managers. *Journal of Applied Social Psychology, 20*(1), 46–67.

Fuchs, C., & Rehm, L. (1977). A self-control behavior therapy program for depression. *Journal of Consulting and Clinical Psychology, 45,* 206–215.

Fuller, B. (1969). *Utopia or oblivion: The prospects for humanity.* New York: Bantam Matrix.

Fuller, T. D., Edwards, J. N., Vorakitphokatorn, S., & Sermsri, S. (1996). Chronic stress and psychological well-being: Evidence from Thailand on household crowding. *Social Science & Medicine, 42*(2), 265–280.

Furumoto, L., & Scarborough, E. (1986). Placing women in the history of psychology. *American Psychologist, 41,* 35–42.

Gaertner, S. L., Mann, J. A., Dovido, J. E. et al. (1990). How does cooperation reduce intergroup bias? *Journal of Personality & Social Psychology, 59*(4), 692–704.

Gagnon, J. H. (1977). *Human sexualities.* Glenview, IL: Scott, Foresman.

Galanter, E. (1962). Contemporary psychophysics. In *New directions in psychology, Vol. I,* 87–156. New York: Holt, Rinehart & Winston.

Galanti, G. (1993). Cult conversion, deprogramming, and the triune brain. *Cultic Studies Journal, 10*(1), 45–52.

Gallup, G. H., Jr., & Newport, F. (1991). Belief in paranormal phenomena among adult Americans. *Skeptical Inquirer, 15,* 137–146.

Galston, A. W., & Slayman, C. L. (1983). Plant sensitivity and sensation. In G. O. Abell & B. Singer (Eds.), *Science and the paranormal.* New York:

Scribner's.

Gambrill, E. (1992). Self-help books. *Skeptical Inquirer, 16*(Summer), 389–399.

Ganellen, R. J. (1996). Comparing the diagnostic efficiency of the MMPI, MCMI-II, and Rorschach. *Journal of Personality Assessment, 67*(2), 219–243.

Gannon, L. (1993). Menopausal symptoms as consequences of dysrhythmia. *Journal of Behavioral Medicine, 16*(4), 387–402.

Garcia, J., Hankins, W. G., & Rusiniak, K. W. (1974). Behavioral regulation of the milieu interne in man and rat. *Science, 185,* 824–831.

Gardner, H. (1993). *Frames of mind.* New York: Basic.

Gardner, M. (1993). The false memory syndrome. *Skeptical Inquirer, 17*(4), 370–375.

Gardner, R. A., & Gardner, B. T. (1969). Teaching sign language to a chimpanzee. *Science, 165,* 664–672.

Gardner, R. M. & Bokenkamp, E. D. (1996). The role of sensory and nonsensory factors in body size estimations of eating disorders subjects. *Journal of Clinical Psychology, 52*(1), 3–15.

Garland, A. F. & Zigler, E. (1993). Adolescent suicide prevention. *American Psychologist, 48*(2), 169–182.

Garnets, L. & Kimmel, D. (1991). Lesbian and gay male dimensions in the psychological study of human diversity. *Psychological perspectives on human diversity in America.* Washington, D.C.: American Psychological Association.

Garrett, P., Ng'andu, N., & Ferron, J. (1994). Poverty experiences of young children and the quality of their home environments. *Child Development, 65*(April), 331–345.

Garside, B. (1993). Physicians Mutual Aid Group. *Health & Social Work, 18*(4), 259–267.

Garza-Trevino, E. (1994). Neurobiological factors in aggressive behavior. *Hospital & Community Psychiatry, 45*(7), 690–699.

Gates, A. I. (1958). Recitation as a factor in memorizing. In J. Deese (Ed.), *The psychology of learning.* New York: McGraw-Hill.

Gatz, M. (1990). Interpreting behavioral genetic results. *Journal of Counseling & Development, 68*(Jul-Aug), 601–605.

Gatz, M. & Pearson, C. G. (1988). Agesim revised and the provision of psychological services. *American Psychologist, 43*(3), 184–188.

Gauthier, J., Cote, G., & French, D. (1994). The role of home practice in the thermal biofeedback treatment of migraine headache. *Journal of Consulting & Clinical Psychology, 62*(1), 180–184.

Gawin, F. H. (1991). Cocaine addiction: Psychology and neurophysiology. *Science, 251*(5000), 1580–1586.

Gazzaniga, M. S. (1970). *The bisected brain.* New York: Plenum.

Gazzaniga, M. S. (1988). *Mind matters.* Boston: Houghton Mifflin.

Gazzaniga, M. S. (1995). On neural circuits and cognition. *Neural Computation, 7*(1), 1–12.

Geehr, J. L., Burke, M. J., & Sulzer, J. L. (1995). Quality circles: The effects of varying degrees of voluntary participation on employee attitudes and program efficacy. *Educational & Psychological Measurement, 55*(1), 124–134.

Geiger, M. A. (1991) Changing multiple-choice answers: Do students accurately perceive their performance? *Journal of Experimental Education, 59*(3), 250–257.

Geiselman, R. E., Fisher, R. P., MacKinnon, D. P., & Holland, H. L. (1986). Eyewitness memory enhancement with the cognitive interview. *American Journal of Psychology, 99,* 385–401.

Gerbner, G., & Gross, L. (1976). Living with television: The violent profile. *Journal of Communication, 26,* 173–199.

Gersh, R. D. (1982). Learning when not to shoot. *Santa Barbara News Press,* June 20.

Geschwind, N. (1979). Specializations of the human brain. *Scientific American, 241,* 180–199.

Gevins, A. (1989). Dynamic functional topography of cognitive tasks. *Brain Topography, 2*(1–2), 37–56.

Gevins, A. S., Bressler, S. L., Cutillo, B. A., Illes, J. et al. (1990). Effects of prolonged mental work on functional brain topography. *Electroencephalography & Clinical Neurophysiology, 76*(4) 339–350.

Giambra, L. M., Jung, R. E., & Grodsky, A. (1996). Age changes in dream recall in adulthood. *Dreaming: Journal of the Association for the Study of Dreams, 6*(1), 17–31.

Gibson, B. & Werner, C. M. (1994). The airport as a behavior setting: The role of legibility in communicating the setting program. *Journal of Personality and Social Psychology, 66,* 1049–1060.

Gibson, E. J., & Walk, R. D. (1960). The "visual cliff." *Scientific American, 202*(4), 67–71.

Gibson, H. B. & Heap, M. (1991). *Hypnosis in therapy.* Hillsdale, NJ: Erlbaum.

Gierl, M. J. & Rogers, W. T. (1996). A confirmatory factor analysis of the Test Anxiety Inventory using Canadian high school students. *Educational & Psychological Measurement, 56*(2), 315–324.

Gifford, R. (1987). *Environmental psychology.* Boston: Allyn & Bacon.

Gilbert, A. N. & Wysocki, C. J. (1987). The smell survey results. *National Geographic,* Oct., 514–524.

Gilbert, D. G., Stunkard, M. E. Jensen, R. A. Detwiler, F. R. J. (1996). Effects of exam stress on mood, cortisol, and immune functioning. *Personality & Individual Differences, 21*(2), 235–246.

Gilbert, S. (1996). Estrogen patch appears to lift severe depression in new mothers. *The New York Times,* May 1, B–9.

Gilchrist, H., Povey, R., Dickinson, A., & Povey, R. (1995). The Sensation Seeking Scale: Its use in a study of the characteristics of people choosing "adventure holidays." *Personality & Individual Differences, 19*(4), 513–516.

Gill, S. T. (1991). Carrying the war into the never-never land of psi. *Skeptical Inquirer, 15*(1), 269–273.

Gillam, B. (1980). Geometrical illusions. *American Psychologist, 242,* 102–111.

Gilligan, C. (1982). *In a different voice.* Cambridge, MA: Harvard University Press.

Gilligan, C. & Attanucci, J. (1988). Two moral orientations: Gender differences and similarities. *Merrill-Palmer Quarterly, 34*(3), 223–237.

Gilmore, D. C. & Ferris, G. R. (1989). The effects of applicant impression management tactics on interviewer judgments. *Journal of Management, 15*(4), 557–564.

Giniger, S., Dispenzieri, A., & Eisenberg, J. (1983). Age, experience, and performance on speed and skill jobs in an applied setting. *Journal of Applied Psychology, 68,* 469–475.

Ginott, H. G. (1965). *Between parent and child: New solutions to old problems.* New York: Macmillan.

Ginzberg, E. (1984). Career development. In D. Brown & L. Brooks (Eds.), *Career choice and development.* San Francisco: Josey-Bass.

Girodo, M. (1978). *Shy? (You don't have to be!).* New York: Pocket Books.

Gladue, B. A. (1987). Psychobiological contributions. In L. Diamant (Ed.) *Male and female homosexuality: Psychological approaches.* Washington, DC: Hemisphere.

Glass, A. L., Holyoak, K. J., & Santa, J. L. (1979). *Cognition.* Reading, MA: Addison-Wesley.

Glass, T. A., Seeman, T. E., Herzog, A. et al. (1995). Change in productive activity in late adulthood: MacArthur studies of successful aging. *Journals of Gerontology: Series B: Psychological Sciences & Social*

Sciences, 50B(2), S65–S76.

Glik, D. C., Kronenfeld, J. J., & Jackson, K. (1996). Predictors of well role performance behaviors. *American Journal of Health Behavior, 20*(4), 218–228.

Glisky, M. L., Williams, J. M., & Kihlstrom, J. F. (1996). Internal and external mental imagery perspectives and performance on two tasks. *Journal of Sport Behavior, 19*(1), 3–18.

Globus, G. (1987). *Dream life, wake life: The human condition through dreams.* Albany, NY: State University of New York Press.

Glovinsky, P. B., Spielman, A. J., Carroll, P., Weinstein, L. et al. (1990). Sleepiness and REM sleep recurrence: The effects of Stage 2 and REM sleep awakenings. *Psychophysiology, 27*(5), 552–559.

Gluhoski, V. L. (1995). A cognitive perspective on bereavement: Mechanism and treatment. *Journal of Cognitive Psychotherapy, 9*(2), 75–84.

Gobet, F. & Simon, H. A. (1996). Recall of random and distorted chess positions: Implications for the theory of expertise. *Memory & Cognition, 24*(4), 493–503.

Goel, V. & Grafman, J. (1995). Are the frontal lobes implicated in "planning" functions? Interpreting data from the Tower of Hanoi. *Neuropsychologia, 33*(5), 623–642.

Gold, P. E. (1987). Sweet Memories. *American Scientist, 75,* (Mar-Apr), 151–155.

Gold, S. N., Hughes, D., & Hohnecker, L. (1994). Degrees of repression of sexual abuse memories. *American Psychologist, 49*(5), 441–442.

Goldberg, L. R. (1993). The structure of phenotypic personality traits. *American Psychologist, 48*(1), 26–34.

Goldfried, M. R., Greenberg, L. S., & Marmar, C. (1990). Individual psychotherapy: Process and outcome. *Annual Review of Psychology, 41,* 659–688.

Goldiamond, I. (1971). Self-control procedures in personal behavior problems. In M. S. Gazzaniga & E. P. Lovejoy (Eds.), *Good reading in psychology.* Englewood Cliffs, NJ: Prentice-Hall.

Goldstein, E. B. (1989). *Sensation and perception.* Belmont, CA: Wadsworth.

Goldstein, I. L. & Gilliam, P. (1990). Training system issues in the year 2000. *American Psychologist, 45*(2), 134–143.

Goldstein, M. J. (1985). *The UCLA family project.* Presented at NIMH High-Risk Consortium, San Francisco. Cited by Mirsky & Duncan, 1986.

Goleman, D. (1982). Staying up: The rebellion against sleep's gentle tyranny. *Psychology Today,* March, 24–35.

Goleman, D. (1989). Afternoon nap natural. *New York Times.*

Goleman, D. (1995). *Emotional intelligence.* New York: Bantam.

Golombok, S. & Tasker, F. (1996). Do parents influence the sexual orientation of their children? *Developmental Psychology, 32*(1), 3–11.

Golombok, S., Cook, R., Bish, A., & Murray, C. (1995). Families created by the new reproductive technologies: Quality of parenting and social and emotional development of the children. *Child Development, 66*(2), 285–298.

Gomberg, E. L. (1993). Women and alcohol: Use and abuse. *Journal of Nervous and Mental Disease, 18*(4), 211–219.

Gondola, J. C., & Tuckman, B. W. (1982). Psychological mood state in "average" marathon runners. *Perceptual and Motor Skills, 55,* 1295–1300.

Good, M. (1995). A comparison of the effects of jaw relaxation and music on postoperative pain. *Nursing Research, 44*(1), 52–57.

Goodall, J. (1990). *Through a window: My thirty years with the chimpanzees of the Gombe.* Boston: Houghton Mifflin.

Goode, E. (1996). Gender and courtship entitlement: Responses to personal ads. *Sex Roles, 34*(3–4), 141–169.

Goodglass, H. (1980). Disorders of naming following brain injury. *American Scientist, 68,* 647–655.

Goodman, G. (1984). SASHA tapes: Expanding options for help-intended communication. In D. Larson (Ed.), *Teaching psychological skills.* Monterey, CA: Brooks/Cole.

Goodwin, D. W. (1995). Alcohol amnesia. *Addiction, 90*(3), 315–317.

Gordon, C. M. & Carey, M. P. (1996). Alcohol's effects on requisites for sexual risk reduction in men. *Health Psychology, 15*(1), 56–60.

Gordon, T. (1970). *P.E.T. parent effectiveness training: A tested new way to raise children.* New York: Peter H. Wyden.

Gottesman, I. I. (1991). *Schizophrenia genesis: The origins of madness.*

Gottfried, A. E. & Gottfried, A. W. (1988). *Maternal employment and children's development.* New York: Plenum.

Gottfried, A. W. & Gottfried, A. E. (1994). *Gifted IQ.* New York: Plenum.

Gottman, J. (1994). *Why marriages succeed or fail.* New York: Simon & Schuster.

Gottman, J. M. & Krokoff, L. J. (1989). Marital interaction and satisfaction: A longitudinal view. *Journal of Consulting & Clinical Psychology, 57*(1), 47–52.

Gough, H. G., Fioravanti, M., & Lazzari, R. (1983). Some implications of self versus ideal-self congruence on the revised adjective check list. *Journal of Personality & Social Psychology, 44,* 1214–1220.

Gould, D. & Udry, E. (1994). Psychological skills for enhancing performance: Arousal regulation strategies. *Medicine & Science in Sports & Exercise, 26*(4), 478–485.

Gould, R. (1975). Growth toward self-tolerance. *Psychology Today,* Feb.

Gould, S. J. (1976). Biological potential vs. biological determinism. *Natural History, 85*(5).

Grack, C. & Richman, C. L. (1996). Reducing general and specific heterosexism through cooperative contact. *Journal of Psychology & Human Sexuality, 8*(4), 59–68.

Grady, D. (1986). Don't get jittery over caffeine. *Discover,* July, 73–79.

Graeff, T. R. (1996). Image congruence effects on product evaluations: The role of self-monitoring and public/private consumption. *Psychology & Marketing, 13*(5), 481–499.

Graffin, N. F., Ray, W. J., & Lundy, R. (1995). EEG concomitants of hypnosis and hypnotic susceptibility. *Journal of Abnormal Psychology, 104*(1), 123–131.

Graham, S. (1992). Most of the subjects were White and middle class. *American Psychologist, 47,* 629–639.

Green, J. A., & Shellenberger, R. D. (1986). Biofeedback research and the ghost in the box: A reply to Roberts. *American Psychologist,* Sept., 1003–1005.

Greene, A. S. & Saxe, L. (1990). *Tall tales told to teachers.* Unpublished manuscript. Brandeis University.

Greene, D., & Lepper, M. R. (1974). How to turn play into work. *Psychology Today,* Sept., 49.

Greenfield, P. M. & Savage-Rumbaugh, E. S. (1993). Comparing communicative competence in child and chimp: The pragmatics of repetition. *Journal of Child Language, 20*(1), 1–26.

Greenwald, A. G., Spangenberg, E. R., Pratkanis, A. R., & Eskenazi, J. (1991). Double-blind tests of subliminal self-help audiotapes. *Psychological Science, 2*(2), 119–122.

Gregory, R. L. (1990). *Eye and brain: The psychology of seeing.* Princeton, NJ: Princeton University Press.

Grenier, G. & Byers, E. S. (1995). Rapid ejaculation: A review of conceptual, etiological, and treatment issues. *Archives of Sexual Behavior, 24*(4), 447–472.

Griffin, D. R. (1992). *Animal minds.* Chicago: University of Chicago Press.

Grimsley, D. L. & Karriker, M. W. (1996). Bilateral skin temperature, handedness, and the biofeedback control of skin temperature. *Journal of Behavioral Medicine, 19*(1), 87–94.

Grobstein, P., & Chow, K. L. (1975). Perceptive field development and individual experience. *Science, 190,* 352–358.

Grolnick, W. S., Cosgrove, T. J., & Bridges, L. J. (1996). Age-graded change in the initiative of positive affect. *Infant Behavior & Development, 19*(1), 153–157.

Gross, T. F. (1990) General test and state anxiety in real examinations: State is not test anxiety. *Educational Research Quarterly, 14*(3), 11–20.

Grossmann, K. E., & Volkmer, H. (1984). Fathers' presence during birth of their infants and paternal involvement. *International Journal of Behavioral Development, 7,* 157–165.

Groth-Marnat, G. & Schumaker, J. (1995). Psychologists in disease prevention and health promotion: A review of the cost effectiveness literature. *Psychology: A Journal of Human Behavior, 32*(1), 1–10.

Gruder, C. L., Mermelstein, R. J., Kirkendol, S. et al. (1993). Effects of social support and relapse prevention training as adjuncts to a televised smoking-cessation intervention. *Journal of Consulting & Clinical Psychology, 61*(1), 113–120.

Gruner, C. R. & Tighe, M. R. (1995). Semantic differential measurements of connotations of verbal terms and their doublespeak facsimiles in sentence contexts. *Psychological Reports, 77*(3,Pt 1) 778.

Guffey, D. G. (1992). Ritalin: What educators and parents should know. *Journal of Instructional Psychology, 19*(3), 167–169.

Gump, B. B. & Kulik, J. A. (1997). Stress, affiliation, and emotional contagion. *Journal of Personality & Social Psychology, 72*(2), 305–319.

Gustavson, C. R., & Garcia, J. (1974). Pulling a gag on the wily coyote. *Psychology Today,* May, 68–72.

Gutek, B. A. (1981). Experiences of sexual harassment: Results from a representative survey. Paper presented at symposium of the annual convention, American Psychological Association, August, 1981, Los Angeles, California.

Guterl, F. (1997). Celestial mechanics. *Discover,* May, 91–93.

Haas, L. J., Benedict, J. G., & Kobos, J. C. (1996). Psychotherapy by telephone: Risks and benefits for psychologists and consumers. *Professional Psychology: Research & Practice, 27*(2), 154–160.

Haber, R. N. (1969). Eidetic images; with biographical sketches. *Scientific American, 220*(12), 36–44.

Haber, R. N. (1970, May). How we remember what we see. *Scientific American,* 104–112.

Hagekull, B. (1995). Day care quality, family and child characteristics and socioemotional development. *Early Childhood Research Quarterly, 10*(4), 505–526.

Haier, R. J., Siegel, B. V., Nuechterlein, K. H., Hazlett et al. (1988). Cortical glucose metabolic rate correlates of abstract reasoning and attention studied with positron emission tomography. *Intelligence, 12,* 199–217.

Hales, D. (1980). *The complete book of sleep.* Reading, MA: Addison-Wesley.

Hall, B. A. (1996a). The psychiatric model: A critical analysis. *Advances in Nursing Science, 18*(3), 16–26.

Hall, C. (1966a). *The meaning of dreams.* New York: McGraw-Hill.

Hall, C. (1974a). What people dream about. In R. L. Woods & H. B. Greenhouse (Eds.), *The new world of dreams: An anthology.* New York: Macmillan.

Hall, C., Domhoff, G. W., Blick, K. A., & Weesner, K. E. (1982). The dreams of college men and women in 1950 and 1980: A comparison of dream contents and sex differences. *Sleep, 5*(2), 188–194.

Hall, E. T. (1966b). *The hidden dimension.* Garden City, NY: Doubleday.

Hall, E. T. (1974b). *Handbook for proxemic research.* Washington, DC: Social Anthropology and Visual Communication.

Hall, J. A. (1996b). Touch, status, and gender at professional meetings. *Journal of Nonverbal Behavior, 20*(1), 23–44.

Halonen, J. S. (1986). *Teaching critical thinking in psychology.* Milwaukee, WI: Alverno Productions.

Hamer D. H., Hu, S., Magnuson, V. L., Hu, N., & Pattatucci, A. M. (1993). A linkage between DNA markers on the X chromosome and male sexual orientation. *Science, 16:261*(5119), 291–292.

Hamill, J. A. (1995). Dexterity and sexuality: Is there a relationship? *Journal of Homosexuality, 28*(3–4), 375–396.

Hamilton, V. L. & Sanders, J. (1995). Crimes of obedience and conformity in the workplace. *Journal of Social Issues, 51*(3), 67–88.

Hammer, J. C., Fisher, J. D., Fitzgerald, P., & Fisher, W. A. (1996). When two heads aren't better than one: AIDS risk behavior in college-age couples. *Journal of Applied Social Psychology, 26*(5), 375–397.

Hancock, L. (1996). Mother's little helper. *Newsweek, 127*(12), 51–57.

Haney, C., Hurtado, A., & Vega, L. (1994). "Modern" death qualification: New data on its biasing effects. *Law & Human Behavior, 18*(6), 619–633.

Hannon, K. (1996). Upset? Try cybertherapy. *U.S. News and World Report,* May 13, 81–83.

Hansel, C. E. M. (1980). *ESP and parapsychology: A critical reevaluation.* Buffalo, NY: Prometheus.

Hansen, C. H. & Hansen, R. D. (1990). Rock music videos and antisocial behavior. *Basic and Applied Social Psychology, 11*(4), 357–369.

Harder, D. W., Strauss, J. S., Greenwald, D. F., Kokes, R. F. et al. (1989). Life events and psychopathology severity. *Journal of Clinical Psychology, 45*(2), 202–209.

Hardin, G. (1968). The tragedy of the commons. *Science, 162,* 1243–1248.

Hardin, G. (1985). *Filters against folly.* New York: Viking.

Hare, R. D. (1996). Psychopathy: A clinical construct whose time has come. *Criminal Justice and Behavior, 23,* 25–54.

Hare-Mustin, R. T. & Marecek, J. (1988). The meaning of difference. *American Psychologist, 43*(6), 455–464.

Harlow, H. F. (1966). Learning to love. *American Scientist, 54,* 244–272.

Harlow, H. F. (1967). The young monkeys. *Psychology Today, 1*(5), 40–74.

Harlow, H. F., & Harlow, M. K. (1962). Social deprivation in monkeys. *Scientific American, 207,* 136–146.

Harlow, H. F., & Zimmerman, R. R. (1958). The development of affectional responses in infant monkeys. *Proceedings of the American Philosophical Society, 102,* 501–509.

Harlow, J. M. (1868). Recovery from the passage of an iron bar through the head. *Massachusetts Medical Society, 2,* 327.

Harma, M., Laitinen, J., Partinen, M., & Suvanto, S. (1994). The effect of four-day round trip flights over 10 time zones on the circadian variation of salivary melatonin and cortisol in airline flight attendants. *Ergonomics, 37*(9), 1479–1489.

Harris, J. A., Rushton, J. P., Hampson, E., & Jackson, D. N. (1996). Salivary testosterone and self-report aggressive and pro-social personality characteristics in men and women. *Aggressive Behavior, 22*(5), 321–331.

Harris, J. R. & Liebert, R. M. (1991). *The child.* Englewood Cliffs, NJ: Prentice Hall.

Harris, L. J. (1993a). Do left-handers die sooner than right-handers? *Psychological Bulletin, 114*(2), 203–234.

Harris, L. J. (1993b). "Left-handedness and life span": Reply to Halpern and Coren. *Psychological Bulletin, 114*(2), 242–247.

Harrison, G. P. & Katz, D. L. (1987). Letter. *The Lancet, 1,* 863.

Harrison, L. F. & Williams, T. M. (1986). Television and cognitive development. In T. M. Williams (Ed.), *The impact of television: A natural experiment in three communities.* Orlando, FL: Academic.

Harrison, R. H. & Newirth, J. (1990). The effect of sensory deprivation and ego strength on a measure of autistic thinking. *Journal of Personality Assessment, 54*(3–4), 694–703.

Harsch, N. & Neisser, U. (1989). *Substantial and irreversible errors in flashbulb memories of the* Challenger *explosion.* Poster presented at the meeting of the Psychonomic Society, November, 1989, Atlanta, GA.

Hart, B. & Risley, T. R. (1992). American parenting of language-learning children: Persisting differences in family-child interactions observed in natural home environments. *Developmental Psychology, 28*(6), 1096–1105.

Hart, K, Ollendick, T. H. (1985). Prevalence of bulimia in working and university women. *American Journal of Psychiatry, 142*(7), 851–854.

Hartgrove-Freile, J. (1990). *Organizations, communication, and culture.* St. Paul, MN: West.

Harvey, C. A., Curson, D. A., Pantelis, C., & Taylor, J. (1996). Four behavioural syndromes of schizophrenia. *British Journal of Psychiatry, 168*(5), 562–570.

Hatfield, E. & Sprecher, S. (1995). Men's and women's preferences in marital partners in the United States, Russia, and Japan. *Journal of Cross-Cultural Psychology, 26*(6), 728–750.

Hatfield, E., Greenberger, D., Traupmann, J., & Lambert, P. (1982). Equity and sexual satisfaction in recently married couples. *Journal of Sex Research, 18,* 18–32.

Hathaway, S. R. & McKinley, J. C. (1989). *MMPI–2: Manual for administration and scoring.* Minneapolis, MN: University of Minnesota Press.

Hauri, P. & Linde, S. (1990). *No more sleepless nights.* New York: Wiley.

Havighurst, R. J. (1961). Successful aging. *Gerontologist, 1,* 8–13.

Havighurst, R. J. (1979). *Developmental tasks and education.* New York: David McKay.

Hawkins, D. B., & Gruber, J. J. (1982). Little league baseball and players' self-esteem. *Perceptual and Motor Skills, 55,* 1335–1340.

Hawkins, M. J., Gray, C., & Hawkins, W. E. (1995). Gender difference of reported safer sex behaviors within a random sample of college students. *Psychological Reports, 77*(3, Dec, Pt 1), 963–968.

Hawley, T. L. (1996). Children of addicted mothers: Effects of the "crack epidemic" on the caregiving environment and the development of preschoolers. *American Journal of Orthopsychiatry, 65*(3), 364–379.

Hayes, C. (1951). *The ape in our house.* New York: Harper & Row.

Hayne, H. & Rovee-Collier, C. (1995). The organization of reactivated memory in infancy. *Child Development, 66*(3), 893–906.

Haywood, H. C., Meyers, C. E., & Switzby, H. N. (1982). Mental retardation. *Annual Review of Psychology, 33,* 309–342.

Hearold, S. L. (1987). Meta-analysis of the effects of television on social behavior. In G. Comstock (Ed.), *Public communication and behavior: Volume 1.* NY: Academic.

Heath, L. & Gilbert, K. (1996). Mass media and fear of crime. *American Behavioral Scientist, 39*(4), 379–386.

Heath, L., Bresolin, L. B., & Rinaldi, R. C. (1989). Effects of media violence on children: A review of the literature. *Archives of General Psychiatry, 46*(4), 376–379.

Hebb, D. O. (1966). *A textbook of psychology.* Philadelphia: Saunders.

Hecht, M. L., Marston, P. J., & Larkey, L. K. (1994). Love ways and relationship quality in heterosexual relationships. *Journal of Social & Personal Relationships, 11*(1), 25–43.

Heckhausen, J. (1987). Balancing for weaknesses and challenging developmental potential. *Developmental Psychology, 23*(6), 762–770.

Heermann, J. A., Jones, L. C., & Wikoff, R. L. (1994). Measurement of parent behavior during interactions with their infants. *Infant Behavior & Development, 17*(3), 311–321.

Heiby, E. M. (1983). Assessment of frequency of self-reinforcement. *Journal of Personality & Social Psychology, 44,* 1304–1307.

Heimann, M. & Meltzoff, A. N. (1996). Deferred imitation in 9– and 14–month-old infants. *British Journal of Developmental Psychology, 14*(Mar), 55–64.

Heinrich, R. K., Corbine, J. L., & Thomas, K. R. (1990). Counseling Native Americans. *Journal of Counseling and Development, 69*(Nov.-Dec.), 128–133.

Heinrichs, R. W. (1993). Schizophrenia and the brain. *American Psychologist, 48*(3), 221–233.

Held, R. (1971). Plasticity in sensory-motor systems. In *Contemporary psychology.* San Francisco: Freeman.

Heller, J. (1961). *Catch 22.* New York: Simon & Schuster.

Hellige, J. B. (1990). Hemispheric asymmetry. *Annual Review of Psychology, 41,* 55–60.

Hellriegel, D., Slocum, J. W., & Woodman, R. W. (1995). *Organizational behavior.* St. Paul, MN: West.

Helms, J. E. (1992). Why is there no study of cultural equivalence in standardized ability testing? *American Psychologist, 47*(9), 1083–1101.

Helson, H. (1964). *Adaptation-level theory.* New York: Harper & Row.

Hembrooke, H. & Ceci, S. J. (1995). Traumatic memories: Do we need to invoke special mechanisms? *Consciousness & Cognition: An International Journal, 4*(1), 75–82.

Henderson, N. D. (1982). Human behavior genetics. *Annual Review of Psychology, 33,* 403–440.

Hendin, H. (1995). Assisted suicide, euthanasia, and suicide prevention. *Suicide & Life-Threatening Behavior, 25*(1), 193–204.

Hendrick, S. S. & Hendrick, C. (1993). Lovers as friends. *Journal of Social & Personal Relationships, 10*(3), 459–466.

Hennevin, E., Hars, B., Maho, C., & Bloch, V. (1995). Processing of learned information in paradoxical sleep: Relevance for memory. *Behavioural Brain Research, 69*(1–2), 125–135.

Henningfield, J. E. & Heishman, S. J. (1995). The addictive role of nicotine in tobacco use. *Psychopharmacology, 117*(1), 11–13.

Hepburn, D. A., Deary, I. J., & MacLeod, K. M. (1996). Adrenaline and psychometric mood factors: A controlled case study of two patients with bilateral adrenalectomy. *EDRA: Environmental Design Research Association, 20*(4), 451–455.

Heppenheimer, T. A. (1990). Shedding light on inner workings of the brain. *Los Angeles Times,* Feb. 26, B3.

Hepper, P. G. (1990). Origins of fetal handedness.

Nature, 347(6292), 431.

Herbert. T. B. & Cohen, S. (1993). Depression and immunity. *Psychological Bulletin, 113*(3), 472–486.

Hernstein, R. & Murray, C. (1994). *The Bell Curve.* New York: Free Press.

Heron, W. (1957). The pathology of boredom. *Scientific American, 196*, 52–56.

Herrnstein, R. J. (1979). Acquisition, generalization, and discrimination reversal of a natural concept. *Journal of Experimental Psychology: Animal Behavior Processes, 5*, 116–129.

Hershey, J. M., Kopplin, D. A., & Cornell, J. E. (1991). Doctors of Psychology: Their career experiences and attitudes toward degree and training. *Professional Psychology: Research & Practice, 22*(5), 351–356.

Herzog, H. A. (1990). Discussing animal rights and animal research in the classroom. *Teaching of Psychology, 17*(2), 90–94.

Hess, E. H. (1959). Imprinting. *Science, 130*, 133–141.

Hess, E. H. (1975a). *The tell-tale eye: How your eyes reveal hidden thoughts and emotions.* New York: Van Nostrand Reinhold.

Hess, E. H. (1975b). The role of pupil size in communication. *Scientific American*, Nov., 110–119.

Heussenstamm, F. K. (1971). Bumper stickers and the cops. *Transaction, 8*, 32–33.

Heyser, C. J., Spear, N. E., & Spear, L. P. (1992). Effects of prenatal exposure to cocaine on conditional discrimination learning in adult rats. *Behavioral Neuroscience, 106*(5), 837–845.

Higbee, K. L., Clawson, C., DeLano, L., & Campbell, S. (1990). Using the link mnemonic to remember errands. *Psychological Record, 40*(3), 429–436.

Hilgard, E. R. (1968). *The experience of hypnosis.* New York: Harcourt Brace Jovanovich.

Hilgard, E. R. (1977). *Divided consciousness.* New York: Wiley.

Hilgard, E. R. (1978). Hypnosis and pain. In R. A. Sternbach (Ed.), *The psychology of pain.* New York: Raven.

Hill, L. (1990). Effort and reward in college: A replication of some puzzling findings. *Journal of Social Behavior & Personality, 5*(4), 151–161.

Hill, P. (1993). Recent advances in selected aspects of adolescent development. *Journal of Child Psychology & Psychiatry & Allied Disciplines, 34*(1), 69–99.

Hilts, P. J. (1995). *Memory's ghost.* New York: Simon & Schuster.

Hine, D. W. & Gifford, R. (1996). Individual restraint and group efficiency in commons dilemmas. *Journal of Applied Social Psychology, 26*(11), 993–1009.

Hinshaw, K. E. (1991). The effects of mental practice on motor skill performance. *Imagination, Cognition & Personality, 11*(1), 3–35.

Hirshberg, L. M. & Svejda, M. (1990). When infants look to their parents. *Child Development, 61*(4), 1175–1186.

Hirt, M. & Pithers, W. (1991). Selective attention and levels of coding in schizophrenia. *British Journal of Clinical Psychology, 30*(2), 139–149.

Hite, S. (1976). *The Hite report.* New York: Macmillan.

Hodapp, R. M. (1994). Mental retardation. *Encyclopedia of human behavior*, Vol. 3, 175–185.

Hodgson, R., & Miller, P. (1982). *Selfwatching.* New York: Facts on File.

Hoffman, M. L. (1977). Moral internalization: Current theory and research. In L. Berkowitz (Ed.), *Advances in experimental and social psychology*, Vol. 10. New York: Academic Press.

Hogan, R., Hogan, J., & Roberts, B. W. (1996). Personality measurement and employment decisions. *American Psychologist, 51*(5), 469–477.

Hogben, D. & Lawson, M. J. (1992). Superiority of the keyword method for backward recall in vocabulary acquisition. *Psychological Reports, 71*(3, Pt 1),

880–882.

Holden, C. (1980). Twins reunited. *Science 80*, Nov., 55–59.

Holden, G. W., Coleman, S. M., & Schmidt, K. L. (1995). Why 3-year-old children get spanked. *Merrill-Palmer Quarterly, 41*(4), 431–452.

Holland, J. (1985). *Making vocational choices: A theory of careers.* Englewood Cliffs, NJ: Prentice-Hall.

Holland, M. K. (1975, 1985). *Using psychology: Principles of behavior and your life.* Boston: Little, Brown.

Hollon, S. D., DeRubeis, R. J., Evans, M. D. et al. (1992). Cognitive therapy and pharmacology for depression. *Archives of General Psychiatry, 49*(10), 774–781.

Holmes, D. S., Curtright, C. A., McCaul, K. D., & Thissen, D. (1980). Biorhythms: Their utility for predicting postoperative recuperative time, death, and athletic performance. *Journal of Applied Psychology, 65*, 233–236.

Holmes, D. S. (1984). Meditation and somatic arousal reduction: A review of the experimental evidence. *American Psychologist, 39*(1), 1–10.

Holmes, D. S., Solomon, S., Cappo, B. M., & Greenberg, J. L. (1983). Effects of transcendental meditation versus resting on physiological and subjective arousal. *Journal of Personality & Social Psychology, 44*, 1245–1252.

Holmes, T., & Masuda, M. (1972). Psychosomatic syndrome. *Psychology Today*, April, 71.

Holroyd, J. (1996). Hypnosis treatment of clinical pain. *International Journal of Clinical & Experimental Hypnosis, 44*(1), 33–51.

Holtzman, W. (1997). Community psychology and full-service schools in different cultures. *American Psychologist, 52*(4), 381–389.

Holtzworth-Munroe, A. & Hutchinson, G. (1993). Attributing negative intent to wife behavior. *Journal of Abnormal Psychology, 102*(2), 206–211.

Honorton, C. & Bem, D. J. (1994). Does psi exist? *Psychological Bulletin, 115*(1), 4–18.

Honzik, M. P. (1984). Life-span development. *Annual Review of Psychology, 35*, 309–331.

Hopson, J. L. (1986). The unraveling of insomnia. *Psychology Today*, June, 43–49.

Horgan, J. (1995). Get smart, take a test: A long-term rise in IQ scores baffles intelligence experts. *Scientific American*, Nov., 2–14.

Horn, J. C. (1987). Bigger pay for better work. *Psychology Today*, July, 54–57.

Horn, J. C. & Meer, J. (1987). The vintage years. *Psychology Today*, May, 76–93ff.

Horn, J. M., Loehlin, J. C., & Willerman, L. (1979). Intellectual resemblance among adoptive and biological relatives: The Texas adoption project. *Behavior Genetics, 9*, 177–207.

Horn, J. M., Plomin, R., & Rosenman, R. (1976). Heritability of personality traits in adult male twins. *Behavior Genetics, 6*, 17–30.

Horne, J. A. & Reyner, L. A. (1996). Counteracting driver sleepiness: Effects of napping, caffeine, and placebo. *Psychophysiology, 33*(3), 306–309.

Horne, J. A., & Staff, L. H. E. (1983). Exercise and sleep: Body-heating effects. *Sleep, 6*, 36–46.

Horvath, A. 0. & Goheen, M. D. (1990). Factors mediating the success of defiance- and compliance-based interventions. *Journal of Counseling Psychology, 37*(4), 363–371.

Horwitz, W. A., Kestenbaum, C., Person, E., & Jarvik, L. (1965). Identical twin "Idiot savants" calendar calculators. *The American Journal of Psychiatry, 121*, 1075–1079.

Hosch, H. M., & Cooper, D. S. (1982). Victimization as a determinant of eyewitness accuracy. *Journal of Applied Psychology, 67*, 649–652.

Howard, A., Pion, G. M., Gottfredson, G. D., Flattau, P. E. et al. (1986a). The changing face of American

psychology. *American Psychologist, 41*, 1311–1327.

Howard, J. L. & Ferris, G. R. (1996). The employment interview context. *Journal of Applied Social Psychology, 26*(2), 112–136.

Howard, K. I., Kopta, S. M., Krause, M. S., & Orlinsky, D. E. (1986b). The dose-effect relationship in psychotherapy. *American Psychologist, 41*, 159–164.

Howell, W. C., (1993). Engineering psychology in a changing world. In L. W. Porter and M. R. Rosenzweig (Eds.), *Annual Review of Psychology, 44*, 231–263.

Howes, C. & Smith, E. W. (1995). Relations among child care quality, teacher behavior, children's play activities, emotional security, and cognitive activity in child care. *Early Childhood Research Quarterly, 10*(4), 381–404.

Howitt, D., Craven, G., Iveson, C., Kremer, J., McCabe, J., & Rolph, T. (1977). The misdirected letter. *British Journal of Social and Clinical Psychology, 16*, 285–286.

Hsia, Y., & Graham, C. H. (1965). Color blindness. In C. H. Graham (Ed.), *Vision and visual perception.* New York: Wiley.

Hsiung, P. (1990). Expansion of field of view via wide angle imaging. Unpublished document.

Hu, S., Pattatucci, A. M., Patterson, C., Li, L. et al. (1995). Linkage between sexual orientation and chromosome Xq28 in males but not in females. *Nature Genetics 11*(3), 248–256.

Hubel, D. H. (1979a). The brain. *Scientific American, 241*(Sept.), 45–53.

Hubel, D. H. (1979b). The visual cortex of normal and deprived monkeys. *American Scientist, 67*, 532–543.

Hubel, D. H., & Wiesel, T. N. (1979). Brain mechanisms of vision. *Scientific American, 241*, 150–162.

Huesmann, L. R. (1986). Psychological processes promoting the relation between exposure to media violence and aggressive behavior by the viewer. *Journal of Social Issues, 42*(3), 125–139.

Huesmann, L. R., Eron, L., Klein, L., Brice, P., & Fischer, P. (1983). Mitigating the imitation of aggressive behaviors by changing children's attitudes about media violence. *Journal of Personality & Social Psychology, 44*, 899–910.

Hugdahl, K., & Karker, A. C. (1981). Biological vs. experimental factors in phobic conditioning. *Behavior Research and Therapy, 19*, 109–115.

Hughes, J. N. & Hasbrouck, J. E. (1996). Television violence: Implications for violence prevention. *School Psychology Review, 25*(2), 134–151.

Hughes, J. R., Higgins, S. T., Bickel, W. K., Hunt, W. K. et al. (1991). Caffeine self-administration, withdrawal, and adverse effects among coffee drinkers. *Archives of General Psychiatry, 48*(7), 611–617.

Hunt E. (1995). The role of intelligence in modern society. *American Scientist, 83*(July-August), 356–368.

Hurd, P., Johnson, C. A., Pechacek, T., Bast, L. P., Jacobs, D. R., & Luepker, R. V. (1980). Prevention of smoking in seventh grade students. *Journal of Behavioral Medicine, 3*, 15–28.

Hurlbert, D. F. & Apt, C. (1995). The coital alignment technique and directed masturbation: A comparative study on female orgasm. *Journal of Sex & Marital Therapy, 21*(1), 21–29.

Hurley, D. (1989). The search for cocaine's methadone. *Psychology Today*, July/Aug., 59–60.

Hutchison, M. (1984). *The book of floating.* New York: Quill.

Hyde, J. S. (1996). *Understanding human sexuality.* New York: McGraw-Hill.

Hyde, J. S. & Linn, M. C. (1988). Gender differences in verbal ability: A meta-analysis. *Psychological*

Bulletin, 104(1), 53–69.

Hyde, J. S. & Plant, E. S. (1995). Magnitude of psychological gender differences. *American Psychologist, 50*(3), 159–161.

Hyde, J. S., Klein, M. H., Essex, M. J., & Clark, R. (1995). Maternity leave and women's mental health. *Psychology of Women Quarterly, 19*(2), 257–285.

Hyland, M. E. (1989). There is no motive to avoid success: The compromise explanation for success-avoiding behavior. *Journal of Personality, 57*(3), 665–693.

Hyman, R. (1989). *The elusive quarry: A scientific appraisal of psychical research.* Buffalo, NY: Prometheus.

Hyman, R. (1996a). Evaluation of the military's twenty-year program on psychic spying. *Skeptical Inquirer, 20*(2), 21–23.

Hyman, R. (1996b). The evidence for psychic functioning: Claims vs. reality. *Skeptical Inquirer, 20*(2), 24–26.

Hynd, G. W. & Semrud-Clikeman, M. (1989). Dyslexia and brain morphology. *Psychological Bulletin, 106*(3), 447–482.

Hyson, M. G., Hirsh-Pasek, K., Rescorla, L., Cone, J. et al. (1991). Ingredients of parental "pressure" in early childhood. *Journal of Applied Developmental Psychology, 12*(3), 347–365.

Iavecchia, J. H., Iavecchia, H. P., & Roscoe, S. N. (1983). The moon illusion revisited. *Aviation, Space, and Environmental Medicine, 54,* 39–46.

Ickes, W. (1993). Traditional gender roles: Do they make, then break, our relationships? *Journal of Social Issues, 49*(3), 71–86.

Infante-Rivard, C., Fernandez, A., Gauthier, R., David, M., & Rivard, G. E. (1993). Fetal loss associated with caffeine intake before and during pregnancy. *Journal of the American Medical Association, 270*(24), 2940–2943.

Institute of Medicine. (1990). *Broadening the base of treatment for alcohol problems.* Washington, D.C.: National Academy Press.

Isaac, R. J. & Armat, V. C. (1990). *Madness in the streets: How psychiatry & the law abandoned the mentally ill.* New York: Free Press.

Isaak, M. I. & Just, A. (1995). Constraints on thinking in insight and invention. In R. J. Sternberg & J. E. Davidson (Eds.) *The nature of insight.* Cambridge, MA: MIT Press.

Isabella, R. A. (1993). Origins of attachment. *Child Development, 64*(2), 605–621.

Isabella, R. A. & Belsky, J. (1991). Interactional synchrony and the origins of infant-mother attachment. *Child Development, 62,* 373–384.

Isenberg, P. L., & Schatzberg, A. F. (1976). Psychoanalytic contribution to a theory of depression. In J. O. Cole, A. F. Schatzberg, & S. H. Frazier (Eds.), *Depression: Biology, psychodynamics, and treatment.* New York: Plenum.

Isser, N. (1991). Why cultic groups develop and flourish. *Cultic Studies Journal, 8*(2), 104–121.

Ito, T. A., Miller, N., & Pollock, V. E. (1996). Alcohol and aggression. *Psychological Bulletin, 120*(1), 60–82.

Ivey, A. E. & Galvin, M. (1984). Microcounseling: A metamodel for counseling, therapy, business, and medical interviews. In D. Larson (Ed.), *Teaching psychological skills.* Monterey, CA: Brooks/Cole.

Izard, C. E. (1977). *Human emotions.* New York: Plenum.

Izard, C. E. (1990). Facial expressions and the regulation of emotions. *Journal of Personality & Social Psychology, 58*(3), 487–498.

Izard, C. E., Fantauzzo, C. A., Castle, J. M., Haynes, O. M., Rayias, M. F., & Putnam, P. H. (1995). The ontogeny and significance of infants' facial expressions in the first 9 months of life. *Developmental Psychology, 31*(6), 997–1013.

Jackson, B. (1973). Our prisons are criminal. *New York Times Magazine,* Sept. 22, 54, 57.

Jackson, R. J. (1994). A multimodal method for assessing and treating airsickness. *International Journal of Aviation Psychology, 4*(1), 85–96.

Jackson, S. E. (1983). Participation in decision making as a strategy for reducing job-related strain. *Journal of Applied Psychology, 68,* 3–19.

Jacobs, G. D., Benson, H., & Friedman, R. (1993). Home-based central nervous system assessment of multi-factor behavioral intervention for chronic sleep-onset insomnia. *Behavior Therapy, 24*(1), 159–174.

Jacobsen, P. B., Bovbjerg, D. H., Schwartz, M. D. et al., (1993). Formation of food aversions in cancer patients receiving repeated infusions of chemotherapy. *Behavior Research & Therapy, 31*(8), 739–748.

Jahn, R. G. (1982). The persistent paradox of psychic phenomena. *Proceedings of the IEEE, 70*(2), 136–166.

Janis, I. L. (1989). *Crucial decisions.* New York: Free Press.

Janis, I. L., & Mann, L. (1965). Effectiveness of emotional role-playing in modifying smoking habits and attitudes. *Journal of Experimental Research in Personality, 1,* 84–90.

Janis, I. L., & Wheeler, D. (1978). Thinking clearly about career choices. *Psychology Today, 11,* 66–78.

Janofsky, J. S., Dunn, M. H., Roskes, E. J., & Briskin, J. K. (1996). Insanity defense pleas in Baltimore city: An analysis of outcome. *American Journal of Psychiatry, 153*(11), 1464–1468.

Janos, P. M. & Robinson, N. M. (1985). Psychosocial development in intellectually gifted children. In F. D. Horowitz & M. O'Brien (Eds.), *The gifted and talented: Developmental perspectives.* Washington, DC: American Psychological Association.

Janowiak, J. J. & Hackman, R. (1994). Meditation and college students' self-actualization and rated stress. *Psychological Reports, 75*(2), 1007–1010.

Janus, S. S. & Janus, C. L. (1993). *The Janus report.* New York: Wiley.

Jarvik, E. M. (1964). Ciba found. In H. Steinberg et al., *Symposium of animal pharmacology drug action.*

Jarvik, M. E. (1995). "The scientific case that nicotine is addictive": Comment. *Psychopharmacology, 117*(1), 18–20.

Jellinik, E. M. (1960). *The disease concept of alcoholism.* New Haven: Hill House.

Jenkins, J. G., & Dallenbach, K. M. (1924). Oblivescence during sleep and waking. *American Journal of Psychology, 35,* 605–612.

Jensen, J. P., Bergin, A. E., & Greaves, D. W. (1990). The meaning of eclecticism: New survey and analysis of components. *Professional Psychology: Research & Practice, 21*(2), 124–130.

Jensen, M. D., Benson, R. C., & Bobak, I. M. (1981). *Maternity care. The nurse and the family.* St. Louis: Mosby.

Jerabek, I. & Standing, L. (1992). Imagined test situations produce contextual memory enhancement. *Perceptual & Motor Skills, 75*(2), 400.

Jewell, L. N. (1989). *Psychology and effective behavior.* St. Paul, MN: West.

Jewell, L. N. (1990). *Contemporary industrial/organizational psychology.* St. Paul, MN: West.

Johnson, B. T. (1991). Insights about attitudes: Meta-analytic perspectives. *Personality & Social Psychology Bulletin, 17*(3), 289–299.

Johnson, J. S. & Newport, E. L. (1989). Critical period effects in second language learning: The influence of maturational state on the acquisition of English as a second language. *Cognitive Psychology, 21*(1), 60–99.

Johnson, M. K. & Hasher, L. (1987). Human learning and memory. *Annual Review of Psychology, 38,* 631–668.

Johnson, S. M., & White, G. (1971). Self-observation as an agent of behavioral change. *Behavior Therapy, 2,* 488–497.

Johnson, S. P. & Nanez, J. E. (1995). Young infants' perception of object unity in two-dimensional displays. *Infant Behavior & Development, 18*(2), 133–143.

Johnson, W. G., Tsoh, J. Y., & Varnado, P. J. (1996). Eating disorders: Efficacy of pharmacological and psychological interventions. *Clinical Psychology Review, 16*(6), 457–478.

Johnston, W. A. & Dark, V. J. (1986). Selective attention. *Annual Review of Psychology, 37,* 43–75.

Jones, E. E., & Nisbett, R. E. (1971). The actor and observer: Divergent perceptions of the causes of behavior. In E. E. Jones, D. E. Kanouse, H. H. Kelley, R. E. Nisbett, S. Valins, & B. Weiner (Eds.), *Attribution: Perceiving the causes of behavior.* Morristown, NJ: General Learning Press.

Jones, L. & Petruzzi, D. C. (1995). Test anxiety: A review of theory and current treatment. *Journal of College Student Psychotherapy, 10*(1), 3–15.

Jones, L. V. & Appelbaum, M. L. (1989). Psychometric methods. *Annual Review of Psychology, 40,* 23–43.

Jones, R. T. Corbin, S. K., Sheehy, L., & Bruce, S. (1995). Substance refusal: More than "just say no." *Journal of Child & Adolescent Substance Abuse, 4*(2) 1–26.

Jones, S. S., Collins, K., & Hong, H. W. (1991). An audience effect on smile production in 10-month-old infants. *Psychological Science, 2,* 45–49.

Jourard, S. M. (1963). *Personal adjustment.* New York: Macmillan.

Jourard, S. M. (1966). An exploratory study of body-accessibility. *British Journal of Social and Clinical Psychology, 5,* 221–231.

Jourard, S. M. (1974). *Healthy personality.* New York: Macmillan.

Joy, L. A., Kimball, M. M., & Zabrack, M. L. (1986). Television and aggressive behavior. In T. M. Williams (Ed.), *The impact of television: A natural experiment involving three towns.* New York: Academic.

Julesz, B. (1971). *Foundations of cyclopean perception.* Chicago: University of Chicago Press.

Julesz, B. (1975). Experiments in the visual perception of texture. *Scientific American, 232*(April), 34–43.

Julien, R. M. (1995). *A primer of drug action.* San Francisco: Freeman.

Jurma, W. E. & Powell, M. L. (1994). Perceived gender roles of managers and effective conflict management. *Psychological Reports, 74*(1), 104–106.

Jussim, L. & Eccles, J. S. (1992). Teacher expectations. *Journal of Personality & Social Psychology, 63*(6), 947–961.

Juster, H. R. Heimberg, R. G., Frost, R. O., & Holt, C. S. (1996). Social phobia and perfectionism. *Personality & Individual Differences, 21*(3), 403–410.

Kagan, J. (1971). *Change and continuity in infancy.* New York: Wiley.

Kagan, J. (1989). Temperamental contributions to social behavior. *American Psychologist, 44*(4), 668–674.

Kagan, J. (1991). The theoretical utility of constructs for self. *Developmental Review, 11*(3), 244–250.

Kahneman, D., & Tversky, A. (1972). Subjective probability: A judgment of representativeness. *Cognitive Psychology, 3,* 430–454.

Kahneman, D., & Tversky, A. (1973). On the psychology of prediction. *Psychological Review, 80,* 237–251.

Kahneman, D., Slovic, P., & Tversky, A. (1982).

Judgment under uncertainty: Heuristics and biases. Cambridge: Cambridge University Press.

Kaitz, M., Zvi, H., Levy, M., Berger, A. et al. (1995). The uniqueness of mother-own-infant interactions. *Infant Behavior & Development, 18*(2), 247–252.

Kakigi, R., Matsuda, Y., & Kuroda, Y. (1993). Effects of movement-related cortical activities on pain-related somatosensory evoked potentials. *Acta Neurologica Scandinavica, 88*(5), 376–380.

Kaluger, G., & Kaluger, M. F. (1984). *Human development.* St. Louis: Times Mirror/Mosby.

Kamin, L. J. (1981). *The intelligence controversy.* New York: Wiley.

Kamin, L. J. (1985). Genes and behavior: The missing link. *Psychology Today,* Oct., 76–78.

Kamiya, J. (1968). Conscious control of brain waves. *Psychology Today, 1,* 57–66.

Kamphaus, R. W. (1993). *Clinical assessment of children's intelligence.* Needham Heights, MA: Allyn and Bacon.

Kandel, E. R. (1976). *Cellular basis of behavior: An introduction to behavioral neurobiology.* San Francisco: Freeman.

Kane, J. M. (1996). Drug therapy: Schizophrenia. *New England Journal of Medicine, 334*(1), 34–41.

Kaplan, H. S. (1974). *The new sex therapy.* New York: Brunner/Mazel.

Kaplan, M. (1983). The issue of sex bias in DSM-III: Comments on the articles by Spitzer, Williams, and Kass. *American Psychologist, 38,* 802–803.

Kaplan, P. S., & Stein, J. (1984). *Psychology of adjustment.* Belmont, CA: Wadsworth.

Kaplan, P. S., Goldstein, M. H., Huckeby, E. R., & Cooper, R. P. (1995). Habituation, sensitization, and infants' responses to motherese speech. *Developmental Psychobiology, 28*(1), 45–57.

Kapleau, P. (1966). *The three pillars of Zen.* New York: Harper & Row.

Karni, A., Tanne, D., Rubenstien, B. S., Askenasy, J. J. M., et al. (1994). Dependence on REM sleep of overnight improvement of a perceptual skill. *Science, 265*(5172), 679–682.

Kasamatsu, A., & Hirai, T. (1966). An electroencephalographic study of Zen meditation (Zazen). *Folia Psychiatria et Neurologia Japonica, 20,* 315–336. Reprinted in Tart (1975), *Altered states of consciousness.*

Kasper, M. E., Rogers, R., & Adams, P. A. (1996). Dangerousness and command hallucinations. *Bulletin of the American Academy of Psychiatry & the Law, 24*(2), 219–224.

Kasser, T. & Ryan, R. M. (1996). Further examining the American dream: Differential correlates of intrinsic and extrinsic goals. *Personality & Social Psychology Bulletin, 22*(3), 280–287.

Kassin, S. M., Ellsworth, P. C., & Smith, V. L. (1989). The "general acceptance" of psychological research on eyewitness testimony: A survey of the experts. *American Psychologist, 44,* 1089–1098.

Kastenbaum, R., & Aisenberg R. (1972). *The psychology of death.* New York: Springer.

Katerndahl, D. A. (1996). Panic attacks and panic disorder. *Journal of Family Practice, 43*(3), 275–282.

Katz, M. R. (1993). *Computer-assisted career decision making.* Educational Testing Service.

Kaufman, L. & Rock, I. (1989). The moon illusion thirty years later. In Hershenson, M. (Ed.), *The moon illusion.* Hillsdale, NJ: Erlbaum.

Kazdin, A. E. (1975). *Behavior modification in applied settings.* Homewood, IL: Dorsey Press.

Kearney, M. (1984). A comparison of motivation to avoid success in males and females. *Journal of Clinical Psychology, 40,* 1005–1007.

Keefe, F. J. (1982). Behavioral assessment and treatment of chronic pain: Current status and future directions. *Journal of Consulting and Clinical Psychology, 50,* 896–911.

Kellehear, A. (1993). Culture, biology, and the near-death experience. *Journal of Nervous & Mental Disease, 181*(3), 148–156.

Keller, M. C. & Young, R. K. (1996). Mate assortment in dating and married couples. *Personality & Individual Differences, 21*(2), 217–221.

Kellermann, A. L., Rivara, F. P., Rushforth, N. B., Banton, J. G. et al. (1993). Gun ownership as a risk factor for homicide in the home. *New England Journal of Medicine, 329*(15), 1084–1091.

Kelley, H. H. (1950). The warm-cold variable in first impressions of persons. *Journal of Personality, 18,* 431–439.

Kelley, H. H. (1967). Attribution in social psychology. *Nebraska Symposium on Motivation, 15,* 192–238.

Kelly, A. D. & Kanas, N. (1993). Communication between space crews and ground personnel. *Aviation, Space, & Environmental Medicine, 64*(9, Sect. 1), 795–800.

Kelly, G. F. (1996). Using meditative techniques in psychotherapy. *Journal of Humanistic Psychology, 36*(3), 49–66.

Kelly, I. W. & Saklofske, D. H. (1994). Psychology and pseudoscience. *Encyclopedia of human behavior, 3,* 611–618.

Kelly, T. H., Foltin, R. W., Emurian, C. S., & Fischman, M. W. (1990). Multidimensional behavioral effects of marijuana. *Progress in Neuropsychopharmacology & Biological Psychiatry, 14*(6), 885–902.

Kelman, H. C. & Hamilton, V. L. (1989). *Crimes of obedience.* New Haven, CT: Yale University Press.

Kemper, E. (1991). *Antidepressants update.* United States Food and Drug Administration, Paper T91-64.

Kempton, W., Darley, J. M., & Stern, P. C. (1992). Psychological research for the new energy problems. *American Psychologist, 47*(10), 1213–1232.

Kenen, R. H. & Smith, A. C. (1995). Genetic counseling for the next 25 years. *Journal of Genetic Counseling, 4*(2), 115–124.

Kennedy, J. M. (1983). What can we learn about pictures from the blind? *American Scientist, 71,* 19–26.

Kenrick, D. T. & MacFarlane, S. W. (1986). Ambient temperature and horn honking: A field study of the heat/aggression relationship. *Environment and Behavior, 18*(2), 1986, 179–191.

Kessen, W. & Cahan, E. D. (1986). A century of psychology: From subject to object to agent. *American Scientist, 74,* 640–649.

Kessler, R. C., Sonnega, A., & Nelson, C. B. (1995). Posttraumatic stress disorder in the National Comorbidity Survey. *Archives of General Psychiatry, 52*(12), 1048.

Kety, S. S. (1979, Sept.). Disorders of the human brain. *Scientific American, 241,* 202–214.

Keys, A., Brozek, J., Henschel, A., Mickelson, O., & Taylor, H. L. (1950). *The biology of human starvation.* Minneapolis: University of Minnesota Press.

Kiecolt-Glaser, J. K. & Glaser, R. (1992). Psychoneuroimmunology: Can psychological interventions modulate immunity? *Journal of Consulting & Clinical Psychology, 60*(4), 569–575.

Kiewra, K. A., DuBois, N. F., Christian, D., McShane, A. et al. (1991). Note-taking functions and techniques. *Journal of Educational Psychology, 83*(2), 240–245.

Kihlstrom, J. F. (1985). Hypnosis. *Annual Review of Psychology 36,* 385–418.

Kim, A., Martin, D., & Martin, M. (1989). Effects of personality on marital satisfaction. *Family Therapy, 16*(3), 243–248.

Kim, J., Singer, R. N., & Radlo, S. J. (1996). Degree of cognitive demands in psychomotor tasks and the effects of the five-step strategy on achievement. *Human Performance, 9*(2), 155–169.

Kimball, M. M. (1986). Television and sex-role attitudes. In T. M. Williams (Ed.), *The impact of television: A natural experiment in three communities.* Orlando, FL: Academic.

Kimble, D. P. (1990). Functional effects of neural grafting in the mammalian central nervous system. *Psychological Bulletin, 108*(3), 462–479.

Kimble, G. A. (1989). Psychology from the standpoint of a generalist. *American Psychologist, 44*(3), 491–499.

Kimmel, D. C. (1988). Ageism, psychology, and public policy. *American Psychologist, 43*(3), 175–178.

Kimmel, D. C. (1990). *Adulthood and aging.* New York: Wiley & Sons.

King, A. (1992). Comparison of self-questioning, summarizing, and notetaking-review as strategies for learning from lectures. *American Educational Research Journal, 29*(2), 303–323.

King, A. (1995). Cognitive strategies for learning from direct teaching. In E. Wood, V. Woloshyn, and T. Willoughby (Eds.), *Cognitive strategy instruction for middle and high schools,* Brookline, Cambridge, MA.

King, H. E. (1961). Psychological effects of excitation in the limbic system. In D. E. Sheer (Ed.), *Electrical stimulation of the brain.* Austin: University of Texas Press.

Kinsey, A., Pomeroy, W., & Martin, C. (1948). *Sexual behavior in the human male.* Philadelphia: Saunders.

Kinsey, A., Pomeroy, W., & Martin, C. (1953). *Sexual behavior in the human female.* Philadelphia: Saunders.

Kipnis, D. (1987). Psychology and behavioral technology. *American Psychologist, 42,* 30–36.

Kipper, D. A. (1992). The effect of two kinds of role playing on self-evaluation of improved assertiveness. *Journal of Clinical Psychology, 48*(2), 246–250.

Kirk, Mary Ann. (1995). Menopause: A developmental stage, not a deficiency disease. *Psychotherapy, 32*(2), 233–241.

Kirsch, I. & Lynn, S. J. (1995). The altered state of hypnosis. *American Psychologist, 50*(10), 846–858.

Kirsch, I., Montgomery, G., & Sapirstein, G. (1995). Hypnosis as an adjunct to cognitive behavioral psychotherapy: A meta-analysis. *Journal of Consulting and Clinical Psychology, 63,* 214–220.

Kitcher, P. (1985). *Vaulting ambition: Sociobiology and the quest for human nature.* Cambridge, MA: MIT Press.

Klaus, M. H., & Kennell, J. H. (1982). *Parent-infant bonding.* St. Louis: Mosby.

Klein, G., Wolf, S., Militello, L., & Zsambok, C. (1995). Characteristics of skilled option generation in chess. *Organizational Behavior & Human Decision Processes, 62*(1), 63–69.

Kleinke, C. L. (1978). *Self-perception: The psychology of personal awareness.* San Francisco: Freeman.

Kleinke, C. L. (1986). *Meeting and understanding people.* New York: Freeman.

Kleinknecht, R. A. (1986). *The anxious self: Diagnosis and treatment of fears and phobias.* New York: Human Sciences Press.

Kleinplatz, P. J. (1996). The erotic encounter. *Journal of Humanistic Psychology, 36*(3), 105–123.

Klinger, E. (1990). *Daydreaming.* Los Angeles, CA: J. P. Tarcher.

Klonoff-Cohen, H. S., Edelstein, S. L., Lefkowitz, E. S., Srinivasan, I. P., et al. (1995). The effect of passive smoking and tobacco exposure through breast milk on sudden infant death syndrome. *Journal of the American Medical Association, 273*(10), 795–798.

Knesper, D. J., Belcher, B. E., & Cross, J. G. (1989). A market analysis comparing the practices of psychiatrists and psychologists. *Archives of General*

Psychiatry, 46(4), 305–314.

Knowles, J. (1995). HIV/STI update. *Insider*, Feb., 2.

Knox, D. (1984). *Human sexuality*. St. Paul, MN: West.

Knutson, J. (1995). Psychological characteristics of maltreated children. *Annual Review of Psychology, 46*, 401–431.

Koenig, S. M. (1996). Central sleep apnea. *Virginia Medical Quarterly, 123*(4), 247–250.

Kohlberg, L. (1969). The cognitive-developmental approach to socialization. In A. Goslin (Ed.), *Handbook of socialization theory and research*. Chicago: Rand McNally.

Kohlberg, L. (1981a). *Essays on moral development. Vol. I. The philosophy of moral development*. San Francisco: Harper.

Kohlberg, L. (1981b). *The meaning and measurement of moral development*. Worcester, MA: Clark University Press.

Kohler, I. (1962). Experiments with goggles. *Scientific American*, Offprint No. 465, 62–72.

Kohler, W. (1925). *The mentality of apes*. New York: Harcourt Brace Jovanovich.

Kohn, A. (1987). Art for art's sake. *Psychology Today*, Sept., 52–57.

Kohn, A. (1988). Shock therapy makes a comeback. *Los Angeles Times*, March 21, Part II, 5.

Kolb, B. (1989). Brain development, plasticity, and behavior. *American Psychologist, 44*(9), 1203–1212.

Kolbe, L. J., Collins, J., & Cortese, P. (1997). Building the capacity of schools to improve the health of the nation. *American Psychologist, 52*(3), 256–265.

Konner, M. (1991). *Childhood*. Boston: Little, Brown.

Koocher, G. P. (1977). Bathroom behavior and human dignity. *Journal of Personality and Social Psychology, 35*, 120–121.

Koop, C. E. (1988a). *The health consequences of smoking: Addiction*. United States Surgeon General's Report. Washington DC: United States Government Printing Office.

Koop, C. E. (1988b). *Understanding AIDS*. HHS Publication No. (CDC) HHS-88-8404. U.S. Department of Health and Human Services, Rockville, MD.

Korenman, S., Miller, J. E., & Sjaastad, J. E. (1995). Long-term poverty and child development in the United States. *Children & Youth Services Review, 17*(1–2), 127–155.

Korte, C., & Milgram, S. (1970). Acquaintance networks between racial groups. *Journal of Personality & Social Psychology, 15*, 101–108.

Koss, M. P. (1993). Rape. *American Psychologist, 48*(10), 1062–1069.

Koss, M., Gidycz, C. A., & Wisniewski, N. (1987). The scope of rape: Incidence and prevalence of sexual aggression and victimization in a national sample of higher education students. *Journal of Consulting and Clinical Psychology, 55*(2), 162–170.

Kosslyn, S. M. (1983). *Ghosts in the mind's machine*. New York: Norton.

Kosslyn, S. M. (1985). Stalking the mental image. *Psychology Today*, May, 23–28.

Kosslyn, S. M. (1990). Mental imagery. In D. N. Osherson, S. M. Kosslyn, & J. M. Hollerbach (Eds.), *Visual cognition and action*. Cambridge, MA: The MIT Press.

Kosslyn, S. M. (1994). *Image and brain*. Cambridge, MA: The MIT Press.

Kosslyn, S. M., Ball, T. M., & Reiser, B. J. (1978). Visual images preserve metric spatial information: Evidence from studies of image scanning. *Journal of Experimental Psychology: Human Perception and Performance, 4*, 47–60.

Kosslyn, S. M., Seger, C., Pani, J. R., & Hillger, L. A. (1990). When is imagery used in everyday life? A diary study. *Journal of Mental Imagery, 14*(3–4),

131–152.

Kosslyn, S. M., Thompson, W. L., & Alpert, N. N. (1995). Topographical representation of mental images in primary visual cortex. *Nature, 378*(6556), 496.

Kotkin, M., Daviet, C., & Gurin, J. (1996). The Consumer Reports mental health survey. *American Psychologist, 51*(10), 1080–1082.

Kottler, J. A., & Brown, R. W. (1996). *Introduction to therapeutic counseling*. Monterey, CA: Brooks/Cole.

Krakow, B. & Neidhardt, J. (1992). *Conquering bad dreams and nightmares*. Berkley Books.

Krakow, B., Kellner, R., Pathak, D., & Lambert, L. (1995). Imagery rehearsal treatment for chronic nightmares. *Behaviour Research & Therapy, 33*(7), 837–843.

Kramer, P. D. (1993). *Listening to Prozac*. New York: Viking.

Krantz, L. (1995). *Jobs rated almanac*. New York: Wiley.

Kratofil, P. H., Baberg, H. T., & Dimsdale, J. E. (1996). Self-mutilation and severe self-injurious behavior associated with amphetamine psychosis. *General Hospital Psychiatry, 18*(2), 117–120.

Krech, D., Rosenzweig, M. R., & Bennett, E. L. (1962). Relations between brain chemistry and problem solving among rats raised in enriched and impoverished environments. *Journal of Comparative and Physiological Psychology, 55*, 801–807.

Krinsky, Richard, Krinsky, Suzanne G. (1996). Pegword mnemonic instruction. *Contemporary Educational Psychology, 21*(2), 193–207.

Krivascka, J. J., Savin-Williams, R. C., & Slater, B. R. (1992, Nov. 8). *Background paper for the resolution on lesbian, gay, and bisexual youths in the schools*.

Kroll, N. E. A., Schepeler, E. M. & Angin, K. T. (1986). Bizarre imagery: The misremembered mnemonic. *Journal of Experimental Psychology: Learning, Memory, and Cognition, 12*, 42–53.

Kroon, M. B., Van Kreveld, D., & Rabbie, J. M. (1992). Group versus individual decision making: Effects of accountability and gender on groupthink. *Small Group Research, 23*(4), 427–458.

Krosnick, J. A., Betz, A. L., Jussim, L. J., & Lynn, A. R. (1992). Subliminal conditioning of attitudes. *Personality & Social Psychology Bulletin, 18*(2), 152–162.

Krueger, J., Ham, J. J., & Linford, K. M. (1996). Perceptions of behavioral consistency: Are people aware of the actor-observer effect? *Psychological Science, 7*(5), 259–264.

Kruger, L., & Liebeskind, J. C. (eds.). (1984). *Advances in pain research and therapy*. New York: Raven Press.

Krupnick, J. L., Sotsky, S. M. Simmens, S., & Moyer, J. (1996). The role of the therapeutic alliance in psychotherapy and pharmacotherapy outcome. *Journal of Consulting & Clinical Psychology, 64*(3), 532–539.

Kubey, R. & Csikszentmihalyi, M. (1990). *Television and the quality of life*. Hillsdale, NJ: Erlbaum.

Kübler-Ross, E. (1975). *Death: The final stage of growth*. Englewood Cliffs, NJ: Prentice-Hall.

Kulik, J. A., Bangert-Drowns, R. L., & Kulik, C. C. (1984). Effectiveness of coaching for aptitude tests. *Psychological Bulletin, 95*, 179–188.

Kunkel, M. A. (1993). A teaching demonstration involving perceived lunar size. *Teaching of Psychology, 20*(3), 178–180.

Kunzendorf, R. G. (1989). After-images of eidetic images: A developmental study. *Journal of Mental Imagery, 13*(1), 55–62.

Kusseling, F. S., Shapiro, M. F., Greenberg, J. M., & Wenger, N. S. (1996). Understanding why heterosexual adults do not practice safer sex: A comparison of two samples. *AIDS Education & Prevention, 8*(3), 247–257.

La Berge, S. P. (1981). Lucid dreaming: Directing the action as it happens. *Psychology Today*, Jan., 48–57.

La Berge, S.P. (1985). *Lucid dreaming*. Los Angeles: Tarcher.

Laan, E., Everaerd, W., van Bellen, G., & Hanewald, G. J. F. P. (1994). Women's sexual and emotional responses to male- and female-produced erotica. *Archives of Sexual Behavior, 23*(2), 153–169.

Laan, E., Everaerd, W., van der Velde, J., & Geer, J. H. (1995). Determinants of subjective experience of sexual arousal in women. *Psychophysiology, 32*(5), 444–451.

Labbe, R., Firl, A., Jr., Mufson, E. J., & Stein, D. G. (1983). Fetal brain transplants: Reduction of cognitive deficits in rats with frontal cortex lesions. *Science, 221*, 470–472.

Labov, W. (1973). The boundaries of words and their meanings. In C. J. N. Bailey & R. W. Shuy (Eds.) *New ways of analyzing variation in English*. Washington, DC: Georgetown University Press.

Lacayo, A. (1995). Neurologic and psychiatric complications of cocaine abuse. *Neuropsychiatry, Neuropsychology, & Behavioral Neurology, 8*(1), 53–60.

Lackner, J. R. & DiZio, P. (1993). Multisensory, cognitive, and motor influences on human spatial orientation in weightlessness. *Journal of Vestibular Research, 3*(3), 361–372.

Lacks, P. & Morin, C. M. (1992). Recent advances in the assessment and treatment of insomnia. *Journal of Clinical and Consulting Psychology, 60*(4), 586–594.

Laing, R. D. (1970). *The divided self*. New York: Pantheon.

Laird, J. D. (1974). Self-attribution of emotion: The effects of expressive behavior on the quality of emotional experience. *Journal of Personality & Social Psychology, 29*, 475–486.

Laird, J. D. (1984). The real role of facial response in the experience of emotion. *Journal of Personality & Social Psychology, 47*, 909–917.

Lamb, M. R. & Yund, E. W. (1996). Spatial frequency and attention. *Perception & Psychophysics, 58*(3), 363–373.

Lambert, M. J. & Cattani-Thompson, K. (1996). Current findings regarding the effectiveness of counseling. *Journal of Counseling & Development, 74*(6), 601–608.

Lambert, W. E. (1987). The effects of bilingual and bicultural experiences on children's attitudes and social perspectives. In P. Homel, M. Palij, & D. Aaronson (Eds.), *Childhood bilingualism*. Hillsdale, NJ: Erlbaum.

Lamme, V. A. F. (1995). The neurophysiology of figure-ground segregation in primary visual cortex. *Journal of Neuroscience, 15*(2), 1605–1615.

Lance, C. E., LaPointe, J. A., & Stewart, A. M. (1994). A test of the context dependency of three causal models of halo rater error. *Journal of Applied Psychology, 79*(3), 332–340.

Landers, S. (1989). In U.S., mental disorders affect 15 percent of adults. *The APA Monitor*, Jan., 16.

Landers, S. (1989). Judge reiterates I.Q. test ban. *APA Monitor*, Dec., 18.

Landy, F. J., Shankster, L. J., & Kohler, S. S. (1994). Personnel selection and placement. *Annual Review of Psychology, 45*, 261–296.

Lang, V. A. (1995). Relative association, interactiveness, and the bizarre imagery effect. *American Journal of Psychology, 108*(1), 13–35.

Langer, E. J., & Abelson, R. P. (1974). A patient by any other name: Clinician group difference in labeling bias. *Journal of Consulting and Clinical Psychology, 42*(1), 4–9.

Langer, E. J., & Piper, A. I. (1987). Prevention of mindblindness. *Journal of Personality & Social Psychology, 53*, 280–287.

Lanzetta, J. T. & Englis, B. G. (1989). Expectations of

cooperation and competition and their effects on observers' vicarious emotional responses. *Journal of Personality & Social Psychology, 56*(4), 543–554.

Larish, J. E. & Andersen, G. J. (1995). Active control in interrupted dynamic spatial orientation. *Perception & Psychophysics, 57*(4), 533–545.

Larner, A. J., Moss, J., Rossi, M. L., & Anderson, M. (1994). Congenital insensitivity to pain. *Journal of Neurology, Neurosurgery & Psychiatry, 57*(8), 973–974.

Larsen, R. J. & Kasimatis, M. (1990). Individual differences in entrainment of mood to the weekly calendar. *Journal of Personality & Social Psychology, 58*(1), 164–171.

Larson, D. E. (Ed.) (1990). *Mayo Clinic family healthbook.* New York: Morrow.

Larson, M. E., Houlihan, D., & Goernert, P. N. (1995). Effects of informational feedback on aluminum can recycling. *Behavioral Interventions, 10*(2), 111–117.

Latané, L., Nida, S. A., & Wilson, D. W. (1981). The effects of group size on helping behavior. In J. P. Rushton & R. M. Sorrentino (Eds.), *Altruism and helping behavior: Social, personality and developmental perspectives.* Hillsdale, NJ: Erlbaum.

Lattanzi-Licht, M. & Connor, S. (1995). "Care of the dying: The hospice approach." In H. Wass & R. A. Neimeyer (Eds.), *Dying: Facing the facts.* Washington, D.C.: Taylor & Francis.

Latty-Mann, H. & Davis, K. E. (1996). Attachment theory and partner choice. *Journal of Social & Personal Relationships, 13*(1), 5–23.

Laumann, E., Michael, R., Michaels, S., & Gagnon, J. (1994). *The social organization of sexuality.* Chicago: University of Chicago Press.

Laurence, J., & Perry, C. (1983). Hypnotically created memory among highly hypnotizable subjects. *Science, 222*, 523–524.

Lawson, T. J. (1995). Gaining admission into graduate programs in psychology: An update. *Teaching of Psychology, 22*(4), 225–227.

Lazarus, A. H. (1964). The treatment of chronic frigidity by systematic desensitization. In H. J. Eysenck (Ed.), *Experiments in behavior therapy.* New York: Pergamon.

Lazarus, R. S. (1981). Little hassles can be hazardous to health. *Psychology Today,* July, 12–14.

Lazarus, R. S. (1991a). Progress on a cognitive-motivational-relational theory of emotion. *American Psychologist, 46*(8), 819–834.

Lazarus, R. S. (1991b). Cognition and motivation in emotion. *American Psychologist, 46*(4), 352–367.

Lazarus, R. S. (1993). From psychological stress to the emotions: A history of changing outlooks. In L. W. Porter and M. R. Rosenzweig (Eds.), *Annual Review of Psychology, 44*, 1–21.

Lazarus, R. S., DeLongis, A., Folkman, S., & Gruen, R. (1985). Stress and adaptational outcomes. *American Psychologist, 40*, 770–779.

Lea, S. E. G. & Kiley-Worthington, M. (1996). Can animals think? In V. Bruce (Ed.), *Unsolved mysteries of the mind: Tutorial essays in cognition.* Hove, East Sussex: Erlbaum (UK), Taylor & Francis.

LeDoux, J. (1996). *The emotional brain: The mysterious underpinnings of emotional life.* New York: Simon & Schuster.

Lee, C. C. (1991a). Cultural dynamics. In C. C. Lee & B. L. Richardson (Eds.), *Multicultural issues in counseling.* Alexandria, VA: American Association for Counseling and Development.

Lee, C. C. (1991b). New approaches to diversity. In C. C. Lee & B. L. Richardson (Eds.), *Multicultural issues in counseling.* Alexandria, VA: American Association for Counseling and Development.

Lee, M., Zimbardo, P. G., & Bertholf, M. (1977). Shy murderers. *Psychology Today,* Nov.

Lee, R. T. & Ashforth, B. E. (1990). On the meaning of Maslach's three dimensions of burnout. *Journal of Applied Psychology, 75*(6), 743–747.

Lee, T. D. & Carnahan, H. (1990). When to provide knowledge of results during motor learning: Scheduling effects. *Human Performance, 3*(2), 87–105.

Lee, V. E., Brooks-Gunn, J. & Schnur, E. (1988). Does Head Start work? A 1-year follow-up comparison of disadvantaged children attending Head Start, no preschool, and other preschool programs. *Developmental Psychology, 24*(2), 210–222.

Leenaars, A. A. (1995). Suicide. In H. Wass & R. A. Neimeyer (Eds.), *Dying.* Washington, D.C.: Taylor & Francis.

Leeper, R. W. (1935). A study of a neglected portion of the field of learning: The development of sensory organization. *Pedagogical Seminary and Journal of Genetic Psychology, 46*, 41–75.

Lefkowitz, M., Blake, R. R., & Mouton, J. S. (1955). Status factors in pedestrian violation of traffic signals. *Journal of Abnormal and Social Psychology, 51*, 704–706.

Leibel, R. L., Rosenbaum, M., & Hirsch, J. (1995). Changes in energy expenditure resulting from altered body weight. *New England Journal of Medicine, 332*(10), 621–628.

Lemley, B. (1986). I'm not a nerd. *Parade Magazine,* June, 22, 8–9.

Lenzenweger, M. F. & Gottesman, I. I. (1994). Schizophrenia. In V. S. Ramachandran (Ed.), *Encyclopedia of human behavior.* San Diego, CA: Academic.

Lenzenweger, M. F., Cornblatt, B. A., & Putnick, M. (1991). Schizotypy and sustained attention. *Journal of Abnormal Psychology, 100*(1), 84–89.

Leor, J., Poole, W. K., & Kloner, R. A. (1996). Sudden cardiac death triggered by earthquake. *The New England Journal of Medicine, 334*(7), 413.

Lepore, S. J., Evans, G. W., & Schneider, M. L. (1992). Role of control and social support in explaining the stress of hassles and crowding. *Environment & Behavior, 24*(6), 795–811.

Lepper, M. R. (1985). Microcomputers in education. *American Psychologist, 40*, 1–18.

Lepper, M. R., Keavney, M., & Drake, M. (1996). Intrinsic motivation and extrinsic rewards. *Review of Educational Research, 66*(1), 5–32.

Lerner, R. M. & von Eye, A. (1992). Sociobiology and human development: Arguments and evidence. *Human Development, 35*(1), 12–33.

Leslie, K. & Ogilvie, R. (1996). Vestibular dreams: The effect of rocking on dream mentation. Dreaming: *Journal of the Association for the Study of Dreams, 6*(1), 1–16.

Lester, B. M., Corwin, M. L., Sepkoski, C., Seifer, R. et al. (1991). Neurobehavioral syndromes in cocaine-exposed newborn infants. *Child Development, 62*(4), 694–705.

Lester, D. (1990). Biorhythms and the timing of death. *Skeptical Inquirer, 14*(4), 410–411.

Lett, J. (1990). A field guide to critical thinking. *Skeptical Inquirer, 14*(Winter), 153–160.

Lettvin, J. Y. (1961). Two remarks on the visual system of the frog. In W. Rosenblith (Ed.), *Sensory communication.* Cambridge, MA: MIT Press.

Leutwyler, K. (1996). Paying attention. *Scientific American, 275*(2). 12–14.

Levant, R. F. (1996). The new psychology of men. *Professional Psychology: Research & Practice, 27*(3), 259–265.

LeVay, S. (1993). *The sexual brain.* Cambridge, MA: The MIT Press.

Leventhal, E. A., Leventhal, H., Shacham, S., & Easterling, D. V. (1989). Active coping reduces reports of pain from childbirth. *Journal of Consulting & Clinical Psychology, 57*(3), 365–371.

Levine, J. M. & Moreland, R. L. (1990). Progress in small group research. *Annual Review of Psychology, 41*, 485–634.

Levine, M., Toro, P. A., & Perkins, D. V., (1993). Social and community interventions. In L. W. Porter and M. R. Rosenzweig (Eds.), *Annual Review of Psychology, 44*, 525–558.

Levine, R. V. (1990). The pace of life. *American Scientist, 78*(Sept.–Oct.), 450–458.

Levinger, G. (1986). Editor's Page. *Journal of Social Issues, 42*(3).

Levinson, D. J. (1986). A conception of adult development. *American Psychologist, 41*(1), 3–13.

Levinson, D. J., & Levinson, J. D. (1996). *The seasons of a woman's life.* New York: Knopf.

Levis, D. J. (1989). The case for a return to a two-factor theory of avoidance: The failure of non-fear interpretations. In S. B Klein & R. R. Mower (Eds.), *Contemporary learning theories.* Hillsdale, NJ: Erlbaum.

Levy, D. A. (1989). Social support and the media: Analysis of responses by radio psychology talk show hosts. *Professional Psychology: Research & Practice, 20*(2), 73–78.

Levy, J., & Reid, M. (1976). Cerebral organization. *Science,* 337–339.

Lewis, M. (1995). Self-conscious emotions. *American Scientist, 83*(Jan-Feb), 68–78.

Lewis, M., & Brooks-Gunn, J. (1979). *Social cognition and the acquisition of self.* New York: Plenum.

Lewis, P. S., Goodman, S. H., & Fandt, P. M. (1995). *Management.* St Paul, MN: West.

Lewis, R. L. (1996). Interference in short-term memory: The magical number two (or three) in sentence processing. *Journal of Psycholinguistic Research, 25*(1), 93–115.

Lichtenstein, E. (1982). The smoking problem: A behavioral perspective. *Journal of Consulting and Clinical Psychology, 50*, 804–819.

Lieberman, D. A. (1979). Behaviorism and the mind: A (limited) call for a return to introspection. *American Psychologist, 34*, 319–333.

Lightsey, O. R. Jr. (1996). What leads to wellness? The role of psychological resources in well-being. *Counseling Psychologist, 24*(4), 589–759.

Lilienfeld, S. O. (1996). EMDR treatment: Less than meets the eye? *Skeptical Inquirer,* Jan-Feb, 25–31.

Lilly, J. C. (1972). *The center of the cyclone.* New York: Julian Press.

Lindstrom, T. C. (1995). Anxiety and adaptation in bereavement. *Anxiety, Stress & Coping: An International Journal, 8*(3), 251–261.

Lindvall, O. (1994). Clinical application of neuronal grafts in Parkinson's disease. Journal of Neurology, 242(1), 54–56.

Linton, M. (1979). I remember it well. *Psychology Today,* July, 81–86.

Lipman, J. J., Miller, B. E., Mays, K. S., Miller, M. N. et al. (1990). Peak B-endorphin concentration in cerebrospinal fluid: Reduced in chronic pain patients and increased during the placebo response. *Psychopharmacology, 102*(1), 112–116.

Lipschitz, D. S., Kaplan, M. L., Sorkenn, J., & Chorney, P. (1996). Childhood abuse, adult assault, and dissociation. *Comprehensive Psychiatry, 37*(4), 261–266.

Lipsey, M. W. & Wilson, D. B. (1993). The efficacy of psychological, educational, and behavioral treatment. *American Psychologist, 48*(12), 1181–1209.

Lipsitt, L. (1990). Nurture is what affects whether or not the genes get to "play out." *The APA Monitor,* Dec., 13.

Lisak, D. & Ivan, C. (1995). Deficits in intimacy and empathy in sexually aggressive men. *Journal of Interpersonal Violence, 10*(3), 296–308.

Lissner, L., Odell, P. M., D'Agostino, R. B. et al.

(1991). Variability of body weight and health outcomes in the Farmington population. *The New England Journal of Medicine, 324*(26), 1839–1844.

Loeber, R. & Hay, D. (1997). Key issues in the development of aggression and violence from childhood to early adulthood. In J. T. Spence (Ed.), *Annual Review of Psychology, 48,* 371–410.

Loehlin, J. C., Willerman, L., & Horn, J. M. (1988). Human behavior genetics. *Annual Review of Psychology, 39,* 101–133.

Loftus, E. (1977). Shifting human color memory. *Memory & Cognition, 5,* 696–699.

Loftus, E. (1979). Words that could save your life. *Psychology Today,* Nov., 102, 105–106.

Loftus, E. (1980). *Memory.* Reading MA: Addison-Wesley.

Loftus, E. (1993). The reality of repressed memories. *American Psychologist, 48*(5), 518–537.

Loftus, E. & Ketcham, K. (1991). *Witness for the defense.* New York: St. Martin's Press.

Loftus, E. F. (1994). The repressed memory controversy. *American Psychologist, 49*(5), 443–444.

Loftus, E. M. & Ketcham, K. (1994). *The myth of repressed memory.* New York: St. Martin's Press.

Loftus, E. M., Feldman, J., & Dashiell, R. (1995). Reality of illusory memories. In D. Schacter, et al., (Eds.), *Memory distortion.* Cambridge, MA: Harvard University Press.

Loftus, E., & Loftus, G. (1980). On the permanence of stored information in the human brain. *American Psychologist, 35,* 409–420.

Loftus, E., & Palmer, J. C. (1974). Reconstruction of automobile destruction: An example of interaction between language and memory. *Journal of Verbal Learning and Verbal Behavior, 13,* 585–589.

Loftus, G. R. & Mackworth, N. H. (1978). Cognitive determinants of fixation location during picture viewing. *Journal of Experimental Psychology: Human Perception and Performance, 4,* 565–572.

Long, D. M. (1991). Fifteen years of transcutaneous electrical stimulation for pain control. *Stereotactic & Functional Neurosurgery, 56*(1), 2–19.

Long, E. C. & Andrews, D. W. (1990). Perspective taking as a predictor of marital adjustment. *Journal of Personality & Social Psychology, 59*(1), 126–131.

Long, G. M. (1994). Exercises for training vision and dynamic visual acuity among college students. *Perceptual & Motor Skills, 78*(3, Pt 1), 1049–1050.

Long, V. 0. (1989). Relation of masculinity to self-esteem and self-acceptance in male professionals, college students, and clients. *Journal of Counseling Psychology, 36*(1), 84–87.

Lord, L. (1985). Morality. *U.S. News & World Report,* December 9, 52–59.

Lore, R. K. & Schultz, L. A. (1993). Control of human aggression. *American Psychologist, 48*(1), 16–25.

Lorenz, K. (1937). Imprinting. *The Auk, 54,* 245–273.

Lorenz, K. (1962). *King Solomon's ring.* New York: Time.

Lorenz, K. (1966). *On aggression.* Translated by M. Kerr-Wilson. New York: Harcourt Brace Jovanovich.

Lorenz, K. (1974). *The eight deadly sins of civilized man.* Translated by M. Kerr-Wilson. New York: Harcourt Brace Jovanovich.

Lovaas, O., & Simmons, J. (1969). Manipulation of self-destruction in three retarded children. *Journal of Applied Behavior Analysis, 2,* 143–157.

Luborsky, L., Crits-Christoph, P., McLellan, A. T., Woody, G. et al. (1986). Do therapists vary much in their success? *American Journal of Orthopsychiatry, 56*(4), 501–512.

Lucas, F. & Sclafani, A. (1990). Hyperphagia in rats produced by a mixture of fat and sugar. *Physiology & Behavior, 47*(1), 51–55.

Luce, G. G. (1965). *Current research on sleep and dreams.* Health Service Publication, No. 1389. U.S. Department of Health, Education and Welfare.

Luiselli, J. K. (1994). Behavioral medicine. *Encyclopedia of human behavior; Vol. 1,* 359–363.

Lumsden, C., & Wilson, E. O. (1983). *Promethean fire.* Cambridge, MA: Harvard University Press.

Luria, A. R. (1968). *The mind of a mnemonist.* New York: Basic.

Luster, T. & Dubow, E. (1992). Home environment and maternal intelligence as predictors of verbal intelligence. *Merrill-Palmer Quarterly, 38*(2), 151–175.

Luxem, M. & Christophersen, E. (1994). Behavioral toilet training in early childhood: Research, practice, and implications. *Journal of Developmental & Behavioral Pediatrics, 15*(5), 370–378.

Lykken, D. T. (1981). *A tremor in the blood, uses and abuses of the lie detector.* New York: McGraw-Hill.

Lykken, D. T. (1995). *The antisocial personalities.* Hillsdale, NJ: Erlbaum.

Lykken, D. T., McGue, M., Tellegen, A., & Bouchar, T. J. (1992). Emergenesis. *American Psychologist, 47,* 1565–1567.

Lynch, G., & Baudry, M. (1984). The biochemistry of memory: A new and specific hypothesis. *Science, 224,* 1057–1163.

Maccoby, E. E. (1990). Gender and relationships: A developmental account. *American Psychologist, 45*(4), 513–520.

Maccoby, E. E., & Jacklin, C. N. (1974). *The psychology of sex differences.* Stanford, CA: Stanford University Press.

MacCoun, R. J. (1993). Drugs and the law: A psychological analysis of drug prohibition. *Psychological Bulletin, 113*(3), 497–512.

MacDonald, T. K., Zanna, M. P., & Fong, G. T. (1996). Why common sense goes out the window: Effects of alcohol on intentions to use condoms. *Personality & Social Psychology Bulletin, 22*(8), 763–775.

MacHovec, F. (1994). Near-death experiences: Psychotherapeutic aspects. *Psychotherapy in Private Practice, 13*(3), 99–105.

Mack, J. E. (1986). Adolescent suicide: An architectural model. In G. L. Klerman (Ed.), *Suicide and depression among adolescents and young adults.* Washington, DC: American Psychiatric Press.

Mackey, M. C. (1995). Women's evaluation of their childbirth performance. *Maternal-Child Nursing Journal, 23*(2), 57–72.

Macy, P. (1990). Research with animals and the new zeitgeist. *American Psychologist,* Nov., 1269.

Maddi, S. R. & Kobasa, S. C. (1984). *The hardy executive: Health under stress.* Homewood, IL: The Dorsey Press.

Madigan, S. & O'Hara, R. (1992). Short-term memory at the turn of the century. *American Psychologist, 47*(2), 170–174.

Madsen, C. H., Jr., Becher, W. C., Thomas, D. R., Koser, L., & Plager, E. (1968). An analysis of the reinforcing function of "sit down" commands. In R. K. Parker (Ed.), *Readings in educational psychology.* Boston: Allyn & Bacon.

Magee, W. J., Eaton, W. W. Wittchen, H. (1996). Agoraphobia, simple phobia, and social phobia in the national comorbidity survey. *Archives of General Psychiatry, 53*(2), 159–168.

Magid, K. (1988). *High risk: Children without a conscience.* New York: Bantam.

Maier, N. R. F. (1949). *Frustration.* New York: McGraw-Hill.

Main, M., & George, C. (1985). Responses of abused and disadvantaged toddlers to distress and age-mates: A study in day care. *Developmental Psychology, 21,* 407–412.

Major, B., Schmidlin, A. M., & Williams, L. (1990). *Journal of Personality & Social Psychology, 58*(4), 634–643.

Malamuth, N. M., & Donnerstein, E. (1982). The effects of aggressive-pornographic mass media stimuli. In L. Berkowitz (Ed.), *Advances in Experimental Social Psychology, 15,* 103–136. New York: Academic.

Malinosky-Rummell, R. & Hansen, D. R. (1993). Long-term consequences of childhood physical abuse. *Psychological Bulletin, 114*(1), 68–79.

Man tells how rod ran through head, (1981). *Los Angeles Times,* Sept. 24, A3.

Mandler, J. M. (1990). A new perspective on cognitive development in infancy. *American Scientist, 78*(3), 236–243.

Mangun, G. R. (1995). Neural mechanisms of visual selective attention. *Psychophysiology, 32*(1), 4–18.

Manschreck, T. C. (1996). Delusional disorder: The recognition and management of paranoia. *Journal of Clinical Psychiatry, 57*(3, Suppl), 32–38.

Mansouri, A. & Adityanjee. (1995). Delusion of pregnancy in males: A case report and literature review. *Psychopathology, 28*(6), 307–311.

Manton K. G. & Stallard, E. (1991). Cross-sectional estimates of active life expectancy for the U.S. elderly and oldest-old populations. *Journal of Gerontology, 46*(3), 170–182.

Mantyla, T. (1986). Optimizing cue effectiveness: Recall of 600 incidentally learned words. *Journal of Experimental Psychology: Learning, Memory, and Cognition, 12*(1), 66–71.

Marion, S. L., Shayka, J. J., & Marcus, S. C. (1996). A short computer interview for obtaining psychiatric diagnoses. *Psychiatric Services, 47*(3), 293–297.

Marks, D. F. (1990). Comprehensive commentary, insightful criticism. *Skeptical Inquirer, 14*(3), 413–418.

Marks, D. F. & Kammann, R. (1979). *The psychology of the psychic.* Buffalo, NY: Prometheus.

Markson, E. W. (1995). To be or not to be: Assisted suicide revisited. *Omega: Journal of Death & Dying, 31*(3), 221–235.

Markus, H., & Nurius, P. (1986). Possible selves. *American Psychologist, 41,* 954–969.

Marlatt, G. A., & Gordon, J. R. (Eds.). (1985). *Relapse prevention: Maintenance strategies in the treatment of addictive behaviors.* New York: Guilford.

Marlatt, G. A., Baer, J. S., Dononovan, D. M., & Kivlahan, D. R. (1988). Addictive behaviors: Etiology and treatment. *Annual Review of Psychology, 39,* 223–252.

Marmor, J. (ed.) (1980). *Homosexual behavior: A modern reappraisal.* New York: Basic.

Marques, P., Bradley, J., Shappee, J., & Marques, C. (1982). *Bienestar: Health, well-being and lifestyle choices for Pinal County.* Project West Pinal, University of Arizona Health Sciences Center.

Marrs, R. W. (1995). A meta-analysis of bibliotherapy studies. *American Journal of Community Psychology, 23*(6), 843–870.

Martin, M. A. (1985). Students' applications of self-questioning study techniques: An investigation of their efficacy. *Reading Psychology, 6*(1–2), 69–83.

Martin, R. J., White, B. D., & Hulsey, M. G. (1991). The regulation of body weight. *American Scientist, 79*(Nov-Dec), 528–541.

Martin, S. (1995). Field's status unaltered by the influx of women. *APA Monitor,* Jan., 9.

Marx, J. A., Gyorky, Z. K., Royalty, G. M., & Stern, T. E. (1992). Use of self-help books in psychotherapy. *Professional Psychology: Research & Practice, 23*(4), 300–305.

Maslach, C. (1982). *Burnout: The cost of caring.* Englewood Cliffs, NJ: Prentice-Hall.

Maslow, A. H. (1954). *Motivation and personality.* New

York: Harper.

Maslow, A. H. (1967). Self-actualization and beyond. In J. F. T. Bugental (Ed.), *Challenges of humanistic psychology*. New York: McGraw-Hill.

Maslow, A. H. (1969). *The psychology of science*. Chicago: Henry Regnery.

Maslow, A. H. (1970). *Motivation and personality*. New York: Harper & Row.

Maslow, A. H. (1971). *The farther reaches of human nature*. New York: Viking.

Maslow, A. H. (1968). *Toward a psychology of being*. New York: Van Nostrand.

Masse, L. C. & Tremblay, R. E. (1997). Behavior of boys in kindergarten and the onset of substance use during adolescence. *Archives of General Psychiatry, 54*(1), 62.

Masters, W. H., & Johnson, V. E. (1966). *Human sexual response*. Boston: Little, Brown.

Masters, W. H., & Johnson, V. E. (1970). *The pleasure bond: A new look at sexuality and commitment*. Boston: Little, Brown.

Masur, E. F. (1995). Infants' early verbal imitation and their later lexical development. *Merrill-Palmer Quarterly, 41*(3), 286–306.

Matarazzo, J. D. (1984). Behavioral immunogens and pathogens in health and illness. In B. L. Hammonds & C. J. Scheirer (Eds.), *Psychology and health*. Washington, DC: American Psychological Association, 5–43.

Matheny, K. B., Brack, G. L., McCarthy, C. J., Penick, J. M. (1996). The effectiveness of cognitively-based approaches in treating stress-related symptoms. *Psychotherapy, 33*(2), 305–320.

Matias, R. & Cohn, J. F. (1993). Are max-specified infant facial expressions during face-to-face interaction consistent with differential emotions theory? *Developmental Psychology, 29*(3), 524–531.

Matossian, M. K. (1982). Ergot and the Salem witchcraft affair. *American Scientist, 70*, 355–357.

Matson, J. L., Sevin, J. A., Fridley D., & Love, S. R. (1990). Increasing spontaneous language in three autistic children. *Journal of Applied Behavior Analysis, 23*(2), 223–227.

Matsuda, L. A., Lolait, S. J., Brownstein, M. J., Young, A. C., & Bonner, T. I. (1990). Structure of a cannabinoid receptor and functional expression of the cloned cDNA. *Nature, 346*(6284), 561–564.

Matthews, D. B. (1990). A comparison of burnout in selected occupational fields. *Career Development Quarterly, 38*(3), 230–239.

Matthews, K. A., Wing, R. R., Kulkr, L. H. et al. (1990). Influences of natural menopause on psychological characteristics and symptoms of middle-aged healthy women. *Journal of Consulting & Clinical Psychology, 58*(3), 345–351.

Maugh, T. H. (1992). Chemical abnormalities linked to schizophrenia. *Los Angeles Times*, July 9, A3, A22.

Maupin, E. W. (1965). Individual differences in response to a Zen meditation exercise. *Journal of Consulting Psychology, 29*, 139–145.

May, M. (1996). Resistance: Friend or foe? *American Journal of Psychotherapy, 50*(1), 32–44.

Mayer, J. D. & Hanson, E. (1995). Mood-congruent judgment over time. *Personality & Social Psychology Bulletin, 21*(3) 237–244.

Mayer, R. E. (1995). *Thinking, problem solving, and cognition*. New York: Freeman.

Mayes, Linda C., Bornstein, M. H., Chawarska, K., & Haynes, O. M. (1996). Impaired regulation of arousal in 3-month-old infants exposed prenatally to cocaine and other drugs. *Development & Psychopathology, 8*(1), 29–42.

Mazurski, E. J., Bond, N. W., Siddle, D. A., & Lovibond, P. F. (1993). Classical conditioning of autonomic and affective responses to fear-relevant and fear-irrelevant stimuli. *Australian Journal of Psychology, 45*(3), 69–73.

McCabe, M. P. (1992). A program for the treatment of inhibited sexual desire in males. *Psychotherapy, 29*(2), 288–296.

McCann, S. L. & Stewin, L. L. (1988). Worry, anxiety, and preferred length of sleep. *Journal of Genetic Psychology, 149*(3), 413–418.

McCardel, J., & Murray, E. J. (1974). Nonspecific factors in weekend encounter groups. *Journal of Consulting Psychology, 42*, 337–345.

McCarthy, B. W. (1995). Bridges to sexual desire. *Journal of Sex Education & Therapy, 21*(2), 132–141.

McCartney, K., Bernieri, F., & Harris, M. J. (1990). Growing up and growing apart: A developmental meta-analysis of twin studies. *Psychological Bulletin, 107*(2), 226–237.

McCaul, K. D. & Malott, J. M. (1984). Distraction and coping with pain. *Psychological Bulletin, 95*, 516–533.

McCleary, R., Chew, K. S., Hellsten, J. J., & Flynn-Bransford, M. (1991). Age- and sex-specific cycles in United States suicides, 1973 to 1985. *American Journal of Public Health, 81*(11), 1494–1497.

McClelland, D. C. (1958). Risk taking in children with high and low need for achievement. In J. W. Atkinson (Ed.), *Motives in fantasy action and society*. New York: Van Nostrand.

McClelland, D. C. (1961). *The achieving society*. New York: Van Nostrand.

McClelland, D. C. (1965). Achievement and entrepreneurship. *Journal of Personality & Social Psychology, 1*, 389–393.

McClelland, D. C. (1973). Testing for competence rather than "intelligence." *American Psychologist, 28*, 1–14.

McClelland, D. C. (1975). *Power: the inner experience*. New York: Irvington.

McClelland, D. C. (1994). The knowledge-testing-educational complex strikes back. *American Psychologist, 49*(1), 66–69.

McClelland, D. C. & Pilon, D. A. (1983). Sources of adult motives in patterns of parent behavior in early childhood. *Journal of Personality & Social Psychology, 44*, 564–574.

McClelland, L., & Cook, S. W. (1980). Promoting energy conservation in master-metered apartments through group financial incentives. *Journal of Applied and Social Psychology, 10*, 20–31.

McCrae, R. R. (1987). Creativity, divergent thinking, and openness to experience. *Journal of Personality & Social Psychology, 52*(6), 1258–1265.

McCrae, R. R. & Costa, P. T. (1990). *Personality in adulthood*. New York: Guilford.

McDaniel, M. A. & Donnelly, C. (1996). Learning with analogy and elaborative interrogation. *Journal of Educational Psychology, 88*(3), 508–519.

McDaniel, M. A. & Schlager, M. S. (1990). Discovery learning and transfer of problem-solving skills. *Cognition & Instruction, 7*(2), 129–159.

McDonald, S. M. (1989). Sex bias in the representation of male and female characters in children's picture books. *Journal of Genetic Psychology, 150*(4), 389–401.

McEachin, J. J., Smith, T., & Lovaas, O. I. (1993). Long-term outcome for children with autism who received early intensive behavioral treatment. *American Journal of Mental Retardation, 97*(4), 359–372.

McGaugh, J. L. (1983). Hormonal influences on memory. *Annual Review of Psychology, 34*, 297–323.

McGee, M. G., & Snyder, M. (1975). Attribution and behavior: Two field studies. *Journal of Personality & Social Psychology, 32*, 185–190.

McGinnies, E. (1949). Emotionality and perceptual defense. *Psychological Review, 56*, 244–251.

McGinnis, J. M. & Foege, W. H. (1993). Actual causes of death in the United States. *Journal of the American Medical Association, 270*(18), 2207–2212.

McGrady, A. (1994). Effects of group relaxation training and thermal biofeedback on blood pressure and related physiological and psychological variables in essential hypertension. *Biofeedback & Self-Regulation, 19*(1), 51–66.

McGregor, D. (1960). *The human side of enterprise*. New York: McGraw-Hill.

McIntosh, W. D., Harlow, T. F., & Martin, L. L. (1995). Linkers and nonlinkers: Goal beliefs as a moderator of the effects of everyday hassles on rumination, depression, and physical complaints. *Journal of Applied Social Psychology, 25*(14), 1231–1244.

McKean, K. (1984). The fine art of reading voters' minds. *Discover*, May, 66–69.

McKean, K. (1985). Of two minds: Selling the right brain. *Discover*, April, 30–40.

McKean, K. J. (1994). Using multiple risk factors to assess the behavioral, cognitive, and affective effects of learned helplessness. *Journal of Psychology, 128*(2), 177–183.

McKellar, P. (1995). Creative imagination: Hypnagogia and surrealism. *Journal of Mental Imagery, 19*(1–2), 33–42.

McKenzie-Mohr, D. & Oskamp, S. (1995). Psychology and sustainability. *Journal of Social Issues, 51*(4), 1–14.

McKim, W. A. (1997). *Drugs and behavior*. Upper Saddle River, NJ: Prentice Hall.

McKinzie, S. J., Williamson, D. A., & Cubic, B. A. (1993). Stable and reactive body image distortions in bulimia nervosa. *Behavior Therapy, 24*(2), 195–207.

McKnight, J. D. & Glass, D. C. (1995). Perceptions of control, burnout, and depressive symptomatology. *Journal of Consulting & Clinical Psychology, 63*(3), 490–494.

McLatchie, B. H. & Lomp, K. G. (1988). Alcoholics Anonymous affiliation and treatment outcome among a clinical sample of problem drinkers. *American Journal of Drug and Alcohol Abuse, 14*(3), 309–324.

McLauglin, S. & Margolskee, R. F. (1994). The sense of taste. *American Scientist, 82*(Nov-Dec), 538–545.

McLennan, J. (1992). "University blues": Depression among tertiary students during an academic year. *British Journal of Guidance & Counselling, 20*(2), 186–192.

McManus, I. C., Sik, G., Cole, D. R., Muellon, A. F. et al. (1988). The development of handedness in children. *British Journal of Developmental Psychology, 6*(3), 257–273.

McMullan, W. E., & Stocking, J. R. (1978). Conceptualizing creativity in three dimensions. *The Journal of Creative Behavior, 12*, 161–167.

McMurdo, M. E. & Gaskell, A. (1991). Dark adaptation and falls in the elderly. *Gerontology, 37*(4), 221–224.

McReynolds, P. (1989). Diagnosis and clinical assessment: Current status and major issues. *Annual Review of Psychology, 40*, 83–108.

Mead, M. (1935). *Sex and temperament in three primitive societies*. New York: Morrow.

Medin, D. L. & Ross, B. H. (1992). *Cognitive psychology*. Fort Worth: Harcourt Brace Jovanovich.

Mednick, M. T. (1989). On the politics of psychological constructs: Stop the bandwagon, I want to get off. *American Psychologist, 44*(8), 1118–1123.

Mehren, E. (1994). Study finds most child care lacking. *The Los Angeles Times*, April 8, E-5.

Meichenbaum, D., Henshaw, D., & Himel, N. (1982). Coping with stress as a problem-solving process. In H. W. Krohne & L. Laux (Eds.), *Achievement, stress, and anxiety*. New York: Hemisphere.

Meier, R. P. (1991). Language acquisition by deaf children. *American Scientist, 79*(1), 60–70.

Meleshko, K. G. & Alden, L. E. (1993). Anxiety and self-disclosure. *Journal of Personality & Social Psychology, 64*(6), 1000–1009.

Melton, G. B. (1989). Public policy and private prejudice. *American Psychologist, 44*(6), 933–940.

Melton, R. F. (1978). Resolution of conflicting claims concerning the effect of behavioral objectives on student learning. *Review of Educational Research, 48,* 291–302.

Meltzoff, A. N. & Moore, M. K. (1983). Newborn infants imitate adult facial gestures. *Child Development, 54,* 702–709.

Meltzoff, A., & Moore, M. K. (1977). Imitation of facial and manual gestures by human neonates. *Science,* Oct., 75–78.

Melzack, R. (1974). Shutting the gate on pain. *Science Year: The World Book science annual.* Palo Alto, CA: Field.

Melzack, R. (1984). The myth of painless childbirth. *Pain, 19,* 321–337.

Melzack, R. (1993). Pain: Past, present and future. *Canadian Journal of Experimental Psychology, 47*(4), 615–629.

Melzack, R. & Wall, P. D. (1983). *The challenge of pain.* New York: Basic.

Mendolia, M., Moore, J., & Tesser, A. (1996). Dispositional and situational determinants of repression. *Journal of Personality & Social Psychology, 70*(4), 856–867.

Menninger, K. (1964). Psychiatrists use dangerous words. *Saturday Evening Post,* April 25.

Menzies, R. G. & Clarke, J. C. (1993). A comparison of *in vivo* and vicarious exposure in the treatment of childhood water phobia. *Behaviour Research and Therapy, 31*(1), 9–15.

Merenda, P. F. (1996). BASC: Behavior Assessment System for Children. *Measurement & Evaluation in Counseling & Development, 28*(4), 229–232.

Merikle, P. M. & Skanes, H. E. (1992). Subliminal self-help audiotapes: A search for placebo effects. *Journal of Applied Psychology, 77*(5), 772–776.

Mermelstein, R. (1986). Social support and smoking cessation and maintenance. *Journal of Consulting & Clinical Psychology, 54*(4), 447–453.

Merritt, J. M., Stickgold, R., Pace-Schott, E., Williams, J. et al. (1994). Emotion profiles in the dreams of men and women. *Consciousness & Cognition, 3*(1), 46–60.

Mesquita, B. & Frijda, N. H. (1992). Cultural variations in emotions. *Psychological Bulletin, 112*(2), 179–204.

Messick, D. M. & Mackie, D. M. (1989). Intergroup relations. *Annual Review of Psychology, 40,* 45–81.

Messick, D. M., Wilke, H., Brewer, M., Kramer, R. M., Zemke, P. E., & Lui, L. (1983). Individual adaptations and structural change as solutions to social dilemmas. *Journal of Personality & Social Psychology, 44,* 294–309.

Metcalfe, J. (1986). Premonitions of insight predict impending error. *Journal of Experimental Psychology: Learning, Memory, and Cognition, 12,* 623–634.

Metzner, R. J. (1994). Prozac is medicine, not a miracle. *The Los Angeles Times,* March 14, B-7.

Meyer, A. J., Nash, J. D., McAlister, A. L., Maccoby, N., & Farquhar, J. W. (1980). Skills training in a cardiovascular health education campaign. *Journal of Consulting and Clinical Psychology, 48,* 129–142.

Meyer, I. H. (1995). Minority stress and mental health in gay men. *Journal of Health & Social Behavior, 36*(1), 38–56.

Meyer, R. G. & Youngjohn, J. R. (1991). Effects of feedback and validity expectancy on responses in a lie detector interview. *Forensic Reports, 4*(3), 235–244.

Meyer-Bahlburg, H. F. L., Ehrhardt, A. A., Rosen, L. R., Gruen, R. S., et al. (1995). Prenatal estrogens and the development of homosexual orientation. *Developmental Psychology, 31*(1), 12–21.

Meyer-Bisch, C. (1996). Epidemiological evaluation of hearing damage related to strongly amplified music (personal cassette players, discotheques, rock concerts). *Audiology, 35*(3), 121.

Michel, D. E. & Chesky, K. S. (1995). A survey of music therapists using music for pain relief. *Arts in Psychotherapy, 22*(1), 49–51.

Michotte, A. (1963). *The perception of causality.* New York: Methuen/Basic.

Middlemist, R. D., Knowles, E. S., & Matter, C. F. (1976). Personal space invasions in the lavatory: Suggestive evidence for arousal. *Journal of Personality and Social Psychology, 33,* 541–546.

Mikulincer, M. & Nachshon, O. (1991). Attachment styles and patterns of self-disclosure. *Journal of Personality & Social Psychology, 61*(2), 321–331.

Mikulincer, M., Babkoff, H., Caspy, T., & Sing, H. C. (1989). The effects of 72 hours of sleep loss on psychological variables. *British Journal of Psychology, 80*(2), 145–162.

Milgram, S. (1963). Behavioral study of obedience. *Journal of Abnormal and Social Psychology, 67,* 371–378.

Milgram, S. (1965). Some conditions of obedience and disobedience to authority. *Human Relations, 18,* 57–76.

Milgram, S. (1967). The small-world problem. *Psychology Today,* May, 61–67.

Milgram, S. (1970). The experience of living in the cities: A psychological analysis. *Science, 167,* 1461–1468.

Milgram, S. (1974). *Obedience to authority: An experimental view.* New York: Harper & Row.

Milgram, S., Bickman, L., & Berkowitz, L. (1969). Note on the drawing power of crowds of different size. *Journal of Personality & Social Psychology, 13,* 79–82.

Miller, D. T., Turnbull, W., & McFarland, C. (1988). Particularistic and universalistic evaluation in the social comparison process. *Journal of Personality & Social Psychology, 55*(6), 908–917.

Miller, G. (1956). The magical number seven, plus or minus two: Some limits on our capacity for processing information. *Psychological Review, 63,* 81–87.

Miller, G. (1977). *Spontaneous apprentices: children and language.* The Seabury Press.

Miller, L. C. (1990). Intimacy and liking: Mutual influence and the role of unique relationships. *Journal of Personality & Social Psychology, 59*(1), 50–60.

Miller, L. K. (1976). The design of better communities through the application of behavioral principles. In W. E. Craighead, A. E. Kazdin, & M. J. Mahone (Eds.), *Behavior modification: Principles, issues, and applications.* Boston: Houghton-Mifflin.

Miller, L., & Milner, B. (1985). Cognitive risk-taking after frontal or temporal lobectomy, II. The synthesis of phonemic and semantic information. *Neuropsychologia, 23,* 371–379.

Miller, N. E. (1944). Experimental studies of conflict. In J. McV. Hunt (Ed.), *Personality and the behavior disorders,* Vol. I, 431–465. New York: Ronald Press.

Miller, N. E. (1985a). Rx: Biofeedback. *Psychology Today, 19,* 54–59.

Miller, N. E. (1985b). The value of behavioral research on animals. *American Psychologist, 40,* 423–440.

Miller, N. E., & Bugelski. R. (1970). The influence of frustration imposed by the in-group on attitudes expressed toward out-groups. In R. I. Evans & R. M. Rozelle (Eds.), *Social psychology in life.* Boston: Allyn & Bacon.

Miller, T. Q., Smith, T. W., Turner, C. W., & Guijarro, M. L. (1996). Meta-analytic review of research on hostility and physical health. *Psychological Bulletin, 119*(2), 322–348.

Miller, T. Q., Turner, C. W., Tindale, R. S., Posavac, E. J. et al. (1991). Reasons for the trend toward null findings in research on Type A behavior. *Psychological Bulletin, 110*(3), 469–485.

Miller-Jones, D. (1989). Culture and testing. *American Psychologist, 44*(2), 360–366.

Millon, T. (1981) *Disorders of personality: DSM-III: Axis II.* New York: Wiley.

Milner, B. (1965). Memory disturbance after bilateral hippocampal lesions. In P. Milner, & S. Glickman (Eds.), *Cognitive processes and the brain,* 97–111. Princeton, NJ: Van Nostrand.

Milunsky, A. (1992). *Heredity and your family's health.* Boston: Houghton Mifflin.

Miranda, J. (1992). Dysfunctional thinking is activated by stressful life events. *Cognitive Therapy & Research, 16*(4), 473–483.

Mirsky, A. F. & Duncan, C. C. (1986). Etiology and expression of schizophrenia. *Annual Review of Psychology, 37,* 291–319.

Mischel, W. (1968). *Personality and assessment.* New York: Wiley.

Mitchell, C. W. (1995). Effects of subliminally presented auditory suggestions of itching on scratching behavior. *Perceptual & Motor Skills, 80*(1), 87–96.

Mitchell, D. (1987). Firewalking cults: Nothing but hot air. *Laser,* Feb., 7–8.

Mitchell, D. B. (1989). How many memory systems? Evidence from aging. *Journal of Experimental Psychology: Learning, Memory, and Cognition, 15*(1), 31–49.

Mogg, K., Bradley, B. P., Williams, R., & Mathews, A. (1993). Subliminal processing of emotional information in anxiety and depression. *Journal of Abnormal Psychology, 102*(2), 304–311.

Monahan, J. (1992). Mental disorder and violent behavior. *American Psychologist, 47*(4), 511–521.

Money, J. (1987). Sin, sickness, or status? *American Psychologist, 42*(4), 384–399.

Money, J., & Mathews, D. (1982). Prenatal exposure to virilizing progestins: An adult follow-up study of twelve women. *Archives of Sexual Behavior, 11,* 73–83.

Monfort, M., Martin, S. A., & Frederickson, W. (1990). Information-processing differences and laterality of students from different colleges and disciplines. *Perceptual & Motor Skills, 70*(1), 163–172.

Monmaney, T. (1987). Are we led by the nose? *Discover,* Sept., 48–56.

Montague, J. (1996). Counseling families from diverse cultures: A nondeficit approach. *Journal of Multicultural Counseling & Development, 24*(1), 37–41.

Montgomery, G. (1989). The mind in motion. *Discover,* March, 58–68.

Monti-Bloch, L., Jennings-White, C., Dolberg, D. S., & Berliner, D. L. (1994). The human vomeronasal system. *Psychoneuroendocrinology, 19*(5–7), 673–686.

Moody, R. (1975). *Life after life.* Covinda, GA: Mockingbird.

Moore, T. E. (1992). Subliminal perception: Facts and fallacies. *Skeptical Inquirer, 16*(Spring), 273–281.

Moore, T. E. (1995). Subliminal self-help auditory tapes: An empirical test of perceptual consequences. *Canadian Journal of Behavioural Science, 27*(1), 9–20.

Moore-Ede, M. C., Sulzman, F. M., & Fuller, C. A. (1982). *The clocks that time us.* Cambridge, MA: Harvard University Press.

Moos, R. H. & Swindle, R. W. (1990). Stressful life circumstances: Concepts and measures. Special Issue: II-IV. Advances in measuring life stress. *Stress*

Medicine, 6(3), 171–178.

Morain, D. (1988). In figuring, she plays it by the numbers. *Los Angeles Times*, March 1, Part I, 3.

Morelli, G. A., Rogoff, B., Oppenheim, D., & Goldsmith, D. (1992). Cultural variation in infants' sleeping arrangements. *Developmental Psychology, 28*(4), 604–613.

Moreno, J. L. (1953). *Who shall survive?* New York: Beacon.

Morgan, J. D. (1995). "Living our dying and our grieving: Historical and cultural attitudes." In H. Wass & R. A. Neimeyer (Eds.), *Dying: Facing the facts*. Washington, D.C.: Taylor & Francis.

Morgan, M. J., Hole, G. J., & Glennerster, A. (1990). Biases and sensitivities in geometrical illusions. Special Issue: Optics, physiology and vision. *Vision Research, 30*(11), 1793–1810.

Moriarty, T. (1975). A nation of willing victims. *Psychology Today*, April, 43–50.

Morisse, D., Batra, L., Hess, L., & Silverman, R. (1996). A demonstration of a token economy for the real world. *Applied & Preventive Psychology, 5*(1), 41–46.

Moritz, A. P., & Zamchech, N. (1946). Sudden and unexpected deaths of young soldiers. *American Medical Association Archives of Pathology, 42*, 459–494.

Morrow-Tlucak, M., Haude, R. H., & Ernhart, C. B. (1988). Breastfeeding and cognitive development in the first 2 years of life. *Social Science and Medicine, 26*(6), 635–639.

Moser, D. (1965). The nightmare of life with Billy. *Life*, May 7.

Mosher, D. L. & MacIan, P. (1994). College men and women respond to X-rated videos intended for male or female audiences: Gender and sexual scripts. *Journal of Sex Research, 31*(2), 99–113.

Moss, K. (1989). Performing the light-switch task in lucid dreams: A case study. *Journal of Mental Imagery, 13*(2), 135–137.

Moyer, R. S., & Bayer, R. H. (1976). Mental comparison and the symbolic distance effect. *Cognitive Psychology, 8*, 228–246.

Mshelia, A. Y. & Lapidus, L. B. (1990). Depth picture perception in relation to cognitive style and training in non-Western children. *Journal of Cross-Cultural Psychology, 21*(4), 414–433.

Mullen, P. E., Martin, J. L., Anderson, J. C., & Romans, S. E. (1996). The long-term impact of the physical, emotional, and sexual abuse of children: A community study. *Child Abuse & Neglect, 20*(1), 7–21.

Mullington, J. & Broughton, R. (1993). Scheduled naps in the management of daytime sleepiness in narcolepsy-cataplexy. *Sleep, 16*(5) 444–456.

Murphy, L. B., & Moriarty, A. E. (1976). *Vulnerability, coping and growth*. New Haven: Yale University Press.

Murray, B. (1995). Master's program growth spurs educational concerns. *APA Monitor*, April, 47.

Murray, B. (1996). Psychology remains top college major. *APA Monitor*, Feb., 1, 42.

Murray, C. B. & Warden, M. R. (1992). Implications of self-handicapping strategies for academic achievement. *Journal of Social Psychology, 132*(1), 23–37.

Murray, F. S. (1980). Estimation of performance levels by students in introductory psychology. *Teaching of Psychology, 7*, 61–62.

Murray, J. B. (1995). Evidence for acupuncture's analgesic effectiveness and proposals for the physiological mechanisms involved. *Journal of Psychology, 129*(4), 443–461.

Murray, R. M., Jones, P. B., O'Callaghan, E., Takei, Noriyoshi et al. (1992). Genes, viruses and neurodevelopmental schizophrenia. *Journal of Psychiatric Research, 26*(4), 225–235.

Murray, S. H., Touyz, S. W., Beumont, P. J. V. (1996). Awareness and perceived influence of body ideals in the media: A comparison of eating disorder patients and the general community. *Eating Disorders: The Journal of Treatment & Prevention, 4*(1), 33–46.

Murray, S. L. & Holmes, J. G. (1993). Seeing virtues in faults. *Journal of Personality & Social Psychology, 65*(4), 707–722.

Murray, S. L., Holmes, J. G., & Griffin, D. W. (1996). The self-fulfilling nature of positive illusions in romantic relationships. *Journal of Personality & Social Psychology, 71*(6), 1155–1180.

Murray-Smith, D., Kinoshita, S., & McConkey, K. M. (1990). Hypnotic memory and retrieval cues. *British Journal of Experimental and Clinical Hypnosis, 7*(1), 1–8.

Murrell, J., Farlow, M., Ghetti, B., & Benson, M. D. (1991). A mutation in the amyloid precursor protein associated with hereditary Alzheimer's disease. *Science, 254*(5028), 97–98.

Murstein, B. I. & Fontaine, P. A. (1993). The public's knowledge about psychologists and other mental health professionals. *American Psychologist, 48*(7), 839–845.

Mussen, P. H., Conger, J. J., Kagan, J., & Geiwitz, J. (1979). *Psychological development: A life span approach*. New York: Harper & Row.

Muth, K. D., Glynn, S. M., Britton, B. K., & Craves, M. F. (1988). Thinking out loud while studying text: Rehearsing key ideas. *Journal of Educational Psychology, 80*(3), 315–318.

Myers, R. D., Wooten, M. H., Ames, C. D., & Nyce, J. W. (1995). Anorexic action of a new potential neuropeptide Y antagonist (D-Tyr-super(27,36), D-Thr-sup-3-sup-2)-NPY (27-36) infused into the hypothalamus of the rat. *Brain Research Bulletin, 37*(3), 237–245.

Naeye, R. L. (1994). The brain at work. *Discover*, July, 30–31.

Nagel, K. L. & Jones, K. H. (1992). Sociological factors in the development of eating disorders. *Adolescence, 27*(105), 107–113.

Nagy, Z., Esiri, M. M., Jobst, K. A., & Morris, J. H. (1996). Clustering of pathological features in Alzheimer's disease. *Dementia, 7*(3), 121–127.

Naitoh, P., Kelly, T. L., & Englund, C. E. (1989). *Health effects of sleep deprivation*. U.S. Naval Health Research Center Report, No. 89-46.

Nakano, K. (1996). Application of self-control procedures to modifying Type A behavior. *Psychological Record, 46*(4), 595–606.

Naranjo, C. (1970). Present-centeredness: Technique, prescription, and ideal. In J. Fagan & I. L. Shepherd (Eds), *What is Gestalt therapy?* New York: Harper & Row.

Narayan, V. K., & Nath, R. (1982). A field test of some attitudinal and behavioral consequences of flexitime. *Journal of Applied Psychology, 67*, 214–218.

Narby, D. J., Cutler, B. L., & Moran, G. (1993). A meta-analysis of the association between authoritarians and jurors' perceptions of defendant culpability. *Journal of Applied Psychology, 78*, 34–42.

Nardi, P. M. (1992). "Seamless souls": An introduction to men's friendships. In P. M. Nardi (Ed.), *Men's friendships*. Newbury Park, CA: Sage.

Natale, V. & Cicogna, P. (1996). Circadian regulation of subjective alertness in morning and evening types. *EDRA: Environmental Design Research Association, 20*(4), 491–497.

Nathans, J., Thomas, P., Piantandia, R. L., Eddy, T. B., Shows, D. S., & Hogness, D. S. (1986). Molecular genetics of inherited variations in human color vision. *Science, 232*, 203–210.

National Institute of Mental Health. (1982). Television and behavior: Ten years of scientific progress and implications for the eighties. Washington, DC: U.S. Government Printing Office.

National television violence study. (1995–96). Studio City, CA: Mediascope, Inc.

Navarro, M. (1995). Drug sold abroad by prescription becomes widely abused in U.S. *The New York Times*, Dec. 9, 1,9.

Naveh-Benjamin, M. (1990). The acquisition and retention of knowledge: Exploring mutual benefits to memory research and the educational setting. *Applied Cognitive Psychology, 4*(4), 295–320.

Needles, D. J. & Abramson, L. Y. (1990). Positive life events, attributional style, and hopefulness: Testing a model of recovery from depression. *Journal of Abnormal Psychology, 99*(2), 156–165.

Neff, F. (1990). Delivering sport psychology services to a professional sport organization. *Sport Psychologist, 4*(4), 378–385.

Neidert, G. P. & Linder, D. E. (1990). Avoiding social traps. *Social Behaviour, 5*(4), 261–284.

Neisser, U., Boodoo, G., Bouchard, T. J., et al, (1996). Intelligence: Knowns and unknowns. *American Psychologist, 51*(2), 77–101.

Nelson, J. R., Smith, D. J., & Dodd, J. (1990). The moral reasoning of juvenile delinquents. *Journal of Abnormal Child Psychology, 18*(3), 231–239.

Nelson, T. O. (1987). Predictive accuracy of the feeling of knowing across different tasks and across different subject populations and individuals. In M. M. Gruneberg, P. E. Morris, & R. N. Sykes (Eds.), *Practical aspects of memory: Current research and issues*. Chinchester, U.K.: Wiley.

Nesca, M. & Koulack, D. (1994). Recognition memory, sleep and circadian rhythms. *Canadian Journal of Experimental Psychology, 48*(3) 359–379.

Neter, E., & Ben-Shakhar, G. (1989). The predictive validity of graphological inferences: A meta-analytic approach. *Personality and Individual Differences, 10*(7), 737–745.

Neufeld, R. W. (1970). The effect of experimentally altered cognitive appraisal on pain tolerance. *Psychonomic Science, 20*(2), 106–107.

Neugarten, B. (1971). Grow old along with me! The best is yet to be. *Psychology Today*, Dec., 45.

Nevin, J. A. & Fuld, K. (1993). On armament traps and how to get out of them. *Behavior & Social Issues, 3*(1–2) 63–74.

Newell, A. & Simon, H. A. (1972). *Human problem solving*. Englewood Cliffs, NJ: Prentice-Hall.

Newman, B. M. & Newman, P. R. (1987). The impact of high school on social development. *Adolescence, 22*(87), 525–534.

Newman, P. R. (1982). The peer group. In B. B. Wolman, G. Stricker, S. J. Ellman, P. Keith-Spiegel, & D. S. Palermo (Eds.), *Handbook of developmental psychology*. Englewood Cliffs, NJ: Prentice-Hall.

Newman, R. (1994). Electronic therapy raises issues, risks. *APA Monitor*, Aug., 25.

Nicholas, J. M. & Penwell, L. W. (1995). A proposed profile of the effective leader in human spaceflight based on findings from analog environments. *Aviation, Space, & Environmental Medicine, 66*(1), 63–72.

Nickerson, R. S., & Adams, M. J. (1979). Long-term memory for a common object. *Cognitive Psychology, 11*, 287–307.

Nicogossian, A. E., & Parker, J. F. (1982). *Space physiology and medicine*. NASA.

Nielsen, D. M., Metha, A. (1994). Parental behavior and adolescent self-esteem in clinical and nonclinical samples. *Adolescence, 29*(115), 525–542.

Nist, S. L., Sharman, S. J., & Holschuh, J. L. (1996). The effects of rereading, self-selected strategy use, and rehearsal on the immediate and delayed understanding of text. *Reading Psychology, 17*(2), 137–157.

Nixon, M. (1990). Professional training in psychology.

American Psychologist, 45(11), 1257–1262.

Njeri, I. (1991). Beyond the melting pot. *Los Angeles Times*, Jan. 13, E-1, E-8.

Noble, K. D., Subotnik, R. F., & Arnold, K. D. (1996). A new model for adult female talent development. In K. D. Arnold, K. D. Noble, & R. F. Subotnik (Eds.), *Remarkable women*. Cresskill, NJ: Hampton Press.

Noel, J. G., Forsyth, D. R., & Kelley, K. N. (1987). Improving the performance of failing students by overcoming their self-serving attributional biases. *Basic and Applied Social Psychology, 8*(1–2), 151–162.

Noller, P. & Ruzzene, M. (1991). Communication in marriage. In G. J. O. Fletcher & F. D. Fincham (Eds.), *Cognition and close relationships*. Hillsdale, NJ: Erlbaum.

Norris, P. A. (1986). On the status of biofeedback and clinical practice. *American Psychologist*, Sept., 1009–1010.

Norris, R. M. & Weinman, J. A. (1996). Psychological change following a long sail training voyage. *Personality & Individual Differences, 21*(2), 189–194.

North, C. S. (1987). *Welcome silence*. NY: Simon & Schuster.

Nurmi, J. (1992). Age differences in adult life goals, and their temporal extension. *International Journal of Behavioral Development, 80*(4), 487–508.

Nurnberger, J. I., & Zimmerman, J. (1970). Applied analysis of human behaviors: An alternative to conventional motivational inferences and unconscious determination in therapeutic programming. *Behavior Therapy, 1*, 59–69.

Nyberg, L. & Tulving, E. (1996). Classifying human long-term memory: Evidence from converging dissociations. *European Journal of Cognitive Psychology, 8*(2), 163–183.

O'Brien, R. M., Figlerski, R. W., Howard, S. R., & Caggiano, J. (1981). The effects of multi-year, guaranteed contracts on the performance of pitchers in major league baseball. Paper presented at the annual meeting of the American Psychological Association, Los Angeles, Aug. 1981.

O'Leary, K. D., Barling, J., Arias, I., Rosenbaum, A. et al. (1989). Prevalence and stability of physical aggression between spouses: A longitudinal analysis. *Journal of Consulting & Clinical Psychology, 57*(2), 263–268.

O'Malley, M. N., & Andrews, L. (1983). The effect of mood and incentives on helping: Are there some things money can't buy? *Motivation and Emotion*, 7, 179.

O'Sullivan, J. J. & Quevillon, R. P. (1992). 40 years later: Is the Boulder model still alive? *American Psychologist, 47*(1), 67–70.

Oatley, K. & Jenkins, J. M. (1992). Human emotions: Function and dysfunction. In M. R. Rosenzweig and L. W. Porter (Eds.), *Annual Review of Psychology, 45*, 55–85.

Ofshe, R. & Watters, E. (1995). *Making monsters*. Berkeley: University of California Press.

Ohman, A. & Soares, J. J. (1993). On the automatic nature of phobic fear. *Journal of Abnormal Psychology, 102*(1), 121–132.

Ohzawa, I., DeAngelis, G. C., & Freeman, R. D. (1990). Stereoscopic depth discrimination in the visual cortex: Neurons ideally suited as disparity detectors. *Science, 249*(4972), 1037–1041.

Olander, F. (1990). Consumer psychology: Not necessarily a manipulative science. *Applied Psychology: An International Review, 39*(1), 105–126.

Olds, J. (1977). *Drives and reinforcements: Behavioral studies of hypothalamic functions*. New York: Raven Press.

Olds, J., & Milner, P. (1954). Positive reinforcement produced by electrical stimulation of septal area and other regions of rat brain. *Journal of Comparative and Physiological Psychology, 47*, 419–427.

Olds, M. E., & Fobes, J. L. (1981). The central basis of motivation: Intracranial self-stimulation studies. *Annual Review of Psychology, 32*, 523–574.

Oliver, J. E. (1993). Intergenerational transmission of child abuse. *American Journal of Psychiatry, 150*(9), 1315–1324.

Oliver, M. B. & Hyde, J. S. (1993). Gender differences in sexuality. *Psychological Bulletin, 114*(1), 29–51.

Oliwenstein, L. (1993). The gene with two faces. *Discover*, May, 26.

Ollendick, T. H. & King, N. J. (1991). Origins of childhood fears. *Behaviour Research & Therapy, 29*(2), 117–123.

Olmstead, B. (1983). More heavy drinking in colleges. *Los Angeles Times*, Feb. 17.

Olson, J. M. & Zanna, M. P. (1993). Attitudes and attitude change. In L. W. Porter and M. R. Rosenzweig (Eds.), *Annual Review of Psychology, 44*, 117–154.

Olson, R. L. & Roberts, M. W. (1987). Alternative treatments for sibling aggression. *Behavior Therapy, 18*(3), 243–250.

Olson, S. L., Bates, J. E., & Kaskie, B. (1992). Caregiver-infant interaction antecedents of children's school-age cognitive ability. *Merrill-Palmer Quarterly, 38*(3), 309–330.

Omer, H. & London, P. (1988). Metamorphosis in psychotherapy: End of the systems era. *Psychotherapy, 25*(2), 171–180.

Ones, D., Viswesvaran, C., & Schmidt, F. L. (1993). Comprehensive meta-analysis of integrity test validities. *Journal of Applied Psychology, 78*(4), 679–703.

Orlick, T. D. (1975). The sports environment: A capacity to enhance—a capacity to destroy. In B. S. Rushall (Ed.), *The status of psychomotor learning and sport psychology research*. Dartmouth, Nova Scotia: Sport Science Associates.

Orlock, C. (1993). *Inner time*. New York: Birch Lane Press.

Ornstein, R. & Ehrlich, P. (1989). *New world new mind*. New York: Simon & Schuster.

Ornstein, R. E. (1972). *The psychology of consciousness*. San Francisco: Freeman.

Ornstein, S. & Isabella, L. (1990). Age vs. stage models of career attitudes of women: A partial replication and extension. *Journal of Vocational Behavior, 36*, 1–19.

Orpen, C. (1981). Effect of flexible working hours on employee satisfaction and performance: A field experiment. *Journal of Applied Psychology, 66*, 113–115.

Osgood, C. E. (1952). The nature and measurement of meaning. *Psychological Bulletin, 49*, 197–237.

Oskamp, S. (1995a). Applying social psychology to avoid ecological disaster. *Journal of Social Issues, 51*(4), 217–239.

Oskamp, S. (1995b). Resouce conservation and recycling: Behavior and policy. *Journal of Social Issues, 51*(4), 157–177.

Ost, L. (1996). One-session group treatment of spider phobia. *Behaviour Research & Therapy, 34*(9), 707–715.

Overmier, J. B., & Seligman, M. E. P. (1967). Effects of inescapable shock upon subsequent escape and avoidance learning. *Journal of Comparative and Physiological Psychology, 63*, 23–33.

Overton, D. A. (1985). Contextual stimulus effects of drugs and internal states. In P. D. Balsam & A. Tomie (Eds.), *Context and learning*, 357–384. Hillsdale, NJ: Erlbaum.

Owen, J. D. (1976). Flextime: Some problems and solutions. *Industrial and Labor Relations Review, 29*, 152–160.

Oyama, T. & Ichikawa, S. (1990). Some experimental studies on imagery in Japan. *Journal of Mental Imagery, 14*(3–4), 185–195.

Pagano, R. R. (1981). *Understanding statistics*. St. Paul, MN: West.

Palfai, T. & Jankiewicz, H. (1991). *Drugs and human behavior*. Dubuque, IA: Wm. C. Brown.

Palkovitz, R. J., & Lore, R. K. (1980). Note taking and note review: Why students fail questions based on lecture material. *Teaching of Psychology*, 7, 159–160.

Palmer, S. E. (1992). Common region: A new principle of perceptual grouping. *Cognitive Psychology, 24*(3), 436–447.

Papps, F., Walker, M., Trimboli, A., & Trimboli, C. (1995). Parental discipline in Anglo, Greek, Lebanese, and Vietnamese cultures. *Journal of Cross-Cultural Psychology, 26*(1), 49–64.

Park, D. C., Smith, A. D., & Cavanaugh, J. C. (1990). Metamemories of memory researchers. *Memory & Cognition, 18*(3), 321–327.

Parke, R. D., & Sawin, D. B. (1977). Fathering: It's a major role. *Psychology Today*, Nov.

Parkes, C. M. (1979). *Grief: The painful reaction to the loss of a loved one*. Monograph, University of California, San Diego.

Parsons, L. M., Fox, P. T., Downs, J. H., Glass, T., et al. (1995). Use of implicit motor imagery for visual shape discrimination as revealed by PET. *Nature, 375*(6526), 54–58.

Pasachoff, J. (1981). *Contemporary astronomy*. New York: Holt, Rinehart & Winston.

Passman, R. H. (1987). Attachments to inanimate objects: Are children who have security blankets insecure? *Journal of Consulting and Clinical Psychology, 55*(6), 825–830.

Patrick, C. J. & Iacono, W. G. (1989). Psychopathy, threat, and polygraph test accuracy. *Journal of Applied Psychology, 74*(2), 347–355.

Patrick, C. J., Bradley, M. M., & Lang, P. J. (1993). Emotion in the criminal psychopath: Startle reflex modulation. *Journal of Abnormal Psychology, 102*(1), 82–92.

Pattatucci, A. M. & Hamer, D. H. (1995). Development and familiality of sexual orientation in females. *Behavior Genetics 25*(5), 407–420.

Patten, B. M. (1990). The history of memory arts. *Neurology, 40*(2), 346–352.

Patterson, C. H. (1989). Foundations for a systematic eclectic psychotherapy. *Psychotherapy, 26*(4), 427–435.

Patterson, C. J. (1995). Sexual orientation and human development: An overview. *Developmental Psychology, 31*(1), 3–11.

Patterson, G. R. (1982). *Coercive family process*. Eugene, OR: Castilia Press.

Pavlov, I. P. (1927). *Conditioned reflexes*. Translated by G. V. Anrep. New York: Dover.

Pedersen, N. L., Plomin, R., McClearn, G. E., & Friberg, L. (1988). Neuroticism, extraversion, and related traits in adult twins reared apart and reared together. *Journal of Personality & Social Psychology, 55*(6), 950–957.

Peeters, M. C. W., Buunk, B. P., & Schaufeli, W. B. (1995). A micro-analysis exploration of the cognitive appraisal of daily stressful events at work. *Anxiety, Stress & Coping: An International Journal, 8*(2), 127–139.

Pelaez-Nogueras, M., Gewirtz, J. L., Field, T., & Cigales, M. (1996). Infants' preference for touch stimulation in face-to-face interactions. *Journal of Applied Developmental Psychology, 17*(2), 199–213.

Pelton, T. (1983). The shootists. *Science 83, 4*(4), 84–86.

Pendergast, M. (1995). *Victims of memory: Incest accusations and shattered lives*. Hinesburg, VT: Upper Access.

Penfield, W. (1957). Brain's record of past a continuous movie film. *Science News Letter,* April 27, 265.

Penfield, W. (1958). *The excitable cortex in conscious man.* Springfield, IL: Charles C Thomas.

Pennebaker, James W. & Francis, Martha E. (1996). Cognitive, emotional, and language processes in disclosure. *Cognition & Emotion, 10*(6), 601–626.

Pennisi, E. (1992). Valentine bind. *Science News, 141* (Feb. 15), 110–111.

Pepler, D. J. & Craig, W. M. (1995). A peek behind the fence: Naturalistic observations of aggressive children with remote audiovisual recording. *Developmental Psychology, 31*(4), 548–553.

Perin, C. T. (1943). A quantitative investigation of the delay of reinforcement gradient. *Journal of Experimental Psychology, 32,* 37–51.

Perkins, D. (1995). *Outsmarting IQ: The emerging science of learnable intelligence.* New York: Free Press.

Perkins, K. A. (1995). Individual variability in responses to nicotine. *Behavior Genetics, 25*(2), 119–132.

Perlman, D. & Cozby, P. C. (1983). *Social psychology.* NY: Holt, Rinehart & Winston.

Perls, F. (1969). *Gestalt therapy verbatim.* Lafayette, CA: Real People.

Perry, C., Orne, M. T., London, R. W., & Orne, E. C. (1996). Rethinking per se exclusions of hypnotically elicited recall as legal testimony. *International Journal of Clinical & Experimental Hypnosis, 44*(1), 66–81.

Perry, D. G., Perry, L. C., & Weiss, R. J. (1989). Sex differences in the consequences that children anticipate for aggression. *Developmental Psychology, 25*(2), 312–319.

Peters, W. A. (1971). *A class divided.* Garden City, NY: Doubleday.

Petersen, A. C. (1987). Those gangly years. *Psychology Today,* Sept., 28–34.

Petersen, A. C., Kennedy, R. E., & Sullivan, P. (1991). Coping with adolescence. In M. E. Colten & S. Gore, (Eds.), *Adolescent Stress.* New York: Aldine de Gruyter.

Petersen, S. E., Fox, P. T., Posner, M. I., Mintun, M. et al. (1988). Positron emission tomographic studies of the cortical anatomy of single-word processing. *Nature, 331*(6157), 585–589.

Peterson, B. E. & Klohnen, E. C. (1995). Realization of generativity in two samples of women at midlife. *Psychology & Aging, 10*(1), 20–29.

Peterson, J. (1995). How are psychologists perceived by the public? *APA Monitor,* March, 31.

Peterson, L. R., & Peterson, M. J. (1959). Short-term retention of individual verbal items. *Journal of Experimental Psychology, 58,* 193–198.

Peterson, P. L. (1979). Direct instruction: Effective for what and for whom? *Educational Leadership, 37,* 46–48.

Peterson, S. E. (1992). The cognitive functions of underlining as a study technique. *Reading Research & Instruction, 31*(2), 49–56.

Petitto, L. A. & Marentette, P. F. (1991). Babbling in the manual mode: Evidence for the ontogeny of language. *Science, 251*(March 22), 1493–1496.

Petri, H. (1996). *Motivation.* Pacific Grove, CA: Brooks/Cole.

Petrie, T. A. & Diehl, N. S. (1995). Sport psychology in the profession of psychology. *Professional Psychology: Research & Practice, 26*(3), 288–291.

Pettit, G. S. & Bates, J. E. (1989). Family interaction patterns and children's behavior problems from infancy to 4 years. *Developmental Psychology, 25*(3), 413–420.

Pfost, K. S. & Fiore, M. (1990). Pursuit of nontraditional occupations: Fear of success or fear of not being chosen? *Sex Roles, 23*(1–2), 15–24.

Phillips, D. P. & Wills, J. S. (1987). A drop in suicides around major national holidays. *Suicide and Life-Threatening Behavior, 17,* 1–12.

Phillips, J. L. (1969). *Origins of intellect: Piaget's theory.* San Francisco: Freeman.

Phillips, R. B., Sharma, R., Premachandra, B. R., & Vaughn, A. J. (1996). Intrauterine exposure to cocaine: Effect on neurobehavior of neonates. *Infant Behavior & Development, 19*(1), 71–81.

Piaget, J. (1951, original French, 1945). *The psychology of intelligence.* New York: Norton.

Piaget, J. (1952). *The origins of intelligence in children.* New York: International University Press.

Piccione, C., Hilgard, E. R., & Zimbardo, P. G. (1989). On the degree of stability of measured hypnotizability over a 25-year period. *Journal of Personality & Social Psychology, 56*(2), 289–295.

Pierce, J. P. (1991). Progress and problems in international public health efforts to reduce tobacco usage. *Annual Review of Public Health, 12,* 383–400.

Pierrel, R., & Sherman, J. G. (1963). Train your pet the Barnabus way. *Brown Alumni Monthly,* Feb.

Piliavin, I. M., Rodin, J., & Piliavin, J. A. (1969). Good samaritanism: An underground phenomenon? *Journal of Personality & Social Psychology, 13,* 289–299.

Pilkington, N. W. & D'Augelli, A. R. (1995). Victimization of lesbian, gay, and bisexual youth in community settings. *Journal of Community Psychology, 23*(1), 34–56.

Pillow, D. R., Zautra, A. J., & Sandler, I. (1996). Major life events and minor stressors: Identifying mediational links in the stress process. *Journal of Personality & Social Psychology, 70*(2), 381–394.

Pilowsky, L. S., Kerwin, R. W., & Murray, R. M. (1993). Schizophrenia: A neurodevelopmental perspective. *Neuropsychopharmacology, 9*(1), 83–91.

Pinsof, W. M., Wynne, L. C., & Hambright, A. B. (1996). The outcomes of couple and family therapy. *Psychotherapy, 33*(2), 321–331.

Pion, G. M. (1991). Psychologists wanted: Employment trends over the last decade. In R. R. Kilburg (Ed.), *How to manage your career in psychology.* Washington, DC: American Psychological Association.

Pion, G. M., Mednick, M. T., Astin, H. S., Hall, C. C. I. et al. (1996). The shifting gender composition of psychology. *American Psychologist, 51*(5), 509–528.

Pittman, T. & Heller, J. F. (1987). Social motivation. *Annual Review of Psychology, 38,* 461–489.

Piven, J., Arndt, S., & Palmer, P. (1995). An MRI study of brain size in autism. *American Journal of Psychiatry, 152*(8), 1145.

Pliner, P. & Haddock, G. (1996). Perfectionism in weight-concerned and -unconcerned women. *International Journal of Eating Disorders, 19*(4), 381–389.

Pliner, P., Eng, A., & Krishnan, K. (1995). The effects of fear and hunger on food neophobia in humans. *Appetite, 25*(1), 77–87.

Plomin, R. (1989). Environment and genes: Determinants of behavior. *American Psychologist, 44*(2), 105–111.

Plomin, R. & Rende, R. (1991). Human behavioral genetics. In M. R. Rosenzweig & L. W. Porter (Eds.), *Annual Review of Psychology, 42,* 161–190.

Plug, C. & Ross, H. E. (1994). The natural moon illusion: A multifactor angular account. *Perception, 23*(3), 321–333.

Plutchik, R. (1980). *Emotion.* New York: Harper & Row.

Plutchik, R. (1990). Emotions in psychotherapy: A psychoevolutionary perspective. In R. Plutchik & H. Kellerman (Eds.), *Emotion.* San Diego, CA: Academic Press.

Plutchik, R. (1994). *The psychology and biology of emotion.* New York: HarperCollins.

Pogatchnik, S. (1990). Kids' TV gets more violent, study finds. *The Los Angeles Times,* Jan. 26, F, 1, 27.

Pollard, P. (1995). Pornography and sexual aggression. *Current Psychology: Developmental, Learning, Personality, Social, 14*(3), 200–221.

Pollock, V. E., Briere, J., Schneider, L., Knop, J. et al. (1990). Childhood antecedents of antisocial behavior. *American Journal of Psychiatry, 147*(10), 1290–1293.

Pope, H. G. & Yurgelun-Todd, D. (1996). The residual cognitive effects of heavy marijuana use in college students. *Journal of the American Medical Association, 275*(7), 521–527.

Pope, H. G., Gruber, A. J., & Yurgelun-Todd, D. (1995). The residual neuropsychological effects of cannabis. *Drug & Alcohol Dependence, 38*(1), 25–34.

Port, R. L. & Seybold, K. S. (1995). Hippocampal synaptic plasticity as a biological substrate underlying episodic psychosis. *Biological Psychiatry, 37*(5), 318–324.

Porte, H. S. & Hobson, J. A. (1996). Physical motion in dreams: One measure of three theories. *Journal of Abnormal Psychology, 105*(3), 329–335.

Porter, L. S. & Lane, R. C. (1996). Iatrogenic creation of false childhood sexual abuse memories: Controversy, dynamics, fantasy, and reality. *Journal of Contemporary Psychotherapy, 26*(1), 23–42.

Potashkin, B. D. & Beckles, N. (1990). Relative efficacy of Ritalin and biofeedback treatments in the management of hyperactivity. *Biofeedback & Self-Regulation, 15*(4), 305–315.

Potkay, C. R., & Allen, B. P. (1986). *Personality: Theory, research, and applications.* Monterey, CA: Brooks/Cole.

Poulin, J. & Walter, C. (1993). Social worker burnout. *Social Work Research & Abstracts, 29*(4), 5–11.

Poulin-Dubois, D., Graham, S., & Sippola, L. (1995). Early lexical development: The contribution of parental labelling and infants' categorization abilities. *Journal of Child Language, 22*(2), 325–343.

Poulton, R. G. & Andrews, G. (1996). Change in danger cognitions in agoraphobia and social phobia during treatment. *Behaviour Research & Therapy, 34*(5–6), 413–421.

Powell, A. L. & Thelen, M. H. (1996). Emotions and cognitions associated with bingeing and weight control behavior in bulimia. *Journal of Psychosomatic Research, 40*(3), 317–328.

Pratkanis, A. R. (1992). The Cargo-sult science of subliminal persuasion. *Skeptical Inquirer, 16*(Spring), 260–272.

Preiser, R. (1997). Personal space. *Discover,* May, 94–95.

Premack, A. J., & Premack, D. (1972). Teaching language to an ape. *Scientific American,* Oct., 92–99.

Premack, D. (1965). Reinforcement theory. In D. Levine (Ed.), *Nebraska symposium on motivation.* Lincoln: University of Nebraska Press.

Premack, D. (1970). The education of S*A*R*A*H. *Psychology Today,* Sept., 54–58.

Premack, D. (1983). Animal cognition. *Annual Review of Psychology, 34,* 351–362.

Premack, D., & Premack, A. J. (1983). *The mind of an ape.* New York: Norton.

Prentice, D. A. & Miller, D. T. (1993). Pluralistic ignorance of alcohol use on campus. *Journal of Personality and Social Psychology, 64*(2), 243–256.

Pressley, M. (1987). Are key-word method effects limited to slow presentation rates? An empirically based reply to Hall and Fuson (1986). *Journal of Educational Psychology, 79*(3), 333–335.

Pressley, M., Symons, S., McDaniel, M. A., Snyder, B. et al. (1988). Elaborative interrogation facilitates acquisition of confusing facts. *Journal of Educational Psychology, 80*(3), 268–278.

Pritchard, R. M. (1961). A collimator stabilizing system. *Quarterly Journal of Experimental Psychology, 13,* 181–183.

Proite, R., Dannells, M., & Benton, S. L. (1993). Gender, sex-role stereotypes, and the attribution of responsibility for date and acquaintance rape. *Journal of College Student Development, 34*(6), 411–417.

Pursch, J. A. (1983). Cocaine can give you the business. *Los Angeles Times*, June 12, Part VII, 12.

Rader, P. E., & Hicks, R. A. (1987). Jet lag desynchronization and self-assessment of business related performance. Paper presented at the Western Psychological Association meeting in Long Beach, CA, April, 1987.

Radetsky, P. (1992). Straight sex and AIDS vaccines. *Discover*, Jan., 52–53.

Radmacher, S. A. & Latosi-Sawin, E. (1995). Summary writing: A tool to improve student comprehension and writing in psychology. *Teaching of Psychology, 22*(2), 113–115.

Rafaeli, A., & Klimoski, R. J. (1983). Predicting sales success through handwriting analysis: An evaluation of the effects of training and handwriting sample content. *Journal of Applied Psychology, 68,* 212–217.

Rahe, R. H. (1972). Subjects' recent life changes and their near-future illness reports. *Annals of Clinical Research, 4,* 250–265.

Ramachandran, V. S. (1992a). Filling in gaps in perception. *Current directions in psychological science 1*(6), 199–205.

Ramachandran, V. S. (1992b). Blind spots. *Scientific American*, May, 86–91.

Ramachandran, V. S. (1995). 2-D or not 2-D—that is the question. In, R. Gregory, J. Harris, P. Heard, & D. Rose (Eds.), *The artful eye*. Oxford: Oxford University Press.

Ramanaiah, N. V., Detwiler, F. R. J., & Byravan, A. (1995). Sex-role orientation and satisfaction with life. *Psychological Reports, 77*(3, Dec, Pt 2), 1260–1262.

Ramsey, P. H., Ramsey, P. P., & Barnes, M. J. (1987). Effects of student confidence and item difficulty on test score gains due to answer changing. *Teaching of Psychology, 14*(4), 206–209.

Randi, J. (1980). *Flim-flam!* New York: Lippincott & Crowell.

Randi, J. (1983). Science and the chimera. In G. O. Abell & B. Singer (Eds.), *Science and the paranormal*. New York: Scribner's.

Rando, T. A. (1995). "Grief and mourning: Accommodating to loss." In H. Wass & R. A. Neimeyer (Eds.), *Dying: Facing the facts*. Washington, D.C.: Taylor & Francis.

Raven, B. H. (1974). The analysis of power and power preference. In J. T. Tebeschi (Ed.), *Prospectus on social power*. Chicago: Aldine.

Raymond, C. (1991). Pioneering research challenges accepted notions concerning the cognitive abilities of infants. *The Chronicle of Higher Education*, Jan. 23, A5–7.

Read, J. (1995). Female sexual dysfunction. *International Review of Psychiatry, 7*(2), 175–182.

Reed, J. D. & Bruce, D. (1982) Longitudinal tracking of difficult memory retrievals. *Cognitive Psychology, 14,* 280–300.

Reed, S. K. (1996). *Cognition: Theory and applications (3ed)*. Pacific Grove, CA: Brooks/Cole.

Reid, H. M. & Fine, G. A. (1992). Self-disclosure in men's friendships. In P. M. Nardi (Ed.), *Men's friendships*. Newbury Park, CA: Sage.

Reif A. E. (1981). The causes of cancer. *American Scientist, 69,* 437–447.

Reif, L. V., Patton, M. J., & Gold, P. B. (1995). Bereavement, stress, and social support in members of a self-help group. *Journal of Community Psychology, 23*(4), 292–306.

Reifman, A. S., Larrick, R. P., & Fein, S. (1991). Temper and temperature on the diamond: The heat-aggression relationship in major league baseball. *Personality & Social Psychology Bulletin, 17*(5), 580–585.

Reisner, A. D. (1996). Repressed memories: True and false. *Psychological Record, 46*(4), 563–579.

Reiterman, T. (1993). Parallel roads led to Jonestown, Waco. *The Los Angeles Times*, April 23, A-24.

Reker, G. T. (1994). Logotheory and logotherapy. *International Forum for Logotherapy, 17*(1), 47–55.

Remland, M. S., Jones, T. S., & Brinkman, H. (1991). Proxemic and haptic behavior in three European countries. *Journal of Nonverbal Behavior, 15*(4), 215–232.

Rennie, J. (1994). Grading the gene tests. *Scientific American*, June, 88–97.

Renwick, P. A., & Lawler, E. E. (1979). What you really want from your job. *Psychology Today, 11*(12), 53–65.

Research versus animal rights: Is there a middle ground? (1989). A. Newman, *American Scientist*, 77(March–April), 135–137.

Reybowski, J. (1982). Social motivation. *Annual Review of Psychology, 33,* 123–154.

Reynolds, S., Stiles, W. B., Barkham, M., Shapiro, D. A. (1996). Acceleration of changes in session impact during contrasting time-limited psychotherapies. *Journal of Consulting & Clinical Psychology, 64*(3), 577–586.

Reznick, J. S. & Goldfield, B. A. (1992). Rapid change in lexical development in comprehension and production. *Developmental Psychology, 28*(3), 406–413.

Rhine, J. B. (1953). *New world of the mind*. New York: Sloane.

Rhine, J. B. (1977). History of experimental studies. In B. B. Wolman (Ed.), *Handbook of parapsychology*. New York: Van Nostrand Reinhold.

Rhodewalt, F. (1994). Conceptions of ability, achievement goals, and individual differences in self-handicapping behavior. *Journal of Personality, 62*(1), 67–85.

Rhodewalt, F. & Zone, J. B. (1989). Appraisal of life change, depression, and illness in hardy and nonhardy women. *Journal of Personality & Social Psychology, 56*(1), 81–88.

Ricci, L. C. & Wellman, M. W. (1990). Monamines: Biochemical markers of suicide? *Journal of Clinical Psychology, 46*(1), 106–116.

Riccio, C. A., Hynd, G. W., Cohen, M. J. et al. (1993). Neurological basis of attention deficit hyperactivity disorder. *Exceptional Children, 60*(2), 118–124.

Rice, K. M., Blanchard, E. B., & Purcell, M. (1993). Biofeedback treatments of generalized anxiety disorder. *Biofeedback & Self-Regulation, 18*(2), 93–105.

Rice, M. E. (1997). Violent offender research and implications for the criminal justice system. *American Psychologist, 52*(4), 414–423.

Richards, L., Rollerson, B., & Phillips, J. (1991). Perceptions of submissiveness: Implications for victimization. *Journal of Psychology, 125*(4), 407–411.

Richardson, B. I. (1991). Utilizing the resources of the African-American church. In C. C. Lee & B. L. Richardson (Eds.), *Multicultural issues in counseling*. Alexandria, VA: American Association for Counseling and Development.

Richelle, M. N. (1995). *B. F. Skinner: A reappraisal*. Hillsdale: Erlbaum.

Ricketts, M. S., & Galloway, R. E. (1984). Effects of three different one-hour single-session treatments for test anxiety. *Psychological Reports, 54,* 113–119.

Riefer, D. M., Keveri, M. K., & Kramer, D. L. (1995). Name that tune: Eliciting the tip-of-the-tongue experience using auditory stimuli. *Psychological Reports, 77*(3) (Pt 2), 1379–1390.

Rieke, M. L. & Guastello, S. J. (1995). Unresolved issues in honesty and integrity testing. *American Psychologist*, June, 458–459.

Riese, M. L. (1995). Mothers' ratings of infant temperament: Relation to neonatal latency to soothe by pacifier. *Journal of Genetic Psychology, 156*(1), 23–31.

Rincover, A. & Newsom, C. D. (1985). The relative motivational properties of sensory and edible reinforcers in teaching autistic children. *Journal of Applied Behavior Analysis, 18*(3), 237–248.

Ring, K. (1980). *Life at death*. New York: Coward, McCann & Geoghegan.

Ritchie, R. J., & Moses, J. L. (1983). Assessment center correlates of women's advancement into middle management: A 7-year longitudinal analysis. *Journal of Applied Psychology, 68,* 227–231.

Roan, S. (1992). Forever set in your ways at 30? *Los Angeles Times*, Sept. 1, E-1, E-2.

Roan, S. (1993). Growth-drug debate: What is too short? *Los Angeles Times*, Feb. 2, E-1,8.

Roberts, D. F., & Bachen, C. M. (1981). Mass communication effects. *Annual Review of Psychology, 32,* 307–356.

Roberts, R. (1989). Passenger fear of flying: Behavioural treatment with extensive *in-vivo* exposure and group support. *Aviation, Space, & Environmental Medicine, 60*(4), 342–348.

Roberts, S. M. (1995). Applicability of the goodness-of-fit hypothesis to coping with daily hassles. *Psychological Reports, 77*(3, Pt 1), 943–954.

Robertson, T. S. & Kassarjian, H. H. (Eds.). (1991). *Handbook of consumer behavior*. Engelwood Cliffs, NJ: Prentice-Hall.

Robinson, F. P. (1970). *Effective study, 4th ed*. New York: Harper & Row.

Robinson-Riegler, B. & McDaniel, M. (1994). Further constraints on the bizarreness effect: Elaboration at encoding. *Memory & Cognition, 22*(6), 702–712.

Robson, P. (1984). Prewalking locomotor movements and their use in predicting standing and walking. *Child Care, Health & Development, 10,* 317–330.

Rock, I., & Kaufman, L. (1962). The moon illusion II. *Science, 136,* 1023–1031.

Rodin, J. (1981). Current status of the internal-external hypothesis for obesity: What went wrong? *American Psychologist, 36,* 361–372.

Roediger, H. L. (1990). Implicit memory. *American Psychologist, 45*(9), 1043–1056.

Roediger, H. L. & McDermott, K. B. (1995). Creating false memories: Remembering words not presented on lists. *Journal of Experimental Psychology: Learning, Memory, and Cognition, 21*(4), 803–814.

Rogers, C. R. (1959). A theory of therapy, personality, and interpersonal relationships, as developed in the client-centered framework. In S. Koch (Ed.), *Psychology: A study of a science*, Vol.3. New York: McGraw-Hill.

Rogers, C. R. (1961). *On becoming a person: A therapist's view of psychotherapy*. Boston: Houghton Mifflin.

Rogers, C. R. (1980). *A way of being*. Boston: Houghton Mifflin

Rogers, J. M. (1971). Drug abuse—Just what the doctor ordered. *Psychology Today*, Sept., 16–24.

Rogers, J. R. (1990). Female suicide. *Journal of Counseling & Development, 69*(6), 37–38.

Rogers, S. (1996). The horizon-ratio relation as information for relative size in pictures. *Perception & Psychophysics, 58*(1), 142–152.

Rogler, L. H., Cortes, D. E., & Malgady, R. G. (1991). Acculturation and mental health status among Hispanics. *American Psychologist, 46*(6), 585–597.

Rohsenow, D. J., & Smith R. E. (1982). Irrational beliefs as predictors of negative affective states. *Motivation and Emotion, 6,* 299–301.

Rolling, B. L. & Belsky, J. (1992). The contribution of mother-child and father-child relationships to the quality of sibling interaction: A longitudinal study. *Child Development*, 63(5), 1209–1222.

Ronen, T. & Wozner, Y. (1995). A self-control intervention package for the treatment of primary nocturnal enuresis. *Child & Family Behavior Therapy*, 17(1), 1–20.

Ronnett, G. V., Hester, L. D., Nye, J. S., Connors, K., & Snyder, S. H. (1990). Human cortical neuronal cell line: Establishment from a patient with unilateral megalencephaly. *Science*, 248(4955), 603–605.

Roos, P. E. & Cohen, L. H. (1987). Sex roles and social support as moderators of life stress adjustment. *Journal of Personality & Social Psychology*, 52, 576–585.

Rorer, L. G., & Widiger, T. A. (1983). Personality structure and assessment. *Annual Review of Psychology*, 34, 431–463.

Rosch, E. (1977). Classification of real-world objects: Origins and representations in cognition. In P. N. Johnson-Laird & P. C. Wason (Eds.), *Thinking: Reading in cognitive science*. Cambridge: Cambridge University Press.

Roscoe, S. N. (1985). Bigness is in the eye of the beholder. *Human Factors*, 27(6), 615–636.

Rose, K. J. (1984). How animals think. *Science Digest*, 89(Feb.), 59–61.

Rose, R. J. (1995). Genes and human behavior. *Annual Review of Psychology*, 46, 625–654.

Rosenbaum, J. F., Biederman, J., Gersten, M., Hirshfeld, D. R. et al. (1989). Behavioral inhibition in children of parents with panic disorder and agoraphobia: A controlled study. *Annual Progress in Child Psychiatry & Child Development*, 294–315.

Rosenbaum, J. F., Biederman, J., Hirshfeld, D. R., Bolduc, E. A. et al. (1991). Further evidence of an association between behavioral inhibition and anxiety disorders. *Journal of Psychiatric Research*, 25(1–2), 49–65.

Rosenbaum, M. B. (1979). The changing body image of the adolescent girl. In M. Sugar (Ed.), *Female adolescent development*. New York: Brunner/Mazel.

Rosenberg, L. B. (1994). The effect of interocular distance upon depth perception when using stereoscopic displays to perform work within virtual and telepresent environments. USAF AMRL Technical Report (Wright-Patterson), Jul., AL/CF-TR-1994-0052. 30 p.

Rosenblith, J. F. (1992). *In the beginning*. Newbury Park: Sage.

Rosenfeld, P., Giacalone, R. A., & Tedeschi, J. T. (1983). Cognitive dissonance vs. impression management. *Journal of Social Psychology*, 120, 203–211.

Rosenhan, D. L. (1973). On being sane in insane places. *Science*, 179, 250–258.

Rosenman, R. H., Brand, R. J., Jenkins, C. D., Friedman, M., Straus, R., & Wurm, M. (1975). Coronary heart disease in the Western Collaborative Group Study: Final follow-up experience of 8 1/2 years. *Journal of the American Medical Association*, 233, 872–877.

Rosenstiel, T. B. (1991). Americans praise media but still back censorship, postwar poll says. *Los Angeles Times*, March 25, A-9.

Rosenthal, D., & Quinn, O. W. (1977). Quadruplet hallucinations: Phenotypic variations of a schizophrenic genotype. *Archives of General Psychiatry*, 34(7), 817–827.

Rosenthal, N. E. (1993a). *Winter blues: Seasonal affective disorder*. New York: Guilford Press.

Rosenthal, R. (1965). *Clever Hans: A case study of scientific method. Introduction to Clever Hans: (The horse of Mr. Von Osten)*. O. Pfungst. New York: Holt, Rinehart & Winston.

Rosenthal, R. (1973). The Pygmalion effect lives. *Psychology Today*, Sept., 56–63.

Rosenthal, R. (1976). *Experimenter effects in behavioral research*. New York: Appleton-Century-Crofts.

Rosenthal, T. L. (1993b). To soothe the savage breast. *Behavior Research & Therapy*, 31(5), 439–462.

Rosenthal, T. L. & Steffek, B. D. (1991). Modeling methods. In F. H. Kanfer & A. P. Goldstein (Eds.), *Helping people change*. Elmsford, NY: Pergamon.

Rosenthal, T. L., & Rosenthal, R. (1980). The vicious cycle of stress reaction. Copyright, Renate and Ted Rosenthal, Stress Management Clinic, Department of Psychiatry, University of Tennessee College of Medicine, Memphis, Tennessee.

Ross, C. A., Miller, S. D., Reagor, P., Bjornson, L. et al. (1990). Structured interview data on 102 cases of multiple personality disorder from four centers. *American Journal of Psychiatry*, 147(5), 596–601.

Ross, J. (1976). The resources of binocular perception. *Scientific American*, March, 80–86.

Ross, M., Karniol, R., & Rothstein, M. (1976). Reward contingency and intrinsic motivation in children. *Journal of Personality & Social Psychology*, 33, 442–447.

Rossi, P. H. (1990). The old homeless and the new homeless in historical perspective. *American Psychologist*, 45(8), 954–959.

Roth, W. T., Breivik, G., Jorgensen, P. E., & Hofmann. (1996). Activation in novice and expert parachutists while jumping. *Psychophysiology*, 33(1), 63–72.

Rothbaum, B. O., Hodges, L. F., Kooper, R., Opdyke, D., et al. (in press). Virtual reality graded exposue in the treatment of acrophobia: A case report. *Behavior Therapy*, 26(3).

Rothbaum, B. O., Hodges, L. F., Kooper, R., Opdyke, D., et al. (1995). Effectiveness of computer-generated (virtual reality) graded exposure in the treatment of acrophobia. *American Journal of Psychiatry*, 152(4), 626–628.

Rothbaum, B. O., Hodges, L., Watson, B. A., Kessler, G. D. et al. (1996). Virtual reality exposure therapy in the treatment of fear of flying: A case report. *Behaviour Research & Therapy*, 34(5–6), 477–481.

Rothblum, E. D., Solomon, L. J., & Murakami, J. (1986). Affective, cognitive, and behavioral differences between high and low procrastinators. *Journal of Consulting Psychology*, 33(4), 387–394.

Rothspan, S. & Read, S. J. (1996). Present versus future time perspective and HIV risk among heterosexual college students. *Health Psychology*, 15(2), 131–134.

Rotter, J. B., & Hochreich, D. J. (1975). *Personality*. Glenview, IL: Scott, Foresman.

Rotton, J. & Kelly, I. W. (1985). Much ado about the full moon: A meta-analysis of lunar-lunacy research. *Psychological Bulletin*, 97, 286–306.

Rowe, D. C., Chassin, L., Presson, C. C., & Sherman, S. J. (1996). Parental smoking and the "epidemic" spread of cigarette smoking. *Journal of Applied Social Psychology*, 26(5), 437–454.

Rubenstein, C. (1983). The modern art of courtly love. *Psychology Today*, July.

Rubenstein, C. & Tavris, C. (1987). Special survey results: 2600 women reveal the secrets of intimacy. *Redbook*, 159, 147–149ff.

Rubin, D. C. (1985). The subtle deceiver: Recalling our past. *Psychology Today*, Sept., 38–46.

Rubin, V., & Comitas, L. (Eds.). (1975). *Ganja in Jamaica*. The Hague: Mouton.

Rubin, Z. (1970a). Jokers wild in the lab. *Psychology Today*, Dec.

Rubin, Z. (1970b). Measurement of romantic love. *Journal of Personality & Social Psychology*, 16, 265–273.

Rubin, Z. (1973). *Liking and loving: An invitation to social psychology*. New York: Holt.

Ruffin, C. L. (1993). Stress and health: Little hassles vs. major life events. *Australian Psychologist*, 28(3), 201–208.

Rumbaugh, D. M., Hopkins, W. D., Washburn, D. A., & Savage-Rumbaugh, E. S. (1989). Lana chimpanzee learns to count by "numath": A summary of a videotaped experimental report. *Psychological Record*, 39(4), 459–470.

Runco, M. A. & Chand, I. (1995). Cognition and creativity. *Educational Psychology Review*, 7(3), 243–268.

Rush, M. C., Schoel, W. A., & Barnard, S. M. (1995). Psychological resiliency in the public sector: "Hardiness" and pressure for change. *Journal of Vocational Behavior*, 46(1), 17–39.

Rushton, J. P. (1995). Sex and race differences in cranial capacity from international labour office data. *Intelligence*, 19(3), 281–294.

Russell, T. G., Rowe, W., & Smouse, A. D. (1991). Subliminal self-help tapes and academic achievement: An evaluation. *Journal of Counseling and Development*, 69(Mar–Apr), 359–362.

Russo, N. F. (1990). Forging research priorities for women's mental health. *American Psychologist*, 45(3), 368–373.

Ryff, C. D. (1995). Psychological well-being in adult life. *Current Directions in Psychological Science*, 4(4), 99–104.

Ryff, C. D. & Keyes, C. L. (1995). The structure of psychological well-being revisited. *Journal of Personality & Social Psychology*, 69(4), 719–727.

Saariluoma, P. (1994). Location coding in chess. *Quarterly Journal of Experimental Psychology: Human Experimental Psychology*, 47A(3), 607–630.

Sackheim, H. A., Decina, P., Kanzler, M., & Kerr, B. (1987). Effects of electrode placement on the efficacy of titrated, low-dose ECT. *American Journal of Psychiatry*, 144(11), 1449–1455.

Sacks, O. (1990). *Seeing voices*. New York: Harper Perennial.

Sadato, N., Pascual-Leone, A., & Hallett, M. (1996). Activation of the primary visual cortex by Braille reading in blind subjects. *Nature*, 380(6574), 526.

Sadker, M. & Sadker, D. (1994). Failing at fairness: How America's schools cheat girls. New York: Scribner's.

Sadowski, C. & Kelley, M. L. (1993). Social problem solving in suicidal adolescents. *Journal of Consulting and Clinical Psychology*, 61(1), 121–127.

Saegert, S., Swap, W., & Zajonc, R. B. (1973). Exposure, context, and interpersonal attraction. *Journal of Personality & Social Psychology*, 25, 234–242.

Sagan, C. & Turco, R. (1990). Too many weapons in the world. *Parade Magazine*, Feb. 4, 10–13.

Sagi, A. (1990). Attachment theory and research from a cross-cultural perspective. *Human Development*, 33(1), 10–22.

Sales, B. D. & Hafemeister, T. L. (1985). Law and psychology. In Altmeir, E. M. & Meyer, M. E. (Eds.), *Applied specialties in psychology*. NY: Random House.

Salive, M. E., Guralnik, J. M., & Glynn, R. J. (1993). Left-handedness and mortality. *American Journal of Public Health*, 83(2), 265–267.

Salmela, J. H. (1974). An information processing approach to volleyball. *C.V.A. Technical Journal*, 1, 49–62.

Salmela, J. H. (1975). Psycho-motor task demands of artistic gymnastics. In J. H. Salmela (Ed.), *The advanced study of gymnastics: A textbook*. Sundby.

Salmoni, A. W., Schmidt, R. A., & Walter, C. B. (1984). Knowledge of results and motor learning: A review and critical reappraisal. *Psychological Bulletin*, 95, 355–386.

Salovey, P. & Singer, J. A. (1989). Mood congruency effects in recall of childhood versus recent memories. *Journal of Social Behavior & Personality, 4*(2), 99–120.

Salthouse, T. A. (1987). Age, experience, and compensation. In C. Schooler & K. W. Schaie (Eds.), *Cognitive functioning and social structure over the life course*, 142–150. New York: Ablex.

Sampson, E. E. (1993). Identity politics. *American Psychologist, 48*(12), 1219–1230.

Sancho, A. M. & Hewitt, J. (1990). Questioning fear of success. *Psychological Reports, 67*(3, Pt 1), 803–806.

Santrock, J. W. (1995). *Adolescence.* Madison, WI: Brown & Benchmark.

Santrock, J., Minnett, A., & Campbell, B. (1994). *The authoritative guide to self-help books.* New York: Guilford.

Santy, P. A., Holland, A. W., Looper, L., & Marcondes-North, R. (1993). Multicultural factors in the space environment. *Aviation, Space, & Environmental Medicine, 64*(3), 196–200.

Sarason, I. G. (1981). Test anxiety, stress, and social support. *Journal of Personality, 49,* 101–114.

Saunders, T., Driskell, J. E., Johnston, J. H., Salas, E. (1996). The effect of stress inoculation training on anxiety and performance. *Journal of Occupational Health Psychology, 1*(2), 170–186.

Savage-Rumbaugh, E. S., Murphy, J., Sevcik, R. A., Brakke, K. E. et al. (1993). Language comprehension in ape and child. *Monographs of the Society for Research in Child Development, 58*(3–4), v–221.

Savage-Rumbaugh, E. S., Rumbaugh, D. M., Premack, D., & Woodruff, G. (1979). Chimpanzee problem comprehension: Insufficient evidence. *Science, 206*(4423), 1201–1202.

Savage-Rumbaugh, S. & Lewin, R. (1996). *Kanzi.* New York: Wiley.

Savage-Rumbaugh, S., Sevcik, R. A., Brakke, K. E., Rumbaugh, D. M. et al. (1990). Symbols: Their communicative use, comprehension, and combination by bonobos (Pan paniscus). *Advances in Infancy Research, 6,* 221–278.

Savant syndrome. (1995). *Education & Training in Mental Retardation & Developmental Disabilities, 30*(3), 243–253.

Sawyer, R. G. & Smith, N. G. (1996). A survey of situational factors at first intercourse among college students. *American Journal of Health Behavior, 20*(4), 208–217.

Saxe, L. (1991). Lying. *American Psychologist, 46*(4), 409–415.

Saxe, L. (1994). Detection of deception: Polygraph and integrity tests. *Current Directions in Psychological Science, 3*(3), 69–73.

Saxe, L., Dougherty, D., & Cross, T. (1985). The validity of polygraph testing. *American Psychologist, 40,* 355–366.

Scarr, S. & Eisenberg, M. (1993). Child care research: Issues, perspectives, and results. In L. W. Porter and M. R. Rosenzweig (Eds.), *Annual Review of Psychology, 44,* 613–644.

Schachere, K. (1990). Attachment between working mothers and their infants. *American Journal of Orthopsychiatry, 60*(1), 19–34.

Schachter, S. (1959). *Psychology of affiliation.* Stanford, CA: Stanford University Press.

Schachter, S., & Wheeler, L. (1962). Epinephrine, chlorpromazine and amusement. *Journal of Abnormal and Social Psychology, 65,* 121–128.

Schacter, D. L. (1996). *Searching for memory.* New York: Basic.

Schafer, M. & Crichlow, S. (1996). Antecedents of groupthink: A quantitative study. *Journal of Conflict Resolution, 40*(3), 415–435.

Schaie, K. W. (1988). Ageism in psychological research. *American Psychologist, 43*(3), 179–183.

Schaie, K. W. (1994). The course of adult intellectual development. *American Psychologist, 49*(4), 304–313.

Schaller, S. (1991). *A man without words.* New York: Summit.

Schein, E. H., Hill, W. F., Lubin, A., & Williams, H. L. (1957). Distinguishing characteristics of collaborators and resistors among American prisoners of war. *Journal of Abnormal and Social Psychology, 55,* 197–201.

Schein, E. H., Schneier, I., & Barker, C. H. (1961). *Coercive persuasion.* New York: Norton.

Schick, T. & Vaughn, L. (1995). How to think about weird things: Critical thinking for a new age. Mountain View, CA: Mayfield.

Schlosberg, H. (1954). Three dimensions of emotion. *Psychological Review, 61,* 81–88.

Schmidt, F. L., Ones, D. S., & Hunter, J. E. (1992). Personnel selection. *Annual Review of Psychology, 43,* 627–670.

Schmidt, L. A. & Fox, N. A. (1995). Individual differences in young adults' shyness and sociability. *Personality & Individual Differences, 19*(4), 455–462.

Schmitt, D. P. & Buss, D. M. (1996). Strategic self-promotion and competitor derogation. *Journal of Personality & Social Psychology, 70*(6), 1185–1204.

Schneider, C. (1987). *Children's television: The art, the business, and how it works.* Chicago: NTC Business Books.

Schneider, H. G. & Shugar, G. J. (1990). Audience and feedback effects in computer learning. *Computers in Human Behavior, 6*(4), 315–321.

Schoggen, P. (1989). *Behavior settings.* Stanford, CA: Stanford University Press.

Schok, K. & Samuels, C. A. (1992). Neonatal bathing and massage intervention with fathers, behavioural effects 12 weeks after birth of the first baby. *International Journal of Behavioral Development, 15*(1), 67–81.

Schommer, N. (1984). Shrinks on the air. *Discover,* Oct., 68–70.

Schooler, C., Flora, J. A., & Farquhar, J. W. (1993). Moving toward synergy: Media supplementation in the Stanford Five-City Project. *Communication Research, 20*(4), 587–610.

Schotte, D. E., Cools, J., & McNally, R. J. (1990). Film-induced negative affect triggers overeating in restrained eaters. *Journal of Abnormal Psychology, 99*(3), 317–320.

Schouten, S. A. (1994). An overview of quantitatively evaluated studies with mediums and psychics. *Journal of the American Society for Psychical Research, 88*(3), 221–254.

Schredl, M. (1995). Creativity and dream recall. *Journal of Creative Behavior, 29*(1), 16–24.

Schreiber, F. R. (1973). *Sybil.* Chicago: Regency.

Schroeder, J. E. (1995). Self-concept, social anxiety, and interpersonal perception skills. *Personality & Individual Differences, 19*(6), 955–958.

Schuerger, J. M. & Witt, A. C. (1989). The temporal stability of individually tested intelligence. *Journal of Clinical Psychology, 45*(2), 294–302.

Schulz, R. & Heckhausen, J. (1996). A life span model of successful aging. *American Psychologist, 51*(7), 702–714.

Schulz, R. (1978). *The psychology of death, dying and bereavement.* Reading, MA: Addison-Wesley.

Schunk, D. H. (1990). Goal setting and self-efficacy during self-regulated learning. Special issue: Self-regulated learning and academic achievement. *Educational Psychologist, 25*(1), 71–86.

Schutte, N. S., Malouff, J. M., Post-Corden, J. C., & Rodasta, A. L. (1988). Effects of playing video-games on children's aggressive and other behaviors. *Journal of Applied Social Psychology, 18*(5), 454–460.

Schwartz, B. & Robbins, S. J. (1995). *Psychology of learning & behavior.* New York: Norton.

Schwartz, L. L. (1991). The historical dimension of cultic techniques of persuasion and control. *Cultic Studies Journal, 8*(1), 37–45.

Schwartz, P. J., Brown, C., Wehr, T. A., & Rosenthal, N. E. (1996). Winter seasonal affective disorder: A follow-up study of the first 59 patients of the National Institute of Mental Health Seasonal Studies Program. *American Journal of Psychiatry, 153*(8), 1028–1036.

Schweickert, R. (1993). A multinomial processing tree model for degradation and redintegration in immediate recall. *Memory & Cognition, 21*(2), 168–175.

Scientists take stand for animal research, (1989). S. Landers, *APA Monitor,* April, 1, 4.

Sclafani, A., & Springer, D. (1976). Dietary obesity in adult rats: Similarities to hypothalamic and human obesity syndromes. *Psychology and Behavior, 17,* 461–471.

Scott, J. (1996). New chapter for the fat controller. *Nature, 379*(6561) 113–114.

Scott, J. P. & Ginsburg, B. E. (1994). The Seville statement on violence revisited. *American Psychologist, 49*(10), 849–850.

Scott, L. & O'Hara, M. W. (1993). Self-discrepancies in clinically anxious and depressed university students. *Journal of Abnormal Psychology, 102*(2), 282–287.

Scott, N. E. & Borodovsky, L. G. (1990). Effective use of cultural role taking. *Professional Psychology: Research & Practice, 21*(3), 167–170.

Seal, D. W. & Palmer-Seal, D. A. (1996). Barriers to condom use and safer sex talk among college dating couples. *Journal of Community & Applied Social Psychology, 6*(1), 15–33.

Sears, R. R., Maccoby, E. E., & Levin, H. (1957). *Patterns of child rearing.* Evanston, IL: Row, Peterson.

Segraves, R. T. & Segraves, K. B. (1995). Human sexuality and aging. *Journal of Sex Education & Therapy, 21*(2), 88–102.

Seligman, M. E. P. (1972a). For helplessness: Can we immunize the weak? In *Readings in psychology today* (2nd ed.). Del Mar, CA: CRM.

Seligman, M. E. P. (1972b). Phobias and preparedness. In M. E. P. Seligman & J. L. Hager (Eds.), *Biological boundaries of learning.* New York: Appleton-Century-Crofts.

Seligman, M. E. P. (1989). *Helplessness.* New York: Freeman.

Seligman, M. E. P. (1991). *Learned optimism.* New York: Knopf.

Seligman, M. E. P. (1994). *What you can change and what you can't.* New York: Knopf.

Seligman, M. E. P. (1995). The effectiveness of psychotherapy. *American Psychologist, 50*(12), 965–974.

Selye, H. (1956, 1976). *The stress of life.* New York: Knopf.

Selye, H. (1976). *Stress in health and disease.* Boston: Butterworth.

Senden, M. V. (1960). *Space and sight.* Translated by P. Heath. Glencoe, IL: Free Press.

Serbin, L. A., & O'Leary, K. D. (1975). How nursery schools teach girls to shut up. *Psychology Today,* Dec., 57–58, 102–103.

Seto, M. C. & Kuban, M. (1996). Criterion-related validity of a phallometric test for paraphilic rape and sadism. *Behaviour Research & Therapy, 34*(2), 175–183.

Shaffer, J. B. & Galinsky, M. D. (1989). *Models of group therapy.* Englewood Cliffs, NJ: Prentice Hall.

Shafir, E. (1993). Choosing versus rejecting: Why some options are both better and worse than others. *Memory and Cognition, 21,* 546–556.

Shafton, A. (1995). *Dream reader.* Albany, NY: SUNY Press.

Shapiro, F. (1995). *Eye movement desensitization and reprocessing.* New York: Guilford.

Shapiro, J. P. & Bowermaster, D. (1994). The case of Dr. Kevorkian obscures critical issues—and dangers. *US News & World Report,* April 25, online edition.

Shatz, M. (1986). Students' guessing strategies: Do they work? *Psychological Reports, 57*(3), 1167–1168.

Shaver, P. R. & Hazen, C. (1993). Adult romantic attachment. In D. Perlman & W. H. Jones (Eds.), *Advances in personal relationships, 4.* London: Kingsley.

Shaw, J. S. (1996). Increases in eyewitness confidence resulting from postevent questioning. *Journal of Experimental Psychology: Applied, 2*(2), 126–146.

Shaywitz, B. A., Fletcher, J. M., & Shaywitz, S. E. (1995). Defining and classifying learning disabilities and attention deficit hyperactivity disorder. *Journal of Child Neurology, 10*(suppl.), S50.

Shaywitz, S. E. & Gore, J. C. (1995). Sex differences in functional organization of the brain for language. *Nature, 373*(6515), 607.

Shedler, J. & Block, J. (1990). Adolescent drug use and psychological health: A longitudinal inquiry. *American Psychologist, 45*(5), 612–630.

Sheehan, P. W. & Statham, D. (1989). Hypnosis, the timing of its introduction, and acceptance of misleading information. *Journal of Abnormal Psychology, 98*(2), 170–176.

Sheehy, G. (1976). *Passages: Predictable crises from adult life.* New York: Dutton.

Sheehy, M. & Cournos, F. (1992). What Is Mental Illness? In F. I. Kass, J. M. Oldham, & H. Pardes (Eds.), *The Columbia University College of Physicians and Surgeons Complete Home Guide to Mental Health.* New York: Sharpe Communications/Henry Holt.

Shepard, R. N. (1975). Form, formation, and transformation of internal representations. In R. L. Solso (Ed.), *Information processing and cognition: The Loyola Symposium.* Hillsdale, NJ: Erlbaum.

Sherif, M., Harvey, O. J., White, B. J., Hood, W. R., & Sherif, C. W. (1961). *Intergroup conflict and cooperation: The Robbers Cave experiment.* University of Oklahoma, Institute of Group Relations.

Shermer, M. (1992). A skeptical look at cryonic suspension. *Skeptic, 1*(2), 50–51.

Shields, P. L. & Rovee-Collier, C. (1992). Long-term memory for context-specific category information at six months. *Child Development, 63*(2), 245–259.

Shneidman, E. (1987a). At the point of no return. *Psychology Today,* March, 54–58.

Shneidman, E. S. (1987b). Psychological approaches to suicide. In VandenBos, G. R. & Bryant, B. K. (Eds.), *Cataclysms, crises, and catastrophes: Psychology in action.* Washington, DC: American Psychological Association.

Shogren, E. (1994). Treatment against their will. *The Los Angeles Times,* Aug. 18, A-1, A-14, A-15.

Shore, L. A. (1990). Skepticism in light of scientific literacy. *Skeptical Inquirer, 15,* Fall, 3–4.

Short, R. H. & Hess, G. C. (1995). Fetal alcohol syndrome: Characteristics and remedial implications. *Developmental Disabilities Bulletin, 23*(1), 12–29.

Shrum, L. J., Lowrey, T. M., & McCarty, J. A. (1995). Applying social and traditional marketing principles to the reduction of household waste. *American Behavioral Scientist, 38*(4), 646–657.

Shulman, G. I. (1974). Race, sex and violence: A laboratory test of the sexual threat of the black male hypothesis. *American Journal of Sociology, 79,* 1260–1277.

Shurkin, J. N. (1992). *Terman's kids.* Boston, MA: Little, Brown.

Shweder, R. A. & Sullivan, M. A., (1993). Cultural psychology: Who needs it? In L. W. Porter and M. R. Rosenzweig (Eds.), *Annual Review of Psychology, 44,* 497–523.

Siau, Keng L. (1996). Group creativity and technology. *Journal of Creative Behavior, 29*(3), 201–216.

Sieber, J. E. & Saks, M. J., (1989). A census of subject pool characteristics and policies. *American Psychologist, 44*(7), 1053–1061.

Siegal, M. (1987). Are sons and daughters treated more differently by fathers than by mothers? *Developmental Review, 7*(3), 183–209.

Siegel, J. M., Nienhuis, R., Fahringer, H. M. et al. (1991). Neuronal activity in narcolepsy: Identification of cataplexy related cells in the medial medulla. *Science, 252*(5010), 1315–1318.

Siegel, O. (1982). Personality development in adolescence. In B. B. Wolman, G. Stricker, S. J. Ellman, P. Keith-Spiegel, & D. S. Palermo (Eds), *Handbook of developmental psychology.* Englewood Cliffs, NJ: Prentice Hall.

Siegel, S., Hearst, E., George, N., & O'Neal, E. (1968). Generalization gradients obtained from individual subjects following classical conditioning. *Journal of Experimental Psychology, 78,* 171–174.

Siegelman, M. (1987). Kinsey and others: Empirical input. In L. Diamant (Ed.), *Male and female homosexuality: Psychological approaches.* Washington, DC: Hemisphere.

Siegler, R. S. (1989). Mechanisms of cognitive development. *Annual Review of Psychology, 40,* 353–379.

Sigman, M. (1995). Current research findings on childhood autism. *Canadian Journal of Psychiatry, 40*(6), 289–294.

Silva, C. E. & Kirsch, I. (1992). Interpretive sets, expectancy, fantasy proneness, and dissociation as predictors of hypnotic response. *Journal of Personality & Social Psychology, 63*(5), 847–856.

Silver, E., Cirincione, C., & Steadman, H. J. (1994). Demythologizing inaccurate perceptions of the insanity defense. *Law & Human Behavior, 18*(1), 63–70.

Silverman, K., Evans, S. M., Strain, E. C., & Griffiths, R. R. (1992). Withdrawal syndrome after the double-blind cessation of caffeine consumption. *New England Journal of Medicine, 327*(16), 1109–1114.

Silverstein, B. (1989). Enemy images. *American Psychologist, 44*(6), 903–913.

Silverstein, L. B. (1991). Transforming the debate about child care and maternal employment. *American Psychologist, 46*(1), 1025–1032.

Simonton, D. K. (1988). Age and outstanding achievement: What do we know after a century of research? *Psychological Bulletin, 104*(2), 251–267.

Simpson, J. A. (1990). Influence of attachment styles on romantic relationships. *Journal of Personality & Social Psychology, 59*(5), 971–980.

Singer, J. L. (1974). Daydreaming and the stream of thought. *American Scientist, 62,* 417–425.

Singer, M. T. (1979). Coming out of the cults. *Psychology Today,* Jan., 72–82.

Singer, M. T. & Addis, M. E. (1992). Cults, coercion, and contumely. *Cultic Studies Journal, 9*(2), 163–189.

Sirkin, M. I. (1990). Cult involvement: A systems approach to assessment and treatment. *Psychotherapy, 27*(1), 116–123.

Sison, C. E., Alpert, M., Fudge, R., & Stern, R. M. (1996). Constricted expressiveness and psychophysiological reactivity in schizophrenia. *Journal of Nervous & Mental Disease, 184*(10), 589–597.

Skeels, H. M. (1966). Adult status of children with contrasting early life experiences. *Monograph of the Society for Research in Child Development, 31*(3).

Skender, M. L., Goodrick, G. K., Del Junco, D. J., Reeves, R. S., et al. (1996). Comparison of 2–year weight loss trends in behavioral treatments of obesity: diet, exercise, and combination interventions. *Journal of the American Dietetic Association, 96*(4), 342–346.

Skinner, B. F. (1938). *The behavior of organisms.* Englewood Cliffs, NJ: Prentice-Hall.

Skinner, B. F. (1971). *Beyond freedom and dignity.* New York: Bantam.

Skinner, B. F. (1990). Can psychology be a science of mind? *American Psychologist, 45*(11), 1206–1210.

Skoog, I. (1996). Sex and Swedish 85-year-olds. *British Journal of Clinical Psychology, 334*(17), 1140–1141.

Skuy, M., Mentis, M., Durbach, F., & Cockcroft, K. (1995). Crosscultural comparison of effects of instrumental enrichment on children in a South African mining town. *School Psychology International, 16*(3), 265–282.

Slaby, A. E., Garfinkel, B. D., & Garfinkel, L. F. (1994). *No one say my pain.* New York: Norton.

Slater, A., Mattock, A., & Brown, E. (1990). Size constancy at birth: Newborn infants' responses to retinal and real size. *Journal of Experimental Child Psychology, 49*(2), 314–322.

Slater, A., Mattock, A., Brown, E., & Bremner, J. G. (1991). Form perception at birth: Cohen and Younger (1984) revisited. *Journal of Experimental Child Psychology, 51*(3), 395–406.

Sledge, W. H., Tebes, J., Rakfeldt, J., Davidson, L. (1996). Day hospital/crisis respite care versus inpatient care: I. Clinical outcomes. *American Journal of Psychiatry, 153*(8), 1065–1073.

Sleek, S. (1995). Online therapy services raise ethical questions. *APA Monitor,* Nov., 9.

Smith, A., & Sugar, O. (1975). Development of above normal language and intelligence 21 years after left hemispherectomy. *Neurology, 25,* 813–818.

Smith, C. (1995). Sleep states and memory processes. *Behavioural Brain Research, 69*(1–2), 137–145.

Smith, C., Carey, S., & Wiser, M. (1985). On differentiation: A case study of the developement of the concepts of size, weight, and density. *Cognition, 21*(3), 177–237.

Smith, E. E. (1989). Concepts and induction. In M. I. Posner (Ed.), *Foundations of cognitive science,* Cambridge, MA: The MIT Press.

Smith, J. C. (1986). Meditation, biofeedback, and the relaxation controversy: A cognitive-behavioral perspective. *American Psychologist,* Sept., 1007–1009.

Smith, J. D. For whom the bell curves: Old texts, mental retardation, and the persistent argument. *Mental Retardation, 33*(3), 199–202.

Smith, K. H. & Rogers, M. (1994). Effectiveness of subliminal messages in television commercials: Two experiments. *Journal of Applied Psychology, 79*(6), 866–874.

Smith, R. W. & Kounios, J. (1996). Sudden insight: All-or-none processing revealed by speed-accuracy decomposition. *Journal of Experimental Psychology: Learning, Memory, & Cognition, 22*(6), 1443–1462.

Smith, T. W. (1990). *Adult sexual behavior in 1989: Number of partners, frequency, and risk.* Paper presented to the American Association for the Advancement of Science, February, 1990, New Orleans.

Smith, V. L., Kassin, S. M., & Ellsworth, P. C. (1989). Eyewitness accuracy and confidence: Within- versus between-subjects correlations. *Journal of Applied Psychology, 74*(2), 356–359.

Smith, W. P., Compton, W. C., & West, W. B. (1995). Meditation as an adjunct to a happiness enhancement program. *Journal of Clinical Psychology, 51*(2), 269–273.

Snow, C. P. (1961). Either-or. *Progressive,* Feb., 24.

Snow, R. E. (1986). Individual differences and the design of educational programs. *American Psychologist, 41,* 1029–1039.

Snowdon, C. T. (1983). Ethology, comparative psychology, and animal behavior. *Annual Review of Psychology, 34,* 63–94.

Snyder, M. (1987). *Public appearances and private realities.* New York: Freeman.

Snyder, M. & Harkness, A. R. (1984). *E = f(p): The impact of personality on choice of situation.* Paper presented at the annual meeting of the Midwestern Psychological Association, Chicago.

Snyder, M. & Smith, D. (1985). *Self-monitoring and depression: Precipitating events and copying strategies.* Paper presented at the annual meeting of the Midwestern Psychological Association, Chicago.

Snyderman, M. & Rothman, S. (1987). Survey of expert opinion on intelligence and aptitude testing. *American Psychologist, 42*(2), 137–144.

Sobel, E., Shine, D., DiPietro, D., & Rabinowitz, M. (1996). Condom use among HIV/infected patients in South Bronx, New York. *AIDS, 10*(2), 235–236.

Solomon, R. C., & Wynne, L. C. (1953). Traumatic avoidance learning: Acquisition in normal dogs. *Psychological Monographs, 67*(4, Whole No. 354).

Solomon, R. L. (1980). The opponent-process theory of acquired motivation. *American Psychologist,* Aug., 691–721.

Solowij, N., Michie, P. T., & Fox, A. M. (1995). Differential impairments of selective attention due to frequency and duration of cannabis use. *Biological Psychiatry, 37*(10), 731–739.

Somberg, D. R., Stone, G., & Claiborn, C. D. (1993). Informed consent: Therapist's beliefs and practices. *Professional Psychology: Research & Practice, 24*(2), 153–159.

Sorce, J. F., Emde, R. N., Campos, J. J., & Klinnert, M. D. (1985). Maternal emotional signaling: Its effect on the visual cliff behavior of 1-year-olds. *Developmental Psychology, 21,* 195–200.

Spangenberg, J. J. & Lategan, T. P. (1993). Coping, androgyny, and attributional style. *South African Journal of Psychology, 23*(4), 195–203.

Spanos, N. P. (1990). Hypnosis, demonic possession, and multiple personality. In C. A. Ward (Ed.), *Altered states of consciousness and mental health.* Newbury Park, CA: Sage.

Spence, J. T. (1984). Masculinity, femininity, and gender-related traits. In B. A. Maker & W. B. Maker (Eds.), *Progress in experimental personality research: Normal personality processes* (Vol. 13). New York: Academic.

Spencer, M. B. (1990). Development of minority children. *Child Development, 61,* 267–269.

Spencer, M. B. & Markstrom-Adams, C. (1990). Identity processes among racial and ethnic minority children in America. *Child Development, 61,* 290–310.

Sperry, R. W. (1968). Hemisphere deconnection and unity in conscious awareness. *American Psychologist, 23,* 723–733.

Sperry, R. W. (1995). The riddle of consciousness and the changing scientific worldview. *Journal of Humanistic Psychology, 35*(2), 7–33.

Spiegel, D. (1986). Dissociation, double binds, and posttraumatic stress in multiple personality disorder. In B. G. Braun (Ed.), *Treatment of multiple personality disorder.* Washington, DC: American Psychiatric Press.

Spitz, R. A. (1945). Hospitalism: An inquiry into the genesis of psychiatric conditions in early childhood. In *The psychoanalytic study of the child* (Vol. I), 53–74. New York: International University Press.

Sprafka, J. M., Folsom, A. R., Burke, G. L. et al. (1990). Type A behavior and its association with cardiovascular disease prevalence in Blacks and Whites: The Minnesota Heart Survey. *Journal of Behavioral Medicine, 13*(1), 1–13.

Sprecher, S. & Hatfield, E. (1996). Premarital sexual standards among U.S. college students. *Archives of Sexual Behavior, 25*(3), 261–288.

Springer, S. P. & Deutsch, G. (1993). *Left brain, right brain.* New York: Freeman.

Squire, L. R. (1992). Memory and the hippocampus: A synthesis from findings with rats, monkeys, and humans. *Psychological Review, 99*(2), 195–231.

Squire, L. R. & Zola-Morgan, S. (1988). Memory: Brain systems and behavior. *Trends in Neurosciences, 11*(4), 170–175.

Squire, L. R., Knowlton, B., & Musen, G., (1993). The structure and organization of memory. In L. W. Porter & M. R. Rosenzweig (Eds.), *Annual Review of Psychology, 44,* 453–495.

Stacy, A. W., Galaif, E. R., Sussman, S., & Dent, C. W. (1996). Self-generated drug outcomes in high-risk adolescents. *Psychology of Addictive Behaviors, 10*(1), 18–27.

Stalheim-Smith, A. & Fitch, G. K. (1993). *Understanding human anatomy and physiology.* St. Paul, MN: West.

Stanovich, K. E. (1996). *How to think straight about psychology,* 4e. New York: HarperCollins.

Staples, S. L. (1996). Human response to environmental noise. *American Psychologist, 51*(2), 143–150.

Staum, M. J. & Brotons, M. (1992). The influence of auditory subliminals on behavior. *Journal of Music Therapy, 29*(3), 130–185.

Staw, B. M., Sutton, R. I., & Pelled, L. H. (1994). Employee positive emotion and favorable outcomes at the workplace. *Organization Science, 5*(1), 51–71.

Steblay, N. M. (1987). Helping behavior in rural and urban environments: A meta-analysis. *Psychological Bulletin, 102*(3), 346–356.

Steblay, N. M. (1992). A meta-analytic review of the weapon focus effect. *Law and Human Behavior, 16,* 413–424.

Steele, C. M. (1997). A threat in the air. *American Psychologist, 52*(6), 613–629.

Steele, C. M. & Josephs, R. A. (1990). Alcohol myopia. *American Psychologist, 45*(8), 921–933.

Steen, R. G. (1996). *DNA and destiny: nature and nurture in human behavior.* New York: Plenum.

Stefanis, C., Dornbush, R. L., & Fink, M. (1977). *Hashish: A study of long-term use.* New York: Raven.

Stein, G. L., Kimiecik, J. C., Daniels, J., & Jackson, S. A. (1995). Psychological antecedents of flow in recreational sport. *Personality & Social Psychology Bulletin, 21*(2), 125–135.

Stein, M. I. (1974). *Stimulating creativity* (Vol. 1). New York: Academic.

Stein, M., Miller, A. H., & Trestman, R. L. (1990). Depression and the immune system. In R. Ader, N. Cohen, & D. L. Felten (Eds.), *Psychoneuroimmunology II.* New York: Academic Press.

Steinbacher, R. & Gilroy, F. (1990). Sex selection technology: A prediction of its use and effect. *Journal of Psychology, 124*(3), 283–288.

Steinberg, L. D., Catalano, R., & Dooley, P. (1981). Economic antecedents of child abuse and neglect. *Child Development, 52,* 975–985.

Stensaas, L. J., Lavker, R. M., Monti-Bloch, L., Grosser, B. I., & Berliner, D. L. (1991). Ultrastructure of the human vomeronasal organ. *Journal of Steroid Biochemistry and Molecular Biology, 39*(4B), 553–560.

Steriade, M. & McCarley, R. W. (1990). *Brainstem control of wakefulness and sleep.* NY: Plenum.

Sterman, M. B. (1996). Physiological origins and functional correlates of EEG rhythmic activities: Implications for self-regulation. *Biofeedback & Self Regulation, 21*(1), 3–33.

Stern, D. (1982). Some interactive functions of rhythm changes between mother and infant. In M. Davis (Ed.), *Interaction rhythms, periodicity in communicative behavior.* New York: Human Sciences Press.

Stern, R. M., Hu, S., Anderson, R. B., Leibowitz, H. W. et al. (1990). The effects of fixation and restricted visual field on vection-induced motion sickness. *Aviation, Space, & Environmental Medicine, 61*(8), 712–715.

Sternberg, R. J. (1988). *The triangle of love.* New York: Basic.

Sternberg, R. J. (1995). Love as a story. *Journal of Social & Personal Relationships, 12*(4), 541–546.

Sternberg, R. J. & Barnes, M. (1986). Real and ideal others in romantic relationships: Is four a crowd? *Journal of Personality & Social Psychology, 49,* 1586–1608.

Sternberg, R. J. & Lubart, T. I. (1995). *Defying the crowd.* New York: The Free Press.

Sternberg, R. J. (1996). *Successful intelligence.* New York: Simon & Schuster.

Sternberg, R. J., & Davidson, J. D. (1982). The mind of the puzzler. *Psychology Today,* June.

Sternberg, R. J., & Grajek, S. (1984). The nature of love. *Journal of Personality & Social Psychology, 47,* 312–329.

Stewart, J. V. (1996). *Astrology: What's really in the stars.* Amherst, NY: Prometheus.

Stiles, W. B., Shapiro, D. A., & Elliott, R. (1986). Are all psychotherapies equivalent? *American Psychologist, 41,* 165–180.

Stokols, D. (1995). The paradox of environmental psychology. *American Psychologist, 50*(10), 821–837.

Stolerman, I. P. & Jarvis, M. J. (1995). The scientific case that nicotine is addictive. *Psychopharmacology, 117*(1), 2–10.

Stoller, F. H. (1967). The long weekend. *Psychology Today, 1*(7), 28–33.

Story, M. & Brown, J. E. (1987). Do young children instinctively know what to eat? *The New England Journal of Medicine, 316,* 103–106.

Strack. F., Martin, L. L., & Stepper, S. (1988). Inhibiting and facilitating conditions of facial expressions: A non-obtrusive test of the facial feedback hypothesis. *Journal of Personality & Social Psychology, 54,* 768–777.

Strange, J. R. (1965). *Abnormal psychology.* New York: McGraw-Hill.

Streissguth, A.P., Treder, R. P., Barr, H. M., Shepard, T. H., Bleyer, W. A., Sampson, P. D., & Martin, D. C. (1987). Aspirin and acetaminophen use by pregnant women and subsequent child IQ and attention decrements. *Teratology, 35*(2), 211–219.

Streufert, S., Pogash, R., Miller, J., Gingrich, D. et al. (1995). Effects of caffeine deprivation on complex human functioning. *Psychopharmacology, 118*(4), 377–384.

Strickler, E. M. & Verbalis, J. G. (1988). Hormones and behavior: The biology of thirst and sodium appetite. *American Scientist,* May-June, 261–267.

Stroeher, S. K. (1994). Sixteen kindergartners' gender-related views of careers. *Elementary School Journal, 95*(1), 95–103.

Strong, B. & DeVault, C. (1994). *Understanding our sexuality.* St. Paul, MN: West.

Strongman, K. T. (1996). *The psychology of emotion.* New York: Wiley.

Strupp, H. H. (1989). Psychotherapy: Can the practitioner learn from the researcher? *American Psychologist, 44*(4), 717–724.

Stunkard, A. J., Sorenson, T. I. A., Hanis, C., Teasdale, T. et al. (1986). An adoption study of human obesity. *New England Journal of Medicine, 314,* 193–198.

Sue, D. & Sue, D. W. (1991). Counseling strategies for Chinese Americans. In C. C. Lee & B. L. Richardson (Eds.), *Multicultural issues in counseling.* Alexandria, VA: American Association for Counseling and Development.

Sue, D. W. & Sue, D. (1990). *Counseling the culturally*

different: Theory and practice. New York: Wiley.

Sue, D., Sue, D. W., & Sue, S. (1994). *Understanding abnormal behavior*. Boston: Houghton Mifflin.

Suedfeld, P. (1980). *Restricted environmental stimulation: Research and clinical applications*. New York: Wiley-Interscience.

Suedfeld, P., & Piedrahita, L. E. (1984). Intimations of mortality: Integrative simplification as a precursor of death. *Journal of Personality and Social Psychology, 47*, 848–852.

Suedfeld, P., Metcalfe, J., & Bluck, S. (1987). Enhancement of scientific creativity by flotation REST (restricted environmental stimulation technique). *Journal of Environmental Psychology, 7*(3), 219–231.

Suinn, R. M. (1970). *Fundamentals of behavior pathology*. New York: Wiley.

Suinn, R. M. (1975). *Fundamentals of behavior pathology* (2nd ed.). New York: Wiley.

Sullivan, M. A. & O'Leary, S. G. (1990). Maintenance following reward and cost token programs. *Behavior Therapy, 21*(1), 139–149.

Suls, J. (1989). Self-awareness and self-identity in adolescence. In J. Worell & F. Danner, Eds. *The adolescent as decision-maker*. New York: Academic.

Suls, J. & Swain, A. (1994). Type A-Type B personalities. *Encyclopedia of human behavior, Vol. 4*, 427–436. San Diego, CA: Academic.

Sumerlin, J. R. & Bundrick, C. M. (1996). Brief Index of Self-Actualization: A measure of Maslow's model. *Journal of Social Behavior & Personality, 11*(2), 253–271.

Susman-Stillman, A., Kalkose, M., Egeland, B., & Waldman, I. (1996). Infant temperament and maternal sensitivity as predictors of attachment security. *Infant Behavior & Development, 19*(1), 33–47.

Susnick, L. C. & Belcher, J. R. (1996). Why are they homeless? The chronically mentally ill in Washington, D. C. *International Journal of Mental Health, 24*(4), 70–84.

Swain, I. U., Zelazo, P. R., & Clifton, R. K. (1993). Newborn infants' memory for speech sounds retained over 24 hours. *Developmental Psychology, 29*(2), 312–323.

Swan, G. E. & Denk, C. E. (1987). Dynamic models for the maintenance of smoking cessation: Event history analysis of late relapse. *Journal of Behavioral Medicine, 10*(6), 527–554.

Swart, L. C. & Morgan, C. L. (1992). Effects of subliminal backward-recorded messages on attitudes. *Perceptual & Motor Skills, 75*(3, Pt 2), 1107–1113.

Swartz, C. M. (1993). ECT or programmed seizures? *American Journal of Psychiatry, 150*(8), 1274–1275.

Swayze, V. W. (1995). Frontal leukotomy and related psychosurgical procedures in the era before antipsychotics (1935–1954): A historical overview. *American Journal of Psychiatry, 152*(4), 505–515.

Swets, J., Bjork, R. A., Cook, T. D., Davison, G. C. et al. (1988). *Enhancing human performance: Issues, theories, and techniques*. Washington, DC: National Academy Press of the United States National Research Council.

Swim, J. K. & Sanna, L. J. (1996). He's skilled, she's lucky: A meta-analysis of observers' attributions for women's and men's successes and failures. *Personality & Social Psychology Bulletin, 22*(5), 507–519.

Szasz, T. S. (1966). Mental illness is a myth. *The New York Times Magazine*, June 12.

Szasz, T. S. (1983). *Thomas Szasz: Primary values and major contentions*. Buffalo, NY: Prometheus.

Szasz, T. S. (1987). *Insanity: The idea and its consequences*. New York: Wiley.

Taeuber, C. M. (1993). *Sixty-five plus in America*. Washington, DC: United States Bureau of Census.

Takei, N., Sham, P., O'Callaghan, E., Murray, G. K. et al. (1994). Prenatal exposure to influenza and the development of schizophrenia. *American Journal of Psychiatry, 151*(1), 117–119.

Takooshian, H., Haber, S., & Lucido, D. J. (1977). Who wouldn't help a lost child? You, maybe. *Psychology Today*, Feb., 67.

Talley, P. F., Strupp, H. H., & Morey, L. C. (1990). Matchmaking in psychotherapy: Patient-therapist dimensions and their impact on outcome. *Journal of Consulting & Clinical Psychology, 58*(2), 182–188.

Tallis, F. (1996). Compulsive washing in the absence of phobic and illness anxiety. *Behaviour Research & Therapy, 34*(4), 361–362.

Tamis-LeMonvda, C. S. & Bornstein, M. H. (1994). Specificity in mother-toddler language-play relations across the second year. *Developmental Psychology, 30*(2), 283–292.

Tang, S., & Hall, V. C. (1995). The overjustification effect: A meta-analysis. *Applied Cognitive Psychology, 9*(5), 365–404.

Tannenbaum, S. I., & Yukl, G. (1992). Training and development in work organizations. In M. R. Rosenzweig & L. W. Porter (Eds.), *Annual Review of Psychology, 43*, 399–441.

Tanner, J. M. (1973). Growing up. *Scientific American*, Sept., 34–43.

Tardif, T. Z. & Sternberg, R. J. (1988). What do we know about creativity? In R. J. Sternberg (Ed.), *The nature of creativity*. Cambridge University Press.

Tart, C. T. (1986). Consciousness, altered states, and worlds of experience. *Journal of Transpersonal Psychology, 18*(2), 159–170.

Tashkin, D. P., Simmons, M., & Clark, V. (1988). Effect of habitual smoking of marijuana alone and with tobacco on nonspecific airways hyperreactivity. *Journal of Psychoactive Drugs, 20*(1), 21–25.

Tavris, C. (1992). *The mismeasure of woman*. New York: Touchstone/Simon & Schuster.

Tavris, C. (1993). Beware the incest-survivor machine. *New York Times Book Review*, (Jan. 3), 1, 16–17.

Tayloe, (1995). The validity of repressed memories and the accuracy of their recall through hypnosis. *American Journal of Clinical Hypnosis, 37*(3), 25–31.

Taylor, S. E. (1990). Health psychology. *American Psychologist, 45*(1), 40–50.

Taylor, T. E. (1983, March 17). Learning studies of higher cognitive levels in short-term sensory isolation environment. Paper delivered at First International Conference on REST and Self-regulation, Denver, Colorado.

Tedeschi, J. T., Lindskold, S., & Rosenfeld, P. (1985). *Introduction to social psychology*. St. Paul: West Publishing.

Teen sex: Not for love. (1989). *Psychology Today*, May, 10.

Tenenbaum, G., Bar-Eli, M., & Eyal, N. (1996). Imagery orientation and vividness: Their effect on a motor skill performance. *Journal of Sport Behavior, 19*(1), 32–49.

Teplin, L. A., Abram, K. M., & McClelland. (1994). Does psychiatric disorder predict violent crime among released jail detainees? *American Psychologist, 49*(4), 335–342.

Terman, L. M., & Merrill, M. A. (1937, revised, 1960). *Stanford-Binet Intelligence Scale*. Boston: Houghton Mifflin.

Terman, L. M., & Oden, M. (1959). *The gifted group in mid-life. Vol. 5, Genetic studies of genius*. Stanford, CA: Stanford University Press.

Terr, L. C. (1991). Childhood traumas. *American Journal of Psychiatry, 148*(1), 10–20.

Terrace, H. S. (1985). In the beginning was the "name." *American Psychologist, 40*, 1011–1028.

Terry, D. J. & Hogg, M. A. (1996). Group norms and the attitude-behavior relationship. *Personality & Social Psychology Bulletin, 22*(8), 776–793.

Teti, D. M. (1996). And baby makes four: Predictors of attachment security among preschool-age firstborns during the transition to siblinghood. *Child Development, 67*(2), 579–596.

Thase, M. E. & Kupfer, D. L. (1996). Recent developments in the pharmacotherapy of mood disorders. *Journal of Consulting & Clinical Psychology, 64*(4), 646–659.

Thatcher, R. W., Walker, R. A., & Giudice, S. (1987). Human cerebral hemispheres develop at different rates and ages. *Science, 236*, 1110–1113.

Thayer, S. (1988). Close encounters. *Psychology Today*, March, 31–36.

Thelen, E. (1995). Motor development. *American Psychologist, 50*(2), 79–95.

They'd kill for $1 million. (1991). *The Los Angeles Times*, July 1, A-8.

Thibodeau, R. & Aronson, E. (1992). Taking a closer look: Reasserting the role of self-concept in dissonance theory. *Personality and Social Psychology Bulletin, 18*(5), 591–602.

Thies, C. F. & Register, C. A. (1993). Decriminalization of marijuana and the demand for alcohol, marijuana and cocaine. *Social Science Journal, 30*(4), 385–399.

Thigpen, C. H., & Cleckley, H. M. (1957). *The three faces of Eve*. New York: McGraw-Hill.

Thoman, E. B., Davis, D. H., Graham, S., Scholz, J. P. et al. (1988). Infants at risk for sudden infant death syndrome (SIDS): Differential prediction for three siblings of SIDS infants. *Journal of Behavioral Medicine, 11*(6), 565–583.

Thomas, T. N. (1995). Acculturative stress in the adjustment of immigrant families. *Journal of Social Distress & the Homeless, 4*(2), 131–142.

Thompson, C. P., Cowan, T. M., & Frieman, J. (1993). *Memory search by a menorist*. Hillsdale, NJ: Lawrence Erlbaum.

Thompson, R. F. (1985). *The brain*. New York: Freeman.

Thompson, R. F. (1991). Are memory traces localized or distributed? *Neuropsychologia, 29*(6), 571–582.

Thornburg, H. D. (1984). *Introduction to educational psychology*. St. Paul: West.

Thorson, J. A. & Powell, F. C. (1990). Meanings of death and intrinsic religiosity. *Journal of Clinical Psychology, 46*(4), 379–391.

Tidwell, M. O., Reis, H. T., & Shaver, P. R. (1996). Attachment, attractiveness, and social interaction. *Journal of Personality & Social Psychology, 71*(4), 729–745.

Tierny, J. (1987). Stitches: Good news; Better health liked to sin, sloth. *Hippocrates*. Sept./Oct., 30–35.

Tiffany, S. T., Martin, E. M., & Baker, T. B. (1986). Treatments for cigarette smoking: An evaluation of the contributions of aversion and counseling procedures. *Behavior Research & Therapy, 24*(4), 437–452.

Timm, P. R. & Peterson, B. D. (1993). *People at work*. St. Paul, MN: West.

Tollefson, G. D., Fawcett, J., Winokur, G., Beasley, C. et al. (1993). Evaluation of suicidality during pharmacologic treatment of mood and nonmood disorders. *Annals of Clinical Psychiatry, 5*(4), 209–224.

Tolman, E. C., & Honzik, C. H. (1930). Introduction and removal of reward and maze performance in rats. *University of California Publications in Psychology, 4*, 257–275.

Tolman, E. C., Ritchie, B. F., & Kalish, D. (1946). Studies in spatial learning: II. Place learning versus response learning. *Journal of Experimental Psychology, 36*, 221–229.

Tomlinson-Keasey, C. & Little, T. D. (1990). Predicting educational attainment, occupational achievement, intellectual skill, and personal adjustment among gifted men and women. *Journal of Educational Psychology, 82*(3), 442–455.

Torrance, M., Thomas, Glyn V., & Robinson, E. J. (1991). Strategies for answering examination essay questions: Is it helpful to write a plan? *British Journal of Educational Psychology, 61*(1), 46–54.

Torrey, E. F. (1988). *Surviving schizophrenia: A family manual.* New York: Harper & Row.

Torrey, E. F. (1996). *Out of the shadows.* New York: John Wiley & Sons.

Townsend, J. M., Kline, J., & Wasserman, T. H. (1995). Low-investment copulaton. *Ethology & Sociobiology, 16*(1), 25–51.

Trappey, C. (1996). A meta-analysis of consumer choice and subliminal advertising. *Psychology & Marketing, 13*(5), 517–530.

Trehub, S. E., Unyk, A. M., & Trainor, L. J. (1993a). Adults identify infant-directed music across cultures. *Infant Behavior & Development, 16*(2), 193–211.

Trehub, S. E., Unyk, A. M., & Trainor, L. J. (1993b). Maternal singing in cross-cultural perspective. *Infant Behavior & Development, 16*(3), 285–295.

Tresemer, D. W. (1977). *Fear of success: An intriguing set of questions.* New York: Plenum.

Triandis, H. C. (1977). *Interpersonal behavior.* Monterey, CA: Brooks/Cole.

Troutt-Ervin, E. D. (1990). Application of keyword mnemonics to learning terminology in the college classroom. *Journal of Experimental Education, 59*(1), 31–41.

Truax, S. R. (1983). Active search, mediation, and the manipulation of cue dimensions: Emotion attribution in the false feedback paradigm. *Motivation and Emotion, 7,* 41–60.

Truman, D. M., Tokar, D. M. & Fischer, A. R. (1996). Dimensions of masculinity: Relations to date rape supportive attitudes and sexual aggression in dating situations. *Journal of Counseling & Development, 74*(6), 555–562.

Tryon, R. C. (1929). The genetics of learning ability in rats. *University of California Publications in Psychology, 4,* 71–89.

Tucker, P. & Aron, A. (1993). Passionate love and marital satisfaction at key transition points in the family life cycle. *Journal of Social & Clinical Psychology, 12*(2), 135–147.

Tulley, M. & Chiu, L. H. (1995). Student teachers and classroom discipline. *Journal of Educational Research, 88*(3), 164–171.

Tulving, E. (1989). Remembering and knowing the past. *American Scientist, 77*(4), 361–367.

Turco, R. P., Toon, O. B., Ackerman, T. P. Pollack, J. B., & Sagan, C. (1983). Nuclear winter: Global consequences of multiple nuclear explosions. *Science, 222*(1), 283–292.

Turkheimer, E. & Parry, C. D. H. (1992). Why the gap? *American Psychologist, 47*(5), 646–655.

Turkington, C. (1986). Pot and the immune system. *APA Monitor,* Aug., 22.

Turkington, C. (1992). Ruling opens door—a crack—to IQ testing some black kids. *APA Monitor,* Dec., 28–29.

Turnbull, C. M. (1961). Some observations regarding the experiences and behavior of the Bambuti Pygmies. *American Journal of Psychology, 74,* 304–308.

Turner, M. E., Pratkanis, A. R., Probasco, P., & Leve, C. (1992). Threat, cohesion, and group effectiveness: Testing a social identity maintenance perspective on groupthink. *Journal of Personality & Social Psychology, 63*(5), 781–796.

Turton, M. D., O'Shea, D., Gunn, I., Beak, S. A. et al. (1996). A role for glucagon-like peptide-1 in the central regulation of feeding. *Nature, 379*(6560),
69–74.

Turvey, M. T. (1996). Dynamic touch. *American Psychologist, 51*(11), 1134–1152.

Tutkun, H., Yargic, L. I., & Sar, V. (1995). Dissociative identity disorder. *Dissociation: Progress in the Dissociative Disorders, 8*(1), 3–9.

Tversky, A., & Kahneman, D. (1981). The framing of decisions and the psychology of choice. *Science, 211,* 453–458.

Tversky, A., & Kahneman, D. (1982). Judgments of and by representativeness. In D. Kahneman, P. Slovic, & A. Tversky, *Judgment under uncertainty: Heuristics and biases.* Cambridge: Cambridge University Press.

Twins with schizophrenia: Genes or germs? (1995). *Schizophrenia Bulletin, 21*(1), 13–18.

Tye-Murray, N., Spencer, L., & Woodworth, G. G. (1995). Acquisition of speech by children who have prolonged cochlear implant experience. *Journal of Speech & Hearing Research, 38*(2), 327–337.

Tyler, L. E. (1992). Counseling psychology: Why? *Professional Psychology: Research & Practice. 23*(5), 342–344.

Tzeng, M. (1992). The effects of socioeconomic heterogamy and changes on marital dissolution for first marriages. *Journal of Marriage and Family, 54,* 609–619.

Tzuriel, D. & Alfassi, M. (1994). Cognitive and motivational modifiability as a function of the Instrumental Enrichment (IE) program. *Special Services in the Schools, 8*(2), 91–128.

U.S. Bureau of the Census. (1995). *Statistical abstracts of the U.S.* (115th ed.). Washington, DC: Author.

Udry, J. R., & Morris, N. M. (1977). Human sexual behavior at different stages of the menstrual cycle. *Journal of Reproduction and Fertility, 51,* 419.

Ulett, G. A. (1992). 3000 years of acupuncture: From metaphysics to neurophysiology. *Integrative Psychiatry, 8*(2), 91–100.

Ulrich, R. E., Stachnik, T. J., & Stainton, N. R. (1963). Student acceptance of generalized personality interpretations. *Psychological Reports, 131,* 831–834.

Underwood, B. J. (1957). Interference and forgetting. *Psychological Review, 64,* 49–60.

UNESCO. (1990). The Seville statement on violence. *American Psychologist, 45*(10), 1167–1168.

United Nations Population Fund. (1993). *Population issues: Briefing kit.* New York: Author.

Valins, S. (1966). Cognitive effects of false heart-rate feedback. *Journal of Personality & Social Psychology, 4,* 400–408.

Valins, S. (1967). Emotionality and information concerning internal reactions. *Journal of Personality & Social Psychology, 6,* 458–463.

van der Hart, O., Lierens, R., & Goodwin, J. (1996). Jeanne Fery: A sixteenth-century case of dissociative identity disorder. *Journal of Psychohistory, 24*(1), 18–35.

Van Goozen, S. H. M., Cohen-Kettenis, P. T., Gooren, L. J. G., & Frijda, N. H. (1995). Gender differences in behaviour: Activating effects of cross-sex hormones. *Psychoneuroendocrinology, 20*(4), 343–363.

Van Lawick-Goodall, J. (1971). *In the shadow of man.* New York: Houghton Mifflin.

Van Maanen, J., & Schein, E. H. (1977). Career development. In J. R. Hackman & J. L. Suttle (Eds.), *Improving life at work.* Santa Monica, CA: Goodyear.

van Rooij, J. J. F. (1994). Introversion-extraversion: Astrology versus psychology. *Personality & Individual Differences, 16*(6), 985–988.

Van Wyk, P. H. & Geist, C. S. (1995). Biology of bisexuality: Critique and observations. *Journal of*
Homosexuality, 28(3–4), 357–373.

VandenBos, G. R. & Bryant, B. K. (1987). Preface. In VandenBos, G. R. & Bryant, B. K. (Eds.), *Cataclysms, crises, and catastrophes: Psychology in action.* Washington, DC: American Psychological Association.

Vane, J. R. & Guarnaccia, V. J. (1989). Personality theory and personality assessment measures: How helpful to the clinician? *Journal of Clinical Psychology, 45*(1), 5–19.

Velakoulis, D. & Pantelis, C. (1996). What have we learned from functional imaging studies in schizophrenia? *Australian & New Zealand Journal of Psychiatry, 30*(2), 195–209.

Ventura J., Nuechterlein, K. H., Lukow, D., & Hardesty, J. P. (1989). A prospective study of stressful life events and schizophrenic relapse. *Journal of Abnormal Psychology, 98*(4), 407–411.

Vera, E. & Betz, N. E. (1992). Relationships of self-regard and affective self-disclosure to relationship satisfaction in college students. *Journal of College Student Development, 33*(5), 422–430.

Vernoy, M. W. (1989). Simultaneous adaptation to size, distance, and curvature underwater. *Human Factors, 31*(1), 77–85.

Viegener, B. J., Perri, M. G., Nezu, A. M. et al. (1990). Effects of an intermittent, low-fat, low-calorie diet in the behavioral treatment of obesity. *Behavior Therapy, 21*(4), 499–509.

Visalberghi, E., Fragaszy, D. M., & Savage-Rumbaugh, S. (1995). Performance in a tool-using task by common chimpanzees (*Pan troglodytes*), bonobos (*Pan paniscus*), an orangutan (*Pongo pygmaeus*), and capuchin monkeys (*Cebus apella*). *Journal of Comparative Psychology, 109*(1), 52–60.

Vogler, R. E., & Bartz, W. R. (1982). *The better way to drink.* New York: Simon and Schuster.

Vogler, R. E., & Bartz, W. R. (1992). *Teenagers and alcohol.* Philadelphia: Charles Press.

Vogler, R. E., Weissbach, T. A., Compton, J. V., & Martin, G. T. (1977). Integrated behavior change techniques for problem drinkers in the community. *Journal of Consulting and Clinical Psychology, 45,* 267–279.

Vokey, J. R. & Read, J. D. (1985). Subliminal messages: Between the Devil and the media. *American Psychologist, 40*(11), 1231–1239.

Volkow, N. D., Gillespie, H., Mullani, N., & Tancredi, L. (1996). Brain glucose metabolism in chronic marijuana users at baseline and during marijuana intoxication. *Psychiatry Research: Neuroimaging, 67*(1), 29–38.

Volling, B. L. & Feagans, L. V. (1995). Infant day care and children's social competence. *Infant Behavior & Development, 18*(2), 177–188.

Volpicelli, J. R., Ulm, R. R., Altenor, A., & Seligman, M. E. P. (1983). Learned mastery in the rat. *Learning and Motivation, 14,* 204–222.

Von Baumgarten, R., Benson, A., Berthoz, A., Brandt, T. et al. (1984). Spatial orientation in weightlessness and readaptation to earth's gravity. *Science, 225,* 205–225.

Wade, S. E. & Trathen, W. (1989). Effect of self selected study methods on learning. *Journal of Educational Psychology, 81*(1), 40–47.

Wagaman, J. R., Miltenberger, R. G., & Woods, D. (1995). Long-term follow-up of a behavioral treatment for stuttering in children. *Journal of Applied Behavior Analysis, 28*(2), 233–234.

Waid, W. M., & Orne, M. T. (1982). The physiological detection of deception. *American Scientist, 70*(July/Aug.), 402–409.

Wakefield, J. C. (1992). The concept of mental disorder. *American Psychologist, 47*(3), 373–388.

Wakeling, A. (1996). Epidemiology of anorexia

nervosa. *Psychiatry Research, 62*(1), 3–9.

Walden, T. A. & Ogan, T. A. (1988). The development of social referencing. *Child Development, 59*(5), 1230–1240.

Waldvogel, J. A. (1990). The bird's eye view. *American Scientist, 78*(4), 342–353.

Wallach, M. A. (1985). Creativity testing and giftedness. In F. D. Horowitz & M. O'Brien (Eds.), *The gifted and talented: Developmental perspectives*, Washington, DC: American Psychological Association, 99–123.

Wallach, M. A., & Kogan, N. (1965). *Modes of thinking in young children.* New York: Holt.

Walsh, M. F. & Flynn, T. J. (1995). A 54–month evaluation of a popular very low calorie diet program. *Journal of Family Practice, 41*(3), 231–236.

Walsh, R. (1984). An evolutionary model of meditation research. In Shapiro, D. H. & Walsh, R. N. (Eds.), *Meditation: Classic and contemporary perspectives.* New York: Aldine.

Walster, E. (1971). Passionate love. In B. I. Murstein (Ed.), *Theories of attraction and love.* New York: Springer.

Walster, E., & Walster, G. W. (1978). *A new look at love.* Reading, MA: Addison-Wesley.

Walton, C. E., Bower, M. L., & Bower, T. G. (1992). Recognition of familiar faces by newborns. *Infant Behavior & Development, 15*(2), 265–269.

Ward, C. A. (1989). The cross-cultural study of altered states of consciousness and mental health. In C. A. Ward (Ed.), *Altered states of consciousness and mental health.* Newbury Park, CA: Sage.

Ward, E. & Ogden, J. (1994). Experiencing vaginismus: Sufferers' beliefs about causes and effects. *Sexual & Marital Therapy, 9*(1), 33–45.

Ward, P. B., Catts, S. V., Fox, A. M., Michie, P. T. et al. (1991). Auditory selective attention and event-related potentials in schizophrenia. *British Journal of Psychiatry, 158*, 534–539.

Ward, T. B., Finke, R. A., & Smith, S. M. (1995). *Creativity and the mind.* New York: Plenum.

Wark, G. R. & Krebs, D. L. (1996). Gender and dilemma differences in real-life moral judgment. *Developmental Psychology, 32*(2), 220–230.

Warrington, E. K. & McCarthy, R. A. (1995). Multiple meaning systems in the brain: A case for visual semantics. *Neuropsychologia, 32*(12), 1465–1473.

Warwick-Evans, L. & Beaumont, S. (1995). An experimental evaluation of sensory conflict versus postural control theories of motion sickenss. *Ecological Psychology, 7*(3), 163–179.

Watkins, J. G. (1989). Hypnotic hypermnesia and forensic hypnosis: A cross-examination. *American Journal of Clinical Hypnosis, 32*(2), 71–83.

Watson, D. L., & Tharp, R. G. (1996). *Self-directed behavior: Self-modification for personal adjustment, 4th ed.* Monterey, CA: Brooks/Cole.

Watson, D. L., deBortali-Tregerthan, G., & Frank, J. (1984). *Social Psychology: Science and application.* Glenview, IL: Scott, Foresman.

Watson, J. B. (1913). Psychology as the behaviorist views it. *Psychological Review, 20*, 158–177.

Watson, John B. (1994). Psychology as the behaviorist views it. Special Issue: The centennial issue of the Psychological Review. *Psychological Review, 101*(2), 248–253.

Weaver, C. A. (1993). Do you need a "flash" to form a flashbulb memory? *Journal of Experimental Psychology: General, 122*(1), 39–46.

Weaver, C. N. & Matthews, M. D. (1987). What white males want from their jobs: Ten years later. *Personnel, 4*(9), 62–65.

Webb, N. M. & Farivar, S. (1994). Promoting helping behavior in cooperative small groups in middle school mathematics. *American Educational Research Journal, 31*(2), 369–395.

Webb, W. B. (1994). Sleep as a biological rhythm: A historical view. *Sleep, 17*(2), 188–194.

Weinberg, R. A. (1989). Intelligence and IQ. *American Psychologist, 44*(2), 98–104.

Weinberger, M., Hiner, S. L., & Tierney, W. M. (1987). In support of hassles as a measure of stress in predicting health outcomes. *Journal of Behavioral Medicine, 10*(1), 19–31.

Weiner, I. B. (1996). Some observations on the validity of the Rorschach Inkblot Method. *Psychological Assessment, 8*(2), 206–213.

Weintraub, M. I. (1983). *Hysterical conversion reactions.* New York: SP Medical & Scientific Books.

Weintraub, S., Powell, D. H., & Whitla, D. K. (1994). Successful cognitive aging. *Journal of Geriatric Psychiatry, 27*(1), 15–34.

Weisburd, D. E. (1990). Planning a community-based mental health system: Perspective of a family member. *American Psychologist, 45*(11), 1245–1248.

Weisenberg, R. W. (1986). *Creativity.* New York: W. H. Freeman.

Weisfeld, G. E., & Beresford, J. M. (1982). Erectness of posture as an indicator of dominance or success in humans. *Motivation and Emotion, 6*, 113–131.

Weiss, B., Dodge, K. A., Bates, J. E., & Pettit, G. S. (1992). Some consequences of early harsh discipline. *Child Development, 63*(6), 1321–1335.

Weiss, J. (1990). Unconscious mental functioning. *Scientific American*, March, 103–109.

Weiss, J. M. (1972). Psychological factors in stress and disease. *Scientific American, 26*, 104–113.

Weiss, R. (1989). Bypassing the ban. *Science News, 138*, 378–379.

Weiten, W. (1988). Pressure as a form of stress and its relationship to psychological symptomatology. *Journal of Social & Clinical Psychology, 6*(1), 127–139.

Weller, L. & Weller, A. (1995). Menstrual synchrony. *Psychoneuroendocrinology, 20*(4), 377–383.

Wells, G. L. (1993). What do we know about eyewitness identification? *American Psychologist, 48*(5), 553–571.

Wells, G. L., Rydell, S. M., & Seelau, E. P. (1993). The selection of distractors for eyewitness lineups. *Journal of Applied Psychology, 78*(5), 835–844.

Wells, N. (1994). Perceived control over pain: Relation to distress and disability. *Research in Nursing & Health, 17*(4), 295–302.

Wertheimer, M. (1959). *Productive thinking.* New York: Harper & Row.

Wesley, J. C. (1994). Effects of ability, high school achievement, and procrastinatory behavior on college performance. *Educational & Psychological Measurement, 54*(2), 404–408.

West, L. J. (1993). A psychiatric overview of cult-related phenomena. *Journal of the American Academy of Psychoanalysis, 21*(1), 1–19.

West, T. G. (1991). *In the mind's eye.* Buffalo, NY: Prometheus.

Wexler, M. N. (1995). Expanding the groupthink explanation to the study of contemporary cults. *Cultic Studies Journal, 12*(1), 49–71.

Wheeler, L. & Miyake, K. (1992). Social comparison in everyday life. *Journal of Personality & Social Psychology, 62*(5), 760–773.

Wheeler, R. J. & Frank, M. A. (1988). Identification of stress buffers. *Behavioral Medicine, 14*(2), 78–89.

Whimbey, A., with Whimbey, L. S. (1980). *Intelligence can be taught.* New York: Dutton.

Whitbourne, S. K. (1986). *Adult development.* New York: Praeger.

White, B. L. (1990). *The first three years of life.* New York: Prentice-Hall.

White, B. L., & Held, R. (1966). Plasticity of sensorimotor development in the human infant. In J. F. Rosenblith, & W. Allinsmith (Eds.). *The causes of behavior Vol. I.* Boston: Allyn & Bacon.

White, B. L., & Watts, J. C. (1973). *Experience and environment Vol. I.* Englewood Cliffs, NJ: Prentice-Hall.

White, S. D. & DeBlassie, R. R. (1992). Adolescent sexual behavior. *Adolescence, 27*(105), 183–191.

Whitehead, W. E. (1992). Behavioral medicine approaches to gastrointestinal disorders. *Journal of Consulting and Clinical Psychology, 60*(4), 605–612.

Whitfield, C. L. (1995). The forgotten difference: Ordinary memory versus traumatic memory. *Consciousness & Cognition: An International Journal, 4*(1) 88–94.

Whitley, B. E. (1993). Reliability and aspects of the construct validity of Sternberg's Triangular Love Scale. *Journal of Social & Personal Relationships, 10*(3), 475–480.

Wichstrom, L. (1995). Social, psychological and physical correlates of eating problems. *Psychological Medicine, 25*(3), 567–579.

Wichstrom, L., Anderson, A. M. C., Holte, A., & Wynne, L. C. (1996). Disqualifying family communication and childhood social competence as predictors of offspring's mental health and hospitalization. *Journal of Nervous & Mental Disease, 184*(10), 581–588.

Wickett, J. C., Vernon, P. A. & Lee, D. H. (1995). In vivo brain size, head perimeter, and intelligence in a sample of healthy adult females. *Personality & Individual Differences, 16*(6), 831–838.

Widiger, T. A. & Trull, T. J. (1991). Diagnosis and clinical assessment. In M. R. Rosenzweig & L. W. Porter (Eds.), *Annual Review of Psychology, 42*, 109–133.

Wiebe, D. J. (1991). Hardiness and stress moderation. *Journal of Personality & Social Psychology, 60*(1), 89–99.

Wieneke, G. H., Janssen, P., & Brutten, G. J. (1995). Variance of central timing of voiced and voiceless periods among stutterers and nonstutterers. *Journal of Fluency Disorders, 20*(2), 171–189.

Wilder, D. A., Simon, A. F., & Faith, M. (1996). Enhancing the impact of counterstereotypic information. *Journal of Personality & Social Psychology, 71*(2), 276–287.

Wilding, J. & Valentine, E. (1994a). Memory champions. *British Journal of Psychology, 85*(2), 231–244.

Wilding, J. & Valentine, E. (1994b). Mnemonic wizardry with the telephone directory: But stories are another story. *British Journal of Psychology, 85*(4), 501–509.

Wilhelm, J. L. (1976). *The search for superman.* New York: Simon & Schuster.

Williams, B. A. (1984). U.S. approves implants to aid the totally deaf. *Santa Barbara News Press*, Nov. 30, part C, 6.

Williams, C. L. & Berry, J. W. (1991). Primary prevention of acculturative stress among refugees. *American Psychologist, 46*(6), 632–641.

Williams, D. G. & Morris, G. (1996). Crying, weeping or tearfulness in British and Israeli adults. *British Journal of Psychology, 87*(3), 479–505.

Williams, J. M. (1995). Applied sport psychology: Goals, issues, and challenges. *Journal of Applied Sport Psychology, 7*(1), 81–91.

Williams, J., Merritt, J., Rittenhouse, C., & Hobson, J. A. (1992). Bizarreness in dreams and fantasies: Implications for the activation-synthesis hypothesis. *Consciousness & Cognition: An International Journal, 1*(2), 172–185.

Williams, L. J. (1995). Peripheral target recognition and visual field narrowing in aviators and nonaviators. *International Journal of Aviation Psychology, 5*(2), 215–232.

Williams, R. (1989). The trusting heart: Great news about Type A behavior. New York: Random House.

Williams, R. L. (1975). The Bitch-100: A culture-specific test. *Journal of Afro-American Issues, 3*, 103–116.

Williams, R. L. et al. (1964). Sleep patterns in young adults: An EEG study. *Electroencephalography and Clinical Neurophysiology*, 376–381.

Williams, R. L., & Long, J. D. (1991). *Toward a self-managed life style*. Boston: Houghton Mifflin.

Williamson, A. M. & Sanderson, J. W. (1986). Changing the speed of shift rotations: A field study. *Ergonomics, 29*(9), 1085–1095.

Williamson, D. A., Davis, C. J., Goreczny, A. J., & Blouin, D. C. (1989). Body-image disturbances in bulimia nervosa: Influences of actual body size. *Journal of Abnormal Psychology, 98*(1), 97–99.

Willinger, M., Hoffman, H. J., & Hartford, R. B. (1994). Infant sleep position and risk for sudden infant death syndrome. *Pediatrics, 93*(5), 814–819.

Wilson, E. O. (1975). Human decency is animal. *New York Times Magazine*, Oct. 12.

Wilson, F. L. (1995). The effects of age, gender, and ethnic/cultural background on moral reasoning. *Journal of Social Behavior & Personality, 10*(1), 67–78.

Wilson, R. R. (1986). *Don't panic: Taking control of anxiety attacks*. New York: Harper & Row.

Wilson, S. A., Becker, L. A., & Tinker, R. H. (1995). Eye movement desensitization and reprocessing treatment for psychologically traumatized individuals. *Journal of Consulting and Clinical Psychology, 63*(6), 928.

Wilson, W. H. (1989). Reassessment of state hospital patients diagnosed with schizophrenia. *Journal of Neuropsychiatry & Clinical Neurosciences, 1*(4), 394–397.

Winget, C., & Kramer, M. (1979). *Dimensions of dreams*. Gainesville: University Presses of Florida.

Wirz-Justice, A., Graw, P., Krauchi, K., & Sarrafzadeh, A. (1996). "Natural" light treatment of seasonal affective disorder. *Journal of Affective Disorders, 37*(2), 109–120.

Wise, J. (1982). A gentle deterrent to vandalism. *Psychology Today*, Sept., 31–38.

Wise, R. A. & Rompre, P. P. (1989). Brain dopamine and reward. *Annual Review of Psychology, 40*, 191–225.

Witelson, S. F. (1991). Neural sexual mosaicism: Sexual differentiation of the human temporo-parietal region for functional asymmetry. *Psychoneuroendocrinology, 16*(1–3), 131–153.

Withers, N. W., Pulvirenti, L., Koob, G. F., & Gillin, J. C. (1995). Cocaine abuse and dependence. *Journal of Clinical Psychopharmacology, 15*(1), 63–78.

Witherspoon, W. (1994). Disorder consumed her life. *Los Angeles Times*, July 28, C-1.

Woehr, D. J. & Cavell, T. A. (1993). Self-report measures of ability, effort, and nonacademic activity as predictors of introductory psychology test scores. *Teaching of Psychology, 20*(3), 156–160.

Wogalter, M. S., Barlow, T., & Murphy, S. A. (1995). Compliance to owner's manual warnings. *Ergonomics, 38*(6), 1081–1091.

Wolcott, J. H., McNeekin, R. R., Burgin, R. E., & Yanowitch, R. E. (1977). Correlation of general aviation accidents with the biorhythm theory. *Human Factors, 19*, 283–293.

Wolfe, D. A. & Wekerle, C. (1993). Treatment strategies for child physical abuse and neglect. *Clinical Psychology Review, 13*(6), 473–500.

Wolfe, J. B. (1936). Effectiveness of token rewards for chimpanzees. *Comparative Psychology Monographs, 12*(5), Whole No. 60.

Wolitzky, D. L. (1995). The theory and practice of traditional psychoanalytic psychotherapy. In A. S. Gurman & S. B. Messer, *Essential Psychotherapies*. New York: Guilford.

Wolpe, J. (1974). *The practice of behavior therapy (2nd ed.)*. New York: Pergamon.

Wolpin, M., Marston, A., Randolph, C., & Clothier, A. (1992). Individual difference correlates of reported lucid dreaming frequency and control. *Journal of Mental Imagery, 16*(3–4), 231–236.

Wolraich, M. L. (1994). Effects of diets high in sucrose or aspartame on the behavior and cognitive performance of children. *The New England Journal of Medicine, 330*(5), 301–307.

Wolraich, M. L., Wilson, D. B., & White, J. W. (1995). The effect of sugar on behavior or cognition in children. *Journal of the American Medical Association, 274*(20), 1617–1621.

Wong, C. Y., Sommer, R., & Cook, E. J. (1992). The soft classroom 17 years later. *Journal of Environmental Psychology, 12*(4), 337–343.

Wong, J. L. & Whitaker, D. J. (1993). Depressive mood states and their cognitive and personality correlates in college students. *Journal of Clinical Psychology, 49*(5), 615–621.

Woo, E. (1995). Teaching that goes beyond IQ. *Los Angeles Times*, Jan. 20, A-1, A-22, A-23.

Wood, E. & Willoughby, T. (1995). Cognitive strategies for test-taking. In E. Wood, V. Woloshyn, and T. Willoughby (Eds.), *Cognitive strategy instruction for middle and high schools*, Brookline, Cambridge, MA.

Wood, J. M. & Bootzin, R. R. (1990). The prevalence of nightmares and their independence from anxiety. *Journal of Abnormal Psychology, 99*(1), 64–68.

Wood, J. M., Bootzin, R. R., Kihlstrom, J. F., & Schacter, D. L. (1992). Implicit and explicit memory for verbal information presented during sleep. *Psychological Science, 3*(4), 236–239.

Wood, N. L. & Cowan, N. (1995). The cocktail party phenomenon revisited. *Journal of Experimental Psychology: General, 124*(3), 243–262.

Woods, P. J. (Ed.) with C. S. Wilkinson. (1987). *Is psychology the major for you? Planning for your undergraduate years*. Washington, DC: American Psychological Association.

Woodward, J. & Goodstein, D. (1996). Conduct, misconduct and the structure of science. *American Scientist, (84)*, 479–490.

Woody, S. R. (1996). Effects of focus of attention on anxiety levels and social performance of individuals with social phobia. *Journal of Abnormal Psychology, 105*(1), 61–69.

Work in America. (1973). Special Task Force, Department of Health, Education and Welfare. Cambridge, MA: MIT Press.

Worthen, J. B. & Marshall, P. H. (1996). Intralist and extralist sources of distinctiveness and the bizarreness effect. *American Journal of Psychology, 109*(2), 239–263.

Wright, D. B. (1993). Recall of the Hillsborough disaster over time: Systematic biases of "flashbulb" memories. *Applied Cognitive Psychology, 7*(2), 129–138.

Wright, R. (1996). Can machines think? *Time*, March 25, 50–57.

Wursig, B. (1979). Dolphins. *Scientific American, 240*(3), 136–148.

Wyatt, J. W., Posey, A., Welker, W., & Seamonds, C. (1984). Natural levels of similarities between identical twins and between unrelated people. *The Skeptical Inquirer, 9*, 62–66.

Yadama, G. N. & Drake, B. (1995). Confirmatory factor analysis of the Maslach Burnout Inventory. *Social Work Research, 19*(3), 184–192.

Yalom, I. D. (1980). *Existential psychotherapy*. New York: Basic.

Yank, G. R., Bentley, K. J., & Hargrove, D. S. (1993). The vulnerability-stress model of schizophrenia. *American Journal of Orthopsychiatry, 63*(1), 55–69.

Yardley, L. (1992). Motion sickness and perception. *British Journal of Psychology, 83*(4), 449–471.

Yarmey, A. D., Yarmey, M. J., & Yarmey, A. L. (1996). Accuracy of eyewitness identification in showups and lineups. *Law & Human Behavior, 20*(4), 459–477.

Yee, A. H., Fairchild, H. H., Weizmann, F., & Wyatt, G. E. (1993). Addressing psychology's problems with race. *American Psychologist, 48*(11), 1132–1140.

Yontef, G. M. (1995). Gestalt therapy. In A. S. Gurman & S. B. Messer, *Essential Psychotherapies*. New York: Guilford.

Yoshida, M. (1993). Three-dimensional electrophysiological atlas created by computer mapping of clinical responses elicited on stimulation of human subcortical structures. *Stereotactic & Functional Neurosurgery, 60*(1–3), 127–134.

Young, R. L. (1994). The "intelligence" of calendrical calculators. *American Journal on Mental Retardation, 99*(2), 186–200.

Yuille, J. C. & Tollestrup, P. A. (1990). Some effects of alcohol on eyewitness memory. *Journal of Applied Psychology, 75*(3), 268–273.

Zametkin, A. J. (1995). Attention-deficit disorder: born to be hyperactive? *The Journal of the American Medical Association, 273*(23), 1871–1874.

Zayas, L. H., Torres, L. R., Malcolm, J., DesRosiers, F. S. (1996). Clinicians' definitions of ethnically sensitive therapy. *Professional Psychology: Research & Practice, 27*(1), 78–82.

Zeidner, M. (1995). Adaptive coping with test situations: A review of the literature. *Educational Psychologist, 30*(3), 123–133.

Zelkowitz, P. & Milet, T. H. (1995). Screening for postpartum depression in a community sample. *Canadian Journal of Psychiatry, 40*(2), 80–86.

Zellner, D. A., Harner, D. E., & Adler, R. L. (1989). Effects of eating abnormalities and gender on perceptions of desirable body shape. *Journal of Abnormal Psychology, 98*(1), 93–96.

Zetlin, A. & Murtaugh, M. (1990). Whatever happened to those with borderline IQs? *American Journal on Mental Retardation, 94*(5), 463–469.

Zgodzinski, D. (1996). Cybertherapy. *Internet World*, Feb., 50–53.

Zigler, E. (1995). Can we "cure" mild mental retardation among individuals in the lower socioeconomic stratum? *American Journal of Public Health, 85*(3), 302–304.

Zigler, E. & Muenchow, S. (1992). *Head Start: The inside story of America's most successful educational experience*. New York: Basic.

Zigler, E. & Styfco, S. J. (1994). Head start. *American Psychologist, 49*(2), 127–132.

Zilbergeld, B. (1983). *The shrinking of America: Myths of psychological change*. Boston: Little Brown.

Zimbardo, P. G., Haney, C., & Banks, W. C. (1973). A pirandellian prison. *The New York Times Magazine*, April 8.

Zimbardo, P. G., Pilkonis, P. A., & Norwood, R. M. (1978). The social disease called shyness. In *Annual editions, personality and adjustment 78/79*. Guilford CT: Dushkin.

Zimmer, C. (1993). Making senses. *Discover*, June, 79–85.

Zimmerman, B. J. (1996a). Enhancing student academic and health functioning: A self-regulatory perspective. *School Psychology Quarterly, 11*(1), 47–66.

Zimmerman, J. D. (1996b). A prosocial media strategy. *American Journal of Orthopsychiatry, 66*(3), 354–362.

Zimmerman, S. & Zimmerman, A. M. (1990). Genetic effects of marijuana. *International Journal of Addictions, 25*(1A), 19–33.

Zinbarg, R. E., Barlow, D. H., Brown, T. A. & Hertz, R. M. (1992). Cognitive-behavioral approaches to the nature and treatment of anxiety disorders. In M. R. Rosenzweig & L. W. Porter (Eds.), *Annual Review of Psychology, 43,* 235–267.

Zubek, J. (1969). Sensory and perceptual-motor processes. In J. Zubek (Ed.). *Sensory deprivation: Fifteen years of research.* New York: Appleton-Century-Crofts.

Zucker, A. (1995). "Rights and the dying." In H. Wass & R. A. Neimeyer (Eds.), *Dying: Facing the facts.* Washington, D.C.: Taylor & Francis.

Zuckerman, M. (1990). The psychophysiology of sensation seeking. *Journal of Personality, 58*(1), 313–345.

Zuckerman, M. (1996). Item revisions in the Sensation Seeking Scale Form V (SSS-V). *EDRA: Environmental Design Research Association, 20*(4), 515.

Zuckerman, M., & Allison, S. (1976). An objective measure of fear of success: Construction and validation. *Journal of Personality, 40,* 422–430.

Zuckerman, M., Eysenck, S., & Eysenck, H. J. (1978). Sensation seeking in England and America: Cross-cultural, age, and sex comparisons. *Journal of Consulting and Clinical Psychology, 46,* 139–149.

Zuwerink, J. R., Devine, P. G., Monteith, M. J., & Cook, D. A. (1996). Prejudice toward Blacks: With and without compunction? *Basic & Applied Social Psychology, 18*(2), 131–150.

Index

Escape learning, 299–300
Ethics of psychological research, 46–47
Eugenics, 124, 393
Euthanasia, 164
Evolutionary psychology, 660–661
Exhibitionism, 569
Existential theory of anxiety, 577
Existential therapy, 618–619, 634
Experimental group, 34, 35, 36
Experimental method, 28–30, 34–38, 41
Experimental psychologist (research psychologist), 14, 19, 20
Experimenter influence (effect), 37–38
Extinction, 281, 288, 307, 625, 626–627
  effects of punishment on, 298
Extraneous variables, 35–36
Extrasensory perception (ESP), 230–233
Extrinsic motives, 428
Extroversion, 520–521, 522, 532
Eye, structure of, 173–178
  and emotional expression, 432–433
  eye movement desensitization, 624–625
Eyewitness testimony, 227, 228, 320–321
Eysenck, H. J., 522, 617

Facial agnosia, 67
Facial feedback hypothesis, 439–440
Fact memory, 322
Fallacy of positive instances, 25
Familial retardation, 391
Family therapy, 630–631, 634
Fantasy
  and creativity, 365
  as a defense mechanism, 462
Fantz, R., 87–88
Farsightedness (hyperopia), 174, 175
Fear, 70, 310, 431–433, 437–441
Fear of success, 425–426
Feedback (in learning), 291–293, 336, 471–472
Female sexual arousal disorder, 510–511
Festinger, L., 655
Fetal alcohol syndrome, 96
Feuerstein, R., 395
Field experiment, 36
Figure-ground organization, 205
File Transfer Protocol, B2
Five-factor model of personality, 524–525
Fixation, 360–361, 530
Fixed action pattern (FAP), 309
Fixed interval (FI) reinforcement, 295
Fixed ratio (FR) reinforcement, 294, 295
Flat affect, 585
Flexitime, 707
Forebrain, 69–70
Forensic psychologist, 19
Forgetting, 314, 317–318, 328–334
Fouts, D. & R., 357
Fovea, 174, 177
Fragile-*X* syndrome, 392–393
Frankl, V., 619
Free association, Freudian, 615–616
Free will, 14, 619
Frequency distribution, A1, A2
Freud, S., 13, 248, 268, 463, 496, 501, 528–532, 577, 615–617, 618, 708
Friedman, M., 472
Frontal lobe, 64–65
Frontal lobotomy, 38–39, 602
Frustration, 449, 457–459, 479–480
  and aggression hypothesis, 693–694
  how to avoid, 479–480
  reactions to, 458–459
  sources of, 457–458
Fugue, 574–575
Functional fixedness, 360

Functional psychosis, 586, 588–595
Functionalism, 9, 14

Gagnon, J., 495
Galvanic skin response (GSR), 433, 434
Gardner, B., and A. Gardner, 356
Gardner, H., 397
Gating, sensory, 193–194
Gazzaniga, M., 457
Geller, U., 230, 233
Gender
  bias, 40, 560
  development, 486–490
  dimensions of, 485, 487
  disorders, 564, 565
  identity, 490
  psychology of, 6
General adaptation syndrome (G.A.S.), 474–475
General paresis, 587
Generalization, 281, 282, 296, 622, 628
Genes, 91–92
Genetics, 122–125
  behavioral, 394, 526–527, 592
  counseling, 123–124
  engineering, 125–126
Genital stage, 531
Genius, 389–390
Gerontology, 150–151
Gestalt psychology, 11–12, 14, 205–206
Gestalt therapy, 619–620, 634
Giantism, 72
Gilligan, C., 113–114
Ginott, H., 160
Girodo, M., 551
Glandular system (endocrine), 71–74
Globus, G., 270
Glove anesthesia, 575–576
Goals, 407–408
  superordinate, 690–691
Goleman, D., 441–442
Goodall, J., 30–31
Gophers, B1–B2
Gordon, T., 161
Gould, R., 145–146, 147
Graphical statistics, A1
Graphology, 24
Graphs, 33–34
Gregory, R., 203, 221
Grief. *See* Bereavement (grief) and death
Group(s), 648–650, 663–664
  conflict, 687–691
  conformity, 664
  membership, 142–143, 648–650, 678
  membership and attitudes, 678–679
  norms, 649–650
  peer, 142–143
  prejudice, 686, 687–691
  reference, 680
  sanctions, 664
  status, 649
Group therapy, 613, 630–633
  encounter, 631
  family therapy, 630–631, 634
  group awareness training, 631–632
  psychodrama, 630, 634
  sensitivity, 631
Groupthink, 663–664
Growth hormone, 71–73
Growth sequence, human, 92–93
Gwiazada, J., 209–210

Habits, breaking bad, 307–308
Habituation, 223–224, 229
Haier, R. J., 61
Hall, C., 248, 269

Hallucinations, 585
  and illusions, 220
  during sleep deprivation, 236, 239
Hallucinogen, 266
Halo effect, 544, 656
Hand dominance, 75–78
Hansen, C. and R., 679
Hardin, G., 673
Harlow, H. F., 103, 116
Health, 449–482
Health psychology, 450–453
Hearing, 117, 183–187
  absolute thresholds, 171, 185–186
  artificial, 185
  loss, 185–187
  stimulus for, 183
  and temporal lobe, 64
Helping (prosocial behavior), 697–699
Helping a troubled person, 634–636
Helplessness, learned, 464, 597, 693, 716
Hemispheres of the brain, 61–64, 75–78
  specialization, 62–64, 65–66, 75–78
Heredity
  and development, 91–93, 94, 122–125, 526–527
  and homosexuality, 499
  and intelligence, 393–395
  and personality, 526–527
  and schizophrenia, 591–592
Hermaphroditism, 489, 490
Hess, E., 432, 433
Heuristics, 358–359
Hierarchy, constructing, 639
  use in desensitization, 623–624
Hindbrain, 68–69
Hippocampus, and memory, 69, 70, 335
History of psychology, 8–16
HIV, 505–508
Hobson, A., 248
Holmes, T., 467
Homeostasis, 409, 419
Homogamy, 657
Homophobia, 500
Homosexuality, 498–500, 568
Honesty tests, 547–548
Hormones, 71–74
  growth, 71–73
  sex, 71, 73–74, 417, 486–489, 496–497, 499
  and the sex drive, 417
  sleep, 240
Horney, K., 532
Hospice, 163
Hospitalism, 115
Hospitalization, 579–580, 602–604
Hostility, 473
Hsiung, P., 212
Hubel, D., 177, 192
Humanistic psychology, 13–14, 15, 16
Humanistic-existential theory of anxiety, 577
Humanistic theory of personality, 538–541, 542, 543
Humanistic therapies, 618–620
Hunger, 409–416
  causes, 409–412
  cultural factors in, 413
  and the hypothalamus, 410
  and taste, 413–414
Huxley, A., 122
Hydrocephaly, 392
Hyperactivity in children (ADHD), 136–137
Hyperopia (farsightedness), 174, 175
Hypnogogic images, 252
Hypnotism, 249–252
  and memory, 251, 320–321
Hypochondria, 470, 575
Hypoglycemia, 410
Hypothalamus, 68, 69, 73
  and hunger, 410

Text and Illustration Credits

This page constitutes an extension of the copyright page. We have made every effort to trace the ownership of all copyrighted material and to secure permission from copyright holders. In the event of any question arising as to the use of any material, we will be pleased to make the necessary corrections in future printings. Thanks are due to the following authors, publishers, and agents for permission to use the material indicated.

131: Figure 5–1 adapted from "Growing Up," by J. M. Tanner. Copyright © 1973 by Scientific American, Inc. All rights reserved. **211:** Figure 7–12, MAGIC EYE cartoon, copyright 1994 by N. E. Thing Enterprises. Reprinted with permission of Universal Press Syndicate. All rights reserved. **223:** Figure 7–30 from "Cognitive Determinants of Fixation Location During Picture Viewing," by G. R. Loftus & N. H. Mackworth, *Journal of Experimental Psychology: Human Perception and Performance*, 1978, *4*, 565–572. Reprinted by permission. **224:** Figure 7–31 from "Cognitive Masking: The Disruptive Effect of an Emotional Stimulus Upon the Perception of Contiguous Neutral Items," by M. H. Erdelyi and A. G. Appelbaum, *Bulletin of the Psychonomic Society*, 1973, *1*, 59–61. Reprinted by permission. **250:** Table 8–3 adapted from "Stanford Hypnotic Scale," by Weitzenhoffer and Hilgard. Copyright © 1959 Stanford University Press. Reprinted by permission. **254:** Figure 8–10 from "Spectrum of Continuum of Drugs," by Dr. Robert W. Earle, University of California, Irvine. **258:** Illustration courtesy of the National Library of Medicine. **267:** Figure from "Beware Marijuana," courtesy of Dr. Lester Grinspoon, Harvard Medical School. **356:** Figure 11–9 from "Teaching Language to an Ape," by A. J. Premack, and D. Premack. Copyright © 1972 by Scientific American, Inc. All rights reserved. **366:** U.S. Patent No. 556,248. From *Absolutely Mad Inventions*, by A. E. Brown and H. A. Jefcott, Jr., Dover, 1970. **386:** Table 12–4, Wechsler Scale, The Psychological Corporation, 1958. **399:** Figure 12–10, Culture Fair Test Sample Items, from R. B. Cattell, "Are I. Q. Tests Intelligent?" Reprinted by permission of Dr. R. B. Cattell. **453:** Copyright Paul Marques, *Bienestar: Health, Well-being and Lifestyle Choices for Pinal County.* University of Arizona, 1982. **468:** Table 14–5 adapted with permission from "Social Readjustment Rating Scale," by T. H. Holmes and R. H. Rahe, *Journal of Psychosomatic Research*, 1967. Reprinted with permission from Pergamon Press, Ltd. **515–516:** Excerpt from "Where Should You Touch?" by H. E. F. Donohue. Copyright © 1965 Hearst Corpo-

ration. Reprinted by permission. **524:** Figure 16–3 from "Personality Pinned Down," by R. B. Cattell, 1973. Reprinted by permission of Dr. R. B. Cattell. **524:** Figure 16–4 from *Personality in Adulthood*, by R. R. McCrae and P. T. Costa. Copyright © 1990 by Guilford Press. Reprinted by permission. **546:** List courtesy of Art Buchwald, Los Angeles Times. **547:** Figure 16–10 reproduced by permission. Copyright 1943, renewed 1970 by the University of Minnesota. Published by The Psychological Corporation, New York, NY. All rights reserved. **626:** Figure 19–4 from "Manipulation of Self-destruction in Three Retarded Children," by O. I. Lovaas and J. Q. Simmons, *Journal of Applied Behavior Analysis*, 1969, *2*, 143–157. Reprinted by permission. **627:** Figure 19–5, Token Economy photograph, courtesy of Robert Liberman, M.D. **695:** Figure 21–5 from "The Development of Aggressive Behavior from the Perspective of a Developing Behaviorism," by L. D. Eron, *American Psychologist*, 1987, *42*, 435–442. Copyright © 1987 by the American Psychological Association. Reprinted by permission.

Photo Credits

Introduction   xxxvi: © Seth Resnick / Stock Boston.

Chapter 1   1: © Robert Brenner / PhotoEdit; **3:** (top left) © Hank Morgan / Rainbow, (top right) © Jeff Greenberg; **5:** (top left) © Bob Daemmrich / Stock Boston, (bottom right) © Hank Morgan / Rainbow, (top right) © David Austen / Stock Boston, (bottom left) © Pierre Lockett / Rainbow; **7:** © Charles Gupton / Stock Boston; **9:** (both) Archives of the History of American Psychology, University of Akron; **10:** (left) Archives of the History of American Psychology, University of Akron, (right) Nina Leen, Life Magazine © Time Inc.; **11:** (top left) © Ken Robert Buck / Stock Boston, (bottom right) Archives of the History of American Psychology, University of Akron; **12 & 13:** (all) Archives of the History of American Psychology, University of Akron; **15:** © Ted Polumbaum; **16:** © Joseph Sohm / Stock Boston; **23:** Bettmann Archive.

Chapter 2   27: © Jim Pickerell / The Image Works; **28:** © Dan McCoy / Rainbow; **31:** Photograph by Baron Hugo Van Lawick. © National Geographic Society; **37:** © Joel Gordon; **44:** © John Nordell / The Image Works.

Chapter 3   51: © Visuals Unlimited; **56:** © Steve Liss / Gamma Liaison; **57:** Fidia Research Laboratories, Pavda, Italy; **61:** Courtesy of Richard Haier, University of California, Irvine; **67:** © Shaywitz, et al.

1995, NMR Research / Yale Medical School; **71:** © Will and Deni McIntyre / Photo Researchers; **72:** (left) © Dan McCoy / Rainbow, (bottom right) © Keystone / The Image Works; **74:** © Focus on Sports; **76:** © Bob Daemmrich / The Image Works; **77:** © Custom Medical Stock Photo; **80:** (left) Huntington Magnetic Resonance Center, Pasadena, California, (right) © Charles Gupton / Stock Boston; **81:** (top & middle) Graphics by EEG Systems, (bottom) Washington University School of Medicine, St. Louis; **82:** Washington University School of Medicine, St. Louis.

Chapter 4   85: © Robert Ullmann / Design Conceptions; **87:** (top) © Margaret Miller / Photo Researchers, (bottom) From A. N. Meltzoff & M. K. Moore, "Imitation of facial and manual gestures by human neonates," Science, 1977, 198, 75–78.; **88:** "The Looking Chamber," © Robert L. Fanz, © David Linton, 1961, Scientific American, Inc.; **89:** © Michael Newman / PhotoEdit; **91:** © Biophoto Associates / Science Source / Photo Researchers; **94:** © M. Siluk / The Image Works; **95:** © Photo Researchers; **96:** © Ted Wood; **97:** © A. Glauberman / Photo Researchers; **98:** © Jeffry W. Myers / Stock Boston; **100:** © Dan McCoy / Rainbow; **101:** © Nina Leen, 1964, Time, Inc.; **102:** © David Grossman; **107:** Jim Pickerell / The Image Works; **108:** (top) © Tony Freeman / PhotoEdit, (bottom) © Yves Debraine / Black Star; **109:** © Bob Daemmrich / The Image Works; **114:** © Joel Gordon 1996; **116:** © Anna Kaufman Moon / Stock Boston; **117:** (top) Courtesy of Harry F. Harlow, University of Wisconsin Primate Laboratory, (bottom) © Charles Gupton / Stock Boston; **122:** © Mark Richards / PhotoEdit; **123:** © Philippe Phailly / Photo Researchers / © 1993 The Walt Disney Co. Reprinted with permission of Discover Magazine; **124:** Al Seib / © Los Angeles Times.

Chapter 5   128: © David J. Sams / Stock Boston; **130:** (top) © Bettmann Archive, (bottom) © Tom McCarthy / PhotoEdit; **132:** © Jeff Greenberg; **134:** © B. D. Lanphere / Stock Boston; **137:** © Stephen McBrady / PhotoEdit; **139:** Courtesy of the Los Angeles County Department of Children's Services; **141:** (left) Corbis-Bettmann, (right) © David Young-Wolff / PhotoEdit; **142:** © Mary Kate Denny / PhotoEdit; **150:** © R. Maiman / Sygma; **152:** (top) © Hank Morgan / Rainbow, (bottom) © Jeff Greenberg / PhotoEdit; **153:** © Michael Newman / PhotoEdit; **155:** (top) Blackmore, 1993, (bottom) © M. Reinstein / The Image Works; **164:** © Amy E. Powers / Gamma-Liaison.

Chapter 6   168: © Hank Morgan / Rainbow; **176:** © Omikron / Photo Researchers; **178:** (top) © Tom McCarthy / PhotoEdit, (bottom) © Mark Richards/ PhotoEdit; **180:** © PhotoEdit; **182:** © Jon L. Barken /

TO THE OWNER OF THIS BOOK:

I hope that you have found *Introduction to Psychology: Exploration and Application*, Eighth Edition, useful. So that this book can be improved in a future edition, would you take the time to complete this sheet and return it? Thank you.

School and address: _____

Department: _____

Instructor's name: _____

1. What I like most about this book is: _____

_____

_____

2. What I like least about this book is: _____

_____

_____

3. My general reaction to this book is: _____

_____

4. The name of the course in which I used this book is: _____

_____

5. Were all of the chapters of the book assigned for you to read? _____

    If not, which ones weren't? _____

 6. In the space below, or on a separate sheet of paper, please write specific suggestions for improving this book and anything else you'd care to share about your experience in using the book.

_____

_____

_____

_____

_____

_____

_____

_____

Optional:

Your name: _____ Date: _____

May Brooks/Cole quote you, either in promotion for *Introduction to Psychology: Exploration and Application,* Eighth Edition, or in future publishing ventures?

Yes: _____ No: _____

Sincerely,

Dennis Coon

FOLD HERE

- -

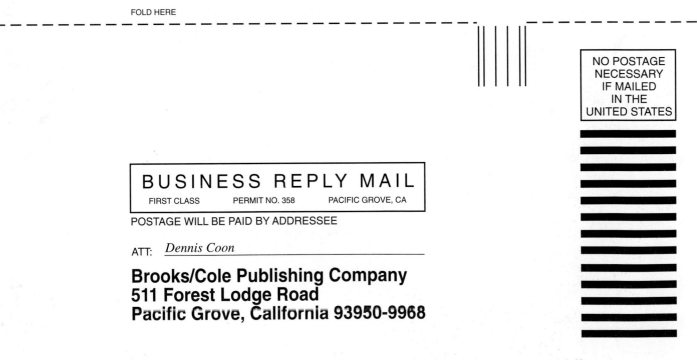

NO POSTAGE
NECESSARY
IF MAILED
IN THE
UNITED STATES

BUSINESS REPLY MAIL

FIRST CLASS   PERMIT NO. 358   PACIFIC GROVE, CA

POSTAGE WILL BE PAID BY ADDRESSEE

ATT: *Dennis Coon* _____

**Brooks/Cole Publishing Company
511 Forest Lodge Road
Pacific Grove, California 93950-9968**

- -

FOLD HERE